Battle Honours
of the British
Empire and
Commonwealth
Land Forces

1662–1991

'Render therefore to all their dues:
tribute to whom tribute is due;
custom to whom custom;
fear to whom fear;
honour to whom honour.'

Rom. 13:7

Battle Honours of the British Empire and Commonwealth Land Forces

1662–1991

Alexander Rodger

The Crowood Press

First published in 2003 by
The Crowood Press Ltd
Ramsbury, Marlborough
Wiltshire SN8 2HR

www.crowood.com

British Library Cataloguing-in-Publication Data
A catalogue record for this book is available from the British Library.

ISBN 1 86126 637 5

Typeset by Phoenix Typesetting, Burley-in-Wharfedale, West Yorkshire

Printed and bound in by The Cromwell Press, Trowbridge

Dedication

This book is dedicated to the men of all races who fought and died to win these battle honours.

And to my wife Janet, who also followed the drum.

Acknowledgements

I wish to acknowledge the invaluable assistance of the staffs of the relevant departments of the Ministry of Defence, Imperial War Museum, National Army Museum and the India Office Library in London; the National Library of Scotland, Edinburgh; the National Defence Headquarters, Ottawa; the Department of Defence, Canberra; the Department of Defence, Pretoria; and the Queen Elizabeth II Army Memorial Museum, Waiouru for their assistance during the preparation of this book.

In addition, I thank Lieutenant Colonel Patric Emerson of The Indian Army Association and Major-General Iftikhar Ali of the Pakistan Army for their contributions on post-Partition battle honours. It was unfortunate that I was unable to contact Major Sarbans Singh, who could have added further details and insight on this period.

Crown copyright material is reproduced with permission of the Controller of Her Majesty's Stationery Office and the Queen's Printer for Scotland.

This book would never have been published without the active encouragement of a large number of people who dealt with my requests for information and clarification and other enquiries with endless patience over twenty years' research; a lack of space precludes me from naming them all, nevertheless, I wish to record my debt to them. Although I have striven to be as accurate as possible in preparing this book, I trust that any errors will be forgiven by them as such errors are mine alone.

Finally, I thank my wife and family for their support and understanding during these years.

Contents

CHAPTER 1   Battle Honours Before The Great War   9

CHAPTER 2   The Great War and the Third Afghan War   77

CHAPTER 3   The Second World War and the Korean Campaign   209

CHAPTER 4   Battle Honours After the Second World War   375

Appendix A   Battles and Other Engagements Fought by the Military
             Forces of the British Empire During The Great War and
             the Third Afghan War   396

Appendix B   Conditions of Award of Battle Honours for The Great
             War 1914-19   425

Appendix C   Battles, Actions and Engagments Fought by the Land
             Forces of the Commonwealth During the Second World
             War and the Korean Campaign   427

Appendix D   Succession of British Battle Honours   463

Appendix E   Succession of Indian Battle Honours   468

Appendix F   Succession of Pakistani Battle Honours   476

Appendix G   Succession of Australian Battle Honours   480

Appendix H   Succession of Canadian Battle Honours   484

Appendix J   Succession of New Zealand Battle Honours   488

Appendix K   Succession of South African Battle Honours   489

Bibliography   492

1

Battle Honours Before The Great War

A Battle Honour is a public commemoration of a battle, action or engagement, of which not only past and present, but future generations of the Regiment can be proud.

Army Council Instruction 58, 28 January 1956

Introduction

On 16 July 1760 near the small German town of Emsdorff, a regiment formed only the previous year – Eliott's or 15th Light Dragoons – so distinguished itself in its first engagement that six years later the regiment inscribed its helmets with:

Five battalions of French defeated and taken by this Regiment with their Colours and nine pieces of cannon at Emsdorff 16th July 1760.

This inscription was confirmed by Royal Warrant dated 19 December 1768, which set out the 'Differences and Distinctions of the several Corps of Cavalry in the Clothing, Horse-Furniture and Standards'. It is, therefore, most likely that this headdress embellishment was considered, at that time, as a dress distinction. Nevertheless, in this manner the battle honours system was introduced, albeit unknowingly at this stage, into the British Army and, in turn, to the land forces of the Empire and Commonwealth. **Emsdorff**, although possibly not the first honorary distinction, is generally recognized as the first officially-named battle honour.

There are two hundred and sixty-three officially-named battle honours commemorating battles and campaigns fought before The Great War. Not all of these honours, however, were awarded before 1914 as, at first, awards were random, irregular and highly selective. It was not until 1965 that the last awards for this period were confirmed by a South African Battle Honours Committee.

By 1914 the badges, mottoes and battle honours of corps were emblazoned on Standards, Guidons or Regimental Colours and were placed on their appointments, such as cap badges, buttons, belt-plates, drums and drum banners: Corps that did not have standards, guidons or colours placed their badges, mottoes and battle honours on their appointments only. Standards, guidons and colours were used by cavalry and infantry corps only. A standard was carried by senior mounted regiments, such as the Household Cavalry, which included the Governor General's Body Guard of the Canadian Militia, and by Dragoon Guards. A guidon was carried by dragoons and some mounted rifle regiments, but not by hussars, lancers nor light horse. All Indian cavalry regiments were classified as lancers, but some carried honorary standards. Most infantry battalions had a King's Colour and a second or regimental colour, except some rifle regiments, which had no colours.

Immediately before the First World War only units of the Household Cavalry, cavalry, yeomanry, light horse, mounted rifles, Indian mountain artillery, sappers and miners, Foot Guards, infantry and Imperial Service Troops provided by the Indian state forces were eligible for the award of battle honours: these units included both regular and part-time, volunteer corps. As this had not always been the case, it is worthwhile to examine briefly the development of the modern battle honours system.

Great Britain and Ireland

The restoration of Charles II led to the disbandment of the existing military structure, largely based on Cromwell's New Model Army, and the formation of the standing army. Regiments of Royal Household troops were formed – all Guards – which were joined later by regiments raised for overseas garrisons, such as Tangier and Bombay. From this modest start, the Army increased in size until, by the end of the Seven Years War, there were three regiments of Household Cavalry, twenty-four of cavalry, three of Foot Guards and seventy of infantry on the Regular Establishment. On its formation, each of these corps was presented with the appropriate standard, guidon or colours, as yet without a single named battle honour.

With the end of the War of American Independence, two further infantry regiments were added to the Regular Establishment, but there were no battle honours for the regiments which had served in North America. The accepted view is that the war did not qualify for awards as it was, in effect, a civil war and all subsequent claims have been disallowed for this reason; however, there was little to commemorate in a war that witnessed British units laying down their arms. To offset this, very obvious defeat, there was a need for an outstanding 'victory'; fortunately, the extension of the war into Europe against France and Spain provided the required battle honour – the Siege of Gibraltar and its gallant defence. An uncharacteristically prompt award to the 1st Battalions of four selected infantry regiments was made on 14 April 1784, instructing the Commanding Officers to place **Gibraltar** on the caps of grenadier and light infantry companies, on accoutrements, drums and also on the Second Colour, below the regimental number at the centre. This battle honour was later enhanced: on 9 December 1836 these same four corps were authorized to add to the Regimental Colour and their appointments the distinction of the badge of The Castle and Key, together with the motto 'Montis Insignia Calpe'. This enhancement was prompted by the increasing numbers of awards – eighty-six battle and campaign honours by 1836 – and the fashionable use of animals, such as The Elephant, with subsequent battle honours, threatening to overshadow the significance of this distinction. The battle honour was extended later to include the Highland Light Infantry for a war-raised 2nd Battalion of 73rd Foot, which had been employed as marines but disbanded in 1783. At that time, disbanded units did not qualify for battle honours.

It is also of interest to note that the Colonel of 15th Light Dragoons and the General who conducted the successful defence of Gibraltar was the same man – General Sir George Augustus Eliott.

By the beginning of the nineteenth century, Britain had been at war with revolutionary France and her allies for seven years without what would be considered at that time an outstanding or decisive engagement to qualify as a battle honour. All the significant battles seemed to be at sea, the Royal Navy's work being supported by a handful of marines, found by detachments from infantry regiments. It was time for another great 'victory'. On 1 January 1801, six infantry battalions were commanded by the King to place **Minden** on their Second Colour to commemorate a battle which took place over fifty years previously, on 1 August 1759. The selection of this distinction seems random, but if examined more closely makes some sense. The battle does not pre-date the Seven Years War – Emsdorff was fought in 1760 – which appears to have been set as the then starting point for battle honours and, possibly more importantly, had been a decisive Anglo- Hanoverian victory against the French, a significant morale factor at that time. Up to this point distinctions had been awarded to 1st Battalions only; however, it was the 2nd Battalion of 20th Foot, raised in 1799, that was selected for the battle honour, as a previously raised 2nd Battalion – Kingsley's Foot, disbanded 1759 – had been present at the battle. This 2nd Battalion, like Kingsley's, was a war-raised battalion and was itself disbanded in 1802. As at that time battle honours were awarded only to the battalion present at the engagement and were emblazoned on the Regimental Colour of that battalion only: distinctions won by war-raised battalions were 'lost' on disbandment. Accordingly, the battle honour followed the 2nd Battalion 'into history'. Later awards for the French Revolutionary Wars and for the Napoleonic Wars, in particular the Peninsula Campaign, included many war-raised battalions, but to avoid the inevitable losses to the corps concerned, a system of retention was devised by the transfer of the award to surviving battalions of the same corps, usually the 1st Battalion. By this device the distinction was restored to 20th Foot in 1820. In 1832 all battalions on establishment were authorized to emblazon all the distinctions of their corps on their Regimental Colour. Thereafter all battle honours were considered to be awards not only to the battalion present but also to the entire corps.

On 16 July 1802, **Egypt**, with the badge of The Sphinx, was awarded to all units which had taken part in the 1801 campaign. This distinction is interesting for several reasons: it was the first to be awarded for a campaign and the first to use a badge to commemorate the award. Also, unlike previous awards, it was not considered necessary for the complete unit to have been present to qualify for the honour. As examples, 11th Light Dragoons had one troop only, albeit as the Commander-in-Chief's escort, and qualified, as did the 1st and the 2nd Battalion of the 40th Foot with the grenadier and light infantry companies only of both present. Moreover, the Staff Corps, disbanded 1836 as the Royal Staff Corps, with a detachment only also qualified. The award to the 2nd Battalion of 1st Foot – the only 2nd Battalion on the Regular Establishment – was extended not only to the 1st Battalion but also to the war-raised 3rd and 4th Battalions in 1812. The award to the Ancient Irish Fencibles is unusual as fencible units were intended for home defence only; however, their terms and conditions of service must have allowed them to volunteer for overseas service. On 1 June 1847, a General Order authorized the issue of the Military General Service Medal, the first to be available to all ranks on application. Of the twenty-nine bars issued with the medal, the first was 'Egypt' with over fourteen hundred successfully claimed. It was well known that the then Duke of Wellington considered that the award of a battle honour should be linked to the issue of a medal or bar; this link was never established officially, although many battle honours are accompanied by the issue of a campaign or service medal.

Although the 1st Battalion of 39th Foot was the first British unit to serve in India, it was the 1st Battalion of 76th Foot that received the first award. On 20 October 1806, **Hindoostan**, the first theatre honour, was awarded for service in India between 1790 and 1805. The following year the badge of The Elephant was authorized as an enhancement, no doubt prompted by the award of **India**, with the badge of The Royal Tiger, to the 1st Battalion, 75th Foot. The award was further enhanced later with the badge of An Elephant with Howdah and Mahout, circumscribed 'Hindoostan', ensigned with the Imperial Crown taken into use by The Duke of Wellington's Regiment, the successor to 76th Foot, to retain the significance of the honour.

At the end of the Napoleonic Wars a large number of corps were disbanded, mainly between 1816 and 1821, and the Regular Establishment was reduced to three regiments of Household Cavalry, seventeen of cavalry, three of Foot Guards and ninety-five regiments of foot; in 1816 the Rifle Brigade was removed from its ranking of 95th Foot and constituted as a separate corps to remain permanently as the 'Left of the Line'.

By 1817 the battle honours system was becoming established, but there were no rules regarding the selection of actions or engagements to be considered suitable as battle honours nor the qualifications required by units to receive such distinctions. Some precedents were set which were used, but, since these were not binding, were not consistently applied. This resulted in a large number of anomalies. Battle honours could be awarded for a significant battle, which included sieges (but it had to be a manifest 'victory'), for a campaign, which had to be successful, or for distinguished service in a particular theatre of operations. These categories of award remained until the First World War. Awards could be retrospective or contemporary. Individual units were selected for the battle honour and, on disbandment, the distinction was not retained by the corps. Eligibility for selection was unrestricted and not limited by the strength of the unit present.

This system remained unchanged until 1832, when the eligibility for the award of a battle honour was reduced when 'Ubique' and 'Quo Fas et Gloria Ducunt' were taken into use by the Royal Regiment of Artillery and by the Corps of Royal Engineers. This distinction ('Everywhere' and 'Whither Right and Glory Lead') was intended as an all-inclusive honour to replace existing distinctions worn on appointments and to indicate participation in every campaign by units of these two arms. This was, at the time, a fashionable solution applied to larger corps with the potential to claim many battle honours. The Royal Marines had been rewarded similarly in 1827 with The Globe encircled within a Laurel Wreath as a distinctive badge and with the motto 'Per Mare per Terram' indicating their world-wide role and valour: the Corps would have qualified for over a hundred battle honours. The Royal Marines, nevertheless, were permitted to place their first battle honour – **Gibraltar** – on their appointments. From this time until awards for the Second Boer War were published, the eligibility for the award of battle honours was restricted to regiments of the Household Cavalry, cavalry, Foot Guards and infantry only.

Following an earlier decision that it was inappropriate for rifle regiments, because of their tactical employment, to carry Colours, Guidons were withdrawn from light cavalry regiments for similar reasons in 1834. Thereafter, the distinctions of these corps were placed on appointments only, primarily on drum banners or, as with 3rd King's Own Light Dragoons, which had no drum banners, inscribed on the silver kettle-drums.

Despite the adoption of 'Ubique' and 'Quo Fas et Gloria Ducunt' ten years earlier, the awards for the First China War included a unit of the Royal Artillery: **China**, with the badge of The Dragon, was worn on officers' appointments by such officers present during the campaign. This distinction was justified as 'personal awards' to the individuals and did not extend to the unit nor its non-commissioned ranks. This was exceptional, was not repeated and, in time, was allowed to lapse.

The first official award with a year-date – **Cabool 1842** – appeared on 20 March

1844. Adding year-dates to battle honours had been used in India by state forces for many years. As the number of battle honours awarded increased, some were becoming duplicated. For example, **St. Lucia** commemorated the capture of the island in both 1796 and 1803, and the addition of a year-date made identification of the award easier. Many existing battle honours had year-dates added as duplication became more evident, and by 1914 all amendments were completed. **New Zealand** alone currently remains undated and continues to cover three separate campaigns.

Also in 1844 the badges, mottos and battle honours of an infantry battalion, which until then could be emblazoned on either one or both Colours, were henceforth to appear on the Regimental Colour: the Queen's Colour was to carry at the centre the number of the regiment beneath the Crown only. Foot Guards, however, were subject to separate regulation and continued to emblazon on both Colours.

The 1850s saw the unlikely extension of battle honours to include yeomanry cavalry and militia units. These corps, unlike the fencibles, which were regarded as regular units, had been raised as part-time units during and after the French Revolutionary Wars for home defence only, and as such were considered unlikely to acquire battle honours. Nevertheless, **Fishguard**, a unique award to the Pembroke Yeomanry Cavalry, is the only battle honour for an action on mainland Britain. This distinction was followed by **Mediterranean** to some militia units embodied for garrison duties in the Mediterranean area during the Crimean War. These awards were well received by the general public, but the Army, which had considered battle honours to be the preserve of the Regular Establishment, thought that such awards to volunteer corps to be inappropriate and diminished the significance of their hard-won battle honours. Although all battle honours are considered to be equal, those awarded to volunteer units were viewed for some time as being of a slightly lower value to those carried by corps on the Regular Establishment. It took the First World War to remove this prejudice when many reserve and war-raised battalions qualified for more individual battle honours than the regular battalions of their corps.

By the end of the Indian Mutiny, with a large number of commitments to be met, mainly overseas, the Regular Establishment had increased to three regiments of Household Cavalry, twenty-five of cavalry, three of Foot Guards and one hundred and one of infantry. Between 1858 and 1861 the transfer of the Honourable East India Company's European regiments to the Crown added a further three cavalry and nine infantry corps. The cavalry regiments had no battle honours on transfer; the infantry regiments retained their distinctions on transfer, but not their seniority due to an old regulation, which set that date on joining the 'English Establishment'. Accordingly, the 1st Bombay Fusiliers, raised 1661 as the Bombay Regiment, became 103rd Foot.

In 1874 corps raised between 1823 and 1858 were permitted to inherit the battle honours of former regiments with the same number that had been disbanded. For example, 20th Hussars took into use **Vimiera** and **Peninsula** awarded to 20th (or Jamaica) Light Dragoons, disbanded 1819, and 96th Foot similarly gained **Egypt** and **Peninsula** from 96th (Queen's Own) Foot, disbanded 1818. In fact, the two battle honours inherited by 96th Foot had been awarded to The Queen's German Regiment and to its successor, the 1st Battalion of 97th Foot, which was renumbered 96th Foot in 1816. It could be argued, therefore, that 97th Foot, rather than 96th Foot, should have inherited the honours. Nevertheless, in this case succession was taken into account and the number of the regiment on disbandment, rather than the unit which had received the award, was taken for inheritance. But the following year the reverse view was taken when 100th Foot, not 99th Foot which it became in 1816, regained **Niagara**. Inconsistent application of precedent had produced a further anomaly.

The Army reorganization of 1881 fell largely on the infantry. By 1858 the senior twenty-five regiments had two regular battalions with the remainder having one battalion, except 60th Foot and the Rifle Brigade which each had four. The single battalion corps, except 79th Foot which continued with one battalion only until 1897, were amalgamated to form forty-one new corps, each of two regular battalions. All corps, less the Rifle Brigade which was unaffected, were given new 'territorial titles' and numbering was discontinued, at least officially. The distinctions of former corps were retained, and, where necessary combined, by the new corps. Each battalion was authorized, as in 1832, to emblazon or to place all the distinctions of the new corps on their Regimental Colour and/or appointments. Militia units, which had been associated with the former corps since 1874, were transferred to the new corps to form consecutively numbered battalions of that corps. For example, the Huntingdonshire Militia became the 5th (Militia) Battalion of The King's Royal Rifle Corps. The militia battalions retained their own distinctions, but did not qualify for the battle honours of their new corps. This ban extended to appointments, such as buttons and badges, if they displayed a corps distinction, but some corps incorporated the old militia badges into their new badges. For example, The Devonshire Regiment added the Castle of Exeter to its new badges and The Queen's Own (Royal West Kent Regiment) went a step further and adopted the old West Kent Militia's badge as the new corps cap badge. Volunteer Rifle Corps units, raised 1859–60, were also integrated into the new corps, except for Irish corps, as volunteer battalions, separately numbered 1st, 2nd and so on, but some, such as 9th Lanarkshire Volunteer Rifle Corps, retained their old titles until 1908. The volunteer battalions, as with the Militia, did not qualify for corps honours.

Such widespread reform, although necessary, was not popular at first, not only with the Regular Establishment, but also with the recently re-formed Volunteers, and it took many years and a world war to prove it a success. The continuing intransigence of the Army to allow the extension of distinctions to new members of their corps was short-sighted and divisive. It should have been clear from the Crimean War when militia units were embodied to relieve regular battalions for Russia and the manpower shortages in both the Ashanti War and the Zulu and Basuto Wars, that such reserves as were now available were not only necessary but essential. Unfortunately, instead of welcoming the new battalions, the Regular Establishment, with few exceptions, showed ill-concealed distaste for the new organization. On the other hand, the militia and volunteer battalions did little to add to the prestige of their new corps at this time, being largely understrength, poorly equipped and undertrained, but they were keen and, possibly more importantly, willing to learn.

One unforeseen result of this reorganization was an increased interest in battle honours by the new corps. Most distinctions emblazoned on Standards, Guidons and Colours or inscribed on appointments were for the years between the Seven Years War and the Zulu and Basuto Wars or for campaigns in India. Earlier wars had not been considered for battle honours. The recently restyled Bedfordshire Regiment, raised 1688, had seen extended service in Flanders and other hard campaigns, but had no battle honours at all. To resolve this, in 1881, the Alison Committee was convened to consider 'claims of Regiments to commemorate certain unrecorded victories', with reference to the campaigns of the Duke of Marlborough and the war against the French in America. Unfortunately, the Committee did not take the opportunity to set some rules for the selection or award of battle honours, but depended on established precedent. The Committee's report, published on 13 March 1882, recommended that the 'successes' – **Blenheim, Ramillies, Oudenarde, Malplaquet, Louisburg** and **Quebec 1759** – were 'to be inscribed on the Colours of such existing Regiments as represent Corps which were engaged in them'.

The pursuit of battle honours did not abate with the publication of the Alison Committee's Report and later that year further retrospective awards were made. The distinction, **South Africa**, which then commemorated three separate campaigns, was reviewed and in July revised awards were made with year-dates added to existing battle honours, including **Cape of Good Hope**, and a further theatre award of **South Africa 1835** was authorized. On 11 September 1882, **Dettingen**, fought on 27 June 1743 and the last battle in which a British monarch personally commanded in the field, was awarded to the surviving representative corps.

In 1886 when the awards for the Nile Campaign of 1884–85 were being considered, it was ruled that only regiments south of Assouan on or before 7 March 1885, in the expedition to relieve General Gordon, would qualify for such awards. This was the first time that the 'battlefield' was defined by what would become known later as 'geographical and chronological limits'.

It is now generally accepted that the Second Boer War was under-rewarded. The Commander-in-Chief, Field Marshal Lord Roberts, laid down that the battle honours awarded should be based on the bars issued with the Queen's South African Medal, 'provided always that the Headquarters and fifty per cent of the Regiment had been present'. Subsequently, it was concluded that twenty-six battle honours was excessive and six battle and one theatre honour only were approved. As previously in the Crimean War, the militia had been embodied, this time to serve in South Africa, to carry out garrison duties in the Mediterranean and to guard Boer prisoners of war on St. Helena. As a result, militia battalions which had served in South Africa qualified for the theatre honour, but **Mediterranean**, with appropriate year-dates, and **St. Helena**, again with appropriate year-dates, were awarded specifically to militia units for the last two tasks. The militia battalions added to the prestige of their corps in this war, with one example from among many: the 3rd Battalion, The Royal Scots were admired for their rapid marching over difficult country and were consequently nicknamed 'The Greyhounds'. Yeomanry regiments and volunteer battalions, under their terms and conditions of service, were unable to serve overseas without lengthy, complex legislation, but they raised companies from volunteers for the Imperial Yeomanry and as reinforcements for their regular battalions serving in South Africa. The fifty per cent ruling, if applied, would have disqualified from award all the Imperial Yeomanry and the volunteer battalions that had provided these sub-units. To overcome this, it was laid down that the theatre honour, with appropriate year-dates, would be awarded to those 'Corps which had furnished parties of 20 or over for service in South Africa'. The final list of awards was published in Special Army Order 3/1905 under four headings: Regular, Militia, Imperial Yeomanry and Volunteer.

The Territorial Force, which was formed on 1 April 1908, was found by the Imperial Yeomanry, now reverted to its former title of Yeomanry, forming fourteen regionally-based mounted brigades and by the volunteer battalions becoming consecutively numbered Territorial Force battalions of their existing corps. In addition, five new Territorial Force infantry regiments, four cyclist battalions and two Officer Training Corps units were established. The Force, which excluded Ireland, was primarily for home defence, but could volunteer for service outside the United Kingdom in a national emergency. In addition to the mounted brigades, the Territorial Force was organized into fourteen peacetime, regionally-based infantry divisions, complete with artillery, engineers and services, with the remaining units retained as Army Troops under War Office control.

A Special Reserve, which included Ireland, was also formed and could serve overseas if mobilized: it was made up of three regiments of horse, transferred from the Yeomanry and by forming reserve battalions within the corps from militia battalions, with the surplus militia battalions being disbanded. Again distinctions were retained on transfer, but corps battle honours remained with the regular battalions.

Together with the increases made between 1900 and 1908, the Regular Establishment, and by including reserves, had expanded to three regiments of Household Cavalry, twenty-eight of cavalry, three of cavalry Special Reserve, fifty-five of yeomanry, four of Foot Guards, seventy-five of infantry, four cyclist Battalions and two Officer Training Corps units, totalling eighty-nine mounted regiments, nine battalions of Foot Guards and four hundred and sixty infantry battalions: the Channel Islands Militia added a further five battalions of light infantry.

Following the Second Boer War, a Standing War Office Committee was set up to consider and to advise on matters relating to all honorary distinctions, including the selection and award of battle honours. This Committee's first task was to review the battle honours awarded for the late war, but no changes were made. The Committee, however, added year-dates to Ghuznee and Candahar, extended **Corunna** to three further corps, **Gibraltar** to the Highland Light Infantry and awarded **Sierra Leone 1898–99** and **Ashanti 1900** to the West Africa Regiment.

Nevertheless, the increasing number of claims from regiments made it necessary for the Committee to meet again in 1909, under the chairmanship of the then Adjutant-General, to examine such retrospective claims. The Ewart Committee, as it became known, applied two criteria to the selection and award of new battle honours – that the headquarters and fifty per cent of the regiment was present and that surviving regiments in direct succession only of the corps engaged should be considered for the awards. These two principles disqualified many corps and the Committee did not comply fully with its own rules: indeed, in some cases, it resorted to a precedent. The Committee's wide-ranging findings were promulgated in a series of Army Orders in 1909 and 1910. **Egypt 1882** was extended to include the recently formed 8th Battalion, The London Regiment (Post Office Rifles) for providing parties as reinforcements to cable and telegraph companies – the first award to a Territorial Force unit. **Warburg** was awarded to commemorate cavalry participation in the Seven Years War; **Tangier**, with appropriate year-dates, was awarded to record the standing army's earliest battle honour and reset the starting point for such distinctions. This was later confirmed when a claim for 'Dunbar 1650' on behalf of Monck's Foot by the Coldstream Guards was refused and was considered by some as mischievous, and the award of **Gibraltar 1704–05** added the appropriate year-dates to **Gibraltar**, previously awarded 1784 and 1908. Two further cavalry awards – **Beaumont** and **Willems** – followed. The long neglected West Indies campaigns of the eighteenth and the early nineteenth century were reviewed: the awards of **Guadaloupe 1759, Martinique 1762, Martinique 1794** and **St. Lucia** 1778 added appropriate year-dates to similarly named battle honours awarded previously in 1817, 1816, 1818 and 1825. **Havannah** was awarded to complement **Moro**, awarded previously in 1827. Service as marine detachments was recognized by the award of **The**

Saints and **The Glorious First of June**, each awarded with the badge of A Naval Crown, superscribed with the appropriate date. The battle honour selected by this Committee to commemorate the War of the Grand Alliance was **Namur 1695**. The recently awarded **Louisburg** was extended to include The Duke of Edinburgh's (Wiltshire Regiment), which as 62nd Foot had served as marine detachments during the expedition, but did not include the badge of A Naval Crown since it was not a sea battle. Finally, **Busaco, Fuentes d'Oñor, Pyrenees** and **Nive** were extended to include several corps, which had been overlooked previously.

In 1910 all corps distinctions were extended to include special reserve battalions, but, possibly reflecting the Regular Establishment's view of past awards to volunteer corps, the militia battle honours were not retained, and allowed to lapse. **South Africa** being an existing corps honour survived, while sadly **Mediterranean**, with or without appropriate year-dates, and **St. Helena** were 'lost'.

The last battle honours awarded before the First World War were **North America 1763–64** and the appropriate year-dates added to **Pekin, Delhi, Afghanistan** and **Ashantee**; however, it was not until after the war that these appeared in the Army Lists.

In August 1914 the United Kingdom entered the First World War and, as before, 'the Army crossed into Flanders and swore horribly'. Nevertheless, the final awards, to date, for the period before The Great War were approved in 1923 with **Somaliland 1901–04** to The King's African Rifles and in 1951 **Salamanca** was extended to include four further corps: the badge of A Naval Crown, superscribed '2nd April 1801' was added to enhance **Copenhagen**, previously awarded 1819 and 1821: a year-date only, not A Naval Crown, was added to **St. Vincent** and **Belleisle**, captured on 7 June 1761, was awarded to eight surviving corps – a reward for persistence.

India

There were Standing Armies in India before the English and other Europeans came to the subcontinent. These belonged to the Indian princes, who were feudal rulers of independent states, which later became bound to British India by treaty. Some units within these armies, later called Indian State Forces, carried Colours on which were emblazoned battle honours, some dating from the fourteenth century. As these distinctions were not awarded by the British nor, as yet, recognized by the present Governments of India and Pakistan on the integration of these forces into their Regular Establishments, the awards are not considered to be 'official' and hence are not included in this section.

Until 1 November 1858 India was administered by the Honourable East India Company, which gradually changed from a trading company into virtually a sovereign state with the rights of such a state: it could raise and maintain armies, make war, conclude treaties and award distinctions without first seeking the approval of the Crown. The Company was organized into three Presidencies – Bengal, Madras and Bombay – each with a separate Army controlled by the Governor General of Bengal and by the Governors of Madras and Bombay, respectively. These Armies started as armed guards, mainly European supported by 'Natives', to protect the trading posts; but in 1668 Bombay was leased to the East India Company and the small garrison raised by Charles II in 1661 became the European Bombay Regiment. Commercial rivalry with France was replaced by serious conflict when the War of Austrian Succession in Europe spread to India in 1744 and continued intermittently until the capture of Pondicherry in 1793 ended all French influence in India. This series of wars required the Company to increase the size of its Armies rapidly. A large number of Native, and a limited number of European, units were raised, or brought into service from allied Indian rulers, as required, during this period. This expansion resulted, in 1796, in the reconstruction of the Armies with the formation of consecutively numbered cavalry and infantry corps, the latter with two battalions. Gradually, each cavalry regiment and each infantry battalion had a Regimental Standard or Colour presented by the East India Company. By 1800 the Bengal Army Establishment was six regiments of cavalry, all Native, fourteen of infantry, two European, with artillery and pioneers; the Madras Army Establishment was six regiments of cavalry, again all Native, sixteen of infantry, one battalion only was European, with artillery and pioneers; the Bombay Army Establishment was eight infantry regiments only, again one battalion was European, supported by artillery and pioneers, cavalry being supplied by allied Indian states.

During the wars against the French and their allies the East India Company started to present Honorary Standards to selected units, usually with an inscription in English and the local language, for some distinguished service, to commemorate a victory or a successful campaign. The 10th Carnatic Battalion received such an Honorary Standard for the defence of Amboor, which was later enhanced by the badge of A Rock Fort worn on appointments; however, when 10th Madras Infantry was disbanded in 1891, the battle honour was not retained by its successor, 1st Burma Battalion, recruited mainly from Gurkhas, as it was thought to be inappropriate for a Nepalese recruited unit to carry early Carnatic battle honours. Nevertheless, with a change of attitude the award was revived and all the battle honours of 10th Madras Infantry were taken into use in 1988 by 10th Princess Mary's Own Gurkha Rifles. Other Honorary Standards were presented for **Sholinghur** to 21st Carnatic Battalion: with the badge of An Embroidered Star and the motto 'Lake and Victory' to the 1st and 2nd Battalions of the 15th Bengal Native Infantry for services under General Gerard Lake in the Deccan; for **Assaye** to commemorate Sir Arthur Wellesley's decisive victory on 23 September 1803 and for **Kelat-i-Ghilzie**, again for the defence of a fort, during the First Afghan War. The last Honorary Standards were presented for service in Scinde in 1843. Later, named awards were made in English, often with some variation in spelling and emblazoned on the Regimental Standard or Colour and/or placed on appointments.

The first overseas campaign battle honour was published on 12 April 1803 when **Egypt**, without the badge of The Sphinx – extended to include Indian corps on 20 May 1823 – was awarded to units of the Bengal, Madras and Bombay Armies for service under Major-General David Baird. This distinction is unique as it is the only pre-Mutiny battle honour approved by the Crown and followed the British Army convention, which was subsequently taken into use by the Company, of making the award to the battalions present at the engagement and not to the corps.

By 1824 the increased size of the territories then administered by the Company, together with the formation of 'irregular' or auxiliary units to provide the necessary additional forces, required a further reorganization of the Armies. In the infantry the two-battalion system from the previous reorganization was replaced by single-battalion corps, with each existing battalion forming a new corps. Distinctions received by former battalions were retained and transferred to the new corps: thereafter, all battle honours were considered as awards to the corps. The Bengal Army Establishment was set at eight regiments of light cavalry, with five of irregular or local horse, all Native, seventy of infantry, two European, fifteen local battalions with increased artillery, pioneers and a recently raised Corps of Sappers and Miners. Also included in this establishment was the Hyderabad Contingent, an auxiliary force of cavalry, infantry and artillery, provided by the Nizam; the Madras Army consisted of eight regiments of Native light cavalry, fifty-three of infantry, one European with two battalions, three local battalions with increased artillery, pioneers and a Corps of Sappers and Miners; the Bombay Army consisted of three regiments of light cavalry, one of irregular horse, twenty-seven of infantry, one European with two battalions and one Native marine battalion, supported by artillery and one company of sappers and miners.

The first battle honours awarded to local units were **Arracan** to Gardner's Horse and **Bhurtpore**, which was extended to two regiments of Skinner's Horse in 1826. The latter distinction was further extended to include Gurkha regiments in 1859 and 1874.

Following the awards for the First Burma War and for the capture of Bhurtpore in 1826, the Bengal Army reviewed previous campaigns and awarded a series of selected, retrospective battle honours to surviving corps in 1829. **Plassey**, fought on 23 June 1757, set the starting point for Indian battle honours and with **Buxar** commemorated the Bengal Wars: **Guzerat** recorded the First Mahratta War; **Carnatic** and **Mysore** were awarded for the Second and the Third Mysore Wars and **Seringapatam** for the Fourth; **Allyghur**, **Delhi**, **Leswarree** and **Deig** were approved for the Second Mahratta War, together with **Java** for the war against the Dutch during the Napoleonic Wars.

Cochin, awarded to 33rd Madras Native Infantry in 1840, was for a brief, little-known but hard-fought campaign. When the corps was disbanded in 1891, the battle honour was renounced by its successor, 3rd Burma Battalion, recruited in the Punjab; however, in 1930 the award was successfully reclaimed by 8th Punjab Regiment.

Reacting to the results of the Bengal Army's review, 1st European Madras Regiment in 1841 successfully claimed **Arcot** – resetting the earliest battle honour to 1751 – **Plassey** with the badge of The Royal Tiger and with the motto 'Spectamur Agendo', **Condore**, **Wandiwash**, **Pondicherry**, **Nundy Droog**, **Amboyna**, **Banda** and **Ternate**. Strangely, apart from **Sholinghur** and **Ava**, which were also awarded, no other Madras regiments were included in any of these awards and, although many were engaged in these actions, their presence remains unrecognized.

On 6 November 1844, **Plassey** and **Buxar** with the badge of The Royal Tiger, **Carnatic** and **Mysore** with the badge of The Elephant and **Guzerat** were extended to include 1st European Bombay Fusiliers.

After the First Sikh War the Company's influence extended into the Punjab, where the defence of the North-West Frontier required further units to be raised locally. The first was the Corps of Guides, Cavalry and Infantry, raised 1846, followed by a Frontier Brigade of five regiments of Punjab cavalry, four of local Sikh infantry and six of Punjab infantry, supported by three mountain batteries. In 1851 this Brigade was restyled the Punjab Irregular Force.

The last battle honours awarded by the East India Company were **Reshire**, **Koosh-ab** and **Persia** in 1858 for operations in the Persian Gulf.

Mutiny was not unknown in India before 1857, but the Company was unprepared for the scale of the Indian (or Great) Mutiny when most of the Bengal Army mutinied. The level of European troops serving in the sub-continent had been reduced by the Crimean War, but fortunately the Madras and the Bombay Armies remained loyal. With these Armies, the rapidly reinforced British garrisons, the loyal remnant of the Bengal Army, the Hyderabad Contingent, the Punjab Irregular Force and newly-raised local units, mainly from the Punjab, the mutiny was successfully put down. On 1 November

1858 the administration of India passed to the Crown, and with this change came a reorganization of the former Company forces. Between 1858 and 1861 all European corps were transferred to the British Army. Distinctions were retained on transfer, except for the artillery whose battle honours lapsed on joining the Royal Artillery. All the mutinous units were disbanded, with all honours and distinctions forfeited: **Korah**, **Allyghur** and **Assam** were 'lost', although **Allyghur** was later reintroduced into the British Army in 1886.

The Bengal Army was reformed in 1861 with nineteen regiments of cavalry, a Corps of Sappers and Miners, forty-four regiments of infantry and four of Gurkhas, now separately numbered. The Madras Army Establishment was four regiments of light cavalry, one Corps of Sappers and Miners and fifty-two regiments of infantry. The Bombay Army Establishment was seven regiments of cavalry, two mountain batteries, one Corps of Sappers and Miners and thirty-one regiments of infantry. The Punjab Irregular Force, soon to be restyled the Punjab Frontier Force, except for the addition of one Gurkha regiment, remained unchanged. The Hyderabad Contingent, now under the control of the Government of India, consisted of four regiments of cavalry, four field batteries and six regiments of infantry. Gradually, new Colours, based on the British Army pattern and presented by the Crown, were to replace the old Company Colours, and a Queen's Colour was introduced for infantry corps.

In 1864 the loyalty of the Hyderabad Contingent was rewarded with retrospective awards for the actions at **Nagpore, Maheidpoor** and **Nowah** during the Third Mahratta (and Pindari) War. These first battle honours were followed by **Central India** in 1866, which was extended to units of the Hyderabad Contingent Artillery in 1878. The last awards confirmed that Indian batteries, unlike their British counterparts, would continue to qualify for the award of battle honours.

After the post-Mutiny reorganization, the basic structure of the Indian Army remained largely unchanged until 1895, when the old Presidency Armies were abolished, with corps retaining their separate identities and distinctions. However, following the Mutiny there was an increasing preference for recruiting from the 'martial races' from Northern India, with the Bengal Army adding a large number of Gurkhas and Garhwalis to its ranks and the Madras and the Bombay corps being filled with Punjabis, Pathans and Baluchis. These changes were soon to be reflected in the description of units and after 1885 the style 'Native' was removed from the titles of all infantry corps.

In 1897 the awards for the Chitral Campaign included for the first time units of the Imperial Service Troops of the Indian State Forces. These units had been formed in 1888, following the threat of war with Russia in 1885, by the rulers of the Native Feudatory States bound by treaty to British India to contribute towards the defence of the sub-continent. These units provided valuable service in an increasing number of frontier and overseas campaigns. The award of **Chitral** and **Defence of Chitral** was soon followed by further battle honours, including **China 1900**.

On 2 October 1903, Field Marshal Lord Kitchener's reorganization of the Indian Army was published in India Army Order 181. The last traces of the Honourable East India Company's Armies were removed by renumbering and by changing unit titles. In addition to the three Body-Guards, which remained unchanged, the new Indian cavalry formed thirty-eight consecutively numbered regiments: the Native Mountain Batteries and the Corps of Sappers and Miners were also renumbered. The new Indian infantry formed one one hundred and thirteen consecutively numbered, single-battalion corps, drawn from the Bengal Infantry, including local infantry and Irregular Force battalions, from the former Punjab Frontier Force, now restyled the Frontier Force, from the Madras Infantry, from the Hyderabad Contingent Infantry and from the Bombay Infantry. Ten Gurkha regiments were taken out of the line and numbered separately. The Queen's Own Corps of Guides remained unchanged. All honours and distinctions were retained by the new corps.

The first, and only, battle honour awarded to the newly renumbered corps was **British East Africa 1901** to 116th Mahrattas, late 16th Bombay Infantry, in 1905.

In 1911 the spelling of fourteen battle honours was changed to conform with the spellings in use with the British Army. It is difficult to see why this was thought necessary as eleven of these distinctions had been awarded by the East India Company before 1858. Nevertheless, the revised spellings were taken into use – some by former European regiments now serving in the British Army – to the dismay of the many corps concerned, including 12th Pioneers, which had to change its title to conform. Appropriate year-dates were added to **Pekin, Delhi** and **Affghanistan** immediately before the First World War, but, as with the British Army, these did not appear in Army Lists until after the war.

In 1932 **Somaliland 1901–04** was approved for units which had taken part in operations against the 'Mad Mullah'.

When new Colours were authorized in 1955, it was directed that the battle honours on the former Colours were to be emblazoned on the new Colours, except for such battle honours that were considered to be 'particularly repugnant to the national sentiments'. This directive was received with little enthusiasm, especially by the regiments and corps which had long histories of service in India and overseas, albeit under British command, and it was virtually ignored. It was felt by Regimental Colonels and Commanding Officers that the politicians were 'trying to rewrite history' and that they took little account of the strong regimental pride in their traditions and distinctions. The directive was repeated in 1958, again with little effect. Consequently, all surviving Indian Army battle honours, except for the most recent awards made by the President, were reviewed by a Ministry of Defence Committee. The report of this Committee was published in 1966 and Army Order 405 listed all the battle honours considered to be 'non-repugnant': only thirty-eight pre-1914 awards were so classified. Henceforth these honours only were to be emblazoned on Standards, Guidons and Colours or worn on appointments. This controversial order was made more unpalatable by being badly drafted, adding to the resentment felt by regiments and corps that the review had been given only scant attention by the Committee. Strangely, the repugnant battle honours were not withdrawn, but would continue to be recorded in the Army Lists. Orders for the emblazonment of Second World War and subsequent battle honours, all of which were considered non-repugnant, were soon published separately. Broadly, these set no limits on the number of battle honours to be emblazoned, but theatre honours were no longer to be carried nor worn on appointments.

Australia

On 1 January 1901 the Federal Commonwealth of Australia was formed by the six colonies of New South Wales, Queensland, Victoria, South Australia, Tasmania and Western Australia, each of which maintained a small force of volunteers or militia. From 1 March all existing forces of the former colonies were unified, for home defence, under the control of the Federal Department of Defence. The Defence Act of 1903 re-organized these forces into regiments of light horse, infantry and other corps and departments, with compulsory registration for service within Australia of all males between the ages of 18 and 60 in time of war.

Encouraged by the 'parties of 20 or over' ruling for South Africa, **Suakin 1885** was successfully claimed on behalf of corps of New South Wales Infantry, which had provided volunteers for the New South Wales Military Contingent in the Second Suakin Expedition during the First Sudan War. The award was published in Military Order 196 of 1907. The distinction was immediately taken into use by 1st, 2nd and 3rd Australian Infantry Regiments as successor corps.

The former colonies, and after 1901, the Commonwealth, sent a total of fifty-seven units to serve in the Second Boer War. Military Order 123 of 1908 awarded **South Africa**, with appropriate year-dates, to the former colonial volunteer and militia units, which had provided volunteers. These awards were also immediately taken into use by successor corps.

Following the introduction of compulsory military training in 1909, a report by Field Marshal Lord Kitchener was placed before the Federal Parliament in 1910 recommending the formation of a small Permanent Force, made up of staff, artillery, engineers and services, with a volunteer, part-time 'citizen army' for home defence. Accordingly, in 1912 the Citizen Military Forces came into being with an establishment of twenty-nine light horse regiments and ninety-three infantry battalions to be found, where possible, from existing units. Nevertheless, during 1913 and 1914 new infantry battalions had to be raised to fill some of the vacancies in the establishment, but the process was incomplete by the outbreak of the First World War. New Guidons and Colours were authorized, including rifle regiments, and battle honours were retained, and even extended where units were divided to form cadres for new corps. **Suakin 1885** was extended to five new successor corps and **South Africa**, with appropriate year-dates, was authorized for twenty light horse regiments and for thirty-six infantry battalions. However, this reorganization was short-lived and did not survive the First World War.

Canada

On 10 February 1763, under the terms of the Treaty of Paris, France renounced all claims to Canada, Nova Scotia and the St. Lawrence River Islands, ending a colonial rivalry which, at times, had led to a series of wars, reflecting the European hostilities, between the French and British settlers. During these wars both sides relied largely on local volunteer or militia forces, supported by a small number of French and British garrisons and a large number of Indian allies. The withdrawal of the French garrisons reduced the troop levels, which were not fully replaced by the British Government, but the local militia forces proved effective in countering American incursions into Canada in 1775–76 and 1812 and dealing with rebellions in both Upper and Lower Canada in 1837–38.

When Upper and Lower Canada were united in 1840, it has been estimated that the Militia numbered some four hundred and twenty-six corps, with universal male liability for service: however, as they mustered for inspection for one day only each year, it is not surprising that the Militia fell into neglect. Further British troop reductions for the Crimean War, resulted in the 1855 Militia Act, which created an active militia of five thousand volunteers, paid for ten days training each year; this proved so popular that a further unpaid category was formed the following year. In 1863 more reforms were introduced, the active militia became unpaid, the volunteer militia, previously set at thirty thousand men, was increased by five thousand and in emergencies militia units could be embodied to operate in their local areas, whereas special units were to be raised from militiamen for service within Canada. Several active and volunteer militia units were successfully mobilized under this legislation for the Fenian raids of 1866.

On 1 July 1867 the Dominion of Canada was created by the union of the Provinces of New Brunswick, Nova Scotia, Quebec and Ontario; by 1905 these provinces had been joined by Manitoba, Saskatchewan, Alberta and British Columbia.

Despite its long history, the first militia battle honour was not awarded until 1870 when **Eccles Hill** was granted to the Missisquoi Battalion for an engagement during the Fenian raids of 1870. The following year the distinction was extended to the Victoria Volunteer Rifles of Montreal, later the Victoria Rifles of Canada; **Trout River** was awarded to the Huntingdon Borderers, later 50th Regiment, Huntingdon and Hemmingford Rangers, for the same campaign in 1879.

In 1883 a small Permanent Force, raised as the Cavalry School Corps, later the Royal Canadian Dragoons, and as the Infantry School Corps, later the Royal Canadian Regiment, was added to the Canadian military establishment. These two corps, together with several mobilized militia battalions, were soon involved in putting down Riel's Rebellion in 1885. The initial immediate award for the campaign was **Batoche** to the Royal Grenadiers only in 1885; by 1906 **Saskatchewan** was approved for the Royal Canadian Regiment and a theatre award – **North-West Canada 1885** – was granted to the Royal Canadian Dragoons and to the Royal Canadian Regiment.

Despite a lack of popular support, over six thousand Canadian volunteers served in South Africa during the Second Boer War. In 1906, **Paardeberg** and **South Africa 1899–1900** were awarded to the Royal Canadian Regiment for its 2nd (Special Service) Battalion, formed from militia volunteers. In addition, the Royal Canadian Dragoons received the award of **South Africa 1900**.

In 1914 successful claims for retrospective awards for Riel's Rebellion were made: **Fish Creek** was authorized and **North-West Canada 1885** was extended to include a further eighteen militia corps. Claims for the Second Boer War were also successful with Lord Strathcona's Horse (Royal Canadians), which had been placed on the Permanent Force establishment in 1901, awarded **South Africa 1900–01** and **South Africa**, with appropriate year-dates, was approved for twenty-seven militia regiments.

Immediately before the outbreak of the First World War the Canadian military forces consisted of a Permanent Force of two cavalry regiments and one infantry corps of one battalion, supported by artillery, engineers and services: the militia, mostly under-strength, of The Governor General's Body Guard and thirty-five consecutively numbered cavalry regiments: The Governor General's Foot Guards, one hundred and two consecutively numbered, single-battalion infantry corps, with supporting artillery, engineers and Services. Each cavalry regiment carried an appropriate Standard or Guidon, except Lord Strathcona's Horse (Royal Canadians) and hussar regiments, and all infantry battalions had a King's Colour and a Regimental Colour, except rifle regiments, which had no Colours.

New Zealand

The Treaty of Waitangi in 1840 promised a large number of Maori chiefs the protection of the Crown and the installation of a British administration, but a differing interpretation of landownership led to Maori discontent, which, in turn, developed into a number of small-scale wars in North Island between 1843 and 1872. The limited British garrisons, reinforced by troops from the Australian garrisons and naval landing parties as required, initially managed to contain the uprisings; however, in time as conflict became more widespread, local forces were raised from existing settlers, forming volunteer units of cavalry and rifle corps. Although a militia was established in 1845, volunteer units, whose members were exempt from militia service, remained the backbone of New Zealand's military forces during this period. A Permanent Force of the New Zealand Armed Constabulary was created in 1867, before the last British troops were withdrawn in 1870, which recruited largely from former volunteers. The threat of war with, and possible invasion by Russia in 1885, led to the formation of the Permanent Militia, a small Regular Army which included the Armed Constabulary, and an increase in the number of volunteer units.

The New Zealand Volunteer Force sent ten contingents of mounted rifles for service in South Africa during the Second Boer War, where it was reported that 'it would hardly be an exaggeration to say that, after they had a little experience, the New Zealanders were by general consent regarded as the best mounted troops in South Africa.' Also, the last recorded shots of the war were fired by two officers of the Ninth Contingent. **South Africa**, with appropriate year-dates, was awarded by General Order 163 to fourteen regiments of mounted rifle volunteers and to eleven battalions of infantry or rifle volunteers in 1907.

New Zealand became a self-governing Dominion in 1907 and the new Government had to consider a revision of national defence. Since 1903 the Permanent Militia, now restyled the New Zealand Permanent Force, had been reduced, for financial reasons, to a small staff and garrison artillery for port defence. Following a review by the seemingly ubiquitous Field Marshal Lord Kitchener in 1910, the Permanent Force was augmented by a part-time Territorial Force of 20,000 men aged from 18 to 25 years, formed, where possible, from existing volunteer force units. To administer this new Force, which was intended for home defence, four Military Districts – Auckland, Canterbury, Otago and Wellington – were established, each with three mounted rifle and four infantry corps. Guidons and Colours were authorized for all units and battle honours were retained on transfer.

Since 1861, when the first colour was presented on behalf of the ladies of the District, the Taranaki Rifle Volunteers had claimed 'Waireka' and 'Mahoetahi', actions during the Second Maori (or First Taranaki) War, as battle honours. These claims had never been recognized; nevertheless, when the first official Colours were presented to The Taranaki Regiment in March 1936, the Regimental Colour was emblazoned with, in addition to **South Africa 1902**, the battle honour **New Zealand** to commemorate these engagements.

South Africa

Before the construction of the Suez Canal, the strategic position of the Cape on the sea-route to India made British occupation inevitable. Following a temporary occupation between 1795 and 1803, a second expeditionary force under General Sir David Baird recaptured the Dutch colony in January 1806, which was officially ceded to Britain by the Netherlands at the end of the Napoleonic Wars in 1815. The small Dutch garrisons were replaced by British troops, the Dutch East India Company's militia and commandos were retained and the recruiting of local forces gradually increased. The early settlers, both Dutch and British, were constantly threatened by native tribes, particularly on the extending eastern frontiers of the new colony. Nine Kaffir (or Cape Frontier) Wars took place between 1779 and 1878, with further peripheral operations until 1897. Differences between the Boers and British led to conflicts in Natal, Griqualand West, the Orange Free State and the Transvaal between 1842 and 1902, and to wars between the British and the Basutos and the Zulus from 1852 until 1879.

Until recently it was believed that the award of **Cape of Good Hope** to the Cape Mounted Rifles in 1841 was the first South African battle honour; however, recent research has shown that this corps, although raised locally, was on the British Army's Regular Establishment until 1870. It was, therefore, not until 9 February 1900 that the first battle honour – **South Africa 1879** – was awarded to four mounted regiments of the Natal Militia Corps and later extended to include the Durban Light Infantry.

All Cape and Natal military forces were mobilized, followed by the raising of a large number of local units, for the Second Boer War. In 1907, because of the sensitive post-war conditions, it was the British Government, with the approval of the Crown, which made direct awards to the Cape and Natal corps for their services during the late war. Surprisingly, none of the loyal commandos nor the many locally war-raised units, by then disbanded, were included in the list.

On 22 September 1908, **Natal 1906** was awarded to eight Natal militia regiments, which 'took part in the suppression of the Native Rebellion, 1906'.

The four colonies of the Cape, Natal, Transvaal and Orange River formed the Union of South Africa on 31 May 1910 and the South African military forces were re-organized by the Defence Act of 1912. By this, a small Permanent Force of five mounted rifle regiments, with an attached artillery brigade, and a part-time Active Citizen Force of twenty mounted rifle regiments, with four independent mounted rifle squadrons, fourteen dismounted rifle regiments, with four independent dismounted rifle squadrons, twelve infantry regiments with artillery, engineers and services was established. The new establishment was to be found, where possible, from former colonial corps and new units to be recruited to meet the shortfall: all distinctions were to be retained on transfer and Guidons and Colours were authorized.

The transfer of battle honours presented some difficulties for the new administration since, except for the Second Boer War, distinctions had been awarded officially to former Natal Militia Corps only. In the past, to correct this oversight, it had become the custom and practice for other corps to select and emblazon their own honours. This situation remained unresolved by the outbreak of the First World War and regiments and corps continued to emblazon both authorized and self-awarded battle honours on their Guidons and Regimental Colours until 1948. This was famously exploited by the Imperial Light Horse, which had been raised in 1899, predominantly from Uitlander (that is, non-Boer) refugees from Johannesburg, and disbanded in 1902, but reformed in 1913 as 5th Mounted Rifles. This unit should have qualified retrospectively for official Second Boer War and Natal Rebellion battle honours, but, being based in Johannesburg in the former Boer colony, without a militia organization, none was awarded. The regiment, therefore, awarded itself 'Elandslaagte', 'Siege of Ladysmith', 'Anglo-Boer War 1899–1902' and 'Native Rebellion 1906', which remained until **Defence of Ladysmith, Relief of Ladysmith, South Africa 1899–1902** and **Natal 1906** were officially substituted in 1948.

In 1965, a South African Battle Honour Committee reviewed the early colonial campaigns and approved the awards of **Umzintzani, Gaika-Gcaleka,** with appropriate year-dates, **Griqualand West 1878, Transkei,** with appropriate year-dates, **Basutoland 1880–81** and **Bechuanaland,** with appropriate year-dates, to successor regiments of the corps engaged in these campaigns.

Battle Honours

The complete list of battle honours before The Great War is shown in Table 1.

Table 1

BATTLE HONOURS BEFORE THE GREAT WAR

1.	**EMSDORFF** 16th July 1760 Seven Years War 1756–63	1766	15th (or King's) Regiment of (Light) Dragoons
2.	**AMBOOR** [1] 10th November–6th December 1767 First Mysore War 1766–69	?	10th Carnatic Battalion [1] Awarded as AMBOOR: the badge of A Rock Fort taken into use 1872.
3.	**SHOLINGHUR** [1] 27th September 1781 Second Mysore War 1780–84	1781 1841 1889 1889	21st Carnatic Battalion 1st European Madras Regiment The Highland Light Infantry; The Royal Munster Fusiliers The 2nd Madras Lancers: The Madras Sappers and Miners (Queen's Own); The 3rd Regiment of Madras Infantry; The 4th Regiment of Madras Infantry; The 5th Regiment of Madras Infantry; The 6th Regiment of Madras Infantry; The 8th Regiment of Madras Infantry; The 9th Regiment of Madras Infantry; The 12th Regiment of Madras Infantry; The 13th Regiment of Madras Infantry; The 14th Regiment of Madras Infantry; The 15th Regiment of Madras Infantry; The 16th Regiment of Madras Infantry; The 17th Regiment of Madras Infantry; The 19th Regiment of Madras Infantry [1] Award considered repugnant to Indian units 1966.
4.	**GIBRALTAR 1779–83** [1] 21st June 1779–6th February 1783 War against France and Spain 1778–83	1784	1st Battalion, 12th (or East Suffolk) Regiment of Foot: 1st Battalion, 39th (or East Middlesex) Regiment of Foot: 1st Battalion, 56th (or West Essex) Regiment of Foot: 1st Battalion, 58th (or Rutlandshire) Regiment of Foot [1] Awarded as GIBRALTAR: the badge of The Castle and Key and with the motto "Montis Insignia Calpe" taken into use 1836: year-dates added 1909.
5.	**MINDEN** 1st August 1759 Seven Years War 1756–63	1801	1st Battalion, 12th (East Suffolk) Regiment of Foot: 2nd Battalion, 20th (East Devonshire) Regiment of Foot: 1st Battalion, 23rd (Royal Welch Fusiliers) Regiment of Foot: 1st Battalion, 25th (Sussex) Regiment of Foot: 1st Battalion, 37th (North Hampshire) Regiment of Foot: 1st Battalion, 51st (2nd Yorkshire, West Riding) Regiment of Foot
6.	**EGYPT** [1] [2] 8th March–26th August 1801 French Revolutionary Wars 1793–1802	1802	11th Regiment of (Light) Dragoons: 12th (Prince of Wales's) Regiment of (Light) Dragoons: 26th Regiment of (Light) Dragoons: 1st Battalion, Coldstream Regiment of Foot Guards: 1st Battalion, Third Regiment of Foot Guards: 2nd Battalion, 1st (Royal) Regiment of Foot: 1st Battalion, 2nd (Queen's Royal) Regiment of Foot: 1st Battalion, 8th (King's) Regiment of Foot: 1st Battalion, 10th (North Lincolnshire) Regiment of Foot: 1st Battalion, 13th (1st Somersetshire) Regiment of Foot: 1st Battalion, 18th (Royal Irish) Regiment of Foot: 1st Battalion, 20th (East Devonshire) Regiment of Foot: 2nd Battalion, 20th (East Devonshire) Regiment of Foot: 1st Battalion, 23rd (Royal Welch Fusiliers) Regiment of Foot: 1st Battalion, 24th (2nd Warwickshire) Regiment of Foot: 1st Battalion, 25th (Sussex) Regiment of Foot: 1st Battalion, 26th (Cameronian) Regiment of Foot: 1st Battalion, 27th (Inniskilling) Regiment of Foot: 2nd Battalion, 27th (Inniskilling) Regiment of Foot: 1st Battalion, 28th (North Gloucestershire) Regiment of Foot: 1st Battalion, 30th (1st Cambridgeshire) Regiment of Foot: 1st Battalion, 40th (2nd Somersetshire) Regiment of Foot: 2nd Battalion, 40th (2nd Somersetshire) Regiment of Foot: 1st Battalion, 42nd (Royal

Highland) Regiment of Foot: 1st Battalion, 44th (East Essex) Regiment of Foot: 1st Battalion, 50th (West Kent) Regiment of Foot: 1st Battalion, 54th (West Norfolk) Regiment of Foot: 2nd Battalion, 54th (West Norfolk) Regiment of Foot: 1st Battalion, 58th (Rutlandshire) Regiment of Foot: 1st Battalion, 61st (South Gloucestershire) Regiment of Foot: 1st Battalion, 79th (Cameronian Volunteers) Regiment of Foot: 1st Battalion, 80th (Staffordshire Volunteers) Regiment of Foot: 1st Battalion, 86th Regiment of Foot: 1st Battalion, 88th (Connaught Rangers) Regiment of Foot: 1st Battalion, 89th Regiment of Foot: 1st Battalion, 90th (Perthshire Volunteers) Regiment of Foot: 1st Battalion, 92nd (Gordon Highlanders) Regiment of Foot: Ancient Irish Fencibles: The Queen's German Regiment: Staff Corps: Royal Corsican Rangers: De Roll's Regiment: De Watteville's Regiment: Dillon's Regiment

1803	Bengal Horse Artillery
1803	Madras Artillery: Madras Pioneers
1803	Bombay Artillery: 2nd Battalion, 1st Regiment of Bombay Native Infantry (Grenadiers): 1st Battalion, 7th Regiment of Bombay Native Infantry

[1] Awarded to British units with the badge of The Sphinx. [2] Awarded to Indian units as EGYPT: the badge of The Sphinx taken into use 1823: award considered repugnant to Indian units 1966.

7. ASSAYE [1][2]
23rd September 1803
Second Mahratta War 1803–05

1803	4th Regiment of Madras Native Cavalry: 5th Regiment of Madras Native Cavalry: 7th Regiment of Madras Native Cavalry: Madras Artillery: Madras Pioneers: 1st Battalion, 2nd Regiment of Madras Native Infantry: 1st Battalion, 4th Regiment of Madras Native Infantry: 1st Battalion, 8th Regiment of Madras Native Infantry: 1st Battalion, 10th Regiment of Madras Native Infantry: 2nd Battalion, 12th Regiment of Madras Native Infantry
1803	Bombay Artillery
1807	19th Regiment of (Light) Dragoons: 1st Battalion, 74th (Highland) Regiment of Foot: 1st Battalion, 78th (Highland) Regiment of Foot (or Ross-shire Buffs)

[1] Awarded with the badge of The Elephant. [2] Award considered repugnant to Indian units 1966.

8. HINDOOSTAN
1st January 1780–31st December 1823
Service in India 1780–1823

1806	1st Battalion, 76th (Hindoostan) Regiment of Foot [1]
1808	24th Regiment of (Light) Dragoons [2]
1821	1st Battalion, 52nd (Oxfordshire) Regiment of Foot (Light Infantry): 1st Battalion, 71st (Highland) Regiment of Foot
1825	8th (The King's Royal Irish) Regiment of (Light) Dragoons (Hussars): 1st Battalion, 17th (Leicestershire) Regiment of Foot [3]
1835	36th (Herefordshire) Regiment of Foot
1837	72nd (The Duke of Albany's Own Highlanders) Regiment of Foot

[1] Awarded as HINDOOSTAN: the badge of The Elephant taken into use 1807: the badge of An Elephant with Howdah and Mahout taken into use ?. [2] Awarded with the badge of The Elephant. [3] Awarded with the badge of The Royal Tiger.

9. MAIDA
4th July 1806
Napoleonic Wars 1803–15

1807	1st Battalion, 20th (East Devonshire) Regiment of Foot: 1st Battalion, 27th (Inniskilling) Regiment of Foot: 1st Battalion, 58th (Rutlandshire) Regiment of Foot: 2nd Battalion, 78th (Highland) Regiment of Foot (or Ross-shire Buffs): 1st Battalion, 81st Regiment of Foot: De Watteville's Regiment
1808	1st Battalion, 35th (Sussex) Regiment of Foot: 1st Battalion, 61st (South Gloucestershire) Regiment of Foot: Royal Engineers
1809	Royal Corsican Rangers

10. INDIA
1st January 1788–31st December 1831
Service in India 1788–1831

1807	1st Battalion, 75th (Highland) Regiment of Foot [1]
1823	1st Battalion, 65th (2nd Yorkshire, North Riding) Regiment of Foot [1]: 1st Battalion, 86th (The Royal County Down) Regiment of Foot
1826	1st Battalion, 69th (South Lincolnshire) Regiment of Foot: 1st Battalion, 67th (South Hampshire) Regiment of Foot [1]

1836   12th (East Suffolk) Regiment of Foot
1838   14th (Buckinghamshire) Regiment of Foot

¹ Awarded with the badge of The Royal Tiger.

11. DOMINICA
22nd February 1805
Napoleonic Wars 1803–15

1808   1st Battalion, 46th (South Devonshire) Regiment of Foot: 1st Battalion, 1st West India Regiment

12. LESWARREE ¹
1st November 1803
Second Mahratta War 1803–05

1808   25th Regiment of (Light) Dragoons ²
1825   8th (The King's Royal Irish) Regiment of (Light) Dragoons (Hussars)
1829   1st Regiment of Bengal Light Cavalry; 2nd Regiment of Bengal Light Cavalry; 3rd Regiment of Bengal Light Cavalry; 4th Regiment of Bengal Light Cavalry; 6th Regiment of Bengal Light Cavalry; Bengal Foot Artillery; 1st Regiment of Bengal Native Infantry; 12th Regiment of Bengal Native Infantry; 21st Regiment of Bengal Native Infantry; 24th Regiment of Bengal Native Infantry; 30th Regiment of Bengal Native Infantry ³: 31st Regiment of Bengal Native Infantry ³: 33rd Regiment of Bengal Native Infantry
1886   The Duke of Wellington's (West Riding Regiment)

¹ Awarded to Indian units as LASWARREE: LESWARREE taken into use 1911: award considered repugnant to Indian units 1966.
² Awarded with the badge of The Elephant. ³ Awarded with the badge of an Embroidered Star with motto "Lake and Victory".

13. BARROSA
5th March 1811
Napoleonic Wars 1803–15

1811   2nd Battalion, 87th (Prince of Wales's Own Irish) Regiment of Foot: 2nd Battalion, First Regiment of Foot Guards
1812   2nd Battalion, Coldstream Regiment of Foot Guards: 2nd Battalion, Third Regiment of Foot Guards
1814   1st Battalion, 28th (North Gloucestershire) Regiment of Foot
1817   2nd Battalion, 67th (South Hampshire) Regiment of Foot
1821   2nd Battalion, Rifle Brigade: 3rd Battalion, Rifle Brigade

14. LINCELLES
18th August 1793
French Revolutionary Wars 1793–1802

1811   1st Battalion, First Regiment of Foot Guards: 1st Battalion, Coldstream Regiment of Foot Guards: 1st Battalion, Third Regiment of Foot Guards

15. CORUNNA
16th January 1809
Napoleonic Wars 1803–15

1811   2nd Battalion, 14th (Buckinghamshire) Regiment of Foot: 1st Battalion, First Regiment of Foot Guards: 3rd Battalion, First Regiment of Foot Guards
1812   1st Battalion, 4th (The King's Own) Regiment of Foot: 1st Battalion, 42nd (Royal Highland) Regiment of Foot: 1st Battalion, 50th (West Kent) Regiment of Foot: 2nd Battalion, 81st Regiment of Foot: 2nd Battalion, 59th (2nd Nottinghamshire) Regiment of Foot
1821   1st Battalion, 43rd (Monmouthshire) Regiment of Foot (Light Infantry): 2nd Battalion, 43rd (Monmouthshire) Regiment of Foot (Light Infantry): 1st Battalion, 52nd (Oxfordshire) Regiment of Foot (Light Infantry): 2nd Battalion, 52nd (Oxfordshire) Regiment of Foot (Light Infantry): 1st Battalion, Rifle Brigade: 2nd Battalion, Rifle Brigade
1823   1st Battalion, 26th (Cameronian) Regiment of Foot
1825   1st Battalion, 5th (Northumberland) Regiment of Foot
1827   1st Battalion, 6th (1st Warwickshire) Regiment of Foot
1830   1st Battalion, 92nd (Gordon Highlanders) Regiment of Foot
1831   1st Battalion, 38th (1st Staffordshire) Regiment of Foot
1832   3rd Battalion, 1st (Royal) Regiment of Foot: 1st Battalion, 28th (North Gloucestershire) Regiment of Foot
1833   91st (Argyllshire) Regiment of Foot: 36th (Herefordshire) Regiment of Foot: 2nd (Queen's Royal) Regiment of Foot
1834   51st (2nd Yorkshire, West Riding) Regiment of Foot (or The King's Own Light Infantry)

	1835	23rd (Royal Welch Fusiliers) Regiment of Foot: 71st (Highland) Regiment of Foot (Light Infantry): 9th (East Norfolk) Regiment of Foot
	1838	20th (East Devonshire) Regiment of Foot
	1842	32nd (Cornwall) Regiment of Foot
	1908	The Duke of Wellington's (West Riding Regiment): The Prince of Wales's Volunteers (South Lancashire Regiment): The Queen's Own Cameron Highlanders
16.	**TALAVERA** 27th–28th July 1809 Napoleonic Wars 1803–15	
	1812	1st Battalion, Coldstream Regiment of Foot Guards: 1st Battalion, Third Regiment of Foot Guards
	1816	23rd Regiment of (Light) Dragoons: 1st Battalion, 48th (Northamptonshire) Regiment of Foot: 2nd Battalion, 48th (Northamptonshire) Regiment of Foot
	1817	1st Battalion, 45th (Nottinghamshire) Regiment of Foot: 2nd Battalion, 24th (2nd Warwickshire) Regiment of Foot: 2nd Battalion, 88th (Connaught Rangers) Regiment of Foot
	1818	16th (The Queen's) Regiment of (Light) Dragoons (Lancers): 1st Battalion, 29th (Worcestershire) Regiment of Foot: 2nd Battalion, 53rd (Shropshire) Regiment of Foot
	1819	4th (Queen's Own) Regiment of Dragoons: 2nd Battalion, 83rd Regiment of Foot: 2nd Battalion, 7th (Royal Fusiliers) Regiment of Foot
	1820	14th (Duchess of York's Own) Regiment of (Light) Dragoons
	1821	5th Battalion, 60th (Royal American) Regiment of Foot: 1st Battalion, 61st (South Gloucestershire) Regiment of Foot
	1823	1st Battalion, 3rd (East Kent) Regiment of Foot (or The Buffs): 2nd Battalion, 31st (Huntingdonshire) Regiment of Foot: 2nd Battalion, 66th (Berkshire) Regiment of Foot
	1824	2nd Battalion, 87th (Prince of Wales's Own Irish) Regiment of Foot: 1st Battalion, 40th (2nd Somersetshire) Regiment of Foot
	1826	3rd (Prince of Wales's) Regiment of Dragoon Guards
17.	**ROLICA** [1] 17th August 1808 Napoleonic Wars 1803–15	
	1812	1st Battalion, 29th (Worcestershire) Regiment of Foot
	1817	1st Battalion, 5th (Northumberland) Regiment of Foot: 1st Battalion, 45th (Nottinghamshire) Regiment of Foot
	1818	1st Battalion, 71st (Highland) Regiment of Foot (Light Infantry)
	1820	1st Battalion, 9th (East Norfolk) Regiment of Foot
	1821	2nd Battalion, Rifle Brigade: 5th Battalion, 60th (Royal American) Regiment of Foot
	1824	1st Battalion, 40th (2nd Somersetshire) Regiment of Foot
	1825	1st Battalion, 82nd (Prince of Wales's Volunteers) Regiment of Foot
	1826	1st Battalion, 32nd (Cornwall) Regiment of Foot
	1827	1st Battalion, 6th (1st Warwickshire) Regiment of Foot
	1831	1st Battalion, 38th (1st Staffordshire) Regiment of Foot
	1833	91st (Argyllshire) Regiment of Foot: 36th (Herefordshire) Regiment of Foot

[1] Awarded as ROLEIA: ROLICA taken into use 1911.

18.	**TARIFA** 31st December 1811 Napoleonic Wars 1803–15	
	1812	2nd Battalion, 87th (Prince of Wales's Own Irish) Regiment of Foot
	1816	2nd Battalion, 47th (Lancashire) Regiment of Foot
19.	**VIMIERA** 21st August 1808 Napoleonic Wars 1803–15	
	1812	1st Battalion, 50th (West Kent) Regiment of Foot
	1816	1st Battalion, 36th (Herefordshire) Regiment of Foot
	1817	1st Battalion, 45th (Nottinghamshire) Regiment of Foot

		1818	1st Battalion, 71st (Highland) Regiment of Foot (Light Infantry): 1st Battalion, 29th (Worcestershire) Regiment of Foot
		1820	1st Battalion, 9th (East Norfolk) Regiment of Foot: 2nd Battalion, 9th (East Norfolk) Regiment of Foot
		1821	1st Battalion, Rifle Brigade: 2nd Battalion, Rifle Brigade: 2nd Battalion, 43rd (Monmouthshire) Regiment of Foot (Light Infantry): 2nd Battalion, 52nd (Oxfordshire) Regiment of Foot (Light Infantry): 5th Battalion, 60th (Royal American) Regiment of Foot
		1824	1st Battalion, 40th (2nd Somersetshire) Regiment of Foot: 1st Battalion, 82nd (Prince of Wales's Volunteers) Regiment of Foot
		1825	1st Battalion, 5th (Northumberland) Regiment of Foot
		1826	1st Battalion, 32nd (Cornwall) Regiment of Foot
		1827	1st Battalion, 6th (1st Warwickshire) Regiment of Foot
		1831	1st Battalion, 38th (1st Staffordshire) Regiment of Foot
		1833	91st (Argyllshire) Regiment of Foot: 2nd (Queen's Royal) Regiment of Foot
		1838	20th (East Devonshire) Regiment of Foot
		1890	20th Hussars
20.	**MANDORA** 13th March 1801 French Revolutionary Wars 1793–1802	1813	1st Battalion, 92nd (Gordon Highlanders) Regiment of Foot [1]
		1817	1st Battalion, 90th (Perthshire Volunteers) Regiment of Foot (Light Infantry)
			[1] *Awarded as MANDARA: MANDORA taken into use 1814.*
21.	**DOURO** 12th May 1809 Napoleonic Wars 1803–15	1813	1st Battalion, 3rd (East Kent) Regiment of Foot (or The Buffs)
		1815	2nd Battalion, 66th (Berkshire) Regiment of Foot
		1818	2nd Battalion, 48th (Northamptonshire) Regiment of Foot
		1827	14th (Duchess of York's Own) Regiment of (Light) Dragoons
22.	**EGMONT-OP-ZEE** 2nd October 1799 French Revolutionary Wars 1793–1802	1814	1st Battalion, 92nd (Gordon Highlanders) Regiment of Foot [1]
		1818	1st Battalion, 79th (Cameron Highlanders) Regiment of Foot
		1819	1st Battalion, 49th (Princess Charlotte of Wales's, Hertfordshire) Regiment of Foot
		1820	1st Battalion, 25th (King's Own Borderers) Regiment of Foot: 1st Battalion, 20th (East Devonshire) Regiment of Foot: 2nd Battalion, 20th (East Devonshire) Regiment of Foot: 15th (The King's) Regiment of (Light) Dragoons (Hussars)
		1821	2nd Battalion, 1st (Royal Scots) Regiment of Foot
		1830	1st Battalion, 63rd (West Suffolk) Regiment of Foot
		1913	Grenadier Guards
			[1] *Awarded as BERGEN-OP-ZOOM: EGMONT-OP-ZEE taken into use 1814.*
23.	**SALAMANCA** 22nd July 1812 Napoleonic Wars 1803–15	1814	5th (Princess Charlotte of Wales's) Regiment of Dragoon Guards: 3rd (King's Own) Regiment of Dragoons: 4th (Queen's Own) Regiment of Dragoons
		1816	1st Battalion, 2nd (Queen's Royal) Regiment of Foot: 1st Battalion, 11th (North Devonshire) Regiment of Foot: 1st Battalion, 32nd (Cornwall) Regiment of Foot: 2nd Battalion, 53rd (Shropshire) Regiment of Foot: 1st Battalion, 61st (South Gloucestershire) Regiment of Foot: 1st Battalion, 36th (Herefordshire) Regiment of Foot
		1817	1st Battalion, 74th Regiment of Foot: 3rd Battalion, 1st (Royal Scots) Regiment of Foot: 1st Battalion, 88th (Connaught Rangers) Regiment of Foot: 2nd Battalion, 5th (Northumberland) Regiment of Foot: 1st Battalion, 5th (Northumberland) Regiment of Foot: 1st Battalion, 45th (Nottinghamshire) Regiment of Foot
		1818	1st Battalion, 48th (Northamptonshire) Regiment of Foot: 1st Battalion, 94th Regiment of Foot: 16th (The Queen's) Regiment of (Light) Dragoons (Lancers): 1st Battalion, 79th (Cameron Highlanders) Regiment of Foot

1819	1st Battalion, 9th (East Norfolk) Regiment of Foot: 2nd Battalion, 83rd Regiment of Foot: 1st Battalion, 7th (Royal Fusiliers) Regiment of Foot
1820	2nd Battalion, 44th (East Essex) Regiment of Foot: 14th (Duchess of York's Own) Regiment of Foot (Light) Dragoons
1821	1st Battalion, Rifle Brigade: 2nd Battalion, Rifle Brigade: 3rd Battalion, Rifle Brigade: 1st Battalion, 43rd (Monmouthshire) Regiment of Foot (Light Infantry): 1st Battalion, 52nd (Oxfordshire) Regiment of Foot (Light Infantry): 2nd Battalion, 58th (Rutlandshire) Regiment of Foot: 1st Battalion, 23rd (Royal Welch Fusiliers) Regiment of Foot: 5th Battalion, 60th (Royal American) Regiment of Foot: 3rd Battalion, 27th (Inniskilling) Regiment of Foot
1823	1st Battalion, 4th (The King's Own) Regiment of Foot: 2nd Battalion, 4th (The King's Own) Regiment of Foot: 1st Battalion, 68th (Durham) Regiment of Foot (Light Infantry)
1824	1st Battalion, 40th (2nd Somersetshire) Regiment of Foot: 2nd Battalion, 24th (2nd Warwickshire) Regiment of Foot
1825	2nd Battalion, 30th (1st Cambridgeshire) Regiment of Foot
1831	1st Battalion, 38th (1st Staffordshire) Regiment of Foot
1834	51st (2nd Yorkshire, West Riding) Regiment of Foot (or The King's Own Light Infantry)
1838	11th Regiment of (Light) Dragoons
1951	12th Royal Lancers (Prince of Wales's): Coldstream Guards: Scots Guards: The Black Watch (Royal Highland Regiment)
24. **PENINSULA** 17th August 1808–14th April 1814 Napoleonic Wars 1803–15	1815 1st Regiment of Life Guards: 2nd Regiment of Life Guards: Royal Horse Guards Blue: 3rd (Prince of Wales's) Regiment of Dragoon Guards: 4th (Royal Irish) Regiment of Dragoon Guards: 5th (Princess Charlotte of Wales's) Regiment of Dragoon Guards: 1st (Royal) Regiment of Dragoons: 3rd (King's Own) Regiment of Dragoons: 4th (Queen's Own) Regiment of Dragoons: 7th (Queen's Own) Regiment of (Light) Dragoons: 9th Regiment of (Light) Dragoons: 10th (Prince of Wales's Own) Royal Regiment of (Light) Dragoons (Hussars): 11th Regiment of (Light) Dragoons: 12th (Prince of Wales's) Regiment of (Light) Dragoons: 13th Regiment of (Light) Dragoons: 14th (Duchess of York's Own) Regiment of (Light) Dragoons: 15th (The King's) Regiment of (Light) Dragoons (Hussars): 16th (The Queen's) Regiment of (Light) Dragoons: 18th Regiment of (Light) Dragoons (Hussars): 20th Regiment of (Light) Dragoons: 23rd Regiment of (Light) Dragoons: Royal Waggon Train: 1st Regiment of Light Dragoons, King's German Legion: 2nd Regiment of Light Dragoons, King's German Legion: 1st Regiment of Hussars, King's German Legion: 2nd Regiment of Hussars, King's German Legion: Brunswick Hussars: 1st Battalion, First Regiment of Foot Guards: 2nd Battalion, First Regiment of Foot Guards: 3rd Battalion, First Regiment of Foot Guards: 1st Battalion, Coldstream Regiment of Foot Guards: 2nd Battalion, Coldstream Regiment of Foot Guards: 1st Battalion, Third Regiment of Foot Guards: 2nd Battalion, Third Regiment of Foot Guards: 3rd Battalion, 1st (Royal Scots) Regiment of Foot: 1st Battalion, 2nd (Queen's Royal) Regiment of Foot: 1st Battalion, 3rd (East Kent) Regiment of Foot (or The Buffs): 1st Battalion, 4th (The King's Own) Regiment of Foot: 1st Battalion, 5th (Northumberland) Regiment of Foot: 2nd Battalion, 5th (Northumberland) Regiment of Foot: 1st Battalion, 6th (1st Warwickshire) Regiment of Foot: 1st Battalion, 7th (Royal Fusiliers) Regiment of Foot: 2nd Battalion, 7th (Royal Fusiliers) Regiment of Foot: 1st Battalion, 9th (East Norfolk) Regiment of Foot: 2nd Battalion, 9th (East Norfolk) Regiment of Foot: 1st Battalion, 10th (North Lincolnshire) Regiment of Foot: 1st Battalion, 11th (North Devonshire) Regiment of Foot: 1st Battalion, 20th (East Devonshire) Regiment of Foot: 1st Battalion, 23rd (Royal Welch Fusiliers) Regiment of Foot: 2nd Battalion, 24th (2nd Warwickshire) Regiment of Foot: 1st Battalion, 27th (Inniskilling) Regiment of Foot: 2nd Battalion, 27th (Inniskilling) Regiment of Foot: 3rd Battalion, 27th (Inniskilling) Regiment of Foot: 1st Battalion, 28th (North Gloucestershire) Regiment of Foot: 2nd Battalion, 28th (North Gloucestershire) Regiment of Foot: 1st Battalion, 29th (Worcestershire) Regiment of Foot: 2nd Battalion, 28th (North Gloucestershire) Regiment of Foot: 2nd Battalion, 31st (Huntingdonshire) Regiment of Foot: 1st Battalion, 30th (1st Cambridgeshire) Regiment of Foot: 1st Battalion, 32nd (Cornwall) Regiment of Foot: 2nd Battalion, 34th (Cumberland) Regiment of Foot: 1st Battalion, 36th (Herefordshire) Regiment of Foot: 1st Battalion, 37th (North Hampshire) Regiment of Foot: 1st Battalion, 38th (1st

Staffordshire) Regiment of Foot: 2nd Battalion, 38th (1st Staffordshire) Regiment of Foot: 1st Battalion, 39th (Dorsetshire) Regiment of Foot: 2nd Battalion, 39th (Dorsetshire) Regiment of Foot: 1st Battalion, 40th (1st Somersetshire) Regiment of Foot: 1st Battalion, 42nd (Royal Highland) Regiment of Foot: 1st Battalion, 43rd (Monmouthshire) Regiment of Foot (Light Infantry): 1st Battalion, 44th (East Essex) Regiment of Foot: 1st Battalion, 44th (East Essex) Regiment of Foot: 2nd Battalion, 45th (Nottinghamshire) Regiment of Foot: 1st Battalion, 48th (Northamptonshire) Regiment of Foot: 2nd Battalion, 48th (Northamptonshire) Regiment of Foot: 1st Battalion, 50th (West Kent) Regiment of Foot: 1st Battalion, 51st (2nd Yorkshire, West Riding) Regiment of Foot (Light Infantry): 1st Battalion, 52nd (Oxfordshire) Regiment of Foot (Light Infantry): 2nd Battalion, 52nd (Oxfordshire) Regiment of Foot (Light Infantry): 2nd Battalion, 53rd (Shropshire) Regiment of Foot: 1st Battalion, 57th (West Middlesex) Regiment of Foot: 1st Battalion, 58th (Rutlandshire) Regiment of Foot: 2nd Battalion, 59th (2nd Nottinghamshire) Regiment of Foot: 5th Battalion, 60th (Royal American) Regiment of Foot: 1st Battalion, 61st (South Gloucestershire) Regiment of Foot: 2nd Battalion, 62nd (Wiltshire) Regiment of Foot: 2nd Battalion, 66th (Berkshire) Regiment of Foot: 2nd Battalion, 67th (South Hampshire) Regiment of Foot: 1st Battalion, 68th (Durham) Regiment of Foot (Light Infantry): 1st Battalion, 71st (Highland) Regiment of Foot (Light Infantry): 1st Battalion, 74th (Highland) Regiment of Foot: 1st Battalion, 76th Regiment of Foot: 1st Battalion, 77th (East Middlesex) Regiment of Foot: 1st Battalion, 79th (Cameron Highlanders) Regiment of Foot: 1st Battalion, 81st Regiment of Foot: 1st Battalion, 82nd (Prince of Wales's Volunteers) Regiment of Foot: 2nd Battalion, 83rd Regiment of Foot: 2nd Battalion, 84th (York and Lancaster) Regiment of Foot: 1st Battalion, 85th (Bucks Volunteers) Regiment of Foot (Light Infantry): 2nd Battalion, 87th (Prince of Wales's Own Irish) Regiment of Foot: 1st Battalion, 88th (Connaught Rangers) Regiment of Foot: 1st Battalion, 91st Regiment of Foot: 1st Battalion, 92nd (Gordon Highlanders) Regiment of Foot: 1st Battalion, 94th Regiment of Foot: 1st Battalion, 95th (Rifle) Regiment of Foot: 2nd Battalion, 95th (Rifle) Regiment of Foot: 3rd Battalion, 95th (Rifle) Regiment of Foot: 1st Battalion, 97th (Queen's Own) Regiment of Foot: Royal Staff Corps: 13th Royal Veteran Battalion: Chasseurs Britanniques: Brunswick Infantry: Dillon's Regiment: De Watteville's Regiment: De Roll's Regiment: 1st Light Infantry Battalion, King's German Legion: 2nd Light Infantry Battalion, King's German Legion: 1st Infantry Battalion, King's German Legion: 4th Infantry Battalion, King's German Legion: 5th Infantry Battalion, King's German Legion: 6th Infantry Battalion, King's German Legion: 7th Infantry Battalion, King's German Legion Royal Engineers

1816

25. **NIAGARA**
18th December 1813
War of 1812 1812–15

1815

19th Regiment of (Light) Dragoons: 1st Battalion, 1st (Royal Scots) Regiment of Foot: 1st Battalion, 8th (King's) Regiment of Foot: 1st Battalion, 41st Regiment of Foot: 2nd Battalion, 89th Regiment of Foot: 1st Battalion, 100th (Prince Regent's, County of Dublin) Regiment of Foot: 1st Battalion, 103rd Regiment of Foot: 1st Battalion, 104th Regiment of Foot: Glengarry Light Infantry Fencibles

1816

1st Battalion, 82nd (Prince of Wales's Volunteers) Regiment of Foot: 1st Battalion, 6th (1st Warwickshire) Regiment of Foot

26. **WATERLOO**
18th June 1815
Napoleonic Wars 1803–15

1815

1st Regiment of Life Guards: 2nd Regiment of Life Guards: Royal Horse Guards Blue: 1st (The King's) Regiment of Dragoon Guards: 1st (Royal) Regiment of Dragoons: 2nd (Royal North British) Regiment of Dragoons: 6th (Inniskilling) Regiment of Dragoons: 7th (Queen's Own) Regiment of (Light) Dragoons (Hussars): 10th (Prince of Wales's Own) Royal Regiment of (Light) Dragoons (Hussars): 11th Regiment of (Light) Dragoons: 12th (Prince of Wales's) Regiment of (Light) Dragoons: 13th Regiment of (Light) Dragoons: 15th (The King's) Regiment of (Light) Dragoons (Hussars): 16th (The Queen's) Regiment of (Light) Dragoons: 18th Regiment of (Light) Dragoons (Hussars): 23rd Regiment of (Light) Dragoons: Royal Waggon Train: Royal Artillery: Royal Engineers: 1st Regiment of Light Dragoons, King's German Legion: 2nd Regiment of Light Dragoons, King's German Legion: 1st Regiment of Hussars, King's German Legion: 3rd Regiment of Hussars, King's German Legion: 2nd

Battalion, First (or Grenadier) Regiment of Foot Guards: 3rd Battalion, First (or Grenadier) Regiment of Foot Guards: 2nd Battalion, Coldstream Regiment of Foot Guards: 2nd Battalion, Third Regiment of Foot Guards: 3rd Battalion, 1st (Royal Scots) Regiment of Foot: 1st Battalion, 4th (The King's Own) Regiment of Foot: 3rd Battalion, 14th (Buckinghamshire) Regiment of Foot: 1st Battalion, 23rd (Royal Welch Fusiliers) Regiment of Foot: 1st Battalion, 27th (Inniskilling) Regiment of Foot: 1st Battalion, 28th (North Gloucestershire) Regiment of Foot: 2nd Battalion, 30th (1st Cambridgeshire) Regiment of Foot: 1st Battalion, 32nd (Cornwall) Regiment of Foot: 1st Battalion, 33rd (1st Yorkshire, West Riding) Regiment of Foot: 1st Battalion, 40th (2nd Somersetshire) Regiment of Foot: 1st Battalion, 42nd (Royal Highland) Regiment of Foot: 2nd Battalion, 44th (East Essex) Regiment of Foot: 1st Battalion, 51st (2nd Yorkshire, West Riding) Regiment of Foot (Light Infantry): 1st Battalion, 52nd (Oxfordshire) Regiment of Foot (Light Infantry): 2nd Battalion, 69th (South Lincolnshire) Regiment of Foot: 1st Battalion, 71st (Highland) Regiment of Foot (Light Infantry): 2nd Battalion, 73rd Regiment of Foot: 1st Battalion, 79th (Cameron Highlanders) Regiment of Foot: 1st Battalion, 92nd (Gordon Highlanders) Regiment of Foot: 1st Battalion, 95th (Rifle) Regiment of Foot: 2nd Battalion, 95th (Rifle) Regiment of Foot: 3rd Battalion, 95th (Rifle) Regiment of Foot: Royal Staff Corps: 1st Light Infantry Battalion, King's German Legion: 2nd Light Infantry Battalion, King's German Legion: 1st Infantry Battalion, King's German Legion: 2nd Infantry Battalion, King's German Legion: 3rd Infantry Battalion, King's German Legion: 4th Infantry Battalion, King's German Legion: 5th Infantry Battalion, King's German Legion: 8th Infantry Battalion, King's German Legion: Artillery, King's German Legion

27. **ALMARAZ**
19th May 1812
Napoleonic Wars 1803–15

1815   1st Battalion, 71st (Highland) Regiment of Foot (Light Infantry): 1st Battalion, 50th (West Kent) Regiment of Foot
1830   1st Battalion, 92nd (Gordon Highlanders) Regiment of Foot

28. **QUEENSTOWN**
13th October 1812
War of 1812 1812–15

1816   1st Battalion, 49th (Hertfordshire) Regiment of Foot: 1st Battalion, 41st Regiment of Foot

29. **ALBUHERA**
16th May 1811
Napoleonic Wars 1803–15

1816   1st Battalion, 57th (West Middlesex) Regiment of Foot: 2nd Battalion, 28th (North Gloucestershire) Regiment of Foot: 2nd Battalion, 31st (Huntingdonshire) Regiment of Foot: 1st Battalion, 7th (Royal Fusiliers) Regiment of Foot: 2nd Battalion, 7th (Royal Fusiliers) Regiment of Foot: 2nd Battalion, 39th (Dorsetshire) Regiment of Foot: 1st Battalion, 23rd (Royal Welch Fusiliers) Regiment of Foot
1817   2nd Battalion, 34th (Cumberland) Regiment of Foot
1818   1st Battalion, 48th (Northamptonshire) Regiment of Foot: 2nd Battalion, 48th (Northamptonshire) Regiment of Foot: 1st Battalion, 29th (Worcestershire) Regiment of Foot
1819   4th (Queen's Own) Regiment of Dragoons
1823   1st Battalion, 3rd (East Kent) Regiment of Foot (or The Buffs): 2nd Battalion, 66th (Berkshire) Regiment of Foot
1825   5th Battalion, 60th (Royal American) Regiment of Foot
1837   3rd (Prince of Wales's) Regiment of Dragoon Guards
1890   13th Hussars

30. **DETROIT**
16th August 1812
War of 1812 1812–15

1816   1st Battalion, 41st Regiment of Foot

31.	**MIAMI** 22nd January 1813 War of 1812 1812–15	1816	1st Battalion, 41st Regiment of Foot

32.	**LEIPZIG** [1] 16th–19th October 1813 Napoleonic Wars 1803–15	1816	2nd Rocket Troop, Royal Horse Artillery

[1] *Awarded as LEIPSIC: LEIPZIG taken into use ?.*

33.	**NIVELLE** 10th November 1813 Napoleonic Wars 1803–15	1816	1st Battalion, 11th (North Devonshire) Regiment of Foot: 1st Battalion, 32nd (Cornwall) Regiment of Foot: 1st Battalion, 36th (Herefordshire) Regiment of Foot: 1st Battalion, 51st (2nd Yorkshire, West Riding) Regiment of Foot (Light Infantry): 1st Battalion, 61st (South Gloucestershire) Regiment of Foot
		1817	1st Battalion, 74th Regiment of Foot: 1st Battalion, 57th (West Middlesex) Regiment of Foot: 1st Battalion, 5th (North-umberland) Regiment of Foot: 1st Battalion, 42nd (Royal Highland) Regiment of Foot: 1st Battalion, 45th (Nottinghamshire) Regiment of Foot
		1818	1st Battalion, 48th (Northamptonshire) Regiment of Foot: 1st Battalion, 94th Regiment of Foot: 1st Battalion, 79th (Cameron Highlanders) Regiment of Foot: 1st Battalion, 91st Regiment of Foot: 1st Battalion, 88th (Connaught Rangers) Regiment of Foot
		1819	1st Battalion, 28th (North Gloucestershire) Regiment of Foot: 1st Battalion, 2nd (Queen's Royal) Regiment of Foot: 2nd Battalion, 83rd Regiment of Foot
		1820	2nd Battalion, 53rd (Shropshire) Regiment of Foot
		1821	1st Battalion, Rifle Brigade: 2nd Battalion, Rifle Brigade: 3rd Battalion, Rifle Brigade: 1st Battalion, 43rd (Monmouthshire) Regiment of Foot (Light Infantry): 1st Battalion, 52nd (Oxfordshire) Regiment of Foot (Light Infantry): 2nd Battalion, 58th (Rutlandshire) Regiment of Foot: 1st Battalion, 23rd (Royal Welch Fusiliers) Regiment of Foot: 5th Battalion, 60th (Royal American) Regiment of Foot: 3rd Battalion, 27th (Inniskilling) Regiment of Foot
		1823	1st Battalion, 3rd (East Kent) Regiment of Foot (or The Buffs): 2nd Battalion, 31st (Huntingdonshire) Regiment of Foot: 2nd Battalion, 66th (Berkshire) Regiment of Foot: 1st Battalion, 68th (Durham) Regiment of Foot (Light Infantry): 2nd Battalion, 34th (Cumberland) Regiment of Foot
		1824	2nd Battalion, 87th (Prince of Wales's Own Irish) Regiment of Foot: 1st Battalion, 40th (2nd Somersetshire) Regiment of Foot: 1st Battalion, 39th (Dorsetshire) Regiment of Foot: 2nd Battalion, 24th (2nd Warwickshire) Regiment of Foot: 1st Battalion, 82nd (Prince of Wales's Volunteers) Regiment of Foot
		1827	1st Battalion, 6th (1st Warwickshire) Regiment of Foot

34.	**TOULOUSE** 10th April 1814 Napoleonic Wars 1803–15	1816	1st Battalion, 11th (North Devonshire) Regiment of Foot: 1st Battalion, 36th (Herefordshire) Regiment of Foot: 1st Battalion, 61st (South Gloucestershire) Regiment of Foot: 1st Battalion, 79th (Cameron Highlanders) Regiment of Foot: 1st Battalion, 91st Regiment of Foot: 1st Battalion, 42nd (Royal Highland) Regiment of Foot: 1st Battalion, 74th Regiment of Foot
		1817	1st Battalion, 88th (Connaught Rangers) Regiment of Foot: 1st Battalion, 45th (Nottinghamshire) Regiment of Foot
		1818	1st Battalion, 48th (Northamptonshire) Regiment of Foot: 1st Battalion, 94th Regiment of Foot: 1st Battalion, 5th (Northumberland) Regiment of Foot
		1819	4th (Queen's Own) Regiment of Dragoons: 1st Battalion, 2nd (Queen's Royal) Regiment of Foot: 1st Battalion, 7th (Royal Fusiliers) Regiment of Foot
		1820	5th (Princess Charlotte of Wales's) Regiment of Dragoon Guards: 2nd Battalion, 53rd (Shropshire) Regiment of Foot: 1st Battalion, 28th (North Gloucestershire) Regiment of Foot

	1821	1st Battalion, Rifle Brigade: 2nd Battalion, Rifle Brigade: 3rd Battalion, Rifle Brigade: 1st Battalion, 43rd (Monmouthshire) Regiment of Foot (Light Infantry): 1st Battalion, 52nd (Oxfordshire) Regiment of Foot (Light Infantry): 1st Battalion, 23rd (Royal Welch Fusiliers) Regiment of Foot: 3rd (King's Own) Regiment of (Light) Dragoons: 3rd Battalion, 27th (Inniskilling) Regiment of Foot: 5th Battalion, 60th (Royal American) Regiment of Foot
	1824	2nd Battalion, 87th (Prince of Wales's Own Irish) Regiment of Foot: 1st Battalion, 40th (2nd Somersetshire) Regiment of Foot
	1826	1st Battalion, 20th (East Devonshire) Regiment of Foot
	1827	2nd Battalion, 83rd Regiment of Foot
	1890	13th Hussars: The Buffs (East Kent Regiment)
35.	**MARTINIQUE 1809** [1]	
	30th January–24th February 1809	1816 1st Battalion, 7th (Royal Fusiliers) Regiment of Foot: 1st Battalion, 8th (King's) Regiment of Foot: 1st Battalion, 23rd (Royal Welch Fusiliers) Regiment of Foot: 1st Battalion, 13th (1st Somersetshire) Regiment of Foot: Royal York Rangers
	Napoleonic Wars 1803–15	1817 1st Battalion, 90th (Perthshire Volunteers) Regiment of Foot (Light Infantry): 1st Battalion, 15th (Yorkshire, East Riding) Regiment of Foot: 3rd Battalion, 60th (Royal American) Regiment of Foot: 1st Battalion, 1st West India Regiment
		1819 1st Battalion, 63rd (West Suffolk) Regiment of Foot: 1st Battalion, 25th (King's Own Borderers) Regiment of Foot
		[1] Awarded as MARTINIQUE: year-date added 1909.
36.	**VITTORIA**	
	21st June 1813	1816 1st Battalion, 28th (North Gloucestershire) Regiment of Foot: 1st Battalion, 51st (2nd Yorkshire, West Riding) Regiment of Foot (Light Infantry)
	Napoleonic Wars 1803–15	1817 1st Battalion, 74th Regiment of Foot: 3rd Battalion, 1st (Royal Scots) Regiment of Foot: 2nd Battalion, 34th (Cumberland) Regiment of Foot: 1st Battalion, 57th (West Middlesex) Regiment of Foot: 1st Battalion, 5th (Northumberland) Regiment of Foot: 1st Battalion, 45th (Nottinghamshire) Regiment of Foot
		1818 1st Battalion, 48th (Northamptonshire) Regiment of Foot: 1st Battalion, 94th Regiment of Foot: 16th The Queen's) Regiment of (Light) Dragoons (Lancers): 2nd Battalion, 59th (2nd Nottinghamshire) Regiment of Foot: 1st Battalion, 71st (Highland) Regiment of Foot (Light Infantry): 2nd Battalion, 47th (Lancashire) Regiment of Foot: 1st Battalion, 88th (Connaught Rangers) Regiment of Foot
		1819 1st Battalion, 9th (East Norfolk) Regiment of Foot: 1st Battalion, 50th (West Kent) Regiment of Foot: 4th (Queen's Own) Regiment of Dragoons: 1st Battalion, 2nd (Queen's Royal) Regiment of Foot: 2nd Battalion, 83rd Regiment of Foot: 1st Battalion, 7th (Royal Fusiliers) Regiment of Foot: 5th (Princess Charlotte of Wales's) Regiment of Dragoon Guards
		1820 14th (Duchess of York's Own) Regiment of (Light) Dragoons: 2nd Battalion, 53rd (Shropshire) Regiment of Foot
		1821 1st Battalion, Rifle Brigade: 2nd Battalion, Rifle Brigade: 3rd Battalion, Rifle Brigade: 1st Battalion, 43rd (Monmouthshire) Regiment of Foot (Light Infantry): 1st Battalion, 52nd (Oxfordshire) Regiment of Foot (Light Infantry): 2nd Battalion, 58th (Rutlandshire) Regiment of Foot: 1st Battalion, 23rd (Royal Welch Fusiliers) Regiment of Foot: 3rd (King's Own) Regiment of (Light) Dragoons: 5th Battalion, 60th (Royal American) Regiment of Foot: 3rd Battalion, 27th (Inniskilling) Regiment of Foot
		1823 1st Battalion, 4th (The King's Own) Regiment of Foot: 2nd Battalion, 31st (Huntingdonshire) Regiment of Foot: 2nd Battalion, 66th (Berkshire) Regiment of Foot: 1st Battalion, 68th (Durham) Regiment of Foot (Light Infantry)
		1824 2nd Battalion, 87th (Prince of Wales's Own Irish) Regiment of Foot: 1st Battalion, 40th (2nd Somersetshire) Regiment of Foot: 2nd Battalion, 39th (Dorsetshire) Regiment of Foot: 2nd Battalion, 24th (2nd Warwickshire) Regiment of Foot: 1st Battalion, 82nd (Prince of Wales's Volunteers) Regiment of Foot
		1826 3rd (Prince of Wales's) Regiment of Dragoon Guards: 1st Battalion, 20th (East Devonshire) Regiment of Foot
		1827 1st Battalion, 6th (1st Warwickshire) Regiment of Foot
		1830 1st Battalion, 92nd (Gordon Highlanders) Regiment of Foot
		1831 1st Battalion, 38th (1st Staffordshire) Regiment of Foot

	1832	15th (The King's) Regiment of (Light) Dragoons (Hussars)
	1890	13th Hussars: The Buffs (East Kent Regiment)

37. BUSACO
27th September 1810
Napoleonic Wars 1803–15

1817	1st Battalion, 45th (Nottinghamshire) Regiment of Foot: 1st Battalion, 74th Regiment of Foot: 3rd Battalion, 1st (Royal Scots) Regiment of Foot: 1st Battalion, 88th (Connaught Rangers) Regiment of Foot
1819	1st Battalion, 9th (East Norfolk) Regiment of Foot
1821	1st Battalion, Rifle Brigade: 1st Battalion, 43rd (Monmouthshire) Regiment of Foot (Light Infantry): 1st Battalion, 52nd (Oxfordshire) Regiment of Foot (Light Infantry)
1825	2nd Battalion, 5th (Northumberland) Regiment of Foot
1827	2nd Battalion, 83rd Regiment of Foot
1831	2nd Battalion, 38th (1st Staffordshire) Regiment of Foot
1879	60th (King's Royal) Rifle Corps
1910	The Royal Fusiliers (City of London Regiment); The South Wales Borderers: The Gloucestershire Regiment: The Black Watch (Royal Highlanders): The Queen's Own Cameron Highlanders

38. GUADALOUPE 1810 [1]
28th January–4th February 1810
Napoleonic Wars 1803–15

1816	Royal York Rangers
1817	1st Battalion, 90th (Perthshire Volunteers) Regiment of Foot (Light Infantry): 1st Battalion, 15th (Yorkshire, East Riding) Regiment of Foot: 1st Battalion, 1st West India Regiment
1819	1st Battalion, 63rd (West Suffolk) Regiment of Foot
1867	70th (Surrey) Regiment

[1] *Awarded as GUADALOUPE: year-date added 1909.*

39. MONTE VIDEO
3rd February 1807
Napoleonic Wars 1803–15

1817	1st Battalion, 38th (1st Staffordshire) Regiment of Foot
1821	2nd Battalion, Rifle Brigade
1824	1st Battalion, 87th (Prince of Wales's Own Irish) Regiment of Foot

40. ST SEBASTIAN [1]
25th July–31st August 1813
Napoleonic Wars 1803–15

1817	1st Battalion, 38th (1st Staffordshire) Regiment of Foot: 3rd Battalion, 1st (Royal Scots) Regiment of Foot
1818	2nd Battalion, 59th (2nd Nottinghamshire) Regiment of Foot: 2nd Battalion, 47th (Lancashire) Regiment of Foot
1819	1st Battalion, 9th (East Norfolk) Regiment of Foot
1823	1st Battalion, 4th (The King's Own) Regiment of Foot

[1] *Awarded as SAN SEBASTIAN: ST SEBASTIAN taken into use ?.*

41. FUENTES D'ONOR
3rd–5th May 1811
Napoleonic Wars 1803–15

1817	1st Battalion, 74th Regiment of Foot: 2nd Battalion, 24th (2nd Warwickshire) Regiment of Foot: 1st Battalion, 88th (Connaught Rangers) Regiment of Foot: 2nd Battalion, 42nd (Royal Highland) Regiment of Foot
1818	16th (The Queen's) Regiment of (Light) Dragoons (Lancers): 1st Battalion, 71st (Highland) Regiment of Foot (Light Infantry): 1st Battalion, 79th (Cameron Highlanders) Regiment of Foot
1819	2nd Battalion, 83rd Regiment of Foot
1820	14th (Duchess of York's Own) Regiment of (Light) Dragoons: 1st Battalion, 45th (Nottinghamshire) Regiment of Foot
1821	1st Battalion, Rifle Brigade: 2nd Battalion, Rifle Brigade: 3rd Battalion, 43rd (Monmouthshire) Regiment of Foot (Light Infantry): 1st Battalion, 52nd (Oxfordshire) Regiment of Foot (Light Infantry): 5th Battalion, 60th (Royal American) Regiment of Foot
1826	1st Battalion, 85th (Duke of York's Own, Bucks Volunteers) Regiment of Foot (Light Infantry)
1830	1st Battalion, 92nd (Gordon Highlanders) Regiment of Foot

42.	**CIUDAD RODRIGO** 9th–19th January 1812 Napoleonic Wars 1803–15	1871 1910	51st (2nd Yorkshire, West Riding, King's Own Light Infantry) Regiment 1st (Royal) Dragoons: Coldstream Guards: Scots Guards
		1817	1st Battalion, 74th Regiment of Foot: 1st Battalion, 88th (Connaught Rangers) Regiment of Foot: 2nd Battalion, 5th (Northumberland) Regiment of Foot: 1st Battalion, 45th (Nottinghamshire) Regiment of Foot: 1st Battalion, 77th (East Middlesex) Regiment of Foot
		1818	1st Battalion, 94th Regiment of Foot
		1819	2nd Battalion, 83rd Regiment of Foot
		1821	1st Battalion, Rifle Brigade: 1st Battalion, 43rd (Monmouthshire) Regiment of Foot (Light Infantry): 1st Battalion, 52nd (Oxfordshire) Regiment of Foot (Light Infantry): 5th Battalion, 60th (Royal American) Regiment of Foot
43.	**BADAJOZ** 17th March–6th April 1812 Napoleonic Wars 1803–15	1817	1st Battalion, 74th Regiment of Foot: 1st Battalion, 45th (Nottinghamshire) Regiment of Foot: 1st Battalion, 77th (East Middlesex) Regiment of Foot
		1818	1st Battalion, 48th (Northamptonshire) Regiment of Foot: 1st Battalion, 94th Regiment of Foot: 2nd Battalion, 5th (Northumberland) Regiment of Foot: 1st Battalion, 88th (Connaught Rangers) Regiment of Foot
		1819	2nd Battalion, 83rd Regiment of Foot: 1st Battalion, 7th (Royal Fusiliers) Regiment of Foot
		1820	2nd Battalion, 44th (East Essex) Regiment of Foot
		1821	1st Battalion, Rifle Brigade: 3rd Battalion, Rifle Brigade: 1st Battalion, 43rd (Monmouthshire) Regiment of Foot (Light Infantry): 1st Battalion, 52nd (Oxfordshire) Regiment of Foot (Light Infantry): 1st Battalion, 23rd (Royal Welch Fusiliers) Regiment of Foot: 5th Battalion, 60th (Royal American) Regiment of Foot: 3rd Battalion, 27th (Inniskilling) Regiment of Foot
		1823	1st Battalion, 4th (The King's Own) Regiment of Foot
		1824	1st Battalion, 40th (2nd Somersetshire) Regiment of Foot
		1825	2nd Battalion, 30th (1st Cambridgeshire) Regiment of Foot
		1831	2nd Battalion, 38th (1st Staffordshire) Regiment of Foot
44.	**PYRENEES** 25th July–2nd August 1813 Napoleonic Wars 1803–15	1817	1st Battalion, 74th Regiment of Foot: 2nd Battalion, 24th (2nd Warwickshire) Regiment of Foot: 1st Battalion, 57th (West Middlesex) Regiment of Foot: 1st Battalion, 20th (East Devonshire) Regiment of Foot: 1st Battalion, 42nd (Royal Highland) Regiment of Foot: 1st Battalion, 45th (Nottinghamshire) Regiment of Foot
		1818	1st Battalion, 6th (1st Warwickshire) Regiment of Foot: 1st Battalion, 48th (Northamptonshire) Regiment of Foot: 1st Battalion, 71st (Highland) Regiment of Foot (Light Infantry): 1st Battalion, 79th (Cameron Highlanders) Regiment of Foot: 1st Battalion, 91st Regiment of Foot
		1819	1st Battalion, 50th (West Kent) Regiment of Foot: 1st Battalion, 28th (North Gloucestershire) Regiment of Foot: 1st Battalion, 2nd (Queen's Royal) Regiment of Foot
		1820	2nd Battalion, 53rd (Shropshire) Regiment of Foot
		1821	2nd Battalion, 58th (Rutlandshire) Regiment of Foot: 1st Battalion, 23rd (Royal Welch Fusiliers) Regiment of Foot: 3rd Battalion, 27th (Inniskilling) Regiment of Foot
		1823	1st Battalion, 3rd (East Kent) Regiment of Foot (or The Buffs): 2nd Battalion, 31st (Huntingdonshire) Regiment of Foot: 2nd Battalion, 66th (Berkshire) Regiment of Foot: 1st Battalion, 61st (South Gloucestershire) Regiment of Foot: 1st Battalion, 68th (Durham) Regiment of Foot (Light Infantry): 2nd Battalion, 34th (Cumberland) Regiment of Foot: 1st Battalion, 11th (North Devonshire) Regiment of Foot: 1st Battalion, 7th (Royal Fusiliers) Regiment of Foot
		1824	1st Battalion, 40th (2nd Somersetshire) Regiment of Foot: 1st Battalion, 39th (Dorsetshire) Regiment of Foot: 82nd (Prince of Wales's Volunteers) Regiment of Foot
		1825	5th Battalion, 60th (Royal American) Regiment of Foot: 1st Battalion, 36th (Herefordshire) Regiment of Foot

Year	Regiments
1826	1st Battalion, 32nd (Cornwall) Regiment of Foot
1830	1st Battalion, 92nd (Gordon Highlanders) Regiment of Foot
1834	51st (2nd Yorkshire, West Riding) Regiment of Foot (or The King's Own Light Infantry)
1910	14th (King's) Hussars: The Oxfordshire and Buckinghamshire Light Infantry: The Connaught Rangers: The Rifle Brigade (The Prince Consort's Own)

45. ORTHES
27th February 1814
Napoleonic Wars 1803–15

Year	Regiments
1817	1st Battalion, 74th Regiment of Foot: 2nd Battalion, 24th (2nd Warwickshire) Regiment of Foot: 1st Battalion, 88th (Connaught Rangers) Regiment of Foot: 1st Battalion, 20th (East Devonshire) Regiment of Foot: 1st Battalion, 42nd (Royal Highland) Regiment of Foot: 1st Battalion, 45th (Nottinghamshire) Regiment of Foot
1818	1st Battalion, 6th (1st Warwickshire) Regiment of Foot: 1st Battalion, 48th (Northamptonshire) Regiment of Foot: 1st Battalion, 94th Regiment of Foot: 1st Battalion, 71st (Highland) Regiment of Foot (Light Infantry): 1st Battalion, 5th (Northumberland) Regiment of Foot: 1st Battalion, 91st Regiment of Foot
1819	1st Battalion, 50th (West Kent) Regiment of Foot: 1st Battalion, 28th (North Gloucestershire) Regiment of Foot: 2nd Battalion, 83rd Regiment of Foot: 1st Battalion, 7th (Royal Fusiliers) Regiment of Foot
1820	14th (Duchess of York's Own) Regiment of (Light) Dragoons
1821	2nd Battalion, Rifle Brigade: 3rd Battalion, Rifle Brigade: 1st Battalion, 52nd (Oxfordshire) Regiment of Foot (Light Infantry): 2nd Battalion, 58th (Rutlandshire) Regiment of Foot: 1st Battalion, 23rd (Royal Welch Fusiliers) Regiment of Foot: 5th Battalion, 60th (Royal American) Regiment of Foot: 3rd Battalion, 27th (Inniskilling) Regiment of Foot
1823	2nd Battalion, 66th (Berkshire) Regiment of Foot: 1st Battalion, 61st (South Gloucestershire) Regiment of Foot: 1st Battalion, 68th (Durham) Regiment of Foot (Light Infantry): 2nd Battalion, 34th (Cumberland) Regiment of Foot: 1st Battalion, 11th (North Devonshire) Regiment of Foot
1824	2nd Battalion, 87th (Prince of Wales's Own Irish) Regiment of Foot: 1st Battalion, 40th (2nd Somersetshire) Regiment of Foot: 1st Battalion, 39th (Dorsetshire) Regiment of Foot: 1st Battalion, 82nd (Prince of Wales's Volunteers) Regiment of Foot
1826	1st Battalion, 32nd (Cornwall) Regiment of Foot
1830	1st Battalion, 92nd (Gordon Highlanders) Regiment of Foot
1834	51st (2nd Yorkshire, West Riding) Regiment of Foot (or The King's Own Light Infantry)
1836	36th (Herefordshire) Regiment of Foot
1847	31st (Huntingdonshire) Regiment of Foot
1890	13th Hussars: The Buffs (East Kent Regiment)
1893	7th (Queen's Own) Hussars

46. NIVE
9th–13th December 1813
Napoleonic Wars 1803–15

Year	Regiments
1817	3rd Battalion, 1st (Royal Scots) Regiment of Foot: 1st Battalion, 57th (West Middlesex) Regiment of Foot: 1st Battalion, 42nd (Royal Highland) Regiment of Foot
1818	2nd Battalion, 84th (York and Lancaster) Regiment of Foot: 16th (The Queen's) Regiment of (Light) Dragoons (Lancers): 2nd Battalion, 59th (2nd Nottinghamshire) Regiment of Foot: 1st Battalion, 71st (Highland) Regiment of Foot (Light Infantry): 1st Battalion, 79th (Cameron Highlanders) Regiment of Foot: 1st Battalion, 91st Regiment of Foot
1819	1st Battalion, 9th (East Norfolk) Regiment of Foot: 1st Battalion, 50th (West Kent) Regiment of Foot: 1st Battalion, 28th (North Gloucestershire) Regiment of Foot
1821	1st Battalion, Rifle Brigade: 2nd Battalion, Rifle Brigade: 3rd Battalion, Rifle Brigade: 1st Battalion, 43rd (Monmouthshire) Regiment of Foot (Light Infantry): 1st Battalion, 52nd (Oxfordshire) Regiment of Foot (Light Infantry)
1823	1st Battalion, 3rd (East Kent) Regiment of Foot (or The Buffs): 4th (The King's Own) Regiment of Foot: 2nd Battalion, 31st (Huntingdonshire) Regiment of Foot: 2nd Battalion, 66th (Berkshire) Regiment of Foot: 1st Battalion, 61st

	(South Gloucestershire) Regiment of Foot: 2nd Battalion, 34th (Cumberland) Regiment of Foot: 1st Battalion, 11th (North Devonshire) Regiment of Foot
1824	1st Battalion, 39th (Dorsetshire) Regiment of Foot
1825	5th Battalion, 60th (Royal American) Regiment of Foot: 1st Battalion, 36th (Herefordshire) Regiment of Foot
1826	1st Battalion, 85th (Duke of York's Own, Bucks Volunteers) Regiment of Foot (Light Infantry)
1830	1st Battalion, 92nd (Gordon Highlanders) Regiment of Foot
1831	1st Battalion, 38th (1st Staffordshire) Regiment of Foot: 1st Battalion, 32nd (Cornwall) Regiment of Foot
1844	62nd (Wiltshire) Regiment of Foot
1845	76th Regiment of Foot
1910	Grenadier Guards: Coldstream Guards: Scots Guards: The Loyal North Lancashire Regiment

47.	**VILLERS-EN-CAUCHIES** [1]	
	24th April 1794	
	French Revolutionary Wars 1793–1802	
	?	15th (The King's) Regiment of (Light) Dragoons (Hussars)
		[1] *Awarded as VILLERS-EN-COUCHE: VILLERS-EN-CAUCHIES taken into use 1911.*

48.	**ST LUCIA 1803** [1]	
	22nd June 1803	
	Napoleonic Wars 1803–15	
	1818	1st Battalion, 64th (2nd Staffordshire) Regiment of Foot
	1821	2nd Battalion, 1st (Royal Scots) Regiment of Foot
		[1] *Awarded as ST LUCIA: year-date added 1909.*

49.	**SURINAM**	
	26th April–5th May 1804	
	Napoleonic Wars 1803–15	
	1818	1st Battalion, 64th (2nd Staffordshire) Regiment of Foot
	1898	The Bedfordshire Regiment

50.	**CORYGAUM** [1]	
	1st–2nd January 1818	
	Third Mahratta (and Pindari) War 1817–18	
	1818	2nd Battalion, 1st Regiment of Bombay Native Infantry (Grenadiers)
	?	Madras Artillery
	1872	Poona Auxiliary Horse
		[1] *Awarded as KOREGAM: CORYGAUM taken into use 1911: award considered repugnant to Indian units 1966.*

51.	**SERINGAPATAM** [1]	
	5th April–4th May 1799	
	Fourth Mysore War 1799	
	1818	19th Regiment of (Light) Dragoons (Lancers): 22nd Regiment of (Light) Dragoons: 1st Battalion, 12th (East Suffolk) Regiment of Foot: 1st Battalion, 33rd (1st Yorkshire, West Riding) Regiment of Foot: 1st Battalion, 73rd Regiment of Foot: 1st Battalion, 74th Regiment of Foot: 1st Battalion, 75th Regiment of Foot: 1st Battalion, 77th (East Middlesex) Regiment of Foot: 1st Battalion, 94th Regiment of Foot [2]
	1820	1st Regiment of Madras Light Cavalry: 2nd Regiment of Madras Light Cavalry: 3rd Regiment of Macras Light Cavalry: 4th Regiment of Madras Light Cavalry: Madras Artillery: Madras Pioneers: 1st Battalion, 1st Regiment of Madras Native Infantry: 2nd Battalion, 2nd Regiment of Madras Native Infantry: 2nd Battalion, 3rd Regiment of Madras Native Infantry: 2nd Battalion, 5th Regiment of Madras Native Infantry: 1st Battalion, 6th Regiment of Madras Native Infantry: 2nd Battalion, 7th Regiment of Madras Native Infantry: 1st Battalion, 8th Regiment of Madras Native Infantry: 2nd Battalion, 9th Regiment of Madras Native Infantry: 1st Battalion, 11th Regiment of Madras Native Infantry: 2nd Battalion, 11th Regiment of Madras Native Infantry: 1st Battalion, 12th Regiment of Madras Native Infantry: 2nd Battalion, 12th Regiment of Madras Native Infantry
		1st Battalion, 1st European Bombay Regiment [2]
	1822	Bombay Artillery: 1st Battalion, 2nd Regiment of Bombay Native Infantry: 2nd Battalion, 2nd Regiment of Bombay Native Infantry: 1st Battalion, 3rd Regiment of Bombay Native Infantry: 2nd Battalion, 3rd Regiment of Bombay Native Infantry: 1st Battalion, 4th Regiment of Bombay Native Infantry: 2nd Battalion, 5th Regiment of Bombay Native Infantry
	1823	
	1829	Bengal Foot Artillery: 14th Regiment of Bengal Native Infantry [3]: 16th Regiment of Bengal Native Infantry [3]: 36th Regiment of

52. **JAVA**
4th August–16th September 1811
Napoleonic Wars 1803–15

1818 — Bengal Native Infantry (Bengal Volunteers) [3]; 37th Regiment of Bengal Native Infantry (Bengal Volunteers) [3]; 38th Regiment of Bengal Native Infantry (Bengal Volunteers); 39th Regiment of Bengal Native Infantry (Bengal Volunteers) [3]

1st Battalion, 14th (Buckinghamshire) Regiment of Foot: 1st Battalion, 59th (2nd Nottinghamshire) Regiment of Foot: 1st Battalion, 69th (South Lincolnshire) Regiment of Foot: 1st Battalion, 78th (Highland) Regiment of Foot (or Ross-shire Buffs);

1820 — 1st Battalion, 89th Regiment of Foot

1829 — Madras Artillery: Madras Pioneers

Governor General's Body-Guard: Bengal Foot Artillery: 25th Regiment of Bengal Native Infantry (Volunteers): 40th Regiment of Bengal Native Infantry (Volunteers)

[1] Award considered repugnant to Indian units 1966. [2] Awarded with the badge of The Elephant. [3] Awarded with the badge of an Embroidered Radiant Star.

53. **COPENHAGEN** [1]
2nd April 1801
French Revolutionary Wars 1793–1802

1819 — 1st Battalion, 49th (Princess Charlotte of Wales's, Hertfordshire) Regiment of Foot

1821 — 1st Battalion, Rifle Brigade

[1] The badge of A Naval Crown superscribed "2nd April 1801" taken into use 1951.

54. **SEETABULDEE**
26th–27th November 1817
Third Mahratta (and Pindari) War 1817–18

1819 — 6th Regiment of Bengal Light Cavalry

1819 — Madras Artillery: 1st Battalion, 1st Regiment of Madras Native Infantry: 1st Battalion, 20th Regiment of Madras Native Infantry

1826 — Governor's Body-Guard, Madras

55. **MAHEIDPOOR** [1]
23rd December 1817
Third Mahratta (and Pindari) War 1817–18

1819 — 3rd Regiment of Madras Light Cavalry: 4th Regiment of Madras Light Cavalry: 8th Regiment of Madras Light Cavalry: Madras Artillery: Madras Pioneers: 1st Battalion, European Madras Regiment: 1st Battalion, 3rd (Palamcottah) Regiment of Madras Native (Light) Infantry: 2nd Battalion, 6th Regiment of Madras Native Infantry: 1st Battalion, 14th Regiment of Madras Native Infantry: 2nd Battalion, 14th Regiment of Madras Native Infantry: 1st Battalion, 16th (Trichonopoly) Regiment of Madras (Light) Infantry: 1st Battalion, Madras Rifle Corps

1823 — 2nd Battalion, 1st (Royal) Regiment of Foot

1864 — 1st Field Battery, Hyderabad Contingent Artillery: 1st Regiment, Hyderabad Contingent Infantry: 2nd Regiment, Hyderabad Contingent Infantry

[1] Awarded to Indian units as MAHIDPORE: MAHEIDPOOR taken into use 1911: award considered repugnant to Indian units 1966.

56. **ARABIA** [1]
3rd–19th December 1819
Operations in Persian Gulf 1819

1823 — 1st Battalion, 65th (2nd Yorkshire, North Riding) Regiment of Foot

57. **NAGPORE** [1]
16th–24th December 1817
Third Mahratta (and Pindari) War 1817–18

1823 — 2nd Battalion, 1st (Royal) Regiment of Foot

1826 — 6th Regiment of Madras Light Cavalry: Madras Artillery: Madras Pioneers: 1st Regiment of Madras Native Infantry: 17th Regiment of Madras Native Infantry: 21st Regiment of Madras Native Infantry: 23rd (Wallajahabad) Regiment of Madras Native (Light) Infantry: 26th Regiment of Madras Native Infantry: 28th Regiment of Madras Native Infantry: 39th Regiment of Madras Native Infantry

1864 — 4th Regiment, Hyderabad Contingent Infantry

1882 — 6th Regiment of Bengal (Light) Infantry

[1] Award considered repugnant to Indian units 1966.

58. SEEDASEER [1]
8th March 1799
Fourth Mysore War 1799

1823 — 1st Battalion, 2nd Regiment of Bombay Native Infantry: 1st Battalion, 3rd Regiment of Bombay Native Infantry: 1st Battalion, 4th Regiment of Bombay Native Infantry

[1] Award considered repugnant to Indian units 1966.

59. KIRKEE [1]
5th November 1817
Third Mahratta (and Pindari) War 1817–18

1823 — Bombay Artillery: 1st Battalion, European Bombay Regiment: 2nd Battalion, 1st Regiment of Bombay Native Infantry (Grenadiers): 2nd Battalion, 6th Regiment of Bombay Native Infantry: 1st Battalion, 7th Regiment of Bombay Native Infantry: 1st Battalion, 12th Regiment of Bombay Native Infantry

[1] Award considered repugnant to Indian units 1966.

60. MANGALORE [1]
9th May 1782–27th January 1784
Second Mysore War 1780–84

1823 — 1st Battalion, 1st Regiment of Bombay Native Infantry (Grenadiers)
? — 1st Battalion, 73rd Regiment of Foot

[1] Award considered repugnant to Indian units 1966.

61. BOURBON
7th–10th July 1810
Napoleonic Wars 1803–15

1823 — 1st Battalion, 86th (Royal County Down) Regiment of Foot: 1st Battalion, 69th (South Lincolnshire) Regiment of Foot
1838 — Madras Artillery: 6th Regiment of Madras Native Infantry: 24th Regiment of Madras Native Infantry
1855 — 4th Regiment of Bombay Native Infantry (Rifle Corps)

62. CAPE OF GOOD HOPE 1806 [1]
6th–10th January 1806
Napoleonic Wars 1803–15

1824 — 1st Battalion, 24th (2nd Warwickshire) Regiment of Foot
1835 — 71st (Highland) Regiment of Foot (Light Infantry): 93rd (Highland) Regiment of Foot
1836 — 59th (2nd Nottinghamshire) Regiment of Foot: 72nd (The Duke of Albany's Own Highlanders) Regiment of Foot: 83rd Regiment of Foot

[1] Awarded as CAPE OF GOOD HOPE; year-date added 1882.

63. KEMMENDINE [1]
1st–9th December 1824
First Burma War 1824–26

1825 — 26th Regiment of Madras Native Infantry

[1] Award considered repugnant to Indian units 1966.

64. NIEUPORT
20th–30th October 1793
French Revolutionary Wars 1793–1802

1825 — 1st Battalion, 53rd (Shropshire) Regiment of Foot

65. TOURNAY
22nd May 1794
French Revolutionary Wars 1793–1802

1825 — 1st Battalion, 53rd (Shropshire) Regiment of Foot
1826 — 1st Battalion, 37th (North Hampshire) Regiment of Foot
1836 — 14th (Buckinghamshire) Regiment of Foot

66. ST LUCIA 1796 [1]
26th April–25th May 1796
French Revolutionary Wars 1793–1802

1825 — 1st Battalion, 53rd (Shropshire) Regiment of Foot
1836 — 27th (Inniskilling) Regiment of Foot

[1] Awarded as ST LUCIA; year-date added 1909.

67. ASSAM
17th January 1824–29th January 1825
First Burma War 1824–26

1826 — 46th Regiment of Bengal Native Infantry: 57th Regiment of Bengal Native Infantry

68. AVA [1]
17th January 1824–24th February 1826
First Burma War 1824–26

1826 — Governor General's Body-Guard: Bengal Horse Artillery: Bengal Foot Artillery: 40th Regiment of Bengal Native Infantry (Volunteers)
1826 — 1st Regiment of Madras Light Cavalry: Madras Artillery: Madras Pioneers: 1st Regiment of Madras Native Infantry: 3rd

	(Palamcottah) Regiment of Madras Native (Light) Infantry: 7th Regiment of Madras Native Infantry: 9th Regiment of Madras Native Infantry: 10th Regiment of Madras Native Infantry: 12th Regiment of Madras Native Infantry: 16th Regiment of Madras Native Infantry: 18th Regiment of Madras Native Infantry: 22nd Regiment of Madras Native Infantry: 26th Regiment of Madras Native Infantry: 28th Regiment of Madras Native Infantry: 30th Regiment of Madras Native Infantry: 32nd Regiment of Madras Native Infantry: 34th (Chicacole) Regiment of Madras Native Infantry: 36th (Nundy) Regiment of Madras Native Infantry: 38th Regiment of Madras Native Infantry: 43rd Regiment of Madras Native Infantry
1826	2nd Battalion, 1st (Royal) Regiment of Foot: 1st Battalion, 13th (1st Somersetshire) Regiment of Foot (Light Infantry): 1st Battalion, 38th (1st Staffordshire) Regiment of Foot: 1st Battalion, 41st Regiment of Foot: 1st Battalion, 44th (East Essex) Regiment of Foot: 1st Battalion, 45th (Nottinghamshire) Regiment of Foot: 1st Battalion, 47th (Lancashire) Regiment of Foot: 1st Battalion, 54th (West Norfolk) Regiment of Foot: 1st Battalion, 87th (Prince of Wales's Own Irish) Regiment of Foot: 1st Battalion, 89th Regiment of Foot
1841	1st European Madras Regiment
	¹ Award considered repugnant to Indian units 1966.

69. ARRACAN ¹
26th March–1st April 1825
First Burma War 1824–26

1826	2nd Regiment of Bengal Local Horse (Gardner's Horse): Bengal Foot Artillery: 26th Regiment of Bengal Native Infantry: 28th Regiment of Bengal Native Infantry: 40th Regiment of Bengal Native Infantry (Volunteers): 42nd Regiment of Bengal Native Infantry: 49th Regiment of Bengal Native Infantry: 62nd Regiment of Bengal Native Infantry
	¹ Award considered repugnant to Indian units 1966.

70. BHURTPORE ¹
17th–18th January 1826
Intervention in Bhurtpore 1825–26

1826	3rd Regiment of Bengal Light Cavalry: 4th Regiment of Bengal Light Cavalry: 6th Regiment of Bengal Light Cavalry: 8th Regiment of Bengal Light Cavalry: 9th Regiment of Bengal Light Cavalry: 10th Regiment of Bengal Light Cavalry: Bengal Horse Artillery: Bengal Foot Artillery: European Bengal Regiment: 6th Regiment of Bengal Native Infantry: 11th Regiment of Bengal Native Infantry: 15th Regiment of Bengal Native Infantry: 18th Regiment of Bengal Native Infantry: 21st Regiment of Bengal Native Infantry: 23rd Regiment of Bengal Native Infantry: 31st Regiment of Bengal Native Infantry: 32nd Regiment of Bengal Native Infantry: 33rd Regiment of Bengal Native Infantry: 35th Regiment of Bengal Native Infantry: 36th Regiment of Bengal Native Infantry (Bengal Volunteers): 37th Regiment of Bengal Native Infantry (Bengal Volunteers): 41st Regiment of Bengal Native Infantry: 58th Regiment of Bengal Native Infantry: 60th Regiment of Bengal Native Infantry: 63rd Regiment of Bengal Native Infantry: 1st Regiment of Bengal Local Horse (Skinner's Horse): 8th Regiment of Bengal Local Horse (Skinner's Horse)
1826	11th Regiment of (Light) Dragoons: 16th (The Queen's) Regiment of (Light) Dragoons (Lancers): 1st Battalion, 14th (Buckinghamshire) Regiment of Foot: 1st Battalion, 59th (2nd Nottinghamshire) Regiment of Foot
1832	Bengal Sappers and Miners
1859	Simoor Rifle Regiment
1874	1st Goorkha Regiment (Light Infantry)
	¹ Award considered repugnant to Indian units 1966.

71. BLADENSBURG
24th August 1814
War of 1812 1812–15

1826	1st Battalion, 85th (Duke of York's Own, Bucks Volunteers) Regiment of Foot (Light Infantry)
1827	1st Battalion, 4th (The King's Own) Regiment of Foot: 1st Battalion, 44th (East Essex) Regiment of
1854	21st (Royal North British Fusiliers) Regiment

72. INDIA 1796-1819 ¹
1st January 1788–31st December 1831
Service in India 1788–1831

1826	1st Battalion, 84th (York and Lancaster) Regiment of Foot
	¹ Awarded as INDIA: year-dates taken into use 1912.

No.	Honour	Year	Units
73.	**MORO** 1st–30th July 1762 Seven Years War 1756–63	1827	1st Battalion, 56th (West Essex) Regiment of Foot
74.	**PLASSEY** 23rd June 1757 Bengal Wars 1756–65	1829 1835 1841 1844	Bengal Foot Artillery: European Bergal Regiment: 1st Regiment of Bengal Native Infantry 39th (Dorsetshire) Regiment of Foot 1st European Madras Regiment 1st European Bombay Regiment
75.	**BUXAR** 23rd October 1764 Bengal Wars 1756–65	1829 1844	Bengal Foot Artillery: European Bengal Regiment: 2nd Regiment of Bengal Native Infantry: 3rd Regiment of Bengal Native Infantry: 5th Regiment of Bengal Native Infantry: 8th Regiment of Bengal Native Infantry: 9th Regiment of Bengal Native Infantry: 10th Regiment of Bengal Native Infantry 1st European Bombay Fusiliers [1] [1] Awarded with the badge of The Royal Tiger.
76.	**KORAH** 10th June 1776 Operations in Oudh 1776	1829	1st Regiment of Bengal Native Infantry: 10th Regiment of Bengal Native Infantry
77.	**GUZERAT** 19th May 1778–17th May 1782 Operations in Guzerat 1778–82	1829 1845	European Bengal Regiment: 2nd Regiment of Bengal Native Infantry: 3rd Regiment of Bengal Native Infantry: 5th Regiment of Bengal Native Infantry: 7th Regiment of Bengal Native Infantry: 11th Regiment of Bengal Native Infantry: 13th Regiment of Bengal Native Infantry 1st European Bombay Fusiliers
78.	**CARNATIC** [1] 1st January 1780–27th January 1784 Second Mysore War 1780–84 and 1st January 1790–16th March 1792 Third Mysore War 1789–92	1829 1844 1889 1889	Bengal Foot Artillery: 4th Regiment of Bengal Native Infantry: 5th Regiment of Bengal Native Infantry: 12th Regiment of Bengal Native Infantry: 22nd Regiment of Bengal Native Infantry: 24th Regiment of Bengal Native Infantry: 26th Regiment of Bengal Native Infantry 1st European Bombay Fusiliers [2] The Highland Light Infantry: Seaforth Highlanders (Ross-shire Buffs, The Duke of Albany's): The Royal Munster Fusiliers The 2nd Madras Lancers: The Madras Sappers and Miners (Queen's Own): The 1st Regiment of Madras Infantry: The 2nd Regiment of Madras Infantry: The 3rd Regiment of Madras Infantry: The 4th Regiment of Madras Infantry: The 5th Regiment of Madras Infantry: The 6th Regiment of Madras Infantry: The 7th Regiment of Madras Infantry: The 8th Regiment of Madras Infantry: The 9th Regiment of Madras Infantry: The 10th Regiment of Madras Infantry: The 12th Regiment of Madras Infantry: The 13th Regiment of Madras Infantry: The 14th Regiment of Madras Infantry: The 15th Regiment of Madras Infantry: The 16th Regiment of Madras Infantry: The 17th Regiment of Madras Infantry: The 19th Regiment of Madras Infantry: The 20th Regiment of Madras Infantry [1] Award considered repugnant to Indian units 1966. [2] Awarded with the badge of The Elephant.
79.	**MYSORE** [1] 29th December 1789–16th March 1792 Third Mysore War 1789–92	1829 1844 1889	Bengal Foot Artillery: 4th Regiment of Bengal Native Infantry [2]: 6th Regiment of Bengal Native Infantry: 13th Regiment of Bengal Native Infantry [2]: 16th Regiment of Bengal Native Infantry [2] 1st European Bombay Fusiliers [3] 19th (Princess of Wales's Own) Hussars: The Worcestershire Regiment: The Duke of Wellington's (West Riding Regiment): The Black Watch (Royal Highlanders): The Oxfordshire Light Infantry: The Duke of Cambridge's Own (Middlesex Regiment): The Highland Light Infantry: Seaforth Highlanders (Ross-shire Buffs, The Duke of Albany's): The Gordon Highlanders

The 1st Madras Lancers: The 2nd Madras Lancers: The 3rd Madras Cavalry: The 4th Madras Cavalry: The Madras Sappers and Miners (Queen's Own): The 1st Regiment of Madras Infantry: The 2nd Regiment of Madras Infantry: The 3rd Regiment of Madras Infantry: The 4th Regiment of Madras Infantry: The 5th Regiment of Madras Infantry: The 6th Regiment of Madras Infantry: The 7th Regiment of Madras Infantry: The 9th Regiment of Madras Infantry: The 10th Regiment of Madras Infantry: The 13th Regiment of Madras Infantry: The 14th Regiment of Madras Infantry: The 15th Regiment of Madras Infantry: The 16th Regiment of Madras Infantry: The 19th Regiment of Madras Infantry: The 20th Regiment of Madras Infantry: The 21st Regiment of Madras Infantry: The 22nd Regiment of Madras Infantry: The 1st Regiment of Bombay Infantry: The 3rd Regiment of Bombay Infantry: The 4th Regiment of Bombay Infantry: The 5th Regiment of Bombay Infantry: The 7th Regiment of Bombay Infantry: The 8th Regiment of Bombay Infantry — **1889**

9th Bombay Infantry — **1891**

[1] *Award considered repugnant to Indian units 1966.* [2] *Awarded with the badge of a Royal Tiger under a Banian Tree.* [3] *Awarded with the badge of The Elephant.*

80. ALLYGHUR
4th September 1803
Second Mahratta War 1803–05
Bengal Foot Artillery: 7th Regiment of Bengal Native Infantry: 23rd Regiment of Bengal Native Infantry: 35th Regiment of Bengal Native Infantry — **1829**
The Duke of Wellington's (West Riding Regiment) — **1886**

81. DELHI 1803 [1]
11th September 1803
Second Mahratta War 1803–05
Bengal Foot Artillery: 2nd Regiment of Bengal Light Cavalry: 3rd Regiment of Bengal Light Cavalry: 1st Regiment of Bengal Native Infantry: 5th Regiment of Bengal Native Infantry: 22nd Regiment of Bengal Native Infantry: 23rd Regiment of Bengal Native Infantry: 28th Regiment of Bengal Native Infantry: 29th Regiment of Bengal Native Infantry: 30th Regiment of Bengal Native Infantry: 31st Regiment of Bengal Native Infantry: 35th Regiment of Bengal Native Infantry — **1829**
The Duke of Wellington's (West Riding Regiment) — **1886**
[1] *Awarded as DELHI: year-date added 1911: award considered repugnant to Indian units 1966.*

82. DEIG [1]
13th November–24th December 1804
Second Mahratta War 1803–05
2nd Regiment of Bengal Light Cavalry: 3rd Regiment of Bengal Light Cavalry: Bengal Horse Artillery: Bengal Foot Artillery: European Bengal Regiment: 5th Regiment of Bengal Native Infantry: 7th Regiment of Bengal Native Infantry: 9th Regiment of Bengal Native Infantry: 30th Regiment of Bengal Native Infantry: 31st Regiment of Bengal Native Infantry: 44th Regiment of Bengal Native Infantry — **1829**
The Duke of Wellington's (West Riding Regiment) — **1886**
[1] *Award considered repugnant to Indian units 1966.*

83. BENI BOO ALLI [1]
2nd March 1821
Operations in Persian Gulf 1821
Bombay Artillery: 1st European Bombay Regiment: 3rd Regiment of Bombay Native Infantry: 4th Regiment of Bombay Native Infantry: 5th Regiment of Bombay Native Infantry: 7th Regiment of Bombay Native Infantry: 13th Regiment of Bombay Native Infantry: 18th Regiment of Bombay Native Infantry: Marine Battalion of Bombay Native Infantry — **1831**
Bombay Sappers and Miners — **1877**
[1] *Awarded as BENI BOO ALLI: BENI BOO ALLI taken into use 1911.*

84. SAHAGUN
21st December 1808
Napoleonic Wars 1803–15
15th (The King's) Regiment of (Light) Dragoons (Hussars) — **1832**

85. WILHELMSTAHL
24th June 1762
Seven Years War 1756–63
5th (Northumberland) Regiment of Foot — **1836**

86.	**GHUZNEE 1839** [*] 23rd July 1839 First Afghan War 1839–42	1839
	2nd Regiment of Bengal Light Cavalry: 3rd Regiment of Bengal Light Cavalry: 4th Regiment of Bengal Local Horse (Skinner's Horse): Bengal Horse Artillery: Bengal Sappers and Miners: 1st European Bengal Regiment: 16th Regiment of Bengal Native Infantry: 35th Regiment of Bengal Native Infantry: 48th Regiment of Bengal Native Infantry	1839
	1st Regiment of Bombay Light Cavalry: Poona Auxiliary Horse: Bombay Artillery: Bombay Sappers and Miners: 19th Regiment of Bombay Native Infantry	
	4th (Queen's Own) Regiment of (Light) Dragoons: 16th (The Queen's) Regiment of (Light) Dragoons (Lancers): 2nd (Queen's Royal) Regiment of Foot: 13th (1st Somersetshire) Regiment of Foot (Light Infantry): 17th (Leicestershire) Regiment of Foot	1840
	[*] *Awarded as GHUZNEE: year-date added 1907.*	
87.	**AFFGHANISTAN 1839** [*] 16th April–7th August 1839 First Afghan War 1839–42	1839
	2nd Regiment of Bengal Light Cavalry: 3rd Regiment of Bengal Light Cavalry: 4th Regiment of Bengal Local Horse (Skinner's Horse): Bengal Horse Artillery: Bengal Foot Artillery: Bengal Sappers and Miners: 1st European Bengal Regiment: 16th Regiment of Bengal Native Infantry: 31st Regiment of Bengal Native Infantry: 35th Regiment of Bengal Native Infantry: 37th Regiment of Bengal Native Infantry (Volunteers): 42nd Regiment of Bengal Native (Light) Infantry: 43rd Regiment of Bengal Native (Light) Infantry: 48th Regiment of Bengal Native Infantry	
	1st Regiment of Bombay Light Cavalry: Poona Auxiliary Horse: Bombay Artillery: Bombay Sappers and Miners: 19th Regiment of Bombay Native Infantry	1839
	4th (Queen's Own) Regiment of (Light) Dragoons: 16th (The Queen's) Regiment of (Light) Dragoons (Lancers): 2nd (Queen's Royal) Regiment of Foot: 13th (1st Somersetshire) Regiment of Foot (Light Infantry): 17th (Leicestershire) Regiment of Foot	1840
	[*] *Awarded as AFGHANISTAN: AFFGHANISTAN taken into use 1911: year-date added 1914.*	
88.	**COCHIN** 19th–21st January 1809 Rebellion in Travancore 1809	1840
	33rd Regiment of Madras Infantry	
89.	**KHELAT** [*] 13th November 1839 First Afghan War 1839–42	1840
	4th Regiment of Bengal Irregular Cavalry (Skinner's Horse): 3rd Regiment of Bengal Native Infantry	1840
	2nd (Queen's Royal) Regiment of Foot: 17th (Leicestershire) Regiment of Foot	1840
	Bombay Artillery: Bombay Sappers and Miners	1841
	[*] *Awarded to Indian units as KELAT: KHELAT taken into use 1911.*	
90.	**ARCOT** 31st August–14th November 1751 Second Carnatic War 1749–54	1841
	1st European Madras Regiment	
91.	**CONDORE** 9th December 1758 Third Carnatic War 1758–63	1841
	1st European Madras Regiment The Royal Munster Fusiliers	1841 1894
92.	**WANDIWASH** [*] 22nd January 1760 Third Carnatic War 1758–63	1841
	1st European Madras Regiment	
	[*] *Awarded as WANDEWASH: WANDIWASH taken into use 1911.*	
93.	**PONDICHERRY** 9th August 1760–15th January 1761 Third Carnatic War 1758–63	1841
	1st European Madras Regiment	

No.	Honour	Year	Unit
94.	**NUNDY DROOG** 18th October 1791 Third Mysore War 1789–92	1841	1st European Madras Regiment
95.	**AMBOYNA** 17th February 1810 Napoleonic Wars 1803–15	1841	1st European Madras Regiment
96.	**BANDA** 9th August 1810 Napoleonic Wars 1803–15	1841	1st European Madras Regiment
97.	**TERNATE** 28th August 1810 Napoleonic Wars 1803–15	1841	1st European Madras Regiment
98.	**ADEN** 19th January 1839 Expedition to Aden 1839	1841	Bombay Artillery: 1st European Bombay Regiment: 24th Regiment of Bombay Native Infantry: Marine Battalion of Bombay Native Infantry
99.	**CAPE OF GOOD HOPE** 21st December 1834–17th December 1835 Sixth Kaffir War 1834–35	1841	Cape Mounted Rifles
100.	**KAHUN** 16th May–28th September 1840 First Afghan War 1839–42	1841	5th Regiment of Bombay Native (Light) Infantry
101.	**MARABOUT** 21st August 1801 French Revolutionary Wars 1793–1802	1841	54th (West Norfolk) Regiment of Foot
102.	**JELLALABAD** [1] 13th November 1841–7th April 1842 First Afghan War 1839–42	1842 1842	13th (1st Somersetshire) Regiment of Foot (Prince Albert's Light Infantry) 5th Regiment of Bengal Light Cavalry: 35th Regiment of Bengal Native Infantry [1] *Awarded with the badge of A Mural Crown.*
103.	**KELAT-I-GHILZIE** [1] 11th February–21st May 1842 First Afghan War 1839–42	1842	Bengal Foot Artillery: Regiment of Kelat-i-Ghilzai [2] [1] *Awarded as KELAT-I-GHILZAI: KELAT-I-GHILZIE taken into use 1911.* [2] *The badge of a Mural Crown superscribed "Invicta" taken into use 1891.*
104.	**CANDAHAR 1842** [1] 10th March 1842 First Afghan War 1839–42	1842 1842	1st Regiment of Bengal Irregular Cavalry (Skinner's Horse): Bengal Foot Artillery: Bengal Sappers and Miners: 2nd Regiment of Bengal Native Infantry: 16th Regiment of Bengal Native Infantry (Bengal Volunteers): 38th Regiment of Bengal Native Infantry: 42nd Regiment of Bengal Native (Light) Infantry: 43rd Regiment of Bengal Native (Light) Infantry: Regiment of Kelat-i-Ghilzai Poona Auxiliary Horse: Bombay Artillery

		1843	41st (Welch) Regiment of Foot
		1844	40th (2nd Somersetshire) Regiment of Foot
			[1] Awarded as CANDAHAR; year-date added 1907.
105.	**GHUZNEE 1842** [1] 7th December 1841–6th March 1842 First Afghan War 1839–42	1842	Bengal Foot Artillery; Bengal Sappers and Miners; 2nd Regiment of Bengal Native Infantry; 38th Regiment of Bengal Native Infantry (Bengal Volunteers); 42nd Regiment of Bengal Native (Light) Infantry; Regiment of Kelat-i-Ghilzai
		1842	3rd Regiment of Bombay Light Cavalry
		1844	40th (2nd Somersetshire) Regiment of Foot: 41st (Welch) Regiment of Foot
			[1] Awarded as GHUZNEE; year-date added 1907.
106.	**CABOOL 1842** 15th September 1842 First Afghan War 1839–42	1842	1st Regiment of Bengal Light Cavalry; 5th Regiment of Bengal Light Cavalry; 10th Regiment of Bengal Light Cavalry; 3rd Regiment of Bengal Irregular Cavalry (1st Rohilla Cavalry); Bengal Horse Artillery; Bengal Foot Artillery; Bengal Sappers and Miners; 2nd Regiment of Bengal Native Infantry; 6th Regiment of Bengal Native Infantry; 16th Regiment of Bengal Native Infantry; 26th Regiment of Bengal Native Infantry; 30th Regiment of Bengal Native Infantry; 31st Regiment of Bengal Native Infantry; 33rd Regiment of Bengal Native Infantry; 35th Regiment of Bengal Native Infantry; 38th Regiment of Bengal Native Infantry (Bengal Volunteers); 42nd Regiment of Bengal Native (Light) Infantry; 43rd Regiment of Bengal Native (Light) Infantry; 53rd Regiment of Bengal Native Infantry; 60th Regiment of Bengal Native Infantry; 64th Regiment of Bengal Native Infantry; Regiment of Kelat-i-Ghilzai
		1842	3rd Regiment of Bombay Light Cavalry
		1844	40th (2nd Somersetshire) Regiment of Foot: 3rd (King's Own) Regiment of (Light) Dragoons; 9th (East Norfolk) Regiment of Foot; 13th (1st Somersetshire) Regiment of Foot (Prince Albert's Light Infantry); 31st (Huntingdonshire) Regiment of Foot; 41st (Welch) Regiment of Foot
107.	**CHINA** [1][2] 4th July 1840–17th August 1842 First China War 1840–42	1842	Madras Artillery; Madras Sappers and Miners; 2nd Regiment of Madras Native Infantry; 6th Regiment of Madras Native Infantry; 14th Regiment of Madras Native Infantry; 36th Regiment of Madras Native Infantry; 37th Regiment of Madras Native Infantry (Grenadiers); 41st Regiment of Madras Native Infantry
		1843	Royal Artillery; 18th (Royal Irish) Regiment of Foot; 26th (Cameronian) Regiment of Foot; 49th (Princess Charlotte of Wales's, Hertfordshire) Regiment of Foot; 55th (Westmorland) Regiment of Foot; 98th Regiment of Foot
			[1] Awarded to Indian units as CHINA, the badge of The Golden Dragon wearing an Imperial Crown taken into use 1843; award considered repugnant to Indian units 1966. [2] Awarded to British units with the badge of The Dragon.
108.	**SCINDE** 6th January–24th March 1843 Scinde Campaign 1843	1843	22nd (Cheshire) Regiment of Foot
109.	**MEEANEE** [1] 17th February 1843 Scinde Campaign 1843	1843	9th Regiment of Bengal Light Cavalry
		1843	Madras Sappers and Miners
		1843	Poona Auxiliary Horse: Scinde Irregular Horse: Bombay Artillery; 12th Regiment of Bombay Native Infantry; 25th Regiment of Bombay Native Infantry
		1844	22nd (Cheshire) Regiment of Foot
			[1] Award considered repugnant to Indian units 1966.

No.	Battle Honour	Year	Regiments
110.	**HYDERABAD** [1] 24th March 1843 Scinde Campaign 1843	1843 1843 1843 1844	9th Regiment of Bengal Light Cavalry Madras Sappers and Miners 3rd Regiment of Bombay Light Cavalry: Poona Auxiliary Horse: Bombay Artillery: 1st Regiment of Bombay Native Infantry: 8th Regiment of Bombay Native Infantry (Grenadiers): 6th Regiment of Bombay Native Infantry: 12th Regiment of Bombay Native Infantry: 21st Regiment of Bombay Native Infantry: 25th Regiment of Bombay Native Infantry 22nd (Cheshire) Regiment of Foot *[1] Award considered repugnant to Indian units 1966.*
111.	**HYDERABAD 1843** [1] 24th March 1843 Scinde Campaign 1843	1843	Scinde Irregular Horse *[1] Award considered repugnant to Indian units 1966.*
112.	**MAHARAJPORE** [1] 29th December 1843 Gwalior Campaign 1843	1844 1844	Governor General's Body-Guard: 1st Regiment of Bengal Light Cavalry: 4th Regiment of Bengal Light Cavalry: 5th Regiment of Bengal Light Cavalry: 8th Regiment of Bengal Light Cavalry: 10th Regiment of Bengal Light Cavalry: 4th Regiment of Bengal Irregular Cavalry (Skinner's Horse); Bengal Horse Artillery: Bengal Foot Artillery: Bengal Sappers and Miners: 2nd Regiment of Bengal Native Infantry: 14th Regiment of Bengal Native Infantry: 16th Regiment of Bengal Native Infantry: 31st Regiment of Bengal Native Infantry: 39th Regiment of Bengal Native Infantry (Bengal Volunteers): 43rd Regiment of Bengal Native (Light) Infantry: 56th Regiment of Bengal Native Infantry: Regiment of Kelat-i-Ghilzai 16th (The Queen's) Regiment of (Light) Dragoons (Lancers): 39th (Dorsetshire) Regiment of Foot: 40th (2nd Somersetshire) Regiment of Foot *[1] Award considered repugnant to Indian units 1966.*
113.	**PUNNIAR** 29th December 1843 Gwalior Campaign 1843	1844 1844	5th Regiment of Bengal Light Cavalry: 8th Regiment of Bengal Light Cavalry: 11th Regiment of Bengal Light Cavalry: 8th Regiment of Bengal Irregular Cavalry: Bengal Horse Artillery: Bengal Sappers and Miners: 39th Regiment of Bengal Native Infantry (Bengal Volunteers): 50th Regiment of Bengal Native Infantry: 51st Regiment of Bengal Native Infantry: 58th Regiment of Bengal Native Infantry: Gwalior Contingent 9th (Queen's Royal) Regiment of (Light) Dragoons (Lancers): 3rd (East Kent) Regiment of Foot (or The Buffs): 50th (Queen's Own) Regiment of Foot
114.	**ARROYO DOS MOLINOS** 28th October 1811 Napoleonic Wars 1803–15	1845	34th (Cumberland) Regiment of Foot
115.	**MOODKEE** [1] 18th December 1845 First Sikh War 1845–46	1846 1847	Governor General's Body-Guard: 4th Regiment of Bengal Light Cavalry: 5th Regiment of Bengal Light Cavalry: 4th Regiment of Bengal Irregular Cavalry (Skinner's Horse): 8th Regiment of Bengal Irregular Cavalry: 9th Regiment of Bengal Irregular Cavalry: Bengal Horse Artillery: Bengal Foot Artillery: 2nd Regiment of Bengal Native Infantry (Grenadiers): 16th Regiment of Bengal Native Infantry (Grenadiers): 24th Regiment of Bengal Native Infantry: 26th Regiment of Bengal Native (Light) Infantry: 43rd Regiment of Bengal Native (Light) Infantry: 45th Regiment of Bengal Native Infantry: 47th Regiment of Bengal Native Infantry (Volunteers): 48th Regiment of Bengal Native Infantry: 73rd Regiment of Bengal Native Infantry 3rd (King's Own) Regiment of (Light) Dragoons: 9th (East Norfolk) Regiment of Foot: 31st (Huntingdonshire) Regiment of Foot: 50th (Queen's Own) Regiment of Foot: 80th (Staffordshire Volunteers) Regiment of Foot *[1] Award considered repugnant to Indian units 1966.*

116.	**FEROZESHAH** [1] 21st–22nd December 1845 First Sikh War 1845–46	1846	Governor General's Body-Guard: 4th Regiment of Bengal Light Cavalry: 5th Regiment of Bengal Light Cavalry: 8th Regiment of Bengal Light Cavalry: 3rd Regiment of Bengal Irregular Cavalry (1st Rohilla Cavalry): 4th Regiment of Bengal Irregular Cavalry (Skinner's Horse): 8th Regiment of Bengal Irregular Cavalry: 9th Regiment of Bengal Irregular Cavalry: Bengal Horse Artillery: Bengal Foot Artillery: Bengal Sappers and Miners: 1st European Bengal Fusiliers: 2nd Regiment of Bengal Native Infantry (Grenadiers): 12th Regiment of Bengal Native Infantry: 14th Regiment of Bengal Native Infantry: 16th Regiment of Bengal Native Infantry (Grenadiers): 24th Regiment of Bengal Native Infantry: 26th Regiment of Bengal Native Infantry: 33rd Regiment of Bengal Native Infantry: 42nd Regiment of Bengal Native Infantry (Light) Infantry: 44th Regiment of Bengal Native Infantry: 45th Regiment of Bengal Native Infantry: 47th Regiment of Bengal Native Infantry (Volunteers): 48th Regiment of Bengal Native Infantry: 54th Regiment of Bengal Native Infantry: 73rd Regiment of Bengal Native Infantry
		1847	3rd (King's Own) Regiment of (Light) Dragoons: 9th (East Norfolk) Regiment of Foot: 29th (Worcestershire) Regiment of Foot: 31st (Huntingdonshire) Regiment of Foot: 50th (Queen's Own) Regiment of Foot: 62nd (Wiltshire) Regiment of Foot: 80th (Staffordshire Volunteers) Regiment of Foot [1] Awarded to Indian units as FEROZESHUHUR: FEROZESHAH taken into use 1911: award considered repugnant to Indian units 1966.
117.	**ALIWAL** [1] 28th January 1846 First Sikh War 1845–46	1846	Governor General's Body-Guard: 1st Regiment of Bengal Light Cavalry: 3rd Regiment of Bengal Light Cavalry: 5th Regiment of Bengal Light Cavalry: 4th Regiment of Bengal Irregular Cavalry (Skinner's Horse): Bengal Horse Artillery: 24th Regiment of Bengal Native Infantry: 30th Regiment of Bengal Native Infantry: 31st Regiment of Bengal Native Infantry: 36th Regiment of Bengal Native Infantry (Bengal Volunteers): 47th Regiment of Bengal Native Infantry (Volunteers): 48th Regiment of Bengal Native Infantry: 4th or Nasiri (Rifle) Battalion of Bengal Local Infantry: 6th (or Sirmoor) Battalion of Bengal Local Infantry: Shekhawati Battalion of Bengal Local Infantry
		1847	16th (The Queen's) Regiment of (Light) Dragoons (Lancers): 31st (Huntingdonshire) Regiment of Foot: 50th (Queen's Own) Regiment of Foot: 53rd (Shropshire) Regiment of Foot [1] Award considered repugnant to Indian units 1966.
118.	**SOBRAON** [1] 10th February 1846 First Sikh War 1845–46	1846	Governor General's Body-Guard: 3rd Regiment of Bengal Light Cavalry: 4th Regiment of Bengal Light Cavalry: 5th Regiment of Bengal Light Cavalry: 2nd Regiment of Bengal Irregular Cavalry (Gardner's Horse): 8th Regiment of Bengal Irregular Cavalry: 9th Regiment of Bengal Irregular Cavalry: Bengal Horse Artillery: Bengal Foot Artillery: Bengal Sappers and Miners: 1st European Bengal Fusiliers: 7th Regiment of Bengal Native Infantry: 12th Regiment of Bengal Native Infantry: 16th Regiment of Bengal Native Infantry (Grenadiers): 26th Regiment of Bengal Native (Light) Infantry: 33rd Regiment of Bengal Native Infantry: 41st Regiment of Bengal Native Infantry: 42nd Regiment of Bengal Native (Light) Infantry: 43rd Regiment of Bengal Native (Light) Infantry: 47th Regiment of Bengal Native Infantry (Volunteers): 59th Regiment of Bengal Native Infantry: 63rd Regiment of Bengal Native Infantry: 68th Regiment of Bengal Native Infantry (Volunteers): 4th or Nasiri (Rifle) Battalion of Bengal Local Infantry: 6th (or Sirmoor) Battalion of Bengal Local Infantry
		1847	3rd (King's Own) Regiment of (Light) Dragoons: 9th (Queen's Royal) Regiment of (Light) Dragoons (Lancers): 16th (The Queen's) Regiment of (Light) Dragoons (Lancers): 9th (East Norfolk) Regiment of Foot: 10th (North Lincolnshire) Regiment of Foot: 29th (Worcestershire) Regiment of Foot: 31st (Huntingdonshire) Regiment of Foot: 50th (Queen's Own) Regiment of Foot: 53rd (Shropshire) Regiment of Foot: 62nd (Wiltshire) Regiment of Foot: 80th (Staffordshire Volunteers) Regiment of Foot [1] Award considered repugnant to Indian units 1966.

119. **MOOLTAN** [1]
7th September 1848–22nd January 1849
Second Sikh War 1848–49

1852: 10th (North Lincolnshire) Regiment: 32nd (Cornwall) Regiment: 60th (The King's Royal Rifle Corps) Regiment

1853: 2nd Regiment of Bengal Light Cavalry: 7th Regiment of Bengal Irregular Cavalry: 11th Regiment of Bengal Irregular Cavalry: 14th Regiment of Bengal Irregular Cavalry: Bengal Horse Artillery: Bengal Foot Artillery: Bengal Sappers and Miners: 8th Regiment of Bengal Native Infantry: 49th Regiment of Bengal Native Infantry: 51st Regiment of Bengal Native Infantry: 72nd Regiment of Bengal Native Infantry: Corps of Guides, Punjab Irregular Force

?: 1st Regiment of Bombay Light Cavalry (Lancers): 1st Regiment of Scinde Irregular Horse: 2nd Regiment of Scinde Irregular Horse: Bombay Artillery: Bombay Sappers and Miners: 1st European Bombay Fusiliers: 3rd Regiment of Bombay Native Infantry: 4th Regiment of Bombay Native Infantry (Rifle Corps): 9th Regiment of Bombay Native Infantry: 19th Regiment of Bombay Native Infantry

[1] Award considered repugnant to Indian units 1966.

120. **CHILLIANWALLAH** [1]
13th January 1849
Second Sikh War 1848–49

1852: 3rd (The King's Own) Light Dragoons: 9th (Queen's Royal) Lancers: 14th (The King's) Light Dragoons: 24th (2nd Warwickshire) Regiment: 29th (Worcestershire) Regiment: 61st (South Gloucestershire) Regiment

1853: 1st Regiment of Bengal Light Cavalry: 5th Regiment of Bengal Light Cavalry: 6th Regiment of Bengal Light Cavalry: 8th Regiment of Bengal Light Cavalry: 3rd Regiment of Bengal Irregular Cavalry (1st Rohilla Cavalry): 9th Regiment of Bengal Irregular Cavalry: Bengal Horse Artillery: Bengal Foot Artillery: Bengal Sappers and Miners: 2nd European Bengal Fusiliers: 15th Regiment of Bengal Native Infantry: 20th Regiment of Bengal Native Infantry: 25th Regiment of Bengal Native Infantry (Volunteers): 30th Regiment of Bengal Native Infantry: 31st Regiment of Bengal Native Infantry: 36th Regiment of Bengal Native Infantry (Bengal Volunteers): 45th Regiment of Bengal Native Infantry: 46th Regiment of Bengal Native Infantry: 56th Regiment of Bengal Native Infantry: 69th Regiment of Bengal Native Infantry: 70th Regiment of Bengal Native Infantry

[1] Awarded to Indian units as CHILLIANWALLA: CHILLIANWALLAH taken into use 1911: award considered repugnant to Indian units 1966.

121. **GOOJERAT** [1]
21st February 1849
Second Sikh War 1848–49

1852: 3rd (The King's Own) Light Dragoons: 9th (Queen's Royal) Lancers: 14th (The King's) Light Dragoons: 10th (North Lincolnshire) Regiment: 24th (2nd Warwickshire) Regiment: 29th (Worcestershire) Regiment: 32nd (Cornwall) Regiment: 53rd (Shropshire) Regiment: 60th (The King's Royal Rifle Corps) Regiment: 61st (South Gloucestershire) Regiment

1853: 1st Regiment of Bengal Light Cavalry: 5th Regiment of Bengal Light Cavalry: 6th Regiment of Bengal Light Cavalry: 8th Regiment of Bengal Light Cavalry: 3rd Regiment of Bengal Irregular Cavalry (1st Rohilla Cavalry): 9th Regiment of Bengal Irregular Cavalry: 11th Regiment of Bengal Irregular Cavalry: 12th Regiment of Bengal Irregular Cavalry: 13th Regiment of Bengal Irregular Cavalry: Bengal Horse Artillery: Bengal Foot Artillery: Bengal Sappers and Miners: 2nd European Bengal Fusiliers: 8th Regiment of Bengal Native Infantry: 13th Regiment of Bengal Native Infantry: 15th Regiment of Bengal Native Infantry (Volunteers): 20th Regiment of Bengal Native Infantry: 25th Regiment of Bengal Native Infantry: 30th Regiment of Bengal Native Infantry: 31st Regiment of Bengal Native Infantry: 36th Regiment of Bengal Native Infantry: 45th Regiment of Bengal Native Infantry: 46th Regiment of Bengal Native Infantry: 51st Regiment of Bengal Native Infantry (Bengal Volunteers): 52nd Regiment of Bengal Native Infantry: 56th Regiment of Bengal Native Infantry: 69th Regiment of Bengal Native Infantry: 70th Regiment of Bengal Native Infantry: 72nd Regiment of Bengal Native Infantry: Corps of Guides, Punjab Irregular Force

1853: 1st Regiment of Scinde Irregular Horse: 2nd Regiment of Scinde Irregular Horse: Bombay Artillery: Bombay Sappers and Miners: 1st European Bombay Fusiliers: 3rd Regiment of Bombay Native Infantry: 19th Regiment of Bombay Native Infantry

[1] Award considered repugnant to Indian units 1966.

122.	**PUNJAUB** [1]	1852

7th September 1848–14th March 1849
Second Sikh War 1848–49

3rd (The King's Own) Light Dragoons: 9th (Queen's Royal) Lancers: 14th (The King's) Light Dragoons: 10th (North Lincolnshire) Regiment: 24th (2nd Warwickshire) Regiment: 29th (Worcestershire) Regiment: 32nd (Cornwall) Regiment: 53rd (Shropshire) Regiment: 60th (The King's Royal Rifle Corps) Regiment: 61st (South Gloucestershire) Regiment: 98th Regiment

		1853

1st Regiment of Bengal Light Cavalry: 2nd Regiment of Bengal Light Cavalry: 5th Regiment of Bengal Light Cavalry: 6th Regiment of Bengal Light Cavalry: 7th Regiment of Bengal Light Cavalry: 8th Regiment of Bengal Light Cavalry: 2nd Regiment of Bengal Irregular Cavalry (Gardner's Horse): 3rd Regiment of Bengal Irregular Cavalry (1st Rohilla Cavalry): 7th Regiment of Bengal Irregular Cavalry: 9th Regiment of Bengal Irregular Cavalry: 11th Regiment of Bengal Irregular Cavalry: 12th Regiment of Bengal Irregular Cavalry: 13th Regiment of Bengal Irregular Cavalry: 14th Regiment of Bengal Irregular Cavalry: 15th Regiment of Bengal Irregular Cavalry: 16th Regiment of Bengal Irregular Cavalry: 17th Regiment of Bengal Irregular Cavalry: Bengal Horse Artillery: Bengal Foot Artillery: Bengal Sappers and Miners: 2nd European Bengal Fusiliers: 1st Regiment of Bengal Native Infantry: 3rd Regiment of Bengal Native Infantry: 4th Regiment of Bengal Native Infantry: 8th Regiment of Bengal Native Infantry: 13th Regiment of Bengal Native Infantry: 15th Regiment of Bengal Native Infantry: 18th Regiment of Bengal Native Infantry: 20th Regiment of Bengal Native Infantry: 22nd Regiment of Bengal Native Infantry: 25th Regiment of Bengal Native Infantry (Volunteers): 29th Regiment of Bengal Native Infantry: 30th Regiment of Bengal Native Infantry: 31st Regiment of Bengal Native Infantry: 36th Regiment of Bengal Native Infantry (Bengal Volunteers): 37th Regiment of Bengal Native Infantry (Bengal Volunteers): 45th Regiment of Bengal Native Infantry: 46th Regiment of Bengal Native Infantry: 49th Regiment of Bengal Native Infantry: 50th Regiment of Bengal Native Infantry: 51st Regiment of Bengal Native Infantry: 52nd Regiment of Bengal Native Infantry: 53rd Regiment of Bengal Native Infantry: 56th Regiment of Bengal Native Infantry: 69th Regiment of Bengal Native Infantry: 70th Regiment of Bengal Native Infantry: 71st Regiment of Bengal Native Infantry: 72nd Regiment of Bengal Native Infantry: 73rd Regiment of Bengal Native Infantry: Corps of Guides, Punjab Irregular Force: 1st Regiment of Sikh Local Infantry, Punjab Irregular Force: 2nd (or Hill) Regiment of Sikh Local Infantry, Punjab Irregular Force

		1853

1st Regiment of Bombay Light Cavalry (Lancers): 1st Regiment of Scinde Irregular Horse: 2nd Regiment of Scinde Irregular Horse: Bombay Artillery: Bombay Sappers and Miners: 1st European Bombay Fusiliers: 3rd Regiment of Bombay Native Infantry: 4th Regiment of Bombay Native Infantry (Rifle Corps): 9th Regiment of Bombay Native Infantry: 19th Regiment of Bombay Native Infantry: 21st Regiment of Bombay Native Infantry

[1] *Awarded to Indian units as PUNJAB: PUNJAUB taken into use 1911: award considered repugnant to Indian units 1966.*

123.	**FISHGUARD**	1853

23rd February 1797
French Revolutionary Wars 1793–1802

Pembroke Yeomanry Cavalry (Castlemartin)

124.	**PEGU** [1]	1853

2nd April 1852–30th June 1853
Second Burma War 1852–53

18th (Royal Irish) Regiment: 51st (2nd Yorkshire, West Riding, King's Own Light Infantry) Regiment: 80th (Staffordshire Volunteers) Regiment

		1855

8th Regiment of Bengal Irregular Cavalry: Bengal Foot Artillery: 1st European Bengal Fusiliers: 2nd European Bengal Fusiliers: 10th Regiment of Bengal Native Infantry: 40th Regiment of Bengal Native Infantry (Volunteers): 67th Regiment of Bengal Native Infantry (Volunteers): 68th Regiment of Bengal Native Infantry (Volunteers): 2nd Regiment of Bengal Local Infantry (Ramgarh Light Infantry): 4th Regiment of Sikh Local Infantry, Punjab Irregular Force

		1855

Madras Sappers and Miners: 1st European Madras Fusiliers: 1st Regiment of Madras Native Infantry: 5th Regiment of Madras Native Infantry: 9th Regiment of Madras Native Infantry: 19th Regiment of Madras Native Infantry: 26th Regiment of Madras Native Infantry: 35th Regiment of Madras Native Infantry: 49th Regiment of Madras Native Infantry

[1] *Award considered repugnant to Indian units 1966.*

No.	Battle Honour	Year	Regiments
125.	**PERSIAN GULF** 3rd–19th December 1819 Operations in Persian Gulf 1819	1854	Marine Battalion of Bombay Native Infantry
126.	**BURMAH** 17th January 1824–24th February 1825 First Burma War 1824–26	1854	Marine Battalion of Bombay Native Infantry
127.	**CUTCHEE** 16th April 1839–15th September 1842 Operations in Scinde 1839–42	1855	1st Regiment of Scinde Irregular Horse: 2nd Regiment of Scinde Irregular Horse
128.	**ALMA** 20th September 1854 Crimean War 1854–56	1855	4th (Queen's Own) Light Dragoons: 8th (King's Royal Irish) Hussars: 11th (Prince Albert's Own) Hussars: 13th Light Dragoons: 17th Lancers: First (or Grenadier) Foot Guards: Coldstream Foot Guards: Scots Fusilier Guards: 1st (Royal) Regiment: 4th (The King's Own) Regiment: 7th (Royal Fusiliers) Regiment: 19th (1st Yorkshire, North Riding) Regiment: 20th (East Devonshire) Regiment: 21st (Royal North British Fusiliers) Regiment: 23rd (Royal Welch Fusiliers) Regiment: 28th (North Gloucestershire) Regiment: 30th (1st Cambridgeshire) Regiment: 33rd (Duke of Wellington's) Regiment: 38th (1st Staffordshire) Regiment: 41st (Welch) Regiment: 42nd (Royal Highland) Regiment: 44th (East Essex) Regiment: 47th (Lancashire) Regiment: 49th (Princess Charlotte of Wales's, Hertfordshire) Regiment: 50th (Queen's Own) Regiment: 55th (Westmorland) Regiment: 63rd (West Suffolk) Regiment: 68th (Durham, Light Infantry) Regiment: 77th (East Middlesex) Regiment: 79th (Cameron Highlanders) Regiment: 88th (Connaught Rangers) Regiment: 93rd (Highland) Regiment: 95th (Derbyshire) Regiment: The Rifle Brigade
129.	**BALAKLAVA** 25th October 1854 Crimean War 1854–56	1855	4th (Royal Irish) Dragoon Guards: 5th (Princess Charlotte of Wales's) Dragoon Guards: 1st (Royal) Dragoons: 2nd (Royal North British) Dragoons: 4th (Queen's Own) Light Dragoons: 6th (Inniskilling) Dragoons: 8th (King's Royal Irish) Hussars: 11th (Prince Albert's Own) Hussars: 13th Light Dragoons: 17th Lancers: 93rd (Highland) Regiment
130.	**INKERMAN** 5th November 1854 Crimean War 1854–56	1855	4th (Queen's Own) Light Dragoons: 8th (King's Royal Irish) Hussars: 11th (Prince Albert's Own) Hussars: 13th Light Dragoons: 17th Lancers: First (or Grenadier) Foot Guards: Coldstream Foot Guards: Scots Fusilier Guards: 1st (Royal) Regiment: 4th (The King's Own) Regiment: 7th (Royal Fusiliers) Regiment: 19th (1st Yorkshire, North Riding) Regiment: 20th (East Devonshire) Regiment: 21st (Royal North British Fusiliers) Regiment: 23rd (Royal Welch Fusiliers) Regiment: 28th (North Gloucestershire) Regiment: 30th (1st Cambridgeshire) Regiment: 33rd (Duke of Wellington's) Regiment: 38th (1st Staffordshire) Regiment: 41st (Welch) Regiment: 44th (East Essex) Regiment: 47th (Lancashire) Regiment: 49th (Princess Charlotte of Wales's, Hertfordshire) Regiment: 50th (Queen' Own) Regiment: 55th (Westmorland) Regiment: 57th (West Middlesex) Regiment: 63rd (West Suffolk) Regiment: 68th (Durham, Light Infantry) Regiment: 77th (East Middlesex) Regiment: 88th (Connaught Rangers) Regiment: 95th (Derbyshire) Regiment: The Rifle Brigade
131.	**SEVASTOPOL** 19th September 1854–8th September 1855 Crimean War 1854–56	1855	1st (King's) Dragoon Guards: 4th (Royal Irish) Dragoon Guards: 5th (Princess Charlotte of Wales's) Dragoon Guards: 6th Dragoon Guards (Carabiniers): 1st (Royal) Dragoons: 2nd (Royal North British) Dragoons: 4th (Queen's Own) Light Dragoons: 6th (Inniskilling) Dragoons: 8th (King's Royal Irish) Hussars: 10th (Prince of Wales's Own Royal) Hussars: 11th (Prince Albert's Own) Hussars: 12th (Prince of Wales's) Lancers: 13th Light Dragoons: 17th Lancers: First (or Grenadier) Foot Guards: Coldstream Foot Guards: Scots Fusilier Guards: 1st (Royal) Regiment: 3rd (East Kent, The Buffs) Regiment: 4th (The King's Own) Regiment: 7th (Royal Fusiliers) Regiment: 9th (East Norfolk) Regiment: 13th (1st Somersetshire, Prince Albert's Light Infantry) Regiment: 14th (Buckinghamshire) Regiment: 17th (Leicestershire) Regiment: 18th (Royal Irish) Regiment: 19th

(1st Yorkshire, North Riding) Regiment: 20th (East Devonshire) Regiment: 21st (Royal North British Fusiliers) Regiment: 23rd (Royal Welch Fusiliers) Regiment: 28th (North Gloucestershire) Regiment: 30th (1st Cambridgeshire) Regiment: 31st (Huntingdonshire) Regiment: 33rd (Duke of Wellington's) Regiment: 34th (Cumberland) Regiment: 38th (1st Staffordshire) Regiment 39th (Dorsetshire) Regiment: 41st (Welch) Regiment: 42nd (Royal Highland) Regiment: 44th (East Essex) Regiment 46th (South Devonshire) Regiment: 47th (Lancashire) Regiment: 48th (Northamptonshire) Regiment: 49th (Princess Charlotte of Wales's, Hertfordshire) Regiment: 50th (Queen's Own) Regiment: 55th (Westmorland) Regiment: 56th (West Essex) Regiment: 57th (West Middlesex) Regiment: 62nd (Wiltshire) Regiment: 63rd (West Suffolk) Regiment: 68th (Durham, Light Infantry) Regiment: 71st (Highland, Light Infantry) Regiment: 72nd (Duke of Albany's Own Highlanders) Regiment: 77th (East Middlesex) Regiment: 79th (Cameron Highlanders) Regiment: 82nd (Prince of Wales's Volunteers) Regiment: 88th (Connaught Rangers) Regiment: 89th Regiment: 90th (Perthshire Volunteers, Light Infantry) Regiment: 93rd (Highland) Regiment 95th (Derbyshire) Regiment: 97th (Earl of Ulster's) Regiment: The Rifle Brigade

132. **MEDITERRANEAN**
28th March 1854–10th March 1856
Crimean War 1854–56

1856
Royal Berkshire Militia: 2nd West Yorkshire Militia (Light Infantry): Royal Wiltshire Militia: 1st Royal Lancashire Militia (Duke of Lancaster's Own): Northamptonshire and Rutland Militia: East Kent Militia: Oxfordshire Militia: 3rd. or Royal Westminster, Middlesex Militia (Light Infantry): The King's Own (1st Staffordshire) Militia: 3rd Royal Lancashire Militia (Duke of Lancaster's Own)

133. **RESHIRE**
7th December 1856
Persian War 1856–57

1858
3rd Regiment of Bombay Light Cavalry: Poona Irregular Horse: Bombay Sappers and Miners: 4th Regiment of Bombay Native Infantry (Rifle Corps): 20th Regiment of Bombay Native Infantry: 2nd Baluch Battalion of Bombay Native Infantry
1859 64th (2nd Staffordshire) Regiment
1861 2nd Bombay Light Infantry

134. **KOOSH-AB**
8th February 1857
Persian War 1856–57

1858
3rd Regiment of Bombay Light Cavalry: Poona Irregular Horse: Bombay Sappers and Miners: 4th Regiment of Bombay Native Infantry (Rifle Corps): 20th Regiment of Bombay Native Infantry: 26th Regiment of Bombay Native Infantry: 2nd Baluch Battalion of Bombay Native Infantry
1859 64th (2nd Staffordshire) Regiment: 78th (Highland, Ross-shire Buffs) Regiment
1861 2nd Bombay Light Infantry

[1] *Awarded to Indian units as KOOSH-AB: KOOSH-AB taken into use 1911.*

135. **PERSIA**
29th November 1856–4th April 1857
Persian War 1856–57

1858 Madras Sappers and Miners
1858 3rd Regiment of Bombay Light Cavalry: Poona Irregular Horse: 1st Regiment of Scinde Irregular Horse: Bombay Sappers and Miners: 4th Regiment of Bombay Native Infantry (Rifle Corps): 11th Regiment of Bombay Native Infantry: 15th Regiment of Bombay Native Infantry: 20th Regiment of Bombay Native Infantry: 23rd Regiment of Bombay Native Infantry (Light) Infantry: 26th Regiment of Bombay Native Infantry: 2nd Baluch Battalion of Bombay Native Infantry
1859 14th (King's) Light Dragoons: 64th (2nd Staffordshire) Regiment: 78th (Highland, Ross-shire Buffs) Regiment
1861 2nd Bombay Light Infantry

136. **BUSHIRE**
12th December 1856
Persian War 1856–57

1859 64th (2nd Staffordshire) Regiment
1861 3rd Regiment of Bombay Light Cavalry: 1st Regiment of Poona Horse: Bombay Sappers and Miners: 4th Regiment of Bombay Native Infantry (Rifle Corps): 20th Regiment of Bombay Native Infantry: 29th Regiment of Bombay Native Infantry (2nd Baluch Battalion): 2nd Bombay Light Infantry

137. **CANTON**
28th December 1857–5th January 1858
Second China War 1857–62

1861 — 59th (2nd Nottinghamshire) Regiment

138. **TAKU FORTS**
21st August 1860
Second China War 1857–62

1861 — 1st (King's) Dragoon Guards: 1st (Royal) Regiment: 2nd (Queen's Royal) Regiment: 3rd (East Kent, The Buffs) Regiment: 31st (Huntingdonshire) Regiment: 44th (East Essex) Regiment: 60th (The King's Royal Rifle Corps) Regiment: 67th (South Hampshire) Regiment

1862 — 11th Regiment of Bengal Cavalry: 19th Regiment of Bengal Cavalry: 20th Regiment of Bengal Native Infantry: 23rd Regiment of Bengal Native Infantry

1870 — Madras Sappers and Miners

139. **PEKIN 1860** [1]
18th September–13th October 1860
Second China War 1857–62

1861 — 1st (King's) Dragoon Guards: 1st (Royal) Regiment: 2nd (Queen's Royal) Regiment: 60th (The King's Royal Rifle Corps) Regiment: 67th (South Hampshire) Regiment: 99th (Lanarkshire) Regiment

1862 — 11th Regiment of Bengal Cavalry: 19th Regiment of Bengal Cavalry: 20th Regiment of Bengal Native Infantry: 23rd Regiment of Bengal Native Infantry

1870 — Madras Sappers and Miners

[1] Awarded as PEKIN; year-date added 1914.

140. **DELHI 1857** [1] [2]
30th May–20th September 1857
Indian Mutiny 1857–58

1863 — 6th Dragoon Guards (Carabiniers): 9th (Queen's Royal) Lancers: 8th (The King's) Regiment: 52nd (Oxfordshire, Light Infantry) Regiment: 60th (The King's Royal Rifle Corps) Regiment: 61st (South Gloucestershire) Regiment: 75th (Stirlingshire) Regiment: 101st (Royal Bengal Fusiliers) Regiment: 104th (Bengal Fusiliers) Regiment

1864 — 9th Regiment of Bengal Cavalry: 10th Regiment of Bengal Cavalry: Bengal Sappers and Miners: 32nd Regiment of Bengal Native Infantry: 2nd Goorkha Regiment: 3rd Goorkha Regiment: 1st Regiment of Punjab Cavalry, Punjab Irregular Force: 2nd Regiment of Punjab Cavalry, Punjab Irregular Force: 5th Regiment of Punjab Cavalry, Punjab Irregular Force: Corps of Guides, Punjab Irregular Force: 4th Regiment of Sikh Infantry, Punjab Irregular Force: 1st Regiment of Punjab Infantry, Punjab Irregular Force: 2nd Regiment of Punjab Infantry, Punjab Irregular Force: 4th Regiment of Punjab Infantry, Punjab Irregular Force

1864 — 27th Regiment of Bombay Native Infantry (1st Baluch Battalion)

[1] Awarded as DELHI; year-date added 1914. [2] Award considered repugnant to Indian units 1966.

141. **LUCKNOW** [1]
30th June 1857–21st March 1858
Indian Mutiny 1857–58

1863 — 2nd (Queen's) Dragoon Guards: 7th (Queen's Own) Hussars: 9th (Queen's Royal) Lancers: 5th (Northumberland Fusiliers) Regiment: 8th (The King's) Regiment: 10th (North Lincolnshire) Regiment: 20th (East Devonshire) Regiment: 23rd (Royal Welch Fusiliers) Regiment: 32nd (Cornwall, Light Infantry) Regiment: 34th (Cumberland) Regiment: 38th (1st Staffordshire) Regiment: 42nd (Royal Highland, The Black Watch) Regiment: 53rd (Shropshire) Regiment: 64th (2nd Staffordshire) Regiment: 75th (Stirlingshire) Regiment: 78th (Highland, Ross-shire Buffs) Regiment: 79th (Cameron Highlanders) Regiment: 82nd (Prince of Wales's Volunteers) Regiment: 84th (York and Lancaster) Regiment: 90th (Perthshire Volunteers, Light Infantry) Regiment: 93rd (Sutherland Highlanders) Regiment: 97th (Earl of Ulster's) Regiment: 101st (Royal Bengal Fusiliers) Regiment: 102nd (Royal Madras Fusiliers) Regiment: The Prince Consort's Own Rifle Brigade

1864 — 9th Regiment of Bengal Cavalry: 10th Regiment of Bengal Cavalry: Bengal Sappers and Miners: 11th Regiment of Bengal Native Infantry (The Lucknow) Regiment: 14th Regiment of Bengal Native Infantry (The Ferozepore): 6th Regiment of Bengal Native Infantry (The Lucknow) [2]: 32nd Regiment of Bengal Native Infantry: 1st Regiment of Punjab Cavalry, Punjab Irregular Force: 2nd Regiment of Punjab Cavalry, Punjab Irregular Force: 5th Regiment of Punjab Cavalry, Punjab Irregular Force: 2nd Regiment of Punjab Infantry, Punjab Irregular Force: 4th Regiment of Punjab Infantry, Punjab Irregular Force

	1864	Madras Sappers and Miners: 27th Regiment of Madras Native Infantry (1st Baluch Battalion)

¹ Award considered repugnant to Indian units 1966. ² The badge of a Turretted Gateway taken into use 1872.

142. **CENTRAL INDIA**¹
8th June 1857–20th September 1858
Indian Mutiny 1857–58

1863	8th (King's Royal Irish) Hussars: 12th (Prince of Wales's Royal) Lancers: 14th (King's) Hussars: 71st (Highland, Light Infantry) Regiment: 72nd (Duke of Albany's Own Highlanders) Regiment: 80th (Staffordshire Volunteers) Regiment: 83rd (County of Dublin) Regiment: 86th (Royal County Down) Regiment: 88th (Connaught Rangers) Regiment: 95th (Derbyshire) Regiment: 108th (Madras Infantry) Regiment: 109th (Bombay Infantry) Regiment
1864	2nd Regiment of Bengal Native (Ligh't) Infantry
1864	Madras Sappers and Miners: 1st Regiment of Madras Native Infantry: 19th Regiment of Madras Native Infantry
1864	1st Regiment of Bombay Light Cavalry: 2nd Regiment of Bombay Light Cavalry: 3rd Regiment of Bombay Light Cavalry: 1st Regiment of Scinde Horse: 3rd Regiment of Scinde Horse: Bombay Sappers and Miners: 4th Regiment of Bombay Native Infantry (Rifle Corps): 10th Regiment of Bombay Native Infantry: 12th Regiment of Bombay Native Infantry: 13th Regiment of Bombay Native Infantry: 24th Regiment of Bombay Native Infantry: 25th Regiment of Bombay Native Infantry
1866	1st Regiment, Hyderabad Contingent Cavalry: 3rd Regiment, Hyderabad Contingent Cavalry: 4th Regiment, Hyderabad Contingent Cavalry: 3rd Regiment, Hyderabad Contingent Infantry: 5th Regiment, Hyderabad Contingent Infantry
1878	1st Field Battery, Hyderabad Contingent Artillery: 2nd Field Battery, Hyderabad Contingent Artillery: 4th Field Battery, Hyderabad Contingent Artillery
1879	17th (Duke of Cambridge's Own) Lancers
1887	Merwara Regiment
1912	42nd Deoli Regiment

¹ Award considered repugnant to Indian units 1966.

143. **NOWAH**
Third Mahratta (and Pindari) War
21st January 1818
1817–18

1864	1st Field Battery, Hyderabad Contingent Artillery: 1st Regiment, Hyderabad Contingent Infantry: 2nd Regiment, Hyderabad Contingent Infantry: 3rd Regiment, Hyderabad Contingent Infantry

144. **ABYSSINIA**
21st October 1867–13th April 1868
Abyssinian War 1867–68

1868	3rd (Prince of Wales's) Dragoon Guards: 4th (The King's Own) Regiment: 26th (Cameronian) Regiment: 33rd (Duke of Wellington's) Regiment: 45th (Nottinghamshire, Sherwood Foresters) Regiment
1869	10th Regiment of Bengal Cavalry: 12th Regiment of Bengal Cavalry: 3rd Regiment of Bombay Light Cavalry: 3rd Regiment of Scinde Horse: No 1 Battery, Native Artillery: Madras Sappers and Miners: Bombay Sappers and Miners: 21st (Punjab) Regiment of Bengal Native Infantry: 23rd (Punjab) Regiment of Bengal Native Infantry (Pioneers): 2nd (Prince of Wales's Own) Regiment of Bombay Native Infantry (Grenadiers): 3rd Regiment of Bombay Native Infantry: 10th Regiment of Bombay Native Infantry (Light) Infantry: 18th Regiment of Bombay Native Infantry: 21st Regiment of Bombay Native Infantry (The Marine Battalion): 25th Regiment of Bombay Native (Light) Infantry: 27th Regiment of Bombay Native Infantry (1st Baluch Regiment)

145. **NEW ZEALAND**
3rd May 1845–20th July 1847
First Maori War 1845–47
6th March 1860–14th March 1861
Second Maori War 1860–61
and 4th May 1863–15th February 1866
Third Maori War 1863–66

1870	12th (East Suffolk) Regiment: 14th (Buckinghamshire) Regiment: 18th (Royal Irish) Regiment: 40th (2nd Somersetshire) Regiment: 43rd (Monmouthshire, Light Infantry) Regiment: 50th (Queen's Own) Regiment: 57th (West Middlesex) Regiment: 58th (Rutlandshire) Regiment: 65th (2nd Yorkshire, North Riding) Regiment: 68th (Durham, Light Infantry) Regiment: 70th (Surrey) Regiment: 96th Regiment: 99th (Lanarkshire) Regiment
?	The Taranaki Regiment

146.	**ECCLES HILL** 25th May 1870 Fenian Raids 1866–70	1870 1871	60th, "Missisquoi Battalion of Infantry" 3rd Battalion, "The Victoria Volunteer Rifles of Montreal"
147.	**DEFENCE OF ARRAH** [1] 30th July–2nd August 1857 Indian Mutiny 1857–58	1874	45th (Rattray's Sikhs) Regiment of Bengal Native Infantry [1] Award considered repugnant to Indian units 1966.
148.	**BEHAR** [1] 16th August 1857 Indian Mutiny 1857–58	1874	45th (Rattray's Sikhs) Regiment of Bengal Native Infantry [1] Award considered repugnant to Indian units 1966.
149.	**ASHANTEE 1873–74** [1] 9th June 1873–6th February 1874 Ashantee War 1873–74	1876 1913	23rd (Royal Welch Fusiliers) Regiment: 42nd (Royal Highland, The Black Watch) Regiment: The Prince Consort's Own Rifle Corps: 1st West India Regiment: 2nd West India Regiment Southern Nigeria Regiment, West African Frontier Force: Gold Coast Regiment, West African Frontier Force [1] Awarded as ASHANTEE: year-dates added 1914.
150.	**TROUT RIVER** 27th May 1870 Fenian Raids 1866–70	1879	50th Battalion, "Huntingdon Borderers"
151.	**ALI MASJID** [1] 21st November 1878 Second Afghan War 1878–80	1881 1881	10th (Prince of Wales's Own Royal) Hussars: 17th (Leicestershire) Regiment: 51st (2nd Yorkshire, West Riding, King's Own Light Infantry) Regiment: 81st (Loyal Lincoln Volunteers) Regiment: Rifle Brigade (The Prince Consort's Own) No 4 (Hazara) Punjab Mountain Battery: Bengal Sappers and Miners: 11th (Prince of Wales' Own) Bengal Lancers: 6th Bengal Native (Light) Infantry: 14th Bengal Native Infantry: 20th Bengal Native Infantry: 27th Bengal Native Infantry: 45th Bengal Native Infantry: 4th Goorkha Regiment: The Queen's Own Corps of Guides: 1st Sikh Infantry [1] Awarded to Indian units as ALI MASJID: ALI MASJID taken into use 1911.
152.	**PEIWAR KOTAL** 2nd December 1878 Second Afghan War 1878–80	1881 1881	8th (The King's) Regiment: 72nd (Duke of Albany's Own Highlanders) Regiment No 1 (Kohat) Punjab Mountain Battery: 12th Bengal Cavalry: 23rd Bengal Native Infantry (Pioneers): 29th Bengal Native Infantry: 5th Goorkha Regiment 2nd Punjab Infantry: 5th Punjab Infantry
153.	**CHARASIAH** [1] 6th October 1879 Second Afghan War 1878–80	1881 1881	67th (South Hampshire) Regiment: 72nd (Duke of Albany's Own Highlanders) Regiment: 92nd (Gordon Highlanders) Regiment No 2 (Derajat) Punjab Mountain Battery: Bengal Sappers and Miners: 12th Bengal Cavalry: 14th Bengal Lancers: 5th Punjab Cavalry: 23rd Bengal Native Infantry (Pioneers): 28th Bengal Native Infantry: 5th Goorkha Regiment: 5th Punjab Infantry [1] Awarded to Indian units as CHARASIA: CHARASIAH taken into use 1911.
154.	**KABUL 1879** 10th–23rd December 1879 Second Afghan War 1878–80	1881 1881	9th (Queen's Royal) Lancers: 9th (East Norfolk) Regiment: 67th (South Hampshire) Regiment: 72nd (Duke of Albany's Own Highlanders) Regiment: 92nd (Gordon Highlanders) Regiment No 1 (Kohat) Punjab Mountain Battery: No 2 (Derajat) Punjab Mountain Battery: No 4 (Hazara) Punjab Mountain Battery: Bengal Sappers and Miners: 12th Bengal Cavalry: 14th Bengal Lancers: 5th Punjab Cavalry: 23rd Bengal Native Infantry (Pioneers): 28th Bengal Native Infantry: 2nd (Prince of Wales' Own) Goorkha Regiment: 4th Goorkha Regiment: 5th Goorkha Regiment: The Queen's Own Corps of Guides: 3rd Sikh Infantry: 5th Punjab Infantry

155.	**AHMAD KHEL**¹ 19th April 1880 Second Afghan War 1878–80	1881 1881	59th (2nd Nottinghamshire) Regiment: 60th (King's Royal) Rifle Corps Bengal Sappers and Miners: 19th Bengal Native Infantry: 1st Punjab Cavalry: 2nd Punjab Cavalry: 15th Bengal Native Infantry: 19th Bengal Native Infantry: 25th Bengal Native Infantry: 3rd Goorkha Regiment: 2nd Sikh Infantry ¹ *Awarded to Indian units as AHMAD KHEL: AHMAD KHEL taken into use 1911.*
156.	**KANDAHAR 1880** 1st September 1880 Second Afghan War 1878–80	1881 1881 1883	9th (Queen's Royal) Lancers: 7th (Royal Fusiliers) Regiment: 60th (King's Royal) Rifle Corps: 66th (Berkshire) Regiment: 72nd (Duke of Albany's Own Highlanders) Regiment: 92nd (Gordon Highlanders) Regiment No 2 (Derajat) Punjab Mountain Battery: 3rd Bengal Cavalry: 3rd Punjab Cavalry: 1st Central India Horse: 2nd Central India Horse: 3rd (Queen's Own) Bombay Light Cavalry: Poona Horse: 3rd Scinde Horse: 15th Bengal Native Infantry: 23rd Bengal Native Infantry (Pioneers): 24th Bengal Native Infantry: 25th Bengal Native Infantry: 2nd (Prince of Wales' Own) Goorkha Regiment: 4th Goorkha Regiment: 5th Goorkha Regiment: 2nd Sikh Infantry: 3rd Sikh Infantry: 1st Bombay Native Infantry (Grenadiers): 4th Bombay Native Infantry (Rifle Corps): 19th Bombay Native Infantry: 28th Bombay Native Infantry: 29th Bombay Native Infantry Bombay Sappers and Miners
157.	**AFGHANISTAN 1878–79** 22nd November 1878–26th May 1879 Second Afghan War 1878–80	1881 1881 1882	10th (Prince of Wales's Own Royal) Hussars: 17th (Leicestershire) Regiment: 70th (Surrey) Regiment: 81st (Loyal Lincoln Volunteers) Regiment: Rifle Brigade (The Prince Consort's Own) No 3 (Peshawar) Punjab Mountain Battery: 11th (Prince of Wales' Own) Bengal Lancers: 6th Bengal Native (Light) Infantry: 12th Bengal Native Infantry: 14th Bengal Native Infantry: 26th Bengal Native Infantry: 1st Sikh Infantry: 1st Punjab Infantry: 2nd Punjab Infantry: Bhopal Battalion: Mhwairwara Battalion 1st Scinde Horse
158.	**AFGHANISTAN 1878–80** 22nd November 1878–20th September 1880 Second Afghan War 1878–80	1881 1881	9th (Queen's Royal) Lancers: 15th (King's) Hussars: 5th (Northumberland Fusiliers) Regiment: 8th (The King's) Regiment: 12th (East Suffolk) Regiment: 25th (King's Own Borderers) Regiment: 51st (2nd Yorkshire, West Riding, King's Own Light Infantry) Regiment: 59th (2nd Nottinghamshire) Regiment: 60th (King's Royal) Rifle Corps: 67th (South Hampshire) Regiment: 72nd (Duke of Albany's Own Highlanders) Regiment: 92nd (Gordon Highlanders) Regiment No 1 (Kohat) Punjab Mountain Battery: No 2 (Derajat) Punjab Mountain Battery: No 4 (Hazara) Punjab Mountain Battery: No 2 Bombay Mountain Battery: Bengal Sappers and Miners: The Queen's Own Madras Sappers and Miners: Bombay Sappers and Miners: 8th Bengal Cavalry: 10th (Duke of Cambridge's Own) Bengal Lancers: 12th Bengal Cavalry: 13th Bengal Lancers: 14th Bengal Lancers: 15th Bengal Cavalry: 19th Bengal Lancers: 1st Punjab Cavalry: 2nd Punjab Cavalry: 5th Punjab Cavalry: 3rd Scinde Horse: 15th Bengal Native Infantry: 19th Bengal Native Infantry: 20th Bengal Native Infantry: 21st Bengal Native Infantry: 23rd Bengal Native Infantry (Pioneers): 24th Bengal Native Infantry: 25th Bengal Native Infantry: 27th Bengal Native Infantry: 28th Bengal Native Infantry: 29th Bengal Native Infantry: 32nd Bengal Native Infantry (Pioneers): 39th Bengal Native Infantry: 45th Bengal Native Infantry: 1st Goorkha Regiment: 2nd (Prince of Wales' Own) Goorkha Regiment: 3rd Goorkha Regiment: 4th Goorkha Regiment: 5th Goorkha Regiment: The Queen's Own Corps of Guides: 2nd Sikh Infantry: 5th Punjab Infantry: 21st Madras Native Infantry: 1st Bombay Native Infantry (Grenadiers): 19th Bombay Native Infantry: 28th Bombay Native Infantry: 29th Bombay Native Infantry: 30th Bombay Native Infantry
159.	**AFGHANISTAN 1879–80** 1st January 1879–20th September 1880 Second Afghan War 1878–80	1881 1881	6th Dragoon Guards (Carabiniers): 8th (King's Royal Irish) Hussars: 7th (Royal Fusiliers) Regiment: 9th (East Norfolk) Regiment: 11th (North Devon) Regiment: 14th (Buckinghamshire, Prince of Wales's Own) Regiment: 15th (York, East Riding) Regiment: 18th (The Royal Irish) Regiment: 63rd (West Suffolk) Regiment: 66th (Berkshire) Regiment: 78th (Highlanders) (Ross-shire Buffs) Regiment: 85th (Bucks Volunteers) (King's Light Infantry) Regiment 1st Bengal Cavalry: 3rd Bengal Cavalry: 4th Bengal Cavalry: 5th Bengal Cavalry: 17th Bengal Cavalry: 18th Bengal Cavalry: 3rd

The following continues from the previous page (the Indian regiment list awarded for the preceding honour):

Punjab Cavalry: 1st Central India Horse: 2nd Central India Horse: 1st Madras Light Cavalry: 2nd Bombay Light Cavalry: 3rd (Queen's Own) Bombay Light Cavalry: Poona Horse: 2nd Scinde Horse: 2nd (Queen's Own) Bengal Native (Light) Infantry: 3rd Bengal Native Infantry: 4th Bengal Native Infantry: 5th Bengal Native (Light) Infantry: 8th Bengal Native Infantry: 9th Bengal Native Infantry: 13th Bengal Native Infantry: 16th Bengal Native Infantry: 17th Bengal Native Infantry: 22nd Bengal Native Infantry: 30th Bengal Native Infantry: 31st Bengal Native Infantry: 41st Bengal Native Infantry: 3rd Sikh Infantry: 4th Punjab Infantry: Infantry of the Deoli Irregular Force: 1st Madras Native Infantry: 4th Madras Native Infantry: 15th Madras Native Infantry: 4th Bombay Native Infantry (Rifle Corps): 5th Bombay Native (Light) Infantry: 8th Bombay Native Infantry: 9th Bombay Native Infantry: 10th Bombay Native (Light) Infantry: 13th Bombay Native Infantry: 15th Bombay Native Infantry: 16th Bombay Native Infantry: 23rd Bombay Native (Light) Infantry: 24th Bombay Native Infantry: 27th Bombay Native (Light) Infantry

No.	Battle Honour / Description	Year	Regiments
160.	**SOUTH AFRICA 1877-78-79** [1] 25th September 1877–2nd December 1879 Zulu and Basuto Wars 1877–79	1881	24th (2nd Warwickshire) Regiment: 88th (Connaught Rangers) Regiment: 90th (Perthshire Volunteers, Light Infantry) Regiment: 94th Regiment [1] *Awarded as SOUTH AFRICA: year-dates added 1882.*
161.	**SOUTH AFRICA 1878-79** [1] 1st January 1878–2nd December 1879 Zulu and Basuto Wars 1877–79	1881	13th (1st Somersetshire, Prince Albert's Light Infantry) Regiment: 80th (Staffordshire Volunteers) Regiment [1] *Awarded as SOUTH AFRICA: year-dates added 1882.*
162.	**SOUTH AFRICA 1879** 1st January–2nd December 1879 Zulu and Basuto Wars 1877–79	1881 1900 ?	1st (King's) Dragoon Guards: 17th (Duke of Cambridge's Own) Lancers: 3rd (East Kent, The Buffs) Regiment: 4th (King's Own Royal) Regiment: 21st (Royal Scots Fusiliers) Regiment: 57th (West Middlesex) Regiment: 58th (Rutlandshire) Regiment: 60th (King's Royal) Rifle Corps: 91st (Princess Louise's Argyllshire Highlanders) Regiment: 99th (Duke of Edinburgh's) Regiment Natal Carbineers: Natal Mounted Rifles: Umvoti Mounted Rifles: Border Mounted Rifles Durban Light Infantry [1] *Awarded to British units as SOUTH AFRICA; year-date added 1882.*
163.	**SOUTH AFRICA 1846-47** 16th March 1846–16th December 1847 Seventh Kaffir War 1846–47	1881 1882	The Prince Consort's Own (Rifle Brigade) [1] The Royal Warwickshire Regiment [1]: 7th (Princess Royal's) Dragoon Guards: The Cameronians (Scottish Rifles): The Royal Inniskilling Fusiliers: The Black Watch (Royal Highlanders): The Sherwood Foresters (Derbyshire Regiment): The Princess Louise's (Argyll and Sutherland Highlanders) [1] *Awarded as SOUTH AFRICA: year-dates added 1882.*
164.	**SOUTH AFRICA 1851-2-3** 24th December 1850–12th March 1853 Eighth Kaffir War 1850–53	1881 1882	The Prince Consort's Own (Rifle Brigade) [1] The Royal Warwickshire Regiment [1]: 12th (Prince of Wales's Royal) Lancers: The Queen's (Royal West Surrey Regiment): The Suffolk Regiment: The Black Watch (Royal Highlanders): The Oxfordshire Light Infantry: The King's Royal Rifle Corps: The Highland Light Infantry: The Princess Louise's (Argyll and Sutherland Highlanders) [1] *Awarded as SOUTH AFRICA: year-dates added 1882.*
165.	**JERSEY 1781** 6th January 1761 War against France and Spain 1778–83	1881	1st (or West) Regiment, Royal Jersey Militia: 2nd (or East) Regiment, Royal Jersey Militia: 3rd (or South) Regiment, Royal Jersey Militia
166.	**BLENHEIM** 13th August 1704 War of the Spanish Succession 1701–14	1882	1st (King's) Dragoon Guards: 3rd (Prince of Wales's) Dragoon Guards: 5th (Princess Charlotte of Wales's) Dragoon Guards: 6th Dragoon Guards (Carabiniers): 7th (Princess Royal's) Dragoon Guards: 2nd Dragoons (Royal Scots Greys): 5th (Royal Irish) Lancers: Grenadier Guards: The Royal Scots (Lothian Regiment): The Buffs (East Kent Regiment): The King's (Liverpool

167. **RAMILLIES**
23rd May 1706
War of the Spanish Succession 1701–14

1882

Regiment); The Lincolnshire Regiment; The East Yorkshire Regiment; The Bedfordshire Regiment; The Royal Irish Regiment; The Royal Scots Fusiliers; The Royal Welsh Fusiliers; The South Wales Borderers; The Cameronians (Scottish Rifles); The Hampshire Regiment

1st (King's) Dragoon Guards; 3rd (Prince of Wales's) Dragoon Guards: 5th (Princess Charlotte of Wales's) Dragoon Guards: 6th Dragoon Guards (Carabiniers); 7th (Princess Royal's) Dragoon Guards: 2nd Dragoons (Royal Scots Greys): 5th (Royal Irish) Lancers; Grenadier Guards: The Buffs (East Kent Regiment); The King's (Liverpool Regiment); The Lincolnshire Regiment; The East Yorkshire Regiment; The Bedfordshire Regiment; The Royal Irish Regiment; The Royal Scots Fusiliers; The Royal Welsh Fusiliers: The South Wales Borderers: The Cameronians (Scottish Rifles); The Gloucestershire Regiment; The Worcestershire Regiment; The Hampshire Regiment

168. **OUDENARDE**
11th July 1708
War of the Spanish Succession 1701–14

1882

1st (King's) Dragoon Guards: 3rd (Prince of Wales's) Dragoon Guards: 5th (Princess Charlotte of Wales's) Dragoon Guards: 6th Dragoon Guards (Carabiniers): 7th (Princess Royal's) Dragoon Guards: 2nd Dragoons (Royal Scots Greys): 5th (Royal Irish) Lancers; Grenadier Guards: Coldstream Guards: The Royal Scots (Lothian Regiment): The Buffs (East Kent Regiment); The King's (Liverpool Regiment); The Lincolnshire Regiment: The East Yorkshire Regiment: The Bedfordshire Regiment: The Royal Irish Regiment: The Royal Scots Fusiliers: The Royal Welsh Fusiliers: The South Wales Borderers: The Cameronians (Scottish Rifles): The Hampshire Regiment

169. **MALPLAQUET**
11th September 1709
War of the Spanish Succession 1701–14

1882

1st (King's) Dragoon Guards: 3rd (Prince of Wales's) Dragoon Guards: 5th (Princess Charlotte of Wales's) Dragoon Guards: 6th Dragoon Guards (Carabiniers): 7th (Princess Royal's) Dragoon Guards: 2nd Dragoons (Royal Scots Greys): 5th (Royal Irish) Lancers; Grenadier Guards: Coldstream Guards: The Royal Scots (Lothian Regiment): The Buffs (East Kent Regiment); The King's (Liverpool Regiment): The Lincolnshire Regiment: The East Yorkshire Regiment: The Bedfordshire Regiment: The Royal Irish Regiment The Princess of Wales's Own (Yorkshire Regiment): The Royal Scots Fusiliers: The Royal Welsh Fusiliers: The South Wales Borderers: The Cameronians (Scottish Rifles): The Hampshire Regiment

170. **LOUISBURG**
8th June–27th July 1758
French and Indian War 1754–63

1882

The Royal Scots (Lothian Regiment): The East Yorkshire Regiment: The Leicestershire Regiment: The Cheshire Regiment: The Gloucestershire Regiment: The Royal Sussex Regiment: The Prince of Wales's Volunteers (South Lancashire Regiment): The Sherwood Foresters (Derbyshire Regiment): The Loyal North Lancashire Regiment: The Northamptonshire Regiment:

1910

The King's Royal Rifle Corps
The Duke of Edinburgh's (Wiltshire Regiment)

171. **QUEBEC 1759**
27th June–18th September 1759
French and Indian War 1754–63

1882

The East Yorkshire Regiment: The Gloucestershire Regiment: The Royal Sussex Regiment: The Oxfordshire Light Infantry: The Loyal North Lancashire Regiment: The Northamptonshire Regiment: The King's Royal Rifle Corps

172. **SOUTH AFRICA 1835**
21st December 1834–17th December 1835
Sixth Kaffir War 1834–35

1882

The Royal Inniskilling Fusiliers: Seaforth Highlanders (Ross-shire Buffs, The Duke of Albany's): The Gordon Highlanders

173. **DETTINGEN**
27th June 1743
War of the Austrian Succession 1740–48

1882

1st Life Guards: 2nd Life Guards: Royal Horse Guards (The Blues): 1st (King's) Dragoon Guards: 7th (Princess Royal's) Dragoon Guards: 1st (Royal) Dragoons: 2nd Dragoons (Royal Scots Greys): 3rd (King's Own) Hussars: 4th (Queen's Own) Hussars: 6th (Inniskilling) Dragoons: 7th (Queen's Own) Hussars: Grenadier Guards: Coldstream Guards: Scots Guards: The Buffs (East Kent Regiment): The King's (Liverpool Regiment): The Devonshire Regiment: The Suffolk Regiment: The Prince Albert's

No.	Battle Honour	Year	Regiments
174.	**CHINA 1860–62** 1st January 1860–20th August 1862 Second China War 1857–62	1882	(Somersetshire Light Infantry): The Lancashire Fusiliers: The Royal Scots Fusiliers: The Royal Welsh Fusiliers: The East Surrey Regiment: The Duke of Cornwall's Light Infantry: The Duke of Wellington's (West Riding Regiment): The Hampshire Regiment
		1882	22nd Bengal Native Infantry ¹: 5th Bombay Native Infantry ¹: 15th Bengal Native Infantry: 27th Bengal Native Infantry ¹ *Awarded as CHINA: year-dates added 1882.*
175.	**CHINA 1858–59** 1st January 1858–31st December 1859 Second China War 1857–62	1882	7th Bengal Native Infantry: 10th Bengal Native Infantry: 11th Bengal Native Infantry
176.	**TEL-EL-KEBIR** 13th September 1882 Revolt of Ali Pasha 1882	1883	1st Life Guards: 2nd Life Guards: Royal Horse Guards: 7th (Princess Royal's) Dragoon Guards: 19th Hussars: Grenadier Guards: Coldstream Guards: Scots Guards: The Royal Irish Regiment: The Duke of Cornwall's Light Infantry: The Black Watch (Royal Highlanders): The King's Royal Rifle Corps: The York and Lancaster Regiment: The Highland Light Infantry: Seaforth Highlanders (Ross-shire Buffs, The Duke of Albany's): The Gordon Highlanders: The Queen's Own Cameron Highlanders: The Princess Victoria's (Royal Irish Fusiliers)
		1883	2nd Bengal Cavalry: 6th Bengal Cavalry: 13th Bengal Lancers: The Madras Sappers and Miners: 7th Bengal Native Infantry: 20th Bengal Native Infantry: 29th Bombay Native Infantry
177.	**EGYPT 1882** ¹ 11th July–23rd September 1882 Revolt of Ali Pasha 1882	1883	1st Life Guards: 2nd Life Guards: Royal Horse Guards: 4th (Royal Irish) Dragoon Guards: 7th (Princess Royal's) Dragoon Guards: 19th Hussars: Grenadier Guards: Coldstream Guards: Scots Guards: The Royal Irish Regiment: The Duke of Cornwall's Light Infantry: The Royal Sussex Regiment: The South Staffordshire Regiment: The Black Watch (Royal Highlanders): The Sherwood Foresters (Derbyshire Regiment): The Princess Charlotte of Wales's (Berkshire Regiment): The King's (Shropshire Light Infantry): The King's Royal Rifle Corps: The Manchester Regiment: The York and Lancaster Regiment: The Highland Light Infantry: Seaforth Highlanders (Ross-shire Buffs, The Duke of Albany's): The Gordon Highlanders: The Queen's Own Cameron Highlanders: The Princess Victoria's (Royal Irish Fusiliers): Royal Malta Fencible Artillery
		1883	2nd Bengal Cavalry: 6th Bengal Cavalry: 13th Bengal Lancers: The Madras Sappers and Miners: 7th Bengal Native Infantry: 20th Bengal Native Infantry: 29th Bombay Native Infantry
		1909	8th (City of London) Battalion, The London Regiment (Post Office Rifles) ¹ *Award considered repugnant to Indian units 1966.*
178.	**EGYPT 1884** 1st February–5th April 1884 Suakin Expedition 1884	1885	10th (Prince of Wales's Own Royal) Hussars: 19th Hussars: The Black Watch (Royal Highlanders): The King's Royal Rifle Corps:The York and Lancaster Regiment: The Gordon Highlanders: Princess Victoria's (Royal Irish Fusiliers)
179.	**BATOCHE** 12th May 1885 Riel's Rebellion 1885	1885 1914	10th Battalion, "Royal Grenadiers" 32nd Manitoba Horse: 90th Regiment "Winnipeg Rifles"
180.	**ABU KLEA** 17th–18th January 1885 First Sudan War 1884–85	1886	19th (Princess of Wales's Own) Hussars: The Royal Sussex Regiment

181.	**KIRBEKAN** 9th February 1885 ¹First Sudan War 1884–85	1886	The South Staffordshire Regiment: The Black Watch (Royal Highlanders)
182.	**NILE 1884–85** 20th August 1884–7th March 1885 First Sudan War 1884–85	1886	19th (Princess of Wales's Own) Hussars: The Royal Irish Regiment: The Duke of Cornwall's Light Infantry: The Royal Sussex Regiment: The South Staffordshire Regiment: The Black Watch (Royal Highlanders): The Essex Regiment: The Queen's Own (Royal West Kent Regiment): The Gordon Highlanders: The Queen's Own Cameron Highlanders
183.	**TOFREK** 23rd March 1885 First Sudan War 1884–85	1886 1886	Princess Charlotte of Wales's (Royal Berkshire Regiment) Queen's Own Madras Sappers and Miners: 15th Bengal Infantry (The Loodianah Sikhs): 17th Bengal Infantry (The Loyal Poorbeah Regiment): 28th Bombay Infantry
184.	**SUAKIN 1885** 1st March–14th May 1885 First Sudan War 1884–85	1886 1886 1907	5th (Royal Irish) Lancers: 20th Hussars: Grenadier Guards: Coldstream Guards: Scots Guards: The East Surrey Regiment: Princess Charlotte of Wales's (Royal Berkshire Regiment): The King's (Shropshire Light Infantry) Queen's Own Madras Sappers and Miners: 9th Bengal Lancers: 15th Bengal Infantry (The Loodianah Sikhs): 17th Bengal Infantry (The Loyal Poorbeah Regiment): 28th Bombay Infantry 1st Regiment, New South Wales Infantry: 2nd Regiment, New South Wales Infantry: 3rd Regiment, New South Wales Infantry
185.	**1800** 1st January–5th September 1800 French Revolutionary Wars 1793–1802	1889	Royal Malta Militia
186.	**BURMA 1885–87** ¹ 14th November 1885–30th April 1887 Third Burma War 1885–87	1890	The Queen's (Royal West Surrey Regiment): The King's (Liverpool Regiment): The Prince Albert's (Somersetshire Light Infantry): The King's (Royal West Surrey Regiment): The Royal Scots Fusiliers: The Royal Welsh Fusiliers: The South Wales Borderers: The Hampshire Regiment: The King's Own (Yorkshire Light Infantry): The Royal Munster Fusiliers: The Rifle Brigade (The Prince Consort's Own)
		1891	No 4 (Hazara) Mountain Battery: No 5 (Bombay) Mountain Battery: No 7 (Bengal) Mountain Battery: No 8 (Bengal) Mountain Battery: The 7th Regiment of Bengal Cavalry: The 1st Regiment of Madras Lancers: The 2nd Regiment of Madras Lancers: The 1st Regiment of Bombay Lancers: The 3rd Regiment of Cavalry, Hyderabad Contingent: The Bengal Sappers and Miners: The Madras Sappers and Miners (Queen's Own): The Bombay Sappers and Miners: The 1st Regiment of Bengal Infantry: The 2nd Regiment of Bengal (Light) Infantry: The 4th Regiment of Bengal Infantry: The 5th Regiment of Bengal (Light) Infantry: The 10th Regiment of Bengal Infantry: The 11th Regiment of Bengal Infantry: The 12th (Kelat-i-Ghilzai) Regiment of Bengal Infantry: The 16th (Lucknow) Regiment of Bengal Infantry: The 18th Regiment of Bengal Infantry: The 26th (Punjab) Regiment of Bengal Infantry: The 27th (Punjab) Regiment of Bengal Infantry: The 33rd (Punjab) Regiment of Bengal Infantry: The 42nd (Gurkha) Regiment of Bengal (Light) Infantry: The 43rd (Gurkha) Regiment of Bengal (Light) Infantry: The 44th (Gurkha) Regiment of Bengal (Light) Infantry: The 3rd Gurkha Regiment: The 1st Regiment of Madras Infantry (Pioneers): The 3rd Regiment of Madras Infantry: The 5th Regiment of Madras Infantry: The 10th Regiment of Madras Infantry: The 12th Regiment of Madras Infantry: The 13th Regiment of Madras Infantry: The 14th Regiment of Madras Infantry: The 15th Regiment of Madras Infantry: The 16th Regiment of Madras Infantry: The 17th Regiment of Madras Infantry: The 21st Regiment of Madras Infantry: The 23rd Regiment of Madras (Light) Infantry: The 25th Regiment of Madras Infantry: The 26th Regiment of Madras Infantry: The 27th Regiment of Madras Infantry: The 30th Regiment of Madras Infantry: The 1st Regiment of Bombay Infantry (Grenadiers): The 5th Regiment of Bombay (Light) Infantry: The 7th Regiment of Bombay Infantry: The 23rd Regiment of Bombay (Light) Infantry: The 27th (1st Baluch) Regiment of Bombay (Light) Infantry: The 25th Regiment of Bombay Infantry: The 2nd Regiment of Infantry, Hyderabad Contingent: The 3rd Regiment of Infantry, Hyderabad Contingent

¹ *Award considered repugnant to Indian units 1966.*

187.	**ST VINCENT 1797** [1] 14th February 1797 French Revoluntionary Wars 1793–1802	1891	The Welsh Regiment [1] *Awarded as ST VINCENT: year-date added 1951.*
188.	**MASULIPATAM** 8th April 1759 Third Carnatic War 1758–63	1894	The Royal Munster Fusiliers
189.	**BADARA** 25th November 1759 Bengal Wars 1756–63	1894	The Royal Munster Fusiliers
190.	**ROHILCUND 1774** 23rd April 1774 First Rohilla War 1774	1894	The Royal Munster Fusiliers
191.	**ROHILCUND 1794** 26th October 1794 Second Rohilla War 1794	1894	The Royal Munster Fusiliers
192.	**WEST AFRICA 1887** 13th November–31st December 1887 Operations in Sierra Leone 1887	1896	West India Regiment
193.	**WEST AFRICA 1892-3-4** 8th March 1892–13th March 1894 Operations in West Africa 1892–94	1896	West India Regiment
194.	**DEFENCE OF CHITRAL** [1] 3rd March–21st April 1895 Chitral Campaign 1895	1897	The 14th (Ferozepore Sikh) Regiment of Bengal Infantry: The 4th Kashmir Rifles [1] *Award considered repugnant to Indian units 1966.*
195.	**CHITRAL** [1] 7th March–15th August 1895 Chitral Campaign 1895	1897	The Buffs (East Kent Regiment): The Bedfordshire Regiment: The King's Own Scottish Borderers: The East Lancashire Regiment: The King's Royal Rifle Corps: Seaforth Highlanders (Ross-shire Buffs, The Duke of Albany's): The Gordon Highlanders
		1897	No 2 (Derajat) Mountain Battery: No 4 (Hazara) Mountain Battery: The 9th Bengal Lancers (Hodson's Horse): The 11th (Prince of Wales' Own) Bengal Lancers: The Madras Sappers and Miners: The Bengal Sappers and Miners (Queen's Own): The 13th (Shekhawati) Regiment of Bengal Infantry: The 15th (Ludhiana Sikh) Regiment of Bengal Infantry: The 23rd (Punjab) Regiment of Bengal Infantry (Pioneers): The 25th (Punjab) Regiment of Bengal Infantry: The 29th (Punjab) Regiment of Bengal Infantry: The 30th (Punjab) Regiment of Bengal Infantry: The 32nd (Punjab) Regiment of Bengal Infantry (Pioneers): The 34th (Punjab) Regiment of Bengal Infantry (Pioneers): The 37th (Dogra) Regiment of Bengal Infantry: The 3rd Gurkha Rifle Regiment: The 4th Gurkha Rifle Regiment: The Corps of Guides (Queen's Own): The 4th Regiment of Sikh Infantry
		1897	The Jeypore Transport Corps: The Gwalior Transport Corps: No 1 Kashmir Mountain Battery: The Kashmir Sappers and Miners [1] *Award considered repugnant to Indian units 1966.*

196.	**HAFIR** 19th–26th September 1896 Second Sudan War 1896–98	1899
197.	**ATBARA** 8th April 1898 Second Sudan War 1896–98	1899
198.	**KHARTOUM** 5th September 1898 Second Sudan War 1896–98	1899
199.	**TIRAH** 2nd October 1897–6th April 1898 Punjab Frontier Revolt 1897–98	1899
		1900
		1900
200.	**MALAKAND** 26th July–2nd August 1897 Punjab Frontier Revolt 1897–98	1900
201.	**SAMANA** 12th September 1897 Punjab Frontier Revolt 1897–98	1900
202.	**PUNJAB FRONTIER** 10th June 1897–6th April 1898 Punjab Frontier Revolt 1897–98	1900

The Prince of Wales's (North Staffordshire Regiment)

The Royal Warwickshire Regiment: The Lincolnshire Regiment: Seaforth Highlanders (Ross-shire Buffs, The Duke of Albany's): The Queen's Own Cameron Highlanders

21st (Empress of India's) Lancers: Grenadier Guards: The Northumberland Fusiliers: The Royal Warwickshire Regiment: The Lincolnshire Regiment: The Lancashire Fusiliers: Seaforth Highlanders (Ross-shire Buffs, The Duke of Albany's): The Queen's Own Cameron Highlanders: The Rifle Brigade (The Prince Consort's Own)

The Queen's (Royal West Surrey Regiment): The Devonshire Regiment: The Princess of Wales's Own (Yorkshire Regiment): The Royal Scots Fusiliers: The King's Own Scottish Borderers: The Dorsetshire Regiment: The Sherwood Foresters (Derbyshire Regiment): The Northamptonshire Regiment: The Gordon Highlanders

The 18th Regiment of Bengal Lancers: No 1 (Kohat) Mountain Battery: No 2 (Derajat) Mountain Battery: No 5 (Bombay) Mountain Battery: The Corps of Bengal Sappers and Miners: The Queen's Own Madras Sappers and Miners: The Corps of Bombay Sappers and Miners: The 15th (Ludhiana Sikh) Regiment of Bengal Infantry: The 30th (Punjab) Regiment of Bengal Infantry: The 36th (Sikh) Regiment of Bengal Infantry: The 1st Gurkha (Rifle) Regiment: The 2nd (Prince of Wales's Own) Gurkha (Rifle) Regiment (Sirmoor Rifles): The 3rd Gurkha (Rifle) Regiment: The 4th Gurkha (Rifle) Regiment: The 3rd Regiment of Sikh Infantry: The 2nd Regiment of Punjab Infantry: The 21st Regiment of Madras Infantry (Pioneers): The 28th Regiment of Bombay Infantry (Pioneers)

The Simmoor Imperial Service Sappers: The Maler-Kotla Imperial Service Sappers: The 1st Patiala Imperial Service Infantry: The Jhind Imperial Service Infantry: The Nabha Imperial Service Infantry: The Kapurthala Imperial Service Infantry: The Jeypore Imperial Service Transport Corps: The Gwalior Imperial Service Transport Corps

The 11th (Prince of Wales' Own) Regiment of Bengal Lancers: No 8 (Bengal) Mountain Battery: The Queen's Own Madras Sappers and Miners: The 24th (Punjab) Regiment of Bengal Infantry: The 31st (Punjab) Regiment of Bengal Infantry: The 35th (Sikh) Regiment of Bengal Infantry: The 38th (Dogra) Regiment of Bengal Infantry: The 45th (Rattray's Sikh) Regiment of Bengal Infantry: The Corps of Guides (Queen's Own)

The 36th (Sikh) Regiment of Bengal Infantry

The 3rd Regiment of Bengal Cavalry: The 6th (Prince of Wales') Regiment of Bengal Cavalry: The 9th Regiment of Bengal Lancers: The 11th (Prince of Wales' Own) Regiment of Bengal Lancers: The 13th (Duke of Connaught's) Regiment of Bengal Lancers: The 18th Regiment of Bengal Lancers: The Central India Horse: No 1 (Kohat) Mountain Battery: No 2 (Derajat) Mountain Battery: No 5 (Bombay) Mountain Battery: No 8 (Bengal) Mountain Battery: The Corps of Bengal Sappers and Miners: The Queen's Own Madras Sappers and Miners: The Corps of Bombay Sappers and Miners: The 9th (Gurkha Rifle) Regiment of Bengal Infantry: The 12th (Kelat-i-Ghilzai) Regiment of Bengal Infantry: The 15th (Ludhiana Sikh) Regiment of Bengal Infantry: The 20th (Duke of Cambridge's Own Punjab) Regiment of Bengal Infantry: The 22nd (Punjab) Regiment of Bengal Infantry: The 24th (Punjab) Regiment of Bengal Infantry: The 30th (Punjab) Regiment of Bengal Infantry: The 31st (Punjab) Regiment of Bengal Infantry: The 34th (Punjab) Regiment of Bengal Infantry (Pioneers): The 35th (Sikh) Regiment of

Bengal Infantry: The 36th (Sikh) Regiment of Bengal Infantry: The 37th (Dogra) Regiment of Bengal Infantry: The 38th (Dogra) Regiment of Bengal Infantry: The 39th (Garhwal Rifle) Regiment of Bengal Infantry: The 45th (Rattray's Sikh) Regiment of Bengal Infantry: The 1st Gurkha (Rifle) Regiment: The 2nd (Prince of Wales's Own) Gurkha (Rifle) Regiment (Sirmoor Rifles): The 3rd Gurkha (Rifle) Regiment: The 4th Gurkha (Rifle) Regiment: The 5th Gurkha (Rifle) Regiment: The Corps of Guides (Queen's Own): The 3rd Regiment of Sikh Infantry: The 2nd Regiment of Punjab Infantry: The 21st Regiment of Madras Infantry (Pioneers): The 28th Regiment of Bombay Infantry (Pioneers)

1900 — No I (Kashmir) Imperial Service Mountain Battery: The Sirmoor Imperial Service Sappers: The Maler-Kotla Imperial Service Sappers: The 1st Patiala Imperial Service Infantry: The Jhind Imperial Service Infantry: The Nabha Imperial Service Infantry: The Kapurthala Imperial Service Infantry: The Jeypore Imperial Service Transport Corps: The Gwalior Imperial Service Transport Corps

¹ Award considered repugnant to Indian units 1966.

203. **BRITISH EAST AFRICA 1896**
27th November–31st December 1896
Operations in East Africa 1896–99
— 1901 — The 24th (Baluchistan: Duchess of Connaught's Own) Regiment of Bombay Infantry

204. **BRITISH EAST AFRICA 1897–99**
1st January 1897–6th May 1899
Operations in East Africa 1896–99
— 1901 — The 27th Regiment (1st Baluch Battalion) of Bombay (Light) Infantry

205. **BRITISH EAST AFRICA 1898** ¹
1st January–31st December 1898
Operations in East Africa 1896–99
— 1901 — The 4th Regiment of Bombay Infantry
¹ Award considered repugnant to Indian units 1966.

206. **PEKIN 1900**
4th–16th August 1900
Boxer Rising 1900
— 1902 — The Royal Welsh Fusiliers
— 1903 — 1st (Duke of York's Own) Bengal Lancers (Skinner's Horse); 7th (Duke of Connaught's Own) Rajput Infantry; 1st Sikh Infantry; 24th Punjab Infantry

207. **SIERRA LEONE 1898**
18th February–31st December 1898
Operations in Sierra Leone 1898–99
— 1903 — West India Regiment

208. **CHINA 1900**
13th June–20th December 1900
Boxer Rising 1900
— 1903 — 16th Bengal Lancers: 3rd (Queen's Own) Bombay Light Cavalry: Queen's Own Madras Sappers and Miners: Bombay Sappers and Miners: Bengal Sappers and Miners: 2nd (Queen's Own) Rajput Light Infantry: 6th Jat Light Infantry: 14th (Ferozepore) Sikh Infantry: 20th (Duke of Cambridge's Own) Punjab Infantry: 34th Punjab Pioneers: 4th Punjab Infantry: 5th Infantry, Hyderabad Contingent: 4th Gurkha Rifles: 1st Madras Pioneers: 3rd (Palamcottah) Madras Light Infantry: 28th Madras Infantry: 31st Burma Light Infantry: 22nd Bombay Infantry: 26th Baluchistan Infantry: 30th Baluch Infantry
— 1903 — Jodhpore Imperial Service Lancers: Malerkotla Imperial Service Sappers: Alwar Imperial Service Infantry: Bikaner Imperial Service Infantry

209. **DEFENCE OF KIMBERLEY**
12th October 1899–15th February 1900
Second Boer War 1899–1902
— 1905 — The Loyal North Lancashire Regiment
— 1907 — Kimberley Regiment

210.	**DEFENCE OF LADYSMITH** 29th October 1899–27th February 1900 Second Boer War 1899–1902	1905	5th (Princess Charlotte of Wales's) Dragoon Guards: 5th (Royal Irish) Lancers: 18th (Princess of Wales's) Hussars: 19th (Alexandra, Princess of Wales's Own) Hussars: The King's (Liverpool Regiment): The Devonshire Regiment: The Leicestershire Regiment: The Gloucestershire Regiment: The King's Royal Rifle Corps: The Manchester Regiment: The Gordon Highlanders: The Rifle Brigade (The Prince Consort's Own)
		1907	Natal Carbineers: Natal Mounted Rifles: Border Mounted Rifles
		1948	Imperial Light Horse
211.	**MODDER RIVER** 28th November 1899 Second Boer War 1899–1902	1905	9th (Queen's Royal) Lancers: Grenadier Guards: Coldstream Guards: Scots Guards: The Northumberland Fusiliers: The Northamptonshire Regiment: The King's Own (Yorkshire Light Infantry): The Highland Light Infantry: Princess Louise's (Argyll and Sutherland Highlanders)
212.	**RELIEF OF KIMBERLEY** 15th February 1900 Second Boer War 1899–1902	1905	1st Life Guards: 2nd Life Guards: Royal Horse Guards: 6th Dragoon Guards (Carabiniers): 2nd Dragoons (Royal Scots Greys): 9th (Queen's Royal) Lancers: 10th (Prince of Wales's Own Royal) Hussars: 12th (Prince of Wales's Royal) Lancers: 16th (Queen's) Lancers: The Buffs (East Kent Regiment): Alexandra, Princess of Wales's Own (Yorkshire Regiment): The Gloucestershire Regiment: The Duke of Wellington's (West Riding Regiment): The Welsh Regiment: The Oxfordshire Light Infantry: The Essex Regiment
213.	**RELIEF OF LADYSMITH** 27th February 1900 Second Boer War 1899–1902	1905	1st (Royal) Dragoons: 13th Hussars: 14th (King's) Hussars: The Queen's (Royal West Surrey Regiment): The King's Own (Royal Lancaster Regiment): The Royal Fusiliers (City of London Regiment): The Devonshire Regiment: The Prince Albert's (Somersetshire Light Infantry): The Prince of Wales's Own (West Yorkshire Regiment): The Lancashire Fusiliers: The Royal Scots Fusiliers: The Royal Welsh Fusiliers: The Cameronians (Scottish Rifles): The Royal Inniskilling Fusiliers: The East Surrey Regiment: The Border Regiment: The Dorsetshire Regiment: The Prince of Wales's Volunteers (South Lancashire Regiment): The Duke of Cambridge's Own (Middlesex Regiment): The King's Royal Rifle Corps: The York and Lancaster Regiment: The Durham Light Infantry: Princess Victoria's (Royal Irish Fusiliers): The Connaught Rangers: The Royal Dublin Fusiliers: The Rifle Brigade (The Prince Consort's Own)
		1907	Umvoti Mounted Rifles: Natal Royal Regiment: Durban Light Infantry
		1948	Imperial Light Horse
214.	**PAARDEBERG** 17th–27th February 1900 Second Boer War 1899–1902	1905	1st Life Guards: 2nd Life Guards: Royal Horse Guards: 6th Dragoon Guards (Carabiniers): 2nd Dragoons (Royal Scots Greys): 9th (Queen's Royal) Lancers: 10th (Prince of Wales's Own Royal) Hussars: 12th (Prince of Wales's Royal) Lancers: 16th (Queen's) Lancers: The Buffs (East Kent Regiment): The Norfolk Regiment: The Lincolnshire Regiment: Alexandra, Princess of Wales's Own (Yorkshire Regiment): The King's Own Scottish Borderers: The Gloucestershire Regiment: The Duke of Cornwall's Light Infantry: The Duke of Wellington's (West Riding Regiment): The Hampshire Regiment: The Welsh Regiment: The Black Watch (Royal Highlanders): The Oxfordshire Light Infantry: The Essex Regiment: The King's (Shropshire Light Infantry): Seaforth Highlanders (Ross-shire Buffs, The Duke of Albany's): The Gordon Highlanders: Princess Louise's (Argyll and Sutherland Highlanders)
		1906	Royal Canadian Regiment
215.	**SOUTH AFRICA 1899–1900** [1] 11th October 1899–31st December 1900 Second Boer War 1899–1902	1905	1st Life Guards: 2nd Life Guards: Royal Horse Guards
		1906	Royal Canadian Regiment
		1907	Southern Rhodesia Volunteers, Western Division
		1908	Australian Horse
		1914	The Governor General's Foot Guards: 1st Regiment "The Grenadier Guards of Canada": 2nd Regiment "Queen's Own Rifles of Canada": 3rd Regiment "Victoria Rifles of Canada": 5th Regiment "Royal Highlanders of Canada": 6th Regiment "The Duke

of Connaught's Own Rifles"; 7th Regiment "Fusiliers"; 8th Regiment "Fusiliers"; 10th Regiment "Royal Rifles"; 10th Regiment "Royal Grenadiers"; 26th Regiment "Middlesex Light Infantry"; 43rd Regiment "The Duke of Cornwall's Own Rifles"; 48th Regiment "Highlanders"; 62nd Regiment "St John Fusiliers"; 63rd Regiment "Halifax Rifles"; 90th Regiment "Winnipeg Rifles"; 66th Regiment "Princess Louise Fusiliers"; 93rd Cumberland Regiment

1 *AFRIQUE DU SUD 1899–1900 taken into use by French-speaking Canadian units 1958.*

216. **SOUTH AFRICA 1899–1902** 1
11th October 1899–31st May 1902
Second Boer War 1899–1902

1905
5th (Princess Charlotte of Wales's) Dragoon Guards: 6th Dragoon Guards (Carabiniers): 1st (Royal) Dragoons: 2nd Dragoons (Royal Scots Greys): 5th (Royal Irish) Lancers: 6th (Inniskilling) Dragoons: 9th (Queen's Royal) Lancers: 10th (Prince of Wales's Own Royal) Hussars: 12th (Prince of Wales's Royal) Lancers: 13th Hussars: 18th (Princess of Wales's) Hussars: 19th (Alexandra, Princess of Wales's Own) Hussars: Grenadier Guards: Coldstream Guards: Scots Guards: The Royal Scots (Lothian Regiment): The Queen's (Royal West Surrey Regiment): The King's Own (Royal Lancaster Regiment): The Northumberland Fusiliers: The Royal Warwickshire Regiment: The Royal Fusiliers (City of London Regiment): The King's (Liverpool Regiment): The Devonshire Regiment: The Suffolk Regiment: The Prince Albert's (Somersetshire Light Infantry): The Prince of Wales's Own (West Yorkshire Regiment): The Leicestershire Regiment: Alexandra, Princess of Wales's Own (Yorkshire Regiment): The Lancashire Fusiliers: The Royal Scots Fusiliers: The Royal Welsh Fusiliers: The Cameronians (Scottish Rifles): The Royal Inniskilling Fusiliers: The Gloucestershire Regiment: The East Surrey Regiment: The Duke of Cornwall's Light Infantry: The Border Regiment: The Dorsetshire Regiment: The Prince of Wales's Volunteers (South Lancashire Regiment): The Welsh Regiment: The Black Watch (Royal Highlanders): The Sherwood Foresters (Nottinghamshire and Derbyshire Regiment): The Loyal North Lancashire Regiment: The Northamptonshire Regiment: Princess Charlotte of Wales's (Royal Berkshire Regiment): The King's Own (Yorkshire Light Infantry): The King's (Shropshire Light Infantry): The King's Royal Rifle Corps: The Manchester Regiment: The York and Lancaster Regiment: The Durham Light Infantry: The Highland Light Infantry: Seaforth Highlanders (Ross-shire Buffs, The Duke of Albany's): The Gordon Highlanders: The Royal Irish Rifles: Princess Victoria's (Royal Irish Fusiliers): The Connaught Rangers: Princess Louise's (Argyll and Sutherland Highlanders): The Royal Munster Fusiliers: The Royal Dublin Fusiliers: The Rifle Brigade (The Prince Consort's Own)

1905
24th Middlesex Volunteer Rifle Corps

1907
No.1 Regiment, Wellington (West Coast) Mounted Rifle Volunteers: 1st Regiment, North Canterbury Mounted Rifle Volunteers: No.1 Regiment, Otago Mounted Rifle Volunteers

1907
Natal Carbineers: Natal Mounted Rifles: Umvoti Mounted Rifles: Border Mounted Rifles: Natal Royal Regiment: Durban Light Infantry: Duke of Edinburgh's Own Volunteer Rifles: Kimberley Regiment: Cape Town Highlanders: Prince Alfred's Volunteer Guard: Kaffrarian Rifles: Uitenhage Volunteer Rifles: Transkei Mounted Rifles: Queenstown Rifle Volunteers: First City Volunteers

1908
New South Wales Lancers: New South Wales Mounted Rifles: Victorian Mounted Rifles: Queensland Mounted Infantry: South Australian Mounted Rifles: 1st Regiment, New South Wales Infantry: 2nd Regiment, New South Wales Infantry: 3rd Regiment, New South Wales Infantry: 1st Battalion, Infantry (Victoria): 2nd Battalion, Infantry (Victoria): 4th Battalion, Infantry (Victoria): 5th Battalion, Infantry (Victoria): Victorian Rangers: 1st Battalion, South Australian Infantry: 2nd Battalion, Western Australian Infantry: 1st Battalion, Tasmanian Infantry Regiment: 2nd Battalion, Tasmanian Infantry Regiment

1948
Imperial Light Horse

217. **SOUTH AFRICA 1900** 1
1st January–31st December 1900
Second Boer War 1899–1902

1905
4th Volunteer Battalion, The Royal Fusiliers (City of London Regiment): 4th Volunteer Battalion, The Gordon Highlanders

1906
Royal Canadian Dragoons

1914
The Governor General's Body Guard: 1st Hussars: 5th Princess Louise Dragoon Guards: 1st Manitoba Dragoons: 17th Duke

of York's Royal Canadian Hussars (Argenteuil Rangers); 13th Royal Regiment; 14th Regiment ''The Princess of Wales' Own Rifles''; 71st York Regiment; 82nd ''Abegweit Light Infantry'' Regiment

1 *AFRIQUE DU SUD 1900 taken into use by French-speaking Canadian units 1958.*

218. SOUTH AFRICA 1900–01 [1]
1st January 1900–31st December 1901
Second Boer War 1899–1902

1905   4th (Militia) Battalion, The King's Own (Royal Lancaster Regiment); 6th (Militia) Battalion, The Royal Warwickshire Regiment; 6th (Militia) Battalion, The Lancashire Fusiliers; 4th (Militia) Battalion, The Cameronians (Scottish Rifles); 4th (Militia) Battalion, The South Staffordshire Regiment; 3rd (Militia) Battalion, The Prince of Wales's Volunteers (South Lancashire Regiment); 4th (Militia) Battalion, The Sherwood Foresters (Nottinghamshire and Derbyshire Regiment); 9th (Militia) Battalion, The King's Royal Rifle Corps; 3rd (Militia) Battalion, The Durham Light Infantry; 4th (Militia) Battalion, Princess Louise's (Argyll and Sutherland Highlanders)

1905   Berks Imperial Yeomanry; Buckinghamshire (Royal Buckinghamshire Hussars) Imperial Yeomanry; Cheshire (Earl of Chester's) Imperial Yeomanry; Denbighshire (-Iussars) Imperial Yeomanry; Derbyshire Imperial Yeomanry; Royal 1st Devon Imperial Yeomanry; Royal North Devon (Hussars) Imperial Yeomanry; Dorset (Queen's Own) Imperial Yeomanry; Fifeshire and Forfarshire Imperial Yeomanry; Gloucestershire (Royal Gloucestershire Hussars) Imperial Yeomanry; Hampshire (Carabiniers) Imperial Yeomanry; Herts Imperial Yeomanry; Royal East Kent (The Duke of Connaught's Own) (Mounted Rifles) Imperial Yeomanry; West Kent (Queen's Own) Imperial Yeomanry; Lanarkshire (Queen's Own Royal Glasgow and Lower Ward of Lanarkshire) Imperial Yeomanry; Lothians and Berwickshire Imperial Yeomanry; Middlesex (Duke of Cambridge's Hussars) Imperial Yeomanry; Oxfordshire 'Queen's Own Oxfordshire Hussars) Imperial Yeomanry; North Somerset Imperial Yeomanry; West Somerset Imperial Yeomanry; Staffordshire (Queen's Own Royal Regiment) Imperial Yeomanry; Suffolk (The Duke of York's Own Loyal Suffolk Hussars) Imperial Yeomanry; Warwickshire Imperial Yeomanry; Westmorland and Cumberland Imperial Yeomanry; Royal Wiltshire (Prince of Wales's Royal Regiment) Imperial Yeomanry

1905   2nd Volunteer Battalion, The King's (Liverpool Regiment); 6th Volunteer Battalion, The King's (Liverpool Regiment); 1st (Exeter and South Devon) Volunteer Battalion, The Devonshire Regiment; 2nd (Prince of Wales's) Volunteer Battalion, The Devonshire Regiment; 4th Volunteer Battalion, The Devonshire Regiment; 5th (Hay Tor) Volunteer Battalion, The Devonshire Regiment: 3rd (Cambridgeshire) Volunteer Battalion, The Suffolk Regiment; Cambridge University Volunteer Rifle Corps: 1st Volunteer Battalion, The Prince Albert's (Somersetshire Light Infantry): 2nd Volunteer Battalion, The Prince Albert's (Somersetshire Light Infantry): 3rd Volunteer Battalion, The Prince Albert's (Somersetshire Light Infantry): 1st Volunteer Battalion, The East Yorkshire Regiment: 2nd Volunteer Battalion, The East Yorkshire Regiment, The Royal Scots Fusiliers: 1st (Brecknockshire) Volunteer Battalion, The South Wales Borderers: 5th Volunteer Battalion, The South Wales Borderers: 1st Volunteer Battalion, The Worcestershire Regiment: 1st Volunteer Battalion, The Duke of Cornwall's Light Infantry: 2nd Volunteer Battalion, The Duke of Cornwall's Light Infantry: 1st Volunteer Battalion, The Royal Sussex Regiment [2]: 5th (Isle of Wght, ''Princess Beatrice's'') Volunteer Battalion, The Hampshire Regiment: 1st Volunteer Battalion, The Dorsetshire Regiment: 2nd Volunteer Battalion, The Prince of Wales's Volunteers (South Lancashire Regiment): 2nd Volunteer Battalion, The Oxfordshire Light Infantry: 1st Wiltshire Volunteer Rifle Corps: 3rd (The Buchan) Volunteer Battalion, The Gordon Highlanders: 4th (Donside Highland) Volunteer Battalion, The Gordon Highlanders: 14th Middlesex (Inns of Court) Volunteer Rifle Corps: 15th Middlesex (The Customs and the Docks) Volunteer Rifle Corps: 20th Middlesex (Artists) Volunteer Rifle Corps

1905   Ceylon Mounted Infantry
1914   Lord Strathcona's Horse (Royal Canadians)

1 *AFRIQUE DU SUD 1900–01 taken into use by French-speaking Canadian units 1958.* 2 *SOUTH AFRICA 1900–02 taken into use 1905.*

219.	**SOUTH AFRICA 1900–02**	1905

1st January 1900–31st May 1902
Second Boer War 1899–1902

1905   7th (Princess Royal's) Dragoon Guards; 8th (King's Royal Irish) Hussars; 14th (King's) Hussars; 16th (Queen's) Lancers; 17th (Duke of Cambridge's Own) Lancers: The Buffs (East Kent Regiment): The Norfolk Regiment: The Lincolnshire Regiment: The East Yorkshire Regiment: The Bedfordshire Regiment: The Royal Irish Regiment: The Cheshire Regiment: The South Wales Borderers: The King's Own Scottish Borderers: The Worcestershire Regiment: The East Lancashire Regiment: The Duke of Wellington's (West Riding Regiment): The Royal Sussex Regiment: The Hampshire Regiment: The South Staffordshire Regiment: The Oxfordshire Light Infantry: The Queen's Own (Royal West Kent Regiment): The Duke of Cambridge's Own (Middlesex Regiment): The Duke of Edinburgh's (Wiltshire Regiment): The Prince of Wales's (North Staffordshire Regiment): The Queen's Own Cameron Highlanders: The Prince of Wales's Leinster Regiment (Royal Canadians)

1905   Honourable Artillery Company of London

1905   3rd (Militia) Battalion, The Royal Scots (Lothian Regiment): 3rd (Militia) Battalion, The Queen's (Royal West Surrey Regiment): 3rd (Militia) Battalion, The Buffs (East Kent Regiment): 3rd (Militia) Battalion, The King's Own (Royal Lancaster Regiment): 3rd (Militia) Battalion, The Norfolk Regiment: 4th (Militia) Battalion, The Prince Albert's (Somersetshire Light Infantry): 4th (Militia) Battalion, The Prince of Wales's Own (West Yorkshire Regiment): 4th (Militia) Battalion, The Bedfordshire Regiment: 3rd (Militia) Battalion, Alexandra, Princess of Wales's Own (Yorkshire Regiment): 4th (Militia) Battalion, The Cheshire Regiment: 3rd (Militia) Battalion, The South Wales Borderers: 3rd (Militia) Battalion, The King's Own Scottish Borderers: 3rd (Militia) Battalion, The East Lancashire Regiment: 3rd (Militia) Battalion, The Duke of Wellington's (West Riding Regiment): 3rd (Militia) Battalion, The Welsh Regiment: 6th (Militia) Battalion, The Duke of Cambridge's Own (Middlesex Regiment): 4th (Militia) Battalion, The Prince of Wales's (North Staffordshire Regiment): 3rd (Militia) Battalion, The Prince of Wales's Leinster Regiment (Royal Canadians): 3rd (Militia) Battalion, The Royal Munster Fusiliers: 5th (Militia) Battalion, The Royal Dublin Fusiliers

1905   Ayrshire (Earl of Carrick's Own) Imperial Yeomanry: Lanarkshire Imperial Yeomanry: Lancashire (Hussars) Imperial Yeomanry: Duke of Lancaster's Own Imperial Yeomanry: Leicestershire (Prince Albert's Own) Imperial Yeomanry: 3rd County of London (Sharpshooters) Imperial Yeomanry: Northumberland (Hussars) Imperial Yeomanry: Nottinghamshire (Sherwood Rangers) Imperial Yeomanry: Nottinghamshire (South Nottinghamshire Hussars) Imperial Yeomanry: Shropshire Imperial Yeomanry: Worcestershire (The Queen's Own Worcestershire Hussars) Imperial Yeomanry: Yorkshire Dragoons (Queen's Own) Imperial Yeomanry: Yorkshire Hussars (Alexandra, Princess of Wales's Own) Imperial Yeomanry

1905   The Queen's Rifle Volunteer Brigade, The Royal Scots (Lothian Regiment): 5th Volunteer Battalion, The Royal Scots (Lothian Regiment): 1st Volunteer Battalion, The Queen's (Royal West Surrey Regiment): 2nd Volunteer Battalion, The Queen's (Royal West Surrey Regiment): 3rd Volunteer Battalion, The Queen's (Royal West Surrey Regiment): 4th Volunteer Battalion, The Queen's (Royal West Surrey Regiment): 1st Volunteer Battalion, The Buffs (East Kent Regiment): 2nd (The Weald of Kent) Volunteer Battalion, The Buffs (East Kent Regiment): 1st Volunteer Battalion, The King's Own (Royal Lancaster Regiment): 2nd Volunteer Battalion, The King's Own (Royal Lancaster Regiment): 1st Volunteer Battalion, The Northumberland Fusiliers: 2nd Volunteer Battalion, The Northumberland Fusiliers: 3rd Volunteer Battalion, The Northumberland Fusiliers: 1st Volunteer Battalion, The Royal Warwickshire Regiment: 2nd Volunteer Battalion, The Royal Warwickshire Regiment: 1st Volunteer Battalion, The Royal Fusiliers (City of London Regiment): 2nd Volunteer Battalion, The Royal Fusiliers (City of London Regiment): 3rd Volunteer Battalion, The Royal Fusiliers (City of London Regiment): 1st Volunteer Battalion, The King's (Liverpool Regiment): 3rd Volunteer Battalion, The King's (Liverpool Regiment): 4th Volunteer Battalion, The King's (Liverpool Regiment): 5th (Irish) Volunteer Battalion, The King's (Liverpool Regiment): 1st Volunteer Battalion, The Norfolk Regiment: 2nd Volunteer Battalion, The Norfolk Regiment: 3rd Volunteer Battalion, The Norfolk Regiment: 4th Volunteer Battalion, The Norfolk Regiment: 1st Volunteer Battalion, The Lincolnshire Regiment: 2nd Volunteer Battalion, The Lincolnshire Regiment: 3rd Volunteer Battalion, The Lincolnshire Regiment: 1st Volunteer Battalion, The Suffolk Regiment: 2nd Volunteer Battalion,

The Suffolk Regiment: 1st Volunteer Battalion, The Prince of Wales's Own (West Yorkshire Regiment): 2nd Volunteer Battalion, The Prince of Wales's Own (West Yorkshire Regiment); 3rd Volunteer Battalion, The Prince of Wales's Own (West Yorkshire Regiment): 1st (Hertfordshire) Volunteer Battalion, The Bedfordshire Regiment: 2nd (Hertfordshire) Volunteer Battalion, The Bedfordshire Regiment: 3rd Volunteer Battalion, The Bedfordshire Regiment: 1st Volunteer Battalion, The Leicestershire Regiment: 1st Volunteer Battalion, Alexandra, Princess of Wales's Own (Yorkshire Regiment): 2nd Volunteer Battalion, Alexandra, Princess of Wales's Own (Yorkshire Regiment): 1st Volunteer Battalion, The Lancashire Fusiliers: 2nd Volunteer Battalion, The Lancashire Fusiliers: 3rd Volunteer Battalion, The Lancashire Fusiliers: 1st Volunteer Battalion, The Royal Scots Fusiliers: 2nd (Earl o⁻ Chester's) Volunteer Battalion, The Cheshire Regiment: 3rd Volunteer Battalion, The Cheshire Regiment: 4th Volunteer Battalion, The Cheshire Regiment: 1st Volunteer Battalion, The Royal Welsh Fusiliers: 2nd Volunteer Battalion, The Royal Welsh Fusiliers: 3rd Volunteer Battalion, The Royal Welsh Fusiliers: 2nd Volunteer Battalion, The South Wales Borderers: 3rd Volunteer Battalion, The South Wales Borderers: 4th Volunteer Battalion, The South Wales Borderers: 1st Roxburgh and Selkirk (The Border) Volunteer Rifle Corps: 2nd (Berwickshire) Volunteer Battalion, The King's Own Scottish Borderers: 3rd (Dumfries) Volunteer Battalion, The King's Own Scottish Borderers: Galloway Volunteer Rifle Corps: 1st Lanarkshire Volunteer Rifle Corps: 2nd Volunteer Battalion, The Cameronians (Scottish Rifles): 3rd Lanarkshire Volunteer Rifle Corps: 4th Volunteer Battalion, The Cameronians (Scottish Rifles): 1st (City of Bristol) Volunteer Battalion, The Gloucestershire Regiment: 2nd Volunteer Battalion, The Gloucestershire Regiment: 2nd Volunteer Battalion, The Worcestershire Regiment: 1st Volunteer Battalion, The East Lancashire Regiment: 1st Surrey (South London) Volunteer Rifle Corps: 2nd Volunteer Battalion, The East Surrey Regiment: 3rd Volunteer Battalion, The East Surrey Regiment: 4th Volunteer Battalion, The East Surrey Regiment: 1st Volunteer Battalion, The Duke of Wellington's (West Riding Regiment): 2nd Volunteer Battalion, The Duke of Wellington's (West Riding Regiment): 3rd Volunteer Battalion, The Duke of Wellington's (West Riding Regiment): 1st (Cumberland) Volunteer Battalion, The Border Regiment: 2nd (Westmorland) Volunteer Battalion, The Border Regiment: 2nd Volunteer Battalion, The Royal Sussex Regiment: 1st Cinque Ports (Cinque Ports and Sussex) Volunteer Rifle Corps: 1st Volunteer Battalion, The Hampshire Regiment: 2nd Volunteer Battalion, The Hampshire Regiment: 3rd (Duke of Connaught's Own) Volunteer Battalion, The Hampshire Regiment: 4th Volunteer Battalion, The Hampshire Regiment: 1st Volunteer Battalion, The South Staffordshire Regiment: 2nd Volunteer Battalion, The South Staffordshire Regiment: 3rd Volunteer Battalion, The South Staffordshire Regiment: 1st Volunteer Battalion, The Prince of Wales's Volunteers (South Lancashire Regiment): 1st (Pembrokeshire) Volunteer Battalion, The Welsh Regiment: 2nd Volunteer Battalion, The Welsh Regiment: 3rd Volunteer Battalion, The Welsh Regiment: 3rd Glamorgan Volunteer Rifle Corps: 1st (City of Dundee) Volunteer Battalion, The Black Watch (Royal Highlanders): 2nd (Angus) Volunteer Battalion, The Black Watch (Royal Highlanders): 3rd (Dundee Highland) Volunteer Battalion, The Black Watch (Royal Highlanders): 4th (Perthshire) Volunteer Battalion, The Black Watch (Royal Highlanders): 5th (Perthshire Highland) Volunteer Battalion, The Black Watch (Royal Highlanders) 6th (Fifeshire) Volunteer Battalion, The Black Watch (Royal Highlanders): 1st Bucks Volunteer Rifle Corps: 1st Volunteer Battalion, The Essex Regiment: 2nd Volunteer Battalion, The Essex Regiment: 3rd Volunteer Battalion, The Essex Regiment 4th Volunteer Battalion, The Essex Regiment: 1st Volunteer Battalion, The Sherwood Foresters (Nottinghamshire and Derbyshire Regiment): 2nd Volunteer Battalion, The Sherwood Foresters (Nottinghamshire and Derbyshire Regiment): 1st Nottinghamshire (Robin Hood) Volunteer Rifle Corps: 4th (Nottinghamshire) Volunteer Battalion, The Sherwood Foresters (Nottinghamshire and Derbyshire Regiment): 1st Volunteer Battalion, The Loyal North Lancashire Regiment: 2nd Volunteer Battalion, The Loyal North Lancashire Regiment: 1st Volunteer Battalion, The Northamptonshire Regiment: 1st Volunteer Battalion, Princess Charlotte of Wales's (Royal Berkshire Regiment): 1st Volunteer Battalion, The Queen's Own (Royal West Kent Regiment): 2nd Volunteer Battalion, The Queen's Own (Royal West Kent Regiment): 1st Volunteer Battalion, The King's Own (Yorkshire Light Infantry): 1st Volunteer Battalion, The King's (Shropshire

Light Infantry): 2nd Volunteer Battalion, The King's (Shropshire Light Infantry): 1st Herefordshire Volunteer Rifle Corps: 1st Volunteer Battalion, The Duke of Cambridge's Own (Middlesex Regiment): 2nd Volunteer Battalion, The Duke of Cambridge's Own (Middlesex Regiment): 17th Middlesex (North Middlesex) Volunteer Rifle Corps: 1st Middlesex (Victoria and St George's) Volunteer Rifle Corps: 2nd Middlesex (South Middlesex) Volunteer Rifle Corps: 4th Middlesex (West London) Volunteer Rifle Corps: 5th Middlesex (West Middlesex) Volunteer Rifle Corps: The Prince of Wales's Own, 12th Middlesex (Civil Service) Volunteer Rifle Corps: 13th Middlesex (Queen's Westminster) Volunteer Rifle Corps: 21st Middlesex (The Finsbury VRC) Volunteer Rifle Corps: 22nd Middlesex (Central London Rangers) Volunteer Rifle Corps: 1st London Volunteer Rifle Corps: 2nd London Volunteer Rifle Corps: 3rd (City of) London Volunteer Rifle Corps: 2nd Volunteer Battalion, The Duke of Edinburgh's (Wiltshire Regiment): 1st Volunteer Battalion, The Manchester Regiment: 2nd Volunteer Battalion, The Manchester Regiment: 3rd Volunteer Battalion, The Manchester Regiment: 4th Volunteer Battalion, The Manchester Regiment: 5th (Ardwick) Volunteer Battalion, The Manchester Regiment: 1st Volunteer Battalion, The Prince of Wales's (North Staffordshire Regiment): 2nd Volunteer Battalion, The Prince of Wales's (North Staffordshire Regiment): 1st (Hallamshire) Volunteer Battalion, The York and Lancaster Regiment: 2nd Volunteer Battalion, The York and Lancaster Regiment: 1st Volunteer Battalion, The Durham Light Infantry: 2nd Volunteer Battalion, The Durham Light Infantry: 3rd (Sunderland) Volunteer Battalion, The Durham Light Infantry: 4th Volunteer Battalion, The Durham Light Infantry: 5th Volunteer Battalion, The Durham Light Infantry: 1st Volunteer Battalion, The Highland Light Infantry: 2nd Volunteer Battalion, The Highland Light Infantry: 3rd (The Blythswood) Volunteer Battalion, The Highland Light Infantry: 9th Lanarkshire Volunteer Rifle Corps: 5th (Glasgow Highland) Volunteer Battalion, The Highland Light Infantry: 1st (Ross Highland) Volunteer Battalion, Seaforth Highlanders (Ross-shire Buffs, The Duke of Albany's): 1st Sutherland Volunteer Rifle Corps: 3rd (Morayshire) Volunteer Battalion, Seaforth Highlanders (Ross-shire Buffs, The Duke of Albany's): 1st Volunteer Battalion, The Gordon Highlanders: 5th (Deeside Highland) Volunteer Battalion, The Gordon Highlanders: 1st (Inverness Highland) Volunteer Battalion, The Queen's Own Cameron Highlanders: 1st (Renfrewshire) Volunteer Battalion, Princess Louise's (Argyll and Sutherland Highlanders): 2nd (Renfrewshire) Volunteer Battalion, Princess Louise's (Argyll and Sutherland Highlanders): 4th (Stirlingshire) Volunteer Battalion, Princess Louise's (Argyll and Sutherland Highlanders): 5th Volunteer Battalion, Princess Louise's (Argyll and Sutherland Highlanders): 1st Dumbartonshire Volunteer Rifle Corps: 7th Middlesex (London Scottish) Volunteer Rifle Corps: 16th Middlesex (London Irish) Volunteer Rifle Corps: 18th Middlesex Volunteer Rifle Corps: 19th Middlesex (St Giles's and St George's, Bloomsbury) Volunteer Rifle Corps: 2nd Tower Hamlets Volunteer Rifle Corps: 6th Volunteer Battalion, The Gordon Highlanders: 2nd Volunteer Battalion, The East Lancashire Regiment: 1st Cadet Battalion, The King's Royal Rifle Corps

1907   No 2 Regiment, Auckland Mounted Rifle Volunteers: 1st Battalion, Auckland Infantry Volunteers ("Countess of Ranfurly's Own"): 2nd Battalion, Auckland (Hauraki) Infantry Volunteers: No 2 Regiment, Wellington (Wairarapa) Mounted Rifle Volunteers: 2nd Battalion, Wellington (West Coast) Rifle Volunteers: 3rd Battalion, Wellington (East Coast) Rifle Volunteers: 1st Regiment, Nelson Mounted Rifle Volunteers: 1st Battalion, Nelson Infantry Volunteers: South Canterbury Battalion of Infantry Volunteers

1908   4th Regiment, New South Wales Infantry: 5th Regiment, New South Wales Infantry: 6th Regiment, New South Wales Infantry: 3rd Battalion, Infantry (Victoria): 1st Queensland (Moreton) Regiment: 3rd Battalion, Tasmanian Infantry Regiment: Queensland Rifles

220.   **SOUTH AFRICA 1901**

1st January–31st December 1901   1905   Montgomeryshire Imperial Yeomanry: Pembroke Imperial Yeomanry
                                   1905   6th Volunteer Battalion, The Royal Scots (Lothian Regiment): 7th Volunteer Battalion, The Royal Scots (Lothian Regiment):
                                           3rd Volunteer Battalion, The Devonshire Regiment

Second Boer War 1899–1902   1908   3rd Queensland (Kennedy) Regiment: 8th Regiment, New South Wales Infantry

221. SOUTH AFRICA 1901–02
1st January 1901–31st May 1902
Second Boer War 1899–1902

1905 — 1st (King's) Dragoon Guards: 2nd Dragoon Guards (Queen's Bays): 3rd (Prince of Wales's) Dragoon Guards: 7th (Queen's Own) Hussars: 20th Hussars

1905 — 5th (Militia) Battalion, The Royal Fusiliers (City of London Regiment): 5th (Militia) Battalion, The Lancashire Fusiliers: 3rd (Militia) Battalion, The Cameronians (Scottish Rifles): 3rd (Militia) Battalion, The East Surrey Regiment: 3rd (Militia) Battalion, The Royal Sussex Regiment: 3rd (Militia) Battalion, The South Staffordshire Regiment: 3rd (Militia) Battalion, The Loyal North Lancashire Regiment: 5th (Militia) Battalion, The Manchester Regiment: 5th (Militia) Battalion, The Royal Irish Rifles

1905 — Lovat's Scouts Imperial Yeomanry [1]: Scottish Horse Imperial Yeomanry [2]

1905 — 4th Volunteer Battalion, The Royal Scots (Lothian Regiment): 8th Volunteer Battalion, The Royal Scots (Lothian Regiment): 9th Volunteer Battalion (Highlanders), The Royal Scots (Lothian Regiment): 1st Volunteer Battalion, The Cheshire Regiment: 3rd (Cumberland) Volunteer Battalion, The Border Regiment: 3rd Volunteer Battalion, The Queen's Own (Royal West Kent Regiment): 6th Volunteer Battalion, The Manchester Regiment: 3rd (Renfrewshire) Volunteer Battalion, Princess Louise's (Argyll and Sutherland Highlanders): 7th (Clackmannan and Kinross) Volunteer Battalion, Princess Louise's (Argyll and Sutherland Highlanders)

1907 — No 1 Regiment, Auckland Mounted Rifle Volunteers: 1st Battalion, Wellington Rifle Volunteers: 1st Battalion, Otago Rifle Volunteers: 2nd Battalion, Otago Rifle Volunteers: 3rd Battalion, Otago Rifle Volunteers

1908 — 7th Regiment, New South Wales Infantry: 1st Battalion, 2nd Regiment, South Australian Infantry: 2nd Battalion, 2nd Regiment, South Australian Infantry: 3rd Battalion, Western Australian Infantry: 4th Battalion, Western Australian Infantry

[1] SOUTH AFRICA 1900–02 taken into use 1908. [2] SOUTH AFRICA 1900–02 taken into use 1905.

222. SOUTH AFRICA 1902 [1]
1st January–31st May 1902
Second Boer War 1899–1902

1905 — 3rd (King's Own) Hussars

1905 — 5th (Militia) Battalion, The Royal Warwickshire Regiment 3rd (Militia) Battalion, The King's (Liverpool Regiment): 4th (Militia) Battalion, The King's (Liverpool Regiment): 3rd (Militia) Battalion, The Lincolnshire Regiment: 3rd (Militia) Battalion, The East Yorkshire Regiment: 3rd (Militia) Battalion, The Leicestershire Regiment: 4th (Militia) Battalion, Alexandra, Princess of Wales's Own (Yorkshire Regiment): 3rd (Militia) Battalion, The Cheshire Regiment: 6th (Militia) Battalion, The Worcestershire Regiment: 4th (Militia) Battalion, The East Surrey Regiment: 3rd (Militia) Battalion, The Essex Regiment: 3rd (Militia) Battalion, The Northamptonshire Regiment: 5th (Militia) Battalion, The Duke of Cambridge's Own (Middlesex Regiment): 6th (Militia) Battalion, The Manchester Regiment: 3rd (Militia) Battalion, The Prince of Wales's (North Staffordshire Regiment): 3rd (Militia) Battalion, The York and Lancaster Regiment: 4th (Militia) Battalion, Princess Louise's (Argyll and Sutherland Highlanders): 4th (Militia) Battalion, The Highland Light Infantry: 3rd (Militia) Battalion, The Durham Light Infantry: 3rd (Militia) Battalion, The Royal Dublin Fusiliers: 5th (Militia) Battalion, The Rifle Brigade (The Prince Consort's Own)

1905 — City of London (Rough Riders) Imperial Yeomanry [2]: 2nd County of London (Westminster Dragoons) Imperial Yeomanry

1905 — 8th (Scottish) Volunteer Battalion, The King's (Liverpool Regiment): 4th Volunteer Battalion, The Queen's Own (Royal West Kent Regiment)

1905 — Ceylon Planters Rifle Corps

1907 — No 3 Regiment, Auckland Mounted Rifle Volunteers: No 4 Regiment, Auckland Mounted Rifle Volunteers: No 3 Regiment, Wellington (Manawatu) Mounted Rifle Volunteers: No 4 Regiment, Wellington (East Coast) Mounted Rifle Volunteers: 2nd Regiment, North Canterbury Mounted Rifle Volunteers: 1st Regiment, South Canterbury Mounted Rifle Volunteers: 1st North Canterbury Battalion of Infantry Volunteers: No 2 Regiment, Otago Mounted Rifle Volunteers

1908 — 5th Battalion, Western Australian Infantry

1914 — 62nd Regiment "St John Fusiliers"

? — The Taranaki Regiment

[1] AFRIQUE DU SUD 1902 taken into use by French-speaking Canadian units 1958. [2] SOUTH AFRICA 1900–02 taken into use 1905.

No.	Battle Honour	Year	Regiments / Notes
223.	**MEDITERRANEAN 1900–01** 1st January 1900–31st December 1901 Second Boer War 1899–1902	1905	5th (Militia) Battalion, The Northumberland Fusiliers: 3rd (Militia) Battalion, The Loyal North Lancashire Regiment: 3rd (Militia) Battalion, The Queen's Own (Royal West Kent Regiment): 3rd (Militia) Battalion, Seaforth Highlanders (Ross-shire Buffs, The Duke of Albany's)
224.	**MEDITERRANEAN 1901** 1st January–31st December 1901 Second Boer War 1899–1902	1905	5th (Militia) Battalion, The Royal Munster Fusiliers
225.	**MEDITERRANEAN 1901–02** 1st January 1901–31st May 1902 Second Boer War 1899–1902	1905	3rd (Militia) Battalion, The Prince of Wales's Own (West Yorkshire Regiment); 3rd (Militia) Battalion, The King's Own (Yorkshire Light Infantry)
226.	**ST HELENA 1900–01** 1st January 1900–31st December 1901 Second Boer War 1899–1902	1905	4th (Militia) Battalion, The Gloucestershire Regiment
227.	**ST HELENA 1901–02** 1st January 1901–31st May 1902 Second Boer War 1899–1902	1905	3rd (Militia) Battalion, The Duke of Edinburgh's (Wiltshire Regiment)
228.	**BRITISH EAST AFRICA 1901** [1] 1st January–30th April 1901 Operations in East Africa 1900–01	1905	116th Mahrattas [1] Award considered repugnant to Indian units 1966.
229.	**SASKATCHEWAN** 24th April–28th May 1885 Riel's Rebellion 1885	1906	Royal Canadian Regiment
230.	**NORTH-WEST CANADA 1885** [1] 24th April–28th May 1885 Riel's Rebellion 1885	1906 1914	Royal Canadian Dragoons; Royal Canadian Regiment The Governor General's Body Guard: 1st Manitoba Dragoons: 15th Light Horse: 16th Light Horse: 21st Alberta Hussars: 32nd Manitoba Horse: The Governor General's Foot Guards: 2nd Regiment "Queen's Own Rifles of Canada": 7th Regiment "Fusiliers": 9th Regiment "Voltigeurs de Quebec": 10th Regiment "Royal Grenadiers": 12th Regiment "York Rangers": 35th Regiment "Simcoe Foresters": 46th Durham Regiment: 52nd Regiment "Prince Albert Volunteers": 63rd Regiment "Halifax Rifles": 65th Regiment "Mount Royal Rifles": 90th Regiment "Winnipeg Rifles": 66th Regiment "Princess Louise Fusiliers" [1] NORD-OUEST DU CANADA 1885 taken into use by French-speaking Canadian units 1958.
231.	**GIBRALTAR 1780–83** [1] 1st January 1780–6th February 1783 War against France and Spain 1778–83	1908	The Highland Light Infantry [1] Awarded with the badge of The Castle and Key superscribed "Gibraltar" and with the motto "Montis Insignia Calpe" underneath: year-dates added 1909.
232.	**SIERRA LEONE 1898–99** 18th February 1898–9th March 1899 Operations in Sierra Leone 1898–99	1908	West African Regiment

233. **ASHANTI 1900**
31st March–25th December 1900
Ashanti Rising 1900
— 1908 — West African Regiment: Southern Nigeria Regiment, West African Frontier Force: Gold Coast Regiment, West African Frontier Force
The King's African Rifles

?

234. **NATAL 1906**
8th February–3rd August 1906
Natal Rebellion 1906
— 1908 — Natal Carbineers: Natal Mounted Rifles: Umvoti Mounted Rifles: Border Mounted Rifles: Northern District Mounted Rifles: Zululand Mounted Rifles: Natal Royal Regiment: Durban Light Infantry

1948 — Imperial Light Horse

235. **TANGIER 1662–80**
30th January 1662–27th October 1680
Defence of Tangier 1662–80
— 1909 — 1st (Royal) Dragoons: The Queen's (Royal West Surrey Regiment)

236. **TANGIER 1680**
1st January–27th October 1680
Defence of Tangier 1662–80
— 1909 — Grenadier Guards: Coldstream Guards: The Royal Scots (Lothian Regiment)

237. **GIBRALTAR 1704–5**
22nd July 1704–7th February 1705
War of the Spanish Succession 1701–14
— 1909 — Grenadier Guards: Coldstream Guards: The King's Own (Royal Lancaster Regiment): The Prince Albert's (Somersetshire Light Infantry): The East Lancashire Regiment: The East Surrey Regiment: The Duke of Cornwall's Light Infantry: The Royal Sussex Regiment

238. **WARBURG**
31st July 1760
Seven Years War 1756–63
— 1909 — Royal Horse Guards (The Blues): 1st (King's) Dragoon Guards: 2nd Dragoon Guards (Queen's Bays): 3rd (Prince of Wales's) Dragoon Guards: 6th Dragoon Guards (Carabiniers): 7th (Princess Royal's) Dragoon Guards: 1st (Royal) Dragoons: 2nd Dragoons (Royal Scots Greys): 6th (Inniskilling) Dragoons: 7th (Queen's Own) Hussars: 10th (Prince of Wales's Own Royal) Hussars: 11th (Prince Albert's Own) Hussars

239. **BEAUMONT**
26th April 1794
French Revolutionary Wars 1793–1802
— 1909 — Royal Horse Guards: 1st (King's) Dragoon Guards: 3rd (Prince of Wales's) Dragoon Guards: 5th (Princess Charlotte of Wales's) Dragoon Guards: 1st (Royal) Dragoons: 7th (Queen's Own) Hussars: 11th (Prince Albert's Own) Hussars: 16th (The Queen's) Lancers

240. **WILLEMS**
10th May 1794
French Revolutionary Wars 1793–1802
— 1909 — Royal Horse Guards: 2nd Dragoon Guards (Queen's Bays): 3rd (Prince of Wales's) Dragoon Guards: 6th Dragoon Guards (Carabiniers): 1st (Royal) Dragoons: 2nd Dragoons (Royal Scots Greys): 6th (Inniskilling) Dragoons: 7th (Queen's Own) Hussars: 11th (Prince Albert's Own) Hussars: 15th (The King's) Hussars: 16th (The Queen's) Lancers

241. **GUADALOUPE 1759**
22nd January–1st May 1759
Seven Years War 1756–63
— 1909 — The Buffs (East Kent Regiment): The King's Own (Royal Lancaster Regiment): The Gloucestershire Regiment: The South Staffordshire Regiment: The Black Watch (Royal Highlanders): The Manchester Regiment: The Prince of Wales's (North Staffordshire Regiment): The York and Lancaster Regiment

242. **MARTINIQUE 1762**
7th January–12th February 1762
Seven Years War 1756–63
— 1909 — The East Yorkshire Regiment: The Leicestershire Regiment: The Cheshire Regiment: The Leicestershire Regiment: The East Yorkshire Regiment: The Gloucestershire Regiment: The Royal Sussex Regiment: The South Staffordshire Regiment: The Prince of Wales's Volunteer (South Lancashire Regiment): The Welsh Regiment: The Black Watch (Royal Highlanders): The Oxfordshire and Buckinghamshire Light Infantry: The Northamptonshire Regiment: The King's Royal Rifle Corps

243. **HAVANNAH**
7th June–14th August 1762
Seven Years War 1756–63
— 1909 — The Royal Scots (Lothian Regiment): The Norfolk Regiment: The East Yorkshire Regiment: The Leicestershire Regiment: The Cheshire Regiment: The Royal Inniskilling Fusiliers: The Border Regiment: The Royal Sussex Regiment: The Prince of Wales's Volunteers (South Lancashire Regiment): The Black Watch (Royal Highlanders): The

			Oxfordshire and Buckinghamshire Light Infantry: The Essex Regiment: The Northamptonshire Regiment: The King's Royal Rifle Corps
244.	**ST LUCIA 1778** 12th–28th December 1778 War against France and Spain 1778–83	1909	The King's Own (Royal Lancaster Regiment): The Northumberland Fusiliers: The East Yorkshire Regiment: The Royal Inniskilling Fusiliers: The Gloucestershire Regiment: The Duke of Cornwall's Light Infantry: The Border Regiment: The Royal Sussex Regiment: The Prince of Wales's Volunteers (South Lancashire Regiment): Princess Charlotte of Wales's (Royal Berkshire Regiment)
245.	**MARTINIQUE 1794** 5th February–23rd March 1794 French Revolutionary Wars 1793–1802	1909	The Royal Warwickshire Regiment: The Norfolk Regiment: The East Yorkshire Regiment: The Royal Scots Fusiliers: The East Surrey Regiment: The Dorsetshire Regiment: The Oxfordshire and Buckinghamshire Light Infantry: The Northamptonshire Regiment: The Prince of Wales's (North Staffordshire Regiment): The York and Lancaster Regiment
246.	**THE SAINTS** ¹ 12th April 1782 War against France and Spain 1778–83	1909	The Welsh Regiment ¹ *Awarded with the badge of A Naval Crown superscribed "'12th April 1782".*
247.	**GLORIOUS FIRST OF JUNE** ¹ 1st June 1794 French Revolutionary Wars 1793–1802	1909	The Queen's (Royal West Surrey Regiment): The Worcestershire Regiment ¹ *Awarded with the badge of A Naval Crown superscribed "1st June 1794".*
248.	**NAMUR 1695** 3rd–6th July 1695 War of the Grand Alliance 1688–97	1910	Grenadier Guards: Coldstream Guards: Scots Guards: The Royal Scots (Lothian Regiment): The Queen's (Royal West Surrey Regiment): The King's Own (Royal Lancaster Regiment): The Royal Warwickshire Regiment: The Royal Fusiliers (City of London Regiment): The Prince of Wales's Own (West Yorkshire Regiment): The Bedfordshire Regiment: The Leicestershire Regiment: The Royal Irish Regiment: The Royal Welsh Fusiliers: The King's Own Scottish Borderers
249.	**NORTH AMERICA 1763–64** 23rd May 1763–10th January 1764 Pontiac's Conspiracy 1763–64	1914	The Black Watch (Royal Highlanders): The King's Royal Rifle Corps
250.	**FISH CREEK** 24th April 1885 Riel's Rebellion 1885	1914	32nd Manitoba Horse: 10th Regiment "Royal Grenadiers": 90th Regiment "Winnipeg Rifles"
251.	**SOMALILAND 1901–04** 22nd May 1901–11th May 1904 Operations in Somaliland 1901–04	1923 1932 1932	The King's African Rifles 8th (Lahore) Mountain Battery: Royal Bombay Sappers and Miners: 4th Bombay Grenadiers: 12th Frontier Force Regiment: 15th Pujab Regiment Bikaner Ganga Risala
252.	**BELLEISLE** 8th April–7th June 1761 Seven Years War 1756–63	1951	The Buffs (Royal East Kent Regiment): The Royal Norfolk Regiment: The Green Howards (Alexandra, Princess of Wales's Own Yorkshire Regiment): The Royal Scots Fusiliers: The Worcestershire Regiment: The East Lancashire Regiment: The Royal Hampshire Regiment: The Welch Regiment
253.	**UMZINTZANI** 2nd December 1877 Zulu and Basuto Wars 1877–79	1965	Prince Alfred's Guard

254.	**GAIKA-GCALEKA 1877** 26th September–31st December 1877 Zulu and Basuto Wars 1877–79	1965	Cape Town Rifles (Dukes)
255.	**GAIKA-GCALEKA 1877–78** 26th September 1877–28th June 1878 Zulu and Basuto Wars 1877–79	1965	Prince Alfred's Guard: First City: Kimberley Regiment
256.	**TRANSKEI 1877–78** 26th September 1877–31st December 1878 Zulu and Basuto Wars 1877–79	1965	Prince Alfred's Guard
257.	**GAIKA-GCALEKA 1878** 1st January–28th June 1878 Zulu and Basuto Wars 1877–79	1965	The Kaffrarian Rifles
258.	**GRIQUALAND WEST 1878** 21st January–13th November 1878 Zulu and Basutom Wars 1877–79	1965	Kimberley Regiment
259.	**TRANSKEI 1879** 1st January–2nd December 1879 Zulu and Basuto Wars 1877–79	1965	Cape Town Rifles (Dukes)
260.	**BASUTOLAND 1880–81** 13th September 1880–27th April 1881 Operations in Cape Colony 1880–81	1965	Cape Town Rifles (Dukes): Prince Alfred's Guard: First City: Kimberley Regiment
261.	**TRANSKEI 1880–81** 13th September 1880–15th May 1881 Operations in Cape Colony 1880–81	1965	Kimberley Regiment
262.	**BECHUANALAND 1896–97** 24th December 1896–30th July 1897 Operations in Bechuanaland 1896–97	1965	The Cape Town Highlanders: Kimberley Regiment
263.	**BECHUANALAND 1897** 1st January–30th July 1897 Operations in Bechuanaland 1896–97	1965	Cape Town Rifles (Dukes): Prince Alfred's Guard: First City: The Kaffrarian Rifles

2

The Great War and the Third Afghan War

Just for a word – 'neutrality', a word which in wartime has so often been disregarded, just for a scrap of paper – Great Britain is going to make war.

Von Bethmann Hollweg

Introduction

The Battles Nomenclature Committee met on Monday, 18 August 1919, with Major-General Sir John Headlam as president and five permanent members, all serving officers, representing the General Staff and the Governments of Australia, Canada, New Zealand and South Africa; there was no Indian Army representative as a permanent member. The first secretary, appointed from the Historical Section of the Committee of Imperial Defence, was Captain C.T. Atkinson of the Oxford University Officer Training Corps. Temporary members, again all serving officers and including three from the Indian Army, were co-opted by the Committee to advise on specific campaigns in the major theatres of war; documentary and supplementary personal evidence was also taken into account.

There were three tasks given to this Committee:

(a) To tabulate the actions fought in this war.

(b) To classify these actions with a definite system of nomenclature which will denote their relative importance.

(c) To define the geographical and chronological limits of each action.

The Report of the Battles Nomenclature Committee was ready by 9 July 1920 and was published the following year without amendment. This report, considering the magnitude of the tasks set, is now rightly accepted as a classic piece of staff work, even the spelling of place names was cleared with the Permanent Committee of Geographical Names, and it sets out the principles and practice of nomenclature and classification on which the current battle honours system is based.

The length and, possibly more importantly the scale, of the war, made the Committee select the tabulation of the engagements, not only chronologically, but separately and completely by each theatre in which they took place: the major theatres, such as France and Flanders, Italy, Macedonia, Dardanelles, Egypt and Palestine and Mesopotamia, were followed by the minor theatres of Persia, India, Russia, Far East and Pacific, East Africa, South-West Africa and West Africa. This sequence was later retained when battle honours were awarded to corps.

From the beginning it was clear to the Committee that the word 'battle' had undergone a change, and that it was now impossible to equate, say, **Minden**, fought in a few hours with any of the great battles of the Somme, which covered months; equally, in some minor theatres engagements were on a smaller scale, but, nonetheless, could be decisive to the course of the campaign. It was, therefore, concluded 'that any attempt to classify the engagements in all the theatres of war on hard-and-fast rules based on the numbers engaged, the casualties suffered, or any similar foundation must work unfairly in practice.' It was decided, therefore, to classify important engagements fought at corps level and above as 'battles', at divisional level as 'actions' and the remaining lesser engagements as 'affairs'. Where there were prolonged operations, such as at Ypres or on the Somme, the series of battles were to be arranged to form a Group of Battles. In the report the term 'capture' implies that actual fighting of some importance took place, whereas 'occupation' means that no such fighting was required. Similarly, a 'passage' is an assault river or canal crossing and 'crossing' is an unopposed river or canal crossing; while 'attack' is an unsuccessful operation, 'defence' is a successful resistance to a 'German or Turkish attack'.

Appropriate names to identify the engagements presented the Committee with some difficulties. Despatches and official accounts had made great use of 'double-barrelled' names, such as 'Ypres– Armentieres', and terms such as 'Second Ypres' or 'Third Gaza', but precedent argued against their use as battle honours. Also, the use of dates as in naval battles, for example, '1st July 1916' to describe the opening attack of the Battles of the Somme, was discounted since it was felt that the significance of the date would, in time, be diminished. Finally, it was decided to continue, as before, with the selection of a local name, followed, if necessary, by the year-date in which the engagement took place; however, no distinction was made when two or more engagements took place at the same location in the same year, as was the case, among others, at Krithia in 1915 or at Bapaume in 1918.

The geographical limits of the 'battle-field' were broadly defined by the Committee as easily recognized features for boundaries, with the outside lines of the infantry assaults determining the flanks and the heavy artillery positions setting the rear line. Nevertheless, all batteries firing on the front of attack, whether or not within these boundaries, were considered to have been present at the engagement.

The Committee also decided that the chronological limits should be defined by the 'day', that is, from midnight to midnight, and should not include the preparatory phase of an operation, but the period of consolidation after an attack should be included.

An extract from the Tabulated List of Engagements is shown at Appendix A.

Great Britain and Ireland

By November 1918 the strength of the Army was nearly three and a half million all ranks; a fourteen-fold increase in the 1914 Regular Establishment. During the four war years the Army had seen great changes – the introduction of conscription for all males between 18 and 41 years, except in Ireland, the conversion of corps from their traditional roles to form much needed cyclist, infantry and machine gun battalions, the increased use of wireless for command and control, mechanization for mobility and the early development of armoured, aerial and chemical warfare.

The three regiments of Household Cavalry remained mounted until 1918, then converted to machine gun battalions; in addition, the Household Cavalry Reserve Regiments, formed in 1914, found the short-lived Guards Divisional Cavalry Squadron, a Household Battalion and a siege battery of the Royal Garrison Artillery. All cavalry regiments remained mounted throughout the war, with no increase in the establishment.

Each of the three regiments of the Cavalry Special Reserve raised three new squadrons, which, together with the original squadrons, provided divisional cavalry squadrons until 1916, and thereafter corps cavalry regiments. In 1918 the North Irish Horse and the South Irish Horse were converted to a corps cyclist battalion and three infantry battalions.

Two further Yeomanry Regiments were raised in 1914 and, together with the pre-war regiments, volunteered with the remainder of the Territorial Force for overseas service, forming Second and Third Line units, which were given fractional designations. Of the First Line units, designated '1/-', only seventeen remained mounted throughout the war, thirty were converted to infantry battalions during 1916–17, nine were converted to machine gun battalions in 1918, one became a corps cyclist battalion in 1918 and one formed a cavalry machine gun squadron in 1916. Most of the Second Line, designated '2/-', were converted to cyclists in 1916, with the remainder either absorbed into Reserve Regiments or providing drafts for the newly-formed Tank Corps. One Second Line unit – 2/1st Northumberland Hussars – crossed to France in March 1917 as a corps cavalry regiment, but six months later was absorbed by 9th Northumberland Fusiliers. The Third Line units, designated '3/-', formed Reserve Regiments. A small number of squadrons, such as C Squadron of the Royal Glasgow Yeomanry, served throughout the war separated from their parent regiments.

It was, however, the Foot Guards and infantry that saw the greatest expansion; by the end of the war a total of one thousand, seven hundred and eighty-nine battalions of all types had been established, although not all survived until 1918. In addition to this establishment, there were eight battalions of Channel Islands Militia, fifteen battalions of the West African Frontier Force, twenty-two battalions of The King's African Rifles and a further twenty-two battalions found by The West India Regiment, The British West Indies Regiment, the West African Regiment, the Rhodesia Regiments and The Royal Newfoundland Regiment.

The Foot Guards, which had no reserve units in 1914, raised four additional front-line battalions, including 1st Welsh Guards, one machine gun battalion, five reserve battalions and two provisional battalions, which were used as demonstration battalions at Aldershot in 1918. The regular infantry establishment was maintained, despite heavy casualties in 1914, throughout the war, except for 2nd Connaught Rangers, the few survivors of which joined the 1st Battalion in December 1914.

The reserve and extra reserve battalions provided garrison troops in Great Britain and Ireland, except for five battalions – 7th Royal Fusiliers, 4th King's Liverpool Regiment, 4th Bedfordshire Regiment, 4th South Staffordshire Regiment and 4th North Staffordshire Regiment – which served in France and Flanders.

The Territorial Force expanded to form Second, Third and a small number of Fourth Line units. All the First Line battalions served overseas, the majority with the fourteen Territorial Force divisions; similarly, the Second Line formed fourteen further Territorial Force divisions, seven of which served overseas. The Third and the Fourth Line formed reserve battalions; however, five units – 3/4th Royal West Surrey Regiment, 3/5th Lancashire Fusiliers, 3/4th Royal West Kent Regiment, 3/10th Middlesex Regiment and 4/5th Loyal North Lancashire Regiment – served on the Western Front.

Five hundred and fifty-seven battalions, including reserve units, were raised by Field Marshal Lord Kitchener's appeal for four 'New Armies' and later by recruiting committees in cities, towns, organizations and even by individuals. These units were called collectively 'New Armies' battalions, but the units raised later were also known as 'locally raised', or sometimes styled 'Pals' battalions. The New Armies units were absorbed by the existing corps, consecutively numbered after existing battalions, and identified by '(Service)' after the number; in addition, locally raised battalions were permitted a further title in brackets to show the city, town, organization or individual which raised them. Consequently, units such as 6th (Service) Battalion, The Border Regiment and 13th (Service) Battalion, The Essex Regiment (West Ham) began increasingly to appear in the Orders of Battle and later Army Lists. A further two hundred and forty-five war-raised battalions were established as garrison – about twenty of which became service battalions in 1918 – labour, transport, docks and other miscellaneous units, many serving overseas.

In addition to the one hundred and eighty-eight squadrons of the newly formed Royal Air Force, which until April 1918 had been found by the Royal Flying Corps, over one hundred machine gun battalions served with the Machine Gun Corps, raised 1915, and the Guards Machine Gun Regiment, raised 1916 as the Machine Gun Guards. Also, eighteen front-line tank battalions served on the Western Front, with a detachment in Egypt and Palestine, formed into the Tank Corps in 1917.

The artillery, engineers and services were correspondingly increased in establishment during the war, mostly by the expansion of the Territorial Force and the formation of New Armies, to provide support at all levels throughout the Army at home and overseas.

Strangely, many of the war-raised battalions were permitted to wear the regulation badges of their new regiments, which, in some cases, included corps honours, whereas this distinction was still denied to units of the Territorial Force. On 22 September 1917, an often overlooked Army Order 298/1917 stated that in 'consideration of the services of the Territorial Force during the war, units were permitted to wear the badges of the Corps, regiment or department of the Regular Forces, including all honours and mottoes incorporated in any of these badges.' This was a significant, if long over-due, change in attitude by the Regular Establishment; possibly, it was now being recognized that after the war the current rules for the award of battle honours, with separate headings as for the Second Boer War, if retained, would be detrimental to the corps.

Following the Armistice, the Army reverted to its pre-1914 Regular Establishment, demobilization of the Special Reserve and Territorial Force began and war-raised units, regiments and corps were disbanded, except for the Welsh Guards, Machine Gun Corps and the Tank Corps, which were retained on the establishment. These processes were completed by the end of 1919 when the last unit – 1/9th Hampshire Regiment – disembarked at Southampton on 5 December 1919 after active service in Russia and Siberia.

During 1920 and 1921 many corps changed their titles to simplify them, to place more emphasis on the territorial affiliations – many local men had fought and died in the 'county regiment' – or to correct what the corps viewed as historical inaccuracies from 1881; all the cavalry titles were restyled. As some examples from many, The Highland Light Infantry became The Highland Light Infantry (City of Glasgow Regiment), the Princess Charlotte of Wales's (Royal Berkshire Regiment) changed to The Royal Berkshire Regiment (Princess Charlotte of Wales's) and The Royal Welsh Fusiliers and The Welsh Regiment again adopted 'Welch' in their titles. Not all these changes were successful: The King's Royal Rifle Corps tried The King's Royal Rifles, felt uncomfortable and reverted to its former title.

The Army was reorganized between 1920 and 1922, which for the first time led to large reductions in the Regular Establishment. Four cavalry regiments were disbanded in 1921, but reconstituted the following year; however, the final reductions were set at 'the equivalent of one regiment of Household Cavalry and eight regiments of Cavalry . . .' The solution was radical, but ingenious, each unit selected for disbandment would pair with another unit to form a composite regiment of four squadrons for the Household Cavalry regiment or of three squadrons for the cavalry regiments, respectively. These new composite regiments were to be considered 'as a complete regiment, but each squadron will retain the name and identity of the original regiment, e.g., 6th Dragoon Guards Squadron, 3rd/6th Dragoon Guards.' This ensured that the individual corps battle honours and other distinctions would be retained and survive separately. Gradually, however, many of the regiments faced the inevitable and became fully amalgamated, new regimental titles were taken into use and battle honours and distinctions were combined. Nevertheless, by the outbreak of the Second World War five composite cavalry regiments remained and battle honours continued to be shown separately in the Army Lists.

Similar reductions in the infantry took place in 1922. With the creation of the Irish Free State, five Irish corps were disbanded and with two corps being paired to form a new corps in which 'battalions of the Corps shall retain the distinctive designations, precedence, traditions, colours and uniforms of The Royal Inniskilling Fusiliers and The Royal Irish Fusiliers (Princess Victoria's)'. In the new corps each regiment had one regular battalion only. Sadly, with the disbandment of The Royal Dublin Fusiliers and The Royal Munster Fusiliers, each with a large number of unique Indian battle honours, there had been no attempt to retain these distinctions, which were thus allowed to disappear from the Army Lists. At the same time, all the remaining corps were reduced to two regular battalions and the Machine Gun Corps was disbanded.

The Special Reserve was not reactivated in 1920, reverting to Militia in 1921 it remained in suspended animation, that is, on establishment but not active, until finally it was disbanded in 1953. The South Irish Horse and King Edward's Horse (The King's Oversea Dominions Regiment) were disbanded in 1922 and 1924, respectively, but the North Irish Horse remained in suspended animation until reactivated in 1939.

The Territorial Force, later restyled the Territorial Army, was reformed in 1920 with a much reduced establishment. The Yeomanry was to provide sixteen mounted regiments for a cavalry division, with the remainder as Army Troops, eight armoured car companies for the Tank Corps, forty-eight batteries for the Royal Artillery and one signal unit for the Royal Engineers Signal Service, soon to become the Royal Corps of Signals; the Lincolnshire Yeomanry was disbanded. All battle honours and other distinctions were retained on conversion and continued in use as yeomanry awards, irrespective of the corps of which they now formed part; indeed, in all cases of conversion to another arm the regiments were the only units to have battle honours. Nevertheless, despite their new roles and possibly being no longer eligible for battle honours, the regiments remained officially as yeomanry. The infantry establishment, based largely on providing for fourteen regionally-based infantry divisions with some additional Army Troops, was reduced from its pre-1914 level by thirty-nine units; this was achieved by amalgamation, by transferring battalions to the Royal Artillery, Royal Engineers and Royal Signals and by disbanding eight battalions. Again, honours and distinctions were retained but, unlike the Yeomanry, the transferred units became fully integrated into their new corps and, as had become the practice with disbanded units, the King's and Regimental Colours were laid up in places of safe keeping, usually churches.

The conditions of award of battle honours were published in Army Order 338 in September 1922. These were contained in six short, concise sub-paragraphs:

1. His Majesty the King has been graciously pleased to approve the award of battle honours to regiments and corps under the following conditions:

   (a) Regiments and corps will have awarded to them, and recorded . . . the honours due to them for taking part in battles enumerated in . . . the tabulated list of engagements given in the report of the Battles Nomenclature Committee.

   (b) Following the honours previously earned and at the head of the List of Honours granted . . . will be placed 'The Great War' and the number of battalions of the regiment taking part.

   (c) Within the meaning of regiments and corps will be included Cavalry and Yeomanry regiments. An infantry regiment or corps will include the Regular, Militia (or Special Reserve), Territorial and Service Battalions . . . There will be only one Honours List for a regiment or corps.

   (d) Regiments of Cavalry and Yeomanry, battalions of Infantry, Regular, Militia (or Special Reserve) and Territorial, will have emblazoned on their Standards, Guidons and Colours not more than 24 honours of which not more than 10 will be 'Great War' honours . . . such honours to be selected by Regimental Committees . . . The honours emblazoned on the Colours will be the same for all units comprising the regiment concerned, and will be shown in the Army List in thicker type.

   (e) The guiding principle in the selection and allotment of battle honours will be that Headquarters and at least 50 per cent of the effective strength of a unit . . . must have been present at the engagement for which the honour is claimed.

   (f) Regimental Committees under the chairmanship of their regimental colonels . . . will be set up to select the particular honours for Regimental Colours.

2. Detailed instructions have been issued to the colonels of regiments and corps concerning . . . claims for the award of battle honours.

It should have been foreseen that the instruction to limit the number of battle honours to not more than twenty-four would bring a swift, strong protest and, in consequence, an amendment was promulgated by Army Order 470 in December 1922:

1. To obviate the necessity of removing honours at present emblazoned on the Colours of Regiments and Corps . . . the following shall be substituted for sub-paragraphs (d) and (f) of paragraph 1 of Army Order 338/1922:

   (d) Regiments of Cavalry and Yeomanry will have emblazoned on their Standards and Guidons battle honours earned by them in The Great War, up to a maximum of 10, in addition to those already carried. Battalions of Infantry, Regular, Militia (or Special Reserve) and Territorial, will have emblazoned on their King's Colour, battle honours up to a maximum of 10 to commemorate their services in The Great War, such honours to be selected by Regimental Committees . . . The honours emblazoned on the King's and Regimental Colours will be the same for all units comprising the regiment concerned, and will be shown in the Army List in thicker type.

   (f) Regimental Committees under the chairmanship of their Regimental Colonels . . . will be set up to select the honours referred to in paragraph (a), and from this list select the particular honours for emblazoning on the Standards, Guidons and King's Colours of the regiments concerned.

It is interesting to note, from sub-paragraph (c), that the eligibility for the award of battle honours applied to the Household Cavalry, cavalry, yeomanry and infantry corps; the war-raised corps – Machine Gun Corps and the Tank Corps – did not qualify to claim for awards. However, units of the Household Cavalry and yeomanry, which had formed machine gun units in 1918 were entitled to claim for the award of battle honours in that role. Similarly, regiments of the Cavalry Special Reserve and yeomanry were also entitled to claim awards as converted cyclist or infantry battalions; indeed, those infantry corps, which the converted units joined, could claim honours on behalf of such units, although not all did so. This generosity extended to disbanded Special Reserve, yeomanry and infantry corps, which could claim posthumously for the award of battle honours. But it was the inclusion of Territorial Army battalions in 'the one Honours List for the regiment or corps', together with the instruction in revised sub-paragraph (d) that the 'honours emblazoned . . . will be the same for all units comprising the regiment concerned . . . ', that had the greatest impact and prepared the way for Territorial Army battalions to become entitled to all their corps honours and distinctions. The former militia battalions had been given this distinction in 1910, largely for their participation in the Second Boer War, now it was to be extended to the Territorial Army on behalf of the Territorial Force for services in The Great War. Claims that this change of policy was forced on the Regular Establishment by the prospect of some highly-prized battle honours being carried separately by the old Volunteers to the exclusion of the corps were dismissed as cynical and ill-informed. Whatever the true reason, whether precedent or recognition of the quality and sacrifice of the Territorial Force, the change was generally well-received and, undoubtedly, considered well-deserved.

The fifty per cent rule was revised to take account of the very high casualty rates, particularly among the 'Old Contemptibles' of the British and Indian Expeditionary Forces in 1914. Before 1914 the fifty per cent was taken to refer to half the personnel on the authorized establishment or 'ration strength' of a unit. However, with the heavy losses during 1914 when battalions were reduced to the size of companies or smaller, units would have failed to qualify for awards under the rule. This, obviously, was not intended when the rule was introduced, and it was corrected by adding 'effective' to mean at least half of the surviving or 'bayonet strength' of a unit. Nevertheless, the amendment did not take fully into account all the effects of authorized establishments, in that it made no allowance for supporting sub-units within such establishments. Until May 1916 an infantry division included a divisional cavalry squadron, provided by cavalry, Special Reserve or yeomanry regiments. In April 1915 the cavalry squadrons were reformed into their regiments, posted to a cavalry division and replaced by yeomanry; however, in May 1916 the remaining squadrons were withdrawn from infantry divisions and formed into corps cavalry regiments, often with sub-units from other regiments. Separated squadrons were thereby disqualified from claiming awards unless two squadrons of the same regiment, albeit often serving with different formations, were present at the same battle. This strict application of the rule affected some yeomanry regiments unfairly; however, this could have been avoided if claims for a campaign or theatre honour had been allowed either by using the 'parties of 20 or over' rule, as for the Second Boer War or under the older precedent set when making awards for the Peninsula, that composite units could also qualify for battle honours or, even in the last resort, the example of the award of **Egypt** to 11th Light Dragoons on behalf of one troop, which was possibly established as the Commander-in-Chief's escort. In the event, no awards were made for these independent sub-units.

The first of ten lists of awards for The Great War was published in February 1924 in Army Order 49; curiously, it contained two battle honours not to be found in the Report of the Battles Nomenclature Committee. **Pursuit to Mons** had been introduced by the Battle Honours Committee as an additional honour to cover operations in Picardy between 17 October and 11 November 1918, and could be claimed only by corps which took part in these operations, but did not qualify for the award of either **Selle**, **Valenciennes** or **Sambre**. Although many individual claims for additional battle honours were disallowed, **Bois des Buttes** was approved for The Devonshire Regiment for the 2nd Battalion's action on 6 June 1918, when IX Corps was under the command of the French Fifth Army. List No 2 also promulgated a second additional award – **Bligny** – to The King's Shropshire Light Infantry on behalf of the 1/4th Battalion, The King's (Shropshire Light Infantry), which carried out a critical counterattack on 6 June 1918, again under IX Corps.

Afghanistan 1919 was awarded to fourteen units 'to be borne on their Standard, Regimental Colours and Appointments' was published separately in Army Order 97/24. Most unusually, 21st Lancers (Empress of India's) and The Hampshire Regiment were included in error among the recipients and the award was subsequently withdrawn.

The Royal Jersey Light Infantry (Militia) had provided a rifle company for the 7th Royal Irish Rifles in 1915 and was awarded **The Great War** in List No 3. The reason for this uncharacteristic distinction is not clear, possibly the usual award of a theatre honour, under the 'parties of 20 or over' was considered as inappropriate in view of the heavy casualties incurred by the battalion; its survivors were absorbed by the 2nd Royal Irish Rifles in 1917.

The Honourable Artillery Company, raised 1537, having convinced the Battle Honours Committee that it was a corps in its own right and not part of the Royal Artillery, was eligible for the award of battle honours. Nonetheless, of the forty-two honours published in List No. 10, twenty-five were won exclusively by artillery batteries.

By November 1924 all ten lists had been published and a Final List for all corps, which cancelled the previous lists, was promulgated in February 1925 by Army Order 55 and no further claims for honours could be submitted. Nevertheless, in July 1925 revised battle honours for four Yeomanry Regiments – Bedfordshire Yeomanry, Essex Yeomanry, Leicestershire Yeomanry (Prince Albert's Own) and The North Somerset Yeomanry – were authorized by Army Order 267. This revision took into account the services of these units after April 1918 when the regiments were broken up and one squadron was attached to each cavalry regiment in the 1st, 3rd, 6th and 9th Cavalry Brigades until the Armistice. This had been previously discounted under the fifty per cent rule, but, as two or more squadrons of each regiment had been present at each subsequent action of these brigades, additional honours were granted. In the same month by Army Order 268 the Northern Rhodesia Police was awarded **SW Africa 1914** and **E Africa 1914–18**.

The Royal Newfoundland Regiment, arguably one of the most distinguished corps in military history, was absent from this series of awards. The regiment, raised as The Newfoundland Regiment in 1915, was redesignated the Royal Newfoundland Regiment in 1918 and disbanded in 1919, but its active service record will never be surpassed and rarely equalled. The corps submission for awards had been made promptly, but the delay was caused by the insistence of the 'Newfoundlanders' to claim 'Beaumont Hamel' for the 1st Battalion on 1 July 1916, when it suffered seven hundred and ten casualties. The Battle Honours Committee at first refused the claim on the grounds that it was not included in the tabulated list of the Battles Nomenclature Committee. The awards of **Bois des Buttes** and **Bligny** did not support this view; and the claimants were determined that the regiment's conduct on that date should be recognized with a battle honour. There matters remained, with much correspondence between the Governor and the then Colonial Office, until a compromise was proposed that the claim should be allowed in the form **Albert (Beaumont Hamel)** 1916, provided that it was specifically approved by the Crown. Accordingly, a royal submission was prepared and presented to George V, who, it is recorded, did not hesitate and the battle honour was granted. The full battle honours of The Royal Newfoundland Regiment were finally published separately in 1925 and are perpetuated today by The Royal Newfoundland Regiment, raised 1949, a regiment of the Royal Canadian Infantry Corps.

There were further disbandments with two corps – the West India Regiment, raised 1795, and the West African Regiment, raised 1898, – disbanded in 1927 and 1928, respectively.

Several amendments had been made to awards published in the Final List, all dealing with changes to the emblazoned battle honours, mainly brought about by amalgamations; but the first correction to awards was made in 1929 when a claim by The Cameronians (Scottish Rifles) for **Gallipoli 1915–16** to replace the earlier award of **Gallipoli 1915** was approved.

Between 1936 and the outbreak of the Second World War the Territorial Army underwent further reorganization. In 1936 two Territorial Army Divisions – 46th and 47th – were disbanded and were replaced by 1st and 2nd Anti-Aircraft Divisions; three further anti-aircraft divisions followed in 1938. A total of fifty infantry battalions either formed searchlight units or were transferred to the Royal Artillery and the Royal Engineers to man the anti-aircraft units in these new divisions. The London Regiment was broken up, new titles were taken into use and the units were transferred to other regiments and corps; the Honourable Artillery Company and the Inns of Court Regiment remained unchanged. All battle honours and distinctions were retained; however, this was largely of academic interest only as, until 1937, all infantry units with battle honours had been transferred to corps, which did not qualify for awards, such as the Royal Artillery or the Royal Tank Corps, and Colours were laid up. Now, for the first time, units carrying battle honours were being transferred to other corps with their own distinctions. Were these units to combine their battle honours with those of their new parent corps, to adopt the distinctions of their new corps or to continue, as before, to carry their current battle honours? It was concluded by the Battle Honours Committee that it would be appropriate for the former units of The London Regiment to retain their own honours and that these should be shown separately in the Army List. In the case of The Liverpool Scottish, transferred to The Queen's Own Cameron Highlanders, the Committee went further and ruled that the battalion should take its own battle honours into use on transfer, which would also be shown separately in the Army List.

In 1937 The Royal Inniskilling Fusiliers and The Royal Irish Fusiliers (Princess Victoria's), which were joined into one corps in 1922, reformed their separate corps and again raised 2nd Battalions.

Although the mechanization of cavalry regiments had begun in 1936, to offset the shortage of armoured units, a further six Territorial Army infantry battalions were transferred to the Royal Tank Corps in November 1938. All honours and distinctions were retained and Colours were laid up on transfer. The following year a new corps – the Royal Armoured Corps – was formed, to which all armoured units were transferred, including the newly retitled Royal Tank Regiment.

In 1939 The Queen's Royal Regiment (West Surrey) absorbed into the corps honours the battle honours of its 6th (Bermondsey) Battalion, late 22nd London Regiment, and 7th (Southwark) Battalion, late 24th London Regiment, which had been shown separately in the Army List for two years. Other corps were to follow this example after the Second World War.

The likelihood of war in Europe brought no increase in the Regular Establishment, but the Territorial Army was doubled virtually overnight by a War Office letter, dated 31 March 1939, which authorized each unit to form a duplicate one; battalions, which had amalgamated in 1921 reformed or, in some cases, Second Line units were recruited.

On 3 September 1939 the United Kingdom declared war on Germany and, as many times before and for a second time in twenty-five years, 'the Army crossed into Flanders and swore horribly'. After the war, in 1951, there were further awards of battle honours for The Great War: **Ypres 1917** was extended to include 42nd Royal Tank Regiment on behalf of the 1/23rd London Regiment, **Khan Baghdadi** to The Dorset Regiment for the 1/4th Battalion, The Dorsetshire Regiment and **Tigris 1916** to The Oxfordshire and Buckinghamshire Light Infantry for the 1st Battalion. The award of **Macedonia 1915–18** to replace the earlier award of **Macedonia 1916–18** to The King's Royal Rifle Corps was also included.

The final awards, to date, were made in 1958 when the Royal Tank Regiment, now eligible as forming part of the Royal Armoured Corps, received its belated battle honours for The Great War.

India

The Indian Army of August 1914 was required to defend the borders of India, particularly the North-West Frontier, and to maintain internal security. Although from 1911 onwards some contingency planning had earmarked a number of Indian divisions for deployment overseas in the event of a war in Europe, it was ill-prepared for a large-scale, modern conflict lasting four years. The Indian Army establishment not only set the number of corps and their strengths, but also controlled the caste or class composition of the units. While a few regiments, such as 14th Murray's Jat Lancers with four squadrons of Jats, were 'class Corps' manned exclusively by one class only, the majority, such as 62nd Punjabis, which had four companies of Punjabi Mussalmans, two of Sikhs and two of Rajputs, operated with each squadron or company recruited separately from selected classes. In addition, the Indian infantry corps were grouped with a Regimental Centre manned by one of the battalions in that group to provide trained recruits for the other battalions. In August 1914 there were forty-three Regimental Centres, and, although the system had worked in peace-time, it was strained with the casualty rates of 1914 and 1915, became dependent on drafts from units remaining in India for reinforcements and finally collapsed in 1916. It was, therefore, not until late 1916 that the war-time expansion of the Indian Army started, which, together with improvements in pay and conditions, national, joint civil–military recruiting with an extension of the class composition and the formation of class reserve battalions, was very successful; over one million men passed through the system between 1916 and 1919.

The Indian cavalry regiments remained mounted throughout the war; seven additional regiments were raised in 1918, three of which served on the North-West Frontier. Detached squadrons also served independently in South Persia, the Gulf and East Africa. The Indian Mountain Artillery increased from twelve pre-war batteries to thirty between 1917 and 1920 and the Sappers and Miners raised fifty-two additional companies, two field squadrons and eight field troops between 1914 and 1919. As with the British Army, it was the infantry that saw the greatest war-time expansion; in August 1914 there were one hundred and fifteen single-battalion and eleven two-battalion corps. By the end of the war the Indian infantry had risen to two hundred and eighty-four battalions; in January 1916 ten Nepalese infantry battalions were taken into British service to make up the shortfall in North-West Frontier garrisons. Between 1916 and 1918 many Indian infantry corps, including the Gurkha Rifles, formed 2nd and 3rd Battalions, some raised a 4th Battalion and 70th Burma Rifles recruited a 5th Battalion. In addition, in 1918 sixteen new infantry and one Gurkha corps were authorized, formed from police battalions, from Indian States Forces and from drafts from battalions serving in the Middle East.

The Imperial Service Troops were mobilized on the outbreak of hostilities and units served, many with distinction, in all the major overseas theatres, in addition to India.

After the war the demobilization of the Indian Army was delayed by events in Afghanistan in 1919 and the continuing requirement to provide troops for garrison duties in the Middle East; however, by 1922 all war-raised units, except for five 2nd Battalions which were retained to form training battalions, had been disbanded. Meanwhile, at the same time the Indian Army, like their British counterparts, was being reorganized. In 1921 the Indian cavalry was reduced to twenty-one regiments, each of three separate class squadrons, by forming eighteen composite regiments and retaining three – 27th and 28th Light Cavalry and the Guides Cavalry; the following year the composite regiments were amalgamated and new numbers and titles were taken into use. The Indian infantry, too, was restructured with corps grouped into twenty, numbered 'large regiments' in 1922; each corps had four or five consecutively-numbered battalions and one training battalion, numbered 10th, later to become the Regimental Centre, with one company for each battalion. Suitable units were selected to form these new corps; for example, the 1st Battalion of 15th Punjab Regiment was found by 25th Punjabis, the 2nd by 26th, the 3rd by 27th, the 4th by 28th and the 10th by 29th; after all units had been allocated to the new establishment the nine remaining Indian infantry corps were disbanded. The Gurkha Rifles remained unchanged, each with two battalions.

Pioneer battalions were removed from the infantry establishment and formed into four separate, numbered corps, with a structure similar to the new Indian infantry corps. The Indian Mountain Batteries became Pack Batteries and were renumbered; the Sappers and Miners raised a fourth corps in 1922 as 4th Burma Sappers and Miners, and in 1923 all corps dropped their numbers and new titles were taken into use. All honours and distinctions remained with their corps, to be combined on amalgamation, reorganization or 'lost' on disbandment.

There had been Volunteers, found by Europeans in Bengal, as early as 1756; it was, however, during the Great Mutiny that a large number of volunteer units, recruited from Europeans and Anglo-Indians, were raised throughout India for the protection of their families and property. Gradually, once the threat was removed, these units became understrength, poorly trained and neglected, many being disbanded, and others survived only by adopting the style of a social club rather than a military organization. The Volunteers, nevertheless, proved a valuable source of additional British officers for the expanded Indian Army during The Great War. In 1917 all surviving units of the Volunteers were transferred to the Indian Defence Force, with compulsory service for all Europeans aged between 18 and 41. In 1920 the Indian Defence Force was replaced by the Auxiliary Force, India, with ten mounted regiments and forty-five infantry battalions, again recruited from mainly Europeans and Anglo-Indians; these units were intended for internal security only and compulsory service was ended. In the same year the Indian Territorial Force was formed with seven battalions, later extended to twenty. These units recruited in or near the training battalions from the same classes as the regular battalions and formed the 11th Battalion of the new corps. Initially, these Indian Territorial Force battalions each had five British officers only, with the remaining ranks filled by Indians, but in time the British element was reduced as suitably qualified Indian officers became available. The Force was specifically excluded from internal security duties, but it could be mobilized in a national emergency and, if necessary, be employed outside India.

When instructions were issued, in March 1923, for the submission of claims for battle honours for The Great War by Indian cavalry, Indian Pioneers and infantry, Indian Pack Batteries, Sappers and Miners and Indian States Forces, the conditions were identical to those issued by the War Office in 1922, except that, unlike in the British Army, disbanded corps were not eligible for the award of honours. To the dismay of the Indian Army, the battle honours were to be awarded, not, as in the past, to the individual units present at the engagement, but, as was the practice in the British Army, to the newly formed corps; this caused great resentment as it was considered unfair to the units of the former regiments which had fought in the action. It was argued strongly by many senior corps that the awards should be made to their units which had been present, and then transferred to the new corps; however, this argument was unsuccessful. Similar instructions in respect of claims for the Third Afghan War were published the following year.

In 1924 the Indian Pack Batteries were transferred to the Royal Artillery, but retained their battle honours and other distinctions and, more importantly, continued to qualify for the award of such honours; curiously, this transfer led to a further distinction, since, forming part of a British regiment, it was granted precedence over the Indian cavalry and made the 'Right of the Line'. In 1927 the units reverted to their old title of Mountain Batteries.

The Governor General's Order 193 of February 1926 made the first awards for the Third Afghan War to Indian Army corps, followed by Order 194/1926 promulgating the award of battle honours for The Great War in six schedules covering the Indian Pack Batteries, cavalry, Sappers and Miners, Indian Pioneers and infantry, Gurkha regiments and Indian States Forces. Later that year the first, and only, correction to the list was made when **France and Flanders 1914–18** replaced **France and Flanders 1916–17** previously awarded to 21st King George's Own Central India Horse. Awards to Indian States Forces for The Third Afghan War were published in Governor General's Order 1409/1926. Additional awards were made in 1927 with **NW Frontier India 1914-15'17** extended to 9th Jat Regiment; three further Gurkha rifle regiments received **Afghanistan 1919**; awards for The Great War to four Indian States Forces units and **Khan Baghdadi** was extended to the Jaipur Transport Corps. The final awards were published in 1928, with **Persia 1918** extended to 101st Royal (Kohat) Indian Mountain Battery (Frontier Force) and **La Bassee 1914, Armentieres 1914, Egypt 1916–17, Kut al Amara 1917** and **Aden** extended to include 3rd Sikh Pioneers.

The withdrawal of troops from the Middle East led to further reductions in the Indian infantry establishment; during 1923–24 and 1926–28 five battalions and then three were disbanded. The axe fell heavily on 3rd Madras Regiment, which lost two battalions in 1923, two more in 1926 and the corps was removed from the Regular Indian Army List when the 1st Battalion was disbanded in 1928; fortunately, the corps had by then four Indian Territorial Force battalions, 11th to 14th, which survived. Between 1930 and 1931 four further battalions were disbanded; this time it was 4th Bombay Grenadiers which bore the brunt with the loss of two battalions and its 10th Battalion was amalgamated with the 10th Battalion of 9th Jat Regiment to form a shared Regimental Centre.

The Burma Sappers and Miners was disbanded in 1929. The Indian Pioneers – the elite of the pre-1914 Indian Army – were also reorganized at the same time; the numbering was removed and the style of corps taken into use; for example, 2nd Bombay Pioneers became the Corps of Bombay Pioneers, with a corps headquarters and two battalions. Four years later, on 10 February 1933, the short-lived Corps of Pioneers were disbanded as the 'retention of an organization which is not fully suited to our needs cannot be justified.' A large number of battle honours, including **Kelat-i-Ghilzie**, 'marched into history' with these corps.

In 1937 Burma was removed from Indian administration and the four regular battalions and one Indian Territorial Force battalion of 20th Burma Rifles were transferred to Burma to form the Burma Rifles. The last infantry disbandment before the Second World War took place in January 1939 when the 4th Battalion, 2nd Punjab Regiment was dispersed after an unfortunate incident when a Muslim sepoy ran amok killing seven officers, both British and Indian; curiously, no subsequent 4th Battalion has, to date, been raised by The Punjab Regiment.

The Indian cavalry had also seen some changes since 1922; in 1936, as mechanization was being planned, the seven cavalry groups set up for administration in the 1922 reorganization were regrouped into three new groups with one regiment in each earmarked to become a permanent training regiment. The regiments selected were 12th Sam Browne's Cavalry (Frontier Force), 15th Lancers and 20th Lancers. The following year the first Indian cavalry regiments – 13th Duke of Connaught's Own Lancers and 14th Scinde Horse – were converted to armoured car units.

By the outbreak of the Second World War the Indian Army consisted of twenty-one cavalry regiments, of which three were training regiments, being mechanized; the recently formed Indian Artillery – the Indian Mountain Batteries were transferred from the Royal Artillery in August 1939 – was being expanded and re-equipped and the Sappers and Miners each had five or six field companies. The Indian infantry was established at one hundred and thirty-six battalions, ninety-seven Regular, seventeen training and twenty-two Indian Territorial Force, including Gurkha rifle regiments. In support, were the Indian States Forces, now nearly fifty States, and the provincial units of the Auxiliary Force, India. In all, over a quarter of a million men, but with outdated equipment, lacking modern weapons and, except for North-West Frontier-type operations, poorly trained in current all-arms tactics. For a second time since 1903, the Indian Army was unprepared to fight a war outside the sub-continent;

nevertheless, it had always shown great flexibility, resourcefulness and fighting qualities and re-equipment was belatedly under way.

Australia

In 1914, unlike the United Kingdom and India which had standing armies, Australia had only a small Permanent Force and the recently formed, but as yet incomplete, part-time Citizen Military Forces, which could not serve outside the Commonwealth. For political and legal reasons, and, in order to fulfil without delay a commitment of twenty thousand men made to the British Government, it was decided to form an all-volunteer expeditionary force of one infantry division and one light horse brigade, to be called the Australian Imperial Force with units identified by the suffix 'AIF'. By 1918 the Force had expanded to two corps headquarters and supporting corps troops and five infantry divisions on the Western Front and part of two mounted divisions in Palestine. In addition, there was a small garrison force occupying former German possessions in Kaiser Wilhelm's Land and the Solomon Islands, which in 1914 had formed the hastily raised Australian Naval and Military Expeditionary Force.

The light horse remained mounted throughout the war, except for the Gallipoli Campaign when the regiments were dismounted and employed as infantry; 4th Light Horse Regiment AIF and 13th Light Horse Regiment AIF provided divisional cavalry until March 1916, and thereafter served as part of II Anzac Corps Cavalry Regiment – the third squadron being found by the Otago Mounted Rifles – and I Anzac Corps Cavalry Regiment, respectively. In January 1917 C Squadron of 4th Light Horse Regiment AIF, which had remained attached to 1st Light Horse Brigade in Egypt, was used to reform the regiment. The light horse establishment was increased from thirteen regiments by the formation of 14th and 15th Light Horse Regiments AIF in July 1918, with Australian personnel from the disbanded 1st and 3rd Battalions of the Imperial Camel Corps Brigade. The infantry establishment finally comprised sixty battalions, each, like the light horse regiments retaining a State identity from which it was recruited; not all, however, survived the war with three, six and one battalions being disbanded in May, September and October 1918, respectively. Five divisional pioneer battalions were established in March 1916 and five divisional machine gun units were formed in February 1918 by grouping the existing companies into battalions. Artillery, engineers and all supporting services at all levels were provided by Australia in France and Flanders and all, except artillery found by Territorial Force Royal Horse Artillery Batteries, in Egypt and Palestine.

It had been foreseen by the Australian Government some time before the Armistice that, unless some method of retention were devised, all honours and distinctions granted in the future to units of the Australian Imperial Force would be 'lost' on disbandment of the Force. Accordingly, on 3 August 1918, Military Order 364 stated that, from 1 October 1918, the Citizen Military Forces would be redesignated to conform to the Australian Imperial Force units 'in order to maintain the traditions and perpetuate the records of the 1914–18 War'. The revised establishment was set at twenty-three consecutively-numbered light horse regiments and sixty, later raised to sixty- two, single-battalion, consecutively-numbered corps. In 1921 the Australian Imperial Force was finally disbanded, but the reorganized and renumbered Citizen Military Forces, soon to become part of the Australian Military Forces, was in place to replicate its former units; for example, the late 9th Light Horse (New South Wales Mounted Rifles) had become 6th Light Horse (New South Wales Mounted Rifles) to maintain the tradtions of 6th Light Horse Regiment AIF, which was recruited from that State and, similarly, the late 78th Infantry (Adelaide Rifles) and the late 79th (Torrens) Infantry had formed 10th Infantry Battalion (Adelaide Rifles) to perpetuate 10th Infantry Battalion AIF from South Australia.

On 9 March 1927, Australian Army Order 112 published 'the award of Battle Honours for The Great War to Cavalry and Infantry units of the Australian Imperial Force . . . '. Fifteen light horse regiments and sixty infantry battalions were listed, but no awards were made to pioneer or machine gun battalions, as there were no equivalent Australian Military Forces battalions on establishment. Nonetheless, not all the awards contained in the order conformed to the then recognized nomenclature for battle honours; the light horse awards included two 'linked' distinctions – **Magdhaba–Rafah** and **Gaza–Beersheba** – and two 'bracketed' honours – **Jordan (Es Salt)** and **Jordan (Amman)**. The infantry awards, also, took some distinctly Australian forms with **Albert 1918 (Chuignes)**, **Sari Bair–Lone Pine** and with **Mont St. Quentin** instead of **Bapaume 1918**. However, it was considered that the selection of these names as honours reflected more accurately the part played by the Australian Imperial Force in these battles and actions and were, hence, more appropriate.

It is interesting to note that 4th Light Horse Regiment was awarded battle honours for both 4th Light Horse Regiment AIF in Palestine and for II Anzac Corps Cavalry Regiment in France and Flanders; furthermore, 14th and 15th Light Horse Regiments were permitted to receive awards on behalf of 1st and 3rd Battalions of the Imperial Camel Corps, the only units from this corps to be so rewarded. The 1st and 2nd Infantry Battalions were also awarded **Herbertshohe** on behalf of 1st and 2nd Battalions of the Australian Naval and Military Expeditionary Force, in addition to awards made to the similarly numbered Australian Imperial Force units.

Following the award of battle honours for The Great War, the order continued;

2. The . . . Battle Honours have been allotted to the units of the Australian Military Forces which have inherited and now hold the titles, designations and traditions of the corresponding units of the Australian Imperial Force.

3. These Battle Honours will be published in the Army List of the AMF under the names of the units concerned, and such units will henceforth be entitled to emblazon on their Guidons or Regimental Colours the ten selected honours which are shown in thick black type . . . '

In 1930 further battle honours for The Great War were published in a terse Australian Army Order 174, which stated that 'approval has been given for the allotment of Battle Honours to the 3rd (Tasmanian Mounted Infantry) Light Horse Regiment, AMF, as having inherited (the title,) designation, and traditions of the 3rd Light Horse Regiment, AIF, in addition to the 3rd (South Australian Mounted Rifles) Light Horse Regiment.' It is strange that there should be two 3rd Light Horse Regiments; although 3rd Light Horse Regiment AIF had been raised in both South Australia and Tasmania, all the honours had accrued to the South Australian Mounted Rifles under the redesignation system for perpetuating such distinctions with none shared with Tasmania. Furthermore, South Australia had three successor light horse regiments of which two – 3rd and 9th – had been allotted battle honours, while the only Tasmanian successor regiment had none. This inequity was corrected under the existing system by simply renumbering temporarily 22nd Light Horse Regiment (Tasmanian Mounted Infantry) to rank 3rd. Accordingly, this device was used, and after the awards had been granted, 3rd (Tasmanian Mounted Infantry) Light Horse Regiment reverted to its former number and title in 1937; not surprisingly, all battle honours and other distinctions were retained on redesignation. This award of battle honours led to further awards, and the last, to date, for The Great War, which were promulgated by Australian Army Order 117 in 1936; **Anzac, Gallipoli 1915, Egypt 1915–17** and **Palestine 1917–18** were extended to include a further seven light horse regiments 'in recognition of the numbers of officers and men supplied by the . . . Regiments and by their regimental areas to Light Horse units of the Australian Imperial Forces.'

Meanwhile, during the 1920s and the 1930s the Australian Military Forces were in decline; with the ending of compulsory training, and a new part-time, paid volunteer force called the Volunteer Militia, with an establishment of twenty-seven thousand all ranks, was formed. However, all the successor light horse and infantry corps were retained by 'linking' units, which were understrength, to avoid amalgamations or disbandments. Despite the neglect, it would appear that within the Australian Military Forces there was a determination that all the traditions and honours of the Australian Imperial Force should survive. By 1939, with a national recruiting campaign the previous year, the volunteer element of the Australian Military Forces had increased to eighty thousand all ranks, which enabled the mechanization of the light horse regiments to be accelerated and the sixty-two infantry battalions to regain their separate identities.

Canada

On 1 August 1914 the Governor General, the Duke of Connaught, offered military assistance to the British Government in the event of war with Germany. It was agreed that a Canadian Expeditionary Force of one infantry division, later expanded to include a cavalry brigade would be provided and that units of this Force would be recognized by use of the suffix 'CEF'. Meanwhile, to the dismay of the Militia, the Minister of Defence and Militia, Samuel Hughes, announced that no part-time militia corps would serve outside Canada and that the Canadian Expeditionary Force would be formed from volunteers only, albeit largely found by drafts from the Militia. As the Force concentrated near Quebec, The Royal Canadian Regiment was despatched to Bermuda and a Montreal businessman, Captain Hamilton Gault, impatient with Hughes's lengthy mobilization, raised the Princess Patricia's Canadian Light Infantry – the first Canadian unit to reach the United Kingdom and then France – at his own expense in Ottawa. The Canadian Expeditionary Force gradually expanded until, in November 1918, it was composed of a corps headquarters and corps troops, four infantry divisions and a cavalry brigade, together with supporting arms and services and some units of the Canadian Railway Troops, on the Western Front, maintained in both Canada and the United Kingdom by a system of provincial depots and reserve battalions. Some Forestry Corps units also served in France and the United Kingdom.

The Canadian Cavalry Brigade served dismounted as infantry with 1st Canadian Division from May until September 1915; in February 1916 the Fort Garry Horse replaced 2nd King Edward's Horse (The King's Overseas Dominions Regiment) and the Cavalry Machine Gun Squadron CEF was added to the establishment. Thereafter the Brigade remained mounted serving with 3rd and 5th Cavalry Divisions. Divisional cavalry squadrons for the 1st and the 2nd Canadian Division were found by 19th Alberta Dragoons and 1st Hussars, respectively until May 1916 when they were withdrawn, and joined by squadrons found by 16th Light Horse and the Royal North-West Mounted Police, formed the Canadian Corps Cavalry Regiment, later restyled the Canadian Light Horse in 1917. The 1st and 2nd Canadian Mounted Rifles Brigades were attached, dismounted, to the Canadian Cavalry Brigade from September to December 1915, then formed the infantry battalions of 8th Canadian Brigade.

By 1918, two hundred and fifty-eight consecutively-numbered Canadian Expeditionary Force infantry battalions had been raised, with two further battalions formed in 1918 for service in North Russia with 16th Canadian Brigade. Many battalions did not survive the war, being broken up to provide reinforcement drafts from both Canada and the United Kingdom for the units in France and Flanders; others were employed as pioneer battalions from 1916 until June 1918, when all divisional pioneer battalions were absorbed by the Canadian Engineer Brigades. Motor Machine Gun Brigades, which were mounted in armoured cars armed with Colt guns, were attached to each division until 1916, then withdrawn to form 1st Motor Machine Gun Brigade CEF, a corps troops formation, which in 1918 was reorganized into two brigades. Machine gun companies replaced the Motor Machine Gun Brigades within the divisions until 1918 when machine gun battalions were formed by grouping the companies.

The Canadian Expeditionary Force was disbanded in 1919 and for the next ten years the Militia experienced minor changes. The disbanded Princess Patricia's Canadian Light Infantry and 22nd (Canadien Francais) Battalion CEF were reformed as regiments of the Permanent Active Militia; the latter to become the Royal 22^e Regiment. A Canadian Machine Gun Corps was established, consisting of 1st and 2nd Motor Machine Gun Brigades, 1st Cavalry Machine Gun Squadron and thirteen numbered machine gun battalions. A Permanent Motor Machine Gun Brigade was also formed, but disbanded in 1923 as the Royal Canadian Permanent Motor Machine Gun Brigade.

In 1920–21 the Militia was 'reconstituted' with some cavalry regiments being renumbered to fill vacancies in the establishment, while others were restyled with new titles taken into use. Despite the renumbering the regiments retained their former seniority, for example, 5th Princess Louise Dragoon Guards became The Princess Louise Dragoon Guards on 15 March 1920, and 31st Regiment (British Columbia Horse) changed to 5th British Columbia Light Horse on 1 November 1920, but the former continued to rank 5th and the latter remained at 31st. Similarly, the 24th changed to the 9th, the 25th was renumbered the 10th, the 27th became the 14th and the 29th became the 18th. Unlike the universal trend towards cavalry reductions, no regiments were amalgamated and only 35th Central Alberta Horse, raised 1913, was disbanded. The Non-Permanent Militia infantry corps dropped the numbered regiment designation and new titles were taken into use, mainly to reflect their territorial associations; for example, 7th Regiment Fusiliers changed to The Western Ontario Regiment and 103rd Regiment Calgary Rifles became The Calgary Regiment. Twelve regiments amalgamated to form six new corps, one regiment was disbanded and four new regiments were raised. Between 1922 and 1928 there were further changes of titles, one cavalry regiment – 10th Queen's Own Canadian Hussars, disbanded 1913 – was reformed, eight new infantry corps were raised, a further six battalions were formed or reformed by disbanding three recently formed corps and one additional corps was formed by amalgamation.

Like the Australians, the Canadian Government had for some time been aware that, in order not to lose any future honours and distinctions earned by units of the Canadian Expeditionary Force in the late war, some means of perpetuating these would have to be introduced. It was evident that units of the Force would receive honours and that selected Militia units would have to be allocated these honours to ensure their continuity. However, in many cases more than one Militia unit had contributed to the formation of a Canadian Expeditionary Force unit and to its maintenance at the front; it would, therefore not be possible to apply the Australian solution or, at least, it would be unfair to do so.

It was not until 1928 that the conditions of award of battle honours for The Great War were published on 1 February in General Order 6. To ensure that every contribution by units of the Militia was recognized and rewarded, the conditions at first appeared to be complicated, but were, in fact, quite logical, comprehensive and detailed.

The conditions of award of battle honours for The Great War 1914–19 are shown in Appendix B.

On the same date, General Order 7 was published, which was based, with amendments to some boundaries, on the Report of the Battles Nomenclature Committee, listing the 'engagements of The Great War in which troops of the Canadian Expeditionary Force took part . . . '; this order was subject to some minor amendments to the boundaries and by the addition of the details for **Beaurevoir** later in 1928.

Between 1929 and 1931 five lists were published in General Orders promulgating the battle honours awarded for The Great War to corps of the Permanent and Non-Permanent Active Militia and units of the Canadian Expeditionary Force; to date, no amendments to these distinctions have been made. However, additional awards were published in 1960 with **Mount Sorrel, Somme 1916** and **France and Flanders 1915–16** extended to include 8th Canadian Hussars (Princess Louise's) and 8th Canadian Hussars (Princess Louise's) (Militia) to perpetuate 6th Regiment, Canadian Mounted Rifles CEF. Similarly, in 1961, Le Regiment de Maisonneuve received **Mount Sorrel, Somme 1916, Arras 1917, Hill 70, Ypres 1917** and **Amiens** in order to perpetuate 41st Canadian Infantry Battalion CEF.

The Non-Permanent Militia saw major changes between 1935 and the outbreak of the Second World War with reductions to both the cavalry and the infantry. By September 1939 seventeen cavalry regiments only remained; reductions brought about by amalgamation, transfers to the Royal Canadian Artillery and disbandments. The infantry made similar reductions, resulting in a total of ninety corps; five regiments formed tank units while remaining on the infantry establishment. The Canadian Machine Gun Corps, formed 1919, was disbanded in 1936; 1st and 2nd Motor Machine Gun Brigades formed 1st and 2nd Armoured Car Regiments, the former being absorbed by 6th Duke of York's Royal Canadian Hussars, with 1st Machine Gun Squadron posted to 2nd Armoured Car Regiment and the remaining machine gun battalions transferred by companies to the Royal Canadian Artillery, to infantry battalions and to form a sixth tank unit – The New Brunswick Regiment (Tank). All battle honours and distinctions were retained on transfer and combined on amalgamation.

New Zealand

The New Zealand Expeditionary Force, formed in August 1914, consisted of a divisional headquarters, with a divisional cavalry regiment and an artillery brigade of three batteries only, a mounted rifles brigade and an infantry brigade; units were identified by the suffix 'NZEF'. As there was no standing army, the Military Districts were required to fill this establishment with volunteers from units of the Territorial Force. Each corps was required to provided one squadron or one company towards a Provincial Regiment or Battalion. Accordingly, the Auckland Mounted Rifles NZEF was found by squadrons from 3rd (Auckland) Mounted Rifles, 4th (Waikato) Mounted Rifles and 11th (North Auckland) Mounted Rifles; the Canterbury Mounted Rifles NZEF by 1st Mounted Rifles (Canterbury Yeomanry Cavalry), 8th (South Canterbury) Mounted Rifles and 10th (Nelson) Mounted Rifles and the Wellington Mounted Rifles NZEF by Queen Alexandra's 2nd (Wellington West Coast) Mounted Rifles, 6th (Manawatu) Mounted Rifles and 9th (Wellington East Coast) Mounted Rifles. The Otago Mounted Rifles NZEF, which was the divisional cavalry regiment, was formed by squadrons from 5th Mounted Rifles (Otago Hussars), 7th (Southland) Mounted Rifles and 12th (Otago) Mounted Rifles. The mounted rifles remained mounted throughout the war, except for the Gallipoli Campaign when they were employed as infantry. Similarly, the Auckland Battalion NZEF was formed by companies from 3rd (Auckland) Regiment (Countess of Ranfurly's Own), 6th (Hauraki) Regiment, 15th (North Auckland) Regiment and 16th (Waikato) Regiment; the Canterbury Battalion NZEF by 1st (Canterbury) Regiment, 2nd (South Canterbury) Regiment, 12th (Nelson) Regiment and 13th (North Canterbury and Westland) Regiment; the Otago Battalion NZEF by 4th (Otago Rifles) Regiment, 8th (Southland Rifles) Regiment, 10th (North Otago Rifles) Regiment and 14th (South Otago Rifles) Regiment and the Wellington Battalion NZEF by 7th (Wellington West Coast Rifles) Regiment, 9th (Hawke's Bay) Regiment, 11th Regiment (Taranaki Rifles) and 17th (Ruahine) Regiment. The 17th Regiment was formed from the 2nd Battalion, 9th (Wellington East Coast Rifles) Regiment – the 1st Battalion having been re-designated 9th (Hawke's Bay) Regiment – and replaced 5th (Wellington Rifles) Regiment, which had provided most of the personnel for the force which occupied the German possessions in Samoa on 29 August 1914. A Maori battalion was also raised from volunteers in October 1914.

The New Zealand Expeditionary Force sailed on 15 October join the Australian Imperial Force at Albany, Western Australia and arrived in Egypt on 3 December 1914.

In May 1915 The Trentham Regiment (Earl of Liverpool's Own), later to become The New Zealand Rifle Brigade (Earl of Liverpool's Own), was raised, mainly from personnel of the Wellington Rifles returning from Samoa.

The New Zealand Expeditionary Force was reorganized after the Gallipoli Campaign in March 1916; the mounted rifles brigade remained unchanged, except for the addition of 1st New Zealand Machine Gun Squadron. A New Zealand Division was established with the Provincial Battalions expanded to form 1st and 2nd Battalions of the now restyled Provincial Regiments, with the third brigade made up of four battalions of The New Zealand Rifle Brigade. The Otago Mounted Rifles was reduced to one squadron and found the divisional cavalry squadron, until July 1916 when it became the third squadron of II Anzac Corps Cavalry Regiment; the remaining two squadrons, together with the Maori battalion, formed the divisional pioneer battalion. A fourth brigade of 3rd Battalions of the Provincial Regiments served with the Division from May 1917 until February 1918, when the Brigade was disbanded. That same month a New Zealand Machine Gun Battalion was formed from existing machine gun companies.

All war-raised units were demobilized by the end of 1919, but the New Zealand Expeditionary Force was not officially disbanded until 1921.

That same year the Territorial Force was reorganized; the mounted rifles establishment was reduced from twelve to nine regiments and new titles – New Zealand Mounted Rifles – were taken into use. No regiments were disbanded, but reduction was achieved by the amalgamation of five regiments to form two New Zealand mounted rifles regiments and by renumbering 9th, 10th and 11th Mounted Rifles as 7th, 8th and 9th New Zealand Mounted Rifles, respectively. The seventeen infantry regiments were reduced to ten new corps; again, no corps were disbanded, but three of the new corps were the result of the amalgamation of six regiments, with two 2nd Battalions of the new corps by the amalgamation of four. In addition, the use of numbers was dropped and new titles were taken into use. All honours and distinctions were retained.

In 1923 The Hawke's Bay Regiment and The Nelson, Marlborough, and West Coast Regiment were reformed from the 2nd Battalions of The Wellington Regiment and The Canterbury Regiment, respectively.

In October 1926 the first list of battle honours was published in General Order 389:

His Majesty the King has been pleased to approve the award of battle honours for The Great War to New Zealand regiments as follows:-

Where the existing regiment is the result of amalgamation of two or more regiments, battle honours have been awarded for each of the regiments so amalgamated.

The honours as published herein will be shown in the NZ Army List.

The honours in heavy type in the attached lists have been approved for emblazoning on the regimental colours of the infantry regiments concerned.

The order listed the then nine mounted rifle regiments, with 1st New Zealand Mounted Rifles (Canterbury Yeomanry Cavalry) showing awards to the former 1st Mounted Rifles and 8th Mounted Rifles and 5th New Zealand Mounted Rifles (Otago Hussars) showing awards to the former 5th Mounted Rifles, 7th Mounted Rifles and 12th Mounted Rifles. The twelve infantry corps listed all the awards to the former corps with The Hawke's Bay Regiment showing awards to 9th (Hawke's Bay) Regiment and 17th (Ruahine) Regiment; The Canterbury Regiment showing awards to 1st (Canterbury) Regiment and 2nd (South Canterbury) Regiment; The Nelson, Marlborough and West Coast Regiment showing awards to 12th (Nelson and Marlborough) Regiment and 13th (North Canterbury and Westland) Regiment; The Otago Regiment showing awards to 4th (Otago) Regiment and 10th (North Otago) Regiment and The Southland Regiment showing awards to 8th (Southland) Regiment and 14th (South Otago) Regiment. No awards were made to the New Zealand Pioneers nor to the New Zealand Machine Gun Battalion. In effect, the awards were made to the original twelve mounted rifle and seventeen infantry corps which had contributed to the war-raised units of the Expeditionary Force.

The New Zealand Mounted Rifles showed seven honours only to be emblazoned, but there was no authority to do so in the order, while the infantry regiments were authorized to emblazon ten selected battle honours on their Regimental Colours. It is not clear why this inconsistency arose, but a possible reason is that the battle honours, which were about to be awarded to the Australian light horse regiments were not the same, despite their having served in the same formations. As the New Zealand Mounted Rifles Brigade had served jointly with Australians in Gallipoli with the New Zealand and Australian Division and subsequently in Egypt and Palestine with the Australian and New Zealand Mounted Division, it was felt that it would be more appropriate, and historically more accurate, if the same battle honours were awarded.

In 1927 the designation of the New Zealand Mounted Rifles, which was never popular, was abolished and new titles, based on former territorial titles, were taken into use. This was followed, in May 1928, by the publication of a second list in General Order 139, which stated:

> With reference to General Order 389/1926, His Majesty the King has been graciously pleased to approve of the following revised lists of battle honours for The Great War for the New Zealand Mounted Rifles Regiments, in substitution of those published in the above-quoted General Order, which is hereby amended accordingly.
>
> The honours in heavy type in the attached lists have been approved for emblazoning on the regimental colours of the Mounted Rifles regiments concerned . . .

The awards included ten selected honours to be emblazoned for each regiment, or former regiment if amalgamated, but **Suvla, Rafah, Gaza** and **Jordan** had been replaced by **Hill 60 (Anzac)**, **Maghdaba– Rafah**, **Gaza–Beersheba** and **Jordan (Amman)**. The Nelson-Marlborough Mounted Rifles, however, retained **Gaza** as the war-raised squadron had not been present at the capture of Beersheba on 31 October 1917. The reference to 'regimental colours of the Mounted Rifles' is confusing, particularly as General Order 138 confirmed that these regiments had permission to carry Guidons. It is possible that this was simply poor drafting or that 'regimental colours' was understood to include Guidons.

The Territorial Force became neglected during the inter-war years, and from 1931, with the ending of compulsory service – which had been in force since 1909, it failed to attract sufficient recruits to maintain its establishment. By 1939 the Force had no armoured units, although there had been a little mechanization in some regiments, and the mounted rifles and the infantry battalions were seriously understrength.

South Africa

On the outbreak of war South Africa was requested by the British Government to occupy the German ports and wireless stations in German South West Africa. To provide troops for this undertaking the Permanent Force was mobilized, later joined by units of the Active Citizen Force and a large number of Commandos, which had been embodied on 24 August 1914. Following the end of the campaign in July 1915, the Active Citizen Force and Commandos, together with the small number of war-raised units, were demobilized, while the regiments of the Permanent Force remained in South West Africa as garrison troops.

Along with the other Dominions, the South African Defence Force was not permitted, under its terms and conditions of service, to serve outside the Union – the recent campaign being an exception due to the external threat of invasion – and from November 1915 units were raised for 'Imperial Service' from individual volunteers and from drafts found by existing corps. Ten mounted regiments of South African horse, twelve infantry battalions and five field batteries were formed, in addition to other individual regiments, such as the South African Rifles and the Cape Corps. Five siege batteries of Royal Garrison Artillery were also manned by South African volunteers. These units served with distinction in British formations in France and Flanders, Egypt and Palestine and East Africa. By 1919 all war-raised units were disbanded.

In 1922 the Defence Force was placed on a formal establishment, with, in addition to the South African Mounted Rifles, an increased Permanent Force with a staff corps and supporting arms and services; the Active Citizen Force, largely unchanged, was retained.

On 21 April 1926 the first battle honours for the Union of South Africa Defence Forces were published in General Order 5997, with awards to units of the South African Permanent Force, Active Citizen Force and units raised for The Great War, which included artillery and, uniquely, two field ambulances of the South African Medical Corps. This was followed by a second, additional list in November 1927 promulgating further awards to the Coast Garrison Artillery, Active Citizen Force and units raised for the war. Both General Orders authorized a maximum of ten battle honours, shown in black type, to be borne on Regimental Standards and Colours. Strangely, and to the dismay of many Active Citizen Force units, which had provided drafts for the Imperial Service units, the battle honours of such war-raised corps were not perpetuated. Successive claims by corps have been, to date, unsuccessful. However, in 1964 the South African Coloured Corps was raised as a successor unit to the Cape Corps and embodied as part of the Permanent Force; it later took into use the title of the South African Cape Corps and was permitted to inherit The Great War battle honours of the Cape Corps, raised 1915 and disbanded 1919. This distinction, however, was short-lived as the Corps was disbanded in the early 1990s.

Between 1926 and 1934 the South African Defence Force was subjected to successive reductions; the South African Mounted Rifles were disbanded and the Permanent Force was cut to an establishment of one thousand four hundred all ranks; all Active Citizen Force training was suspended and forty-nine regiments, mostly those raised in 1913, were disbanded. The surviving Active Citizen Force units, all pre-dating 1913, became increasingly so understrength that the corps were virtually reduced to cadres. In 1934, in an attempt to increase home defence, the Active Citizen Force was revived with part-time training resumed, fifteen corps reformed and nine new regiments, recruited from Afrikaans-speaking volunteers, raised. These new regiments carried old Dutch-style titles, such as Regiment Botha and Regiment President Steyn, and replaced the Commandos, which had also fallen into neglect.

Battle Honours

The complete list of battle honours for The Great War and the Third Afghan War are shown in Tables 2 and 3, respectively.

Table 2

BATTLE HONOURS FOR THE GREAT WAR

1.

MONS

23rd–24th August 1914
The Retreat from Mons

1925   1st Life Guards: 2nd Life Guards: Royal Horse Guards (The Blues): The Queen's Bays (2nd Dragoon Guards): 4th Royal Irish Dragoon Guards: 5th Dragoon Guards (Princess Charlotte of Wales's): The Carabiniers (6th Dragoon Guards): The Royal Scots Greys (2nd Dragoons): 3rd The King's Own Hussars: 4th Queen's Own Hussars: 5th Royal Irish Lancers: 9th Queen's Royal Lancers: 11th Hussars (Prince Albert's Own): 12th Royal Lancers (Prince of Wales's): 15th The King's Hussars: 16th The Queen's Lancers: 18th Royal Hussars (Queen Mary's Own): 20th Hussars: Grenadier Guards: Coldstream Guards: Irish Guards: The Royal Scots (The Royal Regiment): The Queen's Royal Regiment (West Surrey): The Northumberland Fusiliers: The Royal Fusiliers (City of London Regiment): The King's Regiment (Liverpool): The Norfolk Regiment: The Lincolnshire Regiment: The Suffolk Regiment: The Bedfordshire and Hertfordshire Regiment: The Royal Irish Regiment: The Royal Scots Fusiliers: The Cheshire Regiment: The Royal Welch Fusiliers: The South Wales Borderers: The King's Own Scottish Borderers: The Cameronians (Scottish Rifles): The Gloucestershire Regiment: The Worcestershire Regiment: The East Surrey Regiment: The Duke of Cornwall's Light Infantry: The Duke of Wellington's Regiment (West Riding): The Royal Sussex Regiment: The South Staffordshire Regiment: The Dorsetshire Regiment: The Prince of Wales's Volunteers (South Lancashire): The Welch Regiment: The Oxfordshire and Buckinghamshire Light Infantry: The Loyal Regiment (North Lancashire): The Northamptonshire Regiment: The Royal Berkshire Regiment (Princess Charlotte of Wales's): The Queen's Own Royal West Kent Regiment: The King's Own Yorkshire Light Infantry: The Middlesex Regiment (Duke of Cambridge's Own): The King's Royal Rifle Corps: The Wiltshire Regiment (Duke of Edinburgh's): The Manchester Regiment: The Highland Light Infantry (City of Glasgow Regiment): The Gordon Highlanders: The Royal Ulster Rifles: The Connaught Rangers: The Argyll and Sutherland Highlanders (Princess Louise's)

2.

LE CATEAU

26th August 1914
The Retreat from Mons

1925   1st Life Guards: 2nd Life Guards: Royal Horse Guards (The Blues): The Queen's Bays (2nd Dragoon Guards): 4th Royal Irish Dragoon Guards: 5th Dragoon Guards (Princess Charlotte of Wales's): The Carabiniers (6th Dragoon Guards): 3rd The King's Own Hussars: 4th Queen's Own Hussars: 5th Royal Irish Lancers: 9th Queen's Royal Lancers: 11th Hussars (Prince Albert's Own): 16th The Queen's Lancers: 18th Royal Hussars (Queen Mary's Own): 19th Royal Hussars (Queen Alexandra's Own): The Royal Scots (The Royal Regiment): The King's Own Royal Regiment (Lancaster): The Northumberland Fusiliers: The Royal Warwickshire Regiment: The Royal Fusiliers (City of London Regiment): The Norfolk Regiment: The Lincolnshire Regiment: The Suffolk Regiment: The Somerset Light Infantry (Prince Albert's): The Bedfordshire and Hertfordshire Regiment: The Royal Irish Regiment: The Lancashire Fusiliers: The Royal Scots Fusiliers: The Cheshire Regiment: The Royal Welch Fusiliers: The King's Own Scottish Borderers: The Cameronians (Scottish Rifles): The Royal Inniskilling Fusiliers: The Worcestershire Regiment: The East Surrey Regiment: The East Lancashire Regiment: The Duke of Cornwall's Light Infantry: The Duke of Wellington's Regiment (West Riding): The Hampshire Regiment: The Dorsetshire Regiment: The Prince of Wales's Volunteers (South Lancashire): The Essex Regiment: The Queen's Own Royal West Kent Regiment: The King's Own Yorkshire Light Infantry: The Middlesex Regiment (Duke of Cambridge's Own): The Wiltshire Regiment (Duke of Edinburgh's): The Manchester Regiment: The Seaforth Highlanders (Ross-shire Buffs, The Duke of Albany's): The Gordon Highlanders: The Royal Ulster Rifles: The Royal Irish Fusiliers (Princess Victoria's): The Argyll and Sutherland Highlanders (Princess Louise's): The Royal Dublin Fusiliers: The Rifle Brigade (Prince Consort's Own)

3. **RETREAT FROM MONS**
   23rd August–5th September 1914
   The Retreat from Mons

1925   1st Life Guards: 2nd Life Guards: Royal Horse Guards (The Blues): The Queen's Bays (2nd Dragoon Guards): 4th Royal Irish Dragoon Guards: 5th Dragoon Guards (Princess Charlotte of Wales's): The Carabiniers (6th Dragoon Guards): The Royal Scots Greys (2nd Dragoons): 3rd The King's Own Hussars: 4th Queen's Own Hussars: 5th Royal Irish Lancers: 9th Queen's Royal Lancers: 11th Hussars (Prince Albert's Own): 12th Royal Lancers (Prince of Wales's): 15th The King's Hussars: 16th The Queen's Lancers: 18th Royal Hussars (Queen Mary's Own): 19th Royal Hussars (Queen Alexandra's Own): 20th Hussars: North Irish Horse: Grenadier Guards: Coldstream Guards: Scots Guards: Irish Guards: The Royal Scots (The Royal Regiment): The Queen's Royal Regiment (West Surrey): The King's Own Royal Regiment (Lancaster): The Northumberland Fusiliers: The Royal Warwickshire Regiment: The Royal Fusiliers (City of London Regiment): The King's Regiment (Liverpool): The Norfolk Regiment: The Lincolnshire Regiment: The Suffolk Regiment: The Somerset Light Infantry (Prince Albert's): The Bedfordshire and Hertfordshire Regiment: The Royal Irish Regiment: The Lancashire Fusiliers: The Royal Scots Fusiliers: The Cheshire Regiment: The Royal Welch Fusiliers: The South Wales Borderers: The King's Own Scottish Borderers: The Cameronians (Scottish Rifles): The Royal Inniskilling Fusiliers: The Gloucestershire Regiment: The Worcestershire Regiment: The East Lancashire Regiment: The East Surrey Regiment: The Duke of Cornwall's Light Infantry: The Duke of Wellington's Regiment (West Riding): The Royal Sussex Regiment: The Hampshire Regiment: The South Staffordshire Regiment: The Dorsetshire Regiment: The Prince of Wales's Volunteers (South Lancashire): The Welch Regiment: The Black Watch (Royal Highlanders): The Oxfordshire and Buckinghamshire Light Infantry: The Essex Regiment: The Loyal Regiment (North Lancashire): The Northamptonshire Regiment: The Royal Berkshire Regiment (Princess Charlotte of Wales's): The Queen's Own Royal West Kent Regiment: The King's Own Yorkshire Light Infantry: The Middlesex Regiment (Duke of Cambridge's Own): The King's Royal Rifle Corps: The Wiltshire Regiment (Duke of Edinburgh's): The Manchester Regiment: The Highland Light Infantry (City of Glasgow Regiment): The Seaforth Highlanders (Ross-shire Buffs, The Duke of Albany's): The Gordon Highlanders: The Queen's Own Cameron Highlanders: The Royal Ulster Rifles: The Royal Irish Fusiliers (Princess Victoria's): The Connaught Rangers: The Argyll and Sutherland Highlanders (Princess Louise's): The Royal Munster Fusiliers: The Royal Dublin Fusiliers: The Rifle Brigade (Prince Consort's Own)

4. **MARNE 1914**
   7th–10th September 1914
   The Advance to the Aisne

1925   1st Life Guards: 2nd Life Guards: Royal Horse Guards (The Blues): The Queen's Bays (2nd Dragoon Guards): 4th Royal Irish Dragoon Guards: 5th Dragoon Guards (Princess Charlotte of Wales's): The Carabiniers (6th Dragoon Guards): The Royal Scots Greys (2nd Dragoons): 3rd The King's Own Hussars: 4th Queen's Own Hussars: 5th Royal Irish Lancers: 9th Queen's Royal Lancers: 11th Hussars (Prince Albert's Own): 12th Royal Lancers (Prince of Wales's): 15th The King's Hussars: 16th The Queen's Lancers: 18th Royal Hussars (Queen Mary's Own): 19th Royal Hussars (Queen Alexandra's Own): 20th Hussars: North Irish Horse: Grenadier Guards: Coldstream Guards: Scots Guards: Irish Guards: The Royal Scots (The Royal Regiment): The Queen's Royal Regiment (West Surrey): The King's Own Royal Regiment (Lancaster): The Northumberland Fusiliers: The Royal Warwickshire Regiment: The Royal Fusiliers (City of London Regiment): The King's Regiment (Liverpool): The Norfolk Regiment: The Lincolnshire Regiment: The Suffolk Regiment: The Somerset Light Infantry (Prince Albert's): The Bedfordshire and Hertfordshire Regiment: The Royal Irish Regiment: The Lancashire Fusiliers: The Royal Scots Fusiliers: The Cheshire Regiment: The Royal Welch Fusiliers: The South Wales Borderers: The King's Own Scottish Borderers: The Cameronians (Scottish Rifles): The Royal Inniskilling Fusiliers: The Gloucestershire Regiment: The Worcestershire Regiment: The East Lancashire Regiment: The East Surrey Regiment: The Duke of Cornwall's Light Infantry: The Duke of Wellington's Regiment (West Riding): The Royal Sussex Regiment: The Hampshire Regiment: The South Staffordshire Regiment: The Dorsetshire Regiment: The Prince of Wales's Volunteers (South Lancashire): The Welch Regiment: The Black Watch (Royal Highlanders): The Oxfordshire and Buckinghamshire Light Infantry: The Essex Regiment: The Loyal Regiment (North Lancashire): The Northamptonshire Regiment: The Royal Berkshire Regiment (Princess Charlotte of Wales's): The Queen's Own Royal West Kent Regiment: The King's Own Yorkshire Light Infantry: The Middlesex Regiment (Duke of Cambridge's Own): The King's

Royal Rifle Corps: The Wiltshire Regiment (Duke of Edinburgh's): The Manchester Regiment: The Highland Light Infantry (City of Glasgow Regiment): The Seaforth Highlanders (Ross-shire Buffs, The Duke of Albany's): The Gordon Highlanders: The Queen's Own Cameron Highlanders: The Royal Ulster Rifles: The Royal Irish Fusiliers (Princess Victoria's): The Connaught Rangers: The Argyll and Sutherland Highlanders (Princess Louise's): The Royal Munster Fusiliers: The Royal Dublin Fusiliers: The Rifle Brigade (Prince Consort's Own)

5. **AISNE 1914**

12th–15th September 1914

The Advance to the Aisne

1925   1st Life Guards: 2nd Life Guards: Royal Horse Guards (The Blues): The Queen's Bays (2nd Dragoon Guards): 4th Royal Irish Dragoon Guards: 5th Dragoon Guards (Princess Charlotte of Wales's): The Carabiniers (6th Dragoon Guards): The Royal Scots Greys (2nd Dragoons): 3rd The King's Own Hussars: 4th Queen's Own Hussars: 5th Royal Irish Lancers: 9th Queen's Royal Lancers: 11th Hussars (Prince Albert's Own): 12th Royal Lancers (Prince of Wales's): 15th The King's Hussars: 16th The Queen's Lancers: 18th Royal Hussars (Queen Mary's Own): 19th Royal Hussars (Queen Alexandra's Own): 20th Hussars: North Irish Horse: Grenadier Guards: Coldstream Guards: Scots Guards: Irish Guards: The Royal Scots (The Royal Regiment): The Queen's Royal Regiment (West Surrey): The Buffs (East Kent Regiment): The King's Own Royal Regiment (Lancaster): The Northumberland Fusiliers: The Royal Warwickshire Regiment: The Royal Fusiliers (City of London Regiment): The King's Regiment (Liverpool): The Norfolk Regiment: The Lincolnshire Regiment: The Devonshire Regiment: The Suffolk Regiment: The Somerset Light Infantry (Prince Albert's): The West Yorkshire Regiment (The Prince of Wales's Own): The East Yorkshire Regiment: The Bedfordshire and Hertfordshire Regiment: The Leicestershire Regiment: The Royal Irish Regiment: The Lancashire Fusiliers: The Royal Scots Fusiliers: The Cheshire Regiment: The Royal Welch Fusiliers: The South Wales Borderers: The King's Own Scottish Borderers: The Cameronians (Scottish Rifles): The Royal Inniskilling Fusiliers: The Gloucestershire Regiment: The Worcestershire Regiment: The East Lancashire Regiment: The East Surrey Regiment: The Duke of Cornwall's Light Infantry: The Duke of Wellington's Regiment (West Riding): The Royal Sussex Regiment: The Hampshire Regiment: The South Staffordshire Regiment: The Dorsetshire Regiment: The Prince of Wales's Volunteers (South Lancashire): The Welch Regiment: The Black Watch (Royal Highlanders): The Oxfordshire and Buckinghamshire Light Infantry: The Essex Regiment: The Sherwood Foresters (Nottinghamshire and Derbyshire Regiment): The Loyal Regiment (North Lancashire): The Northamptonshire Regiment: The Royal Berkshire Regiment (Princess Charlotte of Wales's): The Queen's Own Royal West Kent Regiment: The King's Own Yorkshire Light Infantry: The King's Shropshire Light Infantry: The Middlesex Regiment (Duke of Cambridge's Own): The King's Royal Rifle Corps: The Wiltshire Regiment (Duke of Edinburgh's): The Manchester Regiment: The North Staffordshire Regiment: The Highland Light Infantry (City of Glasgow Regiment): The Seaforth Highlanders (Ross-shire Buffs, The Duke of Albany's): The Gordon Highlanders: The Queen's Own Cameron Highlanders: The Royal Ulster Rifles: The Royal Irish Fusiliers (Princess Victoria's): The Connaught Rangers: The Argyll and Sutherland Highlanders (Princess Louise's): The Prince of Wales's Leinster Regiment (Royal Canadians): The Royal Munster Fusiliers: The Royal Dublin Fusiliers: The Rifle Brigade (Prince Consort's Own)

6. **LA BASSEE 1914**

10th October–2nd November 1914

Operations in Flanders 1914

1925   4th Royal Irish Dragoon Guards: 5th Dragoon Guards (Princess Charlotte of Wales's): 7th Dragoon Guards (Princess Royal's): 9th Queen's Royal Lancers: 18th Royal Hussars (Queen Mary's Own): The Royal Scots (The Royal Regiment): The Northumberland Fusiliers: The Royal Fusiliers (City of London Regiment): The Norfolk Regiment: The Lincolnshire Regiment: The Devonshire Regiment: The Suffolk Regiment: The Bedfordshire and Hertfordshire Regiment: The Leicestershire Regiment: The Royal Irish Regiment: The Royal Scots Fusiliers: The Cheshire Regiment: The Royal Welch Fusiliers: The King's Own Scottish Borderers: The Cameronians (Scottish Rifles): The Worcestershire Regiment: The East Surrey Regiment: The Duke of Cornwall's Light Infantry: The Duke of Wellington's Regiment (West Riding): The Dorsetshire Regiment: The Prince of Wales's Volunteers (South Lancashire): The Black Watch (Royal Highlanders): The Queen's Own Royal West Kent Regiment:

	1926	The King's Own Yorkshire Light Infantry; The Middlesex Regiment (Duke of Cambridge's Own); The Wiltshire Regiment (Duke of Edinburgh's); The Manchester Regiment; The Seaforth Highlanders (Ross-shire Buffs, The Duke of Albany's); The Gordon Highlanders; The Royal Ulster Rifles; The Argyll and Sutherland Highlanders (Princess Louise's)
		2nd Lancers (Gardner's Horse); 17th Queen Victoria's Own Poona Horse; King George's Own Bengal Sappers and Miners; Royal Bombay Sappers and Miners 9th Jat Regiment; 11th Sikh Regiment; 13th Frontier Force Rifles; 16th Punjab Regiment; 17th Dogra Regiment; 18th Royal Garhwal Rifles; 2nd King Edward's Own Gurkha Rifles (The Sirmoor Rifles); 3rd Queen Alexandra's Own Gurkha Rifles; 8th Gurkha Rifles; 9th Gurkha Rifles
	1928	3rd Sikh Pioneers
7.		**MESSINES 1914**
		12th October–2nd November 1914
		Operations in Flanders 1914
	1925	1st Life Guards; 2nd Life Guards; Royal Horse Guards (The Blues); The Queen's Bays (2nd Dragoon Guards); 4th Royal Irish Dragoon Guards; 5th Dragoon Guards (Princess Charlotte of Wales's); The Carabiniers (6th Dragoon Guards); The Royal Scots Greys (2nd Dragoons); 3rd The King's Own Hussars; 4th Queen's Own Hussars; 5th Royal Irish Lancers; 9th Queen's Royal Lancers; 11th Hussars (Prince Albert's Own); 12th Royal Lancers (Prince of Wales's); 16th The Queen's Lancers; 18th Royal Hussars (Queen Mary's Own); 20th Hussars; Oxfordshire Yeomanry (Queen's Own Oxfordshire Hussars); The Royal Welch Northumberland Fusiliers; The Royal Fusiliers (City of London Regiment); The Lincolnshire Regiment; The Royal Welch Fusiliers; The King's Own Scottish Borderers; The Cameronians (Scottish Rifles); The Royal Inniskilling Fusiliers; The Prince of Wales's Volunteers (South Lancashire); The Essex Regiment; The Queen's Own Royal West Kent Regiment; The King's Own Yorkshire Light Infantry; The Middlesex Regiment (Duke of Cambridge's Own); The Wiltshire Regiment (Duke of Edinburgh's); The Gordon Highlanders; The Royal Ulster Rifles; The Connaught Rangers; The Argyll and Sutherland Highlanders (Princess Louise's); 14th London Regiment (London Scottish)
	1926	10th Baluch Regiment; 13th Frontier Force Rifles; 16th Punjab Regiment
8.		**ARMENTIERES 1914**
		13th October–2nd November 1914
		Operations in Flanders 1914
	1925	1st Life Guards; 2nd Life Guards; Royal Horse Guards (The Blues); The Queen's Bays (2nd Dragoon Guards); 4th Royal Irish Dragoon Guards; 5th Dragoon Guards (Princess Charlotte of Wales's); The Carabiniers (6th Dragoon Guards); 3rd The King's Own Hussars; 4th Queen's Own Hussars; 9th Queen's Royal Lancers; 11th Hussars (Prince Albert's Own); 16th The Queen's Lancers; 18th Royal Hussars (Queen Mary's Own); 19th Royal Hussars (Queen Alexandra's Own); North Irish Horse; Oxfordshire Yeomanry (Queen's Own Oxfordshire Hussars); The Buffs (East Kent Regiment); The King's Own Royal Regiment (Lancaster); The Northumberland Fusiliers; The Royal Warwickshire Regiment; The Royal Fusiliers (City of London Regiment); The Lincolnshire Regiment; The Devonshire Regiment; The Somerset Light Infantry (Prince Albert's); The West Yorkshire Regiment (The Prince of Wales's Own); The East Yorkshire Regiment; The Leicestershire Regiment; The Lancashire Fusiliers; The Cheshire Regiment; The Royal Welch Fusiliers; The Cameronians (Scottish Rifles); The Royal Inniskilling Fusiliers; The Worcestershire Regiment; The East Lancashire Regiment; The East Surrey Regiment; The Duke of Cornwall's Light Infantry; The Hampshire Regiment; The Dorsetshire Regiment; The Prince of Wales's Volunteers (South Lancashire); The Essex Regiment; The Sherwood Foresters (Nottinghamshire and Derbyshire Regiment); The King's Shropshire Light Infantry; The Middlesex Regiment (Duke of Cambridge's Own); The Wiltshire Regiment (Duke of Edinburgh's); The Manchester Regiment; The North Staffordshire Regiment (The Prince of Wales's); The York and Lancaster Regiment; The Durham Light Infantry; The Seaforth Highlanders (Ross-shire Buffs, The Duke of Albany's); The Gordon Highlanders; The Royal Ulster Rifles; The Royal Irish Fusiliers (Princess Victoria's); The Connaught Rangers; The Argyll and Sutherland Highlanders (Princess Louise's); The Prince of Wales's Leinster Regiment (Royal Canadians); The Royal Dublin Fusiliers; The Rifle Brigade (Prince Consort's Own)
	1926	17th Queen Victoria's Own Poona Horse; Royal Bombay Sappers and Miners; 10th Baluch Regiment; 11th Sikh Regiment;

13th Frontier Force Rifles: 16th Punjab Regiment: 18th Royal Garhwal Rifles: 3rd Queen Alexandra's Own Gurkha Rifles: 9th Gurkha Rifles

1928   3rd Sikh Pioneers

9.   YPRES 1914
19th October–22nd November 1914
Operations in Flanders 1914

1925   1st Life Guards: 2nd Life Guards: Royal Horse Guards (The Blues): The Queen's Bays (2nd Dragoon Guards): 3rd Dragoon Guards (Prince of Wales's): 4th Royal Irish Dragoon Guards: 5th Dragoon Guards (Princess Charlotte of Wales's): 1st The Royal Dragoons: The Royal Scots Greys (2nd Dragoons): 3rd The King's Own Hussars: 4th Queen's Own Hussars: 5th Royal Irish Lancers: 9th Queen's Royal Lancers (Prince of Wales's): 10th Royal Hussars (Prince of Wales's Own): 11th Hussars (Prince Albert's Own): 12th Royal Lancers (Prince of Wales's): 15th The King's Hussars: 16th The Queen's Lancers: 18th Royal Hussars (Queen Mary's Own): 20th Hussars: The Northumberland Hussars (Yeomanry): Grenadier Guards: Coldstream Guards: Scots Guards: Irish Guards: The Queen's Royal Regiment (West Surrey): The Northumberland Fusiliers: The Royal Warwickshire Regiment: The Royal Fusiliers (City of London Regiment): The King's Regiment (Liverpool): The Norfolk Regiment: The Lincolnshire Regiment: The Bedfordshire and Hertfordshire Regiment: The Green Howards (Alexandra, Princess of Wales's Own Yorkshire Regiment): The Royal Scots Fusiliers: The Cheshire Regiment: The Royal Welch Fusiliers: The South Wales Borderers: The King's Own Scottish Borderers: The Gloucestershire Regiment: The Worcestershire Regiment: The Duke of Wellington's Regiment (West Riding): The Border Regiment: The Royal Sussex Regiment: The South Staffordshire Regiment: The Prince of Wales's Volunteers (South Lancashire): The Welch Regiment: The Black Watch (Royal Highlanders): The Oxfordshire and Buckinghamshire Light Infantry: The Loyal Regiment (North Lancashire): The Northamptonshire Regiment: The Royal Berkshire Regiment (Princess Charlotte of Wales's): The Queen's Own Royal West Kent Regiment: The King's Own Yorkshire Light Infantry: The King's Royal Rifle Corps: The Wiltshire Regiment (Duke of Edinburgh's): The Highland Light Infantry (City of Glasgow Regiment): The Gordon Highlanders: The Queen's Own Cameron Highlanders: The Royal Ulster Rifles: The Hertfordshire Regiment: The Connaught Rangers: The Royal Munster Fusiliers: 14th London Regiment (London Scottish): The Hertfordshire Regiment: The Leicestershire Yeomanry (Prince Albert's Own) (Hussars): The North Somerset Yeomanry (Dragoons)

1926   10th Baluch Regiment

10.   LANGEMARCK 1914
21st–24th October 1914
Operations in Flanders 1914

1925   1st Life Guards: 2nd Life Guards: Royal Horse Guards (The Blues): 1st The Royal Dragoons: 4th Queen's Own Hussars: 10th Royal Hussars (Prince of Wales's Own): 15th The King's Hussars: The Northumberland Hussars (Yeomanry): Grenadier Guards: Coldstream Guards: Scots Guards: Irish Guards: The Queen's Royal Regiment (West Surrey): The Royal Warwickshire Regiment: The King's Regiment (Liverpool): The Bedfordshire and Hertfordshire Regiment: The Green Howards (Alexandra, Princess of Wales's Own Yorkshire Regiment): The Royal Scots Fusiliers: The Royal Welch Fusiliers: The South Wales Borderers: The Gloucestershire Regiment: The Worcestershire Regiment: The Border Regiment: The South Staffordshire Regiment: The Welch Regiment: The Black Watch (Royal Highlanders): The Oxfordshire and Buckinghamshire Light Infantry: The Loyal Regiment (North Lancashire): The Northamptonshire Regiment: The Royal Berkshire Regiment (Princess Charlotte of Wales's): The King's Royal Rifle Corps: The Wiltshire Regiment (Duke of Edinburgh's): The Highland Light Infantry (City of Glasgow Regiment): The Gordon Highlanders: The Queen's Own Cameron Highlanders: The Connaught Rangers: The Royal Munster Fusiliers

11.   GHELUVELT
29th–31st October 1914
Operations in Flanders 1914

1925   1st Life Guards: 2nd Life Guards: Royal Horse Guards (The Blues): 1st The Royal Dragoons: The Royal Scots Greys (2nd Dragoons): 3rd The King's Own Hussars: 4th Queen's Own Hussars: 5th Royal Irish Lancers: 10th Royal Hussars (Prince of Wales's Own): 15th The King's Hussars: 16th The Queen's Lancers: The Northumberland Hussars (Yeomanry): The Royal Warwickshire Regiment: Grenadier Guards: Coldstream Guards: Scots Guards: Irish Guards: The Queen's Royal Regiment (West Surrey): The Royal Warwickshire Regiment: The King's Regiment (Liverpool): The Bedfordshire and Hertfordshire Regiment: The Green Howards (Alexandra, Princess of Wales's Own Yorkshire Regiment): The Royal Scots Fusiliers: The Royal Welch Fusiliers: The South Wales

Borderers: The Gloucestershire Regiment: The Worcestershire Regiment: The Border Regiment: The Royal Sussex Regiment: The South Staffordshire Regiment: The Welch Regiment: The Black Watch (Royal Highlanders): The Oxfordshire and Buckinghamshire Light Infantry: The Loyal Regiment (North Lancashire): The Northamptonshire Regiment: The Royal Berkshire Regiment (Princess Charlotte of Wales's): The King's Royal Rifle Corps: The Highland Light Infantry (City of Glasgow Regiment): The Gordon Highlanders: The Queen's Own Cameron Highlanders: The Connaught Rangers: The Royal Munster Fusiliers: 14th London Regiment (London Scottish)

1926
10th Baluch Regiment

12. NONNE BOSSCHEN 1914
11th November 1914
Operations in Flanders 1914

1925
1st Life Guards: 2nd Life Guards: Royal Horse Guards (The Blues): 3rd Dragoon Guards (Prince of Wales's): 1st The Royal Dragoons: 10th Royal Hussars (Prince of Wales's Own): 15th The King's Hussars: Grenadier Guards: Coldstream Guards: Scots Guards: Irish Guards: The Norhumberland Fusiliers: The Royal Fusiliers (City of London Regiment): The King's Regiment (Liverpool): The Lincolnshire Regiment: The Bedfordshire and Hertfordshire Regiment: The Royal Scots Fusiliers: The Cheshire Regiment: The South Wales Borcerers: The Gloucestershire Regiment: The Worcestershire Regiment: The Duke of Wellington's Regiment (West Riding): The Royal Sussex Regiment: The South Staffordshire Regiment: The Prince of Wales's Volunteers (South Lancashire): The Welch Regiment: The Black Watch (Royal Highlanders): The Oxfordshire and Buckinghamshire Light Infantry: The Loyal Regiment (North Lancashire): The Northamptonshire Regiment: The Royal Berkshire Regiment (Princess Charlotte of Wales's): The King's Royal Rifle Corps: The Wiltshire Regiment (Duke of Edinburgh's): The Highland Light Infantry (City of Glasgow Regiment): The Gordon Highlanders: The Queen's Own Cameron Highlanders: The Royal Ulster Rifles: The Connaught Rangers: The Royal Munster Fusiliers: 14th London Regiment (London Scottish): The Hertfordshire Regiment

13. FESTUBERT 1914
23rd–24th November 1914
Winter Operations 1914–15

1925
17th Lancers (Duke of Cambridge's Own): The Leicestershire Regiment: The Seaforth Highlanders (Ross-shire Buffs, The Duke of Albany's): The Connaught Rangers

1926
King George's Own Bengal Sappers and Miners: Royal Bombay Sappers and Miners: 2nd Bombay Pioneers: 3rd Sikh Pioneers: 9th Jat Regiment: 10th Baluch Regiment: 13th Frontier Force Rifles: 16th Punjab Regiment: 17th Dogra Regiment: 18th Royal Garhwal Rifles: 2nd King Edward's Own Gurkha Rifles (The Sirmoor Rifles): 3rd Queen Alexandra's Own Gurkha Rifles: 8th Gurkha Rifles: 9th Gurkha Rifles

14. GIVENCHY 1914
20th–21st December 1914
and
25th January 1915
Winter Operations 1914–15

1925
7th Dragoon Guards (Princess Royal's): 8th King's Royal Irish Hussars: Coldstream Guards: Scots Guards: The Suffolk Regiment: The Royal Welch Fusiliers: The South Wales Borderers: The Gloucestershire Regiment: The Royal Sussex Regiment: The Welch Regiment: The Black Watch (Royal Highlanders): The Loyal Regiment (North Lancashire): The Northamptonshire Regiment: The King's Royal Rifle Corps: The Manchester Regiment: The Highland Light Infantry (City of Glasgow Regiment): The Seaforth Highlanders (Ross-shire Buffs, The Duke of Albany's): The Queen's Own Cameron Highlanders: The Connaught Rangers: The Royal Munster Fusiliers: 14th London Regiment (London Scottish)

1926
2nd Lancers (Gardner's Horse): 4th Duke of Cambridge's Own Hodson's Horse: 8th King George's Own Light Cavalry: 9th Royal Deccan Horse: King George's Own Bengal Sappers and Miners: Royal Bombay Sappers and Miners: 2nd Bombay Pioneers: 3rd Sikh Pioneers: 6th Ra,putana Rifles: 10th Baluch Regiment: 11th Sikh Regiment: 13th Frontier Force Rifles: 16th Punjab Regiment: 17th Dogra Regiment: 1st King George's Own Gurkha Rifles (The Malaun Regiment): 2nd King Edward's Own Gurkha Rifles (The Sirmoor Rifles): 3rd Queen Alexandra's Own Gurkha Rifles: 4th Prince of Wales's Own Gurkha Rifles: 8th Gurkha Rifles: 9th Gurkha Rifles

15.	**NEUVE CHAPELLE** 10th–13th March 1915 Summer Operations 1915	1925	The Royal Scots Greys (2nd Dragoons): 12th Royal Lancers (Prince of Wales's): 20th Hussars: Northamptonshire Yeomanry (Dragoons): The Northumberland Hussars (Yeomanry): Grenadier Guards: Coldstream Guards: Scots Guards: The Royal Scots (The Royal Regiment): The Royal Warwickshire Regiment: The King's Regiment (Liverpool): The Lincolnshire Regiment: The Devonshire Regiment: The Suffolk Regiment: The West Yorkshire Regiment (The Prince of Wales's Own): The Bedfordshire and Hertfordshire Regiment: The Leicestershire Regiment: The Green Howards (Alexandra, Princess of Wales's Own Yorkshire Regiment): The Royal Scots Fusiliers: The Royal Welch Fusiliers: The Cameronians (Scottish Rifles): The Worcestershire Regiment: The East Lancashire Regiment: The Border Regiment: The South Staffordshire Regiment: The Black Watch (Royal Highlanders): The Sherwood Foresters (Nottinghamshire and Derbyshire Regiment): The Northamptonshire Regiment: The Royal Berkshire Regiment (Princess Charlotte of Wales's): The Middlesex Regiment (Duke of Cambridge's Own): The Wiltshire Regiment (Duke of Edinburgh's): The Manchester Regiment: The Highland Light Infantry (City of Glasgow Regiment): The Seaforth Highlanders (Ross-shire Buffs, The Duke of Albany's): The Gordon Highlanders: The Queen's Own Cameron Highlanders: The Royal Ulster Rifles: The Connaught Rangers: The Rifle Brigade (Prince Consort's Own): 3rd City of London Regiment (The Royal Fusiliers): 4th City of London Regiment (Princess Louise's Kensington Regiment)
		1926	2nd Lancers (Gardner's Horse): 20th Lancers: King George's Own Bengal Sappers and Miners: Royal Bombay Sappers and Miners: 2nd Bombay Pioneers: 3rd Sikh Pioneers: 6th Rajputana Rifles: 9th Jat Regiment: 10th Baluch Regiment: 11th Sikh Regiment: 13th Frontier Force Rifles: 17th Dogra Regiment: 18th Royal Garhwal Rifles: 1st King George's Own Gurkha Rifles (The Malaun Regiment): 2nd King Edward's Own Gurkha Rifles (The Sirmoor Rifles): 3rd Queen Alexandra's Own Gurkha Rifles: 4th Prince of Wales's Own Gurkha Rifles: 8th Gurkha Rifles: 9th Gurkha Rifles
		1926	Malerkotla Sappers
		1927	Holkar's Transport Corps (Indore)
16.	**HILL 60** 17th–22nd April 1915 Summer Operations 1915	1925	The Devonshire Regiment: The Bedfordshire and Hertfordshire Regiment: The King's Own Scottish Borderers: The East Surrey Regiment: The Duke of Wellington's Regiment (West Riding): The Queen's Own Royal West Kent Regiment: The King's Own Yorkshire Light Infantry: The Queen's Own Cameron Highlanders: 9th London Regiment (Queen Victoria's Rifles)
17.	**YPRES 1915** 22nd April–25th May 1915 Summer Operations 1915	1925	1st Life Guards: 2nd Life Guards: Royal Horse Guards (The Blues): The Queen's Bays (2nd Dragoon Guards): 3rd Dragoon Guards (Prince of Wales's): 4th Royal Irish Dragoon Guards: 5th Dragoon Guards (Princess Charlotte of Wales's): The Carabiniers (6th Dragoon Guards): 1st The Royal Dragoons: The Royal Scots Greys (2nd Dragoons): 3rd The King's Own Hussars: 4th Queen's Own Hussars: 5th Royal Irish Lancers: 9th Queen's Royal Lancers: 10th Royal Hussars (Prince of Wales's Own): 11th Hussars (Prince Albert's Own): 12th Royal Lancers (Prince of Wales's): 15th The King's Hussars: 16th The Queen's Lancers: 18th Royal Hussars (Queen Mary's Own): 19th Royal Hussars (Queen Alexandra's Own): 20th Hussars: Northamptonshire Yeomanry (Dragoons): Oxfordshire Yeomanry (Queen's Own Oxfordshire Hussars): Surrey Yeomanry (Queen Mary's Regiment) (Lancers): Honourable Artillery Company: The Northumberland Fusiliers: The Royal Warwickshire Regiment: The King's Own Royal Regiment (Lancaster): The Buffs (East Kent Regiment): The King's Own Royal Regiment (Lancaster): The Northumberland Fusiliers: The Royal Warwickshire Regiment: The Royal Fusiliers (City of London Regiment): The King's Regiment (Liverpool): The Norfolk Regiment: The Lincolnshire Regiment: The Devonshire Regiment: The Suffolk Regiment: The Somerset Light Infantry (Prince Albert's): The East Yorkshire Regiment: The Bedfordshire and Hertfordshire Regiment: The Royal Irish Regiment: The Green Howards (Alexandra, Princess of Wales's Own Yorkshire Regiment): The Lancashire Fusiliers: The Cheshire Regiment: The King's Own Scottish Borderers: The Gloucestershire Regiment: The Worcestershire Regiment: The East Lancashire Regiment: The East Surrey Regiment: The Duke of Cornwall's Light Infantry: The Duke of Wellington's Regiment (West Riding): The Border Regiment: The Hampshire Regiment: The Dorsetshire Regiment: The Prince of Wales's Volunteers (South Lancashire): The

Welch Regiment: The Essex Regiment: The Queen's Own Royal West Kent Regiment: The King's Own Yorkshire Light Infantry: The King's Shropshire Light Infantry: The Middlesex Regiment (Duke of Cambridge's Own): The King's Royal Rifle Corps: The Manchester Regiment: The York and Lancaster Regiment: The Durham Light Infantry: The Highland Light Infantry (City of Glasgow Regiment): The Seaforth Highlanders (Ross-shire Buffs, The Duke of Albany's): The Gordon Highlanders: The Queen's Own Cameron Highlanders: The Royal Ulster Rifles: The Royal Irish Fusiliers (Princess Victoria's): The Connaught Rangers: The Argyll and Sutherland Highlanders (Princess Louise's): The Prince of Wales's Leinster Regiment (Royal Canadians): The Royal Dublin Fusiliers: The Rifle Brigade (Prince Consort's Own): The Monmouthshire Regiment: The Cambridgeshire Regiment 4th City of London Regiment (The Royal Fusiliers): 5th City of London Regiment (London Rifle Brigade): 9th London Regiment (Queen Victoria's Rifles): 12th London Regiment (Rangers): Essex Yeomanry (Dragoons): The Leicestershire Yeomanry (Prince Albert's Own) (Hussars): The North Somerset Yeomanry (Dragoons)

1926   Royal Bombay Sappers and Miners: 3rd Sikh Pioneers: 10th Baluch Regiment: 11th Sikh Regiment: 13th Frontier Force Rifles: 14th Punjab Regiment: 16th Punjab Regiment: 1st King George's Own Gurkha Rifles (The Malaun Regiment): 4th Prince of Wales's Own Gurkha Rifles

1926   Malerkotla Sappers

1929   16th Canadian Light Horse: The Canadian Grenadier Guards: The Queen's Own Rifles of Canada: The Victoria Rifles of Canada: The Royal Highlanders of Canada: The Royal Grenadiers: The Royal Hamilton Light Infantry: The Canadian Fusiliers (City of London Regiment): The Dufferin Rifles of Canada: The Peterborough Rangers: The Winnipeg Rifles: The Essex Scottish: The 48th Regiment (Highlanders): 1st British Columbia Regiment (Duke of Connaught's Own): The Lake Superior Regiment: The Winnipeg Grenadiers: The Queen's Own Cameron Highlanders of Canada: The Calgary Highlanders: The Calgary Regiment: The Winnipeg Light Infantry: The Saskatoon Light Infantry: The Canadian Scottish Regiment: The Royal Montreal Regiment: The Toronto Regiment: 1st Canadian Infantry Battalion CEF: 4th Canadian Infantry Battalion CEF: 5th Canadian Infantry Battalion CEF: 8th Canadian Infantry Battalion CEF: 13th Canadian Infantry Battalion CEF: 14th Canadian Infantry Battalion CEF: 15th Canadian Infantry Battalion CEF: 16th Canadian Infantry Battalion CEF: Princess Patricia's Canadian Light Infantry: The North British Columbia Regiment: 2nd Canadian Infantry Battalion CEF: 3rd Canadian Infantry Battalion CEF: 10th Canadian Infantry Battalion CEF

1930   5th British Columbia Light Horse: 2th Manitoba Dragoons: 18th Canadian Light Horse: 19th Alberta Dragoons: The Royal Rifles of Canada: The York Rangers: The Perth Regiment: The Peel and Dufferin Regiment: The Lincoln and Welland Regiment: Les Carabiniers Mont-Royal: The York Regiment: The Pictou Highlanders: The Edmonton Fusiliers: The Irish Fusiliers of Canada: 7th Canadian Infantry Battalion CEF

1931   14th Canadian Light Horse: The Seaforth Highlanders of Canada: The Algonquin Regiment

1925   9th Queen's Royal Lancers: 18th Royal Hussars (Queen Mary's Own): The Royal Scots (The Royal Regiment): The Buffs (East Kent Regiment): The King's Own Royal Regiment (Lancaster): The Northumberland Fusiliers: The Royal Fusiliers (City of London Regiment): The King's Regiment (Liverpool): The Norfolk Regiment: The Royal Irish Regiment: The Cheshire Regiment: The King's Own Scottish Borderers: The Gloucestershire Regiment: The East Surrey Regiment: The Duke of Cornwall's Light Infantry: The Duke of Wellington's Regiment (West Riding): The Dorsetshire Regiment: The Welch Regiment: The Queen's Own Royal West Kent Regiment: The King's Own Yorkshire Light Infantry: The King's Shropshire Light Infantry: The Middlesex Regiment (Duke of Cambridge's Own): The King's Royal Rifle Corps: The Manchester Regiment: The York and Lancaster Regiment: The Durham Light Infantry: The Queen's Own Cameron Highlanders: The Royal Irish Fusiliers (Princess Victoria's): The Argyll and Sutherland Highlanders (Princess Louise's): The Prince of Wales's Leinster Regiment (Royal Canadians): The Rifle Brigade (Prince Consort's Own): The Monmouthshire Regiment: The Cambridgeshire Regiment: 9th London Regiment (Queen Victoria's Rifles): 12th London Regiment (Rangers)

18.   **GRAVENSTAFEL**
22nd–23rd April 1915
Summer Operations 1915

	1929	The Queen's Own Rifles of Canada: The Royal Highlanders of Canada: The Canadian Fusiliers (City of London Regiment): The Dufferin Rifles of Canada: The Peterborough Rangers: The Winnipeg Rifles: The 48th Regiment (Highlanders): 1st British Columbia Regiment (Duke of Connaught's Own): The Calgary Highlanders: The Winnipeg Light Infantry: The Saskatoon Light Infantry: The Canadian Scottish Regiment: The Royal Montreal Regiment: The Toronto Regiment: 1st Canadian Infantry Battalion CEF: 4th Canadian Infantry Battalion CEF: 5th Canadian Infantry Battalion CEF: 8th Canadian Infantry Battalion CEF: 13th Canadian Infantry Battalion CEF: 14th Canadian Infantry Battalion CEF: 15th Canadian Infantry Battalion CEF: 16th Canadian Infantry Battalion CEF: 2nd Canadian Infantry Battalion CEF: 3rd Canadian Infantry Battalion CEF: 10th Canadian Infantry Battalion CEF
	1930	19th Alberta Dragoons: 7th Canadian Infantry Battalion CEF
19.	**ST JULIEN**	1st Life Guards: 2nd Life Guards: Royal Horse Guards (The Blues): 4th Royal Irish Dragoon Guards: The Carabiniers (6th Dragoon Guards): The Royal Scots Greys (2nd Dragoons): 3rd The King's Own Hussars: 4th Queen's Own Hussars: 5th Royal Irish Lancers: 9th Queen's Royal Lancers: 12th Royal Lancers (Prince of Wales's): 16th The Queen's Lancers: 18th Royal Hussars (Queen Mary's Own): 20th Hussars: Oxfordshire Yeomanry (Queen's Own Oxfordshire Hussars): The Royal Scots (The Royal Regiment): The Buffs (East Kent Regiment): The King's Own Royal Regiment (Lancaster): The Northumberland Fusiliers: The Royal Warwickshire Regiment: The Royal Fusiliers (City of London Regiment): The King's Regiment (Liverpool): The Norfolk Regiment: The Lincolnshire Regiment: The Devonshire Regiment: The Suffolk Regiment: The Somerset Light Infantry (Prince Albert's): The East Yorkshire Regiment: The Bedfordshire and Hertfordshire Regiment: The Royal Irish Regiment: The Green Howards (Alexandra, Princess of Wales's Own Yorkshire Regiment): The Lancashire Fusiliers: The Cheshire Regiment: The King's Own Scottish Borderers: The Gloucestershire Regiment: The East Lancashire Regiment: The East Surrey Regiment: The Duke of Cornwall's Light Infantry: The Duke of Wellington's Regiment (West Riding): The Hampshire Regiment: The Dorsetshire Regiment: The Prince of Wales's Volunteers (South Lancashire): The Welch Regiment: The Essex Regiment: The Queen's Own Royal West Kent Regiment: The King's Own Yorkshire Light Infantry: The King's Shropshire Light Infantry: The Middlesex Regiment (Duke of Cambridge's Own): The King's Royal Rifle Corps: The Manchester Regiment: The York and Lancaster Regiment: The Durham Light Infantry: The Highland Light Infantry (City of Glasgow Regiment): The Seaforth Highlanders (Ross-shire Buffs, The Duke of Albany's): The Queen's Own Cameron Highlanders: The Royal Irish Fusiliers (Princess Victoria's): The Connaught Rangers: The Argyll and Sutherland Highlanders (Princess Louise's): The Prince of Wales's Leinster Regiment (Royal Canadians): The Royal Dublin Fusiliers: The Rifle Brigade (Prince Consort's Own): The Monmouthshire Regiment: The Cambridgeshire Regiment: 4th City of London Regiment (The Royal Fusiliers): 5th City of London Regiment (London Rifle Brigade): 9th London Regiment (Queen Victoria's Rifles): 12th London Regiment (Rangers): Essex Yeomanry (Dragoons): The Leicestershire Yeomanry (Prince Albert's Own) (Hussars)
	24th April–4th May 1915 Summer Operations 1915	
	1926	Royal Bombay Sappers and Miners: 2nd Sikh Pioneers: 10th Baluch Regiment: 11th Sikh Regiment: 13th Frontier Force Rifles: 14th Punjab Regiment: 16th Punjab Regiment: 1st King George's Own Gurkha Rifles (The Malaun Regiment): 4th Prince of Wales's Own Gurkha Rifles
	1929	The Queen's Own Rifles of Canada: The Royal Highlanders of Canada: The Royal Hamilton Light Infantry: The Canadian Fusiliers (City of London Regiment): The Dufferin Rifles of Canada: The Peterborough Rangers: The Winnipeg Rifles: The 48th Regiment (Highlanders): 1st British Columbia Regiment (Duke of Connaught's Own): The Calgary Highlanders: The Winnipeg Light Infantry: The Saskatoon Light Infantry: The Canadian Scottish Regiment: The Royal Montreal Regiment: The Toronto Regiment: 1st Canadian Infantry Battalion CEF: 4th Canadian Infantry Battalion CEF: 5th Canadian Infantry Battalion CEF: 8th Canadian Infantry Battalion CEF: 13th Canadian Infantry Battalion CEF: 14th Canadian Infantry Battalion CEF: 15th Canadian Infantry Battalion CEF: 16th Canadian Infantry Battalion CEF: 2nd Canadian Infantry Battalion CEF: 3rd Canadian Infantry Battalion CEF: 10th Canadian Infantry Battalion CEF

	1930	19th Alberta Dragoons: 7th Canadian Infantry Battalion CEF

SAINT-JULIEN taken into use by French-speaking Canadian units 1958.

20.	**FREZENBERG** 8th–13th May 1915 Summer Operations 1915	1925	1st Life Guards: 2nd Life Guards: Royal Horse Guards (The Blues); The Queen's Bays (2nd Dragoon Guards): 3rd Dragoon Guards (Prince of Wales's): 4th Royal Irish Dragoon Guards: 5th Dragoon Guards (Princess Charlotte of Wales's): 1st The Royal Dragoons: 9th Queen's Royal Lancers: 10th Royal Hussars (Prince of Wales's Own): 11th Hussars (Prince Albert's Own): 15th The King's Hussars: 18th Royal Hussars (Queen Mary's Own): 19th Royal Hussars (Queen Alexandra's Own): The Royal Scots (The Royal Regiment): The Buffs (East Kent Regiment): The King's Own Royal Regiment (Lancaster): The Northumberland Fusiliers: The Royal Warwickshire Regiment: The Royal Fusiliers (City of London Regiment): The King's Regiment (Liverpool): The Norfolk Regiment: The Lincolnshire Regiment: The Devonshire Regiment: The Suffolk Regiment: The Somerset Light Infantry (Prince Albert's): The East Yorkshire Regiment: The Bedfordshire and Hertfordshire Regiment: The Royal Irish Regiment: The Green Howards (Alexandra, Princess of Wales's Own Yorkshire Regiment): The Cheshire Regiment: The King's Own Scottish Borderers: The Gloucestershire Regiment: The East Lancashire Regiment: The East Surrey Regiment: The Duke of Cornwall's Light Infantry: The Border Regiment: The Hampshire Regiment: The Prince of Wales's Volunteers (South Lancashire): The Welch Regiment: The Essex Regiment: The Queen's Own Royal West Kent Regiment: The King's Own Yorkshire Light Infantry: The King's Shropshire Light Infantry: The Middlesex Regiment (Duke of Cambridge's Own): The King's Royal Rifle Corps: The Manchester Regiment: The York and Lancaster Regiment: The Durham Light Infantry: The Seaforth Highlanders (Ross-shire Buffs, The Duke of Albany's): The Gordon Highlanders: The Queen's Own Cameron Highlanders: The Royal Ulster Rifles: The Prince of Wales's Leinster Regiment (Royal Canadians): The Argyll and Sutherland Highlanders (Princess Louise's): The Royal Irish Fusiliers (Princess Victoria's): The Royal Dublin Fusiliers: The Rifle Brigade (Prince Consort's Own): The Monmouthshire Regiment: The Cambridgeshire Regiment: 5th City of London Regiment (London Rifle Brigade): 9th London Regiment (Queen Victoria's Rifles): 12th London Regiment (Rangers): Essex Yeomanry (Dragoons): The Leicestershire Yeomanry (Prince Albert's Own) (Hussars): The North Somerset Yeomanry (Dragoons)
		1929	Princess Patricia's Canadian Light Infantry
21.	**BELLEWAARDE** 24th–25th May 1915 16th June 1915 and 25th–26th September 1915 Summer Operations 1915	1925	The Queen's Bays (2nd Dragoon Guards): 4th Royal Irish Dragoon Guards: 5th Dragoon Guards (Princess Charlotte of Wales's): The Carabiniers (6th Dragoon Guards): The Royal Scots Greys (2nd Dragoons): 3rd The King's Own Hussars: 4th Queen's Own Hussars: 5th Royal Irish Lancers: 9th Queen's Royal Lancers: 11th Hussars (Prince Albert's Own): 12th Royal Lancers (Prince of Wales's): 15th The King's Hussars: 16th The Queen's Lancers: 18th Royal Hussars (Queen Mary's Own): 19th Royal Hussars (Queen Alexandra's Own): 20th Hussars: Oxfordshire Yeomanry (Queen's Own Oxfordshire Hussars): The Royal Scots (The Royal Regiment): The Buffs (East Kent Regiment): The King's Own Royal Regiment (Lancaster): The Northumberland Fusiliers: The Royal Warwickshire Regiment: The Royal Fusiliers (City of London Regiment): The King's Regiment (Liverpool): The Norfolk Regiment: The Lincolnshire Regiment: The Suffolk Regiment: The Somerset Light Infantry (Prince Albert's): The East Yorkshire Regiment: The Bedfordshire and Hertfordshire Regiment: The Royal Irish Regiment: The Green Howards (Alexandra, Princess of Wales's Own Yorkshire Regiment): The Cheshire Regiment: The King's Own Scottish Borderers: The Gloucestershire Regiment: The East Lancashire Regiment: The East Surrey Regiment: The Duke of Cornwall's Light Infantry: The Border Regiment: The Hampshire Regiment: The Dorsetshire Regiment: The Prince of Wales's Volunteers (South Lancashire): The Welch Regiment: The Essex Regiment: The King's Own Yorkshire Light Infantry: The King's Shropshire Light Infantry: The Middlesex Regiment (Duke of Cambridge's Own): The King's Royal Rifle Corps: The Manchester Regiment: The York and Lancaster Regiment: The Durham Light Infantry: The Seaforth Highlanders (Ross-shire Buffs, The Duke of Albany's): The Gordon Highlanders:

The Royal Irish Fusiliers (Princess Victoria's): The Argyll and Sutherland Highlanders (Princess Louise's): The Royal Dublin Fusiliers: The Rifle Brigade (Prince Consort's Own): The Monmouthshire Regiment: 9th London Regiment (Queen Victoria's Rifles)

1929   Princess Patricia's Canadian Light Infantry

1937   The Liverpool Scottish, The Queen's Own Cameron Highlanders (TA)

22. **AUBERS**

9th May 1915

Summer Operations 1915

1925   Grenadier Guards: Coldstream Guards: Scots Guards: The Royal Scots (The Royal Regiment): The Queen's Royal Regiment (West Surrey): The Royal Warwickshire Regiment: The King's Regiment (Liverpool): The Lincolnshire Regiment: The Devonshire Regiment: The Suffolk Regiment: The West Yorkshire Regiment (The Prince of Wales's Own): The Bedfordshire and Hertfordshire Regiment: The Leicestershire Regiment: The Green Howards (Alexandra, Princess of Wales's Own Yorkshire Regiment): The Royal Scots Fusiliers: The Royal Welch Fusiliers: The South Wales Borderers: The Cameronians (Scottish Rifles): The Royal Inniskilling Fusiliers: The Gloucestershire Regiment: The Worcestershire Regiment: The East Lancashire Regiment: The Duke of Wellington's Regiment (West Riding): The Border Regiment: The Royal Sussex Regiment: The South Staffordshire Regiment: The Welch Regiment: The Black Watch (Royal Highlanders): The Oxfordshire and Buckinghamshire Light Infantry: The Sherwood Foresters (Nottinghamshire and Derbyshire Regiment): The Loyal Regiment (North Lancashire): The Northamptonshire Regiment: The Royal Berkshire Regiment (Princess Charlotte of Wales's): The Middlesex Regiment (Duke of Cambridge's Own): The King's Royal Rifle Corps: The Wiltshire Regiment (Duke of Edinburgh's): The Manchester Regiment: The Highland Light Infantry (City of Glasgow Regiment): The Seaforth Highlanders (Ross-shire Buffs, The Duke of Albany's): The Gordon Highlanders: The Queen's Own Cameron Highlanders: The Royal Ulster Rifles: The Connaught Rangers: The Royal Munster Fusiliers: The Rifle Brigade (Prince Consort's Own): 1st City of London Regiment (The Royal Fusiliers): 3rd City of London Regiment (The Royal Fusiliers): 4th City of London Regiment (The Royal Fusiliers): 13th London Regiment (Princess Louise's Kensington Regiment): 14th London Regiment (London Scottish): 17th London Regiment (Poplar and Stepney Rifles): 21st London Regiment (First Surrey Rifles): 22nd London Regiment (The Queen's): 24th London Regiment (The Queen's)

1926   King George's Own Bengal Sappers and Miners: Royal Bombay Sappers and Miners: 2nd Bombay Pioneers: 6th Rajputana Rifles: 11th Sikh Regiment: 13th Frontier Force Rifles: 14th Punjab Regiment: 16th Punjab Regiment: 17th Dogra Regiment: 18th Royal Garhwal Rifles: 2nd King Edward's Own Gurkha Rifles (The Sirmoor Rifles): 3rd Queen Alexandra's Own Gurkha Rifles: 4th Prince of Wales's Own Gurkha Rifles: 8th Gurkha Rifles: 9th Gurkha Rifles

23. **FESTUBERT 1915**

15th–25th May 1915

Summer Operations 1915

1925   Grenadier Guards: Coldstream Guards: Scots Guards: Irish Guards: The Royal Scots (The Royal Regiment): The Queen's Royal Regiment (West Surrey): The King's Own Royal Regiment (Lancaster): The Royal Warwickshire Regiment: The King's Regiment (Liverpool): The Bedfordshire and Hertfordshire Regiment: The Leicestershire Regiment: The Green Howards (Alexandra, Princess of Wales's Own Yorkshire Regiment): The Royal Scots Fusiliers: The Royal Welch Fusiliers: The Royal Inniskilling Fusiliers: The Worcestershire Regiment: The Border Regiment: The South Staffordshire Regiment: The Black Watch (Royal Highlanders): The Oxfordshire and Buckinghamshire Light Infantry: The Loyal Regiment (North Lancashire): The Royal Berkshire Regiment (Princess Charlotte of Wales's): The King's Royal Rifle Corps: The Wiltshire Regiment (Duke of Edinburgh's): The Highland Light Infantry (City of Glasgow Regiment): The Seaforth Highlanders (Ross-shire Buffs, The Duke of Albany's): The Gordon Highlanders: The Queen's Own Cameron Highlanders: The Argyll and Sutherland Highlanders (Princess Louise's): 3rd City of London Regiment (The Royal Fusiliers): 4th City of London Regiment (The Royal Fusiliers): 6th City of London Regiment (City of London Rifles): 7th City of London Regiment: 8th (City of London) Battalion, The London Regiment (Post Office Rifles): 15th (County of London) Battalion, The London Regiment (Prince of Wales's Own, Civil Service Rifles): 17th London Regiment (Poplar and Stepney Rifles): 18th London Regiment (London Irish Rifles): 19th

London Regiment (St Pancras): 20th London Regiment (The Queen's Own): 21st London Regiment (First Surrey Rifles): 22nd London Regiment (The Queen's): 23rd London Regiment: 24th London Regiment (The Queen's): The Hertfordshire Regiment

1926 2nd Lancers (Gardner's Horse): King George's Own Bengal Sappers and Miners: Royal Bombay Sappers and Miners: 2nd Bombay Pioneers: 6th Rajputana Rifles: 9th Jat Regiment: 11th Sikh Regiment: 13th Frontier Force Rifles: 17th Dogra Regiment: 18th Royal Garhwal Rifles: 1st King George's Own Gurkha Rifles (The Malaun Regiment): 2nd King Edward's Own Gurkha Rifles (The Sirmoor Rifles): 3rd Queen Alexandra's Own Gurkha Rifles: 4th Prince of Wales's Own Gurkha Rifles: 8th Gurkha Rifles: 9th Gurkha Rifles

1926 Malerkotla Sappers: Garhwal Rajya Sappers

1929 16th Canadian Light Horse: The Canadian Grenadier Guards: The Queen's Own Rifles of Canada: The Victoria Rifles of Canada: The Royal Highlanders of Canada: The Royal Grenadiers: The Royal Hamilton Light Infantry: The Canadian Fusiliers (City of London Regiment): The Dufferin Rifles of Canada: The Peterborough Rangers: The Winnipeg Rifles: The Essex Scottish: The 48th Regiment (Highlanders): 1st British Columbia Regiment (Duke of Connaught's Own): The Lake Superior Regiment: The Winnipeg Grenadiers: The Queen's Own Cameron Highlanders of Canada: The Calgary Highlanders: The Calgary Regiment: The Winnipeg Light Infantry: The Saskatoon Light Infantry: The Canadian Scottish Regiment: The Royal Montreal Regiment: The Toronto Regiment: 1st Canadian Infantry Battalion CEF: 4th Canadian Infantry Battalion CEF: 5th Canadian Infantry Battalion CEF: 8th Canadian Infantry Battalion CEF: 13th Canadian Infantry Battalion CEF: 14th Canadian Infantry Battalion CEF: 15th Canadian Infantry Battalion CEF: 16th Canadian Infantry Battalion CEF: The North British Columbia Regiment: 2nd Canadian Infantry Battalion CEF: 3rd Canadian Infantry Battalion CEF: 10th Canadian Infantry Battalion CEF

1930 5th British Columbia Light Horse: 12th Manotoba Dragoons: 8th Canadian Light Horse: The Royal Rifles of Canada: The York Rangers: The Perth Regiment: The Peel and Dufferin Regiment: The Lincoln and Welland Regiment: Les Carabiniers Mont-Royal: The York Regiment: The Pictou Highlanders: The Edmonton Fusiliers: The Irish Fusiliers of Canada: 7th Canadian Infantry Battalion CEF

1931 The Royal Canadian Dragoons: 14th Canadian Light Horse: The Seaforth Highlanders of Canada: Lord Strathcona's Horse (Royal Canadians): The Algonquin Regiment

24. **HOOGE 1915**
19th and 30th July 1915 and
9th August 1915
Summer Operations 1915

1925 The Buffs (East Kent Regiment): The Royal Fusiliers (City of London Regiment): The Suffolk Regiment: The Somerset Light Infantry (Prince Albert's): The West Yorkshire Regiment (The Prince of Wales's Own): The East Yorkshire Regiment: The Leicestershire Regiment: The Duke of Cornwall's Light Infantry: The Oxfordshire and Buckinghamshire Light Infantry: The Sherwood Foresters (Nottinghamshire and Derbyshire Regiment): The King's Own Yorkshire Light Infantry: The King's Shropshire Light Infantry: The Middlesex Regiment (Duke of Cambridge's Own): The King's Royal Rifle Corps: The York and Lancaster Regiment: The Durham Light Infantry: The Gordon Highlanders: The Rifle Brigade (Prince Consort's Own): 16th London Regiment (Queen's Westminster Rifles)

25. **LOOS**
25th September–8th October 1915
Summer Operations 1915

1925 Royal Horse Guards (The Blues): 3rd Dragoon Guards (Prince of Wales's): 1st The Royal Dragoons: 10th Royal Hussars (Prince of Wales's Own): South Irish Horse: King Edward's Horse (The King's Oversea Dominions Regiment): The Northumberland Hussars (Yeomanry): Queen's Own Royal Glasgow Yeomanry (Dragoons): Grenadier Guards: Coldstream Guards: Scots Guards: Irish Guards: Welsh Guards: The Royal Scots (The Royal Regiment): The Queen's Royal Regiment (West Surrey): The Buffs (East Kent Regiment): The King's Own Royal Regiment (Lancaster): The Northumberland Fusiliers: The Royal Warwickshire Regiment: The Royal Fusiliers (City of London Regiment): The King's Regiment (Liverpool): The Norfolk Regiment: The Lincolnshire Regiment: The Devonshire Regiment: The Suffolk Regiment: The Somerset Light Infantry (Prince Albert's): The West Yorkshire Regiment (The Prince of Wales's Own): The East Yorkshire Regiment: The Bedfordshire and Hertfordshire Regiment: The Green Howards (Alexandra, Princess of Wales's Own Yorkshire Regiment): The Royal Scots Fusiliers: The Cheshire Regiment: The Royal Welch Fusiliers: The South Wales Borderers: The King's Own Scottish Borderers: The Cameronians (Scottish Rifles): The Gloucestershire Regiment: The Worcestershire Regiment: The East Surrey Regiment: The Border Regiment: The Royal Sussex Regiment: The South Staffordshire Regiment: The Welch Regiment: The Black Watch (Royal Highlanders): The Oxfordshire and Buckinghamshire Light Infantry: The Essex Regiment: The Sherwood Foresters (Nottinghamshire and Derbyshire Regiment): The Loyal Regiment (North Lancashire): The Northamptonshire Regiment: The Royal Berkshire Regiment (Princess Charlotte of Wales's): The Queen's Own Royal West Kent Regiment: The King's Own Yorkshire Light Infantry: The Middlesex Regiment (Duke of Cambridge's Own): The King's Royal Rifle Corps: The Wiltshire Regiment (Duke of Edinburgh's): The North Staffordshire Regiment (The Prince of Wales's): The York and Lancaster Regiment: The Durham Light Infantry: The Highland Light Infantry (City of Glasgow Regiment): The Seaforth Highlanders (Ross-shire Buffs, The Duke of Albany's): The Gordon Highlanders: The Queen's Own Cameron Highlanders: The Argyll and Sutherland Highlanders (Princess Louise's): The Royal Munster Fusiliers: 6th City of London Regiment (City of London Rifles): 7th City of London Regiment: 8th (City of London) Battalion, The London Regiment (Post Office Rifles): 14th London Regiment (London Scottish): 15th (County of London) Battalion, The London Regiment (Prince of Wales's Own, Civil Service Rifles): 17th London Regiment (Poplar and Stepney Rifles): 18th London Regiment (London Irish Rifles): 19th London Regiment (St Pancras): 20th London Regiment (The Queen's Own): 21st London Regiment (First Surrey Rifles): 22nd London Regiment (The Queen's): 23rd London Regiment 24th London Regiment (The Queen's): The Hertfordshire Regiment: Essex Yeomanry (Dragoons): The North Somerset Yeomanry (Dragoons)

1926 King George's Own Bengal Sappers and Miners: 2nd Bombay Pioneers: 2nd Punjab Regiment: 8th Punjab Regiment: 13th Frontier Force Rifles: 15th Punjab Regiment: 16th Punjab Regiment: 1st King George's Own Gurkha Rifles (The Malaun Regiment): 2nd King Edward's Own Gurkha Rifles (The Sirmoor Rifles): 9th Gurkha Rifles

1925 Coldstream Guards: The Somerset Light Infantry (Prince Albert's): The Duke of Cornwall's Light Infantry: The Oxfordshire and Buckinghamshire Light Infantry: The King's Shropshire Light Infantry

1929 The Royal Canadian Regiment: Royal 22e Regiment: The Mississauga Horse: The Saskatchewan Mounted Rifles: The British Columbia Dragoons: The Eastern Townships Mounted Rifles: The Canadian Grenadier Guards: The Queen's Own Rifles of Canada: The Victoria Rifles of Canada: The Royal Highlanders of Canada: The Royal Grenadiers: The Royal Hamilton Light Infantry: The Princess of Wales' Own Regiment: The Canadian Fusiliers (City of London Regiment): The Dufferin Rifles of Canada: The Peterborough Rangers: The Carleton Light Infantry: The Saint John Fusiliers: The Ottawa Highlanders: The Winnipeg Rifles: The Essex Scottish: The 48th Regiment (Highlanders): 1st British Columbia Regiment (Duke of Connaught's Own): The Argyll and Sutherland Highlanders of Canada (Princess Louise's): The Lake Superior Regiment: The Regina Rifle Regiment: The Winnipeg Grenadiers: The Queen's Own Cameron Highlanders of Canada: The Colchester and Hants Regiment: The Calgary Highlanders: The Calgary Regiment: The Westminster Regiment: The Winnipeg Light Infantry: The Saskatoon Light Infantry: The Canadian Scottish Regiment: The King's Own Rifles of Canada: The Kootenay Regiment: The Royal Montreal Regiment: The Toronto Regiment: The Queen's Rangers, 1st American Regiment: The South Alberta Regiment: The North Alberta Regiment: The Edmonton Regiment: 1st Motor Machine Gun Brigade: 1st Canadian Mounted Rifles Battalion CEF: 2nd Canadian Mounted Rifles Battalion CEF: 4th Canadian Mounted Rifles Battalion CEF: 5th Canadian Mounted Rifles Battalion CEF: 1st Canadian Infantry Battalion CEF: 4th Canadian Infantry Battalion CEF: 5th Canadian Infantry Battalion CEF: 8th Canadian Infantry Battalion CEF: 13th Canadian Infantry Battalion CEF: 14th Canadian Infantry Battalion CEF: 15th Canadian Infantry Battalion CEF: 16th Canadian Infantry Battalion CEF: 18th Canadian Infantry Battalion CEF: 19th Canadian Infantry Battalion CEF: 20th Canadian Infantry Battalion CEF: 24th Canadian Infantry

26. **MOUNT SORREL** [1]
2nd–13th June 1916
Local Operations 1916

Battalion CEF: 26th Canadian Infantry Battalion CEF: 28th Canadian Infantry Battalion CEF: 31st Canadian Infantry Battalion CEF: 42nd Canadian Infantry Battalion CEF: 43rd Canadian Infantry Battalion CEF: 49th Canadian Infantry Battalion CEF: 58th Canadian Infantry Battalion CEF: 60th Canadian Infantry Battalion CEF: 3rd Pioneer Battalion (48th Canadians) CEF: 1st Canadian Motor Machine Gur Brigade CEF: Princess Patricia's Canadian Light Infantry: The North British Columbia Regiment: The Manitoba Regiment: 2nd Canadian Infantry Battalion CEF: 3rd Canadian Infantry Battalion CEF: 10th Canadian Infantry Battalion CEF: 21st Canadian Infantry Battalion CEF: 25th Canadian Infantry Battalion CEF: 27th Canadian Infantry Battalion CEF: 29th Canad an Infantry Battalion CEF: 52nd Canadian Infantry Battalion CEF: 2nd Canadian Pioneer Battalion CEF

1930 The Governor General's Body Guard: The Princess Louise Dragoon Guards: 12th Manitoba Dragoons: 15th Canadian Light Horse: King's Canadian Hussars: The Halifax Rifles: The Royal Rifles of Canada: Les Voltigeurs de Quebec: The Hastings and Prince Edward Regiment: The York Rangers: The Highland Light Infantry of Canada: The Halton Rifles: The Northumberland Regiment: The York Regiment: The New Brunswick Rangers: The Pictou Highlanders: The Manitoba Rangers: The Edmonton Fusiliers: The Prince Albert Volunteers: The Vancouver Regiment: 7th Canadian Infantry Battalion CEF

1931 The Manitoba Mounted Rifles: The Alberta Mounted Rifles: 1st Canadian Pioneer Battalion CEF

? 7th Hussars: 11th Hussars

1960 8th Canadian Hussars (Princess Louise's): 8th Canadian Hussars (Princess Louise's) (Militia): 6th Regiment, Canadian Mounted Rifles CEF

1961 Le Regiment de Maisonneuve: 41st Battalion CEF

¹ *MONT-SORREL taken into use by French-speaking Canadian units 1958.*

27. **SOMME 1916**
1st July–18th November 1916
Operations on the Somme

1925 1st Life Guards: 2nd Life Guards: 1st King's Dragoon Guards: The Queen's Bays (2nd Dragoon Guards): 4th Royal Irish Dragoon Guards: 5th Dragoon Guards (Princess Charlotte of Wales's): 7th Dragoon Guards (Princess Royal's): The Inniskillings (6th Dragoons): 8th King's Royal Irish Hussars: 9th Queen's Royal Lancers: 11th Hussars (Prince Albert's Own): 15th The King's Hussars: 17th Lancers (Duke of Cambridge's Own): 18th Royal Hussars (Queen Mary's Own): 19th Royal Hussars (Queen Alexandra's Own): North Irish Horse: South Irish Horse: The Lancashire Hussars Yeomanry: The Duke of Lancaster's Own Yeomanry (Dragoons): Honourable Artillery Company: Grenadier Guards: Coldstream Guards: Scots Guards: Irish Guards: Welsh Guards: The Royal Scots (The Royal Regiment): The Queen's Royal Regiment (West Surrey): The Buffs (East Kent Regiment): The King's Own Royal Regiment (Lancaster): The Northumberland Fusiliers: The Royal Warwickshire Regiment: The Royal Fusiliers (City of London Regiment): The King's Regiment (Liverpool): The Norfolk Regiment: The Lincolnshire Regiment: The Devonshire Regiment: The Suffolk Regiment: The Somerset Light Infantry (Prince Albert's): The West Yorkshire Regiment (The Prince of Wales's Own): The East Yorkshire Regiment: The Bedfordshire and Hertfordshire Regiment: The Leicestershire Regiment: The Royal Irish Regiment: The Green Howards (Alexandra, Princess of Wales's Own Yorkshire Regiment): The Lancashire Fusiliers: The Royal Scots Fusiliers: The Cheshire Regiment: The Royal Welch Fusiliers: The South Wales Borderers: The King's Own Scottish Borderers: The Cameronians (Scottish Rifles): The Royal Inniskilling Fusiliers: The Gloucestershire Regiment: The Worcestershire Regiment: The East Lancashire Regiment: The East Surrey Regiment: The Duke of Cornwall's Light Infantry: The Duke of Wellington's Regiment (West Riding): The Border Regiment: The Royal Sussex Regiment: The Hampshire Regiment: The South Staffordshire Regiment: The Dorsetshire Regiment: The Prince of Wales's Volunteers (South Lancashire): The Welch Regiment: The Black Watch (Royal Highlanders): The Oxfordshire and Buckinghamshire Light Infantry: The Essex Regiment: The Sherwood Foresters (Nottinghamshire and Derbyshire Regiment): The Loyal Regiment (North Lancashire): The Northamptonshire Regiment: The Royal Berkshire Regiment (Princess Charlotte of Wales's): The Queen's Own Royal West Kent Regiment: The King's Own Yorkshire Light Infantry: The King's Shropshire Light Infantry: The Middlesex Regiment (Duke of Cambridge's Own): The King's Royal Rifle Corps: The Wiltshire Regiment

(Duke of Edinburgh's); The Manchester Regiment: The North Staffordshire Regiment (The Prince of Wales's): The York and Lancaster Regiment: The Durham Light Infantry: The Highland Light Infantry (City of Glasgow Regiment): The Seaforth Highlanders (Ross-shire Buffs, The Duke of Albany's): The Gordon Highlanders: The Queen's Own Cameron Highlanders: The Royal Ulster Rifles: The Royal Irish Fusiliers (Princess Victoria's): The Connaught Rangers: The Argyll and Sutherland Highlanders (Princess Louise's): The Prince of Wales's Leinster Regiment (Royal Canadians): The Royal Munster Fusiliers: The Royal Dublin Fusiliers: The Rifle Brigade (Prince Consort's Own): The Monmouthshire Regiment: The Cambridgeshire Regiment: 1st City of London Regiment (The Royal Fusiliers): 2nd City of London Regiment (The Royal Fusiliers): 3rd City of London Regiment (The Royal Fusiliers): 4th City of London Regiment (The Royal Fusiliers): 5th City of London Regiment (London Rifle Brigade): 6th City of London Regiment (City of London Rifles): 7th City of London Regiment: 8th (City of London) Battalion, The London Regiment (Post Office Rifles): 9th London Regiment (Queen Victoria's Rifles): 12th London Regiment (Rangers): 13th London Regiment (Princess Louise's Kensington Regiment): 14th London Regiment (London Scottish): 15th (County of London) Battalion, The London Regiment (Prince of Wales's Own, Civil Service Rifles): 16th London Regiment (Queen's Westminster Rifles): 17th London Regiment (Poplar and Stepney Rifles): 18th London Regiment (London Irish Rifles): 19th London Regiment (St Pancras): 20th London Regiment (The Queen's Own): 21st London Regiment (First Surrey Rifles): 22nd London Regiment (The Queen's): 23rd London Regiment: 24th London Regiment (The Queen's): The Hertfordshire Regiment: Bedfordshire Yeomanry (Lancers)

1925   The Royal Newfoundland Regiment
1926   2nd Lancers (Gardner's Horse): 4th Duke of Cambridge's Own Hodson's Horse: 9th Royal Deccan Horse: 14th Prince of Wales's Own Scinde Horse: 17th Queen Victoria's Own Poona Horse: 18th King Edward's Own Cavalry: 19th King George's Own Lancers: 21st King George's Own Central India Horse

1926   71st (Transvaal) Siege Battery, Royal Garrison Artillery: 72nd (Griqualand West) Siege Battery, Royal Garrison Artillery: 73rd (Cape) Siege Battery, Royal Garrison Artillery: 74th (Eastern Province) Siege Battery, Royal Garrison Artillery: 75th (Natal) Siege Battery, Royal Garrison Artillery: 125th (Transvaal) Siege Battery, Royal Garrison Artillery: 1st South African Infantry (Cape of Good Hope Regiment): 2nd South African Infantry (Natal and Orange Free State Regiment): 3rd South African Infantry (Transvaal and Rhodesian Regiment): 4th South African Infantry (South African Scottish Regiment): 1st South African Field Ambulance

1926   The Auckland Regiment (Countess of Ranfurly's Own): The Hauraki Regiment: The North Auckland Regiment: The Waikato Regiment: The Wellington Regiment: The Wellington West Coast Regiment: The Hawke's Bay Regiment: The Taranaki Regiment: The Canterbury Regiment: The Nelson, Marlborough, and West Coast Regiment: The Otago Regiment: The Southland Regiment

1927   13th Light Horse Regiment: 1st Battalion: 2nd Battalion: 3rd Battalion: 4th Battalion: 5th Battalion: 6th Battalion: 7th Battalion: 8th Battalion: 9th Battalion: 10th Battalion: 11th Battalion: 12th Battalion: 13th Battalion: 14th Battalion: 15th Battalion: 16th Battalion: 17th Battalion: 18th Battalion: 19th Battalion: 20th Battalion: 21st Battalion: 22nd Battalion: 23rd Battalion: 24th Battalion: 25th Battalion: 26th Battalion: 27th Battalion: 28th Battalion: 29th Battalion: 30th Battalion: 31st Battalion: 32nd Battalion: 45th Battalion: 46th Battalion: 47th Battalion: 48th Battalion: 49th Battalion: 50th Battalion: 51st Battalion: 52nd Battalion: 53rd Battalion: 54th Battalion: 55th Battalion: 56th Battalion: 57th Battalion: 58th Battalion: 59th Battalion: 60th Battalion

1928   The Otago Mounted Rifles
1929   The Royal Canadian Regiment: Royal 22e Regiment: 16th Canadian Light Horse: The Mississauga Horse: The Saskatchewan Mounted Rifles: The British Columbia Dragoons: The Eastern Townships Mounted Rifles: The Canadian Grenadier Guards: The Queen's Own Rifles of Canada: The Victoria Rifles of Canada: The Royal Highlanders of Canada: The Royal Grenadiers:

The Royal Hamilton Light Infantry; The Princess of Wales' Own Regiment; The Canadian Fusiliers (City of London Regiment); The Dufferin Rifles of Canada; The Peterborough Rangers; The Carleton Light Infantry; The Saint John Fusiliers; The Ottawa Highlanders; The Winnipeg Rifles; The Essex Scottish; The 48th Regiment (Highlanders); 1st British Columbia Regiment (Duke of Connaught's Own); The Argyll and Sutherland Highlanders of Canada (Princess Louise's); The Lake Superior Regiment; The Regina Rifle Regiment; The Winnipeg Grenadiers; The Queen's Own Cameron Highlanders of Canada; The Colchester and Hants Regiment; The Calgary Highlanders; The Calgary Regiment; The Westminster Regiment; The Winnipeg Light Infantry; The Saskatoon Light Infantry; The Canadian Scottish Regiment; The King's Own Rifles of Canada; The Kootenay Regiment; The Royal Montreal Regiment; The Toronto Regiment; The Queen's Rangers, 1st American Regiment; The South Alberta Regiment; The North Alberta Regiment; The Edmonton Regiment; The Toronto Scottish Regiment; 1st Motor Machine Gun Brigade; 1st Canadian Mounted Rifles Battalion CEF; 2nd Canadian Mounted Rifles Battalion CEF; 4th Canadian Mounted Rifles Battalion CEF; 5th Canadian Mounted Rifles Battalion CEF; 1st Canadian Infantry Battalion CEF; 4th Canadian Infantry Battalion CEF; 5th Canadian Infantry Battalion CEF; 8th Canadian Infantry Battalion CEF; 13th Canadian Infantry Battalion CEF; 14th Canadian Infantry Battalion CEF; 15th Canadian Infantry Battalion CEF; 16th Canadian Infantry Battalion CEF; 18th Canadian Infantry Battalion CEF; 19th Canadian Infantry Battalion CEF; 20th Canadian Infantry Battalion CEF; 24th Canadian Infantry Battalion CEF; 26th Canadian Infantry Battalion CEF; 28th Canadian Infantry Battalion CEF; 31st Canadian Infantry Battalion CEF; 42nd Canadian Infantry Battalion CEF; 43rd Canadian Infantry Battalion CEF; 44th Canadian Infantry Battalion CEF; 46th Canadian Infantry Battalion CEF; 47th Canadian Infantry Battalion CEF; 49th Canadian Infantry Battalion CEF; 60th Canadian Infantry Battalion CEF; 50th Canadian Infantry Battalion CEF; 54th Canadian Infantry Battalion CEF; 58th Canadian Infantry Battalion CEF; 78th Canadian Infantry Battalion CEF; 73rd Canadian Infantry Battalion CEF; 75th Canadian Infantry Battalion CEF; 102nd Canadian Infantry Battalion CEF; 3rd Pioneer Battalion (48th Canadians) CEF; 1st Canadian Motor Machine Gun Brigade CEF; Princess Patricia's Canadian Light Infantry; The North British Columbia Regiment; The Ontario Regiment; The Manitoba Regiment; 2nd Canadian Infantry Battalion CEF; 3rd Canadian Infantry Battalion CEF; 10th Canadian Infantry Battalion CEF; 21st Canadian Infantry Battalion CEF; 25th Canadian Infantry Battalion CEF; 27th Canadian Infantry Battalion CEF; 29th Canadian Infantry Battalion CEF; 38th Canadian Infantry Battalion CEF; 52nd Canadian Infantry Battalion CEF; 2nd Canadian Pioneer Battalion CEF; 67th Canadian (Pioneer) Battalion CEF

1930   The Governor General's Body Guard: 1st Hussars: 12th Manitoba Dragoons: 15th Canadian Light Horse: 19th Alberta Dragoons: King's Canadian Hussars: The Governor General's Foot Guards: The Halifax Rifles: The Royal Rifles of Canada: Les Voltigeurs de Quebec: The Hastings and Prince Edward Regiment: The Lincoln Regiment: The York Rangers: The Elgin Regiment: The Lambton Regiment: The Highland Light Infantry of Canada: The Peel and Dufferin Regiment: The Halton Rifles: The Northumberland Regiment: The Princess Louise Fusiliers: The York Regiment: The New Brunswick Rangers: The Pictou Les Carabiniers Mont-Royal: The Princess Louise Fusiliers: The York Regiment: The New Brunswick Rangers: The Pictou Highlanders: The Kenora Light Infantry: The Manitoba Rangers: The Edmonton Fusiliers: The Prince Albert Volunteers: The Irish Fusiliers of Canada: The Vancouver Regiment: 7th Canadian Infantry Battalion CEF

1931   The Royal Canadian Dragoons: The Fort Garry Horse: The Manitoba Mounted Rifles: The Seaforth Highlanders of Canada: 1st Cavalry Machine Gun Squadron: 72nd Canadian Infantry Battalion CEF: Machine Gun Squadron, Canadian Cavalry Brigade CEF: Lord Strathcona's Horse (Royal Canadians): The South Alberta Horse: 1st Canadian Pioneer Battalion CEF

?   7th Hussars: 11th Hussars
1937   The Liverpool Scottish, The Queen's Own Cameron Highlanders (TA)
1958   Royal Tank Regiment

	1960	8th Canadian Hussars (Princess Louise's): 8th Canadian Hussars (Princess Louise's) (Militia): 6th Regiment, Canadian Mounted Rifles CEF
	1961	Le Regiment de Maisonneuve: 41st Battalion CEF
28.	**ALBERT 1916** 1st–13th July 1916 Operations on the Somme	
	1925	1st Life Guards: 2nd Life Guards: North Irish Horse: South Irish Horse: The Lancashire Hussars Yeomanry: The Duke of Lancaster's Own Yeomanry (Dragoons): The Royal Scots (The Royal Regiment): The Queen's Royal Regiment (West Surrey): The Buffs (East Kent Regiment): The King's Own Royal Regiment (Lancaster): The Northumberland Fusiliers: The Royal Warwickshire Regiment: The Royal Fusiliers (City of London Regiment): The King's Regiment (Liverpool): The Norfolk Regiment: The Lincolnshire Regiment: The Devonshire Regiment: The Suffolk Regiment: The Somerset Light Infantry (Prince Albert's): The West Yorkshire Regiment (The Prince of Wales's Own): The East Yorkshire Regiment: The Bedfordshire and Hertfordshire Regiment: The Royal Irish Regiment: The Green Howards (Alexandra, Princess of Wales's Own Yorkshire Regiment): The Lancashire Fusiliers: The Royal Scots Fusiliers: The Cheshire Regiment: The Royal Welch Fusiliers: The South Wales Borderers: The King's Own Scottish Borderers: The Cameronians (Scottish Rifles): The Royal Inniskilling Fusiliers: The Gloucestershire Regiment: The Worcestershire Regiment: The East Lancashire Regiment: The East Surrey Regiment: The Duke of Wellington's Regiment (West Riding): The Border Regiment: The Royal Sussex Regiment: The Hampshire Regiment: The South Staffordshire Regiment: The Dorsetshire Regiment: The Prince of Wales's Volunteers (South Lancashire): The Welch Regiment: The Black Watch (Royal Highlanders): The Oxfordshire and Buckinghamshire Light Infantry: The Essex Regiment: The Sherwood Foresters (Nottinghamshire and Derbyshire Regiment): The Loyal Regiment (North Lancashire): The Northamptonshire Regiment: The Royal Berkshire Regiment (Princess Charlotte of Wales's): The Queen's Own Royal West Kent Regiment: The King's Own Yorkshire Light Infantry: The King's Shropshire Light Infantry: The Middlesex Regiment (Duke of Cambridge's Own): The King's Royal Rifle Corps: The Wiltshire Regiment (Duke of Edinburgh's): The Manchester Regiment: The North Staffordshire Regiment (The Prince of Wales's): The York and Lancaster Regiment: The Durham Light Infantry: The Highland Light Infantry (City of Glasgow Regiment): The Seaforth Highlanders (Ross-shire Buffs, The Duke of Albany's): The Gordon Highlanders: The Queen's Own Cameron Highlanders: The Royal Ulster Rifles: The Royal Irish Fusiliers (Princess Victoria's): The Argyll and Sutherland Highlanders (Princess Louise's): The Royal Munster Fusiliers: The Royal Dublin Fusiliers: The Rifle Brigade (Prince Consort's Own): The Monmouthshire Regiment: 1st City of London Regiment (The Royal Fusiliers): 2nd City of London Regiment (The Royal Fusiliers): 3rd City of London Regiment (The Royal Fusiliers): 4th City of London Regiment (The Royal Fusiliers): 5th City of London Regiment (London Rifle Brigade): 9th London Regiment (Queen Victoria's Rifles): 12th London Regiment (Rangers): 13th London Regiment (Princess Louise's Kensington Regiment): 14th London Regiment (London Scottish): 16th London Regiment (Queen's Westminster Rifles)
	1926	72nd (Griqualand West) Siege Battery, Royal Garrison Artillery: 74th (Eastern Province) Siege Battery, Royal Garrison Artillery: 75th (Natal) Siege Battery, Royal Garrison Artillery
29.	**ALBERT (BEAUMONT HAMEL) 1916** 1st July 1916 Operations on the Somme	
	1925	The Royal Newfoundland Regiment
30.	**BAZENTIN** 14th–17th July 1916 Operations on the Somme	
	1925	7th Dragoon Guards (Princess Royal's): 8th King's Royal Irish Hussars: The Royal Scots (The Royal Regiment): The Queen's Royal Regiment (West Surrey): The Buffs (East Kent Regiment): The King's Own Royal Regiment (Lancaster): The Northumberland Fusiliers: The Royal Warwickshire Regiment: The Royal Fusiliers (City of London Regiment): The King's Regiment (Liverpool): The Lincolnshire Regiment: The Devonshire Regiment: The Suffolk Regiment: The West Yorkshire Regiment (The Prince of Wales's Own): The East Yorkshire Regiment: The Bedfordshire and Hertfordshire Regiment: The

Leicestershire Regiment: The Royal Irish Regiment: The Green Howards (Alexandra, Princess of Wales's Own Yorkshire Regiment): The Lancashire Fusiliers: The Royal Scots Fusiliers: The Cheshire Regiment: The Royal Welch Fusiliers: The South Wales Borderers: The King's Own Scottish Borderers: The Cameronians (Scottish Rifles): The Royal Inniskilling Fusiliers: The Gloucestershire Regiment: The Worcestershire Regiment: The East Lancashire Regiment: The East Surrey Regiment: The Duke of Wellington's Regiment (West Riding): The Border Regiment: The Royal Sussex Regiment: The South Staffordshire Regiment: The Prince of Wales's Volunteers (South Lancashire): The Welch Regiment: The Black Watch (Royal Highlanders): The Oxfordshire and Buckinghamshire Light Infantry: The Essex Regiment: The Sherwood Foresters (Nottinghamshire and Derbyshire Regiment): The Loyal Regiment (North Lancashire): The Northamptonshire Regiment: The Royal Berkshire Regiment (Princess Charlotte of Wales's): The Queen's Own Royal West Kent Regiment: The King's Own Yorkshire Light Infantry: The King's Shropshire Light Infantry: The Middlesex Regiment (Duke of Cambridge's Own): The King's Royal Rifle Corps: The Wiltshire Regiment (Duke of Edinburgh's): The Manchester Regiment: The North Staffordshire Regiment (The Prince of Wales's): The Durham Light Infantry: The Highland Light Infantry (City of Glasgow Regiment): The Seaforth Highlanders (Ross-shire Buffs, The Duke of Albany's): The Gordon Highlanders: The Queen's Own Cameron Highlanders: The Royal Ulster Rifles: The Argyll and Sutherland Highlanders (Princess Louise's): The Royal Munster Fusiliers: The Rifle Brigade (Prince Consort's Own)

1926   4th Duke of Cambridge's Own Hodson's Horse: 9th Royal Deccan Horse: 17th Queen Victoria's Own Poona Horse: 19th King George's Own Lancers

1926   71st (Transvaal) Siege Battery, Royal Garrison Artillery: 72nd (Griqualand West) Siege Battery, Royal Garrison Artillery: 73rd (Cape) Siege Battery, Royal Garrison Artillery: 75th (Natal) Siege Battery, Royal Garrison Artillery

1931   The Royal Canadian Dragoons: The Fort Garry Horse: 1st Cavalry Machine Gun Squadron: Machine Gun Squadron, Canadian Cavalry Brigade CEF: Lord Strathcona's Horse (Royal Canadians)

31.

DELVILLE WOOD
15th July–3rd September 1916
Operations on the Somme

1925   The Queen's Royal Regiment (West Surrey): The Buffs (East Kent Regiment): The King's Own Royal Regiment (Lancaster): The Northumberland Fusiliers: The Royal Warwickshire Regiment: The Royal Fusiliers (City of London Regiment): The King's Regiment (Liverpool): The Norfolk Regiment: The Lincolnshire Regiment: The Devonshire Regiment: The Suffolk Regiment: The Somerset Light Infantry (Prince Albert's): The East Yorkshire Regiment: The Bedfordshire and Hertfordshire Regiment: The Royal Irish Regiment: The Lancashire Fusiliers: The Royal Scots Fusiliers: The Cheshire Regiment: The Royal Welsh Fusiliers: The King's Own Scottish Borderers: The Gloucestershire Regiment: The Worcestershire Regiment: The East Surrey Regiment: The Royal Sussex Regiment: The South Staffordshire Regiment: The Duke of Wellington's Regiment (West Riding): The Border Regiment: The Royal Sussex Regiment: The South Staffordshire Regiment: The Essex Regiment: The Sherwood Foresters (Nottinghamshire and Derbyshire Regiment): The Black Watch (Royal Highlanders): The Oxfordshire and Buckinghamshire Light Infantry: The Essex Regiment: The Sherwood Foresters (Nottinghamshire and Derbyshire Regiment): The Northamptonshire Regiment: The Royal Berkshire Regiment (Princess Charlotte of Wales's): The Queen's Own Royal West Kent Regiment: The King's Own Yorkshire Light Infantry: The King's Royal Rifle Corps: The Manchester Regiment: The Middlesex Regiment (Duke of Cambridge's Own): The King's Shropshire Light Infantry: The North Staffordshire Regiment (The Prince of Wales's): The Durham Light Infantry: The Highland Light Infantry (City of Glasgow Regiment): The Seaforth Highlanders (Ross-shire Buffs, The Duke of Albany's): The Gordon Highlanders: The Queen's Own Cameron Highlanders: The Argyll and Sutherland Highlanders (Princess Louise's): The Prince of Wales's Leinster Regiment (Royal Canadians): The Rifle Brigade (Prince Consort's Own)

1926   9th Royal Deccan Horse

1926   1st South African Infantry (Cape of Good Hope Regiment): 2nd South African Infantry (Natal and Orange Free State Regiment): 3rd South African Infantry (Transvaal and Rhodesian Regiment): 4th South African Infantry (South African Scottish Regiment): 1st South African Field Ambulance

32.	**POZIERES** 23rd July–3rd September 1916 Operations on the Somme	1925	9th Queen's Royal Lancers: The Royal Scots (The Royal Regiment): The Queen's Royal Regiment (West Surrey): The Buffs (East Kent Regiment): The King's Own Royal Regiment (Lancaster): The Northumberland Fusiliers: The Royal Warwickshire Regiment: The Royal Fusiliers (City of London Regiment): The Norfolk Regiment: The Lincolnshire Regiment: The Suffolk Regiment: The West Yorkshire Regiment (The Prince of Wales's Own): The East Yorkshire Regiment: The Bedfordshire and Hertfordshire Regiment: The Green Howards (Alexandra, Princess of Wales's Own Yorkshire Regiment): The Lancashire Fusiliers: The Royal Scots Fusiliers: The Cheshire Regiment: The Royal Welch Fusiliers: The South Wales Borderers: The King's Own Scottish Borderers: The Cameronians (Scottish Rifles): The Gloucestershire Regiment: The Worcestershire Regiment: The East Lancashire Regiment: The East Surrey Regiment: The Duke of Wellington's Regiment (West Riding): The Border Regiment: The Royal Sussex Regiment: The South Staffordshire Regiment: The Prince of Wales's Volunteers (South Lancashire): The Welch Regiment: The Black Watch (Royal Highlanders): The Oxfordshire and Buckinghamshire Light Infantry: The Essex Regiment: The Sherwood Foresters (Nottinghamshire and Derbyshire Regiment): The Loyal Regiment (North Lancashire): The Northamptonshire Regiment: The Royal Berkshire Regiment (Princess Charlotte of Wales's): The Queen's Own Royal West Kent Regiment: The King's Own Yorkshire Light Infantry: The Middlesex Regiment (Duke of Cambridge's Own): The King's Royal Rifle Corps: The Wiltshire Regiment (Duke of Edinburgh's): The North Staffordshire Regiment (The Prince of Wales's): The York and Lancaster Regiment: The Durham Light Infantry: The Highland Light Infantry (City of Glasgow Regiment): The Seaforth Highlanders (Ross-shire Buffs, The Duke of Albany's): The Gordon Highlanders: The Queen's Own Cameron Highlanders: The Royal Ulster Rifles: The Argyll and Sutherland Highlanders (Princess Louise's): The Royal Munster Fusiliers
		1926	71st (Transvaal) Siege Battery, Royal Garrison Artillery: 72nd (Griqualand West) Siege Battery, Royal Garrison Artillery: 73rd (Cape) Siege Battery, Royal Garrison Artillery: 74th (Eastern Province) Siege Battery, Royal Garrison Artillery: 75th (Natal) Siege Battery, Royal Garrison Artillery
		1927	13th Light Horse Regiment: 1st Battalion: 2nd Battalion: 3rd Battalion: 4th Battalion: 5th Battalion: 6th Battalion: 7th Battalion: 8th Battalion: 9th Battalion: 10th Battalion: 11th Battalion: 12th Battalion: 13th Battalion: 14th Battalion: 15th Battalion: 16th Battalion: 17th Battalion: 18th Battalion: 19th Battalion: 20th Battalion: 21st Battalion: 22nd Battalion: 23rd Battalion: 24th Battalion: 25th Battalion: 26th Battalion: 27th Battalion: 28th Battalion: 45th Battalion: 46th Battalion: 47th Battalion: 48th Battalion: 49th Battalion: 50th Battalion: 51st Battalion: 52nd Battalion
		1929	The Queen's Own Rifles of Canada: The Royal Highlanders of Canada: The Royal Hamilton Light Infantry: The Canadian Fusiliers (City of London Regiment): The Dufferin Rifles of Canada: The Peterborough Rangers: The 48th Regiment (Highlanders): The Canadian Scottish Regiment: The Royal Montreal Regiment: The Toronto Regiment: 1st Canadian Infantry Battalion CEF: 4th Canadian Infantry Battalion CEF: 13th Canadian Infantry Battalion CEF: 14th Canadian Infantry Battalion CEF: 15th Canadian Infantry Battalion CEF: 16th Canadian Infantry Battalion CEF: 2nd Canadian Infantry Battalion CEF: 3rd Canadian Infantry Battalion CEF
		1931	The Royal Canadian Dragoons: The Fort Garry Horse: Lord Strathcona's Horse (Royal Canadians)
33.	**GUILLEMONT** 3rd–6th September 1916 Operations on the Somme	1925	The Queen's Royal Regiment (West Surrey): The King's Own Royal Regiment (Lancaster): The Royal Warwickshire Regiment: The King's Regiment (Liverpool): The Norfolk Regiment: The Devonshire Regiment: The Somerset Light Infantry (Prince Albert's):The Bedfordshire and Hertfordshire Regiment: The Royal Irish Regiment: The Cheshire Regiment: The Royal Welch Fusiliers: The King's Own Scottish Borderers: The Royal Inniskilling Fusiliers: The Gloucestershire Regiment: The East Surrey Regiment: The Duke of Cornwall's Light Infantry: The Border Regiment: The Hampshire Regiment: The Prince of Wales's Volunteers (South Lancashire): The Oxfordshire and Buckinghamshire Light Infantry: The Loyal Regiment (North Lancashire): The Queen's Own Royal West Kent Regiment: The King's Own Yorkshire Light Infantry: The King's Shropshire Light Infantry: The King's Royal Rifle Corps: The Manchester Regiment: The North Staffordshire Regiment (The Prince of Wales's): The

Durham Light Infantry; The Gordon Highlanders; The Royal Ulster Rifles: The Royal Irish Fusiliers (Princess Victoria's); The Connaught Rangers: The Prince of Wales's Leinster Regiment (Royal Canadians): The Royal Munster Fusiliers: The Royal Dublin Fusiliers: The Rifle Brigade (Prince Consort's Own): 2nd City of London Regiment (The Royal Fusiliers); 4th City of London Regiment (The Royal Fusiliers): 5th City of London Regiment (London Rifle Brigade); 9th London Regiment (Queen Victoria's Rifles); 12th London Regiment (Rangers): 13th London Regiment (Princess Louise's Kensington Regiment): 14th London Regiment (London Scottish): 16th London Regiment (Queen's Westminster Rifles)

1928   The Otago Mounted Rifles

34.   **GINCHY**

9th September 1916
Operations on the Somme

1925   Grenadier Guards; Welsh Guards: The King's Own Royal Regiment (Lancaster): The King's Regiment (Liverpool): The Royal Irish Regiment: The Lancashire Fusiliers: The Royal Inniskilling Fusiliers: The Hampshire Regiment: The Prince of Wales's Volunteers (South Lancashire): The Sherwood Foresters (Nottinghamshire and Derbyshire Regiment): The Loyal Regiment (North Lancashire): The Middlesex Regiment (Duke of Cambridge's Own): The Royal Ulster Rifles: The Royal Irish Fusiliers (Princess Victoria's); The Connaught Rangers: The Prince of Wales's Leinster Regiment (Royal Canadians): The Royal Munster Fusiliers: The Royal Dublin Fusiliers: 2nd City of London Regiment (The Royal Fusiliers): 3rd City of London Regiment (The Royal Fusiliers): 4th City of London Regiment (The Royal Fusiliers): 5th City of London Regiment (London Rifle Brigade): 9th London Regiment (Queen Victoria's Rifles): 12th London Regiment (Rangers): 13th London Regiment (Princess Louise's Kensington Regiment): 14th London Regiment (London Scottish): 16th London Regiment (Queen's Westminster Rifles)

1928   The Otago Mounted Rifles
1937   The Liverpool Scottish, The Queen's Own Cameron Highlanders (TA)

35.   **FLERS-COURCELETTE**

15th–22nd September 1916
Operations on the Somme

1925   The Queen's Bays (2nd Dragoon Guards): 4th Royal Irish Dragoon Guards: 5th Dragoon Guards (Princess Charlotte of Wales's): 7th Dragoon Guards (Princess Royal's): 8th King Royal Irish Hussars: 9th Queen's Royal Lancers: 11th Hussars (Prince Albert's Own): 15th The King's Hussars: 18th Royal Hussars (Queen Mary's Own): 19th Royal Hussars (Queen Alexandra's Own): Grenadier Guards: Coldstream Guards: Scots Guards: Irish Guards: Welsh Guards: The Royal Scots (The Royal Regiment): The Queen's Royal Regiment (West Surrey): The Buffs (East Kent Regiment): The King's Own Royal Regiment (Lancaster): The Northumberland Fusiliers: The Royal Warwickshire Regiment: The Royal Fusiliers (City of London Regiment): The King's Regiment (Liverpool): The Norfolk Regiment: The Lincolnshire Regiment: The Devonshire Regiment: The Suffolk Regiment: The Somerset Light Infantry (Prince Albert's): The West Yorkshire Regiment (The Prince of Wales's Own): The East Yorkshire Regiment: The Bedfordshire and Hertfordshire Regiment: The Leicestershire Regiment: The Green Howards (Alexandra, Princess of Wales's Own Yorkshire Regiment): The Lancashire Fusiliers: The Royal Scots Fusiliers: The Cheshire Regiment: The Royal Welch Fusiliers: The South Wales Borderers: The King's Own Scottish Borderers: The Cameronians (Scottish Rifles): The Gloucestershire Regiment: The East Surrey Regiment: The Duke of Cornwall's Light Infantry: The Duke of Wellington's Regiment (West Riding): The Border Regiment: The Royal Sussex Regiment: The Hampshire Regiment: The South Staffordshire Regiment: The Dorsetshire Regiment: The Prince of Wales's Volunteers (South Lancashire): The Welch Regiment: The Black Watch (Royal Highlanders): The Oxfordshire and Buckinghamshire Light Infantry: The Essex Regiment: The Sherwood Foresters (Nottinghamshire and Derbyshire Regiment): The Loyal Regiment (North Lancashire): The Northamptonshire Regiment: The Royal Berkshire Regiment (Princess Charlotte of Wales's): The Queen's Own Royal West Kent Regiment: The King's Own Yorkshire Light Infantry: The King's Shropshire Light Infantry: The Middlesex Regiment (Duke of Cambridge's Own): The King's Royal Rifle Corps: The Manchester Regiment: The York and Lancaster Regiment: The Durham Light Infantry: The Highland Light Infantry (City of Glasgow Regiment): The Seaforth Highlanders (Ross-shire Buffs, The Duke of Albany's): The Gordon Highlanders: The Queen's Own Cameron Highlanders: The Argyll and Sutherland

Highlanders (Princess Louise's): The Royal Munster Fusiliers: The Rifle Brigade (Prince Consort's Own): 1st City of London Regiment (The Royal Fusiliers): 2nd City of London Regiment (The Royal Fusiliers): 3rd City of London Regiment (The Royal Fusiliers): 4th City of London Regiment (The Royal Fusiliers): 5th City of London Regiment (London Rifle Brigade): 6th City of London Regiment (City of London Rifles): 7th City of London Regiment: 8th (City of London) Battalion, The London Regiment (Post Office Rifles): 9th London Regiment (Queen Victoria's Rifles): 12th London Regiment (Rangers): 13th London Regiment (Princess Louise's Kensington Regiment): 14th London Regiment (London Scottish): 15th (County of London) Battalion, The London Regiment (Prince of Wales's Own, Civil Service Rifles): 16th London Regiment (Queen's Westminster Rifles): 17th London Regiment (Poplar and Stepney Rifles): 18th London Regiment (London Irish Rifles): 19th London Regiment (St Pancras): 20th London Regiment (The Queen's Own): 21st London Regiment (First Surrey Rifles): 22nd London Regiment (The Queen's): 23rd London Regiment: 24th London Regiment (The Queen's): Bedfordshire Yeomanry (Lancers): 4th Duke of Cambridge's Own Hodson's Horse: 9th Royal Deccan Horse: 17th Queen Victoria's Own Poona Horse: 19th King George's Own Lancers

1926   71st (Transvaal) Siege Battery, Royal Garrison Artillery: 72nd (Griqualand West) Siege Battery, Royal Garrison Artillery: 73rd (Cape) Siege Battery, Royal Garrison Artillery: 74th (Eastern Province) Siege Battery, Royal Garrison Artillery: 75th (Natal) Siege Battery, Royal Garrison Artillery: 125th (Transvaal) Siege Battery, Royal Garrison Artillery

1926   The Auckland Regiment (Countess of Ranfurly's Own): The Hauraki Regiment: The North Auckland Regiment: The Waikato Regiment: The Wellington Regiment: The Wellington West Coast Regiment: The Hawke's Bay Regiment: The Taranaki Regiment: The Canterbury Regiment: The Nelson, Marlborough, and West Coast Regiment: The Otago Regiment: The Southland Regiment

1928   The Otago Mounted Rifles

1929   The Royal Canadian Regiment: Royal 22e Regiment: 16th Canadian Light Horse: The Mississauga Horse: The Saskatchewan Mounted Rifles: The British Columbia Dragoons: The Eastern Townships Mounted Rifles: The Queen's Own Rifles of Canada: The Victoria Rifles of Canada: The Royal Highlanders of Canada: The Royal Grenadiers: The Royal Hamilton Light Infantry: The Princess of Wales' Own Regiment: The Canadian Fusiliers (City of London Regiment): The Dufferin Rifles of Canada: The Peterborough Rangers: The Saint John Fusiliers: The Essex Scottish: The Argyll and Sutherland Highlanders of Canada (Princess Louise's): The Lake Superior Regiment: The Regina Rifle Regiment: The Queen's Own Cameron Highlanders of Canada: The Colchester and Hants Regiment: The Canadian Scottish Regiment: The Toronto Regiment: The Queen's Rangers, 1st American Regiment: The South Alberta Regiment: The North Alberta Regiment: The Edmonton Regiment: 1st Motor Machine Gun Brigade: 1st Canadian Mounted Rifles Battalion CEF: 2nd Canadian Mounted Rifles Battalion CEF: 4th Canadian Mounted Rifles Battalion CEF: 5th Canadian Mounted Rifles Battalion CEF: 1st Canadian Infantry Battalion CEF: 4th Canadian Infantry Battalion CEF: 18th Canadian Infantry Battalion CEF: 19th Canadian Infantry Battalion CEF: 20th Canadian Infantry Battalion CEF: 24th Canadian Infantry Battalion CEF: 26th Canadian Infantry Battalion CEF: 28th Canadian Infantry Battalion CEF: 31st Canadian Infantry Battalion CEF: 42nd Canadian Infantry Battalion CEF: 43rd Canadian Infantry Battalion CEF: 49th Canadian Infantry Battalion CEF: 58th Canadian Infantry Battalion CEF: 60th Canadian Infantry Battalion CEF: 3rd Pioneer Battalion (48th Canadians) CEF: 1st Canadian Motor Machine Gun Brigade CEF: Princess Patricia's Canadian Light Infantry: The Manitoba Regiment: 2nd Canadian Infantry Battalion CEF: 3rd Canadian Infantry Battalion CEF: 21st Canadian Infantry Battalion CEF: 25th Canadian Infantry Battalion CEF: 27th Canadian Infantry Battalion CEF: 29th Canadian Infantry Battalion CEF: 52nd Canadian Infantry Battalion CEF: 2nd Canadian Pioneer Battalion CEF

1930   1st Hussars: 19th Alberta Dragoons: The Vancouver Regiment

1931   The Royal Canadian Dragoons: The Fort Garry Horse: The Manitoba Mounted Rifles: 1st Cavalry Machine Gun Squadron:

Machine Gun Squadron, Canadian Cavalry Brigade CEF: Lord Strathcona's Horse (Royal Canadians): 1st Canadian Pioneer Battalion CEF

? 7th Hussars: 11th Hussars

36. **MORVAL**
25th–28th September 1916
Operations on the Somme

1925 1st King's Dragoon Guards: The Inniskillings (6th Dragoons): 17th Lancers (Duke of Cambridge's Own): Grenadier Guards: Coldstream Guards: Scots Guards: Irish Guards: Welsh Guards: The Queen's Royal Regiment (West Surrey): The Buffs (East Kent Regiment): The King's Own Royal Regiment (Lancaster): The Northumberland Fusiliers: The Royal Warwickshire Regiment: The King's Regiment (Liverpool): The Norfolk Regiment: The Lincolnshire Regiment: The Devonshire Regiment: The Suffolk Regiment: The Somerset Light Infantry (Prince Albert's): The West Yorkshire Regiment (The Prince of Wales's Own): The East Yorkshire Regiment: The Bedfordshire and Hertfordshire Regiment: The Leicestershire Regiment: The Green Howards (Alexandra, Princess of Wales's Own Yorkshire Regiment): The Lancashire Fusiliers: The Cheshire Regiment: The Royal Welch Fusiliers: The South Wales Borderers: The King's Own Scottish Borderers: The Gloucestershire Regiment: The East Surrey Regiment: The Duke of Cornwall's Light Infantry: The Duke of Wellington's Regiment (West Riding): The Border Regiment: The Royal Sussex Regiment: The South Staffordshire Regiment: The Prince of Wales's Volunteers (South Lancashire): The Welch Regiment: The Black Watch (Royal Highlanders): The Oxfordshire and Buckinghamshire Light Infantry: The Essex Regiment: The Sherwood Foresters (Nottinghamshire and Derbyshire Regiment): The Loyal Regiment (North Lancashire): The Northamptonshire Regiment: The Royal Berkshire Regiment (Princess Charlotte of Wales's): The Queen's Own Royal West Kent Regiment: The King's Own Yorkshire Light Infantry: The King's Shropshire Light Infantry: The Middlesex Regiment (Duke of Cambridge's Own): The King's Royal Rifle Corps: The York and Lancaster Regiment: The Durham Light Infantry: The Queen's Own Cameron Highlanders: The Argyll and Sutherland Highlanders (Princess Louise's): The Royal Munster Fusiliers: The Rifle Brigade (Prince Consort's Own): 1st City of London Regiment (The Royal Fusiliers): 2nd City of London Regiment (The Royal Fusiliers): 3rd City of London Regiment (London Rifle Brigade): 9th London Regiment (Queen Victoria's Rifles): 12th London Regiment (Rangers): 13th London Regiment (Princess Louise's Kensington Regiment): 14th London Regiment (London Scottish): 16th London Regiment (Queen's Westminster Rifles): 17th London Regiment (Poplar and Stepney Rifles): 18th London Regiment (London Irish Rifles): 19th London Regiment (St Pancras): 20th London Regiment (The Queen's Own)

1926 2nd Lancers (Gardner's Horse): 14th Prince of Wales's Own Scinde Horse: 18th King Edward's Own Cavalry: 19th King George's Own Lancers: 21st King George's Own Central India Horse

1926 125th (Transvaal) Siege Battery, Royal Garrison Artillery

1926 The Auckland Regiment (Countess of Ranfurly's Own): The Hauraki Regiment: The North Auckland Regiment: The Waikato Regiment: The Wellington Regiment: The Wellington West Coast Regiment: The Hawke's Bay Regiment: The Taranaki Regiment: The Canterbury Regiment: The Nelson, Marlborough, and West Coast Regiment: The Otago Regiment: The Southland Regiment

1928 The Otago Mounted Rifles

1937 The Liverpool Scottish, The Queen's Own Cameron Highlanders (TA)

37. **THIEPVAL**
26th–28t September 1916
Operations on the Somme

1925 The Queen's Royal Regiment (West Surrey): The Buffs (East Kent Regiment): The Northumberland Fusiliers: The Royal Fusiliers (City of London Regiment): The Norfolk Regiment: The Lincolnshire Regiment: The Suffolk Regiment: The West Yorkshire Regiment (The Prince of Wales's Own): The East Yorkshire Regiment: The Bedfordshire and Hertfordshire Regiment: The Green Howards (Alexandra, Princess of Wales's Own Yorkshire Regiment): The Lancashire Fusiliers: The Cheshire Regiment: The East Surrey Regiment: The Duke of Wellington's Regiment (West Riding): The Border Regiment: The Royal Sussex Regiment: The Hampshire Regiment: The South Staffordshire Regiment: The Dorsetshire Regiment: The

Black Watch (Royal Highlanders): The Essex Regiment: The Sherwood Foresters (Nottinghamshire and Derbyshire Regiment): The Northamptonshire Regiment: The Royal Berkshire Regiment (Princess Charlotte of Wales's): The Queen's Own Royal West Kent Regiment: The Middlesex Regiment (Duke of Cambridge's Own): The Manchester Regiment: The York and Lancaster Regiment: The Cambridgeshire Regiment: The Hertfordshire Regiment

1926

71st (Transvaal) Siege Battery, Royal Garrison Artillery: 72nd (Griqualand West) Siege Battery, Royal Garrison Artillery: 73rd (Cape) Siege Battery, Royal Garrison Artillery: 74th (Eastern Province) Siege Battery, Royal Garrison Artillery: 75th (Natal) Siege Battery, Royal Garrison Artillery: 125th (Transvaal) Siege Battery, Royal Garrison Artillery

1929

Royal 22e Regiment: The Victoria Rifles of Canada: The Royal Highlanders of Canada: The Princess of Wales' Own Regiment: The Saint John Fusiliers: The Winnipeg Rifles: The Essex Scottish: The 48th Regiment (Highlanders): 1st British Columbia Regiment (Duke of Connaught's Own): The Argyll and Sutherland Highlanders of Canada (Princess Louise's): The Regina Rifle Regiment: The Colchester and Hants Regiment: The Calgary Highlanders: The Winnipeg Light Infantry: The Saskatoon Light Infantry: The Canadian Scottish Regiment: The Royal Montreal Regiment: The Queen's Rangers, 1st American Regiment: The South Alberta Regiment: The North Alberta Regiment: 1st Motor Machine Gun Brigade: 5th Canadian Infantry Battalion CEF: 8th Canadian Infantry Battalion CEF: 13th Canadian Infantry Battalion CEF: 14th Canadian Infantry Battalion CEF: 15th Canadian Infantry Battalion CEF: 16th Canadian Infantry Battalion CEF: 18th Canadian Infantry Battalion CEF: 19th Canadian Infantry Battalion CEF: 20th Canadian Infantry Battalion CEF: 24th Canadian Infantry Battalion CEF: 26th Canadian Infantry Battalion CEF: 28th Canadian Infantry Battalion CEF: 31st Canadian Infantry Battalion CEF: 3rd Pioneer Battalion (48th Canadians) CEF: 1st Canadian Motor Machine Gun Brigade CEF: The Manitoba Regiment: 10th Canadian Infantry Battalion CEF: 21st Canadian Infantry Battalion CEF: 25th Canadian Infantry Battalion CEF: 27th Canadian Infantry Battalion CEF: 29th Canadian Infantry Battalion CEF

1930

The Vancouver Regiment: 7th Canadian Infantry Battalion CEF

38. LE TRANSLOY
1st–18th October 1916
Operations on the Somme

1925

The Royal Scots (The Royal Regiment): The Queen's Royal Regiment (West Surrey): The Buffs (East Kent Regiment): The King's Own Royal Regiment (Lancaster): The Northumberland Fusiliers: The Royal Warwickshire Regiment: The Royal Fusiliers (City of London Regiment): The King's Regiment (Liverpool): The Norfolk Regiment: The Suffolk Regiment: The Somerset Light Infantry (Prince Albert's): The West Yorkshire Regiment (The Prince of Wales's Own): The Bedfordshire and Hertfordshire Regiment: The Leicestershire Regiment: The Green Howards (Alexandra, Princess of Wales's Own Yorkshire Regiment): The Lancashire Fusiliers: The Royal Scots Fusiliers: The Cheshire Regiment: The Royal Welch Fusiliers: The King's Own Scottish Borderers: The Cameronians (Scottish Rifles): The East Lancashire Regiment: The East Surrey Regiment: The Duke of Cornwall's Light Infantry: The Duke of Wellington's Regiment (West Riding): The Border Regiment: The Royal Sussex Regiment: The Hampshire Regiment: The Prince of Wales's Volunteers (South Lancashire): The Black Watch (Royal Highlanders): The Oxfordshire and Buckinghamshire Light Infantry: The Essex Regiment: The Sherwood Foresters (Nottinghamshire and Derbyshire Regiment): The Northamptonshire Regiment: The Royal Berkshire Regiment (Princess Charlotte of Wales's): The Queen's Own Royal West Kent Regiment: The King's Own Yorkshire Light Infantry: The King's Shropshire Light Infantry: The Middlesex Regiment (Duke of Cambridge's Own): The King's Royal Rifle Corps: The Wiltshire Regiment (Duke of Edinburgh's): The Manchester Regiment: The York and Lancaster Regiment: The Durham Light Infantry: The Highland Light Infantry (City of Glasgow Regiment): The Seaforth Highlanders (Ross-shire Buffs, The Duke of Albany's): The Gordon Highlanders: The Queen's Own Cameron Highlanders: The Royal Irish Fusiliers (Princess Victoria's): The Argyll and Sutherland Highlanders (Princess Louise's): The Royal Dublin Fusiliers: The Rifle Brigade (Prince Consort's Own): 1st City of London Regiment (The Royal Fusiliers): 2nd City of London Regiment (The Royal Fusiliers): 3rd City of London Regiment (The Royal Fusiliers): 4th City of London Regiment (The Royal Fusiliers): 5th City of London Regiment (London Rifle Brigade): 6th City of London Regiment (City of London Rifles): 7th City of London Regiment: 8th (City of London) Battalion, The

London Regiment (Post Office Rifles): 9th London Regiment (Queen Victoria's Rifles): 12th London Regiment (Rangers): 13th London Regiment (Princess Louise's Kensington Regiment): 14th London Regiment (London Scottish): 15th (County of London) Battalion, The London Regiment (Prince of Wales's Own, Civil Service Rifles): 16th London Regiment (Queen's Westminster Rifles): 17th London Regiment (Poplar and Stepney Rifles): 18th London Regiment (London Irish Rifles): 19th London Regiment (St Pancras): 20th London Regiment (The Queen's Own): 21st London Regiment (First Surrey Rifles): 22nd London Regiment (The Queen's): 23rd London Regiment: 24th London Regiment (The Queen's)

1925	The Royal Newfoundland Regiment
1926	125th (Transvaal) Siege Battery, Royal Garrison Artillery: 1st South African Infantry (Cape of Good Hope Regiment): 2nd South African Infantry (Natal and Orange Free State Regiment): 3rd South African Infantry (Transvaal and Rhodesian Regiment): 4th South African Infantry (South African Scottish Regiment)
1926	The Auckland Regiment (Countess of Ranfurly's Own): The Hauraki Regiment: The North Auckland Regiment: The Waikato Regiment: The Wellington Regiment: The Wellington West Coast Regiment: The Hawke's Bay Regiment: The Taranaki Regiment: The Canterbury Regiment: The Nelson, Marlborough, and West Coast Regiment: The Otago Regiment: The Southland Regiment
1928	The Otago Mounted Rifles

<table>
<tr><td>39.</td><td>ANCRE HEIGHTS [1]
1st October–11th November 1916
Operations on the Somme</td><td>1925</td><td>Honourable Artillery Company: The Royal Scots (The Royal Regiment): The Queen's Royal Regiment (West Surrey): The Buffs (East Kent Regiment): The King's Own Royal Regiment (Lancaster): The Northumberland Fusiliers: The Royal Warwickshire Regiment: The Royal Fusiliers (City of London Regiment): The Norfolk Regiment: The Suffolk Regiment: The West Yorkshire Regiment (The Prince of Wales's Own): The East Yorkshire Regiment: The Bedfordshire and Hertfordshire Regiment: The Green Howards (Alexandra, Princess of Wales's Own Yorkshire Regiment): The Lancashire Fusiliers: The Royal Scots Fusiliers: The Cheshire Regiment: The Royal Welch Fusiliers: The South Wales Borderers: The King's Own Scottish Borderers: The Cameronians (Scottish Rifles): The Gloucestershire Regiment: The Worcestershire Regiment: The East Lancashire Regiment: The East Surrey Regiment: The Duke of Wellington's Regiment (West Riding): The Border Regiment: The Royal Sussex Regiment: The Hampshire Regiment: The Prince of Wales's Volunteers (South Lancashire): The Welch Regiment: The Black Watch (Royal Highlanders): The Oxfordshire and Buckinghamshire Light Infantry: The Essex Regiment: The Sherwood Foresters (Nottinghamshire and Derbyshire Regiment): The Loyal Regiment (North Lancashire): The Northamptonshire Regiment: The Royal Berkshire Regiment (Princess Charlotte of Wales's): The Queen's Own Royal West Kent Regiment: The Middlesex Regiment (Duke of Cambridge's Own): The King's Royal Rifle Corps: The Wiltshire Regiment (Duke of Edinburgh's): The Manchester Regiment: The North Staffordshire Regiment (The Prince of Wales's): The York and Lancaster Regiment: The Durham Light Infantry: The Highland Light Infantry (City of Glasgow Regiment): The Seaforth Highlanders (Ross-shire Buffs, The Duke of Albany's): The Queen's Own Cameron Highlanders: The Royal Ulster Rifles: The Argyll and Sutherland Highlanders (Princess Louise's): The Rifle Brigade (Prince Consort's Own): The Cambridgeshire Regiment: The Hertfordshire Regiment</td></tr>
<tr><td></td><td></td><td>1926</td><td>71st (Transvaal) Siege Battery, Royal Garrison Artillery: 72nd (Griqualand West) Siege Battery, Royal Garrison Artillery: 73rd (Cape) Siege Battery, Royal Garrison Artillery: 74th (Eastern Province) Siege Battery, Royal Garrison Artillery: 75th (Natal) Siege Battery, Royal Garrison Artillery: 125th (Transvaal) Siege Battery, Royal Garrison Artillery</td></tr>
<tr><td></td><td></td><td>1929</td><td>The Royal Canadian Regiment: Royal 22e Regiment: 16th Canadian Light Horse: The Mississauga Horse: The Saskatchewan Mounted Rifles: The British Columbia Dragoons: The Eastern Townships Mounted Rifles: The Canadian Grenadier Guards: The Queen's Own Rifles of Canada: The Victoria Rifles of Canada: The Royal Highlanders of Canada: The Royal Grenadiers: The Royal Hamilton Light Infantry: The Princess of Wales's Own Regiment: The Canadian Fusiliers (City of London Regiment): The Dufferin Rifles of Canada: The Peterborough Rangers: The Carleton Light Infantry: The Saint John Fusiliers: The Ottawa</td></tr>
</table>

Highlanders: The Winnipeg Rifles: The Essex Scottish: The 48th Regiment (Highlanders): 1st British Columbia Regiment (Duke of Connaught's Own): The Argyll and Sutherland Highlanders of Canada (Princess Louise's): The Lake Superior Regiment: The Regina Rifle Regiment: The Winnipeg Grenadiers: The Queen's Own Cameron Highlanders of Canada: The Colchester and Hants Regiment: The Calgary Highlanders: The Calgary Regiment: The Westminster Regiment: The Winnipeg Light Infantry: The Saskatoon Light Infantry: The Canadian Scottish Regiment: The King's Own Rifles of Canada: The Kootenay Regiment: The Royal Montreal Regiment: The Toronto Regiment: The Queen's Rangers, 1st American Regiment: The South Alberta Regiment: The North Alberta Regiment: The Edmonton Regiment: The Toronto Scottish Regiment: 1st Canadian Mounted Rifles Battalion CEF: 2nd Canadian Mounted Rifles Battalion CEF: 4th Canadian Mounted Rifles Battalion CEF: 5th Canadian Mounted Rifles Battalion CEF: 1st Canadian Infantry Battalion CEF: 4th Canadian Infantry Battalion CEF: 5th Canadian Infantry Battalion CEF: 8th Canadian Infantry Battalion CEF: 13th Canadian Infantry Battalion CEF: 14th Canadian Infantry Battalion CEF: 15th Canadian Infantry Battalion CEF: 16th Canadian Infantry Battalion CEF: 18th Canadian Infantry Battalion CEF: 19th Canadian Infantry Battalion CEF: 20th Canadian Infantry Battalion CEF: 24th Canadian Infantry Battalion CEF: 26th Canadian Infantry Battalion CEF: 28th Canadian Infantry Battalion CEF: 31st Canadian Infantry Battalion CEF: 42nd Canadian Infantry Battalion CEF: 43rd Canadian Infantry Battalion CEF: 44th Canadian Infantry Battalion CEF: 46th Canadian Infantry Battalion CEF: 47th Canadian Infantry Battalion CEF: 49th Canadian Infantry Battalion CEF: 50th Canadian Infantry Battalion CEF: 54th Canadian Infantry Battalion CEF: 58th Canadian Infantry Battalion CEF: 60th Canadian Infantry Battalion CEF: 73rd Canadian Infantry Battalion CEF: 75th Canadian Infantry Battalion CEF: 78th Canadian Infantry Battalion CEF: 87th Canadian Infantry Battalion CEF: 102nd Canadian Infantry Battalion CEF: 3rd Pioneer Battalion (48th Canadians) CEF: Princess Patricia's Canadian Light Infantry: The North British Columbia Regiment: The Manitoba Regiment: 2nd Canadian Infantry Battalion CEF: 3rd Canadian Infantry Battalion CEF: 10th Canadian Infantry Battalion CEF: 21st Canadian Infantry Battalion CEF: 25th Canadian Infantry Battalion CEF: 27th Canadian Infantry Battalion CEF: 29th Canadian Infantry Battalion CEF: 38th Canadian Infantry Battalion CEF: 52nd Canadian Infantry Battalion CEF: 2nd Canadian Pioneer Battalion CEF: 67th Canadian (Pioneer) Battalion CEF

1930   1st Hussars: 19th Alberta Dragoons: The Vancouver Regiment: 7th Canadian Infantry Battalion CEF
1931   The Manitoba Mounted Rifles: The Seaforth Highlanders of Canada: 72nd Canadian Infantry Battalion CEF: 1st Canadian Pioneer Battalion CEF

?   7th Hussars: 11th Hussars
   ¹ HAUTEURS D'ANCRE taken into use by French-speaking Canadian units 1958.

1925   Honourable Artillery Company: The Royal Scots (The Royal Regiment): The Queen's Royal Regiment (West Surrey): The Buffs (East Kent Regiment): The King's Own Royal Regiment (Lancaster): The Northumberland Fusiliers: The Royal Warwickshire Regiment: The Royal Fusiliers (City of London Regiment): The King's Regiment (Liverpool): The Norfolk Regiment: The Lincolnshire Regiment: The Suffolk Regiment: The Somerset Light Infantry (Prince Albert's): The West Yorkshire Regiment (The Prince of Wales's Own): The East Yorkshire Regiment: The Bedfordshire and Hertfordshire Regiment: The Green Howards (Alexandra, Princess of Wales's Own Yorkshire Regiment): The Lancashire Fusiliers: The Royal Scots Fusiliers: The Cheshire Regiment: The Royal Welch Fusiliers: The South Wales Borderers: The Royal Inniskilling Fusiliers: The Gloucestershire Regiment: The Worcestershire Regiment: The East Lancashire Regiment: The East Surrey Regiment: The Duke of Cornwall's Light Infantry: The Border Regiment: The Royal Sussex Regiment: The Hampshire Regiment: The South Staffordshire Regiment: The Dorsetshire Regiment: The Prince of Wales's Volunteers (South Lancashire): The Welch Regiment: The Black Watch (Royal Highlanders): The Oxfordshire and Buckinghamshire Light Infantry: The Essex Regiment: The Sherwood Foresters (Nottinghamshire and Derbyshire Regiment): The Loyal Regiment (North Lancashire): The Northamptonshire Regiment: The Royal Berkshire Regiment (Princess Charlotte of Wales's): The Queen's Own Royal West Kent Regiment: The King's Own

40.   **ANCRE 1916**
   13th–18th November 1916
   Operations on the Somme

Yorkshire Light Infantry: The King's Shropshire Light Infantry: The Middlesex Regiment (Duke of Cambridge's Own): The King's Royal Rifle Corps: The Wiltshire Regiment (Duke of Edinburgh's); The Manchester Regiment: The North Staffordshire Regiment (The Prince of Wales's): The York and Lancaster Regiment: The Highland Light Infantry (City of Glasgow Regiment): The Seaforth Highlanders (Ross-shire Buffs, The Duke of Albany's): The Gordon Highlanders: The Argyll and Sutherland Highlanders (Princess Louise's): The Royal Dublin Fusiliers: The Rifle Brigade (Prince Consort's Own): The Cambridgeshire Regiment: The Hertfordshire Regiment

1926 72nd (Griqualand West) Siege Battery, Royal Garrison Artillery: 73rd (Cape) Siege Battery, Royal Garrison Artillery: 74th (Eastern Province) Siege Battery, Royal Garrison Artillery: 75th (Natal) Siege Battery, Royal Garrison Artillery: 125th (Transvaal) Siege Battery, Royal Garrison Artillery

1929 The Canadian Grenadier Guards: The Royal Highlanders of Canada: The Carleton Light Infantry: The Ottawa Highlanders: The Winnipeg Grenadiers: The Calgary Regiment: The Westminster Regiment: The Canadian Scottish Regiment: The King's Own Rifles of Canada: The Kootenay Regiment: The Toronto Scottish Regiment: 44th Canadian Infantry Battalion CEF: 46th Canadian Infantry Battalion CEF: 47th Canadian Infantry Battalion CEF: 50th Canadian Infantry Battalion CEF: 54th Canadian Infantry Battalion CEF: 73rd Canadian Infantry Battalion CEF: 75th Canadian Infantry Battalion CEF: 78th Canadian Infantry Battalion CEF: 87th Canadian Infantry Battalion CEF: 102nd Canadian Infantry Battalion CEF: The North British Columbia Regiment: 38th Canadian Infantry Battalion CEF: 67th Canadian (Pioneer) Battalion CEF
The Seaforth Highlanders of Canada: 72nd Canadian Infantry Battalion CEF

41. **BAPAUME 1917**
17th March 1917
German Retreat to the Hindenburg Line

1925 The King's Regiment (Liverpool): The Duke of Cornwall's Light Infantry: The South Staffordshire Regiment: The Oxfordshire and Buckinghamshire Light Infantry: The Essex Regiment: The Northamptonshire Regiment: The Middlesex Regiment (Duke of Cambridge's Own)

1926 71st (Transvaal) Siege Battery, Royal Garrison Artillery: 75th (Natal) Siege Battery, Royal Garrison Artillery
1927 13th Light Horse Regiment: 17th Battalion: 18th Battalion: 19th Battalion: 20th Battalion: 21st Battalion: 22nd Battalion: 23rd Battalion: 24th Battalion: 29th Battalion: 30th Battalion: 31 st Battalion: 32nd Battalion

42. **ARRAS 1917**
9th April–4th May 1917
The Arras Offensive

1925 1st Life Guards: 2nd Life Guards: Royal Horse Guards (The Blues): The Queen's Bays (2nd Dragoon Guards): 3rd Dragoon Guards (Prince of Wales's): 4th Royal Irish Dragoon Guards: 5th Dragoon Guards (Princess Charlotte of Wales's): The Carabiniers (6th Dragoon Guards): 1st The Royal Dragoons: The Royal Scots Greys (2nd Dragoons): 3rd The King's Own Hussars: 4th Queen's Own Hussars: 5th Royal Irish Lancers: 9th Queen's Royal Lancers: 10th Royal Hussars (Prince of Wales's Own): 11th Hussars (Prince Albert's Own): 12th Royal Lancers (Prince of Wales's): 16th The Queen's Lancers: 18th Royal Hussars (Queen Mary's Own): 20th Hussars: Northamptonshire Yeomanry (Dragoons): Oxfordshire Yeomanry (Queen's Own Oxfordshire Hussars): Honourable Artillery Company: The Royal Scots (The Royal Regiment): The Queen's Royal Regiment (West Surrey): The Buffs (East Kent Regiment): The King's Own Royal Regiment (Lancaster): The Northumberland Fusiliers: The Royal Warwickshire Regiment: The Royal Fusiliers (City of London Regiment): The King's Regiment (Liverpool): The Norfolk Regiment: The Lincolnshire Regiment: The Devonshire Regiment: The Suffolk Regiment: The Somerset Light Infantry (Prince Albert's): The West Yorkshire Regiment (The Prince of Wales's Own): The East Yorkshire Regiment: The Bedfordshire and Hertfordshire Regiment: The Green Howards (Alexandra, Princess of Wales's Own Yorkshire Regiment): The Lancashire Fusiliers: The Royal Scots Fusiliers: The Cheshire Regiment: The Royal Welch Fusiliers: The South Wales Borderers: The King's Own Scottish Borderers: The Cameronians (Scottish Rifles): The Royal Inniskilling Fusiliers: The Gloucestershire Regiment: The Worcestershire Regiment: The East Lancashire Regiment: The East Surrey Regiment: The Duke of Cornwall's Light Infantry: The Duke of Wellington's Regiment (West Riding): The Border Regiment: The Royal Sussex Regiment: The Hampshire Regiment: The South Staffordshire Regiment: The Dorsetshire Regiment: The Prince of Wales's

Volunteers (South Lancashire): The Black Watch (Royal Highlanders): The Oxfordshire and Buckinghamshire Light Infantry: The Essex Regiment: The Sherwood Foresters (Nottinghamshire and Derbyshire Regiment): The Loyal Regiment (North Lancashire): The Northamptonshire Regiment: The Royal Berkshire Regiment (Princess Charlotte of Wales's): The Queen's Own Royal West Kent Regiment: The King's Own Yorkshire Light Infantry: The King's Shropshire Light Infantry: The Middlesex Regiment (Duke of Cambridge's Own): The King's Royal Rifle Corps: The Wiltshire Regiment (Duke of Edinburgh's): The Manchester Regiment: The North Staffordshire Regiment (The Prince of Wales's): The York and Lancaster Regiment: The Durham Light Infantry: The Highland Light Infantry (City of Glasgow Regiment): The Seaforth Highlanders (Ross-shire Buffs, The Duke of Albany's): The Gordon Highlanders: The Queen's Own Cameron Highlanders: The Royal Irish Fusiliers (Princess Victoria's): The Argyll and Sutherland Highlanders (Princess Louise's): The Prince of Wales's Leinster Regiment (Royal Canadians): The Royal Dublin Fusiliers: The Rifle Brigade (Prince Consort's Own): The Monmouthshire Regiment: 1st City of London Regiment (Royal Fusiliers): 2nd City of London Regiment (The Royal Fusiliers): 3rd City of London Regiment (The Royal Fusiliers): 4th City of London Regiment (The Royal Fusiliers): 5th City of London Regiment (London Rifle Brigade): 9th London Regiment (Queen Victoria's Rifles): 12th London Regiment (Rangers): 13th London Regiment (Princess Louise's Kensington Regiment): 14th London Regiment (London Scottish): 16th London Regiment (Queen's Westminster Rifles): Essex Yeomanry (Dragoons): The Leicestershire Yeomanry (Prince Albert's Own) (Hussars): The North Somerset Yeomanry (Dragoons)

1925   The Royal Newfoundland Regiment
1926   72nd (Griqualand West) Siege Battery, Royal Garrison Artillery: 73rd (Cape) Siege Battery, Royal Garrison Artillery: 74th (Eastern Province) Siege Battery, Royal Garrison Artillery: 125th (Transvaal) Siege Battery, Royal Garrison Artillery: 1st South African Infantry (Cape of Good Hope Regiment): 2nd South African Infantry (Natal and Orange Free State Regiment): 3rd South African Infantry (Transvaal and Rhodesian Regiment): 4th South African Infantry (South African Scottish Regiment): 1st South African Field Ambulance

1927   13th Light Horse Regiment
1929   The Royal Canadian Regiment: Royal 22e Regiment: 16th Canadian Light Horse: The Mississauga Horse: The Saskatchewan Mounted Rifles: The British Columbia Dragoons: The Eastern Townships Mounted Rifles: The Canadian Grenadier Guards: The Queen's Own Rifles of Canada: The Victoria Rifles of Canada: The Royal Highlanders of Canada: The Royal Grenadiers: The Royal Hamilton Light Infantry: The Princess of Wales' Own Regiment: The Canadian Fusiliers (City of London Regiment): The Dufferin Rifles of Canada: The Peterborough Rangers: The Carleton Light Infantry: The Cape Breton Highlanders: The Saint John Fusiliers: The Ottawa Highlanders: The Winnipeg Rifles: The Essex Scottish: The 48th Regiment (Highlanders): 1st British Columbia Regiment (Duke of Connaught's Own): The Argyll and Sutherland Highlanders of Canada (Princess Louise's): The Lake Superior Regiment: The Regina Rifle Regiment: The Winnipeg Grenadiers: The Queen's Own Cameron Highlanders of Canada: The Colchester and Hants Regiment: The Calgary Highlanders: The Calgary Regiment: The Westminster Regiment: The Winnipeg Light Infantry: The Saskatoon Light Infantry: The Canadian Scottish Regiment: The King's Own Rifles of Canada: The Kootenay Regiment: The Royal Montreal Regiment: The Toronto Regiment: The Queen's Rangers, 1st American Regiment: The South Alberta Regiment: The North Alberta Regiment: The Edmonton Regiment: The Toronto Scottish Regiment: 1st Motor Machine Gun Brigade: 1st Canadian Mounted Rifles Battalion CEF: 2nd Canadian Mounted Rifles Battalion CEF: 4th Canadian Mounted Rifles Battalion CEF: 5th Canadian Mounted Rifles Battalion CEF: 1st Canadian Infantry Battalion CEF: 4th Canadian Infantry Battalion CEF: 5th Canadian Infantry Battalion CEF: 8th Canadian Infantry Battalion CEF: 13th Canadian Infantry Battalion CEF: 14th Canadian Infantry Battalion CEF: 15th Canadian Infantry Battalion CEF: 16th Canadian Infantry Battalion CEF: 18th Canadian Infantry Battalion CEF: 19th Canadian Infantry Battalion CEF: 20th Canadian Infantry Battalion CEF: 24th Canadian Infantry Battalion CEF: 26th Canadian Infantry Battalion CEF: 28th Canadian Infantry

Battalion CEF: 31st Canadian Infantry Battalion CEF: 42nd Canadian Infantry Battalion CEF: 43rd Canadian Infantry Battalion CEF: 44th Canadian Infantry Battalion CEF: 46th Canadian Infantry Battalion CEF: 47th Canadian Infantry Battalion CEF: 49th Canadian Infantry Battalion CEF: 50th Canadian Infantry Battalion CEF: 54th Canadian Infantry Battalion CEF: 58th Canadian Infantry Battalion CEF: 60th Canadian Infantry Battalion CEF: 73rd Canadian Infantry Battalion CEF: 75th Canadian Infantry Battalion CEF: 78th Canadian Infantry Battalion CEF: 85th Canadian Infantry Battalion CEF: 87th Canadian Infantry Battalion CEF: 102nd Canadian Infantry Battalion CEF: 116th Canadian Infantry Battalion CEF: 3rd Pioneer Battalion (48th Canadians) CEF: 1st Canadian Motor Machine Gun Brigade CEF: Princess Patricia's Canadian Light Infantry: The North British Columbia Regiment: The Ontario Regiment: The Manitoba Regiment: 2nd Canadian Infantry Battalion CEF: 3rd Canadian Infantry Battalion CEF: 10th Canadian Infantry Battalion CEF: 21st Canadian Infantry Battalion CEF: 25th Canadian Infantry Battalion CEF: 27th Canadian Infantry Battalion CEF: 29th Canadian Infantry Battalion CEF: 38th Canadian Infantry Battalion CEF: 52nd Canadian Infantry Battalion CEF: 2nd Canadian Pioneer Battalion CEF: 67th Canadian (Pioneer) Battalion CEF: 107th Canadian Pioneer Battalion CEF: 123rd Canadian Pioneer Battalion CEF: 124th Canadian Pioneer Battalion CEF

1930   The Governor General's Body Guard: 1st Hussars: 19th Alberta Dragoons: The Prince Edward Island Light Horse: The Governor General's Foot Guards: The Halifax Rifles: The Royal Rifles of Canada: Les Voltigeurs de Quebec: The Argyll Light Infantry: The Hastings and Prince Edward Regiment: The Lincoln Regiment: The Oxford Rifles: The York Rangers: The Elgin Regiment: The Middlesex Light Infantry: The Lambton Regiment: The Highland Light Infantry of Canada: The Simcoe Foresters: The Peel and Dufferin Regiment: The Halton Rifles: The Norfolk Regiment of Canada: The Northumberland Regiment: The Lanark and Renfrew Scottish Regiment: The Lincoln and Welland Regiment: The Victoria and Haliburton Regiment: The Durham Regiment: The Frontenac Regiment: The Sherbrooke Regiment: Les Carabiniers Mont-Royal: The Princess Louise Fusiliers: The York Regiment: The Annapolis Regiment: The North Shore (New Brunswick) Regiment: The New Brunswick Rangers: The Lunenburg Regiment: The Cumberland Highlanders: The Wentworth Regiment: The Prince Edward Island Highlanders: Fusiliers du St Laurent: The Northern Pioneers: The Kenora Light Infantry: The Manitoba Rangers: The Edmonton Fusiliers: The Rocky Mountain Rangers: The Prince Albert Volunteers: The Irish Fusiliers of Canada: The Sault Ste Marie Regiment: The Vancouver Regiment: The Irish Regiment: The Weyburn Regiment: The Saskatchewan Border Regiment: The Yorkton Regiment: 7th Canadian Infantry Battalion CEF

1931   14th Canadian Light Horse: The Manitoba Mounted Rifles: The Seaforth Highlanders of Canada: 72nd Canadian Infantry Battalion CEF: The South Alberta Horse

?   7th Hussars: 11th Hussars: McGill University Contingent

1958   Royal Tank Regiment

1961   Le Regiment de Maisonneuve: 41st Battalion CEF

43.   **VIMY 1917**
9th–14th April 1917
The Arras Offensive

1925   The Royal Warwickshire Regiment: The Royal Fusiliers (City of London Regiment): The Devonshire Regiment: The Somerset Light Infantry (Prince Albert's): The Bedfordshire and Hertfordshire Regiment: The Cheshire Regiment: The King's Own Scottish Borderers: The Gloucestershire Regiment: The East Lancashire Regiment: The East Surrey Regiment: The Duke of Cornwall's Light Infantry: The Royal Sussex Regiment: The Hampshire Regiment: The Black Watch (Royal Highlanders): The Oxfordshire and Buckinghamshire Light Infantry: The Sherwood Foresters (Nottinghamshire and Derbyshire Regiment): The Northamptonshire Regiment: The Queen's Own Royal West Kent Regiment: The Middlesex Regiment (Duke of Cambridge's Own): The Highland Light Infantry (City of Glasgow Regiment): The Seaforth Highlanders (Ross-shire Buffs, The Duke of Albany's): The Gordon Highlanders: The Prince of Wales's Leinster Regiment (Royal Canadians): The Rifle Brigade (Prince Consort's Own)

1926   72nd (Griqualand West) Siege Battery, Royal Garrison Artillery: 73rd (Cape) Siege Battery, Royal Garrison Artillery: 74th (Eastern Province) Siege Battery, Royal Garrison Artillery

1929 The Royal Canadian Regiment: Royal 22e Regiment: 16th Canadian Light Horse: The Mississauga Horse: The Saskatchewan Mounted Rifles: The British Columbia Dragoons: The Eastern Townships Mounted Rifles: The Canadian Grenadier Guards: The Queen's Own Rifles of Canada: The Victoria Rifles of Canada: The Royal Highlanders of Canada: The Royal Grenadiers: The Royal Hamilton Light Infantry: The Princess of Wales' Own Regiment: The Canadian Fusiliers (City of London Regiment): The Dufferin Rifles of Canada: The Peterborough Rangers: The Carleton Light Infantry: The Cape Breton Highlanders: The Saint John Fusiliers: The Ottawa Highlanders: The Winnipeg Rifles: The Essex Scottish: The 48th Regiment (Highlanders): 1st British Columbia Regiment (Duke of Connaught's Own): The Argyll and Sutherland Highlanders of Canada (Princess Louise's): The Lake Superior Regiment: The Regina Rifle Regiment: The Winnipeg Grenadiers: The Queen's Own Cameron Highlanders of Canada: The Colchester and Hants Regiment: The Calgary Highlanders: The Calgary Regiment: The Westminster Regiment: The Winnipeg Light Infantry: The Saskatoon Light Infantry: The Canadian Scottish Regiment: The King's Own Rifles of Canada: The Kootenay Regiment: The Royal Montreal Regiment: The Toronto Regiment: The Edmonton Regiment: The Queen's Rangers, 1st American Regiment: The South Alberta Regiment: The North Alberta Regiment: The Toronto Scottish Regiment: 1st Motor Machine Gun Brigade: 1st Canadian Mounted Rifles Battalion CEF: 2nd Canadian Mounted Rifles Battalion CEF: 4th Canadian Mounted Rifles Battalion CEF: 5th Canadian Mounted Rifles Battalion CEF: 1st Canadian Infantry Battalion CEF: 4th Canadian Infantry Battalion CEF: 5th Canadian Infantry Battalion CEF: 8th Canadian Infantry Battalion CEF: 13th Canadian Infantry Battalion CEF: 14th Canadian Infantry Battalion CEF: 15th Canadian Infantry Battalion CEF: 16th Canadian Infantry Battalion CEF: 18th Canadian Infantry Battalion CEF: 19th Canadian Infantry Battalion CEF: 20th Canadian Infantry Battalion CEF: 24th Canadian Infantry Battalion CEF: 26th Canadian Infantry Battalion CEF: 28th Canadian Infantry Battalion CEF: 31st Canadian Infantry Battalion CEF: 42nd Canadian Infantry Battalion CEF: 43rd Canadian Infantry Battalion CEF: 44th Canadian Infantry Battalion CEF: 46th Canadian Infantry Battalion CEF: 47th Canadian Infantry Battalion CEF: 49th Canadian Infantry Battalion CEF: 50th Canadian Infantry Battalion CEF: 54th Canadian Infantry Battalion CEF: 58th Canadian Infantry Battalion CEF: 60th Canadian Infantry Battalion CEF: 73rd Canadian Infantry Battalion CEF: 75th Canadian Infantry Battalion CEF: 78th Canadian Infantry Battalion CEF: 85th Canadian Infantry Battalion CEF: 87th Canadian Infantry Battalion CEF: 102nd Canadian Infantry Battalion CEF: 116th Canadian Infantry Battalion CEF: 3rd Pioneer Battalion (48th Canadians) CEF: 1st Canadian Motor Machine Gun Brigade CEF: Princess Patricia's Canadian Light Infantry: The North British Columbia Regiment: The Ontario Regiment: The Manitoba Regiment: 2nd Canadian Infantry Battalion CEF: 3rd Canadian Infantry Battalion CEF: 10th Canadian Infantry Battalion CEF: 21st Canadian Infantry Battalion CEF: 25th Canadian Infantry Battalion CEF: 27th Canadian Infantry Battalion CEF: 29th Canadian Pioneer Battalion CEF: 38th Canadian Infantry Battalion CEF: 52nd Canadian Infantry Battalion CEF: 2nd Canadian Pioneer Battalion CEF: 67th Canadian (Pioneer) Battalion CEF: 107th Canadian Pioneer Battalion CEF: 123rd Canadian Pioneer Battalion CEF: 124th Canadian Pioneer Battalion CEF

1930 1st Hussars: 19th Alberta Dragoons: The Vancouver Regiment: 7th Canadian Infantry Battalion CEF
1931 The Manitoba Mounted Rifles: The Seaforth Highlanders of Canada: 72nd Canadian Infantry Battalion CEF
? 7th Hussars: 11th Hussars

44. **SCARPE 1917**
9th–14th April 1917
23rd–24th April 1917
and
3rd–4th May 1917
The Arras Offensive

1925 1st Life Guards: 2nd Life Guards: Royal Horse Guards (The Blues): The Queen's Bays (2nd Dragoon Guards): 3rd Dragoon Guards (Prince of Wales's): 4th Royal Irish Dragoon Guards: 5th Dragoon Guards (Princess Charlotte of Wales's): The Carabiniers (6th Dragoon Guards): 1st The Royal Dragoons: The Royal Scots Greys (2nd Dragoons): 3rd The King's Own Hussars: 4th Queen's Own Hussars: 5th Royal Irish Lancers: 9th Queen's Royal Lancers: 10th Royal Hussars (Prince of Wales's Own): 11th Hussars (Prince Albert's Own): 12th Royal Lancers (Prince of Wales's): 16th The Queen's Lancers: 18th Royal Hussars (Queen Mary's Own): 20th Hussars: Northamptonshire Yeomanry (Dragoons): Oxfordshire Yeomanry (Queen's Own Oxfordshire Hussars): Honourable Artillery Company: The Royal Scots (The Royal Regiment): The Queen's Royal Regiment (West Surrey): The Buffs (East Kent Regiment): The King's Own Royal Regiment (Lancaster): The Northumberland

Fusiliers: The Royal Warwickshire Regiment: The Royal Fusiliers (City of London Regiment): The King's Regiment (Liverpool): The Norfolk Regiment: The Lincolnshire Regiment: The Devonshire Regiment: The Suffolk Regiment: The Somerset Light Infantry (Prince Albert's): The West Yorkshire Regiment (The Prince of Wales's Own): The East Yorkshire Regiment: The Bedfordshire and Hertfordshire Regiment: The Green Howards (Alexandra, Princess of Wales's Own Yorkshire Regiment): The Lancashire Fusiliers: The Royal Scots Fusiliers: The Cheshire Regiment: The Royal Welch Fusiliers: The South Wales Borderers: The King's Own Scottish Borderers: The Cameronians (Scottish Rifles): The Royal Inniskilling Fusiliers: The Gloucestershire Regiment: The Worcestershire Regiment: The East Lancashire Regiment: The East Surrey Regiment: The Duke of Cornwall's Light Infantry: The Duke of Wellington's Regiment (West Riding): The Border Regiment: The Royal Sussex Regiment: The Hampshire Regiment: The South Staffordshire Regiment: The Dorsetshire Regiment: The Prince of Wales's Volunteers (South Lancashire): The Black Watch (Royal Highlanders): The Oxfordshire and Buckinghamshire Light Infantry: The Essex Regiment: The Sherwood Foresters (Nottinghamshire and Derbyshire Regiment): The Loyal Regiment (North Lancashire): The Northamptonshire Regiment: The Royal Berkshire Regiment (Princess Charlotte of Wales's): The Queen's Own Royal West Kent Regiment: The King's Own Yorkshire Light Infantry: The King's Shropshire Light Infantry: The Middlesex Regiment (Duke of Cambridge's Own): The King's Royal Rifle Corps: The Wiltshire Regiment (Duke of Edinburgh's): The Manchester Regiment: The North Staffordshire Regiment (The Prince of Wales's): The York and Lancaster Regiment: The Durham Light Infantry: The Highland Light Infantry (City of Glasgow Regiment): The Seaforth Highlanders (Ross-shire Buffs, The Duke of Albany's): The Gordon Highlanders: The Queen's Own Cameron Highlanders: The Royal Irish Fusiliers (Princess Victoria's): The Argyll and Sutherland Highlanders (Princess Louise's): The Royal Dublin Fusiliers: The Rifle Brigade (Prince Consort's Own): The Monmouthshire Regiment: 1st City of London Regiment (The Royal Fusiliers): 2nd City of London Regiment (The Royal Fusiliers): 3rd City of London Regiment (The Royal Fusiliers): 4th City of London Regiment (The Royal Fusiliers): 5th City of London Regiment (London Rifle Brigade): 9th London Regiment (Queen Victoria's Rifles): 12th London Regiment (Rangers): 13th London Regiment (Princess Louise's Kensington Regiment): 14th London Regiment (London Scottish): 16th London Regiment (Queen's Westminster Rifles): Essex Yeomanry (Dragoons): The Leicestershire Yeomanry (Prince Albert's Own) (Hussars): The North Somerset Yeomanry (Dragoons)

1925 The Royal Newfoundland Regiment

1926 74th (Eastern Province) Siege Battery, Royal Garrison Artillery: 125th (Transvaal) Siege Battery, Royal Garrison Artillery: 1st South African Infantry (Cape of Good Hope Regiment): 2nd South African Infantry (Natal and Orange Free State Regiment): 3rd South African Infantry (Transvaal and Rhodesian Regiment): 4th South African Infantry (South African Scottish Regiment): 1st South African Field Ambulance

1929 Royal 22e Regiment: The Queen's Own Rifles of Canada: The Victoria Rifles of Canada: The Royal Highlanders of Canada: The Royal Grenadiers: The Royal Hamilton Light Infantry: The Canadian Fusiliers (City of London Regiment): The Dufferin Rifles of Canada: The Peterborough Rangers: The Saint John Fusiliers: The 48th Regiment (Highlanders): The Regina Rifle Regiment: The Colchester and Hants Regiment: The Canadian Scottish Regiment: The Royal Montreal Regiment: The Toronto Regiment: The South Alberta Regiment: The North Alberta Regiment: 1st Canadian Infantry Battalion CEF: 4th Canadian Infantry Battalion CEF: 13th Canadian Infantry Battalion CEF: 14th Canadian Infantry Battalion CEF: 15th Canadian Infantry Battalion CEF: 16th Canadian Infantry Battalion CEF: 24th Canadian Infantry Battalion CEF: 26th Canadian Infantry Battalion CEF: 28th Canadian Infantry Battalion CEF: 31st Canadian Infantry Battalion CEF: The Manitoba Regiment: 2nd Canadian Infantry Battalion CEF: 3rd Canadian Infantry Battalion CEF: 25th Canadian Infantry Battalion CEF: 27th Canadian Infantry Battalion CEF: 29th Canadian Infantry Battalion CEF: 2nd Canadian Pioneer Battalion CEF: 107th Canadian Pioneer Battalion CEF: 123rd Canadian Pioneer Battalion CEF

1930 The Vancouver Regiment

45. **ARLEUX**
28th–29th April 1917
The Arras Offensive

1925 — Honourable Artillery Company: The Royal Scots (The Royal Regiment): The King's Own Royal Regiment (Lancaster): The Northumberland Fusiliers: The Royal Warwickshire Regiment: The Royal Fusiliers (City of London Regiment): The King's Regiment (Liverpool): The Norfolk Regiment: The Lincolnshire Regiment: The Bedfordshire and Hertfordshire Regiment: The Suffolk Regiment: The Somerset Light Infantry (Prince Albert's): The East Yorkshire Regiment: The Bedfordshire and Hertfordshire Regiment: The Lancashire Fusiliers: The Royal Scots Fusiliers: The Royal Welch Fusiliers: The King's Own Scottish Borderers: The Cameronians (Scottish Rifles): The Worcestershire Regiment: The East Lancashire Regiment: The Duke of Cornwall's Light Infantry: The Duke of Wellington's Regiment (West Riding): The Royal Sussex Regiment: The South Staffordshire Regiment: The Black Watch (Royal Highlanders): The Oxfordshire and Buckinghamshire Light Infantry: The Essex Regiment: The Loyal Regiment (North Lancashire): The Northamptonshire Regiment: The Royal Berkshire Regiment (Princess Charlotte of Wales's): The King's Shropshire Light Infantry: The Middlesex Regiment (Duke of Cambridge's Own): The King's Royal Rifle Corps: The North Staffordshire Regiment (The Prince of Wales's): The York and Lancaster Regiment: The Durham Light Infantry: The Highland Light Infantry (City of Glasgow Regiment): The Seaforth Highlanders (Ross-shire Buffs, The Duke of Albany's): The Gordon Highlanders: The Queen's Own Cameron Highlanders: The Argyll and Sutherland Highlanders (Princess Louise's): The Royal Dublin Fusiliers: The Rifle Brigade (Prince Consort's Own)

1926 — 72nd (Griqualand West) Siege Battery, Royal Garrison Artillery: 73rd (Cape) Siege Battery, Royal Garrison Artillery

1929 — Royal 22e Regiment: The Queen's Own Rifles of Canada: The Victoria Rifles of Canada: The Royal Highlanders of Canada: The Royal Grenadiers: The Canadian Fusiliers (City of London Regiment): The Dufferin Rifles of Canada: The Peterborough Rangers: The Saint John Fusiliers: The Winnipeg Rifles: The 48th Regiment (Highlanders): 1st British Columbia Regiment (Duke of Connaught's Own): The Colchester and Hants Regiment: The Calgary Highlanders: The Winnipeg Light Infantry: The Saskatoon Light Infantry: The Canadian Scottish Regiment: The Royal Montreal Regiment: The Toronto Regiment: The South Alberta Regiment: The North Alberta Regiment: 1st Canadian Infantry Battalion CEF: 4th Canadian Infantry Battalion CEF: 5th Canadian Infantry Battalion CEF: 8th Canadian Infantry Battalion CEF: 13th Canadian Infantry Battalion CEF: 14th Canadian Infantry Battalion CEF: 15th Canadian Infantry Battalion CEF: 16th Canadian Infantry Battalion CEF: 24th Canadian Infantry Battalion CEF: 26th Canadian Infantry Battalion CEF: 31st Canadian Infantry Battalion CEF: 42nd Canadian Infantry Battalion CEF: Princess Patricia's Canadian Light Infantry: The Manitoba Regiment: 2nd Canadian Infantry Battalion CEF: 3rd Canadian Infantry Battalion CEF: 10th Canadian Infantry Battalion CEF: 25th Canadian Infantry Battalion CEF: 27th Canadian Infantry Battalion CEF: 2nd Canadian Pioneer Battalion CEF: 67th Canadian (Pioneer) Battalion CEF: 107th Canadian Pioneer Battalion CEF: 123rd Canadian Pioneer Battalion CEF

1930 — 7th Canadian Infantry Battalion CEF

46. **OPPY**
28th June 1917
Capture of Oppy Wood

1925 — The Royal Warwickshire Regiment: The Norfolk Regiment: The East Yorkshire Regiment: The Bedfordshire and Hertfordshire Regiment: The Cheshire Regiment: The East Lancashire Regiment: The Queen's Own Royal West Kent Regiment: The York and Lancaster Regiment

1926 — 72nd (Griqualand West) Siege Battery, Royal Garrison Artillery: 73rd (Cape) Siege Battery, Royal Garrison Artillery: 74th (Eastern Province) Siege Battery, Royal Garrison Artillery: 125th (Transvaal) Siege Battery, Royal Garrison Artillery

47. **BULLECOURT**
11th April 1917
and
3rd–17th May 1917
Flanking Operations round Bullecourt

1925 — Honourable Artillery Company: The Queen's Royal Regiment (West Surrey): The Royal Warwickshire Regiment: The Devonshire Regiment: The West Yorkshire Regiment (The Prince of Wales's Own): The Royal Welch Fusiliers: The Duke of Wellington's Regiment (West Riding): The Border Regiment: The South Staffordshire Regiment: The Manchester Regiment: The Gordon Highlanders: 1st City of London Regiment (The Royal Fusiliers): 2nd City of London Regiment (The Royal Fusiliers): 3rd City of London Regiment (The Royal Fusiliers): 4th City of London Regiment (The Royal Fusiliers): 5th City of

	1926	London Regiment (London Rifle Brigade): 8th (City of London) Battalion, The London Regiment (Post Office Rifles): 11th London Regiment (Finsbury Rifles)
	1927	71st (Transvaal) Siege Battery, Royal Garrison Artillery 1st Battalion: 2nd Battalion: 3rd Battalion: 4th Battalion: 5th Battalion: 6th Battalion: 7th Battalion: 8th Battalion: 9th Battalion: 10th Battalion: 11th Battalion: 12th Battalion: 13th Battalion: 14th Battalion: 15th Battalion: 16th Battalion: 17th Battalion: 18th Battalion: 19th Battalion: 20th Battalion: 21st Battalion: 22nd Battalion: 23rd Battalion: 24th Battalion: 25th Battalion: 26th Battalion: 27th Battalion: 28th Battalion: 29th Battalion: 30th Battalion: 31st Battalion: 32nd Battalion: 45th Battalion: 46th Battalion: 47th Battalion: 48th Battalion: 49th Battalion: 50th Battalion: 51st Battalion: 52nd Battalion: 53rd Battalion: 54th Battalion: 55th Battalion: 56th Battalion: 57th Battalion: 58th Battalion: 59th Battalion: 60th Battalion
48.	**HILL 70** [1] 15th–25th August 1917 Flanking Operations towards Lens	
	1925	The West Yorkshire Regiment (The Prince of Wales's Own): The South Staffordshire Regiment: The King's Shropshire Light Infantry: The Durham Light Infantry
	1926	72nd (Griqualand West) Siege Battery, Royal Garrison Artillery: 125th (Transvaal) Siege Battery, Royal Garrison Artillery
	1929	The Royal Canadian Regiment: Royal 22e Regiment: The Mississauga Horse: The Saskatchewan Mounted Rifles: The British Columbia Dragoons: The Eastern Townships Mounted Rifles: The Canadian Grenadier Guards: The Queen's Own Rifles of Canada: The Victoria Rifles of Canada: The Royal Highlanders of Canada: The Royal Grenadiers: The Royal Hamilton Light Infantry: The Princess of Wales' Own Regiment: The Canadian Fusiliers (City of London Regiment): The Dufferin Rifles of Canada: The Peterborough Rangers: The Carleton Light Infantry: The Saint John Fusiliers: The Winnipeg Rifles: The Essex Scottish: The 48th Regiment (Highlanders): 1st British Columbia Regiment (Duke of Connaught's Own): The Argyll and Sutherland Highlanders of Canada (Princess Louise's): The Lake Superior Regiment: The Regina Rifle Regiment: The Winnipeg Grenadiers: The Queen's Own Cameron Highlanders of Canada: The Colchester and Hants Regiment: The Calgary Highlanders: The Calgary Regiment: The Westminster Regiment: The Winnipeg Light Infantry: The Saskatoon Light Infantry: The Canadian Scottish Regiment: The King's Own Rifles of Canada: The Kootenay Regiment: The Royal Montreal Regiment: The Toronto Regiment: The Queen's Rangers, 1st American Regiment: The South Alberta Regiment: The North Alberta Regiment: The Edmonton Regiment: The Toronto Scottish Regiment: 1st Motor Machine Gun Brigade: 1st Canadian Mounted Rifles Battalion CEF: 2nd Canadian Mounted Rifles Battalion CEF: 4th Canadian Mounted Rifles Battalion CEF: 5th Canadian Mounted Rifles Battalion CEF: 1st Canadian Infantry Battalion CEF: 4th Canadian Infantry Battalion CEF: 5th Canadian Infantry Battalion CEF: 8th Canadian Infantry Battalion CEF: 13th Canadian Infantry Battalion CEF: 14th Canadian Infantry Battalion CEF: 15th Canadian Infantry Battalion CEF: 16th Canadian Infantry Battalion CEF: 18th Canadian Infantry Battalion CEF: 19th Canadian Infantry Battalion CEF: 20th Canadian Infantry Battalion CEF: 24th Canadian Infantry Battalion CEF: 26th Canadian Infantry Battalion CEF: 28th Canadian Infantry Battalion CEF: 31st Canadian Infantry Battalion CEF: 42nd Canadian Infantry Battalion CEF: 43rd Canadian Infantry Battalion CEF: 44th Canadian Infantry Battalion CEF: 46th Canadian Infantry Battalion CEF: 47th Canadian Infantry Battalion CEF: 49th Canadian Infantry Battalion CEF: 50th Canadian Infantry Battalion CEF: 54th Canadian Infantry Battalion CEF: 58th Canadian Infantry Battalion CEF: 75th Canadian Infantry Battalion CEF: 87th Canadian Infantry Battalion CEF: 102nd Canadian Infantry Battalion CEF: 116th Canadian Infantry Battalion CEF: 1st Canadian Motor Machine Gun Brigade CEF: Princess Patricia's Canadian Light Infantry: The North British Columbia Regiment: The Ontario Regiment: The Manitoba Regiment: 2nd Canadian Infantry Battalion CEF: 3rd Canadian Infantry Battalion CEF: 10th Canadian Infantry Battalion CEF: 21st Canadian Infantry Battalion CEF: 25th Canadian Infantry Battalion CEF: 27th Canadian Infantry Battalion CEF: 29th Canadian Infantry Battalion CEF: 52nd Canadian Infantry Battalion CEF: 2nd Canadian Pioneer Battalion CEF: 107th Canadian Pioneer Battalion CEF: 123rd Canadian Pioneer Battalion CEF: 124th Canadian Pioneer Battalion CEF
	1930	The Governor General's Body Guard: The Governor General's Foot Guards: The Halifax Rifles: The Royal Rifles of Canada: Les Voltigeurs de Quebec: The Argyll Light Infantry: The Hastings and Prince Edward Regiment: The Lincoln Regiment: The

Oxford Rifles: The York Rangers: The Middlesex Light Infantry: The Highland Light Infantry of Canada: The Grey Regiment: The Simcoe Foresters: The Peel and Dufferin Regiment: The Halton Rifles: The Haldimand Rifles: The Norfolk Regiment of Canada: The Northumberland Regiment: The Lincoln and Welland Regiment: The Victoria and Haliburton Regiment: The Frontenac Regiment: The Sherbrooke Regiment: The Stormont Dundas and Glengarry Highlanders: Les Carabiniers Mont-Royal: The Princess Louise Fusiliers: The York Regiment: The Annapolis Regiment: The North Shore (New Brunswick) Regiment: The New Brunswick Rangers: The Wentworth Regiment: The Northern Pioneers: The Kenora Light Infantry: The Manitoba Rangers: The Edmonton Fusiliers: The Rocky Mountain Rangers: The Prince Albert Volunteers: The Irish Fusiliers of Canada: The Sault Ste Marie Regiment: The Irish Canadian Rangers: The Vancouver Regiment: The Irish Regiment: The Weyburn Regiment: The Saskatchewan Border Regiment: The Yorkton Regiment: 7th Canadian Infantry Battalion CEF

1931   14th Canadian Light Horse: The Manitoba Mounted Rifles: The South Alberta Horse
?   7th Hussars: 11th Hussars: McGill University Contingent
1961   Le Regiment de Maisonneuve: 41st Battalion CEF

¹ COTE 70 taken into use by French-speaking Canadian units 1958.

1925   North Irish Horse: Hampshire (Carabiniers) (Dragoons): The Queen's Royal Regiment (West Surrey): The Buffs (East Kent Regiment): The King's Own Royal Regiment (Lancaster): The Northumberland Fusiliers: The Royal Warwickshire Regiment: The Royal Fusiliers (City of London Regiment): The Lincolnshire Regiment: The West Yorkshire Regiment (The Prince of Wales's Own): The East Yorkshire Regiment: The Bedfordshire and Hertfordshire Regiment: The Royal Irish Regiment: The Green Howards (Alexandra, Princess of Wales's Own Yorkshire Regiment): The Lancashire Fusiliers: The Royal Scots Fusiliers: The Cheshire Regiment: The Royal Welch Fusiliers: The South Wales Borderers: The Royal Inniskilling Fusiliers: The Gloucestershire Regiment: The Worcestershire Regiment: The East Lancashire Regiment: The East Surrey Regiment: The Duke of Wellington's Regiment (West Riding): The Border Regiment: The Royal Sussex Regiment: The Hampshire Regiment: The South Staffordshire Regiment: The Dorsetshire Regiment: The Prince of Wales's Volunteers (South Lancashire): The Welch Regiment: The Sherwood Foresters (Nottinghamshire and Derbyshire Regiment): The Loyal Regiment (North Lancashire): The Northamptonshire Regiment: The Queen's Own Royal West Kent Regiment: The King's Own Yorkshire Light Infantry: The Middlesex Regiment (Duke of Cambridge's Own): The King's Royal Rifle Corps: The Wiltshire Regiment (Duke of Edinburgh's): The Manchester Regiment: The North Staffordshire Regiment (The Prince of Wales's): The York and Lancaster Regiment: The Durham Light Infantry: The Royal Ulster Rifles: The Royal Irish Fusiliers (Princess Victoria's): The Connaught Rangers: The Prince of Wales's Leinster Regiment (Royal Canadians): The Royal Munster Fusiliers: The Royal Dublin Fusiliers: The Rifle Brigade (Prince Consort's Own): 6th City of London Regiment (City of London Rifles): 7th City of London Regiment: 8th (City of London) Battalion, The London Regiment (Post Office Rifles): 15th (County of London) Battalion, The London Regiment (Prince of Wales's Own), Civil Service Rifles): 17th London Regiment (Poplar and Stepney Rifles): 8th London Regiment (London Irish Rifles): 19th London Regiment (St Pancras): 20th London Regiment (The Queen's Own): 21st London Regiment (First Surrey Rifles): 22nd London Regiment (The Queen's): 23rd London Regiment: 24th London Regiment (The Queen's): The British West Indies Regiment

        74th (Eastern Province) Siege Battery, Royal Garrison Artillery

1926   The Auckland Regiment (Countess of Ranfurly's Own): The Hauraki Regiment: The North Auckland Regiment: The Waikato
1926   Regiment: The Wellington Regiment: The Wellington West Coast Regiment: The Hawke's Bay Regiment: The Taranaki Regiment: The Canterbury Regiment: The Nelson, Marlborough, and West Coast Regiment: The Otago Regiment: The Southland Regiment

1927   4th Light Horse Regiment: 13th Battalion: 14th Battalion: 15th Battalion: 16th Battalion: 33rd Battalion: 34th Battalion: 35th

49.   **MESSINES 1917**
        7th–14th June 1917
        The Flanders Offensive

Battalion: 36th Battalion: 37th Battalion: 38th Battalion: 39th Battalion: 40th Battalion: 41st Battalion: 42nd Battalion: 43rd Battalion: 44th Battalion: 45th Battalion: 46th Battalion: 47th Battalion: 48th Battalion: 49th Battalion: 50th Battalion: 51st Battalion: 52nd Battalion

The Otago Mounted Rifles

Royal Tank Regiment

1928
1958

50. **YPRES 1917**
31st July–10th November 1917
The The Flanders Offensive

1925

1st Life Guards: 2nd Life Guards: Royal Horse Guards (The Blues): North Irish Horse: King Edward's Horse (The King's Oversea Dominions Regiment): Queen's Own Royal Glasgow Yeomanry (Dragoons): Lancashire Hussars Yeomanry: The Duke of Lancaster's Own Yeomanry (Dragoons): Westmorland and Cumberland Yeomanry (Hussars): The Royal Wiltshire Yeomanry (Prince of Wales's Own) (Hussars): Honourable Artillery Company: Grenadier Guards: Coldstream Guards: Scots Guards: Irish Guards: Welsh Guards: The Royal Scots (The Royal Regiment): The Queen's Royal Regiment (West Surrey): The Buffs (East Kent Regiment): The King's Own Royal Regiment (Lancaster): The Northumberland Fusiliers: The Royal Warwickshire Regiment: The Royal Fusiliers (City of London Regiment): The King's Regiment (Liverpool): The Norfolk Regiment: The Lincolnshire Regiment: The Devonshire Regiment: The Suffolk Regiment: The Somerset Light Infantry (Prince Albert's): The West Yorkshire Regiment (The Prince of Wales's Own): The East Yorkshire Regiment: The Bedfordshire and Hertfordshire Regiment: The Leicestershire Regiment: The Royal Irish Regiment: The Green Howards (Alexandra, Princess of Wales's Own Yorkshire Regiment): The Lancashire Fusiliers: The Royal Scots Fusiliers: The Cheshire Regiment: The Royal Welch Fusiliers: The South Wales Borderers: The King's Own Scottish Borderers: The Cameronians (Scottish Rifles): The Royal Inniskilling Fusiliers: The Gloucestershire Regiment: The Worcestershire Regiment: The East Lancashire Regiment: The East Surrey Regiment: The Duke of Cornwall's Light Infantry: The Duke of Wellington's Regiment (West Riding): The Border Regiment: The Royal Sussex Regiment: The Hampshire Regiment: The South Staffordshire Regiment: The Dorsetshire Regiment: The Prince of Wales's Volunteers (South Lancashire): The Welch Regiment: The Black Watch (Royal Highlanders): The Oxfordshire and Buckinghamshire Light Infantry: The Essex Regiment: The Sherwood Foresters (Nottinghamshire and Derbyshire Regiment): The Loyal Regiment (North Lancashire): The Northamptonshire Regiment: The Royal Berkshire Regiment (Princess Charlotte of Wales's): The Queen's Own Royal West Kent Regiment: The King's Own Yorkshire Light Infantry: The King's Shropshire Light Infantry: The Middlesex Regiment (Duke of Cambridge's Own): The King's Royal Rifle Corps: The Wiltshire Regiment (Duke of Edinburgh's): The Manchester Regiment: The North Staffordshire Regiment (The Prince of Wales's): The York and Lancaster Regiment: The Durham Light Infantry: The Highland Light Infantry (City of Glasgow Regiment): The Seaforth Highlanders (Ross-shire Buffs, The Duke of Albany's): The Gordon Highlanders: The Queen's Own Cameron Highlanders: The Royal Ulster Rifles: The Royal Irish Fusiliers (Princess Victoria's): The Connaught Rangers: The Argyll and Sutherland Highlanders (Princess Louise's): The Prince of Wales's Leinster Regiment (Royal Canadians): The Royal Munster Fusiliers: The Royal Dublin Fusiliers: The Rifle Brigade (Prince Consort's Own): The Monmouthshire Regiment: The Cambridgeshire Regiment: 1st City of London Regiment (The Royal Fusiliers): 2nd City of London Regiment (The Royal Fusiliers): 3rd City of London Regiment (The Royal Fusiliers): 4th City of London Regiment (The Royal Fusiliers): 5th City of London Regiment (London Rifle Brigade): 6th City of London Regiment (City of London Rifles): 7th City of London Regiment: 8th (City of London) Battalion, The London Regiment (Post Office Rifles): 9th London Regiment (Queen Victoria's Rifles): 10th London Regiment (Hackney): 11th London Regiment (Finsbury Rifles): 12th London Regiment (Rangers): 13th London Regiment (Princess Louise's Kensington Regiment): 14th London Regiment (London Scottish): 15th (County of London) Battalion, The London Regiment (Prince of Wales's Own, Civil Service Rifles): 16th London Regiment (Queen's Westminster Rifles): 17th London Regiment (Poplar and Stepney Rifles): 18th London Regiment (London Irish Rifles): 19th London Regiment (St Pancras): 20th London Regiment (The Queen's Own): 21st London Regiment (First Surrey Rifles): 22nd London

Regiment (The Queen's); 24th London Regiment (The Queen's); 28th London Regiment (Artists' Rifles); The Hertfordshire Regiment: The British West Indies Regiment: Royal Guernsey Militia (Light Infantry)

1925
1926 The Royal Newfoundland Regiment

71st (Transvaal) Siege Battery, Royal Garrison Artillery; 72nd (Griqualand West) Siege Battery, Royal Garrison Artillery: 73rd (Cape) Siege Battery, Royal Garrison Artillery: 74th (Eastern Province) Siege Battery, Royal Garrison Artillery: 75th (Natal) Siege Battery, Royal Garrison Artillery; 125th (Transvaal) Siege Battery, Royal Garrison Artillery: 1st South African Infantry (Cape of Good Hope Regiment); 2nd South African Infantry (Natal and Orange Free State Regiment): 3rd South African Infantry (Transvaal and Rhodesian Regiment): 4th South African Infantry (South African Scottish Regiment); 1st South African Field Ambulance

1926 The Auckland Regiment (Countess of Ranfurly's Own): The Hauraki Regiment: The North Auckland Regiment: The Waikato Regiment: The Wellington Regiment: The Wellington West Coast Regiment: The Hawke's Bay Regiment: The Taranaki Regiment: The Canterbury Regiment: The Nelson, Marlborough, and West Coast Regiment: The Otago Regiment: The Southland Regiment

1927 4th Light Horse Regiment: 13th Light Horse Regiment: 1st Battalion: 2nd Battalion: 3rd Battalion: 4th Battalion: 5th Battalion: 6th Battalion: 7th Battalion: 8th Battalion: 9th Battalion: 10th Battalion: 11th Battalion: 12th Battalion: 13th Battalion: 14th Battalion: 15th Battalion: 16th Battalion: 17th Battalion: 18th Battalion: 19th Battalion: 20th Battalion: 21st Battalion: 22nd Battalion: 23rd Battalion: 24th Battalion: 25th Battalion: 26th Battalion: 27th Battalion: 28th Battalion: 29th Battalion: 30th Battalion: 31st Battalion: 32nd Battalion: 33rd Battalion: 34th Battalion: 35th Battalion: 36th Battalion: 37th Battalion: 38th Battalion: 39th Battalion: 40th Battalion: 41st Battalion: 42nd Battalion: 43rd Battalion: 44th Battalion: 45th Battalion: 46th Battalion: 47th Battalion: 48th Battalion: 49th Battalion: 50th Battalion: 51st Battalion: 52nd Battalion: 53rd Battalion: 54th Battalion: 55th Battalion: 56th Battalion: 57th Battalion: 58th Battalion: 59th Battalion: 60th Battalion

1928
1929 The Otago Mounted Rifles

The Royal Canadian Regiment: Royal 22e Regiment: The Mississauga Horse: The Saskatchewan Mounted Rifles: The British Columbia Dragoons: The Eastern Townships Mounted Rifles: The Canadian Grenadier Guards: The Queen's Own Rifles of Canada: The Victoria Rifles of Canada: The Royal Highlanders of Canada: The Royal Grenadiers: The Royal Hamilton Light Infantry: The Princess of Wales' Own Regiment: The Canadian Fusiliers (City of London Regiment): The Dufferin Rifles of Canada: The Peterborough Rangers: The Carleton Light Infantry: The Cape Breton Highlanders: The Saint John Fusiliers: The Ottawa Highlanders: The Winnipeg Rifles: The Essex Scottish: The 48th Regiment (Highlanders): 1st British Columbia Regiment (Duke of Connaught's Own): The Argyll and Sutherland Highlanders of Canada (Princess Louise's): The Lake Superior Regiment: The Regina Rifle Regiment: The Winnipeg Grenadiers: The Queen's Own Cameron Highlanders of Canada: The Colchester and Hant Regiment: The Calgary Highlanders: The Calgary Regiment: The Westminster Regiment: The Winnipeg Light Infantry: The Saskatoon Light Infantry: The Canadian Scottish Regiment: The King's Own Rifles of Canada: The Kootenay Regiment: The Royal Montreal Regiment: The Toronto Regiment: The Queen's Rangers, 1st American Regiment: The South Alberta Regiment: The North Alberta Regiment: The Edmonton Regiment: The Toronto Scottish Regiment: 1st Motor Machine Gun Brigade: 1st Canadian Mounted Rifles Battalion CEF: 2nd Canadian Mounted Rifles Battalion CEF: 4th Canadian Mounted Rifles Battalion CEF: 5th Canadian Mounted Rifles Battalion CEF: 1st Canadian Infantry Battalion CEF: 4th Canadian Infantry Battalion CEF: 5th Canadian Infantry Battalion CEF: 8th Canadian Infantry Battalion CEF: 13th Canadian Infantry Battalion CEF: 14th Canadian Infantry Battalion CEF: 15th Canadian Infantry Battalion CEF: 16th Canadian Infantry Battalion CEF: 18th Canadian Infantry Battalion CEF: 19th Canadian Infantry Battalion CEF: 20th Canadian Infantry Battalion CEF: 24th Canadian Infantry Battalion CEF: 26th Canadian Infantry Battalion CEF: 28th Canadian Infantry Battalion CEF: 31st Canadian Infantry Battalion CEF: 42nd Canadian Infantry Battalion CEF: 43rd Canadian Infantry Battalion CEF: 44th

Canadian Infantry Battalion CEF: 46th Canadian Infantry Battalion CEF: 47th Canadian Infantry Battalion CEF: 49th Canadian Infantry Battalion CEF: 50th Canadian Infantry Battalion CEF: 54th Canadian Infantry Battalion CEF: 58th Canadian Infantry Battalion CEF: 75th Canadian Infantry Battalion CEF: 78th Canadian Infantry Battalion CEF: 85th Canadian Infantry Battalion CEF: 87th Canadian Infantry Battalion CEF: 102nd Canadian Infantry Battalion CEF: 116th Canadian Infantry Battalion CEF: 1st Canadian Motor Machine Gun Brigade CEF: Princess Patricia's Canadian Light Infantry: The North British Columbia Regiment: The Ontario Regiment: The Manitoba Regiment: 2nd Canadian Infantry Battalion CEF: 3rd Canadian Infantry Battalion CEF: 10th Canadian Infantry Battalion CEF: 21st Canadian Infantry Battalion CEF: 25th Canadian Infantry Battalion CEF: 27th Canadian Infantry Battalion CEF: 29th Canadian Infantry Battalion CEF: 38th Canadian Infantry Battalion CEF: 52nd Canadian Infantry Battalion CEF: 2nd Canadian Pioneer Battalion CEF: 107th Canadian Pioneer Battalion CEF: 123rd Canadian Pioneer Battalion CEF: 124th Canadian Pioneer Battalion CEF

1930   The Governor General's Body Guard: The Prince Edward Island Light Horse: The Governor General's Foot Guards: The Halifax Rifles: The Royal Rifles of Canada: Les Voltigeurs de Quebec: The Argyll Light Infantry: The Hastings and Prince Edward Regiment: The Lincoln Regiment: The Oxford Rifles: The York Rangers: The Elgin Regiment: The Middlesex Light Infantry: The Lambton Regiment: The Highland Light Infantry of Canada: The Grey Regiment: The Simcoe Foresters: The Peel and Dufferin Regiment: The Halton Rifles: The Haldimand Rifles: The Northumberland Regiment: The Lanark and Renfrew Scottish Regiment: The Lincoln and Welland Regiment: The Victoria and Haliburton Regiment: The Frontenac Regiment: The Sherbrooke Regiment: The Stormont Dundas and Glengarry Highlanders: Les Carabiniers Mont-Royal: The Princess Louise Fusiliers: The York Regiment: The Annapolis Regiment: The North Shore (New Brunswick) Regiment: The New Brunswick Rangers: The Lunenburg Regiment: The Cumberland Highlanders: The Wentworth Regiment: The Prince Edward Island Highlanders: The Kent Regiment: The Northern Pioneers: The Kenora Light Infantry: The Manitoba Rangers: The Edmonton Fusiliers: The Rocky Mountain Rangers: The Prince Albert Volunteers: The Irish Fusiliers of Canada: The Sault Ste Marie Regiment: The Irish Canadian Rangers: The Vancouver Regiment: The Irish Regiment: The Yorkton Regiment: 7th Canadian Infantry Battalion CEF: 127th Canadian Infantry Battalion CEF

14th Canadian Light Horse: The Manitoba Mounted Rifles: The Seaforth Highlanders of Canada: 72nd Canadian Infantry Battalion CEF

1931   1st Canadian Pioneer Battalion CEF

?   7th Hussars: 11th Hussars: McGill University Contingent

1937   The Liverpool Scottish, The Queen's Own Cameron Highlanders (TA)

1951   42nd Royal Tank Regiment

1958   Royal Tank Regiment

1961   Le Regiment de Maisonneuve: 41st Battalion CEF

51.   PILCKEM
31st July–2nd August 1917
The Flanders Offensive

1925   North Irish Horse: King Edward's Horse (The King's Oversea Dominions Regiment): The Lancashire Hussars Yeomanry: Honourable Artillery Company: Grenadier Guards: Coldstream Guards: Scots Guards: Irish Guards: Welsh Guards: The Royal Scots (The Royal Regiment): The Queen's Royal Regiment (West Surrey): The Buffs (East Kent Regiment): The King's Own Royal Regiment (Lancaster): The Northumberland Fusiliers: The Royal Warwickshire Regiment: The Royal Fusiliers (City of London Regiment): The King's Regiment (Liverpool): The Norfolk Regiment: The Lincolnshire Regiment: The Devonshire Regiment: The Suffolk Regiment: The West Yorkshire Regiment (The Prince of Wales's Own): The East Yorkshire Regiment: The Bedfordshire and Hertfordshire Regiment: The Green Howards (Alexandra, Princess of Wales's Own Yorkshire Regiment): The Lancashire Fusiliers: The Royal Scots Fusiliers: The Cheshire Regiment: The Royal Welch Fusiliers: The South Wales Borderers: The King's Own Scottish Borderers: The Cameronians (Scottish Rifles): The Royal Inniskilling Fusiliers: The Gloucestershire Regiment: The Worcestershire Regiment: The East Lancashire Regiment: The East Surrey Regiment: The Border Regiment: The Royal Sussex Regiment: The Hampshire Regiment: The Prince of Wales's

Volunteers (South Lancashire): The Welch Regiment: The Black Watch (Royal Highlanders): The Essex Regiment: The Sherwood Foresters (Nottinghamshire and Derbyshire Regiment): The Loyal Regiment (North Lancashire): The Northamptonshire Regiment: The Royal Berkshire Regiment (Princess Charlotte of Wales's): The Queen's Own Royal West Kent Regiment: The Middlesex Regiment (Duke of Cambridge's Own): The King's Royal Rifle Corps: The Wiltshire Regiment (Duke of Edinburgh's): The Manchester Regiment: The North Staffordshire Regiment (The Prince of Wales's): The Durham Light Infantry: The Highland Light Infantry (City of Glasgow Regiment): The Seaforth Highlanders (Ross-shire Buffs, The Duke of Albany's): The Gordon Highlanders: The Queen's Own Cameron Highlanders: The Royal Ulster Rifles: The Argyll and Sutherland Highlanders (Princess Louise's): The Prince of Wales's Leinster Regiment (Royal Canadians): The Rifle Brigade (Prince Consort's Own): The Monmouthshire Regiment: The Cambridgeshire Regiment: The Hertfordshire Regiment

1926 75th (Natal) Siege Battery, Royal Garrison Artillery
1930 The York Rangers: 127th Canadian Infantry Battalion CEF
1937 The Liverpool Scottish, The Queen's Own Cameron Highlanders (TA)

52. **LANGEMARCK 1917**
16th–18th August 1917
The Flanders Offensive

1925 The Royal Scots (The Royal Regiment): The Northumberland Fusiliers: The Royal Warwickshire Regiment: The Royal Fusiliers (City of London Regiment): The King's Regiment (Liverpool): The Norfolk Regiment: The Lincolnshire Regiment: The Devonshire Regiment: The Suffolk Regiment: The Somerset Light Infantry (Prince Albert's): The West Yorkshire Regiment (The Prince of Wales's Own): The East Yorkshire Regiment: The Bedfordshire and Hertfordshire Regiment: The Royal Irish Regiment: The Green Howards (Alexandra, Princess of Wales's Own Yorkshire Regiment): The Lancashire Fusiliers: The Cheshire Regiment: The Royal Welch Fusiliers: The South Wales Borderers: The King's Own Scottish Borderers: The Cameronians (Scottish Rifles): The Royal Inniskilling Fusiliers: The Gloucestershire Regiment: The Worcestershire Regiment: The East Lancashire Regiment: The East Surrey Regiment: The Duke of Cornwall's Light Infantry: The Duke of Wellington's Regiment (West Riding): The Border Regiment: The Royal Sussex Regiment: The Hampshire Regiment: The South Staffordshire Regiment: The Dorsetshire Regiment: The Prince of Wales's Volunteers (South Lancashire): The Welch Regiment: The Oxfordshire and Buckinghamshire Light Infantry: The Essex Regiment: The Sherwood Foresters (Nottinghamshire and Derbyshire Regiment): The Northamptonshire Regiment: The Royal Berkshire Regiment (Princess Charlotte of Wales's): The Queen's Own Royal West Kent Regiment: The King's Own Yorkshire Light Infantry: The King's Shropshire Light Infantry: The Middlesex Regiment (Duke of Cambridge's Own): The King's Royal Rifle Corps: The Manchester Regiment: The North Staffordshire Regiment (The Prince of Wales's): The York and Lancaster Regiment: The Durham Light Infantry: The Highland Light Infantry (City of Glasgow Regiment): The Royal Ulster Rifles: The Royal Irish Fusiliers (Princess Victoria's): The Connaught Rangers: The Prince of Wales's Leinster Regiment (Royal Canadians): The Royal Munster Fusiliers: The Royal Dublin Fusiliers: The Rifle Brigade (Prince Consort's Own): The Monmouthshire Regiment: 1st City of London Regiment (The Royal Fusiliers): 2nd City of London Regiment: 3rd City of London Regiment (The Royal Fusiliers): 4th City of London Regiment (The Royal Fusiliers): 5th City of London Regiment (London Rifle Brigade): 9th London Regiment (Queen Victoria's Rifles): 12th London Regiment (Rangers): 13th London Regiment (Princess Louise's Kensington Regiment): 14th London Regiment (London Scottish): 16th London Regiment (Queen's Westminster Rifles): 17th London Regiment (Poplar and Stepney Rifles): 18th London Regiment (London Irish Rifles): 19th London Regiment (St Pancras): 20th London Regiment (The Queen's Own)

1925 The Royal Newfoundland Regiment
1926 75th (Natal) Siege Battery, Royal Garrison Artillery
1930 The York Rangers: 127th Canadian Infantry Battalion CEF
1931 1st Canadian Pioneer Battalion CEF

53.	**MENIN ROAD** [1] 20th–25th September 1917 The Flanders Offensive	1925	Grenadier Guards: Coldstream Guards: The Royal Scots (The Royal Regiment): The Queen's Royal Regiment (West Surrey): The King's Own Royal Regiment (Lancaster): The Northumberland Fusiliers: The Royal Warwickshire Regiment: The Royal Fusiliers (City of London Regiment): The King's Regiment (Liverpool): The Lincolnshire Regiment: The Suffolk Regiment: The Somerset Light Infantry (Prince Albert's): The West Yorkshire Regiment (The Prince of Wales's Own): The East Yorkshire Regiment: The Green Howards (Alexandra, Princess of Wales's Own Yorkshire Regiment): The Lancashire Fusiliers: The Royal Scots Fusiliers: The Cheshire Regiment: The Royal Welch Fusiliers: The South Wales Borderers: The King's Own Scottish Borderers: The Cameronians (Scottish Rifles): The Gloucestershire Regiment: The Worcestershire Regiment: The East Lancashire Regiment: The East Surrey Regiment: The Duke of Cornwall's Light Infantry: The Duke of Wellington's Regiment (West Riding): The Royal Sussex Regiment: The Hampshire Regiment: The South Staffordshire Regiment: The Prince of Wales's Volunteers (South Lancashire): The Welch Regiment: The Black Watch (Royal Highlanders): The Oxfordshire and Buckinghamshire Light Infantry: The Essex Regiment: The Sherwood Foresters (Nottinghamshire and Derbyshire Regiment): The Loyal Regiment (North Lancashire): The Queen's Own Royal West Kent Regiment: The King's Own Yorkshire Light Infantry: The King's Shropshire Light Infantry: The Middlesex Regiment (Duke of Cambridge's Own): The King's Royal Rifle Corps: The Wiltshire Regiment (Duke of Edinburgh's): The Manchester Regiment: The North Staffordshire Regiment (The Prince of Wales's): The York and Lancaster Regiment: The Durham Light Infantry: The Highland Light Infantry (City of Glasgow Regiment): The Seaforth Highlanders (Ross-shire Buffs, The Duke of Albany's): The Gordon Highlanders: The Queen's Own Cameron Highlanders: The Argyll and Sutherland Highlanders (Princess Louise's): The Rifle Brigade (Prince Consort's Own): The Cambridgeshire Regiment: 1st City of London Regiment (The Royal Fusiliers): 2nd City of London Regiment (The Royal Fusiliers): 3rd City of London Regiment (The Royal Fusiliers): 4th City of London Regiment (The Royal Fusiliers): 5th City of London Regiment (London Rifle Brigade): 6th City of London Regiment (City of London Rifles): 7th City of London Regiment: 8th (City of London) Battalion, The London Regiment (Post Office Rifles): 9th London Regiment (Queen Victoria's Rifles): 10th London Regiment (Hackney): 11th London Regiment (Finsbury Rifles): 12th London Regiment (Rangers): The Hertfordshire Regiment
		1926	71st (Transvaal) Siege Battery, Royal Garrison Artillery: 73rd (Cape) Siege Battery, Royal Garrison Artillery: 74th (Eastern Province) Siege Battery, Royal Garrison Artillery: 1st South African Infantry (Cape of Good Hope Regiment): 2nd South African Infantry (Natal and Orange Free State Regiment): 3rd South African Infantry (Transvaal and Rhodesian Regiment): 4th South African Infantry (South African Scottish Regiment): 1st South African Field Ambulance
		1926	The Wellington Regiment
		1927	1st Battalion: 2nd Battalion: 3rd Battalion: 4th Battalion: 5th Battalion: 6th Battalion: 7th Battalion: 8th Battalion: 9th Battalion: 10th Battalion: 11th Battalion: 12th Battalion: 13th Battalion: 14th Battalion: 15th Battalion: 16th Battalion: 17th Battalion: 18th Battalion: 19th Battalion: 20th Battalion: 21st Battalion: 22nd Battalion: 23rd Battalion: 24th Battalion: 25th Battalion: 26th Battalion: 27th Battalion: 28th Battalion: 29th Battalion: 30th Battalion: 31st Battalion: 32nd Battalion: 45th Battalion: 46th Battalion: 47th Battalion: 48th Battalion: 49th Battalion: 50th Battalion: 51st Battalion: 52nd Battalion: 53rd Battalion: 54th Battalion: 55th Battalion: 56th Battalion: 57th Battalion: 58th Battalion: 59th Battalion: 60th Battalion
		1930	The York Rangers: 127th Canadian Infantry Battalion CEF
		1931	1st Canadian Pioneer Battalion CEF
		1937	The Liverpool Scottish, The Queen's Own Cameron Highlanders (TA)
			[1] *CHEMIN DE MENIN taken into use by French-speaking Canadian units 1958.*
54.	**POLYGON WOOD** [1] 26th September–3rd October 1917 The Flanders Offensive	1925	The Royal Wiltshire Yeomanry (Prince of Wales's Own) (Hussars): Honourable Artillery Company: The Royal Scots (The Royal Regiment): The Queen's Royal Regiment (West Surrey): The King's Own Royal Regiment (Lancaster): The Northumberland Fusiliers: The Royal Warwickshire Regiment: The Royal Fusiliers (City of London Regiment): The King's Regiment (Liverpool): The Norfolk Regiment: The Lincolnshire Regiment: The Devonshire Regiment: The Suffolk Regiment: The

Somerset Light Infantry (Prince Albert's): The West Yorkshire Regiment (The Prince of Wales's Own): The East Yorkshire Regiment: The Bedfordshire and Hertfordshire Regiment: The Leicestershire Regiment: The Green Howards (Alexandra, Princess of Wales's Own Yorkshire Regiment): The Lancashire Fusiliers: The Royal Scots Fusiliers: The Cheshire Regiment: The Royal Welch Fusiliers: The South Wales Borderers: The King's Own Scottish Borderers: The Cameronians (Scottish Rifles): The Royal Inniskilling Fusiliers: The Gloucestershire Regiment: The Worcestershire Regiment: The East Lancashire Regiment: The East Surrey Regiment: The Duke of Cornwall's Light Infantry: The Duke of Wellington's Regiment (West Riding): The Border Regiment: The Royal Sussex Regiment: The Hampshire Regiment: The South Staffordshire Regiment: The Dorsetshire Regiment: The Prince of Wales's Volunteers (South Lancashire): The Welch Regiment: The Black Watch (Royal Highlanders): The Oxfordshire and Buckinghamshire Light Infantry: The Sherwood Foresters (Nottinghamshire and Derbyshire Regiment): The Loyal Regiment (North Lancashire): The Royal Berkshire Regiment (Princess Charlotte of Wales's): The Queen's Own Royal West Kent Regiment: The King's Own Yorkshire Light Infantry: The King's Shropshire Light Infantry: The Middlesex Regiment (Duke of Cambridge's Own): The King's Royal Rifle Corps: The Wiltshire Regiment (Duke of Edinburgh's): The Manchester Regiment: The North Staffordshire Regiment (The Prince of Wales's): The York and Lancaster Regiment: The Durham Light Infantry: The Highland Light Infantry (City of Glasgow Regiment): The Seaforth Highlanders (Ross-shire Buffs, The Duke of Albany's): The Gordon Highlanders: The Queen's Own Cameron Highlanders: The Argyll and Sutherland Highlanders (Princess Louise's): The Royal Dublin Fusiliers: The Rifle Brigade (Prince Consort's Own): The Cambridgeshire Regiment: 1st City of London Regiment (The Royal Fusiliers): 2nd City of London Regiment (The Royal Fusiliers): 3rd City of London Regiment (The Royal Fusiliers): 4th City of London Regiment (City of London Rifles): 7th City of London Regiment: 9th London Regiment (Queen Victoria's Rifles): 10th London Regiment (Hackney): 11th London Regiment (Finsbury Rifles): 12th London Regiment (Rangers): The Hertfordshire Regiment: The British West Indies Regiment

1926	71st (Transvaal) Siege Battery, Royal Garrison Artillery: 73rd (Cape) Siege Battery, Royal Garrison Artillery: 74th (Eastern Province) Siege Battery, Royal Garrison Artillery
1926	The Auckland Regiment (Countess of Ranfurly's Own): The Hauraki Regiment: The North Auckland Regiment: The Waikato Regiment: The Wellington Regiment: The Wellington West Coast Regiment: The Hawke's Bay Regiment: The Taranaki Regiment: The Canterbury Regiment: The Nelson, Marlborough, and West Coast Regiment: The Otago Regiment: The Southland Regiment
1927	1st Battalion: 2nd Battalion: 3rd Battalion: 4th Battalion: 5th Battalion: 6th Battalion: 7th Battalion: 8th Battalion: 9th Battalion: 10th Battalion: 11th Battalion: 12th Battalion: 13th Battalion: 14th Battalion: 15th Battalion: 16th Battalion: 17th Battalion: 18th Battalion: 19th Battalion: 20th Battalion: 21st Battalion: 22nd Battalion: 23rd Battalion: 24th Battalion: 25th Battalion: 26th Battalion: 27th Battalion: 28th Battalion: 29th Battalion: 30th Battalion: 31st Battalion: 32nd Battalion: 33rd Battalion: 34th Battalion: 35th Battalion: 36th Battalion: 37th Battalion: 38th Battalion: 39th Battalion: 40th Battalion: 41st Battalion: 42nd Battalion: 43rd Battalion: 44th Battalion: 45th Battalion: 46th Battalion: 47th Battalion: 48th Battalion: 49th Battalion: 50th Battalion: 51st Battalion: 52nd Battalion: 53rd Battalion: 54th Battalion: 55th Battalion: 56th Battalion: 57th Battalion: 58th Battalion: 59th Battalion: 60th Battalion
1930	The York Rangers: 127th Canadian Infantry Battalion CEF
1931	1st Canadian Pioneer Battalion CEF
	[1] BOIS DU POLYGONE taken into use by French-speaking Canadian units 1958.
1925	1st Life Guards: 2nd Life Guards: Royal Horse Guards (The Blues): The Royal Wiltshire Yeomanry (Prince of Wales's Own) (Hussars): Honourable Artillery Company: The Queen's Royal Regiment (West Surrey): The King's Own Royal Regiment (Lancaster): The Northumberland Fusiliers: The Royal Warwickshire Regiment: The Royal Fusiliers (City of London

55. **BROODSEINDE**
4th October 1917
The Flanders Offensive

Regiment): The Norfolk Regiment: The Lincolnshire Regiment: The Devonshire Regiment: The Somerset Light Infantry (Prince Albert's): The East Yorkshire Regiment: The Bedfordshire and Hertfordshire Regiment: The Green Howards (Alexandra, Princess of Wales's Own Yorkshire Regiment): The Lancashire Fusiliers: The Cheshire Regiment: The Royal Welch Fusiliers: The South Wales Borderers: The King's Own Scottish Borderers: The Royal Inniskilling Fusiliers: The Gloucestershire Regiment: The Worcestershire Regiment: The East Lancashire Regiment: The East Surrey Regiment: The Duke of Cornwall's Light Infantry: The Duke of Wellington's Regiment (West Riding): The Border Regiment: The Royal Sussex Regiment: The Hampshire Regiment: The South Staffordshire Regiment: The Dorsetshire Regiment: The Welch Regiment: The Oxfordshire and Buckinghamshire Light Infantry: The Essex Regiment: The Sherwood Foresters (Nottinghamshire and Derbyshire Regiment): The Royal Berkshire Regiment (Princess Charlotte of Wales's): The Queen's Own Royal West Kent Regiment: The King's Own Yorkshire Light Infantry: The Middlesex Regiment (Duke of Cambridge's Own): The King's Royal Rifle Corps: The Wiltshire Regiment (Duke of Edinburgh's): The Manchester Regiment: The North Staffordshire Regiment (The Prince of Wales's): The York and Lancaster Regiment: The Durham Light Infantry: The Seaforth Highlanders (Ross-shire Buffs, The Duke of Albany's): The Gordon Highlanders: The Argyll and Sutherland Highlanders (Princess Louise's): The Rifle Brigade (Prince Consort's Own): The Cambridgeshire Regiment: The Hertfordshire Regiment: The British West Indies Regiment

1926	71st (Transvaal) Siege Battery, Royal Garrison Artillery: 73rd (Cape) Siege Battery, Royal Garrison Artillery: 74th (Eastern Province) Siege Battery, Royal Garrison Artillery
1926	The Auckland Regiment (Countess of Ranfurly's Own): The Hauraki Regiment: The North Auckland Regiment: The Waikato Regiment: The Wellington Regiment: The Wellington West Coast Regiment: The Hawke's Bay Regiment: The Taranaki Regiment: The Canterbury Regiment: The Nelson, Marlborough, and West Coast Regiment: The Otago Regiment: The Southland Regiment
1927	4th Light Horse Regiment: 1st Battalion: 2nd Battalion: 3rd Battalion: 4th Battalion: 5th Battalion: 6th Battalion: 7th Battalion: 8th Battalion: 9th Battalion: 10th Battalion: 11th Battalion: 12th Battalion: 17th Battalion: 18th Battalion: 19th Battalion: 20th Battalion: 21st Battalion: 22nd Battalion: 23rd Battalion: 24th Battalion: 25th Battalion: 26th Battalion: 27th Battalion: 28th Battalion: 33rd Battalion: 34th Battalion: 35th Battalion: 36th Battalion: 37th Battalion: 38th Battalion: 39th Battalion: 40th Battalion: 41st Battalion: 42nd Battalion: 43rd Battalion: 44th Battalion
1928	The Otago Mounted Rifles
1930	The York Rangers: 127th Canadian Infantry Battalion CEF

56. **POELCAPPELLE**
9th October 1917
The Flanders Offensive

1925	1st Life Guards: 2nd Life Guards: Royal Horse Guards (The Blues): Westmorland and Cumberland Yeomanry (Hussars): The Royal Wiltshire Yeomanry (Prince of Wales's Own) (Hussars): Honourable Artillery Company: Grenadier Guards: Coldstream Guards: Scots Guards: Irish Guards: Welsh Guards: The Royal Scots (The Royal Regiment): The King's Own Royal Regiment (Lancaster): The Royal Warwickshire Regiment: The Royal Fusiliers (City of London Regiment): The King's Regiment (Liverpool): The Norfolk Regiment: The Lincolnshire Regiment: The West Yorkshire Regiment (The Prince of Wales's Own): The East Yorkshire Regiment: The Bedfordshire and Hertfordshire Regiment: The Green Howards (Alexandra, Princess of Wales's Own Yorkshire Regiment): The Lancashire Fusiliers: The Cheshire Regiment: The Royal Welch Fusiliers: The South Wales Borderers: The King's Own Scottish Borderers: The Royal Inniskilling Fusiliers: The Gloucestershire Regiment: The Worcestershire Regiment: The East Lancashire Regiment: The East Surrey Regiment: The Duke of Cornwall's Light Infantry: The Duke of Wellington's Regiment (West Riding): The Border Regiment: The Royal Sussex Regiment: The Hampshire Regiment: The South Staffordshire Regiment: The Dorsetshire Regiment: The Welch Regiment: The Black Watch (Royal Highlanders): The Oxfordshire and Buckinghamshire Light Infantry: The Essex Regiment: The Sherwood Foresters (Nottinghamshire and Derbyshire Regiment): The Loyal Regiment (North Lancashire): The Royal Berkshire Regiment (Princess Charlotte of Wales's):

The King's Own Yorkshire Light Infantry: The Middlesex Regiment (Duke of Cambridge's Own): The King's Royal Rifle Corps: The Wiltshire Regiment (Duke of Edinburgh's): The Manchester Regiment: The North Staffordshire Regiment (The Prince of Wales's): The York and Lancaster Regiment: The Seaforth Highlanders (Ross-shire Buffs, The Duke of Albany's): The Gordon Highlanders: The Queen's Own Cameron Highlanders: The Argyll and Sutherland Highlanders (Princess Louise's): The Rifle Brigade (Prince Consort's Own): The Monmouthshire Regiment: The Cambridgeshire Regiment: The Hertfordshire Regiment: The British West Indies Regiment

1925 The Royal Newfoundland Regiment

1926 75th (Natal) Siege Battery, Royal Garrison Artillery

1927 1st Battalion: 2nd Battalion: 3rd Battalion: 4th Battalion: 5th Battalion: 6th Battalion: 7th Battalion: 8th Battalion: 9th Battalion: 10th Battalion: 11th Battalion: 12th Battalion: 17th Battalion: 18th Battalion: 19th Battalion: 20th Battalion: 21st Battalion: 22nd Battalion: 23rd Battalion: 24th Battalion: 25th Battalion: 26th Battalion: 27th Battalion: 28th Battalion: 29th Battalion: 30th Battalion: 31st Battalion: 32nd Battalion: 33rd Battalion: 34th Battalion: 35th Battalion: 36th Battalion: 37th Battalion: 38th Battalion: 39th Battalion: 40th Battalion: 41st Battalion: 42nd Battalion: 43rd Battalion: 44th Battalion: 53rd Battalion: 54th Battalion: 55th Battalion: 56th Battalion: 57th Battalion: 58th Battalion: 59th Battalion: 60th Battalion

1930 The York Rangers: 127th Canadian Infantry Battalion CEF

57. PASSCHENDAELE
12th October 1917
and
26th October–10th November 1917
The Flanders Offensive

1925 1st Life Guards: 2nd Life Guards: Royal Horse Guards (The Blues): Queen's Own Royal Glasgow Yeomanry (Dragoons): The Duke of Lancaster's Own Yeomanry (Dragoons): Westmorland and Cumberland Yeomanry (Hussars): The Royal Wiltshire Yeomanry (Prince of Wales's Own) (Hussars): Honourable Artillery Company: Grenadier Guards: Coldstream Guards: Scots Guards: Irish Guards: Welsh Guards: The Royal Scots (The Royal Regiment): The Queen's Royal Regiment (West Surrey): The Buffs (East Kent Regiment): The King's Own Royal Regiment (Lancaster): The Northumberland Fusiliers: The Royal Warwickshire Regiment: The Royal Fusiliers (City of London Regiment): The King's Regiment (Liverpool): The Norfolk Regiment: The Lincolnshire Regiment: The Devonshire Regiment: The Suffolk Regiment: The Somerset Light Infantry (Prince Albert's): The West Yorkshire Regiment (The Prince of Wales's Own): The East Yorkshire Regiment: The Bedfordshire and Hertfordshire Regiment: The Green Howards (Alexandra, Princess of Wales's Own Yorkshire Regiment): The Lancashire Fusiliers: The Cheshire Regiment: The Royal Welch Fusiliers: The South Wales Borderers: The King's Own Scottish Borderers: The Cameronians (Scottish Rifles): The Gloucestershire Regiment: The Worcestershire Regiment: The East Lancashire Regiment: The East Surrey Regiment: The Duke of Cornwall's Light Infantry: The Duke of Wellington's Regiment (West Riding): The Border Regiment: The Royal Sussex Regiment: The Hampshire Regiment: The South Staffordshire Regiment: The Dorsetshire Regiment: The Prince of Wales's Volunteers (South Lancashire): The Welch Regiment: The Black Watch (Royal Highlanders): The Oxfordshire and Buckinghamshire Light Infantry: The Essex Regiment: The Sherwood Foresters (Nottinghamshire and Derbyshire Regiment): The Loyal Regiment (North Lancashire): The Northamptonshire Regiment: The Royal Berkshire Regiment (Princess Charlotte of Wales's): The Queen's Own Royal West Kent Regiment: The King's Own Yorkshire Light Infantry: The King's Shropshire Light Infantry: The Middlesex Regiment (Duke of Cambridge's Own): The King's Royal Rifle Corps: The Wiltshire Regiment (Duke of Edinburgh's): The Manchester Regiment: The North Staffordshire Regiment: The Durham Light Infantry: The Highland Light Infantry (City of Glasgow Regiment): The Seaforth Highlanders (Ross-shire Buffs, The Duke of Albany's): The Gordon Highlanders: The Queen's Own Cameron Highlanders: The Argyll and Sutherland Highlanders (Princess Louise's): The Royal Munster Fusiliers: The Rifle Brigade (Prince Consort's Own): The Cambridgeshire Regiment: 1st City of London Regiment (The Royal Fusiliers): 2nd City of London Regiment (The Royal Fusiliers): 3rd City of London Regiment (The Royal Fusiliers): 4th City of London Regiment (The Royal Fusiliers): 5th City of London Regiment (London Rifle Brigade): 6th City of London Regiment (City of London Rifles): 7th City of London Regiment: 8th (City of London) Battalion, The London Regiment (Post Office

Rifles): 9th London Regiment (Queen Victoria's Rifles): 10th London Regiment (Hackney): 11th London Regiment (Finsbury Rifles): 12th London Regiment (Rangers): 28th London Regiment (Artists' Rifles): The Hertfordshire Regiment: The British West Indies Regiment: Royal Guernsey Militia (Light Infantry)

1926 71st (Transvaal) Siege Battery, Royal Garrison Artillery: 72nd (Griqualand West) Siege Battery, Royal Garrison Artillery: 73rd (Cape) Siege Battery, Royal Garrison Artillery: 74th (Eastern Province) Siege Battery, Royal Garrison Artillery: 75th (Natal) Siege Battery, Royal Garrison Artillery: 3rd South African Infantry (Transvaal and Rhodesian Regiment): 1st South African Field Ambulance

1926 The Auckland Regiment (Countess of Ranfurly's Own): The Hauraki Regiment: The North Auckland Regiment: The Waikato Regiment: The Wellington Regiment: The Wellington West Coast Regiment: The Hawke's Bay Regiment: The Taranaki Regiment: The Canterbury Regiment: The Nelson, Marlborough, and West Coast Regiment: The Otago Regiment: The Southland Regiment

1927 4th Light Horse Regiment: 1st Battalion: 2nd Battalion: 3rd Battalion: 4th Battalion: 5th Battalion: 6th Battalion: 7th Battalion: 8th Battalion: 9th Battalion: 10th Battalion: 11th Battalion: 12th Battalion: 13th Battalion: 14th Battalion: 15th Battalion: 16th Battalion: 17th Battalion: 18th Battalion: 19th Battalion: 20th Battalion: 21st Battalion: 22nd Battalion: 23rd Battalion: 24th Battalion: 25th Battalion: 26th Battalion: 27th Battalion: 28th Battalion: 29th Battalion: 30th Battalion: 31st Battalion: 32nd Battalion: 33rd Battalion: 34th Battalion: 35th Battalion: 36th Battalion: 37th Battalion: 38th Battalion: 39th Battalion: 40th Battalion: 41st Battalion: 42nd Battalion: 43rd Battalion: 44th Battalion: 45th Battalion: 46th Battalion: 47th Battalion: 48th Battalion: 49th Battalion: 50th Battalion: 51st Battalion: 52nd Battalion: 53rd Battalion: 54th Battalion: 55th Battalion: 56th Battalion: 57th Battalion: 58th Battalion: 59th Battalion: 60th Battalion

The Otago Mounted Rifles

1928

1929 The Royal Canadian Regiment: Royal 22e Regiment: The Mississauga Horse: The Saskatchewan Mounted Rifles: The British Columbia Dragoons: The Eastern Townships Mounted Rifles: The Canadian Grenadier Guards: The Queen's Own Rifles of Canada: The Victoria Rifles of Canada: The Royal Highlanders of Canada: The Royal Grenadiers: The Royal Hamilton Light Infantry: The Princess of Wales' Own Regiment: The Canadian Fusiliers (City of London Regiment): The Dufferin Rifles of Canada: The Peterborough Rangers: The Carleton Light Infantry: The Cape Breton Highlanders: The Saint John Fusiliers: The Ottawa Highlanders: The Winnipeg Rifles: The Essex Scottish: The 48th Regiment (Highlanders): 1st British Columbia Regiment (Duke of Connaught's Own): The Argyll and Sutherland Highlanders of Canada (Princess Louise's): The Lake Superior Regiment: The Regina Rifle Regiment: The Winnipeg Grenadiers: The Queen's Own Cameron Highlanders of Canada: The Colchester and Hants Regiment: The Calgary Highlanders: The Calgary Regiment: The Westminster Regiment: The Winnipeg Light Infantry: The Saskatoon Light Infantry: The Canadian Scottish Regiment: The King's Own Rifles of Canada: The Kootenay Regiment: The Royal Montreal Regiment: The North Alberta Regiment: The Edmonton Regiment: The Toronto Scottish Regiment: The South Alberta Regiment: 1st Canadian Mounted Rifles Battalion CEF: 2nd Canadian Mounted Rifles Battalion CEF: 4th Canadian Mounted Rifles Battalion CEF: 5th Canadian Mounted Rifles Battalion CEF: 1st Canadian Infantry Battalion CEF: 4th Canadian Infantry Battalion CEF: 5th Canadian Infantry Battalion CEF: 8th Canadian Infantry Battalion CEF: 13th Canadian Infantry Battalion CEF: 14th Canadian Infantry Battalion CEF: 15th Canadian Infantry Battalion CEF: 16th Canadian Infantry Battalion CEF: 18th Canadian Infantry Battalion CEF: 19th Canadian Infantry Battalion CEF: 20th Canadian Infantry Battalion CEF: 24th Canadian Infantry Battalion CEF: 26th Canadian Infantry Battalion CEF: 28th Canadian Infantry Battalion CEF: 31st Canadian Infantry Battalion CEF: 42nd Canadian Infantry Battalion CEF: 43rd Canadian Infantry Battalion CEF: 44th Canadian Infantry Battalion CEF: 46th Canadian Infantry Battalion CEF: 47th Canadian Infantry Battalion CEF: 49th Canadian Infantry Battalion CEF: 50th Canadian Infantry Battalion CEF: 54th Canadian Infantry Battalion CEF: 58th Canadian Infantry

Battalion CEF: 75th Canadian Infantry Battalion CEF: 78th Canadian Infantry Battalion CEF: 85th Canadian Infantry Battalion CEF: 87th Canadian Infantry Battalion CEF: 102nd Canadian Infantry Battalion CEF: 116th Canadian Infantry Battalion CEF: 1st Canadian Motor Machine Gun Brigade CEF: Princess Patricia's Canadian Light Infantry: The North British Columbia Regiment: The Ontario Regiment: The Manitoba Regiment: 2nd Canadian Infantry Battalion CEF: 3rd Canadian Infantry Battalion CEF: 10th Canadian Infantry Battalion CEF: 21st Canadian Infantry Battalion CEF: 25th Canadian Infantry Battalion CEF: 27th Canadian Infantry Battalion CEF: 29th Canadian Infantry Battalion CEF: 38th Canadian Infantry Battalion CEF: 52nd Canadian Infantry Battalion CEF: 2nd Canadian Pioneer Battalion CEF: 107th Canadian Pioneer Battalion CEF: 123rd Canadian Pioneer Battalion CEF: 124th Canadian Pioneer Battalion CEF

1930	The York Rangers: The Vancouver Regiment: 7th Canadian Infantry Battalion CEF: 127th Canadian Infantry Battalion CEF
1931	The Manitoba Mounted Rifles: The Seaforth Highlanders of Canada: 72nd Canadian Infantry Battalion of Canada: 1st Canadian Pioneer Battalion CEF
?	7th Hussars: 11th Hussars
1937	The Liverpool Scottish, The Queen's Own Cameron Highlanders (TA)

58. **CAMBRAI 1917**
20th November–3rd December 1917
The Cambrai Operations

1925 The Queen's Bays (2nd Dragoon Guards): 4th Royal Irish Dragoon Guards: 5th Dragoon Guards (Princess Charlotte of Wales's): The Carabiniers (6th Dragoon Guards): 7th Dragoon Guards (Princess Royal's): The Royal Scots Greys (2nd Dragoons): 3rd The King's Own Hussars: 4th Queen's Own Hussars: 5th Royal Irish Lancers: The Inniskillings (6th Dragoons): 8th King's Royal Irish Hussars: 9th Queen's Royal Lancers: 11th Hussars (Prince Albert's Own): 12th Royal Lancers (Prince of Wales's): 15th The King's Hussars: 16th The Queen's Lancers: 17th Lancers (Duke of Cambridge's Own): 18th Royal Hussars (Queen Mary's Own): 19th Royal Hussars (Queen Alexandra's Own): 20th Hussars: King Edward's Horse (The King's Oversea Dominions Regiment): The Northumberland Hussars (Yeomanry): Oxfordshire Yeomanry (Queen's Own Oxfordshire Hussars): The Yorkshire Dragoons Yeomanry (Queen's Own): Grenadier Guards: Coldstream Guards: Scots Guards: Irish Guards: Welsh Guards: The Royal Scots (The Royal Regiment): The Queen's Royal Regiment (West Surrey): The Buffs (East Kent Regiment): The King's Own Royal Regiment (Lancaster): The Northumberland Fusiliers: The Royal Warwickshire Regiment: The Royal Fusiliers (City of London Regiment): The King's Regiment (Liverpool): The Norfolk Regiment: The Lincolnshire Regiment: The Suffolk Regiment: The Somerset Light Infantry (Prince Albert's): The West Yorkshire Regiment (The Prince of Wales's Own): The East Yorkshire Regiment: The Bedfordshire and Hertfordshire Regiment: The Leicestershire Regiment: The Green Howards (Alexandra, Princess of Wales's Own Yorkshire Regiment): The Lancashire Fusiliers: The Cheshire Regiment: The Royal Welch Fusiliers: The South Wales Borderers: The King's Own Scottish Borderers: The Royal Inniskilling Fusiliers: The Gloucestershire Regiment: The Worcestershire Regiment: The East Surrey Regiment: The Duke of Cornwall's Light Infantry: The Duke of Wellington's Regiment (West Riding): The Border Regiment: The Royal Sussex Regiment: The Hampshire Regiment: The South Staffordshire Regiment: The Prince of Wales's Volunteers (South Lancashire): The Welch Regiment: The Black Watch (Royal Highlanders): The Oxfordshire and Buckinghamshire Light Infantry: The Essex Regiment: The Sherwood Foresters (Nottinghamshire and Derbyshire Regiment): The Loyal Regiment (North Lancashire): The Northamptonshire Regiment: The Royal Berkshire Regiment (Princess Charlotte of Wales's): The Queen's Own Royal West Kent Regiment: The King's Own Yorkshire Light Infantry: The King's Shropshire Light Infantry: The Middlesex Regiment (Duke of Cambridge's Own): The King's Royal Rifle Corps: The North Staffordshire Regiment (The Prince of Wales's): The York and Lancaster Regiment: The Durham Light Infantry: The Highland Light Infantry (City of Glasgow Regiment): The Seaforth Highlanders (Ross-shire Buffs, The Duke of Albany's): The Gordon Highlanders: The Royal Ulster Rifles: The Royal Irish Fusiliers (Princess Victoria's): The Argyll and Sutherland Highlanders (Princess Louise's): The Royal Dublin Fusiliers: The Rifle Brigade (Prince Consort's Own): The Monmouthshire Regiment: 1st City of London Regiment (The Royal Fusiliers): 2nd City of London Regiment (The Royal Fusiliers): 3rd City of London Regiment (The Royal Fusiliers): 4th City of London

Regiment (The Royal Fusiliers); 5th City of London Regiment (London Rifle Brigade); 6th City of London Regiment (City of London Rifles); 7th City of London Regiment: 8th (City of London) Battalion, The London Regiment (Post Office Rifles); 9th London Regiment (Queen Victoria's Rifles); 12th London Regiment (Rangers); 13th London Regiment (Princess Louise's Kensington Regiment); 14th London Regiment (London Scottish); 15th (County of London) Battalion, The London Regiment (Prince of Wales's Own, Civil Service Rifles); 16th London Regiment (Queen's Westminster Rifles); 17th London Regiment (Poplar and Stepney Rifles); 18th London Regiment (London Irish Rifles); 19th London Regiment (St Pancras); 20th London Regiment (The Queen's Own); 21st London Regiment (First Surrey Rifles); 22nd London Regiment (The Queen's); 23rd London Regiment; 24th London Regiment (The Queen's); Bedfordshire Yeomanry (Lancers); Royal Guernsey Militia (Light Infantry)

1925 The Royal Newfoundland Regiment
1926 2nd Lancers (Gardner's Horse); 4th Duke of Cambridge's Own Hodson's Horse; 9th Royal Deccan Horse; 14th Prince of Wales's Own Scinde Horse; 17th Queen Victoria's Own Poona Horse; 18th King Edward's Own Cavalry; 19th King George's Own Lancers; 21st King George's Own Central India Horse
Jodhpur Sardar Risala

1926 71st (Transvaal) Siege Battery, Royal Garrison Artillery; 125th (Transvaal) Siege Battery, Royal Garrison Artillery
1926 The Royal Canadian Dragoons: The Fort Garry Horse: 1st Cavalry Machine Gun Squadron: Machine Gun Squadron, Canadian
1931 Cavalry Brigade CEF: Lord Strathcona's Horse (Royal Canadians)
1937 The Liverpool Scottish, The Queen's Own Cameron Highlanders (TA)
1958 Royal Tank Regiment

59. **SOMME 1918**

21st March–5th April 1918 The German Offensive in Picardy and

21st August–3rd September 1918 The Advance in Picardy

1925 2nd Life Guards: The Queen's Bays (2nd Dragoon Guards): 3rd Dragoon Guards (Prince of Wales's): 4th Royal Irish Dragoon Guards: 5th Dragoon Guards (Princess Charlotte of Wales's): The Carabiniers (6th Dragoon Guards): 7th Dragoon Guards (Princess Royal's): 1st The Royal Dragoons: The Royal Scots Greys (2nd Dragoons): 3rd The King's Own Hussars: 4th Queen's Own Hussars: 5th Royal Irish Lancers: The Inniskillings (6th Dragoons): 8th King's Royal Irish Hussars: 9th Queen's Royal Lancers: 10th Royal Hussars (Prince of Wales's Own): 11th Hussars (Prince Albert's Own): 12th Royal Lancers (Prince of Wales's): 15th The King's Hussars: 16th The Queen's Lancers: 17th Lancers (Duke of Cambridge's Own): 18th Royal Hussars (Queen Mary's Own): 19th Royal Hussars (Queen Alexandra's Own): 20th Hussars: North Irish Horse: South Irish Horse: The Cheshire Yeomanry (Earl of Chester's) (Hussars): Royal 1st Devon Yeomanry (Hussars): Royal North Devon Yeomanry (Hussars): Fife and Forfar Yeomanry: Glamorgan Yeomanry (Dragoons): Hampshire (Carabiniers) (Dragoons): Royal East Kent Yeomanry (The Duke of Connaught's Own) (Mounted Rifles) (Hussars): West Kent Yeomanry (Queen's Own) (Hussars): Queen's Own Royal Glasgow Yeomanry (Dragoons): The Lancashire Hussars Yeomanry: The Duke of Lancaster's Own Yeomanry (Dragoons): Montgomeryshire Yeomanry (Dragoons): The Northumberland Hussars (Yeomanry): Oxfordshire Yeomanry (Queen's Own Oxfordshire Hussars): Pembroke Yeomanry (Castlemartin) (Hussars): Shropshire Yeomanry (Dragoons): West Somerset Yeomanry (Hussars): Suffolk Yeomanry (The Duke of York's Own Loyal Suffolk Hussars): Sussex Yeomanry (Prince of Wales's Own) (Hussars): Welsh Horse (Lancers): Westmorland and Cumberland Yeomanry (Hussars): The Royal Wiltshire Yeomanry (Prince of Wales's Own) (Hussars): Honourable Artillery Company: Grenadier Guards: Coldstream Guards: Scots Guards: Irish Guards: Welsh Guards: The Royal Scots (The Royal Regiment): The Queen's Royal Regiment (West Surrey): The Buffs (East Kent Regiment): The King's Own Royal Regiment (Lancaster): The Northumberland Fusiliers: The Royal Warwickshire Regiment: The Royal Fusiliers (City of London Regiment): The King's Regiment (Liverpool): The Norfolk Regiment: The Lincolnshire Regiment: The Devonshire Regiment: The Suffolk Regiment: The Somerset Light Infantry (Prince Albert's): The West Yorkshire Regiment (The Prince of Wales's Own): The East Yorkshire Regiment: The Bedfordshire and Hertfordshire Regiment: The Leicestershire Regiment: The Royal Irish Regiment: The Green Howards (Alexandra, Princess of Wales's Own Yorkshire Regiment); The Lancashire Fusiliers; The Royal Scots Fusiliers; The Cheshire Regiment; The Royal Welch Fusiliers; The South Wales Borderers; The King's Own Scottish Borderers; The Cameronians (Scottish Rifles); The Royal Inniskilling Fusiliers; The Gloucestershire Regiment; The Worcestershire Regiment; The East Lancashire Regiment; The East Surrey Regiment; The Duke of Cornwall's Light Infantry; The Duke of Wellington's Regiment (West Riding); The Border Regiment; The Royal Sussex Regiment; The Hampshire Regiment; The South Staffordshire Regiment; The Dorsetshire Regiment; The Prince of Wales's Volunteers (South Lancashire); The Welch Regiment; The Black Watch (Royal Highlanders); The Oxfordshire and Buckinghamshire Light Infantry; The Essex Regiment; The Sherwood Foresters (Nottinghamshire and Derbyshire Regiment); The Loyal Regiment (North Lancashire); The Northamptonshire Regiment; The Royal Berkshire Regiment (Princess Charlotte of Wales's); The Queen's Own Royal West Kent Regiment; The King's Own Yorkshire Light Infantry; The King's Shropshire Light Infantry; The Middlesex Regiment (Duke of Cambridge's Own); The King's Royal Rifle Corps; The Wiltshire Regiment (Duke of Edinburgh's); The Manchester Regiment; The North Staffordshire Regiment (The Prince of Wales's); The York and Lancaster Regiment; The Durham Light Infantry; The Highland Light Infantry (City of Glasgow Regiment); The Seaforth Highlanders (Ross-shire Buffs, The Duke of Albany's); The Gordon Highlanders; The Queen's Own Cameron Highlanders; The Royal Ulster Rifles; The Royal Irish Fusiliers (Princess Victoria's); The Connaught Rangers; The Argyll and Sutherland Highlanders (Princess Louise's); The Prince of Wales's Leinster Regiment (Royal Canadians); The Royal Munster Fusiliers; The Royal Dublin Fusiliers; The Rifle Brigade (Prince Consort's Own); The Cambridgeshire Regiment; 1st City of London Regiment (The Royal Fusiliers); 2nd City of London Regiment (The Royal Fusiliers); 3rd City of London Regiment (The Royal Fusiliers); 4th City of London Regiment (The Royal Fusiliers); 5th City of London Regiment (London Rifle Brigade); 6th City of London Regiment (City of London Rifles); 7th City of London Regiment; 8th (City of London) Battalion, The London Regiment (Post Office Rifles); 9th London Regiment (Queen Victoria's Rifles); 10th London Regiment (Hackney); 12th London Regiment (Rangers); 13th London Regiment (Princess Louise's Kensington Regiment); 14th London Regiment (London Scottish); 15th (County of London) Battalion, The London Regiment (Prince of Wales's Own, Civil Service Rifles); 16th London Regiment (Queen's Westminster Rifles); 17th London Regiment (Poplar and Stepney Rifles); 18th London Regiment (London Irish Rifles); 19th London Regiment (St Pancras); 20th London Regiment (The Queen's Own); 21st London Regiment (First Surrey Rifles); 22nd London Regiment (The Queen's); 23rd London Regiment; 24th London Regiment (The Queen's); 28th London Regiment (Artists' Rifles); The Hertfordshire Regiment; Bedfordshire Yeomanry (Lancers); Essex Yeomanry (Dragoons)

1926   72nd (Griqualand West) Siege Battery, Royal Garrison Artillery; 74th (Eastern Province) Siege Battery, Royal Garrison Artillery; 75th (Natal) Siege Battery, Royal Garrison Artillery

1926   The Auckland Regiment (Countess of Ranfurly's Own); The Hauraki Regiment; The North Auckland Regiment; The Waikato Regiment; The Wellington Regiment; The Wellington West Coast Regiment; The Hawke's Bay Regiment; The Taranaki Regiment; The Canterbury Regiment; The Nelson, Marlborough, and West Coast Regiment; The Otago Regiment; The Southland Regiment

1927   13th Light Horse Regiment; 1st Battalion; 2nd Battalion; 3rd Battalion; 4th Battalion; 5th Battalion; 6th Battalion; 7th Battalion; 8th Battalion; 9th Battalion; 10th Battalion; 11th Battalion; 12th Battalion; 13th Battalion; 14th Battalion; 15th Battalion; 16th Battalion; 17th Battalion; 18th Battalion; 19th Battalion; 20th Battalion; 21st Battalion; 22nd Battalion; 23rd Battalion; 24th Battalion; 25th Battalion; 26th Battalion; 27th Battalion; 28th Battalion; 29th Battalion; 30th Battalion; 31st Battalion; 32nd Battalion; 33rd Battalion; 34th Battalion; 35th Battalion; 36th Battalion; 37th Battalion; 38th Battalion; 39th Battalion; 40th Battalion; 41st Battalion; 42nd Battalion; 43rd Battalion; 44th Battalion; 45th Battalion; 46th Battalion; 47th Battalion; 48th Battalion; 49th Battalion; 50th Battalion; 51st Battalion; 52nd Battalion; 53rd Battalion; 54th Battalion; 55th Battalion; 56th Battalion; 57th Battalion; 58th Battalion; 59th Battalion; 60th Battalion

1928	The Otago Mounted Rifles
1929	Royal 22e Regiment: The Victoria Rifles of Canada: The Royal Grenadiers: The Princess of Wales' Own Regiment: The Saint John Fusiliers: The Essex Scottish: The Argyll and Sutherland Highlanders of Canada (Princess Louise's): The Regina Rifle Regiment: The Colchester and Hants Regiment: The Queen's Rangers, 1st American Regiment: The South Alberta Regiment: The North Alberta Regiment: 1st Motor Machine Gun Brigade: 18th Canadian Infantry Battalion CEF: 19th Canadian Infantry Battalion CEF: 20th Canadian Infantry Battalion CEF: 24th Canadian Infantry Battalion CEF: 26th Canadian Infantry Battalion CEF: 28th Canadian Infantry Battalion CEF: 31st Canadian Infantry Battalion CEF: 1st Canadian Motor Machine Gun Brigade CEF: The Manitoba Regiment: 21st Canadian Infantry Battalion CEF: 25th Canadian Infantry Battalion CEF: 27th Canadian Infantry Battalion CEF: 29th Canadian Infantry Battalion CEF: 2nd Canadian Pioneer Battalion CEF: 107th Canadian Pioneer Battalion CEF
1930	The York Rangers: The Vancouver Regiment: 127th Canadian Infantry Battalion CEF
1931	The Royal Canadian Dragoons: The Fort Garry Horse: 1st Cavalry Machine Gun Squadron: Machine Gun Squadron, Canadian Cavalry Brigade CEF: 228th Canadian Infantry Battalion CEF: Lord Strathcona's Horse (Royal Canadians): The Algonquin Regiment: 1st Canadian Pioneer Battalion CEF
1958	Royal Tank Regiment
60. ST QUENTIN 21st–23rd March 1918 The German Offensive in Picardy 1925	The Queen's Bays (2nd Dragoon Guards): 3rd Dragoon Guards (Prince of Wales's): 4th Royal Irish Dragoon Guards: 5th Dragoon Guards (Princess Charlotte of Wales's): The Carabiniers (6th Dragoon Guards): 7th Dragoon Guards (Princess Royal's): 1st The Royal Dragoons: 3rd The King's Own Hussars: 5th Royal Irish Lancers: The Inniskillings (6th Dragoons): 8th King's Royal Irish Hussars: 9th Queen's Royal Lancers: 10th Royal Hussars (Prince of Wales's Own): 11th Hussars (Prince Albert's Own): 12th Royal Lancers (Prince of Wales's): 15th The King's Hussars: 17th Lancers (Duke of Cambridge's Own): 18th Royal Hussars (Queen Mary's Own): 19th Royal Hussars (Queen Alexandra's Own): 20th Hussars: North Irish Horse: South Irish Horse: Hampshire (Carabiniers) (Dragoons): The Lancashire Hussars Yeomanry: The Duke of Lancaster's Own Yeomanry (Dragoons): The Northumberland Hussars (Yeomanry): Oxfordshire Yeomanry (Queen's Own Oxfordshire Hussars): Westmorland and Cumberland Yeomanry (Hussars): The Royal Wiltshire Yeomanry (Prince of Wales's Own) (Hussars): Grenadier Guards: Coldstream Guards: Scots Guards: Irish Guards: The Royal Scots (The Royal Regiment): The Queen's Royal Regiment (West Surrey): The Buffs (East Kent Regiment): The King's Own Royal Regiment (Lancaster): The Northumberland Fusiliers: The Royal Warwickshire Regiment: The Royal Fusiliers (City of London Regiment): The King's Regiment (Liverpool): The Norfolk Regiment: The Lincolnshire Regiment: The Suffolk Regiment: The Somerset Light Infantry (Prince Albert's): The West Yorkshire Regiment (The Prince of Wales's Own): The East Yorkshire Regiment: The Bedfordshire and Hertfordshire Regiment: The Leicestershire Regiment: The Royal Irish Regiment: The Green Howards (Alexandra, Princess of Wales's Own Yorkshire Regiment): The Lancashire Fusiliers: The Royal Scots Fusiliers: The Cheshire Regiment: The Royal Welch Fusiliers: The South Wales Borderers: The King's Own Scottish Borderers: The Cameronians (Scottish Rifles): The Royal Inniskilling Fusiliers: The Gloucestershire Regiment: The Worcestershire Regiment: The East Lancashire Regiment: The East Surrey Regiment: The Duke of Cornwall's Light Infantry: The Duke of Wellington's Regiment (West Riding): The Border Regiment: The Royal Sussex Regiment: The Hampshire Regiment: The South Staffordshire Regiment: The Dorsetshire Regiment: The Prince of Wales's Volunteers (South Lancashire): The Welch Regiment: The Black Watch (Royal Highlanders): The Oxfordshire and Buckinghamshire Light Infantry: The Essex Regiment: The Sherwood Foresters (Nottinghamshire and Derbyshire Regiment): The Loyal Regiment (North Lancashire): The Northamptonshire Regiment: The Royal Berkshire Regiment (Princess Charlotte of Wales's): The Queen's Own Royal West Kent Regiment: The King's Own Yorkshire Light Infantry: The King's Shropshire Light Infantry: The Middlesex Regiment (Duke of Cambridge's Own): The King's Royal Rifle Corps: The Wiltshire Regiment (Duke of Edinburgh's): The Manchester Regiment: The North Staffordshire Regiment (The

Prince of Wales's): The York and Lancaster Regiment: The Durham Light Infantry: The Highland Light Infantry (City of Glasgow Regiment): The Seaforth Highlanders (Ross-shire Buffs, The Duke of Albany's): The Gordon Highlanders: The Queen's Own Cameron Highlanders: The Royal Ulster Rifles: The Royal Irish Fusiliers (Princess Victoria's): The Connaught Rangers: The Argyll and Sutherland Highlanders (Princess Louise's): The Prince of Wales's Leinster Regiment (Royal Canadians): The Royal Munster Fusiliers: The Royal Dublin Fusiliers: The Rifle Brigade (Prince Consort's Own): The Cambridgeshire Regiment: 2nd City of London Regiment (The Royal Fusiliers): 3rd City of London Regiment (The Royal Fusiliers): 4th City of London Regiment (The Royal Fusiliers): 6th City of London Regiment (City of London Rifles): 8th (City of London) Battalion, The London Regiment (Post Office Rifles): 15th (County of London) Battalion, The London Regiment (Prince of Wales's Own, Civil Service Rifles): 17th London Regiment (Poplar and Stepney Rifles): 18th London Regiment (London Irish Rifles): 19th London Regiment (St Pancras): 20th London Regiment (The Queen's Own): 21st London Regiment (First Surrey Rifles): 22nd London Regiment (The Queen's): 23rd London Regiment: 24th London Regiment (The Queen's): 28th London Regiment (Artists' Rifles): The Hertfordshire Regiment

1930   The York Rangers: 127th Canadian Infantry Battalion CEF

1931   The Royal Canadian Dragoons: The Fort Garry Horse: 1st Cavalry Machine Gun Squadron: Machine Gun Squadron, Canadian Cavalry Brigade CEF: 228th Canadian Infantry Battalion CEF: Lord Strathcona's Horse (Royal Canadians)

¹ *SAINT-QUENTIN taken into use by French-speaking Canadian units 1958.*

1958   Royal Tank Regiment

61. **ST QUENTIN 1918**
21st–23rd March 1918
The German Offensive in Picardy

62. **BAPAUME 1918**
24th–25th March 1918
The German Offensive in Picardy
and
31st August–3rd September 1918
The Advance in Picardy

1925   2nd Life Guards: The Queen's Bays (2nd Dragoon Guards): The Carabiniers (6th Dragoon Guards): The Royal Scots Greys (2nd Dragoons): 3rd The King's Own Hussars: 8th King's Royal Irish Hussars: 15th The King's Hussars: 19th Royal Hussars (Queen Alexandra's Own): 20th Hussars: North Irish Horse: The Cheshire Yeomanry (Earl of Chester's) (Hussars): Royal 1st Devon Yeomanry (Hussars): Royal North Devon Yeomanry (Hussars): Fife and Forfar Yeomanry: Glamorgan Yeomanry (Dragoons): Hampshire (Carabiniers) (Dragoons): Royal East Kent Yeomanry (The Duke of Connaught's Own) (Mounted Rifles) (Hussars): West Kent Yeomanry (Queen's Own) (Hussars): Queen's Own Royal Glasgow Yeomanry (Dragoons): The Duke of Lancaster's Own Yeomanry (Dragoons): Montgomeryshire Yeomanry (Dragoons): Oxfordshire Yeomanry (Queen's Own Oxfordshire Hussars): Pembroke Yeomanry (Castlemartin) (Hussars): Shropshire Yeomanry (Dragoons): West Somerset Yeomanry (Hussars): Suffolk Yeomanry (The Duke of York's Own Loyal Suffolk Hussars): Sussex Yeomanry (Dragoons): Welsh Horse (Lancers): Westmorland and Cumberland Yeomanry (Hussars): The Royal Wiltshire Yeomanry (Prince of Wales's Own) (Hussars): Honourable Artillery Company: Grenadier Guards: Coldstream Guards: Scots Guards: Irish Guards: Welsh Guards: The Royal Scots (The Royal Regiment): The Queen's Royal Regiment (West Surrey): The Buffs (East Kent Regiment): The King's Own Royal Regiment (Lancaster): The Northumberland Fusiliers: The Royal Warwickshire Regiment: The Royal Fusiliers (City of London Regiment): The King's Regiment (Liverpool): The Norfolk Regiment: The Lincolnshire Regiment: The Devonshire Regiment: The Suffolk Regiment: The Somerset Light Infantry (Prince Albert's): The West Yorkshire Regiment (The Prince of Wales's Own): The East Yorkshire Regiment: The Bedfordshire and Hertfordshire Regiment: The Leicestershire Regiment: The Green Howards (Alexandra, Princess of Wales's Own Yorkshire Regiment): The Lancashire Fusiliers: The Royal Scots Fusiliers: The Cheshire Regiment: The Royal Welch Fusiliers: The South Wales Borderers: The King's Own Scottish Borderers: The Gloucestershire Regiment: The Worcestershire Regiment: The East Lancashire Regiment: The East Surrey Regiment: The Duke of Cornwall's Light Infantry: The Duke of Wellington's

Regiment (West Riding); The Border Regiment; The Royal Sussex Regiment; The Hampshire Regiment; The South Staffordshire Regiment; The Dorsetshire Regiment; The Prince of Wales's Volunteers (South Lancashire); The Welch Regiment; The Black Watch (Royal Highlanders); The Oxfordshire and Buckinghamshire Light Infantry; The Essex Regiment; The Sherwood Foresters (Nottinghamshire and Derbyshire Regiment); The Loyal Regiment (North Lancashire); The Northamptonshire Regiment; The Royal Berkshire Regiment (Princess Charlotte of Wales's); The Queen's Own Royal West Kent Regiment; The King's Own Yorkshire Light Infantry; The King's Shropshire Light Infantry; The Middlesex Regiment (Duke of Cambridge's Own); The King's Royal Rifle Corps; The Wiltshire Regiment (Duke of Edinburgh's); The Manchester Regiment; The North Staffordshire Regiment (The Prince of Wales's); The York and Lancaster Regiment; The Durham Light Infantry; The Highland Light Infantry (City of Glasgow Regiment); The Seaforth Highlanders (Ross-shire Buffs, The Duke of Albany's); The Gordon Highlanders; The Queen's Own Cameron Highlanders; The Connaught Rangers; The Argyll and Sutherland Highlanders (Princess Louise's); The Prince of Wales's Leinster Regiment (Royal Canadians); The Royal Munster Fusiliers; The Royal Dublin Fusiliers; The Cambridgeshire Regiment: 2nd City of London Regiment (The Royal Fusiliers); 3rd City of London Regiment (The Royal Fusiliers); 4th City of London Regiment (The Royal Fusiliers); 6th City of London Regiment (City of London Rifles); 7th City of London Regiment: 8th (City of London) Battalion, The London Regiment (Post Office Rifles); 9th London Regiment (Queen Victoria's Rifles); 10th London Regiment (Hackney); 12th London Regiment (Rangers); 15th (County of London) Battalion, The London Regiment (Prince of Wales's Own, Civil Service Rifles); 17th London Regiment (Poplar and Stepney Rifles); 18th London Regiment (London Irish Rifles); 19th London Regiment (St Pancras); 20th London Regiment (The Queen's Own); 21st London Regiment (First Surrey Rifles); 22nd London Regiment (The Queen's); 23rd London Regiment: 24th London Regiment (The Queen's); 28th London Regiment (Artists' Rifles); The Hertfordshire Regiment

1926   The Auckland Regiment (Countess of Ranfurly's Own); The Hauraki Regiment; The North Auckland Regiment; The Waikato Regiment; The Wellington Regiment; The Wellington West Coast Regiment; The Hawke's Bay Regiment; The Taranaki Regiment; The Canterbury Regiment; The Nelson, Marlborough, and West Coast Regiment; The Otago Regiment; The Southland Regiment

1929   1st Motor Machine Gun Brigade; 1st Canadian Motor Machine Gun Brigade CEF
1931   228th Canadian Infantry Battalion CEF; The Algonquin Regiment; 1st Canadian Pioneer Battalion CEF
1958   Royal Tank Regiment

63.   **ROSIERES**
       26th–27th March 1918
       The German Offensive in Picardy

1925   The Queen's Bays (2nd Dragoon Guards); 4th Royal Irish Dragoon Guards; 5th Dragoon Guards (Princess Charlotte of Wales's); 8th King's Royal Irish Hussars; 9th Queen's Royal Lancers; 11th Hussars (Prince Albert's Own); 15th The King's Hussars; 18th Royal Hussars (Queen Mary's Own); 19th Royal Hussars (Queen Alexandra's Own); South Irish Horse; The Lancashire Hussars Yeomanry; The Royal Scots (The Royal Regiment); The Queen's Royal Regiment (West Surrey); The Northumberland Fusiliers; The Royal Warwickshire Regiment; The Royal Fusiliers (City of London Regiment); The King's Regiment (Liverpool); The Devonshire Regiment; The Somerset Light Infantry (Prince Albert's); The West Yorkshire Regiment (The Prince of Wales's Own); The East Yorkshire Regiment; The Bedfordshire and Hertfordshire Regiment; The Royal Irish Regiment; The Green Howards (Alexandra, Princess of Wales's Own Yorkshire Regiment); The Lancashire Fusiliers; The Royal Scots Fusiliers; The Cheshire Regiment; The Cameronians (Scottish Rifles); The Royal Inniskilling Fusiliers; The Gloucestershire Regiment; The Worcestershire Regiment; The East Lancashire Regiment; The East Surrey Regiment; The Duke of Cornwall's Light Infantry; The Border Regiment; The Royal Sussex Regiment; The Hampshire Regiment; The Prince of Wales's Volunteers (South Lancashire); The Black Watch (Royal Highlanders); The Oxfordshire and Buckinghamshire Light Infantry; The Sherwood Foresters (Nottinghamshire and Derbyshire Regiment); The Northamptonshire Regiment; The Royal Berkshire Regiment (Princess Charlotte of Wales's); The Queen's Own Royal West Kent Regiment; The King's Shropshire Light Infantry; The Middlesex Regiment (Duke of Cambridge's Own); The King's Royal Rifle Corps; The Manchester Regiment; The North

Staffordshire Regiment (The Prince of Wales's): The Durham Light Infantry: The Gordon Highlanders: The Royal Ulster Rifles: The Royal Irish Fusiliers (Princess Victoria's): The Connaught Rangers: The Argyll and Sutherland Highlanders (Princess Louise's): The Prince of Wales's Leinster Regiment (Royal Canadians): The Royal Munster Fusiliers: The Royal Dublin Fusiliers: The Rifle Brigade (Prince Consort's Own): The Cambridgeshire Regiment: The Hertfordshire Regiment

1929   1st Motor Machine Gun Brigade: 1st Canadian Motor Machine Gun Brigade CEF

64.   **ARRAS 1918**
28th March 1918
The German Offensive in Picardy
and
26th August–3rd September 1918
The Breaking of the Hindenburg Line

1925   1st Life Guards: 10th Royal Hussars (Prince of Wales's Own): Berks Yeomanry (Hungerford) (Dragoons): Buckinghamshire Yeomanry (Royal Bucks Hussars): Hampshire (Carabiniers) (Dragoons): The Yorkshire Hussars Yeomanry (Alexandra, Princess of Wales's Own): Honourable Artillery Company: Grenadier Guards: Coldstream Guards: Scots Guards: Irish Guards: Welsh Guards: The Royal Scots (The Royal Regiment): The Queen's Royal Regiment (West Surrey): The King's Own Royal Regiment (Lancaster): The Northumberland Fusiliers: The Royal Warwickshire Regiment: The Royal Fusiliers (City of London Regiment): The King's Regiment (Liverpool): The Lincolnshire Regiment: The Suffolk Regiment: The Somerset Light Infantry (Prince Albert's): The West Yorkshire Regiment (The Prince of Wales's Own): The East Yorkshire Regiment: The Bedfordshire and Hertfordshire Regiment: The Royal Irish Regiment: The Green Howards (Alexandra, Princess of Wales's Own Yorkshire Regiment): The Lancashire Fusiliers: The Royal Scots Fusiliers: The Cheshire Regiment: The South Wales Borderers: The King's Own Scottish Borderers: The Cameronians (Scottish Rifles): The Gloucestershire Regiment: The East Lancashire Regiment: The East Surrey Regiment: The Duke of Wellington's Regiment (West Riding): The Border Regiment: The Royal Sussex Regiment: The Hampshire Regiment: The South Staffordshire Regiment: The Prince of Wales's Volunteers (South Lancashire): The Welch Regiment: The Black Watch (Royal Highlanders): The Essex Regiment: The Sherwood Foresters (Nottinghamshire and Derbyshire Regiment): The Loyal Regiment (North Lancashire): The Northamptonshire Regiment: The Royal Berkshire Regiment (Princess Charlotte of Wales's): The Queen's Own Royal West Kent Regiment: The King's Own Yorkshire Light Infantry: The King's Shropshire Light Infantry: The Middlesex Regiment (Duke of Cambridge's Own): The King's Royal Rifle Corps: The Manchester Regiment: The York and Lancaster Regiment: The Durham Light Infantry: The Highland Light Infantry (City of Glasgow Regiment): The Seaforth Highlanders (Ross-shire Buffs, The Duke of Albany's): The Gordon Highlanders: The Queen's Own Cameron Highlanders: The Argyll and Sutherland Highlanders (Princess Louise's): The Royal Munster Fusiliers: The Rifle Brigade (Prince Consort's Own): 1st City of London Regiment (The Royal Fusiliers): 2nd City of London Regiment (The Royal Fusiliers): 4th City of London Regiment (London Rifle Brigade): 5th City of London Regiment (London Rifle Brigade): 13th London Regiment (Princess Louise's Kensington Regiment): 14th London Regiment (London Scottish): 16th London Regiment (Queen's Westminster Rifles): 28th London Regiment (Artists' Rifles)

1926   72nd (Griqualand West) Siege Battery, Royal Garrison Artillery: 74th (Eastern Province) Siege Battery, Royal Garrison Artillery: 75th (Natal) Siege Battery, Royal Garrison Artillery

1926   The Auckland Regiment (Countess of Ranfurly's Own): The Hauraki Regiment: The North Auckland Regiment: The Waikato Regiment: The Wellington Regiment: The Wellington West Coast Regiment: The Hawke's Bay Regiment: The Taranaki Regiment: The Canterbury Regiment: The Nelson, Marlborough, and West Coast Regiment: The Otago Regiment: The Southland Regiment

1927   13th Battalion: 14th Battalion: 15th Battalion: 16th Battalion
1928   The Otago Mounted Rifles
1929   The Royal Canadian Regiment: Royal 22e Regiment: 16th Canadian Light Horse: The Mississauga Horse: The Saskatchewan Mounted Rifles: The British Columbia Dragoons: The Eastern Townships Mounted Rifles: The Canadian Grenadier Guards: The Queen's Own Rifles of Canada: The Victoria Rifles of Canada: The Royal Highlanders of Canada: The Royal Hamilton Light Infantry: The Princess of Wales' Own Regiment: The Canadian Fusiliers (City of London Regiment): The Dufferin Rifles of Canada: The Peterborough Rangers: The Carleton Light Infantry: The Cape Breton Highlanders: The Saint John Fusiliers:

The Ottawa Highlanders: The Winnipeg Rifles: The Essex Scottish: The 48th Regiment (Highlanders); 1st British Columbia Regiment (Duke of Connaught's Own): The Argyll and Sutherland Highlanders of Canada (Princess Louise's): The Lake Superior Regiment: The Regina Rifle Regiment: The Winnipeg Grenadiers: The Queen's Own Cameron Highlanders of Canada: The Colchester and Hants Regiment: The Calgary Highlanders: The Calgary Regiment: The Westminster Regiment: The Winnipeg Light Infantry: The Saskatoon Light Infantry: The Canadian Scottish Regiment: The King's Own Rifles of Canada: The Kootenay Regiment: The Royal Montreal Regiment: The Toronto Regiment: The Queen's Rangers, 1st American Regiment: The South Alberta Regiment: The North Alberta Regiment: The Edmonton Regiment: The Toronto Scottish Regiment: 1st Motor Machine Gun Brigade: 1st Canadian Mounted Rifles Battalion CEF: 2nd Canadian Mounted Rifles Battalion CEF: 4th Canadian Mounted Rifles Battalion CEF: 5th Canadian Mounted Rifles Battalion CEF: 1st Canadian Infantry Battalion CEF: 4th Canadian Infantry Battalion CEF: 5th Canadian Infantry Battalion CEF: 8th Canadian Infantry Battalion CEF: 13th Canadian Infantry Battalion CEF: 14th Canadian Infantry Battalion CEF: 15th Canadian Infantry Battalion CEF: 16th Canadian Infantry Battalion CEF: 18th Canadian Infantry Battalion CEF: 19th Canadian Infantry Battalion CEF: 20th Canadian Infantry Battalion CEF: 24th Canadian Infantry Battalion CEF: 26th Canadian Infantry Battalion CEF: 28th Canadian Infantry Battalion CEF: 3 lst Canadian Infantry Battalion CEF: 42nd Canadian Infantry Battalion CEF: 43rd Canadian Infantry Battalion CEF: 44th Canadian Infantry Battalion CEF: 46th Canadian Infantry Battalion CEF: 47th Canadian Infantry Battalion CEF: 49th Canadian Infantry Battalion CEF: 50th Canadian Infantry Battalion CEF: 54th Canadian Infantry Battalion CEF: 58th Canadian Infantry Battalion CEF: 75th Canadian Infantry Battalion CEF: 78th Canadian Infantry Battalion CEF: 85th Canadian Infantry Battalion CEF: 1st Canadian Infantry Battalion CEF: 102nd Canadian Infantry Battalion CEF: 116th Canadian Infantry Battalion CEF: The North British Columbia Regiment: The Ontario Regiment: The Manitoba Regiment: 1st Machine Gun Battalion: 2nd Machine Gun Battalion: 3rd Machine Gun Battalion: 4th Machine Gun Battalion: 2nd Canadian Infantry Battalion CEF: 3rd Canadian Infantry Battalion CEF: 10th Canadian Infantry Battalion CEF: 21st Canadian Infantry Battalion CEF: 25th Canadian Infantry Battalion CEF: 27th Canadian Infantry Battalion CEF: 29th Canadian Infantry Battalion CEF: 38th Canadian Infantry Battalion CEF: 52nd Canadian Infantry Battalion CEF: 2nd Canadian Pioneer Battalion CEF: 107th Canadian Pioneer Battalion CEF: 1st Battalion, Canadian Machine Gun Corps CEF: 2nd Battalion, Canadian Machine Gun Corps CEF: 3rd Battalion, Canadian Machine Gun Corps CEF: 4th Battalion, Canadian Machine Gun Corps CEF

1930 | 1st Hussars: 19th Alberta Dragoons: The Prince Edward Island Light Horse: The Governor General's Foot Guards: The Halifax Rifles: The Argyll Light Infantry: The Lincoln Regiment: The Oxford Rifles: The York Rangers: The Middlesex Light Infantry: The Lambton Regiment: The Highland Light Infantry of Canada: The Wellington Rifles: The Grey Regiment: The Bruce Regiment: The Huron Regiment: The Simcoe Foresters: The Peel and Dufferin Regiment: The Halton Rifles: The Northumberland Regiment: The Brockville Rifles: The Lanark and Renfrew Scottish Regiment: The Sherbrooke Regiment: The Stormont Dundas and Glengarry Highlanders: Les Carabiniers Mont-Royal: The York Regiment: The Annapolis Regiment: The North Shore (New Brunswick) Regiment: The New Brunswick Rangers: The Lunenburg Regiment: The Cumberland Highlanders: The Prince Edward Island Highlanders: The Kenora Light Infantry: The Manitoba Rangers: The Edmonton Fusiliers: The Rocky Mountain Rangers: The Prince Albert Volunteers: The Irish Fusiliers of Canada: The Sault Ste Marie Regiment: The Vancouver Regiment: The Irish Regiment: The Yorkton Regiment: The Assiniboia Regiment: The Battleford Light Infantry: 2nd Motor Machine Gun Brigade: 7th Canadian Infantry Battalion CEF: 2nd Canadian Motor Machine Gun Brigade CEF

1931 | 14th Canadian Light Horse: The Manitoba Mounted Rifles: The Seaforth Highlanders of Canada: 72nd Canadian Infantry Battalion CEF

? | 7th Hussars: 11th Hussars

1958 | Royal Tank Regiment

65. **AVRE**
4th April 1918
The German Offensive in Picardy

1925

3rd Dragoon Guards (Prince of Wales's): 7th Dragoon Guards (Princess Royal's): 1st The Royal Dragoons: The Inniskillings (6th Dragoons): 9th Queen's Royal Lancers: 10th Royal Hussars (Prince of Wales's Own): 17th Lancers (Duke of Cambridge's Own): South Irish Horse: The Queen's Royal Regiment (West Surrey): The Buffs (East Kent Regiment): The Royal Fusiliers (City of London Regiment): The King's Regiment (Liverpool): The Somerset Light Infantry (Prince Albert's): The Bedfordshire and Hertfordshire Regiment: The Cameronians (Scottish Rifles): The Gloucestershire Regiment: The East Surrey Regiment: The Royal Sussex Regiment: The Oxfordshire and Buckinghamshire Light Infantry: The Essex Regiment: The Northamptonshire Regiment: The Royal Berkshire Regiment (Princess Charlotte of Wales's): The Queen's Own Royal West Kent Regiment: The Middlesex Regiment (Duke of Cambridge's Own): The King's Royal Rifle Corps: The North Staffordshire Regiment (The Prince of Wales's): The Royal Munster Fusiliers: The Rifle Brigade (Prince Consort's Own): 6th City of London Regiment (City of London Rifles): 7th City of London Regiment

1927
1929

33rd Battalion: 34th Battalion: 35th Battalion: 36th Battalion: 57th Battalion: 58th Battalion: 59th Battalion: 60th Battalion CEF
1st Motor Machine Gun Brigade: 1st Canadian Motor Machine Gun Brigade CEF

66. **ANCRE 1918**
5th April 1918
The German Offensive in Picardy

1925

Queen's Own Royal Glasgow Yeomanry (Dragoons): The Royal Scots (The Royal Regiment): The Queen's Royal Regiment (West Surrey): The Buffs (East Kent Regiment): The Royal Fusiliers (City of London Regiment): The Norfolk Regiment: The Lincolnshire Regiment: The Suffolk Regiment: The Somerset Light Infantry (Prince Albert's): The Bedfordshire and Hertfordshire Regiment: The Lancashire Fusiliers: The Royal Welch Fusiliers: The East Lancashire Regiment: The Duke of Wellington's Regiment (West Riding): The Royal Sussex Regiment: The Dorsetshire Regiment: The Welch Regiment: The Essex Regiment: The Northamptonshire Regiment: The Royal Berkshire Regiment (Princess Charlotte of Wales's): The Queen's Own Royal West Kent Regiment: The Middlesex Regiment (Duke of Cambridge's Own): The King's Royal Rifle Corps: The Manchester Regiment: The Highland Light Infantry (City of Glasgow Regiment): The Rifle Brigade (Prince Consort's Own): 15th (County of London) Battalion, The London Regiment (Prince of Wales's Own, Civil Service Rifles): 17th London Regiment (Poplar and Stepney Rifles): 18th London Regiment (London Irish Rifles): 19th London Regiment (St Pancras): 20th London Regiment (The Queen's Own): 21st London Regiment (First Surrey Rifles): 22nd London Regiment (The Queen's): 23rd London Regiment: 24th London Regiment (The Queen's): 28th London Regiment (Artists' Rifles)

1926

The Auckland Regiment (Countess of Ranfurly's Own): The Hauraki Regiment: The North Auckland Regiment: The Waikato Regiment: The Wellington Regiment: The Wellington West Coast Regiment: The Hawke's Bay Regiment: The Taranaki Regiment: The Canterbury Regiment: The Nelson, Marlborough, and West Coast Regiment: The Otago Regiment: The Southland Regiment

1927

13th Battalion: 14th Battalion: 15th Battalion: 16th Battalion: 29th Battalion: 30th Battalion: 31st Battalion: 32nd Battalion: 37th Battalion: 38th Battalion: 39th Battalion: 40th Battalion: 41st Battalion: 42nd Battalion: 43rd Battalion: 44th Battalion: 45th Battalion: 46th Battalion: 47th Battalion: 48th Battalion: 49th Battalion: 50th Battalion: 51st Battalion: 52nd Battalion: 53rd Battalion: 54th Battalion: 55th Battalion: 56th Battalion

67. **VILLERS BRETONNEUX**
24th–25th April 1918
Actions of Villers Bretonneux

1925

The Queen's Royal Regiment (West Surrey): The Royal Fusiliers (City of London Regiment): The Devonshire Regiment: The West Yorkshire Regiment (The Prince of Wales's Own): The Bedfordshire and Hertfordshire Regiment: The Worcestershire Regiment: The East Lancashire Regiment: The Essex Regiment: The Sherwood Foresters (Nottinghamshire and Derbyshire Regiment): The Northamptonshire Regiment: The Royal Berkshire Regiment (Princess Charlotte of Wales's): The Queen's Own Royal West Kent Regiment: The Middlesex Regiment (Duke of Cambridge's Own): The Rifle Brigade (Prince Consort's Own): 2nd City of London Regiment (The Royal Fusiliers): 3rd City of London Regiment (The Royal Fusiliers): 4th City of London Regiment (The Royal Fusiliers): 7th City of London Regiment: 9th London Regiment (Queen Victoria's Rifles): 10th London Regiment (Hackney): 12th London Regiment (Rangers)

	1927	49th Battalion: 50th Battalion: 51st Battalion: 52nd Battalion: 53rd Battalion: 54th Battalion: 55th Battalion: 56th Battalion: 57th Battalion: 58th Battalion: 59th Battalion: 60th Battalion: Royal Tank Regiment
	1958	
68.	1927	13th Battalion: 14th Battalion: 15th Battalion: 16th Battalion: 17th Battalion: 18th Battalion: 19th Battalion: 20th Battalion: 21st Battalion: 22nd Battalion: 23rd Battalion: 24th Battalion: 41st Battalion: 42nd Battalion: 43rd Battalion: 44th Battalion: 45th Battalion: 46th Battalion: 48th Battalion: 49th Battalion: 50th Battalion: 51st Battalion

68. HAMEL
4th July 1918
Capture of Hamel

69. LYS
9th–29th April 1918
The German Offensive in Flanders — 1925

The Carabiniers (6th Dragoon Guards): 7th Dragoon Guards (Princess Royal's): The Royal Scots Greys (2nd Dragoons): 3rd The King's Own Hussars: The Inniskilings (6th Dragoons): 12th Royal Lancers (Prince of Wales's): 17th Lancers (Duke of Cambridge's Own): 20th Hussars: King Edward's Horse (The King's Oversea Dominions Regiment): The Lancashire Hussars Yeomanry: Oxfordshire Yeomanry (Queen's Own Oxfordshire Hussars): The Royal Wiltshire Yeomanry (Prince of Wales's Own) (Hussars): Grenadier Guards: Coldstream Guards: Irish Guards: The Royal Scots (The Royal Regiment): The Queen's Royal Regiment (West Surrey): The King's Own Royal Regiment (Lancaster): The Northumberland Fusiliers: The Royal Warwickshire Regiment: The Royal Fusiliers (City of London Regiment): The King's Regiment (Liverpool): The Norfolk Regiment: The Lincolnshire Regiment: The Devonshire Regiment: The Suffolk Regiment: The Somerset Light Infantry (Prince Albert's): The West Yorkshire Regiment (The Prince of Wales's Own): The East Yorkshire Regiment: The Bedfordshire and Hertfordshire Regiment: The Leicestershire Regiment: The Green Howards (Alexandra, Princess of Wales's Own Yorkshire Regiment): The Lancashire Fusiliers: The Royal Scots Fusiliers: The Cheshire Regiment: The Royal Welch Fusiliers: The South Wales Borderers: The King's Own Scottish Borderers: The Cameronians (Scottish Rifles): The Gloucestershire Regiment: The Worcestershire Regiment: The East Lancashire Regiment: The East Surrey Regiment: The Duke of Cornwall's Light Infantry: The Duke of Wellington's Regiment (West Riding): The Border Regiment: The Royal Sussex Regiment: The Hampshire Regiment: The South Staffordshire Regiment: The Prince of Wales's Volunteers (South Lancashire): The Welch Regiment: The Black Watch (Royal Highlanders): The Oxfordshire and Buckinghamshire Light Infantry: The Essex Regiment: The Sherwood Foresters (Nottinghamshire and Derbyshire Regiment): The Loyal Regiment (North Lancashire): The Royal Berkshire Regiment (Princess Charlotte of Wales's): The Queen's Own Royal West Kent Regiment: The King's Own Yorkshire Light Infantry: The King's Shropshire Light Infantry: The Middlesex Regiment (Duke of Cambridge's Own): The King's Royal Rifle Corps: The Wiltshire Regiment (Duke of Edinburgh's): The York and Lancaster Regiment: The Durham Light Infantry: The Highland Light Infantry (City of Glasgow Regiment): The Seaforth Highlanders (Ross-shire Buffs, The Duke of Albany's): The Gordon Highlanders: The Queen's Own Cameron Highlanders: The Royal Ulster Rifles: The Royal Irish Fusiliers (Princess Victoria's): The Argyll and Sutherland Highlanders (Princess Louise's): The Rifle Brigade (Prince Consort's Own): The Monmouthshire Regiment: The Cambridgeshire Regiment: The Hertfordshire Regiment: Royal Guernsey Militia (Light Infantry)

1925 — The Royal Newfoundland Regiment

1926 — 71st (Transvaal) Siege Battery, Royal Garrison Artillery: 73rd (Cape) Siege Battery, Royal Garrison Artillery: 125th (Transvaal) Siege Battery, Royal Garrison Artillery: 1st South African Infantry (Cape of Good Hope Regiment): 2nd South African Infantry (Natal and Orange Free State Regiment): 4th South African Infantry (South African Scottish Regiment)

1927 — 4th Light Horse Regiment: 1st Battalion: 2nd Battalion: 3rd Battalion: 4th Battalion: 5th Battalion: 6th Battalion: 7th Battalion: 8th Battalion: 9th Battalion: 10th Battalion: 11th Battalion: 12th Battalion

1928 — The Otago Mounted Rifles

1937 — The Liverpool Scottish, The Queen's Own Cameron Highlanders (TA)

70.	**ESTAIRES** 9th–11th April 1918 The German Offensive in Flanders	1925	King Edward's Horse (The King's Oversea Dominions Regiment): The King's Own Royal Regiment (Lancaster): The Northumberland Fusiliers: The Royal Fusiliers (City of London Regiment): The King's Regiment (Liverpool): The Lincolnshire Regiment: The Suffolk Regiment: The Green Howards (Alexandra, Princess of Wales's Own Yorkshire Regiment): The Lancashire Fusiliers: The Royal Scots Fusiliers: The Cheshire Regiment: The South Wales Borderers: The King's Own Scottish Borderers: The Gloucestershire Regiment: The Worcestershire Regiment: The East Lancashire Regiment: The East Surrey Regiment: The Duke of Cornwall's Light Infantry: The Duke of Wellington's Regiment (West Riding): The Border Regiment: The Hampshire Regiment: The Prince of Wales's Volunteers (South Lancashire): The Welch Regiment: The Black Watch (Royal Highlanders): The Loyal Regiment (North Lancashire): The King's Shropshire Light Infantry: The Middlesex Regiment (Duke of Cambridge's Own): The Durham Light Infantry: The Highland Light Infantry (City of Glasgow Regiment): The Seaforth Highlanders (Ross-shire Buffs, The Duke of Albany's): The Gordon Highlanders: The Queen's Own Cameron Highlanders: The Argyll and Sutherland Highlanders (Princess Louise's): Royal Guernsey Militia (Light Infantry)
		1926	71st (Transvaal) Siege Battery, Royal Garrison Artillery: 73rd (Cape) Siege Battery, Royal Garrison Artillery: 125th (Transvaal) Siege Battery, Royal Garrison Artillery
		1937	The Liverpool Scottish, The Queen's Own Cameron Highlanders (TA)
71.	**MESSINES 1918** 10th–11th April 1918 The German Offensive in Flanders	1925	The Royal Wiltshire Yeomanry (Prince of Wales's Own) (Hussars): The Royal Scots (The Royal Regiment): The Northumberland Fusiliers: The Royal Warwickshire Regiment: The King's Regiment (Liverpool): The Lincolnshire Regiment: The Suffolk Regiment: The West Yorkshire Regiment (The Prince of Wales's Own): The East Yorkshire Regiment: The Green Howards (Alexandra, Princess of Wales's Own Yorkshire Regiment): The Cheshire Regiment: The Royal Welch Fusiliers: The South Wales Borderers: The Gloucestershire Regiment: The Worcestershire Regiment: The Duke of Wellington's Regiment (West Riding): The Border Regiment: The South Staffordshire Regiment: The Prince of Wales's Volunteers (South Lancashire): The Welch Regiment: The Black Watch (Royal Highlanders): The King's Own Yorkshire Light Infantry: The King's Shropshire Light Infantry: The Middlesex Regiment (Duke of Cambridge's Own): The King's Royal Rifle Corps: The Wiltshire Regiment (Duke of Edinburgh's): The North Staffordshire Regiment (The Prince of Wales's): The York and Lancaster Regiment: The Highland Light Infantry (City of Glasgow Regiment): The Seaforth Highlanders (Ross-shire Buffs, The Duke of Albany's): The Queen's Own Cameron Highlanders: The Royal Ulster Rifles: The Royal Irish Fusiliers (Princess Victoria's): The Argyll and Sutherland Highlanders (Princess Louise's): The Monmouthshire Regiment
		1926	1st South African Infantry (Cape of Good Hope Regiment): 2nd South African Infantry (Natal and Orange Free State Regiment): 4th South African Infantry (South African Scottish Regiment)
72.	**HAZEBROUCK** 12th–15th April 1918 The German Offensive in Flanders	1925	The Carabiniers (6th Dragoon Guards): 7th Dragoon Guards (Princess Royal's): The Royal Scots Greys (2nd Dragoons): 3rd The King's Own Hussars: The Inniskillings (6th Dragoons): 12th Royal Lancers (Prince of Wales's): 17th Lancers (Duke of Cambridge's Own): 20th Hussars: King Edward's Horse (The King's Oversea Dominions Regiment): Oxfordshire Yeomanry (Queen's Own Oxfordshire Hussars): Grenadier Guards: Coldstream Guards: Irish Guards: The Royal Scots (The Royal Regiment): The Queen's Royal Regiment (West Surrey): The King's Own Royal Regiment (Lancaster): The Northumberland Fusiliers: The Royal Warwickshire Regiment: The Royal Fusiliers (City of London Regiment): The Devonshire Regiment: The Suffolk Regiment: The Somerset Light Infantry (Prince Albert's): The West Yorkshire Regiment (The Prince of Wales's Own): The East Yorkshire Regiment: The Bedfordshire and Hertfordshire Regiment: The Green Howards (Alexandra, Princess of Wales's Own Yorkshire Regiment): The Lancashire Fusiliers: The Royal Scots Fusiliers: The Cheshire Regiment: The South Wales Borderers: The King's Own Scottish Borderers: The Cameronians (Scottish Rifles): The Gloucestershire Regiment: The South Wales Borderers: The King's Own Scottish Borderers: The Cameronians (Scottish Rifles): The Gloucestershire Regiment: The Worcestershire Regiment: The East Lancashire Regiment: The East Surrey Regiment: The Duke of Cornwall's Light Infantry:

The Duke of Wellington's Regiment (West Riding): The Border Regiment: The Hampshire Regiment: The Prince of Wales's Volunteers (South Lancashire): The Welch Regiment: The Black Watch (Royal Highlanders): The Oxfordshire and Buckinghamshire Light Infantry: The Essex Regiment: The Royal Berkshire Regiment (Princess Charlotte of Wales's): The Queen's Own Royal West Kent Regiment: The King's Own Yorkshire Light Infantry: The King's Shropshire Light Infantry: The Middlesex Regiment (Duke of Cambridge's Own): The York and Lancaster Regiment: The Durham Light Infantry: The Highland Light Infantry (City of Glasgow Regiment): The Seaforth Highlanders (Ross-shire Buffs, The Duke of Albany's): The Gordon Highlanders: The Argyll and Sutherland Highlanders (Princess Louise's): The Rifle Brigade (Prince Consort's Own): Royal Guernsey Militia (Light Infantry)

1927   1st Battalion: 2nd Battalion: 3rd Battalion: 4th Battalion: 5th Battalion: 6th Battalion: 7th Battalion: 8th Battalion: 9th Battalion: 10th Battalion: 11th Battalion: 12th Battalion

73.

BAILLEUL
13th–15th April 1918
The German Offensive in Flanders

1925   The Royal Wiltshire Yeomanry (Prince of Wales's Own) (Hussars): The Royal Scots (The Royal Regiment): The Queen's Royal Regiment (West Surrey): The Northumberland Fusiliers: The Royal Warwickshire Regiment: The King's Regiment (Liverpool): The Norfolk Regiment: The Lincolnshire Regiment: The Suffolk Regiment: The West Yorkshire Regiment (The Prince of Wales's Own): The Leicestershire Regiment: The Lancashire Fusiliers: The Royal Scots Fusiliers: The Cheshire Regiment: The Royal Welch Fusiliers: The South Wales Borderers: The Cameronians (Scottish Rifles): The Gloucestershire Regiment: The Worcestershire Regiment: The East Lancashire Regiment: The Duke of Wellington's Regiment (West Riding): The Border Regiment: The Hampshire Regiment: The South Staffordshire Regiment: The Prince of Wales's Volunteers (South Lancashire): The Welch Regiment: The Sherwood Foresters (Nottinghamshire and Derbyshire Regiment): The Loyal Regiment (North Lancashire): The King's Own Yorkshire Light Infantry: The King's Shropshire Light Infantry: The Middlesex Regiment (Duke of Cambridge's Own): The King's Royal Rifle Corps: The Wiltshire Regiment (Duke of Edinburgh's): The North Staffordshire Regiment (The Prince of Wales's): The York and Lancaster Regiment: The Durham Light Infantry: The Highland Light Infantry (City of Glasgow Regiment): The Seaforth Highlanders (Ross-shire Buffs, The Duke of Albany's): The Royal Ulster Rifles: The Royal Irish Fusiliers (Princess Victoria's): The Argyll and Sutherland Highlanders (Princess Louise's)

1925   The Royal Newfoundland Regiment
1928   The Otago Mounted Rifles

74.

KEMMEL
17th–19th April 1918
and
25th–26th April 1918
The German Offensive in Flanders

1925   The Lancashire Hussars Yeomanry: The Royal Wiltshire Yeomanry (Prince of Wales's Own) (Hussars): The Royal Scots (The Royal Regiment): The Queen's Royal Regiment (West Surrey): The Northumberland Fusiliers: The Royal Warwickshire Regiment: The King's Regiment (Liverpool): The Norfolk Regiment: The Lincolnshire Regiment: The Suffolk Regiment: The West Yorkshire Regiment (The Prince of Wales's Own): The East Yorkshire Regiment: The Leicestershire Regiment: The Green Howards (Alexandra, Princess of Wales's Own Yorkshire Regiment): The Lancashire Fusiliers: The Cheshire Regiment: The Royal Welch Fusiliers: The South Wales Borderers: The King's Own Scottish Borderers: The Cameronians (Scottish Rifles): The Gloucestershire Regiment: The Worcestershire Regiment: The East Lancashire Regiment: The Duke of Wellington's Regiment (West Riding): The Border Regiment: The Royal Sussex Regiment: The Hampshire Regiment: The South Staffordshire Regiment: The Prince of Wales's Volunteers (South Lancashire): The Welch Regiment: The Black Watch (Royal Highlanders): The Sherwood Foresters (Nottinghamshire and Derbyshire Regiment): The Loyal Regiment (North Lancashire): The Queen's Own Royal West Kent Regiment: The King's Own Yorkshire Light Infantry: The King's Shropshire Light Infantry: The Middlesex Regiment (Duke of Cambridge's Own): The King's Royal Rifle Corps: The Wiltshire Regiment (Duke of Edinburgh's): The Manchester Regiment: The North Staffordshire Regiment (The Prince of Wales's): The York and Lancaster Regiment: The Durham Light Infantry: The Highland Light Infantry (City of Glasgow Regiment): The Seaforth Highlanders (Ross-shire Buffs, The Duke of Albany's): The Queen's Own Cameron Highlanders: The Royal Ulster Rifles: The Royal Irish

Fusiliers (Princess Victoria's): The Argyll and Sutherland Highlanders (Princess Louise's): The Cambridgeshire Regiment: The Hertfordshire Regiment

1925 The Royal Newfoundland Regiment

1926 1st South African Infantry (Cape of Good Hope Regiment): 2nd South African Infantry (Natal and Orange Free State Regiment): 4th South African Infantry (South African Scottish Regiment)

1927 4th Light Horse Regiment: 9th Battalion: 10th Battalion

1928 The Otago Mounted Rifles

75. **BETHUNE**
18th April 1918
The German Offensive in Flanders

1925 The Royal Scots (The Royal Regiment): The King's Own Royal Regiment (Lancaster): The Northumberland Fusiliers: The Royal Warwickshire Regiment: The Royal Fusiliers (City of London Regiment): The King's Regiment (Liverpool): The Suffolk Regiment: The Somerset Light Infantry (Prince Albert's): The Lancashire Fusiliers: The Royal Scots Fusiliers: The South Wales Borderers: The Gloucestershire Regiment: The Duke of Wellington's Regiment (West Riding): The Hampshire Regiment: The Welch Regiment: The Black Watch (Royal Highlanders): The Oxfordshire and Buckinghamshire Light Infantry: The Essex Regiment: The Loyal Regiment (North Lancashire): The Royal Berkshire Regiment (Princess Charlotte of Wales's): The King's Shropshire Light Infantry: The King's Royal Rifle Corps: The Seaforth Highlanders (Ross-shire Buffs, The Duke of Albany's): The Gordon Highlanders: The Queen's Own Cameron Highlanders: The Argyll and Sutherland Highlanders (Princess Louise's): The Rifle Brigade (Prince Consort's Own)

1926 71st (Transvaal) Siege Battery, Royal Garrison Artillery: 73rd (Cape) Siege Battery, Royal Garrison Artillery: 125th (Transvaal) Siege Battery, Royal Garrison Artillery

76. **SCHERPENBERG**
29th April 1918
The German Offensive in Flanders

1925 The Lancashire Hussars Yeomanry: The Northumberland Fusiliers: The King's Regiment (Liverpool): The Suffolk Regiment: The East Yorkshire Regiment: The Bedfordshire and Hertfordshire Regiment: The Leicestershire Regiment: The Green Howards (Alexandra, Princess of Wales's Own Yorkshire Regiment): The Lancashire Fusiliers: The Royal Scots Fusiliers: The Cheshire Regiment: The Royal Welch Fusiliers: The South Wales Borderers: The Cameronians (Scottish Rifles): The Worcestershire Regiment: The Duke of Wellington's Regiment (West Riding): The Border Regiment: The Royal Sussex Regiment: The South Staffordshire Regiment: The Prince of Wales's Volunteers (South Lancashire): The Welch Regiment: The Black Watch (Royal Highlanders): The Sherwood Foresters (Nottinghamshire and Derbyshire Regiment): The Loyal Regiment (North Lancashire): The King's Own Yorkshire Light Infantry: The Middlesex Regiment (Duke of Cambridge's Own): The Wiltshire Regiment (Duke of Edinburgh's): The York and Lancaster Regiment: The Durham Light Infantry: The Cambridgeshire Regiment

1928 The Otago Mounted Rifles

77. **AISNE 1918**
27th May–6th June 1918
The German Offensive in Champagne

1925 The Northumberland Fusiliers: The Royal Warwickshire Regiment: The Lincolnshire Regiment: The Devonshire Regiment: The West Yorkshire Regiment (The Prince of Wales's Own): The East Yorkshire Regiment: The Leicestershire Regiment: The Green Howards (Alexandra, Princess of Wales's Own Yorkshire Regiment): The Lancashire Fusiliers: The Cheshire Regiment: The Royal Welch Fusiliers: The South Wales Borderers: The Gloucestershire Regiment: The Worcestershire Regiment: The East Lancashire Regiment: The Border Regiment: The South Staffordshire Regiment: The Prince of Wales's Volunteers (South Lancashire): The Welch Regiment: The Sherwood Foresters (Nottinghamshire and Derbyshire Regiment): The Loyal Regiment (North Lancashire): The Northamptonshire Regiment: The Royal Berkshire Regiment (Princess Charlotte of Wales's): The King's Shropshire Light Infantry: The King's Own Yorkshire Light Infantry: The Middlesex Regiment (Duke of Cambridge's Own): The Wiltshire Regiment (Duke of Edinburgh's): The North Staffordshire Regiment (The Prince of Wales's): The Durham Light Infantry: The Rifle Brigade (Prince Consort's Own)

78. BLIGNY
6th June 1918
The German Offensive in Champagne

1925 — The King's Shropshire Light Infantry

79. BOIS DES BUTTES
6th June 1918
The German Offensive in Champagne

1925 — The Devonshire Regiment

80. MARNE 1918
20th July–2nd August 1918
The Counter Attack in Champagne

1925 — The Royal Scots (The Royal Regiment); The Queen's Royal Regiment (West Surrey); The Devonshire Regiment; The Somerset Light Infantry (Prince Albert's); The West Yorkshire Regiment (The Prince of Wales's Own); The Cheshire Regiment; The King's Own Scottish Borderers; The Cameronians (Scottish Rifles); The Duke of Wellington's Regiment (West Riding); The Royal Sussex Regiment; The Hampshire Regiment: The Black Watch (Royal Highlanders); The Loyal Regiment (North Lancashire); The King's Own Yorkshire Light Infantry; The York and Lancaster Regiment; The Durham Light Infantry; The Seaforth Highlanders (Ross-shire Buffs, The Duke of Albany's); The Gordon Highlanders; The Queen's Own Cameron Highlanders; The Argyll and Sutherland Highlanders (Princess Louise's); The Herefordshire Regiment

1927 — 4th Light Horse Regiment
1928 — The Otago Mounted Rifles

81. SOISSONNAIS-OURCQ
23rd July–2nd August 1918
The Counter Attack in Champagne

1925 — The Royal Scots (The Royal Regiment); The Queen's Royal Regiment (West Surrey); The Somerset Light Infantry (Prince Albert's); The Cheshire Regiment: The King's Own Scottish Borderers: The Cameronians (Scottish Rifles); The Royal Sussex Regiment: The Black Watch (Royal Highlanders); The Loyal Regiment (North Lancashire); The Seaforth Highlanders (Ross-shire Buffs, The Duke of Albany's); The Gordon Highlanders; The Queen's Own Cameron Highlanders; The Argyll and Sutherland Highlanders (Princess Louise's); The Herefordshire Regiment

82. TARDENOIS
20th–31st July 1918
The Counter Attack in Champagne

1925 — The Royal Scots (The Royal Regiment); The Devonshire Regiment: The West Yorkshire Regiment (The Prince of Wales's Own); The Duke of Wellington's Regiment (West Riding); The Hampshire Regiment: The Black Watch (Royal Highlanders); The King's Own Yorkshire Light Infantry: The York and Lancaster Regiment: The Durham Light Infantry: The Seaforth Highlanders (Ross-shire Buffs, The Duke of Albany's); The Gordon Highlanders; The Argyll and Sutherland Highlanders (Princess Louise's)

1927 — 4th Light Horse Regiment
1928 — The Otago Mounted Rifles

83. AMIENS
8th–11th August 1918
The Advance in Picardy

1925 — The Queen's Bays (2nd Dragoon Guards); 3rd Dragoon Guards (Prince of Wales's); 4th Royal Irish Dragoon Guards: 5th Dragoon Guards (Princess Charlotte of Wales's); The Carabiniers (6th Dragoon Guards); 7th Dragoon Guards (Princess Royal's): 1st The Royal Dragoons: The Royal Scots Greys (2nd Dragoons): 3rd The King's Own Hussars: 4th Queen's Own Hussars: 5th Royal Irish Lancers: The Inniskillings (6th Dragoons): 8th King's Royal Irish Hussars: 9th Queen's Royal Lancers: 10th Royal Hussars (Prince of Wales's Own): 11th Hussars (Prince Albert's Own): 12th Royal Lancers (Prince of Wales's): 15th The King's Hussars: 16th The Queen's Lancers: 17th Lancers (Duke of Cambridge's Own): 18th Royal Hussars (Queen Mary's Own): 19th Royal Hussars (Queen Alexandra's Own): 20th Hussars: The Duke of Lancaster's Own Yeomanry (Dragoons): Oxfordshire Yeomanry (Queen's Own Oxfordshire Hussars): Westmorland and Cumberland Yeomanry (Hussars): Honourable Artillery Company: The Royal Scots (The Royal Regiment): The Queen's Royal Regiment (West Surrey): The Buffs (East Kent Regiment): The Royal Fusiliers (City of London Regiment): The Norfolk Regiment: The Lincolnshire Regiment: The Suffolk Regiment: The West Yorkshire Regiment (The Prince of Wales's Own): The East Yorkshire

Regiment: The Bedfordshire and Hertfordshire Regiment: The Lancashire Fusiliers: The East Surrey Regiment: The Duke of Wellington's Regiment (West Riding): The Border Regiment: The Royal Sussex Regiment: The Dorsetshire Regiment: The Essex Regiment: The Sherwood Foresters (Nottinghamshire and Derbyshire Regiment): The Northamptonshire Regiment: The Royal Berkshire Regiment (Princess Charlotte of Wales's): The Queen's Own Royal West Kent Regiment: The King's Own Yorkshire Light Infantry: The Manchester Regiment: The Highland Light Infantry (City of Glasgow Regiment): The Argyll and Sutherland Highlanders (Princess Louise's): The Cambridgeshire Regiment: 2nd City of London Regiment (The Royal Fusiliers): 4th City of London Regiment (The Royal Fusiliers): 6th City of London Regiment (City of London Rifles): 7th City of London Regiment: 8th (City of London) Battalion, The London Regiment (Post Office Rifles): 9th London Regiment (Queen Victoria's Rifles): 10th London Regiment (Hackney): 12th London Regiment (Rangers): 15th (County of London) Battalion, The London Regiment (Prince of Wales's Own, Civil Service Rifles): 21st London Regiment (First Surrey Rifles): Bedfordshire Yeomanry (Lancers): Essex Yeomanry (Dragoons): The Leicestershire Yeomanry (Prince Albert's Own) (Hussars): The North Somerset Yeomanry (Dragoons)

1927   1st Battalion: 2nd Battalion: 3rd Battalion: 4th Battalion: 5th Battalion: 6th Battalion: 7th Battalion: 8th Battalion: 9th Battalion: 10th Battalion: 11th Battalion: 12th Battalion: 13th Battalion: 14th Battalion: 15th Battalion: 16th Battalion: 17th Battalion: 18th Battalion: 19th Battalion: 20th Battalion: 21st Battalion: 22nd Battalion: 23rd Battalion: 24th Battalion: 25th Battalion: 26th Battalion: 27th Battalion: 28th Battalion: 29th Battalion: 30th Battalion: 31st Battalion: 32nd Battalion: 33rd Battalion: 34th Battalion: 35th Battalion: 37th Battalion: 38th Battalion: 39th Battalion: 40th Battalion: 41st Battalion: 42nd Battalion: 43rd Battalion: 44th Battalion: 45th Battalion: 46th Battalion: 48th Battalion: 49th Battalion: 50th Battalion: 51st Battalion: 53rd Battalion: 54th Battalion: 55th Battalion: 56th Battalion: 57th Battalion: 58th Battalion: 59th Battalion: 60th Battalion

1929   The Royal Canadian Regiment: Royal 22e Regiment: 16th Canadian Light Horse: The Mississauga Horse: The Saskatchewan Mounted Rifles: The British Columbia Dragoons: The Eastern Townships Mounted Rifles: The Canadian Grenadier Guards: The Queen's Own Rifles of Canada: The Victoria Rifles of Canada: The Royal Highlanders of Canada: The Royal Grenadiers: The Royal Hamilton Light Infantry: The Princess of Wales' Own Regiment: The Canadian Fusiliers (City of London Regiment): The Dufferin Rifles of Canada: The Peterborough Rangers: The Carleton Light Infantry: The Cape Breton Highlanders: The Saint John Fusiliers: The Ottawa Highlanders: The Winnipeg Rifles: The Essex Scottish: The 48th Regiment (Highlanders): 1st British Columbia Regiment (Duke of Connaught's Own): The Argyll and Sutherland Highlanders of Canada (Princess Louise's): The Lake Superior Regiment: The Regina Rifle Regiment: The Winnipeg Grenadiers: The Queen's Own Cameron Highlanders of Canada: The Colchester and Hants Regiment: The Calgary Highlanders: The Canadian Scottish Regiment: The Westminster Regiment: The Winnipeg Light Infantry: The Saskatoon Light Infantry: The Canadian Scottish Regiment: The King's Own Rifles of Canada: The Kootenay Regiment: The Royal Montreal Regiment: The North Alberta Regiment: The Edmonton Regiment: The Toronto Scottish Regiment: The South Alberta Regiment: 1st Canadian Machine Gun Brigade: 1st Canadian Mounted Rifles Battalion CEF: 2nd Canadian Mounted Rifles Battalion CEF: 4th Canadian Mounted Rifles Battalion CEF: 5th Canadian Mounted Rifles Battalion CEF: 1st Canadian Infantry Battalion CEF: 4th Canadian Infantry Battalion CEF: 5th Canadian Infantry Battalion CEF: 8th Canadian Infantry Battalion CEF: 13th Canadian Infantry Battalion CEF: 14th Canadian Infantry Battalion CEF: 15th Canadian Infantry Battalion CEF: 16th Canadian Infantry Battalion CEF: 18th Canadian Infantry Battalion CEF: 19th Canadian Infantry Battalion CEF: 20th Canadian Infantry Battalion CEF: 24th Canadian Infantry Battalion CEF: 26th Canadian Infantry Battalion CEF: 28th Canadian Infantry Battalion CEF: 31st Canadian Infantry Battalion CEF: 42nd Canadian Infantry Battalion CEF: 43rd Canadian Infantry Battalion CEF: 44th Canadian Infantry Battalion CEF: 46th Canadian Infantry Battalion CEF: 47th Canadian Infantry Battalion CEF: 49th Canadian Infantry Battalion CEF: 50th Canadian Infantry Battalion CEF: 54th Canadian Infantry Battalion CEF: 58th Canadian Infantry Battalion CEF: 75th Canadian Infantry Battalion CEF: 78th Canadian Infantry Battalion CEF: 85th Canadian Infantry Battalion

CEF: 87th Canadian Infantry Battalion CEF: 102nd Canadian Infantry Battalion CEF: 116th Canadian Infantry Battalion CEF: 1st Canadian Motor Machine Gun Brigade CEF: Princess Patricia's Canadian Light Infantry: The North British Columbia Regiment: The Ontario Regiment: The Manitoba Regiment: 1st Machine Gun Battalion: 2nd Machine Gun Battalion: 3rd Machine Gun Battalion: 4th Machine Gun Battalion: 2nd Canadian Infantry Battalion CEF: 3rd Canadian Infantry Battalion CEF: 10th Canadian Infantry Battalion CEF: 21st Canadian Infantry Battalion CEF: 25th Canadian Infantry Battalion CEF: 27th Canadian Infantry Battalion CEF: 29th Canadian Infantry Battalion CEF: 38th Canadian Infantry Battalion CEF: 52nd Canadian Infantry Battalion CEF: 1st Battalion, Canadian Machine Gun Corps CEF: 2nd Battalion, Canadian Machine Gun Corps CEF: 3rd Battalion, Canadian Machine Gun Corps CEF: 4th Battalion, Canadian Machine Gun Corps CEF

1930 1st Hussars: 19th Alberta Dragoons: The Prince Edward Island Light Horse: The Governor General's Foot Guards: The Halifax Rifles: The Royal Rifles of Canada: Les Voltigeurs de Quebec: The Argyll Light Infantry: The Hastings and Prince Edward Regiment: The Lincoln Regiment: The Oxford Rifles: The York Rangers: The Elgin Regiment: The Middlesex Light Infantry: The Lambton Regiment: The Highland Light Infantry of Canada: The Wellington Rifles: The Grey Regiment: The Bruce Regiment: The Huron Regiment: The Simcoe Foresters: The Peel and Dufferin Regiment: The Halton Rifles: The Northumberland Regiment: The Brockville Rifles: The Lanark and Renfrew Scottish Regiment: The Sherbrooke Regiment: The Stormont Dundas and Glengarry Highlanders: Les Carabiniers Mont-Royal: The Princess Louise Fusiliers: The York Regiment: The Annapolis Regiment: The North Shore (New Brunswick) Regiment: The New Brunswick Rangers: The Lunenburg Regiment: The Three Rivers Regiment: The Pictou Highlanders: The Cumberland Highlanders: The Prince Edward Island Highlanders: The Kenora Light Infantry: The Manitoba Rangers: The Edmonton Fusiliers: The Rocky Mountain Rangers: Les Carabiniers de Sherbrooke: The Prince Albert Volunteers: The Irish Fusiliers of Canada: The Sault Ste Marie Regiment: The Irish Canadian Rangers: The Vancouver Regiment: The Irish Regiment: The Yorkton Regiment: The Assiniboia Regiment: The Battleford Light Infantry: 2nd Motor Machine Gun Brigade: 7th Canadian Infantry Battalion CEF: 2nd Canadian Motor Machine Gun Brigade CEF

1931 The Royal Canadian Dragoons: 14th Canadian Light Horse: The Fort Garry Horse: The Manitoba Mounted Rifles: The Seaforth Highlanders of Canada: 1st Cavalry Machine Gun Squadron: 72nd Canadian Infantry Battalion CEF: Machine Gun Squadron, Canadian Cavalry Brigade CEF: Lord Strathcona's Horse (Royal Canadians): The South Alberta Horse

? 7th Hussars: 11th Hussars: McGill University Contingent

1958 Royal Tank Regiment

1961 Le Regiment de Maisonneuve: 41st Battalion CEF

84. **AMIENS 1918**
8th–11th August 1918
The Advance in Picardy

1927 13th Light Horse Regiment

85. **ALBERT 1918**
21st–23rd August 1918
The Advance in Picardy

1925 The Queen's Bays (2nd Dragoon Guards): 4th Royal Irish Dragoon Guards: 5th Dragoon Guards (Princess Charlotte of Wales's): The Royal Scots Greys (2nd Dragoons): 8th King's Royal Irish Hussars: 9th Queen's Royal Lancers: 11th Hussars (Prince Albert's Own): 12th Royal Lancers (Prince of Wales's): 15th The King's Hussars: 18th Royal Hussars (Queen Mary's Own): 19th Royal Hussars (Queen Alexandra's Own): 20th Hussars: The Duke of Lancaster's Yeomanry (Dragoons): The Northumberland Hussars (Yeomanry): Westmorland and Cumberland Yeomanry (Hussars): Honourable Artillery Company: Grenadier Guards: Coldstream Guards: Scots Guards: Irish Guards: Welsh Guards: The Royal Scots (The Royal Regiment): The Queen's Royal Regiment (West Surrey): The Buffs (East Kent Regiment): The King's Own Royal Regiment (Lancaster): The Northumberland Fusiliers: The Royal Warwickshire Regiment: The Royal Fusiliers (City of London Regiment): The King's Regiment (Liverpool): The Lincolnshire Regiment: The Norfolk Regiment: The Suffolk Regiment: The Somerset

Light Infantry (Prince Albert's): The West Yorkshire Regiment (The Prince of Wales's Own): The East Yorkshire Regiment: The Bedfordshire and Hertfordshire Regiment: The Leicestershire Regiment: The Royal Irish Regiment: The Lancashire Fusiliers: The Royal Scots Fusiliers: The Cheshire Regiment: The Royal Welch Fusiliers: The South Wales Borderers: The King's Own Scottish Borderers: The Gloucestershire Regiment: The East Lancashire Regiment: The East Surrey Regiment: The Duke of Cornwall's Light Infantry: The Duke of Wellington's Regiment (West Riding): The Border Regiment: The Royal Sussex Regiment: The South Staffordshire Regiment: The Dorsetshire Regiment: The Welch Regiment: The Oxfordshire and Buckinghamshire Light Infantry: The Essex Regiment: The Sherwood Foresters (Nottinghamshire and Derbyshire Regiment): The Northamptonshire Regiment: The Royal Berkshire Regiment (Princess Charlotte of Wales's): The Queen's Own Royal West Kent Regiment: The King's Own Yorkshire Light Infantry: The King's Shropshire Light Infantry: The Middlesex Regiment (Duke of Cambridge's Own): The King's Royal Rifle Corps: The Wiltshire Regiment (Duke of Edinburgh's): The Manchester Regiment: The North Staffordshire Regiment (The Prince of Wales's): The Durham Light Infantry: The Highland Light Infantry (City of Glasgow Regiment): The Gordon Highlanders: The Argyll and Sutherland Highlanders (Princess Louise's): The Rifle Brigade (Prince Consort's Own): The Cambridgeshire Regiment: 1st City of London Regiment (The Royal Fusiliers): 2nd City of London Regiment (The Royal Fusiliers): 3rd City of London Regiment (The Royal Fusiliers): 4th City of London Regiment (The Royal Fusiliers): 6th City of London Regiment (City of London Rifles): 7th London Regiment: 8th (City of London) Battalion, The London Regiment (Post Office Rifles): 9th London Regiment (Queen Victoria's Rifles): 10th London Regiment (Hackney): 12th London Regiment (Rangers): 13th London Regiment (Princess Louise's Kensington Regiment): 14th London Regiment (London Scottish): 15th (County of London) Battalion, The London Regiment (Prince of Wales's Own, Civil Service Rifles): 17th London Regiment (Poplar and Stepney Rifles): 18th London Regiment (London Irish Rifles): 19th London Regiment (St Pancras): 20th London Regiment (The Queen's Own): 21st London Regiment (First Surrey Rifles): 22nd London Regiment (The Queen's): 23rd London Regiment: 24th London Regiment (The Queen's): 28th London Regiment (Artists' Rifles): The Hertfordshire Regiment: Bedfordshire Yeomanry (Lancers): Essex Yeomanry (Dragoons)

1926   The Auckland Regiment (Countess of Ranfurly's Own): The Hauraki Regiment: The North Auckland Regiment: The Waikato Regiment: The Wellington Regiment: The Wellington West Coast Regiment: The Hawke's Bay Regiment: The Taranaki Regiment: The Canterbury Regiment: The Nelson, Marlborough, and West Coast Regiment: The Otago Regiment: The Southland Regiment

1927   13th Light Horse Regiment: 5th Battalion: 6th Battalion: 8th Battalion: 9th Battalion: 10th Battalion: 11th Battalion: 12th Battalion: 13th Battalion: 14th Battalion: 15th Battalion: 16th Battalion: 17th Battalion: 18th Battalion: 19th Battalion: 20th Battalion: 21st Battalion: 22nd Battalion: 23rd Battalion: 24th Battalion: 25th Battalion: 26th Battalion: 27th Battalion: 28th Battalion: 29th Battalion: 30th Battalion: 31st Battalion: 32nd Battalion: 33rd Battalion: 34th Battalion: 35th Battalion: 37th Battalion: 38th Battalion: 39th Battalion: 40th Battalion: 41st Battalion: 42nd Battalion: 43rd Battalion: 44th Battalion: 45th Battalion: 46th Battalion: 48th Battalion: 49th Battalion: 50th Battalion: 51st Battalion: 53rd Battalion: 54th Battalion: 55th Battalion: 56th Battalion: 57th Battalion: 58th Battalion: 59th Battalion: 60th Battalion

1931   1st Canadian Pioneer Battalion CEF

86. **ALBERT 1918 (CHUIGNES)**
21st–23rd August 1918
The Advance in Picardy

1927   1st Battalion: 2nd Battalion: 3rd Battalion: 4th Battalion: 7th Battalion

87. **MONT ST QUENTIN**
31st August–3rd September 1918
The Advance in Picardy

1927   17th Battalion: 18th Battalion: 19th Battalion: 20th Battalion: 21st Battalion: 22nd Battalion: 23rd Battalion: 24th Battalion: 25th Battalion: 26th Battalion: 27th Battalion: 28th Battalion: 29th Battalion: 30th Battalion: 31st Battalion: 32nd Battalion: 33rd Battalion: 34th Battalion: 35th Battalion: 37th Battalion: 38th Battalion: 39th Battalion: 40th Battalion: 41st Battalion:

42nd Battalion: 43rd Battalion: 44th Battalion: 53rd Battalion: 54th Battalion: 55th Battalion: 56th Battalion: 57th Battalion: 58th Battalion: 59th Battalion: 60th Battalion

1925

1st Life Guards: Berks Yeomanry (Hungerford) (Dragoons): Buckinghamshire Yeomanry (Royal Bucks Hussars): The Yorkshire Hussars Yeomanry (Alexandra, Princess of Wales's Own): Honourable Artillery Company: Grenadier Guards: Coldstream Guards: Irish Guards: The Royal Scots (The Royal Regiment): The King's Own Royal Regiment (Lancaster): The Northumberland Fusiliers: The Royal Warwickshire Regiment: The King's Regiment (Liverpool): The Lincolnshire Regiment: The Suffolk Regiment: The Somerset Light Infantry (Prince Albert's): The West Yorkshire Regiment (The Prince of Wales's Own): The East Yorkshire Regiment: The Green Howards (Alexandra, Princess of Wales's Own Yorkshire Regiment): The Lancashire Fusiliers: The Royal Scots Fusiliers: The Cheshire Regiment: The King's Own Scottish Borderers: The Cameronians (Scottish Rifles): The East Lancashire Regiment: The Duke of Wellington's Regiment (West Riding): The Hampshire Regiment: The South Staffordshire Regiment: The Prince of Wales's Volunteers (South Lancashire): The Black Watch (Royal Highlanders): The Essex Regiment: The Sherwood Foresters (Nottinghamshire and Derbyshire Regiment): The Northamptonshire Regiment: The Royal Berkshire Regiment (Princess Charlotte of Wales's): The Middlesex Regiment (Duke of Cambridge's Own): The York and Lancaster Regiment: The Highland Light Infantry (City of Glasgow Regiment): The Seaforth Highlanders (Ross-shire Buffs, The Duke of Albany's): The Gordon Highlanders: The Argyll and Sutherland Highlanders (Princess Louise's): The Royal Munster Fusiliers: The Rifle Brigade (Prince Consort's Own): 1st City of London Regiment (The Royal Fusiliers): 2nd City of London Regiment (Royal Fusiliers): 4th City of London Regiment (The Royal Fusiliers): 5th City of London Regiment (London Rifle Brigade): 13th London Regiment (Princess Louise's Kensington Regiment): 14th London Regiment (London Scottish): 16th London Regiment (Queen's Westminster Rifles)

88.   **SCARPE 1918**
26th–30th August 1918
The Breaking of the Hindenburg Line

1926

72nd (Griqualand West) Siege Battery, Royal Garrison Artillery: 74th (Eastern Province) Siege Battery, Royal Garrison Artillery: 75th (Natal) Siege Battery, Royal Garrison Artillery

1929

The Royal Canadian Regiment: Royal 22e Regiment: 16th Canadian Light Horse: The Mississauga Horse: The Saskatchewan Mounted Rifles: The British Columbia Dragoons: The Eastern Townships Mounted Rifles: The Canadian Grenadier Guards: The Queen's Own Rifles of Canada: The Victoria Rifles of Canada: The Royal Highlanders of Canada: The Royal Grenadiers: The Royal Hamilton Light Infantry: The Princess of Wales' Own Regiment: The Canadian Fusiliers (City of London Regiment): The Dufferin Rifles of Canada: The Peterborough Rangers: The Carleton Light Infantry: The Cape Breton Highlanders: The Saint John Fusiliers: The Ottawa Highlanders: The Winnipeg Rifles: The Essex Scottish: The 48th Regiment (Highlanders): 1st British Columbia Regiment (Duke of Connaught's Own): The Argyll and Sutherland Highlanders of Canada (Princess Louise's): The Lake Superior Regiment: The Regina Rifle Regiment: The Winnipeg Grenadiers: The Queen's Own Cameron Highlanders of Canada: The Colchester and Hants Regiment: The Calgary Highlanders: The Westminster Regiment: The Winnipeg Light Infantry: The Saskatoon Light Infantry: The Canadian Scottish Regiment: The King's Own Rifles of Canada: The Kootenay Regiment: The Royal Montreal Regiment: The Toronto Regiment: The Queen's Rangers, 1st American Regiment: The South Alberta Regiment: The North Alberta Regiment: The Edmonton Regiment: The Toronto Scottish Regiment: 1st Motor Machine Gun Brigade: 1st Canadian Mounted Rifles Battalion CEF: 2nd Canadian Mounted Rifles Battalion CEF: 4th Canadian Mounted Rifles Battalion CEF: 5th Canadian Mounted Rifles Battalion CEF: 1st Canadian Infantry Battalion CEF: 4th Canadian Infantry Battalion CEF: 5th Canadian Infantry Battalion CEF: 8th Canadian Infantry Battalion CEF: 13th Canadian Infantry Battalion CEF: 14th Canadian Infantry Battalion CEF: 15th Canadian Infantry Battalion CEF: 16th Canadian Infantry Battalion CEF: 18th Canadian Infantry Battalion CEF: 19th Canadian Infantry Battalion CEF: 20th Canadian Infantry Battalion CEF: 24th Canadian Infantry Battalion CEF: 26th Canadian Infantry Battalion CEF: 28th Canadian Infantry Battalion CEF: 31st Canadian Infantry Battalion CEF: 42nd Canadian Infantry Battalion CEF: 43rd Canadian Infantry Battalion CEF: 44th Canadian Infantry Battalion CEF: 46th Canadian Infantry Battalion CEF: 47th Canadian Infantry Battalion CEF: 49th Canadian

Infantry Battalion CEF: 50th Canadian Infantry Battalion CEF: 54th Canadian Infantry Battalion CEF: 58th Canadian Infantry Battalion CEF: 75th Canadian Infantry Battalion CEF: 78th Canadian Infantry Battalion CEF: 85th Canadian Infantry Battalion CEF: 87th Canadian Infantry Battalion CEF: 102nd Canadian Infantry Battalion CEF: 116th Canadian Infantry Battalion CEF: 1st Canadian Motor Machine Gun Brigade CEF: Princess Patricia's Canadian Light Infantry: The North British Columbia Regiment: The Ontario Regiment: The Manitoba Regiment: 1st Machine Gun Battalion: 2nd Machine Gun Battalion: 3rd Machine Gun Battalion: 4th Machine Gun Battalion: 2nd Canadian Infantry Battalion CEF: 3rd Canadian Infantry Battalion CEF: 10th Canadian Infantry Battalion CEF: 21st Canadian Infantry Battalion CEF: 25th Canadian Infantry Battalion CEF: 27th Canadian Infantry Battalion CEF: 29th Canadian Infantry Battalion CEF: 38th Canadian Infantry Battalion CEF: 52nd Canadian Infantry Battalion CEF: 1st Battalion, Canadian Machine Gun Corps CEF: 2nd Battalion, Canadian Machine Gun Corps CEF: 3rd Battalion, Canadian Machine Gun Corps CEF: 4th Battalion, Canadian Machine Gun Corps CEF

1930   1st Hussars: 19th Alberta Dragoons: The Vancouver Regiment: 2nd Motor Machine Gun Regiment: 2nd Motor Machine Gun Brigade: 7th Canadian Infantry Battalion CEF: 2nd Canadian Motor Machine Gun Brigade CEF

1931   The Manitoba Mounted Rifles: The Seaforth Highlanders of Canada: 72nd Canadian Infantry Battalion CEF

?   7th Hussars: 11th Hussars

89. DROCOURT-QUEANT
2nd–3rd September 1918
The Breaking of the Hindenburg Line

1925   10th Royal Hussars (Prince of Wales's Own): The Yorkshire Hussars Yeomanry (Alexandra, Princess of Wales's Own): Honourable Artillery Company: Coldstream Guards: Scots Guards: Irish Guards: Welsh Guards: The Royal Scots (The Royal Regiment): The King's Own Royal Regiment (Lancaster): The Northumberland Fusiliers: The Royal Warwickshire Regiment: The Royal Fusiliers (City of London Regiment): The King's Regiment (Liverpool): The Lincolnshire Regiment: The Somerset Light Infantry (Prince Albert's): The West Yorkshire Regiment (The Prince of Wales's Own): The Bedfordshire and Hertfordshire Regiment: The Royal Irish Regiment: The Green Howards (Alexandra, Princess of Wales's Own Yorkshire Regiment): The Lancashire Fusiliers: The Royal Scots Fusiliers: The South Wales Borderers: The King's Own Scottish Borderers: The Cameronians (Scottish Rifles): The Gloucestershire Regiment: The Duke of Wellington's Regiment (West Riding): The Royal Sussex Regiment: The Hampshire Regiment: The South Staffordshire Regiment: The Prince of Wales's Volunteers (South Lancashire): The Welch Regiment: The Black Watch (Royal Highlanders): The Essex Regiment: The Sherwood Foresters (Nottinghamshire and Derbyshire Regiment): The Loyal Regiment (North Lancashire): The Northamptonshire Regiment: The King's Royal Rifle Corps: The York and Lancaster Regiment: The Highland Light Infantry (City of Glasgow Regiment): The Seaforth Highlanders (Ross-shire Buffs, The Duke of Albany's): The Queen's Own Cameron Highlanders: The Royal Munster Fusiliers: The Rifle Brigade (Prince Consort's Own): 28th London Regiment (Artists' Rifles)

1926   72nd (Griqualand West) Siege Battery, Royal Garrison Artillery: 74th (Eastern Province) Siege Battery, Royal Garrison Artillery: 75th (Natal) Siege Battery, Royal Garrison Artillery

1929   16th Canadian Light Horse: The Canadian Grenadier Guards: The Queen's Own Rifles of Canada: The Royal Highlanders of Canada: The Royal Grenadiers: The Royal Hamilton Light Infantry: The Princess of Wales' Own Regiment: The Canadian Fusiliers (City of London Regiment): The Dufferin Rifles of Canada: The Peterborough Rangers: The Carleton Light Infantry: The Cape Breton Highlanders: The Ottawa Highlanders: The Winnipeg Rifles: The 48th Regiment (Highlanders): 1st British Columbia Regiment (Duke of Connaught's Own): The Argyll and Sutherland Highlanders of Canada (Princess Louise's): The Lake Superior Regiment: The Regina Rifle Regiment: The Winnipeg Grenadiers: The Queen's Own Cameron Highlanders of Canada: The Calgary Highlanders: The Calgary Regiment: The Westminster Regiment: The Winnipeg Light Infantry: The Saskatoon Light Infantry: The Canadian Scottish Regiment: The King's Own Rifles of Canada: The Kootenay Regiment: The South Alberta Regiment: The North Alberta Regiment: The Toronto Regiment: The Toronto Scottish Regiment: The Queen's Rangers, 1st American Regiment: The South Alberta Regiment: The North Alberta Regiment: 1st Motor Machine Gun Brigade: 1st Canadian Infantry Battalion CEF: 4th Canadian Infantry Battalion CEF: 5th Canadian Infantry Battalion CEF: 8th Canadian Infantry Battalion

CEF: 13th Canadian Infantry Battalion CEF: 14th Canadian Infantry Battalion CEF: 15th Canadian Infantry Battalion CEF: 16th Canadian Infantry Battalion CEF: 19th Canadian Infantry Battalion CEF: 20th Canadian Infantry Battalion CEF: 28th Canadian Infantry Battalion CEF: 31st Canadian Infantry Battalion CEF: 43rd Canadian Infantry Battalion CEF: 44th Canadian Infantry Battalion CEF: 46th Canadian Infantry Battalion CEF: 47th Canadian Infantry Battalion CEF: 50th Canadian Infantry Battalion CEF: 54th Canadian Infantry Battalion CEF: 58th Canadian Infantry Battalion CEF: 75th Canadian Infantry Battalion CEF: 78th Canadian Infantry Battalion CEF: 85th Canadian Infantry Battalion CEF: 87th Canadian Infantry Battalion CEF: 102nd Canadian Infantry Battalion CEF: 116th Canadian Infantry Battalion CEF: 1st Canadian Motor Machine Gun Brigade CEF: The North British Columbia Regiment: The Ontario Regiment: The Manitoba Regiment: 1st Machine Gun Battalion: 2nd Machine Gun Battalion: 4th Machine Gun Battalion: 2nd Canadian Infantry Battalion CEF: 3rd Canadian Infantry Battalion CEF: 10th Canadian Infantry Battalion CEF: 21st Canadian Infantry Battalion CEF: 27th Canadian Infantry Battalion CEF: 29th Canadian Infantry Battalion CEF: 38th Canadian Infantry Battalion CEF: 52nd Canadian Infantry Battalion CEF: 1st Battalion, Canadian Machine Gun Corps CEF: 2nd Battalion, Canadian Machine Gun Corps CEF: 4th Battalion, Canadian Machine Gun Corps CEF

1930 1st Hussars: 19th Alberta Dragoons: The Vancouver Regiment: 2nd Motor Machine Gun Brigade: 7th Canadian Infantry Battalion CEF: 2nd Canadian Motor Machine Gun Brigade CEF

1931 The Seaforth Highlanders of Canada: 72nd Canadian Infantry Battalion CEF

90. **HINDENBURG LINE**[1]
12th September–9th October 1918
The Breaking of the Hindenburg Line

1925 1st Life Guards: 2nd Life Guards: Royal Horse Guards (The Blues): The Queen's Bays (2nd Dragoon Guards): 3rd Dragoon Guards (Prince of Wales's): 4th Royal Irish Dragoon Guards: 5th Dragoon Guards (Princess Charlotte of Wales's): The Carabiniers (6th Dragoon Guards): 7th Dragoon Guards (Princess Royal's): 1st The Royal Dragoons: The Royal Scots Greys (2nd Dragoons): 3rd The King's Own Hussars: 4th Queen's Own Hussars: 5th Royal Irish Lancers: The Inniskillings (6th Dragoons): 8th King's Royal Irish Hussars: 9th Queen's Royal Lancers: 10th Royal Hussars (Prince of Wales's Own): 11th Hussars (Prince Albert's Own): 12th Royal Lancers (Prince of Wales's): 15th The King's Hussars: 16th The Queen's Lancers: 17th Lancers (Duke of Cambridge's Own): 18th Royal Hussars (Queen Mary's Own): 19th Royal Hussars (Queen Alexandra's Own): 20th Hussars: North Irish Horse: The Cheshire Yeomanry (Earl of Chester's) (Hussars): Royal 1st Devon Yeomanry (Hussars): Royal North Devon Yeomanry (Hussars): Fife and Forfar Yeomanry: Glamorgan Yeomanry (Dragoons): Royal East Kent Yeomanry (The Duke of Connaught's Own) (Mounted Rifles) (Hussars): West Kent Yeomanry (Queen's Own) (Hussars): The Lancashire Hussars Yeomanry: The Duke of Lancaster's Own Yeomanry (Dragoons): Montgomeryshire Yeomanry (Dragoons): Nottinghamshire Yeomanry (South Nottinghamshire Hussars): Oxfordshire Yeomanry (Queen's Own Oxfordshire Hussars): Pembroke Yeomanry (Castlemartin) (Hussars): The Scottish Horse: Shropshire Yeomanry (Dragoons): West Somerset Yeomanry (Yeomanry): Suffolk Yeomanry (The Duke of York's Own Loyal Suffolk Hussars): Sussex Yeomanry (Dragoons): The Warwickshire Yeomanry (Hussars): Welsh Horse (Lancers): Westmorland and Cumberland Yeomanry (Hussars): The Yorkshire Hussars Yeomanry (Alexandra, Princess of Wales's Own): Honourable Artillery Company: Grenadier Guards: Coldstream Guards: Scots Guards: Irish Guards: Welsh Guards: The Royal Scots (The Royal Regiment): The Queen's Royal Regiment (West Surrey): The Buffs (East Kent Regiment): The King's Own Royal Regiment (Lancaster): The Northumberland Fusiliers: The Royal Warwickshire Regiment: The Royal Fusiliers (City of London Regiment): The King's Regiment (Liverpool): The Norfolk Regiment: The Lincolnshire Regiment: The Devonshire Regiment: The Suffolk Regiment: The Somerset Light Infantry (Prince Albert's): The West Yorkshire Regiment (The Prince of Wales's Own): The East Yorkshire Regiment: The Bedfordshire and Hertfordshire Regiment: The Leicestershire Regiment: The Royal Irish Regiment: The Green Howards (Alexandra, Princess of Wales's Own Yorkshire Regiment): The Lancashire Fusiliers: The Royal Scots Fusiliers: The Cheshire Regiment: The Royal Welch Fusiliers: The South Wales Borderers: The King's Own Scottish Borderers: The Cameronians (Scottish Rifles): The Royal Inniskilling Fusiliers: The Gloucestershire Regiment: The Worcestershire Regiment: The East Lancashire Regiment: The East Surrey Regiment: The Duke of Cornwall's Light Infantry: The Duke of Wellington's

Regiment (West Riding): The Border Regiment: The Royal Sussex Regiment: The Hampshire Regiment: The South Staffordshire Regiment: The Dorsetshire Regiment: The Prince of Wales's Volunteers (South Lancashire): The Welch Regiment: The Black Watch (Royal Highlanders): The Oxfordshire and Buckinghamshire Light Infantry: The Essex Regiment: The Sherwood Foresters (Nottinghamshire and Derbyshire Regiment): The Loyal Regiment (North Lancashire): The Northamptonshire Regiment: The Royal Berkshire Regiment (Princess Charlotte of Wales's): The Queen's Own Royal West Kent Regiment: The King's Own Yorkshire Light Infantry: The King's Shropshire Light Infantry: The Middlesex Regiment (Duke of Cambridge's Own): The King's Royal Rifle Corps: The Wiltshire Regiment (Duke of Edinburgh's): The Manchester Regiment: The North Staffordshire Regiment (The Prince of Wales's): The York and Lancaster Regiment: The Durham Light Infantry: The Highland Light Infantry (City of Glasgow Regiment): The Seaforth Highlanders (Ross-shire Buffs, The Duke of Albany's): The Gordon Highlanders: The Queen's Own Cameron Highlanders: The Connaught Rangers: The Argyll and Sutherland Highlanders (Princess Louise's): The Royal Munster Fusiliers: The Royal Dublin Fusiliers: The Rifle Brigade (Prince Consort's Own): The Monmouthshire Regiment: The Cambridgeshire Regiment: 1st City of London Regiment (The Royal Fusiliers): 2nd City of London Regiment (The Royal Fusiliers): 3rd City of London Regiment (The Royal Fusiliers): 4th City of London Regiment (The Royal Fusiliers): 5th City of London Regiment (London Rifle Brigade): 6th City of London Regiment (City of London Rifles): 7th City of London Regiment: 8th (City of London) Battalion, The London Regiment (Post Office Rifles): 9th London Regiment (Queen Victoria's Rifles): 10th London Regiment (Hackney): 12th London Regiment (Rangers): 13th London Regiment (Princess Louise's Kensington Regiment): 14th London Regiment (London Scottish): 16th London Regiment (Queen's Westminster Rifles): 20th London Regiment (The Queen's Own): 24th London Regiment (The Queen's): 28th London Regiment (Artists' Rifles): The Hertfordshire Regiment: Bedfordshire Yeomanry (Lancers): Essex Yeomanry (Dragoons): The Leicestershire Yeomanry (Prince Albert's Own) (Hussars): The North Somerset Yeomanry (Dragoons)

1926 72nd (Griqualand West) Siege Battery, Royal Garrison Artillery: 74th (Eastern Province) Siege Battery, Royal Garrison Artillery: 75th (Natal) Siege Battery, Royal Garrison Artillery: 1st South African Infantry (Cape of Good Hope Regiment): 2nd South African Infantry (Natal and Orange Free State Regiment): 4th South African Infantry (South African Scottish Regiment): 1st South African Field Ambulance

1926 The Auckland Regiment (Countess of Ranfurly's Own): The Hauraki Regiment: The North Auckland Regiment: The Waikato Regiment: The Wellington Regiment: The Wellington West Coast Regiment: The Hawke's Bay Regiment: The Taranaki Regiment: The Canterbury Regiment: The Nelson, Marlborough, and West Coast Regiment: The Otago Regiment: The Southland Regiment

1927 1st Battalion: 2nd Battalion: 3rd Battalion: 4th Battalion: 5th Battalion: 6th Battalion: 7th Battalion: 8th Battalion: 9th Battalion: 10th Battalion: 11th Battalion: 12th Battalion: 13th Battalion: 14th Battalion: 15th Battalion: 16th Battalion: 17th Battalion: 18th Battalion: 19th Battalion: 20th Battalion: 21st Battalion: 22nd Battalion: 23rd Battalion: 24th Battalion: 25th Battalion: 26th Battalion: 27th Battalion: 28th Battalion: 29th Battalion: 30th Battalion: 31st Battalion: 32nd Battalion: 33rd Battalion: 34th Battalion: 35th Battalion: 37th Battalion: 38th Battalion: 39th Battalion: 40th Battalion: 41st Battalion: 42nd Battalion: 43rd Battalion: 44th Battalion: 45th Battalion: 46th Battalion: 48th Battalion: 49th Battalion: 50th Battalion: 51st Battalion: 53rd Battalion: 54th Battalion: 55th Battalion: 56th Battalion: 57th Battalion: 58th Battalion: 59th Battalion: 60th Battalion

1929 The Royal Canadian Regiment: Royal 22e Regiment: 16th Canadian Light Horse: The Mississauga Horse: The Saskatchewan Mounted Rifles: The British Columbia Dragoons: The Eastern Townships Mounted Rifles: The Canadian Grenadier Guards: The Queen's Own Rifles of Canada: The Victoria Rifles of Canada: The Royal Highlanders of Canada: The Royal Grenadiers: The Royal Hamilton Light Infantry: The Princess of Wales' Own Regiment: The Canadian Fusiliers (City of London Regiment): The Dufferin Rifles of Canada: The Peterborough Rangers: The Carleton Light Infantry: The Cape Breton Highlanders: The Saint John Fusiliers: The Ottawa Highlanders: The Winnipeg Rifles: The Essex Scottish: The 48th Regiment (Highlanders): 1st

British Columbia Regiment (Duke of Connaught's Own): The Argyll and Sutherland Highlanders of Canada (Princess Louise's): The Lake Superior Regiment: The Regina Rifle Regiment: The Winnipeg Grenadiers: The Queen's Own Cameron Highlanders of Canada: The Colchester and Hants Regiment: The Calgary Regiment: The Westminster Regiment: The Winnipeg Light Infantry: The Saskatoon Light Infantry: The Canadian Scottish Regiment: The King's Own Rifles of Canada: The Kootenay Regiment: The Royal Montreal Regiment: The Toronto Regiment: The Queen's Rangers, 1st American Regiment: The South Alberta Regiment: The North Alberta Regiment: The Edmonton Regiment: The Toronto Scottish Regiment: 1st Motor Machine Gun Brigade: 1st Canadian Mounted Rifles Battalion CEF: 2nd Canadian Mounted Rifles Battalion CEF: 4th Canadian Mounted Rifles Battalion CEF: 5th Canadian Mounted Rifles Battalion CEF: 1st Canadian Infantry Battalion CEF: 4th Canadian Infantry Battalion CEF: 5th Canadian Infantry Battalion CEF: 8th Canadian Infantry Battalion CEF: 13th Canadian Infantry Battalion CEF: 14th Canadian Infantry Battalion CEF: 15th Canadian Infantry Battalion CEF: 16th Canadian Infantry Battalion CEF: 18th Canadian Infantry Battalion CEF: 19th Canadian Infantry Battalion CEF: 20th Canadian Infantry Battalion CEF: 24th Canadian Infantry Battalion CEF: 26th Canadian Infantry Battalion CEF: 28th Canadian Infantry Battalion CEF: 31st Canadian Infantry Battalion CEF: 42nd Canadian Infantry Battalion CEF: 43rd Canadian Infantry Battalion CEF: 44th Canadian Infantry Battalion CEF: 46th Canadian Infantry Battalion CEF: 47th Canadian Infantry Battalion CEF: 49th Canadian Infantry Battalion CEF: 50th Canadian Infantry Battalion CEF: 54th Canadian Infantry Battalion CEF: 58th Canadian Infantry Battalion CEF: 75th Canadian Infantry Battalion CEF: 78th Canadian Infantry Battalion CEF: 85th Canadian Infantry Battalion CEF: 87th Canadian Infantry Battalion CEF: 102nd Canadian Infantry Battalion CEF: 116th Canadian Infantry Battalion CEF: 1st Canadian Motor Machine Gun Brigade CEF: Princess Patricia's Canadian Light Infantry: The North British Columbia Regiment: The Ontario Regiment: The Manitoba Regiment: 1st Machine Gun Battalion: 2nd Machine Gun Battalion: 3rd Machine Gun Battalion: 4th Machine Gun Battalion: 2nd Canadian Infantry Battalion CEF: 3rd Canadian Infantry Battalion CEF: 10th Canadian Infantry Battalion CEF: 21st Canadian Infantry Battalion CEF: 25th Canadian Infantry Battalion CEF: 27th Canadian Infantry Battalion CEF: 29th Canadian Infantry Battalion CEF: 38th Canadian Infantry Battalion CEF: 52nd Canadian Infantry Battalion CEF: 1st Battalion, Canadian Machine Gun Corps CEF: 2nd Battalion, Canadian Machine Gun Corps CEF: 3rd Battalion, Canadian Machine Gun Corps CEF: 4th Battalion, Canadian Machine Gun Corps CEF

1930 1st Hussars: 19th Alberta Dragoons: The Prince Edward Island Light Horse: The Halifax Rifles: The Hastings and Prince Edward Regiment: The Lincoln Regiment: The Oxford Rifles: The York Rangers: The Middlesex Light Infantry: The Lambton Regiment: The Highland Light Infantry of Canada: The Wellington Rifles: The Grey Regiment: The Bruce Regiment: The Huron Regiment: The Simcoe Foresters: The Peel and Dufferin Regiment: The Halton Rifles: The Northumberland Regiment: The Brockville Rifles: The Lanark and Renfrew Scottish Regiment: The Stormont Dundas and Glengary Highlanders: Les Carabiniers Mont-Royal: The York Regiment: The Annapolis Regiment: The North Shore (New Brunswick) Regiment: The New Brunswick Rangers: The Lunenburg Regiment: The Cumberland Highlanders: The Prince Edward Island Highlanders: The Kenora Light Infantry: The Manitoba Rangers: The Edmonton Fusiliers: The Rocky Mountain Rangers: The Prince Albert Volunteers: The Irish Fusiliers of Canada: The Sault Ste Marie Regiment: The Vancouver Regiment: The Irish Regiment: The Yorkton Regiment: 2nd Motor Machine Gun Brigade: 7th Canadian Infantry Battalion CEF: 2nd Canadian Motor Machine Gun Brigade CEF

1931 The Royal Canadian Dragoons: 14th Canadian Light Horse: The Fort Garry Horse: The Manitoba Mounted Rifles: The Seaforth Highlanders of Canada: 1st Cavalry Machine Gun Squadron: 72nd Canadian Infantry Battalion CEF: Machine Gun Squadron, Canadian Cavalry Brigade CEF: 228th Canadian Infantry Battalion CEF: Lord Strathcona's Horse (Royal Canadians): The Algonquin Regiment: 1st Canadian Pioneer Battalion CEF

? 7th Hussars: 11th Hussars: McGill University Contingent

1958 Royal Tank Regiment

LIGNE HINDENBURG taken into use by French-speaking Canadian units 1958.

91.	**HAVRINCOURT** 12th September 1918 The Breaking of the Hindenburg Line	1925	Grenadier Guards: Coldstream Guards: Scots Guards: Welsh Guards: The Royal Fusiliers (City of London Regiment): The Devonshire Regiment: The Somerset Light Infantry (Prince Albert's): The West Yorkshire Regiment (The Prince of Wales's Own): The Royal Welch Fusiliers: The South Wales Borderers: The Duke of Cornwall's Light Infantry: The Duke of Wellington's Regiment (West Riding): The Hampshire Regiment: The South Staffordshire Regiment: The Oxfordshire and Buckinghamshire Light Infantry: The Essex Regiment: The Royal Berkshire Regiment (Princess Charlotte of Wales's): The King's Own Yorkshire Light Infantry: The King's Royal Rifle Corps: The North Staffordshire Regiment (The Prince of Wales's): The York and Lancaster Regiment: The Durham Light Infantry: The Highland Light Infantry (City of Glasgow Regiment): The Rifle Brigade (Prince Consort's Own): 20th London Regiment (The Queen's Own): The Hertfordshire Regiment
		1926	The Auckland Regiment (Countess of Ranfurly's Own): The Hauraki Regiment: The North Auckland Regiment: The Waikato Regiment: The Wellington Regiment: The Wellington West Coast Regiment: The Hawke's Bay Regiment: The Taranaki Regiment
92.	**EPEHY** 18th September 1918 The Breaking of the Hindenburg Line	1925	2nd Life Guards: North Irish Horse: The Cheshire Yeomanry (Earl of Chester's) (Hussars): Royal 1st Devon Yeomanry (Hussars): Royal North Devon Yeomanry (Hussars): Fife and Forfar Yeomanry: Glamorgan Yeomanry (Dragoons): Royal East Kent Yeomanry (The Duke of Connaught's Own) (Mounted Rifles) (Hussars): West Kent Yeomanry (Queen's Own) (Hussars): The Duke of Lancaster's Own Yeomanry (Dragoons): Montgomeryshire Yeomanry (Dragoons): Nottinghamshire Yeomanry (South Nottinghamshire Hussars): Pembroke Yeomanry (Castlemartin) (Hussars): Shropshire Yeomanry (Dragoons): West Somerset Yeomanry (Hussars): Suffolk Yeomanry (The Duke of York's Own Loyal Suffolk Hussars): Sussex Yeomanry (Dragoons): The Warwickshire Yeomanry (Hussars): Welsh Horse (Lancers): Westmorland and Cumberland Yeomanry (Hussars): Honourable Artillery Company: The Queen's Royal Regiment (West Surrey): The Buffs (East Kent Regiment): The Northumberland Fusiliers: The Royal Warwickshire Regiment: The Royal Fusiliers (City of London Regiment): The King's Regiment (Liverpool): The Norfolk Regiment: The Lincolnshire Regiment: The Devonshire Regiment: The Suffolk Regiment: The Somerset Light Infantry (Prince Albert's): The West Yorkshire Regiment (The Prince of Wales's Own): The East Yorkshire Regiment: The Bedfordshire and Hertfordshire Regiment: The Leicestershire Regiment: The Lancashire Fusiliers: The Royal Welch Fusiliers: The South Wales Borderers: The King's Own Scottish Borderers: The Cameronians (Scottish Rifles): The Gloucestershire Regiment: The East Surrey Regiment: The Duke of Wellington's Regiment (West Riding): The Border Regiment: The Royal Sussex Regiment: The Dorsetshire Regiment: The Welch Regiment: The Black Watch (Royal Highlanders): The Essex Regiment: The Sherwood Foresters (Nottinghamshire and Derbyshire Regiment): The Loyal Regiment (North Lancashire): The Northamptonshire Regiment: The Royal Berkshire Regiment (Princess Charlotte of Wales's): The Queen's Own Royal West Kent Regiment: The King's Own Yorkshire Light Infantry: The King's Shropshire Light Infantry: The King's Royal Rifle Corps: The Wiltshire Regiment (Duke of Edinburgh's): The Manchester Regiment: The York and Lancaster Regiment: The Durham Light Infantry: The Queen's Own Cameron Highlanders: The Argyll and Sutherland Highlanders (Princess Louise's): The Cambridgeshire Regiment: 2nd City of London Regiment (The Royal Fusiliers): 3rd City of London Regiment (The Royal Fusiliers): 6th City of London Regiment (City of London Rifles): 7th City of London Regiment: 8th (City of London) Battalion, The London Regiment (Post Office Rifles): 9th London Regiment (Queen Victoria's Rifles): 10th London Regiment (Hackney): 12th London Regiment (Rangers): 24th London Regiment (The Queen's)
		1927	1st Battalion: 2nd Battalion: 3rd Battalion: 4th Battalion: 5th Battalion: 6th Battalion: 7th Battalion: 8th Battalion: 9th Battalion: 10th Battalion: 11th Battalion: 12th Battalion: 13th Battalion: 14th Battalion: 15th Battalion: 16th Battalion: 45th Battalion: 46th Battalion: 48th Battalion: 49th Battalion: 50th Battalion: 51st Battalion
		1931	228th Canadian Infantry Battalion CEF: The Algonquin Regiment
		1958	Royal Tank Regiment

93. **CANAL DU NORD**
27th September–1st October 1918
The Breaking of the Hindenburg Line

1925   The Carabiniers (6th Dragoon Guards): 3rd The King's Own Hussars: 4th Queen's Own Hussars: 5th Royal Irish Lancers: 16th The Queen's Lancers: Oxfordshire Yeomanry (Queen's Own Oxfordshire Hussars): The Yorkshire Hussars Yeomanry (Alexandra, Princess of Wales's Own): Grenadier Guards: Coldstream Guards: Scots Guards: Irish Guards: Welsh Guards: The Royal Scots (The Royal Regiment): The King's Own Royal Regiment (Lancaster): The Northumberland Fusiliers: The Royal Warwickshire Regiment: The Royal Fusiliers (City of London Regiment): The King's Regiment (Liverpool): The Norfolk Regiment: The Lincolnshire Regiment: The Devonshire Regiment: The Suffolk Regiment: The Somerset Light Infantry (Prince Albert's): The West Yorkshire Regiment (The Prince of Wales's Own): The East Yorkshire Regiment: The Bedfordshire and Hertfordshire Regiment: The Royal Irish Regiment: The Green Howards (Alexandra, Princess of Wales's Own Yorkshire Regiment): The Lancashire Fusiliers: The Royal Scots Fusiliers: The Cheshire Regiment: The King's Own Scottish Borderers: The Cameronians (Scottish Rifles): The Gloucestershire Regiment: The Worcestershire Regiment: The East Lancashire Regiment: The East Surrey Regiment: The Duke of Cornwall's Light Infantry: The Duke of Wellington's Regiment (West Riding): The Hampshire Regiment: The South Staffordshire Regiment: The Dorsetshire Regiment: The Prince of Wales's Volunteers (South Lancashire): The Oxfordshire and Buckinghamshire Light Infantry: The Sherwood Foresters (Nottinghamshire and Derbyshire Regiment): The Loyal Regiment (North Lancashire): The Royal Berkshire Regiment (Princess Charlotte of Wales's): The Queen's Own Royal West Kent Regiment: The King's Own Yorkshire Light Infantry: The King's Shropshire Light Infantry: The Middlesex Regiment (Duke of Cambridge's Own): The King's Royal Rifle Corps: The Wiltshire Regiment (Duke of Edinburgh's): The Manchester Regiment: The North Staffordshire Regiment (The Prince of Wales's): The York and Lancaster Regiment: The Durham Light Infantry: The Highland Light Infantry (City of Glasgow Regiment): The Gordon Highlanders: The Argyll and Sutherland Highlanders (Princess Louise's): The Royal Munster Fusiliers: The Rifle Brigade (Prince Consort's Own): 1st City of London Regiment (The Royal Fusiliers): 2nd City of London Regiment (London Rifle Brigade): 3rd London Regiment (Princess Louise's Kensington Regiment): 14th London Regiment (London Scottish): 16th London Regiment (Queen's Westminster Rifles): 20th London Regiment (The Queen's Own): 28th London Regiment (Artists' Rifles): The Leicestershire Yeomanry (Prince Albert's Own) (Hussars)

1926   72nd (Griqualand West) Siege Battery, Royal Garrison Artillery: 74th (Eastern Province) Siege Battery, Royal Garrison Artillery: 75th (Natal) Siege Battery, Royal Garrison Artillery

1926   The Auckland Regiment (Countess of Ranfurly's Own): The Hauraki Regiment: The North Auckland Regiment: The Waikato Regiment: The Wellington Regiment: The Wellington West Coast Regiment: The Hawke's Bay Regiment: The Taranaki Regiment: The Canterbury Regiment: The Nelson, Marlborough, and West Coast Regiment: The Otago Regiment: The Southland Regiment

1929   The Royal Canadian Regiment: Royal 22e Regiment: 16th Canadian Light Horse: The Mississauga Horse: The Saskatchewan Mounted Rifles: The British Columbia Dragoons: The Eastern Townships Mounted Rifles: The Canadian Grenadier Guards: The Queen's Own Rifles of Canada: The Victoria Rifles of Canada: The Royal Highlanders of Canada: The Royal Grenadiers: The Royal Hamilton Light Infantry: The Princess of Wales' Own Regiment: The Canadian Fusiliers (City of London Regiment): The Dufferin Rifles of Canada: The Peterborough Rangers: The Carleton Light Infantry: The Cape Breton Highlanders: The Saint John Fusiliers: The Ottawa Highlanders: The Winnipeg Rifles: The Essex Scottish: The 48th Regiment (Highlanders): 1st British Columbia Regiment (Duke of Connaught's Own): The Argyll and Sutherland Highlanders of Canada (Princess Louise's): The Lake Superior Regiment: The Regina Rifle Regiment: The Winnipeg Grenadiers: The Queen's Own Cameron Highlanders of Canada: The Colchester and Hants Regiment: The Calgary Highlanders: The Calgary Regiment: The Westminster Regiment: The Winnipeg Light Infantry: The Saskatoon Light Infantry: The Canadian Scottish Regiment: The King's Own Rifles of Canada: The Kootenay Regiment: The Royal Montreal Regiment: The Toronto Regiment: The Queen's Rangers, 1st American

Regiment: The South Alberta Regiment: The North Alberta Regiment: The Edmonton Regiment: The Toronto Scottish Regiment: 1st Motor Machine Gun Brigade: 1st Canadian Mounted Rifles Battalion CEF: 2nd Canadian Mounted Rifles Battalion CEF: 4th Canadian Mounted Rifles Battalion CEF: 5th Canadian Mounted Rifles Battalion CEF: 1st Canadian Infantry Battalion CEF: 4th Canadian Infantry Battalion CEF: 5th Canadian Infantry Battalion CEF: 8th Canadian Infantry Battalion CEF: 13th Canadian Infantry Battalion CEF: 14th Canadian Infantry Battalion CEF: 15th Canadian Infantry Battalion CEF: 16th Canadian Infantry Battalion CEF: 18th Canadian Infantry Battalion CEF: 19th Canadian Infantry Battalion CEF: 20th Canadian Infantry Battalion CEF: 24th Canadian Infantry Battalion CEF: 26th Canadian Infantry Battalion CEF: 28th Canadian Infantry Battalion CEF: 31st Canadian Infantry Battalion CEF: 42nd Canadian Infantry Battalion CEF: 43rd Canadian Infantry Battalion CEF: 44th Canadian Infantry Battalion CEF: 46th Canadian Infantry Battalion CEF: 47th Canadian Infantry Battalion CEF: 49th Canadian Infantry Battalion CEF: 50th Canadian Infantry Battalion CEF: 54th Canadian Infantry Battalion CEF: 58th Canadian Infantry Battalion CEF: 75th Canadian Infantry Battalion CEF: 78th Canadian Infantry Battalion CEF: 85th Canadian Infantry Battalion CEF: 1st Canadian Infantry Battalion CEF: 87th Canadian Infantry Battalion CEF: 102nd Canadian Infantry Battalion CEF: 116th Canadian Infantry Battalion CEF: 1st Canadian Motor Machine Gun Brigade: Princess Patricia's Canadian Light Infantry: The North British Columbia Regiment: The Ontario Regiment: The Manitoba Regiment: 1st Machine Gun Battalion: 2nd Machine Gun Battalion: 3rd Machine Gun Battalion: 4th Machine Gun Battalion: 2nd Canadian Infantry Battalion CEF: 3rd Canadian Infantry Battalion CEF: 10th Canadian Infantry Battalion CEF: 21st Canadian Infantry Battalion CEF: 25th Canadian Infantry Battalion CEF: 27th Canadian Infantry Battalion CEF: 29th Canadian Infantry Battalion CEF: 38th Canadian Infantry Battalion CEF: 52nd Canadian Infantry Battalion CEF: 1st Battalion, Canadian Machine Gun Corps CEF: 2nd Battalion, Canadian Machine Gun Corps CEF: 3rd Battalion, Canadian Machine Gun Corps CEF: 4th Battalion, Canadian Machine Gun Corps CEF

1930	1st Hussars: 19th Alberta Dragoons: The Vancouver Regiment: 2nd Motor Machine Gun Brigade: 7th Canadian Infantry Battalion CEF: 2nd Canadian Motor Machine Gun Brigade CEF
1931	The Manitoba Mounted Rifles: The Seaforth Highlanders of Canada: 72nd Canadian Infantry Battalion CEF: 1st Canadian Pioneer Battalion CEF
?	7th Hussars: 11th Hussars

94.	**ST QUENTIN CANAL** [1]
	29th September–2nd October 1918
	The Breaking of the Hindenburg Line
1925	2nd Life Guards: The Queen's Bays (2nd Dragoon Guards): 5th Dragoon Guards (Princess Charlotte of Wales's): 7th Dragoon Guards (Princess Royal's): The Royal Scots Greys (2nd Dragoons): The Inniskillings (6th Dragoons): 8th King's Royal Irish Hussars: 11th Hussars (Prince Albert's Own): 12th Royal Lancers (Prince of Wales's): 15th The King's Hussars: 17th Lancers (Duke of Cambridge's Own): 19th Royal Hussars (Queen Alexandra's Own): 20th Hussars: North Irish Horse: Nottinghamshire Yeomanry (South Nottinghamshire Hussars): The Scottish Horse: The Warwickshire Yeomanry (Hussars): The Honourable Artillery Company: The Royal Scots (The Royal Regiment): The Queen's Royal Regiment (West Surrey): The Buffs (East Kent Regiment): The Northumberland Fusiliers: The Royal Fusiliers (City of London Regiment): The Norfolk Regiment: The Lincolnshire Regiment: The East Yorkshire Regiment: The Bedfordshire and Hertfordshire Regiment: The Leicestershire Regiment: The Royal Welch Fusiliers: The South Wales Borderers: The Cameronians (Scottish Rifles): The Gloucestershire Regiment: The Worcestershire Regiment: The East Surrey Regiment: The Border Regiment: The Royal Sussex Regiment: The South Staffordshire Regiment: The Dorsetshire Regiment: The Welch Regiment: The Black Watch (Royal Highlanders): 11th Hussars (Prince Albert's Own): The Essex Regiment: The Sherwood Foresters (Nottinghamshire and Derbyshire Regiment): The Loyal Regiment (North Lancashire): The Northamptonshire Regiment: The Royal Berkshire Regiment (Princess Charlotte of Wales's): The Queen's Own Royal West Kent Regiment: The King's Own Yorkshire Light Infantry: The Middlesex Regiment (Duke of Cambridge's Own): The King's Royal Rifle Corps: The Wiltshire Regiment (Duke of Edinburgh's): The Manchester Regiment: The North Staffordshire Regiment (The Prince of Wales's): The Durham Light Infantry: The Highland Light Infantry (City of Glasgow Regiment): The Queen's Own Cameron Highlanders: The Argyll and Sutherland Highlanders (Princess Louise's): The

	1927	Royal Munster Fusiliers: The Royal Dublin Fusiliers: The Monmouthshire Regiment: The Cambridgeshire Regiment: Bedfordshire Yeomanry (Lancers): Essex Yeomanry (Dragoons)
		29th Battalion: 30th Battalion: 31st Battalion: 32nd Battalion: 33rd Battalion: 34th Battalion: 35th Battalion: 37th Battalion: 38th Battalion: 39th Battalion: 40th Battalion: 41st Battalion: 42nd Battalion: 43rd Battalion: 44th Battalion: 53rd Battalion: 54th Battalion: 55th Battalion: 56th Battalion: 57th Battalion: 58th Battalion: 59th Battalion
	1931	The Royal Canadian Dragoons: The Fort Garry Horse: 1st Cavalry Machine Gun Squadron: Machine Gun Squadron, Canadian Cavalry Brigade CEF: 228th Canadian Infantry Battalion CEF: Lord Strathcona's Horse (Royal Canadians): The Algonquin Regiment
		¹ CANAL DE SAINT-QUENTIN taken into use by French-speaking Canadian units 1958.
95.	**BEAUREVOIR** 3rd–5th October 1918 The Breaking of the Hindenburg Line	1925
	1925	2nd Life Guards: The Queen's Bays (2nd Dragoon Guards): 3rd Dragoon Guards (Prince of Wales's): 5th Dragoon Guards (Princess Charlotte of Wales's): 7th Dragoon Guards (Princess Royal's): 1st The Royal Dragoons: The Royal Scots Greys (2nd Dragoons): The Inniskillings (6th Dragoons): 8th King's Royal Irish Hussars: 10th Royal Hussars (Prince of Wales's Own): 11th Hussars (Prince Albert's Own): 12th Royal Lancers (Prince of Wales's): 15th The King's Hussars: 17th Lancers (Duke of Cambridge's Own): 19th Royal Hussars (Queen Alexandra's Own): 20th Hussars: Nottinghamshire Yeomanry (South Nottinghamshire Hussars): The Scottish Horse: The Warwickshire Yeomanry (Hussars): The Royal Scots (The Royal Regiment): The Northumberland Fusiliers: The Royal Warwickshire Regiment: The Royal Fusiliers (City of London Regiment): The Norfolk Regiment: The Lincolnshire Regiment: The Devonshire Regiment: The Leicestershire Regiment: The Royal Irish Regiment: The Green Howards (Alexandra, Princess of Wales's Own Yorkshire Regiment): The Royal Welch Fusiliers: The South Wales Borderers: The Royal Inniskilling Fusiliers: The Gloucestershire Regiment: The Worcestershire Regiment: The Border Regiment: The Royal Sussex Regiment: The South Staffordshire Regiment: The Dorsetshire Regiment: The Welch Regiment: The Black Watch (Royal Highlanders): The Sherwood Foresters (Nottinghamshire and Derbyshire Regiment): The King's Own Yorkshire Light Infantry: The King's Royal Rifle Corps: The Wiltshire Regiment (Duke of Edinburgh's): The Manchester Regiment: The North Staffordshire Regiment (The Prince of Wales's): The Durham Light Infantry: The Highland Light Infantry (City of Glasgow Regiment): The Argyll and Sutherland Highlanders (Princess Louise's): The Royal Munster Fusiliers: The Royal Dublin Fusiliers: The Monmouthshire Regiment: Bedfordshire Yeomanry (Lancers): Essex Yeomanry (Dragoons): The North Somerset Yeomanry (Dragoons)
	1926	1st South African Field Ambulance
	1927	17th Battalion: 18th Battalion: 19th Battalion: 20th Battalion: 21st Battalion: 22nd Battalion: 23rd Battalion: 24th Battalion: 25th Battalion: 26th Battalion: 27th Battalion: 28th Battalion
	1931	The Royal Canadian Dragoons: The Fort Garry Horse: 1st Cavalry Machine Gun Squadron: Machine Gun Squadron, Canadian Cavalry Brigade CEF: 228th Canadian Infantry Battalion CEF: Lord Strathcona's Horse (Royal Canadians): The Algonquin Regiment
96.	**CAMBRAI 1918** 8th–9th October 1918 The Breaking of the Hindenburg Line	1925
	1925	1st Life Guards: 2nd Life Guards: Royal Horse Guards (The Blues): The Queen's Bays (2nd Dragoon Guards): 3rd Dragoon Guards (Prince of Wales's): 4th Royal Irish Dragoon Guards: 5th Dragoon Guards (Princess Charlotte of Wales's): The Carabiniers (6th Dragoon Guards): 7th Dragoon Guards (Princess Royal's): 1st The Royal Dragoons: The Royal Scots Greys (2nd Dragoons): 3rd The King's Own Hussars: The Inniskillings (6th Dragoons): 8th King's Royal Irish Hussars: 9th Queen's Royal Lancers: 10th Royal Hussars (Prince of Wales's Own): 11th Hussars (Prince Albert's Own): 12th Royal Lancers (Prince of Wales's): 15th The King's Hussars: 17th Lancers (Duke of Cambridge's Own): 18th Royal Hussars (Queen Mary's Own): 19th Royal Hussars (Queen Alexandra's Own): 20th Hussars: North Irish Horse: The Lancashire Hussars Yeomanry: The Duke of Lancaster's Own Yeomanry (Dragoons): Oxfordshire Yeomanry (Queen's Own Oxfordshire Hussars): The Scottish

Horse: Westmorland and Cumberland Yeomanry (Hussars): The Yorkshire Hussars Yeomanry (Alexandra, Princess of Wales's Own): Honourable Artillery Company: Grenadier Guards: Coldstream Guards: Scots Guards: Irish Guards: Welsh Guards: The Queen's Royal Regiment (West Surrey): The Buffs (East Kent Regiment): The King's Own Royal Regiment (Lancaster): The Northumberland Fusiliers: The Royal Warwickshire Regiment: The Royal Fusiliers (City of London Regiment): The King's Regiment (Liverpool): The Norfolk Regiment: The Lincolnshire Regiment: The Devonshire Regiment: The Suffolk Regiment: The Somerset Light Infantry (Prince Albert's): The West Yorkshire Regiment (The Prince of Wales's Own): The East Yorkshire Regiment: The Bedfordshire and Hertfordshire Regiment: The Leicestershire Regiment: The Royal Irish Regiment: The Green Howards (Alexandra, Princess of Wales's Own Yorkshire Regiment): The Lancashire Fusiliers: The Cheshire Regiment: The Royal Welch Fusiliers: The South Wales Borderers: The King's Own Scottish Borderers: The Cameronians (Scottish Rifles): The Royal Inniskilling Fusiliers: The Gloucestershire Regiment: The Worcestershire Regiment: The East Lancashire Regiment: The East Surrey Regiment: The Duke of Cornwall's Light Infantry: The Duke of Wellington's Regiment (West Riding): The Border Regiment: The Royal Sussex Regiment: The Hampshire Regiment: The South Staffordshire Regiment: The Dorsetshire Regiment: The Prince of Wales's Volunteers (South Lancashire): The Welch Regiment: The Black Watch (Royal Highlanders): The Oxfordshire and Buckinghamshire Light Infantry: The Essex Regiment: The Sherwood Foresters (Nottinghamshire and Derbyshire Regiment): The Loyal Regiment (North Lancashire): The Northamptonshire Regiment: The Royal Berkshire Regiment (Princess Charlotte of Wales's): The Queen's Own Royal West Kent Regiment: The King's Own Yorkshire Light Infantry: The King's Shropshire Light Infantry: The Middlesex Regiment (Duke of Cambridge's Own): The King's Royal Rifle Corps: The Wiltshire Regiment (Duke of Edinburgh's): The Manchester Regiment: The North Staffordshire Regiment (The Prince of Wales's): The York and Lancaster Regiment: The Durham Light Infantry: The Highland Light Infantry (City of Glasgow Regiment): The Seaforth Highlanders (Ross-shire Buffs, The Duke of Albany's): The Gordon Highlanders: The Connaught Rangers: The Argyll and Sutherland Highlanders (Princess Louise's): The Royal Munster Fusiliers: The Royal Dublin Fusiliers: The Rifle Brigade (Prince Consort's Own): The Monmouthshire Regiment: 4th City of London Regiment (The Royal Fusiliers): 13th London Regiment (Princess Louise's Kensington Regiment): 14th London Regiment (London Scottish): 20th London Regiment (The Queen's Own): 28th London Regiment (Artists' Rifles): The Hertfordshire Regiment: Essex Yeomanry (Dragoons): The North Somerset Yeomanry (Dragoons)

1926 72nd (Griqualand West) Siege Battery, Royal Garrison Artillery: 74th (Eastern Province) Siege Battery, Royal Garrison Artillery: 75th (Natal) Siege Battery, Royal Garrison Artillery: 1st South African Infantry (Cape of Good Hope Regiment): 2nd South African Infantry (Natal and Orange Free State Regiment): 4th South African Infantry (South African Scottish Regiment)

1926 The Auckland Regiment (Countess of Ranfurly's Own): The Hauraki Regiment: The North Auckland Regiment: The Waikato Regiment: The Wellington Regiment: The Wellington West Coast Regiment: The Hawke's Bay Regiment: The Taranaki Regiment: The Canterbury Regiment: The Nelson, Marlborough, and West Coast Regiment: The Otago Regiment: The Southland Regiment

1929 Royal 22e Regiment: 16th Canadian Light Horse: The Mississauga Horse: The Saskatchewan Mounted Rifles: The British Columbia Dragoons: The Eastern Townships Mounted Rifles: The Victoria Rifles of Canada: The Royal Grenadiers: The Princess of Wales' Own Regiment: The Saint John Fusiliers: The Essex Scottish: The Argyll and Sutherland Highlanders of Canada (Princess Louise's): The Lake Superior Regiment: The Regina Rifle Regiment: The Queen's Own Cameron Highlanders of Canada: The Colchester and Hants Regiment: The Queen's Rangers, 1st American Regiment: The South Alberta Regiment: The North Alberta Regiment: 1st Motor Machine Gun Brigade: 1st Canadian Mounted Rifles Battalion CEF: 2nd Canadian Mounted Rifles Battalion CEF: 4th Canadian Mounted Rifles Battalion CEF: 5th Canadian Mounted Rifles Battalion CEF: 18th Canadian Infantry Battalion CEF: 19th Canadian Infantry Battalion CEF: 20th Canadian Infantry Battalion CEF: 24th Canadian Infantry Battalion CEF: 26th Canadian Infantry Battalion CEF: 28th Canadian Infantry Battalion CEF: 31st Canadian Infantry

Battalion CEF: 43rd Canadian Infantry Battalion CEF: 58th Canadian Infantry Battalion CEF: 116th Canadian Infantry Battalion CEF: 1st Canadian Motor Machine Gun Brigade CEF: The Ontario Regiment: The Manitoba Regiment: 2nd Machine Gun Battalion: 3rd Machine Gun Battalion: 21st Canadian Infantry Battalion CEF: 25th Canadian Infantry Battalion CEF: 27th Canadian Infantry Battalion CEF: 29th Canadian Infantry Battalion CEF: 52nd Canadian Infantry Battalion CEF: 2nd Battalion, Canadian Machine Gun Corps CEF: 3rd Battalion, Canadian Machine Gun Corps CEF

1930 1st Hussars: 19th Alberta Dragoons: The Vancouver Regiment: 2nd Motor Machine Gun Brigade: 2nd Canadian Motor Machine Gun Brigade CEF

1931 The Royal Canadian Dragoons: The Fort Garry Horse: The Manitoba Mounted Rifles: 1st Cavalry Machine Gun Squadron: Machine Gun Squadron, Canadian Cavalry Brigade CEF: 228th Canadian Infantry Battalion CEF: Lord Strathcona's Horse (Royal Canadians): The Algonquin Regiment

? 7th Hussars: 11th Hussars

97. **YPRES 1918**
29th September–2nd October 1918
The Final Advance

1925 South Irish Horse: The Ayrshire Yeomanry (Earl of Carrick's Own) (Hussars): Berks Yeomanry (Hungerford) (Dragoons): Buckinghamshire Yeomanry (Royal Bucks Hussars): Denbighshire Yeomanry (Hussars): Hampshire (Carabiniers) (Dragoons): The Lanarkshire Yeomanry (Lancers): Queen's Own Royal Glasgow Yeomanry (Dragoons): Norfolk Yeomanry (The King's Own Royal Regiment) (Dragoons): The Royal Scots (The Royal Regiment): The Queen's Royal Regiment (West Surrey): The Northumberland Fusiliers: The Royal Fusiliers (City of London Regiment): The Norfolk Regiment: The Suffolk Regiment: The Somerset Light Infantry (Prince Albert's): The West Yorkshire Regiment (The Prince of Wales's Own): The East Yorkshire Regiment: The Royal Irish Regiment: The Lancashire Fusiliers: The Royal Scots Fusiliers: The Cheshire Regiment: The Royal Welch Fusiliers: The South Wales Borderers: The King's Own Scottish Borderers: The Cameronians (Scottish Rifles): The Royal Inniskilling Fusiliers: The Worcestershire Regiment: The East Lancashire Regiment: The East Surrey Regiment: The Border Regiment: The Royal Sussex Regiment: The Hampshire Regiment: The Prince of Wales's Volunteers (South Lancashire): The Black Watch (Royal Highlanders): The Sherwood Foresters (Nottinghamshire and Derbyshire Regiment): The Loyal Regiment (North Lancashire): The Queen's Own Royal West Kent Regiment: The King's Own Yorkshire Light Infantry: The Middlesex Regiment (Duke of Cambridge's Own): The King's Royal Rifle Corps: The Manchester Regiment: The North Staffordshire Regiment (The Prince of Wales's): The York and Lancaster Regiment: The Durham Light Infantry: The Highland Light Infantry (City of Glasgow Regiment): The Seaforth Highlanders (Ross-shire Buffs, The Duke of Albany's): The Queen's Own Cameron Highlanders: The Royal Ulster Rifles: The Royal Irish Fusiliers (Princess Victoria's): The Argyll and Sutherland Highlanders (Princess Louise's): The Prince of Wales's Leinster Regiment (Royal Canadians): The Royal Dublin Fusiliers: The Monmouthshire Regiment: 14th London Regiment (London Scottish): 15th (County of London) Battalion, The London Regiment (Prince of Wales's Own, Civil Service Rifles): 16th London Regiment (Queen's Westminster Rifles): 17th London Regiment (Poplar and Stepney Rifles): 23rd London Regiment: The Herefordshire Regiment

1925 The Royal Newfoundland Regiment

98. **COURTRAI**
14th–19th October 1918
The Final Advance

1925 South Irish Horse: Berks Yeomanry (Hungerford) (Dragoons): Buckinghamshire Yeomanry (Royal Bucks Hussars): Queen's Own Royal Glasgow Yeomanry (Dragoons): Hampshire (Carabiniers) (Dragoons): 2nd County of London Yeomanry (Westminster Dragoons): The Yorkshire Dragoons Yeomanry (Queen's Own): The Royal Scots (The Royal Regiment): The Queen's Royal Regiment (West Surrey): The Northumberland Fusiliers: The Royal Fusiliers (City of London Regiment): The Suffolk Regiment: The Somerset Light Infantry (Prince Albert's): The Royal Irish Regiment: The Lancashire Fusiliers: The Royal Scots Fusiliers: The Cheshire Regiment: The King's Own Scottish Borderers: The Cameronians (Scottish Rifles): The Royal Inniskilling Fusiliers: The Worcestershire Regiment: The East Surrey Regiment: The Border Regiment: The Royal Sussex Regiment: The Hampshire Regiment: The Prince of Wales's Volunteers (South Lancashire): The Black Watch

(Royal Highlanders): The Sherwood Foresters (Nottinghamshire and Derbyshire Regiment): The Loyal Regiment (North Lancashire): The Queen's Own Royal West Kent Regiment: The Middlesex Regiment (Duke of Cambridge's Own): The King's Royal Rifle Corps: The Manchester Regiment: The North Staffordshire Regiment (The Prince of Wales's): The Durham Light Infantry: The Highland Light Infantry (City of Glasgow Regiment): The Seaforth Highlanders (Ross-shire Buffs, The Duke of Albany's): The Queen's Own Cameron Highlanders: The Royal Ulster Rifles: The Royal Irish Fusiliers (Princess Victoria's): The Argyll and Sutherland Highlanders (Princess Louise's): The Prince of Wales's Leinster Regiment (Royal Canadians): The Royal Dublin Fusiliers: The Monmouthshire Regiment: 14th London Regiment (London Scottish): 15th (County of London) Battalion, The London Regiment (Prince of Wales's Own, Civil Service Rifles): 16th London Regiment (Queen's Westminster Rifles): 17th London Regiment (Poplar and Stepney Rifles): 23rd London Regiment: The Herefordshire Regiment

The Royal Newfoundland Regiment

1925

1925   **SELLE**
       17th–25th October 1918
       The Final Advance

99.

2nd Life Guards: The Carabiniers (6th Dragoon Guards): 3rd The King's Own Hussars: 11th Hussars (Prince Albert's Own): North Irish Horse: The Lancashire Hussars Yeomanry: The Duke of Lancaster's Own Yeomanry (Dragoons): Lincolnshire Yeomanry (Lancers): The Northumberland Hussars (Yeomanry): Nottinghamshire Yeomanry (South Nottinghamshire Hussars): Oxfordshire Yeomanry (Queen's Own Oxfordshire Hussars): The Scottish Horse: The Warwickshire Yeomanry (Hussars): Westmorland and Cumberland Yeomanry (Hussars): The Yorkshire Hussars Yeomanry (Alexandra, Princess of Wales's Own): East Riding of Yorkshire Yeomanry (Lancers): Honourable Artillery Company: Grenadier Guards: Coldstream Guards: Scots Guards: Irish Guards: Welsh Guards: The Royal Scots (The Royal Regiment): The Queen's Royal Regiment (West Surrey): The Buffs (East Kent Regiment): The King's Own Royal Regiment (Lancaster): The Northumberland Fusiliers: The Royal Warwickshire Regiment: The Royal Fusiliers (City of London Regiment): The King's Regiment (Liverpool): The Norfolk Regiment: The Lincolnshire Regiment: The Devonshire Regiment: The Suffolk Regiment: The Somerset Light Infantry (Prince Albert's): The West Yorkshire Regiment (The Prince of Wales's Own): The East Yorkshire Regiment: The Bedfordshire and Hertfordshire Regiment: The Leicestershire Regiment: The Green Howards (Alexandra, Princess of Wales's Own Yorkshire Regiment): The Lancashire Fusiliers: The Royal Scots Fusiliers: The Cheshire Regiment: The Royal Welch Fusiliers: The South Wales Borderers: The King's Own Scottish Borderers: The Cameronians (Scottish Rifles): The Royal Inniskilling Fusiliers: The Duke of Cornwall's Light Infantry: The Worcestershire Regiment: The East Lancashire Regiment: The East Surrey Regiment: The Duke of Wellington's Regiment (West Riding): The Border Regiment: The Royal Sussex Regiment: The Prince of Wales's Volunteers (South Lancashire): The Welch Regiment: The Black Watch (Royal Highlanders): The Oxfordshire and Buckinghamshire Light Infantry: The Essex Regiment: The Sherwood Foresters (Nottinghamshire and Derbyshire Regiment): The Loyal Regiment (North Lancashire): The Northamptonshire Regiment: The Royal Berkshire Regiment (Princess Charlotte of Wales's): The Queen's Own Royal West Kent Regiment: The King's Own Yorkshire Light Infantry: The King's Shropshire Light Infantry: The Middlesex Regiment (Duke of Cambridge's Own): The King's Royal Rifle Corps: The Wiltshire Regiment (Duke of Edinburgh's): The Manchester Regiment: The North Staffordshire Regiment (The Prince of Wales's): The York and Lancaster Regiment: The Durham Light Infantry: The Highland Light Infantry (City of Glasgow Regiment): The Seaforth Highlanders (Ross-shire Buffs, The Duke of Albany's): The Gordon Highlanders: The Queen's Own Cameron Highlanders: The Connaught Rangers: The Argyll and Sutherland Highlanders (Princess Louise's): The Royal Munster Fusiliers: The Royal Dublin Fusiliers: The Rifle Brigade (Prince Consort's Own): 20th London Regiment (The Queen's Own): The Hertfordshire Regiment

1926   1st South African Infantry (Cape of Good Hope Regiment): 2nd South African Infantry (Natal and Orange Free State Regiment): 1st South African Field Ambulance

1926   The Auckland Regiment (Countess of Ranfurly's Own): The Hauraki Regiment: The North Auckland Regiment: The Waikato Regiment: The Wellington Regiment: The Wellington West Coast Regiment: The Hawke's Bay Regiment: The Taranaki

		Regiment: The Canterbury Regiment: The Nelson, Marlborough, and West Coast Regiment: The Otago Regiment: The Southland Regiment
	1931	1st Canadian Pioneer Battalion CEF
	1958	Royal Tank Regiment
100.	**VALENCIENNES** 1st–2nd November 1918 The Final Advance	
	1925	Lincolnshire Yeomanry (Lancers): The Yorkshire Hussars Yeomanry (Alexandra, Princess of Wales's Own): East Riding of Yorkshire Yeomanry (Lancers): The King's Own Royal Regiment (Lancaster): The Northumberland Fusiliers: The Royal Warwickshire Regiment: The Suffolk Regiment: The Somerset Light Infantry (Prince Albert's): The West Yorkshire Regiment (The Prince of Wales's Own): The Green Howards (Alexandra, Princess of Wales's Own Yorkshire Regiment): The Cheshire Regiment: The Royal Welch Fusiliers: The South Wales Borderers: The Gloucestershire Regiment: The Worcestershire Regiment: The East Lancashire Regiment: The Duke of Wellington's Regiment (West Riding): The Hampshire Regiment: The Welch Regiment: The Oxfordshire and Buckinghamshire Light Infantry: The Royal Berkshire Regiment (Princess Charlotte of Wales's): The King's Own Yorkshire Light Infantry: The King's Shropshire Light Infantry: The Middlesex Regiment (Duke of Cambridge's Own): The North Staffordshire Regiment (The Prince of Wales's): The York and Lancaster Regiment: The Seaforth Highlanders (Ross-shire Buffs, The Duke of Albany's): The Rifle Brigade (Prince Consort's Own): 1st City of London Regiment (The Royal Fusiliers): 2nd City of London Regiment (Royal Fusiliers): 4th City of London Regiment (The Royal Fusiliers): 5th City of London Regiment (London Rifle Brigade): 13th London Regiment (Princess Louise's Kensington Regiment): 14th London Regiment (London Scottish): 16th London Regiment (Queen's Westminster Rifles)
	1929	The Mississauga Horse: The Saskatchewan Mounted Rifles: The Eastern Townships Mounted Rifles: The Canadian Grenadier Guards: The Carleton Light Infantry: The Cape Breton Highlanders: The Ottawa Highlanders: The Lake Superior Regiment: The Winnipeg Grenadiers: The Calgary Regiment: The Westminster Regiment: The King's Own Rifles of Canada: The Kootenay Regiment: The Toronto Scottish Regiment: 1st Motor Machine Gun Brigade: 1st Canadian Mounted Rifles Battalion CEF: 4th Canadian Mounted Rifles Battalion CEF: 5th Canadian Mounted Rifles Battalion CEF: 44th Canadian Infantry Battalion CEF: 46th Canadian Infantry Battalion CEF: 47th Canadian Infantry Battalion CEF: 50th Canadian Infantry Battalion CEF: 54th Canadian Infantry Battalion CEF: 75th Canadian Infantry Battalion CEF: 78th Canadian Infantry Battalion CEF: 85th Canadian Infantry Battalion CEF: 87th Canadian Infantry Battalion CEF: 102nd Canadian Infantry Battalion CEF: 116th Canadian Infantry Battalion CEF: 1st Canadian Motor Machine Gun Brigade CEF: The North British Columbia Regiment: The Ontario Regiment: 4th Machine Gun Battalion: 38th Canadian Infantry Battalion CEF: 52nd Canadian Infantry Battalion CEF: 4th Battalion, Canadian Machine Gun Corps CEF
	1930	The Rocky Mountain Rangers: The Irish Fusiliers of Canada
	1931	The Manitoba Mounted Rifles: The Seaforth Highlanders of Canada: 72nd Canadian Infantry Battalion CEF
	?	7th Hussars: 11th Hussars
101.	**SAMBRE** 4th November 1918 The Final Advance	
	1925	Royal Horse Guards (The Blues): The Carabiniers (6th Dragoon Guards): 3rd The King's Own Hussars: 12th Royal Lancers (Prince of Wales's): 20th Hussars: North Irish Horse: The Duke of Lancaster's Own Yeomanry (Dragoons): Lincolnshire Yeomanry (Lancers): The Northumberland Hussars (Yeomanry): Nottinghamshire Yeomanry (South Nottinghamshire Hussars): Oxfordshire Yeomanry (Queen's Own Oxfordshire Hussars): The Scottish Horse: The Warwickshire Yeomanry (Hussars): Westmorland and Cumberland Yeomanry (Hussars): The Yorkshire Hussars Yeomanry (Alexandra, Princess of Wales's Own): East Riding of Yorkshire Yeomanry (Lancers): Honourable Artillery Company: Grenadier Guards: Coldstream Guards: Scots Guards: Irish Guards: Welsh Guards: The Royal Scots (The Royal Regiment): The Queen's Royal Regiment (West Surrey): The Buffs (East Kent Regiment): The King's Own Royal Regiment (Lancaster): The Northumberland Fusiliers: The Royal Warwickshire Regiment: The Royal Fusiliers (City of London Regiment): The King's Regiment (Liverpool): The

Norfolk Regiment: The Lincolnshire Regiment: The Devonshire Regiment: The Suffolk Regiment: The Somerset Light Infantry (Prince Albert's): The West Yorkshire Regiment (The Prince of Wales's Own): The East Yorkshire Regiment: The Bedfordshire and Hertfordshire Regiment: The Leicestershire Regiment: The Green Howards (Alexandra, Princess of Wales's Own Yorkshire Regiment): The Lancashire Fusiliers: The Cheshire Regiment: The Royal Welch Fusiliers: The South Wales Borderers: The King's Own Scottish Borderers: The Cameronians (Scottish Rifles): The Royal Inniskilling Fusiliers: The Gloucestershire Regiment: The Worcestershire Regiment: The East Lancashire Regiment: The East Surrey Regiment: The Duke of Cornwall's Light Infantry: The Duke of Wellington's Regiment (West Riding): The Border Regiment: The Royal Sussex Regiment: The Hampshire Regiment: The South Staffordshire Regiment: The Dorsetshire Regiment: The Prince of Wales's Volunteers (South Lancashire): The Welch Regiment: The Black Watch (Royal Highlanders): The Essex Regiment: The Sherwood Foresters (Nottinghamshire and Derbyshire Regiment): The Loyal Regiment (North Lancashire): The Northamptonshire Regiment: The Royal Berkshire Regiment (Princess Charlotte of Wales's): The Queen's Own Royal West Kent Regiment: The King's Own Yorkshire Light Infantry: The King's Shropshire Light Infantry: The Middlesex Regiment (Duke of Cambridge's Own): The King's Royal Rifle Corps: The Wiltshire Regiment (Duke of Edinburgh's): The Manchester Regiment: The North Staffordshire Regiment (The Prince of Wales's): The York and Lancaster Regiment: The Durham Light Infantry: The Highland Light Infantry (City of Glasgow Regiment): The Gordon Highlanders: The Queen's Own Cameron Highlanders: The Argyll and Sutherland Highlanders (Princess Louise's): The Royal Munster Fusiliers: The Royal Dublin Fusiliers: The Rifle Brigade (Prince Consort's Own): The Monmouthshire Regiment 1st City of London Regiment (The Royal Fusiliers): 2nd City of London Regiment (The Royal Fusiliers): 4th City of London Regiment (The Royal Fusiliers): 5th City of London Regiment (London Rifle Brigade): 13th London Regiment (Princess Louise's Kensington Regiment): 14th London Regiment (London Scottish): 16th London Regiment (Queen's Westminster Rifles): The Hertfordshire Regiment

1st South African Field Ambulance

The Auckland Regiment (Countess of Ranfurly's Own): The Hauraki Regiment: The North Auckland Regiment: The Waikato Regiment: The Wellington West Coast Regiment: The Hawke's Bay Regiment: The Taranaki Regiment: The Canterbury Regiment: The Nelson, Marlborough, and West Coast Regiment: The Otago Regiment: The Southland Regiment

The Mississauga Horse: The Eastern Townships Mounted Rifles: The Canadian Grenadier Guards: The Cape Breton Highlanders: The Ottawa Highlanders: The Winnipeg Grenadiers: The Kootenay Regiment: The Toronto Scottish Regiment: 1st Motor Machine Gun Brigade: 4th Canadian Mounted Rifles Battalion CEF: 5th Canadian Mounted Rifles Battalion CEF: 54th Canadian Infantry Battalion CEF: 75th Canadian Infantry Battalion CEF: 78th Canadian Infantry Battalion CEF: 85th Canadian Infantry Battalion CEF: 87th Canadian Infantry Battalion CEF: 1st Canadian Motor Machine Gun Brigade CEF: 4th Machine Gun Battalion: 38th Canadian Infantry Battalion CEF: 4th Battalion, Canadian Machine Gun Corps CEF

The Seaforth Highlanders of Canada: 72nd Canadian Infantry Battalion CEF

7th Hussars: 11th Hussars

The Wellington Regiment

The Queen's Bays (2nd Dragoon Guards): 3rd Dragoon Guards (Prince of Wales's): 4th Royal Irish Dragoon Guards: 5th Dragoon Guards (Princess Charlotte of Wales's): 7th Dragoon Guards (Princess Royal's): 1st The Royal Dragoons: The Royal Scots Greys (2nd Dragoons): 4th Queen's Own Hussars: 5th Royal Irish Lancers: The Inniskillings (6th Dragoons): 8th King's Royal Irish Hussars: 9th Queen's Royal Lancers: 10th Royal Hussars (Prince of Wales's Own): 15th The King's Hussars: 16th The Queen's Lancers: 17th Lancers (Duke of Cambridge's Own): 18th Royal Hussars (Queen Mary's Own): 19th Royal

1926	
1926	
1929	
1931	
?	

102. SAMBRE (LE QUESNOY)
4th November 1918
The Final Advance

| 1926 |

103. PURSUIT TO MONS [1]
17th October–11th November 1918
The Final Advance

| 1925 |

Hussars (Queen Alexandra's Own): King Edward's Horse (The King's Oversea Dominions Regiment): The Cheshire Yeomanry (Earl of Chester's) (Hussars): Royal 1st Devon Yeomanry (Hussars): Royal North Devon Yeomanry (Hussars): Fife and Forfar Yeomanry: Glamorgan Yeomanry (Dragoons): Royal East Kent Yeomanry (The Duke of Connaught's Own) (Mounted Rifles) (Hussars): West Kent Yeomanry (Queen's Own) (Hussars): City of London Yeomanry (Rough Riders) (Lancers): 3rd County of London Yeomanry (Sharpshooters) (Hussars): Montgomeryshire Yeomanry (Dragoons): Pembroke Yeomanry (Castlemartin) (Hussars): Shropshire Yeomanry (Dragoons): West Somerset Yeomanry (Hussars): Suffolk Yeomanry (The Duke of York's Own Loyal Suffolk Hussars): Sussex Yeomanry (Dragoons): Welsh Horse (Lancers): The Cambridgeshire Regiment: 3rd City of London Regiment (The Royal Fusiliers): 6th City of London Regiment (City of London Rifles): 7th City of London Regiment 8th (City of London) Battalion, The London Regiment (Post Office Rifles): 9th London Regiment (Queen Victoria's Rifles): 10th London Regiment (Hackney): 12th London Regiment (Rangers): 18th London Regiment (London Irish Rifles): 19th London Regiment (St Pancras): 21st London Regiment (First Surrey Rifles): 22nd London Regiment (The Queen's): 24th London Regiment (The Queen's): 28th London Regiment (Artists' Rifles): The British West Indies Regiment: Bedfordshire Yeomanry (Lancers): Essex Yeomanry (Dragoons): The Leicestershire Yeomanry (Prince Albert's Own) (Hussars): The North Somerset Yeomanry (Dragoons)

1926   71st (Transvaal) Siege Battery, Royal Garrison Artillery: 72nd (Griqualand West) Siege Battery, Royal Garrison Artillery: 73rd (Cape) Siege Battery, Royal Garrison Artillery: 74th (Eastern Province) Siege Battery, Royal Garrison Artillery: 75th (Natal) Siege Battery, Royal Garrison Artillery: 125th (Transvaal) Siege Battery, Royal Garrison Artillery: 4th South African Infantry (South African Scottish Regiment)

1929   The Royal Canadian Regiment: Royal 22e Regiment: 16th Canadian Light Horse: The British Columbia Dragoons: The Queen's Own Rifles of Canada: The Victoria Rifles of Canada: The Royal Highlanders of Canada: The Royal Grenadiers: The Royal Hamilton Light Infantry: The Princess of Wales' Own Regiment: The Canadian Fusiliers (City of London Regiment): The Dufferin Rifles of Canada: The Peterborough Rangers: The Saint John Fusiliers: The Winnipeg Rifles: The Essex Scottish: The 48th Regiment (Highlanders): 1st British Columbia Regiment (Duke of Connaught's Own): The Argyll and Sutherland Highlanders of Canada (Princess Louise's): The Regina Rifle Regiment: The Queen's Own Cameron Highlanders of Canada: The Colchester and Hants Regiment: The Calgary Highlanders: The Winnipeg Light Infantry: The Saskatoon Light Infantry: The Canadian Scottish Regiment: The Royal Montreal Regiment: The Toronto Regiment: The Queen's Rangers, 1st American Regiment: The South Alberta Regiment: The North Alberta Regiment: The Edmonton Regiment: 2nd Canadian Mounted Rifles Battalion CEF: 1st Canadian Infantry Battalion CEF: 4th Canadian Infantry Battalion CEF: 5th Canadian Infantry Battalion CEF: 8th Canadian Infantry Battalion CEF: 13th Canadian Infantry Battalion CEF: 14th Canadian Infantry Battalion CEF: 15th Canadian Infantry Battalion CEF: 16th Canadian Infantry Battalion CEF: 18th Canadian Infantry Battalion CEF: 19th Canadian Infantry Battalion CEF: 20th Canadian Infantry Battalion CEF: 24th Canadian Infantry Battalion CEF: 26th Canadian Infantry Battalion CEF: 28th Canadian Infantry Battalion CEF: 31st Canadian Infantry Battalion CEF: 42nd Canadian Infantry Battalion CEF: 43rd Canadian Infantry Battalion CEF: 49th Canadian Infantry Battalion CEF: 58th Canadian Infantry Battalion CEF: Princess Patricia's Canadian Light Infantry: The Manitoba Regiment 1st Machine Gun Battalion: 2nd Machine Gun Battalion: 3rd Machine Gun Battalion: 2nd Canadian Infantry Battalion CEF: 3rd Canadian Infantry Battalion CEF: 10th Canadian Infantry Battalion CEF: 21st Canadian Infantry Battalion CEF: 25th Canadian Infantry Battalion CEF: 27th Canadian Infantry Battalion CEF: 29th Canadian Infantry Battalion CEF: 1st Battalion, Canadian Machine Gun Corps CEF: 2nd Battalion, Canadian Machine Gun Corps CEF: 3rd Battalion, Canadian Machine Gun Corps CEF

1930   1st Hussars: 19th Alberta Dragoons: The Prince Edward Island Light Horse: The Halifax Rifles: The Hastings and Prince Edward Regiment: The Lincoln Regiment: The Oxford Rifles: The York Rangers: The Middlesex Light Infantry: The Lambton Regiment: The Highland Light Infantry of Canada: The Wellington Rifles: The Grey Regiment: The Bruce Regiment: The Huron Regiment:

The Simcoe Foresters: The Peel and Dufferin Regiment: The Halton Rifles: The Northumberland Regiment: The Brockville Rifles: The Lanark and Renfrew Scottish Regiment: The Stormont Dundas and Glengarry Highlanders: Les Carabiniers Mont-Royal: The York Regiment: The Annapolis Regiment: The North Shore (New Brunswick) Regiment: The New Brunswick Rangers: The Lunenburg Regiment: The Cumberland Highlanders: The Prince Edward Island Highlanders: The Kenora Light Infantry: The Manitoba Rangers: The Edmonton Fusiliers: The Prince Albert Volunteers: The Sault Ste Marie Regiment: The Vancouver Regiment: The Irish Regiment: The Yorkton Regiment: 2nd Motor Machine Gun Brigade: 7th Canadian Infantry Battalion CEF: 2nd Canadian Motor Machine Gun Brigade CEF

| 1931 | The Royal Canadian Dragoons: 14th Canadian Light Horse: The Fort Garry Horse: 1st Cavalry Machine Gun Squadron: Machine Gun Squadron, Canadian Cavalry Brigade CEF: Lord Strathcona's Horse (Royal Canadians) |
| ? | McGill University Contingent |

¹ *POURSUITE A MONS taken into use by French-speaking Canadian units 1958.*

104.	**FRANCE AND FLANDERS 1914–15**	1926	20th Lancers: Queen Victoria's Own Madras Sappers and Miners: King George's Own Bengal Sappers and Miners: Royal Bombay Sappers and Miners: 2nd Bombay Pioneers: 3rd Sikh Pioneers: 6th Rajputana Rifles: 9th Jat Regiment: 10th Baluch Regiment: 11th Sikh Regiment: 13th Frontier Force Rifles: 16th Punjab Regiment: 17th Dogra Regiment: 18th Royal Garhwal Rifles: 1st King George's Own Gurkha Rifles (The Malaun Regiment): 2nd King Edward's Own Gurkha Rifles (The Sirmoor Rifles): 3rd Queen Alexandra's Own Gurkha Rifles: 4th Prince of Wales's Own Gurkha Rifles: 8th Gurkha Rifles: 9th Gurkha Rifles
	4th August 1914–31st December 1915		
	Service in France and Flanders 1914–18		
		1926	Bharatpur Transport Corps
		1927	Holkar's Transport Corps (Indore)
105.	**FRANCE AND FLANDERS 1914–16**	1925	13th Hussars
	4th August 1914–31st December 1916	1926	1st Duke of York's Own Skinner's Horse: 8th King George's Own Light Cavalry
	Service in France and Flanders 1914–18		
106.	**FRANCE AND FLANDERS 1914–17**	1925	1st King's Dragoon Guards: Northamptonshire Yeomanry (Dragoons)
	4th August 1914– 31st December 1917		
	Service in France and Flanders 1914–18		
107.	**FRANCE AND FLANDERS 1914–18** ¹	1925	1st Life Guards: 2nd Life Guards: Royal Horse Guards (The Blues): The Queen's Bays (2nd Dragoon Guards); 3rd Dragoon Guards (Prince of Wales's): 4th Royal Irish Dragoon Guards: 5th Dragoon Guards (Princess Charlotte of Wales's): The Carabiniers (6th Dragoon Guards): 7th Dragoon Guards (Princess Royal's): 1st The Royal Dragoons: The Royal Scots Greys (2nd Dragoons): 3rd The King's Own Hussars: 4th Queen's Own Hussars: 5th Royal Irish Lancers: The Inniskillings (6th Dragoons): 8th King's Royal Irish Hussars: 9th Queen's Royal Lancers: 10th Royal Hussars (Prince of Wales's Own): 11th Hussars (Prince Albert's Own): 12th Royal Lancers (Prince of Wales's): 15th The King's Hussars: 16th The Queen's Lancers: 17th Lancers (Duke of Cambridge's Own): 18th Royal Hussars (Queen Mary's Own): 19th Royal Hussars (Queen Alexandra's Own): 20th Hussars: North Irish Horse: The Northumberland Hussars (Yeomanry): Oxfordshire Yeomanry (Queen's Own Oxfordshire Hussars): Honourable Artillery Company: Grenadier Guards: Coldstream Guards: Scots Guards: Irish Guards: The Royal Scots (The Royal Regiment): The Queen's Royal Regiment (West Surrey): The Buffs (East Kent Regiment): The King's Own Royal Regiment (Lancaster): The Northumberland Fusiliers: The Royal Warwickshire Regiment: The Royal Fusiliers (City of London Regiment): The King's Regiment (Liverpool): The Norfolk Regiment: The Lincolnshire Regiment: The Devonshire Regiment: The Suffolk Regiment: The Somerset Light Infantry (Prince Albert's): The West Yorkshire Regiment
	4th August 1914–11th November 1918		
	Service in France and Flanders 1914–18		

(The Prince of Wales's Own): The East Yorkshire Regiment: The Bedfordshire and Hertfordshire Regiment: The Leicestershire Regiment: The Royal Irish Regiment: The Green Howards (Alexandra, Princess of Wales's Own Yorkshire Regiment): The Lancashire Fusiliers: The Royal Scots Fusiliers: The Cheshire Regiment: The Royal Welch Fusiliers: The South Wales Borderers: The King's Own Scottish Borderers: The Cameronians (Scottish Rifles): The Royal Inniskilling Fusiliers: The Gloucestershire Regiment: The Worcestershire Regiment: The East Lancashire Regiment: The East Surrey Regiment: The Duke of Cornwall's Light Infantry: The Duke of Wellington's Regiment (West Riding): The Border Regiment: The Royal Sussex Regiment: The Hampshire Regiment: The South Staffordshire Regiment: The Dorsetshire Regiment: The Prince of Wales's Volunteers (South Lancashire): The Welch Regiment: The Black Watch (Royal Highlanders): The Oxfordshire and Buckinghamshire Light Infantry: The Essex Regiment: The Sherwood Foresters (Nottinghamshire and Derbyshire Regiment): The Loyal Regiment (North Lancashire): The Northamptonshire Regiment: The Royal Berkshire Regiment (Princess Charlotte of Wales's): The Queen's Own Royal West Kent Regiment: The King's Own Yorkshire Light Infantry: The King's Shropshire Light Infantry: The Middlesex Regiment (Duke of Cambridge's Own): The King's Royal Rifle Corps: The Wiltshire Regiment (Duke of Edinburgh's): The Manchester Regiment: The North Staffordshire Regiment (The Prince of Wales's): The York and Lancaster Regiment: The Durham Light Infantry: The Highland Light Infantry (City of Glasgow Regiment): The Seaforth Highlanders (Ross-shire Buffs, The Duke of Albany's): The Gordon Highlanders: The Queen's Own Cameron Highlanders: The Royal Ulster Rifles: The Royal Irish Fusiliers (Princess Victoria's): The Connaught Rangers: The Argyll and Sutherland Highlanders (Princess Louise's): The Prince of Wales's Leinster Regiment (Royal Canadians): The Royal Munster Fusiliers: The Royal Dublin Fusiliers: The Rifle Brigade (Prince Consort's Own): The Monmouthshire Regiment: 5th City of London Regiment (London Rifle Brigade): 9th London Regiment (Queen Victoria's Rifles): 12th London Regiment (Rangers): 13th London Regiment (Princess Louise's Kensington Regiment): 14th London Regiment (London Scottish): 16th London Regiment (Queen's Westminster Rifles): 28th London Regiment (Artists' Rifles): The Hertfordshire Regiment: Essex Yeomanry (Dragoons): The Leicestershire Yeomanry (Prince Albert's Own) (Hussars): The North Somerset Yeomanry (Dragoons)

1926 — 2nd Lancers (Gardner's Horse): 4th Duke of Cambridge's Own Hodson's Horse: 9th Royal Deccan Horse: 14th Prince of Wales's Own Scinde Horse: 17th Queen Victoria's Own Poona Horse: 18th King Edward's Own Cavalry: 19th King George's Own Lancers

1926 — Jodhpur Sardar Risala
1929 — Princess Patricia's Canadian Light Infantry
1937 — The Liverpool Scottish, The Queen's Own Cameron Highlanders (TA)

[1] FRANCE ET FLANDRES 1914–18 taken into use by French-speaking Canadian units 1958.

108. FRANCE AND FLANDERS 1915 [1]
1st January–31st December 1915
Service in France and Flanders 1914–18

1925 — Lothians and Border Horse (Dragoons): Surrey Yeomanry (Queen Mary's Regiment) (Lancers)
1926 — 2nd Punjab Regiment: 8th Punjab Regiment: 14th Punjab Regiment: 15th Punjab Regiment
1926 — Malerkotla Sappers: Garhwal Rajya Sappers
1929 — 3rd Regiment, Canadian Mounted Rifles CEF: 6th Regiment, Canadian Mounted Rifles CEF [2]
1931 — The Algonquin Regiment

[1] FRANCE ET FLANDRES 1915 taken into use by French-speaking Canadian units 1958. [2] FRANCE AND FLANDERS 1915–16 taken into use 1960.

109. FRANCE AND FLANDERS 1915–16 [1]
1st January 1915–31st December 1916
Service in France and Flanders 1914–18

1930 — King's Canadian Hussars
1931 — The Alberta Mounted Rifles
1960 — 8th Canadian Hussars (Princess Louise's): 8th Canadian Hussars (Princess Louise's) (Militia)

[1] FRANCE ET FLANDRES 1915–16 taken into use by French-speaking Canadian units 1958.

110.	**FRANCE AND FLANDERS 1915–17** 1st January 1915–31st December 1917 Service in France and Flanders 1914–18	1925

1925 — King Edward's Horse (The King's Oversea Dominions Regiment)

111.	**FRANCE AND FLANDERS 1915–18** [1] 1st January 1915–11th November 1918 Service in France and Flanders 1914–18	1925

1925 — South Irish Horse: Queen's Own Royal Glasgow Yeomanry (Dragoons): The Duke of Lancaster's Own Yeomanry (Dragoons): The Yorkshire Dragoons Yeomanry (Queen's Own): The Yorkshire Westmorland and Cumberland Yeomanry (Hussars): The Yorkshire Dragoons Yeomanry (Queen's Own): The Yorkshire Hussars Yeomanry (Alexandra, Princess of Wales's Own): Welsh Guards: The Cambridgeshire Regiment: 1st City of London Regiment (The Royal Fusiliers): 2nd City of London Regiment (The Royal Fusiliers): 3rd City of London Regiment (The Royal Fusiliers): 4th City of London Regiment (The Royal Fusiliers): 6th City of London Regiment (City of London Rifles): 7th City of London Regiment: 8th (City of London) Battalion, The London Regiment (Post Office Rifles): 15th (County of London) Battalion, The London Regiment (Prince of Wales's Own, Civil Service Rifles): 17th London Regiment (Poplar and Stepney Rifles): 18th London Regiment (London Irish Rifles): 19th London Regiment (St Pancras): 20th London Regiment (The Queen's Own): 21st London Regiment (First Surrey Rifles): 22nd London Regiment (The Queen's): 23rd London Regiment: 24th London Regiment (The Queen's): Bedfordshire Yeomanry (Lancers)

1929 — The Royal Canadian Regiment: Royal 22e Regiment: 16th Canadian Light Horse: The Mississauga Horse: The Saskatchewan Mounted Rifles: The British Columbia Dragoons: The Eastern Townships Mounted Rifles: The Canadian Grenadier Guards: The Queen's Own Rifles of Canada: The Victoria Rifles of Canada: The Royal Highlanders of Canada: The Royal Grenadiers: The Royal Hamilton Light Infantry: The Princess of Wales's Own Regiment: The Canadian Fusiliers (City of London Regiment): The Dufferin Rifles of Canada: The Peterborough Rangers: The Saint John Fusiliers: The Winnipeg Rifles: The Essex Scottish: The 48th Regiment (Highlanders): 1st British Columbia Regiment (Duke of Connaught's Own): The Argyll and Sutherland Highlanders of Canada (Princess Louise's): The Lake Superior Regiment: The Regina Rifle Regiment: The Winnipeg Grenadiers: The Queen's Own Cameron Highlanders of Canada: The Colchester and Hants Regiment: The Calgary Highlanders: The Calgary Regiment: The Winnipeg Light Infantry: The Saskatoon Light Infantry: The Canadian Scottish Regiment: The Royal Montreal Regiment: The Toronto Regiment: The Queen's Rangers, 1st American Regiment: The South Alberta Regiment: The North Alberta Regiment: The Edmonton Regiment: 1st Motor Machine Gun Brigade: 1st Canadian Mounted Rifles Battalion CEF: 2nd Canadian Mounted Rifles Battalion CEF: 4th Canadian Mounted Rifles Battalion CEF: 5th Canadian Mounted Rifles Battalion CEF: 1st Canadian Infantry Battalion CEF: 4th Canadian Infantry Battalion CEF: 5th Canadian Infantry Battalion CEF: 8th Canadian Infantry Battalion CEF: 13th Canadian Infantry Battalion CEF: 14th Canadian Infantry Battalion CEF: 15th Canadian Infantry Battalion CEF: 16th Canadian Infantry Battalion CEF: 18th Canadian Infantry Battalion CEF: 19th Canadian Infantry Battalion CEF: 20th Canadian Infantry Battalion CEF: 24th Canadian Infantry Battalion CEF: 26th Canadian Infantry Battalion CEF: 28th Canadian Infantry Battalion CEF: 31st Canadian Infantry Battalion CEF: 42nd Canadian Infantry Battalion CEF: 49th Canadian Infantry Battalion CEF: 1st Canadian Motor Machine Gun Brigade CEF: The North British Columbia Regiment: The Manitoba Regiment: 2nd Canadian Infantry Battalion CEF: 3rd Canadian Infantry Battalion CEF: 10th Canadian Infantry Battalion CEF: 21st Canadian Infantry Battalion CEF: 25th Canadian Infantry Battalion CEF: 27th Canadian Infantry Battalion CEF: 29th Canadian Infantry Battalion CEF

1930 — 1st Hussars: 19th Alberta Dragoons: The York Rangers: The Vancouver Regiment: 7th Canadian Infantry Battalion CEF

1931 — The Royal Canadian Dragoons: The Manitoba Mounted Rifles: The Seaforth Highlanders of Canada: Lord Strathcona's Horse (Royal Canadians)

? — 7th Hussars: 11th Hussars

[1] *FRANCE ET FLANDRES 1915–18 taken into use by French-speaking Canadian units 1958.*

112.	**FRANCE AND FLANDERS 1916–17** [1]	
	1st January 1916–31st December 1917	
	Service in France and Flanders 1914–18	
		1925	Hampshire (Carabiniers) (Dragoons)
		1926	21st King George's Own Central India Horse [2]
		1929	60th Canadian Infantry Battalion CEF: 3rd Pioneer Battalion (48th Canadians) CEF: 67th Canadian (Pioneer) Battalion CEF
			[1] *FRANCE ET FLANDRES 1916–17 taken into use by French-speaking Canadian units 1958.* [2] *FRANCE AND FLANDERS 1914–18 taken into use 1926.*
113.	**FRANCE AND FLANDERS 1916–18** [1]	
	1st January 1916–11th November 1918	
	Service in France and Flanders 1914–18	
		1925	The Lancashire Hussars Yeomanry: The Lovat Scouts: The Royal Wiltshire Yeomanry (Prince of Wales's Own) (Hussars): The British West Indies Regiment
		1925	The Royal Newfoundland Regiment
		1926	71st (Transvaal) Siege Battery, Royal Garrison Artillery: 72nd (Griqualand West) Siege Battery, Royal Garrison Artillery: 73rd (Cape) Siege Battery, Royal Garrison Artillery: 74th (Eastern Province) Siege Battery, Royal Garrison Artillery: 75th (Natal) Siege Battery, Royal Garrison Artillery: 125th (Transvaal) Siege Battery, Royal Garrison Artillery: 1st South African Infantry (Cape of Good Hope Regiment): 2nd South African Infantry (Natal and Orange Free State Regiment): 3rd South African Infantry (Transvaal and Rhodesian Regiment): 4th South African Infantry (South African Scottish Regiment): 1st South African Field Ambulance
		1926	The Auckland Regiment (Countess of Ranfurly's Own): The Hauraki Regiment: The North Auckland Regiment: The Waikato Regiment: The Wellington Regiment: The Wellington West Coast Regiment: The Hawke's Bay Regiment: The Taranaki Regiment: The Canterbury Regiment: The Nelson, Marlborough, and West Coast Regiment: The Otago Regiment: The Southland Regiment
		1927	4th Light Horse Regiment: 13th Light Horse Regiment: 1st Battalion: 2nd Battalion: 3rd Battalion: 4th Battalion: 5th Battalion: 6th Battalion: 7th Battalion: 8th Battalion: 9th Battalion: 10th Battalion: 11th Battalion: 12th Battalion: 13th Battalion: 14th Battalion: 15th Battalion: 16th Battalion: 17th Battalion: 18th Battalion: 19th Battalion: 20th Battalion: 21st Battalion: 22nd Battalion: 23rd Battalion: 24th Battalion: 25th Battalion: 26th Battalion: 27th Battalion: 28th Battalion: 29th Battalion: 30th Battalion: 31st Battalion: 32nd Battalion: 33rd Battalion: 34th Battalion: 35th Battalion: 36th Battalion: 37th Battalion: 38th Battalion: 39th Battalion: 40th Battalion: 41st Battalion: 42nd Battalion: 43rd Battalion: 44th Battalion: 45th Battalion: 46th Battalion: 47th Battalion: 48th Battalion: 49th Battalion: 50th Battalion: 51st Battalion: 52nd Battalion: 53rd Battalion: 54th Battalion: 55th Battalion: 56th Battalion: 57th Battalion: 58th Battalion: 59th Battalion: 60th Battalion
		1928	The Otago Mounted Rifles
		1929	The Carleton Light Infantry: The Ottawa Highlanders: The Westminster Regiment: The King's Own Rifles of Canada: The Kootenay Regiment: The Toronto Scottish Regiment: 43rd Canadian Infantry Battalion CEF: 44th Canadian Infantry Battalion CEF: 46th Canadian Infantry Battalion CEF: 47th Canadian Infantry Battalion CEF: 50th Canadian Infantry Battalion CEF: 54th Canadian Infantry Battalion CEF: 58th Canadian Infantry Battalion CEF: 75th Canadian Infantry Battalion CEF: 78th Canadian Infantry Battalion CEF: 87th Canadian Infantry Battalion CEF: 102nd Canadian Infantry Battalion CEF: The Ontario Regiment: 38th Canadian Infantry Battalion CEF: 52nd Canadian Infantry Battalion CEF: 2nd Canadian Pioneer Battalion CEF
		1931	The Fort Garry Horse: 1st Cavalry Machine Gun Squadron: 72nd Canadian Infantry Battalion CEF: Machine Gun Squadron, Canadian Cavalry Brigade CEF: 1st Canadian Pioneer Battalion CEF
		1958	Royal Tank Regiment
			[1] *FRANCE ET FLANDRES 1916–18 taken into use by French-speaking Canadian units 1958.*

114.	FRANCE AND FLANDERS 1917–18		

114. FRANCE AND FLANDERS 1917–18
1st January 1917–11th November 1918
Service in France and Flanders 1914–18

1925 10th London Regiment (Hackney); 11th London Regiment (Finsbury Rifles); Royal Guernsey Militia (Light Infantry)
1929 The Cape Breton Highlanders; 85th Canadian Infantry Battalion CEF; 116th Canadian Infantry Battalion CEF; 107th Canadian Pioneer Battalion CEF; 123rd Canadian Pioneer Battalion CEF; 124th Canadian Pioneer Battalion CEF
1930 127th Canadian Infantry Battalion CEF
1931 228th Canadian Infantry Battalion CEF; The Algonquin Regiment
¹ FRANCE ET FLANDRES 1917–18 taken into use by French-speaking Canadian units 1958.

115. FRANCE AND FLANDERS 1918 ¹
1st January–11th November 1918
Service in France and Flanders 1914–18

1925 King Edward's Horse (The King's Oversea Dominions Regiment); The Ayrshire Yeomanry (Earl of Carrick's Own) (Hussars); Berks Yeomanry (Hungerford) (Dragoons); Buckinghamshire Yeomanry (Royal Bucks Hussars); The Cheshire Yeomanry (Earl of Chester's) (Hussars); Denbighshire Yeomanry (Hussars); Royal 1st Devon Yeomanry (Hussars); Royal North Devon Yeomanry (Hussars); Fife and Forfar Yeomanry (The Duke of Connaught's Own) (Mounted Rifles) (Hussars); West Kent Yeomanry (Queen's Own) (Hussars); The Lanarkshire Yeomanry (Lancers); Lincolnshire Yeomanry (Lancers); City of London Yeomanry (Rough Riders) (Lancers); 2nd County of London Yeomanry (Westminster Dragoons); 3rd County of London Yeomanry (Sharpshooters) (Hussars); Montgomeryshire Yeomanry (Dragoons); Norfolk Yeomanry (The King's Own Royal Regiment) (Dragoons); Nottinghamshire Yeomanry (South Nottinghamshire Hussars); Pembroke Yeomanry (Castlemartin) (Hussars); The Scottish Horse: Shropshire Yeomanry (Dragoons); Suffolk Yeomanry (The Duke of York's Own Loyal Suffolk Hussars); Sussex Yeomanry (Dragoons); The Warwickshire Yeomanry (Hussars); Welsh Horse (Lancers); East Riding of Yorkshire Yeomanry (Lancers); The Herefordshire Regiment
1929 1st Machine Gun Battalion: 2nd Machine Gun Battalion: 3rd Machine Gun Battalion: 4th Machine Gun Battalion: 1st Battalion, Canadian Machine Gun Corps CEF: 2nd Battalion, Canadian Machine Gun Corps CEF: 3rd Battalion, Canadian Machine Gun Corps CEF: 4th Battalion, Canadian Machine Gun Corps CEF
1930 2nd Motor Machine Gun Brigade: 2nd Canadian Motor Machine Gun Brigade CEF
¹ FRANCE ET FLANDRES 1918 taken into use by French-speaking Canadian units 1958.

116. PIAVE
15th–24th June 1918
The Austrian Offensive 1918

1925 Honourable Artillery Company; The Queen's Royal Regiment (West Surrey); The Northumberland Fusiliers; The Royal Warwickshire Regiment; The Devonshire Regiment; The West Yorkshire Regiment (The Prince of Wales's Own); The Green Howards (Alexandra, Princess of Wales's Own); The Royal Welch Fusiliers; The Gloucestershire Regiment; The Worcestershire Regiment; The Duke of Wellington's Regiment (West Riding); The Border Regiment; The Royal Sussex Regiment; The South Staffordshire Regiment: The Oxfordshire and Buckinghamshire Light Infantry; The Sherwood Foresters (Nottinghamshire and Derbyshire Regiment); The Royal Berkshire Regiment (Princess Charlotte of Wales's); The King's Own Yorkshire Light Infantry; The Manchester Regiment; The York and Lancaster Regiment; The Durham Light Infantry; The Gordon Highlanders

117. VITTORIO VENETO
24th October–4th November 1918
The Italian Offensive 1918

1925 Northamptonshire Yeomanry (Dragoons); Honourable Artillery Company; The Queen's Royal Regiment (West Surrey); The Northumberland Fusiliers; The Royal Warwickshire Regiment: The Devonshire Regiment: The West Yorkshire Regiment (The Prince of Wales's Own); The Green Howards (Alexandra, Princess of Wales's Own Yorkshire Regiment); The Royal Welch Fusiliers: The Gloucestershire Regiment: The Worcestershire Regiment: The Duke of Wellington's Regiment (West Riding); The Border Regiment: The Royal Sussex Regiment: The South Staffordshire Regiment: The Oxfordshire and Buckinghamshire Light Infantry: The Royal Berkshire Regiment (Princess Charlotte of Wales's): The King's Own Yorkshire Light Infantry: The Manchester Regiment: The York and Lancaster Regiment: The Durham Light Infantry: The Gordon Highlanders

118.	**ITALY 1917–18** 12th May 1917–4th November 1918 Service in Italy 1917–18	1925	King Edward's Horse (The King's Oversea Dominions Regiment); Hampshire (Carabiniers) (Dragoons): Northamptonshire Yeomanry (Dragoons): Honourable Artillery Company: The Queen's Royal Regiment (West Surrey): The Northumberland Fusiliers: The Royal Warwickshire Regiment: The Royal Fusiliers (City of London Regiment): The Norfolk Regiment: The Devonshire Regiment: The West Yorkshire Regiment (The Prince of Wales's Own). The Bedfordshire and Hertfordshire Regiment: The Green Howards (Alexandra, Princess of Wales's Own Yorkshire Regiment): The Cheshire Regiment: The Royal Welch Fusiliers: The King's Own Scottish Borderers: The Gloucestershire Regiment: The Worcestershire Regiment: The East Surrey Regiment: The Duke of Cornwall's Light Infantry: The Duke of Wellington's Regiment (West Riding): The Border Regiment: The Royal Sussex Regiment: The Hampshire Regiment: The South Staffordshire Regiment: The Oxfordshire and Buckinghamshire Light Infantry: The Sherwood Foresters (Nottinghamshire and Derbyshire Regiment): The Royal Berkshire Regiment (Princess Charlotte of Wales's): The Queen's Own Royal West Kent Regiment: The King's Own Yorkshire Light Infantry: The Middlesex Regiment (Duke of Cambridge's Own): The King's Royal Rifle Corps: The Manchester Regiment: The York and Lancaster Regiment: The Durham Light Infantry: The Gordon Highlanders: The Argyll and Sutherland Highlanders (Princess Louise's): The Royal Munster Fusiliers
119.	**ITALY 1918** 1st January–4th November 1918 Service in Italy 1917–18	1925	The British West Indies Regiment
120.	**KOSTURINO** 7th–8th December 1915 Retreat from Serbia on Salonika	1925	The Royal Inniskilling Fusiliers: The East Lancashire Regiment: The Hampshire Regiment: The Royal Ulster Rifles: The Royal Irish Fusiliers (Princess Victoria's): The Connaught Rangers: The Prince of Wales's Leinster Regiment (Royal Canadians): The Royal Munster Fusiliers: The Royal Dublin Fusiliers
121.	**STRUMA** 30th September–31st October 1916 Operations in the Struma Valley	1925	Derbyshire Yeomanry (Dragoons): The Nottinghamshire Yeomanry (Sherwood Rangers) (Hussars): Nottinghamshire Yeomanry (South Nottinghamshire Hussars): Surrey Yeomanry (Queen Mary's Regiment) (Lancers): The Royal Scots (The Royal Regiment): The Buffs (East Kent Regiment): The King's Own Royal Regiment (Lancaster): The Northumberland Fusiliers: The Royal Fusiliers (City of London Regiment): The Suffolk Regiment: The East Yorkshire Regiment: The Royal Irish Regiment: The Cheshire Regiment: The Royal Inniskilling Fusiliers: The Gloucestershire Regiment: The East Surrey Regiment: The Duke of Cornwall's Light Infantry: The Hampshire Regiment: The Welch Regiment: The King's Own Yorkshire Light Infantry: The Middlesex Regiment (Duke of Cambridge's Own): The York and Lancaster Regiment: The Queen's Own Cameron Highlanders: The Royal Ulster Rifles: The Royal Irish Fusiliers (Princess Victoria's): The Connaught Rangers: The Argyll and Sutherland Highlanders (Princess Louise's): The Prince of Wales's Leinster Regiment (Royal Canadians): The Royal Munster Fusiliers: The Royal Dublin Fusiliers
122.	**DOIRAN 1917** 24th–25th April 1917 and 8th–9th May 1917 1917 Offensive	1925	The King's Own Royal Regiment (Lancaster): The King's Regiment (Liverpool): The Devonshire Regiment: The East Yorkshire Regiment: The Lancashire Fusiliers: The Royal Scots Fusiliers: The Cheshire Regiment: The Royal Welch Fusiliers: The South Wales Borderers: The Cameronians (Scottish Rifles): The Gloucestershire Regiment: The Worcestershire Regiment: The East Lancashire Regiment: The Duke of Cornwall's Light Infantry: The Border Regiment: The Hampshire Regiment: The Prince of Wales's Volunteers (South Lancashire): The Welch Regiment: The Black Watch (Royal Highlanders): The Oxfordshire and Buckinghamshire Light Infantry: The Loyal Regiment (North Lancashire): The Royal Berkshire Regiment (Princess Charlotte of Wales's): The King's Shropshire Light Infantry: The Wiltshire Regiment (Duke of Edinburgh's): The Manchester Regiment: The York and Lancaster Regiment: The Argyll and Sutherland Highlanders (Princess Louise's): 13th London Regiment (Princess Louise's Kensington Regiment): 14th London Regiment (London Scottish): 15th (County of London) Battalion, The London Regiment (Prince of Wales's Own, Civil Service Rifles): 16th London Regiment (Queen's Westminster Rifles): 17th London

Regiment (Poplar and Stepney Rifles): 18th London Regiment (London Irish Rifles): 19th London Regiment (St Pancras): 20th London Regiment (The Queen's Own): 21st London Regiment (First Surrey Rifles): 22nd London Regiment (The Queen's): 23rd London Regiment: 24th London Regiment (The Queen's)

123. DOIRAN 1918
18th–19th September 1918
1918 Offensive

1925

Lothians and Border Horse (Dragoons): The Buffs (East Kent Regiment): The King's Own Royal Regiment (Lancaster): The Devonshire Regiment: The Suffolk Regiment: The Cheshire Regiment: The Royal Welch Fusiliers: The South Wales Borderers: The Cameronians (Scottish Rifles): The Worcestershire Regiment: The East Lancashire Regiment: The East Surrey Regiment: The Duke of Cornwall's Light Infantry: The Border Regiment: The Hampshire Regiment: The Prince of Wales's Volunteers (South Lancashire): The Welch Regiment: The Oxfordshire and Buckinghamshire Light Infantry: The Royal Berkshire Regiment (Princess Charlotte of Wales's): The King's Shropshire Light Infantry: The Middlesex Regiment (Duke of Cambridge's Own): The Argyll and Sutherland Highlanders (Princess Louise's)

124. MACEDONIA 1915–17
5th October 1915–31st December 1917
Service in Macedonia 1915–18

1925

The Royal Irish Regiment: The Royal Inniskilling Fusiliers: The King's Own Yorkshire Light Infantry: The Royal Ulster Rifles: The Royal Irish Fusiliers (Princess Victoria's): The Connaught Rangers: The Prince of Wales's Leinster Regiment (Royal Canadians): The Royal Munster Fusiliers: The Royal Dublin Fusiliers

125. MACEDONIA 1915–18
5th October 1915–30th September 1918
Service in Macedonia 1915–18

1925

Lothians and Border Horse (Dragoons): The Royal Scots (The Royal Regiment): The Buffs (East Kent Regiment): The King's Own Royal Regiment (Lancaster): The Northumberland Fusiliers: The Royal Fusiliers (City of London Regiment): The Lancashire Fusiliers: The King's Regiment (Liverpool): The Devonshire Regiment: The Suffolk Regiment: The East Yorkshire Regiment: The Cheshire Regiment: The Royal Welch Fusiliers: The South Wales Borderers: The Cameronians (Scottish Rifles): The Gloucestershire Regiment: The Worcestershire Regiment: The East Lancashire Regiment: The East Surrey Regiment: The Duke of Cornwall's Light Infantry: The Border Regiment: The Hampshire Regiment: The Welch Regiment: The Black Watch (Royal Highlanders): The Oxfordshire and Buckinghamshire Light Infantry: The Royal Berkshire Regiment (Princess Charlotte of Wales's): The King's Shropshire Light Infantry: The Middlesex Regiment (Duke of Cambridge's Own): The Wiltshire Regiment (Duke of Edinburgh's): The Manchester Regiment: The York and Lancaster Regiment: The Queen's Own Cameron Highlanders: The Argyll and Sutherland Highlanders (Princess Louise's): The Rifle Brigade (Prince Consort's Own)

126. MACEDONIA 1916–17
1st January 1916–31st December 1917
Service in Macedonia 1915–18

1925

City of London Yeomanry (Rough Riders) (Lancers): 1st County of London Yeomanry (Middlesex, Duke of Cambridge's Hussars): 3rd County of London Yeomanry (Sharpshooters) (Hussars): The Nottinghamshire Yeomanry (Sherwood Rangers) (Hussars): Nottinghamshire Yeomanry (South Nottinghamshire Hussars): 13th London Regiment (Princess Louise's Kensington Regiment): 14th London Regiment (London Scottish): 15th (County of London) Battalion, The London Regiment (Prince of Wales's Own, Civil Service Rifles): 16th London Regiment (Queen's Westminster Rifles): 17th London Regiment (Poplar and Stepney Rifles): 18th London Regiment (London Irish Rifles): 19th London Regiment (St Pancras): 20th London Regiment (The Queen's Own): 21st London Regiment (First Surrey Rifles): 22nd London Regiment (The Queen's): 23rd London Regiment: 24th London Regiment (The Queen's)

127. MACEDONIA 1916–18
1st January 1916–30th September 1918
Service in Macedonia 1915–18

1925
1926
1927

Derbyshire Yeomanry (Dragoons): The Lovat Scouts: The Scottish Horse: Surrey Yeomanry (Queen Mary's Regiment) (Lancers): The Royal Scots Fusiliers: The King's Royal Rifle Corps ¹: The Durham Light Infantry
Bharatpur Transport Corps
Holkar's Transport Corps (Indore)
¹ *MACEDONIA 1915–18 taken into use 1951.*

No.	Battle / Operations	Year	Regiments
128.	**MACEDONIA 1917** 1st January–31st December 1917 Service in Macedonia 1915–18	1925	The Loyal Regiment (North Lancashire)
129.	**MACEDONIA 1917–18** 1st January 1917–30th September 1918 Service in Macedonia 1915–18	1925	The Seaforth Highlanders (Ross-shire Buffs, The Duke of Albany's)
130.	**MACEDONIA 1918** 1st January–30th September 1918 Service in Macedonia 1915–18	1926	7th Rajput Regiment: 8th Punjab Regiment: 14th Punjab Regiment: 16th Punjab Regiment: 18th Royal Garhwal Rifles
131.	**HELLES** 25th April–6th June 1915 Helles Operations	1925	The Royal Scots (The Royal Regiment): The Royal Fusiliers (City of London Regiment): The Lancashire Fusiliers: The Royal Scots Fusiliers: The South Wales Borderers: The King's Own Scottish Borderers: The Royal Inniskilling Fusiliers: The Worcestershire Regiment: The East Lancashire Regiment: The Border Regiment: The Hampshire Regiment: The Essex Regiment: The Manchester Regiment: The Royal Munster Fusiliers: The Royal Dublin Fusiliers
		1926	2nd Punjab Regiment: 8th Punjab Regiment: 11th Sikh Regiment: 5th Royal Gurkha Rifles (Frontier Force): 6th Gurkha Rifles: 10th Gurkha Rifles
		1926	The Auckland Regiment (Countess of Ranfurly's Own): The Hauraki Regiment: The North Auckland Regiment: The Waikato Regiment: The Wellington West Coast Regiment: The Hawke's Bay Regiment: The Taranaki Regiment: The Canterbury Regiment: The Nelson, Marlborough, and West Coast Regiment: The Otago Regiment: The Southland Regiment
		1927	5th Battalion: 6th Battalion: 7th Battalion: 8th Battalion
132.	**LANDING AT HELLES** 25th–26th April 1915 Helles Operations	1925	The Royal Scots (The Royal Regiment): The Royal Fusiliers (City of London Regiment): The Lancashire Fusiliers: The South Wales Borderers: The King's Own Scottish Borderers: The Royal Inniskilling Fusiliers: The Worcestershire Regiment: The Border Regiment: The Hampshire Regiment: The Essex Regiment: The Royal Munster Fusiliers: The Royal Dublin Fusiliers
133.	**KRITHIA** 28th April 1915 6th–8th May 1915 and 4th June 1915 Helles Operations	1925	The Royal Scots (The Royal Regiment): The Royal Fusiliers (City of London Regiment): The Lancashire Fusiliers: The South Wales Borderers: The King's Own Scottish Borderers: The Royal Inniskilling Fusiliers: The Worcestershire Regiment: The East Lancashire Regiment: The Border Regiment: The Hampshire Regiment: The Essex Regiment: The Manchester Regiment: The Royal Munster Fusiliers: The Royal Dublin Fusiliers
		1926	2nd Punjab Regiment: 8th Punjab Regiment: 11th Sikh Regiment: 5th Royal Gurkha Rifles (Frontier Force): 6th Gurkha Rifles: 10th Gurkha Rifles
		1926	The Auckland Regiment (Countess of Ranfurly's Own): The Hauraki Regiment: The North Auckland Regiment: The Waikato Regiment: The Wellington West Coast Regiment: The Hawke's Bay Regiment: The Taranaki Regiment: The Canterbury Regiment: The Nelson, Marlborough, and West Coast Regiment: The Otago Regiment: The Southland Regiment
		1927	5th Battalion: 6th Battalion: 7th Battalion: 8th Battalion
134.	**ANZAC** 25th April–30th June 1915 Anzac and Suvla Operations	1926	101st Royal (Kohat) Pack Battery (Frontier Force): 106th (Jacob's) Pack Battery
		1926	The Auckland Regiment (Countess of Ranfurly's Own): The Hauraki Regiment: The North Auckland Regiment: The Waikato Regiment: The Wellington West Coast Regiment: The Hawke's Bay Regiment: The Taranaki Regiment: The Canterbury Regiment: The Nelson, Marlborough, and West Coast Regiment: The Otago Regiment: The Southland Regiment
		1927	1st Light Horse Regiment: 2nd Light Horse Regiment: 3rd Light Horse Regiment: 4th Light Horse Regiment: 5th Light Horse Regiment: 6th Light Horse Regiment: 7th Light Horse Regiment: 8th Light Horse Regiment: 9th Light Horse Regiment: 10th

Light Horse Regiment: 1st Battalion: 2nd Battalion: 3rd Battalion: 4th Battalion: 5th Battalion: 6th Battalion: 7th Battalion: 8th Battalion: 9th Battalion: 10th Battalion: 11th Battalion: 12th Battalion: 13th Battalion: 14th Battalion: 15th Battalion: 16th Battalion

1928   The Canterbury Yeomanry Cavalry: Queen Alexandra's Wellington West Coast Mounted Rifles: The Auckland Mounted Rifles: The Waikato Mounted Rifles: The Otago Mounted Rifles: The Manawatu Mounted Rifles: The Wellington East Coast Mounted Rifles: The Nelson-Marlborough Mounted Rifles: The North Auckland Mounted Rifles

1930   3rd (Tasmanian Mounted Infantry) Light Horse Regiment AMF

1936   16th Light Horse Regiment: 17th Light Horse Regiment: 18th Light Horse Regiment: 19th Light Horse Regiment: 20th Light Horse Regiment: 21st Light Horse Regiment: 23rd Light Horse Regiment

135. LANDING AT ANZAC
25th–26th April 1915
Anzac and Suvla Operations

1926   101st Royal (Kohat) Pack Battery (Frontier Force): 106th (Jacob's) Pack Battery

1926   The Auckland Regiment (Countess of Ranfurly's Own): The Hauraki Regiment: The North Auckland Regiment: The Waikato Regiment: The Wellington West Coast Regiment: The Hawke's Bay Regiment: The Taranaki Regiment: The Canterbury Regiment: The Nelson, Marlborough, and West Coast Regiment: The Otago Regiment: The Southland Regiment

1927   1st Battalion: 2nd Battalion: 3rd Battalion: 4th Battalion: 5th Battalion: 6th Battalion: 7th Battalion: 8th Battalion: 9th Battalion: 10th Battalion: 11th Battalion: 12th Battalion: 13th Battalion: 14th Battalion: 15th Battalion: 16th Battalion

136. DEFENCE OF ANZAC
19th–21st May 1915
Anzac and Suvla Operations

1926   101st Royal (Kohat) Pack Battery (Frontier Force): 106th (Jacob's) Pack Battery

1926   The Auckland Regiment (Countess of Ranfurly's Own): The Hauraki Regiment: The North Auckland Regiment: The Waikato Regiment: The Wellington West Coast Regiment: The Hawke's Bay Regiment: The Taranaki Regiment: The Canterbury Regiment: The Nelson, Marlborough, and West Coast Regiment: The Otago Regiment: The Southland Regiment

1927   1st Light Horse Regiment: 2nd Light Horse Regiment: 3rd Light Horse Regiment: 4th Light Horse Regiment: 5th Light Horse Regiment: 6th Light Horse Regiment: 7th Light Horse Regiment: 8th Light Horse Regiment: 9th Light Horse Regiment: 10th Light Horse Regiment: 1st Battalion: 2nd Battalion: 3rd Battalion: 4th Battalion: 5th Battalion: 6th Battalion: 7th Battalion: 8th Battalion: 9th Battalion: 10th Battalion: 11th Battalion: 12th Battalion: 13th Battalion: 14th Battalion: 15th Battalion: 16th Battalion

1928   The Canterbury Yeomanry Cavalry: Queen Alexandra's Wellington West Coast Mounted Rifles: The Auckland Mounted Rifles: The Waikato Mounted Rifles: The Otago Mounted Rifles: The Manawatu Mounted Rifles: The Wellington East Coast Mounted Rifles: The Nelson-Marlborough Mounted Rifles: The North Auckland Mounted Rifles

1930   3rd (Tasmanian Mounted Infantry) Light Horse Regiment AMF

137. SUVLA
6th–21st August 1915
Anzac and Suvla Operations

1925   Berks Yeomanry (Hungerford) (Dragoons): Buckinghamshire Yeomanry (Royal Bucks Hussars): Derbyshire Yeomanry (Dragoons): Dorset Yeomanry (Queen's Own): Gloucestershire Yeomanry (Royal Gloucestershire Hussars): Herts Yeomanry (Dragoons): City of London Yeomanry (Rough Riders) (Lancers): 1st County of London Yeomanry (Middlesex, Duke of Cambridge's Hussars): 2nd County of London Yeomanry (Westminster Dragoons): 3rd County of London Yeomanry (Sharpshooters) (Hussars): The Nottinghamshire Yeomanry (Sherwood Rangers) (Hussars): Nottinghamshire Yeomanry (South Nottinghamshire Hussars): The Warwickshire Yeomanry (Hussars): Worcestershire Yeomanry (The Queen's Own Worcestershire Hussars): The Royal Scots (The Royal Regiment): The Queen's Royal Regiment (West Surrey): The King's Own Royal Regiment (Lancaster): The Northumberland Fusiliers: The Royal Warwickshire Regiment: The Royal Fusiliers (City of London Regiment): The Norfolk Regiment: The Lincolnshire Regiment: The Suffolk Regiment: The West Yorkshire Regiment (The Prince of Wales's Own): The East Yorkshire Regiment: The Bedfordshire and Hertfordshire Regiment: The Royal Irish Regiment: The Green Howards (Alexandra, Princess of Wales's Own Yorkshire Regiment): The Lancashire Fusiliers: The Cheshire Regiment: The Royal Welch Fusiliers: The South Wales Borderers: The King's Own Scottish Borderers: The Royal Inniskilling Fusiliers: The Gloucestershire Regiment: The Worcestershire Regiment: The East Lancashire Regiment:

The Duke of Wellington's Regiment (West Riding): The Border Regiment: The Royal Sussex Regiment: The Hampshire Regiment: The South Staffordshire Regiment: The Dorsetshire Regiment: The Prince of Wales's Volunteers (South Lancashire): The Welch Regiment: The Essex Regiment: The Sherwood Foresters (Nottinghamshire and Derbyshire Regiment): The Loyal Regiment (North Lancashire): The Northamptonshire Regiment: The Queen's Own Royal West Kent Regiment: The Middlesex Regiment (Duke of Cambridge's Own): The Wiltshire Regiment (Duke of Edinburgh's): The Manchester Regiment: The North Staffordshire Regiment (The Prince of Wales's): The York and Lancaster Regiment: The Royal Ulster Rifles: The Royal Irish Fusiliers (Princess Victoria's): The Connaught Rangers: The Prince of Wales's Leinster Regiment (Royal Canadians): The Royal Munster Fusiliers: The Royal Dublin Fusiliers: 10th London Regiment (Hackney): 11th London Regiment (Finsbury Rifles): The Herefordshire Regiment

1926   101st Royal (Kohat) Pack Battery (Frontier Force): 106th (Jacob's) Pack Battery: 11th Sikh Regiment: 5th Royal Gurkha Rifles (Frontier Force): 6th Gurkha Rifles: 10th Gurkha Rifles

1926   Bharatpur Transport Corps

1926   The Auckland Regiment (Countess of Ranfurly's Own): The Hauraki Regiment: The North Auckland Regiment: The Waikato Regiment: The Wellington West Coast Regiment: The Hawke's Bay Regiment: The Taranaki Regiment: The Canterbury Regiment: The Nelson, Marlborough, and West Coast Regiment: The Otago Regiment: The Southland Regiment

1927   1st Light Horse Regiment: 2nd Light Horse Regiment: 3rd Light Horse Regiment: 4th Light Horse Regiment 5th Light Horse Regiment: 6th Light Horse Regiment: 7th Light Horse Regiment: 8th Light Horse Regiment: 9th Light Horse Regiment: 10th Light Horse Regiment: 11th Light Horse Regiment: 12th Light Horse Regiment: 1st Battalion: 2nd Battalion: 3rd Battalion: 4th Battalion: 5th Battalion: 6th Battalion: 7th Battalion: 8th Battalion: 9th Battalion: 10th Battalion: 11th Battalion: 12th Battalion: 13th Battalion: 14th Battalion: 15th Battalion: 16th Battalion: 17th Battalion: 18th Battalion: 19th Battalion: 20th Battalion

1927   Holkar's Transport Corps (Indore)

1930   3rd (Tasmanian Mounted Infantry) Light Horse Regiment AMF

138. SARI BAIR
6th–10th August 1915
Anzac and Suvla Operations

1925   The King's Own Royal Regiment (Lancaster): The Royal Warwickshire Regiment: The Cheshire Regiment: The Royal Welch Fusiliers: The South Wales Borderers: The Gloucestershire Regiment: The Worcestershire Regiment: The East Lancashire Regiment: The Hampshire Regiment: The Prince of Wales's Volunteers (South Lancashire): The Welch Regiment: The Loyal Regiment (North Lancashire): The Wiltshire Regiment (Duke of Edinburgh's): The North Staffordshire Regiment (The Prince of Wales's): The Royal Ulster Rifles: The Connaught Rangers: The Prince of Wales's Leinster Regiment (Royal Canadians): The Royal Dublin Fusiliers

1926   101st Royal (Kohat) Pack Battery (Frontier Force): 106th (Jacob's) Pack Battery: 11th Sikh Regiment: 5th Royal Gurkha Rifles (Frontier Force): 6th Gurkha Rifles: 10th Gurkha Rifles

1926   The Auckland Regiment (Countess of Ranfurly's Own): The Hauraki Regiment: The North Auckland Regiment: The Waikato Regiment: The Wellington West Coast Regiment: The Hawke's Bay Regiment: The Taranaki Regiment: The Canterbury Regiment: The Nelson, Marlborough, and West Coast Regiment: The Otago Regiment: The Southland Regiment

1927   1st Light Horse Regiment: 2nd Light Horse Regiment: 3rd Light Horse Regiment: 4th Light Horse Regiment: 5th Light Horse Regiment: 6th Light Horse Regiment: 7th Light Horse Regiment: 8th Light Horse Regiment: 9th Light Horse Regiment: 10th Light Horse Regiment: 11th Light Horse Regiment: 12th Light Horse Regiment: 13th Battalion: 14th Battalion: 15th Battalion: 16th Battalion

1928   The Canterbury Yeomanry Cavalry: Queen Alexandra's Wellington West Coast Mounted Rifles: The Auckland Mounted Rifles: The Waikato Mounted Rifles: The Otago Mounted Rifles: The Manawatu Mounted Rifles: The Wellington East Coast Mounted Rifles: The Nelson-Marlborough Mounted Rifles: The North Auckland Mounted Rifles

1930   3rd (Tasmanian Mounted Infantry) Light Horse Regiment AMF

139.	**SARI BAIR-LONE PINE** 6th–10th August 1915 Anzac and Suvla Operations	1927	1st Battalion: 2nd Battalion: 3rd Battalion: 4th Battalion: 7th Battalion: 12th Battalion
140.	**LANDING AT SUVLA** 6th–15th August 1915 Anzac and Suvla Operations	1925	The Queen's Royal Regiment (West Surrey): The Northumberland Fusiliers: The Norfolk Regiment: The Lincolnshire Regiment: The Suffolk Regiment: The West Yorkshire Regiment (The Prince of Wales's Own): The East Yorkshire Regiment: The Bedfordshire and Hertfordshire Regiment: The Royal Irish Regiment: The Green Howards (Alexandra, Princess of Wales's Own Yorkshire Regiment): The Lancashire Fusiliers: The Cheshire Regiment: The Royal Welch Fusiliers: The Royal Inniskilling Fusiliers: The Duke of Wellington's Regiment (West Riding): The Border Regiment: The Royal Sussex Regiment: The Hampshire Regiment: The South Staffordshire Regiment: The Dorsetshire Regiment: The Welch Regiment: The Essex Regiment: The Sherwood Foresters (Nottinghamshire and Derbyshire Regiment): The Northamptonshire Regiment: The Queen's Own Royal West Kent Regiment: The Middlesex Regiment (Duke of Cambridge's Own): The Manchester Regiment: The York and Lancaster Regiment: The Royal Irish Fusiliers (Princess Victoria's): The Royal Munster Fusiliers: The Royal Dublin Fusiliers: 10th London Regiment (Hackney): 11th London Regiment (Finsbury Rifles): The Herefordshire Regiment
		1926 1927	Bharatpur Transport Corps Holkar's Transport Corps (Indore)
141.	**SCIMITAR HILL** 21st August 1915 Anzac and Suvla Operations	1925	Berks Yeomanry (Hungerford) (Dragoons): Buckinghamshire Yeomanry (Royal Bucks Hussars): Derbyshire Yeomanry (Dragoons): Dorset Yeomanry (Queen's Own): Gloucestershire Yeomanry (Royal Gloucestershire Hussars): Herts Yeomanry (Dragoons): City of London Yeomanry (Rough Riders) (Lancers): 1st County of London Yeomanry (Middlesex, Duke of Cambridge's Hussars): 2nd County of London Yeomanry (Westminster Dragoons): 3rd County of London Yeomanry (Sharpshooters) (Hussars): The Nottinghamshire Yeomanry (Sherwood Rangers) (Hussars): Nottinghamshire Yeomanry (South Nottinghamshire Hussars): The Warwickshire Yeomanry (Hussars): Worcestershire Yeomanry (The Queen's Own Worcestershire Hussars): The Royal Scots (The Royal Regiment): The Queen's Royal Regiment (West Surrey): The Northumberland Fusiliers: The Royal Fusiliers (City of London Regiment): The Norfolk Regiment: The Lincolnshire Regiment: The Suffolk Regiment: The West Yorkshire Regiment (The Prince of Wales's Own): The East Yorkshire Regiment: The Bedfordshire and Hertfordshire Regiment: The Green Howards (Alexandra, Princess of Wales's Own Yorkshire Regiment): The Lancashire Fusiliers: The Cheshire Regiment: The Royal Welch Fusiliers: The South Wales Borderers: The King's Own Scottish Borderers: The Royal Inniskilling Fusiliers: The Border Regiment: The Royal Sussex Regiment: The Hampshire Regiment: The Duke of Wellington's Regiment (West Riding): The Dorsetshire Regiment: The Welch Regiment: The Essex Regiment: The Sherwood Foresters (Nottinghamshire and Derbyshire Regiment): The Northamptonshire Regiment: The Queen's Own Royal West Kent Regiment: The Middlesex Regiment (Duke of Cambridge's Own): The Manchester Regiment: The York and Lancaster Regiment: The Royal Irish Fusiliers (Princess Victoria's): The Connaught Rangers: The Royal Munster Fusiliers: The Royal Dublin Fusiliers: 10th London Regiment (Hackney): 11th London Regiment (Finsbury Rifles): The Herefordshire Regiment
		1926 1927	Bharatpur Transport Corps Holkar's Transport Corps (Indore)
142.	**HILL 60 (ANZAC)** 21st and 27th August 1915 Anzac and Suvla Operations	1928	The Canterbury Yeomanry Cavalry: Queen Alexandra's Wellington West Coast Mounted Rifles: The Auckland Mounted Rifles: The Waikato Mounted Rifles: The Otago Mounted Rifles: The Manawatu Mounted Rifles: The Wellington East Coast Mounted Rifles: The Nelson-Marlborough Mounted Rifles: The North Auckland Mounted Rifles

143.	**GALLIPOLI 1915** 25th April–31st December 1915 Service in the Dardanelles 1915–16	1925	The Ayrshire Yeomanry (Earl of Carrick's Own) (Hussars): Berks Yeomanry (Hungerford) (Dragoons): Buckinghamshire Yeomanry (Royal Bucks Hussars): Derbyshire Yeomanry (Dragoons): Royal 1st Devon Yeomanry (Hussars): Royal North Devon Yeomanry (Hussars): Dorset Yeomanry (Queen's Own): Fife and Forfar Yeomanry: Gloucestershire Yeomanry (Royal Gloucestershire Hussars): Herts Yeomanry (Dragoons): Royal East Kent Yeomanry (The Duke of Connaught's Own) (Mounted Rifles) (Hussars): West Kent Yeomanry (Queen's Own) (Hussars): The Lanarkshire Yeomanry (Lancers): City of London Yeomanry (Rough Riders) (Lancers): 1st County of London Yeomanry (Middlesex, Duke of Cambridge's Hussars): 2nd County of London Yeomanry (Westminster Dragoons): 3rd County of London Yeomanry (Sharpshooters) (Hussars): The Lovat Scouts: Norfolk Yeomanry (The King's Own Royal Regiment) (Dragoons): The Nottinghamshire Yeomanry (Sherwood Rangers) (Hussars): Nottinghamshire Yeomanry (South Nottinghamshire Hussars): The Scottish Horse: West Somerset Yeomanry (Hussars): Suffolk Yeomanry (The Duke of York's Own Loyal Suffolk Hussars): Sussex Yeomanry (Dragoons): The Warwickshire Yeomanry (Hussars): Welsh Horse (Lancers): Worcestershire Yeomanry (The Queen's Own Worcestershire Hussars): The Queen's Royal Regiment (West Surrey): The King's Own Royal Regiment (Lancaster): The Northumberland Fusiliers: The Norfolk Regiment: The Lincolnshire Regiment: The Suffolk Regiment: The West Yorkshire Regiment (The Prince of Wales's Own): The East Yorkshire Regiment: The Bedfordshire and Hertfordshire Regiment: The Royal Irish Regiment: The Green Howards (Alexandra, Princess of Wales's Own Yorkshire Regiment): The Lancashire Fusiliers: The Cheshire Regiment: The Cameronians (Scottish Rifles)`: The East Lancashire Regiment: The Duke of Wellington's Regiment (West Riding): The Royal Sussex Regiment: The South Staffordshire Regiment: The Dorsetshire Regiment: The Prince of Wales's Volunteers (South Lancashire): The Welch Regiment: The Sherwood Foresters (Nottinghamshire and Derbyshire Regiment): The Loyal Regiment (North Lancashire): The Northamptonshire Regiment: The Queen's Own Royal West Kent Regiment: The Middlesex Regiment (Duke of Cambridge's Own): The Manchester Regiment: The York and Lancaster Regiment: The Royal Ulster Rifles: The Royal Irish Fusiliers (Princess Victoria's): The Connaught Rangers: The Prince of Wales's Leinster Regiment (Royal Canadians): 3rd City of London Regiment (The Royal Fusiliers): 10th London Regiment (Hackney): 101st London Regiment (Finsbury Rifles): The Herefordshire Regiment
		1926	101st Royal (Kohat) Pack Battery (Frontier Force): 106th (Jacob's) Pack Battery: 2nd Punjab Regiment: 8th Punjab Regiment: 11th Sikh Regiment: 4th Prince of Wales's Own Gurkha Rifles: 5th Royal Gurkha Rifles (Frontier Force): 6th Gurkha Rifles: 10th Gurkha Rifles
		1926	Bharatpur Transport Corps
		1926	The Auckland Regiment (Countess of Ranfurly's Own): The Hauraki Regiment: The North Auckland Regiment: The Waikato Regiment: The Wellington West Coast Regiment: The Hawke's Bay Regiment: The Taranaki Regiment: The Canterbury Regiment: The Nelson, Marlborough, and West Coast Regiment: The Otago Regiment: The Southland Regiment
		1927	1st Light Horse Regiment: 2nd Light Horse Regiment: 3rd Light Horse Regiment: 4th Light Horse Regiment: 5th Light Horse Regiment: 6th Light Horse Regiment: 7th Light Horse Regiment: 8th Light Horse Regiment: 9th Light Horse Regiment: 10th Light Horse Regiment: 11th Light Horse Regiment: 12th Light Horse Regiment: 13th Light Horse Regiment: 1st Battalion: 2nd Battalion: 3rd Battalion: 4th Battalion: 5th Battalion: 6th Battalion: 7th Battalion: 8th Battalion: 9th Battalion: 10th Battalion: 11th Battalion: 12th Battalion: 13th Battalion: 14th Battalion: 15th Battalion: 16th Battalion: 17th Battalion: 18th Battalion: 19th Battalion: 20th Battalion: 21st Battalion: 22nd Battalion: 23rd Battalion: 24th Battalion: 25th Battalion: 26th Battalion: 27th Battalion: 28th Battalion
		1927	Holkar's Transport Corps (Indore)
		1928	The Canterbury Yeomanry Cavalry: Queen Alexandra's Wellington West Coast Mounted Rifles: The Auckland Mounted Rifles: The Waikato Mounted Rifles: The Otago Mounted Rifles: The Manawatu Mounted Rifles: The Wellington East Coast Mounted Rifles: The Nelson-Marlborough Mounted Rifles: The North Auckland Mounted Rifles

	1930 3rd (Tasmanian Mounted Infantry) Light Horse Regiment AMF
	1936 16th Light Horse Regiment: 17th Light Horse Regiment: 18th Light Horse Regiment: 19th Light Horse Regiment: 20th Light Horse Regiment: 21st Light Horse Regiment: 23rd Light Horse Regiment
	' GALLIPOLI 1915–16 taken into use 1929.

<table>
<tr><td>144.</td><td>GALLIPOLI 1915–16
25th April 1915–8th/9th January 1916
Service in the Dardanelles 1915–16</td><td>1925</td><td>The Royal Scots (The Royal Regiment): The Royal Warwickshire Regiment: The Royal Fusiliers (City of London Regiment): The Royal Scots Fusiliers: The Royal Welch Fusiliers: The South Wales Borderers: The King's Own Scottish Borderers: The Royal Inniskilling Fusiliers: The Gloucestershire Regiment: The Worcestershire Regiment: The Border Regiment: The Hampshire Regiment: The Essex Regiment: The Wiltshire Regiment (Duke of Edinburgh's): The North Staffordshire Regiment (The Prince of Wales's): The Highland Light Infantry (City of Glasgow Regiment): The Argyll and Sutherland Highlanders (Princess Louise's): The Royal Munster Fusiliers: The Royal Dublin Fusiliers: 1st City of London Regiment (The Royal Fusiliers): 2nd City of London Regiment (The Royal Fusiliers): 4th City of London Regiment (The Royal Fusiliers)</td></tr>
<tr><td></td><td></td><td>1925</td><td>The Royal Newfoundland Regiment</td></tr>
<tr><td>145.</td><td>AGAGIYA
26th February 1916
Operations against the Senussi</td><td>1925
1926</td><td>Dorset Yeomanry (Queen's Own)
1st South African Infantry (Cape of Good Hope Regiment): 3rd South African Infantry (Transvaal and Rhodesian Regiment)</td></tr>
<tr><td>146.</td><td>SUEZ CANAL
3rd–4th February 1915
Defence of the Suez Canal</td><td>1925
1926</td><td>Herts Yeomanry (Dragoons): 2nd County of London Yeomanry (Westminster Dragoons)
101st Royal (Kohat) Pack Battery (Frontier Force): 106th (Jacob's) Pack Battery: Queen Victoria's Own Madras Sappers and Miners: 2nd Bombay Pioneers: 1st Punjab Regiment: 2nd Punjab Regiment: 7th Rajput Regiment: 8th Punjab Regiment: 11th Sikh Regiment: 12th Frontier Force Regiment: 13th Frontier Force Rifles: 14th Punjab Regiment: 15th Punjab Regiment: 16th Punjab Regiment: 5th Royal Gurkha Rifles (Frontier Force): 6th Gurkha Rifles: 10th Gurkha Rifles</td></tr>
<tr><td></td><td></td><td>1926</td><td>Patiala (Rajindra) Lancers: Bhavnagar Lancers: Hyderabad Imperial Service Lancers: Mysore Lancers: 1st Patiala (Rajindra Sikhs) Infantry: 4th Gwalior Maharaja Bahadur Battalion: 1st Bahawalpur Sadiq Infantry: Bikaner Ganga Risala: Sadul Light Infantry</td></tr>
<tr><td></td><td></td><td>1926</td><td>The Auckland Regiment (Countess of Ranfurly's Own): The Hauraki Regiment: The North Auckland Regiment: The Waikato Regiment: The Wellington West Coast Regiment: The Hawke's Bay Regiment: The Taranaki Regiment: The Canterbury Regiment: The Nelson, Marlborough, and West Coast Regiment: The Otago Regiment: The Southland Regiment</td></tr>
<tr><td></td><td></td><td>1927</td><td>7th Battalion: 8th Battalion</td></tr>
<tr><td>147.</td><td>RUMANI
4th–5th August 1916
Defence of the Suez Canal</td><td>1925</td><td>The Ayrshire Yeomanry (Earl of Carrick's Own) (Hussars): Gloucestershire Yeomanry (Royal Gloucestershire Hussars): City of London Yeomanry (Rough Riders) (Lancers): The Scottish Horse: The Warwickshire Yeomanry (Hussars): Worcestershire Yeomanry (The Queen's Own Worcestershire Hussars): The Royal Scots (The Royal Regiment): The Queen's Royal Regiment (West Surrey): The Lancashire Fusiliers: The Royal Scots Fusiliers: The Royal Welch Fusiliers: The King's Own Scottish Borderers: The Cameronians (Scottish Rifles): The East Lancashire Regiment: The Royal Sussex Regiment: The Essex Regiment: The Queen's Own Royal West Kent Regiment: The Middlesex Regiment (Duke of Cambridge's Own): The Manchester Regiment: The Highland Light Infantry (City of Glasgow Regiment): The Argyll and Sutherland Highlanders (Princess Louise's): The Herefordshire Regiment: The British West Indies Regiment</td></tr>
<tr><td></td><td></td><td>1927</td><td>1st Light Horse Regiment: 2nd Light Horse Regiment: 3rd Light Horse Regiment: 5th Light Horse Regiment: 6th Light Horse Regiment: 7th Light Horse Regiment: 8th Light Horse Regiment: 9th Light Horse Regiment: 10th Light Horse Regiment: 11th Light Horse Regiment: 12th Light Horse Regiment: 14th Light Horse Regiment: 15th Light Horse Regiment</td></tr>
<tr><td></td><td></td><td>1928</td><td>The Canterbury Yeomanry Cavalry: Queen Alexandra's Wellington West Coast Mounted Rifles: The Auckland Mounted</td></tr>
</table>

148. MAGDHABA-RAFAH
23rd December 1916 and 9th January 1917
Operations in the Sinai Peninsula

1930 — Rifles: The Waikato Mounted Rifles: The Manawatu Mounted Rifles: The Wellington East Coast Mounted Rifles: The Nelson-Marlborough Mounted Rifles: The North Auckland Mounted Rifles: 3rd (Tasmanian Mounted Infantry) Light Horse Regiment AMF

1927 — 1st Light Horse Regiment: 2nd Light Horse Regiment: 3rd Light Horse Regiment: 8th Light Horse Regiment: 9th Light Horse Regiment: 10th Light Horse Regiment: 14th Light Horse Regiment: 15th Light Horse Regiment

1930 — 3rd (Tasmanian Mounted Infantry) Light Horse Regiment AMF

149. MAGHDABA-RAFAH
23rd December 1916 and 9th January 1917
Operations in the Sinai Peninsula

1928 — The Canterbury Yeomanry Cavalry: Queen Alexandra's Wellington West Coast Mounted Rifles: The Auckland Mounted Rifles: The Waikato Mounted Rifles: The Manawatu Mounted Rifles: The Wellington East Coast Mounted Rifles: The Nelson-Marlborough Mounted Rifles: The North Auckland Mounted Rifles

150. RAFAH
9th January 1917
Operations in the Sinai Peninsula

1925 — Gloucestershire Yeomanry (Royal Gloucestershire Hussars): The Warwickshire Yeomanry (Hussars): Worcestershire Yeomanry (The Queen's Own Worcestershire Hussars): Honourable Artillery Company

151. EGYPT 1915
26th January–31st December 1915
Service in Egypt 1915–17

1925 — Surrey Yeomanry (Queen Mary's Regiment) (Lancers): The East Surrey Regiment

1926 — 2nd Lancers (Gardner's Horse): 2nd Bombay Pioneers: 1st Punjab Regiment: 2nd Punjab Regiment: 6th Rajputana Rifles: 7th Rajput Regiment: 8th Punjab Regiment: 10th Baluch Regiment: 12th Frontier Force Regiment: 14th Punjab Regiment: 15th Punjab Regiment: 17th Dogra Regiment: 2nd King Edward's Own Gurkha Rifles (The Sirmoor Rifles): 7th Gurkha Rifles: 10th Gurkha Rifles

1926 — Bharatpur Transport Corps

1927 — Holkar's Transport Corps (Indore)

152. EGYPT 1915–16
26th January 1915–31st December 1916
Service in Egypt 1915–17

1925 — Derbyshire Yeomanry (Dragoons): Herts Yeomanry (Dragoons): City of London Yeomanry (Rough Riders) (Lancers): 1st County of London Yeomanry (Middlesex, Duke of Cambridge's Hussars): 3rd County of London Yeomanry (Sharpshooters) (Hussars): The Lovat Scouts: The Nottinghamshire Yeomanry (Sherwood Rangers) (Hussars): Nottinghamshire Yeomanry (South Nottinghamshire Hussars): The Scottish Horse: The Royal Scots (The Royal Regiment): The Queen's Royal Regiment (West Surrey): The West Yorkshire Regiment (The Prince of Wales's Own): The East Yorkshire Regiment: The Queen's Own Royal West Kent Regiment: The King's Own Yorkshire Light Infantry: The Durham Light Infantry: 2nd City of London Regiment (The Royal Fusiliers): 3rd City of London Regiment (The Royal Fusiliers)

The Royal Newfoundland Regiment

1925 — 101st Royal (Kohat) Pack Battery (Frontier Force): 106th (Jacob's) Pack Battery: 11th Sikh Regiment: 16th Punjab Regiment: 18th Royal Garhwal Rifles: 3rd Queen Alexandra's Own Gurkha Rifles (Frontier Force): 6th Gurkha Rifles: 8th Gurkha Rifles

1926 — Patiala (Rajindra) Lancers: 4th Gwalior Maharaja Bahadur Battalion

1926 — The Auckland Regiment (Countess of Ranfurly's Own): The Hauraki Regiment: The North Auckland Regiment: The Waikato Regiment: The Wellington Regiment: The Wellington West Coast Regiment: The Hawke's Bay Regiment: The Taranaki Regiment: The Canterbury Regiment: The Nelson, Marlborough, and West Coast Regiment: The Otago Regiment: The Southland Regiment

1927 — 13th Light Horse Regiment: 1st Battalion: 2nd Battalion: 3rd Battalion: 4th Battalion: 5th Battalion: 6th Battalion: 7th Battalion: 8th Battalion: 9th Battalion: 10th Battalion: 11th Battalion: 12th Battalion: 13th Battalion: 14th Battalion: 15th Battalion: 16th

	Battalion: 17th Battalion: 18th Battalion: 19th Battalion: 20th Battalion: 21st Battalion: 22nd Battalion: 23rd Battalion: 24th Battalion: 25th Battalion: 26th Battalion: 27th Battalion: 28th Battalion: 29th Battalion: 30th Battalion: 31st Battalion: 32nd Battalion
1928	The Otago Mounted Rifles
153.	**EGYPT 1915–17** 26th January 1915–8th February 1917 Service in Egypt 1915–17
1925	Berks Yeomanry (Hungerford) (Dragoons): Buckinghamshire Yeomanry (Royal Bucks Hussars): Dorset Yeomanry (Queen's Own): Fife and Forfar Yeomanry: Gloucestershire Yeomanry (Royal Gloucestershire Hussars): Lincolnshire Yeomanry (Lancers): 2nd County of London Yeomanry (Westminster Dragoons): Norfolk Yeomanry (The King's Own Royal Regiment) (Dragoons): The Staffordshire Yeomanry (Queen's Own Royal Regiment) (Hussars): Suffolk Yeomanry (The Duke of York's Own Loyal Suffolk Hussars): The Warwickshire Yeomanry (Hussars): Welsh Horse (Lancers): Worcestershire Yeomanry (The Queen's Own Worcestershire Hussars): East Riding of Yorkshire Yeomanry (Lancers): Honourable Artillery Company: The Norfolk Regiment: The Suffolk Regiment: The Bedfordshire and Hertfordshire Regiment: The Lancashire Fusiliers: The Cheshire Regiment: The Royal Welch Fusiliers: The East Lancashire Regiment: The Royal Sussex Regiment: The Hampshire Regiment: The Welch Regiment: The Essex Regiment: The Northamptonshire Regiment: The Middlesex Regiment (Duke of Cambridge's Own): The Manchester Regiment: 10th London Regiment (Hackney): 11th London Regiment (Finsbury Rifles)
1926	Queen Victoria's Own Madras Sappers and Miners: 13th Frontier Force Rifles
1926	Bhavnagar Lancers: Hyderabad Imperial Service Lancers: Mysore Lancers: 1st Patiala (Rajindra Sikhs) Infantry: Alwar Jey Paltan: 1st Bahawalpur Sadiq Infantry: Bikaner Ganga Risala: Khairpur Faiz Infantry: Sadul Infantry
1927	1st Light Horse Regiment: 2nd Light Horse Regiment: 3rd Light Horse Regiment: 4th Light Horse Regiment: 5th Light Horse Regiment: 6th Light Horse Regiment: 7th Light Horse Regiment: 8th Light Horse Regiment: 9th Light Horse Regiment: 10th Light Horse Regiment: 11th Light Horse Regiment: 12th Light Horse Regiment
1928	The Canterbury Yeomanry Cavalry: Queen Alexandra's Wellington West Coast Mounted Rifles: The Auckland Mounted Rifles: The Waikato Mounted Rifles: The Manawatu Mounted Rifles: The Wellington East Coast Mounted Rifles: The Nelson-Marlborough Mounted Rifles: The North Auckland Mounted Rifles
1930	3rd (Tasmanian Mounted Infantry) Light Horse Regiment AMF
1936	16th Light Horse Regiment: 17th Light Horse Regiment: 18th Light Horse Regiment: 19th Light Horse Regiment: 20th Light Horse Regiment: 21st Light Horse Regiment: 23rd Light Horse Regiment
154.	**EGYPT 1916** 1st January–31st December 1916 Service in Egypt 1915–17
1925	The King's Own Royal Regiment (Lancaster): The Royal Fusiliers (City of London Regiment): The Lincolnshire Regiment: The Green Howards (Alexandra, Princess of Wales's Own Yorkshire Regiment): The South Wales Borderers: The King's Own Scottish Borderers: The Royal Inniskilling Fusiliers: The Gloucestershire Regiment: The Worcestershire Regiment: The Duke of Wellington's Regiment (West Riding): The Border Regiment: The South Staffordshire Regiment: The Dorsetshire Regiment: The Prince of Wales's Volunteers (South Lancashire): The Black Watch (Royal Highlanders): The Sherwood Foresters (Nottinghamshire and Derbyshire Regiment): The Loyal Regiment (North Lancashire): The North Staffordshire Regiment (The Prince of Wales's): The York and Lancaster Regiment: The Highland Light Infantry (City of Glasgow Regiment): The Argyll and Sutherland Highlanders (Princess Louise's): The Royal Munster Fusiliers: The Royal Dublin Fusiliers: 1st City of London Regiment (The Royal Fusiliers): 4th City of London Regiment (The Royal Fusiliers)
1926	4th Prince of Wales's Own Gurkha Rifles
1926	1st South African Infantry (Cape of Good Hope Regiment): 2nd South African Infantry (Natal and Orange Free State Regiment): 3rd South African Infantry (Transvaal and Rhodesian Regiment): 4th South African Infantry (South African Scottish Regiment): 1st South African Field Ambulance

	1927	45th Battalion: 46th Battalion: 47th Battalion: 48th Battalion: 49th Battalion: 50th Battalion: 51st Battalion: 52nd Battalion: 53rd Battalion: 54th Battalion: 55th Battalion: 56th Battalion: 57th Battalion: 58th Battalion: 59th Battalion: 60th Battalion
155.	**EGYPT 1916–17** 1st January 1916–8th February 1917 Service in Egypt 1915–17	1925	The Ayrshire Yeomanry (Earl of Carrick's Own) (Hussars): The Cheshire Yeomanry (Earl of Chester's) (Hussars): Denbighshire Yeomanry (Royal Bucks Hussars): Royal North Devon Yeomanry (Hussars): Glamorgan Yeomanry (Dragoons): Royal East Kent Yeomanry (The Duke of Connaught's Own) (Mounted Rifles) (Hussars): West Kent Yeomanry (Queen's Own) (Hussars): The Lanarkshire Yeomanry (Lancers): Montgomeryshire Yeomanry (Dragoons): Pembroke Yeomanry (Castlemartin) (Hussars): Shropshire Yeomanry (Dragoons): West Somerset Yeomanry (Hussars): Sussex Yeomanry (Dragoons): The Northumberland Fusiliers: The Devonshire Regiment: The Royal Scots Fusiliers: The Cameronians (Scottish Rifles): The Herefordshire Regiment: The British West Indies Regiment
		1926 1927 1928	4th Bombay Grenadiers 14th Light Horse Regiment: 15th Light Horse Regiment 3rd Sikh Pioneers
156.	**GAZA** 26th–27th March 1917 17th–19th April 1917 The First Offensive and 27th October–7th November 1917 The Second Offensive	1925	The Ayrshire Yeomanry (Earl of Carrick's Own) (Hussars): Berks Yeomanry (Hungerford) (Dragoons): Buckinghamshire Yeomanry (Royal Bucks Hussars): The Cheshire Yeomanry (Earl of Chester's) (Hussars): Denbighshire Yeomanry (Hussars): Royal 1st Devon Yeomanry (Hussars): Royal North Devon Yeomanry (Hussars): Dorset Yeomanry (Queen's Own): Fife and Forfar Yeomanry: Glamorgan Yeomanry (Dragoons): Gloucestershire Yeomanry (Royal Gloucestershire Hussars): Royal East Kent Yeomanry (The Duke of Connaught's Own) (Mounted Rifles) (Hussars): West Kent Yeomanry (Queen's Own) (Hussars): The Lanarkshire Yeomanry (Lancers): Lincolnshire Yeomanry (Lancers): City of London Yeomanry (Rough Riders) (Lancers): 1st County of London Yeomanry (Middlesex, Duke of Cambridge's Hussars): 2nd County of London Yeomanry (Westminster Dragoons): 3rd County of London Yeomanry (Sharpshooters) (Hussars): Montgomeryshire Yeomanry (Dragoons): Norfolk Yeomanry (The King's Own Royal Regiment) (Dragoons): The Nottinghamshire Yeomanry (Sherwood Rangers) (Hussars): Nottinghamshire Yeomanry (South Nottinghamshire Hussars): Pembroke Yeomanry (Castlemartin) (Hussars): Shropshire Yeomanry (Dragoons): West Somerset Yeomanry (Hussars): The Staffordshire Yeomanry (Queen's Own Royal Regiment) (Hussars): Suffolk Yeomanry (The Duke of York's Own Loyal Suffolk Hussars): Sussex Yeomanry (Dragoons): The Warwickshire Yeomanry (Hussars): Welsh Horse (Lancers): Worcestershire Yeomanry (The Queen's Own Worcestershire Hussars): East Riding of Yorkshire Yeomanry (Lancers): Honourable Artillery Company: The Royal Scots (The Royal Regiment): The Queen's Royal Regiment (West Surrey): The Buffs (East Kent Regiment): The Norfolk Regiment: The Devonshire Regiment: The Suffolk Regiment: The Somerset Light Infantry: The Cheshire Regiment: The Royal Welch Fusiliers: The King's Own Scottish Borderers: The Cameronians (Scottish Rifles): The Royal Inniskilling Fusiliers: The Duke of Cornwall's Light Infantry: The Royal Sussex Regiment: The Hampshire Regiment: The Dorsetshire Regiment: The Welch Regiment: The Black Watch (Royal Highlanders): The Essex Regiment: The Loyal Regiment (North Lancashire): The Northamptonshire Regiment: The Queen's Own Royal West Kent Regiment: The King's Shropshire Light Infantry: The Middlesex Regiment (Duke of Cambridge's Own): The Wiltshire Regiment (Duke of Edinburgh's): The Highland Light Infantry (City of Glasgow Regiment): The Royal Ulster Rifles: The Royal Irish Fusiliers (Princess Victoria's): The Connaught Rangers: The Argyll and Sutherland Highlanders (Princess Louise's): The Prince of Wales's Leinster Regiment (Royal Canadians): The Royal Munster Fusiliers: The Royal Dublin Fusiliers: 10th London Regiment (Hackney): 11th London Regiment (Finsbury Rifles): 13th London Regiment (Princess Louise's Kensington Regiment): 14th London Regiment (London Scottish): 15th (County of London) Battalion, The London Regiment (Prince of Wales's Own, Civil Service Rifles): 16th London Regiment (Queen's Westminster Rifles): 17th London Regiment (Poplar and Stepney Rifles): 18th London Regiment (London Irish Rifles): 19th

London Regiment (St Pancras): 20th London Regiment (The Queen's Own): 21st London Regiment (First Surrey Rifles): 22nd London Regiment (The Queen's): 23rd London Regiment: 24th London Regiment (The Queen's): The Herefordshire Regiment: The British West Indies Regiment

1926   Queen Victoria's Own Madras Sappers and Miners: 3rd Sikh Pioneers: 4th Bombay Grenadiers: 6th Rajputana Rifles: 13th Frontier Force Rifles: 3rd Queen Alexandra's Own Gurkha Rifles

1926   Bhavnagar Lancers: Hyderabad Imperial Service Lancers: Mysore Lancers: 1st Patiala (Rajindra Sikhs) Infantry: 4th Gwalior Maharaja Bahadur Battalion: Alwar Jey Paltan: 1st Bahawalpur Sadiq Infantry: Khairpur Faiz Light Infantry

1926   1st Battery, South African Field Artillery: 2nd Battery, South African Field Artillery: 4th Battery, South African Field Artillery
1928   The Nelson-Marlborough Mounted Rifles
1958   Royal Tank Regiment

157.   **GAZA-BEERSHEBA**
26th–27th March 1917
17th–19th April 1917
The First Offensive
and
27th October–7th November 1917
The Second Offensive

1927   1st Light Horse Regiment: 2nd Light Horse Regiment: 3rd Light Horse Regiment: 4th Light Horse Regiment: 5th Light Horse Regiment: 6th Light Horse Regiment: 7th Light Horse Regiment: 8th Light Horse Regiment: 9th Light Horse Regiment: 10th Light Horse Regiment: 11th Light Horse Regiment: 12th Light Horse Regiment: 14th Light Horse Regiment: 15th Light Horse Regiment

1928   The Canterbury Yeomanry Cavalry: Queen Alexandra's Wellington West Coast Mounted Rifles: The Auckland Mounted Rifles: The Waikato Mounted Rifles: The Manawatu Mounted Rifles: The Wellington East Coast Mounted Rifles: The North Auckland Mounted Rifles

1930   3rd (Tasmanian Mounted Infantry) Light Horse Regiment AMF

158.   **EL MUGHAR**
13th November 1917
The Second Offensive

1925   Berks Yeomanry (Hungerford) (Dragoons): Buckinghamshire Yeomanry (Royal Bucks Hussars): Dorset Yeomanry (Queen's Own): Gloucestershire Yeomanry (Royal Gloucestershire Hussars): Lincolnshire Yeomanry (Lancers): City of London Yeomanry (Rough Riders) (Lancers): 1st County of London Yeomanry (Middlesex, Duke of Cambridge's Hussars): 2nd County of London Yeomanry (Westminster Dragoons): 3rd County of London Yeomanry (Sharpshooters) (Hussars): The Nottinghamshire Yeomanry (Sherwood Rangers) (Hussars): Nottinghamshire Yeomanry (South Nottinghamshire Hussars): The Staffordshire Yeomanry (Queen's Own Royal Regiment) (Hussars): The Warwickshire Yeomanry (Hussars): Worcestershire Yeomanry (The Queen's Own Worcestershire Hussars): East Riding of Yorkshire Yeomanry (Lancers): Honourable Artillery Company: The Royal Scots (The Royal Regiment): The Queen's Royal Regiment (West Surrey): The Norfolk Regiment: The Suffolk Regiment: The Somerset Light Infantry (Prince Albert's): The Bedfordshire and Hertfordshire Regiment: The Royal Scots Fusiliers: The Cheshire Regiment: The Royal Welch Fusiliers: The King's Own Scottish Borderers: The Cameronians (Scottish Rifles): The Royal Sussex Regiment: The Hampshire Regiment: The Dorsetshire Regiment: The Welch Regiment: The Northamptonshire Regiment: The Queen's Own Royal West Kent Regiment: The Middlesex Regiment (Duke of Cambridge's Own): The Highland Light Infantry (City of Glasgow Regiment): The Argyll and Sutherland Highlanders (Princess Louise's): 10th London Regiment (Hackney): 11th London Regiment (Finsbury Rifles): 13th London Regiment (Princess Louise's Kensington Regiment): 14th London Regiment (London Scottish): 15th (County of London) Battalion, The London Regiment (Prince of Wales's Own, Civil Service Rifles): 16th London Regiment (Queen's Westminster Rifles): 17th London Regiment (Poplar and Stepney Rifles): 18th London Regiment (London Irish Rifles): 19th London Regiment (St Pancras): 20th London Regiment (The Queen's Own): 21st London Regiment (First Surrey Rifles): 22nd London Regiment (The Queen's): 23rd London Regiment: 24th London Regiment (The Queen's): The Herefordshire Regiment: The British West Indies Regiment

1926   13th Frontier Force Rifles: 3rd Queen Alexandra's Own Gurkha Rifles
1926   1st Battery, South African Field Artillery: 2nd Battery, South African Field Artillery: 4th Battery, South African Field Artillery

	1927	1st Light Horse Regiment: 2nd Light Horse Regiment: 3rd Light Horse Regiment: 4th Light Horse Regiment: 5th Light Horse Regiment: 6th Light Horse Regiment: 7th Light Horse Regiment: 8th Light Horse Regiment: 9th Light Horse Regiment: 10th Light Horse Regiment: 11th Light Horse Regiment: 12th Light Horse Regiment: 14th Light Horse Regiment: 15th Light Horse Regiment
	1930	3rd (Tasmanian Mounted Infantry) Light Horse Regiment AMF
159.	**NEBI SAMWIL** 17th–24th November 1917 Jerusalem Operations	1925	Berks Yeomanry (Hungerford) (Dragoons): Buckinghamshire Yeomanry (Royal Bucks Hussars): Dorset Yeomanry (Queen's Own): Gloucestershire Yeomanry (Royal Gloucestershire Hussars): Lincolnshire Yeomanry (Lancers): City of London Yeomanry (Rough Riders) (Lancers): 1st County of London Yeomanry (Middlesex, Duke of Cambridge's Hussars): 3rd County of London Yeomanry (Sharpshooters) (Hussars): The Nottinghamshire Yeomanry (Sherwood Rangers) (Hussars): Nottinghamshire Yeomanry (South Nottinghamshire Hussars): The Staffordshire Yeomanry (Queen's Own Royal Regiment) (Hussars): The Warwickshire Yeomanry (Hussars): Worcestershire Yeomanry (The Queen's Own Worcestershire Hussars): East Riding of Yorkshire Yeomanry (Lancers): The Royal Scots (The Royal Regiment): The Norfolk Regiment: The Devonshire Regiment: The Suffolk Regiment: The Somerset Light Infantry (Prince Albert's): The Bedfordshire and Hertfordshire Regiment: The Royal Scots Fusiliers: The King's Own Scottish Borderers: The Cameronians (Scottish Rifles): The Duke of Cornwall's Light Infantry: The Hampshire Regiment: The Dorsetshire Regiment: The Loyal Regiment (North Lancashire): The Northamptonshire Regiment: The Wiltshire Regiment (Duke of Edinburgh's): The Highland Light Infantry (City of Glasgow Regiment): The Argyll and Sutherland Highlanders (Princess Louise's): 10th London Regiment (Hackney): 11th London Regiment (Finsbury Rifles): 13th London Regiment (Princess Louise's Kensington Regiment): 14th London Regiment (London Scottish): 15th (County of London) Battalion, The London Regiment (Prince of Wales's Own, Civil Service Rifles): 16th London Regiment (Queen's Westminster Rifles): 17th London Regiment (Poplar and Stepney Rifles): 18th London Regiment (London Irish Rifles): 19th London Regiment (St Pancras): 20th London Regiment (The Queen's Own): 21st London Regiment (First Surrey Rifles): 22nd London Regiment (The Queen's): 23rd London Regiment: 24th London Regiment (The Queen's): The British West Indies Regiment
	1926	6th Rajputana Rifles: 13th Frontier Force Rifles: 3rd Queen Alexandra's Own Gurkha Rifles
	1926	Hyderabad Imperial Service Lancers
	1926	1st Battery, South African Field Artillery: 2nd Battery, South African Field Artillery: 4th Battery, South African Field Artillery
	1927	1st Light Horse Regiment: 2nd Light Horse Regiment: 3rd Light Horse Regiment: 4th Light Horse Regiment: 5th Light Horse Regiment: 6th Light Horse Regiment: 7th Light Horse Regiment: 8th Light Horse Regiment: 9th Light Horse Regiment: 10th Light Horse Regiment: 11th Light Horse Regiment: 12th Light Horse Regiment: 14th Light Horse Regiment: 15th Light Horse Regiment
	1930	3rd (Tasmanian Mounted Infantry) Light Horse Regiment AMF
160.	**JERUSALEM** 7th–9th December 1917 and 26th–30th December 1917 Jerusalem Operations	1925	The Ayrshire Yeomanry (Earl of Carrick's Own) (Hussars): The Cheshire Yeomanry (Earl of Chester's) (Hussars): Denbighshire Yeomanry (Hussars): Royal 1st Devon Yeomanry (Hussars): Royal North Devon Yeomanry (Hussars): Fife and Forfar Yeomanry: Glamorgan Yeomanry (Dragoons): Gloucestershire Yeomanry (Royal Gloucestershire Hussars): Royal East Kent Yeomanry (The Duke of Connaught's Own) (Mounted Rifles) (Hussars): West Kent Yeomanry (Queen's Own) (Hussars): The Lanarkshire Yeomanry (Lancers): 2nd County of London Yeomanry (Westminster Dragoons): Montgomeryshire Yeomanry (Dragoons): Norfolk Yeomanry (The King's Own Royal Regiment) (Dragoons): Pembroke Yeomanry (The Castlemartin) (Hussars): Shropshire Yeomanry (Dragoons): West Somerset Yeomanry (Hussars): Suffolk Yeomanry (The Duke of York's Own Loyal Suffolk Hussars): Sussex Yeomanry (Dragoons): The Warwickshire Yeomanry (Hussars): Welsh Horse (Lancers): Worcestershire Yeomanry (The Queen's Own Worcestershire Hussars): Honourable Artillery Company:

The Queen's Royal Regiment (West Surrey): The Buffs (East Kent Regiment): The Norfolk Regiment: The Devonshire Regiment: The Suffolk Regiment: The Somerset Light Infantry (Prince Albert's): The Bedfordshire and Hertfordshire Regiment: The Royal Irish Regiment: The Royal Scots Fusiliers: The Cheshire Regiment: The Royal Welch Fusiliers: The Royal Inniskilling Fusiliers: The Duke of Cornwall's Light Infantry: The Royal Sussex Regiment: The Hampshire Regiment: The Dorsetshire Regiment: The Welch Regiment: The Black Watch (Royal Highlanders): The Loyal Regiment (North Lancashire): The Northamptonshire Regiment: The Queen's Own Royal West Kent Regiment: The King's Shropshire Light Infantry: The Middlesex Regiment (Duke of Cambridge's Own): The Wiltshire Regiment (Duke of Edinburgh's): The Royal Ulster Rifles: The Royal Irish Fusiliers (Princess Victoria's): The Connaught Rangers: The Prince of Wales's Leinster Regiment (Royal Canadians): The Royal Munster Fusiliers: The Royal Dublin Fusiliers: 10th London Regiment (Hackney): 11th London Regiment (Finsbury Rifles): 13th London Regiment (Princess Louise's Kensington Regiment): 14th London Regiment (London Scottish): 15th (County of London) Battalion, The London Regiment (Prince of Wales's Own, Civil Service Rifles): 16th London Regiment (Queen's Westminster Rifles): 17th London Regiment (Poplar and Stepney Rifles): 18th London Regiment (London Irish Rifles): 19th London Regiment (St Pancras): 20th London Regiment (The Queen's Own): 21st London Regiment (First Surrey Rifles): 22nd London Regiment (The Queen's): 23rd London Regiment: 24th London Regiment (The Queen's): The Herefordshire Regiment: The British West Indies Regiment

1926 6th Rajputana Rifles: 13th Frontier Force Rifles: 3rd Queen Alexandra's Own Gurkha Rifles
1926 4th Gwalior Maharaja Bahadur Battalion
1927 1st Light Horse Regiment: 2nd Light Horse Regiment: 3rd Light Horse Regiment: 4th Light Horse Regiment: 5th Light Horse Regiment: 6th Light Horse Regiment: 7th Light Horse Regiment: 8th Light Horse Regiment: 9th Light Horse Regiment: 10th Light Horse Regiment: 11th Light Horse Regiment: 12th Light Horse Regiment: 14th Light Horse Regiment: 15th Light Horse Regiment

1928 The Canterbury Yeomanry Cavalry: Queen Alexandra's Wellington West Coast Mounted Rifles: The Auckland Mounted Rifles: The Waikato Mounted Rifles: The Manawatu Mounted Rifles: The Wellington East Coast Mounted Rifles: The Nelson-Marlborough Mounted Rifles: The North Auckland Mounted Rifles
1930 3rd (Tasmanian Mounted Infantry) Light Horse Regiment AMF

161. **JAFFA**
21st–22nd December 1917
Jerusalem Operations

1925 The Royal Scots (The Royal Regiment): The Norfolk Regiment: The Suffolk Regiment: The Bedfordshire and Hertfordshire Regiment: The Royal Scots Fusiliers: The King's Own Scottish Borderers: The Cameronians (Scottish Rifles): The Hampshire Regiment: The Essex Regiment: The Loyal Regiment (North Lancashire): The Northamptonshire Regiment: The Highland Light Infantry (City of Glasgow Regiment): The Argyll and Sutherland Highlanders (Princess Louise's): 10th London Regiment (Hackney): 11th London Regiment (Finsbury Rifles): The British West Indies Regiment
1927 1st Light Horse Regiment: 2nd Light Horse Regiment: 3rd Light Horse Regiment
1928 The Canterbury Yeomanry Cavalry: Queen Alexandra's Wellington West Coast Mounted Rifles: The Auckland Mounted Rifles: The Waikato Mounted Rifles: The Manawatu Mounted Rifles: The Wellington East Coast Mounted Rifles: The Nelson-Marlborough Mounted Rifles: The North Auckland Mounted Rifles
1930 3rd (Tasmanian Mounted Infantry) Light Horse Regiment AMF

162. **JERICHO**
19th–21st February 1918
Operations in and beyond the Jordan Valley

1925 The Cheshire Yeomanry (Earl of Chester's) (Hussars): Denbighshire Yeomanry (Hussars): Glamorgan Yeomanry (Dragoons): Montgomeryshire Yeomanry (Dragoons): Pembroke Yeomanry (Castlemartin) (Hussars): Shropshire Yeomanry (Dragoons): Welsh Horse (Lancers): The Queen's Royal Regiment (West Surrey): The Cheshire Regiment: The Royal Welch Fusiliers: The Royal Sussex Regiment: The Welch Regiment: The Queen's Own Royal West Kent Regiment: The King's Shropshire Light Infantry: The Middlesex Regiment (Duke of Cambridge's Own): 13th London Regiment (Princess Louise's

	1927	Kensington Regiment): 14th London Regiment (London Scottish): 15th (County of London) Battalion, The London Regiment (Prince of Wales's Own, Civil Service Rifles): 16th London Regiment (Queen's Westminster Rifles): 17th London Regiment (Poplar and Stepney Rifles): 18th London Regiment (London Irish Rifles): 19th London Regiment (St Pancras): 20th London Regiment (The Queen's Own): 21st London Regiment (First Surrey Rifles): 22nd London Regiment (The Queen's): 23rd London Regiment: 24th London Regiment (The Queen's)
	1928	1st Light Horse Regiment: 2nd Light Horse Regiment: 3rd Light Horse Regiment The Canterbury Yeomanry Cavalry: Queen Alexandra's Wellington West Coast Mounted Rifles: The Auckland Mounted Rifles: The Waikato Mounted Rifles: The Manawatu Mounted Rifles: The Wellington East Coast Mounted Rifles: The Nelson-Marlborough Mounted Rifles: The North Auckland Mounted Rifles
	1930	3rd (Tasmanian Mounted Infantry) Light Horse Regiment AMF
163.	**JORDAN** 21st March–4th May 1918 Operations in and beyond the Jordan Valley	1925	Honourable Artillery Company: The Middlesex Regiment (Duke of Cambridge's Own): 13th London Regiment (Princess Louise's Kensington Regiment): 14th London Regiment (London Scottish): 15th (County of London) Battalion, The London Regiment (Prince of Wales's Own, Civil Service Rifles): 16th London Regiment (Queen's Westminster Rifles): 17th London Regiment (Poplar and Stepney Rifles): 18th London Regiment (London Irish Rifles): 19th London Regiment (St Pancras): 20th London Regiment (The Queen's Own): 21st London Regiment (First Surrey Rifles): 22nd London Regiment (The Queen's): 23rd London Regiment: 24th London Regiment (The Queen's)
164.	**JORDAN (ES SALT)** 24th–25th March 1918 and 30th April–4th May 1918 Operations in and beyond the Jordan valley	1927	1st Light Horse Regiment: 2nd Light Horse Regiment: 3rd Light Horse Regiment: 4th Light Horse Regiment: 5th Light Horse Regiment: 6th Light Horse Regiment: 7th Light Horse Regiment: 8th Light Horse Regiment: 9th Light Horse Regiment: 10th Light Horse Regiment: 11th Light Horse Regiment: 12th Light Horse Regiment: 14th Light Horse Regiment: 15th Light Horse Regiment AMF
	1930	3rd (Tasmanian Mounted Infantry) Light Horse Regiment
165.	**JORDAN (AMMAN)** 27th–30th March 1918 Operations in and beyond the Jordan Valley	1927	1st Light Horse Regiment: 2nd Light Horse Regiment: 3rd Light Horse Regiment: 5th Light Horse Regiment: 6th Light Horse Regiment: 7th Light Horse Regiment: 14th Light Horse Regiment: 15th Light Horse Regiment
	1928	The Canterbury Yeomanry Cavalry: Queen Alexandra's Wellington West Coast Mounted Rifles: The Auckland Mounted Rifles: The Waikato Mounted Rifles: The Manawatu Mounted Rifles: The Wellington East Coast Mounted Rifles: The Nelson-Marlborough Mounted Rifles: The North Auckland Mounted Rifles
	1930	3rd (Tasmanian Mounted Infantry) Light Horse Regiment AMF
166.	**TELL'ASUR** 8th–12th March 1918 Local Operations 1918	1925	The Ayrshire Yeomanry (Earl of Carrick's Own) (Hussars): The Cheshire Yeomanry (Earl of Chester's) (Hussars): Denbighshire Yeomanry: Royal 1st Devon Yeomanry (Hussars): Royal North Devon Yeomanry (Hussars): Fife and Forfar Yeomanry: Glamorgan Yeomanry (Dragoons): Royal East Kent Yeomanry (The Duke of Connaught's Own) (Mounted Rifles) (Hussars): West Kent Yeomanry (Queen's Own) (Hussars): The Lanarkshire Yeomanry (Lancers): Montgomeryshire Yeomanry (Dragoons): Norfolk Yeomanry (The King's Own Royal Regiment) (Dragoons): Pembroke Yeomanry (Castlemartin) (Hussars): Shropshire Yeomanry (Dragoons): West Somerset Yeomanry (Hussars): Suffolk Yeomanry (The Duke of York's Own Loyal Suffolk Hussars): Sussex Yeomanry (Dragoons): The Queen's Royal Regiment (West Surrey): The Buffs (East Kent Regiment): The Norfolk Regiment: The Devonshire Regiment: The Suffolk Regiment: The Bedfordshire and Hertfordshire Regiment: The Royal Irish Regiment: The Royal Scots Fusiliers: The Cheshire Regiment: The Royal Welch Fusiliers: The Royal Inniskilling Fusiliers: The Duke of Cornwall's Light Infantry: The Royal Sussex Regiment: The Hampshire Regiment: The Dorsetshire Regiment: The Welch Regiment: The Black Watch (Royal Highlanders): The Loyal Regiment

(North Lancashire): The Northamptonshire Regiment: The Queen's Own Royal West Kent Regiment: The King's Shropshire Light Infantry: The Middlesex Regiment (Duke of Cambridge's Own): The Royal Ulster Rifles: The Royal Irish Fusiliers (Princess Victoria's): The Connaught Rangers: The Prince of Wales's Leinster Regiment (Royal Canadians): The Royal Munster Fusiliers: The Royal Dublin Fusiliers: 10th London Regiment (Hackney): 11th London Regiment (Finsbury Rifles): 14th London Regiment (London Scottish): 15th (County of London) Battalion, The London Regiment (Prince of Wales's Own, Civil Service Rifles): 16th London Regiment (Queen's Westminster Rifles): 17th London Regiment (Poplar and Stepney Rifles): 21st London Regiment (First Surrey Rifles): 22nd London Regiment (The Queen's): 23rd London Regiment: 24th London Regiment (The Queen's)

1926   1st Battery, South African Field Artillery: 2nd Battery, South African Field Artillery: 3rd Battery, South African Field Artillery: 4th Battery, South African Field Artillery: 5th Battery, South African Field Artillery

1925   Dorset Yeomanry (Queen's Own): Gloucestershire Yeomanry (Royal Gloucestershire Hussars): Herts Yeomanry (Dragoons): 1st County of London Yeomanry (Middlesex, Duke of Cambridge's Hussars): The Nottinghamshire Yeomanry (Sherwood Rangers) (Hussars): The Staffordshire Yeomanry (Queen's Own Royal Regiment) (Hussars): Worcestershire Yeomanry (The Queen's Own Worcestershire Hussars): Honourable Artillery Company: The Royal Fusiliers (City of London Regiment): The Norfolk Regiment: The Suffolk Regiment: The Somerset Light Infantry (Prince Albert's): The Bedfordshire and Hertfordshire Regiment: The Leicestershire Regiment: The Royal Irish Regiment: The Royal Welch Fusiliers: The Duke of Cornwall's Light Infantry: The Hampshire Regiment: The Dorsetshire Regiment: The Welch Regiment: The Black Watch (Royal Highlanders): The Essex Regiment: The Northamptonshire Regiment: The Wiltshire Regiment (Duke of Edinburgh's): The Manchester Regiment: The Seaforth Highlanders (Ross-shire Buffs, The Duke of Albany's): The Royal Irish Fusiliers (Princess Victoria's): The Connaught Rangers: The Prince of Wales's Leinster Regiment (Royal Canadians): 10th London Regiment (Hackney): 11th London Regiment (Finsbury Rifles): 13th London Regiment (Princess Louise's Kensington Regiment): 19th London Regiment (St Pancras): 22nd London Regiment (The Queen's): The British West Indies Regiment

167.   **MEGIDDO**
19th–25th September 1918
The Final Offensive

1926   109th (Murree) Pack Battery: 112th (Poonch) Pack Battery: 119th (Maymyo) Pack Battery: 2nd Lancers (Gardner's Horse): 4th Duke of Cambridge's Own Hodson's Horse: 9th Royal Deccan Horse: 14th Prince of Wales's Own Scinde Horse: 17th Queen Victoria's Own Poona Horse: 18th King Edward's Own Cavalry: 19th King George's Own Lancers: 21st King George's Own Central India Horse: Queen Victoria's Own Madras Sappers and Miners: King George's Own Bengal Sappers and Miners: Royal Bombay Sappers and Miners: 2nd Bombay Pioneers: 3rd Sikh Pioneers: 2nd Punjab Regiment: 4th Bombay Grenadiers: 5th Mahratta Light Infantry: 6th Rajputana Rifles: 8th Punjab Regiment: 10th Baluch Regiment: 11th Sikh Regiment: 12th Frontier Force Regiment: 13th Frontier Force Rifles: 14th Punjab Regiment: 15th Punjab Regiment: 16th Punjab Regiment: 17th Dogra Regiment: 19th Hyderabad Regiment: 1st King George's Own Gurkha Rifles (The Malaun Regiment): 3rd Queen Alexandra's Own Gurkha Rifles: 7th Gurkha Rifles: 8th Gurkha Rifles

1926   Jodhpur Sardar Risala: Bhavnagar Lancers: Hyderabad Imperial Service Lancers: Mysore Lancers: 1st Kashmir Raghupartap Battalion: 3rd Kashmir Raghunath Rifle Battalion: 4th Gwalior Maharaja Bahadur Battalion: Alwar Jey Pattan: 1st Bahawalpur Sadiq Infantry: Khairpur Faiz Light Infantry

1926   1st Battery, South African Field Artillery: 2nd Battery, South African Field Artillery: 3rd Battery, South African Field Artillery: 4th Battery, South African Field Artillery: 5th Battery, South African Field Artillery

1927   1st Light Horse Regiment: 2nd Light Horse Regiment: 3rd Light Horse Regiment: 4th Light Horse Regiment: 5th Light Horse Regiment: 6th Light Horse Regiment: 7th Light Horse Regiment: 8th Light Horse Regiment: 9th Light Horse Regiment: 10th Light Horse Regiment: 11th Light Horse Regiment: 12th Light Horse Regiment: 14th Light Horse Regiment: 15th Light Horse Regiment

1928   The Canterbury Yeomanry Cavalry: Queen Alexandra's Wellington West Coast Mounted Rifles: The Auckland Mounted

	1930	Rifles; The Waikato Mounted Rifles; The Manawatu Mounted Rifles; The Wellington East Coast Mounted Rifles; The Nelson-Marlborough Mounted Rifles; The North Auckland Mounted Rifles; 3rd (Tasmanian Mounted Infantry) Light Horse Regiment AMF
168.	**SHARON** 19th–25th September 1918 The Final Offensive	
	1925	Dorset Yeomanry (Queen's Own); Gloucestershire Yeomanry (Royal Gloucestershire Hussars); Herts Yeomanry (Dragoons); 1st County of London Yeomanry (Middlesex, Duke of Cambridge's Hussars); The Nottinghamshire Yeomanry (Sherwood Rangers) (Hussars); The Staffordshire Yeomanry (Queen's Own Royal Regiment) (Hussars); Honourable Artillery Company; The Norfolk Regiment; The Suffolk Regiment; The Somerset Light Infantry (Prince Albert's); The Bedfordshire and Hertfordshire Regiment; The Leicestershire Regiment; The Duke of Cornwall's Light Infantry; The Hampshire Regiment; The Dorsetshire Regiment; The Black Watch (Royal Highlanders); The Essex Regiment; The Northamptonshire Regiment; The Wiltshire Regiment (Duke of Edinburgh's); The Manchester Regiment The Seaforth Highlanders (Ross-shire Buffs, The Duke of Albany's); The Connaught Rangers; 10th London Regiment (Hackney); 11th London Regiment (Finsbury Rifles); 13th London Regiment (Princess Louise's Kensington Regiment); 19th London Regiment (St Pancras); 22nd London Regiment (The Queen's)
	1926	2nd Lancers (Gardner's Horse); 4th Duke of Cambridge's Own Hodson's Horse; 9th Royal Deccan Horse; 14th Prince of Wales's Own Scinde Horse; 17th Queen Victoria's Own Poona Horse; 18th King Edward's Own Cavalry; 19th King George's Own Lancers; 21st King George's Own Central India Horse; Queen Victoria's Own Madras Sappers and Miners; King George's Own Bengal Sappers and Miners; Royal Bombay Sappers and Miners; 2nd Bombay Pioneers; 3rd Sikh Pioneers; 2nd Punjab Regiment; 5th Mahratta Light Infantry; 6th Rajputana Rifles; 8th Punjab Regiment; 10th Baluch Regiment; 11th Sikh Regiment; 12th Frontier Force Regiment; 13th Frontier Force Rifles; 14th Punjab Regiment; 15th Punjab Regiment; 19th Hyderabad Regiment; 1st King George's Own Gurkha Rifles (The Malaun Regiment); 3rd Queen Alexandra's Own Gurkha Rifles; 7th Gurkha Rifles; 8th Gurkha Rifles
	1926	Jodhpur Sardar Risala; Bhavnagar Lancers; Hyderabad Imperial Service Lancers; Mysore Lancers; 3rd Kashmir Raghunath Rifle Battalion
	1926	1st Battery, South African Field Artillery; 2nd Battery, South African Field Artillery; 3rd Battery, South African Field Artillery; 4th Battery, South African Field Artillery; 5th Battery, South African Field Artillery
	1927	4th Light Horse Regiment; 8th Light Horse Regiment; 9th Light Horse Regiment; 10th Light Horse Regiment; 11th Light Horse Regiment; 12th Light Horse Regiment
169.	**NABLUS** 19th–25th September 1918 The Final Offensive	
	1925	Worcestershire Yeomanry (The Queen's Own Worcestershire Hussars); The Royal Fusiliers (City of London Regiment); The Royal Welch Fusiliers (Royal Canadians); The British West Indies Regiment
	1926	109th (Murree) Pack Battery; 112th (Poonch) Pack Battery; 119th (Maymyo) Pack Battery; Royal Bombay Sappers and Miners; 3rd Sikh Pioneers; 2nd Punjab Regiment; 4th Bombay Grenadiers; 5th Mahratta Light Infantry; 12th Frontier Force Regiment; 14th Punjab Regiment; 16th Punjab Regiment; 7th Dogra Regiment
	1926	1st Kashmir Raghupartap Battalion; 4th Gwalior Maharaja Bahadur Battalion; Alwar Jey Paltan; 1st Bahawalpur Sadiq Infantry; Khairpur Faiz Light Infantry
	1926	1st Battalion, Cape Corps
	1927	1st Light Horse Regiment; 2nd Light Horse Regiment; 3rd Light Horse Regiment; 5th Light Horse Regiment; 6th Light Horse Regiment; 7th Light Horse Regiment; 14th Light Horse Regiment; 15th Light Horse Regiment
	1928	The Canterbury Yeomanry Cavalry; Queen Alexandra's Wellington West Coast Mounted Rifles; The Auckland Mounted

Rifles: The Waikato Mounted Rifles: The Manawatu Mounted Rifles: The Wellington East Coast Mounted Rifles: The Nelson-Marlborough Mounted Rifles: The North Auckland Mounted Rifles

1930   3rd (Tasmanian Mounted Infantry) Light Horse Regiment AMF

170.   **DAMASCUS**
1st October 1918
The Final Offensive

1925   Dorset Yeomanry (Queen's Own): Gloucestershire Yeomanry (Royal Gloucestershire Hussars): Herts Yeomanry (Dragoons): 1st County of London Yeomanry (Middlesex, Duke of Cambridge's Hussars): The Nottinghamshire Yeomanry (Sherwood Rangers) (Hussars): The Staffordshire Yeomanry (Queen's Own Royal Regiment) (Hussars): Worcestershire Yeomanry (The Queen's Own Worcestershire Hussars): Honourable Artillery Company: The Leicestershire Regiment: The Black Watch (Royal Highlanders)

1926   2nd Lancers (Gardner's Horse): 4th Duke of Cambridge's Own Hodson's Horse: 9th Royal Deccan Horse: 14th Prince of Wales's Own Scinde Horse: 17th Queen Victoria's Own Poona Horse: 18th King Edward's Own Cavalry: 19th King George's Own Lancers: 21st King George's Own Central India Horse: King George's Own Bengal Sappers and Miners: Royal Bombay Sappers and Miners

Jodhpur Sardar Risala: Bhavnagar Lancers: Hyderabad Imperial Service Lancers: Mysore Lancers

1926   4th Light Horse Regiment: 8th Light Horse Regiment: 9th Light Horse Regiment: 10th Light Horse Regiment: 11th Light Horse
1927   Regiment: 12th Light Horse Regiment: 14th Light Horse Regiment: 15th Light Horse Regiment

171.   **PALESTINE 1917-18**
26th March 1917-31st October 1918
Service in Palestine 1917-18

1925   The Ayrshire Yeomanry (Earl of Carrick's Own) (Hussars): Berks Yeomanry (Hungerford) (Dragoons): Buckinghamshire Yeomanry (Royal Bucks Hussars): The Cheshire Yeomanry (Earl of Chester's) (Hussars): Denbighshire Yeomanry (Hussars): Royal 1st Devon Yeomanry (Hussars): Royal North Devon Yeomanry (Hussars): Dorset Yeomanry (Queen's Own): Fife and Forfar Yeomanry: Glamorgan Yeomanry (Dragoons): Gloucestershire Yeomanry (Royal Gloucestershire Hussars): Royal East Kent Yeomanry (The Duke of Connaught's Own) (Mounted Rifles) (Hussars): West Kent Yeomanry (Queen's Own) (Hussars): The Lanarkshire Yeomanry (Lancers): Lincolnshire Yeomanry (Lancers): City of London Yeomanry (Rough Riders) (Lancers): 1st County of London Yeomanry (Middlesex, Duke of Cambridge's Hussars): 2nd County of London Yeomanry (Westminster Dragoons): 3rd County of London Yeomanry (Sharpshooters) (Hussars): Montgomeryshire Yeomanry (Dragoons): Norfolk Yeomanry (The King's Own Royal Regiment) (Dragoons): The Nottinghamshire Yeomanry (Sherwood Rangers) (Hussars): Nottinghamshire Yeomanry (South Nottinghamshire Hussars): Pembroke Yeomanry (Castlemartin) (Hussars): Shropshire Yeomanry (Dragoons): West Somerset Yeomanry (Hussars): The Staffordshire Yeomanry (Queen's Own Royal Regiment) (Hussars): Suffolk Yeomanry (The Duke of York's Own Loyal Suffolk Hussars): Sussex Yeomanry (Dragoons): The Warwickshire Yeomanry (Hussars): Welsh Horse (Lancers): Worcestershire Yeomanry (The Queen's Own Worcestershire Hussars): East Riding of Yorkshire Yeomanry (Lancers): Honourable Artillery Company: The Royal Scots (The Royal Regiment): The Queen's Royal Regiment (West Surrey): The Buffs (East Kent Regiment): The Norfolk Regiment: The Devonshire Regiment: The Suffolk Regiment: The Somerset Light Infantry: The Cheshire Regiment: The Royal Welch Fusiliers: The King's Own Scottish Borderers: The Cameronians (Scottish Rifles): The Royal Inniskilling Fusiliers: The Duke of Cornwall's Light Infantry: The Royal Sussex Regiment: The Hampshire Regiment: The Dorsetshire Regiment: The Welch Regiment: The Black Watch (Royal Highlanders): The Essex Regiment: The Loyal Regiment (North Lancashire): The Northamptonshire Regiment: The Queen's Own Royal West Kent Regiment: The King's Shropshire Light Infantry: The Middlesex Regiment (Duke of Cambridge's Own): The Wiltshire Regiment (Duke of Edinburgh's): The Highland Light Infantry (City of Glasgow Regiment): The Royal Ulster Rifles: The Royal Irish Fusiliers (Princess Victoria's): The Connaught Rangers: The Argyll and Sutherland Highlanders (Princess Louise's): The Prince of Wales's Leinster Regiment (Royal Canadians): The

Royal Munster Fusiliers: The Royal Dublin Fusiliers: 10th London Regiment (Hackney): 11th London Regiment (Finsbury Rifles): 13th London Regiment (Princess Louise's Kensington Regiment): 14th London Regiment (London Scottish): 15th (County of London) Battalion, The London Regiment (Prince of Wales's Own, Civil Service Rifles): 16th London Regiment (Queen's Westminster Rifles): 17th London Regiment (Poplar and Stepney Rifles): 18th London Regiment (London Irish Rifles): 19th London Regiment (St Pancras): 20th London Regiment (The Queen's Own): 21st London Regiment (First Surrey Rifles): 22nd London Regiment (The Queen's): 23rd London Regiment: 24th London Regiment (The Queen's): The Herefordshire Regiment: The British West Indies Regiment

1926 Queen Victoria's Own Madras Sappers and Miners: 3rd Sikh Pioneers: 4th Bombay Grenadiers: 6th Rajputana Rifles: 13th Frontier Force Rifles: 3rd Queen Alexandra's Own Gurkha Rifles

1926 Bhavnagar Lancers: Hyderabad Imperial Service Lancers: Mysore Lancers: 1st Patiala (Rajindra Sikhs) Infantry: 4th Gwalior Maharaja Bahadur Battalion: Alwar Jey Paltan: 1st Bahawalpur Sadiq Infantry: Khairpur Faiz Light Infantry

1926 1st Battery, South African Field Artillery: 2nd Battery, South African Field Artillery: 4th Battery, South African Field Artillery

1927 1st Light Horse Regiment: 2nd Light Horse Regiment: 3rd Light Horse Regiment: 4th Light Horse Regiment: 5th Light Horse Regiment: 6th Light Horse Regiment: 7th Light Horse Regiment: 8th Light Horse Regiment: 9th Light Horse Regiment: 10th Light Horse Regiment: 11th Light Horse Regiment: 12th Light Horse Regiment: 14th Light Horse Regiment: 15th Light Horse Regiment

1928 The Canterbury Yeomanry Cavalry: Queen Alexandra's Wellington West Coast Mounted Rifles: The Auckland Mounted Rifles: The Waikato Mounted Rifles: The Manawatu Mounted Rifles: The Wellington East Coast Mounted Rifles: The Nelson-Marlborough Mounted Rifles: The North Auckland Mounted Rifles

1930 3rd (Tasmanian Mounted Infantry) Light Horse Regiment AMF

1936 16th Light Horse Regiment: 17th Light Horse Regiment: 18th Light Horse Regiment: 19th Light Horse Regiment: 20th Light Horse Regiment: 21st Light Horse Regiment: 23rd Light Horse Regiment

172. PALESTINE 1918
1st January–31st October 1918

1925 Herts Yeomanry (Dragoons): The Royal Fusiliers (City of London Regiment): The Leicestershire Regiment: The Manchester Regiment: The Seaforth Highlanders (Ross-shire Buffs, The Duke of Albany's): The West India Regiment

Service in Palestine 1917–18

1926 109th (Murree) Pack Battery: 112th (Poonch) Pack Battery: 119th (Maymyo) Pack Battery: 2nd Lancers (Gardner's Horse): 4th Duke of Cambridge's Own Hodson's Horse: 9th Royal Deccan Horse: 14th Prince of Wales's Own Scinde Horse: 17th Queen Victoria's Own Poona Horse: 18th King Edward's Own Cavalry: 19th King George's Own Lancers: 21st King George's Own Central India Horse: King George's Own Bengal Sappers and Miners: Royal Bombay Sappers and Miners: 2nd Bombay Pioneers: 2nd Punjab Regiment: 5th Mahratta Light Infantry: 8th Punjab Regiment: 10th Baluch Regiment: 11th Sikh Regiment: 12th Frontier Force Regiment: 14th Punjab Regiment: 15th Punjab Regiment: 16th Punjab Regiment: 17th Dogra Regiment: 19th Hyderabad Regiment: 1st King George's Own Gurkha Rifles (The Malaun Regiment): 7th Gurkha Rifles: 8th Gurkha Rifles

1926 Jodhpur Sardar Risala: 1st Kashmir Raghupartap Battalion: 3rd Kashmir Raghunath Rifle Battalion

1926 3rd Battery, South African Field Artillery: 5th Battery, South African Field Artillery: 1st Battalion, Cape Corps

173. ADEN
3rd July 1915–31st October 1918

1925 Honourable Artillery Company: The Buffs (East Kent Regiment): The East Surrey Regiment: The Duke of Cornwall's Light Infantry: The Hampshire Regiment: The Monmouthshire Regiment

Defence of Aden

1926 8th King George's Own Light Cavalry: Aden Troop: King George's Own Bengal Sappers and Miners: Royal Bombay Sappers and Miners: 1st Punjab Regiment: 2nd Punjab Regiment: 3rd Madras Regiment: 4th Bombay Grenadiers: 7th Rajput Regiment: 10th Baluch Regiment: 13th Frontier Force Rifles: 16th Punjab Regiment

1928 3rd Sikh Pioneers

No.	Battle honour	Year	Units
174.	**BASRA** 6th November 1914–14th April 1915 Basra Operations	1925 1926	The Dorsetshire Regiment 103rd (Peshawar) Pack Battery (Frontier Force): 110th (Abbottabad) Pack Battery: Royal Bombay Sappers and Miners: 2nd Bombay Pioneers: 5th Mahratta Light Infantry: 6th Rajputana Rifles: 7th Rajput Regiment: 14th Punjab Regiment
175.	**SHAIBA** 12th–14th April 1915 Basra Operations	1925 1926 1927	The Norfolk Regiment: The Hampshire Regiment: The Dorsetshire Regiment 103rd (Peshawar) Pack Battery (Frontier Force): 110th (Abbottabad) Pack Battery: 6th Duke of Connaught's Own Lancers (Watson's Horse): 17th Queen Victoria's Own Poona Horse: 18th King Edward's Own Cavalry: Royal Bombay Sappers and Miners: 2nd Bombay Pioneers: 1st Punjab Regiment: 5th Mahratta Light Infantry: 6th Rajputana Rifles: 9th Jat Regiment: 14th Punjab Regiment: 7th Gurkha Rifles Jaipur Transport Corps
176.	**KUT AL AMARA 1915** 28th September 1915 Advance up the Tigris 1915	1925 1926 1927	The Norfolk Regiment: The Hampshire Regiment: The Dorsetshire Regiment: The Oxfordshire and Buckinghamshire Light Infantry 6th Duke of Cambridge's Own Lancers (Watson's Horse): 18th King Edward's Own Cavalry: King George's Own Bengal Sappers and Miners: Royal Bombay Sappers and Miners: 2nd Bombay Pioneers: 1st Punjab Regiment: 5th Mahratta Light Infantry: 6th Rajputana Rifles: 7th Rajput Regiment: 14th Punjab Regiment: 7th Gurkha Rifles Jaipur Transport Corps
177.	**CTESIPHON** 22nd–24th November 1915 Advance on Baghdad 1915	1925 1926 1927	The Norfolk Regiment: The Dorsetshire Regiment: The Oxfordshire and Buckinghamshire Light Infantry 6th Duke of Connaught's Own Lancers (Watson's Horse): 17th Queen Victoria's Own Poona Horse: 18th King Edward's Own Cavalry: King George's Own Bengal Sappers and Miners: Royal Bombay Sappers and Miners: 2nd Bombay Pioneers: 1st Punjab Regiment: 5th Mahratta Light Infantry: 6th Rajputana Rifles: 7th Rajput Regiment: 9th Jat Regiment: 14th Punjab Regiment: 7th Gurkha Rifles Jaipur Transport Corps
178.	**DEFENCE OF KUT AL AMARA** 7th December 1915–28th April 1916 Advance on Baghdad 1915	1925 1926 1926	The Norfolk Regiment: The Dorsetshire Regiment: The Oxfordshire and Buckinghamshire Light Infantry: The Queen's Own Royal West Kent Regiment King George's Own Bengal Sappers and Miners: Royal Bombay Sappers and Miners: 2nd Bombay Pioneers: 1st Punjab Regiment: 2nd Punjab Regiment: 5th Mahratta Light Infantry: 6th Rajputana Rifles: 7th Rajput Regiment: 9th Jat Regiment: 14th Punjab Regiment: 7th Gurkha Rifles Simmoor Sappers
179.	**TIGRIS 1916** 4th January–24th April 1916 Attempts to relieve Kut	1925 1926	14th King's Hussars: The Buffs (East Kent Regiment): The King's Own Royal Regiment (Lancaster): The Royal Warwickshire Regiment: The Devonshire Regiment: The Somerset Light Infantry (Prince Albert's): The Leicestershire Regiment: The Cheshire Regiment: The Royal Welch Fusiliers: The South Wales Borderers: The Gloucestershire Regiment: The Worcestershire Regiment: The East Lancashire Regiment: The Hampshire Regiment: The Prince of Wales's Volunteers (South Lancashire): The Welch Regiment: The Black Watch (Royal Highlanders): The Loyal Regiment (North Lancashire): The Wiltshire Regiment (Duke of Edinburgh's): The Manchester Regiment: The North Staffordshire Regiment (The Prince of Wales's): The Highland Light Infantry (City of Glasgow Regiment): The Seaforth Highlanders (Ross-shire Buffs, The Duke of Albany's): The Connaught Rangers 103rd (Peshawar) Pack Battery (Frontier Force): 2nd Lancers (Gardner's Horse): 6th Duke of Connaught's Own Lancers (Watson's Horse): 17th Queen Victoria's Own Poona Horse: 18th King Edward's Own Cavalry: Queen Victoria's Own Madras Sappers and Miners: King George's Own Bengal Sappers and Miners: Royal Bombay Sappers and Miners: 2nd Bombay Pioneers: 3rd Sikh Pioneers: 1st Punjab Regiment: 4th Bombay Grenadiers: 6th Rajputana Rifles: 7th Rajput Regiment: 8th Punjab

Regiment: 9th Jat Regiment: 11th Sikh Regiment: 12th Frontier Force Regiment: 13th Frontier Force Rifles: 15th Punjab Regiment: 16th Punjab Regiment: 17th Dogra Regiment: 19th Hyderabad Regiment: 1st King George's Own Gurkha Rifles (The Malaun Regiment): 2nd King Edward's Own Gurkha Rifles (The Sirmoor Rifles): 4th Prince of Wales's Own Gurkha Rifles: 8th Gurkha Rifles: 9th Gurkha Rifles

1927 Jaipur Transport Corps: Mysore Transport Corps
1951 The Oxfordshire and Buckinghamshire Light Infantry

180. **KUT AL AMARA 1917**
9th January–24th February 1917
The Operations for the Capture of Kut 1917

1925 13th Hussars: 14th King's Hussars: The Buffs (East Kent Regiment): The King's Own Royal Regiment (Lancaster): The Royal Warwickshire Regiment: The Norfolk Regiment: The Devonshire Regiment: The Leicestershire Regiment: The Cheshire Regiment: The Royal Welch Fusiliers: The South Wales Borderers: The Gloucestershire Regiment: The Worcestershire Regiment: The East Lancashire Regiment: The Hampshire Regiment: The Dorsetshire Regiment: The Prince of Wales's Volunteers (South Lancashire): The Welch Regiment: The Black Watch (Royal Highlanders): The Loyal Regiment (North Lancashire): The Wiltshire Regiment (Duke of Edinburgh's): The Manchester Regiment: The North Staffordshire Regiment (The Prince of Wales's): The Highland Light Infantry (City of Glasgow Regiment): The Seaforth Highlanders (Ross-shire Buffs, The Duke of Albany's): The Connaught Rangers

1926 6th Duke of Connaught's Own Lancers (Watson's Horse): 11th Prince Albert Victor's Own Cavalry (Frontier Force): 12th Cavalry (Frontier Force): 13th Duke of Connaught's Own Bombay Lancers: 20th Lancers: Queen Victoria's Own Madras Sappers and Miners: King George's Own Bengal Sappers and Miners: Royal Bombay Sappers and Miners: Burma Sappers and Miners: 1st Madras Pioneers: 2nd Bombay Pioneers: 1st Punjab Regiment: 2nd Punjab Regiment: 4th Bombay Grenadiers: 5th Mahratta Light Infantry: 6th Rajputana Rifles: 8th Punjab Regiment: 10th Baluch Regiment: 11th Sikh Regiment: 12th Frontier Force Regiment: 13th Frontier Force Rifles: 14th Punjab Regiment: 15th Punjab Regiment: 16th Punjab Regiment: 17th Dogra Regiment: 1st King George's Own Gurkha Rifles (The Malaun Regiment): 2nd King Edward's Own Gurkha Rifles (The Sirmoor Rifles): 4th Prince of Wales's Own Gurkha Rifles: 7th Gurkha Rifles: 8th Gurkha Rifles: 9th Gurkha Rifles

1926 Garhwal Rajya Sappers
1927 Jaipur Transport Corps: Mysore Transport Corps
1928 3rd Sikh Pioneers

181. **BAGHDAD**
25th February–30th April 1917
Operations for the consolidation of the position at Baghdad

1925 13th Hussars: 14th King's Hussars: The Buffs (East Kent Regiment): The King's Own Royal Regiment (Lancaster): The Royal Warwickshire Regiment: The Leicestershire Regiment: The Cheshire Regiment: The Royal Welch Fusiliers: The South Wales Borderers: The Gloucestershire Regiment: The Worcestershire Regiment: The East Lancashire Regiment: The Hampshire Regiment: The Dorsetshire Regiment: The Prince of Wales's Volunteers (South Lancashire): The Welch Regiment: The Black Watch (Royal Highlanders): The Loyal Regiment (North Lancashire): The Wiltshire Regiment (Duke of Edinburgh's): The Manchester Regiment: The North Staffordshire Regiment (The Prince of Wales's): The Seaforth Highlanders (Ross-shire Buffs, The Duke of Albany's): The Connaught Rangers

1926 6th Duke of Connaught's Own Lancers (Watson's Horse): 11th Prince Albert Victor's Own Cavalry (Frontier Force): 12th Cavalry (Frontier Force): 13th Duke of Connaught's Own Bombay Lancers: Queen Victoria's Own Madras Sappers and Miners: King George's Own Bengal Sappers and Miners: Royal Bombay Sappers and Miners: Burma Sappers and Miners: 1st Madras Pioneers: 2nd Bombay Pioneers: 3rd Sikh Pioneers: 1st Punjab Regiment: 2nd Punjab Regiment: 4th Bombay Grenadiers: 5th Mahratta Light Infantry: 6th Rajputana Rifles: 8th Punjab Regiment: 10th Baluch Regiment: 11th Sikh Regiment: 12th Frontier Force Regiment: 13th Frontier Force Rifles: 14th Punjab Regiment: 15th Punjab Regiment: 16th Punjab Regiment: 17th Dogra Regiment: 1st King George's Own Gurkha Rifles (The Malaun Regiment): 2nd King Edward's Own Gurkha Rifles (The Sirmoor Rifles): 4th Prince of Wales's Own Gurkha Rifles: 7th Gurkha Rifles: 8th Gurkha Rifles: 9th Gurkha Rifles

No.	Battle Honour	Year	Units
		1927	Jaipur Transport Corps: Mysore Transport Corps
182.	**KHAN BAGHDADI** 26th–27th March 1918 Euphrates Operations 1917–18	1925	7th Queen's Own Hussars: The Queen's Royal Regiment (West Surrey): The Oxfordshire and Buckinghamshire Light Infantry 4th Duke of Cambridge's Own Hodson's Horse: 10th Queen Victoria's Own Corps of Guides Cavalry (Frontier Force): 11th Prince Albert Victor's Own Cavalry (Frontier Force): King George's Own Bengal Sappers and Miners: 2nd Bombay Pioneers: 8th Punjab Regiment: 9th Jat Regiment: 14th Punjab Regiment: 18th Royal Garhwal Rifles: 19th Hyderabad Regiment: 5th Royal Gurkha Rifles (Frontier Force): 6th Gurkha Rifles
		1926	Jaipur Transport Corps
		1927	The Dorset Regiment
		1951	
183.	**SHARQAT** 28th–30th October 1918 Advance on Mosul	1925	7th Queen's Own Hussars: 13th Hussars: The Somerset Light Infantry (Prince Albert's): The Hampshire Regiment: The Queen's Own Royal West Kent Regiment: The Highland Light Infantry (City of Glasgow Regiment)
		1926	105th (Bombay) Pack Battery: 114th (Rajputana) Pack Battery: 6th Duke of Connaught's Own Lancers (Watson's Horse): 10th Queen Victoria's Own Corps of Guides Cavalry (Frontier Force): 11th Prince Albert Victor's Own Cavalry (Frontier Force): 13th Duke of Connaught's Own Bombay Lancers: 20th Lancers: King George's Own Bengal Sappers and Miners: 3rd Sikh Pioneers: 4th Bombay Grenadiers: 5th Mahratta Light Infantry: 11th Sikh Regiment: 12th Frontier Force Regiment: 18th Royal Garhwal Rifles: 3rd Queen Alexandra's Own Gurkha Rifles: 7th Gurkha Rifles: 10th Gurkha Rifles Malerkotla Sappers: Garhwal Rajya Sappers
184.	**MESOPOTAMIA 1914–16** 6th November 1914–31st December 1916 Service in Mesopotamia 1914–18	1926	103rd (Peshawar) Pack Battery (Frontier Force): 110th (Abbottabad) Pack Battery: 17th Queen Victoria's Own Poona Horse
185.	**MESOPOTAMIA 1914–18** 6th November 1914–31st October 1918 Service in Mesopotamia 1914–18	1925	The Norfolk Regiment: The Dorsetshire Regiment: The Oxfordshire and Buckinghamshire Light Infantry Royal Bombay Sappers and Miners: 2nd Bombay Pioneers: 5th Mahratta Light Infantry: 6th Rajputana Rifles: 7th Rajput Regiment: 9th Jat Regiment: 14th Punjab Regiment
		1926	Sirmoor Sappers
186.	**MESOPOTAMIA 1915–16** 1st January 1915–31st December 1916 Service in Mesopotamia 1914–18	1926	2nd Lancers (Gardner's Horse): 18th King Edward's Own Cavalry
187.	**MESOPOTAMIA 1915–17** 1st January 1915–31st December 1917 Service in Mesopotamia 1914–18	1925	The Black Watch (Royal Highlanders)
188.	**MESOPOTAMIA 1915–18** 1st January 1915–31st October 1918 Service in Mesopotamia 1914–18	1925	14th King's Hussars: The Queen's Royal Regiment (West Surrey): The Buffs (East Kent Regiment): The Leicestershire Regiment: The Hampshire Regiment: The Queen's Own Royal West Kent Regiment: The Seaforth Highlanders (Ross-shire Buffs, The Duke of Albany's)
		1926	5th King Edward's Own Probyn's Horse: 6th Duke of Connaught's Own Lancers (Watson's Horse): 11th Prince Albert Victor's Own Cavalry (Frontier Force): Queen Victoria's Own Madras Sappers and Miners: King George's Own Bengal Sappers and Miners: 1st Punjab Regiment: 2nd Punjab Regiment: 3rd Madras Regiment: 4th Bombay Grenadiers: 8th Punjab Regiment: 12th Frontier Force Regiment: 15th Punjab Regiment: 16th Punjab Regiment: 17th Dogra Regiment: 19th Hyderabad Regiment: 7th Gurkha Rifles
		1926	Holkar's Mounted Escort
		1927	Jaipur Transport Corps

189.	**MESOPOTAMIA 1916–17** 1st January 1916–31st December 1917 Service in Mesopotamia 1914–18	1925 1926	The East Lancashire Regiment 8th Gurkha Rifles
190.	**MESOPOTAMIA 1916–18** 1st January 1916–31st October 1918 Service in Mesopotamia 1914–18	1925	13th Hussars: The King's Own Royal Regiment (Lancaster): The Royal Warwickshire Regiment: The Devonshire Regiment: The Somerset Light Infantry (Prince Albert's): The Cheshire Regiment: The Royal Welch Fusiliers: The South Wales Borderers: The Gloucestershire Regiment: The Worcestershire Regiment: The Prince of Wales's Volunteers (South Lancashire): The Welch Regiment: The Loyal Regiment (North Lancashire): The Wiltshire Regiment (Duke of Edinburgh's): The Manchester Regiment: The North Staffordshire Regiment (The Prince of Wales's): The Highland Light Infantry (City of Glasgow Regiment): The Connaught Rangers
		1926	101st Royal (Kohat) Pack Battery (Frontier Force): 106th (Jacob's) Pack Battery: 4th Duke of Cambridge's Own Hodson's Horse: 12th Cavalry (Frontier Force): 13th Duke of Connaught's Own Bombay Lancers: 20th Lancers: Burma Sappers and Miners: 1st Madras Pioneers: 3rd Sikh Pioneers: 10th Baluch Regiment: 11th Sikh Regiment: 13th Frontier Force Rifles: 1st King George's Own Gurkha Rifles (The Malaun Regiment): 2nd King Edward's Own Gurkha Rifles (The Sirmoor Rifles): 4th Prince of Wales's Own Gurkha Rifles: 5th Royal Gurkha Rifles (Frontier Force): 6th Gurkha Rifles: 9th Gurkha Rifles: 10th Gurkha Rifles
		1926 1927	Patiala (Rajindra) Lancers: Malerkotla Sappers: Garhwal Rajya Sappers Mysore Transport Corps
191.	**MESOPOTAMIA 1917–18** 1st January 1917–31st October 1918 Service in Mesopotamia 1914–18	1925 1926	7th Queen's Own Hussars: The East Surrey Regiment: The Middlesex Regiment (Duke of Cambridge's Own) 3rd Cavalry: 10th Queen Victoria's Own Corps of Guides Cavalry (Frontier Force): 18th Royal Garhwal Rifles: 3rd Queen Alexandra's Own Gurkha Rifles
192.	**MESOPOTAMIA 1918** 1st January–31st October 1918 Service in Mesopotamia 1914–18	1926 1927	105th (Bombay) Pack Battery: 111th (Dehra Dun) Pack Battery: 114th (Rajputana) Pack Battery: 4th Hazara Pioneers Gwalior Transport Corps
193.	**MERV** 1st November 1918 Operations in Trans-Caspia against the Bolsheviks	1926	7th Light Cavalry: 2nd Bombay Pioneers: 14th Punjab Regiment
194.	**BAKU** 26th August–15th September 1918 Caspian Operations	1925	The Royal Warwickshire Regiment: The Worcestershire Regiment: The North Staffordshire Regiment (The Prince of Wales's)
195.	**PERSIA 1915–18** 10th January 1915–31st December 1918 Service in Persia and Central Asia 1915–19	1926	7th Rajput Regiment: 10th Baluch Regiment: 19th Hyderabad Regiment
196.	**PERSIA 1915–19** 10th January 1915–8th August 1919 Service in Persia and Central Asia 1915–19	1926	7th Light Cavalry: 14th Punjab Regiment

		Year	Regiments
197.	**PERSIA 1916–19** 1st January 1916–8th August 1919 Service in Persia and Central Asia 1915–19	1926	20th Lancers
198.	**PERSIA 1918** 1st January–31st December 1918 Service in Persia and Central Asia 1915–19	1925	14th King's Hussars: The Royal Warwickshire Regiment: The Gloucestershire Regiment: The Worcestershire Regiment: The North Staffordshire Regiment (The Prince of Wales's)
		1926	106th (Jacob's) Pack Battery: 111th (Dehra Dun) Pack Battery: 115th (Jhelum) Pack Battery: 116th (Zhob) Pack Battery: Queen Victoria's Own Madras Sappers and Miners: King George's Own Bengal Sappers and Miners: Burma Sappers and Miners: 1st Madras Pioneers: 5th Mahratta Light Infantry: 6th Rajputana Rifles: 11th Sikh Regiment: 15th Punjab Regiment: 2nd King Edward's Own Gurkha Rifles (The Sirmoor Rifles): 6th Gurkha Rifles
		1928	101st Royal (Kohat) Indian Mountain Battery (Frontier Force)
199.	**PERSIA 1918–19** 1st January 1918–8th August 1919 Service in Persia and Central Asia 1915–19	1925	The Hampshire Regiment
		1926	Royal Bombay Sappers and Miners: 2nd Bombay Pioneers: 13th Frontier Force Rifles
200.	**NW FRONTIER INDIA 1914** 28th November–31st December 1914 Service on the North-West Frontier 1914–17	1926	11th Sikh Regiment
201.	**NW FRONTIER INDIA 1914–15** 28th November 1914–28th October 1915 Service on the North-West Frontier 1914–17	1926	109th (Murree) Pack Battery: 12th Cavalry (Frontier Force): 14th Prince of Wales's Own Scinde Horse: Queen Victoria's Own Madras Sappers and Miners: 5th Mahratta Light Infantry: 12th Frontier Force Regiment: 19th Hyderabad Regiment
		1927	9th Jat Regiment
202.	**NW FRONTIER INDIA 1915** 1st January–28th October 1915 Service on the North-West Frontier 1914–17	1925	21st Lancers (Empress of India's): The King's Regiment (Liverpool): The Somerset Light Infantry (Prince Albert's): The Royal Sussex Regiment: The North Staffordshire Regiment (The Prince of Wales's): The Durham Light Infantry
		1926	105th (Bombay) Pack Battery: 1st Duke of York's Own Skinner's Horse: 6th Duke of Connaught's Own Lancers (Watson's Horse): 10th Queen Victoria's Own Corps of Guides Cavalry (Frontier Force): 20th Lancers: King George's Own Bengal Sappers and Miners: 1st Madras Pioneers: 1st Punjab Regiment: 2nd Punjab Regiment: 7th Rajput Regiment: 11th Sikh Regiment: 14th Punjab Regiment: 16th Punjab Regiment: 17th Dogra Regiment: 1st King George's Own Gurkha Rifles (The Malaun Regiment): 6th Gurkha Rifles
203.	**NW FRONTIER INDIA 1916** 30th September–31st December 1916 Service on the North-West Frontier 1914–17	1925	21st Lancers (Empress of India's)
		1926	14th Prince of Wales's Own Scinde Horse
204.	**NW FRONTIER INDIA 1916–17** 30th September 1916–10th August 1917 Service on the North-West Frontier 1914–17	1925	The Queen's Royal Regiment (West Surrey): The Border Regiment: The Royal Sussex Regiment: The Durham Light Infantry
		1926	King George's Own Bengal Sappers and Miners: Royal Bombay Sappers and Miners: 2nd Bombay Pioneers: 2nd Punjab Regiment: 11th Sikh Regiment: 12th Frontier Force Regiment: 16th Punjab Regiment: 19th Hyderabad Regiment

205.	**NW FRONTIER INDIA 1917** 1st January–10th August 1917 Service on the North-West Frontier 1914–17	1925 1926	25th (County of London) Cyclist Battalion, The London Regiment: The Kent Cyclist Battalion 103rd (Peshawar) Pack Battery (Frontier Force): 109th (Murree) Pack Battery: 110th (Abbottabad) Pack Battery: 13th Duke of Connaught's Own Bombay Lancers: Queen Victoria's Own Madras Sappers and Miners: 5th Mahratta Light Infantry: 7th Rajput Regiment: 10th Baluch Regiment: 13th Frontier Force Rifles: 14th Punjab Regiment: 15th Punjab Regiment: 17th Dogra Regiment: 1st King George's Own Gurkha Rifles (The Malaun Regiment): 4th Prince of Wales's Own Gurkha Rifles: 5th Royal Gurkha Rifles (Frontier Force)
		1926 1927	Alwar Mangel Lancers: Bahawalpur Camel Transport Corps: Khairpur Camel Transport Corps 9th Jat Regiment
206.	**BALUCHISTAN 1915–16** 1st June 1915–25th June 1916 Service in Baluchistan 1915–16	1926	4th Hazara Pioneers
207.	**BALUCHISTAN 1918** 18th February–8th April 1918 Service in Baluchistan 1918	1925 1926 1926	The Prince of Wales's Volunteers (South Lancashire): The Kent Cyclist Battalion 103rd (Peshawar) Pack Battery (Frontier Force): 1st Duke of York's Own Skinner's Horse: King George's Own Bengal Sappers and Miners: Royal Bombay Sappers and Miners: 1st Madras Pioneers: 2nd Bombay Pioneers: 13th Frontier Force Rifles: 2nd King Edward's Own Gurkha Rifles (The Simmoor Rifles): 4th Prince of Wales's Own Gurkha Rifles Bahawalpur Camel Transport Corps
208.	**MURMAN 1918–19** 29th June 1918–12th October 1919 Service in Murman 1918–19	1925	The Royal Sussex Regiment
209.	**MURMAN 1919** 1st January–12th October 1919 Service in Murman 1918–19	1925	The East Surrey Regiment: The Middlesex Regiment (Duke of Cambridge's Own): The Highland Light Infantry (City of Glasgow Regiment)
210.	**TROITSA** 10th August 1919 Operations to cover withdrawal	1925	The Royal Fusiliers (City of London Regiment)
183.	**ARCHANGEL 1918** 1st August- 31st December 1918 Service in Archangel 1918–19	1925	The Green Howards (Alexandra, Princess of Wales's Own Yorkshire Regiment)
212.	**ARCHANGEL 1918–19** 1st August 1918–27th September 1919 Service in Archangel 1918–19	1925	The Royal Scots (The Royal Regiment): The King's Regiment (Liverpool): The Durham Light Infantry
213.	**ARCHANGEL 1919** 1st January–27th September 1919 Service in Archangel 1918–19	1925	The Royal Fusiliers (City of London Regiment): The Hampshire Regiment: The Oxfordshire and Buckinghamshire Light Infantry: The Highland Light Infantry (City of Glasgow Regiment)
214.	**DUKHOVSKAYA** 23rd–24th August 1918 Ussuri Operations	1925	The Middlesex Regiment (Duke of Cambridge's Own)

No.	Battle Honour / Details	Year	Regiments / Units
215.	**SIBERIA 1918–19** [1] 8th August 1918– ? June 1919 Service in Siberia 1918–19	1925 1929	The Hampshire Regiment: The Middlesex Regiment (Duke of Cambridge's Own) 259th Battalion (Canadian Rifles) CEF: 260th Battalion (Canadian Rifles) CEF ¹ SIBERIE 1918–19 taken into use by French-speaking Canadian units 1958.
216.	**TSINGTAO** 23rd September–7th November 1914 Siege of Tsing-Tau	1925 1926	The South Wales Borderers 11th Sikh Regiment
217.	**HERBERTSHOHE** 12th–21st September 1914 Operations of the Australian Naval and Military Expeditionary Force	1927	1st Battalion: 2nd Battalion
218.	**KILIMANJARO** 5th–21st March 1916 Kilimanjaro Operations	1925 1926 1926 1926 1927	The Royal Fusiliers (City of London Regiment): The Loyal Regiment (North Lancashire): The King's African Rifles 107th (Bengal) Pack Battery: 108th (Lahore) Pack Battery: Royal Bombay Sappers and Miners: 1st Madras Pioneers: 10th Baluch Regiment: 15th Punjab Regiment Faridkot Sappers: 2nd Kashmir Bodyguard Rifle Battalion: 3rd Kashmir Raghunath Rifle Battalion: Bharatpur Infantry 1st Battery, South African Field Artillery: 2nd Battery, South African Field Artillery: 3rd Battery, South African Field Artillery: 4th Battery, South African Field Artillery: 5th Battery, South African Field Artillery: 3rd South African Horse (3de Zuidafrikaanse Ruiters): 5th South African Infantry (Cape Regiment): 6th South African Infantry (Natal, Orange Free State, and Eastern Provinces Regiment): 7th South African Infantry (Transvaal Regiment): 9th South African Infantry (Sportsmen's Regiment): 10th South African Infantry (Railways and Workers Regiment): 11th South African Infantry (Cape and Natal Regiment): 1st Battalion, Cape Corps 4th South African Horse (4de Zuidafrikaanse Ruiters): 8th South African Infantry (Railways and Workers Regiment)
219.	**BEHOBEHO** 3rd–4th January 1917 Advance to the Rufiji	1925 1926 1926 1926	The Royal Fusiliers (City of London Regiment): Nigeria Regiment, West African Frontier Force 10th Baluch Regiment: 16th Punjab Regiment Faridkot Sappers: 2nd Kashmir Bodyguard Rifle Battalion: 3rd Kashmir Raghunath Rifle Battalion 6th South African Infantry (Natal, Orange Free State, and Eastern Provinces Regiment): 1st Battalion, Cape Corps
220.	**NARUNGOMBE** 19th July 1917 Operations in the Kilwa and Lindi Areas, and advance to the Portuguese Frontier	1925 1926 1926 1927	Gold Coast Regiment, West African Frontier Force: The King's African Rifles 102nd (Derajat) Pack Battery (Frontier Force): 107th (Bengal) Pack Battery: 14th Punjab Regiment: 16th Punjab Regiment 7th South African Infantry (Transvaal Regiment) 8th South African Infantry (Railways and Workers Regiment)
221.	**NYANGAO** 16th–19th October 1917 Operations in the Kilwa and Lindi Areas, and advance to the Portuguese Frontier	1925 1926 1926 1926 1927	The Royal Fusiliers (City of London Regiment): Nigeria Regiment, West African Frontier Force: Gambia Company, West African Frontier Force: The King's African Rifles 107th (Bengal) Pack Battery: 16th Punjab Regiment 1st Kashmir Pack Battery: Bharatpur Infantry 10th South African Horse (10de Zuidafrikaanse Ruiters): 7th South African Infantry (Transvaal Regiment): 1st Battalion, Cape Corps 8th South African Infantry (Railways and Workers Regiment)

No.	Honour	Year	Units
222.	**E AFRICA 1914** 15th August–31st December 1914 Service in East Africa 1914–18	1926	6th Rajputana Rifles
223.	**E AFRICA 1914-16** 15th August 1914–31st December 1916 Service in East Africa 1914–18	1925	The Loyal Regiment (North Lancashire)
		1926	4th Bombay Grenadiers
224.	**E AFRICA 1914-17** 15th August 1914–31st December 1917 Service in East Africa 1914–18	1926	108th (Lahore) Pack Battery: 15th Punjab Regiment
		1926	Jind Infantry Battalion: Kapurthala Jagatjit Infantry: 2nd Kashmir Bodyguard Rifle Battalion: 3rd Kashmir Raghunath Rifle Battalion: 3rd Gwalior Maharaja Scindia's Own Battalion
225.	**E AFRICA 1914-18** 15th August 1915–25th November 1918 Service in East Africa 1914–18	1925	The King's African Rifles: Northern Rhodesia Police
		1926	107th (Bengal) Pack Battery: Royal Bombay Sappers and Miners: 1st Madras Pioneers: 19th Hyderabad Regiment
		1926	Faridkot Sappers: Rampur Pioneers
226.	**E AFRICA 1915-17** 1st January 1915–31st December 1917 Service in East Africa 1914–18	1925	The Royal Fusiliers (City of London Regiment)
		1926	Bharatpur Infantry
		1927	South African Rifles (Nyassaland Imperial Service Contingent)
227.	**E AFRICA 1915-18** 1st January 1915–25th November 1918 Service in East Africa 1914–18	1926	10th Baluch Regiment
		1926	5th Mountain Battery (South African Mounted Riflemen): 5th South African Infantry (Cape Regiment)
228.	**E AFRICA 1916** 1st January–31st December 1916 Service in East Africa 1914–18	1926	1st Battery, South African Field Artillery: 2nd Battery, South African Field Artillery: 4th Battery, South African Field Artillery: 3rd South African Horse (3de Zuidafrikaanse Ruiters)
		1927	12th South African Infantry (Transvaal and Orange Free State Regiment)
229.	**E AFRICA 1916-17** 1st January 1916–31st December 1917 Service in East Africa 1914–18	1926	3rd Battery, South African Field Artillery: 5th Battery, South African Field Artillery: 9th South African Horse (9de Zuidafrikaanse Ruiters): 10th South African Horse (10de Zuidafrikaanse Ruiters): 6th South African Infantry (Natal, Orange Free State, and Eastern Provinces Regiment): 7th South African Infantry (Transvaal Regiment): 9th South African Infantry (Sportsmen's Regiment): 10th South African Infantry (Railways and Workers Regiment): 11th South African Infantry (Cape and Natal Regiment): 1st Battalion, Cape Corps
		1927	4th South African Horse (4de Zuidafrikaanse Ruiters): 8th South African Infantry (Railways and Workers Regiment)
230.	**E AFRICA 1916-18** 1st January 1916–25th November 1918 Service in East Africa 1914–18	1925	The West India Regiment: Nigeria Regiment, West African Frontier Force: Gold Coast Regiment, West African Frontier Force
		1926	102nd (Derajat) Pack Battery (Frontier Force): 13th Frontier Force Rifles: 14th Punjab Regiment
		1926	1st Kashmir Pack Battery
231.	**E AFRICA 1917** 1st January–31st December 1917 Service in East Africa 1914–18	1926	12th Cavalry (Frontier Force)
		1927	8th South African Horse (8ste Zuidafrikaanse Ruiters)
232.	**E AFRICA 1917-18** 1st January 1917–25th November 1918 Service in East Africa 1914–18	1925	Gambia Company, West African Frontier Force
		1926	104th (Hazara) Pack Battery (Frontier Force): 16th Punjab Regiment
		1927	2nd Cape Corps

No.	Honour	Year	Units
233.	**E AFRICA 1918** 1st January–25th November 1918 Service in East Africa 1914–18	1926	Queen Victoria's Own Madras Sappers and Miners
234.	**GIBEON** 25th–26th April 1915 Southern Operations	1926	1st Mounted Rifles (Natal Carbineers): 3rd Mounted Rifles (Natal Mounted Rifles): 4th Mounted Rifles (Umvoti Mounted Rifles): 2nd Imperial Light Horse
		1927	2nd Mounted Rifles (Natal Carbineers)
235.	**SW AFRICA 1914** 20th August–31st December 1914 Service in South-West Africa 1914–15	1925	Northern Rhodesia Police
236.	**SW AFRICA 1914–15** 20th August 1914–9th July 1915 Service in South-West Africa 1914–15	1926	1st Regiment, South African Mounted Riflemen: 2nd Regiment, South African Mounted Riflemen: 3rd Regiment, South African Mounted Riflemen: 4th Regiment, South African Mounted Riflemen: 5th Regiment, South African Mounted Riflemen: Field Artillery Brigade (South African Mounted Riflemen): 8th Citizen Battery (Transvaal Horse Artillery): 1st Mounted Rifles (Natal Carbineers): 3rd Mounted Rifles (Natal Mounted Rifles): 4th Mounted Rifles (Umvoti Mounted Rifles): 17th Mounted Rifles (Western Province Mounted Rifles): 18th Mounted Rifles (Griqualand West Ruiters): 20th Mounted Rifles (Graaff-Reinet Ruiters): 1st Infantry (Durban Light Infantry): 4th Infantry (1st Eastern Rifles): 5th Infantry (Kaffrarian Rifles): 7th Infantry (Kimberley Regiment): 8th Infantry (Transvaal Scottish): 10th Infantry (Witwatersrand Rifles): 12th Infantry (Pretoria Regiment): 9th Dismounted Rifles (Bechuanaland Rifles): 1st Field Ambulance, South African Medical Corps: 2nd Imperial Light Horse
		1927	7th Citizen Battery (Natal Field Artillery): Nos 2 and 6 Companies, 1st Division, South African Garrison Artillery (Cape Garrison Artillery): 2nd Mounted Rifles (Natal Carbineers): 5th Mounted Rifles (Imperial Light Horse): 6th Dismounted Rifles (Midlandse Skutters): 2nd Infantry (Duke of Edinburgh's Own Rifles): 11th Infantry (Rand Light Infantry): South African Heavy Artillery: 2nd Battalion, Transvaal Scottish: South African Irish: Rand Rifles
237.	**SW AFRICA 1915** 1st January–9th July 1915 Service in South-West Africa 1914–15	1926	6th Citizen Battery (Prince Alfred's Own Cape Field Artillery): 6th Infantry (Duke of Connaught and Strathearn's Own Capetown Highlanders): 3rd Regiment, 5th Mounted Brigade (Brand's Vrijstaatse Skutters): Botha's Hogeveld Ruiters: Hartigan's Horse: Southern Rifles
		1927	8th Mounted Rifles (Midlandse Ruiters): 11th Mounted Rifles (Potchefstroom Ruiters): Northern Transvaal Ruiters
238.	**KAMINA** 8th–26th August 1914 Advance to Kamina	1925	Gold Coast Regiment, West African Frontier Force
239.	**DUALA** 26th–27th September 1914 Duala Operations	1925	West African Regiment: Nigeria Regiment, West African Frontier Force: Gold Coast Regiment, West African Frontier Force: Sierra Leone Battalion, West African Frontier Force
240.	**GARUA** 31st May–10th June 1915 Operations for the Central Plateau	1925	Nigeria Regiment, West African Frontier Force
241.	**BANYO** 4th–6th November 1915 Operations for the Central Plateau	1925	Nigeria Regiment, West African Frontier Force

242.	**CAMEROONS 1914–16** 6th August 1914–17th February 1916 Service in the Cameroons 1914–16	1925	West African Regiment: Nigeria Regiment, West African Frontier Force: Gold Coast Regiment, West African Frontier Force: Sierra Leone Battalion, West African Frontier Force
243.	**CAMEROONS 1915–16** 1st January 1915–17th February 1916 Service in the Cameroons 1914–16	1925	The West India Regiment: Gambia Company, West African Frontier Force
244.	**THE GREAT WAR** 4th August 1914–11th November 1918 Service by Volunteers	1925	Royal Jersey Light Infantry (Militia)
245.	**THE GREAT WAR 1914–15** 4th August 1914–31st December 1915 Service out of Canada 1914–18	1929	6th Canadian Infantry Battalion CEF
246.	**THE GREAT WAR 1914–17** 4th August 1914–31st December 1917 Service out of Canada 1914–18	1929	11th Canadian Infantry Battalion CEF: 9th Canadian Infantry Battalion CEF: 12th Canadian Infantry Battalion CEF: 17th Canadian Infantry Battalion CEF
247.	**THE GREAT WAR 1915** 1st January–31st December 1915 Service out of Canada 1914–18	1929	7th Regiment, Canadian Mounted Rifles CEF
248.	**THE GREAT WAR 1915–16** 1st January 1915–31st December 1916 Service out of Canada 1914–18	1929	37th Canadian Infantry Battalion CEF: 8th Regiment, Canadian Mounted Rifles CEF: 9th Regiment, Canadian Mounted Rifles CEF: 12th Regiment, Canadian Mounted Rifles CEF: 34th Canadian Infantry Battalion CEF: 41st Canadian Infantry Battalion CEF: 55th Canadian Infantry Battalion CEF *MOUNT SORREL, SOMME 1916, ARRAS 1917, HILL 70, YPRES 1917 and AMIENS taken into use 1961.*
249.	**THE GREAT WAR 1915–17** 1st January 1915–31st December 1917 Service out of Canada 1914–18	1929	30th Canadian Infantry Battalion CEF: 35th Canadian Infantry Battalion CEF: 36th Canadian Infantry Battalion CEF: 23rd Canadian Infantry Battalion CEF: 32nd Canadian Infantry Battalion CEF: 39th Canadian Infantry Battalion CEF: 40th Canadian Infantry Battalion CEF
250.	**THE GREAT WAR 1916** 1st January–31st December 1916 Service out of Canada 1914–18	1929	33rd Canadian Infantry Battalion CEF: 56th Canadian Infantry Battalion CEF: 61st Canadian Infantry Battalion CEF: 62nd Canadian Infantry Battalion CEF: 71st Canadian Infantry Battalion CEF: 82nd Canadian Infantry Battalion CEF: 83rd Canadian Infantry Battalion CEF: 84th Canadian Infantry Battalion CEF: 86th Machine Gun Battalion CEF: 88th Canadian Infantry Battalion CEF: 89th Canadian Infantry Battalion CEF: 91st Canadian Infantry Battalion CEF: 99th Canadian Infantry Battalion CEF: 101st Canadian Infantry Battalion CEF: 113th Canadian Infantry Battalion CEF: 114th Canadian Infantry Battalion CEF: 129th Canadian Infantry Battalion CEF: 131st Canadian Infantry Battalion CEF: 135th Canadian Infantry Battalion CEF: 142nd Canadian Infantry Battalion CEF: 151st Canadian Infantry Battalion CEF: 170th Canadian Infantry Battalion CEF: 179th Canadian Infantry Battalion CEF: 192nd Canadian Infantry Battalion CEF: 10th Regiment, Canadian Mounted Rifles CEF: 13th Regiment, Canadian Mounted Rifles CEF: 45th Canadian Infantry Battalion CEF: 57th Canadian Infantry Battalion CEF: 59th Canadian Infantry Battalion CEF: 63rd Canadian Infantry Battalion CEF: 65th Canadian Infantry Battalion CEF: 66th Canadian Infantry Battalion CEF: 68th Canadian Infantry Battalion CEF: 70th Canadian Infantry Battalion CEF: 74th Canadian Infantry Battalion CEF: 76th Canadian Infantry Battalion CEF: 77th Canadian Infantry Battalion CEF: 79th Canadian Infantry Battalion CEF: 80th Canadian Infantry Battalion

CEF: 81st Canadian Infantry Battalion CEF: 90th Canadian Infantry Battalion CEF: 93rd Canadian Infantry Battalion CEF: 94th Canadian Infantry Battalion CEF: 96th Canadian Infantry Battalion CEF: 97th Canadian Infantry Battalion CEF: 98th Canadian Infantry Battalion CEF: 106th Canadian Infantry Battalion CEF: 109th Canadian Infantry Battalion CEF: 111th Canadian Infantry Battalion CEF: 115th Canadian Infantry Battalion CEF: 126th Canadian Infantry Battalion CEF: 130th Canadian Infantry Battalion CEF: 133rd Canadian Infantry Battalion CEF: 136th Canadian Infantry Battalion CEF: 138th Canadian Infantry Battalion CEF: 146th Canadian Infantry Battalion CEF: 139th Canadian Infantry Battalion CEF: 140th Canadian Infantry Battalion CEF: 145th Canadian Infantry Battalion CEF: 146th Canadian Infantry Battalion CEF: 152nd Canadian Infantry Battalion CEF: 155th Canadian Infantry Battalion CEF: 157th Canadian Infantry Battalion CEF: 171st Canadian Infantry Battalion CEF: 184th Canadian Infantry Battalion CEF: 189th Canadian Infantry Battalion CEF: 195th Canadian Infantry Battalion CEF: 209th Canadian Infantry Battalion CEF: 224th Canadian Forestry Battalion CEF: 238th Canadian Forestry Battalion CEF: 4th Canadian Pioneer Battalion CEF

251. **THE GREAT WAR 1916–17**
1st January 1916–31st December 1917
Service out of Canada 1914–18

1929 — 95th Canadian Infantry Battalion CEF: 100th Canadian Infantry Battalion CEF: 103rd Canadian Infantry Battalion CEF: 203rd Canadian Infantry Battalion CEF: 211th Canadian Infantry Battalion CEF: 213th Canadian Infantry Battalion CEF: 218th Railway Construction Battalion CEF: 219th Canadian Infantry Battalion CEF: 242nd Canadian Forestry Battalion CEF

1931 — 5th Canadian Pioneer Battalion CEF

252. **THE GREAT WAR 1916–18**
1st January 1916–11th November 1918
Service out of Canada 1914–18

1929 — 119th Canadian Infantry Battalion CEF: 125th Canadian Infantry Battalion CEF: 134th Canadian Infantry Battalion CEF: 160th Canadian Infantry Battalion CEF: 161st Canadian Infantry Battalion CEF: 104th Canadian Infantry Battalion CEF: 150th Canadian Infantry Battalion CEF: 156th Canadian Infantry Battalion CEF: 185th Canadian Infantry Battalion CEF

253. **THE GREAT WAR 1917**
1st January–31st December 1917
Service out of Canada 1914–18

1929 — 122nd Canadian Infantry Battalion CEF: 143rd Canadian Infantry Battalion CEF: 174th Canadian Infantry Battalion CEF: 176th Canadian Infantry Battalion CEF: 177th Canadian Infantry Battalion CEF: 182nd Canadian Infantry Battalion CEF: 186th Canadian Infantry Battalion CEF: 191st Canadian Infantry Battalion CEF: 204th Canadian Infantry Battalion CEF: 225th Canadian Infantry Battalion CEF: 227th Canadian Infantry Battalion CEF: 231st Canadian Infantry Battalion CEF: 241st Canadian Infantry Battalion CEF: 255th Canadian Infantry Battalion CEF: 118th Canadian Infantry Battalion CEF: 141st Canadian Infantry Battalion CEF: 149th Canadian Infantry Battalion CEF: 153rd Canadian Infantry Battalion CEF: 165th Canadian Infantry Battalion CEF: 178th Canadian Infantry Battalion CEF: 181st Canadian Infantry Battalion CEF: 190th Canadian Infantry Battalion CEF: 197th Canadian Infantry Battalion CEF: 200th Canadian Infantry Battalion CEF: 207th Canadian Infantry Battalion CEF: 210th Canadian Infantry Battalion CEF: 214th Canadian Infantry Battalion CEF: 215th Canadian Infantry Battalion CEF: 216th Canadian Infantry Battalion CEF: 217th Canadian Infantry Battalion CEF: 220th Canadian Infantry Battalion CEF: 221st Canadian Infantry Battalion CEF: 223rd Canadian Infantry Battalion CEF: 229th Canadian Infantry Battalion CEF: 230th Canadian Forestry Battalion CEF: 232nd Canadian Infantry Battalion CEF: 234th Canadian Infantry Battalion CEF: 235th Canadian Infantry Battalion CEF: 240th Canadian Infantry Battalion CEF: 243rd Canadian Infantry Battalion CEF: 244th Canadian Infantry Battalion CEF: 245th Canadian Infantry Battalion CEF: 246th Canadian Infantry Battalion CEF: 248th Canadian Infantry Battalion CEF: 252nd Canadian Infantry Battalion CEF: 253rd Canadian Infantry Battalion CEF: 254th Canadian Infantry Battalion CEF: 258th Canadian Infantry Battalion CEF

254. **THE GREAT WAR 1917–18**
1st January 1917–11th November 1918
Service out of Canada 1914–18

1929 — 164th Canadian Infantry Battalion CEF: 198th Canadian Infantry Battalion CEF: 208th Canadian Infantry Battalion CEF: 236th Canadian Infantry Battalion CEF

255. **THE GREAT WAR 1918**
1st January–11th November 1918
Service out of Canada 1914–18

1929 — 249th Canadian Infantry Battalion CEF

Table 3

BATTLE HONOURS FOR THE THIRD AFGHAN WAR

1.

AFGHANISTAN 1919 6th May–8th August 1919 Operations in Afghanistan 1919	1924	1st King's Dragoon Guards: The Queen's Royal Regiment (West Surrey): The King's Regiment (Liverpool): The Somerset Light Infantry (Prince Albert's): The Green Howards (Alexandra, Princess of Wales's Own Yorkshire Regiment): The Duke of Wellington's Regiment (West Riding): The Border Regiment: The Royal Sussex Regiment: The Prince of Wales's Volunteers (South Lancashire): The Queen's Own Royal West Kent Regiment: The North Staffordshire Regiment (The Prince of Wales's): The Durham Light Infantry: 25th Bn The London Regiment: 1st Kent Cyclist Battalion
	1926	1st Duke of York's Own Skinner's Horse: 2nd Lancers (Gardner's Horse): 6th Duke of Connaught's Own Lancers (Watson's Horse): 7th Light Cavalry: 8th King George's Own Light Cavalry: 11th Prince Albert Victor's Own Cavalry (Frontier Force): 12th Cavalry (Frontier Force): 13th Duke of Connaught's Own Bombay Lancers: 15th Lancers: 16th Light Cavalry: 17th Queen Victoria's Own Poona Horse: 103rd (Peshawar) Pack Battery (Frontier Force) (Howitzer): 107th (Bengal) Pack Battery (Howitzer): 108th (Lahore) Pack Battery: 115th (Jhelum) Pack Battery: Queen Victoria's Own Madras Sappers and Miners: King George's Own Bengal Sappers and Miners: Royal Bombay Sappers and Miners: Burma Sappers and Miners: 1st Madras Pioneers: 2nd Bombay Pioneers: 3rd Sikh Pioneers: 1st Punjab Regiment: 2nd Punjab Regiment: 4th Bombay Grenadiers: 5th Mahratta Light Infantry: 6th Rajputana Rifles: 7th Rajput Regiment: 8th Punjab Regiment: 9th Jat Regiment: 10th Baluch Regiment: 11th Sikh Regiment: 12th Frontier Force Regiment: 13th Frontier Force Rifles: 14th Punjab Regiment: 16th Punjab Regiment: 17th Dogra Regiment: 18th Royal Garhwal Rifles: 19th Hyderabad Regiment: 1st King George's Own Gurkha Rifles (The Malaun Regiment): 2nd King Edward's Own Gurkha Rifles (The Sirmoor Rifles): 4th Prince of Wales's Own Gurkha Rifles: 7th Gurkha Rifles: 8th Gurkha Rifles: 9th Gurkha Rifles: 10th Gurkha Rifles
	1926	Patiala (Rajindra) Lancers: Alwar Lancers: Bhopal (Victoria) Lancers: No 1 Kashmir Mountain Battery: No 2 Kashmir Mountain Battery: Faridkot Sappers: Sirmoor Sappers: Tehri-Garhwal Sappers: Malerkotla Sappers: Jind Infantry: Nabha Infantry: 1st Patiala Infantry: 1st Kashmir Infantry: 3rd Gwalior Infantry: Kapurthala Infantry (Jagatjit Regiment): Bharatpur Transport Corps: Gwalior Transport Corps: Holkar's Transport Corps (Indore)
	1927	3rd Queen Alexandra's Own Gurkha Rifles: 5th Royal Gurkha Rifles (Frontier Force): 6th Gurkha Rifles

3

The Second World War and the Korean Campaign

While the battles the British fight may differ in the widest possible ways, they have invariably two common characteristics – they are always fought uphill and always at the junction of two or more map sheets.

Field Marshal Viscount Slim

Introduction

The system used for the award of battle honours for The Great War, which had proved so successful, was again adopted for the Second World War.

The Battles Nomenclature Committee, appointed in May 1946, held its first meeting in June, with General Sir Harold Franklyn as chairman and sixteen members, fifteen of whom were serving officers, representing the General Staff, senior war-time commanders, the Historical Section of the Cabinet Office, the India Office, the High Commissioners for Australia, Canada, New Zealand, South Africa and Southern Rhodesia and the Trade Commissioner for Newfoundland: two secretaries were provided by the Army Council Secretariat and the General Staff (Military Operations).

The Committee's tasks were identical to those given to the previous committee: it had been expected to complete these tasks quickly by using a series of sub-committees, each dealing with an individual campaign concurrently. It soon became clear, however, that this process would require detailed research, which would duplicate work already being undertaken by the Historical Section of the Cabinet Office in the preparation of the official histories of the war. It was, therefore, agreed that the Committee would rely on the Historical Section for its documentary evidence; unfortunately, such evidence could not be provided in a suitable, detailed form immediately and, as a result, meetings of the Committee were suspended in January 1947.

It was not until April 1953, when the necessary information from the Historical Section became available, that the Committee was reconvened, again under the chairmanship of General Franklyn, but with a revised composition of fifteen members. The General Staff representation had been reduced by one, the India Office replaced by representatives of the High Commissioners for India and Pakistan, Southern Rhodesia had been replaced by a member for the Federation of Rhodesia and Nyasaland, and Newfoundland was no longer represented separately; these changes reflected changes within the Commonwealth. In addition to the material provided by the Cabinet Office, oral or written evidence was given to the Committee by forty-four senior officers with special knowledge of particular operations.

The first part of the report by the Committee was completed on 23 December 1955 and published the following year. Its contents, which did not include operations in the

South Pacific and the South-West Pacific, were similar to those of the previous report on The Great War: it classified operations as battles, actions and engagements, but defined these categories, not as in the past by the number of troops involved, but by the results of the operations and their importance to the situation at the time. To be classified as a battle, for example, the Committee took into account the following factors:

(i)   size of force and degree of concentration, having regard to the time when the operation took place during the war years (1939–45);
(ii)   intensity of fighting;
(iii) duration;
(iv)   strategical or tactical importance of results;
(v)   relation of episode to size of campaign;
(vi)   public sentiment and popular designation.

Operations of a lesser magnitude or importance were classified as actions, whereas engagements were regarded as 'particularly meritorious operations by units or small formations, sometimes representing independent contributions towards the general plan and at others isolated incidents deserving of special mention.' The Committee classified actions and engagements, not only as separate actions and engagements, but also those included in a battle, as 'many units and formations would also like to consider as a battle honour the place-name which identifies them with this lesser operation, in which they perhaps took a predominant part.'

The Committee tried to avoid using names which were associated with The Great War, and, if necessary, a year-date was added to distinguish between these operations; where separate operations took place at the same location in the same year, 'I' or 'II' was added to differentiate between such operations. If it was impossible to use any identifiable geographical or other feature to describe the action or engagement, a 'descriptive or even fanciful name by which the locality was know by the troops' was used. Similarly, there were included a few examples of alternative names to actions and engagements with which forces, mainly Commonwealth, could more readily identify.

As with The Great War, the chronological limits remained defined by the day from midnight to midnight and the limits shown indicated from 'the initial combat to the final combat' in that operation.

Defining the geographical limits proved difficult due to the amount of movement during many operations in the war: to attempt to record a large geographical area, in the view of the Committee, might have excluded units or formations which took part or have included some units or formations which had no role in the operation. It was concluded, therefore, that it would be more reliable to use the Order of Battle recorded by Historical Sections, and hence no geographical limits were included in the report.

Following the publication of the first part of the report, a smaller Committee with the same chairman and eight members representing the General Staff, the Historical Section of the Cabinet Office, the High Commissioners for Australia, New Zealand, Canada, Rhodesia and Nyasaland, India and Pakistan continued with the classification of operations by Australian and New Zealand forces in the South Pacific and the South-West Pacific. In attendance were the Secretary of the Battle Honours Committee, a member of the Historical Section of the Cabinet Office and two staff liaison officers from the Australian and the Canadian Army, all serving or retired officers: Secretaries continued to be provided by the Army Council Secretariat and the General Staff (Military Operations). Meanwhile, in March 1956 the Committee had been instructed further to make a similar report on the recent operations in the Korean Campaign. The final part of the report was completed on 1 October 1957 and, having been approved by the Army Council, was published the following year.

An extract from the Tabulated List of Operations is shown at Appendix C.

Great Britain and Northern Ireland

There were nearly three million men and women, largely conscripts, serving in the Army in August 1945; it was, moreover, an Army that was very different from the small, poorly equipped force of September 1939. When the Army was reformed after the Dunkirk evacuation in 1940, the immediate requirement for greater numbers of armoured, artillery, engineer and signal regiments was met initially by converting a large number of units, both Regular and Territorial Army, to these roles. Later new corps were raised for the War Establishment. Airborne Forces were introduced with The Parachute Corps, later The Parachute Regiment, being formed in June 1940 and The Glider Pilot Regiment the following year: these two regiments formed the Army Air Corps in February 1942, which was to include, from April 1944, the Special Air Service Regiment, which had been raised as 'L' Detachment in 1941. A Special Raiding Force, soon to be known as the Commandos, later to include the Royal Marines, was also raised in June 1940 'to carry the war to the enemy.' The Brigade Reconnaissance Groups, which were formed in 1940, were in January 1941 transferred to a newly-formed Reconnaissance Corps, which became part of the Royal Armoured Corps in 1944.

On mobilization the Household Cavalry, as in 1914, formed a composite regiment, which was intended to form two 'lorried infantry' or motor battalions; however, by 1941 it had become 1st and 2nd Household Cavalry Regiments, both of which served as armoured car units for the remainder of the war. The cavalry establishment, now part of the Royal Armoured Corps, was increased by three newly-raised regiments in late 1940 and by a further three in 1941; these new cavalry regiments were numbered 22nd to 27th. The Prime Minister, Winston Churchill, himself a former cavalry officer, echoed the cavalry's dismay when he commented:

> Surely it was a very odd thing to create these outlandish regiments of Dragoons, Hussars and Lancers, none of which has carbines, swords or lances, when there exists already telescoped up the 18th, 20th and 19th Hussars, 5th Lancers and 21st Lancers. Surely all these should have been revived before creating these unreal and artificial titles.

The Royal Tank Regiment in 1940, now augmented by twelve converted, pre-war Territorial Army units, expanded by reforming four battalions disbanded in 1919–20. The Reconnaissance Corps formed twenty-three units and the Royal Armoured Corps itself acquired a further thirty-four armoured regiments in 1941–42 by the conversion of Territorial Army infantry battalions. The North Irish Horse was reactivated in the Supplementary Reserve in 1939 and equipped with armoured cars. The Inns of Court Regiment was also equipped with armoured cars on conversion and transfer to the Royal Armoured Corps in 1940.

The Yeomanry met all the extraordinary demands made on it, finding at various times during the war, sixteen mounted regiments – The Cheshire Yeomanry (Earl of Chester's) being the last non- ceremonial mounted regiment in the British Army – eight of which served in the Middle East, five units of 'lorried' or motorized infantry, twenty armoured regiments, fifty-three regiments of artillery, four signal regiments and two infantry units, one of which was later converted to a parachute battalion. Few regiments, however, can match the record of The Sherwood Rangers Yeomanry for versatility: mobilized as a mounted regiment in 1939, dismounted and converted to 'lorried infantry' in the Middle East in 1940, used to man coast artillery batteries at Tobruk and Crete in 1941 and, finally, in 1942–43 as an armoured regiment in North Africa and in North-West Europe in 1944–45.

The Foot Guards expanded during the war from ten battalions to twenty-seven, of which eight had been converted to armoured battalions by 1941 and five remained as reserve or holding battalions. The infantry establishment rose to one hundred and twenty-eight regular battalions, three hundred and ninety-one Territorial Army Battalions and one hundred and ninety war-raised units, including home defence, reserve or holding battalions; however, of these seven hundred and nine battalions, thirty-two were converted to armoured units, eight transferred to the Reconnaissance Corps, fifty-nine to the Royal Artillery and seven to The Parachute Regiment; sixteen Army Commandos were also raised from this War Establishment. The Army Air Corps added a further fourteen units, excluding the Territorial Army conversions to parachute battalions. As in The Great War, the strength of the Regular Establishment was maintained, but many other battalions did not survive the war. An additional ninety-six units were provided by The King's African Rifles, the Royal West African Frontier Force and by battalions from Northern Rhodesia, Southern Rhodesia, Malta, Singapore, Malaya, Palestine, Sudan, Cyprus and Mauritius.

At the end of the war in August 1945, as the Territorial Army was being demobilized and war-raised units disbanded, the Army was required to meet not only its pre-war commitments but also a large number of additional tasks, such as troops for peace-keeping and for occupation forces in Europe, the Middle East and the Far East. Although burdened by large international debts, to meet these immediate commitments a larger than pre-war Regular Establishment of two Household Cavalry and thirty-four Royal Armoured Corps Regiments, five regiments of Foot Guards, sixty-six of infantry, and two regiments of Army Air Corps, in addition to other arms and services was necessary. The Reconnaissance Corps and all units of the Special Air Service Regiment were at first included in this establishment, but both were disbanded in 1946. Male conscription, introduced in 1939, was retained to ensure that the manning levels required by such an establishment, particularly the one hundred and forty-five units of Guards, infantry and Army Air Corps, could be maintained. 'National Service', as it was now called, despite subsequent reductions in establishments, did not end until 1962.

When the Territorial Army was reactivated in January 1947, the duplicated units authorized in March 1939 were either amalgamated with, or absorbed by, their original units or disbanded; a few, however, such as 2/4th Battalion, The South Lancashire Regiment (Prince of Wales's Volunteers) survived to be converted to a unit of the Royal Artillery. The strength of the Territorial Army was set at three regiments of the Royal Tank Regiment and twenty-eight of Yeomanry, thirteen of which were re-converted from other arms, and also included the North Irish Horse and the Inns of Court Regiment. The infantry was reduced from its pre-war level to eighty-eight battalions, with the surplus converted to form sixteen units of the Royal Artillery, two of The Parachute Regiment and one of the Royal Mechanical and Electrical Engineers, a new corps raised in 1942. The Army Air Corps consisted of nine battalions of The Parachute Regiment and, although not retained on the Regular Establishment, one battalion of the Special Air Service Regiment, formed by the conversion of The Artists' Rifles.

On 1 January 1948 the Regular Establishment was increased by the addition of four Gurkha regiments, each of two battalions, from the Indian Army; all honours and distinctions were retained on transfer. Nevertheless, despite increasing Communist activity in Malaya, it was concluded later in the year that the end of overseas commitments in the Dutch East Indies, Trieste, India, Pakistan, Burma, Palestine and Japan was sufficient for the remaining sixty-four infantry corps to lose their 2nd Battalions, raised since 1686, together with the disbandment of the six cavalry Regiments, raised 1940–41, The Lowland Regiment, The Highland Regiment and The Palestine Regiment, all raised in 1942.

Between 1949 and 1956 in addition to the Korean Campaign, the Army was engaged in counter-terrorist operations in Malaya, Kenya, the Suez Canal Zone and Cyprus. In Malaya, the successes of a special jungle warfare unit – the Malayan Scouts, raised in 1950 – led to the reintroduction of the Special Air Service Regiment to the Regular Establishment in 1952.

On 28 January 1956, a Special Army Order, headed 'Battle Honours', was published and stated:

> 1. Her Majesty the Queen has been graciously pleased to approve the award of Battle Honours to Regiments as outlined below.
> 2. Regiments will have awarded to them, and recorded . . . the honours due to them for taking part in the operations enumerated in the tabulated lists . . . given in the Report of the Battles Nomenclature Committee.
> Theatre Honours will also be awarded.
> The Report of the Battles Nomenclature Committee . . . from which claims for Honours may be made . . . covers the operations of all the Armies within the Commonwealth and Empire during the Second World War.
> 3. Following the honours previously earned and at the head of the list of honours now granted . . . will be placed the words 'The Second World War'.
> 4. Regiments . . . eligible for the award of Battle Honours are those of the Cavalry, Royal Armoured Corps and Infantry Arms listed . . . in the Corps Warrant dated 24th September 1951. For Infantry Regiments, honours may be awarded for operations in which Territorial or Service Battalions . . . as well as for those in which Regular Battalions were engaged. There will only be one Honours List for a Regiment.
> 5. Regiments of the Cavalry and Royal Armoured Corps Arms will have emblazoned on their standards and guidons. Battle Honours up to a maximum of 10, to commemorate their services in the Second World War. Battalions of Infantry, Regular and Territorial, will have emblazoned on their Queen's Colour the Battle Honours up to a maximum of 10, to commemorate their services in the Second World War.
> The new Honours to be emblazoned will be additional to those already carried.
> 6. The Honours for emblazonment, which will be the same for all units comprising the regiment concerned, will be selected by Regimental Committees . . . and will be shown in the Army List in heavy type.
> 7. Certain units of Yeomanry and Infantry Regiments, which were converted to other Arms during the War, but which have since resumed their original status within their

regiments, may be awarded an Honorary Distinction in the form of a badge in place of Honours to denote their service in another Arm. Such badges will be carried solely on the Regimental Colour of the unit concerned.

8. The qualifying rules and conditions governing the award of Battle and Theatre Honours, and of Honorary Distinctions, are notified separately in an Army Council Instruction . . . for the guidance of the Regimental Committees referred to in paragraph 6 above.

The introduction of a badge as an honorary distinction highlighted the increasing problem of eligibility for the award of battle honours faced by the Battle Honours Committee; the extension of qualification to include the Royal Tank Regiment and the three new regular regiments of the former Army Air Corps, disbanded 1950, was agreed by the Committee. It was also agreed, in an uncharacteristically generous decision by the Committee, that this extension was to include the Army Commandos, disbanded 1947, despite the fact that it was never a corps nor even part of a corps, usually a prerequisite for such qualification. The Commando Association, an ex-service body formed after the war, would perpetuate the traditions and honours of the Army Commandos. In addition, as for The Great War, disbanded corps would again qualify for the award of battle honours. Furthermore, the Committee agreed to a submission that, under certain circumstances, sub-units of a regiment would be permitted to claim battle honours, thereby modifying the revised fifty per cent rule by taking into account establishments and tactical grouping on the battlefield. This ensured that the claims of battle honours for corps, such as The Cheshire Regiment, which had provided machine gun battalions, mostly employed during the war as independent companies, and regiments, such as 3rd Carabiniers (Prince of Wales's Dragoon Guards), which had fought rarely as a complete unit in Burma during 1944–45, would not be inadmissible.

The Committee's generosity, however, had a limit when considering the possible claims by regiments and units of the Territorial Army, which had been converted to other arms before and during the war. The Committee concluded that such units would be bound by the rules for the eligibility of those arms for the award of battle honours; however, units which had been converted to other arms, but since 1947 had returned to the Yeomanry or their former infantry corps, would not qualify to claim battle honours, but would be granted the honorary distinction of a badge to record their war service in that arm. The infantry were little affected by this ruling as a battalion, on return to its regiment, would carry all corps honours on its Colours, in addition to the badge. The Yeomanry, not surprisingly, did not welcome this ruling as it was held that regiments had the qualification to claim battle honours in whatever temporary role they had fought. This view was based on the precedent of awards made to yeomanry regiments converted to form infantry and Machine Gun Corps units in The Great War. The Committee, therefore, should have taken this precedent into account, and confirmed that these regiments were eligible to claim for battle honours. It is difficult to understand why this case was not presented; it is possible, perhaps, that the eomanry was never given the opportunity to argue it. Nevertheless, the ruling was reluctantly accepted by the regiments concerned, although, on reflection, claims for theatre honours based on the 'parties of 20 or over' rule may have been more acceptable, had these been recognized as admissible by the Committee. However, the honorary distinction was never popular and in 1961 when three yeomanry regiments returned from the Royal Artillery, no retrospective claims for the award were submitted.

Army Council Instruction 58 dated 28 January 1956, set out the details for the submission of claims for awards, the qualifying rules and conditions for the award of battle and theatre honours and honorary distinctions.

Fourteen lists of awards for the Second World War were published between 1956 and 1958. Unlike after The Great War, no consolidated list was published and, despite some errors in drafting, no corrections to awards were considered necessary. List No. 4 included, to the further dismay of the Yeomanry, particularly the regiments which had served as units of the Royal Artillery, seventeen well-earned battle honours to the Honorable Artillery Company, all won by artillery units, claimed on the precedent that similar awards had been made for The Great War. Intermingled with these lists were separate Army Orders disbanding The Glider Pilot Regiment in 1957 and publishing the Royal Tank Regiment's retrospective awards for The Great War in 1958.

In 1958, following the lists for the Second World War, a separate list of awards for the Korean Campaign was published, with authority to emblazon two selected battle honours. One final ruling by the Battle Honours Committee was published in Army Order 79/1958, which stated that the battle honours of 'all amalgamated regiments' were to be combined and no longer to be shown separately in the Army List.

Following this series of awards, it was decided that all units of the Royal Armoured Corps, both regular and Territorial Army, except those already carrying a Standard or a Guidon, should receive Guidons to be issued and maintained at public expense. After one hundred and twenty-five years, Guidons were again to be carried by hussar and lancer regiments, with the addition of units of the Royal Tank Regiment and the Yeomanry.

A major Defence Review was carried out in 1957, following the ill-fated occupation of Port Said in 1956 and the consequent unrest in the Middle East, aimed at achieving substantial cuts in defence expenditure, which, in turn, required fewer overseas commitments. A new defence policy was adopted with, apart from West Germany now considered as a 'home posting', a reduced number of smaller overseas garrisons, to be reinforced by air in an emergency by lightly equipped, airportable units from a Strategic Command based in the United Kingdom. Further future cuts in establishments seemed possible when it was also announced that National Service was to be 'phased out in the near future'. As the emergencies in Malaya, Kenya and Cyprus and operations in the Arabian Peninsula and the Gulf drew to a close, by 1960 the Regular Establishment had been reduced to two regiments of Household Cavalry, the Royal Armoured Corps formed by sixteen cavalry regiments and the Royal Tank Regiment, a total of twenty-three units. The Foot Guards remained at five regiments, although the 3rd Battalion, Coldstream Guards was placed in suspended animation, fifty-one corps of infantry, grouped into fourteen brigades, The Parachute Regiment, four Gurkha regiments, the Special Air Service Regiment, totalling seventy-three battalions, and the Army Air Corps, which had been reformed in 1957. There were no disbandments, the reductions being the result of amalgamations; all honours and distinctions were retained, except for The Royal Highland Fusiliers (Princess Margaret's Own Glasgow and Ayrshire Regiment), formed 1959. The Royal Scots Fusiliers had been awarded **Meijel** for the Second World War, while the Highland Light Infantry (City of Glasgow Regiment) had successfully claimed **Asten**, the alternative name for the same action; two battle honours for the same action are not permitted, therefore **Asten** had to be withdrawn in favour of the senior regiment's honour.

Each infantry corps within these new brigades now wore a common cap-badge; this resulted in the loss of some honours worn on such appointments. However, the East Anglian Brigade badge incorporated The Castle and Key, and the Green Jackets Brigade badge included **Peninsula**, both battle honours being common to all three corps making up each brigade.

A revised establishment for the Territorial Army was set at the Honourable Artillery Company, nineteen regiments of yeomanry and one of the Royal Tank Regiment formed the Royal Armoured Corps, sixty-nine corps of infantry, including The Suffolk and Cambridgeshire Regiment and The Bedfordshire and Hertfordshire Regiment, recently formed by amalgamations, The Parachute Regiment and the Special Air Service Regiment, making a total of ninety-one battalions. The Yeomanry reductions were achieved by amalgamations; any increases in infantry numbers were by reconversion of units within the existing establishment, except for 23rd Special Air Service Regiment, raised 1959. All honours and distinctions were retained on amalgamation or transfer. The changes in the regular infantry establishment were not reflected in this establishment: corps retained their pre-1956 titles, badges and Colours. It did not pass unnoticed that, in many cases, it was now the Territorial Army, not the regular, battalions which perpetuated all the corps honours and distinctions.

There were also changes overseas as former colonies gained independence. On 1 August 1960 the Royal West African Frontier Force was disbanded: the Gold Coast, now Ghana, had become independent in 1957 with The Gold Coast Regiment renamed the Ghana Regiment. Within five years all the Royal West African Frontier Force regiments had been incorporated into the security forces of newly created West African states. Similarly, in East Africa Tanganyika became independent in 1961 and the 6th and 26th Battalions of The King's African Rifles were restyled the 1st and 2nd Battalions of the Tanganika Rifles. In all cases the traditions, honours and distinctions were inherited by the new corps.

The new defence policy was tested in 1961, when a reinforced brigade was rapidly deployed by air to Kuwait when Iraq threatened invasion. In the Far East a revolt in Brunei was quickly suppressed in 1962, which led to 'confrontation' with Indonesia in the former British Borneo territories and later on the Malayan Peninsula.

In October 1962 Uganda became independent with the 4th Battalion of The King's African Rifles reverting to its former title of the Uganda Rifles. In 1963 Kenya and Zanzibar followed Uganda: the 3rd, 5th and 11th Battalions of The King's African Rifles were later redesignated the 1st, 2nd and 3rd Battalions of the Kenya Rifles. Again, all honours and distinctions were retained on transfer.

By the end of 1963, the post-war Army, largely made up of National Servicemen, was replaced by a volunteer 'all-regular Army'; apart from the Korean Campaign it had gained no battle honours, despite having seen active service every year since 1945, sustained casualties, qualified for campaign medals and won some gallantry awards.

It would be a further twenty years before more battle honours were to be awarded. Meanwhile, in 1974, as a result of the numerous amalgamations which had taken place, there was a review of all battle honours. This resulted in **Lamone Bridgehead** being replaced by **Defence of Lamone Bridgehead** and taken into use by the successor Corps, except for The King's Own Royal Border Regiment; revised spellings of **Deir El Munassib** and **Santa Lucia** were also approved. There was a further minor change in 1985 when **Djebel Bou Aoukaz 1943**, without a suffix, was substituted for the previous awards: however, the Scots Guards retained **Djebel Bou Aoukaz 1943 I**.

India

By the end of the Second World War India had the largest volunteer army in the world, with over two million men serving in all theatres, except north-west Europe. The Indian Army in 1945 was a modern, technical force of all arms, no longer recruited on a strictly selected basis but manned by representatives from nearly every race and class in India, capable of fighting in all terrains and in all conditions against a well-equipped enemy.

A severe shortage of equipment restricted the expansion of the Indian cavalry throughout the war. By the end of 1940 mechanization was complete, but regiments were equipped with either obsolescent light tanks and armoured cars, inherited from the British Army, or fifteen-hundredweight trucks, the latter to be employed as motor battalions. As modern armoured vehicles became available, the outdated equipment was replaced, with priority given to regiments in active theatres overseas: it was not until 1941 that seven additional regiments were raised for the newly-formed Indian Armoured Corps, with a further three units raised in 1942. However, due to the continuing lack of equipment, eight of these regiments were disbanded by 1943. Similarly, four regiments earmarked by conversion of infantry battalions in 1942 had, within months, reverted to their former corps. By 1945 only three further armoured regiments had been added to the Indian Armoured Corps establishment.

The recently formed Indian Artillery by 1940 had two field regiments; from cadres supplied by these and the pre-war mountain batteries, by the conversion of twelve infantry battalions in 1942 and by raising new units, in 1944 sixty-four regiments of all types were on establishment. There was a corresponding increase in the Sappers and Miners, now forming part of the Corps of Indian Engineers, which required ten additional Engineer Training Centres to be formed in 1940 to meet this expansion. It was, however, the Indian infantry which saw the largest increase in numbers. On mobilization, the twenty-two Indian Territorial Force battalions were embodied and a further three were authorized; the Auxiliary Force, India, although not mobilized, again provided the extra officers needed by an expanded Indian Army and units of the Indian States Forces were 'placed at the disposal of The King-Emperor'. Regimental Centres replaced the 10th Battalions for training the one hundred and sixty-nine war-raised units; in 1941 3rd Madras Regiment returned to the Regular Indian Army List with the two senior Indian Territorial Force battalions forming the 1st and 2nd Battalions. That same year The Indian Parachute Regiment, The Bihar Regiment, The Assam Regiment, The Mahar Regiment and the Lingayat Battalion were raised. Also raised in 1941, from lower-caste Sikhs not considered suitable for 11th Sikh Regiment, was the Mazhbi and Ramdassia Sikh Regiment, later to be retitled The Sikh Light Infantry. On formation, as this corps had strong traditional links with the old 23rd Bengal Native Infantry, it inherited the traditions and honours of the 1st Battalion, 3rd Sikh Pioneers, disbanded 1933. In 1942 The Ajmar Regiment, The Chamar Regiment, the Afridi Battalion and the Coorg Battalion were raised. It is interesting to note that many of the battalions of these war-raised corps were recruited from tribes and classes not hitherto considered as suitable for military service. The Gurkha Rifles raised twenty-three additional rifle, one parachute, two garrison, and five training battalions.

By the end of the war the Indian infantry establishment had risen to three hundred and twenty-two battalions of all types, including Gurkha regiments. The Indian States Forces added a further four mechanized cavalry units and one Camel regiment, seven units of artillery, both mountain and field, five field companies of Sappers and Miners and thirty-three infantry battalions of various types.

In October 1945, as demobilization started, the Indian Infantry Corps, except 1st, 2nd, 8th, 14th, 15th and 16th Punjab Regiments, removed their regimental numbers and 4th Bombay Grenadiers and 19th Hyderabad Regiment were redesignated The Indian Grenadiers and The Kumaon Regiment, respectively; the Gurkha regiments retained their numbers.

The Indian Army's temporary post-war establishment, which was under review, was set at the Viceregal and old Presidential Bodyguards, seventeen Indian Armoured Corps regiments, twenty-eight regiments of artillery, ninety-five units of engineers, twenty-nine infantry regiments, totalling one hundred and six battalions and ten Gurkha regiments, each with two battalions. The Madras Regiment, The Sikh Light Infantry, The Bihar Regiment, The Assam Regiment and The Mahar Regiment were placed on the Regular Establishment and the Afridi Battalion was disbanded to reform The Kyber Rifles, disbanded 1919. The Indian Parachute Regiment, The Ajmar Regiment and The Chamar Regiment, although initially retained on establishment, were disbanded in 1946 and the Lingayat Battalion and the Coorg Battalion were transferred to the recently restyled Royal Indian Artillery.

In 1946 the Indian Armoured Corps Trade Training Centre and the Indian Armoured Corps Recruit Training Centre were established, inheriting the battle honours of Sam Brown's Cavalry (12th Frontier Force) and 15th Lancers, which had amalgamated in 1940, and 20th Lancers, respectively, having formed their predecessors, No 1 and No 2 Indian Armoured Corps Training Centres in 1940.

On 15 August 1947 Partition created the new Dominions of India and Pakistan: the existing Indian Army was divided along 'communal lines', the Indian Territorial Force, except for four units now forming regular battalions with The Madras and The Dogra Regiments, and the Auxiliary Force, India were disbanded, and the Indian States Forces units, although all but three of the states had already agreed to accede to one or other of the Dominions, had returned to their respective state's control.

On Partition the new Indian Army received The Governor General's Body-Guard, twelve Indian Armoured Corps regiments, fifteen Indian infantry corps and six Gurkha regiments. India also received nineteen regiments of Royal Indian Artillery, sixty-one units of Royal Indian Engineers, together with a number of services units and administrative and training establishments. Full regimental and corps titles were retained on transfer to the new Dominion, as were all the Colours, traditions, honours and distinctions.

Amid all the activity of transfers and cross-postings caused by the Partition, the disbandment of the ceremonial Governor's Body-Guards of Madras and Bombay passed almost unnoticed: these Corps were some of the oldest in the Indian Army, the earliest raised in 1778, and with them a unique battle honour, **Seetabuldee**, awarded to the Governor's Body-Guard, Madras in 1826 for an action on 26 November 1817 during the Third Mahratta and Pindari War, disappeared from the Army Lists.

By the end of 1949 there had been further changes to the Regular Establishment. The Indian Armoured Corps training establishments had been reorganized to form the Indian Armoured Corps Centre and School, thereby releasing 20th Lancers to be reformed as an active unit. The Indian Armoured Corps Centre and School retained the honours of the Indian Armoured Corps Trade Training Centre, while 20th Lancers had recovered its battle honours. The 11th Gurkha Rifles had been raised, with three regular battalions, to absorb the officers and men who had opted to remain with the Indian Army when four Gurkha regiments were transferred to the British Army. The Brigade of the Guards, a new 'all class' elite corps, had been recently established with 1st Rajputana Rifles forming its 3rd Battalion; 1st Rajput Regiment, 2/2nd Punjab Regiment and 1st Grenadiers soon followed to form the 4th, 1st and 2nd Battalions, respectively. The corps took precedence over 2nd Punjab Regiment to become the senior Indian Infantry corps and each battalion retained its former corps battle honours on transfer. A reserve establishment was filled by recruiting an 'all-arms' Indian Territorial Army, similar to the British Territorial Army, with units integrated into their regular regiments. The Indian Territorial Army Infantry Battalions were numbered from 101st and adopted their corps badges and other dress distinctions, but no Colours were issued. Furthermore, the Jammu and Kashmir Militia had been recently formed from irregular volunteer units, mainly scouts, raised after Partition to replace the Frontier Corps for local frontier defence and internal unrest control.

On 26 January 1950 India became a Republic, which resulted in yet further changes in the Army, which, although mainly administrative, were nevertheless widespread. The Army replaced the Navy as the senior Service, the Imperial Crown was replaced by the three Ashoka Lions, the prefix 'Royal', together with sub-titles, and the word 'Indian' were withdrawn from all regimental and corps designations. The following revised titles were taken into use by the Armoured Corps, infantry and Gurkha regiments and corps:

> The President's Body Guard, 16th Light Cavalry, 7th Light Cavalry, 8th Light Cavalry, 1 Horse, 2nd Lancers, The Poona Horse, The Deccan Horse, The Scinde Horse, 3rd Cavalry, 4 Horse, The Central India Horse, 20 Lancers.

> The Brigade of the Guards, The Punjab Regiment, The Madras Regiment, The Grenadiers, The Maratha Light Infantry, The Rajputana Rifles, The Rajput Regiment, The Jat Regiment, The Sikh Regiment, The Sikh Light Infantry, The Dogra Regiment, The Garhwal Rifles, The Kumaon Regiment, The Assam Regiment, The Bihar Regiment, The Mahar Regimen, 1st Gorkha Rifles, 3rd Gorkha Rifles, 4th Gorkha Rifles, 5th Gorkha Rifles, 8th Gorkha Rifles, 9th Gorkha Rifles, 11th Gorkha Rifles.

In addition, the Sappers and Miners, a distinguished title with origins dating from 1780, fell victim to modernization and became the Madras Engineer Group, the Bengal Engineer Group and the Bombay Engineer Group of the Corps of Engineers. The new Armoured Corps order of precedence was based on the seniority of the former Madras Native Cavalry, unbroken from 1784, rather than the preference given to the Bengal Native Cavalry's successors, which were reformed in 1861. A further, visible link with the past was broken when all the King's Colours were laid up, with full honours, in the Indian Military Academy at Dehra Dun on 23 November 1950. The old Regimental Colours, however, remained in use.

In 1952 The Parachute Regiment was reformed with the 1st, 2nd and 3rd Battalions found by the transfer of the 1st (Parachute) Punjab Regiment, 3rd (Parachute) Maratha Light Infantry and 1st (Parachute) Kumaon Regiment, respectively. To indicate its origin each battalion was permitted to add a suffix to its new title – '(Punjab)', '(Maratha)' and '(Kumaon)' – until these were removed in 1963. The maroon beret and other corps dress distinctions were retained by each battalion, as were their traditions and battle honours. Regimental Colours bearing their former corps battle honours and distinctions, as with The Brigade of the Guards, also remained in use. This new corps took precedence over The Punjab Regiment to become the second senior Infantry corps.

Following the accession of the Indian States into the Republic, all Indian States Forces units were at first retained, were grouped regionally and assessed; those units considered to be unsuitable were disbanded, which included many that had received battle honours for service on the North-West Frontier, China and The Great War. In 1951 the surviving units were amalgamated, given new titles and affiliated to suitable regular regiments and corps of the Indian Army. By 1957 these units, now one mounted cavalry regiment, six artillery batteries, six engineer field companies, twenty-three infantry battalions and one mule transport company, had been integrated into the Regular Establishment. To record their origins, the former Indian States Forces units were permitted to add a suitable regional suffix to their new titles; for example, The Bikanir Sadul Light Infantry, raised 1461, became the 19th Battalion (Bikanir), The Rajput Regiment. The Jammu and Kashmir Infantry, exceptionally, was not integrated into an existing corps, but was transferred to the Regular Establishment in 1957, with six battalions. All State standards and Colours remained in use and battle honours were retained on transfer, but not combined with the distinctions of their new corps.

With the introduction, in 1955, of Standards, Guidons and new Colours to corps of the cavalry, Armoured Corps, Armoured Corps Centre and the infantry, including Regimental Centres, the exclusive use of English on such Standards, Guidons and Colours or on appointments was ended and replaced by local languages.

In 1958 a Battle Honours Committee convened, under Lieutenant General Sant Singh, to consider the award of battle honours for the Second World War, given the additional task, ruled that the individual battalion battle honours of the units transferred to form The Brigade of the Guards and The Parachute Regiment could be taken into use by these two corps. It proved to be a controversial decision, and there was the inevitable, but unsuccessful, storm of protest from the former corps concerned. It is unlikely that the Committee was aware of the precedent set in 1937 when The Liverpool Scottish transferred to The Queen's Own Cameron Highlanders and the battalion took its own battle honours into use, which were shown separately in the Army List, while the battle honours of its former corps – The King's Regiment (Liverpool) – remained unchanged.

The instructions, published in 1959, for the submission of claims for battle honours and honorary distinctions for service in the Second World War and the qualifying rules and conditions were nearly identical to those issued by the War Office in 1956. The battle honours to be awarded were based on the Report of the Battles Nomenclature Committee, with the addition of **Tiddim Road** to commemorate the actions there between 31 July and 14 September 1944. The engineers continued to be eligible for awards, but the artillery was now restricted to claim for honour titles only; the infantry corps were permitted to claim for war-raised, Indian Territorial Force and Indian States Forces battalions, in addition to the regular units. Disbanded corps, however, as for The Great War, continued to be disqualified for the award of battle honours. The Brigade of the Guards and The Parachute Regiment were to qualify exclusively for the battle honours awarded to their present battalions, although these battalions had been in other corps at the time of the engagements. This produced further protest, but there were no claims for honorary distinctions by the regiments concerned. The subsequent awards to the 3rd Battalion of the Maratha Light Infantry are, therefore, puzzling, but it must be assumed that this unit perpetuates the 4th (Mahratta) Anti-tank Regiment, formerly the 8th Battalion, which later reformed the 3rd Battalion. Sadly, The Indian Parachute Regiment, disbanded 1946, would have successfully claimed the awards of **Sangshak** and **Burma 1942–45,** on behalf of 152nd Indian Parachute Battalion and 153rd Gurkha Parachute Battalion, had it not been disqualified under the disbanded-corps rule.

Special Army Order 7/S/62, published on 27 March 1962, contained twelve lists showing the battle honours awarded 'to units for service during the Second World War, 1939–45.' The layout of the Annexes to the Special Order was a departure from the by now accepted format, in which each corps with its awards underneath was set out as shown in the Army List. In this case, each list was for a specific campaign and was laid out as a table of six columns showing the corps or regiment, each unit of that corps or regiment present, its battle honours, its theatre honour, its honour title and remarks. It was not only a simple and effective method of presentation in which the unit present at the action for which an award was made, but was also a return to the pre-1914 system of battle honours being awarded first to the unit and not the corps. This can best be shown as the entry for The Rajputana Rifles' awards for the North African Campaign:

The Rajputana Rifles 4th Bn	SIDI BARRANI ALEM HAMZA RUWEISAT RIDGE EL ALAMEIN MATMATA HILLS AKARIT DJEBEL GARCI	NORTH AFRICA 1940–43
17th Bn (Sawai Man)		NORTH AFRICA 1940–43
MG Bn	AKARIT	NORTH AFRICA 1940–43

It should be noted that all the theatre honours awarded record the length of the campaign and do not relate to the time served by each unit in the theatre. Strangely, **British Somaliland** was awarded to The Parachute Regiment with no year-date.

The Special Army Order concluded with:

2 Certain claims, received from units by the Battle Honours Committee, were rejected as not being sufficiently strong. The Regiments/Corps concerned have been informed of such rejections and those wishing to submit appeals have been allowed to do so. The results of the appeals will be announced later.

3 Separate instructions are under issue regarding the adoption and emblazonment of World War II Battle Honours. Pending receipt of these instructions, units will not adopt or emblazon any of these Battle Honours.

The results of the appeals were published in another Special Army Order the following year with the additional awards of **Agordat, Keren-Asmara Road, Keren, Amba Alagi, Malaya 1941–42, El Mechili, Sidi Suleiman, Defence of Alamein Line, North Africa**

1940–43, Mogaung, Chindits 1944, Burma 1942–45, Imphal, Tamu Road, Meiktila and **Rangoon Road.**

In 1963 The Jammu and Kashmir Infantry was restyled The Jammu and Kashmir Rifles and the Ladakh Scouts, a specialist mountain unit to be stationed permanently on the North-West Frontier, was formed from the 7th and 14th Battalions of the Jammu and Kashmir Militia. Originally intended to be a paramilitary unit, the Ladakh Scouts soon joined the Regular Establishment, ranking after the Gorkha Rifles.

Pakistan

There is an undeserving lack of published material regarding the Pakistan Army since 1947, which presents problems to those wishing to carry out any research on this subject. This section, therefore, is based on the best, if limited, information of the Pakistan Army currently available.

Before 1947, there were no exclusive Muslim units in the Indian Army; nevertheless, on Partition the new Dominion, then divided into West Pakistan and East Pakistan, was allocated the following regiments and corps:

> Probyn's Horse (5th King Edward VII's Own Lancers); 6th Duke of Connaught's Own Lancers (Watson's Horse); the Guides Cavalry (10th Queen Victoria's Own Frontier Force); Prince Albert Victor's Own Cavalry (11th Frontier Force); 13th Duke of Connaught's Own Lancers; 19th King George V's Own Lancers;

> 1st Punjab Regiment; 8th Punjab Regiment; the Baluch Regiment; the Frontier Force Regiment; the Frontier Force Rifles; 14th Punjab Regiment; 15th Punjab Regiment; 16th Punjab Regiment.

This allotment required the Sikh, Dogra, Jat and Rajput squadrons and companies to be transferred to the Indian Army in exchange for the Punjabi Mussalman, Hindustani Mussalman, Kaimkhani and Ranghar squadrons and companies.

In addition, nine artillery regiments were transferred to form the Royal Pakistan Artillery and thirty-four engineer units to create the Royal Pakistan Engineers; furthermore, some service and support units and a few adminstrative and training establishments then located within the new boundaries, were handed over to the Pakistan Army. All Colours, battle honours and distinctions were retained on transfer.

Within months of Partition the Bahawalpur Regiment, with four battalions, and formed from the Bahawalpur State Forces – the only state to cede to Pakistan – was placed on the Regular Infantry Establishment, the State Colour with battle honours was retained on transfer. The formation of The Pathan Regiment (Frontier Force), three battalions strong, from units of The Frontier Force Regiment and the raising of the East Bengal Regiment, established for ten battalions, soon followed. The need for more armoured units led subsequently to Sam Browne's Cavalry (12th Frontier Force) and 15th Lancers being reformed, with each regiment recovering its battle honours. It is interesting to note that these same battle honours are also used by the Armoured Corps Centre and School in India.

On 23 March 1956 Pakistan became a Republic: the Imperial Crown was replaced by the Star or the Star and Crescent, the prefix 'Royal', together with corps and unit sub-titles associated with the Imperial past, and the word 'Pakistan' were removed from regimental and corps designations. New titles were taken into use by the Armoured Corps to become 5th Horse, 6th Lancers, Guides Cavalry (Frontier Force), 11th Cavalry (Frontier Force), 12th Cavalry (Frontier Force), 13th Lancers, 15th Lancers and 19th Lancers. The King's Colours – no Queen's Colours had as yet been issued – were laid up, possibly in the Staff College, Quetta, and replacement Standards, Guidons and colours were authorized.

The Pakistan Army was also reorganized, the effects being felt mainly by the infantry. Strangely, despite the initial antipathy caused by the introduction of 'large regiments' in 1922, even larger corps were created. The 1st, 14th, 15th and 16th Punjab Regiments were amalgamated to form The Punjab Regiment; 8th Punjab Regiment and the Bahawalpur Regiment were absorbed by The Baluch Regiment, and The Frontier Force Regiment was formed by the merger of The Frontier Force Regiment, The Frontier Force Rifles and The Pathan Regiment. The East Bengal Regiment remained unchanged. All honours and distinctions were retained on reorganization.

In April 1959, the 19th Battalion, The Baluch Regiment became the cadre for a new Special Services Group, an elite parachute-commando force.

It is not known when the awards of battle honours for the Second World War were made nor in what form they were published. The only documentary evidence that such awards were granted is an Annex to letter No. 30/4/66/Hist Sec, dated 3 June 1968, headed 'List of the Battle Honours awarded during World War II to Regiments and Units now comprising Pakistan Army'; no authority for the awards is given. From this list, however, it is possible to deduce that the qualifying rules and conditions for the award of battle and theatre honours were similar to those issued by the War Office in 1956. The battle honours were taken from the Report of the Battles Nomenclature Committee, on which Brigadier Shaukit Ali Shah represented the High Commissioner for Pakistan, and were awarded to units of the Armoured Corps and infantry arms only: no honorary distinctions were awarded. The titles used in the list were pre-1956 and disbanded units were included; typical entries for The Baluch Regiment were:

5th Bn (Burma) 8th Punjab Regiment

1.   DONBAIK
2.   BURMA 1942–45

2nd Bn the Baluch Regiment

1.   NORTH MALAYA
2.   MACHANG
3.   SINGAPORE ISLAND
4.   MALAYA 1941–42

The theatre honours, like the Indian awards, show the length of the campaign and not the time served by the unit in the theatre.

The Annex also records instructions for ten selected battle or theatre honours to be emblazoned on the Regimental Colours of 'active battalions' in a series of ten lists. Four lists detail the honours to be emblazoned by battalions of the former 1st, 14th, 15th and 16th Punjab Regiments, by each battalion of The Baluch Regiment and by each battalion of the former Frontier Force Regiment and the former Frontier Force Rifles.

Three lists showed the thirty-seven battle honours to be emblazoned on the new Regimental Colours of the Regimental Centres of The Punjab Regiment, of The Baluch Regiment and of The Frontier Force Regiment. No instructions for the emblazonment of battle honours for the Armoured Corps were included. The ten battle honours authorized to be emblazoned by the battalions were Second World War awards only, and it is not clear whether or not these were in addition to the honours previously carried. Since the award of battle honours for the Second World War was the first approved by a President of Pakistan, it is possible that these are the first to be borne on the new Colours. However, the battle honours authorized for the Regimental Centres were selected from the combined awards of all the former regiments forming the new corps. Also, it is most unlikely that the battle honours would continue to be emblazoned in English and it is not known whether or not emblazoned battle honours, such as **Assaye** and **China**, continued to be enhanced with the badges of The Elephant or The Golden Dragon wearing an Imperial Crown, respectively.

Australia

As Australian Military Forces units remained unable to serve overseas in 1939, a second Australian Imperial Force was raised from volunteers, mainly drawn from the Militia. The units serving in the Force were distinguished by the prefix 21-, the suffix 'AIF' and the coloured shoulder patches worn by the original Australian Imperial Force, with a narrow grey border added. By 1940 6th Australian Division was serving with the Western Desert Force, to be joined in 1941 in the Middle East by 7th and 9th Australian Divisions. En route, 18th Brigade of 7th Australian Division was diverted and briefly deployed on the South-East coast of England as part of the Home Forces, before taking part with 9th Australian Division in the Siege of Tobruk. The 8th Australian Division, which was serving in Malaya, was ordered to surrender at the fall of Singapore on 15 February 1942; the Division was not reformed.

The rapid Japanese advances in South-East Asia and the South-West Pacific during 1941–42 posed a real threat of invasion on the Northern and the North-Eastern coast and the Government was required to recall its troops from the Middle East and to prepare for the defence of Australia. The 6th, 7th and 9th Australian Divisions were rapidly moved to New Guinea to counter Japanese penetration and were soon reinforced by 1st and 4th Australian Armoured Brigades. Additionally in 1942, in order to meet the increased manpower required, conscription for service in the South-West Pacific area was introduced and selected militia units, into which the conscripts were drafted, were mobilized for overseas service. As these militia units were not considered to be part of the second Australian Imperial Force, they did not qualify initially for the prefix 21- nor the suffix 'AIF'; however, if subsequently a militia unit had at least seventy-five per cent of 'overseas volunteers' on its strength, the unit would be granted the suffix. The 3rd and 5th Australian Divisions and later 11th Australian Division, in which the mobilized units of both designations served, nevertheless, acquitted themselves well in much hard and bitter fighting in New Guinea and the Solomons. The light horse regiments, which together with the remainder of the Militia had been embodied in 1939, were reorganized to form two motor, later to be redesignated armoured divisions. The 2nd and 3rd Armoured Divisions and 3rd Army Tank Brigade, together with 1st, 2nd, 4th, 10th and 12th Australian Divisions, also formed during 1941–43, remained in Australia. Local forces in Papua and New Guinea were also restructured and brought up to War Establishment. By August 1945 all Australian units serving overseas were located in the South-West Pacific area.

After final victory over Japan, and as Australian Military Forces and second Australian Imperial Force units were beginning demobilization, Army Headquarters started to plan and to implement a far-reaching programme of major reforms to modernize the forces. During the war a small number of militia regiments had been disbanded and this practice was continued in 1945–46 with a further thirty-one corps, mainly infantry, removed from the Regular Establishment. The second Australian Imperial Force was formally disbanded in 1946 and a new regular, volunteer corps, the Australian Regiment, later the Royal Australian Regiment, was raised to provide for future overseas commitments worldwide. The Pacific Islands Regiment, raised 1940 as the Papuan Infantry Battalion, was retained and placed on the Australian Military Forces Establishment, as was the Papuan and New Guinea Volunteer Rifles. Conscription was replaced by compulsory service in the part-time Militia, to be retitled the Citizen Military Forces in 1949, but for home defence duties only.

Australia reacted quickly to the United Nations request for troops to counter Communist aggression and in September 1950 moved the 3rd Battalion, Royal Australian Regiment from occupation duties in Japan to South Korea to join 27th Brigade, newly arrived from Hong Kong; the battalion was relieved in March 1952 but the commitment lasted until 1957. In that same year Australian servicemen were deployed to assist in the Malayan emergency.

On 30 March 1959, Australian Army Order No. 24 was published and included the following paragraphs:

> 2. Armoured and Infantry units of the AMF will have awarded to them, and recorded ... the Honours due to them for taking part in the operations enumerated in the tabulated list of battles, actions and engagements of the Second World War (1939–45) and Korean Campaign (1950–53) given in the Report of the UK Battles Nomenclature Committee. Theatre Honours will also be awarded.

> 3. An extract from the Report ... giving the list of AMF operations for which claims can be made, is attached at Annex A.

> 5. Units of the Royal Australian Armoured Corps will have emblazoned on their Guidons, Battle Honours up to a maximum of ten to commemorate their service in the Second World War. Battalions of Infantry will have emblazoned on their Regimental Colours, Battle Honours up to a maximum of ten to commemorate their service in the Second World War and a maximum of two to commemorate their service in Korea. The new Honours will be additional to those already emblazoned.

> 6. The Honours for emblazonment, which will be the same for all units comprising a regiment, will be shown in the Army List in heavy type.

An Army Headquarters Battle Honours Committee, with Major-General Sir George Wootten and two members, was also appointed 'to examine claims ... and make recommendations to the Military Board on these claims and on any other matters relating to the award of these Honours which the Committee considers should be decided.'

Annex A listed the engagements by each theatre of war in which units of the

Australian Military Forces took part, but the sequence used in the Report of the Battles Nomenclature Committee, published in 1956, was changed with North Africa 1940–43 shown before Syria 1941 and this sequence was retained when battle honours were awarded to the regiments and corps. The Annex also showed four changes to the tabulated list dealing with the South-West Pacific 1942–1945 in the Final Report of the Battles Nomenclature Committee, published in 1958. An additional engagement, **Goodenough Island**, was added to record the fighting by 2/12th Australian Infantry Battalion AIF between 22 and 26 October 1942: 'Dumpu' was renamed **Ramu Valley**, the chronological limits of **Shaggy Ridge** were extended to 6 October 1943–31 January 1944, thereby including the engagement of 'Finesterres I' and the action of 'Kankiryo Saddle', and consequently 'Finesterres II' was amended to **Finesterres**.

The qualifying rules and conditions governing claims for the award of battle honours were published in Military Board Instructions 105/1959. As for The Great War, battle honours earned by second Australian Imperial Force units were to be awarded to, and perpetuated by, Citizen Military Forces regiments and corps with the same number. However, second Australian Imperial Force units without a Citizen Military Forces equivalent, such as the divisional Cavalry regiments, later dismounted to become 'Cavalry Commando' for amphibious operations in the South-West Pacific, and machine gun and pioneer battalions, previously unqualified, were also to be eligible for awards. In addition to perpetuating second Australian Imperial Force awards, mobilized militia units, which had served in the South-West Pacific, were to be permitted to claim for battle honours in their own right. Hence, corps such as 24th Infantry Battalion (The Kooyong Regiment) would be qualified to receive awards on behalf of both 2/24th Australian Infantry Battalion AIF and 24th Infantry Battalion. The Pacific Islands Regiment was, as a successor unit, to be awarded the battle honours earned by the locally-raised Papuan Infantry Battalion.

In 1960 and 1961 a series of seven lists awarding battle honours for the Second World War and Korea were published. Until 1960 it had been generally accepted that the theatre honour would be shown after any battle honour awarded for that theatre: these lists, however, showed a change in that the theatre honour preceded any of the subsequent battle honours. It is possible that this was considered to be a more accurate presentation of the tabulated lists where the theatre and year-dates are used as a heading.

Concurrently, the reorganization of the Australian Military Forces, started in 1946, was completed: the Regular Army Establishment was greatly increased and the Citizen Military Forces, since 1958 a volunteer organization, become the Army Reserve with a limited overseas capability. With effect from 1 June 1960, the reserve establishment was set at seven regiments of light horse and six 'large regiments' of infantry. All corps honours and distinctions were retained on reorganization.

The rules for the emblazonment of Second World War battle honours were changed by Australian Army Order 113/61, which amended paragraph 5 of Order 24/1959 to:

> 5. Units of the Royal Australian Armoured Corps will have emblazoned on their Guidons, Battle Honours up to a maximum of ten to commemorate their service in the Second World War. Battalions of Infantry with the exception of the Pacific Islands Regiment will have emblazoned on the Queen's Colours, Battle Honours up to a maximum of ten to commemorate their service in the Second World War. The new Honours will be in addition to those already emblazoned. Of the Honours for the

Second World War awarded to the Pacific Islands Regiment, a maximum of ten will be emblazoned on the Regimental Colour. A maximum of two Honours awarded to the Royal Australian Regiment to commemorate its service in KOREA will be emblazoned on the Regimental Colour of Battalions of the Royal Australian Regiment.

As a result of these changes, a final list of awards for all Regiments and Corps, which superseded all previous lists, was promulgated on 28 December 1961 by Australian Army Order 135/61. This was followed by the publication of a further consolidated list of battle honours on 28 November 1962 in Order 85/1962. The order showed the battle honours of the armoured and infantry corps, which were on the Order of Battle from 1 July 1960.

Meanwhile, in 1962, Australia's involvement in South Vietnam began with the formation and deployment of the Australian Army Training Team Vietnam to provide training for the South Vietnamese Army. While carrying out its task this remarkable team, initially with a strength of thirty, later rising to over two hundred, all-ranks, won four Victoria Crosses.

In 1963 Australian Army Order 135/61 was amended to extend the battle honours previously awarded to 52nd Infantry Battalion (The Gippsland Regiment), 53rd Infantry Battalion (The West Sydney Regiment) and 60th Infantry Battalion (The Heidelberg Regiment) to 37th Infantry Battalion (The Henty Regiment), 55th Infantry Battalion (The New South Wales Rifle Regiment) and 57th Infantry Battalion (The Merri Regiment). As these units had fought as composite battalions in the South-West Pacific area, battle honours should have been awarded to both units combined to form the composite battalion. This long-standing precedent was established when awards were made for the Peninsular War.

On 16 March 1994 approval was given by the Governor-General for the award of **Maryang-San** to the Royal Australian Regiment on behalf of the 3rd Battalion; in November the corps was permitted, as a further distinction, to emblazon this battle honour on its Regimental Colour, in addition to the two battle honours previously authorized for the Korean Campaign.

Canada

On 17 December 1939 the first units of 1st Canadian Division, part of the recently formed Canadian Active Service Force, disembarked on the Clyde in Scotland. This was made possible by the Canadian Government's action on 1 September 1939, when the Canadian Active Service Force was formed by the mobilization of the Permanent Force, together with twenty-seven militia regiments, and the remainder of the Militia was embodied with details activated for local defence duties. Some units of the Canadian Active Service Force were to remain in Canada, but, as in 1914, only volunteers could serve outside the Dominion. Nevertheless, the mobilized units, which retained their regimental titles with the distinguishing suffix 'CASF' added, were soon at War Establishment. During August and September 1940 2nd Canadian Division arrived in England to join 1st Canadian Division in a counter-invasion role on the South-East coast.

Meanwhile, in Canada the need for more mechanized units was met by cavalry regiments being transferred in 1941 to the Canadian Armoured Corps, formed 1940, and redesignated as numbered armoured regiments with a sub-title added to retain their identity. The 1st Canadian Armoured Division, later 5th Canadian Armoured Division, and 3rd Canadian Division, both of which included Militia units mobilized in May 1940, were embarked for the United Kingdom during June and July 1941. In October two infantry battalions were sent to Hong Kong to reinforce the garrison.

In January 1942 4th Canadian Armoured Division was raised and to provide for the shortfall in armoured regiments ten infantry units were converted to armoured regiments and transferred to the Canadian Armoured Corps; 4th Canadian Armoured Division moved to England in the autumn of 1942.

On 1 January 1943 1st and 2nd Canadian Armoured Brigades were formed from armoured regiments in the United Kingdom. Later that year I Canadian Corps, with 1st Canadian Division and 1st Canadian Armoured Brigade, shortly joined by 5th Canadian Armoured Division, moved to the Mediterranean. The following year 1st Special Service Battalion, raised 1942, arrived in Italy. This remarkable, joint Canadian–American unit was disbanded in Nice in 1944.

In England 1st Canadian Parachute Battalion, raised 1942, joined 6th Airborne Division in August 1943. On D-Day this unit and the First Canadian Army, consisting of II Canadian Corps, 2nd and 3rd Canadian Divisions, 4th Canadian Armoured Division and 2nd Canadian Armoured Brigade, formed part of 21st Army Group for the Normandy landings. After the breakout from the beachhead the First Canadian Army formed the left flank of the Army Group throughout the remainder of the campaign. In October 1944 1st Canadian Armoured Personnel Carrier Regiment was established under command of 79th Armoured Division. However, by November 1944, although a limited form of conscription had been introduced in 1940 for service in Canada, the need to replace casualties made it necessary to extend this to overseas service for the remainder of the war.

During March and April 1945 I Canadian Corps was transferred from Italy to Holland for the final assault on Germany. By the end of the war on 5 May 1945 all Canadian combat units were serving in North-West Europe.

As in The Great War, a number of Canadian units served in the United Kingdom: some remained to form depots and other administrative establishments or were soon disbanded to provide reinforcements, particularly after October 1943. Other regiments provided garrisons for Newfoundland and the West Indies until 1944.

In 1946 the Canadian Active Service Force was disbanded and its units demobilized. The post-war strength of the Canadian Forces was then set at twenty-three regiments forming the Royal Canadian Armoured Corps and sixty-eight regiments forming the Canadian Infantry Corps, of which two and three were Permanent Force, respectively. Four militia cavalry regiments and eight militia infantry units were transferred to the Royal Canadian Artillery, and The Middlesex and Huron Regiment, formed 1936, was disbanded. In 1947 24th Armoured Regiment (Three Rivers Regiment) and 25th Armoured Regiment (Queen's York Rangers) were added to the Royal Canadian Armoured Corps Militia Establishment, and two years later all Royal Canadian Armoured Corps units took new titles into use. All honours and distinctions were retained.

In April 1949 the British colony of Newfoundland, together with Labrador, became Canada's tenth Province. On 24 October 1949 The Newfoundland Regiment, later The Royal Newfoundland Regiment, was raised and added to the Canadian Infantry Corps Militia Establishment. This corps perpetuates the regiment raised for The Great War and has inherited its honours and distinctions.

In 1950 to provide units for the Korean Campaign and the Canadian forces serving in West Germany, 2nd and 3rd Battalions were raised by the three infantry regiments of the former Permanent Force, now known as the Regular Army. This increase was extended in 1953 by the raising of The Regiment of Canadian Guards, a new corps of four regular battalions and the raising of 1st and 2nd Battalions by The Queen's Own Rifles of Canada and by The Black Watch (Royal Highland Regiment) of Canada. The corresponding militia battalions were renumbered accordingly. The honours and distinctions of the five regiments were taken into use by the regular battalions.

Three months after the 2nd Battalion, Princess Patricia's Canadian Light Infantry was raised, it embarked for South Korea to join 27th Brigade. By May 1951 the Canadian contribution to the United Nations force had been increased to a Brigade Group.

Between 1954 and 1956, following the end of the fighting in Korea, a further series of reorganizations took place: the Royal Canadian Armoured Corps Militia Establishment was increased by the conversion and redesignation of The Algonquin Regiment (26th Armoured Regiment), The Elgin Regiment (27th Armoured Regiment), The Grey and Simcoe Foresters (28th Armoured Regiment) and The South Alberta Light Horse (29th Armoured Regiment). The light horse regiment, as a successor unit, took into use the honours and distinctions of 15th Alberta Light Horse and The South Alberta Regiment. The Canadian Infantry Corps also saw some changes: two 3rd Battalions, raised 1950, were disbanded and were replaced by The London and Oxford Fusiliers (3rd Battalion, The Royal Canadian Regiment), which was formed by the amalgamation of The Canadian Fusiliers (City of London Regiment) and the Oxford Rifles, and The Loyal Edmonton Regiment (3rd Battalion, Princess Patricia's Canadian Light Infantry). The Royal Canadian Regiment and its new 3rd Battalion took into use their combined battle honours; the new 3rd Battalion of the Princess Patricia's Canadian Light Infantry, however, retained the honours and distinctions of The Loyal Edmonton Regiment separately. The Royal 22^e Regiment, although none of its regular battalions were disbanded, formed new 4th, 5th and 6th Battalions by amalgamating with Le Regiment de Chateauguay, Les Fusiliers du St.-Laurent, which had absorbed Le Regiment de Montmagny, and Le Regiment de St.-Hyacinthe, respectively. The battalions took into use the honours and distinctions of the Royal 22^e Regiment on amalgamation. None of these new battalions were regular units and they remained on the militia establishment. In addition, a further eighteen units were amalgamated or absorbed to form eight regiments; all battle honours were combined and taken into use by the new regiments.

In 1956 Canada's strong commitment to United Nations operations began with the arrival of a Reconnaissance Squadron in Egypt for service with the United Nations Emergency Force. Later observer teams were provided for Lebanon and Jordan, Congo, Western New Guinea and the Yemen.

On 16 September 1956 Supplement Issue No. 508 to Canadian Army Order 33-1, which set out the rules and conditions for the award of battle honours for the Second World War, was published. The list of operations in the table did not follow the sequence used in the Report of the Battles Nomenclature Committee, with South-East Asia 1941–42 and North-West Europe 1940–42 being shown before Sicily 1943 and Italy 1943–45 and ending with North-West Europe 1944–45; this sequence was retained when awards were made to regiments of the Canadian Army. Several amendments to correct minor drafting errors, mainly the spelling of place names and changes to chronological limits, were issued later in 1956 and 1957. A further amendment to record the expedition to Spitzbergen between 25 August and 3 September 1941 was also shown, but whether or not this additional action was authorized or was simply an annotation is not clear. However, as it was a detachment only of The Loyal Edmonton Regiment which was present, and no such award was made, it is solely of academic interest.

On 28 January 1957 an increase in the Royal Canadian Armoured Corps Establishment was authorized with 8th Princess Louise's (New Brunswick) Hussars forming a regular unit styled 1/8th Canadian Hussars (Princess Louise's) and the militia component designated 2/8th Canadian Hussars (Princess Louise's); later these titles were changed to 8th Canadian Hussars (Princess Louise's) and 8th Canadian Hussars (Princess Louise's)(Militia).

In 1957 thirteen Supplements awarding battle honours for the Second World War were published, followed by four Supplements in 1958 and a further four in 1959. Included in these were three honorary distinctions. The theatre honours awarded in these Supplements used the full year-dates, rather than the shorter form, which hitherto had been the accepted convention. But, unlike the awards made for The Great War, other service outside Canada went unrewarded. There was one amendment made to awards published in the Supplements when **North-West Europe 1944–1945,** approved for the Prince Edward Island Regiment (17th Reconnaissance Regiment), was replaced by **North-West Europe 1945**.

Another long-standing convention also changed in 1958, when French-speaking corps were permitted to emblazon battle honours in French, instead of English, and that all such honours henceforth were to be promulgated in French in the French Supplements to Canadian Army Orders; the necessary amendments to paragraphs 15 and 23 of Supplement Issue 56/508 were authorized by 58/611.

On 19 May 1958 all armoured regiments reverted to their pre-1939 titles, except where changes to such titles had been authorized, converted infantry units added the suffix '(RCAC)' and in September 6th Duke of Connaught's Royal Canadian Hussars and 17th Duke of York's Royal Canadian Hussars amalgamated to form The Royal Canadian Hussars (Montreal). During 1958–59 the militia infantry was increased by the return from the Royal Canadian Artillery of the Irish Fusiliers of Canada (The Vancouver Regiment), The Brockville Rifles, The Lanark and Renfrew Scottish Regiment and The Scots Fusiliers of Canada and by The Perth and Waterloo Regiment (Highland Light Infantry of Canada), formed 1954, reverting to The Perth Regiment and The Highland Light Infantry of Canada; additionally Le Regiment de Quebec was absorbed by Les Voltigeurs de Quebec (Motor).

The awards for the Korean Campaign, which authorized the emblazonment of two battle honours, were included in Supplement Issue 59/634. Full year-dates were again used for theatre honours.

In 1960 **Coriano, Misano Ridge, Casale, Naviglio Canal** and **Italy 1944–45** were extended to include The Lanark and Renfrew Scottish Regiment. In Italy in 1944 The Lanark and Renfrew Scottish Regiment CASF was formed by the conversion of 1st Light Anti-Aircraft Regiment, Royal Canadian Artillery; however, it reverted to the Royal Canadian Artillery on transfer to North-West Europe in 1945. The regiment remained with the Royal Canadian Artillery until 1 December 1959 when it returned to the militia infantry and a retrospective claim by the Regiment for the award of battle honours in its 'infantry role' was successful.

New Zealand

The second New Zealand Expeditionary Force was raised in September 1939 from volunteers, mainly from the embodied Territorial Force which, together with the small Permanent Force, had been mobilized on the outbreak of war. Units for 2nd New Zealand Division, identified by the use of the suffix 'NZEF' were found, as in The Great War, by each Territorial Force infantry regiment in the Military Districts providing one company for a Provincial Battalion, which was numbered. In addition, 27 (Machine Gun) Battalion NZEF and 1st Battalion, The New Zealand Scottish Regiment NZEF were raised. By the end of December 1939 advance elements of 2nd New Zealand Division were in Egypt, but much of the Division was diverted, while in transit, to England to defend the South-East coast against invasion.

In 1940, when 3rd New Zealand Division was mobilized as part of the second New Zealand Expeditionary Force the same grouping of Territorial Force infantry regiments had provided six battalions, with the balance of units being raised by the reintroduction of full-time military service by conscription within the Dominion and overseas. Despite being exempt from conscription, large numbers of Maoris had volunteered for overseas service and 28 (Maori) Battalion NZEF was raised and in 1941 1st Battalion, The Ruahine Regiment NZEF was reformed from 2nd Battalion, The Hawke's Bay Regiment. By November 1941 units of the Division were deployed to Fiji and several surrounding islands to counter the threat of Japanese invasion.

It was not until March 1941 that 2nd New Zealand Division was complete and up to strength in Egypt. The Division saw action in the ill-fated defence and withdrawal from Greece and Crete, during which it suffered heavy casualties, and in subsequent operations with the Eighth and First Armies throughout the remainder of the North African Campaign. In September 1942 it was decided that the Division should have its own supporting armour and 4th New Zealand Brigade was withdrawn to the Delta to become 4th New Zealand Armoured Brigade; the infantry battalions were converted and, while retaining their original numbers, were redesignated as armoured regiments of the recently formed New Zealand Armoured Corps. In November 1943 2nd New Zealand Division rejoined the Eighth Army in Italy, where it remained for the rest of the war.

Meanwhile in the South Pacific in July 1943 15th New Zealand Brigade was disbanded to reinforce the two remaining brigades of 3rd New Zealand Division, which were understrength and earmarked for operations in the Solomon Islands. By November 1944, following the success of these operations, the Division was disbanded.

The second New Zealand Expeditionary Force was disbanded in 1946 and its units demobilized: The New Zealand Scottish Regiment and The Ruahine Regiment were retained on the Territorial Force Establishment. The post-war reorganization began almost immediately and continued with a series of changes until 1953. In 1948 The Otago Regiment and The Southland Regiment amalgamated to form The Otago and Southland Regiment, and The Wellington West Coast Regiment and The Taranaki Regiment formed The Wellington West Coast and Taranaki Regiment. The Waikato Regiment and The Ruahine Regiment were disbanded. The New Zealand Scottish Regiment was transferred to the recently restyled Royal New Zealand Armoured Corps Establishment as 1st Divisional Regiment (New Zealand Scottish). Although disbanded two years earlier, The Waikato Regiment was amalgamated in 1950 with 1st Armoured Regiment, formed in 1944 from The

Auckland (East Coast) Mounted Rifles, The Waikato Mounted Rifles and The North Auckland Mounted Rifles, and retitled 1st Armoured Regiment (Waikato). The 2nd and 3rd Armoured Regiments had also been formed in 1944 from Queen Alexandra's (Wellington West Coast) Mounted Rifles, The Manawatu Mounted Rifles and The Wellington East Coast Mounted Rifles, and from The Canterbury Yeomanry Cavalry, The Otago Mounted Rifles and The Nelson-Marlborough Mounted Rifles, respectively. None of these armoured regiments served outside New Zealand.

In 1950, following the reintroduction of compulsory part-time training in the Territorial Force, the New Zealand Army Act replaced all earlier Acts and Regulations and the term 'New Zealand Army' was taken into use officially. Later that year 16th Field Regiment, Royal New Zealand Artillery, arguably one of the finest 'Gunner' regiments of its time, embarked for South Korea to join 27th Brigade.

The following year the reorganization continued with The North Auckland Regiment restyled The Northland Regiment, and in 1953 the Divisional Regiment, Royal New Zealand Armoured Corps was formed from the Wellington East Coast Squadron of 2nd Armoured Regiment. In 1956 there were further changes to the armoured establishment, with 2nd and 3rd Armoured Regiments placed in 'recess' or suspended animation, the Divisional Regiment retitled 4th Armoured Regiment and 1st Divisional Regiment (New Zealand Scottish) restyled 1st Armoured Car Regiment (New Zealand Scottish).

Following the publication of the Report of the Battles Nomenclature Committee in 1956, a New Zealand Battle Honours Committee was set up with four members and a secretary, all serving officers, under the chairmanship of Major-General Sir Howard Kippenberger, who, after his untimely death, was replaced by Brigadier M.C. Fairbrother. The task of this Committee was to compile 'lists of Battle Honours earned by armoured and infantry regiments in the Second World War, 1939–45'. The Committee's work was completed shortly after the publication of the Final Report of the Battle Nomenclature Committee in 1958. The lists compiled the battle and theatre honours earned by each second New Zealand Expeditionary Force unit by title, with Greece 1941 and Middle East 1941–44 preceding North Africa 1940–43 and Italy 1943–45 and ending with South Pacific 1942–44. The theatre honours used the shortened form, but the year-dates recorded the length of the campaign and did not relate to the time served by each unit in theatre. To perpetuate these battle honours the awards were 'allocated' to nominated Territorial Force mounted rifles and infantry corps, in a system considered so complex that it required an explanatory Inheritance Table to determine the link between the second New Zealand Expeditionary Force unit and the 'Designation of the Inheritor Regiment'.

In 1957 1st Battalion, New Zealand Regiment, raised earlier that year as a regular single-battalion corps, was sent to Malaya to replace the New Zealand Special Air Service Squadron, raised 1955, and 16th Field Regiment, Royal New Zealand Artillery returned from Korea.

On 15 May 1958 the award of Battle Honours for the Second World War to New Zealand armoured and infantry regiments was promulgated by New Zealand Army Order 22/58. The order set out the then 'Inheritor Regiments' of four armoured regiments, two of which were in recess, and one armoured car cegiment of the Royal New Zealand Armoured Corps and the nine infantry regiments of the Royal New Zealand Infantry Corps; it also included five disbanded, war-raised infantry units, including the Machine Gun Battalion NZEF. The layout of the list was further divided, where appropriate, into the Territorial Force regiments and corps which made up the current

'Inheritor Regiment' and it was to these latter regiments that the unit battle honours were allocated.

Although no mounted rifle regiment served overseas, the battle honours of 18 Armoured Regiment NZEF were allocated to The Auckland (East Coast) Mounted Rifles, to The Waikato Mounted Rifles and to The North Auckland Mounted Rifles of 1st Armoured Regiment (Waikato). Similarly, the honours of 19 Armoured Regiment NZEF and 3rd Division Tank Squadron NZEF were taken into use by Queen Alexandra's (Wellington West Coast) Mounted Rifles and by The Manawatu Mounted Rifles of 2nd Armoured Regiment NZAC and by The Wellington East Coast Mounted Rifles of 4th Armoured Regiment (Wellington East Coast). 20 Armoured Regiment NZEF honours were taken into use by The Canterbury Yeomanry Cavalry and by The Otago Mounted Rifles and by The Nelson-Marlborough Mounted Rifles of 3rd Armoured Division. The Divisional Cavalry NZEF and 1st Battalion, New Zealand Scottish Regiment NZEF battle honours were perpetuated by The New Zealand Scottish Regiment, recently designated 1st Armoured Car Regiment (New Zealand Scottish).

The Territorial Force infantry regiments which provided companies for second New Zealand Expeditionary Force units received the battle honours of these battalions: The Auckland Regiment (Countess of Ranfurly's Own), the Hauraki Regiment, The Northland Regiment and The Waikato Regiment were each allocated the combined honours of 18, 21, 24 and 29 Battalions NZEF; similarly, The Wellington Regiment (City of Wellington's Own), The Wellington West Coast Regiment, The Taranaki Regiment and The Hawke's Bay Regiment received the combined honours of 19, 22, 25 and 36 Battalions NZEF; and The Canterbury Regiment, The Otago Regiment, The Southland Regiment and The Nelson, Marlborough and West Coast Regiment received the combined honours of 20, 23, 26, 30 and 37 Battalions NZEF.

The battle honours of units disbanded between 1946 and 1948 were also included in the list, with The Ruahine Regiment taking into use the combined honours of 19, 22, 25 Battalions NZEF and 1st Battalion, The Ruahine Regiment. The battle honours of 27 (Machine Gun) Battalion NZEF, 28 (Maori) Battalion NZEF, 34 Battalion NZEF and 35 Battalion NZEF were recorded, but not perpetuated.

A maximum of ten battle honours were approved to be emblazoned on Regimental Colours or Guidons of the regiments concerned.

The compulsory part-time training in the Territorial Force, introduced in 1949, was ended in 1959; it was replaced in 1962 with selection by annual ballot of 3,000 young men for part-time training with the Territorial Force for three years.

South Africa

In response to the South African Government's appeal in September 1939 for volunteers to serve in defence of the Union and outside the Dominion within Africa, if required, one in three white South Africans of military age – and many well past it – answered the call. At the same time the Permanent Force and Active Citizen Force units were mobilized or embodied. By October 1940 three infantry divisions, manned by the Permanent Force and embodied Active Citizen Force units made up to War Establishment by the volunteers, and supported by divisional troops had been formed. Units of 1st South African Division, formed in Kenya, spearheaded the invasion of Italian Somaliland and the consequent pursuit that led to the successful reconquest of

Abyssinia. The Division next saw action in the Western Desert, where it was soon joined by 2nd South African Division; both of these suffered heavy casualties in the 1942 desert battles and further losses were recorded when units of 2nd South African Division, as part of the ill-fated Tobruk Garrison, were ordered to surrender on 21 June 1942. The 1st South African Division and the few remnants of 2nd South African Division remained with the Eighth Army until December 1942. The heavy casualties and lack of reinforcements caused these much depleted Divisions to be withdrawn to South Africa, later to be disbanded.

The 3rd South African Division remained in South Africa for home defence, garrison duties and to provide reinforcements for the active service divisions in the Middle East. On 4 April 1942 the Division was redesignated 3rd South African Armoured Division; one Brigade of this Division took part in the occupation of Madagascar before the Division was disbanded in October 1942.

In 1943 6th South African Armoured Division – no 4th nor 5th South African Divisions existed – was raised from new volunteers now required to serve overseas. These volunteers, many of whom had fought previously with 1st or 2nd South African Divisions, were to form composite regiments, such as the Imperial Light Horse/Kimberley Regiment, First City/Cape Town Highlanders, the Witwatersrand Rifles/Regiment de la Rey and the Natal Mounted Rifles/South African Air Force Regiment, or as reinforcements to 1 Special Service Battalion, The Royal Natal Carbineers, the Royal Durban Light Infantry, Prince Alfred's Guard and the Pretoria Regiment (Princess Alice's Own). After training in South Africa and Egypt, the Division landed in Italy in April 1944 and remained there until the end of the war.

By 1946 all units had returned to South Africa, war-raised units were officially disbanded, except for 2nd Battalion, Transvaal Scottish and 2 Regiment Botha, later Regiment Christiaan Beyers, which were retained and the Permanent Force and the Active Citizen Force returned to their pre-1939 establishments. In 1948 the South African Irish Regiment was converted to form a unit of the South African Artillery.

A South African Battle Honours Committee was appointed in May 1956 with a chairman, Colonel E.J. de Wet, and three members, all serving officers from the South African Staff Corps representing each of the three services, and a secretary; an adviser from the Union Histories Section of the Prime Minister's Office was in attendance. The task of this Committee was to consider the 'award of battle honours to units and ships of the Union Defence Forces which took part in the Second World War, 1939–45 and the Korean War, 1950–53'.

The conclusions of this Committee were published, in English and Afrikaans, on 1 November 1957 in Union Defence Forces Order 159/57. This Order, even at that time of increasing Afrikaner nationalism, is an extraordinary document, which dealt with the awards to all three services individually and listed the battle honours in three separate appendices. It also set out in further appendices the 'Nomenclature and Classifications of Operations' and 'Rules governing the Award of Battle Honours' upon which the awards had been determined. After this preamble the Order concluded with:

> 6. In the South African Army . . . honours shall be emblazoned on Regimental or Queen's Colours or both . . .

> 7. Rather than impose any numerical restriction on the number of battle honours to be displayed, units . . . are permitted to make their own unrestricted selection from their

entitlements, having regard to space available and the necessity to obviate drastic redesign and major readjustments to colours . . . as a result of possible future entitlements.

8. The Battle Honours to which units are entitled will be emblazoned, as appropriate, in the language medium of the unit concerned. In the case of bilingual units the language medium to be used for this purpose will be determined with due regard to the wishes of the majority of serving members.

From the introduction of battle honours to the British, Imperial and Commonwealth Armies until 1950, when India became a Republic, it had been the custom to submit the lists of awards for approval to the Crown or to some alternative, delegated authority, such as the Honourable East India Company or the Viceroy of India as the Governor General. In Union Defence Forces Order 159/57 there is no record of a submission to the Queen, nor indeed to any authority, requesting approval for these awards; it must be assumed, therefore, that the publication of these battle honours was without the required Royal consent and was sanctioned by the then South African Government.

Despite having been represented on the Battles Nomenclature Committee, the South African Battle Honours Committee concluded in the appendix dealing with 'Nomenclature and Classification of Operations' that 'Although the . . . War Office . . . lists have been used as a guide, certain changes have been made to them.' These 'certain changes' were, in fact, extensive and required **East Africa 1940–41** and **Western Desert 1941–43** to replace **Abyssinia 1940–41** and **North Africa 1941–43**, respectively. In addition **Mega, Combolcia, Sidi Rezegh, Bardia, Tobruk** and **Monte Stanco** were upgraded to the status of 'Battle' and the chronological limits changed, where necessary, to conform strictly with the actual participation of South African units. **Diredawa, Marsa Belafarit, Alem Hamza, Pt 204, Best Post, Acroma Keep, Alamein Defence, Alamein Box, Chiusi, Sarteano, La Foce, Florence, Monte Querciabella, The Greve, Monte Pezza, Sole/Caprara, Po Valley, Finale** and fourteen further battles, actions and engagements for which no awards were made appeared in the operations table, which were additional to those listed in the Report of the Battles Nomenclature Committee. These amendments were justified by the Committee as the

> definition of a Battle differs slightly from the British definition and consequently some operations have been included under the heading of Battle whereas the British classed them as Actions. This and the upgrading of certain Engagements to the status of Actions have been done as the result of information supplied by the Union War Histories Section and in order to emphasise the relative importance of certain operations as national achievements.

A comparison of the definitions in the Report of the Battles Nomenclature Committee and Order 159/57 shows them to be almost identical: no explanation of the high number of additional battles, actions and engagements included in the operational table was given. The appendix did, however, add that 'not all incidents, raids and skirmishes have been included.' It is difficult to understand why these differing views were not discussed and some agreement reached at the meetings of the Battles Nomenclature Committee in London.

The appendix on 'Rules governing the Award of Battle Honours' in the introduction states that it 'is of primary importance that battle honours should retain their value. The fact that in some cases the field of selection of honours to be awarded is very large makes it most desirable that the rules for their award should not only be strict but strictly applied.' Armoured and armoured car and infantry units only were to be eligible for battle honours and that qualification was based on such units having been actively engaged with enemy ground troops and taken a creditable part in the fighting, that the recently modified fifty per cent rule applied and that theatre honours would be awarded to units which had qualified for battle honours in that theatre or had served for one day in the theatre and have creditably performed an allotted task.

Appendix C to Order 159/57 listed the battle honours awarded for the Second World War to the twenty-one existing corps of the South African Army. Subsequent claims extended **The Greve** to include The Royal Natal Carbineers, First City, The Queen's Own Cape Town Highlanders, Witswatersrand Rifles, Regiment de la Rey, Natal Mounted Rifles and Prince Alfred's Guard, and **Mega** was extended to the Transvaal Scottish. In 1961 the latter regiment was also permitted to substitute **Sollum** for **Bardia** as it was considered to be a more representative of the action fought by 2nd Battalion, Transvaal Scottish on 11 and 12 January 1942. In 1960 the South African Irish Regiment returned to the infantry establishment thereby becoming 'entitled to their original honours' on transfer. The last recorded awards for the Second World War were made when the newly raised Regiment Vrystaat took into use the battle honours of the disbanded 4th Armoured Car Regiment and the Regiment Grootkaroo took into use the distinctions of Die Middellandse Regiment on change of title.

The Defence Act of 1957 replaced outdated legislation, changed the title of the Union Defence Forces to the South African Defence Force and introduced new uniforms and rank insignia. A new system of honours and awards replaced the British decorations previously awarded.

On 31 May 1961 South Africa declared itself a Republic and left the Commonwealth.

Battle Honours and Honorary Distinctions

The complete lists of battle honours and honorary distinctions for the Second World War are shown in Tables 4 and 5, respectively; battle honours for the Korean Campaign are shown in Table 6.

Table 4

BATTLE HONOURS FOR THE SECOND WORLD WAR

1.	**VIST** 21st–22nd April 1940 Operations based on Namsos	1957	The Royal Lincolnshire Regiment
2.	**KVAM** 25th–26th April 1940 Operations based on Andalsnes	1957	The King's Own Yorkshire Light Infantry
3.	**OTTA** 28th April 1940 Operations based on Andalsnes	1957	The Green Howards (Alexandra, Princess of Wales's Own Yorkshire Regiment)
4.	**STIEN** 17th–18th May 1940 Operations leading to the Capture of Narvik	1957	Scots Guards
5.	**POTHUS** 25th–26th May 1940 Operations leading to the Capture of Narvik	1956	Irish Guards
6.	**VAAGSO** 27th December 1941 Raid on Fish-oil Factories and Shipping	1957	The Commando Association
7.	**NORWAY 1940** 21st April–31st December 1940 Service in Norway 1940–41	1956 1957 1958	Irish Guards; The Royal Leicestershire Regiment; The York and Lancaster Regiment The Green Howards (Alexandra, Princess of Wales's Own Yorkshire Regiment); The Sherwood Foresters (Nottinghamshire and Derbyshire Regiment); The King's Own Yorkshire Light Infantry; Scots Guards; The Royal Lincolnshire Regiment The South Wales Borderers
8.	**NORWAY 1941** 1st January–27th December 1941 Service in Norway 1940–41	1957	The Commando Association
9.	**DYLE** 10th–16th May 1940 Withdrawal to Dunkirk	1956 1957 1958	4th/7th Royal Dragoon Guards 13th/18th Royal Hussars (Queen Mary's Own); Grenadier Guards; The Cheshire Regiment; The Royal Welch Fusiliers; 12th Royal Lancers (Prince of Wales's); The Royal Ulster Rifles; Coldstream Guards; The Royal Berkshire Regiment (Princess Charlotte of Wales's); The Middlesex Regiment (Duke of Cambridge's Own); The Durham Light Infantry; The Manchester Regiment; The North Staffordshire Regiment (The Prince of Wales's) The Royal Scots (The Royal Regiment)

10. **WITHDRAWAL TO ESCAUT**
17th–19th May 1940
Withdrawal to Dunkirk

1956 15th/19th The King's Royal Hussars
1957 13th/18th Royal Hussars (Queen Mary's Own); The East Riding Yeomanry, Royal Armoured Corps (TA); 5th Royal Inniskilling Dragoon Guards; The Cheshire Regiment; The Gordon Highlanders; The East Yorkshire Regiment (The Duke of York's Own); The Manchester Regiment
1958 The Royal Irish Fusiliers (Princess Victoria's)

11. **DEFENCE OF ESCAUT**
19th–22nd May 1940
Withdrawal to Dunkirk

1956 The Duke of Cornwall's Light Infantry; The Buffs (Royal East Kent Regiment); The Royal Sussex Regiment
1957 The Royal Warwickshire Regiment; The Gloucestershire Regiment; The East Lancashire Regiment; The Lancashire Fusiliers; The Royal Welch Fusiliers; The Oxfordshire and Buckinghamshire Light Infantry; The Queen's Royal Regiment (West Surrey); The Queen's Own Royal West Kent Regiment; The Border Regiment; The Northamptonshire Regiment; The King's Shropshire Light Infantry; The Queen's Own Cameron Highlanders; The East Surrey Regiment; Coldstream Guards; The Royal Norfolk Regiment; The Middlesex Regiment (Duke of Cambridge's Own); The East Yorkshire Regiment (The Duke of York's Own); The Manchester Regiment; The Worcestershire Regiment; The North Staffordshire Regiment (The Prince of Wales's)
1958 The Royal Scots (The Royal Regiment); The Royal Northumberland Fusiliers

12. **AMIENS 1940**
20th May 1940
Withdrawal to Dunkirk

1956 The Royal Sussex Regiment

13. **DEFENCE OF ARRAS**
19th–24th May 1940
Withdrawal to Dunkirk

1956 The Wiltshire Regiment (Duke of Edinburgh's)
1957 12th Royal Lancers (Prince of Wales's); The Green Howards (Alexandra, Princess of Wales's Own Yorkshire Regiment); The Royal Inniskilling Fusiliers; The Northamptonshire Regiment; Welsh Guards; The Black Watch (Royal Highland Regiment); The East Yorkshire Regiment (The Duke of York's Own); The Manchester Regiment
1958 The Royal Scots Fusiliers

14. **ARRAS COUNTER ATTACK**
21st May 1940
Withdrawal to Dunkirk

1957 12th Royal Lancers (Prince of Wales's); The Durham Light Infantry
1958 Royal Tank Regiment; The Royal Northumberland Fusiliers

15. **BOULOGNE 1940**
22nd–25th May 1940
Withdrawal to Dunkirk

1956 Irish Guards
1957 Welsh Guards

16. **CALAIS 1940**
22nd–26th May 1940
Withdrawal to Dunkirk

1957 The Rifle Brigade (Prince Consort's Own); The King's Royal Rifle Corps: Queen Victoria's Rifles, The King's Royal Rifle Corps (TA)
1958 Royal Tank Regiment

17. **FRENCH FRONTIER 1940**
23rd–27th May 1940
Withdrawal to Dunkirk

1957 The East Yorkshire Regiment (The Duke of York's Own)

18. **ST OMER-LA BASSEE**
23rd–29th May 1940
Withdrawal to Dunkirk

1956 The Buffs (Royal East Kent Regiment); The Royal Sussex Regiment
1957 The East Riding Yeomanry, Royal Armoured Corps (TA); The Gloucestershire Regiment; 5th Royal Inniskilling Dragoon Guards; The Lancashire Fusiliers; The Cheshire Regiment; The Royal Welch Fusiliers; The Dorset Regiment; The Sherwood Foresters (Nottinghamshire and Derbyshire Regiment); The Queen's Own Cameron Highlanders; The King's Own Royal Regiment

19. **WORMHOUDT**
28th May 1940
Withdrawal to Dunkirk

1958 — (Lancaster): The Royal Norfolk Regiment: The Royal Berkshire Regiment (Princess Charlotte of Wales's): Welsh Guards: The Essex Regiment: The Durham Light Infantry: The Manchester Regiment: The Worcestershire Regiment

Royal Tank Regiment: The Royal Irish Fusiliers (Princess Victoria's): The Royal Scots (The Royal Regiment): The Royal Northumberland Fusiliers

20. **CASSEL**
27th–29th May 1940
Withdrawal to Dunkirk

1957 — The Royal Warwickshire Regiment: The Gloucestershire Regiment: The Cheshire Regiment: The Worcestershire Regiment

1957 — The East Riding Yeomanry, Royal Armoured Corps (TA): The Gloucestershire Regiment: The Cheshire Regiment: The Oxfordshire and Buckinghamshire Light Infantry

21. **FORET DE NIEPPE**
27th–28th May 1940
Withdrawal to Dunkirk

1956 — The Royal Sussex Regiment
1957 — The Queen's Own Royal West Kent Regiment

22. **YPRES-COMINES CANAL**
26th–28th May 1940
Withdrawal to Dunkirk

1956 — The Wiltshire Regiment (Duke of Edinburgh's): The Cameronians (Scottish Rifles)
1957 — 13th/18th Royal Hussars (Queen Mary's Own): The Royal Warwickshire Regiment: The Oxfordshire and Buckinghamshire Light Infantry: Seaforth Highlanders (Ross-shire Buffs, The Duke of Albany's): The Gordon Highlanders: The Sherwood Foresters (Nottinghamshire and Derbyshire Regiment): The Royal Inniskilling Fusiliers: The Northamptonshire Regiment: The Black Watch (Royal Highland Regiment): The Middlesex Regiment (Duke of Cambridge's Own): The East Yorkshire Regiment (The Duke of York's Own): The Manchester Regiment: The North Staffordshire Regiment (The Prince of Wales's)

1958 — The Royal Scots Fusiliers

23. **DUNKIRK 1940**
26th May–3rd June 1940
Withdrawal to Dunkirk

1956 — The Duke of Wellington's Regiment (West Riding): The Fife and Forfar Yeomanry, Royal Armoured Corps (TA): 4th/7th Royal Dragoon Guards: The Royal Fusiliers (City of London Regiment): The East Lancashire Regiment: 5th Royal Inniskilling Dragoon Guards: Grenadier Guards: The Cheshire Regiment: The Gordon Highlanders: 12th Royal Lancers (Prince of Wales's): The Bedfordshire and Hertfordshire Regiment: The Green Howards (Alexandra, Princess of Wales's Own Yorkshire Regiment): The King's Own Scottish Borderers: The Sherwood Foresters (Nottinghamshire and Derbyshire Regiment): The Border Regiment: The Loyal Regiment (North Lancashire): The King's Shropshire Light Infantry: The King's Own Royal Regiment (Lancaster): The Suffolk Regiment: The East Surrey Regiment: The Royal Hampshire Regiment: The South Lancashire Regiment (The Prince of Wales's Volunteers): The Royal Ulster Rifles: Coldstream Guards: The Royal Lincolnshire Regiment: The Royal Berkshire Regiment (Princess Charlotte of Wales's): The Black Watch (Royal Highland Regiment): The Middlesex Regiment (Duke of Cambridge's Own): The Durham Light Infantry: The East Yorkshire Regiment (The Duke of York's Own)

1958 — The Royal Northumberland Fusiliers

24. **SOMME 1940**
24th May–5th June 1940
Fighting South of the Somme

1956 — 9th Queen's Royal Lancers
1957 — The Queen's Bays (2nd Dragoon Guards): Seaforth Highlanders (Ross-shire Buffs, The Duke of Albany's): The Gordon Highlanders: The Argyll and Sutherland Highlanders (Princess Louise's): 10th Royal Hussars (Prince of Wales's): The Border Regiment: The Queen's Own Cameron Highlanders: 1st/2nd Lothians and Border Horse, Royal Armoured Corps (TA): The Black Watch (Royal Highland Regiment)

1958 — Royal Tank Regiment: The Royal Scots Fusiliers

Battle Honours for the Second World War

25.	**WITHDRAWAL TO SEINE** 6th–10th June 1940 Fighting South of the Somme	1956 1957 1958	9th Queen's Royal Lancers; The Buffs (Royal East Kent Regiment) The Queen's Bays (2nd Dragoon Guards); Seaforth Highlanders (Ross-shire Buffs, The Duke of Albany's); 1st/2nd Lothians and Border Horse, Royal Armoured Corps (TA) The Royal Scots Fusiliers
26.	**WITHDRAWAL TO CHERBOURG** 9th–18th June 1940 Fighting South of the Somme	1957	The Highland Light Infantry (City of Glasgow Regiment)
27.	**ST VALERY-EN-CAUX** 10th–12th June 1940 Fighting South of the Somme	1956 1957	The Duke of Wellington's Regiment (West Riding); Princess Louise's Kensington Regiment (TA) Seaforth Highlanders (Ross-shire Buffs, The Duke of Albany's); The Gordon Highlanders; The Queen's Own Cameron Highlanders; The Royal Norfolk Regiment: 1st/2nd Lothians and Border Horse, Royal Armoured Corps (TA); The Black Watch (Royal Highland Regiment)
28.	**SAAR** 13th May 1940 Position Warfare in the Saar Region	1956 1957	Princess Louise's Kensington Regiment (TA) The Black Watch (Royal Highland Regiment)
29.	**BRUNEVAL** 27th–28th February 1942 Raiding Operations	1956	The Parachute Regiment
30.	**ST NAZAIRE** 27th–28th March 1942 Raiding Operations	1957	The Commando Association
31.	**DIEPPE** 19th August 1942 Raiding Operations	1957 1957 1959	The Commando Association The Essex and Kent Scottish; The Royal Hamilton Light Infantry (Wentworth Regiment); Les Fusiliers Mont-Royal; The Toronto Scottish Regiment; The Queen's Own Cameron Highlanders of Canada (Motor); The Royal Regiment of Canada: The South Saskatchewan Regiment The King's Own Calgary Regiment (RCAC)
32.	**NORMANDY LANDING** ' 6th June 1944 The Assault	1956 1957 1957	Westminster Dragoons (2nd County of London Yeomanry), Royal Armoured Corps (TA); 4th/7th Royal Dragoon Guards; The Devonshire Regiment; The Parachute Regiment 13th/18th Royal Hussars (Queen Mary's Own); The East Riding Yeomanry, Royal Armoured Corps (TA); The Inns of Court Regiment, Royal Armoured Corps (TA); The Royal Warwickshire Regiment; The King's Regiment (Liverpool); The Glider Pilot Regiment; The Cheshire Regiment; The Oxfordshire and Buckinghamshire Light Infantry; The Staffordshire Yeomanry (Queen's Own Royal Regiment), Royal Armoured Corps (TA); The Green Howards (Alexandra, Princess of Wales's Own Yorkshire Regiment); The Dorset Regiment: The Hertfordshire Regiment (TA); The King's Shropshire Light Infantry; The Sherwood Rangers Yeomanry, Royal Armoured Corps (TA); The Suffolk Regiment; The Royal Hampshire Regiment; The South Lancashire Regiment (The Prince of Wales's Volunteers); The Royal Ulster Rifles; 22nd Dragoons; The Royal Norfolk Regiment; The Royal Lincolnshire Regiment; The Royal Berkshire Regiment (Princess Charlotte of Wales's); The Middlesex Regiment (Duke of Cambridge's Own); The East Yorkshire Regiment (The Duke of York's Own); The Commando Association Les Fusiliers de Sherbrooke; The Queen's Own Rifles of Canada: Le Regiment de la Chaudiere: 1st Hussars (6th Armoured Regiment); The Highland Light Infantry of Canada: The Royal Winnipeg Rifles: The Regina Rifle Regiment: The Cameron

Highlanders of Ottawa (MG); Fort Garry Horse (10th Armoured Regiment); The Stormont, Dundas and Glengarry Highlanders (MG): 1st Battalion, The Royal New Brunswick Regiment (Carleton and York); 2nd Battalion, The Royal New Brunswick Regiment (North Shore)

1958 The South Wales Borderers

1958 The First Canadian Parachute Battalion; The Sherbrooke Regiment (RCAC); 1st Battalion, The Nova Scotia Highlanders (North); 2nd Battalion, The Nova Scotia Highlanders (Cape Breton)

1959 The Canadian Scottish Regiment (Princess Mary's)

¹ DEBARQUEMENT EN NORMANDIE taken into use by French-speaking Canadian units 1958.

33. **PEGASUS BRIDGE**
6th June 1944
The Assault
1956 The Parachute Regiment
1957 The Glider Pilot Regiment; The Oxfordshire and Buckinghamshire Light Infantry

34. **MERVILLE BATTERY**
6th June 1944
The Assault
1956 The Parachute Regiment
1957 The Glider Pilot Regiment

35. **PORT EN BESSIN**
7th–8th June 1944
The Expansion of the Bridgehead
1956 The Devonshire Regiment

36. **AUTHIE**
7th June 1944
The Expansion of the Bridgehead
1957 Les Fusiliers de Sherbrooke
1958 The Sherbrooke Regiment (RCAC); 1st Battalion, The Nova Scotia Highlanders (North); 2nd Battalion, The Nova Scotia Highlanders (Cape Breton)

37. **SULLY**
8th–9th June 1944
The Expansion of the Bridgehead
1958 The South Wales Borderers

38. **CAMBES**
9th June 1944
The Expansion of the Bridgehead
1957 The East Riding Yeomanry, Royal Armoured Corps (TA); The King's Own Scottish Borderers; The Royal Ulster Rifles; The Royal Lincolnshire Regiment; The Middlesex Regiment (Duke of Cambridge's Own)

39. **PUTOT EN BESSIN**
8th June 1944
The Expansion of the Bridgehead
1956 24th Lancers
1957 1st Hussars (6th Armoured Regiment); The Royal Winnipeg Rifles
1959 The Canadian Scottish Regiment (Princess Mary's)

40. **BRETTEVILLE-L'ORGUEILLEUSE**
8th–9th June 1944
The Expansion of the Bridgehead
1957 The Regina Rifle Regiment

41. **LE MESNIL-PATRY**
11th June 1944
The Expansion of the Bridgehead
1957 The Queen's Own Rifles of Canada; 1st Hussars (6th Armoured Regiment)

42.	**BREVILLE** 10th–13th June 1944 The Expansion of the Bridgehead	1956 1957	The Parachute Regiment 13th/18th Royal Hussars (Queen Mary's Own):The Black Watch (Royal Highland Regiment):The Middlesex Regiment (Duke of Cambridge's Own)
43.	**VILLERS BOCAGE** 8th–15th June 1944 The Expansion of the Bridgehead	1956 1957	Westminster Dragoons (2nd County of London Yeomanry), Royal Armoured Corps (TA): 24th Lancers 3rd/4th County of London Yeomanry (Sharpshooters), Royal Armoured Corps (TA): The Gloucestershire Regiment: The Queen's Royal Regiment (West Surrey):The Dorset Regiment: 8th King's Royal Irish Hussars:The Sherwood Rangers Yeomanry, Royal Armoured Corps (TA): 11th Hussars (Prince Albert's Own): The Rifle Brigade (Prince Consort's Own): The Durham Light Infantry
44.	**TILLY SUR SEULLES** 14th–19th June 1944 The Expansion of the Bridgehead	1956 1957	The Duke of Wellington's Regiment (West Riding): Princess Louise's Kensington Regiment (TA): 24th Lancers:The Devonshire Regiment The Green Howards (Alexandra, Princess of Wales's Own Yorkshire Regiment):The Dorset Regiment:The Royal Hampshire Regiment:The Essex Regiment:The Durham Light Infantry:The East Yorkshire Regiment (The Duke of York's Own)
45.	**ODON** 25th June–2nd July 1944 The Odon Bridgehead	1956 1957	The Duke of Wellington's Regiment (West Riding): The Wiltshire Regiment (Duke of Edinburgh's): The York and Lancaster Regiment: Princess Louise's Kensington Regiment (TA): 4th/7th Royal Dragoon Guards: 24th Lancers: The Cameronians (Scottish Rifles) 3rd/4th County of London Yeomanry (Sharpshooters), Royal Armoured Corps (TA): The Northamptonshire Yeomanry, Royal Armoured Corps (TA): Seaforth Highlanders (Ross-shire Buffs, The Duke of Albany's): The Gordon Highlanders: The Argyll and Sutherland Highlanders (Princess Louise's): 23rd Hussars: The Somerset Light Infantry (Prince Albert's): The King's Own Scottish Borderers: The King's Shropshire Light Infantry: The Herefordshire Light Infantry (TA): The Sherwood Rangers Yeomanry, Royal Armoured Corps (TA): The Suffolk Regiment: The South Lancashire Regiment (The Prince of Wales's Volunteers): 22nd Dragoons: The Highland Light Infantry (City of Glasgow Regiment): The Rifle Brigade (Prince Consort's Own):The Black Watch (Royal Highland Regiment):The Middlesex Regiment (Duke of Cambridge's Own):The East Yorkshire Regiment (The Duke of York's Own): London Rifle Brigade, The Rifle Brigade (Prince Consort's Own) (TA):The Monmouthshire Regiment (TA): The Worcestershire Regiment
		1958	Royal Tank Regiment:The Royal Scots (The Royal Regiment):The Royal Northumberland Fusiliers:The Royal Scots Fusiliers
46.	**FONTENAY LE PESNIL** 25th–27th June 1944 The Odon Bridgehead	1956 1957 1958	The Duke of Wellington's Regiment (West Riding):The York and Lancaster Regiment: 24th Lancers The King's Own Yorkshire Light Infantry:The Sherwood Rangers Yeomanry, Royal Armoured Corps (TA):The Royal Lincoln- shire Regiment:The Black Watch (Royal Highland Regiment) The Royal Scots Fusiliers
47.	**CHEUX** 26th–27th June 1944 The Odon Bridgehead	1956 1957 1958	The Fife and Forfar Yeomanry, Royal Armoured Corps (TA):The Duke of Cornwall's Light Infantry:The Cameronians (Scottish Rifles) The Northamptonshire Yeomanry, Royal Armoured Corps (TA): Seaforth Highlanders (Ross-shire Buffs, The Duke of Albany's): The King's Own Scottish Borderers:The Highland Light Infantry (City of Glasgow Regiment) The Royal Scots (The Royal Regiment):The Royal Scots Fusiliers
48.	**TOURMAUVILLE BRIDGE** 27th June 1944 The Odon Bridgehead	1957	The Argyll and Sutherland Highlanders (Princess Louise's)

49.	**DEFENCE OF RAURAY** 29th June–2nd July 1944 The Odon Bridgehead	
	1956	24th Lancers
	1957	3rd/4th County of London Yeomanry (Sharpshooters), Royal Armoured Corps (TA): The Northamptonshire Yeomanry, Royal Armoured Corps (TA): The King's Own Scottish Borderers: The Herefordshire Light Infantry (TA): The Sherwood Rangers Yeomanry, Royal Armoured Corps (TA): The Royal Lincolnshire Regiment: The Black Watch (Royal Highland Regiment): The Durham Light Infantry
	1958	The Royal Scots (The Royal Regiment): The Royal Scots Fusiliers
50.	**CAEN** 4th–18th July 1944 The Capture of Caen	
	1956	The Royal Scots Greys (2nd Dragoons): The Wiltshire Regiment (Duke of Edinburgh's): The York and Lancaster Regiment: The Devonshire Regiment: The Cameronians (Scottish Rifles)
	1957	13th/18th Royal Hussars (Queen Mary's Own): 3rd/4th County of London Yeomanry (Sharpshooters), Royal Armoured Corps (TA): The East Riding Yeomanry, Royal Armoured Corps (TA): The Inns of Court Regiment, Royal Armoured Corps (TA): The Royal Warwickshire Regiment: The East Lancashire Regiment: The Northamptonshire Yeomanry, Royal Armoured Corps (TA): Seaforth Highlanders The Lancashire Fusiliers: The Royal Welch Fusiliers: The Oxfordshire and Buckinghamshire Light Infantry: Seaforth Highlanders (Ross-shire Buffs, The Duke of Albany's): The Argyll and Sutherland Highlanders (Princess Louise's): The Staffordshire Yeomanry (Queen's Own Royal Regiment), Royal Armoured Corps (TA): The Somerset Light Infantry (Prince Albert's): The King's Own Scottish Borderers: The Dorset Regiment: The King's Own Royal Regiment: The King's Shropshire Light Infantry: The Royal Hampshire Regiment: The Royal Ulster Rifles: 22nd Dragoons: The Royal Norfolk Regiment: The Royal Lincolnshire Regiment: The Black Watch (Royal Highland Regiment): The Middlesex Regiment (Duke of Cambridge's Own): The East Yorkshire Regiment (The Duke of York's Own): The Manchester Regiment: The North Staffordshire Regiment (The Prince of Wales's)
	1957	14th Canadian Hussars (8th Armoured Regiment): Les Fusiliers de Sherbrooke: The Queen's Own Rifles of Canada: Le Regiment de la Chaudiere: 1st Hussars (6th Armoured Regiment): The Highland Light Infantry of Canada: The Royal Winnipeg Rifles: The Regina Rifle Regiment: The Cameron Highlanders of Ottawa (MG): Fort Garry Horse (10th Armoured Regiment): The Stormont, Dundas and Glengarry Highlanders (MG): 1st Battalion, The Royal New Brunswick Regiment (Carleton and York): 2nd Battalion, The Royal New Brunswick Regiment (North Shore)
	1958	Royal Tank Regiment: The South Wales Borderers: The South Staffordshire Regiment: The Royal Scots (The Royal Regiment): The Royal Northumberland Fusiliers
	1958	17th Duke of York's Royal Canadian Hussars (7th Reconnaissance Regiment): The Sherbrooke Regiment (RCAC): 1st Battalion, The Nova Scotia Highlanders (North): 2nd Battalion, The Nova Scotia Highlanders (Cape Breton)
	1959	The Canadian Scottish Regiment (Princess Mary's)
51.	**CARPIQUET** 4th–5th July 1944 The Capture of Caen	
	1957	The Queen's Own Rifles of Canada: Le Regiment de la Chaudiere: The Royal Winnipeg Rifles: The Cameron Highlanders of Ottawa (MG): Fort Garry Horse (10th Armoured Regiment): 1st Battalion, The Royal New Brunswick Regiment (Carleton and York): 2nd Battalion, The Royal New Brunswick Regiment (North Shore)
52.	**ORNE** 8th–9th July 1944 The Capture of Caen	
	1957	The Royal Lincolnshire Regiment: The Middlesex Regiment (Duke of Cambridge's Own): The North Staffordshire Regiment (The Prince of Wales's)
53.	**THE ORNE** [1] 8th–9th July 1944 The Capture of Caen	
	1957	Les Fusiliers de Sherbrooke: 1st Hussars (6th Armoured Regiment): The Royal Winnipeg Rifles: The Regina Rifle Regiment: The Cameron Highlanders of Ottawa (MG)
	1958	The Sherbrooke Regiment (RCAC): 1st Battalion, The Nova Scotia Highlanders, The Nova Scotia Highlanders (North): 2nd Battalion, The Nova Scotia Highlanders (Cape Breton)
	1959	The Canadian Scottish Regiment (Princess Mary's)

[1] 'L'ORNE taken into use by French-speaking Canadian units 1958.

54.	**THE ORNE (BURON)** 8th–9th July 1944 The Capture of Caen	1957	The Highland Light Infantry of Canada: The Stormont, Dundas and Glengarry Highlanders (MG) 'L'ORNE (BURON) taken into use by French-speaking Canadian units 1958.
55.	**HILL 112** 10th–11th July 1944 The Capture of Caen	1956 1957	The Royal Scots Greys (2nd Dragoons): The Duke of Cornwall's Light Infantry: The Wiltshire Regiment (Duke of Edinburgh's) The Somerset Light Infantry (Prince Albert's): The Royal Hampshire Regiment: The Middlesex Regiment (Duke of Cambridge's Own)
56.	**ESQUAY** 15th–17th July 1944 The Capture of Caen	1957 1958	The Royal Welch Fusiliers: The Oxfordshire and Buckinghamshire Light Infantry: The Argyll and Sutherland Highlanders (Princess Louise's): The King's Own Scottish Borderers: The Highland Light Infantry (City of Glasgow Regiment): The Manchester Regiment The Royal Scots (The Royal Regiment)
57.	**NOYERS** 15th–18th July 1944 The Capture of Caen	1957 1958	The Northamptonshire Yeomanry, Royal Armoured Corps (TA): The North Staffordshire Regiment (The Prince of Wales's) The South Staffordshire Regiment
58.	**BOURGUEBUS RIDGE** 18th–23rd July 1944 The Capture of Caen	1956 1957 1957 1958 1958	The Fife and Forfar Yeomanry, Royal Armoured Corps (TA): The Wiltshire Regiment (Duke of Edinburgh's) 13th/18th Royal Hussars (Queen Mary's Own): 3rd/4th County of London Yeomanry (Sharpshooters), Royal Armoured Corps (TA): The East Riding Yeomanry, Royal Armoured Corps (TA): The Inns of Court Regiment, Royal Armoured Corps (TA): Honourable Artillery Company (TA): The Royal Warwickshire Regiment: The Northamptonshire Yeomanry, Royal Armoured Corps (TA): 23rd Hussars: The King's Shropshire Light Infantry: The Herefordshire Light Infantry (TA): The South Lancashire Regiment (The Prince of Wales's Volunteers): 11th Hussars (Prince Albert's): The Royal Lincolnshire Regiment: The Rifle Brigade (Prince Consort's Own): Welsh Guards: The Middlesex Regiment (Duke of Cambridge's Own): The East Yorkshire Regiment (The Duke of York's Own): London Rifle Brigade, The Rifle Brigade (Prince Consort's Own) (TA): The Monmouthshire Regiment (TA): The Worcestershire Regiment The Essex and Kent Scottish: Les Fusiliers de Sherbrooke: The Queen's Own Rifles of Canada: Le Regiment de la Chaudiere: Les Fusiliers Mont-Roial: 1st Hussars (6th Armoured Regiment): The Toronto Scottish Regiment: The Highland Light Infantry of Canada: The Royal Winnipeg Rifles: The Black Watch (Royal Highland Regiment) of Canada: The Regina Rifle Regiment: The Queen's Own Cameron Highlanders of Canada (Motor): The Royal Regiment of Canada: The Cameron Highlanders of Ottawa (MG): The Calgary Highlanders: The South Saskatchewan Regiment: The Stormont, Dundas and Glengarry Highlanders (MG): 1st Battalion, The Royal New Brunswick Regiment (Carleton and York): 2nd Battalion, The Royal New Brunswick Regiment (North Shore): Le Regiment de Maisonneuve Royal Tank Regiment The Sherbrooke Regiment (RCAC): 1st Battalion, The Nova Scotia Highlanders (North): 2nd Battalion, The Nova Scotia Highlanders (Cape Breton) 'CRETE DE BOURGUEBUS taken into use by French-speaking Canadian units 1958.
59.	**CAGNY** 18th–19th July 1944 The Capture of Caen	1956 1957 1958	Irish Guards The Inns of Court Regiment, Royal Armoured Corps (TA): Grenadier Guards: The Herefordshire Light Infantry (TA): Coldstream Guards: Welsh Guards The Royal Northumberland Fusiliers

60.	**TROARN** 18th–21st July 1944 The Capture of Caen	1957	Seaforth Highlanders (Ross-shire Buffs, The Duke of Albany's): The Staffordshire Yeomanry (Queen's Own Royal Regiment), Royal Armoured Corps (TA): The King's Own Scottish Borderers: The South Lancashire Regiment (The Prince of Wales's Volunteers): The Royal Ulster Rifles: The Royal Lincolnshire Regiment: The Middlesex Regiment (Duke of Cambridge's Own): The East Yorkshire Regiment (The Duke of York's Own)
61.	**FAUBOURG DE VAUCELLES** 18th–19th July 1944 The Capture of Caen	1957	Les Fusiliers de Sherbrooke: The Queen's Own Rifles of Canada: Le Regiment de la Chaudiere: 1st Hussars (6th Armoured Regiment): The Highland Light Infantry of Canada: The Black Watch (Royal Highland Regiment) of Canada: The Regina Rifle Regiment: The Royal Regiment of Canada: The Cameron Highlanders of Ottawa (MG): The Calgary Highlanders: The Stormont, Dundas and Glengarry Highlanders (MG): 1st Battalion, The Royal New Brunswick Regiment (Carleton and York): 2nd Battalion, The Royal New Brunswick Regiment (North Shore): Le Regiment de Maisonneuve
		1958	The Sherbrooke Regiment (RCAC): 1st Battalion, The Nova Scotia Highlanders (North): 2nd Battalion, The Nova Scotia Highlanders (Cape Breton)
62.	**ST ANDRE-SUR-ORNE** [1] 19th–23rd July 1944 The Capture of Caen	1957	The Essex and Kent Scottish: Les Fusiliers de Sherbrooke: Les Fusiliers Mont-Royal: The Toronto Scottish Regiment: The Queen's Own Cameron Highlanders of Canada (Motor): The South Saskatchewan Regiment
		1958	The Sherbrooke Regiment (RCAC) [1] *SAINT-ANDRE-SUR-ORNE taken into use by French-speaking Canadian units 1958.*
63.	**MALTOT** 22nd–23rd July 1944 The Capture of Caen	1956 1957 1957	The Wiltshire Regiment (Duke of Edinburgh's) The Worcestershire Regiment Le Regiment de Maisonneuve
64.	**VERRIERES RIDGE – TILLY-LA-CAMPAGNE** [1] 25th July 1944 The Holding Attack	1957	The Royal Hamilton Light Infantry (Wentworth Regiment): Les Fusiliers Mont-Royal: 1st Hussars (6th Armoured Regiment): The Toronto Scottish Regiment: The Black Watch (Royal Highland Regiment) of Canada: The Queen's Own Cameron Highlanders of Canada (Motor): The Royal Regiment of Canada: The Calgary Highlanders: Le Regiment de Maisonneuve
		1958	1st Battalion, The Nova Scotia Highlanders (North): 2nd Battalion, The Nova Scotia Highlanders (Cape Breton) [1] *CRETE DE VERRIERES – TILLY-LA-CAMPAGNE taken into use by French-speaking Canadian units 1958.*
65.	**MONT PINCON** 30th July–9th August 1944 The Capture of Mont Pincon	1956	The Life Guards: Royal Horse Guards: Irish Guards: The Duke of Cornwall's Light Infantry: The Wiltshire Regiment (Duke of Edinburgh's): 4th/7th Royal Dragoon Guards: The Cameronians (Scottish Rifles)
		1957	13th/18th Royal Hussars (Queen Mary's Own): The Royal Warwickshire Regiment: The Gloucestershire Regiment: 5th Royal Inniskilling Dragoon Guards: The Northamptonshire Yeomanry, Royal Armoured Corps (TA): Grenadier Guards: The Cheshire Regiment: Seaforth Highlanders (Ross-shire Buffs, The Duke of Albany's): The Argyll and Sutherland Highlanders (Princess Louise's): The Queen's Royal Regiment (West Surrey): The Somerset Light Infantry (Prince Albert's): The King's Own Scottish Borderers: The Dorset Regiment: 8th King's Royal Irish Hussars: The King's Shropshire Light Infantry: The Herefordshire Light Infantry (TA): The Sherwood Rangers Yeomanry, Royal Armoured Corps (TA): Scots Guards: The Royal Hampshire Regiment: 11th Hussars (Prince Albert's Own): Coldstream Guards: The Highland Light Infantry (City of Glasgow Regiment): The Rifle Brigade (Prince Consort's Own): Welsh Guards: The Middlesex Regiment (Duke of Cambridge's Own): The East Yorkshire Regiment (The Duke of York's Own): London Rifle Brigade, The Rifle Brigade (Prince Consort's Own) (TA): The Monmouthshire Regiment (TA): The Worcestershire Regiment: The King's Royal Rifle Corps: The Queen's Westminsters, The King's Royal Rifle Corps (TA): The North Staffordshire Regiment (The Prince of Wales's)
		1958	Royal Tank Regiment: The Royal Scots (The Royal Regiment): The Royal Scots Fusiliers

66.	**QUARRY HILL** 30th July–2nd August 1944 The Capture of Mont Pincon	1957	Seaforth Highlanders (Ross-shire Buffs, The Duke of Albany's): The Argyll and Sutherland Highlanders (Princess Louise's): Scots Guards: Coldstream Guards: The Highland Light Infantry (City of Glasgow Regiment)
67.	**JURQUES** 30th July–4th August 1944 The Capture of Mont Pincon	1957	The Sherwood Rangers Yeomanry, Royal Armoured Corps (TA): The Royal Hampshire Regiment: 11th Hussars (Prince Albert's Own): The Worcestershire Regiment
68.	**LA VARINIERE** 4th–9th August 1944 The Capture of Mont Pincon	1956 1957	The Wiltshire Regiment (Duke of Edinburgh's) The Worcestershire Regiment
69.	**SOULEUVRE** 30th July–1st August 1944 The Capture of Mont Pincon	1956 1957	The Life Guards: Royal Horse Guards The King's Shropshire Light Infantry: The Herefordshire Light Infantry (TA): The Monmouthshire Regiment (TA)
70.	**CATHEOLLES** 2nd–5th August 1944 The Capture of Mont Pincon	1957	The Inns of Court Regiment, Royal Armoured Corps (TA)
71.	**LE PERIER RIDGE** 2nd–8th August 1944 The Capture of Mont Pincon	1956 1957	The Fife and Forfar Yeomanry, Royal Armoured Corps (TA) 23rd Hussars: The King's Shropshire Light Infantry: The Royal Norfolk Regiment: The Rifle Brigade (Prince Consort's Own): London Rifle Brigade, The Rifle Brigade (Prince Consort's Own) (TA): The Monmouthshire Regiment (TA)
72.	**BRIEUX BRIDGEHEAD** 6th–8th August 1944 The Capture of Mont Pincon	1957	The Royal Norfolk Regiment: The North Staffordshire Regiment (The Prince of Wales's)
73.	**ST PIERRE LA VIELLE** 9th–16th August 1944 The Advance beyond Falaise to Close the Gap	1956 1957	The Devonshire Regiment 13th/18th Royal Hussars (Queen Mary's Own): 5th Royal Inniskilling Dragoon Guards: The Cheshire Regiment: The Green Howards (Alexandra, Princess of Wales's Own Yorkshire Regiment): The Dorset Regiment: The Royal Hampshire Regiment: The Durham Light Infantry: The East Yorkshire Regiment (The Duke of York's Own)
74.	**ESTRY** 6th–12th August 1944 The Advance beyond Falaise to Close the Gap	1956 1957 1958	The Cameronians (Scottish Rifles) The Argyll and Sutherland Highlanders (Princess Louise's): The King's Own Scottish Borderers: Scots Guards: Coldstream Guards: The Highland Light Infantry (City of Glasgow Regiment) The Royal Scots Fusiliers
75.	**NOIREAU CROSSING** 14th–17th August 1944 The Advance beyond Falaise to Close the Gap	1956 1957	The Life Guards: Royal Horse Guards: The Duke of Cornwall's Light Infantry The Somerset Light Infantry (Prince Albert's): The Sherwood Rangers Yeomanry, Royal Armoured Corps (TA): The Worcestershire Regiment
76	**FALAISE** 7th–22nd August 1944 The Advance beyond Falaise to Close the Gap	1956 1957	The Royal Scots Greys (2nd Dragoons) 3rd/4th County of London Yeomanry (Sharpshooters), Royal Armoured Corps (TA): The Royal Warwickshire Regiment: The Gloucestershire Regiment: The East Lancashire Regiment: The Northamptonshire Yeomanry, Royal Armoured Corps (TA): The Royal Welch Fusiliers: Seaforth Highlanders (Ross-shire Buffs, The Duke of Albany's): The Argyll and Sutherland Highlanders

(Princess Louise's); The King's Shropshire Light Infantry; The Queen's Own Cameron Highlanders; The Herefordshire Light Infantry (TA); The Suffolk Regiment; The South Lancashire Regiment (The Prince of Wales's Volunteers); 22nd Dragoons; The Highland Light Infantry (City of Glasgow Regiment); The Rifle Brigade (Prince Consort's Own); 1st/2nd Lothians and Border Horse, Royal Armoured Corps (TA); The Welch Regiment; The Black Watch (Royal Highland Regiment); The Middlesex Regiment (Duke of Cambridge's Own); The Manchester Regiment; London Rifle Brigade, The Rifle Brigade (Prince Consort's Own) (TA); The Monmouthshire Regiment (TA); The King's Royal Rifle Corps

1957   14th Canadian Hussars (8th Armoured Regiment); The Essex and Kent Scottish; The British Columbia Regiment (Duke of Connaught's Own) (13th Armoured Regiment); Les Fusiliers de Sherbrooke; The Canadian Grenadier Guards (6th Battalion, The Canadian Guards); The Queen's Own Rifles of Canada; The Royal Hamilton Light Infantry (Wentworth Regiment); The Lincoln and Welland Regiment Le Regiment de la Chaudiere; The Lake Superior Scottish Regiment (Motor); Les Fusiliers Mont-Royal: 1st Hussars (6th Armoured Regiment); The Toronto Scottish Regiment; The Highland Light Infantry of Canada; The Royal Winnipeg Rifles; The Black Watch (Royal Highland Regiment) of Canada; The Regina Rifle Regiment; The Queen's Own Cameron Highlanders of Canada (Motor); The Governor General's Foot Guards (5th Canadian Guards); The Royal Regiment of Canada; The Cameron Highlanders of Ottawa (MG); Fort Garry Horse (10th Armoured Regiment); Argyll and Sutherland Highlanders of Canada (Princess Louise's); The Stormont, Dundas and Glengarry Highlanders (MG): 1st Battalion, The Royal New Brunswick Regiment (Carleton and York): 2nd Battalion, The Royal New Brunswick Regiment (North Shore); South Alberta Light Horse (29th Armoured Regiment); Le Regiment de Maisonneuve

1958   Royal Tank Regiment; The South Wales Borderers; The South Staffordshire Regiment; The Royal Northumberland Fusiliers; The Royal Scots Fusiliers

1958   12th Manitoba Dragoons (18th Armoured Regiment): 17th Duke of York's Royal Canadian Hussars (7th Reconnaissance Regiment); The Sherbrooke Regiment (RCAC): 1st Battalion, The Nova Scotia Highlanders (North): 2nd Battalion, The Nova Scotia Highlanders (Cape Breton)

1959   The Canadian Scottish Regiment (Princess Mary's)

1957   The Northamptonshire Yeomanry, Royal Armoured Corps (TA): Seaforth Highlanders (Ross-shire Buffs, The Duke of Albany's); The Queen's Own Cameron Highlanders: 1st/2nd Lothians and Border Horse, Royal Armoured Corps (TA): The Black Watch (Royal Highland Regiment)

1957   14th Canadian Hussars (8th Armoured Regiment): The Essex and Kent Scottish: The British Columbia Regiment (Duke of Connaught's Own) (13th Armoured Regiment); Les Fusiliers de Sherbrooke: The Canadian Grenadier Guards (6th Battalion, The Canadian Guards); The Royal Hamilton Light Infantry (Wentworth Regiment); The Lincoln and Welland Regiment: The Lake Superior Scottish Regiment (Motor): Les Fusiliers Mont-Royal: 1st Hussars (6th Armoured Regiment); The Toronto Scottish Regiment; The Queen's Own Cameron Highlanders of Canada (Motor); The Governor General's Foot Guards (5th Canadian Guards); The Royal Regiment of Canada: Fort Garry Horse (10th Armoured Regiment): Argyll and Sutherland Highlanders of Canada (Princess Louise's): The Calgary Highlanders: The South Saskatchewan Regiment: The Algonquin Regiment (26th Armoured Regiment): 1st Battalion, The Royal New Brunswick Regiment (Carleton and York): 2nd Battalion, The Royal New Brunswick Regiment (North Shore): South Alberta Light Horse (29th Armoured Regiment): Le Regiment de Maisonneuve

1958   12th Manitoba Dragoons (18th Armoured Regiment): The Sherbrooke Regiment (RCAC)

77.   **FALAISE ROAD**[1]
7th–9th August 1944
The Advance beyond Falaise to Close the Gap

[1] *ROUTE DE LA FALAISE taken into use by French-speaking Canadian units 1958.*

78. **QUESNAY WOOD** ¹
10th–11th August 1944
The Advance beyond Falaise to Close
the Gap

1957 The Queen's Own Rifles of Canada: 1st Hussars (6th Armoured Regiment);The Cameron Highlanders of Ottawa (MG): 1st Battalion, The Royal New Brunswick Regiment (Carleton and York): 2nd Battalion, The Royal New Brunswick Regiment (North Shore)
¹ *BOIS DE QUESNAY taken into use by French-speaking Canadian units 1958.*

79. **CLAIR TIZON**
11th–13th August 1944
The Advance beyond Falaise to Close
the Gap

1957 14th Canadian Hussars (8th Armoured Regiment): The Essex and Kent Scottish: Les Fusiliers de Sherbrooke: The Royal Hamilton Light Infantry (Wentworth Regiment);The Toronto Scottish Regiment:The Black Watch (Royal Highland Regiment) of Canada:The Royal Regiment of Canada:The Calgary Highlanders

1958 The Sherbrooke Regiment (RCAC)

80. **LAISON**
14th–17th August 1944
The Advance beyond Falaise to Close
the Gap

1957 1st/2nd Lothians and Border Horse, Royal Armoured Corps (TA)

81. **THE LAISON** ¹
14th–17th August 1944
The Advance beyond Falaise to Close
the Gap

1957 14th Canadian Hussars (8th Armoured Regiment): The British Columbia Regiment (Duke of Connaught's Own) (13th Armoured Regiment); Les Fusiliers de Sherbrooke:The Canadian Grenadier Guards (6th Battalion,The Canadian Guards): The Queen's Own Rifles of Canada:The Lincoln and Welland Regiment: Le Regiment de la Chaudiere:The Lake Superior Scottish Regiment (Motor): Les Fusiliers Mont-Royal: 1st Hussars (6th Armoured Regiment):The Highland Light Infantry of Canada:The Royal Winnipeg Rifles:The Regina Rifle Regiment:The Queen's Own Cameron Highlanders of Canada (Motor); The Governor General's Foot Guards (5th Canadian Guards):The Cameron Highlanders of Ottawa (MG): Fort Garry Horse (10th Armoured Regiment): The South Saskatchewan Regiment:The Algonquin Regiment (26th Armoured Regiment):The Stormont, Dundas and Glengarry Highlanders (MG): 1st Battalion,The Royal New Brunswick Regiment (Carleton and York): 2nd Battalion, The Royal New Brunswick Regiment (North Shore): South Alberta Light Horse (29th Armoured Regiment)

1958 12th Manitoba Dragoons (18th Armoured Regiment): 17th Duke of York's Royal Canadian Hussars (7th Reconnaissance Regiment):The Sherbrooke Regiment (RCAC): 1st Battalion,The Nova Scotia Highlanders (North): 2nd Battalion,The Nova Scotia Highlanders (Cape Breton)

1959 The Canadian Scottish Regiment (Princess Mary's)
¹ *LA LAISON taken into use by French-speaking Canadian units 1958.*

82. **CHAMBOIS**
18th–22nd August 1944
The Advance beyond Falaise to Close
the Gap

1957 The British Columbia Regiment (Duke of Connaught's Own) (13th Armoured Regiment): The Canadian Grenadier Guards (6th Battalion,The Canadian Guards):The Lincoln and Welland Regiment: Le Regiment de la Chaudiere:The Lake Superior Scottish Regiment (Motor): 1st Hussars (6th Armoured Regiment):The Highland Light Infantry of Canada: The Governor General's Foot Guards (5th Canadian Guards):The Algonquin Regiment (26th Armoured Regiment):The Stormont, Dundas and Glengarry Highlanders (MG): 1st Battalion,The Royal New Brunswick Regiment (Carleton and York): 2nd Battalion,The Royal New Brunswick Regiment (North Shore)

1958 12th Manitoba Dragoons (18th Armoured Regiment): 1st Battalion,The Nova Scotia Highlanders (North): 2nd Battalion,The Nova Scotia Highlanders (Cape Breton)

83. **ST LAMBERT-SUR-DIVES** ¹
19th–22nd August 1944
The Advance beyond Falaise to Close
the Gap

1957 Argyll and Sutherland Highlanders of Canada (Princess Louise's): South Alberta Light Horse (29th Armoured Regiment)
¹ *SAINT-LAMBERT-SUR-DIVES taken into use by French-speaking Canadian units 1958.*

84. **DIVES CROSSING**¹
17th–20th August 1944
Pursuit to the River Seine

- The Derbyshire Yeomanry, Royal Armoured Corps (TA): The Parachute Regiment — 1956
- The Northamptonshire Yeomanry, Royal Armoured Corps (TA): Seaforth Highlanders (Ross-shire Buffs, The Duke of Albany's): The Argyll and Sutherland Highlanders (Princess Louise's): 8th King's Royal Irish Hussars: 11th Hussars (Prince Albert's Own): The Commando Association — 1957
- The First Canadian Parachute Battalion — 1958

¹ *TRAVERSEE DE LA DIVES taken into use by French-speaking Canadian units 1958.*

85. **LA VIE CROSSING**
18th–20th August 1944
Pursuit to the River Seine

- The Derbyshire Yeomanry, Royal Armoured Corps (TA): The York and Lancaster Regiment — 1956
- The East Riding Yeomanry, Royal Armoured Corps (TA): Seaforth Highlanders (Ross-shire Buffs, The Duke of Albany's): The Gordon Highlanders: The Queen's Own Cameron Highlanders: 11th Hussars (Prince Albert's Own): The Black Watch (Royal Highland Regiment) — 1957
- The Royal Scots Fusiliers — 1958

86. **LISIEUX**
21st–23rd August 1944
Pursuit to the River Seine

- The Derbyshire Yeomanry, Royal Armoured Corps (TA) — 1956
- The East Riding Yeomanry, Royal Armoured Corps (TA): 5th Royal Inniskilling Dragoon Guards: The Northamptonshire Yeomanry, Royal Armoured Corps (TA): Seaforth Highlanders (Ross-shire Buffs, The Duke of Albany's): 11th Hussars (Prince Albert's Own) — 1957

87. **LA TOUQUES CROSSING**
22nd–23rd August 1944
Pursuit to the River Seine

- The York and Lancaster Regiment: The Parachute Regiment — 1956
- 11th Hussars (Prince Albert's Own) — 1957
- The Royal Scots Fusiliers — 1958

88. **RISLE CROSSING**
25th–27th August 1944
Pursuit to the River Seine

- The Gloucestershire Regiment: 5th Royal Inniskilling Dragoon Guards: 11th Hussars (Prince Albert's Own) — 1957
- The South Wales Borderers — 1958

89. **FORET DE BRETONNE**
28th–30th August 1944
Pursuit to the River Seine

- The York and Lancaster Regiment — 1956
- The East Riding Yeomanry, Royal Armoured Corps (TA) — 1957

90. **FORET DE LA LONDE**
27th–29th August 1944
Pursuit to the River Seine

- The Essex and Kent Scottish: The Royal Hamilton Light Infantry (Wentworth Regiment): Les Fusiliers Mont-Royal: The Black Watch (Royal Highland Regiment) of Canada: The Queen's Own Cameron Highlanders of Canada (Motor): The Royal Regiment of Canada: The Calgary Highlanders: The South Saskatchewan Regiment: Le Regiment de Maisonneuve — 1957

91. **SEINE 1944**
25th–28th August 1944
The Seine Crossing and Pursuit to Antwerp

- 15th/19th The King's Royal Hussars: The Wiltshire Regiment (Duke of Edinburgh's): 4th/7th Royal Dragoon Guards — 1956
- The Somerset Light Infantry (Prince Albert's): The Sherwood Rangers Yeomanry, Royal Armoured Corps (TA): The Highland Light Infantry (City of Glasgow Regiment): The Middlesex Regiment (Duke of Cambridge's Own): The Worcestershire Regiment — 1957

92. **THE SEINE 1944**¹
25th–28th August 1944
The Seine Crossing and Pursuit to Antwerp

- 14th Canadian Hussars (8th Armoured Regiment): The Lincoln and Welland Regiment: The Royal Winnipeg Rifles: The Regina Rifle Regiment: Argyll and Sutherland Highlanders of Canada (Princess Louise's): The Algonquin Regiment (26th Armoured Regiment): 1st Battalion, The Royal New Brunswick Regiment (Carleton and York): 2nd Battalion, The Royal New Brunswick Regiment (North Shore) — 1957

¹ *LA SEINE 1944 taken into use by French-speaking Canadian units 1958.*

No.	Battle	Year	Regiments
93.	**AMIENS 1944** 31st August 1944 The Seine Crossing and Pursuit to Antwerp	1956 1957	The Life Guards: Royal Horse Guards The Inns of Court Regiment, Royal Armoured Corps (TA): 23rd Hussars
94.	**BRUSSELS** 3rd September 1944 The Seine Crossing and Pursuit to Antwerp	1956 1957	The Life Guards: Royal Horse Guards Welsh Guards
95.	**ANTWERP** 4th–7th September 1944 The Seine Crossing and Pursuit to Antwerp	1957	The Inns of Court Regiment, Royal Armoured Corps (TA): Honourable Artillery Company (TA): 23rd Hussars: The King's Shropshire Light Infantry: The Herefordshire Light Infantry (TA): The Rifle Brigade (Prince Consort's Own): London Rifle Brigade, The Rifle Brigade (Prince Consort's Own) (TA):The Monmouthshire Regiment (TA)
96.	**MOERBRUGGE** 8th–10th September 1944 The Seine Crossing and Pursuit to Antwerp	1957	The Lincoln and Welland Regiment: Argyll and Sutherland Highlanders of Canada (Princess Louise's): 1st Battalion, The Royal New Brunswick Regiment (Carleton and York): 2nd Battalion, The Royal New Brunswick Regiment (North Shore); South Alberta Light Horse (29th Armoured Regiment)
97.	**HECHTEL** 7th–12th September 1944 From Brussels to the Nederrijn	1956 1957	15th/19th The King's Royal Hussars The Inns of Court Regiment, Royal Armoured Corps (TA):The Herefordshire Light Infantry (TA):The Rifle Brigade (Prince Consort's Own):Welsh Guards: London Rifle Brigade, The Rifle Brigade (Prince Consort's Own) (TA)
98.	**GHEEL** 8th–11th September 1944 From Brussels to the Nederrijn	1957	The Cheshire Regiment: The Green Howards (Alexandra, Princess of Wales's Own Yorkshire Regiment): The Sherwood Rangers Yeomanry, Royal Armoured Corps (TA): The Durham Light Infantry: The East Yorkshire Regiment (The Duke of York's Own)
99.	**HEPPEN** 8th–9th September 1944 From Brussels to the Nederrijn	1957	Coldstream Guards
100.	**NEERPELT** 10th September 1944 From Brussels to the Nederrijn	1956	The Life Guards: Royal Horse Guards: Irish Guards
101.	**AART** 14th–20th September 1944 From Brussels to the Nederrijn	1957 1958	The Argyll and Sutherland Highlanders (Princess Louise's): The King's Own Scottish Borderers: The Highland Light Infantry (City of Glasgow Regiment) The Royal Scots (The Royal Regiment):The Royal Scots Fusiliers
102.	**NEDERRIJN** 17th–27th September 1944 From Brussels to the Nederrijn	1956 1957	The Life Guards: Royal Horse Guards: 1st The Royal Dragoons: 15th/19th The King's Royal Hussars:The Duke of Cornwall's Light Infantry:The Wiltshire Regiment (Duke of Edinburgh's): 4th/7th Royal Dragoon Guards: The Devonshire Regiment:The Cameronians (Scottish Rifles) The East Lancashire Regiment:The Cheshire Regiment:The Royal Welch Fusiliers (Ross-shire Buffs, The Duke of Albany's):The Somerset Light Infantry (Prince Albert's):The Green Howards (Alexandra, Princess of Wales's Own Yorkshire Regiment);The King's Own Scottish Borderers: 8th King's Royal Irish Hussars:The King's Shropshire Light Infantry:

103. **ARNHEM 1944**
17th–26th September 1944
From Brussels to the Nederrijn

The Sherwood Rangers Yeomanry, Royal Armoured Corps (TA); The Royal Hampshire Regiment: Coldstream Guards: The Royal Lincolnshire Regiment: The Highland Light Infantry (City of Glasgow Regiment): The Rifle Brigade (Prince Consort's Own): Welsh Guards: The Middlesex Regiment (Duke of Cambridge's Own): The East Yorkshire Regiment (The Duke of York's Own): The Manchester Regiment: London Rifle Brigade, The Rifle Brigade (Prince Consort's Own) (TA): The Monmouthshire Regiment (TA): The Worcestershire Regiment

1958 Royal Tank Regiment: The Royal Scots (The Royal Regiment): The Royal Northumberland Fusiliers: The Royal Scots Fusiliers

1956 The Parachute Regiment
1957 The Glider Pilot Regiment: The King's Own Scottish Borderers: The Dorset Regiment: The Border Regiment
1958 The South Staffordshire Regiment

104. **NIJMEGEN**
19th–20th September 1944
From Brussels to the Nederrijn

1956 The Life Guards: Royal Horse Guards: Irish Guards
1957 Grenadier Guards

105. **VEGHEL**
22nd–23rd September 1944
From Brussels to the Nederrijn

1956 1st The Royal Dragoons

106. **BEST**
22nd–27th September 1944
From Brussels to the Nederrijn

1956 The Cameronians (Scottish Rifles)
1957 Seaforth Highlanders (Ross-shire Buffs, The Duke of Albany's): The King's Own Scottish Borderers: 8th King's Royal Irish Hussars: The Highland Light Infantry (City of Glasgow Regiment)
1958 The Royal Scots (The Royal Regiment): The Royal Scots Fusiliers

107. **DUNKIRK 1944** '
8th–15th September 1944
The Channel Ports

1957 Les Fusiliers Mont-Royal: The Toronto Scottish Regiment: The Black Watch (Royal Highland Regiment) of Canada: The Queen's Own Cameron Highlanders of Canada (Motor): The Royal Regiment of Canada: The Calgary Highlanders: The South Saskatchewan Regiment: Le Regiment de Maisonneuve
' DUNKERQUE 1944 taken into use by French-speaking Canadian units 1958.

108. **LE HAVRE**
10th–12th September 1944
The Channel Ports

1956 The York and Lancaster Regiment
1957 Honourable Artillery Company (TA): The Gloucestershire Regiment: The Northamptonshire Yeomanry, Royal Armoured Corps (TA): Seaforth Highlanders (Ross-shire Buffs, The Duke of Albany's): The King's Own Yorkshire Light Infantry: The Queen's Own Cameron Highlanders: 22nd Dragoons: The Royal Lincolnshire Regiment: 1st/2nd Lothians and Border Horse, Royal Armoured Corps (TA): The Black Watch (Royal Highland Regiment): The Essex Regiment: The Middlesex Regiment (Duke of Cambridge's Own)
1958 The South Wales Borderers: The Royal Scots Fusiliers
1959 First Canadian Armoured Personnel Carrier Regiment

109. **BOULOGNE 1944**
17th–22nd September 1944
The Channel Ports

1957 1st/2nd Lothians and Border Horse, Royal Armoured Corps (TA)
1957 The Queen's Own Rifles of Canada: Le Regiment de la Chaudiere: The Highland Light Infantry of Canada: The Cameron Highlanders of Ottawa (MG): Fort Garry Horse (10th Armoured Regiment): The Stormont, Dundas and Glengarry Highlanders (MG): 1st Battalion, The Royal New Brunswick Regiment (Carleton and York): 2nd Battalion, The Royal New Brunswick Regiment (North Shore)
1958 1st Battalion, The Nova Scotia Highlanders (North): 2nd Battalion, The Nova Scotia Highlanders (Cape Breton)
1959 First Canadian Armoured Personnel Carrier Regiment

110.	**CALAIS 1944**	1957	1st/2nd Lothians and Border Horse, Royal Armoured Corps (TA)
	25th September–1st October 1944	1957	The Royal Montreal Regiment:The Queen's Own Rifles of Canada: Le Regiment de la Chaudiere: 1st Hussars (6th Armoured
	The Channel Ports		Regiment);The Highland Light Infantry of Canada:The Royal Winnipeg Rifles:The Regina Rifle Regiment: 1st Battalion,The Royal
			New Brunswick Regiment (Carleton and York); 2nd Battalion,The Royal New Brunswick Regiment (North Shore)
		1958	1st Battalion,The Nova Scotia Highlanders (North); 2nd Battalion,The Nova Scotia Highlanders (Cape Breton)
		1959	The Canadian Scottish Regiment (Princess Mary's)
111.	**MOERKERKE**	1957	The Algonquin Regiment (26th Armoured Regiment): 1st Battalion,The Royal New Brunswick Regiment (Carleton and York);
	13th–14th September 1944		2nd Battalion,The Royal New Brunswick Regiment (North Shore)
	Opening the Port of Antwerp		
112.	**WYNEGHEM**	1957	The Calgary Highlanders
	21st–22nd September 1944		
	Opening the Port of Antwerp		
113.	**ANTWERP-TURNHOUT CANAL**	1956	The Royal Leicestershire Regiment:The York and Lancaster Regiment: Princess Louise's Kensington Regiment (TA)
	24th–29th September 1944	1957	The King's Own Yorkshire Light Infantry;The Royal Lincolnshire Regiment:The Essex Regiment
	Opening the Port of Antwerp	1957	14th Canadian Hussars (8th Armoured Regiment); Les Fusiliers de Sherbrooke: Les Fusiliers Mont-Royal:TheToronto Scottish
			Regiment:The Black Watch (Royal Highland Regiment) of Canada: Fort Garry Horse (10th Armoured Regiment);The Calgary
			Highlanders:The South Saskatchewan Regiment: Le Regiment de Maisonneuve
		1958	The South Wales Borderers:The Royal Scots Fusiliers
		1959	The Sherbrooke Regiment (RCAC)
	¹ ANVERS-CANAL DE TURNHOUT taken into use by French-speaking Canadian units 1958.		
114.	**SCHELDT**	1956	The Fife and Forfar Yeomanry, Royal Armoured Corps (TA): The Royal Leicestershire Regiment:The York and Lancaster
	1st October–8th November 1944		Regiment:The Cameronians (Scottish Rifles)
	Opening the Port of Antwerp	1957	The King's Own Scottish Borderers:The Highland Light Infantry (City of Glasgow Regiment): 1st/2nd Lothians and Border
			Horse, Royal Armoured Corps (TA):The Essex Regiment:The Manchester Regiment
		1958	Royal Tank Regiment:The South Wales Borderers:The Royal Scots (The Royal Regiment):The Royal Scots Fusiliers
115.	**THE SCHELDT** ¹	1957	14th Canadian Hussars (8th Armoured Regiment):The Essex and Kent Scottish:The Royal Montreal Regiment: Les Fusiliers
	1st October–8th November 1944		de Sherbrooke:The Canadian Grenadier Guards (6th Battalion, The Canadian Guards);The Queen's Own Rifles of Canada:
	Opening the Port of Antwerp		The Royal Hamilton Light Infantry (Wentworth Regiment):The Lincoln and Welland Regiment: Le Regiment de la Chaudiere:
			The Lake Superior Scottish Regiment (Motor): Les Fusiliers Mont-Royal:The Toronto Scottish Regiment:The Highland Light
			Infantry of Canada: The Royal Winnipeg Rifles: The Black Watch (Royal Highland Regiment) of Canada: The Regina Rifle
			Regiment:The Queen's Own Cameron Highlanders of Canada (Motor):The Governor General's Foot Guards (5th Canadian
			Guards):The Royal Regiment of Canada:The Cameron Highlanders of Ottawa (MG):The British Columbia Regiment (Duke
			of Connaught's Own) (13th Armoured Regiment): Fort Garry Horse (10th Armoured Regiment): Argyll and Sutherland
			Highlanders of Canada (Princess Louise's): The Calgary Highlanders: The South Saskatchewan Regiment: The Algonquin
			Regiment (26th Armoured Regiment):The Stormont, Dundas and Glengarry Highlanders (MG): 1st Battalion,The Royal New
			Brunswick Regiment (Carleton and York); 2nd Battalion,The Royal New Brunswick Regiment (North Shore); South Alberta
			Light Horse (29th Armoured Regiment): Le Regiment de Maisonneuve
		1958	17th Duke ofYork's Royal Canadian Hussars (7th Reconnaissance Regiment):The Sherbrooke Regiment (RCAC): 1st Battalion,
			The Nova Scotia Highlanders (North); 2nd Battalion,The Nova Scotia Highlanders (Cape Breton)

1959 | The Canadian Scottish Regiment (Princess Mary's)
' L' ESCAUT taken into use by French-speaking Canadian units 1958.

116. LEOPOLD CANAL '
6th–16th October 1944
Opening the Port of Antwerp

1957 | The Royal Montreal Regiment: The Royal Winnipeg Rifles: The Regina Rifle Regiment
1959 | The Canadian Scottish Regiment (Princess Mary's)
' CANAL LEOPOLD taken into use by French-speaking Canadian units 1958.

117. WOENSDRECHT
1st–27th October 1944
Opening the Port of Antwerp

1957 | 14th Canadian Hussars (8th Armoured Regiment): The Essex and Kent Scottish: The Royal Hamilton Light Infantry (Wentworth Regiment): Les Fusiliers Mont-Royal: The Toronto Scottish Regiment: The Black Watch (Royal Highland Regiment) of Canada: The Queen's Own Cameron Highlanders of Canada (Motor): The Royal Regiment of Canada: Fort Garry Horse (10th Armoured Regiment): The Calgary Highlanders: The South Saskatchewan Regiment: South Alberta Light Horse (29th Armoured Regiment): Le Regiment de Maisonneuve

118. SAVOJAARDS PLAAT
9th–10th October 1944
Opening the Port of Antwerp

1957 | The Highland Light Infantry of Canada: The Stormont, Dundas and Glengarry Highlanders (MG)
1958 | 1st Battalion, The Nova Scotia Highlanders (North): 2nd Battalion, The Nova Scotia Highlanders (Cape Breton)

119. BRESKENS POCKET '
11th October–3rd November 1944
Opening the Port of Antwerp

1957 | The Queen's Own Rifles of Canada: The Lincoln and Welland Regiment: Le Regiment de la Chaudiere: The Highland Light Infantry of Canada: The Royal Winnipeg Rifles: The Regina Rifle Regiment: The Cameron Highlanders of Ottawa (MG): Argyll and Sutherland Highlanders of Canada (Princess Louise's): The Algonquin Regiment (26th Armoured Regiment): The Stormont, Dundas and Glengarry Highlanders (MG): 1st Battalion, The Royal New Brunswick Regiment (Carleton and York): 2nd Battalion, The Royal New Brunswick Regiment (North Shore)
1958 | 17th Duke of York's Royal Canadian Hussars (7th Reconnaissance Regiment): 1st Battalion, The Nova Scotia Highlanders (North): 2nd Battalion, The Nova Scotia Highlanders (Cape Breton)
1959 | The Canadian Scottish Regiment (Princess Mary's)
' POCHE DE BRESKENS taken into use by French-speaking Canadian units 1958.

120. SOUTH BEVELAND
24th–31st October 1944
Opening the Port of Antwerp

1956 | The Cameronians (Scottish Rifles)
1957 | The Highland Light Infantry (City of Glasgow Regiment)
1957 | 14th Canadian Hussars (8th Armoured Regiment): The Essex and Kent Scottish: The Royal Hamilton Light Infantry (Wentworth Regiment): Les Fusiliers Mont-Royal: The Toronto Scottish Regiment: The Black Watch (Royal Highland Regiment) of Canada: The Queen's Own Cameron Highlanders of Canada (Motor): The Royal Regiment of Canada: South Saskatchewan Regiment: Le Regiment de Maisonneuve
1958 | The Royal Scots Fusiliers

121. WALCHEREN CAUSEWAY '
31st October–4th November 1944
Opening the Port of Antwerp

1956 | The Cameronians (Scottish Rifles)
1957 | The Highland Light Infantry (City of Glasgow Regiment): The Manchester Regiment
1957 | The Black Watch (Royal Highland Regiment) of Canada: The Calgary Highlanders: Le Regiment de Maisonneuve
' CHAUSSEE DE WALCHEREN taken into use by French-speaking Canadian units 1958.

122. FLUSHING
1st–4th November 1944
Opening the Port of Antwerp

1957 | The King's Own Scottish Borderers: The Manchester Regiment: The Commando Association
1958 | The Royal Scots (The Royal Regiment)

123.	**WESTKAPELLE** 1st–3rd November 1944 Opening the Port of Antwerp	1957	1st/2nd Lothians and Border Horse, Royal Armoured Corps (TA); The Commando Association
124.	**LOWER MAAS** 20th October–7th November 1944 Opening the Port of Antwerp	1956 1957	The Derbyshire Yeomanry, Royal Armoured Corps (TA); The York and Lancaster Regiment 3rd/4th County of London Yeomanry (Sharpshooters), Royal Armoured Corps (TA); The East Riding Yeomanry, Royal Armoured Corps (TA); The East Lancashire Regiment; 5th Royal Inniskilling Dragoon Guards; The Northamptonshire Yeomanry, Royal Armoured Corps (TA); The Royal Welch Fusiliers: The Oxfordshire and Buckinghamshire Light Infantry: Seaforth Highlanders (Ross-shire Buffs, The Duke of Albany's); The Gordon Highlanders; The Argyll and Sutherland Highlanders (Princess Louise's); The Queen's Royal Regiment (West Surrey); The King's Own Yorkshire Light Infantry; 8th King's Royal Irish Hussars; The Queen's Own Cameron Highlanders; 22nd Dragoons; The Highland Light Infantry (City of Glasgow Regiment); The Rifle Brigade (Prince Consort's Own); The Welch Regiment; The Black Watch (Royal Highland Regiment); The Middlesex Regiment (Duke of Cambridge's Own); The Manchester Regiment; The Monmouthshire Regiment (TA)
		1958	The Royal Scots Fusiliers
125.	**THE LOWER MAAS** ¹ 20th October–7th November 1944 Opening the Port of Antwerp	1957	The British Columbia Regiment (Duke of Connaught's Own) (13th Armoured Regiment); Les Fusiliers de Sherbrooke; The Canadian Grenadier Guards (6th Battalion, The Canadian Guards); The Lincoln and Welland Regiment; The Lake Superior Scottish Regiment (Motor): 1st Hussars (6th Armoured Regiment); The Governor General's Foot Guards (5th Canadian Guards); Argyll and Sutherland Highlanders of Canada (Princess Louise's); The Algonquin Regiment (26th Armoured Regiment); 1st Battalion, The Royal New Brunswick Regiment (Carleton and York): 2nd Battalion, The Royal New Brunswick Regiment (North Shore); South Alberta Light Horse (29th Armoured Regiment)
		1958	The Sherbrooke Regiment (RCAC)
		1959	First Canadian Armoured Personnel Carrier Regiment ¹ *LE LOWER MAAS taken into use by French-speaking Canadian units 1958.*
126.	**AAM** 1st–4th October 1944 Preparation for the Thrust to the Ruhr	1956 1957	Irish Guards The Cheshire Regiment; The Dorset Regiment; The East Yorkshire Regiment (The Duke of York's Own)
127.	**OPHEUSDEN** 5th–7th October 1944 Preparation for the Thrust to the Ruhr	1956	The Duke of Cornwall's Light Infantry
128.	**VENRAIJ** 12th–18th October 1944 Preparation for the Thrust to the Ruhr	1956 1957	15th/19th The King's Royal Hussars; Westminster Dragoons (2nd County of London Yeomanry), Royal Armoured Corps (TA) The Royal Warwickshire Regiment: 23rd Hussars: The King's Own Scottish Borderers: The King's Shropshire Light Infantry; The Herefordshire Light Infantry (TA); The Suffolk Regiment; The South Lancashire Regiment (The Prince of Wales's Volunteers); Coldstream Guards: The Royal Norfolk Regiment: The Royal Lincolnshire Regiment: The Middlesex Regiment (Duke of Cambridge's Own); The East Yorkshire Regiment (The Duke of York's Own)
129.	**ASTEN** 27th October–5th November 1944 Preparation for the Thrust to the Ruhr	1956 1957	The Cameronians (Scottish Rifles) The Highland Light Infantry (City of Glasgow Regiment)

130.	**MEIJEL** 27th October–5th November 1944 Preparation for the Thrust to the Ruhr	1956 1957 1958	Westminster Dragoons (2nd County of London Yeomanry), Royal Armoured Corps (TA) Seaforth Highlanders (Ross-shire Buffs, The Duke of Albany's); The Argyll and Sutherland Highlanders (Princess Louise's); The King's Own Scottish Borderers: Coldstream Guards: The Middlesex Regiment (Duke of Cambridge's Own) The Royal Scots (The Royal Regiment): The Royal Scots Fusiliers
131.	**GEILENKIRCHEN** 18th–23rd November 1944 Preparation for the Thrust to the Ruhr	1956 1957	The Duke of Cornwall's Light Infantry: 4th/7th Royal Dragoon Guards 13th/18th Royal Hussars (Queen Mary's Own): The Somerset Light Infantry (Prince Albert's): The Dorset Regiment: The Sherwood Rangers Yeomanry, Royal Armoured Corps (TA): 1st/2nd Lothians and Border Horse, Royal Armoured Corps (TA): The Middlesex Regiment (Duke of Cambridge's Own): The Worcestershire Regiment
132.	**VENLO POCKET** 14th November–3rd December 1944 Preparation for the Thrust to the Ruhr	1956 1957 1958	The Royal Scots Greys (2nd Dragoons): Westminster Dragoons (2nd County of London Yeomanry), Royal Armoured Corps (TA): Princess Louise's Kensington Regiment (TA) The East Riding Yeomanry, Royal Armoured Corps (TA): The Northamptonshire Yeomanry, Royal Armoured Corps (TA): The Royal Welch Fusiliers: Seaforth Highlanders (Ross-shire Buffs, The Duke of Albany's): The Gordon Highlanders: The Argyll and Sutherland Highlanders (Princess Louise's): 23rd Hussars: The King's Own Scottish Borderers: The Queen's Own Cameron Highlanders: The Herefordshire Light Infantry (TA): Scots Guards: The Royal Ulster Rifles: 22nd Dragoons: The Royal Lincolnshire Regiment: The Black Watch (Royal Highland Regiment): The Middlesex Regiment (Duke of Cambridge's Own): The Manchester Regiment: The Monmouthshire Regiment (TA) Royal Tank Regiment: The Royal Scots (The Royal Regiment): The Royal Scots Fusiliers
133.	**KAPELSCHE VEER** 31st December 1944–31st January 1945 Preparation for the Thrust to the Ruhr	1957	The Lincoln and Welland Regiment: Argyll and Sutherland Highlanders of Canada (Princess Louise's): 1st Battalion, The Royal New Brunswick Regiment (Carleton and York): 2nd Battalion, The Royal New Brunswick Regiment (North Shore): South Alberta Light Horse (29th Armoured Regiment)
134.	**ROER** 16th–31st January 1945 Preparation for the Thrust to the Ruhr	1956 1957 1958	Westminster Dragoons (2nd County of London Yeomanry), Royal Armoured Corps (TA): The Wiltshire Regiment (Duke of Edinburgh's): 4th/7th Royal Dragoon Guards: The Devonshire Regiment: The Cameronians (Scottish Rifles) 13th/18th Royal Hussars (Queen Mary's Own): 5th Royal Inniskilling Dragoon Guards: The Queen's Royal Regiment (West Surrey): The Somerset Light Infantry (Prince Albert's): The King's Own Scottish Borderers: 8th King's Royal Irish Hussars: The Sherwood Rangers Yeomanry, Royal Armoured Corps (TA): The Royal Hampshire Regiment: 11th Hussars (Prince Albert's Own): Coldstream Guards: The Highland Light Infantry (City of Glasgow Regiment): The Rifle Brigade (Prince Consort's Own): 1st/2nd Lothians and Border Horse, Royal Armoured Corps (TA): The Durham Light Infantry: The Manchester Regiment: The King's Royal Rifle Corps: The Queen's Westminsters, The King's Royal Rifle Corps (TA) The Royal Scots (The Royal Regiment): The Royal Scots Fusiliers
135.	**ZETTEN** 18th–21st January 1945 Preparation for the Thrust to the Ruhr	1956 1957 1958	The Royal Leicestershire Regiment: Princess Louise's Kensington Regiment (TA) The Gloucestershire Regiment: The Essex Regiment The South Wales Borderers
136.	**OURTHE** 3rd–14th January 1945 The Ardennes	1956 1957	The Derbyshire Yeomanry, Royal Armoured Corps (TA): The Fife and Forfar Yeomanry, Royal Armoured Corps (TA): The East Lancashire Regiment: The Northamptonshire Yeomanry, Royal Armoured Corps (TA): The Parachute Regiment The East Riding Yeomanry, Royal Armoured Corps (TA): The Royal Welch Fusiliers: The Oxfordshire and Buckinghamshire Light Infantry: Seaforth

		Highlanders (Ross-shire Buffs, The Duke of Albany's);The Argyll and Sutherland Highlanders (Princess Louise's): 23rd Hussars: The Highland Light Infantry (City of Glasgow Regiment): The Black Watch (Royal Highland Regiment): The Manchester Regiment:The Monmouthshire Regiment (TA)
137.	**RHINELAND** 8th February–10th March 1945 The Rhineland	1956
		1957

137. **RHINELAND**
8th February–10th March 1945
The Rhineland

1956   Irish Guards: 15th/19th The King's Royal Hussars:The Derbyshire Yeomanry, Royal Armoured Corps (TA):The Fife and Forfar Yeomanry, Royal Armoured Corps (TA):The Duke of Cornwall's Light Infantry:The Wiltshire Regiment (Duke of Edinburgh's): 4th/7th Royal Dragoon Guards:The Cameronians (Scottish Rifles)

1957   13th/18th Royal Hussars (Queen Mary's Own): 3rd/4th County of London Yeomanry (Sharpshooters), Royal Armoured Corps (TA): The Royal Warwickshire Regiment: The East Lancashire Regiment: The Royal Welch Fusiliers: The Oxfordshire and Buckinghamshire Light Infantry: Seaforth Highlanders (Ross-shire Buffs, The Duke of Albany's):The Gordon Highlanders:The Argyll and Sutherland Highlanders (Princess Louise's):The Queen's Own Cameron Highlanders:The Herefordshire Light Infantry (TA):The Sherwood Rangers Yeomanry, Royal Armoured Corps (TA): Scots Guards:The Royal Hampshire Regiment:The South Lancashire Regiment (The Prince of Wales's Volunteers): Coldstream Guards: The Royal Norfolk Regiment: The Royal Lincolnshire Regiment:The Highland Light Infantry (City of Glasgow Regiment):Welsh Guards:The Black Watch (Royal Highland Regiment):The Middlesex Regiment (Duke of Cambridge's Own):The East Yorkshire Regiment (The Duke of York's Own): The Manchester Regiment:The Monmouthshire Regiment (TA):The Worcestershire Regiment:The King's Royal Rifle Corps: The Queen's Westminsters,The King's Royal Rifle Corps (TA)

1958   Royal Tank Regiment:The Royal Scots (The Royal Regiment):The Royal Northumberland Fusiliers:The Royal Scots Fusiliers

138. **THE RHINELAND** [1]
8th February–10th March 1945
The Rhineland

1957   14th Canadian Hussars (8th Armoured Regiment): The Essex and Kent Scottish: The British Columbia Regiment (Duke of Connaught's Own) (13th Armoured Regiment): Les Fusiliers de Sherbrooke:The Canadian Grenadier Guards (6th Battalion, The Canadian Guards):The Queen's Own Rifles of Canada:The Royal Hamilton Light Infantry (Wentworth Regiment):The Lincoln and Welland Regiment: Le Regiment de la Chaudiere:The Lake Superior Scottish Regiment (Motor):Les Fusiliers Mont-Royal: 1st Hussars (6th Armoured Regiment):The Toronto Scottish Regiment:The Highland Light Infantry of Canada:The Royal Winnipeg Rifles: The Black Watch (Royal Highland Regiment) of Canada: The Regina Rifle Regiment: The Queen's Own Cameron Highlanders of Canada (Motor):The Governor General's Foot Guards (5th Canadian Guards):The Royal Regiment of Canada:The Cameron Highlanders of Ottawa (MG): Fort Garry Horse (10th Armoured Regiment): Argyll and Sutherland Highlanders of Canada (Princess Louise's): The Calgary Highlanders: The South Saskatchewan Regiment: The Algonquin Regiment (26th Armoured Regiment):The Stormont, Dundas and Glengarry Highlanders (MG): 1st Battalion,The Royal New Brunswick Regiment (Carleton and York): 2nd Battalion,The Royal New Brunswick Regiment (North Shore): South Alberta Light Horse (29th Armoured Regiment): Le Regiment de Maisonneuve

1958   12th Manitoba Dragoons (18th Armoured Regiment): 17th Duke of York's Royal Canadian Hussars (7th Reconnaissance Regiment):The Sherbrooke Regiment (RCAC): 1st Battalion,The Nova Scotia Highlanders (North): 2nd Battalion,The Nova Scotia Highlanders (Cape Breton)

1959   The Canadian Scottish Regiment (Princess Mary's); First Canadian Armoured Personnel Carrier Regiment

[1] *LA RHENANIE taken into use by French-speaking Canadian units 1958.*

139. **REICHSWALD**
8th–13th February 1945
The Rhineland

1956   The Derbyshire Yeomanry, Royal Armoured Corps (TA):The Cameronians (Scottish Rifles)

1957   The East Lancashire Regiment: Grenadier Guards: The Royal Welch Fusiliers: The Oxfordshire and Buckinghamshire Light Infantry: Seaforth Highlanders (Ross-shire Buffs, The Duke of Albany's):The Gordon Highlanders:The Argyll and Sutherland Highlanders (Princess Louise's);The King's Own Scottish Borderers:The Queen's Own Cameron Highlanders: Scots Guards: 22nd Dragoons: Coldstream Guards:The Highland Light Infantry (City of Glasgow Regiment): 1st/2nd Lothians and Border

No.	Battle Honour	Year	Units
140.	**THE REICHSWALD** [1] 8th–13th February 1945 The Rhineland		Horse, Royal Armoured Corps (TA): The Welch Regiment: The Black Watch (Royal Highland Regiment): The Middlesex Regiment (Duke of Cambridge's Own): The Manchester Regiment: The Monmouthshire Regiment (TA)
		1958	The Royal Scots (The Royal Regiment): The Royal Scots Fusiliers
		1957	The Toronto Scottish Regiment: The Calgary Highlanders: Le Regiment de Maisonneuve
		1959	First Canadian Armoured Personnel Carrier Regiment [1] LE REICHSWALD taken into use by French-speaking Canadian units 1958.
141.	**WAAL FLATS** 8th–15th February 1945 The Rhineland	1957	13th/18th Royal Hussars (Queen Mary's Own)
		1957	The Queen's Own Rifles of Canada: Le Regiment de la Chaudiere: The Highland Light Infantry of Canada: The Royal Winnipeg Rifles: The Regina Rifle Regiment: The Cameron Highlanders of Ottawa (MG): The Stormont, Dundas and Glengarry Highlanders (MG): 1st Battalion, The Royal New Brunswick Regiment (Carleton and York): 2nd Battalion, The Royal New Brunswick Regiment (North Shore)
		1958	1st Battalion, The Nova Scotia Highlanders (North): 2nd Battalion, The Nova Scotia Highlanders (Cape Breton)
		1959	The Canadian Scottish Regiment (Princess Mary's)
142.	**CLEVE** 9th–11th February 1945 The Rhineland	1956	The Wiltshire Regiment (Duke of Edinburgh's): 4th/7th Royal Dragoon Guards
		1957	The Gordon Highlanders: The Somerset Light Infantry (Prince Albert's): The King's Own Scottish Borderers: The Sherwood Rangers Yeomanry, Royal Armoured Corps (TA): Scots Guards: Coldstream Guards: The King's Royal Rifle Corps: The Queen's Westminsters, The King's Royal Rifle Corps (TA)
		1958	The Royal Scots (The Royal Regiment): The Royal Scots Fusiliers
		1959	First Canadian Armoured Personnel Carrier Regiment
143.	**GOCH** 12th–21st February 1945 The Rhineland	1956	The Duke of Cornwall's Light Infantry: The Wiltshire Regiment (Duke of Edinburgh's)
		1957	13th/18th Royal Hussars (Queen Mary's Own): The Royal Welch Fusiliers: Seaforth Highlanders (Ross-shire Buffs, The Duke of Albany's): The Gordon Highlanders: The Somerset Light Infantry (Prince Albert's): The King's Own Scottish Borderers: The Dorset Regiment: The Queen's Own Cameron Highlanders: The Highland Light Infantry (City of Glasgow Regiment): The Black Watch (Royal Highland Regiment): The Middlesex Regiment (Duke of Cambridge's Own): The Manchester Regiment: The Royal Hampshire Regiment: Coldstream Guards: The Worcestershire Regiment: The King's Royal Rifle Corps: The Queen's Westminsters, The King's Royal Rifle Corps (TA)
		1958	The Royal Scots (The Royal Regiment): The Royal Scots Fusiliers
144.	**MOYLAND** 14th–21st February 1945 The Rhineland	1956	The Cameronians (Scottish Rifles)
		1957	Seaforth Highlanders (Ross-shire Buffs, The Duke of Albany's): Scots Guards: Coldstream Guards
145.	**MOYLAND WOOD** [1] 14th–21st February 1945 The Rhineland	1957	The Highland Light Infantry (City of Glasgow Regiment)
		1957	The Royal Winnipeg Rifles: The Regina Rifle Regiment
		1958	The Canadian Scottish Regiment (Princess Mary's)
		1959	First Canadian Armoured Personnel Carrier Regiment [1] BOIS DE MOYLAND taken into use by French-speaking Canadian units 1958.
146.	**GOCH-CALCAR ROAD** [1] 19th–21st February 1945 The Rhineland	1957	The Essex and Kent Scottish: The Royal Hamilton Light Infantry (Wentworth Regiment): The Toronto Scottish Regiment: The Royal Regiment of Canada: Fort Garry Horse (10th Armoured Regiment)
		1959	First Canadian Armoured Personnel Carrier Regiment [1] ROUTE DE GOCH-CALCAR taken into use by French-speaking Canadian units 1958.

147.	**WEEZE** 24th February–2nd March 1945 The Rhineland	1957	The East Lancashire Regiment: The Royal Welch Fusiliers: The Sherwood Rangers Yeomanry, Royal Armoured Corps (TA): The Highland Light Infantry (City of Glasgow Regiment): The Manchester Regiment: The Monmouthshire Regiment (TA)
148.	**HOCHWALD** 24th February–4th March 1945 The Rhineland	1956 1957	The Royal Scots Greys (2nd Dragoons): Irish Guards: 15th/19th The King's Royal Hussars 3rd/4th County of London Yeomanry (Sharpshooters), Royal Armoured Corps (TA): The Somerset Light Infantry (Prince Albert's): The King's Shropshire Light Infantry: The Herefordshire Light Infantry (TA): Scots Guards: The South Lancashire Regiment (The Prince of Wales's Volunteers): Coldstream Guards: The Royal Norfolk Regiment: The Royal Lincolnshire Regiment: The Monmouthshire Regiment (TA): The King's Royal Rifle Corps
149.	**THE HOCHWALD** [1] 24th February–4th March 1945 The Rhineland	1957	The Essex and Kent Scottish: The British Columbia Regiment (Duke of Connaught's Own) (13th Armoured Regiment): Les Fusiliers de Sherbrooke: The Canadian Grenadier Guards (6th Battalion, The Canadian Guards): The Queen's Own Rifles of Canada: The Royal Hamilton Light Infantry (Wentworth Regiment): The Lincoln and Welland Regiment: Le Regiment de la Chaudiere: The Lake Superior Scottish Regiment (Motor): Les Fusiliers Mont-Royal: 1st Hussars (6th Armoured Regiment): The Toronto Scottish Regiment: The Highland Light Infantry of Canada: The Black Watch (Royal Highland Regiment) of Canada: The Queen's Own Cameron Highlanders of Canada (Motor): The Governor General's Foot Guards (5th Canadian Guards): The Royal Regiment of Canada: The Cameron Highlanders of Ottawa (MG): Fort Garry Horse (10th Armoured Regiment): Argyll and Sutherland Highlanders of Canada (Princess Louise's): The Calgary Highlanders: The South Saskatchewan Regiment: The Algonquin Regiment (26th Armoured Regiment): The Stormont, Dundas and Glengarry Highlanders (MG): 1st Battalion, The Royal New Brunswick Regiment (Carleton and York): 2nd Battalion, The Royal New Brunswick Regiment (North Shore): South Alberta Light Horse (29th Armoured Regiment): Le Regiment de Maisonneuve
		1958	The Sherbrooke Regiment (RCAC): 1st Battalion, The Nova Scotia Highlanders (North): 2nd Battalion, The Nova Scotia Highlanders (Cape Breton)
		1959	First Canadian Armoured Personnel Carrier Regiment [1] *LE HOCHWALD taken into use by French-speaking Canadian units 1958.*
150.	**SCHADDENHOF** 27th–28th February 1945 The Rhineland	1957	The East Yorkshire Regiment (The Duke of York's Own)
151.	**XANTEN** 8th–9th March 1945 The Rhineland	1956 1957 1957	The Wiltshire Regiment (Duke of Edinburgh's) The Somerset Light Infantry (Prince Albert's) The Essex and Kent Scottish: Les Fusiliers de Sherbrooke: The Royal Hamilton Light Infantry (Wentworth Regiment): Les Fusiliers Mont-Royal: The Toronto Scottish Regiment: The Black Watch (Royal Highland Regiment) of Canada: The Queen's Own Cameron Highlanders of Canada (Motor): The Royal Regiment of Canada: The Calgary Highlanders: The South Saskatchewan Regiment: Le Regiment de Maisonneuve
		1958 1959	The Sherbrooke Regiment (RCAC) First Canadian Armoured Personnel Carrier Regiment
152.	**VEEN** 6th–10th March 1945 The Rhineland	1957	The British Columbia Regiment (Duke of Connaught's Own) (13th Armoured Regiment): The Canadian Grenadier Guards (6th Battalion, The Canadian Guards): The Lincoln and Welland Regiment: The Lake Superior Scottish Regiment (Motor): The Governor General's Foot Guards (5th Canadian Guards): Argyll and Sutherland Highlanders of Canada (Princess Louise's): The Algonquin Regiment (26th Armoured Regiment): South Alberta Light Horse (29th Armoured Regiment)

153.	**RHINE** 23rd March–1st April 1945 The Crossing of the River Rhine	**1956** 1st The Royal Dragoons: Irish Guards: 15th/19th The King's Royal Hussars: The Fife and Forfar Yeomanry, Royal Armoured Corps (TA): The Duke of Cornwall's Light Infantry: The Wiltshire Regiment (Duke of Edinburgh's): 4th/7th Royal Dragoon Guards: The Devonshire Regiment: The Cameronians (Scottish Rifles): The Parachute Regiment **1957** 13th/18th Royal Hussars (Queen Mary's Own): 3rd/4th County of London Yeomanry (Sharpshooters), Royal Armoured Corps (TA): The East Riding Yeomanry, Royal Armoured Corps (TA): The Inns of Court Regiment, Royal Armoured Corps (TA): Honourable Artillery Company (TA): The East Lancashire Regiment: The Glider Pilot Regiment: The Northamptonshire Yeomanry, Royal Armoured Corps (TA): Grenadier Guards: The Royal Welch Fusiliers: The Oxfordshire and Buckinghamshire Light Infantry: Seaforth Highlanders (Ross-shire Buffs, The Duke of Albany's): The Gordon Highlanders: The Argyll and Sutherland Highlanders (Princess Louise's): The Staffordshire Yeomanry (Queen's Own Royal Regiment), Royal Armoured Corps (TA): The Somerset Light Infantry (Prince Albert's): The King's Own Scottish Borderers: The Dorset Regiment: 8th King's Royal Irish Hussars: The Queen's Own Cameron Highlanders: The Sherwood Rangers Yeomanry, Royal Armoured Corps (TA): Scots Guards: The Royal Hampshire Regiment: The Royal Ulster Rifles: 11th Hussars (Prince Albert's): The Highland Light Infantry (City of Glasgow Regiment): The Royal Berkshire Regiment (Princess Charlotte of Wales's): The Highland Light Infantry (City of Glasgow Regiment): The Manchester Regiment: The Black Watch (Royal Highland Regiment): The Middlesex Regiment (Duke of Cambridge's Own): The Commando Association: The Worcestershire Regiment: The King's Royal Rifle Corps: The Queen's Westminsters, The King's Royal Rifle Corps (TA) **1958** Royal Tank Regiment: The Royal Scots (The Royal Regiment): The Royal Scots Fusiliers
154.	**THE RHINE** ¹ 23rd March–1st April 1945 The Crossing of the River Rhine	**1957** Les Fusiliers de Sherbrooke: The Queen's Own Rifles of Canada: Le Regiment de la Chaudiere: Les Fusiliers Mont-Royal: The Highland Light Infantry of Canada: The Royal Winnipeg Rifles: The Black Watch (Royal Highland Regiment) of Canada: The Regina Rifle Regiment: The Queen's Own Cameron Highlanders of Canada (Motor): The Cameron Highlanders of Ottawa (MG): The Calgary Highlanders: The South Saskatchewan Regiment: The Stormont, Dundas and Glengarry Highlanders (MG): 1st Battalion, The Royal New Brunswick Regiment (Carleton and York): 2nd Battalion, The Royal New Brunswick Regiment (North Shore) **1958** The First Canadian Parachute Battalion: 17th Duke of York's Royal Canadian Hussars (7th Reconnaissance Regiment): The Sherbrooke Regiment (RCAC): 1st Battalion, The Nova Scotia Highlanders (North): 2nd Battalion, The Nova Scotia Highlanders (Cape Breton) **1959** The Canadian Scottish Regiment (Princess Mary's): First Canadian Armoured Personnel Carrier Regiment ¹ *LE RHIN taken into use by French-speaking Canadian units 1958.*
155.	**EMMERICH-HOCH ELTEN** 28th March–1st April 1945 The Crossing of the River Rhine	**1957** Les Fusiliers de Sherbrooke: The Queen's Own Rifles of Canada: Le Regiment de la Chaudiere: The Royal Winnipeg Rifles: The Regina Rifle Regiment: 1st Battalion, The Royal New Brunswick Regiment (Carleton and York): 2nd Battalion, The Royal New Brunswick Regiment (North Shore) **1958** 17th Duke of York's Royal Canadian Hussars (7th Reconnaissance Regiment): The Sherbrooke Regiment (RCAC) **1959** The Canadian Scottish Regiment (Princess Mary's)
156.	**IBBENBUREN** 1st–6th April 1945 Pursuit to the Baltic and North Sea	**1956** 15th/19th The King's Royal Hussars: The Devonshire Regiment **1957** The East Lancashire Regiment: 5th Royal Inniskilling Dragoon Guards: The Royal Welch Fusiliers: The Oxfordshire and Buckinghamshire Light Infantry: The King's Own Scottish Borderers: The King's Shropshire Light Infantry: The Herefordshire Light Infantry (TA): 11th Hussars (Prince Albert's): The Highland Light Infantry (City of Glasgow Regiment): The Durham Light Infantry: The Manchester Regiment: The Monmouthshire Regiment (TA)

157.	**LINGEN** 2nd–5th April 1945 Pursuit to the Baltic and North Sea	1956 1957	The Life Guards: Royal Horse Guards The Royal Warwickshire Regiment: The Staffordshire Yeomanry (Queen's Own Royal Regiment), Royal Armoured Corps (TA): The King's Own Scottish Borderers: The King's Shropshire Light Infantry: Scots Guards: Coldstream Guards: The Royal Norfolk Regiment: The Royal Lincolnshire Regiment: Welsh Guards: The Middlesex Regiment (Duke of Cambridge's Own)
158.	**BENTHEIM** 2nd–3rd April 1945 Pursuit to the Baltic and North Sea	1956	The Life Guards: Royal Horse Guards: Irish Guards
159.	**DREIRWALDE** 4th–8th April 1945 Pursuit to the Baltic and North Sea	1956 1957 1958	The Cameronians (Scottish Rifles) The King's Own Scottish Borderers: The Highland Light Infantry (City of Glasgow Regiment): The Manchester Regiment: The King's Royal Rifle Corps The Royal Scots Fusiliers
160.	**LEESE** 5th–8th April 1945 Pursuit to the Baltic and North Sea	1957	The Inns of Court Regiment, Royal Armoured Corps (TA): The Rifle Brigade (Prince Consort's Own): London Rifle Brigade, The Rifle Brigade (Prince Consort's Own) (TA): The Commando Association
161.	**ALLER** 10th–17th April 1945 Pursuit to the Baltic and North Sea	1956 1957	The Royal Scots Greys (2nd Dragoons): 15th/19th The King's Royal Hussars 3rd/4th County of London Yeomanry (Sharpshooters), Royal Armoured Corps (TA): The Inns of Court Regiment, Royal Armoured Corps (TA): The East Lancashire Regiment: The Cheshire Regiment: The Royal Welch Fusiliers: The King's Shropshire Light Infantry: The Herefordshire Light Infantry (TA): 11th Hussars (Prince Albert's Own): The Highland Light Infantry (City of Glasgow Regiment): The Rifle Brigade (Prince Consort's Own): The Manchester Regiment: London Rifle Brigade, The Rifle Brigade (Prince Consort's Own) (TA): The Monmouthshire Regiment (TA): The Commando Association: The King's Royal Rifle Corps
162.	**BRINKUM** 13th–16th April 1945 Pursuit to the Baltic and North Sea	1957	The Royal Warwickshire Regiment: The Suffolk Regiment: The Royal Norfolk Regiment: The Middlesex Regiment (Duke of Cambridge's Own): The East Yorkshire Regiment (The Duke of York's Own)
163.	**UELZEN** 14th–18th April 1945 Pursuit to the Baltic and North Sea	1957 1958	Seaforth Highlanders (Ross-shire Buffs, The Duke of Albany's): The Argyll and Sutherland Highlanders (Princess Louise's): The King's Own Scottish Borderers: Scots Guards: Coldstream Guards: The Highland Light Infantry (City of Glasgow Regiment) The Royal Scots (The Royal Regiment): The Royal Scots Fusiliers
164.	**BREMEN** 18th–26th April 1945 Pursuit to the Baltic and North Sea	1956 1957 1958	The Royal Scots Greys (2nd Dragoons): The Wiltshire Regiment (Duke of Edinburgh's): 4th/7th Royal Dragoon Guards: The Cameronians (Scottish Rifles) 13th/18th Royal Hussars (Queen Mary's Own): The Royal Warwickshire Regiment: The Somerset Light Infantry (Prince Albert's): The King's Own Scottish Borderers: The King's Shropshire Light Infantry: The South Lancashire Regiment (The Prince of Wales's Volunteers): The Royal Ulster Rifles: The Royal Lincolnshire Regiment: The Highland Light Infantry (City of Glasgow Regiment): The Middlesex Regiment (Duke of Cambridge's Own): The East Yorkshire Regiment (The Duke of York's Own): The Manchester Regiment Royal Tank Regiment: The Royal Scots (The Royal Regiment): The Royal Scots Fusiliers

165. ARTLENBERG
29th–30th April 1945
Pursuit to the Baltic and North Sea

1956	The Cameronians (Scottish Rifles)
1957	Seaforth Highlanders (Ross-shire Buffs, The Duke of Albany's); The Argyll and Sutherland Highlanders (Princess Louise's); The King's Own Scottish Borderers; The Highland Light Infantry (City of Glasgow Regiment)
1958	The Royal Scots (The Royal Regiment); The Royal Scots Fusiliers

166. TWENTE CANAL [1]
2nd–4th April 1945
Pursuit to the Baltic and North Sea

1957	The Dorset Regiment
1957	14th Canadian Hussars (8th Armoured Regiment): The Essex and Kent Scottish: The British Columbia Regiment (Duke of Connaught's Own) (13th Armoured Regiment); The Canadian Grenadier Guards (6th Battalion, The Canadian Guards); The Royal Hamilton Light Infantry (Wentworth Regiment); The Lincoln and Welland Regiment; The Lake Superior Scottish Regiment (Motor); The Toronto Scottish Regiment; The Royal Regiment of Canada; South Alberta Light Horse (29th Armoured Regiment)

[1] *CANAL TWENTE taken into use by French-speaking Canadian units 1958.*

167. ZUTPHEN
6th–8th April 1945
Pursuit to the Baltic and North Sea

1957	Les Fusiliers de Sherbrooke: Le Regiment de la Chaudiere: The Highland Light Infantry of Canada: The Cameron Highlanders of Ottawa (MG); The Stormont, Dundas and Glengarry Highlanders (MG); 1st Battalion, The Royal New Brunswick Regiment (Carleton and York); 2nd Battalion, The Royal New Brunswick Regiment (North Shore)
1958	17th Duke of York's Royal Canadian Hussars (7th Reconnaissance Regiment); The Sherbrooke Regiment (RCAC): 1st Battalion, The Nova Scotia Highlanders (North): 2nd Battalion, The Nova Scotia Highlanders (Cape Breton)

168. DEVENTER
8th–11th April 1945
Pursuit to the Baltic and North Sea

1957	Les Fusiliers de Sherbrooke: The Queen's Own Rifles of Canada: The Royal Winnipeg Rifles: The Regina Rifle Regiment: The Cameron Highlanders of Ottawa (MG)
1958	17th Duke of York's Royal Canadian Hussars (7th Reconnaissance Regiment); The Sherbrooke Regiment (RCAC)
1959	The Canadian Scottish Regiment (Princess Mary's)

169. ARNHEM 1945
12th–14th April 1945
Pursuit to the Baltic and North Sea

1956	The York and Lancaster Regiment: Princess Louise's Kensington Regiment (TA)
1957	The Royal Lincolnshire Regiment: The Essex Regiment
1958	The South Wales Borderers
1958	The Ontario Regiment (11th Armoured Regiment)

170. GRONINGEN
13th–16th April 1945
Pursuit to the Baltic and North Sea

1957	14th Canadian Hussars (8th Armoured Regiment): The Essex and Kent Scottish: The Royal Hamilton Light Infantry (Wentworth Regiment); Les Fusiliers Mont-Royal: The Toronto Scottish Regiment: The Black Watch (Royal Highland Regiment) of Canada: The Royal Canadian Dragoons (1st Armoured Regiment); The Queen's Own Cameron Highlanders of Canada (Motor); The Royal Regiment of Canada: Fort Garry Horse (10th Armoured Regiment); The Calgary Highlanders: The South Saskatchewan Regiment: Le Regiment de Maisonneuve
1959	First Canadian Armoured Personnel Carrier Regiment

171. FRIESOYTHE
14th April 1945
Pursuit to the Baltic and North Sea

1957	The Lincoln and Welland Regiment: The Lake Superior Scottish Regiment (Motor): Argyll and Sutherland Highlanders of Canada (Princess Louise's)

172. APELDOORN
11th–17th April 1945
Pursuit to the Baltic and North Sea

1957	The Hastings and Prince Edward Regiment: 48th Highlanders of Canada: 1st Hussars (6th Armoured Regiment): Princess Patricia's Canadian Light Infantry: West Nova Scotia Regiment (Machine Gun); The Seaforth Highlanders of Canada: 1st Battalion, The Royal New Brunswick Regiment (Carleton and York): 2nd Battalion, The Royal New Brunswick Regiment (North Shore); The Royal 22e Regiment
1958	The Loyal Edmonton Regiment (3rd Battalion, Princess Patricia's Canadian Light Infantry): The Royal Canadian Regiment
1959	Le Regiment de Trois Rivieres: The North Saskatchewan Regiment

173.	**IJSSELMEER** 15th–18th April 1945 Pursuit to the Baltic and North Sea	1957 1958 1959	1/8th Canadian Hussars (Princess Louise's): 2/8th Canadian Hussars (Princess Louise's): The Westminster Regiment: The Governor-General's Horse Guards (3rd Armoured Regiment) The British Columbia Dragoons (9th Reconnaissance Regiment); Lord Strathcona's Horse (Royal Canadians): 1st Battalion, The Nova Scotia Highlanders (North): 2nd Battalion, The Nova Scotia Highlanders (Cape Breton) The Perth Regiment; The Irish Regiment of Canada
174.	**KUSTEN CANAL** [1] 17th–24th April 1945 Pursuit to the Baltic and North Sea	1957	The British Columbia Regiment (Duke of Connaught's Own) (13th Armoured Regiment): The Lake Superior Scottish Regiment (Motor); Argyll and Sutherland Highlanders of Canada (Princess Louise's); The Algonquin Regiment (26th Armoured Regiment): 1st Battalion, The Royal New Brunswick Regiment (Carleton and York): 2nd Battalion, The Royal New Brunswick Regiment (North Shore) [1] *CANAL KUSTEN taken into use by French-speaking Canadian units 1958.*
175.	**LEER** 28th–29th April 1945 Pursuit to the Baltic and North Sea	1957 1958	The Highland Light Infantry of Canada: The Cameron Highlanders of Ottawa (MG); The Stormont, Dundas and Glengarry Highlanders (MG) 1st Battalion, The Nova Scotia Highlanders (North): 2nd Battalion, The Nova Scotia Highlanders (Cape Breton)
176.	**DELFZIJL POCKET** [1] 23rd April–2nd May 1945 Pursuit to the Baltic and North Sea	1957 1958 1959	The Princess Louise Fusiliers (MG); 1/8th Canadian Hussars (Princess Louise's): 2/8th Canadian Hussars (Princess Louise's): The Westminster Regiment The British Columbia Dragoons (9th Reconnaissance Regiment): 1st Battalion, The Nova Scotia Highlanders (North): 2nd Battalion, The Nova Scotia Highlanders (Cape Breton) The Perth Regiment; The Irish Regiment of Canada [1] *POCHE DE DELFZIJL taken into use by French-speaking Canadian units 1958.*
177.	**BAD ZWISCHENAHN** 25th April–4th May 1945 Pursuit to the Baltic and North Sea	1957 1958	The British Columbia Regiment (Duke of Connaught's Own) (13th Armoured Regiment): The Canadian Grenadier Guards (6th Battalion, The Canadian Guards): The Lake Superior Scottish Regiment (Motor): 1st Hussars (6th Armoured Regiment): The Royal Canadian Dragoons (1st Armoured Regiment); The Governor-General's Foot Guards (5th Canadian Guards); Argyll and Sutherland Highlanders of Canada (Princess Louise's); The Algonquin Regiment (26th Armoured Regiment): 1st Battalion, The Royal New Brunswick Regiment (Carleton and York): 2nd Battalion, The Royal New Brunswick Regiment (North Shore): South Alberta Light Horse (29th Armoured Regiment) 12th Manitoba Dragoons (18th Armoured Regiment)
178.	**OLDENBURG** 27th April–5th May 1945 Pursuit to the Baltic and North Sea	1957	14th Canadian Hussars (8th Armoured Regiment): The Essex and Kent Scottish: The Royal Hamilton Light Infantry (Wentworth Regiment): Les Fusiliers Mont-Royal: The Toronto Scottish Regiment: The Black Watch (Royal Highland Regiment) of Canada: The Queen's Own Cameron Highlanders of Canada (Motor): The Royal Regiment of Canada: Fort Garry Horse (10th Armoured Regiment): The Calgary Highlanders: The South Saskatchewan Regiment: Le Regiment de Maisonneuve
179.	**SOUTHERN FRANCE** [1] 15th–28th August 1944 The Invasion of the South of France	1956 1957 1957	The Parachute Regiment The Glider Pilot Regiment 1st Special Service Battalion [1] *SUD DE LA FRANCE taken into use by French-speaking Canadian units 1958.*
180.	**NORTH-WEST EUROPE 1940** 10th May–31st December 1940 Service in North-West Europe 1940–42	1956	The Duke of Wellington's Regiment (West Riding): 9th Queen's Royal Lancers: 15th/19th The King's Royal Hussars: The Fife and Forfar Yeomanry, Royal Armoured Corps (TA): The Duke of Cornwall's Light Infantry: The Wiltshire Regiment (Duke of Edinburgh's): The York and Lancaster Regiment: Princess Louise's Kensington Regiment (TA): 4th/7th Royal Dragoon Guards: The Buffs (Royal East Kent Regiment): The Cameronians (Scottish Rifles): The Royal Sussex Regiment

1957 | The Queen's Bays (2nd Dragoon Guards): 13th/18th Royal Hussars (Queen Mary's Own): The East Riding Yeomanry, Royal Armoured Corps (TA): The Royal Warwickshire Regiment: The Royal Fusiliers (City of London Regiment): The Gloucestershire Regiment: The East Lancashire Regiment: 5th Royal Inniskilling Dragoon Guards: Grenadier Guards: The Lancashire Fusiliers: The Cheshire Regiment: The Royal Welch Fusiliers: The Oxfordshire and Buckinghamshire Light Infantry: Seaforth Highlanders (Ross-shire Buffs, The Duke of Albany's): The Gordon Highlanders: The Argyll and Sutherland Highlanders (Princess Louise's): 12th Royal Lancers (Prince of Wales's): The Queen's Royal Regiment (West Surrey): The West Yorkshire Regiment (The Prince of Wales's Own): The Bedfordshire and Hertfordshire Regiment: The Green Howards (Alexandra, Princess of Wales's Own Yorkshire Regiment): The King's Own Scottish Borderers: The Dorset Regiment: The Sherwood Foresters (Nottinghamshire and Derbyshire Regiment): The Queen's Own Royal West Kent Regiment: 10th Royal Hussars (Prince of Wales's Own): The Royal Inniskilling Fusiliers: The Border Regiment: The Loyal Regiment (North Lancashire): The Northamptonshire Regiment: The King's Shropshire Light Infantry: The Queen's Own Cameron Highlanders: The King's Own Royal Regiment (Lancaster): The Suffolk Regiment: The East Surrey Regiment: The Royal Hampshire Regiment: The South Lancashire Regiment (The Prince of Wales's Volunteers): The Royal Ulster Rifles: Coldstream Guards: The Royal Norfolk Regiment: The Royal Lincolnshire Regiment: The Royal Berkshire Regiment (Princess Charlotte of Wales's): The Highland Light Infantry (City of Glasgow Regiment): The Rifle Brigade (Prince Consort's Own): 1st/2nd Lothians and Border Horse, Royal Armoured Corps (TA): Welsh Guards: The Black Watch (Royal Highland Regiment): The Essex Regiment: The Middlesex Regiment (Duke of Cambridge's Own): The Durham Light Infantry: The East Yorkshire Regiment (The Duke of York's Own): The Manchester Regiment: The Worcestershire Regiment: The King's Royal Rifle Corps: Queen Victoria's Rifles, The King's Royal Rifle Corps (TA): The North Staffordshire Regiment (The Prince of Wales's)

1958 | Royal Tank Regiment: The South Staffordshire Regiment: The Royal Scots (The Royal Regiment): The Royal Northumberland Fusiliers: The Royal Scots Fusiliers

181. NORTH-WEST EUROPE 1942 [1]
1st January–19th August 1942
Service in North-West Europe 1940–42

1956 | The Parachute Regiment
1957 | The Commando Association
1957 | The Essex and Kent Scottish: The Royal Hamilton Light Infantry (Wentworth Regiment): Les Fusiliers Mont-Royal: The Toronto Scottish Regiment: The Queen's Own Cameron Highlanders of Canada (Motor): The Royal Regiment of Canada: The South Saskatchewan Regiment
1959 | The King's Own Calgary Regiment (RCAC)

[1] *NORD-OUEST DE L'EUROPE 1942 taken into use by French-speaking Canadian units 1958.*

182. NORTH-WEST EUROPE 1944 [1]
6th June–31st December 1944
Service in North-West Europe 1944–45

1956 | 24th Lancers
1957 | The King's Regiment (Liverpool): The Lancashire Fusiliers: The Hertfordshire Regiment (TA): The Border Regiment: The North Staffordshire Regiment (The Prince of Wales's)
1957 | 1st Special Service Battalion
1958 | The South Staffordshire Regiment

[1] *NORD-OUEST DE L'EUROPE 1944 taken into use by French-speaking Canadian units 1958.*

183. NORTH-WEST EUROPE 1944-45 [1]
6th June 1944–7th May 1945
Service in North-West Europe 1944-45

1956 | The Life Guards: Royal Horse Guards: 1st The Royal Dragoons: The Royal Scots Greys (2nd Dragoons): Irish Guards: The Duke of Wellington's Regiment (West Riding): 15th/19th The King's Royal Hussars: The Derbyshire Yeomanry, Royal Armoured Corps (TA): The Fife and Forfar Yeomanry, Royal Armoured Corps (TA): Westminster Dragoons (2nd County of London Yeomanry), Royal Armoured Corps (TA): The Royal Leicestershire Regiment: The Duke of Cornwall's Light Infantry: The Wiltshire Regiment (Duke of Edinburgh's): The York and Lancaster Regiment: Princess Louise's Kensington Regiment (TA): The Parachute Regiment: 4th/7th Royal Dragoon Guards: The Devonshire Regiment: The Cameronians (Scottish Rifles): The Parachute Regiment

1957 | 13th/18th Royal Hussars (Queen Mary's Own); 3rd/4th County of London Yeomanry (Sharpshooters), Royal Armoured Corps (TA); The East Riding Yeomanry, Royal Armoured Corps (TA); The Inns of Court Regiment, Royal Armoured Corps (TA); Honourable Artillery Company (TA); The Royal Warwickshire Regiment; The Gloucestershire Regiment; The East Lancashire Regiment; The Glider Pilot Regiment; 5th Royal Inniskilling Dragoon Guards; The Northamptonshire Yeomanry, Royal Armoured Corps (TA); Grenadier Guards; The Cheshire Regiment; The Royal Welch Fusiliers; The Oxfordshire and Buckinghamshire Light Infantry; Seaforth Highlanders (Ross-shire Buffs, The Duke of Albany's); The Gordon Highlanders; The Argyll and Sutherland Highlanders (Princess Louise's); 23rd Hussars; The Staffordshire Yeomanry (Queen's Own Royal Regiment), Royal Armoured Corps (TA); The Queen's Royal Regiment (West Surrey); The Somerset Light Infantry (Prince Albert's); The Green Howards (Alexandra, Princess of Wales's Own Yorkshire Regiment); The King's Own Scottish Borderers; The Dorset Regiment; The King's Own Yorkshire Light Infantry; 8th King's Royal Irish Hussars; The King's Shropshire Light Infantry; The Queen's Own Cameron Highlanders; The Herefordshire Light Infantry (TA); The Sherwood Rangers Yeomanry, Royal Armoured Corps (TA); Scots Guards; The Suffolk Regiment; The Royal Hampshire Regiment; The South Lancashire Regiment (The Prince of Wales's Volunteers); The Royal Ulster Rifles; 11th Hussars (Prince Albert's Own); 22nd Dragoons; Coldstream Guards; The Royal Norfolk Regiment; The Royal Lincolnshire Regiment; The Royal Berkshire Regiment (Princess Charlotte of Wales's); The Highland Light Infantry (City of Glasgow Regiment); The Rifle Brigade (Prince Consort's Own); 1st/2nd Lothians and Border Horse, Royal Armoured Corps (TA); Welsh Guards; The Welch Regiment; The Black Watch (Royal Highland Regiment); The Essex Regiment; The Middlesex Regiment (Duke of Cambridge's Own); The Durham Light Infantry; The East Yorkshire Regiment (The Duke of York's Own); The Manchester Regiment; London Rifle Brigade, The Rifle Brigade (Prince Consort's Own) (TA); The Monmouthshire Regiment (TA); The Commando Association; The Worcestershire Regiment; The King's Royal Rifle Corps; The Queen's Westminsters, The King's Royal Rifle Corps (TA); Special Air Service Regiment

1958 | Royal Tank Regiment; The South Wales Borderers; The Royal Scots (The Royal Regiment); The Royal Northumberland Fusiliers; The Royal Scots Fusiliers

---

184. | **NORTH-WEST EUROPE 1944–1945** [1] | 1957 | 14th Canadian Hussars (8th Armoured Regiment); The Essex and Kent Scottish; The Royal Montreal Regiment; The British Columbia Regiment (Duke of Connaught's Own) (13th Armoured Regiment); Les Fusiliers de Sherbrooke; The Elgin Regiment (27th Armoured Regiment); The Canadian Grenadier Guards (6th Battalion, The Canadian Guards); The Queen's Own Rifles of Canada; The Royal Hamilton Light Infantry (Wentworth Regiment); The Lincoln and Welland Regiment; Le Regiment de la Chaudiere; The Lake Superior Scottish Regiment (Motor); Les Fusiliers Mont-Royal; 1st Hussars (6th Armoured Regiment); The Toronto Scottish Regiment; The Highland Light Infantry of Canada; The Royal Winnipeg Rifles; The Black Watch (Royal Highland Regiment) of Canada; The Regina Rifle Regiment; The Queen's Own Cameron Highlanders of Canada (Motor); The Governor General's Foot Guards (5th Canadian Guards); The Royal Regiment of Canada; The Cameron Highlanders of Ottawa (MG); Fort Garry Horse (10th Armoured Regiment); Argyll and Sutherland Highlanders of Canada (Princess Louise's); The Calgary Highlanders; The South Saskatchewan Regiment; The Algonquin Regiment (26th Armoured Regiment); The Stormont, Dundas and Glengarry Highlanders (MG); 1st Battalion, The Royal New Brunswick Regiment (Carleton and York); 2nd Battalion, The Royal New Brunswick Regiment (North Shore); South Alberta Light Horse (29th Armoured Regiment); Prince Edward Island Regiment (17th Reconnaissance Regiment) [2]; Le Regiment de Maisonneuve

6th June 1944–7th May 1945
Service in North-West Europe 1944–45 | |

| | | 1958 | The First Canadian Parachute Battalion; 12th Manitoba Dragoons (18th Armoured Regiment); 17th Duke of York's Royal Canadian Hussars (7th Reconnaissance Regiment); The Sherbrooke Regiment (RCAC); 1st Battalion, The Nova Scotia Highlanders (North); 2nd Battalion, The Nova Scotia Highlanders (Cape Breton)

| | | 1959 | The Lorne Scots (Peel, Dufferin and Halton Regiment); The Canadian Scottish Regiment (Princess Mary's); First Canadian Armoured Personnel Carrier Regiment

[1] NORD-OUEST DE L'EUROPE 1944–1945 taken into use by French-speaking Canadian units 1958. [2] NORTH-WEST EUROPE 1945 taken into use.

185.	**NORTH-WEST EUROPE 1945** [?] 1st January–7th May 1945 Service in North-West Europe 1944-45	1957 1957 1958 1959	The Northamptonshire Regiment The Hastings and Prince Edward Regiment: 48th Highlanders of Canada: The Princess Louise Fusiliers (MG): Princess Patricia's Canadian Light Infantry: West Nova Scotia Regiment (Machine Gun): The Royal Canadian Dragoons (1st Armoured Regiment): 1/8th Canadian Hussars (Princess Louise's): 2/8th Canadian Hussars (Princess Louise's): The Westminster Regiment: The Governor General's Horse Guards (3rd Armoured Regiment): The Seaforth Highlanders of Canada: The Royal 22e Regiment The British Columbia Dragoons (9th Reconnaissance Regiment): The Ontario Regiment (11th Armoured Regiment): 4th Princess Louise Dragoon Guards (4th Armoured Car Regiment): The Loyal Edmonton Regiment (3rd Battalion, Princess Patricia's Canadian Light Infantry): The Royal Canadian Regiment: Lord Strathcona's Horse (Royal Canadians) Le Regiment de Trois Rivieres: The North Saskatchewan Regiment: The Perth Regiment: The King's Own Calgary Regiment (RCAC): The Irish Regiment of Canada [?] *NORD-OUEST DE L'EUROPE 1945 taken into use by French-speaking Canadian units 1958.*
186.	**GALLABAT** 6th–7th November 1940 Sudan Border (Northern Campaign)	1962 ?	3rd Battalion, The Garhwal Rifles 4th Battalion (Duke of Connaught's Own), The Baluch Regiment: 3rd Royal Battalion, The Frontier Force Regiment
187.	**TEHAMIYAN WELLS** 11th November 1940 Sudan Border (Northern Campaign)	?	3rd Royal Battalion, The Frontier Force Regiment
188.	**GASH DELTA** 23rd December 1940 Sudan Border (Northern Campaign)	?	6th Royal Battalion (Scinde), The Frontier Force Rifles
189.	**JEBEL DAFEIS** 10th January 1941 Sudan Border (Northern Campaign)	1957	The West Yorkshire Regiment (The Prince of Wales's Own)
190.	**JEBEL SHIBA** 21st–23rd January 1941 Eritrea (Northern Campaign)	1957	The Highland Light Infantry (City of Glasgow Regiment)
191.	**GOGNI** 26th January 1941 Eritrea (Northern Campaign)	1957	The Worcestershire Regiment
192.	**UM HAGAR** 21st–31st January 1941 Eritrea (Northern Campaign)	?	3rd Royal Battalion, The Frontier Force Regiment
193.	**AGORDAT** 28th January–1st February 1941 Eritrea (Northern Campaign)	1957 1962 1963 ?	The Royal Fusiliers (City of London Regiment): The Queen's Own Cameron Highlanders 1 Horse: 4th Battalion, The Sikh Regiment 3rd Battalion, The Brigade of the Guards 3rd Battalion, 1st Punjab Regiment: 3rd Battalion, 14th Punjab Regiment: 3rd Royal Battalion, The Frontier Force Regiment

194.	**BARENTU** 27th January–2nd February 1941 Eritrea (Northern Campaign)	1957 1962 ?	The Highland Light Infantry (City of Glasgow Regiment); The Worcestershire Regiment 3rd Battalion, The Garhwal Rifles 4th Battalion (Duke of Connaught's Own), The Baluch Regiment: 6th Royal Battalion (Scinde), The Frontier Force Rifles: 3rd Royal Battalion, The Frontier Force Regiment
195.	**KARORA-MARSA TACLAI** 9th–10th February 1941 Eritrea (Northern Campaign)	1956	The Royal Sussex Regiment
196.	**CUB CUB** 23rd February 1941 Eritrea (Northern Campaign)	1956	The Royal Sussex Regiment
197.	**MESCELIT PASS** 1st March 1941 Eritrea (Northern Campaign)	1956 ?	The Royal Sussex Regiment 4th Battalion (Bhopal), 16th Punjab Regiment
198.	**KEREN** 3rd February–31st March 1941 Eritrea (Northern Campaign)	1956 1957 1962 1963 ?	The Royal Sussex Regiment The Royal Fusiliers (City of London Regiment); The West Yorkshire Regiment (The Prince of Wales's Own); The Queen's Own Cameron Highlanders; The Highland Light Infantry (City of Glasgow Regiment); The Worcestershire Regiment 1 Horse: 3rd Battalion, The Brigade of the Guards: 2nd Battalion, The Parachute Regiment: 3rd Battalion, The Punjab Regiment: 2nd Battalion, The Maratha Light Infantry: 4th Battalion, The Rajputana Rifles: 4th Battalion, The Sikh Regiment: 3rd Battalion, The Garhwal Rifles The Central India Horse 3rd Battalion, 1st Punjab Regiment: 3rd Battalion, 14th Punjab Regiment: 4th Battalion (Duke of Connaught's Own), The Baluch Regiment: 6th Royal Battalion (Scinde), The Frontier Force Rifles: 3rd Royal Battalion, The Frontier Force Regiment
199.	**MT ENGIAHAT** 12th–15th March 1941 Eritrea (Northern Campaign)	1956 ?	The Royal Sussex Regiment 4th Battalion (Bhopal), 16th Punjab Regiment
200.	**KEREN-ASMARA ROAD** 28th–29th March 1941 Eritrea (Northern Campaign)	1963	The Central India Horse
201.	**AD TECLESAN** 30th–31st March 1941 Eritrea (Northern Campaign)	1957 1962 ?	The West Yorkshire Regiment (The Prince of Wales's Own) 3rd Battalion, The Punjab Regiment 6th Royal Battalion (Scinde), The Frontier Force Rifles
202.	**MASSAWA** 8th April 1941 Eritrea (Northern Campaign)	1956 1957 1962 ?	The Royal Sussex Regiment The Highland Light Infantry (City of Glasgow Regiment) 3rd Battalion, The Garhwal Rifles 4th Battalion (Bhopal), 16th Punjab Regiment: 4th Battalion (Duke of Connaught's Own), The Baluch Regiment

No.	Battle Honour	Regiment	Year
203.	**AMBA ALAGI** 20th April–16th May 1941 Eritrea (Northern Campaign)	The Worcestershire Regiment	1957
		The Royal Natal Carbineers: Duke of Edinburgh's Own Rifles: Transvaal Scottish	1957
		3rd Battalion, The Punjab Regiment: 3rd Battalion, The Garhwal Rifles	1962
		1 Horse	1963
		6th Royal Battalion (Scinde), The Frontier Force Rifles: 3rd Royal Battalion, The Frontier Force Regiment	?
204.	**AFODU** 9th March 1941 Subsidiary Campaigns in Western Abyssinia	The King's African Rifles	1957
205.	**GAMBELA** 22nd March 1941 Subsidiary Campaigns in Western Abyssinia	The King's African Rifles	1957
206.	**WOLCHEFIT** 13th April–27th September 1941 Subsidiary Campaigns in Northern Abyssinia	3rd Battalion, 14th Punjab Regiment	?
207.	**MOYALE** 1st–15th July 1940 Kenya Border (Southern Campaign)	The King's African Rifles	1957
208.	**WAL GARIS** 10th and 12th September 1940 Kenya Border (Southern Campaign)	The Gold Coast Regiment, Royal West African Frontier Force	1957
209.	**EL WAK** 15th–17th December 1940 Kenya Border (Southern Campaign)	The Gold Coast Regiment, Royal West African Frontier Force	1957
		The Royal Natal Carbineers: Duke of Edinburgh's Own Rifles: Transvaal Scottish	1957
210.	**MEGA** 15th–18th February 1941 Southern Abyssinia (Southern Campaign)	Transvaal Scottish: South African Irish Regiment	?
211.	**TODENYANG-NAMARAPUTH** 9th February 1941 Southern Abyssinia (Southern Campaign)	The King's African Rifles	1957
212.	**SOROPPA** 31st March 1941 Southern Abyssinia (Southern Campaign)	The King's African Rifles	1957

213.	**JUBA** 4th–26th February 1941 Juba River	1957	The King's African Rifles: The Queen's Own Nigeria Regiment, Royal West African Frontier Force: The Gold Coast Regiment, Royal West African Frontier Force
214.	**THE JUBA**[1] 4th–26th February 1941 Juba River	1957	The Royal Natal Carbineers: Duke of Edinburgh's Own Rifles: Transvaal Scottish [1] *DIE JUBA taken into use by Afrikaans-speaking South African units 1957.*
215.	**BELLES GUGANI** 4th February 1941 Juba River	1957	The King's African Rifles
216.	**BULO ERILLO** 13th February 1941 Juba River	1957	The Gold Coast Regiment, Royal West African Frontier Force
217.	**YONTE** 18th–19th February 1941 Juba River	1957	Transvaal Scottish
218.	**GELIB** 21st–22nd February 1941 Juba River	1957	The Gold Coast Regiment, Royal West African Frontier Force
219.	**ALESSANDRA** 22nd February 1941 Juba River	1957	The Gold Coast Regiment, Royal West African Frontier Force
220.	**GOLUIN** 24th February 1941 Juba River	1957	The Queen's Own Nigeria Regiment, Royal West African Frontier Force
221.	**DIREDAWA** 27th–29th March 1941 Juba River	1957	Transvaal Scottish
222.	**BERBERA** 16th March 1941 Advance to Addis Ababa	1962 ?	1st Battalion, The Parachute Regiment 3rd Battalion, 15th Punjab Regiment
223.	**MARDA PASS** 21st–22nd March 1941 Advance to Addis Ababa	1957	The Queen's Own Nigeria Regiment, Royal West African Frontier Force
224.	**BABILE GAP** 23rd–25th March 1941 Advance to Addis Ababa	1957	The Queen's Own Nigeria Regiment, Royal West African Frontier Force

225.	**BISIDIMO** 26th March 1941 Advance to Addis Ababa	1957	The Queen's Own Nigeria Regiment, Royal West African Frontier Force
226.	**AWASH** 2nd and 3rd April 1941 Advance to Addis Ababa	1957	The King's African Rifles
227.	**FIKE** 1st May 1941 Northern Battle of Lakes	1957	The King's African Rifles
228.	**THE DADABA** [1] 13th May 1941 Northern Battle of Lakes	1957	Natal Mounted Rifles [1] DIE DADABA taken into use by Afrikaans-speaking South African units 1957.
229.	**COLITO** 19th May 1941 Northern Battle of Lakes	1957	The King's African Rifles: The Queen's Own Nigeria Regiment, Royal West African Frontier Force
230.	**GIARSO** 9th April 1941 Southern Battle of Lakes	1957	The Northern Rhodesia Regiment
231.	**WADARA** 8th April–10th May 1941 Southern Battle of Lakes	1957	The Gold Coast Regiment, Royal West African Frontier Force
232.	**OMO** 31st May–6th June 1941 Galla Sidamo	1957	The King's African Rifles: The Queen's Own Nigeria Regiment, Royal West African Frontier Force
233.	**LECHEMTI** 15th June 1941 Galla Sidamo	1957	The Queen's Own Nigeria Regiment, Royal West African Frontier Force
234.	**COMBOLCIA** 17th–26th April 1941 NE Abyssinia	1957	The Royal Natal Carbineers: Duke of Edinburgh's Own Rifles: Transvaal Scottish
235.	**ASSAB** 11th June 1941 NE Abyssinia	?	3rd Battalion, 15th Punjab Regiment
236.	**GONDAR** 15th October–28th November 1941 Gondar	1957	The King's African Rifles

237.	**AMBAZZO** 15th October–28th November 1941 Gondar	1957	The King's African Rifles
238.	**KULKABER** 13th and 21st November 1941 Gondar	1957	The King's African Rifles
239.	**ABYSSINIA 1940** 13th June–31st December 1940 Service in Abyssinia 1940–41	1957 1958	The Essex Regiment Royal Tank Regiment
240.	**ABYSSINIA 1940–41** 13th June 1940–28th November 1941 Service in Abyssinia 1940–41	1957 1957 1962 ?	The West Yorkshire Regiment (The Prince of Wales's Own); The Worcestershire Regiment The King's African Rifles; The Gold Coast Regiment, Royal West African Frontier Force I Horse; The Central India Horse; 12 Field Company, Madras Engineer Group; 20 Field Company, Bombay Engineer Group; 21 Field Company, Bombay Engineer Group; 3rd Battalion, The Brigade of the Guards; 1st Battalion, The Parachute Regiment; 2nd Battalion, The Parachute Regiment; 3rd Battalion, The Punjab Regiment; 14th Battalion (Nabha), The Punjab Regiment; 2nd Battalion, The Maratha Light Infantry; 4th Battalion, The Rajputana Rifles; 17th Battalion (Sawai Man), The Rajputana Rifles; 4th Battalion, The Sikh Regiment; 3rd Battalion, The Garhwal Rifles 3rd Battalion, 1st Punjab Regiment; 3rd Battalion, 14th Punjab Regiment; 15th Punjab Regiment; 4th Battalion (Bhopal), 16th Punjab Regiment; 4th Battalion (Duke of Connaught's Own), The Baluch Regiment; 6th Royal Battalion (Scinde), The Frontier Force Rifles; 3rd Royal Battalion, The Frontier Force Regiment
241.	**EAST AFRICA 1940–41** 13th June 1940–28th November 1941 Service in Abyssinia 1940–41	1957 ? '	The Royal Natal Carbineers; Duke of Edinburgh's Own Rifles; Transvaal Scottish; 2 Regiment Botha; Natal Mounted Rifles; Regiment President Steyn South African Irish Regiment; Regiment Vrystaat OOS-AFRIKA 1940–41 taken into use by Afrikaans-speaking South African units 1957.
242.	**ABYSSINIA 1941** 1st January–28th November 1941 Service in Abyssinia 1940–41	1956 1957 1957	The Royal Sussex Regiment The Argyll and Sutherland Highlanders (Princess Louise's); The Queen's Own Cameron Highlanders; The Highland Light Infantry (City of Glasgow Regiment) The Northern Rhodesia Regiment; The Queen's Own Nigeria Regiment, Royal West African Frontier Force
243.	**TUG ARGAN** 11th–15th August 1940 Enemy Invasion of British Somaliland	1957 ?	The King's African Rifles; The Northern Rhodesia Regiment 3rd Battalion, 15th Punjab Regiment
244.	**BARKASAN** 17th August 1940 Enemy Invasion of British Somaliland	1957	The Black Watch (Royal Highland Regiment)
245.	**BRITISH SOMALILAND 1940** 4th–17th August 1940 Service in British Somaliland 1940	1957 1957 ?	The Black Watch (Royal Highland Regiment) The King's African Rifles; The Northern Rhodesia Regiment 3rd Battalion, 15th Punjab Regiment

246.	**BRITISH SOMALILAND** 4th–17th August 1940 Service in British Somaliland 1940	1962	1st Battalion, The Parachute Regiment
247.	**DEFENCE OF HABBANIYA** 2nd–6th May 1941 Operations against the Iraqi Rebels	1957	The King's Own Royal Regiment (Lancaster)
248.	**FALLUJA** 19th–22nd May 1941 Operations against the Iraqi Rebels	1957	The King's Own Royal Regiment (Lancaster): The Essex Regiment
249.	**BAGHDAD 1941** 28th–31st May 1941 Operations against the Iraqi Rebels	1956 1957	The Life Guards: Royal Horse Guards The Essex Regiment
250.	**IRAQ 1941** 2nd–31st May 1941 Service in Iraq 1941	1956 1957 1962	The Life Guards: Royal Horse Guards: The Royal Wiltshire Yeomanry (Prince of Wales's Own), Royal Armoured Corps (TA): 10th Princess Mary's Own Gurkha Rifles The Warwickshire Yeomanry, Royal Armoured Corps (TA): The King's Own Royal Regiment (Lancaster): The Essex Regiment 9 Field Company, Madras Engineer Group: 10 Field Company, Madras Engineer Group: 3rd Battalion, The Sikh Regiment: 2nd Battalion, 4th Gorkha Rifles: 2nd Battalion, 8th Gorkha Rifles
251.	**SYRIAN FRONTIER** 7th–8th June 1941 Syria and Lebanon	1961	14th Infantry Battalion (The Prahran Regiment): 16th Infantry Battalion (The Cameron Highlanders of West Australia): 31st Infantry Battalion (The Kennedy Regiment): 33rd Infantry Battalion (The New England Regiment)
252.	**LITANI** 9th–10th June 1941 Syria and Lebanon	1957	The Commando Association
253.	**THE LITANI** 9th–10th June 1941 Syria and Lebanon	1961	16th Infantry Battalion (The Cameron Highlanders of West Australia): 27th Infantry Battalion (The South Australian Scottish Regiment)
254.	**MERJAYUN** 9th–27th June 1941 Syria and Lebanon	1956 1957 1961	The Royal Scots Greys (2nd Dragoons) The King's Own Royal Regiment (Lancaster) 6th Cavalry (Commando) Regiment: 5th Infantry Battalion (The Victorian Scottish Regiment): 25th Infantry Battalion (The Darling Downs Regiment): 31st Infantry Battalion (The Kennedy Regiment): 33rd Infantry Battalion (The New England Regiment): 2nd Pioneer Battalion
255.	**ADLUN** 10th–12th June 1941 Syria and Lebanon	1961	6th Cavalry (Commando) Regiment: 14th Infantry Battalion (The Prahran Regiment): 27th Infantry Battalion (The South Australian Scottish Regiment)
256.	**SIDON** 13th–15th June 1941 Syria and Lebanon	1961	6th Cavalry (Commando) Regiment: 9th Cavalry (Commando) Regiment: 16th Infantry Battalion (The Cameron Highlanders of West Australia): 27th Infantry Battalion (The South Australian Scottish Regiment): 3rd Machine Gun Battalion

257.	**JEZZINE** 14th–24th June 1941 Syria and Lebanon	1961	14th Infantry Battalion (The Prahran Regiment); 31st Infantry Battalion (The Kennedy Regiment); 3rd Machine Gun Battalion
258.	**DAMASCUS** 16th–21st June 1941 Syria and Lebanon	1961 1962 ?	3rd Infantry Battalion (The Werriwa Regiment) 4th Battalion, The Rajputana Rifles 13th Duke of Connaught's Own Lancers: 3rd Battalion, 1st Punjab Regiment
259.	**WADI ZEINI** 19th June 1941 Syria and Lebanon	1961	9th Cavalry (Commando) Regiment: 16th Infantry Battalion (The Cameron Highlanders of West Australia)
260.	**PALMYRA** 21st June–3rd July 1941 Syria and Lebanon	1956	The Life Guards: Royal Horse Guards: The Royal Wiltshire Yeomanry (Prince of Wales's Own), Royal Armoured Corps (TA)
261.	**DIMAS** 22nd–28th June 1941 Syria and Lebanon	1957 1961	The Essex Regiment 3rd Infantry Battalion (The Werriwa Regiment)
262.	**CHEMIN AND RHARIFE** 26th June–3rd July 1941 Syria and Lebanon	1961	25th Infantry Battalion (The Darling Downs Regiment)
263.	**DEIR EZ ZOR** 1st–3rd July 1941 Syria and Lebanon	1956 ?	10th Princess Mary's Own Gurkha Rifles 13th Duke of Connaught's Own Lancers: 4th Battalion (Wilde's), The Frontier Force Rifles
264.	**DAMOUR** 6th–12th July 1941 Syria and Lebanon	1961	6th Cavalry (Commando) Regiment: 3rd Infantry Battalion (The Werriwa Regiment): 5th Infantry Battalion (The Victorian Scottish Regiment): 14th Infantry Battalion (The Prahran Regiment): 16th Infantry Battalion (The Cameron Highlanders of West Australia): 25th Infantry Battalion (The Darling Downs Regiment): 27th Infantry Battalion (The South Australian Scottish Regiment): 31st Infantry Battalion (The Kennedy Regiment): 3rd Machine Gun Battalion: 2nd Pioneer Battalion
265.	**MAZRAAT ECH CHOUF** 7th–8th July 1941 Syria and Lebanon	1961	25th Infantry Battalion (The Darling Downs Regiment): 2nd Pioneer Battalion
266.	**HILL 1069** 8th July 1941 Syria and Lebanon	1961	31st Infantry Battalion (The Kennedy Regiment)
267.	**BADARENE** 9th–10th July 1941 Syria and Lebanon	1961	31st Infantry Battalion (The Kennedy Regiment)

268. RAQAA
9th–10th July 1941
Syria and Lebanon

? — 13th Duke of Connaught's Own Lancers: 4th Battalion (Wilde's), The Frontier Force Rifles

269. JEBEL MAZAR
10th–12th July 1941
Syria and Lebanon

1956 — The Royal Leicestershire Regiment: The North Somerset Yeomanry, Royal Armoured Corps (TA)

1957 — The King's Own Royal Regiment (Lancaster)

1961 — 9th Cavalry (Commando) Regiment: 3rd Machine Gun Battalion

270. SYRIA 1941
7th June–12th July 1941
Service in Syria 1941

1956 — The Life Guards: Royal Horse Guards: 1st The Royal Dragoons: The Royal Scots Greys (2nd Dragoons): The Royal Wiltshire Yeomanry (Prince of Wales's Own), Royal Armoured Corps (TA): The Cheshire Yeomanry (Earl of Chester's), Royal Armoured Corps (TA): The Royal Leicestershire Regiment: The North Somerset Yeomanry, Royal Armoured Corps (TA): 10th Princess Mary's Own Gurkha Rifles

1957 — The Royal Fusiliers (City of London Regiment): The Warwickshire Yeomanry, Royal Armoured Corps (TA): The Staffordshire Yeomanry (Queen's Own Royal Regiment), Royal Armoured Corps (TA): The Queen's Own Yorkshire Dragoons, Royal Armoured Corps (TA): The Queen's Royal Regiment (West Surrey): The King's Own Royal Regiment (Lancaster): The Essex Regiment: The Durham Light Infantry: The Commando Association

1961 — 6th Cavalry (Commando) Regiment: 9th Cavalry (Commando) Regiment: 3rd Infantry Battalion (The Werriwa Regiment): 5th Infantry Battalion (The Victorian Scottish Regiment): 14th Infantry Battalion (The Prahran Regiment): 16th Infantry Battalion (The Cameron Highlanders of West Australia): 25th Infantry Battalion (The Darling Downs Regiment): 27th Infantry Battalion (The South Australian Scottish Regiment): 31st Infantry Battalion (The Kennedy Regiment): 33rd Infantry Battalion (The New England Regiment): 3rd Machine Gun Battalion: 2nd Pioneer Battalion

1962 — 9 Field Company, Madras Engineer Group: 18 Field Company, Bombay Engineer Group: 4th Battalion, The Rajputana Rifles: 2nd Battalion, 4th Gorkha Rifles

? — 13th Duke of Connaught's Own Lancers: 3rd Battalion, 1st Punjab Regiment: 4th Battalion (Wilde's), The Frontier Force Rifles: 5th Battalion (Vaughan's), The Frontier Force Rifles

271. EGYPTIAN FRONTIER 1940
12th June–12th September 1940
Operations of Western Desert Force and 13th Corps

1956 — 7th Queen's Own Hussars

1957 — 8th King's Royal Irish Hussars: 11th Hussars (Prince Albert's Own): Coldstream Guards: The Rifle Brigade (Prince Consort's Own): The King's Royal Rifle Corps

272. WITHDRAWAL TO MATRUH
13th–17th September 1940
Operations of Western Desert Force and 13th Corps

1957 — 11th Hussars (Prince Albert's Own)

273. BIR ENBA
19th November 1940
Operations of Western Desert Force and 13th Corps

1957 — 11th Hussars (Prince Albert's Own)

274.	**SIDI BARRANI** 8th–11th December 1940 Operations of Western Desert Force and 13th Corps	1956 1957 1958 1962 ?	The Royal Leicestershire Regiment The Royal Fusiliers (City of London Regiment): The Cheshire Regiment: The Argyll and Sutherland Highlanders (Princess Louise's): The Queen's Royal Regiment (West Surrey): 8th King's Royal Irish Hussars: The Queen's Own Cameron Highlanders: Princess 11th Hussars (Prince Albert's Own): Coldstream Guards: 3rd The King's Own Hussars: The King's Royal Rifle Corps Royal Tank Regiment: The South Staffordshire Regiment: The Royal Northumberland Fusiliers 4th Battalion, The Rajputana Rifles 3rd Battalion, 1st Punjab Regiment: 4th Battalion (Bhopal), 16th Punjab Regiment
275.	**BUQ BUQ** 11th December 1940 Operations of Western Desert Force and 13th Corps	1957	8th King's Royal Irish Hussars: 11th Hussars (Prince Albert's Own): 3rd The King's Own Hussars
276.	**BARDIA 1941** 3rd–5th January 1941 Operations of Western Desert Force and 13th Corps	1957 1961	11th Hussars (Prince Albert's Own) 6th Cavalry (Commando) Regiment: 1st Infantry Battalion (Commando) (City of Sydney's Own Regiment): 2nd Infantry Battalion (City of Newcastle Regiment): 3rd Infantry Battalion (The Werriwa Regiment): 5th Infantry Battalion (The Victorian Scottish Regiment): 6th Infantry Battalion (The Royal Melbourne Regiment): 8th Infantry Battalion: 7th Infantry Battalion: 11th Infantry Battalion
277.	**CAPTURE OF TOBRUK** 21st–22nd January 1941 Operations of Western Desert Force and 13th Corps	1957 1961	The Cheshire Regiment: 11th Hussars (Prince Albert's Own) 6th Cavalry (Commando) Regiment: 1st Infantry Battalion (Commando) (City of Sydney's Own Regiment): 2nd Infantry Battalion (City of Newcastle Regiment): 3rd Infantry Battalion (The Werriwa Regiment): 4th Infantry Battalion (Australian Rifles): 5th Infantry Battalion (The Victorian Scottish Regiment): 6th Infantry Battalion (The Royal Melbourne Regiment): 8th Infantry Battalion: 7th Infantry Battalion: 11th Infantry Battalion
278.	**DERNA** 27th–30th January 1941 Operations of Western Desert Force and 13th Corps	1961	6th Cavalry (Commando) Regiment: 4th Infantry Battalion (Australian Rifles): 8th Infantry Battalion: 11th Infantry Battalion
279.	**BEDA FOMM** 5th–8th February 1941 Operations of Western Desert Force and 13th Corps	1956 1957 1958	7th Queen's Own Hussars 1st King's Dragoon Guards: 11th Hussars (Prince Albert's Own): The Rifle Brigade (Prince Consort's Own): 3rd The King's Own Hussars Royal Tank Regiment
280.	**GIARABUB** 19th–21st March 1941 Operations of Western Desert Force and 13th Corps	1961	6th Cavalry (Commando) Regiment: 9th Infantry Battalion (The Moreton Regiment)
281.	**MERSA EL BREGA** 31st March 1941 Operations of Western Desert Force and 13th Corps	1957	The Rifle Brigade (Prince Consort's Own): Tower Hamlets Rifles (TA)

282.	**AGEDABIA** 2nd April 1941 Operations of Western Desert Force and 13th Corps	1957	The Rifle Brigade (Prince Consort's Own):Tower Hamlets Rifles (TA)
283.	**ER REGIMA** 4th April 1941 Operations of Western Desert Force and 13th Corps	1961	13th Infantry Battalion (The Macquarie Regiment)
284.	**EL MECHILI** 6th–8th April 1941 Operations of Western Desert Force and 13th Corps	1962 1963 ?	18th Cavalry 2nd Lancers Prince Albert Victor's Own Cavalry (11th Frontier Force)
285.	**DERNA AERODROME** 7th April 1941 Operations of Western Desert Force and 13th Corps	1957	The Rifle Brigade (Prince Consort's Own):Tower Hamlets Rifles (TA):The King's Royal Rifle Corps
286.	**HALFAYA 1941** 15th–27th May 1941 Operations of Western Desert Force and 13th Corps	1957 ?	Scots Guards: 11th Hussars (Prince Albert's Own): Coldstream Guards:The Durham Light Infantry Prince Albert Victor's Own Cavalry (11th Frontier Force)
287.	**SIDI SULEIMAN** 15th–17th June 1941 Operations of Western Desert Force and 13th Corps	1956 1957 1958 1963	The Buffs (Royal East Kent Regiment) Scots Guards: 11th Hussars (Prince Albert's Own): 3rd The King's Own Hussars Royal Tank Regiment 3rd Battalion,The Brigade of the Guards: 2nd Battalion,The Maratha Light Infantry
288.	**DEFENCE OF TOBRUK** 8th April–10th December 1941 Operations of Western Desert Force and 13th Corps	1957 1958 1961 1962	1st King's Dragoon Guards The Royal Northumberland Fusiliers 9th Infantry Battalion (The Moreton Regiment): 10th Infantry Battalion (The Adelaide Rifles): 12th Infantry Battalion (The Launceston Regiment): 13th Infantry Battalion (The Macquarie Regiment): 15th Infantry Battalion (The Oxley Regiment): 17th Infantry Battalion: 23rd Infantry Battalion (The City of Geelong Regiment): 24th Infantry Battalion (The Kooyong Regiment): 28th Infantry Battalion (The Swan Regiment): 43rd Infantry Battalion: 48th Infantry Battalion: 32nd Infantry Battalion: 1st Pioneer Battalion 18th Cavalry
289.	**EL ADEM ROAD** 13th–14th April 1941 Operations of Western Desert Force and 13th Corps	1961	13th Infantry Battalion (The Macquarie Regiment): 15th Infantry Battalion (The Oxley Regiment): 17th Infantry Battalion: 48th Infantry Battalion

290. **THE SALIENT 1941**
30th April–4th May 1941
Operations of Western Desert Force and 13th Corps

1961: 9th Infantry Battalion (The Moreton Regiment); 10th Infantry Battalion (The Adelaide Rifles); 12th Infantry Battalion (The Launceston Regiment); 15th Infantry Battalion (The Oxley Regiment); 23rd Infantry Battalion (The City of Geelong Regiment); 24th Infantry Battalion (The Kooyong Regiment); 48th Infantry Battalion; 1st Pioneer Battalion

291. **TOBRUK 1941**
18th November–10th December 1941
Relief of Tobruk

1956: The Royal Gloucestershire Hussars, Royal Armoured Corps (TA); The Royal Leicestershire Regiment; The York and Lancaster Regiment

1957: 3rd/4th County of London Yeomanry (Sharpshooters), Royal Armoured Corps (TA); 1st King's Dragoon Guards; The Queen's Royal Regiment (West Surrey); The Bedfordshire and Hertfordshire Regiment; The Border Regiment; The Queen's Own Cameron Highlanders; Scots Guards; The King's Own Royal Regiment (Lancaster); 11th Hussars (Prince Albert's Own); Coldstream Guards; The Durham Light Infantry; Tower Hamlets Rifles (TA); The King's Royal Rifle Corps; Special Air Service Regiment

1958: Royal Tank Regiment; The Royal Northumberland Fusiliers

1958: The Waikato Regiment; The New Zealand Scottish Regiment; The Canterbury Regiment; The Auckland Regiment (Countess of Ranfurly's Own); The Otago Regiment; The Southland Regiment; The Wellington Regiment (City of Wellington's Own); The Hauraki Regiment; The Wellington West Coast Regiment; The Taranaki Regiment; The Hawke's Bay Regiment; The Nelson, Marlborough, and West Coast Regiment; The Northland Regiment: 27 (MG) Battalion; 28 (Maori) Battalion

1961: 13th Infantry Battalion (The Macquarie Regiment)
1962: 2nd Battalion, The Maratha Light Infantry

292. **TOBRUK**
18th November–10th December 1941
Relief of Tobruk

1958: The Ruahine Regiment

293. **GUBI I**
19th November 1941
Relief of Tobruk

1956: The Royal Gloucestershire Hussars, Royal Armoured Corps (TA)
1957: 3rd/4th County of London Yeomanry (Sharpshooters), Royal Armoured Corps (TA); 11th Hussars (Prince Albert's Own)

294. **GABR SALEH**
19th–21st November 1941
Relief of Tobruk

1957: 3rd/4th County of London Yeomanry (Sharpshooters), Royal Armoured Corps (TA); 11th Hussars (Prince Albert's Own)

295. **SIDI REZEGH 1941**
19th–23rd November 1941
Relief of Tobruk

1956: 7th Queen's Own Hussars; The Royal Gloucestershire Hussars, Royal Armoured Corps (TA)

1957: 3rd/4th County of London Yeomanry (Sharpshooters), Royal Armoured Corps (TA); 8th King's Royal Irish Hussars; 11th Hussars (Prince Albert's Own); The Rifle Brigade (Prince Consort's Own); The King's Royal Rifle Corps

1958: Royal Tank Regiment

1958: The Waikato Regiment; The Auckland Regiment (Countess of Ranfurly's Own); The Wellington Regiment (City of Wellington's Own); The Hauraki Regiment; The Wellington West Coast Regiment; The Taranaki Regiment; The Hawke's Bay Regiment; The Nelson, Marlborough, and West Coast Regiment; The Northland Regiment; The Ruahine Regiment

296. **SIDI REZEGH**
19th–23rd November 1941
Relief of Tobruk

1957: The Royal Natal Carbineers; Duke of Edinburgh's Own Rifles; Transvaal Scottish: 2 Regiment Botha; Regiment President Steyn

1958: The Canterbury Regiment; The Otago Regiment; The Southland Regiment

?: South African Irish Regiment; Regiment Vrystaat

297.	**TOBRUK SORTIE 1941** 21st–23rd November 1941 Relief of Tobruk	1956	The York and Lancaster Regiment
298.	**TOBRUK SORTIE** 21st–23rd November 1941 Relief of Tobruk	1957	1st King's Dragoon Guards: The Queen's Royal Regiment (West Surrey): The Bedfordshire and Hertfordshire Regiment: The King's Own Royal Regiment (Lancaster): The Black Watch (Royal Highland Regiment)
299.	**SIDI AZEIZ** 21st–30th November 1941 Relief of Tobruk	1958	The New Zealand Scottish Regiment: The Canterbury Regiment: The Southland Regiment: The Otago Regiment: The Wellington Regiment (City of Wellington's Own): The Wellington West Coast Regiment: The Taranaki Regiment: The Hawke's Bay Regiment: The Nelson, Marlborough, and West Coast Regiment: The Ruahine Regiment: 27 (MG) Battalion: 28 (Maori) Battalion
300.	**OMARS** 22nd November–2nd December 1941 Relief of Tobruk	1956 1958 1962 ?	The Royal Sussex Regiment The Waikato Regiment: The Auckland Regiment (Countess of Ranfurly's Own): The Hauraki Regiment: The Northland Regiment 4th Battalion, The Sikh Regiment 3rd Battalion, 1st Punjab Regiment: 4th Battalion (Bhopal), 16th Punjab Regiment
301.	**TAIEB EL ESSEM** 24th–25th November 1941 Relief of Tobruk	1957	11th Hussars (Prince Albert's Own)
302.	**BELHAMED** 25th November–1st December 1941 Relief of Tobruk	1957 1958 1958	The Bedfordshire and Hertfordshire Regiment: The Essex Regiment Royal Tank Regiment: The Royal Northumberland Fusiliers The Waikato Regiment: The Canterbury Regiment: The Auckland Regiment (Countess of Ranfurly's Own): The Otago Regiment: The Southland Regiment: The Wellington Regiment (City of Wellington's Own): The Hauraki Regiment: The Wellington West Coast Regiment: The Taranaki Regiment: The Hawke's Bay Regiment: The Nelson, Marlborough, and West Coast Regiment: The Northland Regiment: The Ruahine Regiment
		1961	13th Infantry Battalion (The Macquarie Regiment)
303.	**ZEMLA** 3rd December 1941 Relief of Tobruk	1958	The New Zealand Scottish Regiment: The Wellington Regiment (City of Wellington's Own): The Wellington West Coast Regiment: The Taranaki Regiment: The Hawke's Bay Regiment: The Ruahine Regiment: 28 (Maori) Battalion
304.	**GUBI II** 4th–6th December 1941 Relief of Tobruk	1957 1962	The Queen's Own Cameron Highlanders: 11th Hussars (Prince Albert's Own) 2nd Battalion, The Maratha Light Infantry
305.	**RELIEF OF TOBRUK 1941** 7th–10th December 1941 Relief of Tobruk	1962	The Central India Horse
306.	**RELIEF OF TOBRUK** 7th–10th December 1941 Relief of Tobruk	1957	1st King's Dragoon Guards: 8th King's Royal Irish Hussars: 11th Hussars (Prince Albert's Own): The Durham Light Infantry

307.	**MARSA BELAFARIT** 9th December 1941 Relief of Tobruk	1957	Imperial Light Horse
308.	**ALEM HAMZA** 14th–16th December 1941 Pursuit to Agedabia	1956 1958 1962	The Buffs (Royal East Kent Regiment) The Canterbury Regiment: The Otago Regiment: The Southland Regiment: The Wellington Regiment (City of Wellington's Own): The Wellington West Coast Regiment: The Taranaki Regiment: The Hawke's Bay Regiment: The Nelson, Marlborough, and West Coast Regiment: The Ruahine Regiment: 28 (Maori) Battalion 4th Battalion, The Rajputana Rifles
309.	**CHOR ES SUFAN** 27th–30th December 1941 Pursuit to Agedabia	1956 1957	The Royal Gloucestershire Hussars, Royal Armoured Corps (TA) 3rd/4th County of London Yeomanry (Sharpshooters), Royal Armoured Corps (TA): 12th Royal Lancers (Prince of Wales's): The Rifle Brigade (Prince Consort's Own): Tower Hamlets Rifles (TA)
310.	**BARDIA 1942** 31st December 1941–2nd January 1942 Pursuit to Agedabia	1958	The New Zealand Scottish Regiment
311.	**BARDIA** 31st December 1941–2nd January 1942 Pursuit to Agedabia	1957	Royal Durban Light Infantry: The Kaffrarian Rifles: Rand Light Infantry: Imperial Light Horse: Die Middellandse Regiment
312.	**SOLLUM** [1] 11th–12th January 1942 Pursuit to Agedabia	1957	Transvaal Scottish [1] *Awarded as BARDIA: SOLLUM taken into use 1961.*
313.	**SAUNNU** 23rd January 1942 Enemy Counter Offensive	1956 1957	9th Queen's Royal Lancers 10th Royal Hussars (Prince of Wales's Own): 11th Hussars (Prince Albert's Own): The Rifle Brigade (Prince Consort's Own)
314.	**MSUS** 25th January 1942 Enemy Counter Offensive	1956 1957	1st The Royal Dragoons The Queen's Bays (2nd Dragoon Guards): 11th Hussars (Prince Albert's Own): Coldstream Guards
315.	**BENGHAZI** 27th–29th January 1942 Enemy Counter Offensive	1956 1957 ?	The Royal Sussex Regiment The Welch Regiment 1st Battalion, 1st Punjab Regiment: 4th Battalion (Bhopal), 16th Punjab Regiment
316.	**CARMUSA** 29th January–5th February 1942 Enemy Counter Offensive	1957	The Queen's Own Cameron Highlanders
317.	**GAZALA** 26th May–21st June 1942 Resumption of Enemy Offensive	1956 1957	1st The Royal Dragoons: 9th Queen's Royal Lancers: The Royal Gloucestershire Hussars, Royal Armoured Corps (TA): The Duke of Cornwall's Light Infantry The Queen's Bays (2nd Dragoon Guards): 3rd/4th County of London Yeomanry (Sharpshooters), Royal Armoured Corps (TA): The Cheshire Regiment: 1st King's Dragoon Guards: The Green Howards (Alexandra, Princess of Wales's Own Yorkshire

Regiment):The Sherwood Foresters (Nottinghamshire and Derbyshire Regiment): 8th King's Royal Irish Hussars: 10th Royal Hussars (Prince of Wales's Own):The Queen's Own Cameron Highlanders: Scots Guards: 4th Queen's Own Hussars:The Highland Light Infantry (City of Glasgow Regiment):The Rifle Brigade (Prince Consort's Own):The Durham Light Infantry:The East Yorkshire Regiment (The Duke of York's Own):Tower Hamlets Rifles (TA):The Worcestershire Regiment:The King's Royal Rifle Corps:The Rangers, The King's Royal Rifle Corps (TA)

1957 The Royal Natal Carbineers: Royal Durban Light Infantry: Duke of Edinburgh's Own Rifles: The Queen's Own Cape Town Highlanders:Transvaal Scottish: Rand Light Infantry: 2 Regiment Botha: Natal Mounted Rifles: Imperial Light Horse: Regiment President Steyn: Die Middellandse Regiment

1958 Royal Tank Regiment:The South Wales Borderers

? Regiment Vrystaat

? 13th Duke of Connaught's Own Lancers: 3rd Battalion, 1st Punjab Regiment: 3rd Royal Battalion,The Frontier Force Regiment: 4th Battalion (Wilde's),The Frontier Force Rifles

318. **PT 171**
27th May 1942
Resumption of Enemy Offensive

1962 2nd Lancers

319. **RETMA**
27th May 1942
Resumption of Enemy Offensive

1957 The Rangers, The King's Royal Rifle Corps (TA)

320. **BIR EL IGELA**
27th May 1942
Resumption of Enemy Offensive

1957 8th King's Royal Irish Hussars

321. **BIR EL ASLAGH**
27th–31st May 1942
Resumption of Enemy Offensive

1956 9th Queen's Royal Lancers:The Royal Gloucestershire Hussars, Royal Armoured Corps (TA)
1957 The Queen's Bays (2nd Dragoon Guards); 10th Royal Hussars (Prince of Wales's Own)

322. **BIR HACHEIM**
27th May–11th June 1942
Resumption of Enemy Offensive

1957 1st King's Dragoon Guards:The King's Royal Rifle Corps:The Rangers, The King's Royal Rifle Corps (TA)
? 13th Duke of Connaught's Own Lancers:The Guides Cavalry (10th Queen Victoria's Own Frontier Force); Prince Albert Victor's Own Cavalry (11th Frontier Force): 3rd Royal Battalion, The Frontier Force Regiment

323. **ALEM HAMZA**
28th May 1942
Resumption of Enemy Offensive

1957 Duke of Edinburgh's Own Rifles:The Queen's Own Cape Town Highlanders:Transvaal Scottish

324. **CAULDRON**
5th–6th June 1942
Resumption of Enemy Offensive

1956 The Royal Gloucestershire Hussars, Royal Armoured Corps (TA)
1957 The Queen's Bays (2nd Dragoon Guards): 3rd/4th County of London Yeomanry (Sharpshooters), Royal Armoured Corps (TA):The West Yorkshire Regiment (The Prince of Wales's Own):The Highland Light Infantry (City of Glasgow Regiment)
1958 Royal Tank Regiment:The Royal Northumberland Fusiliers

325. **THE CAULDRON**
5th–6th June 1942
Resumption of Enemy Offensive

1962 2nd Battalion, 4th Gorkha Rifles
? 4th Battalion (Duke of Connaught's Own),The Baluch Regiment

326.	**PT 204** 5th June 1942 Resumption of Enemy Offensive	1957	The Royal Natal Carbineers
327.	**KNIGHTSBRIDGE** 6th–7th June 1942 and 11th–13th June 1942 Resumption of Enemy Offensive	1956 1957 1958	1st The Royal Dragoons The Queen's Bays (2nd Dragoon Guards); Honourable Artillery Company (TA); Scots Guards: Coldstream Guards:The Rifle Brigade (Prince Consort's Own);The King's Royal Rifle Corps Royal Tank Regiment
328.	**HAGIAG ER RAML** 11th–13th June 1942 Resumption of Enemy Offensive	1957	3rd/4th County of London Yeomanry (Sharpshooters), Royal Armoured Corps (TA)
329.	**GABR EL FACHRI** 14th June 1942 Resumption of Enemy Offensive	1957	The Durham Light Infantry
330.	**VIA BALBIA** 14th June 1942 Resumption of Enemy Offensive	1957	The Queen's Bays (2nd Dragoon Guards);The Worcestershire Regiment
331.	**BEST POST** 14th June 1942 Resumption of Enemy Offensive	1957	The Queen's Own Cape Town Highlanders: Natal Mounted Rifles
332.	**ZT EL MRASSES** 15th June 1942 Resumption of Enemy Offensive	1957	The Durham Light Infantry
333.	**EL ADEM** 15th–17th June 1942 Resumption of Enemy Offensive	?	13th Duke of Connaught's Own Lancers: 3rd Royal Battalion,The Frontier Force Regiment
334.	**SIDI REZEGH 1942** 17th June 1942 Resumption of Enemy Offensive	1956 ?	9th Queen's Royal Lancers 13th Duke of Connaught's Own Lancers: 4th Battalion (Wilde's), The Frontier Force Rifles
335.	**GAMBUT** 18th June 1942 Resumption of Enemy Offensive	?	13th Duke of Connaught's Own Lancers: 4th Battalion (Wilde's), The Frontier Force Rifles
336.	**TOBRUK 1942** 20th–21st June 1942 Resumption of Enemy Offensive	1957 1962 ?	The Queen's Own Cameron Highlanders: 7th Gurkha Rifles: Coldstream Guards 2nd Battalion,The Maratha Light Infantry 13th Duke of Connaught's Own Lancers

337.	**ACROMA KEEP** 6th–18th June 1942 Resumption of Enemy Offensive	1957	Transvaal Scottish
338.	**THE KENNELS** 24th June 1942 Resumption of Enemy Offensive	1962	18th Cavalry
339.	**MERSA MATRUH** 26th–30th June 1942 Resumption of Enemy Offensive	1957 1958 1962 ?	The Queen's Bays (2nd Dragoon Guards): 3rd/4th County of London Yeomanry (Sharpshooters), Royal Armoured Corps (TA): The Cheshire Regiment: 8th King's Royal Irish Hussars: The Highland Light Infantry (City of Glasgow Regiment): The Essex Regiment: The Durham Light Infantry: The East Yorkshire Regiment (The Duke of York's Own) The Waikato Regiment: The Canterbury Regiment: The Auckland Regiment (Countess of Ranfurly's Own): The Otago Regiment: The Southland Regiment: The Wellington Regiment (City of Wellington's Own): The Hauraki Regiment: The Wellington West Coast Regiment: The Taranaki Regiment: The Hawke's Bay Regiment: The Nelson, Marlborough, and West Coast Regiment: The Northland Regiment: The Ruahine Regiment: 27 (MG) Battalion: 28 (Maori) Battalion 61 Field Company, Madras Engineer Group: 2nd Battalion, The Parachute Regiment: 2nd Battalion, The Sikh Regiment 3rd Battalion (Queen Mary's Own), The Baluch Regiment: 4th Battalion (Wilde's), The Frontier Force Rifles
340.	**POINT 174** 27th June 1942 Resumption of Enemy Offensive	1957	The Durham Light Infantry
341.	**MINQAR QAIM** 27th–28th June 1942 Resumption of Enemy Offensive	1957 1958 ?	3rd/4th County of London Yeomanry (Sharpshooters), Royal Armoured Corps (TA) The Waikato Regiment: The Canterbury Regiment: The Auckland Regiment (Countess of Ranfurly's Own): The Otago Regiment: The Southland Regiment: The Wellington Regiment (City of Wellington's Own): The Hauraki Regiment: The Wellington West Coast Regiment: The Taranaki Regiment: The Hawke's Bay Regiment: The Nelson, Marlborough, and West Coast Regiment: The Northland Regiment: The Ruahine Regiment: 27 (MG) Battalion: 28 (Maori) Battalion The Guides Cavalry (10th Queen Victoria's Own Frontier Force)
342.	**FUKA** 28th June 1942 Resumption of Enemy Offensive	1957 ?	The Highland Light Infantry (City of Glasgow Regiment) 13th Duke of Connaught's Own Lancers
343.	**KILO 23** 28th June 1942, Resumption of Enemy Offensive	?	4th Battalion (Wilde's), The Frontier Force Rifles
344.	**DEFENCE OF ALAMEIN LINE** 1st–27th July 1942 Enemy Offensive Halted	1956 1957 1958 1958	1st The Royal Dragoons: 9th Queen's Royal Lancers 3rd/4th County of London Yeomanry (Sharpshooters), Royal Armoured Corps (TA): The Cheshire Regiment: 1st King's Dragoon Guards: The West Yorkshire Regiment (The Prince of Wales's Own): The Green Howards (Alexandra, Princess of Wales's Own Yorkshire Regiment): Scots Guards: 4th Queen's Own Hussars: 11th Hussars (Prince Albert's Own): Coldstream Guards: The Rifle Brigade (Prince Consort's Own): The Essex Regiment: The East Yorkshire Regiment (The Duke of York's Own): Tower Hamlets Rifles (TA): The King's Royal Rifle Corps: The Rangers, The King's Royal Rifle Corps (TA) Royal Tank Regiment The Waikato Regiment: The New Zealand Scottish Regiment: The Canterbury Regiment: The Auckland Regiment (Countess

of Ranfurly's Own); The Otago Regiment; The Southland Regiment; The Wellington Regiment (City of Wellington's Own); The Hauraki Regiment; The Wellington West Coast Regiment; The Taranaki Regiment; The Hawke's Bay Regiment; The Nelson, Marlborough, and West Coast Regiment; The Northland Regiment; The Ruahine Regiment; 27 (MG) Battalion; 28 (Maori) Battalion

1961 — 9th Cavalry (Commando) Regiment; 13th Infantry Battalion (The Macquarie Regiment); 23rd Infantry Battalion (The City of Geelong Regiment); 24th Infantry Battalion (The Kooyong Regiment); 28th Infantry Battalion (The Swan Regiment); 43rd Infantry Battalion; 48th Infantry Battalion; 32nd Infantry Battalion; 2nd Machine Gun Battalion

1963 — 3rd Battalion, The Rajput Regiment

? — 1st Battalion, 1st Punjab Regiment; 3rd Battalion, 14th Punjab Regiment

345. ALAMEIN DEFENCE
1st–27th July 1942
Enemy Offensive Halted

1957 — The Royal Natal Carbineers; Royal Durban Light Infantry; Duke of Edinburgh's Own Rifles; The Queen's Own Cape Town Highlanders; Transvaal Scottish; Rand Light Infantry; 2 Regiment Botha; Natal Mounted Rifles; Imperial Light Horse; Regiment President Steyn; Die Middellandse Regiment

? — Regiment Vrystaat

¹ *ALAMEIN-VERDEDIGING taken into use by Afrikaans-speaking South African units 1957.*

346. DEIR EL SHEIN
1st July 1942
Enemy Offensive Halted

1957 — 3rd/4th County of London Yeomanry (Sharpshooters), Royal Armoured Corps (TA); The Cheshire Regiment; The Essex Regiment

1962 — 4th Battalion, The Sikh Regiment; 2nd Battalion, 3rd Gorkha Rifles

? — The Guides Cavalry (10th Queen Victoria's Own Frontier Force)

347. RUWEISAT
2nd–4th July 1942
Enemy Offensive Halted

1956 — 9th Queen's Royal Lancers

1957 — 3rd/4th County of London Yeomanry (Sharpshooters), Royal Armoured Corps (TA); 4th Queen's Own Hussars; The Rifle Brigade (Prince Consort's Own); The Essex Regiment; The King's Royal Rifle Corps; The Rangers, The King's Royal Rifle Corps (TA)

348. FUKA AIRFIELD
7th July 1942
Enemy Offensive Halted

1957 — The King's Royal Rifle Corps; The Rangers, The King's Royal Rifle Corps (TA)

349. TELL EL EISA
10th–11th July 1942
Enemy Offensive Halted

1961 — 9th Cavalry (Commando) Regiment; 24th Infantry Battalion (The Kooyong Regiment); 48th Infantry Battalion

350. POINT 93
11th July 1942
Enemy Offensive Halted

1957 — 3rd/4th County of London Yeomanry (Sharpshooters), Royal Armoured Corps (TA)

351. ALAMEIN BOX
13th July 1942
Enemy Offensive Halted

1957 — Royal Durban Light Infantry; Imperial Light Horse

352. RUWEISAT RIDGE
14th–16th July 1942
Enemy Offensive Halted

1956 — 9th Queen's Royal Lancers

1957 — 3rd/4th County of London Yeomanry (Sharpshooters), Royal Armoured Corps (TA); The Essex Regiment

1958 — The Royal Northumberland Fusiliers

No.	Battle	Year	Regiments
		1958	The Waikato Regiment; The New Zealand Scottish Regiment; The Canterbury Regiment; The Auckland Regiment (Countess of Ranfurly's Own); The Otago Regiment; The Southland Regiment; The Wellington Regiment (City of Wellington's Own); The Hauraki Regiment; The Wellington West Coast Regiment; The Taranaki Regiment; The Hawke's Bay Regiment; The Nelson, Marlborough, and West Coast Regiment; The Northland Regiment; The Ruahine Regiment; 27 (MG) Battalion
		1961	2nd Machine Gun Battalion
		1962	4th Battalion, The Rajputana Rifles
		?	3rd Battalion (Queen Mary's Own), The Baluch Regiment
353.	TELL EL MAKH KHAD 17th–18th July 1942 Enemy Offensive Halted	1961	9th Cavalry (Commando) Regiment: 28th Infantry Battalion (The Swan Regiment): 43rd Infantry Battalion: 32nd Infantry Battalion
354.	EL MREIR 21st–22nd July 1942 Enemy Offensive Halted	1958	The Waikato Regiment: The New Zealand Scottish Regiment: The Canterbury Regiment: The Auckland Regiment (Countess of Ranfurly's Own): The Otago Regiment: The Southland Regiment: The Wellington Regiment (City of Wellington's Own): The Hauraki Regiment: The Wellington West Coast Regiment: The Taranaki Regiment: The Hawke's Bay Regiment: The Nelson, Marlborough, and West Coast Regiment: The Northland Regiment: The Ruahine Regiment: 27 (MG) Battalion: 28 (Maori) Battalion
		1961	9th Cavalry (Commando) Regiment: 28th Infantry Battalion (The Swan Regiment): 32nd Infantry Battalion: 2nd Machine Gun Battalion
355.	SANYET EL MITEIRYA 21st–23rd July 1942 Enemy Offensive Halted	1961	28th Infantry Battalion (The Swan Regiment)
356.	QATTARA TRACK 26th–27th July 1942 Enemy Offensive Halted		
357.	ALAM EL HALFA 30th August–7th September 1942 Repulse of Final Enemy Offensive	1956	The Royal Scots Greys (2nd Dragoons); The Derbyshire Yeomanry, Royal Armoured Corps (TA); The Royal Gloucestershire Hussars, Royal Armoured Corps (TA); The Buffs (Royal East Kent Regiment); The Royal Sussex Regiment
		1957	3rd/4th County of London Yeomanry (Sharpshooters), Royal Armoured Corps (TA); 1st King's Dragoon Guards; 12th Royal Lancers (Prince of Wales's); The Staffordshire Yeomanry (Queen's Own Royal Regiment), Royal Armoured Corps (TA); The Queen's Own Royal West Kent Regiment; 8th King's Royal Irish Hussars; 10th Royal Hussars (Prince of Wales's); The Sherwood Rangers Yeomanry, Royal Armoured Corps (TA); 4th Queen's Own Hussars; 11th Hussars (Prince Albert's Own); The Rifle Brigade (Prince Consort's Own); London Rifle Brigade, The Rifle Brigade (Prince Consort's Own) (TA); The King's Royal Rifle Corps
		1958	Royal Tank Corps
		1958	The Waikato Regiment: The New Zealand Scottish Regiment: The Canterbury Regiment: The Auckland Regiment (Countess of Ranfurly's Own): The Otago Regiment: The Southland Regiment: The Wellington Regiment (City of Wellington's Own): The Hauraki Regiment: The Wellington West Coast Regiment: The Taranaki Regiment: The Hawke's Bay Regiment: The Nelson, Marlborough, and West Coast Regiment: The Northland Regiment: The Ruahine Regiment: 27 (MG) Battalion: 28 (Maori) Battalion
		1961	15th Infantry Battalion (The Oxley Regiment): 17th Infantry Battalion
		?	3rd Battalion, 14th Punjab Regiment

358.	**WEST POINT 23** 1st September 1942 Repulse of Final Enemy Offensive	1956 1961	The Royal Gloucestershire Hussars, Royal Armoured Corps (TA) 9th Cavalry (Commando) Regiment: 15th Infantry Battalion (The Oxley Regiment)
359.	**BENGHAZI RAID** 13th–14th September 1942 Repulse of Final Enemy Offensive	1957	Special Air Service Regiment
360.	**DEIR EL MUNASSIB** [1] 30th September 1942 Repulse of Final Enemy Offensive	1957	The Queen's Royal Regiment (West Surrey) [1] *Awarded as DEIR EL MUNASIB: DEIR EL MUNASSIB taken into use 1974.*
361.	**EL ALAMEIN** 23rd October–4th November 1942 The Offensive from Alamein to Tripoli	1956	The Life Guards: Royal Horse Guards: 1st The Royal Dragoons: The Royal Scots Greys (2nd Dragoons): 9th Queen's Royal Lancers: The Royal Wiltshire Yeomanry (Prince of Wales's Own), Royal Armoured Corps (TA): The Derbyshire Yeomanry, Royal Armoured Corps (TA): The Buffs (Royal East Kent Regiment): The Royal Sussex Regiment
		1957	The Queen's Bays (2nd Dragoon Guards): 3rd/4th County of London Yeomanry (Sharpshooters), Royal Armoured Corps (TA): Honourable Artillery Company (TA): The Warwickshire Yeomanry, Royal Armoured Corps (TA): The Cheshire Regiment: Seaforth Highlanders (Ross-shire Buffs, The Duke of Albany's): The Gordon Highlanders: The Argyll and Sutherland Highlanders (Princess Louise's): 12th Royal Lancers (Prince of Wales's): The Staffordshire Yeomanry (Queen's Own Royal Regiment), Royal Armoured Corps (TA): The Queen's Own Yorkshire Dragoons, Royal Armoured Corps (TA): The Queen's Royal Regiment (West Surrey): The Green Howards (Alexandra, Princess of Wales's Own Yorkshire Regiment): The Sherwood Foresters (Nottinghamshire and Derbyshire Regiment): The Queen's Own Royal West Kent Regiment: 8th King's Royal Irish Hussars: 10th Royal Hussars (Prince of Wales's Own): The Queen's Own Cameron Highlanders: The Sherwood Rangers Yeomanry, Royal Armoured Corps (TA): 4th Queen's Own Hussars: 11th Hussars (Prince Albert's Own): The Rifle Brigade (Prince Consort's Own): The Black Watch (Royal Highland Regiment): The Essex Regiment: The Middlesex Regiment (Duke of Cambridge's Own): The Durham Light Infantry: 3rd The King's Own Hussars: The East Yorkshire Regiment (The Duke of York's Own): London Rifle Brigade, The Rifle Brigade (Prince Consort's Own) (TA): The King's Royal Rifle Corps: The Queen's Westminsters, The King's Royal Rifle Corps (TA): 2nd King Edward VII's Own Gurkha Rifles (The Sirmoor Rifles)
		1957	The Royal Natal Carbineers: Royal Durban Light Infantry: Duke of Edinburgh's Own Rifles: The Queen's Own Cape Town Highlanders: Transvaal Scottish: Rand Light Infantry: 2 Regiment Botha: Natal Mounted Rifles: Imperial Light Horse: Regiment President Steyn: Die Middellandse Regiment
		1958	Royal Tank Regiment: The Royal Northumberland Fusiliers
		1958	The Waikato Regiment: The New Zealand Scottish Regiment: The Canterbury Regiment: The Auckland Regiment (Countess of Ranfurly's Own): The Otago Regiment: The Southland Regiment: The Wellington Regiment (City of Wellington's Own): The Hauraki Regiment: The Wellington West Coast Regiment: The Taranaki Regiment: The Hawke's Bay Regiment: The Nelson, Marlborough, and West Coast Regiment: The Northland Regiment: The Ruahine Regiment: 27 (MG) Battalion: 28 (Maori) Battalion
		1961	9th Cavalry (Commando) Regiment: 13th Infantry Battalion (The Macquarie Regiment): 15th Infantry Battalion (The Oxley Regiment): 17th Infantry Battalion: 23rd Infantry Battalion (The City of Geelong Regiment): 24th Infantry Battalion (The Kooyong Regiment): 28th Infantry Battalion (The Swan Regiment): 43rd Infantry Battalion: 48th Infantry Battalion: 32nd Infantry Battalion: 2nd Machine Gun Battalion: 3rd Pioneer Battalion
		1962 ?	4th Battalion, The Rajputana Rifles: 4th Battalion, The Rajput Regiment Regiment Vrystaat

No.	Battle Honour	Year	Units
		?	1st Battalion, 1st Punjab Regiment: 4th Battalion (Bhopal), 16th Punjab Regiment: 3rd Battalion (Queen Mary's Own), The Baluch Regiment
362.	**CAPTURE OF HALFAYA PASS 1942** 10th–11th November 1942 The Offensive from Alamein to Tripoli	1957	The King's Royal Rifle Corps
		1958	The Waikato Regiment: The Auckland Regiment (Countess of Ranfurly's Own): The Hauraki Regiment: The Northland Regiment
363.	**EL AGHEILA** 13th–17th December 1942 The Offensive from Alamein to Tripoli	1956	1st The Royal Dragoons: The Royal Scots Greys (2nd Dragoons): The Buffs (Royal East Kent Regiment)
		1957	1st King's Dragoon Guards: The Staffordshire Yeomanry (Queen's Own Royal Regiment), Royal Armoured Corps (TA): The Sherwood Rangers Yeomanry, Royal Armoured Corps (TA)
		1958	The Waikato Regiment: The New Zealand Scottish Regiment: The Canterbury Regiment: The Auckland Regiment (Countess of Ranfurly's Own): The Otago Regiment: The Southland Regiment: The Wellington Regiment (City of Wellington's Own): The Hauraki Regiment: The Wellington West Coast Regiment: The Taranaki Regiment: The Hawke's Bay Regiment: The Nelson, Marlborough, and West Coast Regiment: The Northland Regiment: The Ruahine Regiment
364.	**NOFILIA** 17th–18th December 1942 The Offensive from Alamein to Tripoli	1956	The Royal Scots Greys (2nd Dragoons)
		1957	The King's Royal Rifle Corps
		1958	The Waikato Regiment: The New Zealand Scottish Regiment: The Canterbury Regiment: The Auckland Regiment (Countess of Ranfurly's Own): The Otago Regiment: The Southland Regiment: The Hauraki Regiment: The Nelson, Marlborough, and West Coast Regiment: The Northland Regiment: 28 (Maori) Battalion
365.	**ADVANCE ON TRIPOLI** 15th–23rd January 1943 The Offensive from Alamein to Tripoli	1956	1st The Royal Dragoons: The Royal Scots Greys (2nd Dragoons): The Buffs (Royal East Kent Regiment)
		1957	Seaforth Highlanders (Ross-shire Buffs, The Duke of Albany's): The Gordon Highlanders: 1st King's Dragoon Guards: 12th Royal Lancers (Prince of Wales's): The Staffordshire Yeomanry (Queen's Own Royal Regiment), Royal Armoured Corps (TA): 11th Hussars (Prince Albert's Own): The Black Watch (Royal Highland Regiment): The Middlesex Regiment (Duke of Cambridge's Own)
		1958	The Royal Northumberland Fusiliers
366.	**ADVANCE TO TRIPOLI** 15th–23rd January 1943 The Offensive from Alamein to Tripoli	1958	The New Zealand Scottish Regiment
367.	**MEDENINE** 6th March 1943 Repulse of Enemy Offensive in Tunisia	1957	The Argyll and Sutherland Highlanders (Princess Louise's): The Queen's Royal Regiment (West Surrey): Scots Guards: Coldstream Guards: The Black Watch (Royal Highland Regiment)
		1958	The Royal Northumberland Fusiliers
368	**MEDININE** 6th March 1943 Repulse of Enemy Offensive in Tunisia	1958	The Waikato Regiment: The New Zealand Scottish Regiment: The Canterbury Regiment: The Auckland Regiment (Countess of Ranfurly's Own): The Otago Regiment: The Southland Regiment: The Hauraki Regiment: The Nelson, Marlborough, and West Coast Regiment: The Northland Regiment: 28 (Maori) Battalion
369.	**ZEMLET EL LEBENE** 6th March 1943 Repulse of Enemy Offensive in Tunisia	1957	The Black Watch (Royal Highland Regiment)

370.	**TADJERA KHIR** 6th March 1943 Repulse of Enemy Offensive in Tunisia	1957	Scots Guards
371.	**MARETH** 16th–23rd March 1943 Advance on Tunis	1957	Grenadier Guards: The Cheshire Regiment: Seaforth Highlanders (Ross-shire Buffs, The Duke of Albany's): The Gordon Highlanders: The Green Howards (Alexandra, Princess of Wales's Own Yorkshire Regiment): The Queen's Own Cameron Highlanders: Coldstream Guards: The Black Watch (Royal Highland Regiment): The Middlesex Regiment (Duke of Cambridge's Own): The Durham Light Infantry: The East Yorkshire Regiment (The Duke of York's Own): 2nd King Edward VII's Own Gurkha Rifles (The Sirmoor Rifles)
		1958 ?	Royal Tank Regiment 4th Battalion (Bhopal), 16th Punjab Regiment
372.	**WADI ZEUSS EAST** 16th–17th March 1943 Advance on Tunis	1957	The Cheshire Regiment
373.	**WADI ZIGZAOU** 20th–23rd March 1943 Advance on Tunis	1957	The Cheshire Regiment: Seaforth Highlanders (Ross-shire Buffs, The Duke of Albany's): The Queen's Own Cameron Highlanders: The East Yorkshire Regiment (The Duke of York's Own)
374.	**TEBAGA GAP** 21st–30th March 1943 Advance on Tunis	1956 1957	9th Queen's Royal Lancers: The Buffs (Royal East Kent Regiment) The Queen's Bays (2nd Dragoon Guards): 1st King's Dragoon Guards: 12th Royal Lancers (Prince of Wales's): The Staffordshire Yeomanry (Queen's Own Royal Regiment), Royal Armoured Corps (TA): The Queen's Own Yorkshire Dragoons, Royal Armoured Corps (TA): The Sherwood Rangers Yeomanry, Royal Armoured Corps (TA): The Rifle Brigade (Prince Consort's Own): London Rifle Brigade, The Rifle Brigade (Prince Consort's Own) (TA): The King's Royal Rifle Corps
		1958	The Waikato Regiment: The New Zealand Scottish Regiment: The Canterbury Regiment: The Auckland Regiment (Countess of Ranfurly's Own): The Otago Regiment: The Southland Regiment: The Wellington Regiment (City of Wellington's Own): The Hauraki Regiment: The Wellington West Coast Regiment: The Taranaki Regiment: The Hawke's Bay Regiment: The Nelson, Marlborough, and West Coast Regiment: The Northland Regiment: The Ruahine Regiment: 27 (MG) Battalion: 28 (Maori) Battalion
375.	**POINT 201 (ROMAN WALL)** 21st–22nd March 1943 Advance on Tunis	1957 1958	1st King's Dragoon Guards: The Staffordshire Yeomanry (Queen's Own Royal Regiment), Royal Armoured Corps (TA): The Sherwood Rangers Yeomanry, Royal Armoured Corps (TA) The New Zealand Scottish Regiment: The Canterbury Regiment: The Otago Regiment: The Southland Regiment: The Wellington Regiment (City of Wellington's Own): The Wellington West Coast Regiment: The Taranaki Regiment: The Hawke's Bay Regiment: The Nelson, Marlborough, and West Coast Regiment: The Ruahine Regiment
376.	**EL HAMMA** 27th–29th March 1943 Advance on Tunis	1956 1957 1958	9th Queen's Royal Lancers: The Buffs (Royal East Kent Regiment) The Queen's Bays (2nd Dragoon Guards): Honourable Artillery Company (TA): 1st King's Dragoon Guards: 12th Royal Lancers (Prince of Wales's): The Staffordshire Yeomanry (Queen's Own Royal Regiment), Royal Armoured Corps (TA): The Queen's Own Yorkshire Dragoons, Royal Armoured Corps (TA): 10th Royal Hussars (Prince of Wales's Own) The Waikato Regiment: The New Zealand Scottish Regiment: The Canterbury Regiment: The Auckland Regiment (Countess of Ranfurly's Own): The Otago Regiment: The Southland Regiment: The Wellington Regiment (City of Wellington's Own): The

			Hauraki Regiment: The Wellington West Coast Regiment: The Taranaki Regiment: The Hawke's Bay Regiment: The Nelson, Marlborough, and West Coast Regiment: The Northland Regiment: The Ruahine Regiment: 27 (MG) Battalion: 28 (Maori) Battalion
377.	**MATMATA HILLS** 25th–28th March 1943 Advance on Tunis	1957 1962	The Essex Regiment 4th Battalion, The Rajputana Rifles
378.	**AKARIT** 6th–7th April 1943 Advance on Tunis	1956 1957	The Buffs (Royal East Kent Regiment): The Royal Sussex Regiment 3rd/4th County of London Yeomanry (Sharpshooters), Royal Armoured Corps (TA): The Cheshire Regiment: Seaforth Highlanders (Ross-shire Buffs, The Duke of Albany's): The Argyll and Sutherland Highlanders (Princess Louise's): 1st King's Dragoon Guards: 12th Royal Lancers (Prince of Wales's): The Staffordshire Yeomanry (Queen's Own Royal Regiment), Royal Armoured Corps (TA): The Green Howards (Alexandra, Princess of Wales's Own Yorkshire Regiment): The Queen's Own Cameron Highlanders: The Black Watch (Royal Highland Regiment): The Essex Regiment: The Middlesex Regiment (Duke of Cambridge's Own): The East Yorkshire Regiment (The Duke of York's Own): 2nd King Edward VII's Own Gurkha Rifles (The Sirmoor Rifles)
		1958 1962 ?	Royal Tank Regiment 4th Battalion, The Rajputana Rifles: MG Battalion, The Rajputana Rifles 4th Battalion (Bhopal), 16th Punjab Regiment
379.	**DJEBEL EL MEIDA** 6th April 1943 Advance on Tunis	1956 1957 1962	The Royal Sussex Regiment 2nd King Edward VII's Own Gurkha Rifles (The Sirmoor Rifles) 1st Battalion, 9th Gorkha Rifles
380.	**WADI AKARIT EAST** 6th–7th April 1943 Advance on Tunis	1957	The Cheshire Regiment: The Black Watch (Royal Highland Regiment)
381.	**DJEBEL ROUMANA** 6th–7th April 1943 Advance on Tunis	1957	3rd/4th County of London Yeomanry (Sharpshooters), Royal Armoured Corps (TA): Seaforth Highlanders (Ross-shire Buffs, The Duke of Albany's): The Queen's Own Cameron Highlanders: The Black Watch (Royal Highland Regiment): The Middlesex Regiment (Duke of Cambridge's Own)
382.	**SEBKRET EN NOUAL** 7th April 1943 Advance on Tunis	1957	The Staffordshire Yeomanry (Queen's Own Royal Regiment), Royal Armoured Corps (TA)
383.	**CHEBKET EN NOUIGES** 8th April 1943 Advance on Tunis	1957	The Sherwood Rangers Yeomanry, Royal Armoured Corps (TA)
384.	**DJEBEL EL TELIL** 9th April 1943 Advance on Tunis	1957	The Staffordshire Yeomanry (Queen's Own Royal Regiment), Royal Armoured Corps (TA)

385.	**ENFIDAVILLE** 19th–29th April 1943 Advance on Tunis	1957	The Cheshire Regiment; The Oxfordshire and Buckinghamshire Light Infantry; The Staffordshire Yeomanry (Queen's Own Royal Regiment), Royal Armoured Corps (TA); The Sherwood Rangers Yeomanry, Royal Armoured Corps (TA); 11th Hussars (Prince Albert's Own); The Essex Regiment; 2nd King Edward VII's Own Gurkha Rifles (The Sirmoor Rifles)
		1958	The Waikato Regiment; The New Zealand Scottish Regiment; The Canterbury Regiment; The Auckland Regiment (Countess of Ranfurly's Own); The Otago Regiment; The Southland Regiment; The Wellington Regiment (City of Wellington's Own); The Hauraki Regiment; The Wellington West Coast Regiment; The Taranaki Regiment; The Hawke's Bay Regiment; The Nelson, Marlborough, and West Coast Regiment; The Northland Regiment; The Ruahine Regiment; 27 (MG) Battalion; 28 (Maori) Battalion
386.	**TAKROUNA** 20th–21st April 1943 Advance on Tunis	1957	The Staffordshire Yeomanry (Queen's Own Royal Regiment), Royal Armoured Corps (TA): The Sherwood Rangers Yeomanry, Royal Armoured Corps (TA)
		1958	The Waikato Regiment; The Canterbury Regiment; The Auckland Regiment (Countess of Ranfurly's Own); The Otago Regiment; The Southland Regiment; The Wellington Regiment (City of Wellington's Own); The Hauraki Regiment; The Wellington West Coast Regiment; The Taranaki Regiment; The Hawke's Bay Regiment; The Nelson, Marlborough, and West Coast Regiment; The Northland Regiment; The Ruahine Regiment; 27 (MG) Battalion; 28 (Maori) Battalion
387.	**DJEBEL GARCI** 20th April 1943 Advance on Tunis	1957 1962 ?	The Essex Regiment 4th Battalion, The Rajputana Rifles: 1st Battalion, 9th Gorkha Rifles 4th Battalion (Bhopal), 16th Punjab Regiment
388.	**DJEBEL TERHOUNA** 25th–29th April 1943 Advance on Tunis	1958	The Canterbury Regiment; The Otago Regiment; The Southland Regiment; The Nelson, Marlborough, and West Coast Regiment
389.	**DJEBEL ES SRAFI** 25th–29th April 1943 Advance on Tunis	1958	The Canterbury Regiment; The Otago Regiment; The Southland Regiment; The Nelson, Marlborough, and West Coast Regiment
390.	**DJEBIBINA** 6th–9th May 1943 Advance on Tunis	1958	The Waikato Regiment; The New Zealand Scottish Regiment; The Canterbury Regiment; The Auckland Regiment (Countess of Ranfurly's Own); The Otago Regiment; The Southland Regiment; The Hauraki Regiment; The Nelson, Marlborough, and West Coast Regiment; The Northland Regiment; 28 (Maori) Battalion
391.	**DJEBEL TEBAGA** 8th–9th May 1943 Advance on Tunis	1957	The Royal Fusiliers (City of London Regiment)
392.	**DJEBEL ABIOD** 17th November 1942 Allied Build-up and Enemy Counter Offensive	1957	The Queen's Own Royal West Kent Regiment
393.	**SOUDIA** 24th November 1942 Allied Build-up and Enemy Counter Offensive	1956	The Parachute Regiment

394.	**MEDJEZ EL BAB** 25th–26th November 1942 Allied Build-up and Enemy Counter Offensive	1956 1957	The Derbyshire Yeomanry, Royal Armoured Corps (TA) The Lancashire Fusiliers; The Rifle Brigade (Prince Consort's Own); Tower Hamlets Rifles (TA)
395.	**TEBOURBA** 27th November 1942 Allied Build-up and Enemy Counter Offensive	1957	The East Surrey Regiment
396.	**DJEDEIDA** 28th–29th November 1942 Allied Build-up and Enemy Counter Offensive	1957	The Northamptonshire Regiment
397.	**DJEBEL AZZAG 1942** 28th–30th November 1942 Allied Build-up and Enemy Counter Offensive	1957	The Argyll and Sutherland Highlanders (Princess Louise's); The Queen's Own Royal West Kent Regiment
398.	**OUDNA** 29th November–3rd December 1942 Allied Build-up and Enemy Counter Offensive	1956	The Parachute Regiment
399.	**TEBOURBA GAP** 1st–10th December 1942 Allied Build-up and Enemy Counter Offensive	1956 1957	17th/21st Lancers; The Derbyshire Yeomanry, Royal Armoured Corps (TA) The Royal Hampshire Regiment
400.	**LONGSTOP HILL 1942** 23rd–25th December 1942 Allied Build-up and Enemy Counter Offensive	1957	Coldstream Guards
401.	**DJEBEL AZZAG 1943** 5th–7th January 1943 Allied Build-up and Enemy Counter Offensive	1956	The Buffs (Royal East Kent Regiment); The Parachute Regiment
402.	**TWO TREE HILL** 13th January 1943 Allied Build-up and Enemy Counter Offensive	1957	The Royal Inniskilling Fusiliers

403.	**BOU ARADA** 18th–25th January 1943 Allied Build-up and Enemy Counter Offensive	1956 1957 1958	17th/21st Lancers: The Derbyshire Yeomanry, Royal Armoured Corps (TA) The Royal Inniskilling Fusiliers: 1st/2nd Lothians and Border Horse, Royal Armoured Corps (TA): London Irish Rifles, The Royal Ulster Rifles (TA) The Royal Irish Fusiliers (Princess Victoria's)
404.	**ROBAA VALLEY** 31st January 1943 Allied Build-up and Enemy Counter Offensive	1956	The Buffs (Royal East Kent Regiment)
405.	**DJEBEL ALLILIGA** 3rd–4th February 1943 Allied Build-up and Enemy Counter Offensive	1956	The Parachute Regiment
406.	**KASSERINE** 14th–25th February 1943 Allied Build-up and Enemy Counter Offensive	1956 1957	17th/21st Lancers: The Derbyshire Yeomanry, Royal Armoured Corps (TA) The Rifle Brigade (Prince Consort's Own): 1st/2nd Lothians and Border Horse, Royal Armoured Corps (TA): Tower Hamlets Rifles (TA): 16th/5th The Queen's Royal Lancers
407.	**SBIBA** 19th–22nd February 1943 Allied Build-up and Enemy Counter Offensive	1957	Honourable Artillery Company (TA): Coldstream Guards
408.	**THALA** 20th–22nd February 1943 Allied Build-up and Enemy Counter Offensive	1956 1957	17th/21st Lancers Honourable Artillery Company (TA): The Rifle Brigade (Prince Consort's Own): 1st/2nd Lothians and Border Horse, Royal Armoured Corps (TA): Tower Hamlets Rifles (TA)
409.	**EL HADJEBA** 26th February 1943 Enemy Thrusts at Allied Communication Centres	1956 1957	The Parachute Regiment London Irish Rifles, The Royal Ulster Rifles (TA)
410.	**DJEBEL DJAFFA** 26th February 1943 Enemy Thrusts at Allied Communication Centres	1957	The Northamptonshire Regiment
411.	**SIDI NSIR** 26th February 1943 Enemy Thrusts at Allied Communication Centres	1957	The Royal Hampshire Regiment

		Year	Regiment
412.	**FORT McGREGOR** 26th–27th February 1943 Enemy Thrusts at Allied Communication Centres	1957	The East Surrey Regiment
413.	**STUKA FARM** 26th–28th February 1943 Enemy Thrusts at Allied Communication Centres	1957 1958	London Irish Rifles, The Royal Ulster Rifles (TA) The Royal Irish Fusiliers (Princess Victoria's)
414.	**STEAMROLLER FARM** 26th February–1st March 1943 Enemy Thrusts at Allied Communication Centres	1956 1957	The Derbyshire Yeomanry, Royal Armoured Corps (TA) Coldstream Guards: The Commando Association
415.	**HUNT'S GAP** 27th–28th February 1943 Enemy Thrusts at Allied Communication Centres	1957	North Irish Horse, Royal Armoured Corps (TA): The Royal Hampshire Regiment
416.	**MONTAGNE FARM** 28th February–2nd March 1943 Enemy Thrusts at Allied Communication Centres	1956 1957	The Royal Leicestershire Regiment The Royal Hampshire Regiment
417.	**KEF OUIBA PASS** 28th February–4th March 1943 Enemy Thrusts at Allied Communication Centres	1957	The Argyll and Sutherland Highlanders (Princess Louise's)
418.	**DJEBEL GUERBA** 2nd March 1943 Enemy Thrusts at Allied Communication Centres	1957	The Sherwood Foresters (Nottinghamshire and Derbyshire Regiment)
419.	**SEDJENANE I** 4th March 1943 Enemy Thrusts at Allied Communication Centres	1957	North Irish Horse, Royal Armoured Corps (TA): The Royal Lincolnshire Regiment: The Durham Light Infantry: The Commando Association
420.	**TAMERA** 5th–15th March 1943 Enemy Thrusts at Allied Communication Centres	1956 1957	The Parachute Regiment North Irish Horse, Royal Armoured Corps (TA): The Sherwood Foresters (Nottinghamshire and Derbyshire Regiment)

421.	**MAKNASSY** 12th–31st March 1943 Enemy Thrusts at Allied Communication Centres	1956	The Derbyshire Yeomanry, Royal Armoured Corps (TA)
422.	**DJEBEL DAHRA** 20th–24th March 1943 Enemy Thrusts at Allied Communication Centres	1956	The Parachute Regiment
423.	**DJEBEL CHOUCHA** 28th March 1943 Allied Counter Offensive	1957	The Commando Association
424.	**KEF EL DEBNA** 28th March 1943 Allied Counter Offensive	1956	The Parachute Regiment
425.	**MINE DE SEDJENANE** 30th–31st March 1943 Allied Counter Offensive	1956 1957	The York and Lancaster Regiment The Argyll and Sutherland Highlanders (Princess Louise's); The King's Own Yorkshire Light Infantry; The Royal Lincolnshire Regiment
426.	**FONDOUK** 7th–11th April 1943 Allied Counter Offensive	1956 1957 1958	17th/21st Lancers; The Derbyshire Yeomanry, Royal Armoured Corps (TA) The Royal Hampshire Regiment; The Rifle Brigade (Prince Consort's Own); 1st/2nd Lothians and Border Horse, Royal Armoured Corps (TA); Welsh Guards; Tower Hamlets Rifles (TA); 16th/5th The Queen's Royal Lancers Royal Tank Regiment
427.	**PICHON** 8th April 1943 Allied Counter Offensive	1957	The Royal Hampshire Regiment
428.	**DJEBEL EL RHORAB** 9th April 1943 Allied Counter Offensive	1957	Welsh Guards
429.	**FONDOUK PASS** 9th April 1943 Allied Counter Offensive	1957	The Rifle Brigade (Prince Consort's Own); Tower Hamlets Rifles (TA)
430.	**SIDI ALI** 10th April 1943 Allied Counter Offensive	1957	1st/2nd Lothians and Border Horse, Royal Armoured Corps (TA)
431.	**KAIROUAN** 10th April 1943 Allied Counter Offensive	1956 1957	The Derbyshire Yeomanry, Royal Armoured Corps (TA) 16th/5th The Queen's Royal Lancers

	Battle Honour	Year	Regiments
432.	**BORDJ** 11th April 1943 Allied Counter Offensive	1957	1st/2nd Lothians and Border Horse, Royal Armoured Corps (TA); 16th/5th The Queen's Royal Lancers
433.	**OUED ZARGA** 7th–15th April 1943 Allied Counter Offensive	1957 1958	The Lancashire Fusiliers; The Queen's Own Royal West Kent Regiment; The Royal Inniskilling Fusiliers; The Northamptonshire Regiment; The East Surrey Regiment The Royal Irish Fusiliers (Princess Victoria's)
434.	**MERGUEB CHAOUACH** 7th April 1943 Allied Counter Offensive	1957	North Irish Horse, Royal Armoured Corps (TA)
435.	**DJEBEL BEL MAHDI** 7th April 1943 Allied Counter Offensive	1957 1958	The Royal Inniskilling Fusiliers The Royal Irish Fusiliers (Princess Victoria's)
436.	**DJEBEL BECH CHEKAOUI** 9th April 1943 Allied Counter Offensive	1956	The Buffs (Royal East Kent Regiment)
437.	**DJEBEL RMEL** 10th April 1943 Allied Counter Offensive	1957	North Irish Horse, Royal Armoured Corps (TA)
438.	**DJEBEL ANG** 14th–15th April 1943 Allied Counter Offensive	1957 1958	The Queen's Own Royal West Kent Regiment; The East Surrey Regiment The Royal Irish Fusiliers (Princess Victoria's)
439.	**DJEBEL TANNGOUCHA** 14th–25th April 1943 Allied Counter Offensive	1957 1958	The Royal Inniskilling Fusiliers; The Northamptonshire Regiment The Royal Irish Fusiliers (Princess Victoria's)
440.	**HEIDOUS** 15th–25th April 1943 Allied Counter Offensive	1956 1957	The Buffs (Royal East Kent Regiment) London Irish Rifles, The Royal Ulster Rifles (TA)
441.	**BANANA RIDGE** 21st April 1943 Allied Counter Offensive	1956 1957	The Duke of Wellington's Regiment (West Riding) The Loyal Regiment (North Lancashire)
442.	**DJEBEL KESSKISS** 21st April 1943 Allied Counter Offensive	1957	The Loyal Regiment (North Lancashire); The North Staffordshire Regiment (The Prince of Wales's)
443.	**DJEBEL DJAFFA PASS** 21st–22nd April 1943 Allied Counter Offensive	1957	The East Surrey Regiment

444.	**EL KOURZIA** 22nd–26th April 1943 Allied Counter Offensive	1956 1957 1958	9th Queen's Royal Lancers: 17th/21st Lancers: The Derbyshire Yeomanry, Royal Armoured Corps (TA) The Queen's Bays (2nd Dragoon Guards): 12th Royal Lancers (Prince of Wales's): The Queen's Own Yorkshire Dragoons, Royal Armoured Corps (TA): 10th Royal Hussars (Prince of Wales's Own): The Royal Hampshire Regiment: The Rifle Brigade (Prince Consort's Own): The Durham Light Infantry: Tower Hamlets Rifles (TA) Royal Tank Regiment
445.	**BER RABAL** 22nd April 1943 Allied Counter Offensive	1957	The Royal Hampshire Regiment
446.	**ARGOUB SELLAH** 22nd April 1943 Allied Counter Offensive	1957	The King's Own Yorkshire Light Infantry: The Royal Lincolnshire Regiment
447.	**MEDJEZ PLAIN** 23rd–30th April 1943 Allied Counter Offensive	1956 1957 1958	Irish Guards: The Duke of Wellington's Regiment (West Riding): The Duke of Cornwall's Light Infantry: The Buffs (Royal East Kent Regiment) Grenadier Guards: The Gordon Highlanders: The Argyll and Sutherland Highlanders (Princess Louise's): The Sherwood Foresters (Nottinghamshire and Derbyshire Regiment): The Queen's Own Royal West Kent Regiment: The Loyal Regiment (North Lancashire): Scots Guards: The East Surrey Regiment: The Black Watch (Royal Highland Regiment): The North Staffordshire Regiment (The Prince of Wales's) Royal Tank Regiment
448.	**GRICH EL OUED** 23rd April 1943 Allied Counter Offensive	1957	Scots Guards
449.	**GUERIAT EL ATACH RIDGE** 23rd–24th April 1943 Allied Counter Offensive	1956 1957	The Duke of Wellington's Regiment (West Riding) The Loyal Regiment (North Lancashire): The King's Shropshire Light Infantry: The North Staffordshire Regiment (The Prince of Wales's)
450.	**LONGSTOP HILL 1943** 23rd–26th April 1943 Allied Counter Offensive	1956 1957	The Buffs (Royal East Kent Regiment) The Argyll and Sutherland Highlanders (Princess Louise's): The Queen's Own Royal West Kent Regiment: North Irish Horse, Royal Armoured Corps (TA): The East Surrey Regiment
451.	**PETERS CORNER** 24th April 1943 Allied Counter Offensive	1957	The Royal Fusiliers (City of London Regiment)
452.	**SI MEDIENE** 25th–26th April 1943 Allied Counter Offensive	1957	The Black Watch (Royal Highland Regiment)
453.	**DJEBEL BOU AOUKAZ 1943** 27th–28th April 1943 and 5th–6th May 1943 Allied Counter Offensive	1956 1957	Irish Guards: The Duke of Wellington's Regiment (West Riding) The Loyal Regiment (North Lancashire) [1]: The King's Shropshire Light Infantry [2] [1] Awarded as DJEBEL BOU AOUKAZ 1943 I: DJEBEL BOU AOUKAZ 1943 taken into use 1985. [2] Awarded as DJEBEL BOU AOUKAZ 1943 II: DJEBEL BOU AOUKAZ 1943 taken into use 1985.

454. **DJEBEL BOU AOUKAZ 1943 I**
27th–28th April 1943
Allied Counter Offensive

1957 Scots Guards

455. **SI ABDALLAH**
27th–30th April 1943
Allied Counter Offensive

1956 The Duke of Cornwall's Light Infantry
1957 The Queen's Own Royal West Kent Regiment

456. **GAB GAB GAP**
28th–30th April 1943
Allied Counter Offensive

1957 The Loyal Regiment (North Lancashire);The North Staffordshire Regiment (The Prince of Wales's)

457. **SIDI AHMED**
28th–30th April 1943
Allied Counter Offensive

1957 The Northamptonshire Regiment

458. **DJEBEL KOURNINE**
25th–30th April 1943
Allied Counter Offensive

1956 The York and Lancaster Regiment
1957 The Queen's Bays (2nd Dragoon Guards): 12th Royal Lancers (Prince of Wales's): 10th Royal Hussars (Prince of Wales's Own);The Rifle Brigade (Prince Consort's Own): 1st/2nd Lothians and Border Horse, Royal Armoured Corps (TA): 16th/5th The Queen's Royal Lancers

459. **ARGOUB MEGAS**
30th April 1943
Allied Counter Offensive

1957 The King's Royal Rifle Corps

460. **TUNIS**
5th–12th May 1943
Allied Counter Offensive

1956 The Duke of Wellington's Regiment (West Riding): 9th Queen's Royal Lancers: 17th/21st Lancers:The Derbyshire Yeomanry, Royal Armoured Corps (TA);The Royal Sussex Regiment
1957 The Queen's Bays (2nd Dragoon Guards): 3rd/4th County of London Yeomanry (Sharpshooters), Royal Armoured Corps (TA): Honourable Artillery Company (TA): 1st King's Dragoon Guards: 12th Royal Lancers (Prince of Wales's):The Queen's Own Yorkshire Dragoons, Royal Armoured Corps (TA):The Queen's Royal Regiment (West Surrey):The Bedfordshire and Hertfordshire Regiment:The Sherwood Foresters (Nottinghamshire and Derbyshire Regiment): 10th Royal Hussars (Prince of Wales's Own):The King's Shropshire Light Infantry: North Irish Horse, Royal Armoured Corps (TA):The East Surrey Regiment: 11th Hussars (Prince Albert's Own):Coldstream Guards:The Rifle Brigade (Prince Consort's Own): 1st/2nd Lothians and Border Horse, Royal Armoured Corps (TA): Welsh Guards: The Black Watch (Royal Highland Regiment): The Essex Regiment: London Rifle Brigade, The Rifle Brigade (Prince Consort's Own) (TA):Tower Hamlets Rifles (TA): 16th/5th The Queen's Royal Lancers:The King's Royal Rifle Corps: 2nd King Edward VII's Own Gurkha Rifles (The Sirmoor Rifles)
1958 Royal Tank Regiment
? 4th Battalion (Bhopal), 16th Punjab Regiment

461. **MONTARNAUD**
6th May 1943
Allied Counter Offensive

1957 The East Surrey Regiment

462.	**RAGOUBET SOUISSI** 6th May 1943 Allied Counter Offensive	1957 1962	The Essex Regiment 1st Battalion, 9th Gorkha Rifles
463.	**HAMMAM LIF** 8th–9th May 1943 Allied Counter Offensive	1956 1957	17th/21st Lancers Coldstream Guards:The Rifle Brigade (Prince Consort's Own): 1st/2nd Lothians and Border Horse, Royal Armoured Corps (TA):Welsh Guards:Tower Hamlets Rifles (TA)
464.	**CRETEVILLE PASS** 8th–11th May 1943 Allied Counter Offensive	1956 1957	9th Queen's Royal Lancers The Queen's Bays (2nd Dragoon Guards): 12th Royal Lancers (Prince of Wales's)
465.	**GROMBALLA** 10th May 1943 Allied Counter Offensive	1957	16th/5th The Queen's Royal Lancers
466.	**BOU FICHA** 11th May 1943 Allied Counter Offensive	1957	1st/2nd Lothians and Border Horse, Royal Armoured Corps (TA): 16th/5th The Queen's Royal Lancers
467.	**NORTH AFRICA 1940** 12th June–31st December 1940 Service in North Africa 1940–43	1957 1958	The Royal Fusiliers (City of London Regiment) The South Staffordshire Regiment
468.	**NORTH AFRICA 1940–41** 12th June 1940–31st December 1941 Service in North Africa 1940–43	1956 1961	The Royal Leicestershire Regiment: 7th Queen's Own Hussars 6th Cavalry (Commando) Regiment: 1st Infantry Battalion (Commando) (City of Sydney's Own Regiment): 2nd Infantry Battalion (City of Newcastle Regiment): 3rd Infantry Battalion (The Werriwa Regiment): 4th Infantry Battalion (Australian Rifles): 5th Infantry Battalion (The Victorian Scottish Regiment): 6th Infantry Battalion (The Royal Melbourne Regiment): 8th Infantry Battalion: 7th Infantry Battalion: 11th Infantry Battalion
469.	**NORTH AFRICA 1940–42** 12th June 1940–31st December 1942 Service in North Africa 1940–43	1957	The West Yorkshire Regiment (The Prince of Wales's Own): 8th King's Royal Irish Hussars:The King's Own Royal Regiment (Lancaster):The Highland Light Infantry (City of Glasgow Regiment):The Welch Regiment: 3rd The King's Own Hussars
470.	**NORTH AFRICA 1940–43** 12th June 1940–12th May 1943 Service in North Africa 1940–43	1956 1957 1958 1958 1962	The Royal Sussex Regiment The Cheshire Regiment: The Argyll and Sutherland Highlanders (Princess Louise's): The Queen's Royal Regiment (West Surrey): The Queen's Own Cameron Highlanders:The Royal Hampshire Regiment: 11th Hussars (Prince Albert's Own): Coldstream Guards:The Rifle Brigade (Prince Consort's Own):The Durham Light Infantry:The King's Royal Rifle Corps: Special Air Service Regiment Royal Tank Regiment:The Royal Northumberland Fusiliers The Waikato Regiment:The New Zealand Scottish Regiment:The Canterbury Regiment:The Auckland Regiment (Countess of Ranfurly's Own):The Otago Regiment:The Southland Regiment:The Wellington Regiment (City of Wellington's Own):The Hauraki Regiment:The Wellington West Coast Regiment:The Taranaki Regiment:The Hawke's Bay Regiment:The Northland Regiment:The Ruahine Regiment: 27 (MG) Battalion: 28 (Maori) Battalion 2nd Lancers:The Poona Horse: 18th Cavalry:The Central India Horse: 9 Field Company, Madras Engineer Group: 12 Field

Company, Madras Engineer Group: 61 Field Company, Madras Engineer Group: 66 Field Company, Bengal Engineer Group: 20 Field Company, Bombay Engineer Group: 21 Field Company, Bombay Engineer Group: 3rd Battalion, The Brigade of the Guards: 1st Battalion, The Parachute Regiment: 2nd Battalion, The Parachute Regiment: 3rd Battalion, The Parachute Regiment: 3rd Battalion, The Punjab Regiment: 9th Battalion, The Grenadiers: 1st Battalion, The Maratha Light Infantry: 2nd Battalion, The Maratha Light Infantry: 4th Battalion, The Rajputana Rifles: 17th Battalion (Sawai Man), The Rajputana Rifles: MG Battalion, The Rajputana Rifles: 4th Battalion, The Rajput Regiment: 3rd Battalion, The Jat Regiment: 2nd Battalion, The Sikh Regiment: 4th Battalion, The Sikh Regiment: 3rd Battalion, The Garhwal Rifles: 2nd Battalion, 3rd Gorkha Rifles: 2nd Battalion, 4th Gorkha Rifles: 2nd Battalion, 8th Gorkha Rifles: 1st Battalion, 9th Gorkha Rifles

1963   3rd Battalion, The Rajput Regiment

?   13th Duke of Connaught's Own Lancers: The Guides Cavalry (10th Queen Victoria's Own Frontier Force): Prince Albert Victor's Own Cavalry (11th Frontier Force): 1st Battalion, 1st Punjab Regiment: 3rd Battalion, 1st Punjab Regiment: 3rd Battalion, 14th Punjab Regiment: 4th Battalion (Bhopal), 16th Punjab Regiment: 3rd Battalion (Queen Mary's Own), The Baluch Regiment: 4th Battalion (Duke of Connaught's Own), The Baluch Regiment: 3rd Royal Battalion, The Frontier Force Regiment: 4th Battalion (Wilde's), The Frontier Force Rifles

471.   **NORTH AFRICA 1941**
1st January–31st December 1941
Service in North Africa 1940–43

1956   The York and Lancaster Regiment
1957   The Bedfordshire and Hertfordshire Regiment
1961   7th Cavalry (Commando) Regiment: 9th Infantry Battalion (The Moreton Regiment): 10th Infantry Battalion (The Adelaide Rifles): 12th Infantry Battalion (The Launceston Regiment): 14th Infantry Battalion (The Prahran Regiment): 16th Infantry Battalion (The Cameron Highlanders of West Australia): 25th Infantry Battalion (The Darling Downs Regiment): 27th Infantry Battalion (The South Australian Scottish Regiment): 33rd Infantry Battalion (The New England Regiment): 1st Pioneer Battalion

472.   **WESTERN DESERT 1941** ¹
1st January–31st December 1941
Service in North Africa 1940–43

?   South African Irish Regiment
¹ WESTELIKE WOESTYN 1941 taken into use by Afrikaans-speaking South African units 1957.

473.   **NORTH AFRICA 1941–42**
1st January–31st December 1942
Service in North Africa 1940–43

1956   The Royal Gloucestershire Hussars, Royal Armoured Corps (TA)
1957   The Worcestershire Regiment
1961   13th Infantry Battalion (The Macquarie Regiment): 15th Infantry Battalion (The Oxley Regiment): 17th Infantry Battalion: 23rd Infantry Battalion (The City of Geelong Regiment): 24th Infantry Battalion (The Kooyong Regiment): 28th Infantry Battalion (The Swan Regiment): 43rd Infantry Battalion: 48th Infantry Battalion: 32nd Infantry Battalion: 2nd Machine Gun Battalion

474.   **NORTH AFRICA 1941–43**
1st January–12th May 1943
Service in North Africa 1940–43

1956   1st The Royal Dragoons: The Buffs (Royal East Kent Regiment)
1957   The Queen's Bays (2nd Dragoon Guards): 3rd/4th County of London Yeomanry (Sharpshooters), Royal Armoured Corps (TA): Honourable Artillery Company (TA): 1st King's Dragoon Guards: 12th Royal Lancers (Prince of Wales's): Scots Guards: The Black Watch (Royal Highland Regiment): The Essex Regiment: Tower Hamlets Rifles (TA)

475.   **WESTERN DESERT 1941–43** ¹
1st January–12th May 1943
Service in North Africa 1940–43

1957   The Royal Natal Carbineers: Royal Durban Light Infantry: Duke of Edinburgh's Own Rifles: The Queen's Own Cape Town Highlanders: Transvaal Scottish: Rand Light Infantry: 2 Regiment Botha: Natal Mounted Rifles: Umvoti Mounted Rifles: Imperial Light Horse: Regiment President Steyn: Die Middellandse Regiment Regiment Vrystaat
?   ¹ WESTELIKE WOESTYN 1941–43 taken into use by Afrikaans-speaking South African units 1957.

Battle Honours for the Second World War

298

476. **NORTH AFRICA 1942**
1st January–31st December 1942
Service in North Africa 1940–43

1956 The Royal Wiltshire Yeomanry (Prince of Wales's Own), Royal Armoured Corps (TA)
1957 The Warwickshire Yeomanry, Royal Armoured Corps (TA): 7th Gurkha Rifles: 4th Queen's Own Hussars: The Queen's Westminsters, The King's Royal Rifle Corps (TA): The Rangers, The King's Royal Rifle Corps (TA)
1958 The South Wales Borderers
1961 9th Cavalry (Commando) Regiment: 3rd Pioneer Battalion

477. **NORTH AFRICA 1942–43**
1st January 1942–12th May 1943
Service in North Africa 1940–43

1956 The Life Guards: Royal Horse Guards: The Royal Scots Greys (2nd Dragoons): 9th Queen's Royal Lancers: 17th/21st Lancers: The Derbyshire Yeomanry, Royal Armoured Corps (TA): The Duke of Cornwall's Light Infantry: The Parachute Regiment
1957 Grenadier Guards: The Lancashire Fusiliers: Seaforth Highlanders (Ross-shire Buffs, The Duke of Albany's): The Gordon Highlanders: The Staffordshire Yeomanry (Queen's Own Royal Regiment), Royal Armoured Corps (TA): The Queen's Own Yorkshire Dragoons, Royal Armoured Corps (TA): The Green Howards (Alexandra, Princess of Wales's Own Yorkshire Regiment): The Sherwood Foresters (Nottinghamshire and Derbyshire Regiment): The Queen's Own Royal West Kent Regiment: 10th Royal Hussars (Prince of Wales's Own): The Royal Inniskilling Fusiliers: The Northamptonshire Regiment: The Sherwood Rangers Yeomanry, Royal Armoured Corps (TA): The Middlesex Regiment (Duke of Cambridge's Own): The East Yorkshire Regiment (The Duke of York's Own): London Rifle Brigade, The Rifle Brigade (Prince Consort's Own) (TA): The Commando Association: 16th/5th The Queen's Royal Lancers: London Irish Rifles, The Royal Ulster Rifles (TA): 2nd King Edward VII's Own Gurkha Rifles (The Sirmoor Rifles)

478. **NORTH AFRICA 1943**
1st January–12th May 1943
Service in North Africa 1940–43

1956 Irish Guards: The Duke of Wellington's Regiment (West Riding): The York and Lancaster Regiment: The York and Lancaster Regiment
1957 The Royal Fusiliers (City of London Regiment): The Oxfordshire and Buckinghamshire Light Infantry: The Bedfordshire and Hertfordshire Regiment: The King's Own Yorkshire Light Infantry: The Loyal Regiment (North Lancashire): The King's Shropshire Light Infantry: North Irish Horse, Royal Armoured Corps (TA): The Royal Lincolnshire Regiment: Welsh Guards: The North Staffordshire Regiment (The Prince of Wales's)

479. **LANDING IN SICILY** [1]
9th–12th July 1943
Assault and Capture of Sicily

1956 The York and Lancaster Regiment: The Devonshire Regiment: The Cameronians (Scottish Rifles)
1957 3rd/4th County of London Yeomanry (Sharpshooters), Royal Armoured Corps (TA): The Glider Pilot Regiment: The Cheshire Regiment: Seaforth Highlanders (Ross-shire Buffs, The Duke of Albany's): The Gordon Highlanders: The Argyll and Sutherland Highlanders (Princess Louise's): The Green Howards (Alexandra, Princess of Wales's Own Yorkshire Regiment): The Dorset Regiment: The Royal Inniskilling Fusiliers: The Border Regiment: The Northamptonshire Regiment: The Royal Hampshire Regiment: The Highland Light Infantry (City of Glasgow Regiment): The Black Watch (Royal Highland Regiment): The Durham Light Infantry: The Commando Association: Special Air Service Regiment
1957 The Hastings and Prince Edward Regiment: 48th Highlanders of Canada: Princess Patricia's Canadian Light Infantry: West Nova Scotia Regiment (Machine Gun): The Seaforth Highlanders of Canada: 1st Battalion, The Royal New Brunswick Regiment (Carleton and York): 2nd Battalion, The Royal New Brunswick Regiment (North Shore): The Royal 22e Regiment
1958 The South Staffordshire Regiment: The Royal Scots Fusiliers
1958 The Loyal Edmonton Regiment (3rd Battalion, Princess Patricia's Canadian Light Infantry): The Royal Canadian Regiment
1959 Le Regiment de Trois Rivieres: The North Saskatchewan Regiment
? 3rd Battalion (Queen Mary's Own), The Baluch Regiment: 3rd Royal Battalion, The Frontier Force Regiment

[1] *DEBARQUEMENT EN SICILE taken into use by French-speaking Canadian units 1958.*

480.	**SOLARINO** 11th–13th July 1943 Assault and Capture of Sicily	1956 1957	The Wiltshire Regiment (Duke of Edinburgh's) The Royal Inniskilling Fusiliers: The Durham Light Infantry
481.	**VIZZINI** 11th–14th July 1943 Assault and Capture of Sicily	1957	The Black Watch (Royal Highland Regiment)
482.	**AUGUSTA** 12th–13th July 1943 Assault and Capture of Sicily	1957	Seaforth Highlanders (Ross-shire Buffs, The Duke of Albany's)
483.	**FRANCOFONTE** 13th–15th July 1943 Assault and Capture of Sicily	1957	Seaforth Highlanders (Ross-shire Buffs, The Duke of Albany's): The Queen's Own Cameron Highlanders: The Middlesex Regiment (Duke of Cambridge's Own)
484.	**LENTINI** 13th–18th July 1943 Assault and Capture of Sicily	1957	3rd/4th County of London Yeomanry (Sharpshooters), Royal Armoured Corps (TA): The Green Howards (Alexandra, Princess of Wales's Own Yorkshire Regiment): London Irish Rifles, The Royal Ulster Rifles (TA)
485.	**PRIMOSOLE BRIDGE** 13th–18th July 1943 Assault and Capture of Sicily	1956 1957 1958	The London Scottish, The Gordon Highlanders (TA): The Parachute Regiment The Cheshire Regiment: The Durham Light Infantry: The East Yorkshire Regiment (The Duke of York's Own) Royal Tank Regiment
486.	**GRAMMICHELE** 15th July 1943 Assault and Capture of Sicily	1957 1959	The Hastings and Prince Edward Regiment Le Regiment de Trois Rivieres
487.	**PIAZZA ARMERINA** [1] 16th–17th July 1943 Assault and Capture of Sicily	1958 1959	The Loyal Edmonton Regiment (3rd Battalion, Princess Patricia's Canadian Light Infantry) Le Regiment de Trois Rivieres [1] *PIAZZA-ARMERINA taken into use by French-speaking Canadian units 1958.*
488.	**SFERRO** 15th–20th July 1943 Assault and Capture of Sicily	1957	The Gordon Highlanders: The Black Watch (Royal Highland Regiment): The Middlesex Regiment (Duke of Cambridge's Own)
489.	**VALGUARNERA** 17th–19th July 1943 Assault and Capture of Sicily	1957 1958 1959	The Hastings and Prince Edward Regiment: 48th Highlanders of Canada: West Nova Scotia Regiment (Machine Gun): 1st Battalion, The Royal New Brunswick Regiment (Carleton and York): 2nd Battalion, The Royal New Brunswick Regiment (North Shore): The Royal 22e Regiment The Royal Canadian Regiment Le Regiment de Trois Rivieres: The North Saskatchewan Regiment
490.	**SIMETO BRIDGEHEAD** 18th–21st July 1943 Assault and Capture of Sicily	1956 1957	The Wiltshire Regiment (Duke of Edinburgh's): The York and Lancaster Regiment: The Cameronians (Scottish Rifles) 3rd/4th County of London Yeomanry (Sharpshooters), Royal Armoured Corps (TA): The Cheshire Regiment: The Royal Inniskilling Fusiliers: London Irish Rifles, The Royal Ulster Rifles (TA)

491.	**GERBINI** 18th–21st July 1943 Assault and Capture of Sicily	1957 1958	The Argyll and Sutherland Highlanders (Princess Louise's):The Black Watch (Royal Highland Regiment) Royal Tank Regiment
492.	**ASSORO** 20th–22nd July 1943 Assault and Capture of Sicily	1957	The Hastings and Prince Edward Regiment: 48th Highlanders of Canada
493.	**LEONFORTE** 21st–22nd July 1943 Assault and Capture of Sicily	1957 1958	Princess Patricia's Canadian Light Infantry The Loyal Edmonton Regiment (3rd Battalion, Princess Patricia's Canadian Light Infantry)
494.	**AGIRA** 24th–28th July 1943 Assault and Capture of Sicily	1957 1957 1958 1959	The Dorset Regiment The Hastings and Prince Edward Regiment: 48th Highlanders of Canada: Princess Patricia's Canadian Light Infantry: The Seaforth Highlanders of Canada The Loyal Edmonton Regiment (3rd Battalion, Princess Patricia's Canadian Light Infantry):The Royal Canadian Regiment Le Regiment de Trois Rivieres:The North Saskatchewan Regiment
495.	**ADRANO** 29th July–7th August 1943 Assault and Capture of Sicily	1957 1957 1958 1958 1959	The Lancashire Fusiliers: Seaforth Highlanders (Ross-shire Buffs, The Duke of Albany's):The Argyll and Sutherland Highlanders (Princess Louise's):The Royal Inniskilling Fusiliers:The Northamptonshire Regiment:The Queen's Own Cameron Highlanders: The East Surrey Regiment:The Black Watch (Royal Highland Regiment): London Irish Rifles,The Royal Ulster Rifles (TA) The Hastings and Prince Edward Regiment: 48th Highlanders of Canada: West Nova Scotia Regiment (Machine Gun):The Seaforth Highlanders of Canada:The Royal 22e Regiment Royal Tank Regiment:The Royal Irish Fusiliers (Princess Victoria's) 4th Princess Louise Dragoon Guards (4th Armoured Car Regiment):The Loyal Edmonton Regiment (3rd Battalion, Princess Patricia's Canadian Light Infantry):The Royal Canadian Regiment Le Regiment de Trois Rivieres:The North Saskatchewan Regiment
496.	**CATENANUOVA** 29th–30th July 1943 Assault and Capture of Sicily	1957	West Nova Scotia Regiment (Machine Gun):The Royal 22e Regiment
497.	**REGALBUTO** 29th July–3rd August 1943 Assault and Capture of Sicily	1956 1957 1957 1958	The Devonshire Regiment The Dorset Regiment:The Royal Hampshire Regiment The Hastings and Prince Edward Regiment: 48th Highlanders of Canada The Royal Canadian Regiment
498.	**SFERRO HILLS** 31st July–3rd August 1943 Assault and Capture of Sicily	1957	Seaforth Highlanders (Ross-shire Buffs, The Duke of Albany's):The Queen's Own Cameron Highlanders:The Black Watch (Royal Highland Regiment):The Middlesex Regiment (Duke of Cambridge's Own)
499.	**CENTURIPE** 31st July–3rd August 1943 Assault and Capture of Sicily	1956 1957 1957	Princess Louise's Kensington Regiment (TA):The Buffs (Royal East Kent Regiment) The Argyll and Sutherland Highlanders (Princess Louise's):The Queen's Own Royal West Kent Regiment:The Royal Inniskilling Fusiliers:The East Surrey Regiment: London Irish Rifles,The Royal Ulster Rifles (TA) West Nova Scotia Regiment (Machine Gun)

		1958	The Royal Irish Fusiliers (Princess Victoria's)
500.	**TROINA VALLEY** [1] 2nd–6th August 1943 Assault and Capture of Sicily	1957 1958 1959	The Seaforth Highlanders of Canada 4th Princess Louise Dragoon Guards (4th Armoured Car Regiment); The Loyal Edmonton Regiment (3rd Battalion, Princess Patricia's Canadian Light Infantry) Le Regiment de Trois Rivieres [1] *VALLEE DE TROINA taken into use by French-speaking Canadian units 1958.*
501.	**SALSO CROSSING** 4th August 1943 Assault and Capture of Sicily	1957 1958	London Irish Rifles, The Royal Ulster Rifles (TA) The Royal Irish Fusiliers (Princess Victoria's)
502.	**SIMETO CROSSING** 5th August 1943 Assault and Capture of Sicily	1957 1958	The Royal Inniskilling Fusiliers: London Irish Rifles, The Royal Ulster Rifles (TA) The Royal Irish Fusiliers (Princess Victoria's)
503.	**MONTE RIVOGLIA** 9th August 1943 Assault and Capture of Sicily	1956 1957	The Buffs (Royal East Kent Regiment) The Queen's Own Royal West Kent Regiment
504.	**MALLETO** 12th–13th August 1943 Assault and Capture of Sicily	1957 1958	London Irish Rifles, The Royal Ulster Rifles (TA) The Royal Irish Fusiliers (Princess Victoria's)
505.	**PURSUIT TO MESSINA** [1] 2nd–17th August 1943 Assault and Capture of Sicily	1956 1957 1958	The York and Lancaster Regiment The Royal Inniskilling Fusiliers: The Royal Berkshire Regiment (Princess Charlotte of Wales's); The Commando Association: London Irish Rifles, The Royal Ulster Rifles (TA) The Ontario Regiment (11th Armoured Regiment) [1] *POURSUITE A MESSINE taken into use by French-speaking Canadian units 1958.*
506.	**SICILY 1943** [1] 9th July–17th August 1943 Assault and Capture of Sicily	1956 1957 1957	1st The Royal Dragoons: The London Scottish; The Gordon Highlanders (TA); The Wiltshire Regiment (Duke of Edinburgh's); Princess Louise's Kensington Regiment (TA); The Buffs (Royal East Kent Regiment); The Devonshire Regiment: The Cameronians (Scottish Rifles); The York and Lancaster Regiment: The Parachute Regiment 3rd/4th County of London Yeomanry (Sharpshooters), Royal Armoured Corps (TA); Honourable Artillery Company (TA); The Glider Pilot Regiment: The Lancashire Fusiliers: The Cheshire Regiment: Seaforth Highlanders (Ross-shire Buffs, The Duke of Albany's); The Gordon Highlanders: The Argyll and Sutherland Highlanders (Princess Louise's); The Green Howards (Alexandra, Princess of Wales's Own Yorkshire Regiment): The Dorset Regiment: The Queen's Own Royal West Kent Regiment: The King's Own Yorkshire Light Infantry: The Royal Inniskilling Fusiliers: The Northamptonshire Regiment: The Queen's Own Cameron Highlanders: The East Surrey Regiment: The Royal Hampshire Regiment: The Royal Berkshire Regiment (Princess Charlotte of Wales's); The Highland Light Infantry (City of Glasgow Regiment): The Welch Regiment: The Black Watch (Royal Highland Regiment): The Middlesex Regiment (Duke of Cambridge's Own): The Durham Light Infantry: The East Yorkshire Regiment (The Duke of York's Own): The Commando Association: London Irish Rifles, The Royal Ulster Rifles (TA): Special Air Service Regiment The Elgin Regiment (27th Armoured Regiment): The Hastings and Prince Edward Regiment: 48th Highlanders of Canada: Princess Patricia's Canadian Light Infantry; West Nova Scotia Regiment (Machine Gun); The Seaforth Highlanders of Canada: 1st

	1958	Battalion,The Royal New Brunswick Regiment (Carleton and York); 2nd Battalion,The Royal New Brunswick Regiment (North Shore);The Royal 22e Regiment
	1958	Royal Tank Regiment;The South Staffordshire Regiment;The Royal Scots Fusiliers
		The Ontario Regiment (11th Armoured Regiment); 4th Princess Louise Dragoon Guards (4th Armoured Car Regiment);The Loyal Edmonton Regiment (3rd Battalion, Princess Patricia's Canadian Light Infantry);The Royal Canadian Regiment
	1959	Le Regiment de Trois Rivieres;The Lorne Scots (Peel, Dufferin and Halton Regiment);The North Saskatchewan Regiment;The King's Own Calgary Regiment (RCAC)
	?	3rd Battalion (Queen Mary's Own),The Baluch Regiment: 3rd Royal Battalion,The Frontier Force Regiment

¹ *SICILE 1943 taken into use by French-speaking Canadian units 1958.*

507. **LANDING AT REGGIO** ¹
3rd September 1943
The Landings in Calabria

1957	The Hastings and Prince Edward Regiment: 48th Highlanders of Canada: West Nova Scotia Regiment (Machine Gun): 1st Battalion, The Royal New Brunswick Regiment (Carleton and York): 2nd Battalion, The Royal New Brunswick Regiment (North Shore);The Royal 22e Regiment
1958	4th Princess Louise Dragoon Guards (4th Armoured Car Regiment):The Royal Canadian Regiment
?	3rd Royal Battalion,The Frontier Force Regiment

¹ *DEBARQUEMENT A REGGIO taken into use by French-speaking Canadian units 1958.*

508. **LANDING AT PORTO SAN VENERE**
8th September 1943
The Landings in Calabria

| 1956 | The Devonshire Regiment |
| 1957 | The Dorset Regiment:The Royal Hampshire Regiment:The Commando Association |

509. **TARANTO**
9th–22nd September 1943
The Landing in the "Heel"

| 1956 | The Parachute Regiment |

510. **POTENZA**
19th–20th September 1943
The Advance towards Ortona

| 1957 | West Nova Scotia Regiment (Machine Gun):The Royal 22e Regiment |

511. **MOTTA MONTECORVINO**
1st–3rd October 1943
The Advance towards Ortona

1957	The Hastings and Prince Edward Regiment
1958	4th Princess Louise Dragoon Guards (4th Armoured Car Regiment):The Royal Canadian Regiment
1959	The King's Own Calgary Regiment (RCAC)

512. **TERMOLI**
3rd–6th October 1943
The Advance towards Ortona

1956	Princess Louise's Kensington Regiment (TA):The Buffs (Royal East Kent Regiment)
1957	3rd/4th County of London Yeomanry (Sharpshooters), Royal Armoured Corps (TA):The Lancashire Fusiliers:The Argyll and Sutherland Highlanders (Princess Louise's):The Queen's Own Royal West Kent Regiment:The Royal Inniskilling Fusiliers:The Commando Association: London Irish Rifles, The Royal Ulster Rifles (TA): Special Air Service Regiment
1958	The Royal Irish Fusiliers (Princess Victoria's)
1959	Le Regiment de Trois Rivieres

513. **MONTE SAN MARCO** ¹
6th–7th October 1943
The Advance towards Ortona

| 1957 | The Seaforth Highlanders of Canada |

¹ *MONTE SAN-MARCO taken into use by French-speaking Canadian units 1958.*

514.	**GAMBATESA** 7th–8th October 1943 The Advance towards Ortona	1957	West Nova Scotia Regiment (Machine Gun): 1st Battalion, The Royal New Brunswick Regiment (Carleton and York): 2nd Battalion, The Royal New Brunswick Regiment (North Shore)
515.	**CAMPOBASSO** 11th–14th October 1943 The Advance towards Ortona	1957 1958	The Hastings and Prince Edward Regiment: 48th Highlanders of Canada The Royal Canadian Regiment
516.	**BARANELLO** 17th–18th October 1943 The Advance towards Ortona	1957	The Seaforth Highlanders of Canada
517.	**COLLE D'ANCHISE** 22nd–24th October 1943 The Advance towards Ortona	1958	The Ontario Regiment (11th Armoured Regiment): The Loyal Edmonton Regiment (3rd Battalion, Princess Patricia's Canadian Light Infantry)
518.	**TRIGNO** 22nd October–5th November 1943 The Advance towards Ortona	1956 1957 1958	The Buffs (Royal East Kent Regiment) The Lancashire Fusiliers: The Royal Inniskilling Fusiliers: The East Surrey Regiment: The Essex Regiment: London Irish Rifles, The Royal Ulster Rifles (TA) The Royal Irish Fusiliers (Princess Victoria's)
519.	**THE TRIGNO** 22nd October–5th November 1943 The Advance towards Ortona	?	6th Duke of Connaught's Own Lancers (Watson's Horse): 3rd Battalion, 8th Punjab Regiment: 6th Royal Battalion (Scinde), The Frontier Force Rifles
520.	**TORELLA** 24th–27th October 1943 The Advance towards Ortona	1957 1958	The Hastings and Prince Edward Regiment: 48th Highlanders of Canada The Royal Canadian Regiment
521.	**TUFILLO** 1st–5th November 1943 The Advance towards Ortona	?	6th Duke of Connaught's Own Lancers (Watson's Horse): 6th Royal Battalion (Scinde), The Frontier Force Rifles
522.	**SAN SALVO** 2nd–3rd November 1943 The Advance towards Ortona	1957	The Queen's Own Royal West Kent Regiment: The Royal Inniskilling Fusiliers
523.	**PERANO** 17th November 1943 The Advance towards Ortona	1958 ?	Queen Alexandra's (Wellington West Coast) Mounted Rifles: The Manawatu Mounted Rifles: The Wellington East Coast Mounted Rifles 3rd Battalion, 8th Punjab Regiment
524.	**SANGRO** 19th November–3rd December 1943 The Advance towards Ortona	1956 1957 1958	Princess Louise's Kensington Regiment (TA): The Buffs (Royal East Kent Regiment) 3rd/4th County of London Yeomanry (Sharpshooters), Royal Armoured Corps (TA): The Royal Fusiliers (City of London Regiment): The Lancashire Fusiliers: The Cheshire Regiment: The Argyll and Sutherland Highlanders (Princess Louise's): The Queen's Own Royal West Kent Regiment: The Royal Inniskilling Fusiliers: The Northamptonshire Regiment: The East Surrey Regiment: The Essex Regiment: The King's Royal Rifle Corps: London Irish Rifles, The Royal Ulster Rifles (TA) The Royal Irish Fusiliers (Princess Victoria's): The Royal Scots Fusiliers

525.	**THE SANGRO**	
	19th November–3rd December 1943	
	The Advance towards Ortona	
		1957	West Nova Scotia Regiment (Machine Gun): 1st Battalion, The Royal New Brunswick Regiment (Carleton and York): 2nd Battalion, The Royal New Brunswick Regiment (North Shore): The Royal 22e Regiment
		1958	The Auckland (East Coast) Mounted Rifles: The Waikato Mounted Rifles: The North Auckland Mounted Rifles: The Waikato Regiment: Queen Alexandra's (Wellington West Coast) Mounted Rifles: The Manawatu Mounted Rifles: The Wellington East Coast Mounted Rifles: The New Zealand Scottish Regiment: The Canterbury Regiment: The Auckland Regiment (Countess of Ranfurly's Own): The Otago Regiment: The Southland Regiment: The Wellington Regiment (City of Wellington's Own): The Hauraki Regiment: The Wellington West Coast Regiment: The Taranaki Regiment: The Hawke's Bay Regiment: The Nelson, Marlborough, and West Coast Regiment: The Northland Regiment: The Ruahine Regiment: 27 (MG) Battalion: 28 (Maori) Battalion
		1962	1st Battalion, The Maratha Light Infantry: 5th Battalion, The Maratha Light Infantry: 1st Battalion, 5th Gorkha Rifles
		?	6th Duke of Connaught's Own Lancers (Watson's Horse): 3rd Battalion, 15th Punjab Regiment: 3rd Battalion, 8th Punjab Regiment: 6th Royal Battalion (Scinde), The Frontier Force Rifles: 1st Battalion, The Frontier Force Regiment

¹ LE SANGRO taken into use by French-speaking Canadian units 1958.

526.	**CASTEL DI SANGRO**	
	23rd–24th November 1943	
	The Advance towards Ortona	
		1957	West Nova Scotia Regiment (Machine Gun)

527.	**MOZZAGROGNA**	
	27th–29th November 1943	
	The Advance towards Ortona	
		1957	The Royal Fusiliers (City of London Regiment)
		?	1st Battalion, The Frontier Force Regiment

528.	**FOSSACESIA**	
	30th November 1943	
	The Advance towards Ortona	
		1957	3rd/4th County of London Yeomanry (Sharpshooters), Royal Armoured Corps (TA): London Irish Rifles, The Royal Ulster Rifles (TA)
		1958	The Royal Irish Fusiliers (Princess Victoria's)

529.	**CASTEL FRENTANO**	
	1st–2nd December 1943	
	The Advance towards Ortona	
		1958	The Auckland (East Coast) Mounted Rifles: The Waikato Mounted Rifles: The North Auckland Mounted Rifles: The Waikato Regiment: Queen Alexandra's (Wellington West Coast) Mounted Rifles: The Manawatu Mounted Rifles: The Wellington East Coast Mounted Rifles: The New Zealand Scottish Regiment: The Canterbury Regiment: The Auckland Regiment (Countess of Ranfurly's Own): The Otago Regiment: The Southland Regiment: The Wellington Regiment (City of Wellington's Own): The Hauraki Regiment: The Wellington West Coast Regiment: The Taranaki Regiment: The Hawke's Bay Regiment: The Nelson, Marlborough, and West Coast Regiment: The Northland Regiment: The Ruahine Regiment: 27 (MG) Battalion: 28 (Maori) Battalion
		?	3rd Battalion (Queen Mary's Own), The Baluch Regiment

530.	**ROMAGNOLI**	
	30th November– 1st December 1943	
	The Advance towards Ortona	
		1957	The Queen's Own Royal West Kent Regiment
		?	1st Battalion, The Frontier Force Regiment

531.	**ORSOGNA**	
	3rd–24th December 1943	
	The Advance towards Ortona	
		1956	The Parachute Regiment
		1958	The Auckland (East Coast) Mounted Rifles: The Waikato Mounted Rifles: The North Auckland Mounted Rifles: The Waikato Regiment: Queen Alexandra's (Wellington West Coast) Mounted Rifles: The Manawatu Mounted Rifles: The Canterbury Yeomanry Cavalry: The Otago Mounted Rifles: The Nelson-Marlborough Mounted Rifles: The Wellington East Coast Mounted Rifles: The New Zealand Scottish Regiment: The Canterbury Regiment: The Auckland Regiment (Countess of Ranfurly's Own):

No.	Battle Honour	Date / Campaign	Year	Regiments
532.	THE MORO	5th–7th December 1943 The Advance towards Ortona	?	The Otago Regiment:The Southland Regiment:The Wellington Regiment (City of Wellington's Own):The Hauraki Regiment:The Wellington-West Coast Regiment:The Taranaki Regiment:The Hawke's Bay Regiment:The Nelson, Marlborough, and West Coast Regiment:The Northland Regiment:The Ruahine Regiment: 27 (MG) Battalion: 28 (Maori) Battalion: 3rd Battalion (Queen Mary's Own),The Baluch Regiment
			1957 ?	The Hastings and Prince Edward Regiment: Princess Patricia's Canadian Light Infantry:The Seaforth Highlanders of Canada 6th Duke of Connaught's Own Lancers (Watson's Horse): 3rd Battalion, 15th Punjab Regiment: 1st Battalion, The Frontier Force Regiment ¹ LA MORO taken into use by French-speaking Canadian units 1958.
533.	IMPOSSIBLE BRIDGE	5th–13th December 1943 The Advance towards Ortona	1957 ?	The Queen's Own Royal West Kent Regiment 6th Royal Battalion (Scinde), The Frontier Force Rifles: 1st Battalion, The Frontier Force Regiment
534.	SAN LEONARDO ¹	8th–9th December 1943 The Advance towards Ortona	1957 1958 1959	The Hastings and Prince Edward Regiment: 48th Highlanders of Canada:The Seaforth Highlanders of Canada The Royal Canadian Regiment The King's Own Calgary Regiment (RCAC) ¹ SAN-LEONARDO taken into use by French-speaking Canadian units 1958.
535.	THE GULLY ¹	10th–19th December 1943 The Advance towards Ortona	1957 1958 1959	The Hastings and Prince Edward Regiment: 48th Highlanders of Canada: Princess Patricia's Canadian Light Infantry:West Nova Scotia Regiment (Machine Gun):The Seaforth Highlanders of Canada: 1st Battalion, The Royal New Brunswick Regiment (Carleton and York): 2nd Battalion, The Royal New Brunswick Regiment (North Shore) The Ontario Regiment (11th Armoured Regiment):The Loyal Edmonton Regiment (3rd Battalion, Princess Patricia's Canadian Light Infantry):The Royal Canadian Regiment Le Regiment de Trois Rivieres:The North Saskatchewan Regiment:The King's Own Calgary Regiment (RCAC) ¹ LE RAVIN taken into use by French-speaking Canadian units 1958.
536.	CASA BERARDI ¹	14th–15th December 1943 The Advance towards Ortona	1957 1958	The Royal 22e Regiment The Ontario Regiment (11th Armoured Regiment) ¹ CASA-BERARDI taken into use by French-speaking Canadian units 1958.
537.	CALDARI	13th–14th December 1943 The Advance towards Ortona	1957 1962	The Royal Fusiliers (City of London Regiment) 1st Battalion, 5th Gorkha Rifles
538.	ORTONA	20th–29th December 1943 The Advance towards Ortona	1957 1958 1959	The Hastings and Prince Edward Regiment: 48th Highlanders of Canada:The Seaforth Highlanders of Canada The Ontario Regiment (11th Armoured Regiment):The Loyal Edmonton Regiment (3rd Battalion, Princess Patricia's Canadian Light Infantry):The Royal Canadian Regiment Le Regiment de Trois Rivieres:The North Saskatchewan Regiment
539.	VILLA GRANDE	22nd–28th December 1943 The Advance towards Ortona	1957 ?	The Queen's Own Royal West Kent Regiment:The Essex Regiment 6th Royal Battalion (Scinde), The Frontier Force Rifles

540.	**SAN NICOLA-SAN TOMMASO** [1] 31st December 1943 The Advance towards Ortona	1957	48th Highlanders of Canada [1] *SAN-NICOLA-SAN-TOMMASO taken into use by French-speaking Canadian units 1958.*
541.	**POINT 59** 29th December 1943–4th January 1944 The Advance towards Ortona	1957 1958	1st Battalion, The Royal New Brunswick Regiment (Carleton and York): 2nd Battalion, The Royal New Brunswick Regiment (North Shore) The Ontario Regiment (11th Armoured Regiment)
542.	**TORRE MUCCHIA** [1] 29th December 1943–4th January 1944 The Advance towards Ortona	1957	The Royal 22e Regiment [1] *TORRE-MUCCHIA taken into use by French-speaking Canadian units 1958.*
543.	**SALERNO** 9th–18th September 1943 The Salerno Landing and Bridgehead	1956 1957 1958	The Royal Scots Greys (2nd Dragoons); The Royal Leicestershire Regiment; The York and Lancaster Regiment The Royal Fusiliers (City of London Regiment); Grenadier Guards: The Cheshire Regiment: The Oxfordshire and Buckinghamshire Light Infantry: The Queen's Royal Regiment (West Surrey): The Sherwood Foresters (Nottinghamshire and Derbyshire Regiment); The King's Own Yorkshire Light Infantry; Scots Guards: The Royal Hampshire Regiment: Coldstream Guards: The Royal Lincolnshire Regiment: The Durham Light Infantry: The Commando Association Royal Tank Regiment: The Royal Northumberland Fusiliers
544.	**ST LUCIA** [1] 9th–16th September 1943 The Salerno Landing and Bridgehead	1957	The Royal Fusiliers (City of London Regiment)
545.	**SANTA LUCIA** [1] 9th–16th September 1943 The Salerno Landing and Bridgehead	1957	The Cheshire Regiment: The Oxfordshire and Buckinghamshire Light Infantry [1] *Awarded as ST LUCIA: SANTA LUCIA taken into use 1974.*
546.	**VIETRI PASS** 9th–16th September 1943 The Salerno Landing and Bridgehead	1956 1957	The York and Lancaster Regiment The Royal Lincolnshire Regiment
547.	**SALERNO HILLS** 9th–17th September 1943 The Salerno Landing and Bridgehead	1957	The Oxfordshire and Buckinghamshire Light Infantry: The King's Own Yorkshire Light Infantry: The Royal Hampshire Regiment
548.	**BATTIPAGLIA** 10th–18th September 1943 The Salerno Landing and Bridgehead	1956 1957	The Royal Scots Greys (2nd Dragoons) The Royal Fusiliers (City of London Regiment): The Cheshire Regiment: Scots Guards: The Royal Hampshire Regiment: Coldstream Guards
549.	**CAPTURE OF NAPLES** 22nd September–1st October 1943 Operations leading to the Capture of Naples	1956 1957	The York and Lancaster Regiment 1st King's Dragoon Guards: 11th Hussars (Prince Albert's Own): The Royal Lincolnshire Regiment
550.	**CAVA DI TIRRENI** 22nd–28th September 1943 Operations leading to the Capture of Naples	1956 1957	The York and Lancaster Regiment The King's Own Yorkshire Light Infantry: The Royal Hampshire Regiment: The Royal Lincolnshire Regiment

551.	**CAPPEZANO** 24th–25th September 1943 Operations leading to the Capture of Naples	1957	Coldstream Guards
552.	**MONTE STELLA** 24th–26th September 1943 Operations leading to the Capture of Naples	1957	The Queen's Royal Regiment (West Surrey)
553.	**SCAFATI BRIDGE** 28th September 1943 Operations leading to the Capture of Naples	1957	1st King's Dragoon Guards: The Queen's Royal Regiment (West Surrey)
554.	**CARDITO** 3rd October 1943 Operations leading to the Capture of Naples	1957	The Rifle Brigade (Prince Consort's Own)
555.	**VOLTURNO CROSSING** 12th–25th October 1943 The Advance to the Winter Line	1956 1957 1958	The Royal Scots Greys (2nd Dragoons): The York and Lancaster Regiment 3rd/4th County of London Yeomanry (Sharpshooters), Royal Armoured Corps (TA): Grenadier Guards: The Cheshire Regiment: The Queen's Royal Regiment (West Surrey): The Sherwood Foresters (Nottinghamshire and Derbyshire Regiment): The King's Own Yorkshire Light Infantry: Scots Guards: The Royal Hampshire Regiment: 11th Hussars (Prince Albert's Own): Coldstream Guards: The Royal Lincolnshire Regiment: The Durham Light Infantry Royal Tank Regiment: The Royal Northumberland Fusiliers
556.	**MONTE MARO** 22nd–23rd October 1943 The Advance to the Winter Line	1957	The Cheshire Regiment
557.	**ROCCHETTA E CROCE** 22nd–23rd October 1943 The Advance to the Winter Line	1957	Scots Guards
558.	**TEANO** 28th–31st October 1943 The Advance to the Winter Line	1956 1957	The London Scottish, The Gordon Highlanders (TA) The Royal Fusiliers (City of London Regiment): The Cheshire Regiment: The Oxfordshire and Buckinghamshire Light Infantry: The Durham Light Infantry: London Irish Rifles, The Royal Ulster Rifles (TA)
559.	**MONTE CAMINO** 5th November–9th December 1943 The Advance to the Winter Line	1956 1957 1957 1958	The London Scottish, The Gordon Highlanders (TA): The York and Lancaster Regiment The Royal Fusiliers (City of London Regiment): Grenadier Guards: The Cheshire Regiment: The Oxfordshire and Buckinghamshire Light Infantry: 1st King's Dragoon Guards: The Queen's Royal Regiment (West Surrey): The Sherwood Foresters (Nottinghamshire and Derbyshire Regiment): Scots Guards: Coldstream Guards: The Royal Berkshire Regiment (Princess Charlotte of Wales's): The Durham Light Infantry: London Irish Rifles, The Royal Ulster Rifles (TA) 1st Special Service Battalion The Royal Northumberland Fusiliers
560.	**CALABRITTO** 5th November–6th December 1943 The Advance to the Winter Line	1956 1957	The London Scottish, The Gordon Highlanders (TA): The Royal Leicestershire Regiment: The York and Lancaster Regiment Coldstream Guards: The Royal Berkshire Regiment (Princess Charlotte of Wales's): London Irish Rifles, The Royal Ulster Rifles (TA)

561.	**MONTE LA DIFENSA-MONTE REMETANEA** 2nd–8th December 1943 The Advance to the Winter Line	1957	1st Special Service Battalion
562.	**MONTE MAJO** 3rd–8th January 1944 The Advance to the Winter Line	1957	1st Special Service Battalion
563.	**COLLE CEDRO** 4th–9th January 1944 The Advance to the Winter Line	1956	The York and Lancaster Regiment
564.	**GARIGLIANO CROSSING** 17th–31st January 1944 The Advance to the Winter Line	1956 1957 1958	The London Scottish, The Gordon Highlanders (TA); The Wiltshire Regiment (Duke of Edinburgh's); The York and Lancaster Regiment; The Cameronians (Scottish Rifles) The Royal Fusiliers (City of London Regiment); The Cheshire Regiment; The Oxfordshire and Buckinghamshire Light Infantry; Seaforth Highlanders (Ross-shire Buffs, The Duke of Albany's); 1st King's Dragoon Guards; The Queen's Royal Regiment (West Surrey); The King's Own Yorkshire Light Infantry; The Royal Inniskilling Fusiliers; The Northamptonshire Regiment; The Royal Hampshire Regiment; Coldstream Guards; The Royal Lincolnshire Regiment; The Royal Berkshire Regiment (Princess Charlotte of Wales's); London Irish Rifles, The Royal Ulster Rifles (TA) Royal Tank Regiment; The Royal Northumberland Fusiliers; The Royal Scots Fusiliers
565.	**MINTURNO** 17th–25th January 1944 The Advance to the Winter Line	1956 1957 1958	The Wiltshire Regiment (Duke of Edinburgh's); The York and Lancaster Regiment The Cheshire Regiment; The Green Howards (Alexandra, Princess of Wales's Own Yorkshire Regiment); The King's Own Yorkshire Light Infantry; The Royal Inniskilling Fusiliers The Royal Scots Fusiliers
566.	**DAMIANO** 18th–30th January 1944 The Advance to the Winter Line	1956 1957	The London Scottish, The Gordon Highlanders (TA) The Royal Fusiliers (City of London Regiment); The Cheshire Regiment; The Oxfordshire and Buckinghamshire Light Infantry; The Royal Hampshire Regiment; The Royal Berkshire Regiment (Princess Charlotte of Wales's); London Irish Rifles, The Royal Ulster Rifles (TA)
567.	**MONTE TUGA** 26th–30th January 1944 The Advance to the Winter Line	1956 1957	The York and Lancaster Regiment The King's Own Yorkshire Light Infantry; The Royal Lincolnshire Regiment; The Durham Light Infantry
568.	**MONTE ORNITO** 2nd–20th February 1944 The Advance to the Winter Line	1957	The Royal Hampshire Regiment; Coldstream Guards; Welsh Guards; The Commando Association
569.	**CERASOLA** 7th–9th February 1944 The Advance to the Winter Line	1957	The Royal Hampshire Regiment

570. ANZIO
22nd January–22nd May 1944
The Anzio Landing and Bridgehead

1956 — Irish Guards: The Duke of Wellington's Regiment (West Riding): The London Scottish, The Gordon Highlanders (TA): The Wiltshire Regiment (Duke of Edinburgh's): The York and Lancaster Regiment: The Buffs (Royal East Kent Regiment): The Cameronians (Scottish Rifles)

1957 — The Royal Fusiliers (City of London Regiment): Grenadier Guards: The Cheshire Regiment: The Oxfordshire and Buckinghamshire Light Infantry: Seaforth Highlanders (Ross-shire Buffs, The Duke of Albany's): The Gordon Highlanders: The Queen's Own Yorkshire Dragoons, Royal Armoured Corps (TA): The Queen's Royal Regiment (West Surrey): The Green Howards (Alexandra, Princess of Wales's Own Yorkshire Regiment): The Sherwood Foresters (Nottinghamshire and Derbyshire Regiment): The King's Own Yorkshire Light Infantry: The Royal Inniskilling Fusiliers: The Loyal Regiment (North Lancashire): The Northamptonshire Regiment: The King's Shropshire Light Infantry: Scots Guards: The Royal Berkshire Regiment (Princess Charlotte of Wales's): The Middlesex Regiment (Duke of Cambridge's Own): The Commando Association: The North Staffordshire Regiment (The Prince of Wales's): London Irish Rifles, The Royal Ulster Rifles (TA)

1957 — 1st Special Service Battalion
1958 — Royal Tank Regiment: The Royal Scots Fusiliers

571. APRILIA
24th–26th January 1944
The Anzio Landing and Bridgehead

1956 — Irish Guards

572. CAMPOLEONE
24th–31st January 1944
The Anzio Landing and Bridgehead

1956 — The Duke of Wellington's Regiment (West Riding)
1957 — The Sherwood Foresters (Nottinghamshire and Derbyshire Regiment): The King's Shropshire Light Infantry: Scots Guards

573. CARROCETO
7th–10th February 1944
The Anzio Landing and Bridgehead

1956 — Irish Guards: The London Scottish, The Gordon Highlanders (TA)
1957 — The King's Shropshire Light Infantry: Scots Guards: The Royal Berkshire Regiment (Princess Charlotte of Wales's): The Middlesex Regiment (Duke of Cambridge's Own): The North Staffordshire Regiment (The Prince of Wales's): London Irish Rifles, The Royal Ulster Rifles (TA)

574. CASSINO I
20th January–25th March 1944
The First Attacks on Cassino

1956 — The Buffs (Royal East Kent Regiment): The Royal Sussex Regiment
1957 — The Queen's Own Cameron Highlanders: 7th Gurkha Rifles: The Essex Regiment: 2nd King Edward VII's Own Gurkha Rifles (The Sirmoor Rifles)

1957 — The Hastings and Prince Edward Regiment: 48th Highlanders of Canada: West Nova Scotia Regiment (Machine Gun): 1st Battalion, The Royal New Brunswick Regiment (Carleton and York): 2nd Battalion, The Royal New Brunswick Regiment (North Shore): The Royal 22e Regiment

1958 — The Ontario Regiment (11th Armoured Regiment): The Royal Canadian Regiment
1958 — The Waikato Regiment: Queen Alexandra's (Wellington West Coast) Mounted Rifles: The Manawatu Mounted Rifles: The Canterbury Yeomanry Cavalry: The Otago Mounted Rifles: The Nelson-Marlborough Mounted Rifles: The Wellington East Coast Mounted Rifles: The New Zealand Scottish Regiment: The Canterbury Regiment: The Auckland Regiment (Countess of Ranfurly's Own): The Otago Regiment: The Southland Regiment: The Wellington Regiment (City of Wellington's Own): The Hauraki Regiment: The Wellington West Coast Regiment: The Taranaki Regiment: The Hawke's Bay Regiment: The Nelson, Marlborough, and West Coast Regiment: The Northland Regiment: The Ruahine Regiment: 27 (MG) Battalion: 28 (Maori) Battalion

1959 — Le Regiment de Trois Rivieres: The North Saskatchewan Regiment: The King's Own Calgary Regiment (RCAC)
1962 — 12 Field Company, Madras Engineer Group: MG Battalion, The Rajputana Rifles: 1st Battalion, 9th Gorkha Rifles
? — 4th Battalion (Bhopal), 16th Punjab Regiment

575.	**CASSINO** ¹ 20th January–25th March 1944 and 11th–18th May 1944 The First Attacks on Cassino The Liri Valley Operations	1957	The Queen's Own Royal West Kent Regiment; The East Surrey Regiment ¹ *Awarded for CASSINO I and CASSINO II.*
576.	**MONASTERY HILL** 15th–18th February 1944 The First Attacks on Cassino	1956 1957 1958 1962	The Royal Sussex Regiment 2nd King Edward VII's Own Gurkha Rifles (The Sirmoor Rifles) 28 (Maori) Battalion 4th Battalion, The Rajputana Rifles
577.	**CASTLE HILL** 15th–24th March 1944 The First Attacks on Cassino	1957 1962	The Queen's Own Royal West Kent Regiment; The Essex Regiment 3rd Battalion, The Brigade of the Guards: 4th Battalion, The Rajputana Rifles
578.	**HANGMAN'S HILL** 15th–25th March 1944 The First Attacks on Cassino	1957 1962	The Essex Regiment 1st Battalion, 9th Gorkha Rifles
579.	**CASSINO RAILWAY STATION** 17th March 1944 The First Attacks on Cassino	1958	The Canterbury Regiment; The Otago Regiment; The Southland Regiment; The Nelson, Marlborough, and West Coast Regiment
580.	**CASSINO II** 11th–18th May 1944 The Liri Valley Operations	1956 1957 1957 1958 1958 1958 1959 1962 ?	17th/21st Lancers; The Derbyshire Yeomanry, Royal Armoured Corps (TA); The Duke of Cornwall's Light Infantry; Princess Louise's Kensington Regiment (TA) Honourable Artillery Company (TA); The Royal Fusiliers (City of London Regiment); The King's Regiment (Liverpool); The Lancashire Fusiliers; The Argyll and Sutherland Highlanders (Princess Louise's); The Somerset Light Infantry (Prince Albert's); The Bedfordshire and Hertfordshire Regiment; The Royal Inniskilling Fusiliers; The Northamptonshire Regiment; The Royal Hampshire Regiment; The Rifle Brigade (Prince Consort's Own); 1st/2nd Lothians and Border Horse, Royal Armoured Corps (TA); The Black Watch (Royal Highland Regiment); Tower Hamlets Rifles (TA); 16th/5th The Queen's Royal Lancers: London Irish Rifles, The Royal Ulster Rifles (TA) The Hastings and Prince Edward Regiment; 48th Highlanders of Canada; West Nova Scotia Regiment (Machine Gun); 1st Battalion, The Royal New Brunswick Regiment (Carleton and York); 2nd Battalion, The Royal New Brunswick Regiment (North Shore); The Royal 22e Regiment The Royal Irish Fusiliers (Princess Victoria's); The Royal Northumberland Fusiliers The Ontario Regiment (11th Armoured Regiment); The Royal Canadian Regiment Queen Alexandra's (Wellington West Coast) Mounted Rifles: The Manawatu Mounted Rifles; The Wellington East Coast Mounted Rifles Le Regiment de Trois Rivieres; The North Saskatchewan Regiment; The King's Own Calgary Regiment (RCAC) 66 Field Company, Bengal Engineer Group: 1st Battalion, 5th Gorkha Rifles 6th Duke of Connaught's Own Lancers (Watson's Horse); 3rd Battalion, 15th Punjab Regiment: 6th Royal Battalion (Scinde), The Frontier Force Rifles: 1st Battalion, The Frontier Force Regiment

581.	**CASINO II** 11th–18th May 1944 The Liri Valley Operations	1957	The Royal Natal Carbineers: Royal Durban Light Infantry; First City: The Queen's Own Cape Town Highlanders: Kimberley Regiment; Witwatersrand Rifles: Regiment De La Rey; Imperial Light Horse
582.	**GUSTAV LINE** [1] 11th–18th May 1944 The Liri Valley Operations	1957	The Hastings and Prince Edward Regiment: 48th Highlanders of Canada: West Nova Scotia Regiment; The Royal New Brunswick Regiment (Carleton and York): 2nd Battalion, The Royal New Brunswick Regiment (North Shore): The Royal 22e Regiment
		1958	The Ontario Regiment (11th Armoured Regiment): The Royal Canadian Regiment
		1958	Queen Alexandra's (Wellington West Coast) Mounted Rifles: The Manawatu Mounted Rifles: The Wellington East Coast Mounted Rifles
		1959	Le Regiment de Trois Rivieres: The North Saskatchewan Regiment: The King's Own Calgary Regiment (RCAC)
		?	3rd Battalion, 8th Punjab Regiment 6th Royal Battalion (Scinde), The Frontier Force Rifles

[1] *LIGNE GUSTAV taken into use by French-speaking Canadian units 1958.*

583.	**SANT'ANGELO IN TEODICE** 13th May 1944 The Liri Valley Operations	1958	The Ontario Regiment (11th Armoured Regiment)
		1962	1st Battalion, 5th Gorkha Rifles
584.	**MASSA VERTECHI** 14th May 1944 The Liri Valley Operations	1957	The Royal Hampshire Regiment
585.	**PIGNATARO** 13th–15th May 1944 The Liri Valley Operations	1959	The King's Own Calgary Regiment (RCAC)
		?	6th Duke of Connaught's Own Lancers (Watson's Horse): 6th Royal Battalion (Scinde), The Frontier Force Rifles: 1st Battalion, The Frontier Force Regiment
586.	**MASSA TAMBOURINI** 15th May 1944 The Liri Valley Operations	1957	The Royal Inniskilling Fusiliers
587.	**CASA SINAGOGGA** 16th May 1944 The Liri Valley Operations	1957	London Irish Rifles, The Royal Ulster Rifles (TA)
588.	**LIRI VALLEY** [1] 18th–30th May 1944 The Liri Valley Operations	1956	The Royal Wiltshire Yeomanry (Prince of Wales's Own), Royal Armoured Corps (TA): The Derbyshire Yeomanry, Royal Armoured Corps (TA): Princess Louise's Kensington Regiment (TA): The Buffs (Royal East Kent Regiment)
		1957	The Argyll and Sutherland Highlanders (Princess Louise's): The Queen's Own Royal West Kent Regiment: The Royal Inniskilling Fusiliers: North Irish Horse, Royal Armoured Corps (TA): The Rifle Brigade (Prince Consort's Own): 1st/2nd Lothians and Border Horse, Royal Armoured Corps (TA): Welsh Guards: The Black Watch (Royal Highland Regiment): Tower Hamlets Rifles (TA): 16th/5th The Queen's Own Royal Lancers: London Irish Rifles, The Royal Ulster Rifles (TA)
		1957	The Hastings and Prince Edward Regiment: 48th Highlanders of Canada: The Princess Louise Fusiliers (MG): Princess Patricia's Canadian Light Infantry: West Nova Scotia Regiment (Machine Gun): The Royal Canadian Dragoons (1st Armoured Regiment): 1/8th Canadian Hussars (Princess Louise's): 2/8th Canadian Hussars (Princess Louise's): The Westminster Regiment: The Governor General's Horse Guards (3rd Armoured Regiment): The Seaforth Highlanders of Canada: 1st Battalion, The Royal

	1958	New Brunswick Regiment (Carleton and York): 2nd Battalion, The Royal New Brunswick Regiment (North Shore): The Royal 22e Regiment
		The Royal Irish Fusiliers (Princess Victoria's)
	1958	The British Columbia Dragoons (9th Reconnaissance Regiment): The Ontario Regiment (11th Armoured Regiment): 4th Princess Louise Dragoon Guards (4th Armoured Car Regiment): The Loyal Edmonton Regiment (3rd Battalion, Princess Patricia's Canadian Light Infantry): The Royal Canadian Regiment: Lord Strathcona's Horse (Royal Canadians): 1st Battalion, The Nova Scotia Highlanders (North): 2nd Battalion, The Nova Scotia Highlanders (Cape Breton)
	1959	Le Regiment de Trois Rivieres: The North Saskatchewan Regiment: The Perth Regiment: The King's Own Calgary Regiment (RCAC): The Irish Regiment of Canada
	?	6th Duke of Connaught's Own Lancers (Watson's Horse)
		[1] VALLEE DE LA LIRI taken into use by French-speaking Canadian units 1958.
589. **HITLER LINE** [1] 18th–24th May 1944 The Liri Valley Operations	1957	North Irish Horse, Royal Armoured Corps (TA)
	1957	The Hastings and Prince Edward Regiment: 48th Highlanders of Canada: Princess Patricia's Canadian Light Infantry: West Nova Scotia Regiment (Machine Gun): The Seaforth Highlanders of Canada: 1st Battalion, The Royal New Brunswick Regiment (Carleton and York): 2nd Battalion, The Royal New Brunswick Regiment (North Shore): The Royal 22e Regiment
	1958	4th Princess Louise Dragoon Guards (4th Armoured Car Regiment): The Loyal Edmonton Regiment (3rd Battalion, Princess Patricia's Canadian Light Infantry): The Royal Canadian Regiment
	1959	Le Regiment de Trios Rivieres: The North Saskatchewan Regiment
		[1] LIGNE HITLER taken into use by French-speaking Canadian units 1958.
590. **AQUINO** 18th–24th May 1944 The Liri Valley Operations	1956	The Derbyshire Yeomanry, Royal Armoured Corps (TA): The Buffs (Royal East Kent Regiment)
	1957	The Argyll and Sutherland Highlanders (Princess Louise's)
	1958	The Ontario Regiment (11th Armoured Regiment)
	1959	The King's Own Calgary Regiment (RCAC)
591. **PIEDIMONTE HILL** 20th–21st May 1944 The Liri Valley Operations	1957	The Queen's Own Royal West Kent Regiment
592. **MELFA CROSSING** [1] 24th–25th May 1944 The Liri Valley Operations	1957	The Rifle Brigade (Prince Consort's Own): Tower Hamlets Rifles (TA)
	1957	The Princess Louise Fusiliers (MG): West Nova Scotia Regiment (Machine Gun): 1/8th Canadian Hussars (Princess Louise's): 2/8th Canadian Hussars (Princess Louise's): The Westminster Regiment: The Governor General's Horse Guards (3rd Armoured Regiment): 1st Battalion, The Royal New Brunswick Regiment (Carleton and York): 2nd Battalion, The Royal New Brunswick Regiment (North Shore)
	1958	The British Columbia Dragoons (9th Reconnaissance Regiment): 4th Princess Louise Dragoon Guards (4th Armoured Car Regiment): Lord Strathcona's Horse (Royal Canadians): 1st Battalion, The Nova Scotia Highlanders (North): 2nd Battalion, The Nova Scotia Highlanders (Cape Breton)
	1959	The Perth Regiment: The Irish Regiment of Canada
		[1] TRAVERSEE DE LA MELFA taken into use by French-speaking Canadian units 1958.
593. **MONTE PICCOLO** 26th–28th May 1944 The Liri Valley Operations	1956	17th/21st Lancers
	1957	Coldstream Guards: 1st/2nd Lothians and Border Horse, Royal Armoured Corps (TA): Welsh Guards: 16th/5th The Queen's Royal Lancers

594.	**CEPRANO** 26th–27th May 1944 The Liri Valley Operations	1957 1958 1959	1/8th Canadian Hussars (Princess Louise's); 2/8th Canadian Hussars (Princess Louise's) 1st Battalion, The Nova Scotia Highlanders (North): 2nd Battalion, The Nova Scotia Highlanders (Cape Breton) The Perth Regiment
595.	**ROCCA D'ARCE** 27th–29th May 1944 The Liri Valley Operations	1962	1st Battalion, 5th Gorkha Rifles
596.	**TORRICE CROSSROADS** [1] 30th May 1944 The Liri Valley Operations	1958	Lord Strathcona's Horse (Royal Canadians) [1] *CARREFOUR TORRICE taken into use by French-speaking Canadian units 1958.*
597.	**ROME** 22nd May–4th June 1944 The Capture of Rome	1956 1957 1957	The Duke of Wellington's Regiment (West Riding): The Wiltshire Regiment (Duke of Edinburgh's): The Buffs (Royal East Kent Regiment) The Cheshire Regiment: The Gordon Highlanders: The Queen's Own Yorkshire Dragoons, Royal Armoured Corps (TA): The Royal Inniskilling Fusiliers: The Loyal Regiment (North Lancashire): The North Staffordshire Regiment (The Prince of Wales's) 1st Special Service Battalion
598.	**ADVANCE TO TIBER** 22nd May–4th June 1944 The Capture of Rome	1956 1957 1958	The Royal Wiltshire Yeomanry (Prince of Wales's Own), Royal Armoured Corps (TA): The Wiltshire Regiment (Duke of Edinburgh's): The York and Lancaster Regiment: The Cameronians (Scottish Rifles) The Sherwood Foresters (Nottinghamshire and Derbyshire Regiment): The Royal Inniskilling Fusiliers: The North Staffordshire Regiment (The Prince of Wales's) The Royal Scots Fusiliers
599.	**ADVANCE TO THE TIBER** [1] 22nd May–4th June 1944 The Capture of Rome	1957	1st Special Service Battalion [1] *PROGRESSION VERS LE TIBRE taken into use by French-speaking Canadian units 1958.*
600.	**THE TIBER** [1] 22nd May–8th June 1944 The Capture of Rome	1957	Natal Mounted Rifles [1] *DIE TIBER taken into use by Afrikaans-speaking South African units 1957.*
601.	**MONTE ROTONDO** 6th–7th June 1944 The Advance to the Arno	1957	The Rifle Brigade (Prince Consort's Own): 1st/2nd Lothians and Border Horse, Royal Armoured Corps (TA): Tower Hamlets Rifles (TA)
602.	**CELLENO** 9th June 1944 The Advance to the Arno	1957	1 Special Service Battalion: Kimberley Regiment: Natal Mounted Rifles: Imperial Light Horse: Prince Alfred's Guard
603.	**BAGNO REGIO** 11th–13th June 1944 The Advance to the Arno	1957	Pretoria Regiment (Princess Alice's Own)
604.	**ALLERONA** 15th June 1944 The Advance to the Arno	1957	Witwatersrand Rifles: Regiment De La Rey

605.	**FICULLE** 15th June 1944 The Advance to the Arno	1957	The Warwickshire Yeomanry, Royal Armoured Corps (TA)
606.	**MONTE GABBIONE** 16th–17th June 1944 The Advance to the Arno	1957	The Northamptonshire Regiment
607.	**CITTA DELLA PIEVE** 16th–19th June 1944 The Advance to the Arno	1956 1957	The Royal Wiltshire Yeomanry (Prince of Wales's Own), Royal Armoured Corps (TA) 3rd The King's Own Hussars
608.	**CAPTURE OF PERUGIA** 18th–20th June 1944 The Advance to the Arno	1956 1957	17th/21st Lancers 1st King's Dragoon Guards: Coldstream Guards: The Rifle Brigade (Prince Consort's Own): 1st/2nd Lothians and Border Horse, Royal Armoured Corps (TA): Welsh Guards: Tower Hamlets Rifles (TA): 16th/5th The Queen's Royal Lancers
609.	**RIPA RIDGE** 18th–19th June 1944 The Advance to the Arno	1957 1962	The Royal Fusiliers (City of London Regiment) 1st Battalion, 5th Gorkha Rifles
610.	**MONTE MALBE** 19th–20th June 1944 The Advance to the Arno	1957	The Rifle Brigade (Prince Consort's Own): London Rifle Brigade, The Rifle Brigade (Prince Consort's Own) (TA)
611.	**TRASIMENE LINE** ¹ 20th–30th June 1944 The Advance to the Arno	1956 1957 1958 1958 1959	The Royal Wiltshire Yeomanry (Prince of Wales's Own), Royal Armoured Corps (TA): The Duke of Cornwall's Light Infantry: The Buffs (Royal East Kent Regiment) The King's Regiment (Liverpool): The Warwickshire Yeomanry, Royal Armoured Corps (TA): The Lancashire Fusiliers: The Somerset Light Infantry (Prince Albert's): The Bedfordshire and Hertfordshire Regiment: The Queen's Own Royal West Kent Regiment: The Royal Inniskilling Fusiliers: The Northamptonshire Regiment: Scots Guards: The Royal Hampshire Regiment: London Irish Rifles, The Royal Ulster Rifles (TA) The Royal Irish Fusiliers (Princess Victoria's) The Ontario Regiment (11th Armoured Regiment) Le Regiment de Trois Rivieres: The King's Own Calgary Regiment (RCAC) ¹ *LIGNE TRASIMENE taken into use by French-speaking Canadian units 1958.*
612.	**SANFATUCCHIO** 20th–21st June 1944 The Advance to the Arno	1957 1958	The Warwickshire Yeomanry, Royal Armoured Corps (TA): London Irish Rifles, The Royal Ulster Rifles (TA) The Ontario Regiment (11th Armoured Regiment)
613.	**CHIUSI** 21st–22nd June 1944 The Advance to the Arno	1957	First City: The Queen's Own Cape Town Highlanders
614.	**SARTEANO** 23rd June 1944 The Advance to the Arno	1957	Pretoria Regiment (Princess Alice's Own)

| 615. | **LA FOCE**
26th June 1944
The Advance to the Arno | 1957 | Pretoria Regiment (Princess Alice's Own) |
| 616. | **GABBIANO**
1st July 1944
The Advance to the Arno | 1957 | The Royal Fusiliers (City of London Regiment) |

617. AREZZO
4th–17th July 1944
The Advance to the Arno

1956	The Life Guards: Royal Horse Guards: The Derbyshire Yeomanry, Royal Armoured Corps (TA)
1957	1st King's Dragoon Guards: The Somerset Light Infantry (Prince Albert's): The Queen's Own Royal West Kent Regiment: Coldstream Guards: The Rifle Brigade (Prince Consort's Own): 1st/2nd Lothians and Border Horse, Royal Armoured Corps (TA): Welsh Guards: London Rifle Brigade, The Rifle Brigade (Prince Consort's Own) (TA): Tower Hamlets Rifles (TA): 16th/5th The Queen's Royal Lancers: The King's Royal Rifle Corps
1958	The Ontario Regiment (11th Armoured Regiment)
1958	The Waikato Regiment: The Canterbury Regiment: The Auckland Regiment (Countess of Ranfurly's Own): The Otago Regiment: The Southland Regiment: The Wellington Regiment (City of Wellington's Own): The Hauraki Regiment: The Wellington West Coast Regiment: The Taranaki Regiment: The Hawke's Bay Regiment: The Nelson, Marlborough, and West Coast Regiment: The Northland Regiment: The Ruahine Regiment
1959	Le Regiment de Trois Rivieres: The King's Own Calgary Regiment (RCAC)
?	3rd Battalion, 1st Punjab Regiment: 3rd Battalion (Queen Mary's Own), The Baluch Regiment

| 618. | **TUORI**
5th July 1944
The Advance to the Arno | 1957 | The King's Regiment (Liverpool) |

619. MONTE LIGNANO
14th July 1944
The Advance to the Arno

1958	The Wellington Regiment (City of Wellington's Own): The Wellington West Coast Regiment: The Taranaki Regiment: The Hawke's Bay Regiment: The Ruahine Regiment

620. ADVANCE TO FLORENCE
17th July–10th August 1944
The Advance to the Arno

1956	The Life Guards: Royal Horse Guards: 17th/21st Lancers: The Royal Wiltshire Yeomanry (Prince of Wales's Own), Royal Armoured Corps (TA): The Derbyshire Yeomanry, Royal Armoured Corps (TA): The Duke of Cornwall's Light Infantry
1957	The Royal Fusiliers (City of London Regiment): The Warwickshire Yeomanry, Royal Armoured Corps (TA): The Somerset Light Infantry (Prince Albert's): The Queen's Own Royal West Kent Regiment: North Irish Horse, Royal Armoured Corps (TA): Scots Guards: The Royal Hampshire Regiment: Coldstream Guards: The Rifle Brigade (Prince Consort's Own): 1st/2nd Lothians and Border Horse, Royal Armoured Corps (TA): Welsh Guards: The Black Watch (Royal Highland Regiment): Tower Hamlets Rifles (TA): 16th/5th The Queen's Royal Lancers
	Royal Tank Regiment
1958	The Ontario Regiment (11th Armoured Regiment)
1958	The Auckland (East Coast) Mounted Rifles: The Waikato Mounted Rifles: The North Auckland Mounted Rifles: The Waikato Regiment: Queen Alexandra's (Wellington West Coast) Mounted Rifles: The Manawatu Mounted Rifles: The Canterbury Yeomanry Cavalry: The Otago Mounted Rifles: The Nelson-Marlborough Mounted Rifles: The Wellington East Coast Mounted Rifles: The New Zealand Scottish Regiment: The Canterbury Regiment: The Auckland Regiment (Countess of Ranfurly's Own):
1958	The Otago Regiment: The Southland Regiment: The Wellington Regiment (City of Wellington's Own): The Hauraki Regiment:

		1959 1962 ?	The Wellington West Coast Regiment: The Taranaki Regiment: The Hawke's Bay Regiment: The Nelson, Marlborough, and West Coast Regiment: The Northland Regiment: The Ruahine Regiment: 27 (MG) Battalion: 28 (Maori) Battalion Le Regiment de Trois Rivieres: The King's Own Calgary Regiment (RCAC) 1st Battalion, The Maratha Light Infantry: 5th Battalion, The Maratha Light Infantry 3rd Battalion, 1st Punjab Regiment: 6th Royal Battalion (Scinde), The Frontier Force Rifles: 1st Battalion, The Frontier Force Regiment: 3rd Royal Battalion, The Frontier Force Regiment ¹ *PROGRESSION VERS FLORENCE taken into use by French-speaking Canadian units 1958.*
621.	**FLORENCE** 17th July–10th August 1944 The Advance to the Arno	1957	1 Special Service Battalion: The Royal Natal Carbineers: Royal Durban Light Infantry: First City: The Queen's Own Cape Town Highlanders: Kimberley Regiment: Witwatersrand Rifles: Regiment De La Rey: Natal Mounted Rifles: Imperial Light Horse: Prince Alfred's Guard: Pretoria Regiment (Princess Alice's Own)
622.	**MONTE SAN MICHELE** 18th–20th July 1944 The Advance to the Arno	1957	Scots Guards
623.	**MONTE QUERCIABELLA** 20th July 1944 The Advance to the Arno	1957	Witwatersrand Rifles: Regiment De La Rey
624.	**MONTE FILI** 21st–23rd July 1944 The Advance to the Arno	1957	Witwatersrand Rifles: Regiment De La Rey
625.	**MONTE DOMINI** 21st–24th July 1944 The Advance to the Arno	1957	Coldstream Guards
626.	**THE GREVE** ¹ 24th July–2nd August 1944 The Advance to the Arno	1957 ?	1 Special Service Battalion: Kimberley Regiment: Imperial Light Horse The Royal Natal Carbineers: Natal Mounted Rifles: Prince Alfred's Guard: First City: The Queen's Own Cape Town Highlanders: Witwatersrand Rifles: Regiment De La Rey ¹ *DIE GREVE taken into use by Afrikaans-speaking South African units 1957.*
627.	**CERBAIA** 27th–29th July 1944 The Advance to the Arno	1958	The Waikato Regiment: Queen Alexandra's (Wellington West Coast) Mounted Rifles: The Manawatu Mounted Rifles: The Wellington East Coast Mounted Rifles: The New Zealand Scottish Regiment: The Canterbury Regiment: The Auckland Regiment (Countess of Ranfurly's Own): The Otago Regiment: The Southland Regiment: The Wellington Regiment (City of Wellington's Own): The Hauraki Regiment: The Wellington West Coast Regiment: The Taranaki Regiment: The Hawke's Bay Regiment: The Nelson, Marlborough, and West Coast Regiment: The Northland Regiment: The Ruahine Regiment: 27 (MG) Battalion
628.	**MONTE SCALARI** 27th–30th July 1944 The Advance to the Arno	1957	The Royal Fusiliers (City of London Regiment): The Queen's Own Royal West Kent Regiment: The Black Watch (Royal Highland Regiment)

629.	**SAN MICHELE** 28th–30th July 1944 The Advance to the Arno	1958	The Auckland (East Coast) Mounted Rifles: The Waikato Mounted Rifles: The North Auckland Mounted Rifles: The Waikato Regiment: Queen Alexandra's (Wellington West Coast) Mounted Rifles: The Manawatu Mounted Rifles: The Canterbury Yeomanry Cavalry: The Otago Mounted Rifles: The Nelson-Marlborough Mounted Rifles: The Wellington East Coast Mounted Rifles: The New Zealand Scottish Regiment: The Canterbury Regiment: The Auckland Regiment (Countess of Ranfurly's Own): The Otago Regiment: The Southland Regiment: The Wellington Regiment (City of Wellington's Own): The Hauraki Regiment: The Wellington West Coast Regiment: The Taranaki Regiment: The Hawke's Bay Regiment: The Nelson, Marlborough, and West Coast Regiment: The Northland Regiment: The Ruahine Regiment: 27 (MG) Battalion: 28 (Maori) Battalion
630.	**PAULA LINE** 30th July–4th August 1944 The Advance to the Arno	1958	The Auckland (East Coast) Mounted Rifles: The Waikato Mounted Rifles: The North Auckland Mounted Rifles: The Waikato Regiment: Queen Alexandra's (Wellington West Coast) Mounted Rifles: The Manawatu Mounted Rifles: The Canterbury Yeomanry Cavalry: The Otago Mounted Rifles: The Nelson-Marlborough Mounted Rifles: The Wellington East Coast Mounted Rifles: The New Zealand Scottish Regiment: The Canterbury Regiment: The Auckland Regiment (Countess of Ranfurly's Own): The Otago Regiment: The Southland Regiment: The Wellington Regiment (City of Wellington's Own): The Hauraki Regiment: The Wellington West Coast Regiment: The Taranaki Regiment: The Hawke's Bay Regiment: The Nelson, Marlborough, and West Coast Regiment: The Northland Regiment: The Ruahine Regiment: 27 (MG) Battalion: 28 (Maori) Battalion
631.	**IL CASTELLO** 3rd–8th August 1944 The Advance to the Arno	1962	2nd Battalion, The Parachute Regiment: 2nd Battalion, 3rd Gorkha Rifles
632.	**INCONTRO** 5th–8th August 1944 The Advance to the Arno	1956	The Duke of Cornwall's Light Infantry
633.	**MONTONE** 5th–7th July 1944 The Advance to the Arno	1957	The King's Own Royal Regiment (Lancaster)
634.	**TRESTINA** 10th July 1944 The Advance to the Arno	1962	2nd Battalion, 4th Gorkha Rifles
635.	**MONTE DELLA GORGACE** 8th–14th July 1944 The Advance to the Arno	1962	2nd Battalion, The Parachute Regiment: 2nd Battalion, 3rd Gorkha Rifles
636.	**MONTE CEDRONE** 13th–18th July 1944 The Advance to the Arno	1956 1962 ?	The Royal Wiltshire Yeomanry (Prince of Wales's Own), Royal Armoured Corps (TA) 2nd Battalion, 4th Gorkha Rifles 4th Battalion (Duke of Connaught's Own), The Baluch Regiment
637.	**CITTA DI CASTELLO** 16th–22nd July 1944 The Advance to the Arno	1956 1957 1962 ?	The Royal Wiltshire Yeomanry (Prince of Wales's Own), Royal Armoured Corps (TA) The King's Own Royal Regiment (Lancaster): 3rd The King's Own Hussars 3rd Battalion, The Garhwal Rifles 4th Battalion (Duke of Connaught's Own), The Baluch Regiment

638.	**PIAN DI MAGGIO** 19th–20th July 1944 The Advance to the Arno	1957	2nd King Edward VII's Own Gurkha Rifles (The Sirmoor Rifles)
639.	**CAMPRIANO** 20th–28th July 1944 The Advance to the Arno	1957 ?	The Warwickshire Yeomanry, Royal Armoured Corps (TA): 7th Gurkha Rifles 3rd Royal Battalion, The Frontier Force Regiment
640.	**CITERNA** 25th–26th July 1944 The Advance to the Arno	1957	12th Royal Lancers (Prince of Wales's)
641.	**POGGIO DEL GRILLO** 4th–8th August 1944 The Advance to the Arno	1957	The Queen's Own Cameron Highlanders: 7th Gurkha Rifles
642.	**FIESOLE** 25th August 1944 The Advance to the Arno	1957	The Loyal Regiment (North Lancashire)
643.	**CERRONE** 25th–31st August 1944 The Advance to the Arno	1959	The King's Own Calgary Regiment (RCAC)
644.	**MONTORSOLI** 1st–5th September 1944 The Advance to the Arno	1957	The Hertfordshire Regiment (TA)
645.	**ANCONA** 2nd–18th July 1944 The Advance to the Arno	1956	7th Queen's Own Hussars
646.	**GOTHIC LINE** [1] [2] 25th August–22nd September 1944 The Gothic Line Operations	1956	The Life Guards: Royal Horse Guards: The London Scottish, The Gordon Highlanders (TA): The Royal Leicestershire Regiment: The York and Lancaster Regiment: The Royal Sussex Regiment
		1957	The Royal Fusiliers (City of London Regiment); Grenadier Guards: The Cheshire Regiment: 1st King's Dragoon Guards: 12th Royal Lancers (Prince of Wales's): The Queen's Royal Regiment (West Surrey): The Sherwood Foresters (Nottinghamshire and Derbyshire Regiment): The Hertfordshire Regiment (TA): The Loyal Regiment (North Lancashire): The King's Shropshire Light Infantry: The Queen's Own Cameron Highlanders: North Irish Horse, Royal Armoured Corps (TA): The Royal Hampshire Regiment: The Royal Lincolnshire Regiment: The Rifle Brigade (Prince Consort's Own): Welsh Guards: The Middlesex Regiment (Duke of Cambridge's Own): The Durham Light Infantry: The Manchester Regiment: London Rifle Brigade, The Rifle Brigade (Prince Consort's Own) (TA): The North Staffordshire Regiment (The Prince of Wales's): 2nd King Edward VII's Own Gurkha Rifles (The Sirmoor Rifles)
		1957	The Hastings and Prince Edward Regiment: 48th Highlanders of Canada: The Princess Louise Fusiliers (MG); Princess Patricia's Canadian Light Infantry: West Nova Scotia Regiment (Machine Gun): The Royal Canadian Dragoons (1st Armoured Regiment); 1/8th Canadian Hussars (Princess Louise's): 2/8th Canadian Hussars (Princess Louise's): The Westminster Regiment: The

Governor General's Horse Guards (3rd Armoured Regiment): The Seaforth Highlanders of Canada: 1st Battalion, The Royal New Brunswick Regiment (Carleton and York): 2nd Battalion, The Royal New Brunswick Regiment (North Shore): The Royal 22e Regiment

1957 1 Special Service Battalion: The Royal Natal Carbineers: Royal Durban Light Infantry: First City: The Queen's Own Cape Town Highlanders: Kimberley Regiment: Witwatersrand Rifles: Regiment De La Rey: Natal Mounted Rifles: Imperial Light Horse: Prince Alfred's Guard: Pretoria Regiment (Princess Alice's Own)

1958 27th Lancers: Royal Tank Regiment: The Royal Scots (The Royal Regiment)

1958 The British Columbia Dragoons (9th Reconnaissance Regiment): 4th Princess Louise Dragoon Guards (4th Armoured Car Regiment): The Loyal Edmonton Regiment (3rd Battalion, Princess Patricia's Canadian Light Infantry): The Royal Canadian Regiment: Lord Strathcona's Horse (Royal Canadians): 1st Battalion, The Nova Scotia Highlanders (North): 2nd Battalion, The Nova Scotis Highlanders (Cape Breton)

1959 The North Saskatchewan Regiment: The Perth Regiment: The Irish Regiment of Canada

1962 The Central India Horse: 1st Battalion, The Maratha Light Infantry: 5th Battalion, The Maratha Light Infantry: MG Battalion, The Rajputana Rifles: 4th Battalion, The Sikh Regiment: 2nd Battalion, 8th Gorkha Rifles

? 3rd Battalion, 1st Punjab Regiment: 3rd Battalion, 15th Punjab Regiment: 3rd Battalion (Queen Mary's Own), The Baluch Regiment: 4th Battalion (Duke of Connaught's Own), The Baluch Regiment: 6th Royal Battalion (Scinde), The Frontier Force Rifles: 1st Battalion, The Frontier Force Regiment: 4th Battalion (Wilde's), The Frontier Force Rifles

[1] LIGNE GOTHIQUE taken into use by French-speaking Canadian units 1958.
[2] GOTTIESE LINIE taken into use by Afrikaans-speaking South African units 1957.

---

647. **MONTECICCARDO**
27th–28th August 1944
The Gothic Line Operations

1958 The Loyal Edmonton Regiment (3rd Battalion, Princess Patricia's Canadian Light Infantry)

648. **MONTE CALVO**
29th–31st August 1944
The Gothic Line Operations

1962 4th Battalion, The Sikh Regiment
? 3rd Battalion (Queen Mary's Own), The Baluch Regiment

649. **MONTECCHIO**
30th–31st August 1944
The Gothic Line Operations

1957 1/8th Canadian Hussars (Princess Louise's): 2/8th Canadian Hussars (Princess Louise's)
1958 1st Battalion, The Nova Scotia Highlanders (North): 2nd Battalion, The Nova Scotia Highlanders (Cape Breton)
1959 The Perth Regiment: The Irish Regiment of Canada

650. **POINT 204**
31st August 1944
The Gothic Line Operations

1959 The Perth Regiment

651. **POZZO ALTO RIDGE** [1]
31st August 1944
The Gothic Line Operations

1957 The Seaforth Highlanders of Canada
1958 The British Columbia Dragoons (9th Reconnaissance Regiment): Lord Strathcona's Horse (Royal Canadians)

[1] CRETE DE POZZO ALTO taken into use by French-speaking Canadian units 1958.

652. **MONTE LURO**
1st September 1944
The Gothic Line Operations

1958 The Loyal Edmonton Regiment (3rd Battalion, Princess Patricia's Canadian Light Infantry)

653.	**BORGO SANTA MARIA** [1] 1st September 1944 The Gothic Line Operations	1957	The Royal 22e Regiment [1] *BORGO SANTA-MARIA taken into use by French-speaking Canadian units 1958.*
654.	**TOMBA DI PESARO** 1st–2nd September 1944 The Gothic Line Operations	1957 1958	1/8th Canadian Hussars (Princess Louise's): 2/8th Canadian Hussars (Princess Louise's) 4th Princess Louise Dragoon Guards (4th Armoured Car Regiment)
655.	**MONTE GRIDOLFO** 30th August–2nd September 1944 The Gothic Line Operations	1956 1957	The Royal Leicestershire Regiment The Royal Hampshire Regiment: The Royal Lincolnshire Regiment: The Manchester Regiment
656.	**TAVOLETO** 1st–4th September 1944 The Gothic Line Operations	1957 1962	The Queen's Own Cameron Highlanders: 7th Gurkha Rifles 1st Battalion, 9th Gorkha Rifles
657.	**MONTEGAUDIO** 28th August 1944 The Gothic Line Operations	1957	The Royal Hampshire Regiment
658.	**PRATELLE PASS** 6th September 1944 The Gothic Line Operations	1962	1st Battalion, The Parachute Regiment
659.	**ALPE DEVITIGLIANO** 12th–15th September 1944 The Gothic Line Operations	1963	1st Battalion, The Maratha Light Infantry
660.	**FEMMINA MORTA** 17th–18th September 1944 The Gothic Line Operations	1962	1st Battalion, 5th Gorkha Rifles
661.	**MONTE PORRO DEL BAGNO** 15th–18th September 1944 The Gothic Line Operations	1957	Kimberley Regiment: Imperial Light Horse
662.	**CORIANO** 3rd–15th September 1944 Operations in 5th (British) Corps and 1st (Canadian) Corps Sectors	1956 1957 1957	The London Scottish, The Gordon Highlanders (TA): 9th Queen's Royal Lancers: The York and Lancaster Regiment: The Buffs (Royal East Kent Regiment): 10th Princess Mary's Own Gurkha Rifles The Queen's Bays (2nd Dragoon Guards): Honourable Artillery Company (TA): The Royal Fusiliers (City of London Regiment): The Cheshire Regiment: The Oxfordshire and Buckinghamshire Light Infantry: The Queen's Own Yorkshire Dragoons, Royal Armoured Corps (TA): The Sherwood Foresters (Nottinghamshire and Derbyshire Regiment): 10th Royal Hussars (Prince of Wales's Own): The Queen's Own Cameron Highlanders: 6th Gurkha Rifles: The Royal Hampshire Regiment: 4th Queen's Own Hussars: The Welch Regiment: The Manchester Regiment: The King's Royal Rifle Corps: London Irish Rifles, The Royal Ulster Rifles (TA): 2nd King Edward VII's Own Gurkha Rifles (The Sirmoor Rifles) The Princess Louise Fusiliers (MG): 1/8th Canadian Hussars (Princess Louise's): 2/8th Canadian Hussars (Princess Louise's): The Westminster Regiment

663. SAN CLEMENTE
3rd–4th September 1944
Operations in 5th (British) Corps and 1st (Canadian) Corps Sectors

Regiment	Year
Royal Tank Regiment	1958
Lord Strathcona's Horse (Royal Canadians): 1st Battalion, The Nova Scotia Highlanders (North); 2nd Battalion, The Nova Scotia Highlanders (Cape Breton)	1958
The Perth Regiment; The Irish Regiment of Canada	1959
The Lanark and Renfrew Scottish Regiment	1960
2nd Battalion, The Sikh Regiment: 2nd Battalion, 8th Gorkha Rifles	1962
3rd Royal Battalion, The Frontier Force Regiment	?
The York and Lancaster Regiment	1956
4th Queen's Own Hussars: The Manchester Regiment	1957

664. POGGIO SAN GIOVANNI
3rd–5th September 1944
Operations in 5th (British) Corps and 1st (Canadian) Corps Sectors

Regiment	Year
2nd King Edward VII's Own Gurkha Rifles (The Sirmoor Rifles)	1957
2nd Battalion, The Sikh Regiment	1962

665. PIAN DI CASTELLO
5th–8th September 1944
Operations in 5th (British) Corps and 1st (Canadian) Corps Sectors

Regiment	Year
The Royal Sussex Regiment	1956
The Queen's Own Cameron Highlanders	1957
3rd Battalion (Queen Mary's Own), The Baluch Regiment	?

666. CROCE
5th–9th September 1944
Operations in 5th (British) Corps and 1st (Canadian) Corps Sectors

Regiment	Year
The London Scottish, The Gordon Highlanders (TA)	1956
The Royal Fusiliers (City of London Regiment); The Welch Regiment; London Irish Rifles, The Royal Ulster Rifles (TA)	1957
3rd Battalion (Queen Mary's Own), The Baluch Regiment	?

667. GEMMANO RIDGE
5th–15th September 1944
Operations in 5th (British) Corps and 1st (Canadian) Corps Sectors

Regiment	Year
The York and Lancaster Regiment	1956
The Cheshire Regiment: The Oxfordshire and Buckinghamshire Light Infantry: The Queen's Royal Regiment (West Surrey): The King's Own Yorkshire Light Infantry: The Royal Lincolnshire Regiment: The Durham Light Infantry: The Manchester Regiment	1957
3rd Battalion (Queen Mary's Own), The Baluch Regiment	?

668. MONTEBELLO-SCORTICATA RIDGE
22nd–24th September 1944
Operations in 5th (British) Corps and 1st (Canadian) Corps Sectors

Regiment	Year
7th Gurkha Rifles	1957
3rd Royal Battalion, The Frontier Force Regiment	?

669. SANTARCANGELO
22nd–24th September 1944
Operations in 5th (British) Corps and 1st (Canadian) Corps Sectors

Regiment	Year
10th Princess Mary's Own Gurkha Rifles	1956
10th Royal Hussars (Prince of Wales's Own): 6th Gurkha Rifles	1957
2nd Battalion, 8th Gorkha Rifles	1962

670.	**MONTE REGGIANO** 24th September–1st October 1944 Operations in 5th (British) Corps and 1st (Canadian) Corps Sectors	1956 1957	The Royal Sussex Regiment The Queen's Own Cameron Highlanders: 2nd King Edward VII's Own Gurkha Rifles (The Sirmoor Rifles)
671.	**SAVIGNANO** 27th–30th September 1944 Operations in 5th (British) Corps and 1st (Canadian) Corps Sectors	1957	The Cheshire Regiment
672.	**SAN MARTINO SOGLIANO** 4th–5th October 1944 Operations in 5th (British) Corps and 1st (Canadian) Corps Sectors	1957 1962	The King's Own Royal Regiment (Lancaster) 1st Battalion, The Parachute Regiment
673.	**MONTE FARNETO** 6th–7th October 1944 Operations in 5th (British) Corps and 1st (Canadian) Corps Sectors	1957 1962 ?	North Irish Horse, Royal Armoured Corps (TA) 2nd Battalion, The Parachute Regiment 2nd Battalion, 3rd Gorkha Rifles 4th Battalion (Duke of Connaught's Own), The Baluch Regiment
674.	**MONTILGALLO** 7th–8th October 1944 Operations in 5th (British) Corps and 1st (Canadian) Corps Sectors	1957	The Royal Hampshire Regiment: The Manchester Regiment
675.	**SAN PAOLO-MONTE SPACCATO** 8th–9th October 1944 Operations in 5th (British) Corps and 1st (Canadian) Corps Sectors	?	4th Battalion (Duke of Connaught's Own), The Baluch Regiment
676.	**CARPINETA** 12th–15th October 1944 Operations in 5th (British) Corps and 1st (Canadian) Corps Sectors	1956 1957	The York and Lancaster Regiment The Queen's Bays (2nd Dragoon Guards): The King's Own Yorkshire Light Infantry
677.	**MONTE CHICCO** 13th–14th October 1944 Operations in 5th (British) Corps and 1st (Canadian) Corps Sectors	1957	6th Gurkha Rifles
678.	**MONTE CAVALLO** 21st–23rd October 1944 Operations in 5th (British) Corps and 1st (Canadian) Corps Sectors	1957 1962	North Irish Horse, Royal Armoured Corps (TA) 2nd Battalion, The Parachute Regiment: 2nd Battalion, 3rd Gorkha Rifles

	Battle Honour	Year	Units
679.	**CAPTURE OF FORLI** 7th–9th November 1944 Operations in 5th (British) Corps and 1st (Canadian) Corps Sectors	1956 1957	9th Queen's Royal Lancers The King's Regiment (Liverpool); 12th Royal Lancers (Prince of Wales's); The Somerset Light Infantry (Prince Albert's); The East Surrey Regiment; The Royal Hampshire Regiment; The Manchester Regiment
680.	**CASA FORTIS** 9th–11th November 1944 Operations in 5th (British) Corps and 1st (Canadian) Corps Sectors	1957	The Royal Fusiliers (City of London Regiment); The Queen's Own Royal West Kent Regiment; North Irish Horse, Royal Armoured Corps (TA); The Black Watch (Royal Highland Regiment)
681.	**MONTE SAN BARTOLO** 11th–14th November 1944 Operations in 5th (British) Corps and 1st (Canadian) Corps Sectors	1962	1st Battalion, 5th Gorkha Rifles
682.	**COSINA CANAL CROSSING** 20th–23rd November 1944 Operations in 5th (British) Corps and 1st (Canadian) Corps Sectors	1957	The Somerset Light Infantry (Prince Albert's); The Sherwood Foresters (Nottinghamshire and Derbyshire Regiment); 10th Royal Hussars (Prince of Wales's Own); The Royal Hampshire Regiment; The Durham Light Infantry
683.	**CASA BETTINI** 24th November–1st December 1944 Operations in 5th (British) Corps and 1st (Canadian) Corps Sectors	1957 1963 ?	North Irish Horse, Royal Armoured Corps (TA) 14th Battalion (Nabha), The Punjab Regiment 4th Battalion (Duke of Connaught's Own), The Baluch Regiment
684.	**LAMONE CROSSING** [1] 2nd–13th December 1944 Operations in 5th (British) Corps and 1st (Canadian) Corps Sectors	1956 1957 1957 1958 1958 1959	9th Queen's Royal Lancers; The York and Lancaster Regiment The Queen's Bays (2nd Dragoon Guards); 6th Gurkha Rifles; North Irish Horse, Royal Armoured Corps (TA); The Royal Hampshire Regiment; The Royal Lincolnshire Regiment; The Manchester Regiment; The King's Royal Rifle Corps The Hastings and Prince Edward Regiment; 48th Highlanders of Canada; The Princess Louise Fusiliers (MG); West Nova Scotia Regiment (Machine Gun); The Royal Canadian Dragoons (1st Armoured Regiment); 1/8th Canadian Hussars (Princess Louise's); 2/8th Canadian Hussars (Princess Louise's); The Westminster Regiment; The Governor General's Horse Guards (3rd Armoured Regiment); 1st Battalion, The Royal New Brunswick Regiment (Carleton and York); 2nd Battalion, The Royal New Brunswick Regiment (North Shore); The Royal 22e Regiment Royal Tank Regiment The British Columbia Dragoons (9th Reconnaissance Regiment); The Royal Canadian Regiment; Lord Strathcona's Horse (Royal Canadians); 1st Battalion, The Nova Scotia Highlanders (North); 2nd Battalion, The Nova Scotia Highlanders (Cape Breton) The North Saskatchewan Regiment; The Perth Regiment; The Irish Regiment of Canada [1] *TRAVERSEE DE LA LAMONE taken into use by French-speaking Canadian units 1958.*
685.	**PIDEURA** 4th–7th December 1944 Operations in 5th (British) Corps and 1st (Canadian) Corps Sectors	1956 1957	9th Queen's Royal Lancers The Royal Hampshire Regiment

686.	**LAMONE BRIDGEHEAD** 9th December 1944 Operations in 5th (British) Corps and 1st (Canadian) Corps Sectors	1957	The King's Own Royal Regiment (Lancaster)
687.	**DEFENCE OF LAMONE BRIDGEHEAD** ¹ 9th December 1944 Operations in 5th (British) Corps and 1st (Canadian) Corps Sectors	1956 1957	9th Queen's Royal Lancers; The York and Lancaster Regiment The Queen's Bays (2nd Dragoon Guards); The King's Own Yorkshire Light Infantry; The Manchester Regiment ¹ *Awarded as LAMONE BRIDGEHEAD: DEFENCE OF LAMONE BRIDGEHEAD taken into use 1974.*
688.	**CELLE** 14th–15th December 1944 Operations in 5th (British) Corps and 1st (Canadian) Corps Sectors	1958	The Auckland (East Coast) Mounted Rifles; The Waikato Mounted Rifles; The North Auckland Mounted Rifles; The Canterbury Regiment; The Otago Regiment; The Southland Regiment; The Wellington Regiment (City of Wellington's Own); The Wellington West Coast Regiment; The Taranaki Regiment; The Hawke's Bay Regiment; The Nelson, Marlborough, and West Coast Regiment; The Ruahine Regiment; 27 (MG) Battalion; 28 (Maori) Battalion
689.	**PERGOLA RIDGE** 14th–16th December 1944 Operations in 5th (British) Corps and 1st (Canadian) Corps Sectors	1957	The Durham Light Infantry
690.	**FAENZA POCKET** 19th–20th December 1944 Operations in 5th (British) Corps and 1st (Canadian) Corps Sectors	1958	The Waikato Regiment; The Canterbury Yeomanry Cavalry; The Otago Mounted Rifles; The Nelson-Marlborough Mounted Rifles; The Canterbury Regiment; The Auckland Regiment (Countess of Ranfurly's Own); The Otago Regiment; The Southland Regiment; The Wellington Regiment (City of Wellington's Own); The Hauraki Regiment; The Wellington West Coast Regiment; The Taranaki Regiment; The Hawke's Bay Regiment; The Nelson, Marlborough, and West Coast Regiment; The Northland Regiment; The Ruahine Regiment; 27 (MG) Battalion
691.	**SENIO POCKET** 4th–5th January 1945 Operations in 5th (British) Corps and 1st (Canadian) Corps Sectors	1956 1957	The London Scottish; The Gordon Highlanders (TA) The Queen's Royal Regiment (West Surrey); 10th Royal Hussars (Prince of Wales's Own); 4th Queen's Own Hussars
692.	**SENIO FLOODBANK** 23rd February–3rd March 1945 Operations in 5th (British) Corps and 1st (Canadian) Corps Sectors	1956 1957 1962	10th Princess Mary's Own Gurkha Rifles The Cheshire Regiment; The Queen's Royal Regiment (West Surrey); 6th Gurkha Rifles; London Irish Rifles, The Royal Ulster Rifles (TA) 1 Horse
693.	**MISANO RIDGE** ¹ 3rd–5th September 1944 Operations in 5th (British) Corps and 1st (Canadian) Corps Sectors	1957 1958 1960	The Hastings and Prince Edward Regiment; 48th Highlanders of Canada; The Princess Louise Fusiliers (MG); The Royal Canadian Dragoons (1st Armoured Regiment); 1/8th Canadian Hussars (Princess Louise's); 2/8th Canadian Hussars (Princess Louise's); The Westminster Regiment; The Governor General's Horse Guards (3rd Armoured Regiment) The Royal Canadian Regiment; Lord Strathcona's Horse (Royal Canadians) The Lanark and Renfrew Scottish Regiment ¹ *CRETE DE MISANO taken into use by French-speaking Canadian units 1958.*

694.	**RIMINI LINE** [1] 14th–21st September 1944 Operations in 5th (British) Corps and 1st (Canadian) Corps Sectors	1956 1957 1957 1958 1958 1959	The London Scottish, The Gordon Highlanders (TA); The York and Lancaster Regiment 7th Queen's Own Hussars: The Queen's Bays (2nd Dragoon Guards); The King's Regiment (Liverpool); The Cheshire Regiment: The Queen's Own Yorkshire Dragoons, Royal Armoured Corps (TA): The Queen's Own Royal West Kent Regiment: The Royal Hampshire Regiment: 4th Queen's Own Hussars: The Welch Regiment: The Black Watch (Royal Highland Regiment); The Manchester Regiment: London Irish Rifles, The Royal Ulster Rifles (TA) The Hastings and Prince Edward Regiment: 48th Highlanders of Canada: Princess Patricia's Canadian Light Infantry; West Nova Scotia Regiment (Machine Gun); The Seaforth Highlanders of Canada: 1st Battalion, The Royal New Brunswick Regiment (Carleton and York); 2nd Battalion, The Royal New Brunswick Regiment (North Shore); The Royal 22e Regiment Royal Tank Regiment The Loyal Edmonton Regiment (3rd Battalion, Princess Patricia's Canadian Light Infantry): The Royal Canadian Regiment The North Saskatchewan Regiment [1] *LIGNE RIMINI taken into use by French-speaking Canadian units 1958.*
695.	**MONTE COLOMBO** 14th September 1944 Operations in 5th (British) Corps and 1st (Canadian) Corps Sectors	1956	The Royal Leicestershire Regiment
696.	**CASA FABBRI RIDGE** 14th September 1944 Operations in 5th (British) Corps and 1st (Canadian) Corps Sectors	1957	The Queen's Royal Regiment (West Surrey); The Black Watch (Royal Highland Regiment)
697.	**MONTESCUDO** 14th–17th September 1944 Operations in 5th (British) Corps and 1st (Canadian) Corps Sectors	1957	The Royal Hampshire Regiment: The Manchester Regiment
698.	**SAN MARTINO-SAN LORENZO** [1] 14th–18th September 1944 Operations in 5th (British) Corps and 1st (Canadian) Corps Sectors	1957 1958	48th Highlanders of Canada: West Nova Scotia Regiment (Machine Gun): The Seaforth Highlanders of Canada: The Royal 22e Regiment The Royal Canadian Regiment [1] *SAN-MARTINO-SAN-LORENZO taken into use by French-speaking Canadian units 1958.*
699.	**FRISONI** 16th–18th September 1944 Operations in 5th (British) Corps and 1st (Canadian) Corps Sectors	1957	The Royal Hampshire Regiment
700.	**SAN MARINO** 17th–20th September 1944 Operations in 5th (British) Corps and 1st (Canadian) Corps Sectors	1956 1957 1962 ?	The York and Lancaster Regiment The Queen's Own Cameron Highlanders: The Royal Lincolnshire Regiment 4th Battalion, The Sikh Regiment: 1st Battalion, 9th Gorkha Rifles 3rd Battalion (Queen Mary's Own), The Baluch Regiment

701.	**CERIANO RIDGE** 17th–21st September 1944 Operations in 5th (British) Corps and 1st (Canadian) Corps Sectors	1956 1957	The London Scottish, The Gordon Highlanders (TA) The Queen's Bays (2nd Dragoon Guards); The Cheshire Regiment; The Queen's Own Yorkshire Dragoons, Royal Armoured Corps (TA); The Welch Regiment: London Irish Rifles, The Royal Ulster Rifles (TA)
702.	**SAN FORTUNATO** [1] 18th–20th September 1944 Operations in 5th (British) Corps and 1st (Canadian) Corps Sectors	1957 1958	The Hastings and Prince Edward Regiment: Princess Patricia's Canadian Light Infantry; West Nova Scotia Regiment (Machine Gun): The Seaforth Highlanders of Canada: 1st Battalion, The Royal New Brunswick Regiment (Carleton and York); 2nd Battalion, The Royal New Brunswick Regiment (North Shore); The Royal 22e Regiment The Loyal Edmonton Regiment (3rd Battalion, Princess Patricia's Canadian Light Infantry) [1] *SAN-FORTUNATO taken into use by French-speaking Canadian units 1958.*
703.	**CASALE** 23rd–25th September 1944 Operations in 5th (British) Corps and 1st (Canadian) Corps Sectors	1957 1958 1960	The Westminster Regiment 4th Princess Louise Dragoon Guards (4th Armoured Car Regiment); Lord Strathcona's Horse (Royal Canadians) The Lanark and Renfrew Scottish Regiment
704.	**RIO FONTANACCIA** 24th–25th September 1944 Operations in 5th (British) Corps and 1st (Canadian) Corps Sectors	1958	The Waikato Regiment: The Canterbury Yeomanry Cavalry; The Otago Mounted Rifles: The Nelson-Marlborough Mounted Rifles: The Canterbury Regiment: The Auckland Regiment (Countess of Ranfurly's Own): The Otago Regiment: The Southland Regiment: The Wellington Regiment (City of Wellington's Own): The Hauraki Regiment: The Wellington West Coast Regiment: The Taranaki Regiment: The Hawke's Bay Regiment: The Nelson, Marlborough, and West Coast Regiment: The Northland Regiment: The Ruahine Regiment
705.	**SANT'ANGELO IN SALUTE** 11th–15th October 1944 Operations in 5th (British) Corps and 1st (Canadian) Corps Sectors	1957 1958	The Royal Canadian Dragoons (1st Armoured Regiment) 4th Princess Louise Dragoon Guards (4th Armoured Car Regiment)
706.	**ST ANGELO IN SALUTE** 11th–15th October 1944 Operations in 5th (British) Corps and 1st (Canadian) Corps Sectors	1958	The Waikato Regiment: Queen Alexandra's (Wellington West Coast) Mounted Rifles: The Manawatu Mounted Rifles: The Canterbury Yeomanry Cavalry: The Otago Mounted Rifles: The Nelson-Marlborough Mounted Rifles: The Wellington East Coast Mounted Rifles: The New Zealand Scottish Regiment: The Canterbury Regiment: The Auckland Regiment (Countess of Ranfurly's Own): The Otago Regiment: The Southland Regiment: The Hauraki Regiment: The Nelson, Marlborough, and West Coast Regiment: The Northland Regiment: 27 (MG) Battalion: 28 (Maori) Battalion
707.	**BULGARIA VILLAGE** 13th–14th October 1944 Operations in 5th (British) Corps and 1st (Canadian) Corps Sectors	1957	The Hastings and Prince Edward Regiment
708.	**CESENA** 15th–20th October 1944 Operations in 5th (British) Corps and 1st (Canadian) Corps Sectors	1957 1957 1959 ?	The Queen's Bays (2nd Dragoon Guards): 10th Royal Hussars (Prince of Wales's Own): The Durham Light Infantry; The Manchester Regiment The Royal 22e Regiment The North Saskatchewan Regiment 4th Battalion (Duke of Connaught's Own), The Baluch Regiment

709. **PISCIATELLO**
16th–19th October 1944
Operations in 5th (British) Corps and 1st (Canadian) Corps Sectors

1958	The Loyal Edmonton Regiment (3rd Battalion, Princess Patricia's Canadian Light Infantry); The Royal Canadian Regiment
1958	The Auckland (East Coast) Mounted Rifles; The Waikato Mounted Rifles; The North Auckland Mounted Rifles; The Waikato Regiment: Queen Alexandra's (Wellington West Coast) Mounted Rifles: The Manawatu Mounted Rifles: The Canterbury Yeomanry Cavalry; The Otago Mounted Rifles; The Nelson-Marlborough Mounted Rifles; The Wellington East Coast Mounted Rifles; The New Zealand Scottish Regiment; The Canterbury Regiment; The Auckland Regiment (Countess of Ranfurly's Own); The Otago Regiment; The Southland Regiment; The Wellington Regiment (City of Wellington's Own); The Hauraki Regiment; The Wellington West Coast Regiment; The Taranaki Regiment; The Hawke's Bay Regiment; The Nelson, Marlborough, and West Coast Regiment; The Northland Regiment; The Ruahine Regiment; 27 (MG) Battalion

710. **SAVIO BRIDGEHEAD** 1
20th–23rd October 1944
Operations in 5th (British) Corps and 1st (Canadian) Corps Sectors

1957	The Royal Fusiliers (City of London Regiment); The Queen's Own Royal West Kent Regiment; The Black Watch (Royal Highland Regiment)
1957	Princess Patricia's Canadian Light Infantry; West Nova Scotia Regiment (Machine Gun); The Seaforth Highlanders of Canada
1958	27th Lancers
1958	The Loyal Edmonton Regiment (3rd Battalion, Princess Patricia's Canadian Light Infantry)
1959	The North Saskatchewan Regiment
?	4th Battalion (Duke of Connaught's Own), The Baluch Regiment

1 *TETES DE PONT DE LA SAVIO taken into use by French-speaking Canadian units 1958.*

711. **CAPTURE OF RAVENNA** 1
3rd–4th December 1944
Operations in 5th (British) Corps and 1st (Canadian) Corps Sectors

1958	27th Lancers
1958	4th Princess Louise Dragoon Guards (4th Armoured Car Regiment)

1 *PRISE DE RAVENNE taken into use by French-speaking Canadian units 1958.*

712. **NAVIGLIO CANAL** 1
12th–15th December 1944
Operations in 5th (British) Corps and 1st (Canadian) Corps Sectors

1957	The Hastings and Prince Edward Regiment: Princess Patricia's Canadian Light Infantry; The Westminster Regiment: The Seaforth Highlanders of Canada: 1st Battalion, The Royal New Brunswick Regiment (Carleton and York): 2nd Battalion, The Royal New Brunswick Regiment (North Shore)
1958	The British Columbia Dragoons (9th Reconnaissance Regiment): 4th Princess Louise Dragoon Guards (4th Armoured Car Regiment); The Loyal Edmonton Regiment (3rd Battalion, Princess Patricia's Canadian Light Infantry); Lord Strathcona's Horse (Royal Canadians)
1959	The North Saskatchewan Regiment
1960	The Lanark and Renfrew Scottish Regiment

1 *CANAL NAVIGLIO taken into use by French-speaking Canadian units 1958.*

713. **FOSSO VECCHIO**
16th–18th December 1944
Operations in 5th (British) Corps and 1st (Canadian) Corps Sectors

1957	The Hastings and Prince Edward Regiment: 48th Highlanders of Canada: The Royal Canadian Dragoons (1st Armoured Regiment)
1958	The Royal Canadian Regiment
1959	The North Saskatchewan Regiment

714. **FOSSO MUNIO**
19th–21st December 1944
Operations in 5th (British) Corps and 1st (Canadian) Corps Sectors

1957	Princess Patricia's Canadian Light Infantry; The Governor General's Horse Guards (3rd Armoured Regiment); The Seaforth Highlanders of Canada
1958	The British Columbia Dragoons (9th Reconnaissance Regiment); The Loyal Edmonton Regiment (3rd Battalion, Princess Patricia's Canadian Light Infantry); Lord Strathcona's Horse (Royal Canadians); 1st Battalion, The Nova Scotia Highlanders (North); 2nd Battalion, The Nova Scotia Highlanders (Cape Breton)
1959	The North Saskatchewan Regiment; The Perth Regiment; The Irish Regiment of Canada

715.	**CONVENTELLO-COMACCHIO** 2nd–6th January 1945 Operations in 5th (British) Corps and 1st (Canadian) Corps Sectors	1957 1957 1958 1959	12th Royal Lancers (Prince of Wales's): 4th Queen's Own Hussars 1/8th Canadian Hussars (Princess Louise's): 2/8th Canadian Hussars (Princess Louise's) The British Columbia Dragoons (9th Reconnaissance Regiment): 1st Battalion, The Nova Scotia Highlanders (North): 2nd Battalion, The Nova Scotia Highlanders (Cape Breton) The Perth Regiment: The Irish Regiment of Canada
716.	**GRANAROLO** 3rd–5th January 1945 Operations in 5th (British) Corps and 1st (Canadian) Corps Sectors	1957	Princess Patricia's Canadian Light Infantry: The Seaforth Highlanders of Canada
717.	**MARRADI** 21st–24th September 1944 Operations by 13th (British) Corps	1957 1958	The North Staffordshire Regiment (The Prince of Wales's) The Royal Scots (The Royal Regiment)
718.	**MONTE GAMBERALDI** 25th–29th September 1944 Operations by 13th (British) Corps	1957 1958	The Hertfordshire Regiment (TA): The Loyal Regiment (North Lancashire) The Royal Scots (The Royal Regiment)
719.	**BATTAGLIA** 2nd–12th October 1944 Operations by 13th (British) Corps	1957	Grenadier Guards: Welsh Guards
720.	**MONTE CASALINO** 2nd–23rd October 1944 Operations by 13th (British) Corps	1957	The Argyll and Sutherland Highlanders (Princess Louise's)
721.	**MONTE CECO** 3rd–17th October 1944 Operations by 13th (British) Corps	1956 1957	The Duke of Wellington's Regiment (West Riding) The Lancashire Fusiliers: The Sherwood Foresters (Nottinghamshire and Derbyshire Regiment): The Hertfordshire Regiment (TA): The Loyal Regiment (North Lancashire): The King's Shropshire Light Infantry
722.	**MONTE LA PIEVE** 13th–19th October 1944 Operations by 13th (British) Corps	1957 1959	The Northamptonshire Regiment Le Regiment de Trois Rivieres
723.	**MONTE PIANOERENO** 17th–23rd October 1944 Operations by 13th (British) Corps	1957	The Queen's Own Royal West Kent Regiment
724.	**MONTE SPADURO** 19th–24th October 1944 Operations by 13th (British) Corps	1956 1957 1958 1959	Princess Louise's Kensington Regiment (TA): The Buffs (Royal East Kent Regiment) The Lancashire Fusiliers: The Argyll and Sutherland Highlanders (Princess Louise's): The Queen's Own Royal West Kent Regiment: The Royal Inniskilling Fusiliers: London Irish Rifles, The Royal Ulster Rifles (TA) The Royal Irish Fusiliers (Princess Victoria's) Le Regiment de Trois Rivieres

		Year	
725.	**ORSARA** 25th–26th October 1944 Operations by 13th (British) Corps	1957	The Rifle Brigade (Prince Consort's Own): London Rifle Brigade, The Rifle Brigade (Prince Consort's Own) (TA)
726.	**MONTE GRANDE** 1st November–12th December 1944 Operations by 13th (British) Corps	1957	The Argyll and Sutherland Highlanders (Princess Louise's): The Hertfordshire Regiment (TA): The Loyal Regiment (North Lancashire): The King's Shropshire Light Infantry: The Middlesex Regiment (Duke of Cambridge's Own): London Irish Rifles, The Royal Ulster Rifles (TA)
		1958	The Royal Irish Fusiliers (Princess Victoria's)
		?	3rd Battalion, 8th Punjab Regiment: 6th Royal Battalion (Scinde), The Frontier Force Rifles: 4th Battalion (Wilde's), The Frontier Force Rifles
727.	**TOSSIGNANO** 12th–16th December 1944 Operations by 13th (British) Corps	1957	The Rifle Brigade (Prince Consort's Own): Tower Hamlets Rifles (TA)
728.	**CATARELTO RIDGE** [1] 28th September–3rd October 1944 Operations by 6th South African Division	1957 1957	Scots Guards: Coldstream Guards Pretoria Regiment (Princess Alice's Own)
			[1] CATERELTO-RIF taken into use by Afrikaans-speaking South African units 1957.
729.	**MONTE VIGESE** 30th September–6th October 1944 Operations by 6th South African Division	1957	The Royal Natal Carbineers: Kimberley Regiment: Imperial Light Horse
730.	**MONTE STANCO** 7th–13th October 1944 Operations by 6th South African Division	1957	The Royal Natal Carbineers: Royal Durban Light Infantry: First City: The Queen's Own Cape Town Highlanders: Witwatersrand Rifles: Regiment De La Rey
		?	4th Battalion (Wilde's), The Frontier Force Rifles
731.	**MONTE PEZZA** 17th October 1944 Operations by 6th South African Division	1957	The Royal Natal Carbineers: Royal Durban Light Infantry: First City: The Queen's Own Cape Town Highlanders
732.	**MONTE SALVARO** 19th–23rd October 1944 Operations by 6th South African Division	1957	Kimberley Regiment: Witwatersrand Rifles: Regiment De La Rey: Imperial Light Horse
733.	**VALLI DI COMACCHIO** 1st–8th April 1945 Final Operations	1956 1957	The London Scottish, The Gordon Highlanders (TA) The Royal Fusiliers (City of London Regiment): The Cheshire Regiment: 10th Royal Hussars (Prince of Wales's Own): North Irish Horse, Royal Armoured Corps (TA): The Commando Association: London Irish Rifles, The Royal Ulster Rifles (TA): Special Air Service Regiment

734.	**SENIO** 9th–12th April 1945 Final Operations	1956 1957	The Buffs (Royal East Kent Regiment) Honourable Artillery Company (TA):The Royal Fusiliers (City of London Regiment):The Lancashire Fusiliers:The Argyll and Sutherland Highlanders (Princess Louise's):The Queen's Own Royal West Kent Regiment: North Irish Horse, Royal Armoured Corps (TA): 4th Queen's Own Hussars
735.	**THE SENIO** 9th–12th April 1945 Final Operations	1958	The Auckland (East Coast) Mounted Rifles:The Waikato Mounted Rifles:The North Auckland Mounted Rifles:The Waikato Regiment: The Canterbury Yeomanry Cavalry: The Otago Mounted Rifles: The Nelson-Marlborough Mounted Rifles: The Canterbury Regiment:The Auckland Regiment (Countess of Ranfurly's Own): The Otago Regiment:The Southland Regiment: The Wellington Regiment (City of Wellington's Own): The Hauraki Regiment: The Wellington West Coast Regiment: The Taranaki Regiment:The Hawke's Bay Regiment:The Nelson, Marlborough, and West Coast Regiment:The Northland Regiment: The Ruahine Regiment: 28 (Maori) Battalion
		1962 ?	1st Battalion, The Maratha Light Infantry: 1st Battalion, 5th Gorkha Rifles 6th Duke of Connaught's Own Lancers (Watson's Horse): 3rd Battalion, 1st Punjab Regiment: 3rd Battalion, 15th Punjab Regiment: 3rd Battalion, 8th Punjab Regiment: 6th Royal Battalion (Scinde), The Frontier Force Rifles: 1st Battalion, The Frontier Force Regiment
736.	**SANTERNO CROSSING** 11th–12th April 1945 Final Operations	1957 1958	The Argyll and Sutherland Highlanders (Princess Louise's): 4th Queen's Own Hussars The Auckland (East Coast) Mounted Rifles:The Waikato Mounted Rifles:The North Auckland Mounted Rifles:The Waikato Regiment: The Canterbury Yeomanry Cavalry: The Otago Mounted Rifles: The Nelson-Marlborough Mounted Rifles: The Canterbury Regiment:The Auckland Regiment (Countess of Ranfurly's Own): The Otago Regiment:The Southland Regiment: The Wellington Regiment (City of Wellington's Own): The Hauraki Regiment: The Wellington West Coast Regiment: The Taranaki Regiment:The Hawke's Bay Regiment:The Nelson, Marlborough, and West Coast Regiment:The Northland Regiment: The Ruahine Regiment: 28 (Maori) Battalion
		?	6th Duke of Connaught's Own Lancers (Watson's Horse): 1st Battalion, The Frontier Force Regiment
737.	**MENATE** 10th–11th April 1945 Final Operations	1957 1958	The Queen's Royal Regiment (West Surrey) 27th Lancers
738.	**FILO** 12th–14th April 1945 Final Operations	1957 1958	The Queen's Royal Regiment (West Surrey) 27th Lancers
739.	**ARGENTA GAP** 13th–31st April 1945 Final Operations	1956 1957	The London Scottish, The Gordon Highlanders (TA): 9th Queen's Royal Lancers: 17th/21st Lancers: The Derbyshire Yeomanry, Royal Armoured Corps (TA): Princess Louise's Kensington Regiment (TA): The Buffs (Royal East Kent Regiment) The Queen's Bays (2nd Dragoon Guards):The Royal Fusiliers (City of London Regiment):The Lancashire Fusiliers:The Argyll and Sutherland Highlanders (Princess Louise's): The Queen's Royal Regiment (West Surrey):The Queen's Own Royal West Kent Regiment: 10th Royal Hussars (Prince of Wales's Own):The Royal Inniskilling Fusiliers:The Northamptonshire Regiment: Scots Guards:The East Surrey Regiment: 4th Queen's Own Hussars: Coldstream Guards:The Rifle Brigade (Prince Consort's Own): 1st/2nd Lothians and Border Horse, Royal Armoured Corps (TA):The Welch Regiment:The Commando Association: 16th/5th The Queen's Royal Lancers:The King's Royal Rifle Corps: London Irish Rifles, The Royal Ulster Rifles (TA)
		1958	27th Lancers: Royal Tank Regiment: The Royal Irish Fusiliers (Princess Victoria's)

740.	**FOSSA CEMBALINA** 20th–21st April 1945 Final Operations	1956 1957	17th/21st Lancers: The Derbyshire Yeomanry, Royal Armoured Corps (TA) The Rifle Brigade (Prince Consort's Own): London Rifle Brigade, The Rifle Brigade (Prince Consort's Own) (TA)
741.	**SAN NICOLO CANAL** 21st April 1945 Final Operations	1958	The Royal Irish Fusiliers (Princess Victoria's)
742.	**BOLOGNA** 14th–21st April 1945 Final Operations	1956 1957 1958 1958 ?	10th Princess Mary's Own Gurkha Rifles 12th Royal Lancers (Prince of Wales's): 14th/20th King's Hussars 27th Lancers The Auckland (East Coast) Mounted Rifles: The Waikato Mounted Rifles: The North Auckland Mounted Rifles: The Waikato Regiment: Queen Alexandra's (Wellington West Coast) Mounted Rifles: The Manawatu Mounted Rifles: The Canterbury Yeomanry Cavalry: The Otago Mounted Rifles: The Nelson-Marlborough Mounted Rifles: The Wellington East Coast Mounted Rifles: The New Zealand Scottish Regiment: The Canterbury Regiment: The Auckland Regiment (Countess of Ranfurly's Own): The Otago Regiment: The Southland Regiment: The Wellington Regiment (City of Wellington's Own): The Hauraki Regiment: The Wellington West Coast Regiment: The Taranaki Regiment: The Hawke's Bay Regiment: The Nelson, Marlborough, and West Coast Regiment: The Northland Regiment: The Ruahine Regiment: 27 (MG) Battalion: 28 (Maori) Battalion 6th Royal Battalion (Scinde), The Frontier Force Rifles: 4th Battalion (Wilde's), The Frontier Force Rifles
743.	**SILLARO CROSSING** 14th–16th April 1945 Final Operations	1956 1957 1958 	10th Princess Mary's Own Gurkha Rifles 12th Royal Lancers (Prince of Wales's): The Durham Light Infantry The Waikato Regiment: Queen Alexandra's (Wellington West Coast) Mounted Rifles: The Manawatu Mounted Rifles: The Canterbury Yeomanry Cavalry: The Otago Mounted Rifles: The Nelson-Marlborough Mounted Rifles: The Wellington East Coast Mounted Rifles: The New Zealand Scottish Regiment: The Canterbury Regiment: The Auckland Regiment (Countess of Ranfurly's Own): The Otago Regiment: The Southland Regiment: The Wellington Regiment (City of Wellington's Own): The Hauraki Regiment: The Wellington West Coast Regiment: The Taranaki Regiment: The Hawke's Bay Regiment: The Nelson, Marlborough, and West Coast Regiment: The Northland Regiment: The Ruahine Regiment: 27 (MG) Battalion
744.	**MONTE SOLE** 15th–18th April 1945 Final Operations	?	4th Battalion (Wilde's), The Frontier Force Rifles
745.	**SOLE/CAPRARA** 15th–18th April 1945 Final Operations	1957	Royal Durban Light Infantry: First City: The Queen's Own Cape Town Highlanders: Witwatersrand Rifles: Regiment De La Rey
746.	**MEDICINA** 16th April 1945 Final Operations	1957	14th/20th King's Hussars: 6th Gurkha Rifles
747.	**GAIANA CROSSING** 17th–19th April 1945 Final Operations	1956 1957 1958 1958	10th Princess Mary's Own Gurkha Rifles 6th Gurkha Rifles 27th Lancers Queen Alexandra's (Wellington West Coast) Mounted Rifles: The Manawatu Mounted Rifles: The Wellington East Coast

748. **IDICE BRIDGEHEAD**
20th–21st April 1945
Final Operations

1962	Mounted Rifles: The New Zealand Scottish Regiment: The Wellington Regiment (City of Wellington's Own): The Wellington West Coast Regiment: The Taranaki Regiment: The Hawke's Bay Regiment: The Ruahine Regiment: 27 (MG) Battalion 2nd Battalion, 8th Gorkha Rifles
1957	12th Royal Lancers (Prince of Wales's)
1958	The Auckland (East Coast) Mounted Rifles: The Waikato Mounted Rifles: The Waikato Regiment: The Canterbury Yeomanry Cavalry: The Otago Mounted Rifles: The Nelson-Marlborough Mounted Rifles: The Canterbury Regiment: The Auckland Regiment (Countess of Ranfurly's Own): The Otago Regiment: The Southland Regiment: The Wellington Regiment (City of Wellington's Own): The Hauraki Regiment: The Wellington West Coast Regiment: The Taranaki Regiment: The Hawke's Bay Regiment: The Nelson, Marlborough, and West Coast Regiment: The Northland Regiment: The Ruahine Regiment: 28 (Maori) Battalion
1962	1st Battalion, The Parachute Regiment: 2nd Battalion, The Parachute Regiment
?	4th Battalion (Duke of Connaught's Own), The Baluch Regiment

749. **TRAGHETTO**
19th–20th April 1945
Final Operations

1957	16th/5th The Queen's Royal Lancers

750. **PO VALLEY** [1]
19th–30th April 1945
Final Operations

1957	1 Special Service Battalion: The Royal Natal Carbineers: Royal Durban Light Infantry: First City: The Queen's Own Cape Town Highlanders: Kimberley Regiment: Witwatersrand Rifles: Regiment De La Rey: Natal Mounted Rifles: Imperial Light Horse: Prince Alfred's Guard: Pretoria Regiment (Princess Alice's Own)

[1] PO-VALLEI taken into use by Afrikaans-speaking South African units 1957.

751. **CAMPOSANTO BRIDGE** [1]
22nd April 1945
Final Operations

1957	Witwatersrand Rifles: Regiment De La Rey

[1] CAMPOSANTO-BRUG taken into use by Afrikaans-speaking South African units 1957.

752. **ITALY 1943**
3rd September–31st December 1943
Service in Italy 1943–45

1956	1st The Royal Dragoons: The Royal Scots Greys (2nd Dragoons): The Devonshire Regiment
1957	3rd/4th County of London Yeomanry (Sharpshooters), Royal Armoured Corps (TA): The Dorset Regiment: 11th Hussars (Prince Albert's Own): The Highland Light Infantry (City of Glasgow Regiment)
1958	The South Staffordshire Regiment

753. **ITALY 1943–44**
3rd September 1943–31st December 1944
Service in Italy 1943–45

1956	Irish Guards: The Wiltshire Regiment (Duke of Edinburgh's): The Cameronians (Scottish Rifles): The Parachute Regiment
1957	Seaforth Highlanders (Ross-shire Buffs, The Duke of Albany's): 1st King's Dragoon Guards: The Green Howards (Alexandra, Princess of Wales's Own Yorkshire Regiment): The Essex Regiment: The Queen's Westminsters, The King's Royal Rifle Corps (TA)
1958	The Royal Scots Fusiliers

754. **ITALY 1943–1944** [1]
3rd September 1943–31st December 1944
Service in Italy 1943–45

1957	1st Special Service Battalion

[1] ITALIE 1943–1944 taken into use by French-speaking Canadian units 1958.

755.	**ITALY 1943–45** 3rd September 1943–22nd April 1945 Service in Italy 1943–45	
	1956	The Duke of Wellington's Regiment (West Riding): The London Scottish, The Gordon Highlanders (TA): The Royal Leicestershire Regiment: The York and Lancaster Regiment: Princess Louise's Kensington Regiment (TA): The Buffs (Royal East Kent Regiment)
	1957	The Royal Fusiliers (City of London Regiment): Grenadier Guards: The Lancashire Fusiliers: The Cheshire Regiment: The Oxfordshire and Buckinghamshire Light Infantry: The Argyll and Sutherland Highlanders (Princess Louise's): The Queen's Royal Regiment (West Surrey): The Sherwood Foresters (Nottinghamshire and Derbyshire Regiment): The Queen's Own Royal West Kent Regiment: The King's Own Yorkshire Light Infantry: The Royal Inniskilling Fusiliers: The Northamptonshire Regiment: The King's Shropshire Light Infantry: Scots Guards: The East Surrey Regiment: The Royal Hampshire Regiment: Coldstream Guards: The Royal Lincolnshire Regiment: The Royal Berkshire Regiment (Princess Charlotte of Wales's): The Rifle Brigade (Prince Consort's Own): The Welch Regiment: The Durham Light Infantry: The Commando Association: The King's Royal Rifle Corps: London Irish Rifles, The Royal Ulster Rifles (TA): Special Air Service Regiment
	1958	Royal Tank Regiment: The Royal Northumberland Fusiliers
	1958	The Auckland (East Coast) Mounted Rifles: The Waikato Mounted Rifles: The North Auckland Mounted Rifles: The Waikato Regiment: Queen Alexandra's (Wellington West Coast) Mounted Rifles: The Manawatu Mounted Rifles: The Canterbury Yeomanry Cavalry: The Otago Mounted Rifles: The Nelson-Marlborough Mounted Rifles: The Wellington East Coast Mounted Rifles: The New Zealand Scottish Regiment: The Canterbury Regiment: The Auckland Regiment (Countess of Ranfurly's Own): The Otago Regiment: The Southland Regiment: The Wellington Regiment (City of Wellington's Own): The Hauraki Regiment: The Wellington West Coast Regiment: The Taranaki Regiment: The Hawke's Bay Regiment: The Nelson, Marlborough, and West Coast Regiment: The Northland Regiment: The Ruahine Regiment: 27 (MG) Battalion: 28 (Maori) Battalion
	1962	I Horse: The Central India Horse: 10 Field Company, Madras Engineer Group: 12 Field Company, Madras Engineer Group: 1 Field Company, Bengal Engineer Group: 7 Field Company, Bengal Engineer Group: 66 Field Company, Bengal Engineer Group: 69 Field Company, Bengal Engineer Group: 21 Field Company, Bombay Engineer Group: 3rd Battalion, The Brigade of the Guards: 1st Battalion, The Parachute Regiment: 2nd Battalion, The Parachute Regiment: 14th Battalion (Nabha), The Punjab Regiment: 1st Battalion, The Maratha Light Infantry: 5th Battalion, The Maratha Light Infantry: 4th Battalion, The Rajputana Rifles: 17th Battalion (Sawai Man), The Rajputana Rifles: MG Battalion, The Rajputana Rifles: 20th Battalion (Jodhpur), The Rajput Regiment: 2nd Battalion, The Sikh Regiment: 4th Battalion, The Sikh Regiment: 3rd Battalion, The Garhwal Rifles: 2nd Battalion, 3rd Gorkha Rifles: 2nd Battalion, 4th Gorkha Rifles: 1st Battalion, 5th Gorkha Rifles: 2nd Battalion, 8th Gorkha Rifles: 1st Battalion, 9th Gorkha Rifles
	?	6th Duke of Connaught's Own Lancers (Watson's Horse): 3rd Battalion, 1st Punjab Regiment: 3rd Battalion, 15th Punjab Regiment: 4th Battalion (Bhopal), 16th Punjab Regiment: 3rd Battalion, 8th Punjab Regiment: 3rd Battalion (Queen Mary's Own), The Baluch Regiment: 4th Battalion (Duke of Connaught's Own), The Baluch Regiment: 6th Royal Battalion (Scinde), The Frontier Force Rifles: 1st Battalion, The Frontier Force Regiment: 3rd Royal Battalion, The Frontier Force Regiment: 4th Battalion (Wilde's), The Frontier Force Rifles
756.	**ITALY 1943–1945** [1] 3rd September 1943–22nd April 1945 Service in Italy 1943–45	
	1957	The Elgin Regiment (27th Armoured Regiment): The Hastings and Prince Edward Regiment: 48th Highlanders of Canada: Princess Patricia's Canadian Light Infantry: West Nova Scotia Regiment (Machine Gun): The Seaforth Highlanders of Canada: 1st Battalion, The Royal New Brunswick Regiment (Carleton and York): 2nd Battalion, The Royal New Brunswick Regiment (North Shore): The Royal 22e Regiment
	1958	The Ontario Regiment (11th Armoured Regiment): 4th Princess Louise Dragoon Guards (4th Armoured Car Regiment): The Loyal Edmonton Regiment (3rd Battalion, Princess Patricia's Canadian Light Infantry): The Royal Canadian Regiment
	1959	Le Regiment de Trois Rivieres: The Lorne Scots (Peel, Dufferin and Halton Regiment): The North Saskatchewan Regiment: The King's Own Calgary Regiment (RCAC): The Irish Regiment of Canada

[1] *ITALIE 1943–1945 taken into use by French-speaking Canadian units 1958.*

No.	Battle Honour	Year	Regiments
757.	**ITALY 1944** 1st January–31st December 1944 Service in Italy 1943–45	1956	The Life Guards: Royal Horse Guards: The Royal Wiltshire Yeomanry (Prince of Wales's Own), Royal Armoured Corps (TA)
		1957	The Warwickshire Yeomanry, Royal Armoured Corps (TA): The Queen's Own Yorkshire Dragoons, Royal Armoured Corps (TA): The Queen's Own Cameron Highlanders: 7th Gurkha Rifles: The Black Watch (Royal Highland Regiment): 3rd The King's Own Hussars: The Manchester Regiment
758.	**ITALY 1944–45** [1] 1st January 1944–22nd April 1945 Service in Italy 1943–45	1956	9th Queen's Royal Lancers: 17th/21st Lancers: The Derbyshire Yeomanry, Royal Armoured Corps (TA): The Duke of Cornwall's Light Infantry: 7th Queen's Own Hussars: The Royal Sussex Regiment: 10th Princess Mary's Own Gurkha Rifles
		1957	The Queen's Bays (2nd Dragoon Guards): Honourable Artillery Company (TA): The King's Regiment (Liverpool): The Gordon Highlanders: 12th Royal Lancers (Prince of Wales's): The Somerset Light Infantry (Prince Albert's): The Bedfordshire and Hertfordshire Regiment: The Hertfordshire Regiment (TA): 10th Royal Hussars (Prince of Wales's Own): The Loyal Regiment (North Lancashire): 6th Gurkha Rifles: North Irish Horse, Royal Armoured Corps (TA): The King's Own Royal Regiment (Lancaster): 4th Queen's Own Hussars: 1st/2nd Lothians and Border Horse, Royal Armoured Corps (TA): Welsh Guards: The Middlesex Regiment (Duke of Cambridge's Own): London Rifle Brigade, The Rifle Brigade (Prince Consort's Own) (TA): Tower Hamlets Rifles (TA): 16th/5th The Queen's Royal Lancers: The North Staffordshire Regiment (The Prince of Wales's): 2nd King Edward VII's Own Gurkha Rifles (The Sirmoor Rifles)
		1957	1 Special Service Battalion: The Royal Natal Carbineers: Royal Durban Light Infantry: First City: The Queen's Own Cape Town Highlanders: Kimberley Regiment: Witwatersrand Rifles: Regiment De La Rey: Natal Mounted Rifles: Imperial Light Horse: Prince Alfred's Guard: Pretoria Regiment (Princess Alice's Own)
		1958	27th Lancers: The Royal Scots (The Royal Regiment)

[1] ITALIE 1944–45 taken into use by Afrikaans-speaking South African units 1957.

No.	Battle Honour	Year	Regiments
759.	**ITALY 1944–1945** [1] 1st January 1944–22nd April 1945 Service in Italy 1943–45	1957	The Princess Louise Fusiliers (MG): The Royal Canadian Dragoons (1st Armoured Regiment): 1/8th Canadian Hussars (Princess Louise's): 2/8th Canadian Hussars (Princess Louise's): The Westminster Regiment: The Governor General's Horse Guards (3rd Armoured Regiment)
		1958	The British Columbia Dragoons (9th Reconnaissance Regiment): Lord Strathcona's Horse (Royal Canadians): 1st Battalion, The Nova Scotia Highlanders (North): 2nd Battalion, The Nova Scotia Highlanders (Cape Breton)
		1959	The Perth Regiment
		1960	The Lanark and Renfrew Scottish Regiment

[1] ITALIE 1944–1945 taken into use by French-speaking Canadian units 1958.

No.	Battle Honour	Year	Regiments
760.	**ITALY 1945** 1st January–22nd April 1945 Service in Italy 1943–45	1957	14th/20th King's Hussars: The Highland Light Infantry (City of Glasgow Regiment)
761.	**MOUNT OLYMPUS** 10th–18th April 1941 The Defence and Withdrawal from Greece	1958	The Waikato Regiment: The New Zealand Scottish Regiment: The Canterbury Regiment: The Auckland Regiment (Countess of Ranfurly's Own): The Otago Regiment: The Southland Regiment: The Wellington Regiment (City of Wellington's Own): The Hauraki Regiment: The Wellington West Coast Regiment: The Taranaki Regiment: The Hawke's Bay Regiment: The Nelson, Marlborough, and West Coast Regiment: The Northland Regiment: The Ruahine Regiment: 28 (Maori) Battalion
		1961	1st Infantry Battalion (Commando) (City of Sydney's Own Regiment): 2nd Infantry Battalion (City of Newcastle Regiment): 3rd Infantry Battalion (The Werriwa Regiment): 8th Infantry Battalion: 1st Machine Gun Battalion
762.	**ALIAKMON BRIDGE** 11th–13th April 1941 The Defence and Withdrawal from Greece	1958	The New Zealand Scottish Regiment

763.	**SERVIA PASS** 13th–18th April 1941 The Defence and Withdrawal from Greece	1958	The Waikato Regiment: The Canterbury Regiment: The Auckland Regiment (Countess of Ranfurly's Own): The Otago Regiment: The Southland Regiment: The Wellington Regiment (City of Wellington's Own): The Hauraki Regiment: The Wellington West Coast Regiment: The Taranaki Regiment: The Hawke's Bay Regiment: The Nelson, Marlborough, and West Coast Regiment: The Northland Regiment: The Ruahine Regiment
		1961	1st Machine Gun Battalion
764.	**PLATAMON TUNNEL** 15th–16th April 1941 The Defence and Withdrawal from Greece	1958	The Waikato Regiment: The Auckland Regiment (Countess of Ranfurly's Own): The Hauraki Regiment: The Northland Regiment
765.	**OLYMPUS PASS** 15th–17th April 1941 The Defence and Withdrawal from Greece	1958	The Canterbury Regiment: The Otago Regiment: The Southland Regiment: The Wellington Regiment (City of Wellington's Own): The Wellington West Coast Regiment: The Taranaki Regiment: The Hawke's Bay Regiment: The Nelson, Marlborough, and West Coast Regiment: The Ruahine Regiment: 28 (Maori) Battalion
766.	**TEMPE GORGE** 18th April 1941 The Defence and Withdrawal from Greece	1958	The Waikato Regiment: The New Zealand Scottish Regiment: The Auckland Regiment (Countess of Ranfurly's Own): The Hauraki Regiment: The Northland Regiment
		1961	2nd Infantry Battalion (City of Newcastle Regiment): 3rd Infantry Battalion (The Werriwa Regiment)
767.	**VEVE** 10th–12th April 1941 The Defence and Withdrawal from Greece	1957 1958 1961	The King's Royal Rifle Corps: The Rangers, The King's Royal Rifle Corps (TA) 27 (MG) Battalion 4th Infantry Battalion (Australian Rifles): 8th Infantry Battalion
768.	**SOTER** 13th April 1941 The Defence and Withdrawal from Greece	1961	4th Infantry Battalion (Australian Rifles)
769.	**PROASTEION** 13th April 1941 The Defence and Withdrawal from Greece	1957	4th Queen's Own Hussars: The Rangers, The King's Royal Rifle Corps (TA)
770.	**ELASSON** 18th April 1941 The Defence and Withdrawal from Greece	1958	The Waikato Regiment: The New Zealand Scottish Regiment: The Auckland Regiment (Countess of Ranfurly's Own): The Wellington Regiment (City of Wellington's Own): The Hauraki Regiment: The Wellington West Coast Regiment: The Taranaki Regiment: The Hawke's Bay Regiment: The Northland Regiment: The Ruahine Regiment
771.	**BRALLOS PASS** 22nd–24th April 1941 The Defence and Withdrawal from Greece	1961	1st Infantry Battalion (Commando) (City of Sydney's Own Regiment): 4th Infantry Battalion (Australian Rifles): 11th Infantry Battalion

772.	**MOLOS** 22nd–25th April 1941 The Defence and Withdrawal from Greece	1958	The Waikato Regiment: The Canterbury Regiment: The Auckland Regiment (Countess of Ranfuly's Own): The Otago Regiment: The Southland Regiment: The Wellington Regiment (City of Wellington's Own): The Hauraki Regiment: The Wellington West Coast Regiment: The Taranaki Regiment: The Hawke's Bay Regiment: The Nelson, Marlborough, and West Coast Regiment: The Northland Regiment: The Ruahine Regiment
773.	**CORINTH CANAL** 26th April 1941 The Defence and Withdrawal from Greece	1957	4th Queen's Own Hussars
774.	**GREECE 1941** 10th–29th April 1941 Service in Greece 1941	1957 1958 1958	4th Queen's Own Hussars: The King's Royal Rifle Corps: The Rangers, The King's Royal Rifle Corps (TA) Royal Tank Regiment The Waikato Regiment: The New Zealand Scottish Regiment: The Canterbury Regiment: The Auckland Regiment (Countess of Ranfurly's Own): The Otago Regiment: The Southland Regiment: The Wellington Regiment (City of Wellington's Own): The Hauraki Regiment: The Wellington West Coast Regiment: The Taranaki Regiment: The Hawke's Bay Regiment: The Nelson, Marlborough, and West Coast Regiment: The Northland Regiment: The Ruahine Regiment: 27 (MG) Battalion: 28 (Maori) Battalion
		1961	1st Infantry Battalion (Commando) (City of Sydney's Own Regiment): 2nd Infantry Battalion (City of Newcastle Regiment): 3rd Infantry Battalion (The Werriwa Regiment): 4th Infantry Battalion (Australian Rifles): 5th Infantry Battalion (The Victorian Scottish Regiment): 6th Infantry Battalion (The Royal Melbourne Regiment): 8th Infantry Battalion: 7th Infantry Battalion: 11th Infantry Battalion: 1st Machine Gun Battalion
775.	**ATHENS** 2nd December 1944–15th January 1945 Operations in Greece in 1944–45	1956 1957 ?	The Parachute Regiment The Royal Fusiliers (City of London Regiment): The King's Regiment (Liverpool): 1st King's Dragoon Guards: The Somerset Light Infantry (Prince Albert's): The Bedfordshire and Hertfordshire Regiment: The Royal Hampshire Regiment: The Highland Light Infantry (City of Glasgow Regiment): The Black Watch (Royal Highland Regiment): The Essex Regiment: The Durham Light Infantry: The Queen's Westminsters, The King's Royal Rifle Corps (TA) 3rd Battalion (Queen Mary's Own), The Baluch Regiment: 3rd Royal Battalion, The Frontier Force Regiment
776.	**GREECE 1944–45** 16th September 1944–15th January 1945 Service in Greece 1944–45	1956 1957 1962 1963 ?	The Parachute Regiment The Royal Fusiliers (City of London Regiment): The King's Regiment (Liverpool): 1st King's Dragoon Guards: The Somerset Light Infantry (Prince Albert's): The Bedfordshire and Hertfordshire Regiment: The Queen's Own Royal West Kent Regiment: The East Surrey Regiment: The Royal Hampshire Regiment: The Highland Light Infantry (City of Glasgow Regiment): The Black Watch (Royal Highland Regiment): The Essex Regiment: The Durham Light Infantry: The Commando Association: The King's Royal Rifle Corps: The Queen's Westminsters, The King's Royal Rifle Corps (TA): 2nd King Edward VII's Own Gurkha Rifles (The Sirmoor Rifles): Special Air Service Regiment 21 Field Company, Bombay Engineer Group: 9th Battalion, The Grenadiers: MG Battalion, The Rajputana Rifles: 2nd Battalion, The Sikh Regiment: 1st Battalion, 9th Gorkha Rifles The Central India Horse 3rd Battalion (Queen Mary's Own), The Baluch Regiment: 3rd Royal Battalion, The Frontier Force Regiment: 14th Battalion, The Frontier Force Regiment

777. **CRETE**
20th May–1st June 1941
The Defence and Withdrawal from Crete

- 1956 — The Royal Leicestershire Regiment: The York and Lancaster Regiment
- 1957 — The Argyll and Sutherland Highlanders (Princess Louise's): The Welch Regiment: The Black Watch (Royal Highland Regiment): 3rd The King's Own Hussars: The Commando Association: The King's Royal Rifle Corps: The Rangers, The King's Royal Rifle Corps (TA)
- 1958 — The Waikato Regiment: The New Zealand Scottish Regiment: The Canterbury Regiment: The Auckland Regiment (Countess of Ranfurly's Own): The Otago Regiment: The Southland Regiment: The Wellington Regiment (City of Wellington's Own): The Hauraki Regiment: The Wellington West Coast Regiment: The Taranaki Regiment: The Hawke's Bay Regiment: The Nelson, Marlborough, and West Coast Regiment: The Northland Regiment: The Ruahine Regiment: 27 (MG) Battalion: 28 (Maori) Battalion
- 1961 — 1st Infantry Battalion (Commando) (City of Sydney's Own Regiment); 4th Infantry Battalion (Australian Rifles); 8th Infantry Battalion: 7th Infantry Battalion: 11th Infantry Battalion: 1st Machine Gun Battalion

778. **MALEME**
20th–23rd May 1941
The Defence and Withdrawal from Crete

- 1958 — The Waikato Regiment: The Canterbury Regiment: The Auckland Regiment (Countess of Ranfurly's Own): The Otago Regiment: The Southland Regiment: The Wellington Regiment (City of Wellington's Own): The Hauraki Regiment: The Wellington West Coast Regiment: The Taranaki Regiment: The Hawke's Bay Regiment: The Nelson, Marlborough, and West Coast Regiment: The Northland Regiment: The Ruahine Regiment 28 (Maori) Battalion

779. **GALATAS**
20th–25th May 1941
The Defence and Withdrawal from Crete

- 1958 — The Waikato Regiment: The New Zealand Scottish Regiment: The Canterbury Regiment: The Auckland Regiment (Countess of Ranfurly's Own): The Otago Regiment: The Wellington Regiment (City of Wellington's Own): The Hauraki Regiment: The Wellington West Coast Regiment: The Taranaki Regiment: The Hawke's Bay Regiment: The Nelson, Marlborough, and West Coast Regiment: The Northland Regiment: The Ruahine Regiment: 27 (MG) Battalion

780. **CANEA**
20th–27th May 1941
The Defence and Withdrawal from Crete

- 1957 — The Welch Regiment: The Rangers, The King's Royal Rifle Corps (TA)
- 1958 — The Waikato Regiment: The New Zealand Scottish Regiment: The Auckland Regiment (Countess of Ranfurly's Own): The Wellington Regiment (City of Wellington's Own): The Hauraki Regiment: The Wellington West Coast Regiment: The Taranaki Regiment: The Hawke's Bay Regiment: The Northland Regiment: The Ruahine Regiment: 28 (Maori) Battalion
- 1961 — 8th Infantry Battalion: 7th Infantry Battalion

781. **HERAKLION**
20th–29th May 1941
The Defence and Withdrawal from Crete

- 1956 — The Royal Leicestershire Regiment: The York and Lancaster Regiment
- 1957 — The Argyll and Sutherland Highlanders (Princess Louise's): The Black Watch (Royal Highland Regiment)
- 1961 — 4th Infantry Battalion (Australian Rifles)

782. **RETIMO**
20th–30th May 1941
The Defence and Withdrawal from Crete

- 1957 — The Rangers, The King's Royal Rifle Corps (TA)
- 1961 — 1st Infantry Battalion (Commando) (City of Sydney's Own Regiment): 11th Infantry Battalion

783. **42ND STREET**
27th May 1941
The Defence and Withdrawal from Crete

- 1958 — The Waikato Regiment: The New Zealand Scottish Regiment: The Canterbury Regiment: The Auckland Regiment (Countess of Ranfurly's Own): The Otago Regiment: The Southland Regiment: The Wellington Regiment (City of Wellington's Own): The Hauraki Regiment: The Wellington West Coast Regiment: The Taranaki Regiment: The Hawke's Bay Regiment: The Nelson, Marlborough, and West Coast Regiment: The Northland Regiment: The Ruahine Regiment 28 (Maori) Battalion
- 1961 — 8th Infantry Battalion: 7th Infantry Battalion

784. **WITHDRAWAL TO SPHAKIA**
28th May–1st June 1941
The Defence and Withdrawal from Crete

- 1957 — The Welch Regiment
- 1958 — The Waikato Regiment: The New Zealand Scottish Regiment: The Canterbury Regiment: The Auckland Regiment (Countess of Ranfurly's Own): The Otago Regiment: The Southland Regiment: The Wellington Regiment (City of Wellington's Own):

			The Hauraki Regiment: The Wellington West Coast Regiment: The Taranaki Regiment: The Hawke's Bay Regiment: The Nelson, Marlborough, and West Coast Regiment: The Northland Regiment: The Ruahine Regiment: 28 (Maori) Battalion
		1961	8th Infantry Battalion: 7th Infantry Battalion
785.	**MADAGASCAR** 5th May–6th November 1942 The Occupation of Madagascar	1957	The East Lancashire Regiment: The Royal Welch Fusiliers: Seaforth Highlanders (Ross-shire Buffs, The Duke of Albany's): The Northamptonshire Regiment: The South Lancashire Regiment (The Prince of Wales's Volunteers): The Commando Association
		1957	The King's African Rifles
		1958	The Royal Scots Fusiliers
786.	**MADAGASCAR 1942** [1] 5th May–6th November 1942 The Occupation of Madagascar	1957	First City: Pretoria Regiment (Princess Alice's Own): Pretoria Highlanders [1] *MADAGASKAR 1942 taken into use by Afrikaans-speaking South African units 1957.*
787.	**COS** 3rd–16th October 1943 Operations in the Aegean Area	1957	The Durham Light Infantry
788.	**LEROS** 12th–16th November 1943 Operations in the Aegean Area	1956	The Buffs (Royal East Kent Regiment)
		1957	The Queen's Own Royal West Kent Regiment
		1958	The Royal Irish Fusiliers (Princess Victoria's)
789.	**ADRIATIC** 18th March–21st November 1944 Operations in the Adriatic Area	1957	The Highland Light Infantry (City of Glasgow Regiment): The Commando Association: Special Air Service Regiment
790.	**MIDDLE EAST 1941** 20th May–31st December 1941 Service in the Middle East 1941–44	1956	The York and Lancaster Regiment
		1957	The Argyll and Sutherland Highlanders (Princess Louise's): The Welch Regiment: The Black Watch (Royal Highland Regiment): The King's Royal Rifle Corps: The Rangers, The King's Royal Rifle Corps (TA)
		1961	1st Infantry Battalion (Commando) (City of Sydney's Own Regiment): 4th Infantry Battalion (Australian Rifles): 8th Infantry Battalion: 7th Infantry Battalion: 11th Infantry Battalion: 1st Machine Gun Battalion
791.	**MIDDLE EAST 1941–44** 20th May 1941–21st November 1944 Service in the Middle East 1941–44	1958	The Waikato Regiment: The New Zealand Scottish Regiment: The Canterbury Regiment: The Auckland Regiment (Countess of Ranfurly's Own): The Otago Regiment: The Southland Regiment: The Wellington Regiment (City of Wellington's Own): The Hauraki Regiment: The Wellington West Coast Regiment: The Taranaki Regiment: The Hawke's Bay Regiment: The Nelson, Marlborough, and West Coast Regiment: The Northland Regiment: The Ruahine Regiment: 27 (MG) Battalion: 28 (Maori) Battalion
792.	**MIDDLE EAST 1942** 1st January–31st December 1942 Service in the Middle East 1941–44	1956	The Wiltshire Regiment (Duke of Edinburgh's)
		1957	The Royal Welch Fusiliers: Seaforth Highlanders (Ross-shire Buffs, The Duke of Albany's): The Royal Inniskilling Fusiliers: The South Lancashire Regiment (The Prince of Wales's Volunteers)
		1957	The King's African Rifles: The Northern Rhodesia Regiment
		1958	The Royal Scots Fusiliers

793.	**MIDDLE EAST 1943** 1st January–31st December 1943 Service in the Middle East 1941–44	1956 1957	The Buffs (Royal East Kent Regiment) The Durham Light Infantry
794.	**MIDDLE EAST 1943–44** 1st January 1943–21st November 1944 Service in the Middle East 1941–44	1957	Special Air Service Regiment
795.	**MIDDLE EAST 1944** 1st January–21st November 1944 Service in the Middle East 1941–44	1957	The Highland Light Infantry (City of Glasgow Regiment)
796.	**MALTA 1940** 11th June–31st December 1940 The Defence of Malta	1957 1958	The Manchester Regiment The Royal Irish Fusiliers (Princess Victoria's)
797.	**MALTA 1940–42** 11th June 1940–20th November 1942 The Defence of Malta	1956 1956 1957	The Buffs (Royal East Kent Regiment);The Devonshire Regiment King's Own Malta Regiment The Dorset Regiment;The Queen's Own Royal West Kent Regiment
798.	**MALTA 1941–42** 1st January 1941–20th November 1942 The Defence of Malta	1957	The Lancashire Fusiliers;The Cheshire Regiment;The King's Own Royal Regiment (Lancaster);The Royal Hampshire Regiment
799.	**MALTA 1942** 1st January–20th November 1942 The Defence of Malta	1957	The Durham Light Infantry
800.	**NORTH MALAYA** 8th–21st December 1941 Operations in Malaya and Singapore Island	1957 1962 ?	The Argyll and Sutherland Highlanders (Princess Louise's); 2nd King Edward VII's Own Gurkha Rifles (The Sirmoor Rifles) 3rd Cavalry; 4th Battalion, The Kumaon Regiment 1st Battalion, 8th Punjab Regiment: 2nd Battalion, The Baluch Regiment; 2nd Battalion, The Frontier Force Regiment: 1st Battalion (Coke's), The Frontier Force Rifles
801.	**KOTA BAHRU** 8th December 1941 Operations in Malaya and Singapore Island	1962 ?	3rd Battalion, The Dogra Regiment 2nd Battalion, The Frontier Force Regiment: 1st Battalion (Coke's), The Frontier Force Rifles
802.	**KROH** 10th–13th December 1941 Operations in Malaya and Singapore Island	?	3rd Battalion, 16th Punjab Regiment
803.	**JITRA** 10th–13th December 1941 Operations in Malaya and Singapore Island	1957 1962 ?	2nd King Edward VII's Own Gurkha Rifles (The Sirmoor Rifles) 2nd Battalion, The Jat Regiment: 2nd Battalion, 1st Gorkha Rifles 1st Battalion, 14th Punjab Regiment: 2nd Battalion, 16th Punjab Regiment: 1st Battalion, 8th Punjab Regiment

804.	**MACHANG** 12th–17th December 1941 Operations in Malaya and Singapore Island	?	2nd Battalion, The Baluch Regiment: 2nd Battalion, The Frontier Force Regiment
805.	**GURUN** 14th–15th December 1941 Operations in Malaya and Singapore Island	?	2nd Battalion, 16th Punjab Regiment: 1st Battalion, 8th Punjab Regiment
806.	**GRIK ROAD** 17th–23rd December 1941 Operations in Malaya and Singapore Island	1957	The Argyll and Sutherland Highlanders (Princess Louise's)
807.	**CENTRAL MALAYA** 26th December 1941–10th January 1942 Operations in Malaya and Singapore Island	1957 1962 ?	The Argyll and Sutherland Highlanders (Princess Louise's); 2nd King Edward VII's Own Gurkha Rifles (The Sirmoor Rifles) 3rd Cavalry; 5th Battalion, The Punjab Regiment 2nd Battalion, The Frontier Force Regiment
808.	**IPOH** 26th–29th December 1941 Operations in Malaya and Singapore Island	1957 1962 ?	The Argyll and Sutherland Highlanders (Princess Louise's) 5th Battalion, The Punjab Regiment 3rd Battalion, 16th Punjab Regiment
809.	**KUANTAN** 27th December 1941–3rd January 1942 Operations in Malaya and Singapore Island	1962 ?	22 Field Company, Bombay Engineer Group: 5th Battalion, The Sikh Regiment: 2nd Battalion, The Garhwal Rifles 2nd Battalion, The Frontier Force Regiment
810.	**KAMPAR** 30th December 1941–3rd January 1942 Operations in Malaya and Singapore Island	1956 1957 1962 ?	The Royal Leicestershire Regiment The East Surrey Regiment: 2nd King Edward VII's Own Gurkha Rifles (The Sirmoor Rifles) 3 Field Company, Bengal Engineer Group: 2nd Battalion, The Jat Regiment: 2nd Battalion, 1st Gorkha Rifles 1st Battalion, 14th Punjab Regiment: 3rd Battalion, 16th Punjab Regiment: 1st Battalion, 8th Punjab Regiment
811.	**SLIM RIVER** 7th January 1942 Operations in Malaya and Singapore Island	1957 1962	The Argyll and Sutherland Highlanders (Princess Louise's); 2nd King Edward VII's Own Gurkha Rifles (The Sirmoor Rifles) 4th Battalion, The Kumaon Regiment
812.	**JOHORE** 14th–31st January 1942 Operations in Malaya and Singapore Island	1957 1961 ?	The Loyal Regiment (North Lancashire); The Cambridgeshire Regiment (TA); The Royal Norfolk Regiment: 2nd King Edward VII's Own Gurkha Rifles (The Sirmoor Rifles) 18th Infantry Battalion: 19th Infantry Battalion (The South Sydney Regiment); 20th Infantry Battalion (The Parramatta and Blue Mountains Regiment); 26th Infantry Battalion (The Logan and Albert Regiment); 29th Infantry Battalion (The East Melbourne Regiment); 30th Infantry Battalion (The New South Wales Scottish Regiment) 1st Battalion, The Bahawalpur Regiment: 1st Battalion (Coke's), The Frontier Force Rifles
813.	**GEMAS** 14th–15th January 1942 Operations in Malaya and Singapore Island	1961 ?	30th Infantry Battalion (The New South Wales Scottish Regiment) 1st Battalion (Coke's), The Frontier Force Rifles

No.	Battle Honour	Year	Regiment
814.	**MUAR** 16th–23rd January 1942 Operations in Malaya and Singapore Island	1957	The Royal Norfolk Regiment
815.	**THE MUAR** 16th–23rd January 1942 Operations in Malaya and Singapore Island	1961 1962 ?	19th Infantry Battalion (The South Sydney Regiment); 29th Infantry Battalion (The East Melbourne Regiment) 4th Battalion, The Jat Regiment 3rd Battalion, 16th Punjab Regiment: 1st Battalion (Coke's), The Frontier Force Rifles
816.	**BATU PAHAT** 21st–26th January 1942 Operations in Malaya and Singapore Island	1957	The Loyal Regiment (North Lancashire); The Cambridgeshire Regiment (TA); The Royal Norfolk Regiment
817.	**NIYOR** 24th–25th January 1942 Operations in Malaya and Singapore Island	1961	5th Battalion, The Sikh Regiment
818.	**JEMALUANG** 26th–27th January 1942 Operations in Malaya and Singapore Island	1961	18th Infantry Battalion
819.	**SINGAPORE ISLAND** 8th–15th February 1942 Operations in Malaya and Singapore Island	1957	The Argyll and Sutherland Highlanders (Princess Louise's): The Bedfordshire and Hertfordshire Regiment: The Sherwood Foresters (Nottinghamshire and Derbyshire Regiment): The Loyal Regiment (North Lancashire): The Suffolk Regiment: The Cambridgeshire Regiment (TA): The Royal Norfolk Regiment: The Manchester Regiment: 2nd King Edward VII's Own Gurkha Rifles (The Sirmoor Rifles)
		1957	The Singapore Volunteer Corps: The Malay Regiment
		1958	The Royal Northumberland Fusiliers
		1961	18th Infantry Battalion: 19th Infantry Battalion (The South Sydney Regiment): 20th Infantry Battalion (The Parramatta and Blue Mountains Regiment): 26th Infantry Battalion (The Logan and Albert Regiment): 29th Infantry Battalion (The East Melbourne Regiment): 30th Infantry Battalion (The New South Wales Scottish Regiment): 4th Machine Gun Battalion
		1962	13th Battalion, The Punjab Regiment
		?	1st Battalion, 14th Punjab Regiment: 3rd Battalion, 16th Punjab Regiment: 6th Battalion, 1st Punjab Regiment: 2nd Battalion, The Baluch Regiment: 1st Battalion, The Bahawalpur Regiment: 2nd Battalion, The Frontier Force Regiment: 1st Battalion (Coke's), The Frontier Force Rifles
820.	**MALAYA 1941–42** 8th December 1941–15th February 1942 Operations in Malaya and Singapore Island	1956 1957	The Royal Leicestershire Regiment The Argyll and Sutherland Highlanders (Princess Louise's): The Loyal Regiment (North Lancashire): The East Surrey Regiment: The Manchester Regiment: 2nd King Edward VII's Own Gurkha Rifles (The Sirmoor Rifles)
		1957 1961	The Singapore Volunteer Corps: The Malay Regiment 18th Infantry Battalion: 19th Infantry Battalion (The South Sydney Regiment): 20th Infantry Battalion (The Parramatta and Blue Mountains Regiment): 26th Infantry Battalion (The Logan and Albert Regiment): 29th Infantry Battalion (The East Melbourne Regiment): 30th Infantry Battalion (The New South Wales Scottish Regiment): 4th Machine Gun Battalion
		1962	3rd Cavalry: 3 Field Company, Bengal Engineer Group: 19 Field Company, Bombay Engineer Group: 22 Field Company, Bombay Engineer Group: 5th Battalion, The Punjab Regiment: 13th Battalion, The Punjab Regiment: 7th Battalion, The Rajputana Rifles: 2nd Battalion, The Jat Regiment: 4th Battalion, The Jat Regiment: 5th Battalion, The Sikh Regiment: 3rd Battalion, The Dogra

	Honour / Dates / Operation	Year	Regiments
			Regiment: 2nd Battalion, The Garhwal Rifles: 4th Battalion, The Kumaon Regiment: 2nd Battalion, 1st Gorkha Rifles: 2nd Battalion, 9th Gorkha Rifles
		1963	13 Field Company, Madras Engineer Group
		?	1st Battalion, 14th Punjab Regiment: 2nd Battalion, 16th Punjab Regiment: 3rd Battalion, 16th Punjab Regiment: 6th Battalion, 1st Punjab Regiment: 1st Battalion, 8th Punjab Regiment: 2nd Battalion, The Baluch Regiment: 1st Battalion, The Bahawalpur Regiment: 2nd Battalion, The Frontier Force Regiment: 1st Battalion (Coke's), The Frontier Force Rifles
821.	**MALAYA 1942** 1st January–15th February 1942 Operations in Malaya and Singapore Island	1957	The Bedfordshire and Hertfordshire Regiment: The Sherwood Foresters (Nottinghamshire and Derbyshire Regiment): The Suffolk Regiment: The Cambridgeshire Regiment (TA): The Royal Norfolk Regiment
822.	**HONG KONG** 8th–25th December 1941 Defence of Kowloon Peninsula and Hong Kong	1956 1957 1957 1962 ?	Royal Hong Kong Defence Force The Middlesex Regiment (Duke of Cambridge's Own) The Winnipeg Grenadiers: The Royal Rifles of Canada 5th Battalion, The Rajput Regiment 2nd Battalion (Duke of Cambridge's Own), 14th Punjab Regiment
823.	**WEST BORNEO 1941–42** 16th December 1941–9th March 1942 Operations of Sarawak Force in Defence of British Borneo	?	2nd Battalion, 15th Punjab Regiment
824.	**SOUTH-EAST ASIA 1941** 8th–31st December 1941 Service in South-East Asia 1941–42	1957 1957 1958 	The Middlesex Regiment (Duke of Cambridge's Own) The Winnipeg Grenadiers: The Royal Rifles of Canada The Royal Scots (The Royal Regiment) *SUD-EST DE L'ASIE 1941 taken into use by French-speaking Canadian units 1958.*
825.	**SOUTH-EAST ASIA 1941–42** 8th December 1941–9th March 1942 Service in South-East Asia 1941–42	1962 ?	5th Battalion, The Rajput Regiment 2nd Battalion (Duke of Cambridge's Own), 14th Punjab Regiment: 2nd Battalion, 15th Punjab Regiment
826.	**MOULMEIN** 30th–31st January 1942 Enemy Invasion of Burma	?	4th Battalion, The Frontier Force Regiment
827.	**KUZEIK** 11th–12th February 1942 Enemy Invasion of Burma	?	7th Battalion, The Baluch Regiment
828.	**SITTANG 1942** 16th–23rd February 1942 Enemy Invasion of Burma	1956 1957 1962 ?	The Duke of Wellington's Regiment (West Riding) The King's Own Yorkshire Light Infantry: 7th Gurkha Rifles 1st Battalion, 3rd Gorkha Rifles: 2nd Battalion, 5th Gorkha Rifles 4th Battalion, The Frontier Force Regiment

No.	Battle Honour	Date	Campaign	Year	Regiments
829.	**PEGU**	6th–7th March 1942	Enemy Invasion of Burma	1956	7th Queen's Own Hussars
830.	**PEGU 1942**	6th–7th March 1942	Enemy Invasion of Burma	1956	The Cameronians (Scottish Rifles)
				1957	The West Yorkshire Regiment (The Prince of Wales's Own): 7th Gurkha Rifles
				1962	1st Battalion, 4th Gorkha Rifles
				?	4th Battalion, The Frontier Force Regiment: 2nd Battalion, The Frontier Force Rifles
831.	**TAUKYAN**	7th–8th March 1942	Enemy Invasion of Burma	1957	The Gloucestershire Regiment
				?	4th Battalion, The Frontier Force Regiment: 2nd Battalion, The Frontier Force Rifles
832.	**PYUNTAZA-SHWEGYIN**	11th March 1942	Enemy Invasion of Burma	?	5th Battalion, 1st Punjab Regiment
833.	**PAUNGDE**	28th–30th March 1942	Enemy Invasion of Burma	1956	The Duke of Wellington's Regiment (West Riding): 7th Queen's Own Hussars: The Cameronians (Scottish Rifles)
				1957	The Gloucestershire Regiment
834.	**YENANGYAUNG 1942**	11th–19th April 1942	Enemy Invasion of Burma	1956	The Cameronians (Scottish Rifles)
				1957	The West Yorkshire Regiment (The Prince of Wales's Own): The Royal Inniskilling Fusiliers
				1962	369 Field Company, Bengal Engineer Group: 1st Battalion, The Garhwal Rifles: 2nd Battalion, 5th Gorkha Rifles
				?	5th Battalion, 1st Punjab Regiment
835.	**KYAUKSE 1942**	28th–29th April 1942	Enemy Invasion of Burma	1957	7th Gurkha Rifles
				1962	1st Battalion, 3rd Gorkha Rifles: 2nd Battalion, 5th Gorkha Rifles
836.	**MONYWA 1942**	30th April–2nd May 1942	Enemy Invasion of Burma	1956	10th Princess Mary's Own Gurkha Rifles
				1957	The Gloucestershire Regiment
				1962	1st Battalion, The Garhwal Rifles
				?	5th Battalion, 1st Punjab Regiment: 2nd Battalion, The Frontier Force Rifles
837.	**SHWEGYIN**	9th–11th May 1942	Enemy Invasion of Burma	1957	7th Gurkha Rifles
				?	4th Battalion, The Frontier Force Regiment: 2nd Battalion, The Frontier Force Rifles
838.	**RATHEDAUNG**	29th December 1942–3rd February 1943	Operations in Arakan and NW Burma	1957	The Lancashire Fusiliers
				1962	8th Battalion, The Rajputana Rifles
				?	1st Battalion, 15th Punjab Regiment
839.	**DONBAIK**	8th January–18th March 1943	Operations in Arakan and NW Burma	1957	The Royal Welch Fusiliers: The Royal Inniskilling Fusiliers: The Royal Lincolnshire Regiment: The Royal Berkshire Regiment (Princess Charlotte of Wales's): The Durham Light Infantry
				1958	The Royal Scots (The Royal Regiment)

| | 1962 | 4th Battalion, The Brigade of the Guards: 1st Battalion, The Dogra Regiment |
| | ? | 2nd Battalion, 1st Punjab Regiment: 9th Battalion, 15th Punjab Regiment: 5th Battalion (Burma), 8th Punjab Regiment |

840. HTIZWE
6th–16th March 1943
Operations in Arakan and NW Burma

| 1957 | The Lancashire Fusiliers |
| ? | 2nd Battalion, 1st Punjab Regiment |

841. POINT 201 (ARAKAN)
28th–29th March 1943
Operations in Arakan and NW Burma

| 1957 | The Royal Lincolnshire Regiment |

842. STOCKADES
26th–27th May 1943
Operations in Arakan and NW Burma

| 1962 | 2nd Battalion, 5th Gorkha Rifles |

843. FORT WHITE
13th–15th November 1943
Operations in Arakan and NW Burma

| ? | 1st Battalion, 16th Punjab Regiment |

844. YU
18th–20th January 1944
Operations in Arakan and NW Burma

| 1957 | The Northamptonshire Regiment |

845. THE YU
18th–20th January 1944
Operations in Arakan and NW Burma

| ? | 5th Battalion (Pathans), 14th Punjab Regiment |

846. MOGAUNG
26th–27th June 1944
Operations in Arakan and NW Burma

| 1963 | 5th Battalion, 5th Gorkha Rifles |

847. NORTH ARAKAN
1st January–12th June 1944
Operations to Clear Arakan and Mayu Peninsula

1956	The Wiltshire Regiment (Duke of Edinburgh's): The York and Lancaster Regiment: The Royal Sussex Regiment
1957	The Gloucestershire Regiment: The East Lancashire Regiment: The Royal Welch Fusiliers: The Queen's Royal Regiment (West Surrey): The Somerset Light Infantry (Prince Albert's): The West Yorkshire Regiment (The Prince of Wales's Own): The King's Own Scottish Borderers: The Queen's Own Royal West Kent Regiment: The Suffolk Regiment: The South Lancashire Regiment (The Prince of Wales's Volunteers): The Royal Lincolnshire Regiment: The Manchester Regiment: 2nd King Edward VII's Own Gurkha Rifles (The Sirmoor Rifles)
1957	The Queen's Own Nigeria Regiment, Royal West African Frontier Force: The Gold Coast Regiment, Royal West African Frontier Force: The Sierra Leone Regiment, Royal West African Frontier Force: The Gambia Regiment, Royal West African Frontier Force
1958	25th Dragoons: The South Wales Borderers: The Royal Scots Fusiliers
1962	1st Battalion, The Garhwal Rifles
1963	7th Battalion, The Punjab Regiment: 2nd Battalion, The Rajput Regiment: 4th Battalion, The Rajput Regiment: 1st Battalion, The Sikh Regiment: 4th Battalion, 5th Gorkha Rifles: 1st Battalion, 8th Gorkha Rifles
?	1st Battalion, 1st Punjab Regiment: 2nd Battalion, 1st Punjab Regiment: 5th Battalion, 1st Punjab Regiment: 3rd Battalion, 14th Punjab Regiment: 4th Battalion, 14th Punjab Regiment, 16th Punjab Regiment: 8th Battalion, The Baluch Regiment:

No.	Battle Honour	Year	Regiments
			8th Battalion, 8th Punjab Regiment: 2nd Battalion, The Frontier Force Rifles: 14th Battalion, The Frontier Force Regiment: MG Battalion, The Frontier Force Regiment: 8th Battalion, The Frontier Force Rifles
848.	**BUTHIDAUNG** 16th January–3rd February and 5th March–8th April 1944 Operations to Clear Arakan and Mayu Peninsula	1957 1958 1962 ?	The Somerset Light Infantry (Prince Albert's): The King's Own Scottish Borderers: The Royal Lincolnshire Regiment 25th Dragoons 7th Battalion, The Punjab Regiment: 1st Battalion, The Sikh Regiment: 4th Battalion, 5th Gorkha Rifles 19th King George V's Own Lancers: 1st Battalion, 1st Punjab Regiment: 2nd Battalion, 1st Punjab Regiment: 3rd Battalion, 14th Punjab Regiment: 4th Battalion, 14th Punjab Regiment: MG Battalion, The Frontier Force Regiment
849.	**RAZABIL** 19th–30th January and 10th–17th March 1944 Operations to Clear Arakan and Mayu Peninsula	1957 1958 1962 ?	The Queen's Own Royal West Kent Regiment 25th Dragoons: The Royal Scots Fusiliers 4th Battalion, The Rajput Regiment: 3rd Battalion, The Jat Regiment 1st Battalion, 1st Punjab Regiment: 2nd Battalion, 1st Punjab Regiment: 3rd Battalion, 14th Punjab Regiment
850.	**KALADAN** 4th February–31st March 1944 Operations to Clear Arakan and Mayu Peninsula	1957 ?	The Queen's Own Nigeria Regiment, Royal West African Frontier Force: The Gold Coast Regiment, Royal West African Frontier Force: The Sierra Leone Regiment, Royal West African Frontier Force: The Gambia Regiment, Royal West African Frontier Force 7th Battalion, 16th Punjab Regiment: 8th Battalion, The Frontier Force Rifles
851.	**POINT 551** 3rd April–22nd May 1944 Operations to Clear Arakan and Mayu Peninsula	1956 ?	The Wiltshire Regiment (Duke of Edinburgh's) 6th Battalion, The Baluch Regiment: 2nd Battalion, The Frontier Force Rifles
852.	**PT 551** 3rd April–22nd May 1944 Operations to Clear Arakan and Mayu Peninsula	1962	1st Battalion, The Brigade of the Guards: 2nd Battalion, The Rajput Regiment: 1st Battalion, 8th Gorkha Rifles
853.	**ALETHANGYAW** 8th March–15th April 1944 Operations to Clear Arakan and Mayu Peninsula	1957	The Commando Association
854.	**MAYU TUNNELS** 15th March–20th April 1944 Operations to Clear Arakan and Mayu Peninsula	1956 1957 1958 ?	The Wiltshire Regiment (Duke of Edinburgh's) The Gloucestershire Regiment: The Queen's Own Royal West Kent Regiment: The South Lancashire Regiment (The Prince of Wales's Volunteers) The South Wales Borderers 2nd Battalion, 1st Punjab Regiment: 5th Battalion, 1st Punjab Regiment: 2nd Battalion, The Frontier Force Rifles: 8th Battalion, The Frontier Force Rifles

855. **MAUNGDAW**
1st January–31st May 1944
Operations to Clear Arakan and Mayu
Peninsula

1956 The York and Lancaster Regiment
1957 The West Yorkshire Regiment (The Prince of Wales's Own)
?   2nd Battalion, 1st Punjab Regiment: 3rd Battalion, 14th Punjab Regiment: 5th Battalion, 16th Punjab Regiment: 6th Battalion, The Baluch Regiment: MG Battalion, The Frontier Force Regiment: 8th Battalion, The Frontier Force Rifles

856. **MOWDOK**
3rd May–12th June 1944
Operations to Clear Arakan and Mayu
Peninsula

1957 The Gambia Regiment, Royal West African Frontier Force

857. **NGAKYEDAUK PASS**
4th February–4th March 1944
Operations to Clear Arakan and Mayu
Peninsula

1956 The Wiltshire Regiment (Duke of Edinburgh's)
1957 The Somerset Light Infantry (Prince Albert's): The King's Own Scottish Borderers: The Royal Lincolnshire Regiment
1958 25th Dragoons
1962 7th Battalion, The Punjab Regiment: 4th Battalion, The Rajput Regiment: 1st Battalion, The Garhwal Rifles
1963 421 Field Company, Madras Engineer Group: 95 Field Company, Bengal Engineer Group
?   2nd Battalion, 1st Punjab Regiment: 3rd Battalion, 14th Punjab Regiment: 4th Battalion, 14th Punjab Regiment: 5th Battalion, 16th Punjab Regiment: 2nd Battalion, The Frontier Force Rifles: MG Battalion, The Frontier Force Regiment

858. **DEFENCE OF SINZWEYA**
5th–29th February 1944
Operations to Clear Arakan and Mayu
Peninsula

1957 The West Yorkshire Regiment (The Prince of Wales's Own)
1962 24 Engineer Battalion, Bombay Engineer Group

859. **IMPHAL**
12th March–22nd June 1944
Enemy Offensive Across the Chinwin

1956 3rd Carabiniers (Prince of Wales's Dragoon Guards): The Devonshire Regiment: 10th Princess Mary's Own Gurkha Rifles
1957 Seaforth Highlanders (Ross-shire Buffs, The Duke of Albany's): The West Yorkshire Regiment (The Prince of Wales's Own): The King's Own Scottish Borderers: The Border Regiment: The Northamptonshire Regiment: The Suffolk Regiment: 7th Gurkha Rifles
1962 3rd Battalion, The Punjab Regiment: 1st Battalion, 3rd Gorkha Rifles: 3rd Battalion, 3rd Gorkha Rifles: 2nd Battalion, 5th Gorkha Rifles: 3rd Battalion, 5th Gorkha Rifles: 3rd Battalion, 8th Gorkha Rifles: 4th Battalion, 8th Gorkha Rifles
1963 7th Light Cavalry
?   2nd Battalion, 1st Punjab Regiment: 3rd Battalion, 14th Punjab Regiment: 16th Punjab Regiment: 4th Battalion, The Frontier Force Regiment: 9th Battalion, The Frontier Force Regiment: 14th Battalion, The Frontier Force Rifles

860. **TUITUM**
16th–24th March 1944
Enemy Offensive Across the Chinwin

1956 10th Princess Mary's Own Gurkha Rifles
1962 1st Battalion, 3rd Gorkha Rifles

861. **SAKAWNG**
18th–25th March 1944
Enemy Offensive Across the Chinwin

1957 The Border Regiment
1962 3rd Battalion, 3rd Gorkha Rifles: 2nd Battalion, 5th Gorkha Rifles
1963 3rd Battalion, 5th Gorkha Rifles

No.	Battle Honour	Year	Units
862.	**TAMU ROAD** 12th March–4th April 1944 Enemy Offensive Across the Chinwin	1956 1957 1962 1963 ?	3rd Carabiniers (Prince of Wales's Dragoon Guards):The Devonshire Regiment: 10th Princess Mary's Own Gurkha Rifles The Border Regiment:The Northamptonshire Regiment 422 Field Company, Madras Engineer Group: 3rd Battalion, 8th Gorkha Rifles 4th Battalion, The Madras Regiment 2nd Battalion, 1st Punjab Regiment: 1st Battalion, 16th Punjab Regiment: 9th Battalion, The Frontier Force Regiment
863.	**SANGSHAK** 16th–26th March 1944 Enemy Offensive Across the Chinwin	1962	4th Battalion, The Maratha Light Infantry
864.	**SHENAM PASS** 1st April–22nd June 1944 Enemy Offensive Across the Chinwin	1956 1957 1962 ?	The Devonshire Regiment: 10th Princess Mary's Own Gurkha Rifles Seaforth Highlanders (Ross-shire Buffs, The Duke of Albany's):The Border Regiment 5th Battalion, The Rajputana Rifles: 3rd Battalion, 1st Gorkha Rifles: 3rd Battalion, 3rd Gorkha Rifles: 3rd Battalion, 5th Gorkha Rifles 5th Battalion (Pathans), 14th Punjab Regiment: 9th Battalion, The Frontier Force Regiment
865.	**NUNGSHIGUM** 5th–13th April 1944 Enemy Offensive Across the Chinwin	1956 1962 ?	3rd Carabiniers (Prince of Wales's Dragoon Guards) 3rd Battalion,The Jat Regiment: 1st Battalion, The Dogra Regiment 3rd Battalion, 14th Punjab Regiment
866.	**LITAN** 12th April–15th May 1944 Enemy Offensive Across the Chinwin	1956 1957 1962 ?	10th Princess Mary's Own Gurkha Rifles Seaforth Highlanders (Ross-shire Buffs, The Duke of Albany's) 15th Battalion, The Punjab Regiment 2nd Battalion, 1st Punjab Regiment: 1st Battalion, 16th Punjab Regiment: 14th Battalion, The Frontier Force Rifles
867.	**BISHENPUR** 14th April–22nd June 1944 Enemy Offensive Across the Chinwin	1956 1957 1962 ?	3rd Carabiniers (Prince of Wales's Dragoon Guards): 10th Princess Mary's Own Gurkha Rifles The West Yorkshire Regiment (The Prince of Wales's Own):The Northamptonshire Regiment: 7th Gurkha Rifles 60 Field Company, Madras Engineer Group: 362 Field Company, Madras Engineer Group: 2nd Battalion,The Kumaon Regiment: 3rd Battalion, 1st Gorkha Rifles: 1st Battalion, 3rd Gorkha Rifles: 1st Battalion, 4th Gorkha Rifles: 2nd Battalion, 5th Gorkha Rifles: 3rd Battalion, 8th Gorkha Rifles 5th Battalion (Pathans), 14th Punjab Regiment: 4th Battalion, The Frontier Force Regiment: 9th Battalion, The Frontier Force Regiment
868.	**KANGLATONGBI** 21st April–22nd June 1944 Enemy Offensive Across the Chinwin	1956 1957 1962 ?	3rd Carabiniers (Prince of Wales's Dragoon Guards) The West Yorkshire Regiment (The Prince of Wales's Own):The King's Own Scottish Borderers 3rd Battalion, The Punjab Regiment: 3rd Battalion,The Jat Regiment: 1st Battalion,The Sikh Regiment: 4th Battalion, 8th Gorkha Rifles 2nd Battalion, 1st Punjab Regiment: 3rd Battalion, 14th Punjab Regiment
869.	**KOHIMA** 27th March–22nd June 1944 Enemy Offensive Across the Chinwin	1956 1957 1958	The Duke of Wellington's Regiment (West Riding) The Lancashire Fusiliers:The Royal Welch Fusiliers: The Queen's Royal Regiment (West Surrey):The Dorset Regiment:The Border Regiment:The Queen's Own Cameron Highlanders:The South Lancashire Regiment (The Prince of Wales's Volunteers):The Royal Norfolk Regiment:The Royal Berkshire Regiment (Princess Charlotte of Wales's):The Essex Regiment:The Durham Light Infantry:The Manchester Regiment:The Worcestershire Regiment The Royal Scots (The Royal Regiment)

No.	Battle / Dates / Campaign	Year	Regiments
870.	**DEFENCE OF KOHIMA** 4th–18th April 1944 Enemy Offensive Across the Chinwin	1962	2nd Battalion, The Grenadiers; 5th Battalion, The Grenadiers
		1963	4th Battalion, The Rajput Regiment
		?	1st Battalion, 1st Punjab Regiment; 2nd Battalion, 1st Punjab Regiment; 4th Battalion, 14th Punjab Regiment
871.	**JESSAMI** 27th March–1st April 1944 Enemy Offensive Across the Chinwin	1957	The Queen's Own Royal West Kent Regiment
		1962	1st Battalion, The Assam Regiment
		?	1st Battalion, 1st Punjab Regiment
		1962	1st Battalion, The Assam Regiment
		?	4th Battalion, 14th Punjab Regiment
872.	**RELIEF OF KOHIMA** 5th–20th April 1944 Enemy Offensive Across the Chinwin	1957	The Queen's Own Cameron Highlanders: The Worcestershire Regiment
		1958	The Royal Scots (The Royal Regiment)
		1962	4th Battalion, The Rajput Regiment
		?	Prince Albert Victor's Own Cavalry (11th Frontier Force): 1st Battalion, 1st Punjab Regiment
873.	**JAIL HILL** 7th–13th May 1944 Enemy Offensive Across the Chinwin	1962	77 Field Company, Bengal Engineer Group
		?	1st Battalion, 1st Punjab Regiment: 4th Battalion, 15th Punjab Regiment
874.	**NAGA VILLAGE** 4th May–4th June 1944 Enemy Offensive Across the Chinwin	1957	The Lancashire Fusiliers: The Queen's Own Cameron Highlanders: The Worcestershire Regiment
		1962	2nd Battalion, The Grenadiers
		?	4th Battalion, 14th Punjab Regiment, 15th Punjab Regiment
875.	**ARADURA** 14th May–6th June 1944 Enemy Offensive Across the Chinwin	1957	The Queen's Own Cameron Highlanders: The Royal Norfolk Regiment
		1958	The Royal Scots (The Royal Regiment)
		1962	1st Battalion, The Assam Regiment
876.	**MAO SONGSANG** 15th–19th June 1944 Enemy Offensive Across the Chinwin	1957	The Royal Berkshire Regiment (Princess Charlotte of Wales's): The Worcestershire Regiment
		?	4th Battalion, 14th Punjab Regiment
877.	**UKHRUL** 24th June–20th July 1944 Enemy Retreat to the Chinwin	1956	The Devonshire Regiment
		1957	The King's Own Scottish Borderers: The Border Regiment
		1962	4th Battalion, The Madras Regiment: 3rd Battalion, 1st Gorkha Rifles
		?	2nd Battalion, 1st Punjab Regiment
878.	**TENGNOUPAL** 21st–28th July 1944 Enemy Retreat to the Chinwin	1956	10th Princess Mary's Own Gurkha Rifles
		1957	Seaforth Highlanders (Ross-shire Buffs, The Duke of Albany's)
		1962	15th Battalion, The Punjab Regiment: 4th Battalion, The Maratha Light Infantry: 6th Battalion, The Maratha Light Infantry: 5th Battalion, The Rajputana Rifles: 3rd Battalion, 3rd Gorkha Rifles
879.	**TIDDIM ROAD** 31st July–11th September 1944 Enemy Retreat to the Chinwin	1962	4th Battalion, The Rajput Regiment

No.	Battle	Year	Regiment
880.	**TONZANG** 14th–22nd September 1944 Enemy Retreat to the Chinwin	1962	3rd Battalion, The Punjab Regiment
881.	**KENNEDY PEAK** 3rd October–7th November 1944 Enemy Retreat to the Chinwin	1956 1962 ?	3rd Carabiniers (Prince of Wales's Dragoon Guards) 3rd Battalion, The Punjab Regiment: 1st Battalion, The Dogra Regiment: 4th Battalion, The Jammu & Kashmir Infantry 1st Battalion, 1st Punjab Regiment: 2nd Battalion, 1st Punjab Regiment
882.	**MAWLAIK** 28th October–10th November 1944 Enemy Retreat to the Chinwin	1957 1962	The King's African Rifles: The Northern Rhodesia Regiment 1st Battalion, The Assam Regiment
883.	**PINWE** 11th–30th November 1944 Enemy Retreat to the Chinwin	1956 1957 1958	The Royal Sussex Regiment The Gloucestershire Regiment: The East Lancashire Regiment: The Manchester Regiment The South Wales Borderers: The Royal Scots Fusiliers
884.	**KALEWA** 13th November–16th December 1944 Enemy Retreat to the Chinwin	1957 1962 ?	The King's African Rifles: The Northern Rhodesia Regiment 3rd Battalion, The Grenadiers 1st Battalion, 1st Punjab Regiment
885.	**HAKA** 9th–10th October 1944 Enemy Retreat to the Chinwin	1962	1st Battalion, The Bihar Regiment
886.	**GANGAW** 11th November 1944–10th January 1945 Enemy Retreat to the Chinwin	1962	1st Battalion, The Bihar Regiment
887.	**SHWEBO** 6th–9th January 1945 Enemy Retreat to the Chinwin	1956 1957 1958 1962 ?	3rd Carabiniers (Prince of Wales's Dragoon Guards) The Queen's Own Cameron Highlanders: 6th Gurkha Rifles: The Royal Berkshire Regiment (Princess Charlotte of Wales's): The Manchester Regiment: The Worcestershire Regiment The Royal Scots (The Royal Regiment) 4th Battalion, 4th Gorkha Rifles 5th Battalion (King George V's Own), The Baluch Regiment
888.	**MONYWA 1945** 7th–22nd January 1945 Enemy Retreat to the Chinwin	1957 ?	The Northamptonshire Regiment Prince Albert Victor's Own Cavalry (11th Frontier Force): 5th Battalion (Pathans), 14th Punjab Regiment
889.	**SHWELI** 1st January–12th February 1945 Offensive Across the Irrawaddy	1956 1957 1958 1962	The Buffs (Royal East Kent Regiment): The Royal Sussex Regiment The Gloucestershire Regiment The South Wales Borderers: The Royal Scots Fusiliers 3rd Battalion, The Parachute Regiment

890.	**THE SHWELI** 1st January–12th February 1945 Offensive Across the Irrawaddy	? 2nd Battalion, 8th Punjab Regiment
891.	**KYAUKMYAUNG BRIDGEHEAD** 9th January–12th February 1945 Offensive Across the Irrawaddy	1957 1962 ? 6th Gurkha Rifles: The Royal Berkshire Regiment (Princess Charlotte of Wales's): The Welch Regiment 7th Light Cavalry: 3rd Battalion, The Rajputana Rifles: 1st Battalion, The Assam Regiment 1st Battalion, 15th Punjab Regiment: 5th Battalion (King George V's Own), The Baluch Regiment: 8th Battalion, The Frontier Force Regiment
892.	**SAGAING** 23rd January–12th February 1945 Offensive Across the Irrawaddy	1956 3rd Carabiniers (Prince of Wales's Dragoon Guards)
893.	**MANDALAY** 12th February–21st March 1945 The Clearing of the Mandalay-Meiktila Plain	1956 1957 1958 1962 ? 3rd Carabiniers (Prince of Wales's Dragoon Guards): 10th Princess Mary's Own Gurkha Rifles The Royal Welch Fusiliers: The Dorset Regiment: The Border Regiment: The Queen's Own Cameron Highlanders: 6th Gurkha Rifles: The Royal Norfolk Regiment: The Royal Berkshire Regiment (Princess Charlotte of Wales's): The Durham Light Infantry: The Worcestershire Regiment The Royal Scots (The Royal Regiment): The Royal Scots Fusiliers 7th Light Cavalry: 3rd Battalion, The Rajputana Rifles: 4th Battalion, 4th Gorkha Rifles: 3rd Battalion, 8th Gorkha Rifles Prince Albert Victor's Own Cavalry (11th Frontier Force): 1st Battalion, 15th Punjab Regiment: 5th Battalion (King George V's Own), The Baluch Regiment: 8th Battalion, The Frontier Force Regiment: 9th Battalion, The Frontier Force Regiment: 14th Battalion, The Frontier Force Rifles
894.	**MYITSON** 13th February–9th March 1945 The Clearing of the Mandalay-Meiktila Plain	1956 1957 1958 ? The Buffs (Royal East Kent Regiment) The Gloucestershire Regiment The South Wales Borderers 2nd Battalion, 8th Punjab Regiment
895.	**AVA** 13th February–20th March 1945 The Clearing of the Mandalay-Meiktila Plain	1956 1957 1962 3rd Carabiniers (Prince of Wales's Dragoon Guards) The Royal Welch Fusiliers: The Queen's Own Cameron Highlanders 4th Battalion, The Madras Regiment
896.	**MYINMU BRIDGEHEAD** 12th February–7th March 1945 The Clearing of the Mandalay-Meiktila Plain	1956 1957 1962 ? The Devonshire Regiment: 10th Princess Mary's Own Gurkha Rifles The Border Regiment: The Northamptonshire Regiment: The Manchester Regiment 92 Field Company, Bombay Engineer Group: 3rd Battalion, 1st Gorkha Rifles: 3rd Battalion, 8th Gorkha Rifles Prince Albert Victor's Own Cavalry (11th Frontier Force): 9th Battalion, The Frontier Force Regiment: 14th Battalion, The Frontier Force Rifles
897.	**FORT DUFFERIN** 9th–20th March 1945 The Clearing of the Mandalay-Meiktila Plain	1957 1962 ? 6th Gurkha Rifles: The Royal Berkshire Regiment (Princess Charlotte of Wales's) 3rd Battalion, The Grenadiers: 3rd Battalion, The Rajputana Rifles 1st Battalion, 15th Punjab Regiment: 8th Battalion, The Frontier Force Regiment

898.	**MAYMYO** 11th–12th March 1945 The Clearing of the Mandalay-Meiktila Plain	1957	6th Gurkha Rifles: The Welch Regiment
899.	**SEIKPYU** 10th–16th February 1945 The Clearing of the Mandalay-Meiktila Plain	1957	The King's African Rifles
900.	**KYAUKSE 1945** 8th–21st March 1945 The Clearing of the Mandalay-Meiktila Plain	1956 ?	The Devonshire Regiment: 10th Princess Mary's Own Gurkha Rifles 5th Battalion (Pathans), 14th Punjab Regiment: 9th Battalion, The Frontier Force Regiment
901.	**KYAUKSE** 8th–21st March 1945 The Clearing of the Mandalay-Meiktila Plain	1962	3rd Battalion, 3rd Gorkha Rifles
902.	**MEIKTILA** 12th February–30th March 1945 The Clearing of the Mandalay-Meiktila Plain	1956 1957 1962 1963 ?	10th Princess Mary's Own Gurkha Rifles The West Yorkshire Regiment (The Prince of Wales's Own): The King's Own Scottish Borderers: The Border Regiment: The South Lancashire Regiment (The Prince of Wales's Volunteers): 7th Gurkha Rifles 16th Light Cavalry: 7th Light Cavalry: 60 Field Company, Madras Engineer Group: 84 Field Company, Bengal Engineer Group: 6th Battalion, The Rajput Regiment: 1st Battalion, 3rd Gorkha Rifles The Deccan Horse Probyn's Horse (5th King Edward VII's Own Lancers): 2nd Battalion, 1st Punjab Regiment: 4th Battalion, 15th Punjab Regiment: 9th Battalion, The Frontier Force Rifles: MG Battalion, The Frontier Force Rifles
903.	**NYAUNGU BRIDGEHEAD** 12th–21st February 1945 The Clearing of the Mandalay-Meiktila Plain	1957 1962 ?	The South Lancashire Regiment (The Prince of Wales's Volunteers) 1st Battalion, The Sikh Regiment 4th Battalion, 14th Punjab Regiment: 4th Battalion, 15th Punjab Regiment: 4th Battalion, The Frontier Force Regiment: 9th Battalion, The Frontier Force Rifles: MG Battalion, The Frontier Force Rifles
904.	**CAPTURE OF MEIKTILA** 28th February–2nd March 1945 The Clearing of the Mandalay-Meiktila Plain	1956 1957 1962 ?	10th Princess Mary's Own Gurkha Rifles The West Yorkshire Regiment (The Prince of Wales's Own): 7th Gurkha Rifles 16th Light Cavalry: The Deccan Horse: The Grenadiers: 6th Battalion, The Rajput Regiment Prince Albert Victor's Own Cavalry (11th Frontier Force): Probyn's Horse (5th King Edward VII's Own Lancers): 6th Battalion, 15th Punjab Regiment: 7th Battalion, The Baluch Regiment: 4th Battalion, The Frontier Force Regiment: 9th Battalion, The Frontier Force Rifles

No.	Battle	Year	Regiments
905.	**DEFENCE OF MEIKTILA** 3rd–29th March 1945 The Clearing of the Mandalay-Meiktila Plain	1956	10th Princess Mary's Own Gurkha Rifles
		1957	The West Yorkshire Regiment (The Prince of Wales's Own): 7th Gurkha Rifles
		1962	16th Light Cavalry: The Deccan Horse: 402 Field Company, Bombay Engineer Group: 3rd Battalion, The Punjab Regiment: 4th Battalion, The Grenadiers: 6th Battalion, The Rajput Regiment: 1st Battalion, The Sikh Light Infantry: 4th Battalion, The Jammu & Kashmir Infantry: 1st Battalion, 3rd Gorkha Rifles
		?	Probyn's Horse (5th King Edward VII's Own Lancers): 1st Battalion, 1st Punjab Regiment: 7th Battalion, The Baluch Regiment: 4th Battalion, The Frontier Force Regiment: 9th Battalion, The Frontier Force Rifles
906.	**TAUNGTHA** 24th February and 14th–28th March 1945 The Clearing of the Mandalay-Meiktila Plain	1957	The Queen's Own Royal West Kent Regiment
		1962	4th Battalion, The Grenadiers: 4th Battalion, The Rajput Regiment
		?	Probyn's Horse (5th King Edward VII's Own Lancers): 1st Battalion, 1st Punjab Regiment: 2nd Battalion, 1st Punjab Regiment: 4th Battalion, 15th Punjab Regiment: MG Battalion, The Frontier Force Rifles
907.	**MYINGYAN** 1st–5th March and 18th–23rd March 1945 The Clearing of the Mandalay-Meiktila Plain	?	4th Battalion, 15th Punjab Regiment: MG Battalion, The Frontier Force Rifles
908.	**LETSE** 23rd February–10th April 1945 The Clearing of the Mandalay-Meiktila Plain	1957 1957 ?	The South Lancashire Regiment (The Prince of Wales's Volunteers) The King's African Rifles 4th Battalion, 14th Punjab Regiment
909.	**SINGU** 18th February–20th March 1945 The Clearing of the Mandalay-Meiktila Plain	1962	4th Battalion, 8th Gorkha Rifles
910.	**IRRAWADDY** 29th March–30th May 1945 Advance through the Irrawaddy Valley	1956	3rd Carabiniers (Prince of Wales's Dragoon Guards): 10th Princess Mary's Own Gurkha Rifles
		1957	The King's Own Scottish Borderers: The Northamptonshire Regiment: The Queen's Own Cameron Highlanders: The South Lancashire Regiment (The Prince of Wales's Volunteers): The Manchester Regiment: The Worcestershire Regiment: 2nd King Edward VII's Own Gurkha Rifles (The Sirmoor Rifles)
911.	**THE IRRAWADDY** 29th March–30th May 1945 Advance through the Irrawaddy Valley	1962	1st Battalion, The Sikh Regiment: 4th Battalion, 5th Gorkha Rifles
		?	Prince Albert Victor's Own Cavalry (11th Frontier Force): 2nd Battalion, 1st Punjab Regiment: 4th Battalion, 15th Punjab Regiment: 8th Battalion, The Baluch Regiment (King George V's Own), The Baluch Regiment: 5th Battalion, The Frontier Force Regiment: 9th Battalion, The Frontier Force Regiment: 14th Battalion, The Frontier Force Regiment
912.	**MT POPA** 2nd–20th April 1945 Advance through the Irrawaddy Valley	1957 1962	The Dorset Regiment: The Queen's Own Cameron Highlanders: The Worcestershire Regiment 1st Battalion, The Madras Regiment

913. **YENANGYAUNG 1945**
18th–25th April 1945
Advance through the Irrawaddy Valley

1956	3rd Carabiniers (Prince of Wales's Dragoon Guards)
1957	The Queen's Royal Regiment (West Surrey)
?	4th Battalion, 15th Punjab Regiment: 14th Battalion, The Frontier Force Rifles

914. **MAGWE**
11th–23rd April 1945
Advance through the Irrawaddy Valley

1957	2nd King Edward VII's Own Gurkha Rifles (The Sirmoor Rifles)
1962	3rd Battalion, The Parachute Regiment: 4th Battalion, The Dogra Regiment
?	4th Battalion, 14th Punjab Regiment: 14th Battalion, The Frontier Force Rifles

915. **SHANDATGYI**
6th–13th May 1945
Advance through the Irrawaddy Valley

| 1962 | 1st Battalion, The Sikh Regiment |
| 1963 | 4th Battalion, 8th Gorkha Rifles |

916. **KAMA**
20th–30th May 1945
Advance through the Irrawaddy Valley

1957	The King's Own Scottish Borderers
1962	3rd Battalion, The Parachute Regiment: 4th Battalion, The Madras Regiment: 1st Battalion, The Sikh Regiment
?	4th Battalion, 15th Punjab Regiment: 2nd Battalion, 8th Punjab Regiment

917. **RANGOON ROAD**
1st April–6th May 1945
Advance and Capture of Rangoon

1956	The York and Lancaster Regiment: 10th Princess Mary's Own Gurkha Rifles
1957	The West Yorkshire Regiment (The Prince of Wales's Own): The Border Regiment: 6th Gurkha Rifles: 7th Gurkha Rifles: The Royal Berkshire Regiment (Princess Charlotte of Wales's): The Welch Regiment
1962	7th Light Cavalry: 6th Battalion, The Rajput Regiment: 1st Battalion, The Sikh Light Infantry: 1st Battalion, 3rd Gorkha Rifles
1963	16th Light Cavalry: The Deccan Horse
?	Prince Albert Victor's Own Cavalry (11th Frontier Force): Probyn's Horse (5th King Edward VII's Own Lancers): 19th King George V's Own Lancers: 1st Battalion, 1st Punjab Regiment: 2nd Battalion, 1st Punjab Regiment: 5th Battalion (Pathans), 14th Punjab Regiment: 4th Battalion, The Frontier Force Regiment: 8th Battalion, The Frontier Force Regiment: 9th Battalion, The Frontier Force Rifles

918. **PYAWBWE**
1st–10th April 1945
Advance and Capture of Rangoon

| 1957 | The West Yorkshire Regiment (The Prince of Wales's Own): The Border Regiment: 7th Gurkha Rifles |
| ? | Probyn's Horse (5th King Edward VII's Own Lancers): 2nd Battalion, 1st Punjab Regiment: 6th Battalion, 15th Punjab Regiment: 4th Battalion, The Frontier Force Regiment |

919. **PYABWE**
1st–10th April 1945
Advance and Capture of Rangoon

| 1962 | The Deccan Horse: 4th Battalion, The Grenadiers: 1st Battalion, The Sikh Light Infantry: 1st Battalion, 3rd Gorkha Rifles |

920. **SHWEMYO BLUFF**
12th–18th April 1945
Advance and Capture of Rangoon

| ? | 1st Battalion, 1st Punjab Regiment: 2nd Battalion, 1st Punjab Regiment |

921. **PYINMANA**
19th–20th April 1945
Advance and Capture of Rangoon

| 1962 | 3rd Battalion, The Punjab Regiment |
| ? | Probyn's Horse (5th King Edward VII's Own Lancers): 1st Battalion, 1st Punjab Regiment |

922. **TOUNGOO**
22nd April–6th May 1945
Advance and Capture of Rangoon

1956	The York and Lancaster Regiment
1957	6th Gurkha Rifles: The Royal Berkshire Regiment (Princess Charlotte of Wales's)
1962	1st Battalion, The Assam Regiment

No.	Battle Honour	Year	Regiments
923.	**PEGU 1945** 27th April–2nd May 1945 Advance and Capture of Rangoon	?	Probyn's Horse (5th King Edward VII's Own Lancers): 1st Battalion, 1st Punjab Regiment: 2nd Battalion, 1st Punjab Regiment: 1st Battalion, 15th Punjab Regiment: 8th Battalion, The Frontier Force Regiment
		1956	10th Princess Mary's Own Gurkha Rifles
		1962	16th Light Cavalry: 4th Battalion, The Grenadiers: 1st Battalion, 3rd Gorkha Rifles
		?	Probyn's Horse (5th King Edward VII's Own Lancers): 1st Battalion, 1st Punjab Regiment: 2nd Battalion, 1st Punjab Regiment: 5th Battalion (Pathans), 14th Punjab Regiment: 6th Battalion, 15th Punjab Regiment: 7th Battalion, The Baluch Regiment: 4th Battalion, The Frontier Force Regiment: 9th Battalion, The Frontier Force Rifles
924.	**SITTANG 1945** 10th May–15th August 1945 Attempted Enemy Breakout in Pegu Yomas	1956	10th Princess Mary's Own Gurkha Rifles
		1957	The Queen's Royal Regiment (West Surrey): The West Yorkshire Regiment (The Prince of Wales's Own): The Queen's Own Royal West Kent Regiment: The Border Regiment: 6th Gurkha Rifles: The Welch Regiment: The East Yorkshire Regiment (The Duke of York's Own): 2nd King Edward VII's Own Gurkha Rifles (The Sirmoor Rifles)
		1962	16th Light Cavalry: 8th Light Cavalry: 3rd Battalion, The Parachute Regiment: 4th Battalion, The Rajput Regiment: 1st Battalion, The Sikh Regiment: 1st Battalion, The Sikh Light Infantry: 4th Battalion, 5th Gorkha Rifles: 4th Battalion, 8th Gorkha Rifles:
		1963	5th Battalion, 5th Gorkha Rifles
		?	1st Battalion, 1st Punjab Regiment: 4th Battalion, 14th Punjab Regiment: 15th Punjab Regiment: 6th Battalion, 15th Punjab Regiment: 5th Battalion (King George V's Own), The Baluch Regiment: 7th Battalion, The Baluch Regiment: 4th Battalion, The Frontier Force Regiment: 8th Battalion, The Frontier Force Regiment: 14th Battalion, The Frontier Force Rifles: 9th Battalion, The Frontier Force Rifles: MG Battalion, The Frontier Force Rifles
925.	**POINT 1433** 8th–12th September 1944 Operations in Arakan by 15th Corps	1957	2nd King Edward VII's Own Gurkha Rifles (The Sirmoor Rifles)
926.	**TINMA** 14th–16th December 1944 Operations in Arakan by 15th Corps	1957	The Gold Coast Regiment, Royal West African Frontier Force
927.	**MAYU VALLEY** 11th–31st December 1944 Operations in Arakan by 15th Corps	1957	The Queen's Own Nigeria Regiment, Royal West African Frontier Force: The Gold Coast Regiment, Royal West African Frontier Force
		?	19th King George V's Own Lancers
928.	**MYOHAUNG** 15th–25th January 1945 Operations in Arakan by 15th Corps	1957	The Queen's Own Nigeria Regiment, Royal West African Frontier Force: The Gold Coast Regiment, Royal West African Frontier Force: The Sierra Leone Regiment, Royal West African Frontier Force: The Gambia Regiment, Royal West African Frontier Force
929.	**ARAKAN BEACHES** 12th January–29th April 1945 Operations in Arakan by 15th Corps	1956	The York and Lancaster Regiment
		1957	The Oxfordshire and Buckinghamshire Light Infantry: The Green Howards (Alexandra, Princess of Wales's Own Yorkshire Regiment): 2nd King Edward VII's Own Gurkha Rifles (The Sirmoor Rifles)
		1957	The King's African Rifles: The Rhodesian African Rifles: The Northern Rhodesia Regiment: The Queen's Own Nigeria Regiment, Royal West African Frontier Force: The Gold Coast Regiment, Royal West African Frontier Force
		?	7th Battalion, 16th Punjab Regiment: 2nd Battalion, The Frontier Force Rifles: 15th Battalion, The Frontier Force Rifles: MG Battalion, The Frontier Force Regiment: 8th Battalion, The Frontier Force Rifles

No.	Battle	Year	Regiments
930.	**MYEBON** 12th–21st January 1945 Operations in Arakan by 15th Corps	1957 ?	The Commando Association: 2nd King Edward VII's Own Gurkha Rifles (The Sirmoor Rifles) 19th King George V's Own Lancers: 2nd Battalion, The Frontier Force Rifles: 15th Battalion, The Frontier Force Rifles
931.	**RAMREE** 21st January–15th February 1945 Operations in Arakan by 15th Corps	1957 1962 ?	The Royal Lincolnshire Regiment 1st Battalion, The Garhwal Rifles 5th Battalion, 1st Punjab Regiment: 2nd Battalion, The Frontier Force Rifles: MG Battalion, The Frontier Force Regiment: 8th Battalion, The Frontier Force Rifles
932.	**KANGAW** 23rd January–17th February 1945 Operations in Arakan by 15th Corps	1957 1957 1962 ?	The Commando Association The Queen's Own Nigeria Regiment, Royal West African Frontier Force: The Gold Coast Regiment, Royal West African Frontier Force 1st Battalion, The Brigade of the Guards: 4th Battalion, The Kumaon Regiment 19th King George V's Own Lancers
933.	**RU-YWA** 17th–23rd February 1945 Operations in Arakan by 15th Corps	1962 ?	17th Battalion, The Maratha Light Infantry 19th King George V's Own Lancers
934.	**DALET** 27th February–4th March 1945 Operations in Arakan by 15th Corps	1957 ?	The Queen's Own Nigeria Regiment, Royal West African Frontier Force 19th King George V's Own Lancers
935.	**TAMANDU** 27th February–11th March 1945 Operations in Arakan by 15th Corps	1957 1957 ?	The Oxfordshire and Buckinghamshire Light Infantry: 2nd King Edward VII's Own Gurkha Rifles (The Sirmoor Rifles) The Queen's Own Nigeria Regiment, Royal West African Frontier Force 19th King George V's Own Lancers
936.	**TAUNGUP** 3rd–29th April 1945 Operations in Arakan by 15th Corps	1957 1962 ?	The King's African Rifles: The Rhodesian African Rifles: The Northern Rhodesia Regiment: The Gold Coast Regiment, Royal West African Frontier Force 1st Battalion, The Garhwal Rifles MG Battalion, The Frontier Force Regiment
937.	**CHINDITS 1943** January–June 1943 1st Wingate Expedition	1957	The King's Regiment (Liverpool): 2nd King Edward VII's Own Gurkha Rifles (The Sirmoor Rifles)
938.	**CHINDITS 1944** February–August 1944 2nd Wingate Expedition	1956 1957 1957 1958 1962 1963	The Duke of Wellington's Regiment (West Riding): The Royal Leicestershire Regiment: The York and Lancaster Regiment: The Cameronians (Scottish Rifles) The King's Regiment (Liverpool): The Lancashire Fusiliers: The Queen's Royal Regiment (West Surrey): The Bedfordshire and Hertfordshire Regiment: The Border Regiment: 6th Gurkha Rifles: The King's Own Royal Regiment (Lancaster): The Black Watch (Royal Highland Regiment): The Essex Regiment The Queen's Own Nigeria Regiment, Royal West African Frontier Force The South Staffordshire Regiment 3rd Battalion, 4th Gorkha Rifles: 3rd Battalion, 9th Gorkha Rifles: 4th Battalion, 9th Gorkha Rifles 5th Battalion, 5th Gorkha Rifles

939. **BURMA 1942**
20th January–31st December 1942
Service in Burma 1942–45

1956   7th Queen's Own Hussars; The Cameronians (Scottish Rifles)
1957   The Gloucestershire Regiment; The King's Own Yorkshire Light Infantry
1958   Royal Tank Regiment

940. **BURMA 1942–43**
20th January 1942–31st December 1943
Service in Burma 1942–45

1957   The Royal Inniskilling Fusiliers

941. **BURMA 1942–44**
20th January 1942–31st December 1944
Service in Burma 1942–45

1956   The Duke of Wellington's Regiment (West Riding)
1957   Seaforth Highlanders (Ross-shire Buffs, The Duke of Albany's)

942. **BURMA 1942–45**
20th January 1942–15th August 1945
Service in Burma 1942–45

1956   10th Princess Mary's Own Gurkha Rifles
1957   The West Yorkshire Regiment (The Prince of Wales's Own); 7th Gurkha Rifles; The Royal Berkshire Regiment (Princess Charlotte of Wales's)
1962   16th Light Cavalry; 7th Light Cavalry; 8th Light Cavalry; The Deccan Horse: 36 Field Squadron, Madras Engineer Group: 60 Field Company, Madras Engineer Group: 62 Field Company, Madras Engineer Group: 63 Field Company, Madras Engineer Group: 362 Field Company, Madras Engineer Group: 422 Field Company, Madras Engineer Group: 424 Field Company, Madras Engineer Group: 425 Field Company, Madras Engineer Group: 428 Field Company, Madras Engineer Group: 429 Field Company, Madras Engineer Group: 23 Engineer Battalion, Bengal Engineer Group: 67 Field Company, Bengal Engineer Group: 72 Field Company, Bengal Engineer Group: 73 Field Company, Bengal Engineer Group: 74 Field Company, Bengal Engineer Group: 75 Field Company, Bengal Engineer Group: 76 Field Company, Bengal Engineer Group: 77 Field Company, Bengal Engineer Group: 80 Field Company, Bengal Engineer Group: 81 Field Company, Bengal Engineer Group: 84 Field Company, Bengal Engineer Group: 368 Field Company, Bengal Engineer Group: 369 Field Company, Bengal Engineer Group: 24 Engineer Battalion, Bombay Engineer Group: 401 Indian Field Squadron, Bombay Engineer Group: 92 Field Company, Bombay Engineer Group: 402 Field Company, Bombay Engineer Group: 481 Field Company, Bombay Engineer Group: 1st Battalion, The Brigade of the Guards: 4th Battalion, The Brigade of the Guards: 3rd Battalion, The Parachute Regiment: 3rd Battalion, The Punjab Regiment: 7th Battalion, The Punjab Regiment: 15th Battalion, The Punjab Regiment: 1st Battalion, The Madras Regiment: 4th Battalion, The Madras Regiment: 2nd Battalion, The Grenadiers: 3rd Battalion, The Grenadiers: 4th Battalion, The Grenadiers: 5th Battalion, The Grenadiers: 4th Battalion, The Maratha Light Infantry: 6th Battalion, The Maratha Light Infantry: 7th Battalion, The Maratha Light Infantry: 3rd Battalion, The Rajputana Rifles: 5th Battalion, The Rajputana Rifles: 8th Battalion, The Rajputana Rifles: 2nd Battalion, The Rajput Regiment: 4th Battalion, The Rajput Regiment: 6th Battalion, The Rajput Regiment: 17th Battalion, The Rajput Regiment: 1st Battalion, The Jat Regiment: 3rd Battalion, The Jat Regiment: 5th Battalion, The Jat Regiment: 6th Battalion, The Jat Regiment: MG Battalion, The Jat Regiment: 1st Battalion, The Sikh Regiment: 1st Battalion, The Dogra Regiment: 4th Battalion, The Dogra Regiment: 1st Battalion, The Garhwal Rifles: 2nd Battalion, The Kumaon Regiment: 4th Battalion, The Kumaon Regiment: 1st Battalion, The Sikh Light Infantry: 1st Battalion, The Bihar Regiment: 4th Battalion, Jammu & Kashmir Infantry: 3rd Battalion, 1st Gorkha Rifles: 1st Battalion, 3rd Gorkha Rifles: 3rd Battalion, 3rd Gorkha Rifles: 1st Battalion, 4th Gorkha Rifles: 3rd Battalion, 4th Gorkha Rifles: 4th Battalion, 4th Gorkha Rifles: 2nd Battalion, 5th Gorkha Rifles: 3rd Battalion, 5th Gorkha Rifles: 4th Battalion, 5th Gorkha Rifles: 1st Battalion, 8th Gorkha Rifles: 3rd Battalion, 8th Gorkha Rifles: 4th Battalion, 8th Gorkha Rifles: 3rd Battalion, 9th Gorkha Rifles: 4th Battalion, 9th Gorkha Rifles
1963   58 Field Company, Madras Engineer Group: 421 Field Company, Madras Engineer Group: 95 Field Company, Bengal Engineer Group: 5th Battalion, 5th Gorkha Rifles: 5th Battalion, 8th Gorkha Rifles
?   Prince Albert Victor's Own Cavalry (11th Frontier Force); Probyn's Horse (5th King Edward VII's Own Lancers): 19th King

943. **BURMA 1943**
1st January–31st December 1943
Service in Burma 1942–45

George V's Own Lancers: 1st Battalion, 1st Punjab Regiment: 2nd Battalion, 1st Punjab Regiment: 5th Battalion, 1st Punjab Regiment: 3rd Battalion, 14th Punjab Regiment: 4th Battalion, 14th Punjab Regiment: 1st Battalion, 15th Punjab Regiment: 4th Battalion, 15th Punjab Regiment: 1st Battalion, 16th Punjab Regiment: 5th Battalion (Pathans), 14th Punjab Regiment: 7th Battalion, 16th Punjab Regiment: 6th Battalion, 15th Punjab Regiment: 7th Battalion, 15th Punjab Regiment: 9th Battalion, 15th Punjab Regiment: 5th Battalion, 16th Punjab Regiment: 2nd Battalion, 8th Punjab Regiment: 5th Battalion (Burma), 8th Punjab Regiment: 5th Battalion (King George V's Own), The Baluch Regiment: 6th Battalion, The Baluch Regiment: 7th Battalion, The Baluch Regiment: 8th Battalion, The Baluch Regiment: 8th Punjab Regiment: 4th Battalion, The Frontier Force Regiment: 2nd Battalion, The Frontier Force Rifles: 14th Battalion, The Frontier Force Regiment: 15th Battalion, The Frontier Force Rifles: 8th Battalion, The Frontier Force Regiment: 9th Battalion, The Frontier Force Regiment: 14th Battalion, The Frontier Force Rifles: MG Battalion, The Frontier Force Regiment: 8th Battalion, The Frontier Force Rifles: 9th Battalion, The Frontier Force Rifles: MG Battalion, The Frontier Force Rifles

1957 The King's Own Scottish Borderers: The North Staffordshire Regiment (The Prince of Wales's)

944. **BURMA 1943–44**
1st January 1943–31st December 1944
Service in Burma 1942–45

1956 The Wiltshire Regiment (Duke of Edinburgh's)
1957 The King's Regiment (Liverpool)

945. **BURMA 1943–45**
1st January 1943–15th August 1945
Service in Burma 1942–45

1956 The York and Lancaster Regiment: The Devonshire Regiment: The Royal Sussex Regiment
1957 The Lancashire Fusiliers: The Royal Welch Fusiliers: The Oxfordshire and Buckinghamshire Light Infantry: The Queen's Royal Regiment (West Surrey): The Somerset Light Infantry (Prince Albert's): The Queen's Own Royal West Kent Regiment: The Border Regiment: The Northamptonshire Regiment: The Suffolk Regiment: The South Lancashire Regiment (The Prince of Wales's Volunteers): The Royal Lincolnshire Regiment: The Essex Regiment: The Durham Light Infantry: 2nd King Edward VII's Own Gurkha Rifles (The Sirmoor Rifles)

1957 The Queen's Own Nigeria Regiment, Royal West African Frontier Force: The Gold Coast Regiment, Royal West African Frontier Force: The Sierra Leone Regiment, Royal West African Frontier Force: The Gambia Regiment, Royal West African Frontier Force: The Royal Scots (The Royal Regiment)

1958 The Royal Scots (The Royal Regiment)

946. **BURMA 1944**
1st January–31st December 1944
Service in Burma 1942–45

1956 The Cameronians (Scottish Rifles)
1957 The Bedfordshire and Hertfordshire Regiment: The King's Own Royal Regiment (Lancaster): The Black Watch (Royal Highland Regiment)
1958 The South Staffordshire Regiment

947. **BURMA 1944–45**
1st January 1944–15th August 1945
Service in Burma 1942–45

1956 3rd Carabiniers (Prince of Wales's Dragoon Guards)
1957 The Gloucestershire Regiment: The East Lancashire Regiment: The Dorset Regiment: The Queen's Own Cameron Highlanders: 6th Gurkha Rifles: The Royal Norfolk Regiment: The Welch Regiment: The Manchester Regiment: The Commando Association: The Worcestershire Regiment

1957 The King's African Rifles: The Rhodesian African Rifles: The Northern Rhodesia Regiment
1958 25th Dragoons: The South Wales Borderers: The Royal Scots Fusiliers

948.	**BURMA 1945** 1st January–15th August 1945 Service in Burma 1942–45	1956 1957	The Buffs (Royal East Kent Regiment) The Royal Warwickshire Regiment; The Green Howards (Alexandra, Princess of Wales's Own Yorkshire Regiment); The King's Own Scottish Borderers; The East Yorkshire Regiment (The Duke of York's Own)
949.	**KOEPANG** 20th–23rd February 1942 Operations in the Outer Islands	1961	40th Infantry Battalion (The Derwent Regiment)
950.	**AMBON** 30th January–3rd February 1942 Operations in the Outer Islands	1961	21st Infantry Battalion (The Victorian Rangers)
951.	**LAHA** 30th January–3rd February 1942 Operations in the Outer Islands	1961	21st Infantry Battalion (The Victorian Rangers)
952.	**RABAUL** 23rd January 1942 Operations in the Outer Islands	1961	22nd Infantry Battalion (The Richmond Regiment); Papuan and New Guinea Volunteer Rifles
953.	**JAVA 1942** 28th February–12th March 1942 Operations in the Outer Islands	1961	3rd Machine Gun Battalion; 2nd Pioneer Battalion
954.	**KOKODA TRAIL** 22nd July–13th November 1942 Operations in Papua	1961	Pacific Islands Regiment; 1st Infantry Battalion (Commando) (City of Sydney's Own Regiment); 2nd Infantry Battalion (City of Newcastle Regiment); 3rd Infantry Battalion (The Werriwa Regiment); 14th Infantry Battalion (The Prahran Regiment); 16th Infantry Battalion (The Cameron Highlanders of West Australia); 25th Infantry Battalion (The Darling Downs Regiment); 27th Infantry Battalion (The South Australian Scottish Regiment); 31st Infantry Battalion (The Kennedy Regiment); 33rd Infantry Battalion (The New England Regiment); 39th Infantry Battalion (The Hawthorn-Kew Regiment)
955.	**KOKODA-DENIKI** 25th July–14th August 1942 Operations in Papua	1961	Pacific Islands Regiment; 39th Infantry Battalion (The Hawthorn-Kew Regiment)
956.	**ISURAVA** 15th–30th August 1942 Operations in Papua	1961	14th Infantry Battalion (The Prahran Regiment); 16th Infantry Battalion (The Cameron Highlanders of West Australia); 39th Infantry Battalion (The Hawthorn-Kew Regiment)
957.	**EORA CREEK-TEMPLETON'S CROSSING I** 31st August–5th September 1942 Operations in Papua	1961	14th Infantry Battalion (The Prahran Regiment); 16th Infantry Battalion (The Cameron Highlanders of West Australia); 39th Infantry Battalion (The Hawthorn-Kew Regiment)
958.	**EFOGI-MENARI** 6th–9th September 1942 Operations in Papua	1961	14th Infantry Battalion (The Prahran Regiment); 16th Infantry Battalion (The Cameron Highlanders of West Australia); 27th Infantry Battalion (The South Australian Scottish Regiment)

959.	**IORIBAIWA** 10th–28th September 1942 Operations in Papua	1961	3rd Infantry Battalion (The Werriwa Regiment): 14th Infantry Battalion (The Prahran Regiment): 16th Infantry Battalion (The Cameron Highlanders of West Australia): 25th Infantry Battalion (The Darling Downs Regiment): 31st Infantry Battalion (The Kennedy Regiment): 33rd Infantry Battalion (The New England Regiment)
960.	**EORA CREEK-TEMPLETON'S CROSSING II** 8th–30th October 1942 Operations in Papua	1961	1st Infantry Battalion (Commando) (City of Sydney's Own Regiment): 2nd Infantry Battalion (City of Newcastle Regiment): 3rd Infantry Battalion (The Werriwa Regiment): 25th Infantry Battalion (The Darling Downs Regiment): 31st Infantry Battalion (The Kennedy Regiment): 33rd Infantry Battalion (The New England Regiment)
961.	**OIVI-GORARI** 4th–13th November 1942 Operations in Papua	1961	1st Infantry Battalion (Commando) (City of Sydney's Own Regiment): 2nd Infantry Battalion (City of Newcastle Regiment): 3rd Infantry Battalion (The Werriwa Regiment): 25th Infantry Battalion (The Darling Downs Regiment): 31st Infantry Battalion (The Kennedy Regiment): 33rd Infantry Battalion (The New England Regiment)
962.	**BUNA-GONA** 16th November 1942–22nd January 1943 Operations in Papua	1961 1963	7th Cavalry (Commando) Regiment: 1st Infantry Battalion (Commando) (City of Sydney's Own Regiment): 2nd Infantry Battalion (City of Newcastle Regiment): 3rd Infantry Battalion (The Werriwa Regiment): 9th Infantry Battalion (The Moreton Regiment): 10th Infantry Battalion (The Adelaide Rifles): 12th Infantry Battalion (The Launceston Regiment): 14th Infantry Battalion (The Prahran Regiment): 16th Infantry Battalion (The Cameron Highlanders of West Australia): 27th Infantry Battalion (The South Australian Scottish Regiment): 31st Infantry Battalion (The Kennedy Regiment): 33rd Infantry Battalion (The New England Regiment): 36th Infantry Battalion (The St George's English Rifle Regiment): 39th Infantry Battalion (The Hawthorn-Kew Regiment): 49th Infantry Battalion (The Stanley Regiment): 53rd Infantry Battalion (The West Sydney Regiment): 6th New South Wales Mounted Rifles 55th Infantry Battalion (The New South Wales Rifle Regiment)
963.	**GONA** 19th November–9th December 1942 Operations in Papua	1961	3rd Infantry Battalion (The Werriwa Regiment): 14th Infantry Battalion (The Prahran Regiment): 16th Infantry Battalion (The Cameron Highlanders of West Australia): 25th Infantry Battalion (The Darling Downs Regiment): 27th Infantry Battalion (The South Australian Scottish Regiment): 31st Infantry Battalion (The Kennedy Regiment): 33rd Infantry Battalion (The New England Regiment): 39th Infantry Battalion (The Hawthorn-Kew Regiment)
964.	**SANANANDA ROAD** 19th November 1942–14th January 1943 Operations in Papua	1961 1963	7th Cavalry (Commando) Regiment: 1st Infantry Battalion (Commando) (City of Sydney's Own Regiment): 2nd Infantry Battalion (City of Newcastle Regiment): 3rd Infantry Battalion (The Werriwa Regiment): 12th Infantry Battalion (The Launceston Regiment): 36th Infantry Battalion (The St George's English Rifle Regiment): 39th Infantry Battalion (The Hawthorn-Kew Regiment): 49th Infantry Battalion (The Stanley Regiment): 53rd Infantry Battalion (The West Sydney Regiment) 55th Infantry Battalion (The New South Wales Rifle Regiment)
965.	**AMBOGA RIVER** 10th–21st December 1942 Operations in Papua	1961	14th Infantry Battalion (The Prahran Regiment): 39th Infantry Battalion (The Hawthorn-Kew Regiment)
966.	**CAPE ENDAIADERE-SINEMI CREEK** 18th December 1942–2nd January 1943 Operations in Papua	1961	9th Infantry Battalion (The Moreton Regiment): 10th Infantry Battalion (The Adelaide Rifles): 12th Infantry Battalion (The Launceston Regiment): 6th New South Wales Mounted Rifles
967.	**SANANANDA-CAPE KILLERTON** 15th–22nd January 1943 Operations in Papua	1961	9th Infantry Battalion (The Moreton Regiment): 10th Infantry Battalion (The Adelaide Rifles): 12th Infantry Battalion (The Launceston Regiment)

No.	Honour	Year	Units
968.	**MILNE BAY** 26th August–7th September 1942 Operations in Papua	1961	9th Infantry Battalion (The Moreton Regiment); 10th Infantry Battalion (The Adelaide Rifles); 12th Infantry Battalion (The Launceston Regiment); 25th Infantry Battalion (The Darling Downs Regiment); 61st Infantry Battalion (The Queensland Cameron Highlanders)
969.	**GOODENOUGH ISLAND** 22nd–26th October 1942 Operations in Papua	1961	12th Infantry Battalion (The Launceston Regiment)
970.	**WAU** 8th March 1942–26th February 1943 Operations in Wau-Salamaua	1961	5th Infantry Battalion (The Victorian Scottish Regiment); 6th Infantry Battalion (The Royal Melbourne Regiment); 7th Infantry Battalion; Papuan and New Guinea Volunteer Rifles
971.	**MUBO I** 22nd April–29th May 1943 Operations in Wau-Salamaua	1961	7th Infantry Battalion
972.	**BOBDUBI I** 22nd April–29th May 1943 Operations in Wau-Salamaua	1961	24th Infantry Battalion (The Kooyong Regiment)
973.	**LABABIA RIDGE** 20th–23rd June 1943 Operations in Wau-Salamaua	1961	6th Infantry Battalion (The Royal Melbourne Regiment)
974.	**BOBDUBI II** 30th June–19th August 1943 Operations in Wau-Salamaua	1961	5th Infantry Battalion (The Victorian Scottish Regiment); 6th Infantry Battalion (The Royal Melbourne Regiment); 7th Infantry Battalion; 24th Infantry Battalion (The Kooyong Regiment); 58th Infantry Battalion; 59th Infantry Battalion (The Hume Regiment)
975.	**NASSAU BAY** 30th June–4th July 1943 Operations in Wau-Salamaua	1961	Pacific Islands Regiment
976.	**MUBO II** 7th–14th July 1943 Operations in Wau-Salamaua	1961	5th Infantry Battalion (The Victorian Scottish Regiment); 6th Infantry Battalion (The Royal Melbourne Regiment)
977.	**MOUNT TAMBU** 16th July–19th August 1943 Operations in Wau-Salamaua	1961	5th Infantry Battalion (The Victorian Scottish Regiment); 42nd Infantry Battalion (The Capricornia Regiment)
978.	**TAMBU BAY** 17th July–29th August 1943 Operations in Wau-Salamaua	1961	Pacific Islands Regiment; 15th Infantry Battalion (The Oxley Regiment); 42nd Infantry Battalion (The Capricornia Regiment); 47th Infantry Battalion (The Wide Bay Regiment)
979.	**KOMIATUM** 16th–21st August 1943 Operations in Wau-Salamaua	1961	5th Infantry Battalion (The Victorian Scottish Regiment); 6th Infantry Battalion (The Royal Melbourne Regiment); 7th Infantry Battalion; 42nd Infantry Battalion (The Capricornia Regiment); 58th Infantry Battalion; 59th Infantry Battalion (The Hume Regiment)

980.	**LAE-NADZAB** 4th–16th September 1943 Operations in New Guinea	1961	13th Infantry Battalion (The Macquarie Regiment); 14th Infantry Battalion (The Oxley Regiment); 17th Infantry Battalion (The City of Geelong Regiment); 24th Infantry Battalion (The Kooyong Regiment); 25th Infantry Battalion (The Darling Downs Regiment); 28th Infantry Battalion (The Swan Regiment);31st Infantry Battalion (The Kennedy Regiment);33rd Infantry Battalion (The New England Regiment);43rd Infantry Battalion: 48th Infantry Battalion: 32nd Infantry Battalion: 2nd Machine Gun Battalion: 2nd Pioneer Battalion
981.	**BUSU RIVER** 8th–12th September 1943 Operations in New Guinea	1961	23rd Infantry Battalion (The City of Geelong Regiment); 24th Infantry Battalion (The Kooyong Regiment); 28th Infantry Battalion (The Swan Regiment): 43rd Infantry Battalion
982.	**LAE ROAD** 11th–15th September 1943 Operations in New Guinea	1961	24th Infantry Battalion (The Kooyong Regiment);25th Infantry Battalion (The Darling Downs Regiment); 31st Infantry Battalion (The Kennedy Regiment); 33rd Infantry Battalion (The New England Regiment); 2nd Pioneer Battalion
983.	**FINSCHHAFEN** 22nd September–8th December 1943 Operations in New Guinea	1961	1st Royal New South Wales Lancers: Pacific Islands Regiment: 13th Infantry Battalion (The Macquarie Regiment): 15th Infantry Battalion (The Oxley Regiment): 17th Infantry Battalion: 22nd Infantry Battalion (The Richmond Regiment): 23rd Infantry Battalion (The City of Geelong Regiment): 24th Infantry Battalion (The Kooyong Regiment): 28th Infantry Battalion (The Swan Regiment): 43rd Infantry Battalion: 48th Infantry Battalion: 32nd Infantry Battalion: 2nd Machine Gun Battalion: 3rd Pioneer Battalion
984.	**SCARLET BEACH** 22nd September 1943 Operations in New Guinea	1961	Pacific Islands Regiment: 13th Infantry Battalion (The Macquarie Regiment); 15th Infantry Battalion (The Oxley Regiment): 17th Infantry Battalion
985.	**BUMI RIVER** 23rd–24th September 1943 Operations in New Guinea	1961	13th Infantry Battalion (The Macquarie Regiment): 15th Infantry Battalion (The Oxley Regiment)
986.	**DEFENCE OF SCARLET BEACH** 16th–28th October 1943 Operations in New Guinea	1961	13th Infantry Battalion (The Macquarie Regiment); 15th Infantry Battalion (The Oxley Regiment); 17th Infantry Battalion: 28th Infantry Battalion (The Swan Regiment): 43rd Infantry Battalion: 48th Infantry Battalion: 32nd Infantry Battalion: 3rd Pioneer Battalion
987.	**JIVENANENG-KUMAWA** 3rd October–3rd November 1943 Operations in New Guinea	1961	13th Infantry Battalion (The Macquarie Regiment): 17th Infantry Battalion
988.	**SIKI COVE** 18th–22nd October 1943 Operations in New Guinea	1961	28th Infantry Battalion (The Swan Regiment): 3rd Pioneer Battalion
989.	**SATTELBERG** 17th–25th November 1943 Operations in New Guinea	1961	1st Royal New South Wales Lancers: 23rd Infantry Battalion (The City of Geelong Regiment); 24th Infantry Battalion (The Kooyong Regiment): 48th Infantry Battalion: 2nd Machine Gun Battalion

990.	**PABU** 19th–26th November 1943 Operations in New Guinea	1961	43rd Infantry Battalion: 32nd Infantry Battalion
991.	**GUSIKA** 29th November 1943 Operations in New Guinea	1961	28th Infantry Battalion (The Swan Regiment)
992.	**WAREO** 1st–8th December 1943 Operations in New Guinea	1961	1st Royal New South Wales Lancers: 23rd Infantry Battalion (The City of Geelong Regiment); 24th Infantry Battalion (The Kooyong Regiment)
993.	**NONGORA** 2nd December 1943 Operations in New Guinea	1961	15th Infantry Battalion (The Oxley Regiment)
994.	**LIBERATION OF AUSTRALIAN NEW GUINEA** 18th September 1943–8th August 1945 Operations in Markham-Ramu Valleys and the Finisterres	1961	6th Cavalry (Commando) Regiment: 1st Royal New South Wales Lancers: 4th Prince of Wales Light Horse: Pacific Islands Regiment: 1st Infantry Battalion (Commando) (City of Sydney's Own Regiment): 2nd Infantry Battalion (City of New-castle Regiment): 3rd Infantry Battalion (The Werriwa Regiment): 4th Infantry Battalion (Australian Rifles): 5th Infantry Battalion (The Victorian Scottish Regiment): 6th Infantry Battalion (The Royal Melbourne Regiment): 8th Infantry Battalion: 7th Infantry Battalion: 9th Infantry Battalion (The Moreton Regiment): 10th Infantry Battalion (The Adelaide Rifles): 11th Infantry Battalion: 12th Infantry Battalion (The Launceston Regiment): 13th Infantry Battalion (The Macquarie Regiment): 14th Infantry Battalion (The Prahran Regiment): 15th Infantry Battalion (The Oxley Regiment): 16th Infantry Battalion (The Cameron Highlanders of West Australia): 17th Infantry Battalion: 19th Infantry Battalion (The South Sydney Regiment): 22nd Infantry Battalion (The Richmond Regiment): 24th Infantry Battalion (The Kooyong Regiment): 25th Infantry Battalion (The Darling Downs Regiment): 26th Infantry Battalion (The Logan and Albert Regiment): 27th Infantry Battalion (The South Australian Scottish Regiment): 29th Infantry Battalion (The East Melbourne Regiment): 30th Infantry Battalion (The New South Wales Scottish Regiment): 31st Infantry Battalion (The Kennedy Regiment): 33rd Infantry Battalion (The New England Regiment): 35th Infantry Battalion (Newcastle's Own Regiment): 36th Infantry Battalion (The St George's English Rifle Regiment): 52nd Infantry Battalion (The Gippsland Regiment): 42nd Infantry Battalion (The Capricornia Regiment): 46th Infantry Battalion (The Brighton Rifles): 47th Infantry Battalion (The Wide Bay Regiment): 51st Infantry Battalion (The Far North Queensland Regiment): 53rd Infantry Battalion (The West Sydney Regiment): 60th Infantry Battalion (The Heidelberg Regiment): 58th Infantry Battalion: 32nd Infantry Battalion: 59th Infantry Battalion (The Hume Regiment): 61st Infantry Battalion (The Queensland Cameron Highlanders): 3rd Machine Gun Battalion: 2nd Pioneer Battalion
		1963	37th Infantry Battalion (The Henty Regiment): 55th Infantry Battalion (The New South Wales Rifle Regiment): 57th Infantry Battalion (The Merri Regiment)
995.	**RAMU VALLEY** 21st September–5th October 1943 Operations in Markham-Ramu Valleys and the Finisterres	1961	14th Infantry Battalion (The Prahran Regiment): 16th Infantry Battalion (The Cameron Highlanders of West Australia): 25th Infantry Battalion (The Darling Downs Regiment): 27th Infantry Battalion (The South Australian Scottish Regiment): 31st Infantry Battalion (The Kennedy Regiment): 33rd Infantry Battalion (The New England Regiment): 2nd Pioneer Battalion

		Year	Units
996.	**SHAGGY RIDGE** 6th October 1943–31st January 1944 Operations in Markham-Ramu Valleys and the Finisterres	1961	9th Infantry Battalion (The Moreton Regiment); 10th Infantry Battalion (The Adelaide Rifles); 12th Infantry Battalion (The Launceston Regiment); 14th Infantry Battalion (The Prahran Regiment); 16th Infantry Battalion (The Cameron Highlanders of West Australia); 25th Infantry Battalion (The Darling Downs Regiment); 27th Infantry Battalion (The South Australian Scottish Regiment); 31st Infantry Battalion (The Kennedy Regiment); 33rd Infantry Battalion (The New England Regiment); 2nd Pioneer Battalion
997.	**FINISTERRES** 1st–28th February 1944 Operations in Markham-Ramu Valleys and the Finisterres	1961	9th Infantry Battalion (The Moreton Regiment); 12th Infantry Battalion (The Launceston Regiment); 24th Infantry Battalion (The Kooyong Regiment); 60th Infantry Battalion (The Heidelberg Regiment); 58th Infantry Battalion: 59th Infantry Battalion (The Hume Regiment)
		1963	57th Infantry Battalion (The Merri Regiment)
998.	**BARUM** 18th March 1944 Operations in Markham-Ramu Valleys and the Finisterres	1961	58th Infantry Battalion: 59th Infantry Battalion (The Hume Regiment)
999.	**BOGADJIM** 13th April 1944 Operations in Markham-Ramu Valleys and the Finisterres	1961	60th Infantry Battalion (The Heidelberg Regiment)
		1963	57th Infantry Battalion (The Merri Regiment)
1000.	**MADANG** 24th April 1944 Operations in Markham-Ramu Valleys and the Finisterres	1961	30th Infantry Battalion (The New South Wales Scottish Regiment)
1001.	**KALUENG RIVER** 3rd December 1943 The Coastal Advance	1961	22nd Infantry Battalion (The Richmond Regiment)
1002.	**WAREO-LAKONA** 9th–17th December 1943 The Coastal Advance	1961	1st Royal New South Wales Lancers: 22nd Infantry Battalion (The Richmond Regiment); 24th Infantry Battalion (The Kooyong Regiment)
1003.	**GUSIKA-FORTIFICATION POINT** 3rd–20th December 1943 The Coastal Advance	1961	1st Royal New South Wales Lancers: 22nd Infantry Battalion (The Richmond Regiment); 29th Infantry Battalion (The East Melbourne Regiment); 52nd Infantry Battalion (The Gippsland Regiment); 46th Infantry Battalion (The Brighton Rifles)
		1963	37th Infantry Battalion (The Henty Regiment)
1004.	**SIO** 21st December 1943–15th January 1944 The Coastal Advance	1961	13th Infantry Battalion (The Macquarie Regiment): 15th Infantry Battalion (The Oxley Regiment): 17th Infantry Battalion
1005.	**SIO-SEPIK RIVER** 25th January–19th June 1944 The Coastal Advance	1961	Pacific Islands Regiment: 30th Infantry Battalion (The New South Wales Scottish Regiment): 35th Infantry Battalion (Newcastle's Own Regiment)

Battle Honours for the Second World War

364

No.	Honour	Year	Units
1006.	**MATAPAU** 17th December 1944–2nd January 1945 Aitape-Wewak Operations	1961	11th Infantry Battalion
1007.	**PEREMBIL**¹ 3rd–4th January 1945 Aitape-Wewak Operations	1961	5th Infantry Battalion (The Victorian Scottish Regiment) ¹ Awarded as PERIMBUL: PEREMBIL taken into use 1962.
1008.	**ABAU-MALIN** 5th–7th January 1945 Aitape-Wewak Operations	1961	6th Cavalry (Commando) Regiment: 8th Infantry Battalion: 11th Infantry Battalion
1009.	**NAMBUT RIDGE** 19th January–19th February 1945 Aitape-Wewak Operations	1961	1st Infantry Battalion (Commando) (City of Sydney's Own Regiment): 3rd Infantry Battalion (The Werriwa Regiment): 3rd Machine Gun Battalion
1010.	**BALIF** 18th January–6th February 1945 Aitape-Wewak Operations	1961	5th Infantry Battalion (The Victorian Scottish Regiment)
1011.	**ANUMB RIVER** 4th–9th March 1945 Aitape-Wewak Operations	1961	6th Cavalry (Commando) Regiment: 3rd Machine Gun Battalion
1012.	**BUT DAGUA**¹ 16th March–5th April 1945 Aitape-Wewak Operations	1961	1st Infantry Battalion (Commando) (City of Sydney's Own Regiment): 2nd Infantry Battalion (City of Newcastle Regiment): 3rd Infantry Battalion (The Werriwa Regiment): 3rd Machine Gun Battalion ¹ Awarded as BUT-DAGUA: BUT DAGUA taken into use 1962.
1013.	**MAPRIK** 8th March–24th April 1945 Aitape-Wewak Operations	1961	6th Cavalry (Commando) Regiment: 6th Infantry Battalion (The Royal Melbourne Regiment): 7th Infantry Battalion
1014.	**HAWAIN RIVER** 9th–29th April 1945 Aitape-Wewak Operations	1961	4th Prince of Wales Light Horse: 1st Infantry Battalion (Commando) (City of Sydney's Own Regiment): 2nd Infantry Battalion (City of Newcastle Regiment): 3rd Infantry Battalion (The Werriwa Regiment)
1015.	**WEWAK** 8th–11th May 1945 Aitape-Wewak Operations	1961	6th Cavalry (Commando) Regiment: 4th Prince of Wales Light Horse: 4th Infantry Battalion (Australian Rifles): 11th Infantry Battalion
1016.	**WIRUI MISSION** 11th–15th May 1945 Aitape-Wewak Operations	1961	6th Cavalry (Commando) Regiment: 4th Prince of Wales Light Horse: 4th Infantry Battalion (Australian Rifles): 11th Infantry Battalion

1017.	**MOUNT SHIBURANGU-MOUNT TAZAKI** 28th May–5th July 1945 Aitape-Wewak Operations	1961	4th Infantry Battalion (Australian Rifles); 8th Infantry Battalion
1018.	**YAMIL-ULUPU** 3rd May–14th July 1945 Aitape-Wewak Operations	1961	5th Infantry Battalion (The Victorian Scottish Regiment); 6th Infantry Battalion (The Royal Melbourne Regiment); 7th Infantry Battalion
1019.	**KABOIBUS-KIARIVU** 15th July–8th August 1945 Aitape-Wewak Operations	1961	Pacific Islands Regiment: 5th Infantry Battalion (The Victorian Scottish Regiment); 6th Infantry Battalion (The Royal Melbourne Regiment); 7th Infantry Battalion
1020.	**TSIMBA RIDGE** 17th January–9th February 1945 Bougainville – Northern Sector	1961	31st Infantry Battalion (The Kennedy Regiment); 51st Infantry Battalion (The Far North Queensland Regiment)
1021.	**BONIS-PORTON** 7th–11th June 1945 Bougainville – Northern Sector	1961	Pacific Islands Regiment: 26th Infantry Battalion (The Logan and Albert Regiment); 31st Infantry Battalion (The Kennedy Regiment); 51st Infantry Battalion (The Far North Queensland Regiment)
1022.	**ARTILLERY HILL** 18th December 1944 Bougainville – Central Sector	1961	9th Infantry Battalion (The Moreton Regiment)
1023.	**PEARL RIDGE** 30th December 1944 Bougainville – Central Sector	1961	25th Infantry Battalion (The Darling Downs Regiment)
1024.	**ADELE RIVER** 19th–29th December 1944 Bougainville – Southern Sector	1961	15th Infantry Battalion (The Oxley Regiment)
1025.	**MAWARAKA** 4th–17th January 1945 Bougainville – Southern Sector	1961	15th Infantry Battalion (The Oxley Regiment); 25th Infantry Battalion (The Darling Downs Regiment); 42nd Infantry Battalion (The Capricornia Regiment); 47th Infantry Battalion (The Wide Bay Regiment)
1026.	**MOSIGETTA** 2nd–15th February 1945 Bougainville – Southern Sector	1961	9th Infantry Battalion (The Moreton Regiment); 25th Infantry Battalion (The Darling Downs Regiment); 61st Infantry Battalion (The Queensland Cameron Highlanders)
1027.	**PURIATA RIVER** 24th January–26th February 1945 Bougainville – Southern Sector	1961	9th Infantry Battalion (The Moreton Regiment); 25th Infantry Battalion (The Darling Downs Regiment); 61st Infantry Battalion (The Wide Bay Regiment)

No.	Honour	Year	Units
1028.	**DARARA** 16th–19th February 1945 Bougainville – Southern Sector	1961	25th Infantry Battalion (The Darling Downs Regiment)
1029.	**SLATER'S KNOLL** 28th March–6th April 1945 Bougainville – Southern Sector	1961	4th Prince of Wales Light Horse: 25th Infantry Battalion (The Darling Downs Regiment)
1030.	**HONGORAI RIVER** 17th April–7th May 1945 Bougainville – Southern Sector	1961 1963	4th Prince of Wales Light Horse: 9th Infantry Battalion (The Moreton Regiment): 24th Infantry Battalion (The Kooyong Regiment): 60th Infantry Battalion (The Heidelberg Regiment): 58th Infantry Battalion: 59th Infantry Battalion (The Hume Regiment) 57th Infantry Battalion (The Merri Regiment)
1031.	**EGAN'S RIDGE-HONGORAI FORD** 13th–22nd May 1945 Bougainville – Southern Sector	1961	4th Prince of Wales Light Horse: 24th Infantry Battalion (The Kooyong Regiment): 58th Infantry Battalion: 59th Infantry Battalion (The Hume Regiment)
1032.	**COMMANDO ROAD** 17th–28th May 1945 Bougainville – Southern Sector	1961 1963	60th Infantry Battalion (The Heidelberg Regiment) 57th Infantry Battalion (The Merri Regiment)
1033.	**HARI RIVER** 2nd–7th June 1945 Bougainville – Southern Sector	1961 1963	4th Prince of Wales Light Horse: 24th Infantry Battalion (The Kooyong Regiment): 60th Infantry Battalion (The Heidelberg Regiment): 58th Infantry Battalion: 59th Infantry Battalion (The Hume Regiment) 57th Infantry Battalion (The Merri Regiment)
1034.	**OGORATA RIVER** 13th–16th June 1945 Bougainville – Southern Sector	1961 1963	24th Infantry Battalion (The Kooyong Regiment): 60th Infantry Battalion (The Heidelberg Regiment): 58th Infantry Battalion (The Hume Regiment) 57th Infantry Battalion (The Merri Regiment)
1035.	**MOBIAI RIVER** 16th–25th June 1945 Bougainville – Southern Sector	1961 1963	60th Infantry Battalion (The Heidelberg Regiment): 58th Infantry Battalion: 59th Infantry Battalion (The Hume Regiment) 57th Infantry Battalion (The Merri Regiment)
1036.	**MIVO RIVER** 26th–30th June 1945 Bougainville – Southern Sector	1961 1963	4th Prince of Wales Light Horse: 24th Infantry Battalion (The Kooyong Regiment): 60th Infantry Battalion (The Heidelberg Regiment): 58th Infantry Battalion: 59th Infantry Battalion (The Hume Regiment) 57th Infantry Battalion (The Merri Regiment)
1037.	**MIVO FORD** 2nd–9th July 1945 Bougainville – Southern Sector	1961	15th Infantry Battalion (The Oxley Regiment): 42nd Infantry Battalion (The Capricornia Regiment): 47th Infantry Battalion (The Wide Bay Regiment)
1038.	**WAITAVOLO** 5th–7th March 1945 New Britain	1961	14th Infantry Battalion (The Prahran Regiment): 16th Infantry Battalion (The Cameron Highlanders of West Australia): 19th Infantry Battalion (The South Sydney Regiment): 32nd Infantry Battalion

1039.	**BORNEO** 1st May–15th August 1945 Operations in Borneo	1961	7th Cavalry (Commando) Regiment: 9th Cavalry (Commando) Regiment: 1st Royal New South Wales Lancers: 9th Infantry Battalion (The Moreton Regiment): 10th Infantry Battalion (The Adelaide Rifles): 12th Infantry Battalion (The Launceston Regiment): 13th Infantry Battalion (The Macquarie Regiment): 14th Infantry Battalion (The Prahran Regiment): 15th Infantry Battalion (The Oxley Regiment): 16th Infantry Battalion (The Cameron Highlanders of West Australia): 17th Infantry Battalion: 23rd Infantry Battalion (The City of Geelong Regiment): 24th Infantry Battalion (The Kooyong Regiment): 25th Infantry Battalion (The Darling Downs Regiment): 27th Infantry Battalion (The South Australian Scottish Regiment): 28th Infantry Battalion (The Swan Regiment): 31st Infantry Battalion (The Kennedy Regiment): 33rd Infantry Battalion (The New England Regiment): 43rd Infantry Battalion: 48th Infantry Battalion: 32nd Infantry Battalion: 1st Machine Gun Battalion: 2nd Machine Gun Battalion: 1st Pioneer Battalion: 3rd Pioneer Battalion: 4th Pioneer Battalion
1040.	**TARAKAN** 1st May–15th August 1945 Operations in Borneo	1961	9th South Australian Mounted Rifles: 23rd Infantry Battalion (The City of Geelong Regiment): 24th Infantry Battalion (The Kooyong Regiment): 48th Infantry Battalion: 3rd Pioneer Battalion
1041.	**BRUNEI** 10th June–8th August 1945 Operations in Borneo	1961	13th Infantry Battalion (The Macquarie Regiment): 15th Infantry Battalion (The Oxley Regiment): 17th Infantry Battalion: 2nd Machine Gun Battalion
1042.	**LABUAN** 10th–21st June 1945 Operations in Borneo	1961	9th Cavalry (Commando) Regiment: 9th South Australian Mounted Rifles: 28th Infantry Battalion (The Swan Regiment): 43rd Infantry Battalion: 2nd Machine Gun Battalion
1043.	**BEAUFORT** 17th–30th June 1945 Operations in Borneo	1961	28th Infantry Battalion (The Swan Regiment): 43rd Infantry Battalion: 32nd Infantry Battalion
1044.	**MIRI** 10th–23rd June 1945 Operations in Borneo	1961	13th Infantry Battalion (The Macquarie Regiment): 15th Infantry Battalion (The Oxley Regiment): 17th Infantry Battalion
1045.	**BALIKPAPAN** 1st–9th July 1945 Operations in Borneo	1961	7th Cavalry (Commando) Regiment: 1st Royal New South Wales Lancers: 9th Infantry Battalion (The Moreton Regiment): 10th Infantry Battalion (The Adelaide Rifles): 12th Infantry Battalion (The Launceston Regiment): 14th Infantry Battalion (The Prahran Regiment): 16th Infantry Battalion (The Cameron Highlanders of West Australia): 25th Infantry Battalion (The Darling Downs Regiment): 27th Infantry Battalion (The South Australian Scottish Regiment): 31st Infantry Battalion (The Kennedy Regiment): 33rd Infantry Battalion (The New England Regiment): 1st Machine Gun Battalion
1046.	**MILFORD HIGHWAY** 10th–22nd July 1945 Operations in Borneo	1961	7th Cavalry (Commando) Regiment: 1st Royal New South Wales Lancers: 25th Infantry Battalion (The Darling Downs Regiment): 31st Infantry Battalion (The Kennedy Regiment): 33rd Infantry Battalion (The New England Regiment): 1st Machine Gun Battalion
1047.	**SOUTH WEST PACIFIC 1942** 20th February–31st December 1942 Service in South West Pacific 1942–45	1961	21st Infantry Battalion (The Victorian Rangers): 40th Infantry Battalion (The Derwent Regiment): 3rd Machine Gun Battalion

1048. **SOUTH WEST PACIFIC 1942–43**
20th February 1942–31st December 1943
Service in South West Pacific 1942–45

1961

7th Cavalry (Commando) Regiment: 39th Infantry Battalion (The Hawthorn-Kew Regiment): 49th Infantry Battalion (The Stanley Regiment): 1st Pioneer Battalion: 6th New South Wales Mounted Rifles: Papuan and New Guinea Volunteer Rifles

1049. **SOUTH WEST PACIFIC 1942–44**
20th February 1942–31st December 1944
Service in South West Pacific 1942–45

1961

62nd Infantry Battalion (The Merauke Regiment)

1050. **SOUTH WEST PACIFIC 1942–45**
20th February 1942–15th August 1945
Service in South West Pacific 1942–45

1961

Pacific Islands Regiment: 1st Infantry Battalion (Commando) (City of Sidney's Own Regiment): 2nd Infantry Battalion (City of Newcastle Regiment): 3rd Infantry Battalion (The Werriwa Regiment): 5th Infantry Battalion (The Victorian Scottish Regiment): 6th Infantry Battalion (The Royal Melbourne Regiment): 7th Infantry Battalion: 9th Infantry Battalion (The Moreton Regiment): 10th Infantry Battalion (The Adelaide Rifles): 12th Infantry Battalion (The Launceston Regiment): 14th Infantry Battalion (The Prahran Regiment): 16th Infantry Battalion (The Cameron Highlanders of West Australia): 22nd Infantry Battalion (The Richmond Regiment): 25th Infantry Battalion (The Darling Downs Regiment): 27th Infantry Battalion (The South Australian Scottish Regiment): 31st Infantry Battalion (The Kennedy Regiment): 33rd Infantry Battalion (The New England Regiment): 36th Infantry Battalion (The St George's English Rifle Regiment): 53rd Infantry Battalion (The West Sydney Regiment): 61st Infantry Battalion (The Queensland Cameron Highlanders): 2nd Pioneer Battalion

1963

55th Infantry Battalion (The New South Wales Rifle Regiment)

1051. **SOUTH WEST PACIFIC 1943**
1st January–31st December 1943
Service in South West Pacific 1942–45

1961

7th Machine Gun Battalion

1052. **SOUTH WEST PACIFIC 1943–44**
1st January 1943–31st December 1944
Service in South West Pacific 1942–45

1961

8th Victorian Mounted Rifles

1053. **SOUTH WEST PACIFIC 1943–45**
1st January 1943–15th August 1945
Service in South West Pacific 1942–45

1961

1st Royal Royal New South Wales Lancers: 13th Infantry Battalion (The Macquarie Regiment): 15th Infantry Battalion (The Cameron Highlanders of West Australia): 17th Infantry Battalion: 23rd Infantry Battalion (The City of Geelong Regiment): 24th Infantry Battalion (The Kooyong Regiment): 26th Infantry Battalion (The Logan and Albert Regiment): 28th Infantry Battalion (The Swan Regiment): 52nd Infantry Battalion (The Gippsland Regiment): 42nd Infantry Battalion (The Capricornia Regiment): 43rd Infantry Battalion: 48th Infantry Battalion: 46th Infantry Battalion (The Brighton Rifles): 47th Infantry Battalion (The Wide Bay Regiment): 51st Infantry Battalion: 58th Infantry Battalion (The Far North Queensland Regiment): 60th Infantry Battalion (The Heidelberg Regiment): 58th Infantry Battalion: 32nd Infantry Battalion: 59th Infantry Battalion (The Hume Regiment): 2nd Machine Gun Battalion: 3rd Pioneer Battalion

1963

37th Infantry Battalion (The Henty Regiment): 57th Infantry Battalion (The Merri Regiment)

1054. **SOUTH WEST PACIFIC 1944–45**
1st January 1944–15th August 1945
Service in South West Pacific 1942–45

1961

6th Cavalry (Commando) Regiment: 20th Victorian Mounted Rifles: 4th Infantry Battalion (Australian Rifles): 8th Infantry Battalion: 11th Infantry Battalion: 29th Infantry Battalion (The East Melbourne Regiment): 30th Infantry Battalion (The New South Wales Scottish Regiment): 35th Infantry Battalion (Newcastle's Own Regiment): 3rd Machine Gun Battalion

1055. **SOUTH WEST PACIFIC 1945**
1st January–15th August 1945
Service in South West Pacific 1942–45

1961

7th Cavalry (Commando) Regiment: 9th Cavalry (Commando) Regiment: 9th South Australian Mounted Rifles: 4th Prince of Wales Light Horse: 19th Infantry Battalion (The South Sydney Regiment): 1st Machine Gun Battalion: 1st Pioneer Battalion: 4th Pioneer Battalion

1056.	**SOLOMONS** 7th August 1942–20th March 1944 Operations in the South Pacific	1958	The Canterbury Regiment: The Auckland Regiment (Countess of Ranfurly's Own): The Otago Regiment: The Southland Regiment: The Wellington Regiment (City of Wellington's Own): The Hauraki Regiment: The Wellington West Coast Regiment: The Taranaki Regiment: The Hawke's Bay Regiment: The Nelson, Marlborough, and West Coast Regiment: The Northland Regiment: 34 Battalion: 35 Battalion
1057.	**VELLA LAVELLA** 31st August–9th October 1943 Operations in the South Pacific	1958	The Canterbury Regiment: The Otago Regiment: The Southland Regiment: The Nelson, Marlborough, and West Coast Regiment: 35 Battalion
1058.	**TREASURY ISLANDS** 27th October–12th November 1943 Operations in the South Pacific	1958	The Auckland Regiment (Countess of Ranfurly's Own): The Wellington Regiment (City of Wellington's Own): The Hauraki Regiment: The Wellington West Coast Regiment: The Taranaki Regiment: The Hawke's Bay Regiment: The Northland Regiment: 34 Battalion
1059.	**GREEN ISLANDS** 30th January–23rd February 1944 Operations in the South Pacific	1958	The Canterbury Regiment: The Otago Regiment: The Southland Regiment: The Nelson, Marlborough, and West Coast Regiment: 35 Battalion
1060.	**SOUTH PACIFIC 1942–44** 7th August 1942–25th June 1944 Service in South Pacific 1942–44	1958	Queen Alexandra's (Wellington West Coast) Mounted Rifles: The Wellington East Coast Mounted Rifles: The New Zealand Scottish Regiment: The Canterbury Regiment: The Auckland Regiment (Countess of Ranfurly's Own): The Otago Regiment: The Southland Regiment: The Wellington Regiment (City of Wellington's Own): The Hauraki Regiment: The Wellington West Coast Regiment: The Taranaki Regiment: The Hawke's Bay Regiment: The Nelson, Marlborough, and West Coast Regiment: The Northland Regiment: The Ruahine Regiment: 34 Battalion: 35 Battalion

Table 5

HONORARY DISTINCTIONS FOR THE SECOND WORLD WAR

1.	A Badge of the Royal Corps of Signals, with year-date "1945", and with one scroll: "North-West Europe"	The Cheshire Yeomanry (Earl of Chester's), Royal Armoured Corps (TA)
2.	A Badge of the Royal Corps of Signals, with year-dates "1942–45", and with four scrolls: "North Africa" "Sicily" "Italy" "North-West Europe"	The North Somerset Yeomanry, Royal Armoured Corps (TA)
3.	A Badge of the Royal Regiment of Artillery, with year-dates "1940–45", and with five scrolls: "North Africa" "Greece" "Middle East" "Sicily" "North-West Europe"	The Northumberland Hussars, Royal Armoured Corps (TA)
4.	A Badge of the Royal Regiment of Artillery, with year-dates "1940,'44-45", and with one scroll: "North-West Europe"	The Queen's Own Worcestershire Hussars, Royal Armoured Corps (TA)
5.	A Badge of the Royal Regiment of Artillery, with year-dates "1940,'42-45", and with four scrolls: "North-West Europe" "North Africa" "Sicily" "Italy"	The Queen's Own Royal Glasgow Yeomanry, Royal Armoured Corps (TA)
6.	A Badge of the Royal Regiment of Artillery, with year-dates "1942–45", and with two scrolls: "North Africa" "Italy"	The City of London Yeomanry (Rough Riders), Royal Armoured Corps (TA)
7.	A Badge of the Durham Light Infantry, with year-dates "1940,'42–45", and with three scrolls: "North-West Europe" "North Africa" "Sicily"	17th Battalion, The Parachute Regiment (TA)
8.	A Badge of the Royal Regiment of Artillery, with year-dates "1943–45", and with two scrolls: "Sicily" "Italy"	The Shropshire Yeomanry, Royal Armoured Corps (TA)
9.	A Badge of the Royal Regiment of Artillery, with year-dates "1942,'44–45", and with three scrolls: "North-West Europe" "North Africa" "Italy"	The Leicestershire Yeomanry (Prince Albert's Own), Royal Armoured Corps (TA)
10.	A Badge of the Reconnaissance Corps, with year-dates "1944–45", and with one scroll: "North-West Europe"	5th Battalion, The Gloucestershire Regiment (TA)
11.	A Badge of the Royal Regiment of Artillery, with year-dates "1942–45", and with three scrolls: "North-West Europe" "North Africa" "Italy"	The Ayrshire Yeomanry (Earl of Carrick's Own), Royal Armoured Corps (TA)
12.	A Badge of the Royal Regiment of Artillery, with year-dates "1944–45", and with two scrolls: "North-West Europe" "Italy"	The Duke of Lancaster's Own Yeomanry, Royal Armoured Corps (TA)
13.	A Badge of the Royal Armoured Corps, with year-dates "1944–45", and with one scroll: "North-West Europe"	5th Battalion, The King's Own Royal Regiment (Lancaster) (TA)
14.	A Badge of the Royal Regiment of Artillery, with year-dates "1941–45", and with four scrolls: "North-West Europe" "Sicily" "Italy" "Malaya"	The Lanarkshire Yeomanry, Royal Armoured Corps (TA)

15.	A Badge of the Royal Regiment of Artillery, with year-dates "1943–45", and with three scrolls: "North-West Europe" "Sicily" "Italy"	The Scottish Horse, Royal Armoured Corps (TA)
16.	A Badge of the Royal Tank Regiment, with year-dates "1942–45", and with two scrolls: "North Africa" "Italy"	7th (Leeds Rifles) Battalion, The West Yorkshire Regiment (The Prince of Wales's Own) (TA)
17.	A Badge of the Royal Tank Regiment, with year-dates "1941–45", and with three scrolls: "North-West Europe" "North Africa" "Italy"	23rd London Regiment (TA)
18.	A Badge of the Reconnaissance Corps, with year-date "1942", and with one scroll: "Malaya"	5th Battalion, The Loyal Regiment (North Lancashire) (TA)
19.	A Badge of the Royal Rifles of Canada, with the year-date "1941"	The Sherbrooke Regiment (RCAC)
20.	A Badge of the Royal Rifles of Canada, with the year-date "1941"	7th/11th Hussars
21.	A Badge of the Stormont, Dundas and Glengarry Highlanders, with the year-dates "1944–45"	The Brockville Rifles

Table 6

BATTLE HONOURS FOR THE KOREAN CAMPAIGN

1.	**NAKTONG BRIDGEHEAD** 16th–25th September 1950 The UN Counter Offensive	1958	The Middlesex Regiment (Duke of Cambridge's Own)
2.	**SARIWON** 17th–18th October 1950 The UN Counter Offensive	1961	Royal Australian Regiment
3.	**YONGJU** 21st–22nd October 1950 The UN Counter Offensive	1961	Royal Australian Regiment
4.	**CHONGJU** 25th–30th October 1950 The UN Counter Offensive	1958 1961	The Middlesex Regiment (Duke of Cambridge's Own) Royal Australian Regiment
5.	**PAKCHON** 4th–5th November 1950 The UN Counter Offensive	1958 1961	The Argyll and Sutherland Highlanders (Princess Louise's) Royal Australian Regiment
6.	**CHONGCHON II** 25th–30th November 1950 Withdrawal from the Yalu	1958	The Middlesex Regiment (Duke of Cambridge's Own)
7.	**UIJONGBU** 1st January 1951 The Chinese Offensive	1961	Royal Australian Regiment
8.	**SEOUL** 2nd–4th January 1951 The Chinese Offensive	1958	8th King's Royal Irish Hussars:The Royal Northumberland Fusiliers:The Royal Ulster Rifles
9.	**CHUAM-NI** 14th–17th February 1951 The Advance to the 38th Parallel	1958 1961	The Middlesex Regiment (Duke of Cambridge's Own) Royal Australian Regiment
10.	**HILL 327** 16th–20th February 1951 The Advance to the 38th Parallel	1958	8th King's Royal Irish Hussars:The Gloucestershire Regiment

11.	**MAEHWA-SAN** 7th–12th March 1951 The Advance to the 38th Parallel	1961	Royal Australian Regiment
12.	**KAPYONG-CHON** 3rd–16th April 1951 The Advance to the 38th Parallel	1958	The Middlesex Regiment (Duke of Cambridge's Own)
13.	**IMJIN** 22nd–25th April 1951 The Battle of the 38th Parallel	1958	8th King's Royal Irish Hussars: The Royal Northumberland Fusiliers: The Gloucestershire Regiment: The Royal Ulster Rifles
14.	**KAPYONG** 22nd–25th April 1951 The Battle of the 38th Parallel	1958 1959 1961	The Middlesex Regiment (Duke of Cambridge's Own) Princess Patricia's Canadian Light Infantry Royal Australian Regiment
15.	**KOWANG-SAN** 3rd–12th October 1951 The Final Phase	1958 1961	8th King's Royal Irish Hussars: The Royal Northumberland Fusiliers: The King's Own Scottish Borderers: The King's Shropshire Light Infantry Royal Australian Regiment
16.	**MARYANG-SAN** 4th–6th November 1951 The Final Phase	1958 1994	The Royal Leicestershire Regiment: The King's Own Scottish Borderers Royal Australian Regiment
17.	**HILL 227 I** 17th–19th November 1951 The Final Phase	1958	The King's Shropshire Light Infantry
18.	**THE HOOK 1952** 18th–19th November 1952 The Final Phase	1958	5th Royal Inniskilling Dragoon Guards: The Black Watch (Royal Highland Regiment)
19.	**THE HOOK 1953** 28th–29th May 1953 The Final Phase	1958	The King's Regiment (Liverpool): The Duke of Wellington's Regiment (West Riding)
20.	**THE SAMICHON** 24th–26th July 1953 The Final Phase	1961	Royal Australian Regiment
21.	**KOREA 1950–51** 1st August 1950–31st December 1951 Service in Korea 1950–53	1958	8th King's Royal Irish Hussars: The Royal Northumberland Fusiliers: The Gloucestershire Regiment: The Middlesex Regiment (Duke of Cambridge's Own): The Royal Ulster Rifles: The Argyll and Sutherland Highlanders (Princess Louise's)
22.	**KOREA 1950–1953** ¹ 1st August 1950–26th July 1953 Service in Korea 1950–53	1959	Princess Patricia's Canadian Light Infantry ¹ COREE 1950-1953 taken into use by French-speaking Canadian units 1959.

23.	**KOREA 1950–53** 1st August 1950–26th July 1953 Service in Korea 1950–53	1961	Royal Australian Regiment
24.	**KOREA 1951–52** 1st January 1951–31st December 1952 Service in Korea 1950–53	1958	5th Royal Inniskilling Dragoon Guards: The Royal Norfolk Regiment: The Royal Leicestershire Regiment: The King's Own Scottish Borderers: The Welch Regiment: The King's Shropshire Light Infantry
25.	**KOREA 1951–53** 1st January 1951–26th July 1953 Service in Korea 1950–53	1958	Royal Tank Regiment
26.	**KOREA 1951–1953** [1] 1st January 1951–26th July 1953 Service in Korea 1950–53	1959	Lord Strathcona's Horse (Royal Canadians): The Royal Canadian Regiment: Royal 22e Regiment [1] *COREE 1951–1953 taken into use by French-speaking Canadian units 1959.*
27.	**KOREA 1952–53** 1st January 1952–26th July 1953 Service in Korea 1950–53	1958	The Royal Fusiliers (City of London Regiment): The King's Regiment (Liverpool): The Duke of Wellington's Regiment (West Riding): The Black Watch (Royal Highland Regiment): The Durham Light Infantry

4

Battle Honours After the
Second World War

*In times of peace we have neglected much, occupied ourselves with
frivolities, flattered the people's love of shows and neglected war.*
                                        Field Marshal August von Gneisenau

Introduction

Strangely, the period between 1963 and 1993 sometimes has been referred to as 'The Thirty Years Peace', although these were not peaceful years. In addition to the seemingly continuous major conflicts throughout the Middle East and South-East Asia, there were numerous 'small wars' and international peacekeeping operations in support of regional defence organizations, such as the North Atlantic Treaty Organization, or on behalf of the United Nations, all of which, at various times, involved units or military personnel of the Commonwealth.

During this same period the Commonwealth itself had undergone change, enlarged with newly created states in Africa, South-East Asia and the Indian and Pacific Oceans, these new members, together with the older, white Dominions, had become less dependent on the United Kingdom in defence matters. By 1975, apart from Gibraltar, Hong Kong and Southern Rhodesia, all the former colonies and protectorates of any significance had gone: in East Africa, Uganda became a self-governing country in 1962 and the 4th Battalion, The King's African Rifles was retitled the Uganda Rifles; in 1963 Kenya became independent and the 3rd, 5th and 11th Battalions of The King's African Rifles formed the 1st, 2nd and 3rd Battalions of the Kenya Rifles. Zanzibar, later to be federated with Tanganyika to form Tanzania, also gained its independence in 1964 and the Tanganyika Rifles, formed 1961, were renamed The People's Defence Force. Also in 1964 Nyasaland became Malawi with the 1st Battalion, The King's African Rifles restyled 1st Malawi Rifles and the 2nd Battalion, The King's African Rifles being disbanded; Northern Rhodesia changed its name to Zambia and The Northern Rhodesia Rifles became 1st Zambia Rifles. In South-East Asia, Malaya, independent since 1962, joined with Singapore, Sarawak and Sabah to form Malaysia in 1963: in addition to the Royal Malay Regiment, 28th Commonwealth Brigade continued to provide a garrison until 1974. In the Indian Ocean, Mauritius gained independence in 1968, followed by the Seychelles in 1971. In the Pacific, Fiji became an independent state in 1970, later to leave the Commonwealth; in 1975 Papua New Guinea finally gained independence having been administered by Australia since 1905 and the Pacific Islands Regiment was restyled the Royal Pacific Islands Regiment. In all cases the honours and distinctions of the corps were retained on transfer.

Although Malta became independent in 1964, the Royal Malta Artillery remained part of the Royal Artillery until 1970 and The King's Own Malta Regiment was disbanded in 1972. Strangely, when Malta became a Republic in 1974 the Royal Malta Artillery retained and kept its title until 1977.

Except for India, Pakistan and South Africa, it was also, generally, a time of cuts in defence budgets, made at every opportunity when it was considered possible by governments, with the attendant reductions in establishments.

Great Britain and Northern Ireland

By 1968, with the conclusion of the emergency in Malaya, declared in 1948, the end of the subsequent 'confrontation' with Indonesia and the fighting withdrawal from South Arabia and Aden, for the first time since the end of the Second World War no unit of the British Army was on active service. This relief, however, was short-lived: following civil unrest in Northern Ireland troops were deployed in 1969 'in aid to the Civil Power', and personnel, mainly the Special Air Service Regiment, were despatched to fight a little publicized campaign in the Djebel Dhofar region of Oman. The former commitment, due to a gradual increase in terrorist activities by both Republican and Loyalist organizations from 1971, remains today, albeit recently much reduced in scale, while the latter campaign ended successfully in 1976.

By the time Argentine forces occupied South Georgia and the Falkland Islands on Good Friday 1982, the British Army had changed. A series of cuts following the 1957 Defence Review had reduced the Regular Establishment to two regiments of Household Cavalry, one of which was an amalgamation in 1969 to form the Blues and Royals (Royal Horse Guards and 1st Dragoons) and thirteen cavalry regiments and four units of the Royal Tank Regiment forming the Royal Armoured Corps. The Foot Guards remained at five regiments and twenty-eight corps of infantry, grouped into six administrative divisions, with The Parachute Regiment, four Gurkha regiments and the Special Air Service Regiment, totalling fifty-six battalions, and the Army Air Corps. In addition, The Ulster Defence Regiment, raised 1970, was established for eleven part-time battalions, but these could serve only in Northern Ireland. Apart from The Cameronians (Scottish Rifles), raised 1689, and The York and Lancaster Regiment, raised 1756, which were disbanded in 1968, with **India 1796-1819** and **Arabia** 'lost', all reductions were the result of amalgamations, some forming 'large regiments' of three battalions; all honours and distinctions were retained.

It was, however, the reserve sstablishment that had seen the most change. In 1967 the Territorial Army and the Army Emergency Reserve were disbanded and replaced by the Territorial and Army Volunteer Reserve. The Class I and Class II units, called 'Volunteers', were to provide immediate reinforcement in a national emergency; the establishment was set at one yeomanry regiment, the Honourable Artillery Company and thirteen infantry battalions, four parachute battalions and two Special Air Service Regiments. To meet this establishment, sub-units representing five yeomanry regiments were grouped to form The Royal Yeomanry Regiment and, similarly using sub-units drawn from Territorial Army infantry regiments, ten new infantry volunteer corps, such as The Light Infantry and Mercian Volunteers, and three volunteer battalions of The Queen's Regiment, The Royal Anglian Regiment and The Royal Green Jackets were formed. Three battalions of The Parachute Regiment and two regiments of the Special Air Service were also formed by the conversion of the existing units to Volunteer status. In 1969 the Class III units, called 'Territorials', which had no liability to serve overseas, were disbanded and surviving units were reduced to a cadre of one officer and eight other ranks to preserve the title, honours and traditions of the former regiments. In 1971 Class II was expanded by four yeomanry regiments and a further sixteen volunteer battalions, formed mainly from the 1967 cadres; by 1982, however, only five of the original infantry volunteer corps remained and the volunteer battalions had increased to twenty. With the formation of volunteer battalions it was ruled that such battalions were permitted to take into use the corps honours of their new regiments; however, this ruling was not extended to include the yeomanry regiments and infantry volunteer corps as the honours and traditions were deemed to be vested in the sub-units making up these regiments.

The award of battle honours for operations in the Falkland Islands was published in Defence Council Instruction (Army) 196/84 and concluded with:

> These Honours will be printed in the Army List as a permanent record with 'Falkland Islands 1982' in heavy type as the Honour to be borne on Colours.

On 2 May 1989 Hungary opened its border with the West, which resulted in a mass migration of East Germans; this in turn led to demonstrations in Leipzig and other East German cities with the collapse of the Communist regime. The dismantling of the Berlin Wall and the subsequent reunification of East and West Germany signalled the end of the Cold War in Europe and removed the threat of the Warsaw Pact. While the Government considered the 'peace dividend', which would have brought further reductions in defence, Iraq first invaded, and then formally annexed, Kuwait. The United Nations condemned this aggression and Coalition Forces, led by the United States, began concentrating in Saudi Arabia. It soon became apparent that to provide an armoured division of two brigades, with supporting services, at War Establishment would require stripping the remainder of the British Army of equipment, spares, ammunition and other supplies. In addition, increased manning levels would require drafts from other regular corps to provide the required additional squadrons and companies and Territorial Army and Volunteer Reserve personnel and units, mainly medical and specialist, to be mobilized. Fortunately, Operation Desert Sabre lasted only one hundred hours and casualties were astonishingly low.

The award of battle honours for operations in Kuwait and Iraq were promulgated in a Directed Letter dated 20 October 1991 from the Director General of Personal Services. Included in the list of awards was the Army Air Corps, now considered eligible for battle honours, on behalf of 654, 659 and 661 Squadrons; in addition, **Falkland Islands 1982** was extended to include that corps on behalf of 656 Squadron. Authority was also given for the theatre honours to be emblazoned on Colours.

India

When it was announced that British India was to be partitioned, the numerous Princely States, which made up fifty per cent of the sub-continent, were required to renounce their independence and to accede to one or other of the new Dominions. By 15 August 1947 only Hyderabad and Jammu and Kashmir remained uncommitted. Kashmir had a predominantly Muslim population with a Hindu ruler, whose indecision led to unrest, riots and finally fighting between the two religious factions, which resulted in the involvement of both India and Pakistan in a long-running and continuing dispute.

Between October 1947 and December 1948 tension between India and its new neighbour led to fighting, which ended with an uneasy United Nations truce and a ceasefire line separating the two sides.

Hyderabad, on the other hand, was occupied by Indian forces without United Nations intervention in September 1948, the Nizam signed the Instrument of Accession on 26 January 1950 and, after the reorganization of Indian States, the former State of Hyderabad ceased to exist.

The Portuguese enclaves of Goa, Damao and Diu were dealt with similarly by occupation on 18 December 1961.

Following Communist China's invasion of Tibet in October 1950, India's North-Eastern frontier was subjected to a series of Chinese border incursions and territorial violations. In October 1962 Chinese troops successfully attacked Indian frontier posts in the North-Eastern Frontier Agency and in Ladakh, afterwards withdrawing to lines which controlled their gains. India was obliged to accept 'a crushing and humiliating defeat on the Indian Army.' This short campaign resulted in a large-scale reform of the Indian Army, with deficiencies in modern equipment and training provided by the United States and the Commonwealth.

The award of battle honours for operations in Jammu and Kashmir in 1947-48 was published in 1965: the Jammu and Kashir Militia were not considered eligible to claim for battle honours, not being on the Regular Establishment, and such claims were disallowed. In 1971 **Srinagar** was extended to include the 4th Battalion, The Kumaon Regiment, which, due to an oversight, had been omitted in the earlier list of awards.

In April 1965 a frontier dispute with Pakistan in the Rann of Kutch developed into a second period of full-scale hostilities on three fronts, which again ended with an United Nations-sponsored ceasefire on 23 September 1965.

In 1970 The Naga Regiment was raised and placed on the Regular Establishment, ranking after the Ladakh Scouts. A 2nd Battalion was formed in 1988.

The proclamation of the independence of East Pakistan as Bangladesh on 25 March 1971 initiated the third conflict between India and Pakistan. On 3 December 1971 India invaded East Pakistan in support of the rebels, and the following day Pakistan countered by invading Jammu and Kashmir, Punjab and Sindh. On 16 December 1971, after much heavy fighting, Dacca, the capital of East Pakistan, surrendered; this ended the war. Both sides accepted a ceasefire, withdrawal to a 'line of actual control' in Kashmir and a return to the recognized international borders elsewhere.

In recognition of its services in the 1971 war the Jammu and Kashmir Militia was restyled the Jammu and Kashir Light Infantry and placed on the Regular Establishment in 1972.

The lists of award of battle honours for the 'Chinese Aggression 1962' and the 'Indo-Pak Conflict 1965' were published in 1975. In 1976 **Jammu and Kashmir 1965** was extended to include the 11th Battalion, Jammu and Kashmir Light Infantry.

Armoured personnel carriers had been in service with the Indian Army since 1966 and battalions equipped with them had been used in the 1971 hostilities against Pakistan. On 1 April 1979 The Mechanised Infantry Regiment was raised by the transfer of thirteen battalions of existing infantry corps and one of Gurkha Rifles, including six 1st Battalions. This new corps took precedence after The Brigade of the Guards and The Parachute Regiment. Inevitably, the question of battle honours arose; however, in 1980 it was ruled that each mechanized unit, while bearing the Colours of the new corps, would retain its own individual battalion battle honours on transfer. In addition, these battalion battle honours would continue to be used by their former corps. The battle honours of The Brigade of the Guards and The Parachute Regiment, however, were not affected by this ruling.

In 1982 the list of awards of battle honours for the 'Indo-Pak Conflict 1971' was published. The eligibility for the award of battle honours was extended to the Jammu and Kashmir Light Infantry and the Ladakh Scouts. Also, awards were made for the first time to engineer regiments in addition to companies of the Madras, Bengal or Bombay Engineers, where companies, irrespective of their engineer groups, had been formed into regiments, to support operations.

Since 1980 the Indian Army has contributed to many United Nations peacekeeping operations, in addition to internal security duties, in Jammu and Kashmir, Punjab, Assam, Gujerat, Manipur, Mizo, Nagaland and Tipura. It has also, during 1988-89, carried out counterinsurgency operations in Sri Lanka and the Maldives at the invitation of both Governments. India maintains a large standing army of over one million volunteers, but details of the Regular Establishment remain highly classified. However, in 1991 it was estimated that the Armoured Corps totalled fifty-six regiments and that there were twenty-two infantry and seven Gurkha regiments and corps providing four hundred and one battalions of all types. All of these units, except for the most recently raised battalions of The Mechanised Infantry Regiment and The Naga Regiment, bear emblazoned battle honours on their Standards, Guidons and Colours.

Pakistan

As with India, the lack of published material on the Pakistan Army after Partition, together with the high national security classification given to such material, restricts the information available on battle honours.

This section is based, therefore, exclusively on a demi-official letter, DO/10990/PA, dated 12 March 1998, from the Director General Military Training in Rawalpindi. This letter, which was authorized for release by the General Headquarters, enclosed a list headed 'Units possessing Battle Honours in various conflicts/wars after 1947' and, in the absence of further detail, is the only source available.

The Azad Kashmir Regiment - The Free Kashmir Regiment - which features prominently in the list was raised from Muslim personnel of the former Jammu and Kashmir State Forces in 1947; it joined the Regular Establishment in 1971.

Pakistan contributed to the Coalition Forces in Saudi Arabia for the Gulf campaign in 1991.

Australia

One unit of the Royal Australian Regiment was already actively engaged in the Borneo confrontation when, in June 1965, the 1st Battalion, Royal Australian Regiment, later reinforced to form a battalion group of all arms with logistical support, arrived in South Vietnam. Later, this commitment was further increased to form 1st Australian Task Force, a tactical formation of approximately sixteen hundred all ranks, which required the regular infantry establishment to be raised to nine battalions, all of which served in South Vietnam. To maintain this increased level in manpower required the introduction of selective conscription in March 1966, which was unpopular. Even with little support for the war in Australia, unit morale remained high in South Vietnam and, despite the difficulties of serving under American command, the regiments returned, in December 1972, with their reputations enhanced. At the same time, selective conscription ended and the infantry establishment was reduced. In 1975 the Australian Armed Forces were grouped to form the Australian Defence Force, under a single Chief of Defence Staff.

The battle honours for the Vietnam War, the first to be approved by the Governor-General on delegated authority from the Queen, were announced in June 1982. Approval was also given for a maximum of one theatre honour and two battle honours to be emblazoned on the Standard, Guidon and Regimental Colour.

Australia has provided support for many United Nations peacekeeping operations and by 1991 personnel had served, or are still serving, with missions in Namiba, Cambodia, the Western Sahara, Somalia, Cyprus and the Middle East.

Canada

A series of reductions in the Militia Establishment began in 1965 with 4th Princess Louise Dragoon Guards, The Halifax Rifles (RCAC), 12th Manitoba Dragoons and 19th Alberta Dragoons placed on the Supplementary Order of Battle, a form of suspended animation: The Sherbrooke Regiment (RCAC) and 7th/11th Hussars were amalgamated to form The Sherbrooke Hussars, and The Algonquin Regiment (RCAC) was converted to an infantry battalion and redesignated The Algonquin Regiment. Also placed on the Supplementary Order of Battle were the Victoria Rifles of Canada raised 1862, The Perth Regiment, Le Regiment de Joliette, The Winnipeg Grenadiers, the Irish Fusiliers of Canada (The Vancouver Regiment) and The Irish Regiment of Canada. The 58th Field Regiment (Sudbury), Royal Canadian Artillery was converted to form the 2nd Battalion of The Irish Regiment of Canada. The Highland Light Infantry of Canada and The Scots Fusiliers of Canada were amalgamated to form The Highland Fusiliers of Canada. All corps honours and distinctions were retained and the newly formed 2nd Battalion took into use the corps honours of The Irish Regiment of Canada. In addition, The Essex and Kent Scottish lost its 2nd Battalion. In 1966 The Royal Rifles of Canada was placed on the Supplementary Order of Battle.

The 1968 Armed Forces Act unified all three services into a single command structure, under a Chief of Defence Staff, and the title of Canadian Armed Forces was taken into use. The changes introduced had little effect on the Army as its titles, badges and distinctions remained unchanged, but the colour of khaki was replaced by a new standard, bottle green uniform and a universal system of rank insignia. There were, however, further changes to the Militia Establishment, with 14th Canadian Hussars, The South Saskatchewan Regiment and The Yukon Regiment being placed on the Supplementary Order of Battle. Les Fusiliers du St.-Laurent (5e Bataillon, Royal 22e Regiment) reverted to Les Fusiliers du St.-Laurent, later Les Fusiliers du Saint-Laurent, and its former corps battle honour was again taken into use; Le Regiment de Trois Rivieres (RCAC) was restyled 12e Regiment Blinde du Canada and later joined the regular Royal Canadian Armoured Corps Establishment. The regular infantry establishment was increased by the raising of The Canadian Airborne Regiment, which inherited the combined battle honours of the disbanded First Canadian Parachute Battalion and 1st Special Service Battalion.

The reduction of force levels in Europe in 1970 resulted in the Fort Garry Horse being placed on the Supplementary Order of Battle, together with the remaining regular battalions, raised in 1953, of The Canadian Guards, The Queen's Own Rifles of Canada and The Black Watch (Royal Highland Regiment) of Canada. These reductions to the regular infantry establishment were off-set by the raising of new 3rd Battalions for The Royal Canadian Regiment and Princess Patricia's Canadian Light Infantry. To conform to these changes in the Regular Establishment the numbering of the corresponding militia regiments was amended accordingly. The Grey and Simcoe Foresters (RCAC) was converted to form an infantry battalion, reverted to its old title of The Grey and Simcoe Foresters and The North Saskatchewan Regiment lost its 2nd Battalion.

In 1970 several units of the Militia were embodied, for the first time since the Reil Rebellion, to assist some mobilized regular units to counter the activities of the Front de Liberation de Quebec, an extremist organization, in the St. Lawrence Valley. And in 1990 units of the Regular Army were deployed 'in aid to the Civil Power', again in Quebec Province, to overcome a Mohawk uprising against a proposed golf course to be built on a sacred tribal site.

By 1991, in addition to its North Atlantic Treaty Organization commitment and despite defence cuts, servicemen and women of the Canadian Armed Forces have served in every United Nations peacekeeping mission since 1956.

New Zealand

In 1964 The Royal New Zealand Regiment amalgamated with The Canterbury Regiment, The Auckland Regiment (Countess of Ranfurly's Own), The Otago and Southland Regiment, The Wellington Regiment (City of Wellington's Own), The Hauraki Regiment, The Wellington West Coast and Taranaki Regiment, The Hawke's Bay Regiment, The Nelson, Marlborough and West Coast Regiment and The Northland Regiment to form The Royal New Zealand Infantry Regiment, a 'large regiment' of eight battalions, of which two were Regular Army units and the remaining six part of the Territorial Force:

    1st Battalion
    2/1st Battalion
    2nd Battalion (Canterbury and Nelson, Marlborough and West Coast)
    3rd Battalion (Auckland (Countess of Ranfurly's Own and Northland)
    4th Battalion (Otago and Southland)
    5th Battalion (Wellington West Coast and Taranaki)
    6th Battalion (Hauraki)
    7th Battalion (Wellington (City of Wellington's Own) and Hawke's Bay).

The new corps took into use all the combined battle honours of the former Territorial Force regiments: however, each battalion was authorized to select and to emblazon a maximum of twenty-one appropriate battle honours on their Regimental Colour, with **New Zealand** borne as an additional honour by the 1st and 5th Battalions only. Also, in that same year New Zealand personnel, all volunteers, arrived in South Vietnam to augment the Australian Army Training Team Vietnam.

The newly formed 1st Battalion, Royal New Zealand Infantry Regiment was on active service in the Borneo confrontation when 161st Field Battery, Royal New Zealand Artillery was deployed to South Vietnam to support the Royal Australian Regiment Battle Group. Later the 1st Battalion provided V and W Companies for Australian and New Zealand Army Corps battalions formed by the 2nd, 4th and 6th

Battalions, Royal Australian Regiment. This commitment ended in 1971 when New Zealand troops were withdrawn from South Vietnam.

By 1971 the Royal New Zealand Armoured Corps Establishment had been reduced to four Territorial Force squadrons with no Regular Army units. In 1972 the annual ballot for part-time training, introduced in 1962, was ended and the regular Army and the Territorial Force became 'all volunteer'.

Military personnel were sent to Zimbabwe in 1979 to supervise the transfer of power and during the following ten years the country continued to support United Nations missions in Sinai, Lebanon, Israel, Iran, Namibia, Pakistan, Cambodia, Angola and Yugoslavia.

A retrospective award of a theatre honour for South Vietnam was approved by the Queen on 2 July 1999.

South Africa

The hasty withdrawal from their African colonies by Belgium, France and, in particular, Portugal, the blockade of Southern Rhodesia, later Zimbabwe, and the United Nations suspension over the future administration of the former German South West Africa left the new Republic feeling isolated and threatened. The external situation, together with unrest within the nation, combined to lead South Africa into a series of protracted counterinsurgency operations against several nationalist groups, supported by the Soviet Union and her Communist allies, in particular Cuba, between 1966 and 1989. Initially, these operations were confined to South West Africa, later Namibia, against the South West Africa People's Organization. From 1975, however, these operations escalated to include direct intervention in Angola in support of the National Union for the Total Independence of Angola in 1975-82 and 1983-84.

By 1990, following extensive negotiations in the last months of 1989 in Geneva, a timetable for Namibian independence and for the withdrawal of Cuban forces from Angola was finally agreed. At the same time within South Africa the ban on opposition parties was lifted and political activity was resumed. These actions reduced anti-Government protests, many violent, which had been a feature of life in South Africa since the early 1960s. In 1994 a democratic black majority Government was elected and shortly afterwards South Africa chose to return to the Commonwealth.

The post-1961 South African Army expanded rapidly to provide the force levels required to carry out the counterinsurgency operations, mainly by raising additional Afrikaans-speaking regiments. By 1980 it was an efficient and well-equipped force with a Permanent Force Establishment of twenty-two infantry and two armoured regiments and a Citizen Force of twenty regiments of artillery and forty-seven infantry and seventeen armoured Regiments. It is understood that claims for the award of battle honours for 'Southern Africa 1966-1989' by these units are being considered by the Department of Defence in Pretoria.

Battle Honours

The complete list of battle honours post-Second World War is shown in Table 7.

Table 7

BATTLE HONOURS AFTER THE SECOND WORLD WAR

1.	**SRINAGAR** 27th October–13th November 1947 Kashmir Dispute 1947–48	1965 1976	7th Light Cavalry: 3rd Battalion, The Parachute Regiment: 1st Battalion, The Sikh Regiment 4th Battalion, The Kumaon Regiment
2.	**NAUSHERA** 24th January–7th February 1948 Kashmir Dispute 1947–48	1965	7th Light Cavalry: 1st Battalion, The Brigade of the Guards: 4th Battalion, The Brigade of the Guards: 2nd Battalion, The Parachute Regiment
3.	**JHANGAR** 15th–18th March 1948 Kashmir Dispute 1947–48	1965	7th Light Cavalry: 2nd Battalion, The Parachute Regiment: 15th Battalion (Patiala), The Punjab Regiment: 4th Battalion, The Dogra Regiment
4.	**RAJAORI** 8th–12th April 1948 Kashmir Dispute 1947–48	1965	The Central India Horse: 37 Assault Field Company, Bombay Engineer Group: 2nd Battalion, The Jat Regiment: 4th Battalion, The Dogra Regiment
5.	**TITHWAL** 17th–23rd May 1948 Kashmir Dispute 1947–48	1965	1st Battalion, The Madras Regiment: 1st Battalion, The Sikh Regiment: 3rd Battalion, The Garhwal Rifles
6.	**URI** 19th May–19th June 1948 Kashmir Dispute 1947–48	1965	2nd Battalion, The Dogra Regiment: 2nd Battalion, 3rd Gorkha Rifles
7.	**PUNCH** 20th November 1947–23rd November 1948 Kashmir Dispute 1947–48	1965	1st Battalion, The Parachute Regiment: 3rd Battalion, The Parachute Regiment: 4th Battalion, The Madras Regiment: 2nd Battalion, The Rajputana Rifles: 5th Battalion, The Rajputana Rifles: 1st Battalion, The Jammu and Kashmir Rifles: 7th Battalion, The Jammu and Kashmir Rifles: 8th Battalion, The Jammu and Kashmir Rifles: 9th Battalion, The Jammu and Kashmir Rifles: 1st Battalion, 4th Gorkha Rifles: 6th Battalion, 8th Gorkha Rifles
8.	**GURAIS** 24th–29th June 1948 Kashmir Dispute 1947–48	1965	2nd Battalion, The Brigade of the Guards: 2nd Battalion, 4th Gorkha Rifles
9.	**SKARDU** 11th February–13th August 1948 Kashmir Dispute 1947–48	1965	6th Battalion, The Jammu and Kashmir Rifles
10.	**ZOJI LA** 3rd September–4th November 1948 Kashmir Dispute 1947–48	1965	7th Light Cavalry: 13 Field Company, Madras Engineer Group: 433 Field Company, Madras Engineer Group: 15th Battalion (Patiala), The Punjab Regiment: 4th Battalion, The Rajput Regiment: 3rd Battalion, The Jat Regiment: 1st Battalion, 5th Gorkha Rifles

Battle Honours After the Second World War

11.	**KARGIL** 5th–24th November 1948 Kashmir Dispute 1947–48	1965	1st Battalion, 5th Gorkha Rifles
12.	**JAMMU AND KASHMIR 1947–48** 27th October 1947–31st December 1948 Kashmir Dispute 1947–48	1965	7th Light Cavalry;The Central India Horse: 12 Field Company, Madras Engineer Group: 13 Field Company, Madras Engineer Group: 14 Field Company, Madras Engineer Group: 433 Field Company, Madras Engineer Group: 32 Assault Field Company, Madras Engineer Group: 36 Parachute Field Company, Madras Engineer Group: 69 Field Company, Bengal Engineer Group: 19 Field Company, Bombay Engineer Group: 21 Field Company, Bombay Engineer Group: 22 Field Company, Bombay Engineer Group: 99 Field Company,Bombay Engineer Group: 37 Assault Field Company, Bombay Engineer Group: 411 Parachute Field Company, Bombay Engineer Group: 1st Battalion, The Brigade of the Guards: 2nd Battalion, The Brigade of the Guards: 4th Battalion, The Brigade of the Guards: 1st Battalion, The Parachute Regiment: 2nd Battalion, The Parachute Regiment: 3rd Battalion, The Parachute Regiment: 15th Battalion (Patiala), The Punjab Regiment: 1st Battalion, The Madras Regiment: 4th Battalion, The Madras Regiment: 2nd Battalion, The Rajputana Rifles: 5th Battalion, The Rajputana Rifles: 6th Battalion, The Rajputana Rifles: 7th Battalion (Sawai Man),The Rajputana Rifles: 3rd Battalion,The Rajput Regiment: 4th Battalion,The Rajput Regiment: 2nd Battalion, The Jat Regiment: 3rd Battalion, The Jat Regiment: 5th Battalion, The Jat Regiment: 1st Battalion, The Sikh Regiment: 5th Battalion, The Sikh Regiment: 2nd Battalion,The Dogra Regiment: 4th Battalion, The Dogra Regiment: 1st Battalion,The Garhwal Rifles: 3rd Battalion, The Garhwal Rifles: 4th Battalion, The Kumaon Regiment: 3rd Battalion, The Assam Regiment: 1st Battalion,The Mahar Regiment: 1st Battalion,The Jammu and Kashmir Rifles:2nd Battalion,The Jammu and Kashmir Rifles: 3rd Battalion,The Jammu and Kashmir Rifles: 5th Battalion, The Jammu and Kashmir Rifles: 6th Battalion,The Jammu and Kashmir Rifles: 7th Battalion,The Jammu and Kashmir Rifles: 8th Battalion, The Jammu and Kashmir Rifles: 9th Battalion, The Jammu and Kashmir Rifles: 2nd Battalion, 3rd Gorkha Rifles: 1st Battalion, 4th Gorkha Rifles: 1st Battalion, 5th Gorkha Rifles: 6th Battalion, 8th Gorkha Rifles
13.	**KASHMIR 1948** July–August 1948 Kashmir Dispute 1947–48	?	11th Cavalry (Frontier Force): 1st Battalion, The Punjab Regiment: 2nd Battalion, The Punjab Regiment: 5th Battalion, The Punjab Regiment: 6th Battalion, The Punjab Regiment: 8th Battalion, The Punjab Regiment: 13th Battalion, The Punjab Regiment: 14th Battalion,The Punjab Regiment: 17th Battalion,The Punjab Regiment: 11th Battalion,The Baluch Regiment: 1st Battalion,The Frontier Force Regiment: 2nd Battalion (Guides), The Frontier Force Regiment: 4th Battalion,The Frontier Force Regiment: 5th Battalion, The Frontier Force Regiment: 7th Battalion (Coke's), The Frontier Force Regiment: 9th Battalion (Wilde's),The Frontier Force Regiment: 10th Battalion,The Frontier Force Regiment: 1st Battalion,The Azad Kashmir Regiment: 2nd Battalion, The Azad Kashmir Regiment: 3rd Battalion, The Azad Kashmir Regiment: 4th Battalion, The Azad Kashmir Regiment: 5th Battalion,The Azad Kashmir Regiment: 6th Battalion,The Azad Kashmir Regiment: 7th Battalion,The Azad Kashmir Regiment: 10th Battalion,The Azad Kashmir Regiment: 11th Battalion,The Azad Kashmir Regiment: 12th Battalion, The Azad Kashmir Regiment: 14th Battalion,The Azad Kashmir Regiment: 17th Battalion,The Azad Kashmir Regiment: 18th Battalion,The Azad Kashmir Regiment: 19th Battalion,The Azad Kashmir Regiment: 29th Battalion,The Azad Kashmir Regiment: 30th Battalion, The Azad Kashmir Regiment: 31st Battalion, The Azad Kashmir Regiment: 32nd Battalion, The Azad Kashmir Regiment: 33rd Battalion,The Azad Kashmir Regiment: 36th Battalion,The Azad Kashmir Regiment: 38th Battalion,The Azad Kashmir Regiment
14.	**NURANANG** 16th–18th November 1962 Chinese Aggression 1962	1975	4th Battalion, The Garhwal Rifles
15.	**REZANG LA** 18th November 1962 Chinese Aggression 1962	1975	13th Battalion, The Kumaon Regiment

No.	Battle Honour	Year	Units
16.	**CHUSHUL** 18th–24th November 1962 Chinese Aggression 1962	1975	1st Battalion, 8th Gorkha Rifles
17.	**LADAKH 1962** 20th October–24th November 1962 Chinese Aggression 1962	1975	5th Battalion, The Jat Regiment: 13th Battalion, The Kumaon Regiment: 1st Battalion, The Mahar Regiment: 1st Battalion, 8th Gorkha Rifles
18.	**HAJIPIR** 26th–31st August 1965 Indo-Pak Conflict 1965	1975	1st Battalion, The Parachute Regiment: 19th Battalion, The Punjab Regiment: 6th Battalion, The Dogra Regiment
19.	**RAJA PICQUET–CHAND TEKRI** 5th–6th September 1965 Indo-Pak Conflict 1965	1975	2nd Battalion, The Sikh Regiment: 3rd Battalion, The Dogra Regiment
20.	**JAURIAN-KALIT** 2nd–5th September 1965 Indo-Pak Conflict 1965	1975	9th Battalion, The Mahar Regiment
21.	**KALIDHAR** 1st September–5th October 1965 Indo-Pak Conflict 1965	1975	9th Battalion, The Punjab Regiment: 1st Battalion, The Madras Regiment: 6th Battalion, The Sikh Light Infantry: 3rd Battalion, The Mahar Regiment: 1st Battalion, 1st Gorkha Rifles
22.	**SANJOI-MIRPUR** 3rd–12th September 1965 Indo-Pak Conflict 1965	1975	4th Battalion, The Kumaon Regiment: 3rd Battalion, 8th Gorkha Rifles
23.	**OP HILL (NL 1053)** 2nd–3rd November 1965 Indo-Pak Conflict 1965	1975	7th Battalion, The Sikh Regiment: 5th Battalion, The Sikh Light Infantry: 2nd Battalion, The Dogra Regiment
24.	**JAMMU AND KASHMIR 1965** 5th August–3rd November 1965 Indo-Pak Conflict 1965	1975	18th Cavalry: 20 Lancers: 13 Field Company, Madras Engineer Group: 68 Field Company, Bengal Engineer Group: 73 Field Company, Bengal Engineer Group: 89 Field Company, Bengal Engineer Group: 369 Field Company, Bengal Engineer Group: 374 Field Company, Bengal Engineer Group: 40 Field Park Company, Bengal Engineer Group: 305 Field Park Company, Bombay Engineer Group: 1st Battalion, The Parachute Regiment: 9th Battalion, The Punjab Regiment: 19th Battalion, The Punjab Regiment: 1st Battalion, The Madras Regiment: 8th Battalion, The Grenadiers: 3rd Battalion, The Rajputana Rifles: 4th Battalion, The Rajput Regiment: 2nd Battalion, The Sikh Regiment: 7th Battalion, The Sikh Regiment: 5th Battalion, The Sikh Light Infantry: 6th Battalion, The Sikh Light Infantry: 2nd Battalion, The Dogra Regiment: 3rd Battalion, The Dogra Regiment: 6th Battalion, The Dogra Regiment: 4th Battalion, The Kumaon Regiment: 14th Battalion (Gwalior), The Kumaon Regiment: 3rd Battalion, The Mahar Regiment: 9th Battalion, The Mahar Regiment: 11th Battalion, The Mahar Regiment: 1st Battalion, 1st Gorkha Rifles: 3rd Battalion, 8th Gorkha Rifles
		1976	11th Battalion, Jammu and Kashmir Militia

25.	**BURKI** 9th–10th September 1965 Indo-Pak Conflict 1965	1975	The Central India Horse: 5th Battalion, The Brigade of the Guards: 16th Battalion (Patiala), The Punjab Regiment 19th Battalion (Kolhapur), The Maratha Light Infantry: 4th Battalion, The Sikh Regiment
26.	**ASAL UTTAR** 9th–11th September 1965 Indo-Pak Conflict 1965	1975	The Deccan Horse: 3rd Cavalry: 4th Battalion, The Grenadiers: 18th Battalion (Saurashtra), The Rajputana Rifles: 1st Battalion, The Dogra Regiment: 2nd Battalion, The Mahar Regiment: 9th Battalion, The Jammu and Kashmir Rifles
27.	**HUSSAINIWALA BRIDGE** 20th September 1965 Indo-Pak Conflict 1965	1975	2nd Battalion, The Maratha Light Infantry
28.	**DOGRAI** 21st–22nd September 1965 Indo-Pak Conflict 1965	1975	The Scinde Horse: 7th Battalion, The Punjab Regiment: 13th Battalion (Jind), The Punjab Regiment: 3rd Battalion, The Jat Regiment: 15th Battalion, The Dogra Regiment
29.	**MAHARAJKE** 7th–8th September 1965 Indo-Pak Conflict 1965	1975	4th Battalion, The Madras Regiment
30.	**CHARWA** 7th–8th September 1965 Indo-Pak Conflict 1965	1975	4th Battalion, The Rajputana Rifles: 2nd Battalion, 5th Gorkha Rifles
31.	**PHILLORA** 11th–13th September 1965 Indo-Pak Conflict 1965	1975	The Poona Horse: 4 Horse: 5th Battalion, The Jat Regiment: 5th Battalion, 9th Gorkha Rifles
32.	**BUTTUR DOGRANDI** 16th–17th September 1965 Indo-Pak Conflict 1965	1975	The Poona Horse: 8th Battalion, The Garhwal Rifles
33.	**TILAKPUR-MUHADIPUR** 18th–19th September 1965 Indo-Pak Conflict 1965	1975	18th Cavalry: 10th Battalion, The Mahar Regiment
34.	**PUNJAB 1965** 6th–23rd September 1965 Indo-Pak Conflict 1965	1975	16th Light Cavalry: 7th Light Cavalry: 8th Light Cavalry: 2nd Lancers: The Poona Horse: The Deccan Horse: The Scinde Horse: 3rd Cavalry: 18th Cavalry: 4 Horse: The Central India Horse: 14 Assault Field Company, Madras Engineer Group: 65 Assault Field Company, Madras Engineer Group: 428 Field Company, Madras Engineer Group: 100 Field Company, Bengal Engineer Group: 5th Battalion, The Brigade of the Guards: 7th Battalion, The Punjab Regiment: 13th Battalion (Jind), The Punjab Regiment: 16th Battalion (Patiala), The Punjab Regiment: 1st Battalion, The Madras Regiment: 3rd Battalion, The Madras Regiment: 4th Battalion, The Madras Regiment: 9th Battalion (Travancore), The Madras Regiment: 4th Battalion, The Grenadiers: 2nd Battalion, The Maratha Light Infantry: 19th Battalion (Kolhapur), The Maratha Light Infantry: 4th Battalion, The Rajputana Rifles: 5th Battalion, The Rajputana Rifles: 18th Battalion (Saurashtra), The Rajputana Rifles: 20th Battalion (Jodhpur), The Rajput Regiment: 3rd Battalion, The Jat Regiment: 5th Battalion, The Jat Regiment: 4th Battalion, The Sikh Regiment: 1st Battalion, The Sikh Light Infantry: 1st Battalion, The Dogra Regiment: 15th Battalion, The Dogra Regiment: 6th Battalion, The Garhwal Rifles: 8th Battalion,

#	Battle Honour	Year	Units
			The Garhwal Rifles: 9th Battalion, The Kumaon Regiment: 2nd Battalion, The Mahar Regiment: 10th Battalion, The Mahar Regiment: 9th Battalion, The Jammu and Kashmir Rifles: 5th Battalion, 4th Gorkha Rifles: 2nd Battalion, 5th Gorkha Rifles: 6th Battalion, 8th Gorkha Rifles: 5th Battalion, 9th Gorkha Rifles
35.	**GADRA ROAD** 8th September 1965 Indo-Pak Conflict 1965	1975	3rd Battalion, The Brigade of the Guards: 1st Battalion, The Garhwal Rifles
36.	**RAJASTHAN 1965** 6th September–2nd December 1965 Indo-Pak Conflict 1965	1975	78 Field Company, Bengal Engineer Group: 85 Field Company, Bengal Engineer Group: 3rd Battalion, The Brigade of the Guards: 3rd Battalion, The Grenadiers: 13th Battalion (Jaisalmer), The Grenadiers: 4th Battalion, The Maratha Light Infantry: 5th Battalion, The Maratha Light Infantry: 1st Battalion, The Garhwal Rifles
37.	**KHEM KARAN 1965** September 1965 Hostilities with India 1965	?	4 Cavalry: 5th Horse: 6th Lancers: 12th Cavalry (Frontier Force): 15th Lancers: 24 Cavalry: 7th Battalion, The Punjab Regiment: 6th Battalion, The Baluch Regiment: 7th Battalion, The Baluch Regiment: 1st Battalion, The Frontier Force Regiment: 2nd Battalion (Guides), The Frontier Force Regiment: 5th Battalion, The Frontier Force Regiment: 10th Battalion, The Frontier Force Regiment
38.	**CHAWINDA 1965** September 1965 Hostilities with India 1965	?	The Guides Cavalry (Frontier Force): 11th Cavalry (Frontier Force): 19th Lancers: 22 Cavalry: 25 Cavalry: 31 Cavalry: 33 Cavalry: 2nd Battalion,The Punjab Regiment: 14th Battalion, The Punjab Regiment: 20th Battalion, The Baluch Regiment: 3rd Battalion, The Frontier Force Regiment: 4th Battalion,The Frontier Force Regiment: 9th Battalion (Wilde's), The Frontier Force Regiment: 13th Battalion, The Frontier Force Regiment: 14th Battalion, The Frontier Force Regiment
39.	**DEVA-CHAMB 1965** September 1965 Hostilities with India 1965	?	11th Cavalry (Frontier Force): 13th Lancers: 9th Battalion, The Punjab Regiment: 8th Battalion, The Baluch Regiment: 6th Battalion, The Frontier Force Regiment: 12th Battalion, The Frontier Force Regiment: 5th Battalion, The Azad Kashmir Regiment: 14th Battalion, The Azad Kashmir Regiment: 19th Battalion, The Azad Kashmir Regiment
40.	**JAURIAN 1965** September 1965 Hostilities with India 1965	?	13th Lancers: 6th Battalion, The Punjab Regiment: 13th Battalion, The Punjab Regiment: 14th Battalion, The Punjab Regiment: 15th Battalion, The Punjab Regiment: 8th Battalion, The Baluch Regiment: 6th Battalion, The Frontier Force Regiment: 12th Battalion, The Frontier Force Regiment: 19th Battalion, The Azad Kashmir Regiment
41.	**SIALKOT 1965** September 1965 Hostilities with India 1965	?	20 Lancers: 31 Cavalry: 1st Battalion, The Punjab Regiment: 19th Battalion (Sher Shah), The Punjab Regiment: 2nd Battalion, The Baluch Regiment: 4th Battalion, The Baluch Regiment: 9th Battalion, The Baluch Regiment
42.	**LAHORE 1965** September 1965 Hostilities with India 1965	?	23rd Cavalry (Frontier Force): 30 Cavalry: 12th Battalion, The Punjab Regiment: 16th Battalion (Pathans), The Punjab Regiment: 17th Battalion, The Punjab Regiment: 1st Battalion, The Baluch Regiment: 3rd Battalion, The Baluch Regiment: 11th Battalion, The Baluch Regiment: 15th Battalion, The Baluch Regiment: 18th Battalion, The Baluch Regiment: 7th Battalion (Coke's), The Frontier Force Regiment: 10th Battalion, The Frontier Force Regiment: 11th Battalion, The Frontier Force Regiment: 15th Battalion, The Frontier Force Regiment
43.	**BEDIAN 1965** September 1965 Hostilities with India 1965	?	32 Cavalry

No.	Battle Honour / Date / Conflict	Awarded	Units
44.	**SULEMANKI 1965** September 1965 Hostilities with India 1965	?	4th Battalion, The Punjab Regiment: 10th Battalion, The Punjab Regiment: 22nd Battalion, The Punjab Regiment: 1st Battalion, The Baluch Regiment
45.	**RANN KUTCH 1965** September 1965 Hostilities with India 1965	?	6th Battalion, The Punjab Regiment: 15th Battalion, The Punjab Regiment: 18th Battalion, The Punjab Regiment: 6th Battalion, The Baluch Regiment: 2nd Battalion (Guides), The Frontier Force Regiment: 8th Battalion, The Frontier Force Regiment
46.	**KASUR 1965** September 1965 Hostilities with India 1965	?	7th Battalion, The Punjab Regiment: 7th Battalion, The Baluch Regiment: 12th Battalion, The Baluch Regiment
47.	**HAJIPIR 1965** September 1965 Hostilities with India 1965	?	20th Battalion, The Punjab Regiment: 10th Battalion, The Baluch Regiment: 4th Battalion, The Azad Kashmir Regiment: 6th Battalion, The Azad Kashmir Regiment: 7th Battalion, The Azad Kashmir Regiment: 10th Battalion, The Azad Kashmir Regiment
48.	**RAJASTHAN 1965** September 1965 Hostilities with India 1965	?	18th Battalion, The Punjab Regiment: 8th Battalion, The Frontier Force Regiment: 23rd Battalion, The Frontier Force Regiment
49.	**MAHL 1965** September 1965 Hostilities with India 1965	?	12th Battalion, The Azad Kashmir Regiment
50.	**TITHWAL-JURA 1965** September 1965 Hostilities with India 1965	?	23rd Battalion, The Azad Kashmir Regiment
51.	**DARSANA** 3rd–20th December 1971 Indo-Pak Conflict 1971	1982	45 Cavalry; 5th Battalion, 1st Gorkha Rifles
52.	**SUADIH** 3rd–20th December 1971 Indo-Pak Conflict 1971	1982	5th Battalion, The Maratha Light Infantry: 9th Battalion, The Dogra Regiment
53.	**MADHUMATI RIVER** 3rd–20th December 1971 Indo-Pak Conflict 1971	1982	22nd Battalion, The Rajput Regiment
54.	**KUMARKHALI** 3rd–20th December 1971 Indo-Pak Conflict 1971	1982	2nd Battalion, 9th Gorkha Rifles
55.	**SYAMGANJ** 3rd–20th December 1971 Indo-Pak Conflict 1971	1982	1st Battalion, The Jammu and Kashmir Rifles

No.	Battle Honour	Year	Units
56.	**SIRAMANI** 3rd–20th December 1971 Indo-Pak Conflict 1971	1982	26th Battalion, The Madras Regiment; 4th Battalion, The Sikh Regiment; 13th Battalion, The Dogra Regiment
57.	**HILLI** 3rd–20th December 1971 Indo-Pak Conflict 1971	1982	8th Battalion, The Brigade of the Guards; 5th Battalion, The Garhwal Rifles
58.	**BHADURIA** 3rd–20th December 1971 Indo-Pak Conflict 1971	1982	17th Battalion, The Kumaon Regiment
59.	**BOGRA** 3rd–20th December 1971 Indo-Pak Conflict 1971	1982	63 Cavalry; 69 Armoured Regiment: 5th Battalion, 11th Gorkha Rifles
60.	**KHANSAMA** 3rd–20th December 1971 Indo-Pak Conflict 1971	1982	21st Battalion, The Rajput Regiment
61.	**SHAMSHER NAGAR** 3rd–20th December 1971 Indo-Pak Conflict 1971	1982	4th Battalion, The Kumaon Regiment: 10th Battalion, The Mahar Regiment
62.	**SYLHET** 3rd–20th December 1971 Indo-Pak Conflict 1971	1982	108 Engineer Regiment, Bombay Engineer Group: 9th Battalion, The Brigade of the Guards: 4th Battalion, 5th Gorkha Rifles
63.	**GANGA SAGAR** 3rd–20th December 1971 Indo-Pak Conflict 1971	1982	14th Battalion, The Brigade of the Guards
64.	**AKHAURA** 3rd–20th December 1971 Indo-Pak Conflict 1971	1982	4th Battalion, The Brigade of the Guards: 18th Battalion (Saurashtra), The Rajput Regiment
65.	**BELONIA** 3rd–20th December 1971 Indo-Pak Conflict 1971	1982	2nd Battalion, The Rajput Regiment
66.	**MIAN BAZAR** 3rd–20th December 1971 Indo-Pak Conflict 1971	1982	7th Light Cavalry
67.	**CHAUDDAGRAM** 3rd–20th December 1971 Indo-Pak Conflict 1971	1982	3rd Battalion, The Dogra Regiment

68.	**MYNAMATI** 3rd–20th December 1971 Indo-Pak Conflict 1971	1982	7th Battalion, The Rajputana Rifles
69.	**JAMALPUR** 3rd–20th December 1971 Indo-Pak Conflict 1971	1982	1st Battalion, The Maratha Light Infantry
70.	**POONGLI BRIDGE** 3rd–20th December 1971 Indo-Pak Conflict 1971	1982	2nd Battalion, The Parachute Regiment
71.	**EAST PAKISTAN 1971** 3rd–20th December 1971 Indo-Pak Conflict 1971	1982	7th Light Cavalry; 63 Cavalry; 45 Cavalry; 69 Armoured Regiment; 3 Engineer Regiment, Madras Engineer Group: 4 Engineer Regiment, Madras Engineer Group: 13 Engineer Regiment, Madras Engineer Group: 52 Engineer Regiment, Bengal Engineer Group: 58 Engineer Regiment, Bengal Engineer Group: 59 Engineer Regiment, Bengal Engineer Group: 62 Engineer Regiment, Bengal Engineer Group: 63 Engineer Regiment, Bengal Engineer Group: 102 Engineer Regiment, Bombay Engineer Group: 108 Engineer Regiment, Bombay Engineer Group: 4th Battalion, The Brigade of the Guards: 5th Battalion, The Brigade of the Guards: 8th Battalion, The Brigade of the Guards: 9th Battalion, The Brigade of the Guards: 14th Battalion, The Brigade of the Guards: 2nd Battalion, The Parachute Regiment: 7th Battalion, The Punjab Regiment: 8th Battalion, The Madras Regiment: 26th Battalion, The Madras Regiment: 1st Battalion, The Maratha Light Infantry: 5th Battalion, The Maratha Light Infantry: 20th Battalion (Baroda), The Maratha Light Infantry: 22nd Battalion (Hyderabad), The Maratha Light Infantry: 7th Battalion, The Rajputana Rifles: 12th Battalion, The Rajputana Rifles: 19th Battalion, The Rajputana Rifles: 2nd Battalion, The Rajput Regiment: 6th Battalion, The Rajput Regiment: 18th Battalion (Saurashtra), The Rajput Regiment: 21st Battalion, The Rajput Regiment: 22nd Battalion, The Rajput Regiment: 4th Battalion, The Jat Regiment: 4th Battalion, The Sikh Regiment: 2nd Battalion, The Sikh Light Infantry: 4th Battalion, The Sikh Light Infantry: 3rd Battalion, The Dogra Regiment: 9th Battalion, The Dogra Regiment: 13th Battalion, The Dogra Regiment: 5th Battalion, The Garhwal Rifles: 3rd Battalion, The Kumaon Regiment: 17th Battalion, The Kumaon Regiment: 9th Battalion, The Kumaon Regiment: 12th Battalion, The Kumaon Regiment: 10th Battalion, The Mahar Regiment: 1st Battalion, The Kumaon Regiment: 10th Battalion, The Bihar Regiment: 2nd Battalion, 5th Gorkha Rifles: 4th Battalion, 5th Gorkha Rifles: Jammu and Kashmir Rifles: 5th Battalion, 1st Gorkha Rifles: 2nd Battalion, 9th Gorkha Rifles: 5th Battalion, 11th Gorkha Rifles
72.	**CHHAMB** 3rd–20th December 1971 Indo-Pak Conflict 1971	1982	72 Armoured Regiment: 5th Battalion, The Assam Regiment
73.	**LALEALI-PICQUET 707** 3rd–20th December 1971 Indo-Pak Conflict 1971	1982	8th Battalion, The Jammu and Kashmir Light Infantry
74.	**DEFENCE OF PUNCH** 3rd–20th December 1971 Indo-Pak Conflict 1971	1982	9th Battalion (Commando), The Parachute Regiment: 6th Battalion, The Sikh Regiment

75.	**THANPIR** 3rd–20th December 1971 Indo-Pak Conflict 1971	1982	13th Battalion, The Mahar Regiment
76.	**GUTRIAN** 3rd–20th December 1971 Indo-Pak Conflict 1971	1982	11th Battalion, The Jammu and Kashmir Light Infantry
77.	**NANGI TEKRI** 3rd–20th December 1971 Indo-Pak Conflict 1971	1982	21st Battalion, The Punjab Regiment
78.	**TURTOK** 3rd–20th December 1971 Indo-Pak Conflict 1971	1982	HQ Ladakh Scouts
79.	**SHINGO RIVER VALLEY** 3rd–20th December 1971 Indo-Pak Conflict 1971	1982	7th Battalion, The Brigade of the Guards: 5th Battalion, 3rd Gorkha Rifles: 2nd Battalion, 11th Gorkha Rifles: 9th Battalion, The Jammu and Kashmir Light Infantry
80.	**BRACHIL PASS AND WALI MALIK** 3rd–20th December 1971 Indo-Pak Conflict 1971	1982	18th Battalion, The Punjab Regiment
81.	**JAMMU AND KASHMIR 1971** 3rd–20th December 1971 Indo-Pak Conflict 1971	1982	72 Armoured Regiment: 14 Engineer Regiment, Madras Engineer Group: 61 Engineer Regiment, Bengal Engineer Group: 105 Engineer Regiment, Bombay Engineer Group: 7th Battalion, The Brigade of the Guards: 11th Battalion, The Brigade of the Guards: 12th Battalion, The Brigade of the Guards: 9th Battalion (Commando), The Parachute Regiment: 18th Battalion, The Punjab Regiment: 21st Battalion, The Punjab Regiment: 8th Battalion, The Jat Regiment: 5th Battalion, The Sikh Regiment: 6th Battalion, The Sikh Regiment: 7th Battalion, The Kumaon Regiment: 5th Battalion, The Assam Regiment: 13th Battalion, The Mahar Regiment: 4th Battalion, 1st Gorkha Rifles: 5th Battalion, 3rd Gorkha Rifles: 4th Gorkha Rifles: 3rd Battalion, 5th Gorkha Rifles: 4th Battalion, 9th Gorkha Rifles: 2nd Battalion, 11th Gorkha Rifles: 7th Battalion, 11th Gorkha Rifles: 8th Battalion, The Jammu and Kashmir Light Infantry: 9th Battalion, The Jammu and Kashmir Light Infantry: 11th Battalion, The Jammu and Kashmir Light Infantry: HQ Ladakh Scouts
82.	**HARAR KALAN** 3rd–20th December 1971 Indo-Pak Conflict 1971	1982	1 Horse: 1st Battalion, The Mahar Regiment
83.	**MALAKPUR** 3rd–20th December 1971 Indo-Pak Conflict 1971	1982	The Scinde Horse
84.	**CHAKRI** 3rd–20th December 1971 Indo-Pak Conflict 1971	1982	8th Battalion, The Grenadiers

85.	**BASANTAR RIVER** 3rd–20th December 1971 Indo-Pak Conflict 1971	1982	The Poona Horse: 4 Horse: 5 Engineer Regiment, Madras Engineer Group: 9 Engineer Regiment, Madras Engineer Group: 6th Battalion, The Madras Regiment: 16th Battalion (Travancore), The Madras Regiment: 18th Battalion (Saurashtra), The Rajputana Rifles
86.	**JARPAL** 3rd–20th December 1971 Indo-Pak Conflict 1971	1982	3rd Battalion, The Grenadiers
87.	**DERA BABA NANAK** 3rd–20th December 1971 Indo-Pak Conflict 1971	1982	10th Battalion, The Dogra Regiment 1st Battalion, 9th Gorkha Rifles
88.	**BURJ** 3rd–20th December 1971 Indo-Pak Conflict 1971	1982	15th Battalion, The Maratha Light Infantry
89.	**FATEHPUR** 3rd–20th December 1971 Indo-Pak Conflict 1971	1982	8th Battalion, The Sikh Light Infantry
90.	**SHEHJRA** 3rd–20th December 1971 Indo-Pak Conflict 1971	1982	3rd Cavalry: 6th Battalion, The Mahar Regiment: 1st Battalion, 5th Gorkha Rifles
91.	**PUNJAB 1971** 3rd–20th December 1971 Indo-Pak Conflict 1971	1982	7th Light Cavalry: 1 Horse: The Poona Horse: The Scinde Horse: 3rd Cavalry: 4 Horse: 66 Armoured Regiment: 5 Engineer Regiment, Madras Engineer Group: 7 Engineer Regiment, Madras Engineer Group: 9 Engineer Regiment, Madras Engineer Group: 201 Engineer Regiment, Madras Engineer Group: 104 Engineer Regiment, Bombay Engineer Group: 110 Engineer Regiment, Bombay Engineer Group: 113 Engineer Regiment, Bombay Engineer Group: 9th Battalion, The Punjab Regiment: 15th Battalion (Patiala), The Punjab Regiment: 22nd Battalion, The Punjab Regiment: 6th Battalion, The Madras Regiment: 16th Battalion (Travancore), The Madras Regiment: 3rd Battalion, The Grenadiers: 8th Battalion, The Grenadiers: 15th Battalion, The Maratha Light Infantry: 18th Battalion (Saurashtra), The Rajputana Rifles: 2nd Battalion, The Sikh Regiment: 8th Battalion, The Sikh Light Infantry: 1st Battalion, The Dogra Regiment: 10th Battalion, The Dogra Regiment: 15th Battalion, The Dogra Regiment: 6th Battalion, The Kumaon Regiment: 1st Battalion, The Mahar Regiment: 6th Battalion, The Mahar Regiment: 1st Battalion, 5th Gorkha Rifles: 1st Battalion, 9th Gorkha Rifles: 3rd Battalion, 9th Gorkha Rifles
92.	**LONGANEWALA** 3rd–20th December 1971 Indo-Pak Conflict 1971	1982	23rd Battalion, The Punjab Regiment
93.	**GADRA CITY** 3rd–20th December 1971 Indo-Pak Conflict 1971	1982	15th Battalion (Indore), The Kumaon Regiment
94.	**KHINSAR** 3rd–20th December 1971 Indo-Pak Conflict 1971	1982	20th Battalion (Jodhpur), The Rajput Regiment

95.	**CHACHRO** 3rd–20th December 1971 Indo-Pak Conflict 1971	1982	10th Battalion (Commando), The Parachute Regiment
96.	**PARBAT ALI** 3rd–20th December 1971 Indo-Pak Conflict 1971	1982	10th Battalion, The Sikh Regiment: 10th Battalion, The Sikh Light Infantry: 2nd Battalion, The Mahar Regiment
97.	**SINDH 1971** 3rd–20th December 1971 Indo-Pak Conflict 1971	1982	75 Armoured Regiment: 57 Engineer Regiment, Bengal Engineer Group: 10th Battalion (Commando), The Parachute Regiment: 23rd Battalion, The Punjab Regiment: 18th Battalion (Mysore), The Madras Regiment: 20th Battalion (Jodhpur), The Rajput Regiment: 10th Battalion, The Sikh Regiment: 10th Battalion, The Sikh Light Infantry: 13th Battalion, The Kumaon Regiment: 15th Battalion (Indore), The Kumaon Regiment: 2nd Battalion, The Mahar Regiment
98.	**SHAKARGARH 1971** December 1971 Hostilities with India 1971	?	20 Lancers: 33 Cavalry: 72 Medium Regiment: 78 Field Regiment: 83 Medium Regiment: 11th Battalion, The Punjab Regiment: 13th Battalion, The Punjab Regiment: 20th Battalion, The Punjab Regiment: 27th Battalion, The Punjab Regiment: 19th Battalion, The Frontier Force Regiment: 23rd Battalion, The Frontier Force Regiment: 27th Battalion, The Frontier Force Regiment
99.	**QAISAR-I-HIND 1971** December 1971 Hostilities with India 1971	?	4 Cavalry: 45 Field Regiment: 170 Independent Mortar Battery: 3rd Battalion, The Punjab Regiment: 9th Battalion, The Punjab Regiment: 19th Battalion (Sher Shah), The Punjab Regiment: 41st Battalion, The Baluch Regiment
100.	**CHHAMB 1971** December 1971 Hostilities with India 1971	?	11th Cavalry (Frontier Force): 26 Cavalry: 28 Cavalry: 11 Field Regiment: 28 Medium Regiment: 39 Field Regiment: 50 Field Regiment: 63 Field Regiment: 64 Medium Regiment: 71 Mountain Regiment: 81 Field Battery, Azad Kashmir: 285 Division Locating Battery: 474 Engineer Battalion: 41 Signal Battalion: 4th Battalion, The Punjab Regiment: 14th Battalion, The Punjab Regiment: 42nd Battalion, The Punjab Regiment: 10th Battalion, The Baluch Regiment: 23rd Battalion, The Baluch Regiment: 3rd Battalion, The Frontier Force Regiment: 17th Battalion, The Frontier Force Regiment: 33rd Battalion, The Frontier Force Regiment: 6th Battalion, The Azad Kashmir Regiment: 13th Battalion, The Azad Kashmir Regiment: 60 Electrical and Mechanical Engineering Battalion
101.	**ZAFARWAL 1971** December 1971 Hostilities with India 1971	?	13th Lancers: 31 Cavalry: 12 Medium Regiment: 17 Corps Locating Regiment: 29 Light Anti-Aircraft Regiment: 33 Heavy Regiment: 46 Field Regiment: 61 (Self Propelled) Field Regiment: 79 Division Locating Battery: 24th Battalion, The Punjab Regiment: 40th Battalion, The Punjab Regiment: 11th Battalion, The Baluch Regiment: 29th Battalion, The Frontier Force Regiment: 33rd Battalion, The Frontier Force Regiment
102.	**LAHORE 1971** December 1971 Hostilities with India 1971	?	4 Field Regiment: 9 Medium Regiment: 18 Field Regiment: 47 Field Regiment: 15th Battalion, The Punjab Regiment: 16th Battalion (Pathans), The Punjab Regiment: 43rd Battalion, The Punjab Regiment: 2nd Battalion, The Baluch Regiment: 3rd Battalion, The Baluch Regiment
103.	**SARGODHA 1971** December 1971 Hostilities with India 1971	?	5 Light Anti-Aircraft Regiment: 52 Heavy Anti-Aircraft Regiment: 52 Light Anti-Aircraft Regiment
104.	**BADIN 1971** December 1971 Hostilities with India 1971	?	58 Light Anti-Aircraft Regiment

105.	**SABUNA 1971** December 1971 Hostilities with India 1971	?	75 Light Anti-Aircraft Regiment; 76 Field Regiment; 46th Battalion, The Punjab Regiment
106.	**LIPA 1971** December 1971 Hostilities with India 1971	?	82 Mountain Battery; 9th Battalion, The Azad Kashmir Regiment
107.	**PAKKA 1971** December 1971 Hostilities with India 1971	?	173 Engineer Battalion: 7th Battalion, The Punjab Regiment
108.	**DARUCHIAN 1971** December 1971 Hostilities with India 1971	?	68 Mountain Regiment: 29th Battalion, The Azad Kashmir Regiment
109.	**LONG TAN** 18th–19th August 1966 Vietnam War 1965–72	1983	3rd Cavalry Regiment: Royal Australian Regiment
110.	**BIEN HOA** 24th January–1st March 1968 Vietnam War 1965–72	1983	3rd Cavalry Regiment: Royal Australian Regiment
111.	**CORAL-BALMORAL** 21st April–7th June 1968 Vietnam War 1965–72	1983	1st Armoured Regiment: 3rd Cavalry Regiment: Royal Australian Regiment
112.	**HAT DICH** 3rd December 1968–19th February 1969 Vietnam War 1965–72	1983	1st Armoured Regiment: 3rd Cavalry Regiment: Royal Australian Regiment
113.	**BINH BA** 31st May–30th June 1969 Vietnam War 1965–72	1983	1st Armoured Regiment: 3rd Cavalry Regiment: Royal Australian Regiment
114.	**VIETNAM 1965–72** 3rd June 1965–18th December 1972 Vietnam War 1965–72	1983	3rd Cavalry Regiment: Royal Australian Regiment
115.	**VIETNAM 1968–72** 1st January 1968–18th December 1972 Vietnam War 1965–72	1983	1st Armoured Regiment
116.	**GOOSE GREEN** 28th–29th May 1982 Falkland Islands Campaign 1982	1984	The Parachute Regiment

117.	**MOUNT LONGDON** 11th–12th June 1982 Falkland Islands Campaign 1982	1984	The Parachute Regiment
118.	**TUMBLEDOWN MOUNTAIN** 13th–14th June 1982 Falkland Islands Campaign 1982	1984	Scots Guards
119.	**WIRELESS RIDGE** 13th–14th June 1982 Falkland Islands Campaign 1982	1984	The Parachute Regiment
120.	**FALKLAND ISLANDS 1982** 2nd April–14th June 1982 Falkland Islands Campaign 1982	1984	The Blues and Royals (Royal Horse Guards and 1st Dragoons): Scots Guards: Welsh Guards: The Parachute Regiment: 7th Duke of Edinburgh's Own Gurkha Rifles: Special Air Service Regiment
		1991	Army Air Corps
121.	**WESTERN IRAQ** 19th January–24th March 1991 Gulf Campaign 1991	1991	Special Air Service Regiment
122.	**WADI AL BATIN** 25th–28th February 1991 Gulf Campaign 1991	1991	The Life Guards: 1st The Queen's Dragoon Guards: The Royal Scots Dragoon Guards (Carabiniers and Greys): The Queen's Royal Irish Hussars: 14th/20th King's Hussars: 16th/5th The Queen's Royal Lancers: Grenadier Guards: The Royal Scots (The Royal Regiment): The Royal Regiment of Fusiliers: The Staffordshire Regiment (The Prince of Wales's): Army Air Corps
123.	**GULF 1991** 16th January–28th February 1991 Gulf Campaign 1991	1991	The Life Guards: 1st The Queen's Dragoon Guards: The Royal Scots Dragoon Guards (Carabiniers and Greys): The Queen's Royal Irish Hussars: 14th/20th King's Hussars: 16th/5th The Queen's Royal Lancers: Grenadier Guards: Coldstream Guards: Scots Guards: The Royal Scots (The Royal Regiment): The Royal Regiment of Fusiliers: The Royal Highland Fusiliers (Princess Margaret's Own Glasgow and Ayrshire Regiment): The King's Own Scottish Borderers: The Staffordshire Regiment (The Prince of Wales's): Queen's Own Highlanders (Seaforth and Camerons): Special Air Service Regiment: Army Air Corps
124.	**VIETNAM 1967–70** 1st January 1967–31st December 1970 Vietnam War 1965–72	1999	Royal New Zealand Infantry Regiment

BATTLES AND OTHER ENGAGEMENTS FOUGHT BY THE MILITARY FORCES OF THE BRITISH EMPIRE DURING THE GREAT WAR AND THE THIRD AFGHAN WAR

FRANCE AND FLANDERS

1. **The Retreat from Mons**

	23rd August–5th September 1914	North of the Seine, and east of the road Paris – Roye – Peronne – Cambrai – Valenciennes – Conde.
BATTLE OF MONS	23rd–24th August 1914	The river d'Estinne to Peissant: thence a line to
Action of Elouges	24th August 1914	Rouveroy – Quevy-le-Petit – Athis – Quievrechain – Conde (exclusive).
Rearguard Action of Solesmes	25th August 1914	Between the rivers St Georges and d'Erclin, north of the line Salesches – Solesmes – St Vaast.
		*
Affair of Landrecies	25th August 1914	Bazuel (exclusive) – St Souplet – Walincourt – Esnes.
BATTLE OF LE CATEAU	26th August 1914	Neighbourhood of the villages of Marbaix and le Grand
Rearguard Affair of le Grande Fayt	26th August 1914	Fayt, and the ground between them.
Rearguard Affair of Etreux	27th August 1914	Neighbourhood of the villages of Fesmy and Etreux, and the ground between them.
		*
Affair of Cerizy	28th August 1914	*
Affair of Nery	1st September 1914	
Rearguard Action of Crepy-en-Valois	1st September 1914	North of Crepy-en-Valois.
Rearguard Actions of Villers Cotterets	1st September 1914	(a) Near Taillefontaine.
		(b) In the forest north of Villers Cotterets.
		(c) Near Pisseleux.

2. **The Advance to the Aisne**

BATTLE OF THE MARNE 1914	6th September–1st October 1914	*
Passage of the Petit Morin	7th–10th September 1914	Chateau Thierry – la Ferte-Gaucher – the river Grand Morin to Crecy: thence a line to Dhuisy.
Passage of the Marne		
BATTLE OF THE AISNE 1914	12th–15th September 1914	Oulches – Maizy – Blanzy – Septmonts – Soissons – Crouy – Allemant.
Passage of the Aisne		
Capture of the Aisne Heights, including the Chemin des Dames		
Actions of the Aisne Heights	20th September 1914	North of the Aisne, between Paissy and Vailly (exclusive).
Action of Chivy	26th September 1914	North of the Aisne, between Troyon and Beaulne.

3.	**The Defence of Antwerp**	4th–10th October 1914	
4.	**Operations in Flanders 1914**		
	BATTLE OF LA BASSEE	10th October–22nd November 1914 10th October–2nd November 1914	Road Noyelles-lez-Vermelles – Beuvry – Bethune (exclusive) – Estaires (exclusive): thence a line to Fournes (exclusive).
	BATTLE OF MESSINES 1914	12th October–2nd November 1914	The river Douve from Warneton to Dranoutre: thence a line to Caestre Station – Abeele Station – Reninghelst – Dickebusch – Voormezeele: thence along the Canal.
	BATTLE OF ARMENTIERES	13th October–2nd November 1914	Fournes – Estaires – Hazebrouck Station – Caestre Station – Dranoutre (exclusive); thence to the river Douve.
	Capture of Meteren	19th October–22nd November 1914	
	THE BATTLES OF YPRES 1914	21st–24th October 1914	The Comines Canal to Ypres: thence the Yser Canal to Steenstraat: from there the road to Bixschoote and, thence along the southern edge of the Houthulst Forest.
	BATTLE OF LANGEMARCK 1914	29th–31st October 1914	
	BATTLE OF GHELUVELT	11th November 1914	
	BATTLE OF NONNE BOSSCHEN		
5.	**Winter Operations 1914–15**	November 1914-February 1915	
	Defence of Festubert	23rd–24th November 1914	Givenchy (exclusive) – Gorre: thence road to le Touret – Rue de l'Epinette – la Quinque Rue.
	Attack on Wytschaete	14th December 1914	Road Wytschaete – Lindenhoek – Mt Kemmel – la Clytte – Hallebast – Vierstraat – Wytschaete.
	Defence of Givenchy 1914	20th–21st December 1914	The la Bassee Canal to Gorre: thence road to le Touret – Rue de l'Epinette – la Quinque Rue.
	First Action of Givenchy 1915	25th January 1915	Road to la Bassee – Annequin – Beuvry – Gorre – Festubert (exclusive).
	Affairs of Guinchy	29th January, 1st and 6th February 1915	Between the road and canal from Beuvry to la Bassee.
6.	**Summer Operations 1915**	March-October 1915	
	BATTLE OF NEUVE CHAPELLE	10th–13th March 1915	Road Richebourg-l'Avoue – Croix Barbee – Pont du Hem – Fauquissart – Aubers.
	Action of St Eloi	14th–15th March 1915	The Comines-Ypres railway as far as Zillebeke Lake, and thence the Zillebeke– Klein Zillebeke road.
	Capture of Hill 60	17th–22nd April 1915	
	THE BATTLES OF YPRES 1915	22nd April–25th May 1915	The Comines-Ypres Canal as far as Voormezeele: thence road to Vlamertinghe Chateau – Elverdinghe Chateau – Boesinghe – Langemarck.
	BATTLE OF GRAVENSTAFEL RIDGE	22nd–23rd April 1915	
	The Gas Attack	24th April–4th May 1915	
	BATTLE OF ST JULIEN	8th–13th May 1915	
	BATTLE OF FREZENBERG RIDGE	24th–25th May 1915	
	BATTLE OF BELLEWAARDE RIDGE	9th May 1915	Road Aubers – Fauquissart – Laventie – Rouge-de-Bout – Fleurbaix (exclusive) – la Boutillerie – Bas Maisnil.
	BATTLE OF AUBERS RIDGE	9th May 1915	
	Attack at Fromelles		

Battles and Engagements of The Great War and the Third Afghan War

Attack at Rue du Bois	9th May 1915	Road la Quinque Rue (exclusive) – le Touret – Lacouture – Croix Barbee: thence a line to the Bois du Biez (South-West Corner).
BATTLE OF FESTUBERT	15th–25th May 1915	The la Bassee Canal to Gorre: thence road to le Touret – Lacouture – Croix Barbee: thence a line to the Bois du Biez (South-West Corner).
Second Action of Givenchy 1915	15th–16th June 1915	Givenchy – Gorre: thence road to le Touret – Rue du l'Epinette – la Quinque Rue (exclusive).
First Attack on Bellewaarde	16th June 1915	Gheluvelt – Zillebeke: thence road to Ypres (exclusive) – Zonnebeke.
Actions of Hooge	19th and 30th July and 9th August 1915	Gheluvelt – Zillebeke: thence road to Ypres (exclusive) – Zonnebeke.
THE BATTLE OF LOOS	25th September–8th October 1915	Road Aix-Noulette – Noeux-les-Mines – Bethune (exclusive) – Gorre – Festubert (exclusive).
Action of Pietre	25th September 1915	Haut Pommereau – Neuve Chapelle (exclusive) – Rouge Croix – Pont du Hem – l'Epinette – Aubers.
Action of Bois Grenier	25th September 1915	Bas Maisnil – Croix-Marechal – Bac-St-Maur – Erquinghem – Bois Grenier – Bois Blancs.
Second Attack on Bellewaarde	25th–26th September 1915	Gheluvelt – Zillebeke: thence road to Ypres (exclusive) – Zonnebeke.
Actions of the Hohenzollern Redoubt	13th–19th October 1915	Road Hulluch – Loos – Fosse No 7 – Noyelles-lez-Vermelles – Cambrin.
7. **Local Operations 1916**		
Actions of The Bluff	February–June 1916 14th–15th February and 2nd March 1916	Between the Ypres-Comines Canal and the Ypres-Comines railway (Ypres exclusive).
Actions of St Eloi Craters	27th March–16th April 1916	Road Wytschaete – Vierstraat – Ypres (exclusive): thence the Ypres-Comines railway.
German Attack on Vimy Ridge	21st May 1916	Thelus – Neuville-St Vaast – Mont-St-Eloy – Carency – Ablain-St Nazaire: thence along the Notre-Dame-de-Lorette ridge to the river Souchez.
BATTLE OF MOUNT SORREL	2nd–13th June 1916	Between the Ypres-Comines Canal and the Ypres-Roulers railway (Ypres exclusive).
		*
8. **Operations on the Somme** THE BATTLES OF THE SOMME 1916 BATTLE OF ALBERT 1916 Capture of Montauban Capture of Mametz Capture of Fricourt Capture of Contalmaison Capture of la Boisselle	1st July–18th November 1916 1st July–18th November 1916 1st–13th July 1916	** The Combles valley to Hardecourt: thence the road to Maricourt – Suzanne – Bray – Albert – Bouzincourt – Hedauville – Forceville – Bertrancourt – Sailly-au-Bois (exclusive) – Hebuterne – Puisieux-au-Mont.

Battle / Engagement	Date	Boundaries
Attack on Gommecourt Salient	1st July 1916	Road Puisieux-au-Mont – Hebuterne – Sailly-au-Bois – Bayencourt – Souastre – Humbercamps – Pommier – Berles-au-Bois – Monchy-au-Bois.
BATTLE OF BAZENTIN RIDGE Capture of Longueval Capture of Trones Wood Capture of Ovillers Attack at Fromelles	14th–17th July 1916	Road Hardecourt – Maricourt – Fricourt – Becourt – Albert (exclusive): thence the river Ancre.
Attacks on High Wood	19th July 1916	Road Aubers – Fauquissart – Laventie – Rouge-de-Bout – Fleurbaix (exclusive) – la Boutillerie – Bas Maisnil.
	20th–25th July 1916	Road Flers – Longueval – Bazentin-le-Grand – Bazentin-le-Petit – Martinpuich.
BATTLE OF DELVILLE WOOD BATTLE OF POZIERES RIDGE	15th July–3rd September 1916 23rd July–3rd September 1916	Delville Wood. Road Bazentin-le-Petit – Contalmaison – Fricourt – Becourt – Albert (exclusive): thence the river Ancre.
Fighting for Mouquet Farm BATTLE OF GUILLEMONT	3rd–6th September 1916 9th September 1916	The Combles valley to Hardecourt: thence road to Maricourt – Montauban – Longueval.
BATTLE OF GINCHY BATTLE OF FLERS-COURCELETTE Capture of Martinpuich	15th–22nd September 1916	The Combles valley to Hardecourt: thence road to Maricourt – Fricourt – Becourt – Albert (exclusive): thence the river Ancre.
BATTLE OF MORVAL Capture of Combles Capture of Lesboeufs Capture of Gueudecourt BATTLE OF THIEPVAL RIDGE	25th–28th September 1916	The Combles valley to Hardecourt: thence road to Maricourt – Fricourt – Becourt – la Boisselle –Bapaume.
	26th–28th September 1916	The Bapaume road to Albert (exclusive): thence road to Martinsart – Englebelmer – Auchonvillers – Serre.
BATTLE OF THE TRANSLOY RIDGES Capture of Eaucourt l'Abbaye Capture of le Sars Attacks on the Butte de Warlencourt	1st–18th October 1916	The valley from Sailly-Saillisel to Combles: thence road to Ginchy – Longueval – Martinpuich – Courcelette: thence the valley to Warlencourt.
BATTLE OF THE ANCRE HEIGHTS Capture of Schwaben Redoubt Capture of Stuff Redoubt Capture of Regina Trench	1st October–11th November 1916	Road Pys – le Sars – Martinpuich – Contalmaison – la Boisselle – Aveluy – Martinsart – Mesnil – Hamel.
BATTLE OF THE ANCRE 1916 Capture of Beaumont Hamel	13th–18th November 1916	The Bapaume road to la Boisselle: thence road to Aveluy – Martinsart – Englebelmer – Mailly-Maillet – Colincamps – Hebuterne – Puisieux-au-Mont.

9. **Operations on the Ancre**

*

Actions of Miraumont Capture of the Thilloys	11th January–13th March 1917 17th and 18th February 1917 25th February–2nd March 1917	Road Pys – Courcelette – Thiepval – Hamel – Beaucourt. Road Bapaume – Gueudecourt (exclusive) – le Sars – Pys (exclusive) – Grevillers.

	Engagement	Dates	Location
	Capture of Irles	10th March 1917	Road Warlencourt – Courcelette – Miraumont: thence the railway to Achiet-le-Grand.
10.	**German Retreat to the Hindenburg Line**		
	Capture of Bapaume	14th March–5th April 1917	*
	Occupation of Peronne	17th March 1917	*
		18th March 1917	*
11.	**The Arras Offensive**		*
	THE BATTLES OF ARRAS 1917	9th April–15th May 1917	*
	BATTLE OF VIMY RIDGE	9th April–4th May 1917	
		9th–14th April 1917	Willerval – Maroeuil – Mont-St-Eloy – Ablain-St Nazaire – Lievin – Lens.
	FIRST BATTLE OF THE SCARPE 1917	9th–14th April 1917	Cherisy – Hamelincourt – Maroeuil (exclusive) – Willerval (exclusive).
	Capture of Monchy-le-Preux		
	Capture of Wancourt Ridge		
	SECOND BATTLE OF THE SCARPE 1917	23rd–24th April 1917	The river Sensee from Vis-en-Artois to Ervillers (exclusive); thence a line to Dainville (exclusive) – Bailleul – Oppy.
	Capture of Guemappe		
	Capture of Gavrelle		
	Attack on la Coulotte	23rd April 1917	Road Mericourt – Vimy – Neuville-St Vaast – la Targette – Souchez: thence the river Souchez.
	BATTLE OF ARLEUX	28th–29th April 1917	Boiry-Notre-Dame – Monchy-le-Preux – Beaurains – Roclincourt – Vimy – Acheville.
	THIRD BATTLE OF THE SCARPE 1917	3rd–4th May 1917	The river Sensee from Vis-en-Artois to St Leger: thence a line to Boyelles – Beaurains – Roclincourt – Vimy – Acheville.
	Capture of Fresnoy		
	Capture of Roeux	13th–14th May 1917	Boiry-Notre-Dame – Monchy-le-Preux – Athies – Fresnes-lez-Montauban.
	Capture of Oppy Wood	28th June 1917	
	Flanking Operations round Bullecourt	11th April–16th June 1917	*
	First Attack on Bullecourt	11th April 1917	*
	German Attack on Lagnicourt	15th April 1917	The railway Havrincourt – Beugny: thence road to Vaulx-Vraucourt – Ecoust-St Mein – Hendecourt.
	BATTLE OF BULLECOURT	3rd–17th May 1917	Road Queant (exclusive) – Noreuil – Vaulx-Vraucourt – l'Homme Mort – Ecoust-St Mein – Hendecourt.
	Actions on the Hindenburg Line	20th May–16th June 1917	Road Queant (exclusive) – Noreuil – Vaulx-Vraucourt – l'Homme Mort – Ecoust-St Mein.
	Flanking Operations towards Lens	3rd June–26th August 1917	*
	Affairs south of the Souchez River	3rd–25th June 1917	Road Mericourt – Vimy – Neuville-St Vaast – la Targette – Souchez: thence the river Souchez.
	Capture of Avion	26th–29th June 1917	Road Mericourt – Vimy – Neuville-St Vaast – la Targette – Souchez: thence the river Souchez.

No.	Battle / Engagement	Date	Location
	BATTLE OF HILL 70	15th–25th August 1917	The river Souchez from Lens to Angres; thence a line to Grenay – Vermelles Station – Vendin-le-Vieil.
12.	**The Flanders Offensive**	7th June–10th November 1917	
	THE BATTLE OF MESSINES 1917	7th–14th June 1917	Road Frelinghien – le Bizet – Petit Pont – Neuve Eglise – Dranoutre – Locre – la Clytte – Dickebusch – Kruisstraat: thence a line to Zillebeke – Gheluvelt.
	Capture of Wytschaete		
			*
	German Attack on Nieuport	10th–11th July 1917	Between the Nieuport Canal and the sea, east of the road from Wulpen to Oost-Dunkerke Bains.
			*
	THE BATTLES OF YPRES 1917	31st July–10th November 1917	The Comines-Ypres Canal as far as Voormezeele: thence road to Vlamertinghe Chateau – Elverdinghe Chateau – Woesten – Bixschoote.
	BATTLE OF PILCKEM RIDGE	31st July–2nd August 1917	
	Capture of Westhoek	10th August 1917	
	BATTLE OF LANGEMARCK 1917	16th–18th August 1917	
	BATTLE OF THE MENIN ROAD RIDGE	20th–25th September 1917	
	BATTLE OF POLYGON WOOD	26th September–3rd October 1917	
	BATTLE OF BROODSEINDE	4th October 1917	
	BATTLE OF POELCAPPELLE	9th October 1917	
	FIRST BATTLE OF PASSCHENDAELE	12th October 1917	
	SECOND BATTLE OF PASSCHENDAELE	26th October–10th November 1917	
			*
13.	**The Cambrai Operations**	20th November–7th December 1917	Road Honnecourt – Villers-Guislain – Gouzeaucourt – Metz – Ruyaulcourt – Beaumetz – Morchies – Lagnicourt – Queant.
	BATTLE OF CAMBRAI 1917	20th November–3rd December 1917	Road Ronssoy – Villers-Faucon – Fins – Ruyaulcourt – Beaumetz – Morchies – Lagnicourt – Queant.
	The Tank Attack	20th–21st November 1917	Road Banteux – Gonnelieu – Gouzeaucourt Station: thence the railway to Marcoing.
	Capture of Bourlon Wood	23rd–28th November 1917	
	The German Counter Attacks	30th November–3rd December 1917	
			*
	Action of Welch Ridge	30th December 1917	
14.	**The German Offensive in Picardy**	21st March–5th April 1918	The river Oise to Chauny: thence road to Guiscard – Ham – Peronne – Bapaume – Boyelles: thence the river Cojeul.
	THE FIRST BATTLES OF THE SOMME 1918	21st March–5th April 1918	
	BATTLE OF ST QUENTIN	21st–23rd March 1918	The line of the Somme from Ham to Hem.
	Actions at the Somme Crossings	24th–25th March 1918	The river Somme to Bray: thence road to Albert – Martinsart – Sailly-au-Bois – Monchy-au-Bois – Arras: thence the river Scarpe.
	FIRST BATTLE OF BAPAUME	24th–25th March 1918	
	BATTLE OF ROSIERES	26th–27th March 1918	Between the rivers Avre and Somme, east of road Pierrepont – Mezieres – Demuin – Villers Bretonneux – Corbie.
	FIRST BATTLE OF ARRAS 1918	28th March 1918	Road Authuille – Bertrancourt – Couin – Gaudiempre – Arras – Oppy.
	BATTLE OF THE AVRE	4th April 1918	Between the rivers Avre and Somme.
	BATTLE OF THE ANCRE 1918	5th April 1918	Road Mericourt l'Abbe – Warloy – Acheux – Souastre – Monchy-au-Bois – Ayette.

	Actions of Villers Bretonneux	24th–25th April 1918	Between the rivers Avre and Somme.
	Capture of Hamel	4th July 1918	Between the road Lamotte – Longueau and the Somme.

*

15.	**The German Offensive in Flanders**		
	THE BATTLES OF THE LYS	9th–29th April 1918	The la Bassee Canal to Bethune: thence road to St Venant:
	BATTLE OF ESTAIRES	9th–29th April 1918	thence a line to Vieux Berquin: from there the road to Bailleul –
	First Defence of Givenchy 1918	9th–11th April 1918	Armentieres (all exclusive).
			Road Armentieres – Bailleul – Locre – Dickebusch –
	BATTLE OF MESSINES 1918	10th–11th April 1918	Voormezeele: thence the Ypres-Comines Canal.
	Loss of Hill 63		The river Lawe from le Casan to Bethune (exclusive);
	BATTLE OF HAZEBROUCK	12th–15th April 1918	thence the railway by Hazebrouck (exclusive) to
	Defence of Hinges Ridge		Caestre: thence road to Mont des Cats – Meteren.
	Defence of Nieppe Forest		Road Meteren – Mont des Cats – Boeschepe –
	BATTLE OF BAILLEUL	13th–15th April 1918	Reninghelst – Ouderdom – Vierstraat – Wytschaete.
	Defence of Neuve Eglise		Road Meteren – Mont des Cats – Boeschepe – Reninghelst –
	FIRST BATTLE OF KEMMEL RIDGE	17th–19th April 1918	Ouderdom – Vierstraat – Wytschaete.
			The la Bassee Canal to Bethune (exclusive): thence
	BATTLE OF BETHUNE	18th April 1918	road to Chocques – Busnes – St Venant – Merville.
	Second Defence of Givenchy 1918		Road Meteren – Mont des Cats – Boeschepe – Reninghelst –
	SECOND BATTLE OF KEMMEL RIDGE	25th–26th April 1918	Vlamertinghe – Ypres (exclusive); thence the Comines Canal.
			Road St Jans Cappel – Boeschepe – Reninghelst – Vlamertinghe
	BATTLE OF THE SCHERPENBERG	29th April 1918	– Ypres (exclusive); thence the Comines Canal.
			The Lys Canal to St Venant (exclusive): thence the road to
	Action of la Becque	28th June 1918	Morbecque: thence a line to Swartenbrouck – Vieux Berquin.
			The Meteren Becque to Fletre: thence a line to Fontaine Houck
	Capture of Meteren	19th July 1918	– Bailleul Station.

*

16.	**The German Offensive in Champagne**		
	BATTLE OF THE AISNE 1918	27th May–6th June 1918	Between the Chemin des Dames and the Montagne de Reims,
		27th May–6th June 1918	east of the line Bouconville – Fismes Verneuil.

*

17.	**The Counter Attack in Champagne**		
	THE BATTLES OF THE MARNE 1918	20th July–2nd August 1918	Between the rivers Ourcq and Aisne, east of the line
	BATTLE OF THE SOISSONNAIS AND OF THE OURCQ	20th July–2nd August 1918	Breny – Vierzy – Pommiers.
	Attack on Buzancy	23rd July–2nd August 1918	
	Capture of Beugneux Ridge	28th July 1918	
	BATTLE OF TARDENOIS	20th–31st July 1918	The Valley of the Ardre above Sarcy.
	The fighting for the Ardre Valley		

18.	**The Advance in Picardy** THE BATTLE OF AMIENS	8th August–3rd September 1918 8th–11th August 1918	Between the roads Amiens – Roye and Amiens – Albert (Amiens exclusive).
	Actions round Damery	15th–17th August 1918	Road Roye – Bouchoir – Rosieres: thence the railway to Puzeaux.
			*
19.	**The Advance in Flanders** Action of Outtersteene Ridge	18th August–6th September 1918 18th August 1918	The railway from Bailleul to Strazeele Station: thence road to Strazeele – Meteren.
			*
20.	**The Advance in Picardy** THE SECOND BATTLES OF THE SOMME 1918	21st August–3rd September 1918 21st August–3rd September 1918	Road Chaulnes – Lamotte – Corbie – Warloy – Acheux – Souastre – Berles-au-Bois – Bretencourt – Heninel.
	BATTLE OF ALBERT 1918 Capture of Chuignes SECOND BATTLE OF BAPAUME	21st–23rd August 1918 31st August–3rd September 1918	Road Athies – Chaulnes – Rosieres – Bray – Miraumont – Hamelincourt – St Leger: thence a line to Noreuil – Moeuvres.
	Capture of Mont St Quentin Occupation of Peronne	1st September 1918	*
21.	**The Breaking of the Hindenburg Line** THE SECOND BATTLES OF ARRAS 1918	26th August–12th October 1918 26th August–3rd September 1918	Noreuil (exclusive) – St Leger (exclusive) – Boisleux-au-Mont – Roclincourt – Bailleul – Oppy.
	Capture of Monchy-le-Preux BATTLE OF THE DROCOURT-QUEANT LINE	26th–30th August 1918 2nd–3rd September 1918	Moeuvres (exclusive) – Noreuil (exclusive) – St Leger (exclusive) – Monchy-le-Preux – Pelves: thence the river Scarpe.
	THE BATTLES OF THE HINDENBURG LINE BATTLE OF HAVRINCOURT	12th September–9th October 1918 12th September 1918	Road Gouzeaucourt – Fins – Ytres – Beaumetz – Morchies: thence a line to Moeuvres.
	BATTLE OF EPEHY	18th September 1918	St Quentin (exclusive) – Beauvois – Cartigny – Manacourt: thence by the southern edge of Havrincourt Wood to Villers Plouich.
	BATTLE OF THE CANAL DU NORD Capture of Bourlon Wood	27th September–1st October 1918	Road Banteux – Gouzeaucourt (exclusive) – Fins (exclusive) – Ytres – Lagnicourt – Vis-en-Artois: thence the river Sensee.
	BATTLE OF THE ST QUENTIN CANAL Passage at Bellenglise Capture of Bellicourt Tunnel Defences BATTLE OF THE BEAUREVOIR LINE	29th September–2nd October 1918	Road St Quentin (exclusive) – Vermand – Roisel – Villers-Faucon – Fins – Gouzeaucourt – Banteux (exclusive).
	BATTLE OF CAMBRAI 1918 Capture of Villers-Outreaux	3rd–5th October 1918	Road Sequehart – Bellenglise – Pontru – Epehy – Vendhuille – Villers-Outreaux.
	Capture of Cambrai	8th–9th October 1918	Road Fresnoy – Sequehart – Bellenglise – Bellicourt – Vendhuille – Villers-Guislain – Villers-Plouich –
	The Pursuit to the Selle	9th–12th October 1918	Graincourt – Bourlon – Oisy-le-Verger: thence the river Sensee.
			*

22. **The Final Advance**

In Flanders

BATTLE OF YPRES 1918   28th September–11th November 1918

     28th September–2nd October 1918   Road Armentieres – Bailleul – Locre – Reninghelst – Vlamertinghe Chateau – Elverdinghe Chateau: thence a line to Moorslede.

BATTLE OF COURTRAI   14th–19th October 1918   Dottignes – Comines – Messines: thence along the ridge to Passchebdaele: thence a line to Moorslede – Lendelede.

Action of Ooteghem   25th October 1918   Road Bossuyt – St Genois – Sweveghem – Nieuwe Kappaart: thence the stream to Waereghem and from there the road to Wortegem.

Action of Tieghem   31st October 1918   The river Escaut to Avelghem: thence road to Heestert – Kattestraat – Vichte – Heirweg – Mooregem – Wortegem.

In Artois

Capture of Douai   2nd October–11th November 1918

In Picardy   17th October 1918

BATTLE OF THE SELLE   17th October–11th November 1918

     17th–25th October 1918   The railway Boue – Busigny – Caudry: thence the stream to its junction with the river Escaut: thence the latter.

BATTLE OF VALENCIENNES   1st–2nd November 1918   The Bavai – Cambrai road as far as Vendegies: thence the stream to its junction with the river Escaut: thence a line to Wailers: thence along the southern edge of the forests of Vicoigne and Raismes.

Capture of Mont Houy

BATTLE OF THE SAMBRE   4th November 1918   The railway Boue – le Cateau (exclusive): thence road to Romeries – Famara – Onnaing: thence the railway to Mons.

Passage of the Sambre-Oise Canal

Capture of le Quesnoy

Passage of the Grand Honnelle   5th–7th November 1918   Between the Bavai – Cambrai road and the Valenciennes – Mons railway, east of the line Wargnies – Onnaing.

Capture of Mons 11th November 1918

ITALY

23. **The Italian Offensives 1917**

TENTH BATTLE OF THE ISONZO   12th May–8th June 1917   Between Gorizia and the sea, east of the Isonzo.

ELEVENTH BATTLE OF THE ISONZO   17th August–12th September 1917   Between Gorizia and the sea, east of the Isonzo.

24. **The Austrian Offensive 1917**

TWELFTH BATTLE OF THE ISONZO   24th October–18th November 1917   Between the Carso and the Piave.

The stand on the Carso

The Retreat to the Piave

MACEDONIA

(table continued)

No.	Battle / Operation	Date	Location
25.	**The Austrian Offensive 1918**		
	THE BATTLE OF THE PIAVE	15th–24th June 1918	From the Astico to the Sea.
	The fighting on the Asiago Plateau	15th–16th June 1918	The Asiago Plateau, north of the line Conco – Cogollo.
			*
26.	**The Italian Offensive 1918**		
	THE BATTLE OF VITTORIO VENETO	24th October–4th November 1918	Between the railways Treviso – Conegliano and Treviso – Oderzo.
	Passage of the Piave	23rd October–4th November 1918	
	The fighting in the Val d'Assa	1st–4th November 1918	The Val d'Assa, north of Asiago.
			*

MACEDONIA

No.	Battle / Operation	Date	Location
27.	**Retreat from Serbia on Salonika**	December 1915	North of the Serbo-Greek frontier.
	Actions of Kosturino	7th–8th December 1915	
28.	**Doiran Operations 1916**	August–September 1916	
	Affairs of Horseshoe Hill	10th–18th August 1916	Between the Gol Ayak and the Selimli Dere.
	Action of Machukovo	13th–14th September 1916	Between the Selimli Dere and the river Vardar.
			*
29.	**Operations in the Struma Valley**	1916–1918	
	Action of the Karajakoï's, including Capture of Yenikoi	30th September–4th October 1916	The Struma Valley above Lake Takhinos.
	Affair of Barakli Juma'a	31st October 1916	The Struma Valley above Lake Takhinos.
30.	**1917 Offensive**	April–May 1917	Between the Doiran – Karasuli railway and the river Vardar.
	BATTLE OF DOIRAN 1917	24th–25th April 1917 and 8th–9th May 1917	
			*
31.	**1918 Offensive**	1st–30th September 1918	Between the Vardar and the line Mayadag – Pardovitsa.
	Capture of the Roche Noir Salient	1st–2nd September 1918	Between the Dova Tepe – Doiran – Karasuli railway and the river Vardar.
	BATTLE OF DOIRAN 1918	18th–19th September 1918	Dova Tepe – Doiran – Karasuli: thence the river Vardar to the confluence of the Koja Dere: thence the latter.
	The Pursuit to the Strumitza Valley	22nd–30th September 1918	

DARDANELLES

No.	Battle / Operation	Date	Location
32.	**Helles Operations**	25th April 1915–8th January 1916	*
	THE BATTLES OF HELLES	25th April–6th June 1915	*

Battle/Engagement	Date	Location
THE LANDING AT CAPE HELLES	25th–26th April 1915	All landings on the southern end of the Gallipoli Peninsula.
Capture of Sedd el Bahr		
Landing at Kum Kale	25th–26th April 1915	Landing by French force on the Asiatic shore.
FIRST BATTLE OF KRITHIA	28th April 1915	From the Straits on the right to the sea on the left.
Actions of Eski Hissarlik	1st–2nd May 1915	
SECOND BATTLE OF KRITHIA	6th–8th May 1915	From the Straits on the right to the sea on the left.
First Action of Kereves Dere		
Affair of Gurkha Bluff	12th May 1915	From Gully Ravine on the right to the sea on the left.
THIRD BATTLE OF KRITHIA	4th June 1915	From the Straits on the right to the sea on the left.
Second Action of Kereves Dere		
Third Action of Kereves Dere	21st June 1915	From the Straits on the right to Achi Baba Nullah on the left.
Action of Gully Ravine	28th June–2nd July 1915	From East Krithia Nullah (exclusive) on the right to the sea on the left.
Fourth Action of Kereves Dere	30th June 1915	From the Straits on the right to Achi Baba Nullah on the left.
Action of Achi Baba Nullah	12th–13th July 1915	From the Straits on the right to the Sedd el Bahr – Krithia road on the left.
Actions of Krithia Vineyard	6th–13th August 1915	From Achi Baba Nullah on the right to Gully Ravine (exclusive) on the left.
Affair of the Krithia Nullahs	29th December 1915	From the Achi Baba Nullah on the right to West Krithia Nullah on the left.
The Evacuation of Helles	7th–8th January 1916	From the Achi Baba Nullah on the right to the sea on the left.
The last Turkish Attacks	7th January 1916	*
33. **Anzac and Suvla Operations**		
THE BATTLES OF ANZAC	25th April–20th December 1915	*
THE LANDING AT ANZAC	25th April–30th June 1915	*
Demonstration in the Gulf of Xeros	25th–26th April 1915	From Gaba Tepe (exclusive) to Fisherman's Hut (exclusive).
Attack on the Chessboard	2nd May 1915	*
Affair of Quinn's Post	10th May 1915	*
THE DEFENCE OF ANZAC	19th–21st May 1915	From Gaba Tepe (exclusive) to Fisherman's Hut (exclusive).
Affair of Holly Ridge	28th June 1915	*
Defence of Walker's Ridge	30th June 1915	*
THE BATTLES OF SUVLA	6th–21st August 1915	
BATTLE OF SARI BAIR	6th–10th August 1915	South of the Azmak Dere.
Capture of Lone Pine		
Attack at Russell's Top		
THE LANDING AT SUVLA	6th–15th August 1915	North of the Azmak Dere.
Capture of Karakol Dagh		
Capture of Chocolate Hill		
Demonstration in the Gulf of Xeros	6th–7th August 1915	*
BATTLE OF SCIMITAR HILL	21st August 1915	North of the Azmak Dere.
Attack on "W" Hill		

Actions of Hill 60 (Anzac) — 21st and 27th August 1915 — Between the Azmak Dere and the Aghil Dere.

The Evacuation of Suvla and Anzac — 19th–20th December 1915

EGYPT AND PALESTINE

SUDAN

34.	**Operations against the Sultan of Darfur**	1st March–31st December 1916	*
	Affair of Beringiya	22nd May 1916	*
	Occupation of El Fasher	23rd May 1916	*
	Affair of Gyuba	6th November 1916	*

WESTERN FRONTIER

35.	**Operations against the Senussi**	23rd November 1915–8th February 1917	*
	Affair of the Wadi Senab	11th–13th December 1915	Area covered by the force under Lt Col JLR Gordon.
	Affair of the Wadi Majid	25th December 1915	Area covered by the two columns under Maj Gen A Wallace.
	Affair of Halazin	23rd January 1916	Area covered by the force under Brig HT Lukin.
	Action of Agagiya	26th February 1916	*
	Affairs in the Dakhla Oasis	17th–22nd October 1916	Siwa Oasis to Munasib.
	Affairs near the Siwa Oasis	3rd–5th February 1917	

EASTERN FRONTIER AND PALESTINE

36.	**Defence of the Suez Canal**	26th January 1915–12th August 1916	*
	Actions on the Suez Canal	3rd–4th February 1915	East of the Suez – Qantara Railway.
	Affair of Qatia	23rd April 1916	East of the Canal and north of El Ferdan Station.
	BATTLE OF RUMANI	4th–5th August 1916	East of the Canal and north of Ismailia.

37.	**Operations in the Sinai Peninsula**	15th November 1916–9th January 1917	*
	Affair of Magdhaba	23rd December 1916	South and east of Bir Lahfan.
	Action of Rafah	9th January 1917	North and east of Sheikh Zowa'id.

38.	**The First Offensive**		*
	FIRST BATTLE OF GAZA	24th March–19th April 1917	
	SECOND BATTLE OF GAZA	26th–27th March 1917	North of the line Beersheba – Bela'.
		17th–19th April 1917	*

39.	**The Second Offensive**		
	THIRD BATTLE OF GAZA	27th October–16th November 1917	North of the Wadi Ghuzze.
	Capture of Beersheba	27th October–7th November 1917	

Engagement	Date	Location
Capture of the Sheria Position	8th November 1917	North of the line Beersheba – Gaza and west of the Beersheba – Jerusalem road.
Affair of Huj	13th November 1917	
Action of El Mughar	14th November 1917	
Occupation of Junction Station		
40. Jerusalem Operations		
BATTLE OF NEBI SAMWIL	17th November–30th December 1917	
Capture of Jerusalem	17th–24th November 1917	*
DEFENCE OF JERUSALEM	7th–9th December 1917	North and east of the line Hebron – Junction Station.
BATTLE OF JAFFA	26th–30th December 1917	
	21st–22nd December 1917	Between the Tul Keram – Junction Station – Jaffa railway and the sea.
41. Operations in and beyond the Jordan Valley		
Capture of Jericho	19th February–4th May 1918	*
	19th–21st February 1918	Between the Bethlehem – Nablus road and the Jordan, north of the line Jerusalem – Dead Sea.
Passage of the Jordan	21st–23rd March 1918	East of the Jordan.
First Action of Es Salt	24th–25th March 1918	
First Attack on Amman	27th–30th March 1918	
Turkish Attack on the Jordan Bridgeheads	11th April 1918	
Second Action of Es Salt	30th April–4th May 1918	
Arab Operations in the Mountains of Moab	March–April 1918	
42. Local Operations 1918		
Actions of Tel Asur	8th–12th March 1918	West of the Jordan, and north of the line Jericho – Ram Allah – Jaffa.
Affair of Abu Telul	14th July 1918	*
43. The Final Offensive		
THE BATTLES OF MEGIDDO	18th September–31st October 1918	
BATTLE OF SHARON	19th–25th September 1918	*
BATTLE OF NABLUS	19th–25th September 1918	*
Actions beyond Jordan	23rd–30th September 1918	Between the Hejaz Railway and the sea, north of the line Dhaba Station – mouth of Jordan – Arsuf.
Capture of Amman	25th September 1918	
Capture of Dera'a	27th September 1918	
The Pursuit through Syria	26th September–31st October 1918	
Capture of Damascus	1st October 1918	North of the Haifa – Dera'a railway.
Affair of Haritan	26th October 1918	
Occupation of Aleppo	26th October 1918	

ARABIA

HEJAZ

44.	**The Arab Revolt**	June–December 1916		
	Attack on Medina	6th June 1916	*	
	Capture of Jidda	9th June 1916	*	
	Capture of Mecca	10th June 1916	*	
	Capture of Yenbo	27th July 1916	*	
	Capture of Taif	22nd September 1916	*	
45.	**Operations against the Hejaz Railway**	October 1916–November 1918	*	From Ma'an to Medina.
46.	**Wejh Operations**	January 1917		North of Yenbo.
	Capture of Yenbo	24th January 1917	*	
47.	**Aqaba Operations**			
	Affair of Aba el Lissan	6th May–21st October 1917	*	
	Occupation of Aqaba	3rd July 1917	*	
	Turkish Attack on Petra	6th July 1917	*	
		21st October 1917	*	Between the Hejaz Railway and the Wadi Araba.
48.	**Tafile Operations**			
	Actions for Et Tafile	January–March 1918	*	
	Seizure of the Turkish Dead Sea Flotilla	1st–28th January 1918		Between the Hejaz Railway and the Wadi Araba.
		27th January 1918	*	El Mezra'a.
49.	**Ma'an Operations**			
	Affair of Shahim Station	April–September 1918	*	
	Affair of Mudawara Station	20th April 1918	*	
	Evacuation of Ma'an	6th August 1918	*	
		23rd September 1918	*	

SOUTHERN ARABIA

50.	**Operations in the Bab el Mandeb**	1914–15		
	Capture of Sheikh Sa'id	10th November 1914	*	Sheikh Sa'id Peninsula.
	Turkish Attack on Perim	14th–15th June 1915		Perim Island (Troops under command of Capt HAC Hutchinson).
51.	**Defence of Aden**	3rd July 1915–31st October 1918		
	Action of Lahej	4th–5th July 1915	*	
	Affair of Sheikh Othman	20th July 1915	*	
	Affair of Jabir	7th December 1917	*	
	Affair of Imad	22nd October 1918	*	

MESOPOTAMIA

52. Basra Operations

Engagement	Date	Location	
Landing at Fao	6th November 1914–14th April 1915	Delta of the Shatt al'Arab up to Basra.	*
Affair of Saihan	6th November 1914		
Affair of Sahil	15th November 1914		
	17th November 1914		
Occupation of Basra	22nd November 1914	The Tigris above Basra.	
First Action of Qurna	4th–8th December 1914	North-west of Ahwaz (exclusive).	
Affair of Ahwaz	3rd March 1915	West of Shaiba (exclusive).	
Affair of Shaiba	3rd March 1915	The inundation west of Basra and to the west of it.	
BATTLE OF SHAIBA	12th–14th April 1915		

53. Advance up the Tigris 1915

Second Action of Qurna	31st May–5th October 1915	The Tigris above Qurna.	*
Occupation of Amara	31st May 1915		
	3rd June 1915		*
BATTLE OF KUT 1915	28th September 1915	The Tigris above Sanna-i-Yat.	*
Operations on the Karkha River	7th May–3rd June 1915		*
Affair of Khafajiya	14th–16th May 1915		

54. Advance up the Euphrates 1915

Actions for Nasiriya	27th June–25th July 1915	The Euphrates west of Khor al Hammar.	*
	5th, 13th–14th, and 24th July 1915		

55. Advance on Baghdad 1915

BATTLE OF CTESIPHON	11th November–6th December 1915		*
Affair of Umm at Tubul	22nd–24th November 1915	The Tigris above Lajj.	
DEFENCE OF KUT	1st December 1915	The Tigris above Kut.	*
The Christmas Eve Attack	7th December 1915–28th April 1916		

56. Attempts to relieve Kut

First Attempt	4th January–24th April 1916		*
Action of Shaikh Sa'ad	4th–23rd January 1916		*
Action of the Wadi	6th–8th January 1916	The Tigris above 'Ali Gharbi.	
First Attack on Hanna	13th–14th January 1916	The Tigris above Shaikh Sa'ad.	
Second Attempt	21st January 1916	The Tigris above the Wadi.	
Attack on the Dujaila Redoubt	7th–10th March 1916		*
Third Attempt	8th March 1916	The Tigris above the Wadi.	
Action of Falahiya, including the Capture of Hanna	1st–24th April 1916		*
First Attack on Sanna-i-Yat	5th April 1916	The Tigris above the Wadi.	
Second Attack on Sanna-i-Yat	6th April 1916		
Action of Bait Aissa	9th April 1916		
Third Attack on Sanna-i-Yat	17th–18th April 1916		
Capitulation of Kut	22nd April 1916		
	29th April 1916		*

57.	**Euphrates Operations 1916**	January–September 1916	North of Nasiriya. *
	Affair of Butaniya	14th January 1916	
	Action of As Sahilan	11th September 1916	
58.	**Operations for the Capture of Kut 1917**		*
	BATTLE OF KUT 1917	13th December 1916–25th February 1917	
	Capture of Khadairi Bend	9th January–24th February 1917	The Tigris above Shaikh Sa'ad.
	Capture of the Hai Salient	9th–19th January 1917	
	Capture of the Dahra Bend	25th January–5th February 1917	
	Capture of Sanna-i-Yat	9th–16th February 1917	
	Passage of the Shumran Bend	17th–24th February 1917	
	Pursuit to Baghdad	23rd–24th February 1917	
	Passage of the Diyala	25th February–10th March 1917	The Tigris above Kut. *
	Occupation of Baghdad	7th–10th March 1917	*
		11th March 1917	*
59.	**Operations for the consolidation of the position at Baghdad**	14th March–30th April 1917	
	Action of Mushaidiya	14th March 1917	The Tigris above Kadhimain.
	First Action of the Jabal Hamrin	25th March 1917	Near Shahraban.
	Affair of Dali 'Abbas	27th–28th March 1917	Right bank of the River Diyala above Ba'quba.
	Affair of Dogame	29th March 1917	The Tigris above Mushaidiya.
	Affairs on the Nahr Khalis	9th–15th April 1917	The Nahr Khalis Canal above Daltawa.
	Passage of the 'Adhaim	18th April 1917	The Tigris above Dogame.
	Action of Istabulat	21st–22nd April 1917	The Tigris above the Shatt al'Adhaim.
	Occupation of Samarra	23rd–24th April 1917	*
	Affairs on the Shatt al'Adhaim	30th April 1917	The Shatt al'Adhaim above its junction with the Tigris.
60.	**Euphrates Operations 1917–18**	8th July 1917–13th April 1918	*
	Attack on Ramadi	11th–14th July 1917	
	Capture of Ramadi	28th–29th September 1917	The Euphrates above Dhibban.
	Action of Khan Baghdadi	26th–27th March 1918	*
	Occupation of Ana	28th March 1918	The Euphrates above Hit. *
	Blockade of Najaf	1st–13th April 1918	*
61.	**Tigris Operations 1917**	1st October–6th December 1917	*
	Second Action of the Jabal Hamrin	18th–20th October 1917	North of Shahraban.
	Actions for Tikrit	24th October, 2nd and 5th November 1917	The Tigris above Al Ajik.
	Third Action of the Jabal Hamrin	3rd–6th December 1917	North of Shahraban.
62.	**Kirkuk Operations**	25th April–24th May 1918	
	Action of Tuz Khurmatli	29th April 1918	North of Kifri. *
63.	**Advance on Mosul**	23rd October–5th November 1918	
	Action of Fatha Gorge	23rd–24th October 1918	The Tigris above Tikrit. *

Battles and Engagements of The Great War and the Third Afghan War

Actions on the Lesser Zab	25th October 1918	
BATTLE OF SHARQAT	28th–30th October 1918	
Affair of Qaiyara	30th October 1918	
Occupation of Mosul	3rd November 1918	* The Tigris above Fatha Gorge.

PERSIA AND CENTRAL ASIA

SOUTH PERSIA AND THE PERSIAN GULF

64.	**Defence of the Gulf Ports 1915**		
	Defence of Muscat	10th–11th January 1915	*
	Defence of Jask	16th–17th April 1915	*
	Defence of Chahbar	2nd–3rd May 1915	*
	Destruction of Dilbar	12th–16th August 1915	*
	Defence of Bushire	9th September 1915	*
	Operations of the Makran Mission	11th April 1916–2nd February 1917	Persian Makran.
65.	**Establishment of order 1916**		
	Capture of Saidabad	28th September 1916	*
	Occupation of Shiraz and formation of the	12th November 1916	* Fars.
	South Persia Rifles		
	Affair of Dasht-i-Arjan	25th December 1916	*
66.	**Opening the trade routes**		
	Affair of Kafta	1st January–30th November 1917	*
	Affairs in the Lashani country	5th July 1917	
	Affairs in the Chabar Rah country	19th–30th September 1917	* The valley on the north side of Lake Niriz.
		1st–21st October 1917	Northern Fars.
67.	**Recrudescence of disorders**		
	Affairs of Gumm	14th December 1917–31st January 1918	*
		24th–27th January 1918	Arainjan district, east of the Shiaz – Deh Bid road.
68.	**Operations in Northern Fars**		
	Affair of Ziarat	3rd–23rd May 1918	*
	Affair of Kuh-i-Khan	13th–14th May 1918	*
		16th May 1918	*
69.	**Qashqai Operations 1918**		
	Action of Deh Shaikh	25th–26th May 1918	*
	Persian Mutiny at Khan-i-Zinian	25th May 1918	*
	Action of Ahmadabad	16th June 1918	*
	Affair of Chanar Rahdar	7th–8th July 1918	*

Defence and Relief of Abadeh	28th June–17th July 1918	*	
Defence and Relief of Firuzabad	16th–24th October 1918		Firuzabad and the Khajai valley.
70. Persian Operations round Isfahan and in Fars 1919		*	
Capture of Kadarjan	10th June 1919	*	
Capture of Feragheh	8th August 1919	*	
71. Establishment of line of communication between Bushire and Shiraz	29th September 1918–10th March 1919	*	
Consolidation of the coastal belt and occupation of Borazjun	29th September–23rd October 1918		Between Bushire and Borazjun.
Affair of Lardeh	31st October 1918	*	
Seizure of the Kamarji Pass	20th December 1918	*	
Occupation of Kazarun	27th January 1919	*	
Junction between the Bushire and Shiraz Columns	28th January 1919		Mian Kotal.
Punitive measures in Southern Fars	11th December 1918–10th March 1919		Area Bushire – Kazarun – Shiraz – Firuzabad.

EAST PERSIA AND TRANS-CASPIA

72. Establishment of the East Persia Cordon	29th July 1915–31st January 1918	*	
Occupation of Birjand and junction with Russian Cordon	7th October 1915		The Nushki – Kacha – Birjand road.
Captures of German agents	17th January and 8th August 1916		Deh Salm and Sehdeh.
Affair of Lirudik	13th–14th April 1916	*	
Affair of Kundi	17th–18th April 1916	*	
Occupation of Kwash (Vasht)	11th May 1916	*	
Affair of the Gusht Defile	19th–21st July 1916	*	
Affair of Kalmas	26th September 1916	*	
73. Extension of the Cordon into Khorasan	1st February–18th July 1918	*	
Occupation of Meshed	3rd March 1918	*	
74. Operations in Trans-Caspia against the Bolsheviks	19th July 1918–15th March 1919	*	
Affairs near Kaakhka	28th August, 11th and 18th September 1918	*	
Action of Dushak	12th October 1918	*	
Occupation of Merv	1st November 1918	*	
Action of Annenkovo	16th January 1919	*	

NORTH-WEST PERSIA AND THE CASPIAN

75.	**Establishment of line of communication between Baghdad and the Caspian**	27th January–29th July 1918	*
	Affair near Zuhab	25th April 1918	*
	Defence of Resht	20th July 1918	*
76.	**Caspian Operations**	August–September 1918	*
	Occupation of Baku	4th August 1918	*
	Occupation of Krasnovodsk	27th August 1918	*
	Defence of Baku	26th August–15th September 1918	*
77.	**Azerbaijan Operations**	September 1918	*
	Rearguard Actions from Mianeh	5th–14th September 1918	North-west of Nikpai.

INDIA

NORTH-WEST FRONTIER

78.	**Operations in the Tochi**	28th November 1914–27th March 1915	*
	Affair of Miran Shah	28th–29th November 1914	*
	Affair of Spina Khaisora	7th January 1915	*
	Action of Dardoni	25th–26th March 1915	*
79.	**Operations against the Mohmands**	14th–19th April 1915	*
	First Affair of Hafiz Kor	18th April 1915	North-west of road Abazai – Shabkadr – Michni.
80.	**Operations against the Mohmands, Bunerwals and Swatis**	17th August–28th October 1915	North-west of road Abazai – Shabkadr – Michni.
	Affair near Rustan	17th August 1915	*
	Affair of Surkhawi	26th August 1915	*
	Affairs of Landakai and Kak Fort	27th–29th August 1915	Swat Valley above Thana.
	Affairs near Malandri	28th–31st August 1915	North-west of road Abazai – Shabkadr – Michni.
	Action of Hafiz Kor	5th September 1915	*
	Second Affair of Hafiz Kor	9th October 1915	Wuch Valley north of Chakdarra (exclusive).
	Affair near Wuch	27th October 1915	
81.	**The Mohmand Blockade**	30th September 1916–19th July 1917	*
	Third Affair of Hafiz Kor	15th November 1916	North-west of road Abazai – Shabkadr – Michni.

No.		Dates	Location
82.	**Operations against the Mahsuds**		
	Defence of Sarwekai	2nd March–10th August 1917	*
	Affairs of the Gwalerai Pass	2nd–8th March 1917	*
	Action of Kharkhwasta	9th April–1st May and 16th May 1917	The Gumal between Nili Kach and Kajuri Kach (both exclusive).
	Actions in the Shahur Valley	9th–10th May 1917	The route between the Khuzma Post and Sarwekai.
		19th–24th June 1917	The Shahur Valley above Haidari Kach, Nanu and the Khaisora.

BALUCHISTAN

83.	**Kalat Operations**		
	Affair of Wadh	1st June–10th July 1915 and	South of Mastung.
		5th June–18th August 1916	
		25th June 1916	
84.	**Operations against the Marri and Khetran tribes**		
	Defence of Gumbaz Post	18th February–8th April 1918	*
	Affair of Fort Munro	19th–20th February 1918	*
	Capture of the Hadb Position	15th March 1918	*
		6th April 1918	*

THE THIRD AFGHAN WAR

No.		Dates	Location
85.	**Chitral Operations**		
	Capture of Arnawai	6th May–8th August 1919	*
	Affair in the Bumboret Valley	23rd–24th May 1919	Kala Drosh (exclusive) to Narai.
		17th July 1919	The Bumboret Valley.
86.	**Khyber Operations**		
	Action of Bagh Springs	6th May–8th August 1919	*
	Occupation of Dakka	9th–11th May 1919	The Khyber; north-west of Landi Kotal.
	Affairs near Ali Masjid	13th May 1919	*
	Action of Dakka	15th and 16th May 1919	The Khyber; between Fort Maude and Gurgura Post.
	Affairs near Fort Maude	16th and 17th May 1919	North-west of Paindi Khakh.
		18th and 19th July 1919	*
87.	**Kurram Operations**		
	Afghan Attack on Thal	6th May–8th August 1919	*
	Relief of Thal	26th–31st May 1919	*
	Affairs in the Upper Kurram	30th May–3rd June 1919	West of Doaba (exclusive).
		27th May–2nd June 1919	The Kurram above Alizai.
88.	**Waziristan and Derajat Operations**		
	Evacuation of Militia Posts and the South Waziristan Posts.	6th May–8th August 1919	*
	Affair near Miran Shah	25th–30th May 1919	The Tochi Posts above Miran Shah and Spinwam line,
	Affair near Draband	1st June 1919	*
	Defence and Relief of Jandola	3rd June 1919	*
		28th May–9th June 1919	The route from Khirgi (exclusive) to Jandola.
89.	**Zhob Operations**		
	Withdrawal from Wana	6th May–8th August 1919	*
		25th–31st May 1919	The route between Wana and Fort Sandeman.

	Affairs round Fort Sandeman	3rd June–14th July 1919	The Lower Zhob.
	Affair near Kapip	15th–17th July 1919	The road between Babar and Kapip.
	Affair of Hindu Bagh	22nd July 1919	*
90.	**Chaman Operations**		
	Capture of Spin Baldak Fort	6th May–8th August 1919	*
		27th May 1919	*

NORTH-EAST FRONTIER AND BURMA

91.	**Punitive measures in the Kachin Hills**	31st December 1914–28th February 1915	The area bounded on the north by latitude 26° 30', on the east by the River Mali Kha from where it cuts 26° 30' to the confluence, and thence the Irrawaddy until it cuts 25° 15'. On the west longitude 96°. On the south latitude 25°.
92.	**Punitive measures in the Chin Hills**	1st December 1917–1st June 1918	Eastern Boundary – Left bank of Chindwin River. Southern Boundary – Bargelai 23° 45', west to longitude 93°.
93.	**Operations in the Kuki Hills**	1st November 1918–15th May 1919	Western Boundary – Longitude 93° to Lakhipur: thence adjoining Lakhipur to Manipur Road Station. Northern Boundary – A line joining Manipur Road Station east to Tuzu River at point of junction 42 miles east by north from Kohima: thence follow river to junction with Chindwin. Troops at Kindat, Mawlaik and Monywa are also included.

RUSSIA

MURMAN

94.	**Seizure of the Railway 1918**		
	Disarmament of the Bolsheviks as far as Soroki	29th and 30th June 1918	Kandalaksha and Kem.
95.	**Operations in Karelia 1918**		
	Capture of Uktinskaya	11th September 1918	*
	Capture of Voknavolotskaya	21st September 1918	*
	Action near Pyavozero Lake	3rd October 1918	*
96.	**Winter Operations 1918–19**		
	Occupation of Rugozerski	16th January 1919	West of the railway and south of Soroki.
	Capture of Segeja	18th February 1919	South of the line Rugozerski – Kem – Sumski Posad.
	Transfer of troops to the Archangel front	February to April 1919	The Soroki – Onega road beyond Sumski Posad.

97.	**Advance to Lake Onega 1919**	
	Capture of Urosozero	11th April 1919	South of the line Rugozerski – Kem – Sumski Posad. *
	Capture of Maselskaya	3rd May 1919	South of the line Olimpi – Sumski Posad – Nyukhotskoe
	Occupation of Povyenets	18th May 1919	South of Maselskaya.
	Capture of Medvyejya Gora	21st May 1919	*
98.	**Lake Onega Operations 1919**	
	Capture of Kyapeselga	5th July 1919	South of Maselskaya.
	Flotilla Actions	5th June, 3rd July, 2nd and 28th August 1919	Lake Onega.
99.	**Operations to cover withdrawal 1919**	
	Action of Syatnavolotski	27th August 1919	South of Maselskaya. *
	Capture of Lijma	14th–16th September 1919	
	The Evacuation	1st–12th October 1919	Murmansk and Kem.

ARCHANGEL

100.	**Seizure of the White Sea ports and Initial Advances**	
	Capture of Archangel	July–October 1918	*
	Affair of Chunovskaya	1st and 2nd August 1918	Mudyug Island to Archangel.
	Affair of Puchuga	3rd August 1918	The Onega – Obozerskaya road.
	Affairs about Obozerskaya	24th August 1918	The Dvina above Seletski.
	Actions of Chamova	31st August and 4th September 1918	The Vologda railway south of the Kenza river.
	Affair on the Yemtsa River	12th–14th September 1918	The Dvina above Bereznik (exclusive).
	Affair of Seletski	16th and 28th–29th September 1918	The Yemtsa above the confluence of the Tyugra.
	Affairs near Chekuevo	11th October 1918	The Dvina above Tulgas (exclusive).
		12th–17th October 1918	The Onega above Chekuevo.
101.	**Defensive Operations 1918–19**	
	Affair of Kleshevo	October 1918–August 1919	*
	On the Onega River and the Vologda Railway	27th December 1918	The Onega above Chekuevo.
	Affairs near Bolshi Ozerki		*
	Defence of Bolshi Ozerki	17th March–18th April 1919	*
	Between the Vologda Railway and the Dvina River	22nd–23rd July 1919	*
	Affairs at Tarasovo		*
	Attack at Kadish	25th and 29th January 1919	*
	Defence of Sredmekhrenga	7th February 1919	Between Kadish and Avdinskaya.
	On the Dvina and Vaga Rivers	8th–11th February 1919	*
	Affair of Tulgas	11th–13th November 1918	The Dvina above Chamova.
	Defence of Shenkursk	16th–25th January 1919	The Vaga above Bereznik (exclusive).
	Affairs round Vistavka	1st–4th and 8th–10th March 1919	The Vaga above Bereznik (exclusive).
	Affair of Ignatyevskoe	26th June 1919	The Vaga above Bereznik.

	On the Pinega River			
	First Affair of Ust-Pocha	1st–3rd June 1919	The Pinega above Pinega.	*
102.	**Operations to cover withdrawal**			
	BATTLE OF TROITSA	August-September 1919	The Dvina above Troitsa.	*
	Affair of Yemtsa	10th August 1919	The Vologda Railway south of Obozerskaya.	
	Second Affair of Ust-Pocha	29th–31st August 1919	The Pinega above Pinega.	
	The Evacuation	4th September 1919	Archangel.	
		27th September 1919		

SIBERIA

103.	**Ussuri Operations**			
	BATTLE OF DUKHOVSKAYA	8th–28th August 1918	Between the lesser Ussuri River and Lake Khanka, north of Dukhovskaya.	*
		23rd–24th August 1918		
104.	**Ufa Operations**	October 1918-June 1919		*

FAR EAST AND PACIFIC

CHINA

105.	**Siege of Tsing-Tau**	23rd September–7th November 1914		*

AUSTRALASIA

106.	**Operations of the New Zealand Expeditionary Force**	14th–30th August 1914		*
	Occupation of Samoa	29th August 1914		*
107.	**Operations of the Australian Naval and Military Expeditionary Force**	11th September–6th November 1914		*
	Affair of Herbertshohe	12th September 1914	Herbertshohe.	*
	Surrender of the German Forces	21st September 1914		

EAST AFRICA

NORTHERN AND EASTERN AREAS

108.	**Defence of the Uganda Railway**		
	German Occupation of Taveta	August-October 1914	*
	Affair of Tsavo	15th August 1914	*
	Affair of Majareni	6th September 1914	*
	Affair of Gazi	23rd September 1914	*
		8th October 1914	*
109.	**First Invasion of German East Africa**		
	Attack on Tanga	2nd–6th November 1914	The port of Tanga.
	Affair of Longido	2nd–5th November 1914	Neighbourhood of Mt Longido, south of Manga (exclusive).
		3rd November 1914	*
110.	**Umba Valley Operations**	10th December 1914–8th February 1915	
	Affair of Jasin	18th–19th January 1915	The Umba Valley.
			*
111.	**Victoria Nyanza Operations**		
	Affairs on the Kagera River	August 1914-July 1916	South of the line Mbarara – Kanyanga.
	Capture of Bukoba	August 1914-July 1916	*
	Occupation of Mwanza	22nd–23rd June 1915	*
		14th July 1916	*
112.	**Operations covering the construction of the Voi-Taveta Railway**	May 1915-February 1916	
	Affair of Mbuyuni	14th July 1915	West of Kampi ya Bibi (exclusive).
	Attack on Salaita Hill	12th February 1916	West of Mbuyuni (exclusive).
113.	**Kilimanjaro Operations**	5th–21st March 1916	*
	Action of Latema Nek	11th–12th March 1916	West of Serengeti Camp (exclusive) on the Taveta line of advance, and south of Longido (exclusive) on that line.
	Action of Kahe	21st March 1921	
114.	**Kondoa Irangi Operations**	3rd April–10th May 1916	
	Capture of Kondoa Irangi	17th–19th April 1916	South-west of Arusha.
	German Attack on Kondoa Irangi	9th–10th May 1916	*
115.	**Operations for the Northern Railway, and Pursuit to the Nguru Hills**	18th May–24th June 1916	
	Affair of German Bridge	30th May 1916	South of the Ruvu (Pangani) River.
	Action of Mkaramo	9th June 1916	*
	Occupation of Handeni	19th June 1916	
116.	**Operations for the Central Railway**		
	Seizure of the Railway from Kilimatinde to Kilosa	24th June–22nd August 1916	South of Kondoa Irangi (exclusive).
			*

	Advance through the Nguru Hills to Morogoro	5th–26th August 1916	South of Msiha Camp (exclusive).
	Affair of Matamondo	10th–11th August 1916	South of Msiha Camp (exclusive).
	Affairs on the Wami River	13th–17th August 1916	
117.	**Clearing of the Uluguru Mountains**	27th August–15th September 1916	*
	Affair of Kisaki	7th September 1916	
	Affair of Dutumi	11th–13th September 1916	
	Affair of Kisangire	9th October 1916	*
118.	**Coast Operations**	January 1915–December 1916	*
	Seizure of Mafia Island	10th–12th January 1915	*
	Destruction of the "Konigsberg"	11th July 1915	River Rufiji.
	Landing at Manza Bay	4th July 1916	*
	Landing at Pangani	23rd July 1916	*
	Landing at Sadani	1st August 1916	*
	Landing at Bagamoyo	15th August 1916	*
	Landings at Konduchi and Msasani Bay	2nd September 1916	*
	Occupation of Dar es Salaam	4th September 1916	*
	Landings at Kilwa Kivinje and Kilwa Kisiwani	7th September 1916	*
	Landings at Lindi, Sudi Bay, and Mikindani	13th–16th September 1916	*

SOUTHERN AND WESTERN AREAS

119.	**Defence of the Nyasaland-Rhodesia Border**	August 1914–24th May 1916	*
	Affairs near Karonga	9th September 1914	*
	Defence of Abercorn	5th–9th September 1914	*
	Defence of Fife	6th–27th December 1914	*
	Affair of Sphinxhaven	30th May 1915	*
	Destruction of the "Hermann von Wissmann"	30th May 1915	*
	Defence of Saisi	28th–29th June and 26th July–2nd August 1915	*
120.	**Operations on Lake Tanganyika**	23rd December 1915–March 1916	*
	Capture of the "Kingani"	26th December 1915	Lake Tanganyika.
	Sinking of the "Hedwig von Wissmann"	9th February 1916	
121.	**Advance from the Nyasa-Tanganyika line**	25th May–23rd June 1916	*
	Occupation of Neu Langenburg	27th May 1916	*
	Occupation of Bismarckburg	8th June 1916	*
	Occupation of Ubena	23rd June 1916	*
122.	**Advance on Iringa**	23rd June–31st October 1916	*
	First Affair of Malangali	24th July 1916	*
	Occupation of Iringa	29th August 1916	*

123.	**Operations on the Ruhuje**		
	Affairs near Mkapire	18th August–31st October 1916	*
		28th September and 30th October 1916	*
124.	**Operations against the Tabora Force**		
	Second Affair of Malangali	8th October–26th November 1916	*
	Defence of Lupembe	8th–12th October 1916	*
	Affairs about Ngominyi and Muhanga	12th–14th November 1916	*
	Capture of Ilembule	19th–29th October 1916	*
		24th–26th November 1916	*
125.	**Operations in the Songea District**		
	Defence of Songea	10th September–31st December 1916	*
		14th November 1916	*
126.	**Advance to the Rufiji**		
	Affairs about Kibata	December 1916–January 1917	*
	Affair of Wiransi	6th–16th December 1916	*
	Action of Beho Beho	1st January 1917	*
	Affair of Kibambawe	3rd–4th January 1917	*
	Capture of Mkindu	6th–7th January 1917	*
	Affair of Nyandete	18th January 1917	*
		24th January 1917	*
127.	**Operations in the Kilwa and Lindi Areas, and advance to the Portuguese Frontier**	April–November 1917	*
	Affair of Ngaura	18th April 1917	*
	Affair of Lutende	30th June 1917	*
	Affair of Mnindi	6th July 1917	*
	Action of Narungombe	19th July 1917	*
	Affair of Tandamuti	3rd August 1917	*
	Affair of Narunyu	18th August 1917	*
	Affair of Bweho Chini	22nd September 1917	*
	Action of Nyangao	16th–19th October 1917	*
	Affair of Lukuledi	21st October 1917	*
	Affairs round Chiwata	6th–18th November 1917	*
	Surrender of Tafel's Force	28th November 1917	The Mwiti Valley.
128.	**Operations in the Songea District and advance on Liwale and Mahenge**	1st January–13th November 1917	*
	Capture of Likuyu	24th January 1917	*
	Affairs near Kitanda	22nd–30th January 1917	*
	Affairs on the Likuyu-Mponda Road	6th July–1st October 1917	*
	Occupation of Tunduru	23rd August 1917	*
	Affair of Likasa	30th August 1917	*
	Affairs of Kalimoto and Mtrika	11th and 22nd September 1917	*
	Occupation of Mahenge	9th October 1917	*
	Occupation of Liwale	29th October 1917	*

	Affair at Liganduka's	1st–2nd November 1917	*
129.	**Pursuit and capture of Wintgens and Naumann**	10th February–1st October 1917	*
	Affair of Tandala	19th–21st February 1917	*
	Affair of St Moritz	21st March 1917	*

PORTUGUESE EAST AFRICA

130.	**Operations in Portuguese Nyasa**	11th January–23rd May 1918	*
	Affair of Nakote	5th May 1918	*
	Affair of Korewa	22nd May 1918	*
131.	**Operations in the Mozambique District**	24th May–6th September 1918	*
	Affair of Nyamakura	1st–3rd July 1918	*
	Affair of Nyamirue	21st–23rd July 1918	*
	Affair of Nyamaroi	24th August 1918	*
	Affair of Lioma	30th–31st August 1918	*
132.	**Pursuit into Rhodesia**	7th September–25th November 1918	*
	Affair of Mpwera	6th September 1918	*
	Affair of Kayambi	6th November 1918	*
	Surrender of the German Forces	25th November 1918	Abercorn.

SOUTH-WEST AFRICA

133.	**Orange River Operations**	20th August–10th November 1914	
	Affairs near Raman's Drift	14th–27th September 1914	North-east of Steinkopf (exclusive).
	Affair of Keimoes	22nd October 1914	The Orange river between Upington and Schuit Drift.
	Affair of Kakamas	24th October 1914	
	Defence of Upington	23rd–24th January 1915	*
134.	**Southern Operations**	15th September 1914–30th April 1915	
	Landing at Luderitz Bay	19th September 1914	*
	Occupation of Aus	30th March 1915	East of Chaukaib.
	Action of Gibeon	25th–26th April 1915	North of Beersheba (exclusive).
135.	**Northern Operations**	21st December 1914–9th July 1915	
	Occupation of Swakopmund	14th January 1915	*
	Advance on Windhuk	22nd February–20th May 1915	East of Swakopmund.
	Actions of Jakalswater	20th March 1915	
	Affair of Trekkopjies	26th April 1915	*
	Occupation of Windhuk	13th May 1915	
	Advance on Otavifontein	19th June–9th July 1915	North of the Elefantsberg.

Capture of Otavifontein	1st July 1915	
Surrender of the German Forces	9th July 1915	

WEST AFRICA

TOGO

136.	**Advance to Kamina**	8th–26th August 1914	North of Lome (exclusive). *
	Affair of Agbeluvoe	15th–16th August 1914	
	Affair of Khra	22nd–23rd August 1914	Amuchu.
	Surrender of the German Forces	26th August 1914	

FRENCH WEST AFRICA

137.	**Tuareg Operations**	5th January–15th May 1917	Beyond the Nigerian Frontier.

CAMEROONS

138.	**Northern Operations**	August-September 1914	*
	Affair of Tepe	25th August 1914	On the Benue river in German territory.
	First Attack on Garua	30th–31st August 1914	
	Affairs of Kuseri	25th August and 20th September 1914	*
	First Attack on Mora	27th August 1914	*
	Affair of Nsanakang	6th September 1914	On the Cross river in German territory.
139.	**Duala Operations**	September-November 1914	*
	Capture of Duala	26th–27th September 1914	*
	The first advances up the Northern and Midland Railways	29th September–15th November 1914	
	Capture of Yabasi	14th October 1914	North and east of Duala (exclusive).
	Occupation of Edea	26th October 1914	North and east of Duala (exclusive).
	Occupation of Muyuka	13th November 1914	
	Capture of Buea and of the Cameroon Mountain	14th–15th November 1914	
140.	**Operations up the Northern Railway**	3rd December 1914–4th March 1915	North of Mujuka (exclusive).
	Capture of Chang	3rd February 1915	
	Affair of Mbureku	3rd February 1915	
	Affair of Harmann's Farm	4th March 1915	

141.	**The German Counter-Offensive**			
	Defence of Edea	January 1915		*
		5th January 1915		*
142.	**Coast Operations 1914–15**			
	At Kribi	19th December 1914		*
	At Kampo	8th July 1915		*
	At Nyong	13th July 1915		*
143.	**First Advance on Yaunde**	12th April–28th June 1915	East of Edea (exclusive).	
	Affair of Ngwe	14th April 1915		
	Affair of Sende	3rd–4th May 1915		
	First Affair of Wum Biagas	3rd–4th May 1915		
144.	**Operations for the Central Plateau**	26th May–31st December 1915	South-east of the Nigerian frontier.	
	Capture of Garua	31st May–10th June 1915		
	Capture of Ngaundere	28th June 1915		
	Capture of Bamenda	22nd October 1915		
	Capture of Banyo	4th–6th November 1915		
	Capture of Fumban	2nd December 1915		
145.	**Blockade of Mora**	8th September 1915–18th February 1916		*
	Second Attack on Mora	8th–9th September 1915		*
	Third Attack on Mora	30th October–4th November 1915		*
	Capitulation of Mora	18th February 1916		*
146.	**Second Advance on Yaunde**	22nd September–31st December 1915	South of the Sanaga River (exclusive).	
	Second Affair of Wum Biagas	9th October 1915		
	Affair at Lesog's	27th November 1915		
	Affair of Chang Mangas	17th December 1915		
	Affair of Mangele	21st December 1915		
	Occupation of Yaunde	1st January 1916		
	Pursuit to the Spanish frontier	1st January–17th February 1916		

CONDITIONS OF AWARD OF BATTLE HONOURS FOR THE GREAT WAR 1914–1919

(1)   Regiments and Corps of the Permanent and Non-Permanent Active Militia will have awarded to them and recorded in the Militia List, in addition to those already shown, the honours due to them in respect to campaigns and battles enumerated in list 'A' issued as an annexure to this order. The geographical and chronological limits of battles are defined in General Order No.7 of 1928.

The term 'Regiments and Corps' shall comprise Regiments of Cavalry or Mounted Troops; Regiments or Battalions of Infantry; Motor Machine Gun Brigades; Cavalry Machine Gun Squadrons and Machine Gun Battalions.

(2)   Honours awarded to Militia Corps for services previous to the Great War shall pass to the reconstituted Militia Regiment and shall be emblazoned on all Regimental Standards, Guidons or Colours.

(3)   There will be one Honours List for each Cavalry or Infantry regiment or Machine Gun unit of the Militia.

(4)   Honours will be awarded to Militia regiments by virtue of services rendered by

        (a) The unit itself in the field:
        (b) Perpetuated CEF regiments, battalions and Machine Gun units which served in France:
        (c) Detachments contributed on organisation to CEF regiments or battalions which fought in France:
        (d) Reinforcements contributed to units at the front by perpetuated CEF regiments or battalions which proceeded to England but did not proceed to France as units:

subject to the conditions laid down below.

(5)   Following the honours previously earned and at the head of the list of honours granted for the Great War to be recorded in the Militia List, will be placed 'THE GREAT WAR'. The honours, including group names, will follow chronologically. In addition to those for earlier campaigns already carried, the number of honours to be selected from this list of Honours for the Great War for emblazonment on the Colours of Militia regiments may not exceed ten, and these will be shown in the Militia List in thicker type. Should a regiment select for emblazonment on its Colours the honours for battles or groups of battles of the same name fought in the same or different years, that name followed by the appropriate year-dates shall constitute one battle honour. For example, 'Ypres 1915, '17' would constitute one Honour.

(6)   Honours will be awarded to Militia regiments which had, or which perpetuate CEF units which had headquarters and 50 per cent of the effective strength (exclusive of drafts which although in the theatre of war had not actually joined the unit), within the prescribed area of the battle during the prescribed period as laid down in GO No. 7 of 1928, vide para. 1, above. The Theatre of War Honour 'France and Flanders', with appropriate year-dates up to 1918 inclusive, will also be awarded to Militia regiments which served, or which perpetuate CEF units which served as units in the campaign, and will be available for selection as one of the honours to be emblazoned on the Standards, Guidons or Colours.

(7)   Honours will be awarded to Militia Cavalry regiments which provided Divisional Cavalry Squadrons and squadrons in the Corps Cavalry Regiment. For the period prior to May 1916 these regiments will receive honours according to the services of the individual squadrons furnished by them. Names of battles in which the squadrons attacked or were attacked will be available for selection to be emblazoned on the Standards or Guidons. For the period May 1916 to November 1918, each of the Militia Cavalry regiments which provided squadrons in the Corps Cavalry Regiment will receive honours according to the services of the Corps Cavalry Regiment. Names of battles in which the Corps Cavalry Regiment attacked or were attacked will be available for selection to be emblazoned on the Standards or Guidons. The Theatre of War Honour 'France and Flanders', with appropriate year-dates up to 1918 inclusive, will also be awarded to these Militia cavalry regiments and will be available for selection as an honour to be emblazoned on the Standards or Guidons.

(8)   A Motor Machine Gun Brigade, Machine Gun Squadron or Machine Gun Battalion shall receive honours only from the date of organization of the perpetuated unit.

(9)   The Honours earned by a CEF unit during the first seven months after its arrival in France will be awarded also (in addition to those to which they may be entitled for other services) to regiments of the reconstituted Militia replacing those Militia Corps which contributed not less than 200 all ranks to the CEF unit on mobilization, except that in the case of battles falling within a group such honours shall be restricted to the group name only.

Subject to this restriction, the names of battles in which the CEF unit attacked or was attacked will be available for selection as honours to be emblazoned on the Standards, Guidons or Colours of the Militia regiment.

(10) A Militia regiment, perpetuating one or more CEF units which left Canada but which did not reach France, will be awarded honours (in addition to those to which it may be entitled for other services) in respect of battles where not less than 250 men originally in the perpetuated unit were present; except that in the case of battles falling within a group such honours shall be restricted to the group name only. If these men were in units which attacked or were attacked, the names of the battles (subject to the restriction to group names, wherever such exist) will be available for selection as honours to be emblazoned on the Colours of the Militia regiment.   If,   however, none of the honours so earned are available for the Colours, that battle in which the largest number of men were present shall be emblazoned on the Colours, subject to the restriction to the use of the group name when the battle falls within a group.

(11) A Militia regiment referred to in para. 10 which does not comply with the conditions for honours laid down therein may be granted an Honour for that battle in which the largest number of men were present; provided that not less than 250 men of the perpetuated CEF unit were taken on strength of CEF Cavalry regiments or Infantry battalions in France. Such honour shall be carried on the Colours of the Militia regiment, except that in the case of battles falling within a group such honour shall be restricted to the group name only.

(12) A Militia regiment, perpetuating a CEF unit which sent reinforcements from Canada or England prior to its own arrival in France, will be awarded honours (in addition to those to which it is entitled for other services) in respect to battles where less than 250 men originally in the perpetuated unit were present; except that in the case of battles falling within a group such honours shall be restricted to the group name only. Subject to this restriction, if these men were in units which attacked or were attacked, the names of the battles will be available for selection as honours to be emblazoned on the Colours of the Militia regiment.

(13) A Militia regiment perpetuating a CEF unit which was disbanded in France will be awarded honours (in addition to those to which it is entitled for other services) in respect to battles, subsequent to the disbandment of the perpetuated unit, where not less than 250 men originally in the perpetuated unit were present, except that in the case of battles falling within a group such honours shall be restricted to the group name only. Subject to this restriction, if these men were in units which attacked or were attacked, the names of the battles will be available for selection as honours to be emblazoned on the Colours of the Militia regiment.

(14) Lists of honours for which Militia regiments are eligible have been compiled at National Defence headquarters from War Diaries and records and will be forwarded to Districts for distribution to the regiments concerned. For the purpose of selecting from these lists the honours to be borne on the Standards, Guidons or Colours, District Officers Commanding shall issue instructions for the formation of Regimental Committees of not less than five members for each Cavalry, Mounted Rifles, and Infantry Regiment concerned within their District. The Commanding Officer of the Militia regiment shall be a member, and all surviving ex-commanding officers of perpetuated units shall be invited to be members. In any case at least one representative of each perpetuated unit shall be on the Committee. The Chairman of each Committee shall forward to National Defence Headquarters, through the usual channel, the list of honours selected to be borne on the Colours of the regiment. No reimbursement from public funds can be made for expenses incurred in connection with these Committees.

(15) In the case of CEF units which no longer exist the following rules as to emblazonment of Battle Honours on Colours will apply:
(a) Upon the Colours of units which fought in France will be emblazoned honours for battles in which the units served and the Theatre of War Honour 'France and Flanders' with year-dates, to a total of ten, inclusive of the Theatre of War Honour. Should a unit select for emblazonment the Colours the honours for battles or groups of battles of the same name fought in the same or different years, that name, followed by the appropriate year-dates, shall constitute one honour. The year-dates to follow the Theatre of War Honour will be determined by the calendar years, up to 1918, inclusive, during any portion of which the unit served as a unit in France and Belgium.
(b) Upon the Colours of battalions of the CEF which served in Siberia will be emblazoned 'Siberia 1918-19'.
(c) Upon the Colours of units which proceeded to England but did not reach France will be emblazoned 'The Great War', followed by year-dates. The year-dates will be determined by the calendar years, up to 1918, inclusive, during any portion of which the unit served as a unit out of Canada.

(16) The selection of honours to be emblazoned on the Colours of CEF battalions, under para. 15(a) shall be left to the surviving members of the battalions. District Officers Commanding in the District where the unit is perpetuated will communicate with the President of Battalion Associations, where such exist, with a view to the matter being decided by these organisations. When no Battalion Associations exist the District Officers Commanding will communicate with surviving ex-commanding officers with a view to a committee of the battalion being formed or a meeting of ex-members being held. District Officers Commanding must use their best endeavours to ensure that the list of honours selected represents the wishes of the majority of the surviving members of the battalion.

BATTLES, ACTIONS AND ENGAGEMENTS FOUGHT BY THE LAND FORCES OF THE COMMONWEALTH DURING THE SECOND WORLD WAR AND THE KOREAN CAMPAIGN

NORWAY 1940–41

1.	**Operations based on Namsos**	Vist	21st–22nd April 1940
2.	**Operations based on Andalsnes**	Tretten	23rd April 1940
		Kvam	25th–26th April 1940
		Otta	28th April 1940
		Dombaas	30th April 1940
3.	**Operations leading to the Capture of Narvik**	Stien	17th–18th May 1940
		Krokstrand	21st–22nd May 1940
		Pothus	25th–26th May 1940
4.	**Raid on Fish-oil Factories and Shipping**	Vaagso	27th December 1941

NORTH-WEST EUROPE 1940–42

5.	**Withdrawal to Dunkirk**	The Dyle	10th–16th May 1940
		Withdrawal to the Escaut	17th–19th May 1940
		Defence of the Escaut	19th–22nd May 1940
		Amiens 1940	20th May 1940
		Abbeville	20th May 1940
		Defence of Arras	19th–24th May 1940
		Arras Counter Attack	21st May 1940
		Boulogne 1940	22nd–25th May 1940
		Calais 1940	23rd–26th May 1940
		French Frontier 1940	23rd–27th May 1940

Battles, Actions and Engagements of the Second World War and the Korean Campaign

	ST OMER-LA BASSEE		
		Morbecque	23rd–29th May 1940
		Wormhoudt	24th May 1940
		Cassel	28th May 1940
		Foret de Nieppe	27th–29th May 1940
	YPRES-COMINES CANAL		27th–28th May 1940
	Dunkirk 1940		26th–28th May 1940
			26th May–3rd June 1940
6.	**Fighting South of the Somme**		
	The Somme 1940		24th May–5th June 1940
	Withdrawal to the Seine		6th–10th June 1940
		Withdrawal to Cherbourg	9th–18th June 1940
		St Valery-en-Caux	10th–12th June 1940
7.	**Position Warfare in the Saar Region**		
		Saar	13th May 1940
8.	**Raiding Operations**		
		Bruneval	27th–28th February 1942
		St Nazaire	27th–28th March 1942
	Dieppe		19th August 1942

NORTH-WEST EUROPE 1944–45

9.	**The Assault**		
	NORMANDY LANDING		
		Pegasus Bridge	6th June 1944
		Merville Battery	6th June 1944
			6th June 1944
10.	**The Expansion of the Bridgehead**		
		Port en Bessin	7th–8th June 1944
		Authie	7th June 1944
		Sully	8th–9th June 1944
		Cambes	9th June 1944
		Putot en Bessin	8th June 1944
		Bretteville L'Orgueilleuse	8th–9th June 1944
		Le Mesnil Patry	11th June 1944
		Breville	10th–13th June 1944
	Villers Bocage		8th–15th June 1944
		Tilly sur Seulles	14th–19th June 1944

11.	**The Odon Bridgehead**		
	THE ODON		25th June–2nd July 1944
		Cheux	25th–27th June 1944
		Fontenay le Pesnil	25th–27th June 1944
		Defence of Rauray	26th–27th June 1944
		Tourmauville Bridge	29th June–2nd July 1944
12.	**The Capture of Caen**		
	CAEN		4th–18th July 1944
		Carpiquet	4th–5th July 1944
		The Orne or Orne (Buron)	8th–9th July 1944
		Hill 112	10th–11th July 1944
		Esquay	15th–17th July 1944
		Noyers	15th–18th July 1944
	BOURGUEBUS RIDGE		18th–23rd July 1944
		Cagny	18th–19th July 1944
		Troarn	18th–21st July 1944
		Faubourg de Vaucelles	18th–19th July 1944
	St Andre sur Orne		19th–23rd July 1944
		Maltot	22nd–23rd July 1944
13.	**The Holding Attack**		
	Verrieres Ridge-Tilly La Campagne		25th July 1944
14.	**The Capture of Mont Pincon**		
	MONT PINCON		30th July–9th August 1944
		Quarry Hill	30th July–2nd August 1944
		Jurques	30th July–4th August 1944
		La Variniere	4th–9th August 1944
		The Souleuvre	30th July–1st August 1944
		Catheoiles	2nd–5th August 1944
		Le Perier Ridge	2nd–8th August 1944
		Brieux Bridgehead	6th–8th August 1944
15.	**The Advance beyond Falaise to Close the Gap**		
		St Pierre la Vielle	9th–16th August 1944
		Estry	6th–12th August 1944
		Noireau Crossing	14th–17th August 1944
	FALAISE		7th–22nd August 1944
		Falaise Road	7th–9th August 1944
		Quesnay Wood	10th–11th August 1944
		Clair Tizon	11th–13th August 1944
		Jort	15th August 1944

Battles, Actions and Engagements of the Second World War and the Korean Campaign

		The Laison	14th–17th August 1944
		Chambois	18th–22nd August 1944
		St Lambert sur Dives	19th–22nd August 1944
16.	**Pursuit to the River Seine**		
		Dives Crossing	17th–20th August 1944
		La Vie Crossing	18th–20th August 1944
		Lisieux	21st–23rd August 1944
		La Touques Crossing	22nd–23rd August 1944
		Risle Crossing	25th–27th August 1944
		Foret de Bretonne	28th–30th August 1944
		Foret de la Londe	27th–29th August 1944
17.	**The Seine Crossing and Pursuit to Antwerp**		
	The Seine 1944		
		Amiens 1944	25th–28th August 1944
		Brussels	31st August 1944
		Antwerp	3rd September 1944
		Moerbrugge	4th–7th September 1944
			8th–10th September 1944
18.	**From Brussels to the Nederrijn**		
		Hechtel	7th–12th September 1944
		Gheel	8th–11th September 1944
		Heppen	8th–9th September 1944
		Neerpelt	10th September 1944
		Aart	14th–20th September 1944
	THE NEDERRIJN		17th–27th September 1944
	Arnhem 1944		17th–26th September 1944
		Nijmegen	19th–20th September 1944
		Veghel	22nd–23rd September 1944
		Best	22nd–27th September 1944
19.	**The Channel Ports**		
		Dunkirk 1944	8th–15th September 1944
		Le Havre	10th–12th September 1944
		Boulogne 1944	17th–22nd September 1944
		Calais 1944	25th September–1st October 1944
20.	**Opening the Port of Antwerp**		
		Terneuzen	12th–22nd September 1944
		Moerkerke	13th–14th September 1944
		Wyneghem	21st–22nd September 1944
		Antwerp-Turnhout Canal	24th–29th September 1944

	THE SCHELDT	Leopold Canal	1st October–8th November 1944
		Woensdrecht	6th–16th October 1944
		Savojaards Plaat	1st–27th October 1944
		Breskens Pocket	9th–10th October 1944
			11th October–3rd November 1944
		South Beveland	24th–31st October 1944
		Walchern Causeway	31st October–4th November 1944
		Flushing	1st–4th November 1944
		Westkapelle	1st–3rd November 1944
		The Lower Maas	20th October–7th November 1944
21.	**Preparation for the Thrust to the Ruhr**	Alphen	29th September–5th October 1944
		Aam	1st–4th October 1944
		Opheusen	5th–7th October 1944
		Venraij	12th–18th October 1944
		Asten or Meijel	27th October–5th November 1944
		Geilenkirchen	18th–23rd November 1944
		Venlo Pocket	14th November–3rd December 1944
		Kapelsche Veer	31st December 1944–31st January 1945
		The Roer	16th–31st January 1945
		Zetten	18th–21st January 1945
22.	**The Ardennes**	The Ourthe	3rd–14th January 1945
23.	**The Rhineland** THE RHINELAND	The Reichswald	8th February–10th March 1945
		Waal Flats	8th–13th February 1945
		Cleve	8th–15th February 1945
			9th–11th February 1945
		Goch	12th–21st February 1945
		Moyland or Moyland Wood	14th–21st February 1945
		Goch-Calcar Road	19th–21st February 1945
		Weeze	24th February–2nd March 1945
		The Hochwald	26th February–4th March 1945
		Schaddenhof	27th–28th February 1945
		Xanten	8th–9th March 1945
		Veen	6th–10th March 1945
24.	**The Crossing of the River Rhine** THE RHINE	Emmerich-Hoch Elten	23rd March–1st April 1945
			28th March–1st April 1945

Battles, Actions and Engagements of the Second World War and the Korean Campaign

25. **Pursuit to the Baltic and North Sea**

Ibbenburen	1st–6th April 1945
Lingen	2nd–5th April 1945
Bentheim	2nd–3rd April 1945
Dreirwalde	4th–8th April 1945
Leese	5th–8th April 1945
The Aller	10th–17th April 1945
Brinkum	13th–16th April 1945
Uelzen	14th–18th April 1945
Bremen	18th–26th April 1945
Artlenberg	29th–30th April 1945
Twente Canal	2nd–4th April 1945
Zutphen	6th–8th April 1945
Deventer	8th–11th April 1945
Arnhem 1945	12th–14th April 1945
Groningen	13th–16th April 1945
Friesoythe	14th April 1945
Apeldoorn	11th–17th April 1945
Ijsselmeer	15th–18th April 1945
Kusten Canal	17th–24th April 1945
The Leda	19th–29th April 1945
Leer	28th–29th April 1945
Delfzijl Pocket	23rd April–2nd May 1945
Bad Zwischenahm	25th April–4th May 1945
Oldenburg	27th April–5th May 1945

26. **The Invasion of the South of France**
SOUTHERN FRANCE

	15th–28th August 1944

27. **Sudan Border (Northern Campaign)**

Sudan Frontier	
Tessenei	17th June–31st October 1940
Kassala	17th–27th June 1940
Adardeb	4th–7th July 1940
Banda Rolle Raid	26th August 1940
Jebel Tendelai	15th–28th October 1940
	5th–6th November 1940
Gallabat	6th–7th November 1940
Tehamiyam Wells	11th November 1940

ABYSSINIA 1940–41

28.	**Eritrea (Northern Campaign)**		
		Gash Delta	23rd December 1940
		The Setit	2nd January 1941
		Jebel Dafeis	10th January 1941
		Gallabat Fort	12th January 1941
		Eribo (Badika)	25th January 1941
		Keru	21st–22nd January 1941
		Jebel Shiba	21st–23rd January 1941
		K 285 Barentu Road	23rd January 1941
		Gogni	26th January 1941
		Tauda	28th January 1941
		Um Hagar	21st–31st January 1941
	Agordat		28th January–1st February 1941
	Barentu		27th January–2nd February 1941
		Arresa Road	2nd–8th February 1941
		Wahni	7th February 1941
		Karora-Marsa Taclai	9th–10th February 1941
		Cubcub	23rd February 1941
		Mescelit Pass	1st March 1941
	KEREN		3rd February–31st March 1941
		Mt Engiahat	12th–15th March 1941
		Zaad Amba	5th–18th March 1941
		Keren-Asmara Road	28th–29th March 1941
		Keren-Asmara Railway	29th–31st March 1941
		Ad Teclesan	30th–31st March 1941
		Adigrat	4th April 1941
	Massawa		8th April 1941
	AMBA ALAGI		20th April–16th May 1941
29.	**Subsidiary Campaigns in Western Abyssinia**		
		Shogali	20th January 1941
		Qeissan	11th February 1941
		Kurmuk	14th February 1941
		Afodu	9th March 1941
		Gambela	22nd March 1941
		Maji	14th February–21st April 1941
		The Bortai	15th April–3rd July 1941
		Kretei	3rd July 1941

Battles, Actions and Engagements of the Second World War and the Korean Campaign

No.	Campaign	Location	Action	Date
30.	**Subsidiary Campaigns in Northern Abyssinia**		Debra Tabor	1st April–6th July 1941
			Wolchefit	13th April–27th September 1941
			Magdala	14th–17th May 1941
			Chilga	17th–19th May 1941
31.	**Gojjam**	Gojjam	Bahrdar Giorgis	12th February–23rd May 1941
			Burye	12th February–28th April 1941
			Cheraka	26th February–8th March 1941
			Debra Markos	6th March 1941
			Mota	11th March–4th April 1941
			Addis Derra	19th–24th April 1941
			Agibar	28th April–16th May 1941
				18th–23rd May 1941
32.	**Kenya Border (Southern Campaign)**		Dif	13th June 1940
			Moyale	1st–15th July 1940
			Korondil-Dobel	29th–30th July 1940
			Wal Garis	10th and 12th September 1940
			Buna	9th October 1940
			Liboi	9th October 1940
			Loruth	27th November 1940
		El Wak		15th–17th December 1940
33.	**Southern Abyssinia (Southern Campaign)**		El Yibo	16th–18th January 1941
			Turbi Road	24th–25th January 1941
			Gorai	1st February 1941
			El Gumu	1st February 1941
			Hobok	2nd February 1941
			Banno	8th–9th February 1941
			Yavello Road	15th February 1941
		Mega		15th–18th February 1941
			Todenyang-Namaraputh	9th February 1941
			Neghelli	20th March 1941
			Soroppa	31st March 1941
34.	**Juba River**	THE JUBA	Beles Gugani	4th–26th February 1941
			Badada	4th February 1941
				6th February 1941

No.	Battle Honour	Action	Engagement	Date
35.	**Advance to Addis Ababa**		Afmadu	6th–11th February 1941
			Bulo Erillo	13th February 1941
			Gobwen	14th February 1941
			Yonte	18th–19th February 1941
			Gelib	21st–22nd February 1941
			Alessandra	22nd February 1941
			Mabungo	22nd February 1941
			Goluin	24th February 1941
		Marda Pass		
36.	**Northern Battle of Lakes**		Berbera	16th March 1941
			Babile Gap	21st–22nd March 1941
			The Bisidimo	23rd–25th March 1941
			Hubeta Pass	26th March 1941
			Collubi	27th March 1941
			The Awash	30th March 1941
			The Awash	2nd and 3rd April 1941
37.	**Southern Battle of Lakes**		Fike	1st May 1941
			Lokole	7th May 1941
			Bubissa	11th May 1941
			Dadaba	13th May 1941
			Colito	19th May 1941
		Wadara	Giarso	9th April 1941
			Budo Magado	8th April–10th May 1941
			Hula	6th–7th May 1941
				20th May 1941
38.	**Galla Sidamo**	The Omo	Lechemti	31st May–6th June 1941
			The Didessa	15th June 1941
				27th June 1941
39.	**NE Abyssinia**	Combolcia	Debra Sina	15th April 1941
			NE Somaliland	17th–26th April 1941
			Assab	20th April–21st May 1941
				11th June 1941
40.	**Gondar** GONDAR			15th October–28th November 1941

Battles, Actions and Engagements of the Second World War and the Korean Campaign

	Ambazzo	15th October–28th November 1941
	Gianda	11th November 1941
	Kulkaber	13th and 21st November 1941
	Yeo Mariam	20th November 1941

BRITISH SOMALILAND 1940

41. **Enemy Invasion of British Somaliland**

	Hargeisa	4th–5th August 1940
	Tug Argan	11th–15th August 1940
	Barkasan	17th August 1940

IRAQ 1941

42. **Operations against the Iraqi Rebels**

	Defence of Habbaniya	2nd–6th May 1941
	Basra	2nd–7th May 1941
	Relief of Habbaniya	13th–18th May 1941
	Falluja	19th–22nd May 1941
	Baghdad 1941	28th–31st May 1941

SYRIA 1941

43. **Syria and the Lebanon**

	Syrian Frontier	7th–8th June 1941
		8th June 1941
	Deraa	8th–9th June 1941
	Cheikh Meskene	9th–10th June 1941
	The Litani	9th–27th June 1941
	Merjayun	10th–12th June 1941
	Adlun	10th–16th June 1941
		13th–15th June 1941
	Kissoue	14th–24th June 1941
	Sidon	15th–17th June 1941
	Jezzine	16th–17th June 1941
	Ezraa	
	Kuneitra	

DAMASCUS

	Wadi Zeini	16th–21st June 1941
		19th June 1941
Palmyra		21st June–3rd July 1941
	Dimas	22nd–28th June 1941
	Chehim and Rharife	26th June–3rd July 1941
	Nebek	30th June 1941
	Deir ez Zor	1st–3rd July 1941
		6th–12th July 1941
DAMOUR	Mazraat ech Chouf	7th–8th July 1941
	Hill 1069	8th July 1941
	Badarene	9th–10th July 1941
	Raqqa	9th–10th July 1941
	Jebel Mazar	10th–12th July 1941

NORTH AFRICA 1940–43

44. **Operations of Western Desert Force and 13th Corps**

Egyptian Frontier 1940		12th June–12th September 1940
	Withdrawal to Matruh	13th–17th September 1940
	Bir Enba	19th November 1940
SIDI BARRANI		8th–11th December 1940
BARDIA 1941		11th December 1940
CAPTURE OF TOBRUK		3rd–5th January 1941
		21st–22nd January 1941
BEDA FOMM	Derna	27th–30th January 1941
		5th–8th February 1941
Giarabub		19th–21st March 1941
	Mersa el Brega	31st March 1941
	Agedabia	2nd April 1941
	Er Regima	4th April 1941
El Mechili		6th–8th April 1941
	Derna Aerodrome	7th April 1941
	Tmimi	7th April 1941
Sidi Suleiman	Halfaya 1941	15th–27th May 1941
		15th–17th June 1941
DEFENCE OF TOBRUK		8th April–10th December 1941
El Adem Road		13th–14th April 1941
The Salient 1941		30th April–4th May 1941

Operations of the Eighth Army

45.	**Relief of Tobruk**			
	TOBRUK 1941			18th November–10th December 1941
			Gubi I	19th November 1941
	Sidi Rezegh 1941			19th–21st November 1941
			Gabr Saleh	19th–23rd November 1941
	Tobruk Sortie 1941			21st–23rd November 1941
			Sidi Azeiz	21st–30th November 1941
	Omars			22nd November–2nd December 1941
			Taieb el Essem	24th–25th November 1941
	Belhamed			25th November–1st December 1941
			Zemla	3rd December 1941
			Gubi II	4th–6th December 1941
	Relief of Tobruk 1941			7th–10th December 1941
46.	**Pursuit to Agedabia**			
	Alem Hamza			14th–16th December 1941
			Chor es Sufan	27th–30th December 1941
	Bardia 1942			31st December 1941–2nd January 1942
			Clayden's Trench (Salum)	11th–12th January 1942
47.	**Enemy Counter Offensive**			
			Mas el Gefera	21st January 1942
	Saunnu			23rd January 1942
			Msus	25th January 1942
			Benghazi	27th–29th January 1942
			Carmusa	29th January–5th February 1942
48.	**Resumption of Enemy Offensive**			
	GAZALA			26th May–21st June 1942
			Pt 171	27th May 1942
			Retma	27th May 1942
			Bir el Igela	27th May 1942
	Bir el Aslagh			27th–31st May 1942
	Bir Hacheim			27th May–11th June 1942
	Sidi Muftah			29th May–1st June 1942
	The Cauldron			5th–6th June 1942
			Knightsbridge	6th–7th June and 11th–13th June 1942
	Hagiag er Raml			11th–13th June 1942
			Gabr el Fachri	14th June 1942
			Via Balbia	14th June 1942

Battle Honour	Action	Date
		Zt el Mrasses — 15th June 1942
		El Adem — 15th–17th June 1942
		Sidi Rezegh 1942 — 17th June 1942
		Gambut — 18th June 1942
MERSA MATRUH	Tobruk 1942	The Kennels — 20th–21st June 1942
		24th June 1942
		Siwa Road — 26th–30th June 1942
		Pt 174 — 26th–27th June 1942
	Minqar Qaim	27th June 1942
		El Sarahna — 27th–28th June 1942
		Fuka — 27th–28th June 1942
		El Zarqa — 28th June 1942
		Kilo 23 — 28th June 1942
		El Casaba — 28th–29th June 1942

49. Enemy Offensive Halted
DEFENCE OF ALAMEIN LINE

Battle Honour	Action	Date
Deir el Shein	Deir el Shein	1st–27th July 1942
Ruweisat	Ruweisat	1st July 1942
		2nd–4th July 1942
	Fuka Airfield	7th July 1942
Tell el Eisa	Tell el Eisa	10th–11th July 1942
		11th July 1942
	Point 93	14th–16th July 1942
Ruweisat Ridge	Ruweisat Ridge	15th–16th July 1942
		17th–18th July 1942
El Mreir	Point 23	21st–22nd July 1942
Sanyet el Miteirya	Tell el Makh Khad	21st–23rd July 1942
Qattara Track		26th–27th July 1942

50. Repulse of Final Enemy Offensive
ALAM EL HALFA

Battle Honour	Action	Date
	West Point 23	30th August–7th September 1942
		1st September 1942
	Tobruk Raid 1942	13th–14th September 1942
	Benghazi Raid	13th–14th September 1942
	Barce Raid	13th–14th September 1942
	Gialo Raid	15th–20th September 1942
Deir el Munassib		30th September 1942

51. The Offensive from Alamein to Tripoli
EL ALAMEIN

Battle Honour	Action	Date
	Capture of Halfaya Pass 1942	23rd October–4th November 1942
	El Agheila	10th–11th November 1942
		13th–17th December 1942

Battles, Actions and Engagements of the Second World War and the Korean Campaign

No.	Battle	Action	Engagement	Date
52.	**Repulse of Enemy Offensive in Tunisia**			
	MEDENINE	Advance on Tripoli	Nofilia	17th–18th December 1942
				15th–23rd January 1943
		Wadi Hachana		6th March 1943
		Zemlet el Lebene		6th March 1943
		Tadjera Khir		6th March 1943
		Metameur		6th March 1943
53.	**Advance on Tunis**			
	MARETH		Wadi Zeuss East	16th–23rd March 1943
			Wadi Zeuss West	16th–17th March 1943
			Si el Guelaa	16th–17th March 1943
			Mestaoua	16th–17th March 1943
		Wadi Zigzaou		18th March 1943
				20th–23rd March 1943
	TEBAGA GAP	Point 201 (Roman Wall)		21st–30th March 1943
		El Hamma		21st–22nd March 1943
				27th–29th March 1943
			Wadi Merteba	28th March 1943
			Gabes	30th March 1943
			Matmata Hills	25th–28th March 1943
	AKARIT	Djebel el Meida		6th–7th April 1943
		Djebel Tebaga Fatnassa		6th April 1943
		Wadi Akarit East		6th April 1943
		Djebel Roumana		6th–7th April 1943
		Wadi Akarit West		6th–7th April 1943
			Sebkret en Noual	6th April 1943
			Chebket en Nouiges	7th April 1943
			Messouna	8th April 1943
			Wadi Chaffar	8th April 1943
			Djebel el Telil	9th April 1943
				9th April 1943
	ENFIDAVILLE	Takrouna		19th–29th April 1943
		Djebel Garci		20th–21st April 1943
				20th April 1943
			Djebel Terhouna	25th–29th April 1943
			Djebel es Srafi	25th–29th April 1943
		Djebel Tebaga	Djebibina	6th–9th May 1943
				8th–9th May 1943

Operations of First Army in Tunisia

54. **Allied Build-up and Enemy Counter Offensive**

		Djebel Abiod	17th November 1942
		Soudia	24th November 1942
	Medjez el Bab		25th–26th November 1942
			27th November 1942
		Tebourba	28th–29th November 1942
		Djedeida	28th–30th November 1942
	Djebel Azzag 1942		
		Oudna	29th November–3rd December 1942
		Sidi el Moudjad	1st–5th December 1942
TEBOURBA GAP			
			1st–10th December 1942
		El Guessa	6th December 1942
		Djebel bou Aoukaz 1942	10th December 1942
	Longstop Hill 1942		23rd–25th December 1942
		El Aroussia	23rd–26th December 1942
	Djebel Azzag 1943		5th–7th January 1943
			13th January 1943
		Two Tree Hill	18th–25th January 1943
BOU ARADA			31st January 1943
		Robaa Valley	3rd–4th February 1943
		Djebel Alliliga	14th–25th February 1943
KASSERINE			
	Sbiba		19th–22nd February 1943
	Thala		20th–22nd February 1943

55. **Enemy Thrusts at Allied Communication Centres**

		El Hadjeba	26th February 1943
		Djebel Djaffa	26th February 1943
		Sidi Nsir	26th February 1943
		Fort McGregor	26th–27th February 1943
		Tally Ho Corner	26th–27th February 1943
		Stuka Farm	26th–28th February 1943
		Steamroller Farm	26th February–1st March 1943
		El Aouana	26th–28th February 1943
	Hunt's Gap		27th–28th February 1943
		Montagne Farm	28th February–2nd March 1943
		Kef Ouiba Pass	28th February–4th March 1943
		Djebel Guerba	2nd March 1943
		Sedjenane I	4th March 1943
		Barka Hill	4th March 1943
		Djebel Touila I	5th March 1943

Battles, Actions and Engagements of the Second World War and the Korean Campaign

	Tamera	5th–15th March 1943
	Oussettia	11th March 1943
	Maknassy	12th–31st March 1943
	Sedjenane II	20th March 1943
	Djebel Dahra	20th–24th March 1943
56.	**Allied Counter Offensive**	
	Djebel Choucha	
	Kef el Debna	28th March 1943
	Djebel el Harch	28th March 1943
	Mine de Sedjenane	29th March 1943
	Faid Pass	30th–31st March 1943
	Argoub en Negrila	3rd April 1943
		9th April 1943
FONDOUK	Pichon	7th–11th April 1943
	Djebel el Rhorab	8th April 1943
	Fondouk Pass	9th April 1943
	Sidi Ali	9th April 1943
	Kairouan	10th April 1943
	Bordj	10th April 1943
		11th April 1943
OUED ZARGA	Djebel el Dourat	7th–15th April 1943
	Mergueb Chaouach	7th April 1943
	Djebel bel Mahdi	7th April 1943
	Toukabeur	7th April 1943
	Djebel bech Chekaoui	8th April 1943
	Chaouach	9th April 1943
	Djebel Rmel	10th April 1943
	Djebel oum Guerinat	10th April 1943
	Djebel Touila II	11th April 1943
	Kef el Coraa	13th April 1943
	Djebel el Hara	14th April 1943
	Djebel Ang	14th–15th April 1943
	Djebel Tanngoucha	14th–25th April 1943
	Heidous	15th–25th April 1943
	Banana Ridge	21st April 1943
	Djebel Kesskiss	21st April 1943
	Djebel Djaffa Pass	21st–22nd April 1943
	Sulutos	21st April 1943
EL KOURZIA	Ber Rabal	22nd–26th April 1943
	Argoub Sellah	22nd April 1943
		22nd April 1943

Section	Battle Honour		Date
		Si Dzifallah	23rd–24th April 1943
		Wadi Enafidet	24th April 1943
		Sebkra Djabeur	24th April 1943
		Si Mabrouk	25th April 1943
		Djebel Rouissate	26th April 1943
MEDJEZ PLAIN	Grich el Oued		23rd–30th April 1943
	Gueriat el Atach Ridge		23rd April 1943
	Longstop Hill 1943		23rd–24th April 1943
			23rd–26th April 1943
			23rd–30th April 1943
		Djebel Rhaouass	24th April 1943
	Peters Corner		25th–26th April 1943
		Si Mediene	26th–27th April 1943
		Si Salem	27th–28th April 1943
	Djebel bou Aoukaz 1943 I		27th–30th April 1943
	Si Abdallah		27th–30th April 1943
		Djebel el Asoud	28th–30th April 1943
		Gab Gab Gap	28th–30th April 1943
		Sidi Ahmed	25th–30th April 1943
		Djebel Kournine	27th April 1943
		Hir el Halouani	30th April 1943
		Argoub el Megas	
TUNIS	Djebel bou Aoukaz 1943 II		5th–12th May 1943
		Djebel Sahbi	5th–6th May 1943
	Montarnaud		5th–6th May 1943
	Ragoubet Souissi		6th May 1943
	Massicault		6th May 1943
		Djebel Sidi Achour	6th May 1943
		Djebel Sidi Salah	6th May 1943
	Hammam Lif		7th May 1943
		Creteville Pass	8th–9th May 1943
		Soliman	8th–11th May 1943
		Gromballa	10th May 1943
	Bou Ficha		10th May 1943
			11th May 1943

SICILY 1943

57. Assault and Capture of Sicily
LANDING IN SICILY — 9th–12th July 1943

	Solarino	11th–13th July 1943
	Vizzini	11th–14th July 1943
	Augusta	12th–13th July 1943
	Sortino	12th–13th July 1943
	Francofonte	13th–15th July 1943
Lentini or Primosole Bridge		13th–18th July 1943
	Grammichele	15th July 1943
	Piazza Armerina	16th–17th July 1943
	Sferro	15th–20th July 1943
	Valguarnera	17th–19th July 1943
	Simeto Bridgehead	18th–21st July 1943
	Gerbini	18th–21st July 1943
	Assoro	20th–22nd July 1943
	Leonforte	21st–22nd July 1943
ADRANO		24th–28th July 1943
Agira		24th–28th July 1943
	Catenanuova	29th July–7th August 1943
	Regalbuto	29th–30th July 1943
Sferro Hills		29th July–3rd August 1943
Centuripe		31st July–3rd August 1943
	Troina Valley	31st July–3rd August 1943
	Salso Crossing	2nd–6th August 1943
	Simeto Crossing	4th August 1943
	Monte Rivoglia	5th August 1943
	Malleto	9th August 1943
Pursuit to Messina		12th–13th August 1943
		2nd–17th August 1943

ITALY 1943–45

Eighth Army Operations

58.	**The Landings in Calabria**		
	Landing at Reggio	Bagnara Calabria	3rd September 1943
	Landing at Porto San Venere		3rd–4th September 1943
			8th September 1943
59.	**The Landing in the "Heel"**		
	Taranto		9th–22nd September 1943

60. **The Advance towards Ortona**

Battle Honour	Action	Date
	Potenza	19th–20th September 1943
	Motta Montecorvino	1st–3rd October 1943
Termoli		3rd–6th October 1943
	Monte San Marco	6th–7th October 1943
	Gambatesa	7th–8th October 1943
Campobasso		11th–14th October 1943
	Baranello	17th–18th October 1943
	Colle d'Anchise	22nd–24th October 1943
The Trigno		22nd October–5th November 1943
	Torella	24th–27th October 1943
	Tufillo	1st–5th November 1943
	San Salvo	2nd–3rd November 1943
	Atessa	7th November 1943
	Perano	17th November 1943
THE SANGRO		19th November–3rd December 1943
	Castel di Sangro	23rd–24th November 1943
Mozzagrogna		27th–29th November 1943
Fossacesia		30th November 1943
Castel Frentano		1st–2nd December 1943
	Romagnoli	30th November–1st December 1943
Orsogna		3rd–24th December 1943
The Moro		5th–7th December 1943
	Moro Bridge or Impossible Bridge	5th–13th December 1943
San Leonardo		8th–9th December 1943
The Gully		10th–19th December 1943
	Casa Berardi	14th–15th December 1943
	Caldari	13th–14th December 1943
Ortona		20th–28th December 1943
Villa Grande		22nd–28th December 1943
	San Nicola-San Tommaso	31st December 1943
	Point 59 or Torre Mucchia	29th December 1943–4th January 1944

Fifth Army Operations

61. **The Salerno Landing and Bridgehead**

Battle Honour	Action	Date
SALERNO		9th–18th September 1943
	Salerno Pass	9th–16th September 1943
	Santa Lucia	9th–16th September 1943
	Vietri Pass	9th–16th September 1943

Battles, Actions and Engagements of the Second World War and the Korean Campaign

62. Operations leading to the Capture of Naples

Salerno Hills	9th–17th September 1943
Battipaglia	10th–18th September 1943
CAPTURE OF NAPLES	22nd September–1st October 1943
Cava di Tirreni	22nd–28th September 1943
Cappezano	24th–25th September 1943
Monte Stella	24th–26th September 1943
Scafati Bridge	28th September 1943
Cardito	3rd October 1943

63. The Advance to the Winter Line

VOLTURNO CROSSING	12th–25th October 1943
Monte Maro	22nd–23rd October 1943
Rocchetta e Croce	22nd–23rd October 1943
Teano	28th–31st October 1943
Mondragone	30th October–2nd November 1943
MONTE CAMINO	5th November–9th December 1943
Calabritto	5th November–6th December 1943
Monte la Difensa–Monte la Remetanea	2nd–8th December 1943
Rocca d'Evandro	7th–9th December 1943
Monte Majo	3rd–8th January 1944
Colle Cedro	4th–9th January 1944
GARIGLIANO CROSSING	17th–31st January 1944
Minturno	17th–25th January 1944
Damiano	18th–30th January 1944
Monte Tuga	26th–30th January 1944
Monte Natale	30th January–1st February 1944
Cerasola	2nd–20th February 1944
Monte Ornito	7th–9th February 1944

64. The Anzio Landing and Bridgehead

ANZIO	22nd January–22nd May 1944
Campoleone	24th–26th January 1944
Carroceto	24th–31st January 1944
Aprilia	7th–10th February 1944

65. The First Attacks on Cassino

CASSINO I	20th January–25th March 1944
Monastery Hill	15th–18th February 1944
Castle Hill	15th–24th March 1944
Hangman's Hill	15th–25th March 1944
Cassino Railway Station	17th March 1944

66. **The Liri Valley Operations**

CASSINO II			11th–18th May 1944
	Gustav Line		11th–18th May 1944
		Sant'Angelo in Teodice	13th May 1944
		Massa Vertechi	14th May 1944
		Pignataro	14th–15th May 1944
		Massa Tambourini	15th May 1944
		Casa Sinagogga	16th May 1944
LIRI VALLEY			18th–30th May 1944
	Hitler Line		18th–24th May 1944
	Aquino		18th–24th May 1944
		Piedimonte Hill	20th–21st May 1944
	Melfa Crossing		24th–25th May 1944
	Monte Piccolo		26th–28th May 1944
		Ceprano	26th–27th May 1944
		Rocca d'Arce	27th–29th May 1944
		Torrice Crossroads	30th May 1944

Central Italy

67. **The Capture of Rome**

ROME		22nd May–4th June 1944
	Advance to the Tiber	22nd May–4th June 1944

68. **The Advance to the Arno**

		Monte Rotondo	6th–7th June 1944
		Celleno	9th June 1944
	Bagnoregio		11th–13th June 1944
		Allerona	15th June 1944
		Ficulle	15th June 1944
		Monte Gabbione	16th–17th June 1944
	Citta della Pieve		16th–19th June 1944
	Capture of Perugia		18th–20th June 1944
		Ripa Ridge	18th–19th June 1944
		Monte Malbe	19th–20th June 1944
TRASIMENE LINE			20th–30th June 1944
		Sanfatucchio	20th–21st June 1944
		Monte Pilonica	26th June 1944
		Gabbiano	1st July 1944
AREZZO			4th–17th July 1944
		Tuori	5th July 1944

Battles, Actions and Engagements of the Second World War and the Korean Campaign

ADVANCE TO FLORENCE

	Monte Lignano	14th July 1944
Monte San Michele		17th July–10th August 1944
		18th–20th July 1944
	Monte Fili	21st–23rd July 1944
	Monte Domini	21st–24th July 1944
Cerbaia		27th–29th July 1944
	Monte Scalari	27th–30th July 1944
	San Michele	28th–30th July 1944
Paula Line		30th July–4th August 1944
Il Castello		3rd–8th August 1944
Incontro		5th–8th August 1944
	Montone	5th–7th July 1944
	Trestina	10th July 1944
	Monte della Gorgace	8th–14th July 1944
	Pezzano	13th–17th July 1944
	Monte Cedrone	13th–18th July 1944
	Citta di Castello	16th–22nd July 1944
	Pian di Maggio	19th–20th July 1944
	Campriano	20th–28th July 1944
Citerna		25th–26th July 1944
	Poggio del Grillo	4th–8th August 1944
	Fiesole	25th August 1944
	Cerrone	25th–31st August 1944
	Montorsoli	1st–5th September 1944
	Monte Calvana	1st–9th September 1944
	Ancona	2nd–18th July 1944
	Metauro	19th–22nd August 1944

69. **The Gothic Line Operations**
GOTHIC LINE

	Monteciccardo	25th August–22nd September 1944
	Monte Calvo	27th–28th August 1944
	Montecchio	29th–31st August 1944
	Point 204 or Pozzo Alto Ridge	30th–31st August 1944
	Monte Luro	31st August 1944
	Borgo Santa Maria	1st September 1944
	Tomba di Pesaro	1st September 1944
Monte Gridolfo		1st–2nd September 1944
		30th August–2nd September 1944
	Tavoleto	1st–4th September 1944
	Santa Teodora	2nd–3rd September 1944
	Montegaudio	28th August 1944
	Pratelle Pass	6th September 1944

Alpe di Vitigliano	12th–15th September 1944
Monte Guivigiana	13th–16th September 1944
Femmina Morta	17th–18th September 1944
Monte Porro del Bagno	15th–18th September 1944

Operations in the Mountains

70. Operations in 5th (British) Corps and 1st (Canadian) Corps Sectors

CORIANO

San Clemente	3rd–15th September 1944
	3rd–4th September 1944
Poggio San Giovanni	3rd–5th September 1944
Pian di Castello	5th–8th September 1944
Croce	5th–9th September 1944
Gemmano Ridge	5th–15th September 1944
Montebello–Scorticata Ridge	22nd–24th September 1944
Poggio Berni	22nd–24th September 1944
Santarcangelo	22nd–24th September 1944
Monte Reggiano	24th September–1st October 1944
Savignano	27th–30th September 1944
San Martino Sogliano	4th–5th October 1944
Monte Farneto	6th–7th October 1944
Montilgallo	7th–8th October 1944
Monte Gattona	7th–8th October 1944
San Paolo–Monte Spaccato	8th–9th October 1944
Carpineta	12th–15th October 1944
Monte Chicco	13th–14th October 1944
Monte Cavallo	21st–23rd October 1944
Capture of Forli	7th–9th November 1944
Cosina Canal Crossing	9th–11th November 1944
Casa Bettini	20th–23rd November 1944
Casa Fortis	24th November–1st December 1944
LAMONE CROSSING	2nd–13th December 1944
Defence of Lamone Bridgehead	4th–7th December 1944
Pideura	9th December 1944
Celle	14th–15th December 1944
Pergola Ridge	14th–16th December 1944
Faenza Pocket	19th–20th December 1944
Senio Pocket	4th–5th January 1945
Senio Floodbank	23rd February–3rd March 1945
Misano Ridge	3rd–5th September 1944

Battles, Actions and Engagements of the Second World War and the Korean Campaign

RIMINI LINE

	Monte Colombo	14th–21st September 1944
	Casa Fabri Ridge	14th September 1944
	Montescudo	14th September 1944
San Martino–San Lorenzo		14th–17th September 1944
		14th–18th September 1944
	Colle il Monte	15th–16th September 1944
	Frisoni	6th–18th September 1944
San Marino		17th–20th September 1944
Ceriano Ridge		17th–21st September 1944
San Fortunato		18th–20th September 1944
	Casale	23rd–25th September 1944
Rio Fontanaccia		24th–25th September 1944
	Sant'Angelo in Salute	11th–15th October 1944
	Bulgaria Village	13th–14th October 1944
Cesena		15th–20th October 1944
Pisciatello		16th–19th October 1944
	Savio Bridgehead	20th–23rd October 1944
Capture of Ravenna		3rd–4th December 1944
Naviglio Canal		12th–15th December 1944
	Fosso Vecchio	16th–18th December 1944
Fosso Munio		19th–21st December 1944
Conventello-Comacchio		2nd–6th January 1945
Granarolo		3rd–5th January 1945

71. Operations by 13th (British) Corps

Marradi		21st–24th September 1944
Monte Gamberaldi		25th–29th September 1944
		25th–29th September 1944
	Monte di Castelnuovo	2nd–12th October 1944
	Battaglia	2nd–23rd October 1944
	Monte Casalino	3rd–17th October 1944
Monte Ceco		13th–19th October 1944
Monte la Pieve		17th–23rd October 1944
Monte Pianoereno		19th–24th October 1944
Monte Spaduro		25th–26th October 1944
	Orsara	
	Monte San Bartolo	11th–14th November 1944
Monte Grande		1st November–12th December 1944
	Tossignano	12th–16th December 1944

72. Operations by 6th South African Division

	Catarelto Ridge	28th September–3rd October 1944
	Monte Vigese	30th September–6th October 1944

73. **Final Operations**

	Monte Stanco	7th–13th October 1944
	Monte Salvaro	19th–23rd October 1944
THE SENIO	Valli di Comacchio	1st–8th April 1945
		9th–12th April 1945
	Santerno Crossing	11th–12th April 1945
	Menate	10th–11th April 1945
	Filo	12th–14th April 1945
ARGENTA GAP	Fossa Cembalina	13th–21st April 1945
	San Nicolo Canal	20th–21st April 1945
		21st April 1945
BOLOGNA	Sillaro Crossing	14th–21st April 1945
	Monte Sole	14th–16th April 1945
	Medicina	15th–18th April 1945
		16th April 1945
	Gaiana Crossing	17th–19th April 1945
	Idice Bridgehead	20th–21st April 1945
	Traghetto	19th–20th April 1945
	Campostano Bridge	22nd April 1945

GREECE 1941

74. **The Defence and Withdrawal from Greece**

MOUNT OLYMPUS		10th–18th April 1941
Servia Pass		11th–13th April 1941
	Aliakmon Bridge	13th–18th April 1941
Olympus Pass		15th–16th April 1941
Tempe Gorge	Platamon Tunnel	15th–17th April 1941
Veve		18th April 1941
		10th–12th April 1941
	Soter	13th April 1941
	Proasteion	13th April 1941
	Elasson	18th April 1941
Brallos Pass		22nd–24th April 1941
Molos		22nd–25th April 1941
	Corinth Canal	26th April 1941
	Kriekouki	26th April 1941
	Marcopoulon	27th April 1941
	Kalami	28th–29th April 1941

Battles, Actions and Engagements of the Second World War and the Korean Campaign

GREECE 1944–45

75. **Operations in Greece in 1944-45**

Athens   2nd December 1944–15th January 1945

MIDDLE EAST 1941–44

76. **The Defence and Withdrawal from Crete**
CRETE

Maleme		20th May–1st June 1941
Galatas		20th–23rd May 1941
		20th–25th May 1941
	Kastelli	20th–26th May 1941
Canea		20th–27th May 1941
Heraklion		20th–29th May 1941
Retimo		20th–30th May 1941
42nd Street		27th May 1941
Withdrawal to Sphakia		28th May–1st June 1941
	Vitsilokoumos	30th May 1941

77. **The Occupation of Madagascar**

Madagascar   5th May–6th November 1942

78. **Operations in the Aegean Area**

Cos   3rd–16th October 1943
Leros   12th–16th November 1943

79. **Operations in the Adriatic Area**

Adriatic   18th March–21st November 1944

MALTA 1940–42

80. **The Defence of Malta**
MALTA

    11th June 1940–20th November 1942

MALAYA 1941–42

81. **Operations in Malaya and Singapore Island**
NORTH MALAYA

    8th–23rd December 1941

	Kota Bharu	8th December 1941
	Kroh	10th–13th December 1941
	Jitra	10th–13th December 1941
	Machang	12th–17th December 1941
	Gurun	14th–15th December 1941
	Grik Road	17th–23rd December 1941
CENTRAL MALAYA	Ipoh	26th December 1941–10th January 1942
	Kuantan	26th–29th December 1941
	Kampar	27th December 1941–3rd January 1942
	Slim River	30th December 1941–3rd January 1942
JOHORE		7th January 1942
	Gemas	14th–31st January 1942
	The Muar	14th–15th January 1942
	Batu Pahat	16th–23rd January 1942
	Niyor	21st–26th January 1942
	Jemaluang	24th–25th January 1942
		26th–27th January 1942
SINGAPORE ISLAND		8th–15th February 1942

SOUTH-EAST ASIA 1941–42

82.	**Defence of Kowloon Peninsula and Hong Kong**	
	Hong Kong	8th–25th December 1941
83.	**Operations of Sarawak Force in Defence of British Boreo**	
	West Borneo 1941–42	16th December 1941–9th March 1942

BURMA 1942–45

Burma 1942

84.	**Enemy Invasion of Burma**	
	Kawkareik	20th–22nd January 1942
	Moulmein	30th–31st January 1942
	Kuzeik	11th–12th February 1942
	Chieng Rai	17th February 1942

Sittang 1942	16th–23rd February 1942
Pegu 1942	6th–7th March 1942
Taukyan	7th–8th March 1942
Pyuntaza-Shwegyin	11th March 1942
Paungde	28th–30th March 1942
Yenangyaung 1942	11th–19th April 1942
Kyaukse 1942	28th–29th April 1942
Monywa 1942	30th April–2nd May 1942
Shwegyin	9th–11th May 1942

Indo-Burmese Border 1942–43

85. Operations in Arakan and NW Burma

Rathedaung	29th December 1942–3rd February 1943
Donbaik	8th January–18th March 1943
Htizwe	6th–16th March 1943
Point 201 (Arakan)	28th–29th March 1943
Stockades	26th–27th March 1943

Indo-Burmese Border 1943–44

Fort White	13th–15th November 1943
The Yu	18th–20th January 1944

86. Operations to Clear Arakan and Mayu Peninsula

NORTH ARAKAN

Buthidaung	1st January–12th June 1944
Razabil	16th January–3rd February and 5th March– 8th April 1944
	19th–30th January and 10th–17th March 1944
Point 551	4th February–31st March 1944
Kaladan	3rd April–22nd May 1944
	8th March–15th April 1944
Alethangyaw	15th March–20th April 1944
Mayu Tunnels	1st January–31st May 1944
Maungdaw	3rd May–12th June 1944
Mowdok	4th February–4th March 1944
NGAKYEDAUK PASS	
Defence of Sinzweya	5th–29th February 1944

87. Enemy Offensive Across the Chinwin

IMPHAL	12th March–22nd June 1944
Tuitum	16th–24th March 1944
Sakawng	18th–25th March 1944
Tamu Road	12th March–4th April 1944
Sangshak	16th–26th March 1944
Shenam Pass	1st April–22nd June 1944
Nungshigum	5th–13th April 1944
Litan	12th April–15th May 1944
Bishenpur	14th April–22nd June 1944
Kanglatongbi	21st April–22nd June 1944
KOHIMA	27th March–22nd June 1944
Defence of Kohima	4th–18th April 1944
Jessami	27th March–1st April 1944
Relief of Kohima	5th–20th April 1944
Jail Hill	7th–13th May 1944
Naga Village	4th May–4th June 1944
Aradura	14th May–6th June 1944
Mao Songsang	15th–19th June 1944

88. Enemy Retreat to the Chinwin

Ukhrul	24th June–20th July 1944
Tengnoupal	21st–28th July 1944
Tongzang	14th–22nd September 1944
Kennedy Peak	3rd October–7th November 1944
Mawlaik	28th October–10th November 1944

Reconquest of Burma 1944–45

Pinwe	11th–30th November 1944
Kalewa	13th November–16th December 1944
Gangaw	11th November 1944–10th January 1945
Shwebo	6th–9th January 1945
Monywa 1945	7th–22nd January 1945

89. Offensive Across the Irrawaddy

The Shweli	1st January–12th February 1945
Kyaukmyaung Bridgehead	9th January–12th February 1945
Sagaing	23rd January–12th February 1945

90.	**The Clearing of the Mandalay–Meiktila Plain**	
	MANDALAY	12th/13th February–21st March 1945
	Myitson	13th February–5th March 1945
	Ava	13th February–20th March 1945
	Myinmu Bridgehead	12th February–7th March 1945
	Fort Dufferin	9th–20th March 1945
	Maymyo	11th–12th March 1945
	Seikpyu	10th–16th February 1945
	Kyaukse 1945	8th–21st March 1945
	MEIKTILA	12th February–30th March 1945
	Nyaungu Bridgehead	12th–21st February 1945
	Capture of Meiktila	28th February–2nd March 1945
	Defence of Meiktila	3rd–29th March 1945
	Taungtha	24th February and 14th–28th March 1945
	Myingyan	1st–5th March and 18th–23rd March 1945
	Letse	23rd February–10th April 1945
	Singu	18th February–20th March 1945
91.	**Advance through the Irrawaddy Valley**	
	THE IRRAWADDY	29th March–30th May 1945
	Mt Popa	2nd–20th April 1945
	Yenangyaung 1945	18th–25th April 1945
	Magwe	11th–23rd April 1945
	Shandatgyi	6th–13th May 1945
	Kama	20th–30th May 1945
92.	**Advance and Capture of Rangoon**	
	RANGOON ROAD	1st April–6th May 1945
	Pyawbwe	1st–10th April 1945
	Shwemyo Bluff	12th–18th April 1945
	Pyinmana	19th–20th April 1945
	Toungoo	22nd April–6th May 1945
	Pegu 1945	27th April–2nd May 1945
93.	**Attempted Enemy Breakout in Pegu Yomas**	
	SITTANG 1945	10th May–15th August 1945
94.	**Operations in Arakan by 15th Corps**	
	Point 1433	8th–12th September 1944
	Tinma	14th–16th December 1944
	ARAKAN BEACHES	11th–31st December 1944
	Mayu Valley	15th–25th January 1945
	Myohaung	12th January–29th April 1945
	Myebon	12th–21st January 1945

	Ramree	21st January–15th February 1945
	Kangaw	23rd January–17th February 1945
	Ru-Ywa	17th–23rd February 1945
	Dalet	27th February–4th March 1945
	Tamandu	27th February–11th March 1945
	Letpan	13th–17th March 1945
	Taungup	3rd–29th April 1945
95.	**1st Wingate Expedition**	
	Chindits 1943	January–June 1943
96.	**2nd Wingate Expedition**	
	Chindits 1944	February–August 1944

SOUTH-WEST PACIFIC 1942–45

97.	**Operations in the Outer Islands**	
	Koepang	20th–23rd February 1942
	Dili	19th–20th February 1942
	Portuguese Timor	20th February 1942–10th February 1943
	Ambon	30th January–3rd February 1942
	Laha	30th January–3rd February 1942
	Rabaul	23rd January 1942
98.	**Operations in Papua**	
	KOKODA TRAIL	
	Kokoda-Deniki	22nd July–13th November 1942
	Isurava	25th July–14th August 1942
		15th–30th August 1942
	Eora Creek-Templeton's Crossing I	31st August–5th September 1942
	Efogi-Menari	6th–9th September 1942
	Ioribaiwa	10th–28th September 1942
	Eora Creek-Templeton's Crossing II	8th–30th October 1942
	Oivi-Gorari	4th–13th November 1942
	BUNA-GONA	
	Gona	16th November 1942–22nd January 1943
		19th November–9th December 1942
	Sanananda Road	19th November 1942–14th January 1943
	Buna Village	22nd November 1942–2nd January 1943
	Amboga River	10th–21st December 1942
	Cape Endaiadere-Sinemi Creek	18th December 1942–2nd January 1943

Battles, Actions and Engagements of the Second World War and the Korean Campaign

Battles, Actions and Engagements of the Second World War and the Korean Campaign

	MILNE BAY		
		Sanananda-Cape Killerton	15th–22nd January 1943
	MILNE BAY		26th August–7th September 1942
99.	**Operations in Wau-Salamaua**		
	Wau		8th March 1942–26th February 1943
		Mubo I	22nd April–29th May 1943
		Bobdubi I	22nd April–29th May 1943
		Lababia Ridge	20th–23rd June 1943
		Nassau Bay	30th June–19th August 1943
	Bobdubi II		30th June–4th July 1943
	Mubo II		7th–14th July 1943
		Mount Tambu	16th July–19th August 1943
		Tambu Bay	17th July–29th August 1943
	Komiatum		16th–21st August 1943
100.	**Operations in New Guinea**		
	LAE-NADZAB		4th–16th September 1943
		Busu River	8th–12th September 1943
		Lae Road	11th–15th September 1943
	FINSCHHAFEN		22nd September–8th December 1943
		Bumi River	22nd September 1943
	Scarlet Beach		23rd–24th September 1943
	Defence of Scarlet Beach		16th–28th October 1943
		Jivenaneng-Kumawa	3rd October–3rd November 1943
		Siki Cove	18th–22nd October 1943
	Sattelberg		17th–25th November 1943
		Pabu	19th–26th November 1943
		Palanko	25th November 1943
		Gusika	29th November 1943
		Wareo	1st–8th December 1943
		Nongora	2nd December 1943
		Bena Bena	27th May–31st October 1943
101.	**Operations in Markham-Ramu Valleys and the Finisterres**		
	LIBERATION OF AUSTRALIAN NEW GUINEA		18th September 1943–8th August 1945
		Kaiapit	18th–20th September 1943
		Dumpu	21st September–5th October 1943
		Finisterres I	6th October–26th December 1943
		Shaggy Ridge	27th December 1943
	Kankiryo Saddle		19th–31st January 1944
		Orgoruna-Mataloi	30th January 1944
		Finisterres II	1st–28th February 1944

102.	**The Coastal Advance**	
	Yokopi	13th March 1944
	Barum	18th March 1944
	Bogadjim	13th April 1944
	Madang	24th April 1944
	Kalueng River	3rd December 1943
	Wareo-Lakona	9th–17th December 1943
	Gusika-Fortification Point	3rd–20th December 1943
	Sio	21st December 1943–15th January 1944
	Sio-Sepik River	25th January–19th June 1944
	Kar Kar Island	2nd June 1944
103.	**Aitape-Wewak Operations**	
	Matapau	17th December 1944–2nd January 1945
	Perembil	3rd–4th January 1945
	Abau-Malin	5th–7th January 1945
	Nambut Ridge	19th January–19th February 1945
	Balif	18th January–6th February 1945
	Anumb River	4th–9th March 1945
	But Dagua	16th March–5th April 1945
	Maprik	8th March–24th April 1945
	Hawain River	9th–29th April 1945
	Wewak	8th–11th May 1945
	Wirui Mission	11th–15th May 1945
	Mount Shiburangu-Mount Tazaki	28th May–5th July 1945
	Yamil-Ulupu	3rd May–14th July 1945
	Kaboibus-Kiarivu	15th July–8th August 1945

Operations in Australian Mandated Territory

104.	**Bougainville-Northern Sector**	
	Tsimba Ridge	17th January–9th February 1945
	Bonis-Porton	7th–11th June 1945
105.	**Bougainville-Central Sector**	
	Artillery Hill	18th December 1944
	Pearl Ridge	30th December 1944
106.	**Bougainville-Southern Sector**	
	Adele River	19th–29th December 1944
	Mawaraka	4th–17th January 1945

Battles, Actions and Engagements of the Second World War and the Korean Campaign

	Mosigetta	2nd–15th February 1945
	Puriata River	24th January–26th February 1945
	Darara	16th–19th February 1945
	Slater's Knoll	28th March–6th April 1945
	Hongorai River	17th April–7th May 1945
	Egan's Ridge-Hongorai Ford	13th–22nd May 1945
	Commando Road	17th–28th May 1945
	Hari River	2nd–7th June 1945
	Ogorata River	13th–16th June 1945
	Mobiai River	16th–25th June 1945
	Mivo River	26th–30th June 1945
	Mivo Ford	2nd–9th July 1945

107. **New Britain**

	Waitavolo	5th–7th March 1945

108. **Operations in Borneo**
BORNEO

	Tarakan	1st May–15th August 1945
	Brunei	1st May–15th August 1945
	Labuan	10th June–8th August 1945
	Beaufort	10th–21st June 1945
	Miri	17th–30th June 1945
	Balikpapan	10th–23rd June 1945
		1st–9th July 1945
	Milford Highway	10th–22nd July 1945

SOUTH PACIFIC 1942–44

109. **Operations in the South Pacific**
SOLOMONS

	Guadalcanal	7th August 1942–20th March 1944
	New Georgia	7th August 1942–10th February 1944
	Vella Lavella	5th July–10th August 1943
	Treasury Islands	31st August–9th October 1943
	Bougainville	27th October–12th November 1943
		21st December 1943–25th June 1944
	Green Islands	30th January–23rd February 1944

KOREA 1950–53

110. Defence of Pusan Perimeter
PUSAN — 1st August–15th September 1950

111. The UN Counter Offensive
NAKTONG BRIDGEHEAD — 16th–25th September 1950
Songju — 21st–25th September 1950
Sariwon — 17th–18th October 1950
Yongju — 21st–22nd October 1950
Chongju — 25th–30th October 1950
Pakchon — 4th–5th November 1950

112. Withdrawal from the Yalu
CHONGCHON I — 11th–25th November 1950
CHONGCHON II — 25th–30th November 1950
Yongwon-Ni — 29th–30th November 1950
HUNGNAM — 27th November–24th December 1950

113. The Chinese Offensive
SEOUL
Uijongbu — 1st January 1951
Chungchung-Dong — 2nd–4th January 1951
— 2nd–4th January 1951

114. The Advance to 38th Parallel
Chuam-Ni — 14th–17th February 1951
Hill 327 — 16th–20th February 1951
Hill 419 — 21st February–3rd March 1951
Maehua-San — 7th–12th March 1951
Kapyong-Chon — 3rd–16th April 1951

115. The Battle of 38th Parallel
The Imjin — 22nd–25th April 1951
Kapyong — 22nd–25th April 1951
Chail-Li — 30th May 1951

116. The Final Phase
Kowang-San
Maryang-San — 3rd–12th October 1951
Hill 227 I — 4th–6th November 1951
Hill 227 II — 17th–19th November 1951
Hill 355 — 23rd–25th November 1951
— 23rd–24th October 1952

Battles, Actions and Engagements of the Second World War and the Korean Campaign

The Hook 1952	18th–19th November 1952
Pochum-Ni	2nd–3rd May 1953
The Hook 1953	28th–29th May 1953
The Samichon	24th–26th July 1953

SUCCESSION OF BRITISH BATTLE HONOURS

Listed below in bold type are the honour-bearing Regiments and Corps on establishment in 1991. Below each are shown the short titles of the Regiments and Corps which have previously been awarded, or some which later have taken into use, the battle honours currently borne by these Regiments and Corps. Regiments and Corps with extant honours retained by other Arms and Services or by sub-units and cadres are not included.

It should be noted, however, that this list is not a comprehensive inheritance table, but is intended to provide basic information to show the succession of battle honours.

The Life Guards
1st Life Guards and 2nd Life Guards formed The Life Guards

The Blues and Royals (Royal Horse Guards and 1st Dragoons)
Royal Horse Guards and 1st Dragoons later The Royal Dragoons formed The Blues and Royals

1st The Queen's Dragoon Guards
1st Dragoon Guards later 1st King's Dragoon Guards and 2nd Dragoon Guards later The Queen's Bays formed The Queen's Dragoon Guards

The Royal Scots Dragoon Guards (Carabiniers and Greys)
3rd Dragoon Guards and 6th Dragoon Guards later The Carabiniers formed 3rd Carabiniers, which with 2nd Dragoons later The Royal Scots Greys formed The Royal Scots Dragoon Guards

4th/7th Royal Dragoon Guards
4th Dragoon Guards later 4th Royal Irish Dragoon Guards and 7th Dragoon Guards formed 4th/7th Dragoon Guards later 4th/7th Royal Dragoon Guards

5th Royal Inniskilling Dragoon Guards
5th Dragoon Guards and 6th Dragoons later The Inniskillings formed 5th Inniskilling Dragoon Guards later 5th Royal Inniskilling Dragoon Guards

The Queen's Own Hussars
3rd Dragoons, 3rd Light Dragoons later 3rd The King's Own Hussars and 7th Light Dragoons later 7th Queen's Own Hussars formed The Queen's Own Hussars

The Queen's Own Royal Irish Hussars
4th Dragoons, 4th Light Dragoons later 4th Queen's Own Hussars and 8th Light Dragoons later 8th King's Own Royal Irish Hussars formed The Queen's Royal Irish Hussars

9th/12th Royal Lancers (Prince of Wales's)
9th Light Dragoons later 9th Queen's Royal Lancers and 12th Light Dragoons later 12th Royal Lancers formed 9th/12th Royal Lancers

The Royal Hussars (Prince of Wales's Own)
10th Light Dragoons later 10th Royal Hussars and 11th Light Dragoons later 11th Hussars formed The Royal Hussars

13th/18th Royal Hussars (Queen Mary's Own)
13th Light Dragoons later 13th Hussars and 18th Hussars (raised 1858) later 18th Royal Hussars formed 13th/18th Hussars later 13th/18th Royal Hussars

14th/20th King's Hussars
14th Light Dragoons later 14th King's Hussars and 20th Hussars (from HEIC 1861) formed 14th/20th Hussars later 14th/20th King's Hussars

15th/19th The King's Royal Hussars
15th Light Dragoons later 15th The King's Hussars and 19th Hussars (from HEIC 1861) later 19th Royal Hussars formed 15th/19th Hussars later 15th/19th The King's Royal Hussars

16th/5th The Queen's Royal Lancers
16th Light Dragoons later 16th The Queen's Lancers and 5th Lancers later 5th Royal Irish Lancers formed 16th/5th Lancers later 16th/5th The Queen's Royal Lancers

17th/21st Lancers
17th Lancers and 21st Lancers (from HEIC 1861) formed 17th/21st Lancers

---

Royal Tank Regiment
  Royal Tank Regiment

Honourable Artillery Company
  Honourable Artillery Company of London later Honourable Artillery Company

Grenadier Guards
  First Foot Guards later Grenadier Guards

Coldstream Guards
  Coldstream Foot Guards later Coldstream Guards

Scots Guards
  Third Foot Guards, Scots Fusilier Guards later Scots Guards

Irish Guards
  Irish Guards

Welsh Guards
  Welsh Guards

The Royal Scots (The Royal Regiment)
  1st Foot later The Royal Scots

The Queen's Regiment
  2nd Foot later The Queen's Royal Regiment with 6th London Regiment, 22nd London Regiment and 24th London Regiment and 31st Foot and 70th Foot later The East Surrey Regiment with 23rd London Regiment formed The Queen's Royal Surrey Regiment: 3rd Foot later The Buffs and 50th Foot and 97th Foot (raised 1824) later The Royal West Kent Regiment formed The Queen's Own Buffs: The Queen's Royal Surrey Regiment and The Queen's Own Buffs with 35th Foot and 107th Foot (from HEIC 1859) later The Royal Sussex Regiment and 57th Foot and 77th Foot later The Middlesex Regiment with 4th London Regiment formed The Queen's Regiment

The King's Own Royal Border Regiment
  4th Foot later The King's Own Royal Regiment and 34th Foot and 55th Foot later The Border Regiment formed The King's Own Royal Border Regiment

The Royal Regiment of Fusiliers
  5th Foot later The Royal Northumberland Fusiliers, 6th Foot, The Royal Warwickshire Regiment later The Royal Warwickshire Fusiliers, 7th Foot later The Royal Fusiliers with 1st London Regiment and 2nd London Regiment and 20th Foot later The Lancashire Fusiliers formed The Royal Regiment of Fusiliers

The King's Regiment
  8th Foot later The King's Regiment and 63rd Foot and 96th Foot (raised 1824) later The Manchester Regiment formed The King's Regiment

The Royal Anglian Regiment
  9th Foot later The Royal Norfolk Regiment and 12th Foot later The Suffolk Regiment formed 1st East Anglian Regiment: 10th Foot later The Royal Lincolnshire Regiment and 48th Foot and 58th Foot later The Northamptonshire Regiment formed 2nd East Anglian Regiment: 16th Foot, The Bedfordshire Regiment later The Bedfordshire and Hertfordshire Regiment and 44th Foot and 56th Foot later The Essex Regiment formed 3rd East Anglian Regiment: 1st East Anglian Regiment, 2nd East Anglian Regiment and 3rd East Anglian Regiment with 17th Foot later The Royal Leicestershire Regiment formed The Royal Anglian Regiment

The Devonshire and Dorset Regiment
  11th Foot later The Devonshire Regiment and 39th Foot and 54th Foot, The Dorsetshire Regiment later The Dorset Regiment formed The Devonshire and Dorset Regiment

The Light Infantry
  13th Foot later The Somerset Light Infantry and 32nd Foot and 46th Foot later The Duke of Cornwall's Light Infantry formed The Somerset and Cornwall Light Infantry, which with 51st Foot and 105th Foot (from HEIC 1859) later The King's Own Yorkshire Light Infantry, 53rd Foot and 85th Foot later The King's Shropshire Light Infantry, 68th Foot and 106th Foot (from HEIC 1859) later The Durham Light Infantry and The Herefordshire Regiment later The Herefordshire Light Infantry formed The Light Infantry

The Prince of Wales's Own Regiment of Yorkshire
  14th Foot later The West Yorkshire Regiment and 15th Foot later The East Yorkshire Regiment formed The Prince of Wales's Own Regiment of Yorkshire

The Green Howards (Alexandra, Princess of Wales's Own Yorkshire Regiment)
  19th Foot, Alexandra, Princess of Wales's Own Yorkshire Regiment later The Green Howards

The Royal Highland Fusiliers (Princess Margaret's Own Glasgow and Ayrshire Regiment)
21st Foot later The Royal Scots Fusiliers and 71st Foot and 74th Foot later The Highland Light Infantry formed The Royal Highland Fusiliers

The Cheshire Regiment
22nd Foot later The Cheshire Regiment

The Royal Welch Fusiliers
23rd Foot, The Royal Welsh Fusiliers later The Royal Welch Fusiliers

The Royal Regiment of Wales (24th/41st Foot)
24th Foot later The South Wales Borderers and 41st Foot and 69th Foot, The Welsh Regiment later The Welch Regiment with The Monmouthshire Regiment formed The Royal Regiment of Wales

The King's Own Scottish Borderers
25th Foot, The King's Own Borderers later The King's Own Scottish Borderers

The Royal Irish Rangers (27th (Inniskilling) 83rd and 87th)
27th Foot and 108th Foot (from HEIC 1859) later The Royal Inniskilling Fusiliers, 83rd Foot and 86th Foot, The Royal Irish Rifles later The Royal Ulster Rifles and 87th Foot and 89th Foot later The Royal Irish Fusiliers formed The Royal Irish Rangers

The Gloucestershire Regiment
28th Foot and 61st Foot later The Gloucestershire Regiment

The Worcestershire and Sherwood Foresters Regiment (29th/45th Foot)
29th Foot and 36th Foot later The Worcestershire Regiment and 45th Foot and 95th (raised 1823) later The Sherwood Foresters formed The Worcestershire and Sherwood Foresters Regiment

The Queen's Lancashire Regiment
30th Foot and 59th Foot later The East Lancashire Regiment and 40th Foot and 82nd Foot later The South Lancashire Regiment formed The Lancashire Regiment, which with 47th Foot and 81st Foot, The Loyal North Lancashire Regiment later The Loyal Regiment formed The Queen's Lancashire Regiment

The Duke of Wellington's Regiment (West Riding)
33rd Foot and 76th Foot later The Duke of Wellington's Regiment

The Royal Hampshire Regiment
37th Foot and 67th Foot later The Royal Hampshire Regiment

The Staffordshire Regiment (The Prince of Wales's)
38th Foot and 80th Foot later The South Staffordshire Regiment and 64th Foot and 98th Foot (raised 1824) later The North Staffordshire Regiment formed The Staffordshire Regiment

The Black Watch (Royal Highland Regiment)
42nd Foot and 73rd Foot later The Black Watch

The Duke of Edinburgh's Royal Regiment (Berkshire and Wiltshire)
49th Foot and 66th Foot later The Royal Berkshire Regiment and 62nd Foot and 99th Foot (raised 1824) later The Wiltshire Regiment formed The Duke of Edinburgh's Royal Regiment

Queen's Own Highlanders (Seaforth and Camerons)
72nd Foot and 78th Foot later Seaforth Highlanders and 79th Foot later The Queen's Own Cameron Highlanders formed The Queen's Own Highlanders

The Gordon Highlanders
75th Foot and 92nd Foot later The Gordon Highlanders

The Argyll and Sutherland Highlanders (Princess Louise's)
91st Foot and 93rd Foot later The Argyll and Sutherland Highlanders

The Parachute Regiment
The Parachute Regiment

2nd King Edward VII's Own Gurkha Rifles (The Sirmoor Rifles)
Sirmoor Rifle Battalion, 6th Bengal Local Battalion, 2nd Goorkha Regiment later 2nd King Edward VII's Own Gurkha Rifles (from IA 1948)

6th Queen Elizabeth's Own Gurkha Rifles
42nd Bengal Native Infantry, 42nd Goorkha Light Infantry, 6th Gurkha Rifles (from IA 1948) later 6th Queen Elizabeth's Own Gurkha Rifles

7th Duke of Edinburgh's Own Gurkha Rifles
7th Gurkha Rifles (from IA 1948) later 7th Duke of Edinburgh's Own Gurkha Rifles

10th Princess Mary's Own Gurkha Rifles
  10th Madras Native Infantry, 10th Gurkha Rifles (from IA 1948) later 10th Princess Mary's Own Gurkha Rifles

The Royal Green Jackets
  43rd Foot and 52nd Foot, The Oxfordshire Light Infantry, The Oxfordshire and Buckinghamshire Light Infantry later 1st Green Jackets, 60th Foot, The King's Royal Rifle Corps later 2nd Green Jackets and 95th (Rifle) Foot, The Rifle Brigade later 3rd Green Jackets formed The Royal Green Jackets

Special Air Service Regiment
  Special Air Service Regiment

Army Air Corps
  Army Air Corps

DISBANDED REGIMENTS AND CORPS

Cavalry

18th Regiment of (Light) Dragoons (Hussars)	disbanded 1821
19th Regiment of (Light) Dragoons (Lancers)	disbanded 1821
20th Regiment of (Light) Dragoons	disbanded 1818
22nd Regiment of (Light) Dragoons	disbanded 1820: no successor
23rd Regiment of (Light) Dragoons (Lancers)	disbanded 1819: no successor
24th Regiment of (Light) Dragoons	disbanded 1819: no successor
25th Regiment of (Light) Dragoons	disbanded 1819: no successor
26th Regiment of (Light) Dragoons	disbanded 1819 as 23rd Light Dragoons

Royal Armoured Corps

22nd Dragoons	disbanded 1948: no successor
23rd Hussars	disbanded 1948: no successor
24th Lancers	disbanded 1948: no successor
25th Dragoons	disbanded 1948: no successor
27th Lancers	disbanded 1948: no successor

Yeomanry

Lincolnshire Yeomanry	disbanded 1920: no successor
Welsh Horse	disbanded 1919: no successor

Special Reserve

South Irish Horse	disbanded 1922: no successor
King Edward's Horse (The King's Oversea Dominions Regiment)	disbanded 1924: no successor

Regiments of Foot

18th (The Royal Irish) Regiment of Foot	disbanded 1922 as The Royal Irish Regiment
26th (Cameronian) Regiment of Foot	disbanded 1968 as The Cameronians
65th (2nd Yorkshire, North Riding) Regiment of Foot	disbanded 1968 as The York and Lancaster Regiment
84th (York and Lancaster) Regiment of Foot	disbanded 1968 as The York and Lancaster Regiment
88th (Connaught Rangers) Regiment of Foot	disbanded 1922 as The Connaught Rangers
90th (Perthshire Volunteers, Light Infantry) Regiment of Foot	disbanded 1968 as The Cameronians
94th Regiment of Foot	disbanded 1818
94th Regiment of Foot (raised 1823)	disbanded 1922 as The Connaught Rangers
96th (Queen's Own) Regiment of Foot	disbanded 1818
97th Regiment of Foot	disbanded 1818 as 96th Foot
99th (Prince Regent's, County of Dublin) Regiment of Foot	disbanded 1818
100th Regiment of Foot	disbanded 1818 as 99th Foot
100th Regiment of Foot (raised 1824)	disbanded 1922 as The Prince of Wales's Leinster Regiment
101st (Royal Bengal Fusiliers) Regiment of Foot (from HEIC 1859)	disbanded 1922 as The Royal Munster Fusiliers
102nd (Royal Madras Fusiliers) Regiment of Foot (from HEIC 1859)	disbanded 1922 as The Royal Dublin Fusiliers
103rd Regiment of Foot	disbanded 1817: no successor
103rd (Royal Bombay Fusiliers) Regiment of Foot (from HEIC 1859)	disbanded 1922 as The Royal Dublin Fusiliers

104th Regiment of Foot	disbanded 1817: no successor
104th (Bengal Fusiliers) Regiment of Foot (from HEIC 1859)	disbanded 1922 as The Royal Munster Fusiliers
109th (Bombay Infantry) Regiment of Foot (from HEIC 1859)	disbanded 1922 as The Prince of Wales's Leinster Regiment

Infantry

The Royal Irish Regiment	disbanded 1922: no successor
The Cameronians (Scottish Rifles)	disbanded 1968: no successor
The York and Lancaster Regiment	disbanded 1968: no successor
The Connaught Rangers	disbanded 1922: no successor
The Prince of Wales's Leinster Regiment (Royal Canadians)	disbanded 1922: no successor
The Royal Munster Fusiliers	disbanded 1922: no successor
The Royal Dublin Fusiliers	disbanded 1922: no successor

Infantry – Territorial Force

18th Middlesex Volunteer Rifle Corps	disbanded 1912 as 10th London Regiment
10th (County of London) Battalion, The London Regiment (Paddington Rifles)	disbanded 1912: no successor

Infantry – Territorial Army

The Suffolk and Cambridgeshire Regiment (raised 1961)	disbanded 1971: no successor
The Bedfordshire and Hertfordshire Regiment (raised 1961)	disbanded 1971: no successor

Army Air Corps

The Glider Pilot Regiment	disbanded 1957: no successor

Channel Islands Militia

The Royal Jersey Light Infantry	disbanded 1947: no successor
Royal Guernsey Light Infantry	disbanded 1920: no successor

Militia

4th Battalion, The King's Own (Royal Lancaster Regiment)	disbanded 1908: no successor
4th Battalion, Prince Albert's (Somerset Light Infantry)	disbanded 1908: no successor
4th Battalion, Alexandra, Princess of Wales's Own (Yorkshire Regiment)	disbanded 1908: no successor
4th Battalion, The Cheshire Regiment	disbanded 1908: no successor
4th Battalion, The Gloucestershire Regiment	disbanded 1908: no successor
9th Battalion, The King's Royal Rifle Corps	disbanded 1908: no successor

Volunteers

3rd Volunteer Battalion, The King's (Liverpool Regiment)	disbanded 1908: no successor
4th Volunteer Battalion, The Queen's Own (Royal West Kent Regiment)	disbanded 1908: no successor

Miscellaneous Corps

Ancient Irish Fencibles	disbanded 1802: no successor
Glengarry Light Infantry Fencibles	disbanded 1816: no successor
The Queen's German Regiment	disbanded 1818 as 96th Foot
Royal Waggon Train	disbanded 1833: no successor
Royal Staff Corps	disbanded 1837: no successor
Royal Veterans Battalions	disbanded 1827: no successor
Chasseurs Britannique	disbanded 1814: no successor
King's German Legion	disbanded 1816: no successor
Duke of Brunswick Corps	disbanded 1816: no successor
Royal Corsican Rangers	disbanded 1816: no successor
Royal York Rangers	disbanded 1818: no successor
De Roll's Regiment	disbanded 1816: no successor
De Watteville's Regiment	disbanded 1816: no successor
Dillon's Regiment	disbanded 1815: no successor

Colonial Forces

Cape Mounted Rifles	disbanded 1870 : no successor
The West India Regiment	disbanded 1927
West African Regiment	disbanded 1928: no successor
The British West Indies Regiment	disbanded 1921: no successor

Appendix E

SUCCESSION OF INDIAN BATTLE HONOURS

Listed below in bold type are the honour bearing Regiments and Corps on establishment in 1991. Below each are shown the short titles of the Regiments and Corps which have previously been awarded, or some which later have taken into use, the battle honours currently borne by these Regiments and Corps. Battalion battle honours of The Mechanised Infantry Regiment are not included.

It should be noted, however, that this list is not a comprehensive inheritance table, but is intended to provide basic information to show the succession of battle honours.

The President's Body Guard
> Governor General's Body-Guard

16th Light Cavalry
> 2nd Madras Light Cavalry, 2nd Madras Lancers, 27th Light Cavalry later 16th Light Cavalry

7th Light Cavalry
> 3rd Madras Light Cavalry, 3rd Madras Lancers, 28th Light Cavalry later 7th Light Cavalry

8th Light Cavalry
> 1st Madras Light Cavalry, 26th Light Cavalry later 26th King George's Own Light Cavalry and 4th Cavalry Hyderabad Contingent, 4th Lancers Hyderabad Contingent later 30th Lancers formed 8th King George's Own Light Cavalry later 8th King George V's Own Light Cavalry

1 Horse (Skinner's Horse)
> 1st Bengal Local Horse, 1st Bengal Irregular Cavalry, 1st Bengal Lancers later 1st Duke of York's Own Lancers and 4th Bengal Local Horse, 4th Bengal Irregular Cavalry, 3rd Bengal Cavalry later 3rd Skinner's Horse formed 1st Duke of York's Own Skinner's Horse later Skinner's Horse

2nd Lancers
> 2nd Bengal Local Horse, 2nd Bengal Irregular Cavalry, 2nd Bengal Lancers later 2nd Lancers and 4th Bengal Lancers, 4th Lancers later 4th Cavalry formed 2nd Lancers later 2nd Royal Lancers

The Poona Horse
> 3rd Bombay Light Cavalry, 3rd Queen's Own Bombay Light Cavalry later 33rd Queen's Own Light Cavalry and Poona Horse, 4th Bombay Cavalry later 34th Prince Albert Victor's Own Poona Horse formed 17th Queen Victoria's Own Poona Horse later The Poona Horse

The Deccan Horse
> 1st Cavalry Hyderabad Contingent, 1st Lancers Hyderabad Contingent, 20th Deccan Horse later 20th Royal Deccan Horse and 2nd Cavalry Hyderabad Contingent, 2nd Lancers Hyderabad Contingent later 29th Lancers formed 9th Royal Deccan Horse later The Royal Deccan Horse

The Scinde Horse
> Scinde Irregular Horse, 1st Scinde Horse, 5th Bombay Cavalry later 35th Scinde Horse and Scinde Irregular Horse, 2nd Scinde Horse, 6th Bombay Cavalry later 36th Jacob's Horse formed 14th Prince of Wales's Own Scinde Horse later The Scinde Horse

3rd Cavalry
> 7th Bengal Irregular Cavalry, 5th Bengal Cavalry later 5th Cavalry and 8th Bengal Cavalry, 8th Lancers later 8th Cavalry formed 3rd Cavalry

18th Cavalry
> 8th Bengal Irregular Cavalry, 6th Bengal Cavalry later 6th King Edward's Own Cavalry and 17th Bengal Irregular Cavalry, 7th Bengal Lancers later 7th Hariana Lancers formed 18th King Edward's Own Cavalry later 18th King Edward VII's Own Cavalry

4 Horse
> 9th Bengal Cavalry, 9th Bengal Lancers later 9th Hodson's Horse and 10th Bengal Cavalry, 10th Bengal Lancers later 10th Duke of Cambridge's Own Lancers formed 4th Duke of Cambridge's Own Hodson's Horse later Hodson's Horse

The Central India Horse
> 1st Central India Horse, 38th Central India Horse later 38th King George's Own Central India Horse and 2nd Central India Horse, 39th Central India Horse later 39th King George's Own Central India Horse formed 21st King George's Own Central India Horse later The Central India Horse

20th Lancers
>14th Bengal Lancers later 14th Murray's Jat Lancers and 15th Bengal Lancers later 15th Lancers formed 20th Lancers

63 Cavalry
>63 Cavalry

61 Cavalry
>Patiala (Rajindra) Lancers, Alwar Mangel Lancers, Jodhpur Imperial Service Lancers, Jodhpur Sardar Risala and Mysore Lancers formed 61 Cavalry

45 Cavalry
>45 Cavalry

66 Armoured Regiment
>66 Armoured Regiment

69 Armoured Regiment
>69 Armoured Regiment

72 Armoured Regiment
>72 Armoured Regiment

75 Armoured Regiment
>75 Armoured Regiment

Armoured Corps Centre and School
>2nd Punjab Cavalry, 22nd Cavalry (FF) later 22nd Sam Browne's Cavalry (FF) and 5th Punjab Cavalry later 25th Cavalry (FF) formed Sam Browne's Cavalry (FF), which with 17th Bengal Cavalry, 17th Cavalry later 15th Lancers formed the Indian Armoured Corps Trade Training Centre

2 Mountain Battery
>No 2 Mountain Battery, 22nd Derajat Mountain Battery (FF) later 102nd Pack Battery (FF)

4 Mountain Battery
>No 4 Mountain Battery, 24th Hazara Mountain Battery (FF) later 104th Pack Battery (FF)

5 Mountain Battery
>No 1 Bombay Mountain Battery, No 5 Mountain Battery, 25th Mountain Battery later 105th Pack Battery

7 Mountain Battery
>No 7 Mountain Battery, 27th Mountain Battery later 107th Pack Battery

9 Mountain Battery
>109th Pack Battery

12 Mountain Battery
>119th Pack Battery

76 Jammu and Kashmir Mountain Battery
>No 1 Kashmir Mountain Battery later 1st Kashmir Mountain Battery

Madras Engineer Group and Centre
>Madras Pioneers, Queen's Own Madras Sappers and Miners, 2nd Queen Victoria's Own Sappers and Miners, Queen Victoria's Own Madras Sappers and Miners later Queen Victoria's Own Madras Sappers and Miners Group

Bengal Engineer Group and Centre
>Bengal Sappers and Miners, 1st Sappers and Miners, 1st King George's Own Sappers and Miners, King George's Own Bengal Sappers and Miners, King George V's Own Bengal Sappers and Miners later King George V's Own Bengal Sappers and Miners Group

Bombay Engineer Group and Centre
>Bombay Sappers and Miners, 3rd Sappers and Miners, 3rd Royal Bombay Sappers an Miners, Royal Bombay Sappers and Miners later Royal Bombay Sappers and Miners Group

The Brigade of the Guards
>9th Madras Native Infantry, 69th Punjabis, 2/2nd Punjab Regiment later 2nd Punjab Regiment, 1st Bombay Native Infantry, 101st Grenadiers, 1/4th Bombay Grenadiers later 1st Grenadiers, 2/2nd Bombay Native Infantry, 4th Bombay Native Infantry, 104th Wellesley's Rifles, 1/6th Rajptana Rifles later 1st Rajputana Rifles and 2/15th Bengal Native Infantry, 31st Bengal Native Infantry, 2nd Queen's Own Rajput Light Infantry, 1/7th Rajput Regiment later 1st Rajput Regiment formed The Brigade of the Guards

The Parachute Regiment

7th Madras Native Infantry, 67th Punjabis, 1/2nd Punjab Regiment later 1st Punjab Regiment, 10th Bombay Native Infantry, 110th Mahratta Light Infantry, 3/5th Mahratta Light Infantry later 3rd Mahratta Light Infantry and 1st Infantry Hyderabad Contingent, 94th Russell's Infantry, 1/19th Hyderabad Regiment later 1st Kumaon Regiment formed The Parachute Regiment

The Punjab Regiment

7th Madras Native Infantry later 67th Punjabis, 9th Madras Native Infantry later 69th Punjabis, 12th Madras Native Infantry later 72nd Punjabis, 2/6th Madras Native Infantry, 14th Madras Native Infantry later 74th Punjabis and 1/14th Madras Native Infantry, 27th Madras Native Infantry later 87th Punjabis formed 2nd Punjab Regiment, which with Jind Infantry, Nabha Infantry and 1st Patiala Infantry formed The Punjab Regiment

The Madras Regiment

2/3rd Madras Native Infantry, 13th Madras Native Infantry later 73rd Carnatic Infantry, 15th Madras Native Infantry later 75th Carnatic Infantry, 2/7th Madras Native Infantry, 19th Madras Native Infantry later 79th Carnaric Infantry, 1/12th Madras Native Infantry, 23rd Madras Native Infantry later 83rd Wallajahbad Light Infantry and 2/13th Madras Native Infantry, 26th Madras Native Infantry later 86th Carnatic Infantry formed 3rd Madras Regiment later The Madras Regiment

The Grenadiers

1st Bombay Native Infantry later 101st Grenadiers, 2/1st Bombay Native Infantry, 2nd Bombay Native Infantry later 102nd King Edward's Own Grenadiers, 8th Bombay Native Infantry later 108th Infantry, 1/5th Bombay Native Infantry, 9th Bombay Native Infantry later 109th Infantry, 2/6th Bombay Native Infantry, 12th Bombay Native Infantry later 112th Infantry and 1/7th Bombay Native Infantry, 13th Bombay Native Infantry later 113th Infantry formed 4th Bombay Grenadiers later Indian Grenadiers, which with Mewar Infantry and Bikaner Ganga Risala formed The Grenadiers

The Maratha Light Infantry

1/2nd Bombay Native Infantry, 3rd Bombay Native Infantry later 103rd Mahratta Light Infantry, 1/3rd Bombay Native Infantry, 5th Bombay Native Infantry later 105th Mahratta Light Infantry, 10th Bombay Native Infantry later 110th Mahratta Light Infantry and 16th Bombay Native Infantry later 116th Mahrattas formed 5th Mahratta Light Infantry later The Maratha Light Infantry

The Rajputana Rifles

2/2nd Bombay Native Infantry, 4th Bombay Native Infantry later 104th Wellesley's Rifles, 20th Bombay Native Infantry later 120th Rajputana Infantry, 22nd Bombay Native Infantry later 122nd Rajputana Infantry, 1/12th Bombay Native Infantry, 23rd Bombay Native Infantry later 123rd Outram's Rifles, 25th Bombay Native Infantry later 125th Napier's Rifles and 13th Bengal Native Infantry later 13th Rajputs formed 6th Rajputana Rifles, which with Sawai Man Guards and Bhavnagar Lancers formed The Rajputana Rifles

The Rajput Regiment

2/15th Bengal Native Infantry, 31st Bengal Native Infantry, 2nd Bengal Native Infantry later 2nd Queen's Own Rajput Light Infantry, 2/16th Bengal Native Infantry, 33rd Bengal Native Infantry, 4th Bengal Native Infantry later 4th Prince Albert Victor's Rajputs, 47th Bengal Native Infantry, 7th Bengal Native Infantry later 7th Duke of Connaught's Own Rajputs, 59th Bengal Native Infantry, 8th Bengal Native Infantry later 8th Rajputs, 70th Bengal Native Infantry, 11th Bengal Native Infantry later 11th Rajputs and 16th Bengal Native Infantry later 16th Rajputs formed 7th Rajput Regiment, which with Sadul Light Infantry formed The Rajput Regiment

The Jat Regiment

1/22nd Bengal Native Infantry, 43rd Bengal Native Infantry, 6th Bengal Native Infantry later 6th Royal Jat Light Infantry, 19th Bombay Native Infantry later 119th Infantry, 10th Bengal Native Infantry later 10th Jats and 18th Bengal Native Infantry later 18th Infantry formed 9th Jat Regiment later The Jat Regiment

The Sikh Regiment

14th Bengal Native Infantry later 14th King George's Own Ferozepore Sikhs, 15th Bengal Native Infantry later 15th Ludhiana Sikhs, 45th Bengal Native Infantry later 45th Rattray's Sikhs, 36th Bengal Infantry later 36th Sikhs and 35th Bengal Infantry later 35th Sikhs formed 11th Sikh Regiment later The Sikh Regiment

The Sikh Light Infantry

23rd Bengal Native Infantry later 23rd Sikh Pioneers

The Dogra Regiment

37th Bengal Infantry later 37th Dogras and 38th Bengal Infantry later 38th Dogras formed 17th Dogra Regiment later The Dogra Regiment

The Garhwal Rifles

39th Bengal Infantry, 39th Royal Garhwal Rifles formed 18th Royal Garhwal Rifles later The Royal Garhwal Rifles

The Kumaon Regiment
1st Infantry Hyderabad Contingent later 94th Russell's Infantry, 3rd Infantry Hyderabad Contingent later 96th Berar Infantry, 4th Infantry Hyderabad Contingent later 97th Deccan Infantry, 5th Infantry Hyderabad Contingent later 98th Infantry and 2nd Infantry Hyderabad Contingent later 95th Russell's Infantry formed 19th Hyderabad Regiment, which with 1st Kumaon Rifles, 4th Gwalior Battalion and Holkar's Transport Corps formed The Kumaon Regiment

The Assam Regiment
The Assam Regiment

The Bihar Regiment
The Bihar Regiment

The Mahar Regiment
The Mahar Regiment

The Jammu and Kashmir Rifles
4th Kashmir Rifles later The Jammu and Kashmir Infantry, which with 1st Kashmir Raghupartap Battalion, 2nd Kashmir Bodyguard Rifle Battalion and 3rd Kashmir Ragunath Rifle Battalion formed The Jammu and Kashmir Rifles

1st Gorkha Rifles
4th Bengal Local Battalion, 66th Bengal Native Infantry, 1st Goorkha Regiment later 1st King George V's Own Gurkha Rifles

3rd Gorkha Rifles
3rd Goorkha Regiment later 3rd Queen Alexandra's Own Gurkha Rifles

4th Gorkha Rifles
4th Goorkha Regiment later 4th Prince of Wales's Gurkha Rifles

5th Gorkha Rifles
5th Goorkha Regiment later 5th Royal Gurkha Rifles (FF)

8th Gorkha Rifles
44th Bengal Infantry, 44th Gurkha Rifles later 8th Gurkha Rifles

9th Gorkha Rifles
32nd Bengal Native Infantry, 63rd Bengal Native Infantry, 9th Bengal Native Infantry later 9th Gurkha Rifles

11th Gorkha Rifles
11th Gorkha Rifles

The Jammu and Kashmir Light Infantry
Jammu and Kashmir Militia later Jammu and Kashmir Light Infantry

Ladakh Scouts
Ladakh Scouts

DISBANDED REGIMENTS AND CORPS

Bengal Cavalry

1st Regiment Light Cavalry	disbanded 1857: no successor
2nd Regiment Light Cavalry	disbanded 1841
2nd Regiment Light Cavalry (raised 1850)	disbanded 1857: no successor
3rd Regiment Light Cavalry	disbanded 1857: no successor
4th Regiment Light Cavalry (Lancers)	disbanded 1857: no successor
5th Regiment Light Cavalry	disbanded 1857: no successor
6th Regiment Light Cavalry	disbanded 1857: no successor
7th Regiment Light Cavalry	disbanded 1857: no successor
8th Regiment Light Cavalry	disbanded 1857: no successor
9th Regiment Light Cavalry	disbanded 1857: no successor
10th Regiment Light Cavalry	disbanded 1857: no successor
11th Regiment Light Cavalry (raised 1842)	disbanded 1857 as 2nd Light Cavalry

Bengal Local Horse

8th Local Horse (Skinner's Horse)	disbanded 1829: no successor

Bengal Irregular Cavalry
3rd Irregualr Cavalry (1st Rohilla Cavalry)	disbanded 1857: no successor
9th Irregular Cavalry	disbanded 1857: no successor
11th Irregular Cavalry	disbanded 1857: no successor
12th Irregular Cavalry	disbanded 1857: no successor
13th Irregular Cavalry	disbanded 1857: no successor
14th Irregular Cavalry	disbanded 1857: no successor
15th Irregular Cavalry	disbanded 1857: no successor
16th Irregular Cavalry	disbanded 1857: no successor

Hyderabad Contingent
3rd Lancers	disbanded 1903: no successor
1st Field Battery	disbanded 1950: no successor
2nd Field Battery	disbanded 1950: no successor
4th Field Battery	disbanded 1950: no successor

Madras Cavalry
4th (Prince of Wales's) Regiment Light Cavalry	disbanded 1891: no successor
5th Regiment Light Cavalry	disbanded 1860: no successor
6th Regiment Light Cavalry	disbanded 1860: no successor
7th Regiment Light Cavalry	disbanded 1860: no successor
8th Regiment Light Cavalry	disbanded 1857: no successor

Bombay Irregular Cavalry
3rd Regiment, Scinde Horse	disbanded 1882: no successor

Indian Cavalry
Governor's Body-Guard, Madras	disbanded 1947: no successor
Aden Troop	disbanded 1929: no successor

Sappers and Miners
Burma Sappers and Miners	disbanded 1929: no successor

Bengal Native Infantry
1st Regiment Native Infantry	disbanded 1857: no successor
2nd (Grenadiers) Regiment Native Infantry	disbanded 1857: no successor
3rd Regiment Native Infantry	disbanded 1857: no successor
3rd Regiment of Bengal Native Infantry (raised 1861)	disbanded 1922 as 3rd Brahmans
4th Regiment Native Infantry	disbanded 1857: no successor
5th Regiment Native Infantry	disbanded 1857: no successor
5th Regiment of Bengal Native (Light) Infantry (raised 1861)	disbanded 1922 as 5th Light Infantry
6th Regiment Native Infantry	disbanded 1857: no successor
7th Regiment Native Infantry	disbanded 1857: no successor
8th Regiment Native Infantry	disbanded 1857: no successor
9th Regiment Native Infantry	disbanded 1857: no successor
10th Regiment Native Infantry	disbanded 1857: no successor
11th Regiment Native Infantry	disbanded 1857: no successor
12th Regiment Native Infantry	disbanded 1857: no successor
12th Regiment of Bengal Native Infantry (raised 1861)	disbanded 1933 as 2nd Bombay Pioneers
13th Regiment Native Infantry	disbanded 1857: no successor
14th Regiment Native Infantry	disbanded 1857: no successor
15th Regiment Native Infantry	disbanded 1857: no successor
16th (Grenadiers) Regiment Native Infantry	disbanded 1857: no successor
17th Regiment of Bengal Native Infantry (raised 1861)	disbanded 1922 as 17th The Loyal Regiment
18th Regiment Native Infantry	disbanded 1857: no successor
20th Regiment Native Infantry	disbanded 1857: no successor
22nd Regiment Native Infantry	disbanded 1857: no successor
23rd Regiment Native Infantry	disbanded 1857: no successor
23rd Regiment of Bengal Native Infantry (raised 1861)	disbanded 1933 as 1st and 10th Sikh Pioneers
24th Regiment Native Infantry	disbanded 1857: no successor
25th Regiment Native Infantry (Volunteers)	disbanded 1857: no successor
26th Regiment Native (Light) Infantry	disbanded 1857: no successor
28th Regiment Native Infantry	disbanded 1857: no successor
29th Regiment Native Infantry	disbanded 1857: no successor
30th Regiment Native Infantry	disbanded 1857: no successor
32nd Regiment Native Infantry	disbanded 1922 as 3rd Brahmans
32nd Regiment of Bengal Native Infantry (raised 1861)	disbanded 1933 as 2nd Sikh Pioneers

35th Regiment Native (Light) Infantry	disbanded 1857: no successor
36th Regiment Native Infantry (Bengal Volunteers)	disbanded 1857: no successor
37th Regiment Native Infantry (Bengal Volunteers)	disbanded 1857: no successor
38th Regiment Native Infantry (Bengal Volunteers)	disbanded 1857: no successor
39th Regiment Native Infantry (Bengal Volunteers)	disbanded 1857: no successor
40th Regiment Native Infantry (Volunteers)	disbanded 1857: no successor
41st Regiment Native Infantry	disbanded 1857: no successor
41st Regiment of Bengal Native Infantry (raised 1861)	disbanded 1882: no successor
42nd Regiment Native (Light) Infantry	disbanded 1922 as 5th Light Infantry
44th Regiment Native Infantry	disbanded 1857: no successor
45th Regiment Native Infantry	disbanded 1857: no successor
46th Regiment Native Infantry	disbanded 1857: no successor
48th Regiment Native Infantry	disbanded 1857: no successor
49th Regiment Native Infantry	disbanded 1857: no successor
50th Regiment Native Infantry	disbanded 1857: no successor
51st Regiment Native Infantry	disbanded 1857: no successor
52nd Regiment Native Infantry	disbanded 1857: no successor
53rd Regiment Native Infantry	disbanded 1857: no successor
54th Regiment Native Infantry	disbanded 1857: no successor
56th Regiment Native Infantry	disbanded 1857: no successor
57th Regiment Native Infantry	disbanded 1857: no successor
58th Regiment Native Infantry	disbanded 1857: no successor
60th Regiment Native Infantry	disbanded 1857: no successor
62nd Regiment Native Infantry	disbanded 1857: no successor
64th Regiment Native Infantry	disbanded 1857: no successor
67th Regiment Native Infantry (Volunteers)	disbanded 1857: no successor
68th Regiment Native Infantry (Volunteers)	disbanded 1857: no successor
69th Regiment Native Infantry	disbanded 1857: no successor
71st Regiment Native Infantry	disbanded 1857: no successor
72nd Regiment Native Infantry	disbanded 1857: no successor
73rd Regiment Native Infantry	disbanded 1857: no successor

Bengal Local Infantry

Ramgarh Light Infantry Battalion	disbanded 1857: no successor

Irregular Contingents

Gwalior Contingent	disbanded 1857: no successor
Deoli Irregular Force	disbanded 1922 as 42nd Deoli Regiment
Mhwairwara Battalion	disbanded 1922 as 44th Merwara Infantry

Madras Native Infantry

1/1st Madras Native Infantry	disbanded 1933 as 1st Madras Pioneers
2/2nd Madras Native Infantry	disbanded 1922 as 80th Carnatic Infantry
3rd (Palamcottah) Native (Light) Infantry	disbanded 1922 as 63rd Palamcottah Light Infantry
1/4th Madras Native Infantry	disbanded 1933 as 2nd Madras Pioneers
5th Regiment Native Infantry	disbanded 1904 as 65th Carnatic Light Infantry
1/8th Madras Native Infantry	disbanded 1902 as 8th Gurkha (Rifle) Regiment
2/9th Madras Native Infantry	disbanded 1904 as 71st Coorg Rifles
10th Carnatic Battalion	disbanded 1891 as 10th Madras Infantry
1/10th Madras Native Infantry	disbanded 1891 as 10th Madras Infantry
1/11th Madras Native Infantry	disbanded 1933 as 10th Madras Pioneers
11th Regiment Native Infantry	disbanded 1904 as 71st Coorg Rifles
1/14th Madras Native Infantry	disbanded 1922 as 88th Carnatic Infantry
17th Regiment Native Infantry	disbanded 1907 as 77th Moplah Rifles
18th Regiment Native Infantry	disbanded 1864: no successor
1/20th Madras Native Infantry	disbanded 1882 as 39th Native Infantry
20th Regiment Native Infantry	disbanded 1922 as 80th Carnatic Infantry
21st Carnatic Battalion	disbanded 1922 as 80th Carnatic Infantry
21st Regiment Native Infantry	disbanded 1933 as 10th Madras Pioneers
25th Regiment of Madras Native Infantry	disbanded 1907 as 78th Moplah Rifles
28th Regiment of Madras Native Infantry	disbanded 1922 as 88th Carnatic Infantry
34th (Chicacole) Regiment Native (Light) Infantry	disbanded 1864: no successor
35th Regiment of Madras Native Infantry	disbanded 1882: no successor
36th (Nundy) Regiment of Madras Native Infantry	disbanded 1882: no successor
37th (Grenadiers) Regiment of Madras Native Infantry	disbanded 1882: no successor
38th Regiment of Madras Native Infantry	disbanded 1882: no successor

39th Regiment of Madras Native Infantry	disbanded 1882: no successor
39th Regiment of Madras Native Infantry	disbanded 1882: no successor
41st Regiment of Madras Native Infantry	disbanded 1882: no successor
43rd Regiment Native Infantry	disbanded 1864: no successor
49th Regiment Native Infantry	disbanded 1864: no successor
Madras Rifle Corps	disbanded 1830: no successor

Bombay Native Infantry

2/3rd Bombay Native Infantry	disbanded 1882 as 6th Bombay Native Infantry
1/4th Bombay Native Infantry	disbanded 1933 as 1st Bombay Pioneers
6th Regiment of Bombay Native Infantry	disbanded 1882: no successor
11th Regiment of Bombay Native Infantry	disbanded 1882: no successor
15th Regiment of Bombay Native Infantry	disbanded 1882: no successor
18th Regiment of Bombay Native Infantry	disbanded 1882: no successor
21st Regiment Native Infantry	disbanded 1857
21st Regiment of Bombay Native Infantry (raised 1861)	disbanded 1933 as 10th Bombay Pioneers
Marine Battalion	disbanded 1933 as 10th Bombay Pioneers

Bengal Infantry

3rd Regiment of Bengal Infantry	disbanded 1922 as 3rd Brahmans
5th Regiment of Bengal (Light) Infantry	disbanded 1922 as 5th Light Infantry
12th (Kelat-i-Ghilzie) Regiment of Bengal Infantry	disbanded 1933 as 2nd Bombay Pioneers
17th (The Loyal) Regiment of Bengal Infantry	disbanded 1922 as 17th The Loyal Regiment
23rd (Punjab) Regiment of Bengal Infantry	disbanded 1933 as 1st and 10th Sikh Pioneers
32nd (Punjab) Regiment of Bengal Infantry (raised 1857)	disbanded 1933 as 2nd Sikh Pioneers
34th (Punjab) Regiment of Bengal Infantry (raised 1887)	disbanded 1933 as 3rd Sikh Pioneers
39th (Aligarh) Regiment of Bengal Infantry	disbanded 1890: no successor

Madras Infantry

1st Regiment of Madras Infantry	disbanded 1933 as 1st Madras Pioneers
3rd (Palamcottah) Regiment of Madras (Light) Infantry	disbanded as 63rd Palamcottah Light Infantry
4th Regiment of Madras Infantry	disbanded 1933 as 2nd Madras Pioneers
5th Regiment of Madras Infantry	disbanded 1904 as 65th Carnatic Light Infantry
8th Regiment of Madras Infantry	disbanded 1902 as 8th Gurkha (Rifle) Regiment
8th Gurkha (Rifle) Regiment	disbanded 1902: no successor
10th Regiment of Madras Infantry	disbanded 1891
11th Regiment of Madras Infantry	disbanded 1904 as 71st Coorg Rifles
17th Regiment of Madras Infantry	disbanded 1907 as 77th Moplah Rifles
20th Regiment of Madras Infantry	disbanded 1922 as 80th Carnatic Infantry
21st Regiment of Madras Infantry	disbanded 1933 as 10th Madras Pioneers
25th Regiment of Madras Infantry	disbanded 1907 as 78th Moplah Rifles
28th Regiment of Madras Infantry	disbanded 1922 as 88th Carnatic Infantry

Bombay Infantry

7th Regiment of Bombay Infantry	disbanded 1933 as 1st Bombay Pioneers
21st Regiment of Bombay Infantry	disbanded 1933 as 10th Bombay Pioneers
28th Regiment of Bombay Infantry (raised 1846)	disbanded 1933 as 3rd Bombay Pioneers

Indian Infantry

3rd Brahmans	disbanded 1922: no successor
5th Light Infantry	disbanded 1922: no successor
17th The Loyal Regiment	disbanded 1922: no successor
42nd Deoli Regiment	disbanded 1922: no successor
44th Merwara Infantry	disbanded 1922: no successor
63rd Palamcottah Light Infantry	disbanded 1922: no successor
65th Carnatic Light Infantry	disbanded 1904: no successor
71st Coorg Rifles	disbanded 1904: no successor
77th Moplah Rifles	disbanded 1907: no successor
78th Moplah Rifles	disbanded 1907: no successor
80th Carnatic Infantry	disbanded 1922: no successor
88th Carnatic Infantry	disbanded 1922: no successor

Pioneers

12th Pioneers (Kelat-i-Ghilzie Regiment)	disbanded 1933 as 2nd Bombay Pioneers
23rd Sikh Pioneers	disbanded 1933 as 1st and 10th Sikh Pioneers
32nd Sikh Pioneers	disbanded 1933 as 2nd Sikh Pioneers
34th Sikh Pioneers	disbanded 1933 as 3rd Sikh Pioneers

61st King George's Own Pioneers	disbanded 1933 as 1st Madras Pioneers
64th Pioneers	disbanded 1933 as 2nd Madras Pioneers
81st Pioneers	disbanded 1933 as 10th Madras Pioneers
106th Hazara Pioneers (raised 1904)	disbanded 1933 as Hazara Pioneers
107th Pioneers	disbanded 1933 as 1st Bombay Pioneers
121st Pioneers	disbanded 1933 as 10th Bombay Pioneers
128th Pioneers	disbanded 1933 as 3rd Bombay Pioneers
Corps of Madras Pioneers	disbanded 1933: no successor
Corps of Bombay Pioneers	disbanded 1933: no successor
Corps of Sikh Pioneers	disbanded 1933: no successor
Corps of Hazara Pioneers	disbanded 1933: no successor

Imperial Service Troops

Hyderabad Imperial Service Lancers	disbanded 1950: no successor
Holkar's Mounted Escort	disbanded ? : no successor
Kashmir Sappers and Miners	disbanded ? : no successor
Faridkot Sappers	disbanded ? : no successor
Malerkotla Sappers	disbanded ? : no successor
Sirmoor Sappers	disbanded ? : no successor
Garhwal Rajya Sappers	disbanded ? : no successor
Karpurthala Jagjit Infantry	disbanded ? : no successor
3rd Gwalior Infantry	disbanded ? : no successor
Alwar Jey Paltan	disbanded ? : no successor
Bharatpur Infantry	disbanded ? : no successor
Rampur Pioneers	disbanded ? : no successor
Bharatpur Transport Corps	disbanded ? : no successor
Gwalior Transport Corps	disbanded ? : no successor
Jaipur Transport Corps	disbanded ? : no successor
Mysore Transport Corps	disbanded ? : no successor

SUCCESSION OF PAKISTANI BATTLE HONOURS

Listed below in bold type are the honour bearing Regiments and Corps estimated to be on establishment in 1991. Below each are shown the short titles of the Regiments and Corps which have previously been awarded, or some which later have taken into use, the battle honours currently borne by these Regiments and Corps.

It should be noted, however, that this list is not a comprehensive inheritance table, but is intended to provide basic information to show the succession of battle honours.

4 Cavalry
> 4 Cavalry

5th Horse
> 11th Bengal Lancers later 11th King Edward's Own Lancers and 12th Bengal Cavalry later 12th Cavalry formed 5th King Edward's Own Probyn's Horse later Probyn's Horse

6th Lancers
> 13th Bengal Lancers later 13th Duke of Connaught's Own Lancers and 16th Bengal Lancers later 16th Cavalry formed 6th Duke of Connaught's Own Lancers

Guides Cavalry (Frontier Force)
> Queen's Own Guides, 10th Queen Victoria's Own Guides Cavalry (FF) later The Guides Cavalry (FF)

11th Cavalry (Frontier Force)
> 1st Punjab Cavalry later 21st Prince Albert Victor's Own Cavalry (FF) and 3rd Punjab Cavalry later 23rd Cavalry (FF) formed 11th Prince Albert Victor's Own Cavalry (FF) later Prince Albert Victor's Own Cavalry (FF)

12th Cavalry (Frontier Force)
> 2nd Punjab Cavalry later 22nd Sam Browne's Cavalry (FF) and 5th Punjab Cavalry later 25th Cavalry (FF) formed Sam Browne's Cavalry (FF)

13th Lancers
> 1st Bombay Light Cavalry, 1st Bombay Lancers later 31st Duke of Connaught's Own Lancers and 2nd Bombay Light Cavalry, 2nd Bombay Lancers later 32nd Lancers formed 13th Duke of Connaught's Own Bombay Lancers later 13th Duke of Connaught's Own Lancers

15th Lancers
> 17th Bengal Cavalry, 17th Lancers later 15th Lancers

19th Lancers
> 18th Bengal Cavalry, 18th Bengal Lancers later 18th Tiwana Lancers and 19th Bengal Lancers later 19th Lancers formed 19th King George's Own Lancers later 19th King George V's Own Lancers

20 Lancers
> 20 Lancers

22 Cavalry
> 22 Cavalry

23 Cavalry (Frontier Force)
> 23 Cavalry (FF)

24 Cavalry
> 24 Cavalry

25 Cavalry
> 25 Cavalry

26 Cavalry
> 26 Cavalry

28 Cavalry
> 28 Cavalry

30 Cavalry
> 30 Cavalry

31 Cavalry
> 31 Cavalry

32 Cavalry
> 32 Cavalry

33 Cavalry
> 33 Cavalry

4 Field Regiment
> 4 Field Regiment

5 Light Anti-Aircraft Regiment
> 5 Light Anti-Aircraft Regiment

9 Medium Regiment
> 9 Medium Regiment

11 Field Regiment
> 11 Field Regiment

12 Medium Regiment
> 12 Medium Regiment

17 Corps Locating Regiment
> 17 Corps Locating Regiment

18 Field Regiment
> 18 Field Regiment

28 Medium Regiment
> 28 Medium Regiment

29 Light Anti-Aircraft Regiment
> 29 Light Anti-Aircraft Regiment

33 Heavy Regiment
> 33 Heavy Regiment

39 Field Regiment
> 39 Field Regiment

45 Field Regiment
> 45 Field Regiment

46 Field Regiment
> 46 Field Regiment

47 Field Regiment
> 47 Field Regiment

50 Field Regiment
> 50 Field Regiment

52 Heavy Anti-Aircraft Regiment
> 52 Heavy Anti-Aircraft Regiment

58 Light Anti-Aircraft Regiment
> 58 Light Anti-Aircraft Regiment

61 (Self Propelled) Field Regiment
> 61 (Self Propelled) Field Regiment

63 Field Regiment
> 63 Field Regiment

64 Medium Regiment
> 64 Medium Regiment

68 Mountain Regiment
> 68 Mountain Regiment

71 Mountain Regiment
> 71 Mountain Regiment

72 Medium Regiment
> 72 Medium Regiment

75 Light Anti-Aircraft Regiment
> 75 Light Anti-Aircraft Regiment

76 Field Regiment
76 Field Regiment

78 Field Regiment
78 Field Regiment

83 Medium Regiment
83 Medium Regiment

1 Mountain Battery
No 1 Mountain Battery, 21st Kohat Mountain Battery (FF) later 101st Royal Pack Battery (FF)

3 Mountain Battery
No 3 Mountain Battery, 23rd Peshawar Mountain Battery (FF) later 103rd Pack Battery (FF)

6 Mountain Battery
No 2 Bombay Mountain Battery, No 6 Mountain Battery, 26th Jacob's Mountain Battery later 106th Pack Battery

8 Mountain Battery
No 2 Bengal Mountain Battery, No 8 Mountain Battery, 28th Mountain Battery later 108th Pack Battery

52 Light Anti-Aircraft Battery
52 Light Anti-Aircraft Battery

79 Division Locating Battery
79 Division Locating Battery

81 Field Battery Azad Kashmir
81 Field Battery Azad Kashmir

82 Mountain Battery
82 Mountain Battery

170 Independent Mortar Battery
170 Independent Mortar Battery

285 Division Locating Battery
285 Division Locating Battery

173 Engineer Battalion
173 Engineer Battalion

474 Engineer Battalion
474 Engineer Battalion

41 Signal Battalion
41 Signal Battalion

The Punjab Regiment
2nd Madras Native Infantry later 62nd Punjabis, 6th Madras Native Infantry later 66th Punjabis, 2/5th Madras Native Infantry, 16th Madras Native Infantry later 76th Punjabis, 2/9th Bengal Native Infantry, 21st Bengal Native Infantry, 1st Bengal Native Infantry later 1st Brahmans, 2/11th Madras Native Infantry, 22nd Madras Native Infantry later 82nd Punjabis and 2/12th Madras Native Infantry, 24th Madras Native Infantry later 84th Punjabis formed 1st Punjab Regiment: 19th Bengal Native Infantry later 19th Punjabis, 20th Bengal Native Infantry later 20th Duke of Cambridge's Own Punjabis, 22nd Bengal Native Infantry later 22nd Punjabis, 24th Bengal Native Infantry later 24th Punjabis and 21st Bengal Native Infantry later 21st Punjabis formed 14th Punjab Regiment: 25th Bengal Native Infantry later 25th Punjabis, 26th Bengal Native Infantry later 26th Punjabis, 27th Bengal Native Infantry later 27th Punjabis, 28th Bengal Native Infantry later 28th Punjabis and 29th Bengal Native Infantry later 29th Punjabis formed 15th Punjab Regiment: 30th Bengal Native Infantry later 30th Punjabis, 31st Bengal Native Infantry later 31st Punjabis, 33rd Bengal Infantry later 33rd Punjabis and Bhopal Battalion later 9th Bhopal Infantry formed 16th Punjab Regiment: 1st Punjab Regiment, 14th Punjab Regiment, 15th Punjab Regiment and 16th Punjab Regiment formed The Punjab Regiment

The Baluch Regiment
30th Madras Native Infantry, 30th Burma Infantry later 90th Punjabis, 16th Madras Native Infantry, 31st Madras Native Infantry, 31st Burma Light Infantry later 91st Punjabis, 32nd Madras Native Infantry, 32nd Burma Infantry later 92nd Punjabis and 33rd Madras Native Infantry later 93rd Burma Infantry formed 8th Punjab Regiment: 24th Bombay Native Infantry later 124th Duchess of Connaught's Own Baluchistan Infantry, 26th Bombay Native Infantry later 126th Baluchistan Infantry, 27th Bombay Native Infantry later 127th Queen Mary's Own Baluch Light Infantry, 2nd Baluch Battalion, 29th Bombay Native Infantry later 129th Duke of Connaught's Own Baluchis and 30th Bombay Infantry later 130th King George's Own Baluchis formed 10th Baluch Regiment later The Baluch Regiment: 8th Punjab Regiment and The Baluch Regiment, with Bahawalpur Regiment formed The Baluch Regiment

The Frontier Force Regiment

Ist Sikh Local Infantry, Ist Sikh Infantry later 51st Prince of Wales's Own Sikhs (FF), 2nd Sikh Local Infantry, 2nd Sikh Infantry later 52nd Sikhs (FF), 3rd Sikh Infantry later 53rd Sikhs (FF), 4th Sikh Local Infantry, 4th Sikh Infantry later 54th Sikhs (FF) and Queen's Own Guides later Queen Victoria's Own Guides Infantry (FF) formed 12th Frontier Force Regiment later The Frontier Force Regiment: Ist Punjab Infantry later 55th Coke's Rifles (FF), 2nd Punjab Infantry later 56th Punjabi Rifles (FF), 4th Punjab Infantry later 57th Wilde's Rifles (FF), 5th Punjab Infantry later 58th Vaughan's Rifles (FF) formed 13th Frontier Force Rifles later The Frontier Force Rifles: The Frontier Force Regiment and The Frontier Force Rifles, with Pathan Regiment formed The Frontier Force Regiment

The Azad Kashmir Regiment

Azad Kashmir Regiment

60 Electrical and Mechanical Engineering Battalion

60 Electrical and Mechanical Engineering Battalion

Appendix G

SUCCESSION OF AUSTRALIAN BATTLE HONOURS

Listed below in bold type are the honour bearing Regiments and Corps on establishment in 1988. Below each are shown the short titles of the Regiments and Corps which have previously been awarded, or some which later have taken into use, the battle honours currently borne by these Regiments and Corps.

It should be noted, however, that this list is not a comprehensive inheritance table, but is intended to provide basic information to show the succession of battle honours.

1st Armoured Regiment
1st Armoured Regiment

1st/15th Royal New South Wales Lancers
New South Wales Lancers, 1st Australian Light Horse Regiment, 7th Light Horse, 1st Light Horse later 1st Royal New South Wales Lancers and New South Wales Mounted Rifles, 5th Australian Light Horse Regiment, 4th Light Horse, 15th Light Horse later 15th Northern Rivers Lancers formed 1st/15th Royal New South Wales Lancers

2nd/14th Queensland Mounted Infantry
Queensland Mounted Infantry, 13th Australian Light Horse Regiment later 2nd Light Horse Regiment and Queensland Mounted Infantry, 15th Australian Light Horse Regiment, 27th Light Horse later 14th Light Horse Regiment formed 2nd/14th Queensland Mounted Infantry

3rd/4th Cavalry Regiment
3rd Cavalry Regiment

3rd/9th South Australian Mounted Rifles
South Australian Mounted Rifles, 16th Australian Light Horse Regiment, 22nd Light Horse later 3rd Light Horse Regiment and South Australian Mounted Rifles, 17th Australian Light Horse Regiment, 24th Light Horse later 9th Light Horse Regiment formed 3rd/9th South Australian Mounted Rifles

4th/19th Prince of Wales Light Horse
Victorian Mounted Rifles, 9th Australian Light Horse Regiment, 20th Light Horse later 4th Light Horse Regiment, Victorian Mounted Rifles, 9th Australian Light Horse Regiment, 17th Light Horse later 17th Prince of Wales's Light Horse and Victorian Mounted Rifles, 9th Australian Light Horse later 19th Light Horse Regiment formed 4th/19th Prince of Wales Light Horse

8th/13th Victorian Mounted Rifles
Victorian Mounted Rifles, 8th Australian Light Horse Regiment, 16th Light Horse later 8th Light Horse Regiment and Victorian Mounted Rifles, 10th Australian Light Horse Regiment later 13th Light Horse Regiment and Victorian Mounted Rifles, 7th Australian Light Horse Regiment, 15th Light Horse later 20th Light Horse Regiment formed 8th/13th Victorian Mounted Rifles

10th Light Horse
Western Australian Mounted Infantry, 18th Australian Light Horse Regiment, 25th Light Horse Regiment, 10th Light Horse Regiment later 10th Light Horse

12th/16th Hunter River Lancers
Australian Horse, 6th Australian Light Horse, 5th Light Horse later 12th Light Horse Regiment and New South Wales Lancers, 4th Australian Light Horse Regiment, 6th Light Horse later 16th Light Horse Regiment formed 12th/16th Hunter River Lancers

Royal Australian Regiment
Royal Australian Regiment

The Royal Queensland Regiment
1st Queensland Regiment, 1/9th Australian Infantry Regiment, 7th Infantry later 9th Infantry Battalion, 25th Infantry Battalion, 3rd Queensland Regiment, 1st Kennedy Infantry Regiment, 2nd Infantry later 31st Infantry Battalion, 41st Infantry Battalion, 42nd Infantry, 47th Infantry Battalion, 49th Infantry Battalion and 2nd Tasmanian Infantry Regiment, 1/12th Australian Battalion Infantry Regiment, 92nd Infantry later 51st Infantry Battalion formed The Royal Queensland Regiment

The Royal New South Wales Regiment
1st New South Wales Infantry Regiment, 1st Australian Infantry Regiment, 21st Infantry later 1st Infantry Battalion, 2nd Infantry Battalion, 2nd New South Wales Infantry Regiment, 2nd Australian Infantry Regiment,

43rd Infantry later 3rd Infantry Battalion, 6th New South Wales Infantry Regiment, 1/1st Australian Rifle Regiment, 29th Infantry later 4th Infantry Battalion, 4th New South Wales Infantry Regiment, 4th Australian Infantry Regiment, 14th Infantry later 13th Infantry Battalion, 3rd New South Wales Infantry Regiment, 3rd Australian Infantry Regiment, 18th Infantry later 17th Infantry Battalion and 18th Infantry Battalion forming 17th/18th Infantry Battalion, 19th Infantry Battalion, 5th New South Wales Infantry Regiment, New South Wales Scottish Regiment, 25th Infantry later 30th Infantry Battalion, 34th Infantry Battalion, 35th Infantry Battalion, 41st Infantry Battalion, 45th Infantry Battalion and New South Wales Mounted Rifles,, 2nd Australian Light Horse Regiment, 9th Light Horse, 6th Light Horse later 6th New South Wales Mounted Rifles formed The Royal New South Wales Regiment

The Royal Victoria Regiment

2nd Militia Infantry Brigade, 6th Australian Infantry Regiment, 51st Infantry later 5th Infantry Battalion, 1st Militia Infantry Brigade, 1/5th Australian Infantry Regiment, 64th Infantry later 6th Infantry Battalion, 3rd Militia Infantry Brigade, 7th Australian Infantry Regiment, 70th Infantry and 71st Infantry later 8th Infantry Battalion and 7th Infantry Battalion forming 8th/7th Infantry Battalion, 2nd Militia Infantry Brigade, 6th Australian Infantry Regiment, 56th Infantry later 22nd Infantry Battalion, 5th Militia Infantry Brigade, 2/8th Australian Infantry Regiment, 67th Infantry later 38th Infantry Battalion, 58th Infantry Battalion and 4th Militia Infantry Brigade, 1/8th Australian Infantry Regiment, 65th Infantry later 32nd Infantry Battalion forming 58th/32nd Infantry Battalion (raised 1948) and 59th Infantry Battalion (raised 1953) formed The Royal Victoria Regiment

The Royal South Australia Regiment

1st South Australian Infantry Regiment, 1/10th Australian Infantry Regiment, 78th Infantry later 10th Infantry Battalion, 2nd South Australian Infantry Regiment, 2/10th Australian Infantry Regiment, 74th Infantry later 27th Infantry Battalion and 43rd Infantry Battalion and 48th Infantry Battalion forming 43th/48th Infantry Battalion formed The Royal South Australia Regiment

The Royal Western Australia Regiment

1st Western Australian Infantry Regiment and 2nd Western Australian Infantry Regiment, 1/11th Australian Infantry Regiment, 88th Infantry later 11th Infantry Battalion and 3rd Western Australian Infantry Regiment and 4th Western Australian Infantry Regiment, 1st Western Australian Infantry Regiment, 86th Infantry forming 11th/44th Infantry Battalion, 5th Western Australian Infantry Regiment, 1st Goldfields Infantry Regiment, 84th Infantry later 16th Infantry Battalion and 28th Infantry Battalion formed The Royal Western Australia Regiment

The Royal Tasmania Regiment

3rd Tasmanian Infantry Regiment, 1st Tasmanian Rangers, 91st Infantry later 12th Infantry Battalion and 1st Tasmanian Infantry Regiment, 1st Derwent Regiment, 93rd Infantry later 40th Infantry Battalion formed The Royal Tasmania Regiment

DISBANDED REGIMENTS AND CORPS

Light Horse

1st (Central Queensland) Light Horse	disbanded 1943 as 5th Motor Regiment
3rd Australian Light Horse Regiment (Australian Horse)	disbanded 1943 as 7th Motor Regiment
3rd (Darling Downs) Light Horse	disbanded 1943 as 11th Motor Regiment
3rd (Tasmanian Mounted Infantry) Light Horse	disbanded 1943 as 22nd Motor Regiment
5th Light Horse (Central Queensland Light Horse)	disbanded 1943 as 5th Motor Regiment
7th Light Horse (Australian Horse)	disbanded 1943 as 7th Motor Regiment
11th Light Horse (Australian Horse)	disbanded 1943 as 7th Motor Regiment
11th Light Horse (Darling Downs)	disbanded 1943 as 11th Motor Regiment
12th Australian Light Horse Regiment (Tasmanian Mounted Infantry)	disbanded 1943 as 22nd Motor Regiment
13th Australian Light Horse Regiment (Queensland Mounted Infantry)	disbanded 1943 as 5th Motor Regiment
14th Australian Light Horse Regiment (Queensland Mounted Infantry)	disbanded 1943 as 11th Motor Regiment
18th Light Horse (Machine Gun)(Adelaide Lancers)	disbanded 1943 as 12th Armoured Regiment
21st Light Horse (Riverina Horse)	disbanded 1943 as 21st Australian Divisional Cavalry Regiment
22nd Light Horse (Tasmanian Mounted Infantry)	disbanded 1943 as 22nd Motor Regiment
23rd Light Horse (Barossa)	disbanded 1942 as 23rd Reconnaissance Company
26th Light Horse (Tasmanian Mounted Infantry)	disbanded 1943 as 22nd Motor Regiment

Cavalry

6th Cavalry (Commando) Regiment	disbanded 1946: no successor
7th Cavalry (Commando) Regiment	disbanded 1946: no successor

9th Cavalry (Commando) Regiment	disbanded 1946: no successor
21st Australian Divisional Cavalry Regiment	
(The Riverina Horse)	disbanded 1943: no successor
23rd Reconnaissance Company (The Barossa Light Horse)	disbanded 1942: no successor

Motor Regiments

5th Motor Regiment (The Wide Bay and Burnett Light Horse)	disbanded 1943: no successor
7th Motor Regiment (The Australian Horse)	disbanded 1943: no successor
11th Motor Regiment (The Darling Downs Light Horse)	disbanded 1943: no successor
18th Motor Regiment (The Adelaide Lancers)	disbanded 1943 as 12th Armoured Regiment
22nd Motor Regiment (The Tasmanian Mounted Infantry)	disbanded 1943: no successor

Armoured Regiments

12th Armoured Regiment (The Adelaide Lancers)	disbanded 1943: no successor

Infantry

Victorian Rangers	disbanded 1945 as 21st Infantry Battalion
1st Queensland (Moreton) Regiment (part)	disbanded 1945 as 15th Infantry Battalion
1st New South Wales Irish Rifle Regiment	disbanded 1945 as 55th Infantry Battalion
1st South Australian Infantry Regiment	disbanded 1945 as 50th Infantry Battalion
1st Militia Infantry Brigade (Victoria)(part)	disbanded 1946 as 60th Infantry Battalion
1st St George's English Rifle Regiment	disbanded 1945 as 36th Infantry Battalion
1/1st Australian Infantry Regiment	disbanded 1945 as 36th Infantry Battalion
2nd Militia Infantry Brigade (Victoria)(part)	disbanded 1945 as 22nd Infantry Battalion
2nd Militia Infantry Brigade (Victoria)(part)	disbanded 1945 as 14th Infantry Battalion
2nd Militia Infantry Brigade (Victoria)(part)	disbanded 1946 as 59th Infantry Battalion
1/2nd and 2/2nd South Australian Infantry	disbanded 1945 as 50th Infantry Battalion
3rd New South Wales Infantry (part)	disbanded 1944 as 20th Infantry Battalion
1/3rd Australian Infantry Regiment	disbanded 1944 as 20th Infantry Battalion
1/6th Australian Infantry Regiment	disbanded 1945 as 14th Infantry Battalion
7th New South Wales Infantry (part)	disbanded 1945 as 36th Infantry Battalion
8th New South Wales Infantry (part)	disbanded 1945 as 55th Infantry Battalion
8th Infantry (Oxley Battalion)	disbanded 1945 as 15th Infantry Battalion
14th Infantry Battalion (The Prahran Regiment)	disbanded 1945: no successor
15th Infantry Battalion (The Oxley Regiment)	disbanded 1945: no successor
19th Infantry Battalion (The South Sydney Regiment)	disbanded 1945: no successor
20th Infantry Battalion	
(The Parramatta and Blue Mountains Regiment)	disbanded 1944: no successor
21st Infantry Battalion (The Victorian Rangers)	disbanded 1945: no successor
22nd Infantry Battalion (The Richmond Regiment)	disbanded 1945: no successor
23rd Infantry Battalion (The City of Geelong Regiment)	disbanded 1943: no successor
24th Infantry Battalion (The Kooyong Regiment)	disbanded 1946: no successor
26th Infantry Battalion (The Logan and Albert Regiment)	disbanded 1946: no successor
29th Infantry Battalion (The East Melbourne Regiment)	disbanded 1946: no successor
31st (Leichardt) Infantry	disbanded 1945 as 36th Infantry Battalion
32nd Infantry Battalion (The Footscray Regiment)	disbanded 1943
33rd Infantry Battalion (The New England Regiment)	disbanded 1943: no successor
35th Infantry Battalion (Newcastle's Own Regiment)	disbanded 1946: no successor
36th Infantry Battalion (The St George's English Rifle Regiment)	disbanded 1945: no successor
37th Infantry Battalion (The Henty Regiment)	disbanded 1946: no successor
39th Infantry (Hawthorn Regiment)	disbanded 1946 as 39th Infantry Battalion
39th Infantry Battalion (The Hawthorn-Kew Regiment)	disbanded 1946: no successor
41st (Blue Mountains) Infantry	disbanded 1944 as 20th Infantry Battalion
46th Infantry Battalion (The Brighton Rifles)	disbanded 1946: no successor
49th (Prahran) Infantry	disbanded 1945 as 14th Infantry Battalion
49th Infantry Battalion (The Stanley Regiment)	disbanded 1943: no successor
50th Infantry (Barrier Regiment)	disbanded 1945 as 50th Infantry Battalion
50th Infantry Battalion (The Tasmanian Rangers)	disbanded 1945: no successor
52nd Infantry Battalion (The Gippsland Regiment)	disbanded 1946: no successor
53rd Infantry Battalion (The West Sydney Regiment)	disbanded 1945: no successor
54th Infantry Battalion (The Lachlan Macquarie Regiment)	disbanded 1944: no successor
55th Infantry (New South Wales Irish Rifles)	disbanded 1945 as 55th Infantry Battalion
55th Infantry Battalion (The New South Wales Rifle Regiment)	disbanded 1945: no successor
56th Infantry (Yarra Borderers)	disbanded 1945 as 22nd Infantry Battalion
56th Infantry Battalion (The Riverina Regiment)	disbanded 1957: no successor
57th Infantry Battalion (The Merri Regiment)	disbanded 1946: no successor

58th Infantry (Essendon Rifles)	disbanded 1943 as 58th Infantry Battalion
58th Infantry Battalion	
(The Essendon-Coburg-Brunswick Regiment)	disbanded 1943
59th Infantry (Coburg-Brunswick Regiment)	disbanded 1946 as 59th Infantry Battalion
59th Infantry Battalion (The Hume Regiment)	disbanded 1946
60th (Prince's Hill) Infantry	disbanded 1946 as 60th Infantry Battalion
60th Infantry (Jika Jika Regiment)	disbanded 1946 as 60th Infantry Battalion
60th Infantry Battalion (The Heidelberg Regiment)	disbanded 1946: no successor
61st Infantry Battalion (The Queensland Cameron Highlanders)	disbanded 1946: no successor
62nd Infantry Battalion (The Merauke Regiment)	disbanded 1944: no successor
73rd Infantry (Victorian Rangers)	disbanded 1945 as 21st Infantry Battalion
81st (Wakefield) Infantry	disbanded 1945 as 50th Infantry Battalion

Machine Gun Battalions

1st Machine Gun Battalion	disbanded 1946: no successor
2nd Machine Gun Battalion	disbanded 1946: no successor
3rd Machine Gun Battalion	disbanded 1946: no successor
4th Machine Gun Battalion	disbanded 1943: no successor
7th Machine Gun Battalion	disbanded 1944: no successor

Pioneers Battalions

1st Pioneer Battalion	disbanded 1946: no successor
2nd Pioneer Battalion	disbanded 1946: no successor
3rd Pioneer Battalion	disbanded 1946: no successor
4th Pioneer Battalion	disbanded 1946: no successor

Appendix H

SUCCESSION OF CANADIAN BATTLE HONOURS

Listed below in bold type are the honour bearing Regiments and Corps on establishment in 1988. Below each are shown the short titles of the Regiments and Corps which have previously been awarded, or some which later have taken into use, the battle honours currently borne by these Regiments and Corps. Regiments and Corps with extant honours retained by other Arms and Services or on the Supplementary Order of Battle are not included.

It should be noted, however, that this list is not a comprehensive inheritance table, but is intended to provide basic information to show the succession of battle honours.

The Royal Canadian Dragoons
> The Royal Canadian Dragoons

Lord Strathcona's Horse (Royal Canadians)
> Lord Strathcona's Horse

8th Canadian Hussars (Princess Louise's)
> 8th Canadian Hussars

12e Regiment Blinde du Canada
> The Three Rivers Regiment, Le Regiment de Trois Riviers later 12e Regiment Blinde du Canada

The Governor General's Horse Guards
> The Governor General's Body Guard and The Mississauga Horse formed The Governor General's Horse Guards

The Elgin Regiment
> The Elgin Regiment

The Queen's York Rangers (1st American Regiment)
> 12th Regiment later The York Rangers and The Queen's Rangers, 1st American Regiment formed The Queen's York Rangers

The Ontario Regiment
> The Ontario Regiment

The Sherbrooke Hussars
> 7th Hussars and 11th Hussars formed 7th/11th Hussars, which with The Sherbrooke Regiment formed The Sherbrooke Hussars

1st Hussars
> 1st Hussars

The Prince Edward Island Regiment
> 82nd Regiment later The Prince Edward Island Highlanders and The Prince Edward Island Light Horse formed The Prince Edward Island Regiment

The Royal Canadian Hussars (Montreal)
> 1st Motor Machine Gun Brigade, 1st Armoured Car Regiment later 6th Duke of Connaught's Royal Canadian Hussars and 17th Duke of York's Royal Canadian Hussars formed The Royal Canadian Hussars

The British Columbia Regiment (Duke of Connaught's Own)
> 6th Regiment, 1st British Columbia Regiment later The British Columbia Regiment

The South Alberta Light Horse
> 15th Light Horse later 15th Canadian Light Horse and The Alberta Mounted Rifles later The South Alberta Light Horse formed 15th Alberta Light Horse, which with The South Alberta Regiment formed The South Alberta Light Horse

The Saskatchewan Dragoons
> The King's Own Rifles of Canada later The Saskatchewan Dragoons

The King's Own Calgary Regiment
> The Calgary Regiment later The King's Own Calgary Regiment

The British Columbia Dragoons
> The British Columbia Dragoons

The Fort Garry Horse
32nd Manitoba Horse later The Manitoba Horse and The Fort Garry Horse formed The Fort Garry Horse

The Royal Canadian Regiment
The Royal Canadian Regiment

Princess Patricia's Canadian Light Infantry
Princess Patricia's Canadian Light Infantry

Royal 22e Regiment
Royal 22e Regiment

The Canadian Airborne Regiment (raised 1968)
First Canadian Parachute Battalion and 1st Special Service Battalion

Governor General's Foot Guards
Governor General's Foot Guards

The Canadian Grenadier Guards
1st Regiment later The Canadian Grenadier Guards

The Queen's Own Rifles of Canada
2nd Regiment later The Queen's Own Rifles of Canada

The Black Watch (Royal Highland Regiment) of Canada
5th Regiment, The Royal Highlanders of Canada later The Black Watch of Canada

Les Voligeurs de Quebec
9th Regiment later Les Voltigeurs de Quebec

The Royal Regiment of Canada
10th Battalion, 10th Regiment later The Royal Grenadiers and The Toronto Regiment formed The Royal Regiment of Toronto Grenadiers later The Royal Regiment of Canada

The Royal Hamilton Light Infantry (Wentworth Regiment)
13th Royal Regiment, The Royal Hamilton Regiment later The Royal Hamilton Light Infantry and The Wentworth Regiment formed The Royal Hamilton Light Infantry

The Princess of Wales' Own Regiment
14th Regiment, The Kingston Regiment later The Princess of Wales' Own Regiment

The Hastings and Prince Edward Regiment
46th Durham Regiment later The Durham Regiment and The Northumberland Regiment formed The Midland Regiment, which with The Argyll Light Infantry and The Hastings and Prince Edward Regiment formed The Hastings and Prince Edward Regiment

The Lincoln and Welland Regiment
The Lincoln Regiment and The Lincoln and Welland Regiment formed The Lincoln and Welland Regiment

4th Battalion, The Royal Canadian Regiment (London and Oxford Fusiliers)
7th Regiment, The Western Ontario Regiment later The Canadian Fusiliers, 2nd Machine Gun Battalion and The Oxford Rifles formed The London and Oxford Fusiliers, which with The Royal Canadian Regiment formed 3rd Royal Canadian Regiment later 4th Royal Canadian Regiment

The Highland Fusiliers of Canada
The Highland Light Infantry of Canada later The Highland Fusiliers of Canada

The Grey and Simcoe Foresters
The Grey Regiment and 35th Regiment later The Simcoe Foresters formed The Grey and Simcoe Forester

The Lorne Scots (Peel, Dufferin and Halton Regiment)
The Peel and Dufferin Regiment and The Halton Rifles later The Lorne Rifles formed The Lorne Scots

The Brockville Rifles
The Brockville Rifles

The Lanark and Renfrew Scottish Regiment
The Lanark and Renfrew Scottish Regiment

Stormont, Dundas and Glengarry Highlanders
The Stormont, Dundas and Glengarry Highlanders

Les Fusiliers du Saint-Laurent
Fusiliers du St Laurent

Le Regiment de la Chaudiere
Le Regiment de la Chaudiere

4e Bataillon, Royal 22e Regiment (Chateauguay)
Royal 22e Regiment

6e Bataillon, Royal 22e Regiment
Royal 22e Regiment

Les Fusiliers Mont-Royal
65th Regiment, Les Carabiniers Mont-Royal later Les Fusiliers Mont-Royal

The Princess Louise Fusiliers
66th Regiment later The Princess Louise Fusiliers

The Royal New Brunswick Regiment
The Carleton Light Infantry and 71st York Regiment later The York Regiment formed The Carleton and York Regiment: 62nd Regiment later The Saint John Fusiliers and The New Brunswick Rangers formed The South New Brunswick Regiment later The New Brunswick Scottish: The Carleton and York and The New Brunswick Scottish, with The North Shore (New Brunswick) Regiment formed The New Brunswick Regiment later The Royal New Brunswick Regiment

The West Nova Scotia Regiment
The Annapolis Regiment and The Lunenburg Regiment formed The West Nova Scotia Regiment

The Nova Scotia Highlanders
93rd Cumberland Regiment later The Cumberland Highlanders and The Colchester and Hants Regiment formed The North Nova Scotia Highlanders, which with The Pictou Highlanders and The Cape Breton Highlanders formed The Nova Scotia Highlanders

Le Regiment de Maisonneuve
Le Regiment de Maisonneuve

The Cameron Highlanders of Ottawa
43rd Regiment, The Ottawa Regiment, The Ottawa Highlanders later The Cameron Highlanders of Ottawa

The Royal Winnipeg Rifles
90th Regiment, The Winnipeg Rifles later The Royal Winnipeg Rifles and The Winnipeg Light Infantry formed The Royal Winnipeg Rifles

The Essex and Kent Scottish
The Essex Scottish and The Kent Regiment formed The Essex and Kent Scottish

48th Highlanders of Canada
48th Regiment, The 48th Regiment later 48th Highlanders of Canada

The Algonquin Regiment
The Algonquin Regiment and The Northern Pioneers formed The Algonquin Regiment

The Argyll and Sutherland Highlanders of Canada (Princess Louise's)
The Argyll and Sutherland Highlanders of Canada and 3rd Machine Gun Battalion

The Lake Superior Scottish Regiment
The Lake Superior Regiment later The Lake Superior Scottish Regiment

The North Saskatchewan Regiment
16th Light Horse later 16th Canadian Light Horse and The Saskatchewan Mounted Rifles formed 16th/22nd Saskatchewan Horse later The Battleford Light Infantry: The Battleford Light Infantry and The Prince Albert Volunteers formed The Prince Albert and Battleford Volunteers, which with The Saskatoon Light Infantry formed The North Saskatchewan Regiment

The Regina Rifle Regiment
The Regina Rifle Regiment

The Rocky Mountain Rangers
The Rocky Mountain Rangers

The Loyal Edmonton Regiment (4th Battalion, Princess Patricia's Canadian Light Infantry)
The Edmonton Regiment later The Loyal Edmonton Regiment

The Queen's Own Cameron Highlanders of Canada
The Queen's Own Cameron Highlanders of Canada

The Royal Westminster Regiment
The Westminster Regiment later The Royal Westminster Regiment

The Calgary Highlanders
> The Calgary Highlanders

Les Fusiliers de Sherbrooke
> Les Carabiniers de Sherbrooke later Les Fusiliers de Sherbrooke

The Seaforth Highlanders of Canada
> The Seaforth Highlanders of Canada

The Canadian Scottish Regiment (Princess Mary's)
> The Canadian Scottish Regiment

The Royal Montreal Regiment
> The Royal Montreal Regiment

2nd Battalion, The Irish Regiment of Canada
> The Irish Regiment later The Irish Regiment of Canada and 1st Machine Gun Battalion

The Toronto Scottish Regiment
> The Toronto Scottish Regiment

The Royal Newfoundland Regiment (raised 1949)
> The Royal Newfoundland Regiment

DISBANDED REGIMENTS AND CORPS

Canadian Armoured Corps

First Canadian Armoured Personnel Carrier Regiment	disbanded 1945: no successor

Militia (Infantry)

The Middlesex Light Infantry	disbanded 1946 as The Middlesex and Huron Regiment
The Middlesex and Huron Regiment	disbanded 1946: no successor
The Wellington Rifles	disbanded 1936 as The Wellington Regiment
The Wellington Regiment	disbanded 1936: no successor
The Bruce Regiment	disbanded 1936: no successor
The Huron Regiment	disbanded 1946 as The Middlesex and Huron Regiment
The Norfolk Regiment of Canada	disbanded 1936: no successor
The Victoria and Haliburton Regiment	disbanded 1936: no successor
50th Battalion of Infantry Huntingdon Borderers	disbanded 1903 as 50th Huntingdon and Hemmingford Rangers
50th Regiment "Huntingdon and Hemmingford Rangers"	disbanded 1903: no successor
The Irish Canadian Rangers	disbanded 1936: no successor
60th Mississquoi Battalion of Infantry	disbanded 1898: no successor
The Manitoba Rangers	disbanded 1936: no successor
The Kootenay Regiment	disbanded 1936: no successor
The North Alberta Regiment	disbanded 1936: no successor
The Yorkton Regiment	disbanded 1936: no successor
The Assinaboia Regiment	disbanded 1936: no successor
The Manitoba Regiment	disbanded 1936: no successor

Infantry

First Canadian Parachute Battalion	disbanded 1946

Special Forces

1st Special Service Battalion	disbanded 1944

SUCCESSION OF NEW ZEALAND BATTLE HONOURS

Listed below in bold type are the honour bearing Regiments and Corps on establishment in 1990. Below each are shown the short titles of the Regiments and Corps which have previously been awarded, or some which later have taken into use, the battle honours currently borne by these Regiments and Corps. Regiments and Corps with extant honours retained by sub-units or in recess are not included.

It should be noted, however, that this list is not a comprehensive inheritance table, but is intended to provide basic information to show the succession of battle honours.

Royal New Zealand Infantry Regiment

1st North Canterbury Infantry Volunteers later 1st Regiment and South Canterbury Infantry Volunteers later 2nd Regiment formed The Canterbury Regiment: 1st Auckland Infantry Volunteers, 3rd Regiment later The Auckland Regiment: 1st Otago Rifle Volunteers later 4th Regiment and 3rd Otago Rifle Volunteers later 10th Regiment formed The Otago Regiment: 1st Wellington Rifle Volunteers, 5th Regiment later The Wellington Regiment: 2nd Auckland Infantry Volunteers, 6th Regiment later The Hauraki Regiment: 2nd Wellington Rifle Volunteers, 7th Regiment later The Wellington West Coast Regiment: 2nd Otago Rifle Volunteers later 8th Regiment and 14th Regiment formed The Southland Regiment: 3rd Wellington Rifle Volunteers later 9th Regiment and 17th Regiment formed The The Hawke's Bay Regiment: 4th Wellington Rifle Volunteers, 11th Regiment later The Taranaki Regiment: 1st Nelson Infantry Volunteers later 12th Regiment and 13th Regiment formed The Nelson, Marlborough and West Coast Regiment: 15th Regiment, The North Auckland Regiment later The Northland Regiment: The Otago Regiment and The Southland Regiment formed The Otago and Southland Regiment: The Wellington West Coast Regiment and The Taranaki Regiment formed The Wellington West Coast and Taranaki Regiment: The Canterbury Regiment, The Auckland Regiment, The Otago and Southland Regiment, The Wellington Regiment, The Hauraki Regiment, The Wellington West Coast and Taranaki Regiment, The Hawke's Bay Regiment, The Nelson, Marlborough, ans West Coast Regiment and The Northland Regiment formed Royal New Zealand Infantry Regiment

DISBANDED REGIMENTS AND CORPS

Rifle Volunteers
No 4 Regiment, Auckland Mounted Rifle Volunteers — disbanded 1911: no successor

Infantry
The Waikato Regiment — disbanded 1948
The Ruahine Regiment — disbanded 1948: no successor
28 (Maori) Battalion — disbanded 1946: no successor
34 Battalion — disbanded 1944: no successor
35 Battalion — disbanded 1944: no successor

Machine Gun
27 (MG) Battalion — disbanded 1946: no successor

SUCCESSION OF SOUTH AFRICAN BATTLE HONOURS

Listed below in bold type are the honour bearing Regiments and Corps on establishment in 1980. Below each are shown the short titles of the Regiments and Corps which have previously been awarded, or some which later have taken into use, the battle honours currently borne by these Regiments and Corps.

It should be noted, however, that this list is not a comprehensive inheritance table, but is intended to provide basic information to show the succession of battle honours.

The Natal Carbineers
Natal Carbineers, 1st Mounted Rifles later The Royal Natal Carbineers

Durban Light Infantry
Durban Light Infantry, 1st Infantry later Royal Durban Light Infantry

Cape Town Rifles (Dukes)
Duke of Edinburgh's Own Volunteer Rifles, Duke of Edinburgh's Own Rifles, 2nd Infantry later Cape Town Rifles

First City Regiment
Queenstown Rifle Volunteers and First City Volunteers formed First Eastern Rifles, 4th Infantry later First City

Kaffrarian Rifles
Kaffrarian Rifles, 5th Infantry later The Kaffrarian Rifles

Cape Town Highlanders
Cape Town Highlanders, Duke of Connaught and Strathearn's Cape Town Highlanders, 6th Infantry later The Queen's Own Cape Town Highlanders

Kimberley Regiment
Kimberley Regiment, 7th Infantry later Kimberley Regiment

Transvaal Scottish Regiment
8th Infantry later Transvaal Scottish

Witwatersrand Rifles
10th Infantry later Witwatersrand Rifles

Rand Light Infantry
11th Infantry later Rand Light Infantry

1 Regiment De La Rey
Regiment De La Rey

South African Irish Regiment
South African Irish later South African Irish Regiment

Regiment Christian Beyers
2 Regiment Botha

Regiment Grootkaroo
Die Middellandse Regiment

2 Regiment De La Rey
Regiment De La Rey

1 Special Service Battalion
1 Special Service Battalion

1 Natal Mounted Rifles
Natal Mounted Rifles and Border Mounted Rifles formed Natal Mounted Rifles, 3rd Mounted Rifles later Natal Mounted Rifles

Umvoti Mounted Rifles
Umvoti Mounted Rifles and Zululand Mounted Rifles formed Umvoti Mounted Rifles, 4th Mounted Rifles later Umvoti Mounted Rifles

1 Light Horse Regiment
5th Mounted Rifles and 2nd Imperial Light Horse later Imperial Light Horse

Prince Alfred's Guard
> Prince Alfred's Volunteer Guard and Uitenhage Volunteer Rifles formed Prince Alfred's Guard, 3rd Infantry later Prince Alfred's Guard

Pretoria Regiment
> 12th Infantry later Pretoria Regiment

Regiment President Steyn
> Regiment President Steyn

Pretoria Highlanders
> Pretoria Highlanders

2 Natal Mounted Rifles
> Natal Mounted Rifles and Border Mounted Rifles formed Natal Mounted Rifles, 3rd Mounted Rifles later Natal Mounted Rifles

2 Light Horse Regiment
> 5th Mounted Rifles and 2nd Imperial Light Horse later Imperial Light Horse

Regiment Vrystaat
> Regiment Vrystaat

DISBANDED REGIMENTS AND CORPS

South African Permanent Force

1st Regiment, South African Mounted Riflemen	disbanded 1926: no successor
2nd Regiment, South African Mounted Riflemen	disbanded 1920: no successor
3rd Regiment, South African Mounted Riflemen	disbanded 1920: no successor
4th Regiment, South African Mounted Riflemen	disbanded 1920: no successor
5th Regiment, South African Mounted Riflemen	disbanded 1920: no successor
Field Artillery Brigade (South African Mounted Riflemen)	disbanded ? : no successor[1]
5th Mountain Battery (South African Mounted Riflemen)	disbanded ? : no successor[1]
South African Cape Corps (raised 1964)	disbanded ? : no successor

Mounted Rifles

Northern District Mounted Rifles	disbanded 1912: no successor

Infantry

Natal Royal Regiment	disbanded 1913: no successor

Active Citizen Force

Transkei Mounted Rifles	disbanded 1929 as Cape Light Horse
6th Mounted Rifles (Cape Light Horse)	disbanded 1929: no successor
8th Mounted Rifles (Midlandse Ruiters)	disbanded 1929: no successor
11th Mounted Rifles (Potchefstroom Ruiters)	disbanded 1929: no successor
17th Mounted Rifles (Western Province Mounted Rifles)	disbanded 1929: no successor
18th Mounted Rifles (Griqualand West Ruiters)	disbanded 1929: no successor
20th Mounted Rifles (Graaff-Reinet Ruiters)	disbanded 1929: no successor
6th Dismounted Rifles (Midlandse Skutters)	disbanded 1926: no successor
9th Dismounted Rifles (Bechuanaland Rifles)	disbanded 1926: no successor
1st Field Ambulance South African Medical Corps	disbanded ? : no successor

Artillery[1]

1st Battery, South African Field Artillery	disbanded 1919: no successor
2nd Battery, South African Field Artillery	disbanded 1919: no successor
3rd Battery, South African Field Artillery	disbanded 1919: no successor
4th Battery, South African Field Artillery	disbanded 1919: no successor
5th Battery, South African Field Artillery	disbanded 1919: no successor
71st (Transvaal) Siege Battery, Royal Garrison Artillery	disbanded 1919: no successor
72nd (Griqualand West) Siege Battery, Royal Garrison Artillery	disbanded 1919: no successor
73rd (Cape) Siege Battery, Royal Garrison Artillery	disbanded 1919: no successor
74th (Eastern Province) Siege Battery, Royal Garrison Artillery	disbanded 1919: no successor
75th (Natal) Siege Battery, Royal Garrison Artillery	disbanded 1919: no successor
125th (Transvaal) Siege Battery, Royal Garrison Artillery	disbanded 1919: no successor

Miscellaneous Corps

Southern Rhodesia Volunteers	disbanded 1901: no successor

3rd South African Horse (3de Zuidafrikaanse Ruiters)	disbanded 1917: no successor
4th South African Horse (4de Zuidafrikaanse Ruiters)	disbanded 1918: no successor
8th South African Horse (8st Zuidafrikaanse Ruiters)	disbanded 1918: no successor
9th South African Horse (9de Zuidafrikaanse Ruiters)	disbanded 1918: no successor
10th South African Horse (10de Zuidafrikaanse Ruiters)	disbanded 1918: no successor
Northern Transvaal Ruiters	disbanded 1915: no successor
3rd Regiment, 5th Mounted Brigade (Brand's Vrijstaatse Skutters)	disbanded 1915: no successor
Botha's Hogeveld Ruiters	disbanded 1915: no successor
Hartigan's Horse	disbanded 1915: no successor
1st South African Infantry (Cape of Good Hope Regiment)	disbanded 1919: no successor
2nd South African Infantry (Natal and Orange Free State Regiment)	disbanded 1919: no successor
3rd South African Infantry (Transvaal and Rhodesian Regiment)	disbanded 1919: no successor
4th South African Infantry (South African Scottish Regiment)	disbanded 1919: no successor
5th South African Infantry (Cape Regiment)	disbanded 1919: no successor
6th South African Infantry (Natal, Orange Free State and Eastern Provinces Regiment)	disbanded 1919: no successor
7th South African Infantry (Transvaal Regiment)	disbanded 1919: no successor
8th South African Infantry (Railways and Workers Regiment)	disbanded 1919: no successor
9th South African Infantry (Sportsmen's Regiment)	disbanded 1919: no successor
10th South African Infantry (Railways and Workers Regiment)	disbanded 1919: no successor
11th South African Infantry (Cape and Natal Regiment)	disbanded 1919: no successor
12th South African Infantry (Transvaal and Orange Free State Regiment)	disbanded 1919: no successor
South African Rifles (Nyassaland Imperial Service Contingent)	disbanded 1918: no successor
Rand Rifles	disbanded 1915: no successor
Southern Rifles	disbanded 1915: no successor
1st Battalion, Cape Corps	disbanded 1918
2nd Cape Corps	disbanded 1919
1st South African Field Ambulance	disbanded 1919: no successor

[1] *South African Artillery units are not permitted to perpetuate battle honours awarded for The Great War, but are currently awarded theatre honours for other campaigns: nevertheless, no details of such awards are available.*

Bibliography

Baker, Anthony, *Battle Honours of the British and Commonwealth Armies* (London, 1986)

Churchill, Winston, *The Second World War* (London, 1948–54)

Cook, H.C.B., *Battle Honours of the British and Indian Armies 1662 to 1982* (London, 1987)

Corbett, D.A., *The Regimental Badges of New Zealand* (Auckland, 1980)

Curson, H.H., *Colours and Honours in South Africa 1783–1948* (Pretoria, 1948)

Dornbusch, C.E., *The Lineages of the Canadian Army 1855–1961* (Cornwallville, 1961)

Edwards, Major T.J., *Regimental Badges* (Aldershot, 1951)

Festberg, Alfred, *Australian Army Lineage Book* (Melbourne, 1965)

Fletcher, Ian, *Wellington's Regiments* (Tunbridge Wells, 1994)

Frederick, J.B.M., *Lineage Book of British Land Forces 1660–1978* (Wakefield, 1984)

Gaylor, John, *Sons of John Company: the Indian and Pakistan Armies 1903–91* (Tunbridge Wells, 1992)

Harfield, Alan, *The Indian Army of the Empress 1861–1903* (Tunbridge Wells, 1990)

Haythornthwaite, Philip J., *The Colonial Wars Source Book* (London, 1995)

—— *The World War One Source Book* (London, 1992)

Haywood, Colonel A. and Brigadier F.A.S. Clarke, *The History of the Royal West African Frontier Force* (Aldershot, 1964)

James, Brigadier E.A., *British Regiments of 1914–18* (London, 1978)

James, Captain E.A., *A Record of the Battles and Engagements of the British Armies in France and Flanders 1914–18* (Aldershot, 1924)

Joslen, Lieutenant Colonel H.F., *Orders of Battle Second World War 1939–1945* (London, 1960)

Leslie, N.B., *Battle Honours of the British and Indian Armies 1695–1914* (London, 1970)

Merewether, Lieutenant Colonel J.W.B. and Sir Frederick Smith, *The Indian Corps in France* (London, 1919)

Mileham, Patrick, *The Scottish Regiments 1633–1996* (Staplehurst, 1996)

Mollo, Boris, *The Indian Army* (Blandford, 1981)

Moyse-Bartlett, Lieutenant Colonel H., *The King's African Rifles* (Aldershot, 1956)

Nevins, Edward M., *Forces of the British Empire 1914* (Arlington, 1992)

Norman, C.B., *Battle Honours of the British Army* (London, 1911)

Perry, F.W., *Order of Battle of Divisions, Part 5A: The Divisions of Australia, Canada and New Zealand and Those in East Africa* (Newport, 1992)

—— *Order of Battle of Divisions, Part 5B: Indian Army Divisions* (Newport, 1993)

Singh, Major Sarbans, *Battle Honours of the Indian Army 1757–1971* (New Delhi, 1993)

Stewart, Charles H., *The Concise Lineages of the Canadian Army* (Toronto, 1982)

Tylden, G., *Armed Forces of South Africa 1695–1947* (Johannesburg, 1954)

Westlake, Ray, *English and Welsh Infantry Regiments: An Illustrated Record of Service 1662–1994* (Staplehurst, 1995)